CW00549106

7TH EDITION

WISDEN

CRICKETERS' ALMANACK

AUSTRALIA

—— 2004-05 ——

Hardie Grant Books

Published in 2004 by
Hardie Grant Books
85 High Street, Prahran, Victoria 3181, Australia
www.hardiegrant.com.au

The Australian edition of the *Wisden Cricketers' Almanack*
published by Hardie Grant Books under licence from
John Wisden & Co Ltd.

Cased edition ISBN 1 74066 181 8
Leather bound edition ISBN 1 74066 217 2
(Limited edition of 100)
ISSN 1441-1725

Typeset by
Melbourne Media Services & Pauline Haas
Printed in Australia by Ligare Book Printer

Preface

Another summer, another 12 months of Australia squashing every opponent in sight, another *Wisden*. Actually, not quite. In the same year that Sourav Ganguly's Indians provided an unexpected hiccup to Steve Waugh's carefully choreographed farewell lap, we have been doing a bit of tinkering with the script ourselves. We started at the very beginning – the first full-colour pictorial cover in the history of *Wisden*. It is the first of several firsts.

Farewells is a new section of lyrical tributes to Australian cricketers – some celebrated, others less so – who have departed the stage. The Wisden Review heralds a longer and livelier back half, with new features on administrators, grounds and a where-are-they-now guide to retired cricketers. Every Australian Test, at home and abroad, is now assigned a different reporter. We sent a correspondent to the Imparja Cup, the national Aboriginal carnival. We have added Darwin to our nationwide coverage of grade cricket.

For the first time there are individual player sketches of Australia's top women cricketers. As for the blokes, we have spiced up their profiles and put them in alphabetical order. Other Cricketing Notables is a new register of the game's most significant off-field contributors. There are more pictures, bigger headlines and a little extra breathing space all round. And yes, in case you're wondering, this is the biggest *Wisden Australia* ever. At 976 pages, we hope you will find it unputdownable but not unpickupable.

We have fiddled with the statistics too. Balls faced and boundaries hit are now incorporated in Test scorecards. The Records section is more arcane and far-reaching than ever, a statistical masterwork by *Wisden*'s resident numbers man Ross Dundas, who was equal to every challenge lumped on him by a new editor with wild ideas and wacky deadlines. Of particular delight are two new tables listing every Australian Test and one-day player in order of appearance. They highlight, at a glance, not only runs and wickets but strike-rates and economy-rates too, the kind of odds and ends you might spend half a day trawling for on the internet.

Our first thanks go to the writers, an unfailingly energetic and eloquent bunch, whose hard slog is much appreciated. Thanks, too, to our typesetters David Spratt and Pauline Haas. Warned of the long and mountainous trek ahead, they paused only to reach for their hiking boots. Peter English was a precious sub, sounding board and proofreader. George Thomas was a valued wordsmith. Gideon Haigh and Tim de Lisle, with his anything-is-possible philosophy, were ideal people to run a hair-brained scheme past. Warwick Franks, editor for the previous three years, was a pillar of comfort and wisdom. Bernard Whimpress and Ken Williams, who put in the hard yards on the Other Cricketing Notables list, worked wonders in hours.

Sandy Grant, the publisher, was an enthusiastic ideas man. For our friends at cricketing associations across the country – at national, local and particularly state level – nothing was ever too much bother. Matthew Engel and Chris Lane, at John Wisden & Co in England, were supportive team-mates and eager advisers when asked. Mary Small at Hardie Grant Books was worldly, rigorous, untiring and sunny. Without her, *Wisden Australia 2004-05* might not have hit the shelves till 3004-05.

We trust you will find it a feisty, provocative read, not afraid to take a broom to some of the dustier crannies of the Australian cricketing empire. After all, *Wisden Australia* is seven years old now, the age at which humans start to develop their adult teeth. We thought we'd do likewise.

CHRISTIAN RYAN
Editor

Contents

1 Comment

2 The Players

3 Records

4 International Summer

5 The Domestic Scene

Contents

6 Australians Abroad

7 History and Law

8 The Wisden Review

Opposite SLOG-SWEEPING ALL
BEFORE HIM: Steve Waugh holes out to
Sachin Tendulkar on the SCG fence,
his final stroke as a Test cricketer.
Picture by Chris McGrath, Getty Images.

1

Comment

Notes by the Editor

Let's begin at the endings. This was the year we farewelled four giants. Between them, they brought change that promises to reverberate down the decades (Steve Waugh) and a shimmering grace that was purely for the moment (Mark Waugh). They carried us on an exhilarating hide-behind-the-couch joyride (Michael Slater) and left us with an excruciating sense of wasted opportunity (Stuart Law). Or at least that's how the softies saw it. For the hardheads, they gave us 24,322 Test runs, 66 hundreds and 119 fifties at an average of 45.89. Take your pick; we will miss them either way.

Seldom have we known upheaval quite like it. In 1911-12 Clem Hill and Victor Trumper, the two punchiest strokeplayers of Australian cricket's first 80 years, played their final Tests. Neil Harvey and Alan Davidson bowed out together in 1962-63. In 1983-84 Dennis Lillee, Greg Chappell and Rod Marsh, one by agonising one, all called it quits within a month of each other. At the time we felt vulnerable and exposed. Compared with 2003-04, they were summers of grinding stability.

Matthew Hayden, with his violent 380 against Zimbabwe, reclaimed then relinquished the world batting record in the space of six months. Michael Bevan started the summer as the world's canniest limited-overs batsman and ended it no longer ranked among Australia's top 25. The domestic game lost curly Jo Angel and burly Darren Berry, its most productive fast bowler and wicket-keeper. The world lost David Hookes. Two new venues, Darwin and Cairns, were welcomed with a flurry of breathless press releases and a pair of less than breathtaking Test matches. At the time of writing there seems every chance that international cricket's newest playing fields are already being put out to pasture.

There were so many goings, in fact, that it was sometimes hard to appreciate the comings, the here and now. Bunged in the middle was a classic Test series for the ages between Australia and India, one buzzing with high drama and audacious batsmanship. It felt bunged in the middle partly because of all these side distractions. And it felt bunged in the middle partly because, well, it was bunged in the middle. It started December 4, ended January 6 and was all over in 34 sleeps.

Now, nobody is asking for a return to the mad old days when the players travelled by boat and an Ashes tour might take a year out of your life. Apart from anything, Glenn McGrath's tour diaries would be torture ("Woke up 6.15. Played deck quoits with Lucy the masseur for the 97th morning in a row."). But in the whirl of recent dust-storms involving bookies, diet pills and mobile phones, plus various others entirely unconnected with Shane Warne, we have lost sight of the bigger catastrophe. The disappearance of the five-Test series threatens to distort beyond recognition the shape of the game we cherish.

There is a simple reason why the five-Test series held sway for cricket's first century and a bit. It works. Five days make a Test and five Tests make a series. The first Test, ideally played on a bouncy or seaming wicket, involves a few nerves, a bit of luck and a lot of probing and poking and sussing each other out. During the second and third Tests the pitches flatten out, the players express themselves and spectators get a feel for their personalities, their idiosyncrasies. It is a time of artistry and attrition, of hard slog and delicious twists and cagey experimentation. It is the sweetest part in a way, with so much at stake yet so much time left, as if summer might linger forever.

The fourth and fifth Tests are tauter occasions. The pitches stay low and take spin, nerves and luck simmer back to the surface, injuries play their part, psychological gashes exposed in the earlier contests bleed for all to see. If it is a truly great series the fifth day of the fifth Test will begin with the outcome a mystery. It is made greater by all that has gone before. To take even one Test away is to upset this delicate balance. The tempo is shattered. A four-Test series and a five-Test series are as different as a square and a pentagon.

Worst of all is the two-Test series – either too short or too long and never just right. But the four-Test series, too, is a curiously unsatisfying beast. It has neither the jagged frenzy of three Tests nor the leisurely suspense of five. Last summer's was only the second four-Test series in Australia in 121 years. Here's hoping it was the last.

Admittedly there was a lot to like about it: the suppleness of V. V. S. Laxman, the unblinking unbowlability of Rahul Dravid and the willpower of Sachin Tendulkar; the vigour of Ricky Ponting's cover drive, the emotional willy-willy engulfing Steve Waugh and the furrowed brow of Stuart MacGill, furrowing more with every snap of the batsmen's wrists. What it lacked was ebb and flow, space to breathe. Rain in Brisbane effectively slashed it to a three-and-a-half-Test series. It did not merely leave us wanting more, as the best series do. It needed more.

Only when Australia play England are we now assured the unique thrill of a five-Test series. And beware the hardheads: with their calculators for brains and cash registers for hearts, they are plotting to take even that away from us. Cricket tampers with its own crazy, bewitching rhythms at its peril.

Time for a brake

What is needed is a Slow Cricket revolution. This has nothing to do with batsmen's run-rates; may the four-an-over juggernaut pioneered by Steve Waugh outlive even his beer-drenched, blood-soaked baggy green cap. It has everything to do with spectators' enjoyment rates. The Slow Cities movement in Europe invites participating cities to build more park benches and friendlier public transport. The Slow Food movement, encompassing more hours in the kitchen, is a riposte to McDonald's.

Slow Cricket is an antidote to McCricket – a rejection of back-to-back Tests, whistlestop tours, two- and four-Test series and all other dunderheaded attempts to jam Test cricket into a polystyrene carton and shove it down our throats as quickly as possible. It is about tasting and savouring the game's richest nuances. In 2004, Slow Cricket was altogether cheaper and easier to achieve – if only fleetingly – than either Slow Cities or Slow Food. All you had to do was switch on the telly when Warne was bowling.

A star is Warne

You often hear it said that Warne ain't the bowler he used to be. It is as if he hit his peak with the humungous leg-break that gazoodled Mike Gatting at Old Trafford in 1993 and has been in steady decline ever since. When did you last see him land a flipper? Does he even have a wrong'un? To suggest there is a lick of difference between his zooter, slider, toppie or back-spinner is considered rank gullibility; swallow that and you'll probably believe those two diet pills really were his mum's fault.

There is an element of truth in all that. Yet from this vantage point Warne, never easy to turn away from, was at his most unturnawayable in 2004. Like the great classical painters he stumbled upon the art of simplicity. More than ever he relied on his two oldest friends, his accuracy and his leg-break. Except that instead of one leg-break he had at least six. There was one that spun an inch, one that spun a foot and one that kept going and going and going. Then there was one drifting in, another sloping out and yet another that sailed gunbarrel straight until it cuffed the pitch. The genius lay in the way he seemed able to vary at will the precise degree of turn, taking chance out of cricket's chanciest occupation: that of the leg-spin bowler. His bowling has never been simpler, nor more effective, nor lovelier to look at.

It was tempting to suppose that his various nadirs were actually integral episodes of some masterplan. His shoulder and finger injuries made him focus on his leg-break. His 12-month ban for ingesting diuretics concentrated his mind and desire. In his first three Tests back, on hostile terrain, a laughing stock among many of his countrymen, he swept aside 26 Sri Lankan batsmen and made Muttiah Muralidaran look a novice by comparison. As comebacks go, this was without parallel.

Few Australians in any walk of life can have polarised opinion the way Warne does. Either he was "born for greatness" with "that coil-like wrist", as the 1950s leg-spinner Rex Sellers contends on page 70, or he is "a giant sleazy hamster with terrible hair", as a female colleague of mine suggested by email earlier this year. Indeed your gender tends to have a lot to do with what you think of him. So does your acquaintance with history. To condemn Warne for shooting off salacious text messages is to forget that cricketers have been known to flirt with pretty admirers and shag themselves silly on tour for decades. His cheap dig at Murali – that he specialises in bowling out bunnies on bunsens – was as graceless as his walk-up trot is graceful. But like all Warne's worst sins, it happened off the field. On it he brings sweet joy.

So long as he keeps spinning the cover off the ball, we'll keep putting him on our cover. He is not only the inaugural cover star of *Wisden Australia*; he is the cover star of our generation. May he bowl on till he's 50.

The neglectful billionaire

Unfortunately, switching on the telly when Warne was bowling sometimes brought nothing but irritation. Had you done so around 5.30 p.m. on July 13, 2004, the only highly paid superstar on display was a quiz show host called Larry, looking as happy as his name implies. The only spinning digits were those on a tacky electronic screen. Warne probed and pouted, sweated and slavered, after the one wicket he needed to equal the world record. And Channel Nine, after several minutes of addled to-ing and fro-ing, had ditched their cricket telecast and crossed to *The Price Is Right*.

The last Australian to hold the record was Dennis Lillee. Several hundred thousand men and women have an imperishable mental picture of Lillee angling wide of the crease and letting rip a leg-cutter outside off. Larry Gomes nibbled at it and Greg Chappell, hiding under a floppy white hat and ginger beard, crouched to his left and pouched the catch. Wicket No. 310 was his. Lillee's bald spot was combed over, his tight white shirt unbuttoned almost to his ribcage, gold chain bobbing in a forest of spidery chest hair. But there were no histrionics. He accepted his team-mates' hugs, slung his sweater over his shoulder and waltzed in a daze towards back-ward point, before realising he was supposed to be at fine leg and shuffling sheepishly in the opposite direction. Pure class.

Twenty-three years later, Warne followed in Lillee's footsteps. Nobody saw it. This was the kind of advertisement for cricket that money can't buy, worth more than all the marketing budgets and hi-tech academies and Kanga Cricket kits put together. Kerry Packer, Channel Nine's owner, had cost Australian cricket untold millions.

I spent most of last summer on the first floor of Packer's Castlereagh Street headquarters in Sydney, editing a magazine called *Inside Edge*. Cricket sometimes felt like an afterthought. Our editorial staff of four was dwarfed by our friends at *Rugby League Week* and the multitude of soft-core slap-and-tickle rags that twist spinifex-like throughout the building. But the Boss's favourite light reading, I was assured, the magazine he kept religiously beside the dunny, was not *Ralph* or *Picture* or *100% Home Girls*. It was *Inside Edge*. And at least Packer reckoned the summer game was worth celebrating, at a time when every other specialist sporting magazine is obsessed with how to renovate your four-wheel drive or improve your putting stroke. Cricket was in good hands here, I figured.

It is becoming less so. Until now, the relationship between crick-et and Packer has mostly been win-win. Packer sped up the arrival of night matches, helmets, big-screen replays and decent player salaries; cricket leant his network prestige and filled his pockets with advertising revenue. Packer's priority has only ever been his own prosperity, not cricket's. But so long as the two went hand in hand, all was hunky-dory.

In the past year, Packer has appeared happy to suck the game dry and give very little back. Channel Nine didn't just miss Warne's moment, it stubbornly refuses to air a half-hour evening highlights package for the hapless mugs who go to work or school. Channel Nine insisted on the ludicrously early 9.30 a.m. start to this year's Tests in Darwin and Cairns, rendering batting tricky and robbing those games of the in-built tension and anticipation that accompanies an 11 o'clock start. The reason, you guessed it, was to cram in a pre-news episode of *The Price Is Right*.

The price, increasingly, is too steep. It makes you wonder whom cricket belongs to: Packer or the people. Maybe it's time Cricket Australia reminded a certain billionaire who's really Boss.

Don't read all about it

With any luck, on that farcical lost evening of July 13, you fought off the urge to hurl the dog at the TV or ring Channel Nine's switchboard. "Only 20" punters did complain, say the network's publicity people, which seems about as plausible as Ricky Ponting scoring "only 20" runs against England this winter. Perhaps you contented yourself with switching the thing off. Never mind, you might have said, I'll read about it in the papers tomorrow. If so, more fool you.

A funny thing has happened to newspaper reports of Test matches in this country. They have stopped describing what happened. Narrative and drama are out. Prefabricated quotes and never-ending statistical drivel are in. And so we are told what Jason Gillespie said – "I'm happy with the way they're coming out" and "taking things six balls at a time" – but not where he bowled, how fast he was, whether he swung it or what he looked like. We are told how many fours Matthew Hayden hit – "whipped" is invariably the preferred cliché – but not where he hit them. To suggest this is what fans want is insane. It is like saying we'd rather read Wayne Carey than Peter Carey, Roland Perry than Ray Robinson.

It is not so much the fault of those in the press box, who love cricket and are chuffed to be eyewitnesses to history, but of the sports editors whose donkey-work they are carrying out. Cricket is treated not as a game but as a breaking news story. Alan McGilvray used to reckon the key to good radio commentary was to imagine you were describing the action to a blind person. A similar logic once applied to cricket writers; their mission was to inform, entertain and analyse, to paint a word picture. Now the newspapers may as well hire robots. They escort a tape recorder into the post-stumps press conference, pick out the raciest quotes and unload them on to their laptops. Maybe chuck in a couple of stats. Then hit send. The blind people McGilvray was talking about could do that themselves.

This frightening trend coincides, ironically, with the internet age. All winter long, a couple of mouse-clicks away, the best English match reporters offer wit, insight, variety and a theatrical flourish. Reading *The Guardian*'s Mike Selvey, elegant and steadfastly cynical, together with *The Sunday Telegraph*'s Scyld Berry, feisty and sagacious, is like devouring a tender sirloin and three veg. In India a pipeline of young scribes, housed at Wisden CricInfo's Mumbai office, polish their adjectives and serve up spicy, pungent finger-food in minutes. In Australia we get brussel sprouts.

It is possible that Australians have never played cricket more swashbucklingly than we do now. It is equally possible that we have never reported on it more tediously.

Careless talk

Still, there are worse things to be than boring. Being plain wrong, for starters. During Fox Sport's coverage of the Sri Lanka v Australia Test in Galle, Jeff Thomson was adamant that under the lbw law a batsman can never, ever be given out if the ball pitches outside off. And Thommo, lest we forget, used to be a bowler.

Bruce Yardley, quite earnestly, was urging Ponting to declare with Australia 260 ahead on a flat pitch with eight hours to go. Ranjit Fernando was gobsmacked that Damien Martyn's spot was in danger because "he's always been a magnificent player of spin bowling" – which was quite a scoop, especially to anyone who had ever seen Martyn bat at the SCG. Allan Border, in town as a national selector and earning a few TV bucks on the side, declined to say anything negative or interesting about anyone or anything, which made him an awfully nice bloke but an awful commentator. Geoff Lawson kept a dignified silence. He presumably thought he'd tripped up the wrong staircase and on to the set of a David Lynch movie.

It would be unfair to pick exclusively on Fox. One ABC radio commentator, all summer long, depicted Laxman and Dravid's success in terms of their "subcontinental wrist" – as if anyone born outside the subcontinent is disadvantaged by the mysterious absence of any kind of joint between their hand and arm. When Sri Lanka toured in the winter and Thilan Samaraweera uncoiled a cover drive, he was still at it: "There's that subcontinental wrist again." There's that queasy bit of unhelpful racial stereotyping again.

Amid such plodding and offensive mediocrity came a reminder of how good cricket commentary can be. Richie Benaud, still curling his bottom lip and uttering not a syllable he hasn't thought about first, witnessed his 500th Test when England played New Zealand at Lord's. Sadly, Benauds come along about as often as Bradmans. It would be foolish to wish for another. But there can be no excuse for employing a selector as a commentator, surely one of the game's uglier conflicts of interest. And it seems reasonable to hope for a commentary box that is not clogged with ex-players who have forgotten more than they ever knew. Worryingly, as mentioned at the top of these Notes, a whole new batch of retired cricketers are on the prowl, with time to kill and facts to murder.

Rats and mice

When a game involves five days of standing around interrupted by sporadic flurries of activity, it is only natural that we spend more time talking about what might happen than actually doing. In 2004 an unearthly number of hours whizzed by discussing two things that never eventuated: the two-Test series scheduled in Zimbabwe, and the likelihood of Muttiah Muralidaran touring Australia. So we'll keep this brief.

It is tempting to skip over Zimbabwe altogether, now that their athletes have competed in the Athens Olympics and their cricketers in September's Champions Trophy. If Australia failed the Zimbabwe test, then the world patently has too. Before we seek shelter in this logic, however, let's remember that it was an Australian commentator, Dean Jones, who said of Zimbabwe's thuggish, tyrannical president Robert Mugabe: "I'm just there to watch the cricket and I don't give a rat's arse what he does about his country." And it was Cricket Australia's public affairs manager, Peter Young, who said of the Zimbabwe tour: "We need to put it behind us, put a tick in that box." A tick in a box? Have Australian cricket administrators no heart, no moral existence at all?

Thuggery and tyranny are not necessarily sufficient reasons to cancel a cricket tour. A cricket tour can be a rainbow of hope in grim times. No, Australia should have stayed home because a brutal government hijacked the national cricket board, gatecrashed the selection panel and started picking a majority of players because they were black and not white. What was our response? Well, the players said it was a matter for Cricket Australia. Cricket Australia said it was a matter for the ICC. The ICC said it was a matter for the politicians. The politicians said it was a matter for the ICC. And so nobody did anything.

Except for Stuart MacGill, a leg-spinner, and the one active member of Australia's cricketing establishment who did give a rat's arse. Once it became evident that going to Zimbabwe meant playing against a team he may not have been eligible to play for because of the colour of his skin, MacGill pulled out. Darren Lehmann, in honour of his belated, unlikely and romantic international purple patch, is *Wisden Australia*'s Cricketer of the Year. Stuart MacGill is our Man of the Year. He didn't have much to beat.

An elbow and a cold shoulder

In England in July, Muttiah Muralidaran wore a tailor-made arm-brace comprised of plaster and steel rods, and bowled in front of five TV cameras. His intention, in his 13th year as a Test cricketer, was to demonstrate that he bowls with a straight arm. Although it was Murali's choice to do this, it was perhaps the most demeaning act any champion bowler has put himself through, the equivalent of John Merrick protesting to the world: "I am not an animal."

In fact, there is a direct cricketing precedent for this. In November 1900, the gifted Aboriginal fast bowler Jack Marsh was called for throwing on the first day of a trial game between NSW and a Colts Fifteen. On the second day he bowled with his right arm bandaged and in splints so that his elbow could not possibly bend at the point of delivery. Marsh, incidentally, was effectively hounded out of cricket and died at 42 after a street brawl outside a pub in Orange. For what it's worth Murali, steel rods and all, wheeled down off-breaks, top-spinners and doosras that day. Some hailed it as proof that he is not a chucker. More certainly, it was confirmation of how little progress we have made in resolving this issue humanely and rationally.

Murali's unusual bowling action and congenitally deformed arm makes determining whether or not he chucks a fuzzy matter. Deciding what to do about this is fuzzier still. What is clear is that anything, everything, should have been done to make sure he felt comfortable about touring Australia in July. Ultimately he elected not to because a couple of Australian umpires, a handful of Australian spectators and one Australian prime minister, John Howard, have said he throws the ball.

"We tried," James Sutherland, Cricket Australia's chief executive, tells a muck-raking Gideon Haigh on page 66, in an interview that scythes through the usual flim-flam shrouding cricket's beancounters. They did not try hard enough. Australia is the only cricketing nation Murali has felt compelled to stay away from. History will judge us accordingly.

U is for unloved

Flicking through the revised third edition of the *Macquarie* dictionary recently, I came across the following entry: **Grout** *noun* **Wally**, 1927-68, Australian Test cricketer. We truly live in a lucky country when a dependable Queensland backstop rates a mention in our national dictionary. Less happily, they gave his nickname as 'The Grix'. He was, of course, 'The Griz', shortened from 'Grizzler', and so-called because of his non-stop chuntering from behind the wicket. Please fix soonest.

Anyway, it set me wondering. Are bowlers, so often unloved and unsung while batsmen wallow in all the glory, under-represented in the dictionary too? Ten minutes of slapdash research later and the answer was a resounding yes. Discounting present-day players, only five of Australia's top 30 Test runscorers are deemed unworthy of entry in the *Macquarie*: Ian Redpath, Kim Hughes, Ian Healy, Graeme Wood and Colin McDonald. Yet no fewer than 12 of our 30 elite wicket-takers fail to make the cut: Graham McKenzie, Geoff Lawson, Terry Alderman, Bill Johnston, Hugh Trumble, Max Walker, Ashley Mallett, Bruce Yardley, Rodney Hogg, Bruce Reid, Paul Reiffel and Alan Connolly.

Some omissions are particularly vexing. Graham McKenzie, who took 246 Test wickets, misses out. William Mackenzie – a Canadian politician, apparently – gets in. There are seven Johnstons – including a jockey, a soccer star, a biologist, a soldier, a novelist and two confederate generals in the American Civil War – but no room for dear old Bill. David Frith, a devoted student of fast bowling, rates Johnston ("all knees and elbows") the equal of Ray Lindwall and Keith Miller.

We live in curious days. Australia could comfortably field three, maybe four, world-class batting line-ups. But if two of our leading bowlers tear hamstrings we are in an almighty fix. The national bowling drought is more striking in some places than others. In Perth, for example, you could once find a dozen muscular tearaways kicking up the sand on any suburban beach. Last season, four of Western Australia's grizzliest fast men were interstate blow-ins: Ben Edmondson, Brad Williams, John Taylor and Paul 'Blocker' Wilson. At the Gabba, Nathan Bracken became Australia's first left-arm quick to make his Test debut since Brendon Julian a decade earlier.

In an age when kids slog away their high-school years in the hope of sneaking into university and shoring up some kind of future, bowling should loom as the more attractive profession. Toss up three long-hops and you're still a shot at snaffling a wicket next ball. In batting, one mistake and you're on your bike – and that's assuming the umpire doesn't puncture your tyres first. Yet for some reason, our brightest young things are all becoming batsmen. This is more than a curiosity, actually. It is the single biggest threat to Australia's supremacy.

Instead of reversing this trend, the authorities are apparently determined to frighten away any person fool enough to flirt with bowling for a living. Last summer's pitches were flatter than Brett Lee's abdominal muscles. In the Pura Cup, 76 individual hundreds – the most ever in a domestic season – were hammered. In the ING Cup, batsmen were offered a bonus free hit whenever a bowler overstepped the popping crease. This seemed designed not merely to penalise bowlers but to mock them. Why not blindfold and dress them up in a grass-skirt, just to make doubly sure they get the message? Bowlers need hugging, not humiliating.

November pain

After Dick Hughes ("jazz pianist and vocalist") and Howard Hughes ("industrialist, aviator, film producer and eccentric") comes **Hughes**, **Mervyn Gregory** (*Merv*). The dictionary makes no mention, alas, of **Hughes**, **Kimberley John**. Back on Boxing Day 1981, this would have seemed unthinkable. On a damp MCG pitch, Kim Hughes had sliced and slugged 100 not out against the nastiest bowling attack ever assembled: Michael Holding, Andy Roberts, Joel Garner, Colin Croft. A fortnight later Merv, a 20-year-old hillbilly with a ridiculously long and convoluted run-up, made his Sheffield Shield debut in Geelong of all places. There seemed no doubt which Hughes was destined for dictionary notoriety. Little did we know.

But, then, who could have foreseen Kim Hughes's fate? November 26 marks the 20th anniversary of his resignation as Australian captain. His goodbye speech is remembered solely for the oddity that he never finished it; the tears were coming too hard and fast. Before giving up, though, he croaked out a farewell line bubbling with a jagged anguish rarely heard in cricketspeak today: "The constant criticism, speculation and innuendo by former players and a section of the media over the past four or five years have finally taken their toll."

It was a fair enough comment, although fault festered on all sides. Australia's selectors were wrong to appoint as captain such an ambitious but fragile youngster. Yet it was he who craved the job so desperately. It was Hughes who couldn't jet out of Heathrow soon enough after Australia thudded out of the 1983 World Cup. It was he who orchestrated the petulant blockathon in Pointe-á-Pierre in 1984 when, in protest at Trinidad & Tobago's refusal to declare, he opened the batting and unfurled two scoring shots in 24 overs.

What happened after November 26, 1984, is the forgotten tragedy. Hughes made 0, 2, 0 and 0. He was reduced to little more than a fluffy toy hanging from Joel Garner's rear-view mirror. He never played another Test. The 20th anniversary will probably pass largely unnoticed. But of all the Australian cricketers who have met with sticky ends, his was the squelchiest fall from grace of all.

And what grace he had. Like Stan McCabe, Hughes was famed for three out-of-this-world innings – that one at the MCG and two at Lord's, when he hit 117 and 84 and tonked Chris Old on to the top deck of the pavilion. He also creamed a fabulous 62 against England in Perth in 1982-83, and chiselled a headstrong 106 against Abdul Qadir on a fifth-day Adelaide pitch in 1983-84.

It was at Lord's that Patrick Eagar took perhaps the most ravishing photograph of an Australian batsman since George W. Beldam immortalised Trumper stepping out to drive in 1905. Hughes has advanced a couple of metres, bent down on his right knee and square cut – *square cut* – Mike Hendrick for four. His eyes are superglued to the ball, his tongue is sticking out, his baggy green is perfectly straight. Everything about him looks exquisitely symmetrical. A man who can play a shot like that deserves our undying affection, if not his own dictionary entry.

The jolly swagger man

Various stick-in-the-muds insist another 1980s dasher, the late David Hookes, was grossly over-glorified in the wake of his senseless death on a St Kilda street in January. They damn him as an average cricketer, someone who played fewer than two-dozen Tests and contributed only 34 runs an innings. This is to let the stats get in the way of a good story. Hookes, the batsman, was a peculiar mix of arrogance and innocence. He had straggly blond hair, a fantastic eye, amazing timing and no fear.

His weakness was footwork, or a lack thereof – a couple of abrupt, jittery, mini-goosesteps, then wham! Perversely, this only added to his attraction. His untutored technique and the fact he didn't give a fig about statistics made him a throwback, of sorts, to a more ramshackle age. So did his love of clobbering sixes, like some left-handed, 20th-century George Bonnor. Three months after Hookes died, the lumberjack-like New Zealander Chris Cairns broke Viv Richards's world record of 84 Test sixes. Cairns did it in half as many games – 60 to 121 – as Viv. Had Hookes played 60 Tests he might have run Cairns close.

Alas, he was granted only 23 matches. Summoned for the Ashes summer of 1982-83, he responded with consecutive knocks of 56, 28, 66 not out, 37, 53, 68, 17, 19 and 143 not out. It was not just how many but how; each of these innings had a jolly swagger about it, culminating in a century in a session in Kandy. His reward was exile. Between February 1983 and October 1985, with Hookes at his free-swinging peak and the national XI in the doghouse, he did not play a single home Test. Few Australian cricketers can have been so shabbily mishandled. Lawrie Sawle – later heralded as a prime architect of Australia's renaissance – was then starting out as a junior selector. Which goes to show that Sawle, like Hookes, wasn't perfect.

It is true that the media beat up both the story and significance of his death. But this says more about the voraciousness of 24-hour rolling news networks and mushrooming newspaper supplements than it does about him or us. Hookes was miles better than average – and his average.

They've got to urn it

Cricket hovers at the cusp of a heavenly, unprecedented trinity: a strong Australia, India and England. Listen to the gibberish of excitable Poms and you'd think the day had arrived already, that the 2005 Ashes are as good as England's. That's what winning seven out of eight Tests against West Indies will do for you. As a book of record, it is our sober duty to point out that Australia have won nine of their past 10 Tests against those same downtrodden opponents. The reaction was not national hysteria but to wonder what the blazes went wrong in Antigua.

At the risk of stating the bleeding obvious, we confidently assert that when Australia play England in July, Andrew Flintoff and Marcus Trescothick will be pegged flatfooted to the crease. Andrew Strauss will discover that teeing off against Edwards, Collymore and Bravo is no rehearsal for seeing off Gillespie, McGrath and Warne. Michael Vaughan's scudding cover drive will pick out the man at extra cover as unerringly as it evaded him two summers ago. Graham Thorpe, missing from 13 of the past 15 Ashes Tests, will again go AWOL against crunch opponents. Ashley Giles will neither rip nor bounce it enough to bother inventive Australian batsmen. The selectors will get in a muddle over whether to pick a batsman-keeper, a keeper-batsman or scuttle back to Alec Stewart. Steve Harmison will be found to be only human. Heaven will have to wait till 2006–07.

Accelerate, regenerate

The clue to another radical, more imminent, transformation can be found on page 967. On February 17, Australia play their first Twenty20 international in Auckland. On June 13, they play another in Southampton. It is possible that one-day cricket as we know it will henceforth shrivel up and disappear.

The appeal of 20-overs-a-side cricket hinges on the flaw of 50-overs cricket, which is that from overs 16 to 45 the bowlers cease trying to take wickets and the batsmen satisfy themselves with nudging ones and twos into massive open expanses. Twenty20 eradicates those 60 mind-curdling overs, keeps the 40 potentially interesting ones, makes every ball count and saves four hours. If Steve Waugh could trade his 325 limited-overs internationals for 325 bite-size bash-fests he would get nearly two months of his life back.

Which invites a new quandary: what to do with all that spare time. Here's a thought. When two high-quality Test sides are scheduled to meet, let's offer them a full five Tests – not four, not three and sure as heck not two – to joust and express themselves. Maybe even give them a breather between games. And play a warm-up match or two. Who'd have imagined it? Fast Cricket saves Slow Cricket. In times of change, cricket's capacity to renew itself is a reassuring constant.

The hurricane hundred

by CHARLES DAVIS

Statistics, it is often said, never tell the whole story. But headway is being made. A long-standing challenge to statisticians is to venture beyond the basics, to better reflect the reasons why cricket is appreciated and remembered. An important but previously elusive dimension in assessing batting careers – the speed of scoring – is now coming into range.

The list over the page is the first serious undertaking in history to calculate the all-time 100 fastest runscorers in Test cricket. It is frequently claimed that Test batting has never been more aggressive and dynamic than it is today, thanks to better bats, smaller grounds, the wider armament of strokes imported from the one-day game and the winning-is-everything ethos of Steve Waugh's Australians. To some extent our top 100 backs this theory up: Adam Gilchrist, sprinting along at 81.9 runs per 100 balls, comes out on top as the most buccaneering batsman in Test history.

No fewer than 30 of the fastest 100 are on the Test scene today. Four of them – Gilchrist, India's Virender Sehwag, England's Andrew Flintoff and Sri Lanka's Sanath Jayasuriya – rank among the top 10. And yet if we strip away the 1,000-run/2,000-ball minimum qualification the swiftest batsman of them all was Gilbert Jessop, that legend of English county cricket. Sadly he only occasionally brought his genius to bear in Test cricket, scoring 569 runs and spending fewer than nine hours at the crease during his 13-year Test career. But while he was out there he scored at a staggering 112 runs per 100 balls, a rate never matched since. And he was doing it a century ago.

Indeed, nestled among some of the familiar modern names are a handful of old-time batsmen who may need some introduction. At No. 4, the South African Jimmy Sinclair is lesser known than most. He was a man of many remarkable feats – not least being his escape from a Boer War prison camp. During his white-knuckle 104 against Australia in Cape Town in 1902-03, he hit 34 runs off two overs; at one stage he smashed more than 50 runs off about 18 balls.

Re-smiting history: Adam Gilchrist, fastest batsman ever.

TEST CRICKET'S FASTEST RUNSCORERS

	Career	Runs per 100 balls	Total runs	Average
1. A. C. Gilchrist (Aus)	1999-	81.9	3,485	52.80
2. Kapil Dev (Ind)	1978-94	80–81	5,248	31.05
3. M. W. Tate (Eng)	1924-35	75–76	1,198	25.48
4. J. H. Sinclair (SAf)	1896-1911	73–74	1,069	23.23
5. V. Sehwag (Ind)	2001-	73.1	1,951	52.72
6. A. Flintoff (Eng)	1998-	69.4	2,012	32.98
7. I. V. A. Richards (WI)	1974-91	68–69	8,540	50.23
8. V. T. Trumper (Aus)	1899-1912	67–68	3,163	39.04
9. S. T. Jayasuriya (SL)	1991-	64.6	5,964	41.70
10. K. Srikkanth (Ind)	1981-92	64–65	2,062	29.88
11. M. L. Hayden (Aus)	1994-	63.5	5,059	58.14
12. I. D. S. Smith (NZ)	1980-92	63.2	1,815	25.56
13. S. M. Patil (Ind)	1980-84	63–64	1,588	36.93
14. G. C. Smith (SAf)	2002-	62.1	2,350	57.31
15. D. S. Lehmann (Aus)	1998-	61.6	1,549	51.63
16. D. G. Bradman (Aus)	1928-48	60–61	6,996	99.94
17. J. M. Gregory (Aus)	1920-28	60–61	1,146	36.96
18. S. J. McCabe (Aus)	1930-38	60–61	2,748	48.21
19. R. S. Kaluwitharana (SL)	1992-	60.8	1,867	26.67
20. I. T. Botham (Eng)	1977-92	60.7	5,200	33.54
21. F. E. Woolley (Eng)	1909-34	60–61	3,283	36.07
22. B. C. Lara (WI)	1990-	60.0	10,094	52.84
23. L. Klusener (SAf)	1996-	59.8	1,906	32.86
24. C. H. Lloyd (WI)	1966-85	59–60	7,515	46.67
25. E. D. Weekes (WI)	1948-58	59–60	4,455	58.61
26. Habibul Bashar (Ban)	2000-	58.9	2,079	35.84
27. V. G. Kambli (Ind)	1993-95	58.7	1,084	54.20
28. F. M. Engineer (Ind)	1961-75	58–59	2,611	31.08
29. C. G. Macartney (Aus)	1907-26	58–59	2,131	41.78
30. C. Hill (Aus)	1896-1912	58–59	3,412	39.21
31. L. R. D. Mendis (SL)	1982-88	58–59	1,329	31.64
32. R. A. McLean (SAf)	1951-64	58–59	2,120	30.28
33. A. L. Logie (WI)	1983-91	58–59	2,470	35.79
34. R. A. Duff (Aus)	1902-05	57–58	1,317	35.59
35. R. T. Ponting (Aus)	1995-	57.8	6,086	54.33
36. M. Azharuddin (Ind)	1984-2000	57–58	6,215	45.03
37. R. J. Hadlee (NZ)	1973-90	57–58	3,124	27.16
38. R. L. Dias (SL)	1982-87	57–58	1,285	36.71
39. D. W. Hookes (Aus)	1977-85	57–58	1,306	34.36
40. C. L. Cairns (NZ)	1989-2004	57.1	3,320	33.53
41. R. G. Pollock (SAf)	1963-70	56–57	2,256	60.97
42. Saeed Anwar (Pak)	1990-2001	55.8	4,052	45.52
43. C. D. McMillan (NZ)	1997-	55.5	3,046	40.07
44. Aamir Sohail (Pak)	1992-2000	55.3	2,823	35.28
45. Zaheer Abbas (Pak)	1969-85	55–56	5,062	44.79
46. D. T. Lindsay (SAf)	1963-70	54–55	1,130	37.66
47. Asif Iqbal (Pak)	1964-80	54–55	3,575	38.85
48. J. Darling (Aus)	1894-1905	54–55	1,657	28.56
49. C. H. Gayle (WI)	2000-	54.3	3,035	38.41
50. S. R. Tendulkar (Ind)	1989-	54.3	9,470	57.39
51. K. C. Sangakkara (SL)	2000-	54.1	3,188	49.04

	Career	Runs per 100 balls	Total runs	Average
52. T. G. Evans (Eng)	1946-59	53–54	2,439	20.49
53. C. L. Walcott (WI)	1948-60	53–54	3,798	56.68
54. M. E. Trescothick (Eng)	2000-	53.5	3,982	42.81
55. M. J. Slater (Aus)	1993-2001	53.3	5,312	42.83
56. S. M. Nurse (WI)	1960-69	53–54	2,523	47.60
57. Inzamam-ul-Haq (Pak)	1992-	53.2	6,899	49.63
58. J. L. Langer (Aus)	1993-	52.8	5,488	44.98
59. G. S. Sobers (WI)	1954-74	52–53	8,032	57.78
60. W. Bardsley (Aus)	1909-26	52–53	2,469	40.47
61. Wasim Akram (Pak)	1985-2002	52–53	2,898	22.64
62. M. E. Waugh (Aus)	1991-2002	52.3	8,029	41.81
63. Wasim Raja (Pak)	1973-85	52–53	2,821	36.16
64. R. R. Lindwall (Aus)	1946-60	51–52	1,502	21.15
65. P. V. Simmons (WI)	1988-97	51.8	1,002	22.26
66. G. S. Chappell (Aus)	1970-84	51–52	7,110	53.86
67. M. P. Vaughan (Eng)	1999-	51.7	3,777	45.50
68. M. V. Boucher (SAf)	1997-	51.6	2,782	30.91
69. G. A. Faulkner (SAf)	1906-24	51–52	1,754	40.79
70. D. P. M. D. Jayawardene (SL)	1997-	51.6	4,633	49.28
71. K. R. Stackpole (Aus)	1966-74	51–52	2,807	37.42
72. D. R. Martyn (Aus)	1992-	51.5	2,875	47.13
73. A. J. Lamb (Eng)	1982-92	51.4	4,656	36.09
74. H. H. Gibbs (SAf)	1996-	51.3	4,697	48.42
75. J. B. Hobbs (Eng)	1908-30	51–52	5,410	56.94
76. S. Abid Ali (Ind)	1967-74	51–52	1,018	20.36
77. Moin Khan (Pak)	1990-	51.2	2,735	29.09
78. V. S. Ransford (Aus)	1907-12	51–52	1,211	37.84
79. S. M. Pollock (SAf)	1995-	50.9	2,932	32.57
80. F. S. Jackson (Eng)	1893-1905	50–51	1,415	48.79
81. K. D. Walters (Aus)	1965-81	50–51	5,357	48.26
82. D. I. Gower (Eng)	1978-92	50.6	8,231	44.25
83. S. B. Styris (NZ)	2002-	50.5	1,072	42.88
84. P. A. de Silva (SL)	1984-2002	50–51	6,361	42.97
85. C. L. Hooper (WI)	1987-2002	50.2	5,762	36.46
86. C. J. Barnett (Eng)	1933-48	50–51	1,098	35.41
87. V. V. S. Laxman (Ind)	1996-	50.0	3,584	46.54
88. S. C. Williams (WI)	1994-2002	50.0	1,183	24.14
89. Intikhab Alam (Pak)	1959-77	49–50	1,493	22.28
90. C. G. Greenidge (WI)	1974-91	49–50	7,558	44.72
91. R. N. Harvey (Aus)	1948-63	49–50	6,149	48.41
92. R. B. Kanhai (WI)	1957-74	49–50	6,227	47.53
93. A. Ranatunga (SL)	1982-2000	49–50	5,105	35.69
94. I. A. Healy (Aus)	1988-99	49.7	4,356	27.39
95. Salim Malik (Pak)	1982-99	49–50	5,768	43.69
96. Younis Khan (Pak)	2000-	49.7	1,680	37.33
97. Majid Khan (Pak)	1964-83	49–50	3,931	38.92
98. B. F. Butcher (WI)	1958-69	49–50	3,104	43.11
99. G. A. Gooch (Eng)	1975-95	49.5	8,900	42.58
100. S. Madan Lal (Ind)	1974-86	49–50	1,042	22.65

Qualification: min 1,000 runs or 2,000 balls faced in Tests, batting average over 20. Where career data for balls faced is less than 100% complete, a rounded result to within one run is given. Data for minutes batted is over 90% complete in the great majority of cases, 100% in most. Data to October 1, 2004.

Chasing leather that day was Victor Trumper, who features at No. 7. Since Trumper, only Viv Richards has ever sustained a better scoring rate at a higher batting average over a full career. It has been said, too often perhaps, that statistics can never measure Trumper's genius. But here, for the first time, we are getting a statistical indication of the qualities that set him apart.

The top 100 is the product of many hours of detective work and countless more hours spent slogging through old match reports and scorebooks. These days, complete information on the balls faced and time batted by every batsman is easily accessible for modern Tests. But balls faced, as a statistic, took a long time – about a century, in fact – to catch on. The legendary Australian scorer Bill Ferguson gave a complete set of balls faced in his 1909 and 1910-11 scorebooks. Apparently no one took any interest so he stopped calculating it thereafter. The statistic only came into widespread use – and then only in some countries – in the 1970s. As recently as the mid-1980s some official scorebooks in England still did not include balls faced.

To make matters worse, many old Test scorebooks have been lost. Others were thrown away. Even the tied Test in Brisbane of 1960-61, between Australia and West Indies, has no known scorebook still in existence. But much survives. An important aim of my research is to bring to light the hidden archives, to allow us to look at old Test matches with the same detail and clarity that we expect from modern records. As more and more Test cricket passes from living memory, this seems a worthwhile goal.

It is remarkable how much historical information can be reconstructed. For all the old scorebooks that have been lost, many others can still be found, some in large archives such as at Lord's or the SCG, others scattered around the libraries at various Test match grounds. Some are in private hands; Jack Cameron, the ABC's Melbourne scorer, has a complete set of MCG Test and first-class scores dating back to the 1950s, many of which are unique now that the official scorebooks have vanished.

When balls have not been recorded, or when no original scorebook is available – which is true of roughly one-quarter of the 1,712 Tests played since 1877 – it is still possible to estimate balls faced. This is done by taking into account the number of minutes batted and applying the prevailing over-rate for each innings. The word *estimate* should be emphasised here – but it is far, far more accurate than might be expected.

For instance, calculating balls faced based on time and over-rates relies on the assumption that each batsman receives 50% of the strike. We know from personal experience that many individual innings do not follow this pattern. However, when averaged out over a whole career any variations tend to balance out. An analysis of leading batsmen since 1998 shows that nearly all average between 48% and 52% of the strike, and a large majority between 49-51%. There is no reason to believe it was any different in earlier eras. Even Don Bradman, who was often accused of hogging the strike, usually averaged 51%. (Interestingly one of Bradman's chief accusers, Jack Fingleton, apparently failed to notice during their record 346-run stand against England in 1936-37 that it was Fingleton who dominated the strike – 58% to 42%. Bradman still scored twice as many runs.)

For some of the early Tests in Australia and South Africa, where the scorebooks are long lost, extraordinary detail can be found in contemporary match reports. Every scoring stroke, and nearly every over, is described. The reports of the very first Test at the MCG in 1877 – which appeared in *The Age*, Melbourne's *Daily Telegraph* and other sources – make an over-by-over reconstruction possible (albeit time-consuming!). This allows educated estimates of balls faced to be made for each batsman. Charles Bannerman, for example, faced about 330 deliveries in his historic 165 not out in the first Test innings. Until now, that figure had remained a mystery.

Ultimately, reliable measures of batting speed have been obtained for more than 98% of all individual Test innings, with up to 75% directly measured in balls faced and the balance estimated from batting times. For some batsmen, notably those from Pakistan in the 1970s and 80s, the percentages are lower. But in every single case there is still a large and representative majority of innings covered. All major batsmen have over 80% career coverage. All those in the Top 25 have better than 90%. The majority have 100%.

The research confirms that today's overall scoring speeds surpass those of Test cricket's previous sustained high point, around 1910 to 1912, during the so-called Golden Age. Some of the amazing feats of earlier years now seem slightly less impressive. Nobody has equalled Bradman's feat of scoring 309 runs in a single day at Leeds in 1930. But 419 balls were bowled at Bradman during that one day – far more than any modern batsman could hope for with the sluggish over-rates of recent decades.

It is fair to say that Gilchrist, taking both batting average and scoring speed into account, is the most dynamic batsman the game has ever seen. One advantage he has, as with Richards in the 1980s, is that he plays in a supremely dominant side. Seldom is he exposed to predicaments demanding fierce resistance or stout defence. But even so, Gilchrist's response to such situations is invariably aggressive. His maiden Test century, 149 off 163 balls against Pakistan to salvage a draw from a fourth-innings crisis in Hobart, is a fine example. Time will tell whether Gilchrist can sustain his pace – a spell out of form could change his outlook, as it might for fellow high-flyers Sehwag and Graeme Smith. But for now his career appears to be on a unique trajectory.

Jessop is not the only famed big-hitter to narrowly miss out on qualification for the top 100. Others include the powerful 19th-century Australian batsman Jack Lyons (68 runs per 100 balls), the graceful West Indian Learie Constantine (82) and the stump-smashing, ball-bashing fast bowler 'Tibby' Cotter (89). The research also uncovers one other batsman of Jessopian potential. In the few Tests played by India in the 1930s, the all-rounder Ladha Amar Singh achieved a scoring rate comparable to Jessop, including an innings of 44 in 26 minutes at The Oval in 1936. However, his opportunities were few – he was limited to 292 Test runs at an average of 22.46 – and he died six months before his 30th birthday.

The other extreme, of course, is the stonewaller batsman. The following list reveals the 12 slowest batsmen in Test history:

THE DAWDLING DOZEN

	Career	Runs per 100 balls	Total runs	Average
1. A. C. Bannerman (Aus)	1879-93	22–23	1,108	23.08
2. W. H. Scotton (Eng)	1881-87	22–23	510	22.17
3. G. O. Rabone (NZ)	1949-55	23–24	562	31.22
4. T. J. Franklin (NZ)	1983-91	26.4	828	23.00
5. T. E. Bailey (Eng)	1949-59	26–27	2,290	29.74
6. A. J. Pithey (SAf)	1957-65	26–27	819	31.50
7. R. G. Barlow (Eng)	1881-87	27–28	591	22.73
8. T. W. Jarvis (NZ)	1965-73	27–28	625	29.76
9. Asif Mujtaba (Pak)	1986-97	28.6	928	24.42
10. J. W. Burke (Aus)	1951-59	28–29	1,280	34.59
11. C. B. Van Ryneveld (SAf)	1951-58	28–29	724	26.81
12. J. M. Brearley (Eng)	1976-81	29.8	1,442	22.88

Qualification as per main table. Data for Barlow and Scotton is only 86-88% complete.
Slowest present-day batsman (min 1,000 runs): G. W. Flower (Zim) 34.5 runs per 100 balls.

The above list contains several of the usual suspects, including those notorious slow-coaches of the 1880s: Australia's Alec Bannerman and England's William Scotton. One of the most exciting discoveries of this project was a fragile old scorebook, unearthed at Cricket NSW, detailing a previously overlooked record from the Sydney Test of 1891-92. It shows that Bannerman, in one of the most extraordinary Test innings ever played, defied the England attack for 620 balls in scoring just 91 runs. For perspective, consider that the slowest century by any Australian is the 378 balls it took Bill Woodfull to reach three figures against England at the MCG in 1928-29; or that Matthew Hayden needed only 437 deliveries to reach 380 against Zimbabwe last year. For prolonged immobility, Bannerman's innings has no parallel in Test history. He was also capable of what might be called stonewalling "cameos", such as facing more than 220 balls for 19 runs in a Test at the SCG in 1886-87 or, with Bill Murdoch, blocking his way through 22 consecutive (four-ball) maiden overs at the MCG in 1882-83.

Tenacity such as Bannerman's can have its uses. After all, Australia came from 163 runs behind to win that aforementioned SCG Test of 1891-92. The speed database can also be used to identify the batsmen most difficult to dismiss by calculating the average number of balls between dismissals (BBD). It makes for an interesting list. While Bradman's position at No. 1 will surprise no one, the narrowness of his lead over the imperturbable English opener Herbert Sutcliffe might shock a few people. The leading positions, logically enough, are mostly occupied by slow scorers with high averages. Modern-day players do not figure prominently, although Rahul Dravid confirms his reputation as the most valuable wicket in world cricket today. And Dravid's is an increasingly valuable scalp: his last 2,000 Test runs have come at a BBD rate of 175, which is better than Bradman.

THE 20 ULTIMATE UNBOWLABLES

	Career	Balls between dismissals	Total runs	Runs per 100 balls
1. D. G. Bradman (Aus)	1928-48	164	6,996	60–61
2. H. Sutcliffe (Eng)	1924-35	163	4,555	37–38
3. B. Mitchell (SAf)	1929-49	151	3,471	31–32
4. S. G. Barnes (Aus)	1938-48	149	1,072	42–43
5. D. R. Jardine (Eng)	1928-34	147	1,296	32–33
6. L. Hutton (Eng)	1937-55	145	6,971	38–39
7. K. F. Barrington (Eng)	1955-68	141	6,806	41–42

	Career	Balls between dismissals	Total runs	Runs per 100 balls
8. C. A. Davis (WI)	1968-73	139	1,301	38–39
9. G. O. Rabone (NZ)	1949-55	139	562	23–24
10. G. A. Headley (WI)	1930-54	139	2,190	43–44
11. R. Dravid (Ind)	1996-	137	6,855	42.5
12. G. M. Turner (NZ)	1969-83	136	2,991	32–33
13. W. M. Woodfull (Aus)	1926-34	136	2,300	33–34
14. G. Boycott (Eng)	1964-82	134	8,114	35–36
15. Hanif Mohammad (Pak)	1952-69	133	3,915	33–34
16. J. F. Reid (NZ)	1979-86	132	1,296	34–35
17. E. Paynter (Eng)	1931-39	131	1,540	45–46
18. C. A. G. Russell (Eng)	1920-23	130	910	43–44
19. J. H. Kallis (SAf)	1995-	129	5,967	41.8
20. W. R. Hammond (Eng)	1927-47	128	7,249	45–46

Qualification as per main table.

At the other end of the scale, the player with the shortest average innings (minimum 2,000 career runs) is none other than Shane Warne with a BBD of 30. The prominence of old-timers in both the slowest and most tenacious lists is another hint of how the game has changed. If it is difficult enough to imagine any batsman beating Bradman's 974 runs in a single Test series, then Hammond's 2,527 balls faced in the 1928-29 Ashes series – including 977 balls in one match in Adelaide – is utterly beyond modern reach. Modern players are far less likely to play sustained defensive innings.

This final list focuses on the major runscorers of Test history, those with 5,000 or more runs, who failed to make the top 100:

LAST BUT NOT LEAST

	Career	Runs per 100 balls	Total runs	Average
111. A. J. Stewart (Eng)	1990-2003	48.7	8,463	39.54
113. S. R. Waugh (Aus)	1985-2004	48.6	10,927	51.06
121. R. B. Richardson (WI)	1983-95	47.8	5,949	44.39
129. Javed Miandad (Pak)	1976-93	47–48	8,832	52.57
143. G. P. Thorpe (Eng)	1993-	46.3	6,349	44.39
150. W. R. Hammond (Eng)	1927-47	45–46	7,249	58.45
165. G. R. Viswanath (Ind)	1969-83	45–46	6,080	41.93
169. S. M. Gavaskar (Ind)	1971-87	44–45	10,122	51.12
170. M. D. Crowe (NZ)	1982-95	44.7	5,444	45.36
174. I. M. Chappell (Aus)	1964-80	44–45	5,345	42.42
176. D. L. Haynes (WI)	1978-94	44–45	7,487	42.29
197. D. B. Vengsarkar (Ind)	1976-92	43–44	6,868	42.13
202. S. P. Fleming (NZ)	1994-	43.5	5,335	38.65
203. G. Kirsten (SAf)	1993-	43.4	7,289	45.27
220. D. C. S. Compton (Eng)	1937-57	42–43	5,807	50.06
225. R. Dravid (Ind)	1996-	42.5	6,855	58.09

	Career	Balls between dismissals	Total runs	Average
226. S. Chanderpaul (WI)	1994-	42.5	5,192	44.37
241. J. H. Kallis (SAf)	1995-	41.8	5,967	53.75
244. K. F. Barrington (Eng)	1955-68	41–42	6,806	58.67
250. M. A. Taylor (Aus)	1989-99	41.5	7,525	43.49
259. A. R. Border (Aus)	1978-94	41–42	11,174	50.56
263. D. C. Boon (Aus)	1984-96	41.0	7,422	43.65
272. N. Hussain (Eng)	1990-2004	40.4	5,764	37.18
275. M. C. Cowdrey (Eng)	1954-75	40–41	7,624	44.06
300. L. Hutton (Eng)	1937-55	38–39	6,971	56.67
322. W. M. Lawry (Aus)	1961-71	38–39	5,234	47.15
336. J. H. Edrich (Eng)	1963-76	37–38	5,138	43.54
338. M. A. Atherton (Eng)	1989-2001	37.3	7,728	37.69
371. G. Boycott (Eng)	1964-82	35–36	8,114	47.72
373. J. G. Wright (NZ)	1978-93	35–36	5,334	37.82

Qualification: 5,000 runs.

Some of the batsmen and rankings here are reassuringly pre-dictable: Bill Lawry at No. 322; Geoff Boycott at No. 371. Others are more surprising. Who would have thought that Denis Compton and Ken Barrington, one a dasher and the other a grafter by reputation, would score at such a similar clip? In truth, Compton's cavalier image obscured the fact that he often scored quite slowly; in Adelaide in 1946-47 he faced 703 balls for his 147 and 103 not out. In his golden year of 1947, Compton's 1,159 runs came at a relatively undramatic 46 runs per 100 balls.

Readers who care to study these tables may find other bizarre twists. Some may even be sceptical, remembering that old saw about lies and statistics. But these figures, even if they still do not tell the whole story, are at least free from preconception. They analyse batsmen as they really were, in every innings, not just the moments we care to remember them by. Ultimately the figures are satisfying in that they provide a good mix of the expected and unexpected. If statistics never surprised us, they could never be so fascinating.

Charles Davis is a Melbourne-based cricket writer and scientist – not to be confused with Charlie Davis, West Indies' most unbowlable batsman.

Forgiven, not forgotten

by JOHN HARMS

It is now 20 years since Kim Hughes led a so-called rebel Australian cricket team on two tours of South Africa. Outswingers still beat the bat, umpires remain loath to give lbw decisions and a whack in the protector still brings tears to your eyes. What has changed is our acceptance of cricket as a commercial enterprise and of cricketers as sellers of their talents. The other thing that has changed is our understanding that the game does not exist outside the political process. Indeed, it never has.

Back then, though, the legacy of more than a century of cricket folklore – however imagined – held firm. In the minds of traditionalists, cricketers were not professional craftsmen who plied their trade; they were men who represented their country. The Australian cricket team was not an enterprise which employed and paid its players; it was an apotheosis of Australian nationhood. Players represented their country the way schoolboys represent their school, as if the institution had some hold over them and they some commitment to it. Or if they didn't, they should.

And so a lot of mud was thrown at the 16 Australian cricketers who chose to tour South Africa. Cricket as run by the Australian Cricket Board was deemed official and legitimate. Hughes and his men were labelled rebels; worse than that, they were mercenaries, willing to forego any moral obligation for a bag of silver. They had turned their backs not only on the Australian cricket team but on the international sporting boycotts in place at the time. Some saw it as a crime against the nation. Others were convinced that sport and politics should always be kept separate.

Now we are more savvy, more suspicious, more alert to the reality that everyone and everything – cricket included – has a political dimension. Now, then, is an appropriate time to revisit those two tours of South Africa. They involved so many people: players, administrators, media proprietors, politicians, the general public. Each individual had his own motives, aspirations, justifications and rationalisations. Yet the spotlight, at the time, fell strictly on the rebels.

Didn't they abhor South Africa's apartheid regime? Didn't they realise their presence might equate to support for an oppressive government? How could they defy their own government, their country, their team-mates, for the sake of money? Twenty years on, as the reflections of some of the protagonists reveal, the situation was much more complex than that. It was more complicated than many of us acknowledged at the time.

This story begins in the 1970s, with Dr Ali Bacher a key figure and South African cricket in an awkward position. Banned from international competition in 1970, they looked to have no chance of returning so long as the country's apartheid policies remained in place. Bacher, as a white citizen, was on the advantaged side of the apartheid divide. Like anyone, he was a product of the culture in which he grew up. He was also an intelligent man with critical faculties, who could adopt or resist the cultural forces at work.

But Bacher had little interest in politics. What motivated him was cricket. For Bacher, the principal issue was not the morality of a sinister system that denied basic civil rights to a majority of the population on the basis of race; it was whether banning a nation from Test cricket was in any way a catalyst to reform that society. If anything, he believed the playing of cricket could work for good.

In the very year they were banned, Bacher captained South Africa to a 4–0 whitewash of Australia. They were a brilliant, talented, aggressive team. Yet by the early 1980s he was adamant that unless players could compete against Test-quality rivals, South African cricket would atrophy; indeed, he thought it would die. He refused to let that happen. He loved cricket too much. The only option was for South Africa to organise their own tours, with neither the ratification nor the blessing of international authorities.

Bacher phoned Tony Greig and asked whether he could assemble a team of elite Australian cricketers. Greig had been employed by Kerry Packer since the World Series Cricket days; if he wanted to keep his job, he could not get involved. But Greig did suggest that Bruce Francis, the former New South Wales and Australian Test opener, might help out.

Francis and Greig were good friends. It was Francis who brought Greig out to Australia to play for Sydney club team Waverley. They had made their Test debuts together at Old Trafford in 1972 and toured Rhodesia (now Zimbabwe) with an international Wanderers side. Francis also played in South Africa in 1973 with Derrick

Robins' XI, a team which included the black West Indian John Shepherd, who was unable to enter white restaurants until dispensation was granted by the government. "I was totally opposed to apartheid at that time," Francis says now, "but you rationalise what you want to rationalise. I was keen to be selected for Australia, so I was probably more conscious of the reasons why I should be playing rather than why I shouldn't be."

Francis made regular visits to South Africa and built many friendships, particularly with Joe Pamensky, a member of the South African Cricket Union's executive. He admired the commitment of men like Pamensky and Bacher to preserving South African cricket. He was intelligent, articulate and capable. Although he understood the arguments of idealists, and was often sympathetic to them, he existed in the world of realpolitik. His economics degree from Sydney University included a major in political science. The hot social issues during his undergraduate days were war in Vietnam and apartheid in South Africa, and he had come to regard himself as a student of South African politics and history. He spent hours every day reading South African newspapers. "From about 1977 I believed South Africa would have to embark on rebel tours," Francis explains. "And I believed that I would be the person who would coordinate and facilitate them from this end."

Francis had no moral problem with organising a cricket tour and so he agreed to help. He knew that what the world wanted was a non-racial political system in South Africa, based on a one-man, one-vote democracy, and that this would make his task difficult – but not impossible. The first moves were made during the 1983 World Cup in England. It was all very secretive. Bacher asked a number of Australian cricketers to visit him in the Mayfair flat where he was staying. He suggested they come in pairs and incognito. Kepler Wessels promptly turned up in his Australian blazer. Despite his initial indiscretion Wessels, with his links to both countries, was later to play an instrumental role in the tours eventuating.

Jeff Thomson was another of the players involved in those early discussions. It was going to take a lot of money to persuade him, though. "I gave Bacher a price which was double everyone else's," says Thomson. His reluctance, like Ian Botham's in England, was based largely out of respect for black West Indian friends such as Viv Richards. "I didn't need the hassle," says Thomson. "I didn't want to go to South Africa and have Viv and all those mates think

I was going against everything I believed in. So I gave a ridiculous price and they knocked it back."

What Thomson did do was encourage his fellow Australians to drive a hard bargain. "I remember 'Hoggy' shittin' himself," Thomson recalls. "I said to him: 'They fuckin' want you, so you put your fuckin' price on.'" An account of these meetings was leaked to Adelaide's evening paper, *The News*. Bacher was convinced David Hookes was the man who had spilled the beans, even suspecting that Hookes was a plant, loyal to the ACB or other cricketing powerbrokers. Everything was off.

But the whispers would not go away. Unofficial tours of South Africa by players from England (1981-82), Sri Lanka (1982-83) and West Indies (1983-84) kept the proposition plausible – and, if reports of the money changing hands could be believed, extremely attractive. Australian players at that time were not on a great wicket. Despite the change in thinking and improvement in conditions heralded by World Series Cricket, they were paid little and had virtually no voice in decisions which affected their lives. And yet they were valuable commodities, both to the board and the broadcaster – Packer's Publishing and Broadcasting Ltd (PBL) – which ran Channel Nine.

Francis's situation was made even more delicate by his personal relationship with the Packer family. Apart from having negotiated Greig's contract with Packer, Francis was the private coach of Packer's son, James, a capable opening batsman at Cranbrook School in Sydney. He had spent a lot of time with Packer, who knew of his interest in organising a South African tour. In November 1983, Francis told James he would be unable to coach him for a few days because he had to go to Brisbane on a business trip. It so happened that this business trip coincided with the Second Test against Pakistan at the Gabba.

"I understand you are going up to Brisbane to sign up a few of my players for South Africa ... Don't waste your time," Packer warned Francis. "I've got them under contract. You'll never sign enough players and even if you do, you'll never get them out of the country." Francis was surprised because any thoughts of a South African tour, at that stage, had been put on the backburner.

But the South Africans had lost none of their enthusiasm. All they needed was an opponent. Francis was encouraged to try again. In September 1984 the Australian squad gathered for a training camp at the Australian Institute of Sport in Canberra. Francis booked a room out of town in the Embassy Motel. He invited some of the players, again two at a time, to visit him. He was after whomever he could get to fill an acceptably talented touring party.

The ACB had recently introduced a three-tier contract system for first-class players, ranging from $11,000 to $4,000. The SACU, through Francis, was offering $200,000 – tax-free – to play two summers in South Africa with an unofficial Australian side. It was a remarkable, persuasive sum that could not be ignored.

Graham Yallop was coming to the end of a successful career. He had captained Australia and played 39 Tests, yet cricket had failed to make him financially secure. "We weren't really true professionals," Yallop says. "I was spending huge amounts of time running indoor sports centres. My cricket was suffering to a small degree. Although I was trying to put as many hours as I could into cricket, trying to hold down jobs as well made it pretty difficult."

His decision was soon made even easier for him. "A few of us had been approached by senior members of the [ACB] selection panel," Yallop explains, "who said that unless we did amazing things our future in the game at the top level may be short-lived. We had to perform all the time or it was all over."

Rodney Hogg, at 33, found himself at a similar stage. "It was perfect timing for me," he says. "My career was near the end. There wasn't too much weighing up. I'd never played cricket for politics before. I've never played cricket for politics since. I just loved playing cricket. This gave me the opportunity to play two more years at international level."

John Maguire, a 28-year-old Queensland fast bowler, addressed other parameters before arriving at his decision. "It was difficult … I trusted the opinion of Bacher and Francis. I talked at length with them about the political situation … But [ultimately] it was a purely professional decision for me. At the time I was a borderline player and that was all I was going to be. I didn't know from one day to the next whether I was going to be playing for Queensland, let alone Australia."

The money had to be considerable because of the possible ramifications. "We were expecting to have a life ban," says Maguire. "The figure was very attractive. But if you looked at it long-term, that could have been the last cricket we played professionally."

In October 1984 the Australians went to India. A waterlogged, essentially meaningless one-day junket assumed special significance on the way home when they stopped off in Singapore, where the players involved in the South African negotiations met with Bacher. Those who had not been in India flew in from Australia. The SACU was anxious to sign them up as soon as possible. But the players were astute and cautious. No contracts were signed until some weeks later when an Australian solicitor signed in South Africa on behalf of all the players. By the time Clive Lloyd's West Indians arrived down under, nine of the 12 Australians picked for the First Test in Perth had agreed to tour South Africa the following summer. Only the signatures of Australia's three leading players – Hughes, Allan Border and Geoff Lawson – were missing. The others had told Francis there was no point asking them.

BUMPY RIDES, SOFT LANDINGS

The squad	Cricketing involvement
Kim Hughes (capt)	Occasional ABC radio commentator. Former chairman of WA selectors, seller of cricket memorabilia.
Terry Alderman	ABC radio commentator
John Dyson	Coach of Sri Lanka
Peter Faulkner	Tasmanian selector
Mike Haysman	TV commentator in South Africa
Tom Hogan	WA selector
Rodney Hogg	Bowling coach – has helped out Zimbabwe and Victoria.
Trevor Hohns	Chairman of Australia's selectors
John Maguire	No cricketing involvement
Rod McCurdy	No cricketing involvement
Carl Rackemann	Occasional ABC radio commentator. Former coach of Zimbabwe.
Steve Rixon	Coach of Surrey. Former coach of New Zealand and NSW.
Greg Shipperd	Coach of Victoria
Steve Smith	Former fitness coach of the Australian team
Mick Taylor	South Melbourne vice-president, co-coach
Graham Yallop	South Melbourne president, co-coach

Lawson didn't sign, he confirms, because he didn't get asked. "I wouldn't have gone anyway", he adds. "At that stage, morally or financially, I wouldn't have had anything to gain from going to South Africa. Those guys got some pretty good tax-free money. Had I been asked the moral question, I don't know what answer I would have come up with … But it didn't surprise me one iota that the guys took the money. We were still getting paid fairly poorly, no contracts. We weren't being treated like genuine employees."

Sensation followed the Second Test in Brisbane. Hughes re-signed as Test captain, Border replaced him and the Australians were hammered yet again by one of the greatest teams in history. Although the South African tour remained a secret, rumours were rife. Still, there was no guarantee it would go ahead. If a couple of players withdrew everything would be in jeopardy. To make it harder for them to change their minds they were each paid $25,000 of their overall fee. For Carl Rackemann, part of the family farming enterprise north of Kingaroy, in Queensland, the money came in handy. "I bought Dad a tractor," he says. "We put ribbon on the steering wheel and hid it over the hill and blindfolded him. We led him about 300 metres, blindfolded. He needed another tractor so it was good to have one."

Murray Bennett, a left-arm orthodox spinner from NSW, was one player who did reconsider his decision. He initially signed because "the money was too good". As a PE teacher he was earning around $30,000 per annum. "But I had all sorts of trouble after I'd signed," he admits. "I'd played cricket all my life for nothing, and here I was making this decision based on money. And I really couldn't come to grips with the life ban hanging over my head. It was also the idea of not going to England in '85 – that had always been a dream, I guess."

Bennett phoned Francis and began the difficult and costly legal process of being released from his contract. Francis was "pretty understanding" but argued that it was up to the other contracted players to decide how difficult it would be for Bennett to opt out. "I believe the reason I wasn't released with any ease," Bennett points out, "was that quite a few of the players were nervous about it. If I was allowed to pull out, others would follow suit and their golden handshake would fall away." The tour would be in jeopardy again.

On March 20, 1985, Australia's Ashes squad to England was announced. It didn't include Hughes. A couple of days later, however, he was in Sharjah with the Australian side on yet another trifling one-day adventure. Hughes made 14 and 11, hardly enough to shore up his future. But during his time away he roomed with Wessels who, it seems, filled him in on what was going to happen in South Africa. It captured his attention.

On April 13, *The Australian* and Adelaide's *Advertiser* named the players who had signed for the rebel tour. Suddenly things got very hot. Bob Hawke, the prime minister, and John Brown, the sports minister, expressed their disgust. For two weeks the debate raged on

TV, in newspapers and on talkback radio. During Question Time in parliament, Hawke announced he was concerned with "the comfort [the cricketers] would give to a racist regime". He made what *The Australian* described as an "emotional appeal" for the players not to tour. He intended to have Australian taxation authorities look "extraordinarily closely" at the financial arrangements. He said the players had breached both government and ACB policy. And he refused to rule out the possibility of cancelling passports.

The board also took action. It was losing its players. It demanded that everyone selected in the Ashes squad sign a statutory declaration promising they would not tour South Africa. Those refusing to sign would not go to England.

Packer acted too, for the ACB players were his players as well. He couldn't afford to lose 16 of them. Channel Nine's ratings were dependent on good cricket, and good cricket required good cricketers. So he took matters into his own hands.

Soon after, there was a turnaround. Dirk Wellham, Wayne Phillips and Graeme Wood, who had all signed for South Africa, suddenly advised Francis they had changed their minds – for various reasons. Hearing of this, the other rebel tourists were upset, disappointed and very, very worried. Rod McCurdy, the fast bowler, had a tense conversation with Phillips, the contents of which are recorded in a statutory declaration made by McCurdy to Victorian police on April 23:

I [McCurdy] said, "Gidday Flipper, what are you doing to us?"

He [Phillips] said, "I had an offer I couldn't refuse."

I said, "Who from, Packer?"

He said, "Yes, the big boss."

I said, "What about the blokes who put their careers and families on the line?"

He said, "Well you have to look after yourself."

Francis had a similar conversation with Phillips. "What about your mates and their families?" Francis asked him. "They could be destroyed." Phillips replied: "It's played on my mind. It hasn't been easy. It's not the most pleasant day of my life." By contrast, Francis was mightily impressed with the integrity of McCurdy, Steve Rixon and Terry Alderman, who were all picked in the 1985 Ashes squad but all stayed true to their word.

Those who remained committed were now in a precarious position. "I was in England," Rackemann recalls, "and Francis called to say the three had pulled out. He said he didn't know what it meant but that it wasn't good. The interesting thing about it, because ultimately we replaced them and went to South Africa with a good side anyway, was that we'd had a meeting months previous where we'd discussed that this might happen – that the ACB or Packer or both of them would try to derail the tour. What they'd probably do was buy people out of it. And that's exactly what happened. Everyone in that room agreed that if they happened to be the target they wouldn't have a bar of it. It was like a commitment to each other. We thought we'd been dealing with blokes who'd stand up. But three of them didn't."

According to Chris Harte and Warwick Hadfield, in their book *Cricket Rebels*, Wellham got a message from Greig: "Kerry Packer wants to see you." Within hours, Wellham had withdrawn from the tour. He says now that he changed his mind because he was unsure whether he had made the right decision. "It was a political issue," he says, "but there was a lot of morality surrounding it and one never knows what is the right way to go." Also, he was "surprised" when he was selected to go to England. Also, he was offered a job with PBL Marketing.

Bennett finally withdrew too, but his case was different. "It agitates me that sometimes I'm bracketed with the three who pulled out … that I also received payment from Packer. Because that was a fairly sensitive period for me." Bennett received nothing.

At the same time Packer targeted several emerging players. Dean Jones, Robbie Kerr, Mike Veletta, Peter Clifford and Steve Waugh were all placed on the PBL books. Waugh was on a youth scholarship in England when he was visited by a woman employed by PBL. He was offered a three-year, five-figure contract – and he couldn't sign quickly enough. "I did nothing over the three years," Waugh recalled in the book *Waugh Declared*. "Just collected the cheques."

Meanwhile, unrest festered within the official Australian team. Not one of the Ashes tourists was happy with the inclusion of Wood, Phillips, Wellham and Bennett, and for a while it looked like the Ashes might even be called off. Certainly a few things had to be sorted out. On the night before flying to England, the team stayed in a Melbourne hotel and the four were given a thorough working over. "I was rooming with Dirk," Bennett remembers. "The four of us were asked to remain in our rooms for some hours, then one by one we were invited down. When it was my turn I passed Dirk in the hallway and he was white as a ghost. I never discussed [what happened] with Dirk. But when I went into the room it was really just a question and answer thing."

Thomson has a somewhat different recollection. "There was 'Henry' [Lawson] and me and someone else, and we gave them a fuckin' pizzling. You know, 'What's your story? You fuckin' pulled out on your fuckin' mates. What are you gunna do on this tour when the shit hits the fan?'" Thomson was equally unhappy with the ACB. "They left it up to us," he says. "Typical of the board: weak as piss. Sat on the sideline. And did nothin'. And left it with the players again."

The tour went ahead and, despite the initial acrimony and Australia's 3–1 defeat, it proved amicable enough. Back in Australia, though, the situation grew tenser when Hughes signed for South Africa. Disillusioned with the summer's events and his exclusion from the Ashes party, he believed he had no future in Australian cricket. Bill O'Reilly, the former champion leg-spinner, was one member of the press box who stood firm in support of Hughes – "a thoughtful, ambitious, well-educated man [who] exercised the right which every Australian considered to be his from birth. He has made his decision to take advantage of an unparalleled offer to set his family up for life."

The Australian government continued to huff and puff, but Maguire recognised an inconsistency in Hawke's outrage. "Around that time Australia was doing millions and millions of dollars of trade with South Africa," Maguire says. "If they were serious about sanctions they would have completely pulled the plug on them. Then Bob Hawke would have had to go and say to the wheat farmers, for example, you can't sell your wheat there." Around this same time Hawke was locked in battle with Queenland's premier Joh Bjelke–Petersen over that state's anti-union legislation. Bill Mitchell produced a cartoon in *The Australian*: "Have you heard – no sporting contact with Queensland."

To Francis, it was blatant hypocrisy. South African cricketers had been permitted to play in Australia during the World Series days. South African tennis players, golfers and surfers were all allowed in the country. Why should touring cricketers be any different? He defended his players publicly.

To the surprise of many, public opinion polls ran two-to-one in favour of Hughes and his rebels. The only negative feedback, says

Maguire, appeared in the media. "Those who were putting the information out had vested interests," he says. "The politicians, the ACB, Channel Nine – I think they were driving the publicity machine around that time. The politicians, they'll do what's best for them. Nobody came up to me in the street and said 'you shouldn't be doing this'. Either people didn't have the courage to front you on it or they didn't care. Or I occasionally got people saying: 'Good on you. I would have done the same thing given the same circumstances.'"

The ACB believed the players had breached their contracts and was intent on taking them to court. Apart from anything, this gave the board an opportunity to test the strength of its player contracts at a time when Packer was buying up cricketers. He already had eight on his books and wanted more. When Geoff Dakin, the SACU president, visited Australia for the court case he got a message from Greig that Packer wanted to see him.

Their meeting is recorded in Bacher's biography: "Packer was very irritated because he said we were poaching players that he wanted for the Australian team, including Mike Haysman. He made his point in no uncertain terms using very colourful language. I reminded him that I had agreed to see him as president of SACU, and I therefore suggested that he address me a little more courteously. He barked at me: 'Listen fella, you may be a rooster today, but tomorrow you're a feather duster.'"

The legal action against the rebels was ultimately settled out of court. The tour was free to go ahead. The ACB banned the players from Sheffield Shield cricket until September 30, 1987, and from Test cricket until exactly one year later. For men who had been anticipating a life ban, this was a relief.

In terms of on-field action and off-field functions, the players say the tour was like any other. The South Africans regarded them as a representative Australian team and the cricket was of international standard. The legendary South African Graeme Pollock showed, even at 42, that he was still a superb batsman. "I don't think people appreciate how good he was," says Maguire. "He was unorthodox: big heavy bat, long handle, feet wide apart. He just timed the ball so well. He wasn't moving his feet much by then but he was just awesome ... He was a bit scratchy early but when he got going he was pretty scary."

In other ways it was a less than typical Test tour. South Africa remained in a state of emergency. Nelson Mandela was still in prison.

The African National Congress used the tour to its own political advantage. Coming in from the airport at Cape Town, the players saw billboards with "Kill the Aussie Cricketers" painted on them.

For the Victorian batsman Mick Taylor, who had never played a Test or one-day international, it was a thrill just to be playing international cricket. Generally he felt untroubled being in South Africa, although: "There were some things which disturbed me. The way that some Afrikaaners spoke to the blacks, they really had been brainwashed into believing the blacks were second-class citizens, that they were inferior mentally. And the effect of the blacks being deprived of education confirmed this perception. But the British and Jewish South Africans were pretty good."

Graham Yallop now has mixed feelings. "I'm pleased that I went from the cricket side," he says. "Hindsight is a great thing. From the political point of view it wasn't the greatest decision, but we were ill-informed I think. We relied on people for the knowledge and maybe we weren't getting the complete truth ... Being on the tour opened our eyes to the political situation. But we couldn't get out of the decision. No matter what I thought personally, we were under contract and it was something I had to complete ... After we returned that made for some difficult moments of conscience."

The Australians were encouraged, on the whole, by the SACU's attempts to ensure cricket was integrated. "We played in the provinces against black cricketers," says Yallop. "They weren't treated differently at all. Not at all. We didn't treat them differently and neither, as far as we could see, were they treated differently by their teams ... I think cricket was at the forefront as an institution of change."

The two-year bans were served concurrently with the two South African tours, which meant the players walked straight back into their Sheffield Shield squads to prepare for the 1987-88 summer. Only the Victorians were not selected: they were told to force their way back in by weight of runs. Taylor promptly went to Tasmania and scored 1,000 runs in the season. He and Yallop are now co-coaches at South Melbourne Cricket Club. "Almost everyone," Taylor observes, "is either currently involved or has been involved to a significant extent in cricket. From that point of view we were accepted back into the fold."

In fact, Thomson is bemused by just how little impact the rebel tour had on the careers of those cricketers. He doesn't begrudge them – but he does make an interesting point about the ongoing unwillingness to award World Series Cricket matches first-class status. "Trevor Hohns is now the chairman of selectors," says Thomson. "This is what makes me fuckin' laugh. Yet us blokes, played for Australia, played World Series Cricket, didn't go against anti-apartheid, and they won't even recognise our wickets and runs. What a load of shit."

Three of the South African tourists – Alderman, Hohns and Rackemann – actually went on to play Test cricket. A surreal situation unfolded after Australia's victory in the Lord's Test of 1989. Bob Hawke was in the dressing room – in front of the cameras – back-slapping the three former rebels as if nothing had happened. Rackemann remembers the day well: "Hawke came in and he was everyone's best mate. I'd had an operation on my knee. I was on the floor doing some straight leg raises with an icepack on. But Hawke made a special point of bending over and shaking my hand, full of good spirits. He'd probably forgotten."

So much of this story is about self-interest and the interaction of competing interests. The SACU, Ali Bacher and his colleagues. Bruce Francis. The players who went to South Africa. The players who didn't go. The players who signed to go but changed their minds. The ACB. Kerry Packer and PBL. The Australian government and Bob Hawke. The ANC. These were just some of the entities involved. All had their own aspirations.

But the final word goes to Nelson Mandela. Interestingly, he accepted an invitation to write the foreword to the recently published biography, *Ali: The Life of Ali Bacher*. With a heart that transcends self-interest, Mandela says that even while incarcerated on Robben Island, he and his friends took pride in the performance of the South African cricket team. "It will always stand to the credit of the game of cricket that its leadership was amongst the first to take steps," Mandela writes. "Even before the political negotiations were concluded they reached out to each other and formed a united South African body to lead and oversee the transformation of the game."

Any participation by professional cricketers, who happen to be Australians, in games of cricket in South Africa is, by comparison, inconsequential.

John Harms is a Melbourne-based sportswriter and the author of Confessions Of A Thirteenth Man. *His next book, a biography of* Steve Renouf, *is out in March.*

WAUGH'S OVER: PART I

The mourning after

by DAVID FRITH

Steve Waugh played 260 Test innings, all around the cricket world, a huge achievement which has the unavoidable effect of defocusing much of what he did. So repeatedly did he punch his team out of difficulty that details tend to merge into one another. What is left is a kind of archetypal image: Waugh parrying a vicious bouncer, ducking another, then out-staring the glaring bowler. Waugh slapping something he's turned into a half-volley all the way to the pickets forward of square. Waugh trotting a single after a thick edge and ignoring the bowler. Waugh poking his bat perfunctorily towards the perimeter as the applause swells for yet another landmark.

And yet the summer-long hysteria that followed Waugh everywhere he went in 2003-04 is unprecedented in all cricket history. It culminated in that crunch moment on the last evening of the last Test, when a pulsating series between Australia and India ended in high drama and a just equality. Waugh's fairytale century against England 12 months earlier was not, after all, to be repeated. Instead he made a canny 80, lofted a catch to Sachin Tendulkar and that evening was carried shoulder-high by team-mates around one full lap of his beloved SCG. Cricket had never seen anything quite like it. I could not help wondering just how many Australians were in need of grief counselling now that his 18-year Test career was finished at long last.

How is this grieving, this obsession with Waugh, to be explained? Perhaps the clue lies in something the sociologist James Bradley uttered as one of the speakers at the Menzies Centre's Bradman Symposium at Lord's in 2001: "By being so silent, Bradman allowed the myths to stick to him and allowed himself to become what Australia wanted him to be." Could it be that Waugh, who always kept his responses to journalists' questions to a reasonable minimum length, also allowed himself to become what Australia wanted him to be?

And if so, what did Australians want of him? It goes without saying that they rejoiced in his phenomenal record as batsman and captain. He was fortunate to be put in charge of a rare crop of all the talents – fast bowlers, faster batsmen, a genius leg-spinner – and he led from the front. His personal image was that of an Aussie battler, a blue-collar cricketer, a working-class boy who had much in common with his predecessor as national hero, Allan Border.

Australians love the word "legend" and its modern interpretation tends to conveniently disregard the "myth" aspect. Don Bradman was no myth; his batting average looks mythical but he existed surely enough. While Victor Trumper's origins prior to his enrolment at Crown Street School are shrouded in mystery, we have a clear picture of the solitary boy Bradman practising with his stump in the backyard in Bowral. We have a powerful image of the likes of Bill O'Reilly and Stan McCabe in other New South Wales bush towns; of Arthur Mailey domiciled and dreaming by the sand dunes of Botany; and of the formidable Chappell clan biting each other's heads off in their suburban Adelaide backyard.

The Revesby–Panania area of south-western Sydney in the mid-1960s was a flat patchwork of building plots, each with a newly erected fibro house and a Hills Hoist out the back, laden with sparkling white nappies. Holdens and Zephyrs zoomed down Beaconsfield Street, the main through road. Light aircraft croaked to and from Bankstown aerodrome. Within a few years Mr and Mrs Waugh's twin boys were being driven to sports ovals all over Sydney's western suburbs. For once, all those forecasts that certain gifted boy cricketers would some day play for Australia were about to be fulfilled. Whether anybody expected Steve and Mark, between them, to register 296 Test appearances, 18,956 runs, 52 centuries, 151 wickets and 293 catches – to say nothing of 569 one-day internationals – is another matter.

Mark, the elegant aristocrat of the crease, could easily have been reckoned a product of the ritzy eastern suburbs. But there was no mistaking no-frills Steve as the boy from the backblocks. Productivity was his keynote. Style, especially in the middle and later stages of his career, did not come into it. Runs in the book were what earned selection, won matches, dominated series, secured immortality. There was nothing glamorous about him. Trumper was pigeon-toed and Bradman a titch; Waugh was identifiable in the field by his Charlie Chaplin walk.

Any war metaphors in our descriptions of cricket are close to obscenity. Waugh himself caused a few cringes when he and his players, en route to England in 2001, decked themselves out in diggers' slouch hats and crouched in the trenches of Gallipoli. We owe it to ourselves and previous generations to uphold the truth that cricket is merely a game (and a rich adjunct to show-business). I prefer to draw comparisons with other sports, in this case boxing. For Waugh often resembled one of the real-life Rockies – Graziano or even Marciano – as he ducked and weaved and counter-punched when the bouncers were flying, all the while staring defiantly back at his tormentors through squinting, impenetrable eyes. His unflinching reaction and short, sharp verbal response as the towering Curtly Ambrose eyeballed him at Port-of-Spain in 1995 was one of the photographic images of the age.

When such an extraordinary cricketer leaves the game, adulation inevitably knows no bounds. When Sir Donald Bradman died in 2001 at the age of 92, the nation's response stretched far beyond expectation. The tragic death of David Hookes outside a St Kilda hotel last January again surprised sociologists by the intensity of the grieving which followed.

But the degree of public anguish that greeted Waugh's farewell last summer, even allowing for its long build-up, was something else again. Was there an element of apprehension that Australia's proud invincibility might end? Did his departure somehow have the same deflating effect as the death of Winston Churchill had on Britons in 1965, even though the bulldog wartime leader was by then 90 years of age? Did fervently patriotic cricket lovers feel exposed and vulnerable now that Waugh was gone? If you were at the SCG on January 6, 2004, you would not consider that an outrageous question.

That he is a family man with a scandal-free image – various biographies have disclosed nothing more than a boozy period in his youth – seems to have added to his appeal among cricket lovers. Many could identify with him because of his ordinariness. But linked to that ordinariness is a career record all other cricketers might only dream of. He featured in an unprecedented number of Tests (168) and captained his country to an unrivalled proportion of victories (41 out of 57). He amassed an astronomical run tally (10,927 – behind only Border) at a handsome average (51.06). His 32 hundreds – and he didn't hit his first, remember, until his 27th Test – left him trailing only Sunil Gavaskar on the day he quit. And his collection of 92 Test wickets is way beyond those of Gavaskar, Tendulkar, Border, Bradman and

Brian Lara combined. He was run out four times and left the arena unbeaten on 46 occasions. Analysts can make of that what they will.

Several marathon efforts rush to mind: his unparted 464-run stand with brother Mark against Western Australia in 1990-91; his 332-run partnership with Border that blew England away at Headingley in 1993; the 385 runs he and Greg Blewett put on in Johannesburg three years later. All were for the fifth wicket, that stage of an innings when the opposition feel a breakthrough now will let them into the match.

But two marks, above all others, take the breath away. One is a team credit: victory, with fleeting help from his deputy Adam Gilchrist, in 16 successive Tests as leader. The other is an individual honour: he is the only batsman to have reached 150 against all nine other Test countries. Might Kenya's elevation to Test status one day tempt him back, even though he may be 50 years of age by then?

KING OF THE BOUNDARY HITTERS

In his final Test innings at the SCG, when he cut Anil Kumble past backward point to move from 70 to 74, Steve Waugh overtook Allan Border as the most prolific boundary-hitter in Australian Test history. It was the second-last boundary he ever struck. The West Indian Brian Lara holds the world record (1,335 fours, 69 sixes, 5,754 runs) ahead of Sachin Tendulkar and Waugh. Matthew Hayden's 63 sixes is the most by an Australian in Test history; Adam Gilchrist, on 54, ranks second. Chris Cairns, from New Zealand, holds the world record with 87 sixes, three more than Viv Richards.

	Fours	Sixes	Boundary runs
S. R. Waugh	1,175	20	4,820
A. R. Border	1,161	28	4,812
M. E. Waugh	844	41	3,622
D. C. Boon	822	2	3,300
G. S. Chappell	755	16	3,116
R. T. Ponting	694	38	3,004
M. A. Taylor	727	9	2,962
M. L. Hayden	618	63	2,850
D. G. Bradman	681*	6	2,760
J. L. Langer	632	30	2,708
M. J. Slater	598	30	2,572

Excludes four of Bradman's innings, for which boundary figures are not available. Figures accurate to September 2004.

Amazing though the figures are, Waugh will be remembered for his image and character. Out of the bleak and painful early 1980s, when Australia wondered from where the successors to Greg Chappell, Dennis Lillee and Rod Marsh might emerge, came this young man whom Bill O'Reilly perceived as a partial reincarnation of Stan McCabe. Some prolific developmental seasons with Somerset presaged his first big Test series. In England in 1989 he broke through with nigh-on 400 runs in the first three Tests before he was finally dismissed. His 92 in the next match at Old Trafford ensured the Ashes were recovered. From then until his emotional farewell-to-the-Poms century in Sydney 14 years later, the little urn was never, metaphorically speaking, out of his pocket. It was as if he had wrapped it in his famous ragged red handkerchief.

That 92 was his third score in the nineties in eight months and one of 10 in his career. He was closer than we suspected to becoming the greatest maker of hundreds the game has known. The most poignant near miss was his 99 not out at the WACA in 1994-95 when his brother, acting as runner, was run out, as if in some mischievous backyard game.

Perhaps his most heroic and skilful performance came in his second Old Trafford Test in 1997. Australia were one-nil down after two Tests and struggling at 3 for 42 in the third. Against a demanding England attack, on a sometimes difficult pitch, and nursing a bruised right hand, Waugh toughed out a century in each innings. He erected the platform upon which Australia levelled proceedings, paving the way for yet another series triumph. Ashes history was being recast, for never before has one side won so many consecutive series – eight – as in the Border-Taylor-Waugh era.

On his final Test visit to England, in 2001, Waugh added to the suspicion that he was made of something beyond conventional flesh and blood. Having had his face smashed in an outfield collision with Jason Gillespie in Kandy in 1999, he now tore a leg muscle with Australia minutes away from securing the Ashes at Trent Bridge. The medical prognosis was grim. But we should have known better than to question Waugh's resolve. Having watched helplessly while Mark Butcher snatched the fourth Test for England, he rematerialised for the fifth Test at The Oval. He limped his way to another century, signalled memorably with a body-surf through the dust to the crease, bat raised while he still lay prone in the dust, giving onlookers a glimpse of the cheeky chap he once was and – away from the public gaze – still is.

'Tugga' Waugh, slightly flashy as a youngster, soon sorted out what he wanted. He got it through force of character. It first showed on the world stage one November evening at Eden Gardens, Kolkata, when he steadied Australia in the nail-biting closing stages of the 1987 World Cup final. The 'Ice Man' they called him then. It showed a year later at the Gabba when he bounced a startled Viv Richards three balls running, the third delivery causing the West Indian dominator to lose his cap and maybe, for the only time in his life, to consider wearing a helmet. It showed in Waugh's only Test double-century when he and his brother weathered fusillades of bouncers to snatch the Worrell Trophy in Jamaica in 1995, and again in his incredible Headingley hundred against South Africa that brought Australia back from the dead in the 1999 World Cup.

Waugh's own threadbare and stained baggy green was eventually reconditioned, and is destined for display in some museum some day. Holy Trinity, Panania, might be an apt site for it. Traditionalists, and in reality Australians everywhere, owe it to him that he restored pride in the Australian Test cap. It is a timeless, wonderful and intimidating sight to behold 11 green caps in the field.

Steve Waugh, even allowing for his charity work, made lots of money out of cricket. Of course he did. Nobody should envy him for that. No such riches would have been there fifty or eighty years ago, but still he would have enjoyed his cricket and played it just as hard, if not perhaps for quite so long. For one thing, Waugh's belief in imposing "mental disintegration" on adversaries – a euphemism for malodorous sledging – would have caused him severe problems.

Australia will – must – come to terms with his retirement, though we shall inevitably hear people invoking his name in times of trouble. That's history for you. Just as he once sat at the knee of Hunter 'Stork' Hendry, listening to tales of yore, so some young blade will one day direct an awed gaze at Waugh's craggy features, questing for reminiscence and trying, probably without success, to discern the secret of such a successful and sustained performance at the gold-seamed coalface.

David Frith has written 26 books on cricket. His latest is The Ross Gregory Story.

WAUGH'S OVER: PART II

Premature evacuation

by MALCOLM KNOX

In a vintage year for delusional world leaders, no performance was more impressive than Nasser Hussain's when he retired from Test cricket in May. The former England captain combined Blair-like denial of the facts with the vanity of his namesake Saddam in summing up his matchwinning 103 not out against New Zealand. "The most important thing for me," he said, "is to end on a high, like I did with my captaincy, so people look back and say: 'Yes, he was a good captain.' ... I want people to look back on me as a good captain and a good player."

At least Hussain was candid about his effort to force public opinion into a shape of his making. He spoke at length about being able to "go out in the way I deserved". He talked about having, in that last Test, pulled off a match-turning run-out, peeled off three straight fours to raise his second-innings century, then finished "with my favourite shot, the cover drive". In a feat of spin that portends a productive future in the media, Hussain said that last day at Lord's typified his entire career.

To point out that he never averaged 40 in Test cricket would have seemed churlish. To mention that his "favourite" cover drive was greeted by good bowlers as a gift from heaven would have been mean. And to balance his glowing self-assessment as a captain with an observation of his tendency to craven gutlessness under pressure – sending Australia in to bat in Brisbane in 2002-03, for starters – might have pricked the balloon even before Hussain could finish blowing it up. What is most interesting about Nasser-in-Wonderland is what it says about how retirements are becoming scripted and choreographed to a reality-defying template.

The cricket year also saw the orchestrated retirement of an authentically great cricketer and captain in Steve Waugh. By the time his last innings rolled around Waugh did not need to rewrite history, Hussain-style. His career record could stand up without assistance and be seen for what it was (as will Hussain's). Yet the manner of Waugh's retirement says as much as Hussain's about how the end of a career is being distorted from something poignant, something marking a natural end, into a stage-managed Event.

In Australia, the management of retirements has its origins in 1983-84, when Greg Chappell, Dennis Lillee and Rod Marsh stepped down at once. A year later 15 of Australia's best went to South Africa and were banned. It left the Test team with a hole that took half a decade to fill. The lesson learned was "never again", and by the mid-1990s it had taken on the rigidity of a dogma. In 1998, when Mark Taylor, Ian Healy and the Waugh twins were breasting their mid-30s, the chairman of selectors Trevor Hohns was quietly hatching a plan to stagger their retirements.

"We've really got to do our best not to let what happened in the 1980s happen again," Hohns told me at the end of 1998. "As selectors, our charter is not only to pick winning teams but to nurture winning teams for the future ... Above all, we've got to make sure people don't get complacent about the future because things can go downhill very quickly." Hohns knew that his legacy as a selector would rest on how this transition was managed. "Australian cricket doesn't tolerate lengthy rebuilding periods," he said. "That's where the pressure might begin to tell in a few years. The public will always expect the Australian cricket team to win."

The staggering of retirements took five years. Taylor went in January 1999, Healy in October. Mark Waugh lasted until 2002, Steve another 18 months. Ageing others such as Colin Miller and Damien Fleming were elbowed out along the way. All the while, the Australian team not only maintained the winning momentum of the Taylor years but improved it. Under Steve Waugh, the best team in the world turned into arguably the best ever.

The job done, Hohns can feel well satisfied. The far shore of the Ponting era has been reached without that "lengthy rebuilding period" in which losses had to be sustained for the long-term good. Nobody who remembers Australian cricket's losing days of the mid-1980s would argue that our game was healthier with its tail between its legs.

But it is worth turning this coin to see if it has a dark side. For all the apparent seamlessness of the managerial theory of retirement, is there anything we have lost?

Taking the recent Big Four retirements individually, the first, Taylor's, was the least fraught. His batting had been on the wane for two years, and his unbeaten 334 in Peshawar in November 1998 was a nice last flourish. By January 1999 his time had come and he knew it. He stepped easily from the crease to the commentary box.

Healy also moved into commentary, but not without leaving a few claw-marks on the dressing-room floor. Having broken the world wicket-keeping record, he was still playing well at 35. His batting and keeping were sound on his last tours, to Sri Lanka and Zimbabwe in 1999. But then came the tap on the shoulder; he could go the easy way or the hard way. Healy begged one last indulgence: a farewell Test at the Gabba against Pakistan. Hohns denied him. The managerial style had no room for sentiment.

With some resentment, Healy accepted retirement rather than risk being dropped. Until then he and Hohns, old Queensland colleagues, had been mates. Both have since conceded their friendship was ruined. At least the outcome seemed smooth because the selectors were lucky enough to have the superlative Adam Gilchrist as Healy's successor. But not even the selectors had any idea Gilchrist would step into the Test arena as prodigiously as he did; if they had, they might have given Healy the nudge a year or two sooner. If Gilchrist hadn't taken the world by surprise, Healy's forced retirement might be remembered with some bitterness.

More strain was evident around the retirement of Mark Waugh. By the end of 2001 both Waughs were suffering inconsistent form. They took turns at pulling their careers out of the fire. One moment the pressure was on Steve, the next on Mark. The younger twin's time ran out in Sharjah in late 2002, just as Steve borrowed a little more with a last-ditch century.

There is no doubt Hohns and his co-selectors wanted to separate the Waughs' retirements. Given the brothers' national popularity, and their contribution to the game, Hohns did not want to be seen to be forcing either out, and certainly not both at once. When this was sensed to be the case in 2002 the reaction was extreme. Steve Waugh's manager, Robert Joske, went so far as to coordinate a "Save Steve" campaign with the Murdoch newspapers that contracted his client.

Mark lacked Steve's stature as captain, and his form ebbed at just the wrong moment – a wrong moment designated by the selectors, that is. Like Healy, and like David Boon back in 1995, he received the tap on the shoulder unwillingly. Few believed his statement that he was "retiring" from Test cricket. He was stepping out of the guillotine's path.

When I interviewed Hohns about his long-range plans in 1998-99, I also spoke to Steve Waugh. He was at his most forceful in denying the relevance of age: "Age is nothing. Allan Border, Graham Gooch and Javed Miandad all played their best cricket over 30. I can't understand how if a guy's taken 10 years to gain his experience and know-how ... then all of a sudden when he's at his peak, you're looking to replace him with another guy who's got to learn that whole thing and go through the 10-year cycle again.

"Once guys are in their 30s, if they're still playing, they have a lot to add to the young guys. We're all still really keen and determined and enjoy the challenge of playing Test and one-day cricket. If we're the best players, we should be picked ... I think it's stupid to write off players because of their age."

By the end of his career, Steve Waugh gave no sign of changing his views. Dropped from the one-day side in 2002, he continued to make himself available for selection. Pressured for his Test place during 2003, he kept fighting back like a caged animal. Steve Waugh had every intention of carrying on to tour India in September 2004. He had lost Test series there in 1998 and 2001. He craved another chance. There was no doubt he wanted to play on.

But he was, in a sense, paid off at the beginning of the 2003-04 season. The money or the box? He could choose to take a secure lap of honour, a farewell tour around the country. Or he could keep fighting for his place and risk the indignity of being dropped.

There's the rub: that word "indignity". Nasser Hussain spoke a lot about the dignity of his retirement, as if dignity was something he could thrust upon himself, like Napoleon seizing his crown from the Pope. As custodians of the national team's fortunes, Hohns and his selection panel, along with the Cricket Australia directors, have little latitude for the bestowal of dignity. What they have learned to do, however, is to help manufacture what is crudely termed a "dignified exit" for senior players, such as they gave Boon, Healy and Mark Waugh, or the "triumphant" one given Steve Waugh.

But followers of the game must by now be examining the meaning of this increasingly hollowed-out and commodified word. Dignity. Steve Waugh's dignity grew organically from an 18-year career: from his courage as a batsman; from his imagination as a captain; from his purpose as an individual. Did it come from being able to raise his bat at every Test ground in Australia during 2003-04? Emphatically not.

FROM WAUGHSOME TO WAUGHFUL

No cricketer in history has been so adored by newspaper sub-editors as Steve Waugh.
Here is a life in puns:

Waugh begins *200 Seasons of Australian Cricket* (1997)
Makes 13 and five on debut.

Waugh hero again *The Sun* (Melbourne): Oct. 20, 1987
Guides Australia to a one-day win over New Zealand in Indore.

Calm exterior – but secretly, a Waugh of nerves *The Courier-Mail*: Dec. 2, 1987
Talks about pressure after winning the World Cup.

Time to salute a declaration of Waugh *Sydney Morning Herald*: Nov. 25, 1988
Bowls three bouncers to Viv Richards at the Gabba.

Steve's Waugh-path silences the knockers *The Sun*: Dec. 28, 1988
Makes 42 against West Indies at the MCG.

Waugh Lord *Sun Herald*: June 10, 1989
Hits maiden Test hundred at Headingley.

Waugh zone *The Sun*: July 6, 1989
Lines up against Ian Botham at Edgbaston.

Waugh Machine *National Nine Tour Guide* (1989-90)
How he deals with the spotlight after his sensational Ashes tour.

A battle without Waugh *Sydney Morning Herald*: Feb. 1, 1990
Told not to bowl against New Zealand because of a back injury.

Civil Waugh: Brothers in arms *Australian Cricket*, Oct. 1990
Australia debates whether to select one Waugh or two.

Waugh Declared Pan Macmillan: 1992
Mark Gately's book on the twins.

True Blue bruise tells Waugh tale *Sydney Morning Herald*: May 2, 1995
Hits 200 v West Indies then plays John Williamson's 'True Blue' in team hotel.

Waugh under the gun, but don't shoot the selectors *Sydney Morning Herald*: Dec. 12, 1997
Loses four of his first five matches as one-day captain.

Images of Waugh HarperCollins: 1998
Book of Waugh photos depicting life on tour.

World Waugh *Sydney Morning Herald*: June 22, 1999
Australia win the World Cup.

Australians lead in gang Waughfare *The Guardian*: Aug. 6, 2001
Why the Aussies stuff the Poms.

Waugh talk stirs troops *Sun Herald*: June 15, 2003
Addresses the NSW State of Origin rugby league team.

Time Waughp *Sun Herald*: Jan. 4, 2004
Caption accompanying picture of a young Steve and Mark.

Hero Waugh-ship news.com.au: Jan. 7, 2004
Tributes flood News Ltd's website.

Waugh goes out fighting *Daily Telegraph*: Jan. 7, 2004
Hits 80 in his final Test innings.

Research: Peter English

Conversely, would it have been undignified for Steve Waugh (and Healy, and Mark Waugh, and the rest) to keep playing on until they were dropped? Would it have been a sad end for Steve Waugh to struggle through an overseas tour and play his last Test in an obscure place in front of empty stands, as his brother did?

To assess these questions, we have to ask whether our concept of dignity rests on what we know of sport and life, or on what is packaged and presented to us. In a 2002 article in *Harper's Magazine* called "The Boys of Winter", the American writer Rich Cohen deplored those who urge stars to "get out on top". He called it "a useless phrase that only diminishes the connection between sports and life; in life, no-one goes out on top. It is a sentiment that reflects the neurosis of our society: the fear of age, the disregard of history. So we drive our veterans off to the golf courses and the television studios, and thereby cheat ourselves of the finest moments in sports."

Cohen listed many such finest moments, in which grizzled old dogs played on past their apparent use-by dates to produce stunning gestures of defiance – not simply shaking their fist at the opponent on the field but at time itself. Cohen said that these moments brought sports back to their universal roots. Rather than worshipping supermen, we were identifying totally with the ageing sportsman, because he or she, like the rest of us, was raging against death, the ultimate foe. What, Cohen asked, can be more inspiring and dignified than this?

Steve Waugh's famous last-ball-of-the-day century against England at the SCG in 2002-03 was one such moment. Should he have quietly retired, at the beginning of that series, with "dignity"? Many thought he should have. Had he done so, we would have missed one of sport's great human moments. Now that Waugh has bowed to the tap on the shoulder, we may be missing many more.

There is no indignity in playing on. Allan Border, who as a national selector has bought into the managerial theory of retirement, should know better. He played on into his late 30s. As a batsman he struggled to middle the ball; as a captain he seemed tired. The staging of his retirement was botched. But was it sad? Was it undignified? Did it take one iota away from his record?

For a day it may have seemed so, but history is making its judgements every day, and the more historical perspective we have the more we understand that a player's record stands forever, and his dignity derives from that record and the spirit in which he played the game, not from the way he retires. It is worth asking ourselves if we're placing too much emphasis on the flourish in the final bow.

Does it really matter how a player goes out? Mark Waugh faded out palely in Sharjah; Nasser Hussain in a blaze of glory at Lord's. Allan Border spat the dummy on a golf course. Steve Waugh hit 80 on a gloomy Sydney afternoon against a limp attack in a drawn Test, then got bowled going for a slog. When history passes judgement on these players, the final day will be the first one forgotten.

Malcolm Knox is literary editor of The Sydney Morning Herald.

WAUGH'S OVER: PART III

The Invisibles

by MAX BONNELL

As Steve Waugh walked from the field after his final Test last summer, plenty in the SCG pavilion were ready to argue that he had led the finest of all cricket teams. The usual benchmarks were offered up for debate: Don Bradman's 1948 Invincibles, Clive Lloyd's relentless mid-1980s West Indian side. Another team, a much older Australian XI, didn't rate a mention. They were versatile, swashbuckling and had one slightly unfair advantage. To paraphrase Woody Allen in his 1985 movie *The Purple Rose of Cairo*: "They were the most wonderful team – they're fictional, but you can't have everything."

The 1917 Ashes tour to England was scheduled but never occurred. It was swamped by World War I and the Australian players who did sail to Europe wore khakis instead of whites. The English historian E. H. Carr famously dismissed "what if" history as a "parlour game" – but it's a peculiarly fascinating one. Let us assume, in choosing the 1917 Australian team which never was, that every player was fit, available and in form, and that the selectors made no colossal blunders. Given all that, they would have ranked among the most powerful sides ever assembled – a match, more than a match perhaps, for Steve Waugh's men.

Consider the spinners. Waugh had the brilliance of Shane Warne plus another leg-spinner, Stuart MacGill, as a high-class understudy. But in 1917 there was not only quality and depth but variety too. Arthur Mailey, already an outstanding leg-spinner by the outbreak of war, spun the ball as hard as any man ever has, joyfully luring batsmen to their destruction without keeping count of the cost. Yet he may well have been relegated to the MacGill role if Herbert Hordern could have been tempted away from his dental practice to make the trip. Still only 34 in 1917, Hordern was Australia's first great googly bowler, striking at a rate of almost seven wickets a Test in his short career.

If the pitches were wet, Bert Ironmonger's left-arm spinners might have wreaked the most damage. Victoria's best bowler immediately before the war, Ironmonger was a relatively youthful

35 in 1917. He ultimately waited until he was 46 before playing for Australia, and even at that advanced age he collected 74 wickets in only 14 Tests. Whichever of those three played would be backed up by Warwick Armstrong, the captain, who turned his leg-break only gently but was cunning, competitive and astonishingly accurate. Two of the batsmen, Charlie Macartney and Bert Collins, could also send down useful orthodox left-armers that reaped plenty of wickets on soft English pitches. Even if we say Waugh's team had the best spinners, the 1917 side unquestionably had the better spin attack.

And what of the fast men? Glenn McGrath, Jason Gillespie and Brett Lee are perhaps more fearsome than their predecessors of two generations ago, but it is a close-run thing. For the 1917 attack would have been led by Ted McDonald. Do not be fooled by this man's modest Test record: he was one of Australia's great bowlers. His Test career was delayed by the war until he was 30, then ended almost at once when he signed a county contract with Lancashire. But his speed, control and movement were devastating. Had the 21-year-old Jack Gregory emerged from Sydney grade cricket by 1917 – which given his extravagant talent seems a fair assumption – then he would have shared the new ball. Gregory bounded in and made the ball fly at a nasty pace.

Coming on at first-change would be Jack Massie, possibly the finest Australian bowler never to play a Test. A giant, muscular left-armer, Massie could make the new ball swing and bounce, then cut or spin it when the turf was slow or wet. He dominated Australian cricket in the two seasons before the war when, to the cost of his long-term reputation, no Tests were played. During the war he served with reckless bravery. He was twice wounded at Gallipoli, but it was a stray bomb falling behind the lines in France that injured his foot badly enough to end his cricketing career. Remember, too, that Jack Ryder, a batsman good enough to average 51 in Test cricket – though not quite good enough to make our first-choice 1917 side – was a genuine pre-war strike bowler for Victoria.

Charlie Macartney

The verdict? Waugh's men had the edge in sheer speed, nobody from 1917 could sledge like McGrath, and when the time comes to celebrate a wicket Lee wins hands down (and up, and shaken all around). But the 1917ers, once again, had greater variety and adaptability.

Waugh's teams have rightly been praised for raising the tempo of Test cricket through their daring, brutal strokeplay. But batting would have been a strength of the 1917 side too. When war broke out in 1917, Warren Bardsley was the world's best left-hander; he remained a Test force until 1926. Armstrong, slimmer and fitter than the 'Big Ship' who captained Australia in 1920-21, was a consistently formidable accumulator of runs. Macartney was an electric strokemaker and Ryder a fierce driver. Johnny Taylor was a graceful stylist. Collins and Charlie Kelleway were dogged grafters. Gregory, clubber of the fastest hundred (70 minutes) in Test history, would have filled Adam Gilchrist's role as a clean-hitting lefty in the lower order.

Then there are the tantalising maybes, the unfulfilled talents who, but for the war, might now be remembered as great cricketers. Norman Callaway was 19 when he played his only game for New South Wales in 1915. He went in at 3 for 17 and the score would have been 5 for 58 had Macartney not been dropped first ball. Callaway, a nuggetty country boy, thrashed 207 in even time, playing all his strokes as if time was running out. It was: that was Callaway's only first-class innings. A few weeks after his 21st birthday he was blasted into the mud near Bullecourt in France, his remains never recovered. There is no telling what he might have done. But he was the most exciting raw talent to emerge in Australia since Victor Trumper.

WAUGH's 1st XI

Justin Langer
Matthew Hayden
Ricky Ponting
Mark Waugh
Steve Waugh (c)
Damien Martyn
Adam Gilchrist (wk)
Shane Warne
Brett Lee
Jason Gillespie
Glenn McGrath

A more sophisticated cricketer was Eric Barbour, a doctor who may have been the most intelligent man ever to play for New South Wales. His technique was flawless and his temperament unflappable. A youthful prodigy, Barbour scored his first two first-class centuries while still at school, and was averaging 51 until war broke out when he was 24. He survived the war but his cricket career did not, and he left the first-class game upon returning from service in Europe.

Owen Rock, another doctor who served in France, was even less fortunate. Caught in the boggy mud of no-man's land, he suffered terrible damage to his right knee. Barely able to run, he returned to cricket after the war with a remodelled technique, in which his back foot scarcely moved and he tried to score in boundaries. Because of his weak fielding he played only six first-class games, in which he thumped 758 runs at an average of 94. What might he have done in 1917, a 20-year-old with two good legs?

There were others, too, whose frustrated careers might have flourished. Claude Tozer was an immaculate opener, who survived dreadful war wounds only to be shot in 1920 by a thwarted lover.

ARMSTRONG'S 1st XI

Warren Bardsley
Bert Collins
Charlie Macartney
Johnny Taylor
Warwick Armstrong (c)
Eric Barbour
Jack Gregory
Bert Oldfield
Ted McDonald
Jack Massie
Bert Ironmonger

Roy Park was a neat Victorian batsman whose one Test innings, after the war, lasted precisely one ball. And Roy Minnett was a graceful all-rounder whose potential was never quite realised in his nine Tests before the war. It is difficult to assess the strength of Australia's batting in 1917 because there are so many imponderables. But it would have been nothing less than outstanding.

The clearest difference between the two teams is in fielding. Here Waugh's team is obviously stronger, although Gregory's slip-fielding – he plucked 15 catches in five Tests in the 1920-21 Ashes series – would have been a match for Mark Waugh. And if the selectors had spotted a 22-year-old Bert Oldfield in time for the 1917 tour, his side may have had a slight advantage behind the stumps. On the other hand a few cumbersome characters, most notably Armstrong and Ironmonger, would need to be hidden.

The pace of change in modern cricket makes it harder than ever to compare teams across generations. After their matches, the players of 1917 would have returned to their day jobs in offices, surgeries and building sites. There were no helmets, few heavy bats and no coaches sliding quotes from Chinese philosophers under hotel doors. But just suppose: what if the teams could be matched against each other?

Waugh's men would surely dominate the first two days, imposing themselves on the game with the sheer speed of their batting and bowling, playing at a tempo nobody could have imagined in the

Bert Oldfield

Jack Gregory

leisurely Edwardian age. On the third day they are looking to extend their first-innings lead. But it rains. The complexion of the game alters utterly. On the uncovered sticky wickets, heavy bats become a liability and men like Ironmonger turn deadly. It's a rout, and Armstrong's men from 1917 are left to chase a modest target. But the pitch is taking spin, and there's Warne to contend with. Maybe Gregory can knock him off his length, and then ...

And then who knows? The 1917 team would have been endlessly adaptable and versatile, with several leading lights capable of turning matches with bat and ball alike. Waugh's men batted with greater fluency, bowled aggressively and fielded like lightning. Maybe they were the best ever. But one thing is certain: Armstrong's 1917 line-up is the greatest team the world never saw.

Max Bonnell is a lawyer, sports historian and the author of How Many More Are Coming? The Short Life of Jack Marsh.

Hamish Blair/Getty Images

CHEERS, TUGGA: Steve Waugh is hoisted on a farewell lap around his beloved SCG.

VERY, VERY SWASHBUCKLING: V.V.S. Laxman hit 937 international runs, none of them ugly.

HAIRY PROPOSITION: Jason Gillespie, Australia's attack leader in 2003-04.

CRICKETER OF THE YEAR: Darren Lehmann

PURA CUP CRICKETER OF THE YEAR: Matthew Elliott

DRAMA IN THE DUSK: All eyes dart to the square-leg umpire as Shane Warne, in fading light in Cairns, has Lloyd Chandpaul stumped and ...

Hamish Blair/Getty Images

SO FAST: As in batting, so in life. David Hookes, who died at 48, had a habit of resting his bat against the stumps, a gesture re-enacted during his funeral at Adelaide Oval.

KEEP AN EYE ON THIS ONE: A boy and a ball in Katherine, Northern Territory, where Steve Waugh ran a coaching session in June 2004.

Still grappling, still squirreling

by GIDEON HAIGH

Cricket, a resolutely nostalgic game, loves its centenaries. But one coming up on May 1, 2005, seems barely to have been noted. Some would think the 100th anniversary of the inaugural meeting of the Australian Board of Control for International Cricket hardly worth celebrating. It is nonetheless certainly worth marking.

To be sure, nobody remembered when the board turned 75 in 1980 either, although that was perhaps because not much had changed. The Australian Cricket Board was still more an address than an organisation. Its senior executive officer was its secretary, the Dickensian figure of Alan Barnes, who answered correspondence from a dusty office in Cricket House in Melbourne. He was nicknamed 'Justa' for his regular response when asked for a document: "Just a minute, just a minute." The files he could not fit in his cabinets – sometimes because of the cartons of cigarettes stored in there – were stacked on the floor, in places as high as the ceiling.

The 100th anniversary will probably slip by for the opposite reason: that the body now known as Cricket Australia is rooted so firmly in the present. Presiding over that first meeting at Wesley College was Lawrence Adamson, the school's 45-year-old headmaster, an old boy of Rugby and lifelong bachelor whose role was of a piece with his other pro bono works, like chairmanship of the Lost Dogs' Home. Its chief executive officer since June 2001, James Sutherland, is a 39-year-old schoolmaster's son with three young children who doesn't look much less fit than he did in the four first-class and nine one-day games he played for Victoria in the early 1990s.

Mind you, if a Melbourne establishment can verifiably be said to exist, Sutherland is a scion of it. He is married to the former Heidi Asimus, daughter of David Asimus, the one-time chairman of the Australian Wheat Board and BHP director. His maternal grandfather, Sir James Darling, was the legendary headmaster of Sutherland's alma mater, Geelong Grammar.

Sir James told the story of how, on coming to Grammar from Charterhouse in England in 1930, he was disconcerted by the sporting earnestness of Australians. "The trouble with you Englishmen," his sportsmaster seethed at him through gritted teeth, "is that you don't know the difference between games and sport." James Sutherland, it would seem, could tell the difference, and came down on the side of games. He was serious about cricket but never wrapped up in it. "There were two reasons," he says. "One, I never had enough belief in my cricket ability to think I could bank on it. Two, while as a cricketer I wanted to be the best I could be, I knew there was a lot more to life than playing cricket."

Broad-shouldered and standing 194 cm, Sutherland had the physical gifts to be a fast bowler but lacked, perhaps, the necessary loose screw. His reputation was as a reliable medium-paced workhorse and a rock-ribbed team player. He found his main cricketing mentor in 1985 when he left Melbourne CC for Melbourne University CC, where Peter Spence was coach. University had been well-run off the field but "a bit of a chopping block" on it. In Sutherland's first season they made the finals. "The thing I learned was that success breeds success," he recalls. "When people start believing in themselves, they begin to take pride in everything around them. They want to take responsibility for committee roles, to organise social functions. The club mag goes from being a sheet that comes out a couple of times a year to 50 pages a month."

Sutherland also recalls his sense of connectedness to the rest of cricket. "I remember the feeling I got from the fact that Malcolm Gray was on the Victorian Cricket Association and chairman of the Australian Cricket Board while he was still vice-president of Melbourne University CC. That resonated with me, that connection to the whole. While it can be argued that it's a weakness of Australian cricket that it has principally been made up of volunteers, there's also a sense in which it's been a great strength that a grassroots cricket administrator can serve cricket at the highest level."

At that stage, Sutherland had "no idea what I wanted to do". Work and cricket ran in parallel. His undergraduate degree was in commerce and he spent five years at Ernst & Young, after qualifying as a chartered accountant; in the meantime he won flags at University in 1990-91, then at his old club Melbourne in 1992-93, before returning to University and leading them to another premiership. This is not by the way. The experience was formative.

"The culture 20 years ago was very supportive of players who worked," he says. "It was accepted. People went: 'Well, we don't pay you a wage as a cricketer that is sufficient for you to get by. You need to work. And on that basis we'll start training at 5 p.m.' If I was a cricketer like me now, I actually think I would have faced some tough decisions about work and cricket. And I've got a problem with that. The fact is that very few cricketers get to a level where they earn sufficient income to set themselves up for the rest of their lives to justify the sacrifices they have made. Ten to 20 at any one time. So that means there are 120 to 130 players making significant sacrifices that mean their transition when their cricket career is over will be difficult. We haven't got it right yet."

Colleagues who knew I was going to interview Sutherland warned me to expect a sort of Bismarck, who proverbially could say nothing in seven languages. I didn't find him so; on the contrary he was personable, candid, sometimes humorous and, on one occasion, decidedly unimpressed. This was when I recounted to him a recent conversation with a talented teenage cricketer, the member of a Pura Cup squad, who told me he had no time to work or study in winter because he was "so busy" going to training and keeping fit.

Sutherland: "That's absolute crap. These guys, they do not know what busy is. That's a great pity. Players at state level shouldn't go round thinking themselves in clover to the extent that they can simply fritter the winter away not furthering themselves, whether that's study, improving their qualifications, getting work experience."

Wisden: "I think this bloke knows that. But he needs someone he respects to give him that advice."

Sutherland: "That's the trouble. We send mixed messages. We tell players: 'We want you to be the best you can be. You need to do this, this and this to improve. We've got a training session at 6 a.m. and we'll be back together at 3 p.m.' But if it prevents players developing in other ways, what is that doing for them in real life?"

An earlier form of this dilemma plagued the ACB when Sutherland was recruited in November 1998 after six years as finance director at the Carlton Football Club. Although the ACB had signed its first Memorandum of Understanding with first-class players, the dust was yet to settle on the industrial unrest caused by the irruption of the Australian Cricketers' Association. "When I was hired there wasn't really a job vacancy," says Sutherland. "It was a created role, because the ACB needed someone with commercial background

Centenary test: Balancing work and life for cricketers is one of James Sutherland's biggest challenges – and "we haven't got it right yet".

who could understand the MOU, but also the cricket experience to talk and deal with the players as a cricketer. The relationship at the time was pretty average. There was a lot of animosity."

Sutherland can take credit for an altogether calmer industrial relations environment than that bequeathed him by Malcolm Speed. But his reservations about full-time professionalism remain, and he is comfortable thinking about them aloud.

Wisden: "The current MOU expires in June 2005. Will the concerns you've just expressed be on the agenda?"

Sutherland: "They're certainly on my agenda. And I think they're on Tim May and Ian Healy's agenda too. I'd like to think we're like-minded on that. It's just that we haven't found the magic recipe to get it right. Because you can't really take people and tell them they're going to do this and this. Well, perhaps you can. Perhaps you can make it part of the contract: that in return for getting paid, there will be an expectation that they will do boom-boom-boom to further their career or set themselves up later. Ideally, I wouldn't want it to get to that stage. But in the absence of other solutions, that might be an extreme we have to explore. It's what I grapple with. Ultimately, people have a choice in the way they choose to live their lives. But in five or 10 years' time, when they're not prepared for a transition, what happens?"

Wisden: "How much do professional cricketers have to be told? How much guidance do they need?"

Sutherland: "That's a tough question."

Sutherland has been prepared to answer it. The initiative most associated with him has been the Spirit of Cricket charter, which Australia's contracted internationals signed last year. Sutherland got there, he explains, by degrees. The bad-tempered Sydney Test of 2002-03, when both Adam Gilchrist and Matthew Hayden were fined for ICC code-of-conduct breaches, disturbed him. Glenn McGrath's *contretemps* with Ramnaresh Sarwan in Antigua five months later infuriated him, to the extent that he rang Steve Waugh from Australia. Interestingly, perhaps, Sutherland does not refer directly to the *politesse* of cricket. His concern was that these incidents clashed with the first of four "strategic priorities" – to strengthen and protect the spirit of cricket – listed in Cricket Australia's strategic plan *From Backyard to Baggy Green*. He might have been recruited because of his cricketing background but he now speaks very much like a manager.

Sutherland: "It was starting to get to me. I thought: 'You're saying that this is important. But how bloody important is it?' If you're going to hold the game up as special, then you've got a problem if your leaders and role models aren't buying to that. Might as well not have it."

Wisden: "Why did we need a process for what used to be thought of as commonsense?"

Sutherland: "The game's different. There's huge amounts of personal income involved. I'm not saying people try any harder than they did. There's just more at stake, commercially and financially."

Wisden: "You're not telling me that McGrath was thinking about his income when he threatened to rip Sarwan's throat out, are you?"

Sutherland: "No. But for whatever reason, there has been a stigma attached to the way the Australian cricket team played the game. And that wasn't consistent with the strategic plan."

Wisden: "That's surely not only a matter of financial stakes."

Sutherland: "No you're right. I think one of the factors was that International Cricket Council referees, for whatever reason, had not been policing the code. Nor, I think, was the code itself clear enough. I think our code of conduct now is very clear. It says you can do this but not that. And that's what players need. Players need battle lines to be drawn because when you get out there, in the heat of battle, you've got a job to do. You want to know where your boundaries are so you can just go for it."

Wisden: "But it's not a battle. And these aren't battle lines. It's a game. The very words we use these days, I think, complicate our understanding of what constitutes suitable aggression."

Sutherland: "That's probably the case. But you can't snap your fingers and change that. It's how it is. Let's take 'battle' out of it. Lines have been drawn. That's important, because people in their uncertainty were pushing the lines and not being pulled up."

Sutherland's approach seems to have paid dividends. The Australian team were recently awarded the 2004 Ausport Prize by the Australian Sports Commission for their contribution to the "integrity, good sports and fair play of Australian sport". In fact, the misbehaviour of players has been less of a concern lately than that of administrators, particularly those at the Zimbabwe Cricket Union. Engulfed by the despot Robert Mugabe's ruling Zanu-PF party, the ZCU triggered a crisis by sacking its leading (mostly white) players in favour of more tractable junior (mostly black) players – a crisis Australia reluctantly wandered into in May on a short but embarrassing tour.

The visit proceeded largely because the ICC's Future Tours Programme threatens those who do not tour with fines and suspensions. Sutherland defended this policy strongly in Cricket Australia's *Insight* magazine: "Cricket clearly does not exist in a vacuum. It is affected by and in turn has an impact on all sorts of other aspects of local and global life. However, Cricket Australia has the task of promoting cricket as its core purpose. The only authority we have … is to focus on that task." The reasoning, I have to confess, did not impress me: Sutherland's concession that cricket does not take place in a vacuum was accompanied by confirmation that this is the way it would be treated.

Wisden: "It seems to me that the role of Cricket Australia expands and shrinks according to what you want to get involved in and don't. 'Promoting cricket' might be Cricket Australia's 'core purpose', but it also has the purpose of representing Australia. The Test team is called 'Australia' not 'Australian Cricketers'. How can we be national representatives one minute and just a group of cricketers the next?"

Sutherland: "I understand your argument. It would have been easy for us to say: 'We're not going'. But the effect of that is a compromise that would have far-reaching consequences in lots and lots of ways. It's a really difficult issue. One of the simple things for me to say is the Australian government should just have said: 'You're not going. We don't want you to go.' And if they'd said that … then we wouldn't have gone. If the government was serious about that and about the issues in Zimbabwe and an association by Australia as a country … then clearly it should have taken a much stronger stance."

Wisden: "But surely that's the essence of our protest about Zimbabwe, that the government of the country shouldn't be bossing the cricket board around. Look, it's fair enough to deplore it when cricket and politics mix. But by going to Zimbabwe, you were helping it mix. You were saying: 'Fill your board with political cronies. Turn your team into an arm of state propaganda. Plunder your exchequer. Do as you please. After all, it's only a game of cricket.'"

Sutherland: "I think you're drawing conclusions about Mugabe having representation on the board."

Wisden: "He is the patron. And haven't there been a host of appointments in the last year with Zanu-PF connections? Isn't that clear?"

Sutherland: "It's not clear to me. In fact, nothing on the Zimbabwe issue is clear to me. The lead-in to that tour was extremely frustrating because we just weren't getting a clear view of the situation. I don't know whether that's because the people at the ZCU didn't know or what it was. But on a daily basis, we were getting advice to the effect that the players were back, then they were sacked, then they were back, then sacked again. If we'd known what was going to happen a long way out, it may well have been easier to make a decision. But, I mean, we were always going to go, weren't we? We telegraphed that by going to Zimbabwe during the World Cup."

"If the government was serious about the issues in Zimbabwe … then clearly it should have taken a much stronger stance"

Wisden: "Everything I've seen coming out of Zimbabwe suggests the game has been intensely politicised since then: at selection, administration, finance, in domestic cricket, club cricket, coaching. I understand that sport and politics mix more freely in some countries than others, but it is seldom that boards are actually taken over in the way that Zanu-PF has devoured the ZCU. If the Australian government demanded control of Cricket Australia – sought a balance of power on your board, took control of your selection, and opposed the involvement in the game of a racial minority – what would you want other countries to do? Would you want them to keep playing with us?"

Sutherland: "That's very much a hypothetical question … Generally speaking, however, given their commitment to the Future Tours Programme, we would expect other Test-playing countries to support the game in our country by continuing to play against us … Anyway, is this a position that a member country should have been placed in in the first place? Or is it an issue for world cricket? One of the things we've not mentioned is that the Future Tours Programme says if a country does not turn up and play without a good reason, specifically related to security, then they get a minimum $US 2 million fine plus any damages … You're saying to me that we shouldn't have gone. But I've also got the commercial consideration that it's going to cost us $US 2 million plus."

Wisden: "Isn't that to imbue the Future Tours Programme with the status of the Ten Commandments?"

Sutherland (smiling): "That's what it is to us, Gideon. Look, if there is a key plank of the financial arrangements of world cricket, it is the knowledge, comfort, security of who is going to be playing here this summer. Without that, we're frantically trying to organise whoever we can get."

Wisden: "And you're back to the old days of bilateral arrangements."

Sutherland: "Which weren't all bad. But the positives of the Future Tours Programme far outweigh the negatives."

Wisden: "Is that primarily because cricket has obligations to sponsors and broadcasters?"

Sutherland: "It's certainly that."

Wisden: "So isn't that the tail wagging the dog?"

Sutherland: "No, it's broader than that. We've got obligations to the cricket community – which includes broadcasters, sponsors, grounds, members of cricket associations, who are fans and players and who expect cricket every summer. And that has a negative impact on the level of interest in the game and the status of the Australian cricket team."

Wisden: "But doesn't it have a negative impact on the status of the Australian cricket team that we're prepared to go to Zimbabwe under present circumstances?"

Sutherland: "The reality is we're in a no-win situation with Zimbabwe. And we chose the lesser of two evils. There was obviously a lot of public comment. A lot of people thought very hard about it round here."

Wisden: "What did you think, James? Not answering as CEO of Cricket Australia but as James Sutherland, private citizen?"

Sutherland (pauses): "I don't think it matters what I think."

Wisden: "But I'm sure you've got your own thoughts on this. I'm giving you the opportunity to take your Cricket Australia hat off and express them."

Sutherland: "It's hard for me to do that because I've been to Zimbabwe, I know some of the people involved in Zimbabwean cricket, I know the game. What I can say is I'm not uncomfortable with the action Cricket Australia took."

Wisden: "You won't take it off will you?"

Sutherland (smiling): "I try to take it off when I go to the footy and watch the Cats. One thing I will say is that I don't think countries should be placed in those difficult situations, where they're even more compromised in their decision-making by the Future Tours Programme."

Wisden: "Do you object to the idea of the programme being a regulation, with the possibility of fines and suspensions?"

Sutherland: "It does seem rather drastic. But when you see the importance of the Future Tours Programme to some countries, you can understand the rationale. There are some countries for which an Indian tour is the main source of revenue. If India does not tour, Zimbabwean cricket is dead meat for five years [because of lost revenue from TV rights]. It's that significant."

Of course, sport and politics sometimes mix in Australia, specifically when prime ministers get involved. It seemed worth asking Sutherland's view of John Howard's infamous gaffe – that Muttiah Muralidaran is a chucker because "they proved it in Perth with that thing" – and Murali's subsequent decision not to play in Darwin and Cairns. Sutherland's remarks were rather more nuanced than Shane Warne's "I-cop-it-sweet-so-should-he" response.

Sutherland: "I think it [Howard's comment] would have been better left unsaid. Needless to say, a prime minister's comment will inevitably get airplay, and those about Muralidaran especially so. But I'm not sure the comments were directly responsible for Murali not touring. I don't think he wanted to come."

Wisden: "Was it beyond the wit of man to find some way to make touring here a little easier for Murali?"

Sutherland: "We tried. The players were encouraging about him coming. I made public comments to the effect that I wanted him to come, and I spoke to Duleep Mendis [the Sri Lankan board's CEO] about it too. But it was pretty clear that he wasn't coming."

Wisden: "In Murali's position, I doubt I'd have wanted to come. There was nothing in it for him."

Sutherland: "I agree."

Wisden: "I think he's had a very rough time out here."

Sutherland: "He has. And he gets a lot of coverage. Yes, I agree."

Zimbabwe presents the ICC with other problems. The Future Tours Programme may be next to godliness but it is also leading to an awful lot of lacklustre, low-intensity cricket being miraculously awarded Test status. The glutted cricket calendar, like the weather, is a subject we all discuss but nobody wants to do anything about. I asked Sutherland about this in the light of the whizzbang ICC Super Series to be held in Australia next October, pitting the world's No. 1 Test nation – Australia – against a Rest of the World XI.

Sutherland: "My personal view is that the amount of cricket being played is about right. The problem has been the amount of mediocre cricket, which has grated on everyone. But this is the best against the best. People can't get enough of the best cricket. You saw that last summer. India and Australia played one of the best summers of cricket that the country's ever seen, and whilst the Australian public have enjoyed the success of the Australian team, they also enjoyed seeing them under the pump, having to come from behind to equalise then go one-all to Sydney."

> "These guys, they do not know what busy is. Players at state level shouldn't think … they can fritter the winter away not furthering themselves"

Cricket Australia is both a very new and a very old institution. The idea of a serious permanent executive and staff is really no more than 10 years old, dating to the end of the board's post-World Series Cricket relationship with Kerry Packer's PBL Marketing. But the concept of a board composed of members elected by the state associations is as old as the body itself: that is, it turns 100 in May 2005. Isn't it time it was revisited?

Wisden: "Australian cricket's structure is historic but unusual, almost as though the paramount body is owned by its subsidiaries. Is it improveable and how?"

Sutherland (smiling): "That's a prick of a question. Depends on the side of the fence you're on. Sometimes we think we run Australian cricket. But if you go to a state association, they'll say: 'Well, we own you.'"

Wisden: "So that's the difference between the board and the associations? The board thinks it runs Australian cricket, the associations know they do."

Sutherland: "They know they own the people who think they run it."

Wisden: "Cricket Australia is governed by 14 directors: three each from New South Wales, Victoria and South Australia; two each from Queensland and Western Australia; one from Tasmania. So the founder states have nine votes. Yet the most successful states of the last 15 years, Queensland and WA, have four. Why?"

Sutherland (sighs): "Next question. Well, it's historical, you know that."

Wisden: "That doesn't mean it's optimal."

Sutherland: "That's true … Look, I'm a big one for worrying about the things I can control and not about those I can't. We executives don't have any input in that. It's for the members. If they believe it's an issue, they'll address it."

The CEO of a listed company knows when he is doing a good job; it's in his profits and his share price. But how is Sutherland to know? The difficulties of his job were illustrated by another of his key initiatives last year: a census of participants in Australian cricket. Setting a stricter definition of participation than most previous censuses, it revealed 281,058 club players, 90,666 school players and 64,601 playing reduced-numbers variations such as Kanga and Have-A-Go cricket – a total of 436,325. While itself not of great use until a comparative census is done in a few years, it does highlight the complexities of the issues confronting cricket at community level.

Sutherland: "What do I feel about that number? I'm glad we have it. Is it a performance indicator? Yes and no. Say you have a club turning over 80 players in a season. If suddenly they have 120 in one season, they're going to suffer capacity constraints. Where do they play? Where do you find grounds? There's no point in us attracting more people to play the game if there aren't the grounds, facilities, umpires, coaches, volunteers. Grounds especially are harder to come by than ever, and more expensive. Housing estates are being built where developers think about pathways for people to walk their dogs, but not ovals to play cricket on. If they have some spare space they might build a little soccer pitch, which is not big enough for cricket or footy. So it's much more of a challenge than incremental increases in participation rates."

Cricket Australia's resources have their own capacity constraints. In seasons 2001-02 and 2002-03, Cricket Australia reported operating surpluses totalling $77 million, about 82% of which was distributed to the states. Is this peculiar status of Cricket Australia – as a partnership of state associations to which it immediately disgorges its surpluses – one that will work in its second century? All Sutherland would say was: "In any organisation owned by its members there is a debate about the right amount of retained earnings." The associations, he was quick to add, were "doing a very good job" and "running a tight ship".

Wisden: "Would you like Cricket Australia to lead a more autonomous existence, with less reference to the states?"

Sutherland: "In an ideal world you'd be in a position where you could manage on a needs basis rather than having to juggle from year to year. But we're just not in that position. We are trying to build our reserves, but the level of distributions to states means the growth is minimal. So we're squirreling a bit away. But whether there's enough there to deal with a disaster is highly debatable."

Nothing has changed very quickly in Australian cricket administration. But perhaps we should give it time. In some respects, it's hardly begun.

Gideon Haigh edited Wisden Cricketers' Almanack Australia *from 1999 to 2000-01. His latest book is* Game for Anything: Writings on Cricket.

That coil-like wrist

Shane Warne is the most written about cricketer of the modern age. He has been the star of seven books, one poem (by John Clarke), a million tributes, two million bucketings, a thousand crowd banners and one never-ending soap opera. In the year of his greatest triumph, when he became the first slow bowler to scale 500 Test wickets and joined Sri Lanka's Muttiah Muralidaran in a breathless duel to become history's greatest wicket-taker, we decided not to ask yet another writer to write yet another thoughtful appreciation. Instead we approached six Australian Test leg-spinners – one from every decade since World War II – and invited them to compare themselves to Warne. What does he do that they couldn't? How does he do it? And can there ever be another like him?

Rex Sellers, 1950s

"I was a novice compared with Warne. I only played one Test and my style of getting wickets was completely different. I used to throw the ball up, land it just inside off stump and the batsmen came down the wicket to me. I hardly ever bowled with a square leg; I had one man behind square, a mid-wicket and a deep mid-on, with everyone else on the off side. It would have been a bad ball for me to be bowling on leg stump because I was far too slow through the air. I think Warne is the forerunner, the benchmark, of pushing the ball through. When I went to England in 1964 I found it difficult. The wickets are slow and you don't get the same bounce, so you have to push the ball through and move your line closer to the leg stump. You become a different bowler – and I found it hard to do that.

That's why the first thing that comes to mind with Warne is his resilience, his adaptability in all facets, in any hemisphere. Then there is his uncomplicated run-up and delivery stride, and his ability to be a shock or stock bowler, which is a testimony to his stamina. And he has that coil-like wrist; he was born for greatness with that first ball he bowled in the UK to Mike Gatting. The biggest spinner I've ever seen, including Warne, was the left-armer David Sincock. His bosie or wrong'un was as big as his stock ball – can you imagine what would Warne be like if he spun it back the other way with the same amount of lateral spin? But David was very inaccurate, the ball used to fly around everywhere. Warne has huge turn and accuracy, which is hard to do. His accuracy, the coil-like spin of his legbreak, his speed through the air and his ability to bowl for so long are what sets him apart.

And he has so many variations. Longevity gives him that. I used to try to learn one new ball a year, so that people hadn't worked me out the next year. I think Warnie has done that too, and he's been playing nearly 15 years, so he's developed lots of balls and variations. I daresay he's got two or three wrong'uns, even though he doesn't have a great one. Then there's his flippers and straight balls and zooters and top-spinners. He definitely has variations of what looks like the same ball.

I couldn't bowl the flipper. My hands were too small to be able to hold over the top of the ball, which is what you have to do. I played around the same time as Richie Benaud and I think Warne is more potent than Richie was. Richie only had a small wrong'un – Bobby Simpson probably bowled a better wrong'un than Richie – but he did have a leg-spinner and a flipper. Warne has got more wickets with his flipper but, gee, Richie's was very good. I think their flippers were on a par; Warnie just uses his more often. Richie was a pastmaster at giving the sucker short leg-spinner – pull! Then another short leg-spinner – pull! And then he'd bowl the flipper which would shoot straight through and get you lbw.

When Warne came back from injury he was really only able to bowl leggies for about 18 months. Batsmen started taking risks against him and getting away with it. But gradually he's lost weight and his strength and his flipper have come back. He's lethal again. He has taken the ability to bowl leg-spin to a new level, I think. He is in the super club. He is unquestionably the best spin bowler ever."

Rex Sellers, whose family migrated from India to Adelaide when he was seven, debuted for South Australia in 1959-60. His solitary Test was in Kolkata in 1964-65; he took 0 for 17 off five overs and then it rained.

John Gleeson, 1960s

"The main thing is his control. Fellows who have been big spinners of the ball – Johnny Martin and David Sincock and Stuart MacGill – their control is not within a bull's roar of this bloke's. The ball can do only three things: it either goes straight or spins from the leg or goes from the off. It can't do anything else. It doesn't disappear or explode. So I think the main thing that sticks to Warne is his control and knowledge of the game. He showed that when he had the captaincy a couple of times.

I didn't see Bill O'Reilly, and apparently he was pretty handy, but this fella has got to be the best leggie since the war, at least. Normally people with Warne's control have to give something up, usually the amount or the variety of spin. But this bloke's got everything – variety and control – although I think a bit of baloney goes on about the eight different balls he says he can bowl. As I said, basically you do three things, so there's a certain amount of bluff there.

But as a spinner you've got to use a bit of guile. It's not as if you can bounce somebody; you've got to be aggressive in different ways, with field placings and thinking about the game. I used to always make people look for something that wasn't there. I reckon I knew two or three fellas who could pick what I was doing most of the time, but that never worried me. I never thought I couldn't get them out. I had one advantage in that I had eight balls an over – Warne's only got six – and that gives you more time to work on a fellow. He's got an edge with all the protection they've got. Guys can field a lot closer and feel confident they won't get hurt, and they intimidate the batsmen. It allows you to get that extra over-spin and make the ball bounce higher, looking for catches.

My biggest problem was we lacked quick bowling, so I did the donkey-work. I wasn't used the way Warne is. Economically we'd probably work out about the same, however he's a far bigger spinner. Also he bowled a flipper – I bowled a sort of a one, but you wouldn't really call it a flipper – so he's got that ammunition I didn't have. For me, the newer the ball and greener the wicket the better. I tried to get the ball off the track as quick as possible, to commit a batsman to a stroke and give him no time to get out of it. The lbw rule was different too. You had to pitch between wicket and wicket, and hit wicket, so lbw was virtually out of the game. The Poms used to kick it through cover quicker than I could hit it. If you struck a bloke on the full or close to the full you had no chance in the world. You wouldn't even have the hide to appeal, let alone bellow, which they do nowadays. I'd like to be playing now. The men with the finger, they throw them up quick smart – more than they should, I believe.

I heard it mentioned that Warne said he might ring me during his year off to work out a new mystery ball, but he never did. I was at

Alan Davidson's farewell lunch a while ago and John Buchanan, the Australian coach, suggested that with the technology they've got they should put a bit of my action on film and keep it for the archives, in case somebody might use it down the line. One day that might occur. But they'd want to start soon – I'm getting too old to start bowling again.

If I could change one thing about Warne I'd make him run through the crease more. Sometimes he just takes one step and stops dead – boom, boom – and then he's an ordinary bowler, you've got him by the short and curlies. I always reckon when you finish four or five steps down the wicket it gives the ball extra vim and vigour. He had a great flipper and a good wrong'un early on, and both of them seem to have disappeared. But he's got away with it. The rest of his game has developed to the extent that he's still as good as he was when he had more variety. Very talented character. I don't think we'll ever see another one like him. We'll see someone who's different, who might even be as productive, but there'll never be another Warne. Never. Like there'll never be another Gleeson."

John Gleeson, one of cricket's most tantalising mystery spinners, bowled leg-breaks that looked like off-breaks with a bent-finger grip based on photographs of Jack Iverson's technique. He took 93 wickets at 36.20 in 29 Tests.

Jim Higgs, 1970s

"I first came in contact with him when he was at St Kilda and Jack Edwards, the club president, asked me to have a few sessions with him. He wasn't bowling the flipper at that stage, he was more fiddling around with it than anything. All I did was show him what I used to do. He got a bit of help from Terry Jenner but everyone works things out for themselves. What is certain is that Shane has always been his own bowler.

It was obvious that he was going to have a huge impact on the game, although not everyone could see it. He was struggling to get a start with Victoria in the early 1990s. I was one of the national selection committee at the time and I had to wonder why. He could do most things with the ball. He developed a few things later on, like the flipper and using the subtleties of back-spin and square-spin to create different flight paths. But the thing that stood out was that he was so strong. Without that, a spinner will struggle. Shane had that – and obviously a bit more.

From a technical point of view, there have been a lot of slow bowlers over the years – some finger-spinners, some leggies – who can bowl accurately and consistently for a long period of time. Then there are those who can spin the bejesus out of it. As far as I've seen, he's the first that's really been able to do both. You look at Anil Kumble. He's consistent but he's nowhere near as potent as Warnie in terms of getting blokes out – and in conditions that are made for batting. That's the key rider.

I used to try to spin the crap out of it and hope it landed in the right place. I'd try to confuse the bloke at the other end. That was a product of the times; we played on hard and fast wickets that offered very little turn, so you had to rip it hard if you were to be any chance of taking wickets. I played at a time when finger-spin wasn't popular and just about every Sheffield Shield team had a leggie. That's gone out because of the need for consistency. Leg-spin has disappeared to the point where only the ones who can bowl accurately survive. Shane is one of those bowlers.

The most intriguing thing about him is the way he has been able to re-invent himself when he's had to. Having had one myself, a shoulder reconstruction is very debilitating. You lose a lot of strength. So he had to change. His brute power was gone. He couldn't just blast them out the way he used to. Now he uses a refined approach whereby he unnerves batsmen until they get themselves out.

He has been a great advertisement for wrist-spin bowling. In the 1970s, the only people who could see what you were doing with the flight of the ball were the ones sitting in the front row of the member's stand. Television has demystified things for the average punter. They can see through slow-motion the curve and flight path of the ball. I think that's been his biggest legacy. He has added a dimension that never used to be there."

Jim Higgs took 66 wickets at 31.16 in his 22 Tests, despite bowling in an era when his craft received little recognition. He later became a national selector and was instrumental in helping Warne develop his flipper.

Bob Holland, 1980s

"I've watched his career with huge interest. What impresses me most is his ability to read a batsman. When he screws his face up after a delivery, as if to say 'that nearly got through', I can see what he's thinking. He sums up a batsman in about three balls. He realises that this guy isn't so good off the back foot or doesn't like to use his feet. Then he hones in. The difference between him and other bowlers is that he bowls exactly the right delivery in exactly the right spot at exactly the right time.

I tried to spin the ball as much as possible so I had my fair share of bad deliveries. If you put a lot of revs on it, you have to control it. Shane has exceptional control all of the time. And a lot of variation. He has a great wrong'un but he doesn't bowl it very much because he usually has the flipper going. There are two deliveries that stand out for me. There's his leg-spinner that drifts from middle to leg and then spins a lot, that's an incredible delivery; and the other one is the flipper that's quick and straight and usually around the mark. They are both lethal.

There was never too much bluff about the way I bowled. It wasn't something I went home to work on. Shane has always conjured up the idea of mystery balls. He's always mentioned new deliveries, like the zooter. I used to bowl a variety of it but at the time it was called a flipper. In essence, they're the same: both spin backwards and go straight, except that one comes out one side of the hand and one comes out the other. He's a strong fella and that allows him to vary his pace. He normally bowls at 82 kph but he can bowl the flipper at 90 to 100 kph. You can basically only bowl leg-breaks, wrong'uns or one that goes straight. It's the degree to which you bowl them that's the key. And that's where a lot of Shane's mystery comes from.

It's been a good time to bowl, of course. He's been in a successful team. He's had runs to bowl to and there are fewer slow bowlers these days, so batsmen aren't getting much practice against leggies. He's also had someone keeping it tight at the other end. When a promising partnership is developing, and Shane is having to work hard, Glenn McGrath is at the other end either keeping them quiet or getting them out. Australia have rarely known success like it. Is it because Shane's there? Or is it just his good luck to have been around at the right time? I'd say it's a bit of both.

It's very unlikely that we'll see a leggie like him again – although it is possible. I went to England in 1985 and someone asked me if I would be the last Australian leg-spinner to tour. I said I hoped not. Almost 20 years later we have a bowler who has revolutionised leg-spin bowling. Now every leggie has a little bit of Warne in them. But I'd like to think he's got a bit of every leggie that came before in him as well."

Bob Holland made his Test debut at 38 and took 34 wickets at 39.76 in 11 Tests. He lives in the Newcastle region and retired from all forms of cricket two years ago, aged 56.

Peter McIntyre, 1990s

"I guess if I had my time again I'd love to be born in a different era. We were together at the Academy in Adelaide for a while – I was part-time, he was full-time – and Terry Jenner, myself and Warnie were standing around spinning balls to ourselves, as you do. The revolutions on his ball were almost twice as much as ours. I remember TJ giving me a nudge and saying: 'Have a look at Warnie when he spins the ball up.' It just kept going and going, it had a lot more noise on it. He wasn't overly fit in those early days – he was a fat boy, and he'll admit that – but he had this enormous strength.

It was a real adventure. We both started out in club cricket, him at St Kilda and me at Essendon, and then we went to Zimbabwe on a Young Australia tour in 1991. Ever since Abdul Qadir there hadn't been any focus on leg-spin. We were discovering all these different balls that had been dormant since Clarrie Grimmett, and batsmen just didn't know what they were. There was this real hype. We were talking about flippers and zooters and back-spinners. We named our flipper 'the Butchie ball' because Ian Butchart, who used to play for Zimbabwe, got cleaned up with it every time – by both of us.

We were both on a par. Then Warnie took a seven-for on that tour and you could almost predict, even then, that he was going to be a freak. But we always had a nice rapport going, it was never a competition. It wasn't about who was better; it was just the whole adventure of leg-spin coming back into vogue.

I had a better wrong'un. He had a pretty unique grip where he held the ball with his forefinger and middle finger together, and it's always difficult to bowl the wrong'un like that. He did have one but he didn't rip it enough for it to be any sort of weapon. But he definitely had a better flipper and back-spinner than me. The other factor was his drift. When he's on, and he's really got some grip on the ball, just watch his drift – that's his biggest weapon. When he really drifts it and then puts the big spin on it too, it's very hard to work out where the ball is going. He's like a swing bowler. Drift is not something you can work on – it's a natural thing – and the fact that he had so many more revolutions on the ball than other leg-spinners is what made it drift more. The ball was grabbing the air as it went down. And his accuracy is probably the best of any bowler ever.

When we played our one Test together in Adelaide there was a lot of conjecture about whether two leg-spinners would work. But we were different kinds of bowlers. He was this big drifting, leg-spinning thing and I was just using a bit of subtle variation, some wrong'uns and back-spin. Before he did his finger, his flipper was a huge weapon. It was well-disguised, he used to drift it and it was bang on target every time. He could bowl it a lot easier because of those two fingers together, he used them as the axis.

I think he had the perfect action too. He still has. If you look at his wrist it's almost square to the batsman every time he bowls, so he gets maximum side-spin. Apparently George Tribe, a left-arm wrist spinner of the 1940s and 50s, was a similar sort of bowler in that he got lots of rip and drift and bounce. Qadir had all those tricks too, especially his wrong'un, but he wasn't as accurate. Warnie is just a unique bowler – we may not see another like him for a very long time. Who'd ever have thought leg-spinners would be used in one-day cricket? He changed that whole thought process. He's set the standard for how leggies will bowl in the future. It was great to go along for the ride."

Peter McIntyre, three years older than Warne, played two Tests – one of them, against England in Adelaide in 1994-95, in tandem with Warne. McIntyre took 2 for 51 and 0 for 36; Warne 2 for 72 and 2 for 82.

Cameron White, 2000s

"I didn't grow up as a kid thinking I wanted to bowl like Shane Warne, although I'm sure there are thousands out there who do. I was more of a batsman who tried to bowl medium-pace occasionally. I didn't start to play around with leg-spin until I was 13, and by then Warnie had really made a name for himself. So I guess my take on him is a bit different to leg-spinners of the past. I've had an opportunity, as a young fan, to grow up watching him on TV – and now, in the last few seasons, to bowl alongside him as a player. I've been able to watch him and get a real insight into how he's done it, and how he's still doing it.

A lot of people have different opinions about why he has had such a big effect on the game. He is obviously a great bowler because of the things he can do with the ball, his different deliveries and his variations on those deliveries. He has every part of the game covered. But for me, what stands out most is his ability to do exactly what he's thinking and the way he prepares to get batsmen out. It's something the average person might not appreciate. When Shane pitches one on middle and it spins sharply and the batsman nicks it to slip, it's easy to think it's simply a great delivery. But being out there in the middle with him, you get to learn how it unfolds. Every game, he's always telling his team-mates that he's going to bowl one here, then another there, then one around there. And then he does exactly that four or five balls later. Sometimes it might be five overs later. He sets a batsman up perfectly. Now he's teaching me to think more about that type of execution.

Usually, spinners either have a lot of accuracy or they can put a lot of spin on the ball – and if they do turn it dramatically they have to put up with bowling plenty of bad ones. But Shane can do both, and he has been doing both for a long time. There were a lot of comparisons between us when I was first coming on, probably because we're both Victorians and we're both leg-spinners. But we are totally different. For me, accuracy is the main thing because I can't spin it as much as him. I have to rely on bounce and drift and my changes of pace.

I really only have three deliveries: the wrong'un, a leg-break and a top-spinner. It would be good to have a bit more mystery to what I'm doing, like Shane's always had. He has been working with me on that. I guess I'm blessed in a way – he's not a bad teacher to have. I don't think I could have hoped for anyone better."

Cameron White was appointed captain of Victoria at 20 and picked in Australia's squad to India at 21, an age when Warne had yet to make his first-class debut.

Interviews by Christian Ryan and Andrew Webster.

A tragic case

by MATT PRICE

In a parliamentary career spanning 30 years, John Howard has been routinely flattered and slandered. For decades he was known as 'Honest John', a sarcastic slight that morphed into an unintended compliment. To George W. Bush he is the 'Man of Steel'; to Mark Latham, his Labor adversary, he is 'Arse-licker'. One sobriquet rests lightest on Howard's shoulders. "I am, as nominated by Mark Taylor, the ultimate cricket tragic," he told a cricket dinner in 2000. "I plead guilty to that. I regard it as a great term of endearment."

The tragic tag stuck in October 1998. Howard had narrowly hung on to the prime minister's job in the GST election, while a runless Taylor had salvaged his own position with a marathon 12-hour knock against Pakistan in Peshawar. When Taylor declared overnight on 334 not out, declining to bat on in deference to Don Bradman's famous mark, Howard wallowed in the symbolism of it all. He rescheduled a cabinet meeting in Sydney and assembled his ministers at dawn, freeing himself up to attend a welcome home luncheon for the returning Test skipper.

Taylor beamed. "The prime minister has been a great supporter of mine through thick and thin. But he is a cricket tragic. That's what we call him in the change-room. He loves the game more than I do." Less than three months later, Howard crowned Taylor as Australian of the Year. Forget conspiracy theories; the prime minister does not nominate but merely signs off on the award-winner. He did, though, apply his rubber stump with undisguised glee.

"There has been no prouder wearer of the baggy green," Howard gushed that day. "Like any truly great sportsman, like any person who truly, over a long period of time, achieves what he or she sets out to achieve in life, he's had his moments of despair and his moments of receiving fierce criticism and his moments wondering what was going to happen next."

A bit like Howard himself, really. The inference was clear: they
were brothers in arms. 'Tubby' and 'Tragic'. Dogged, persistent,
patriotic, unspectacular, unmovable.

As this book was going to press, Howard was in the middle of a
knife-edge federal election campaign. The future of Australia's
third longest-serving PM looked shaky. Equally shaky, among
some of the game's aficionados, were his credentials as a cricket
tragic. Only months earlier, he had expanded on the reasons why he
considered Sri Lanka's Muttiah Muralidaran a chucker – because
"they proved it in Perth with that thing" – without ever suggesting
he had more than the flimsiest grasp of the game's fundamentals.
Even some of his associates mock the tragic label. "Back in his
Treasury days in the 1970s," says one former Liberal Party
colleague, "everyone else would be watching the cricket. And
Howard would be at his desk, the only one working. I'm convinced
it's all contrived."

Howard the politician is a skilful, often slippery operator. He
stonewalls when necessary, is ever alert to potential crises and
always leaves his options open as long as practicable. Howard the
cricket lover, by comparison, seems entirely artless. He loves Australia, loves winning, loves Warnie, loved the Waughs and reckoned
Bradman, until his death, to be the greatest living Australian.

For the sceptics, it has all been a little too picture perfect. The late
Robert Menzies, Howard's political hero and fellow tragic, wrote a
chapter on cricket in his 1967 autobiography *Afternoon Light*. In it,
he professed: "As every experienced politician knows, it is better to
be vigorously hated than to be tepidly admired." There is no
shortage of Howard haters who suspect that, unlike Menzies, he is a
conveniently cultivated, rather than genuinely committed, cricket
fan. That he is not a cricket tragic but a cricket fake.

When I first arrived in Canberra in 2001, this was a matter of
some contention. As the PM's annual Christmas drinks for the parliamentary press gallery approached, a colleague hatched a cunning
plot to determine Howard's cricketing bona fides. The colleague
was of Middle Eastern extraction but could comfortably pass as a
descendant of the subcontinent. His plan was audacious but simple.
We'd conspire to engage Howard in cricket talk, then deftly steer
discussion towards the forthcoming tour of India. At an appropriate
point, we would introduce my colleague's mythical off-spinning
kinsman into the conversation.

Nick Wilson/Getty Images

Not happy John: Watching on with Janette as the PM's XI play West Indies in 2000-01.

Price: "You know his uncle represented India, PM?"
Colleague: "Yes, took 64 wickets in the late 1960s, early 70s."
Price: "Punjab Singh, a tidy off-spinner, wasn't he?"
Colleague: "Yes, you'd remember him, wouldn't you PM?"

A fake tragic wouldn't be able to plead ignorance. But if Howard played along and started waxing lyrical about imaginary Uncle Singh, we'd have pegged him for a fraud. Alas, our scheme never progressed beyond imbecilic theory; we were laughing too much to kick-start the ruse.

Instead we have had to rely on much more circumstantial evidence. Howard invariably has an opinion and is eager to express it on whatever the cricketing hot topic of the day – from who will win the Ashes, to how much Australia will miss Steve Waugh, to whether Murali chucks or not. As the Melbourne writer Martin Flanagan noted last year, cricket "is a large part of his personal and political mythology. Figures such as Don Bradman and Mark Taylor have been key symbols of the Howard years ... [But] when has he said something that actually shows real insight into the game?"

Shortly before the election campaign, during a rare break in a parliamentary sitting week, Howard accepts *Wisden Australia*'s invitation to ruminate on cricket. "My first memories were literally in the backyard," he says. "I had three older brothers and we used to play. I can remember listening to cricket on the radio just after World War II when the MCC, led by Walter Hammond, came to Australia in 1946. Then I started playing cricket in the local church team."

It has been a busy day for a prime minister in unofficial campaign mode, but Howard seems eager to talk cricket. He takes off his coat, sinks into a large leather chair and grins impishly when asked to reflect on Kerry O'Keeffe's description of his bowling action. "Biomechanically faultless," declared O'Keeffe, in what Latham might call a shameless "arse-lick", when the PM joined him in the commentary box in 2001. "Your release point for the off-break is as good as you'd want."

Howard laughs. "I was OK. I played at school and got into the 2nd XI at Canterbury High. I was never as good at cricket as I'd like to have been." Press gallery colleagues confirm this. Back in the 1980s, when he had more time on his hands, Howard was a regular participant in MPs versus Gallery matches. "He was keen and enthusiastic but not much chop with the bat or the ball," recalls one senior correspondent. "When Howard came in to bat, we'd have to get the quicks to ease up for fear of hurting him. The word 'bunny' comes to mind when I recall his technique."

As a nine-year-old, Howard was taken by his father to see Bradman's last first-class innings at the SCG. Growing up, he says his pin-ups were Arthur Morris, Keith Miller and Ray Lindwall. Studying law, he rushed from his final exam to the SCG to watch Garry Sobers belt an elegant 168 in the Third Test of the celebrated 1960-61 series. He kept playing into his late 20s and was still rolling his arm over when he entered parliament in 1974. "I stopped playing then because I found I couldn't commit myself," he says. "In the end it became too hard."

Soon after that Kerry Packer's World Series Cricket split the game in two. Howard felt torn. "I was sort of mixed," he says. "I didn't like the fact that the game got divided. But looking back it's been a good thing, hasn't it? I still like the traditional Test cricket but it's been enhanced by the skills of the one-day game. The fielding and the run-rates are better."

Peter Wells/The Canberra Times

The unhappy hooker: Bob Hawke's back-foot technique lets him down during the Politicians v Press Gallery match in Canberra, 1984.

THE POWER AND THE PASSION

Prime minister	Tragic?	Could he play?	Greatest contribution?
Edmund Barton (1901-03)	Yes. He was club secretary at Sydney University and umpired after he finished playing – two jobs that nobody takes on without a tragic devotion to the game.	A little. He was in the Sydney University first-grade team and once captained a side that included Dave Gregory, Australia's first captain. His highest score was 68 but he was a dismal fielder, usually at long-stop.	Umpired the match between NSW and Lord Harris's England XI in 1879, when the run-out of Billy Murdoch triggered a crowd riot. It was the other umpire, George Coulthard, who made the call.
Stanley Bruce (1923-29)	Not especially, although he did serve as High Commissioner in London for 13 years and often made his way to Lord's.	Up to a point. He was cricket captain at Melbourne Grammar School but didn't play much after that.	Helped start Tibby Cotter's career, succumbing twice to the fast bowler when Melbourne Grammar played Sydney Grammar in 1900.
Robert Menzies (1939-41 and 1949-66)	Obsessively so. He timed his (numerous) trips to England to coincide with the Tests. He wrote forewords for dozens of cricket books, and articles for *Wisden*. And he always found time to get to the MCG. But his judgement was not always accurate; he once paid for Keith Stackpole to receive special coaching – as a leg-spinner.	Not at all. He liked to watch.	Established the tradition of the Prime Minister's XI, which still plays against touring international teams today.
Bob Hawke (1983-91)	Moderately so. Often seen at the SCG during big matches these days but unlikely to remember Steve Waugh's batting average.	Yes. Scored plenty of runs in the University first-grade side in Perth. But he was unable to make Colin Cowdrey's Oxford team during his days as a Rhodes Scholar, probably because his back-foot technique was better suited to fast pitches.	Took a hard line on the South African sports boycott in the 1980s.
John Howard (1996-)	Up there with Menzies.	On mats. In the churches competition. A bit of off-spin (with a straight elbow).	Helped Australia beat Sri Lanka in 2004 by sledging Muttiah Muralidaran before he even made it into the country. Now *that's* border protection.

Research: Max Bonnell

Howard did not attend a single World Series Supertest or one-day match. In this respect, the generational chasm in Australian politics is gaping. For Latham, a fine schoolboy cricketer, was at the SCG on November 28, 1978, to see the inaugural night match between Australia and West Indies. "We had just finished the HSC and with some mates we loaded up a plastic garbage bin full of cans," he told *Inside Sport* magazine recently. "We would have had the first garbage bin full of beers into the SCG under lights. We didn't cause any trouble that night but others did, I can assure you."

Indeed Australians ambivalent about interest rates, national security or Tasmania's forests had the unusual option at the recent election of casting their vote on distinct cricketing lines. Latham was a regular at the SCG Hill before it was turned to concrete; as recently as January 2003, he was spotted in the outer with a dozen western Sydney mates. They wore zinc cream and Hawaiian shirts, drank beer and harangued the Poms. "Always went to the Hill, absolutely," says Latham. "You'd never sit in the stands if you were fair dinkum about cricket."

His opposite number seldom ventures beyond the stands. Howard's way is altogether less frenetic. "It's probably a quaint thing to say but it's probably the gentle constancy of it all," is how he describes the attraction of watching cricket. "I find it a very restful thing, watching a cricket match. Very, very relaxing. I could do it for hours, just sit and watch. There's action and continuity and unexpected excitement."

Howard is a creature of habit. For two decades he, wife Janette and their three children would pack the car every New Year and head north to the New South Wales coastal resort of Hawk's Nest. Eventually the kids grew up and the local newspaper cruelled their holiday by publishing directions to the Howards' beachside chalet. Ever since, he has spent New Year camped at the SCG.

"For probably four of the last five years I've spent the entire five days at the Sydney Test," he says. "Janette's quite a cricket fan, she takes the radio and watches with the ABC commentary in her ear. With me, people are normally chattering away but she sort of isolates herself. A lot of former players come and there are always plenty of people to chat to." He happily admits that "being able to wander into the dressing room" is his most cherished perk of office. "I don't overdo it, I don't do it all the time. But it's rather nice to wander in and see all those baggy greens."

One problem with the notion of Howard as a cricketing fake is that, for all his flaws, he has always been a remarkably gimmick-free politician. He refuses to don silly hats for photographers. He is a diehard St George rugby league fan but has never, unlike his predecessor Paul Keating, feigned to support an Australian Rules side. And despite his dial-a-quote reputation when it comes to cricket, Howard diplomatically sidesteps issues such as Shane Warne's latest shenanigans.

My favourite Howard evasion came in 2003 during the lead-up to war in Iraq. He had caused uproar in the region by speculating about the possibility of launching pre-emptive military strikes on neighbours to protect Australia from terrorists. As angry ambassadors stormed the Foreign Ministry, Howard complained that he had merely been honestly answering an interviewer's question. The next day he was asked whether Steve Waugh should have been left out of the World Cup squad. The PM stayed mum. Having blithely outraged much of the southern hemisphere, Howard didn't want to upset the Australian selectors.

If you are still suspicious about Howard's cricketing credentials, the veteran *Sydney Morning Herald* columnist Alan Ramsey is convincing. A constant and brutal critic of Howard's leadership, Ramsey recalls visiting the Howard family home during the 1980s. "His study was a kind of museum, a testimony to all the things Howard had achieved," says Ramsey. "And in amongst all this memorabilia, including the formal commissions from when he was appointed a minister under Malcolm Fraser, was Howard's cricket gear. The old school cap and pads and gloves, in there amongst all his other achievements. His love of cricket is genuine."

In which case, this next question should be a cinch. Who will win the Ashes in 2005? "I always want Australia to win," Howard replies, "but it's silly to pretend that it's good for things to be so one-sided. I think it's good for it to be close, everybody likes a bit of competition. As long as we win." Spoken like a true tragic.

Matt Price is a journalist in the Canberra press gallery who writes for The Australian.

The man who averaged infinity

by JOHN BIRMINGHAM

Ian Healy, a 119-Test titan of Australia's revival in the 1980s and 90s, has reason to be envious of Stuart Law, a fellow Queenslander with only one Test to his name. While Healy was passing away a few pointless hours in a minor game in St Lucia on Australia's 1994-95 trip to the Caribbean, the tour that won back the Frank Worrell Trophy, Law was making history. He was leading their home state to its first victory in the Sheffield Shield.

It sounds almost a booby prize, a decidedly modest bauble to polish up by comparison, unless you are acquainted with Queensland's poisonous record of heartbreak, madness, desolation and despair. Despite producing some of the finest players ever to pull on a baggy green cap, the deep north had suffered through 68 barren years. Never once had they carved their name on Lord Sheffield's rather ugly looking shield, the prize for winning Australia's domestic four-day competition.

It became a matter of near psychosis for Queensland cricket fans, particularly through the 1970s and 80s, when on numerous occasions they could reasonably claim to have fielded Test-strength sides. Neither local heroes nor expensive imports were able to overcome whatever deep-seated complex robbed them of their manhood whenever the Shield beckoned. Ray Lindwall, Wes Hall, Rusi Surti, Tom Graveney, Majid Khan, Greg Chappell, Jeff Thomson, Viv Richards, Alvin Kallicharran, Kepler Wessels, Allan Border, Graeme Hick and Ian Botham all came. None conquered.

And then at 3.52 p.m. on Tuesday, March 28, 1995, Stuart Law captained a Queensland team which finally and ruthlessly put that legacy to the sword. As Healy would later lament: "It was as if the biggest party in the world was happening in my backyard but I had been called in to the office."

Last February, at the age of 35, Law announced his retirement from the domestic game. Days earlier he had eclipsed Sam Trimble as Queensland's all-time leading runscorer. Days later he clattered Western Australia's bowlers for 203 in his final first-class innings at the Gabba. He had come a long way, this boy who always knew he would be a cricketer. At school he used to stare out the window, dreaming he was out there batting, until one day his French teacher told him French was more important than cricket. "There's not too many times you'll be speaking French out on the cricket field," he replied. "I don't think so, love."

After breaking through for that giddy inaugural triumph in 1994-95, Law and his marauding band of brothers went on to claim four more in the next seven years. Law was the skipper on all five occasions. Only Monty Noble, another grizzly no-nonsense ruler who captained New South Wales to six Sheffield Shields in the 1900s, has done better. Not that Law was universally admired for the feat. Victorians in particular still bear a grudge against the graceful right-hander for what they feel was a less than graceful refusal to play within the spirit of the game.

He robbed them, they are sure, of two championships. Twice in Pura Cup finals, in 1999-2000 and 2000-01, he refused to walk for what the Victorians swear were legitimate and obvious catches behind the wicket. Twice he went on to play crucial match-swinging innings, just when victory seemed within Victoria's grasp. Fate had other intentions. Law came to maturity as a player in the hard-bitten era of super-commercialism, which was the natural outcome of the Packer revolution. He neither asked nor gave quarter to his foe. To this day he is unapologetic and maintains he would do nothing differently.

There is no reason to doubt his sincerity. After all, Law was tutored by Allan Border in the twilight of his legendary career. Border it was who can claim to have worked a total transformation in the doctrine, strategy and tactics of Australian cricket. He turned the national team from a sheltered workshop for neurotic and anxious try-hards into a company of hardhearted gladiators, who were always nothing less than completely ruthless and occasionally quite vengeful when settling old scores.

Winning the Shield during his long reign as Queensland captain was one of the few feats Border never managed. But he stayed on

Jonathon Wood/Getty Images

Top banana: Stuart Law, Queensland idol, signs off from the Gabba with a farewell double-century.

once his Test days were over to mentor Law and the next generation. The pitiless, calculated style of captaincy which won back the Ashes for Australia became the template which first won the Shield for Queensland under the leadership of Law.

'I WAS ON A HIDING TO NOTHING'

"I was brought up the old-fashioned way. If I did something wrong it'd be a clip round the ear. My father had a horrible technique but he was a good first-grader: self-taught, got his coaching certificates. He got me doing things properly. He'd put a ball in a sock and suspend it from a branch. It was all: 'Oi, elbow up.' That was when I was six. When I made 12 in my first game, he said: 'Not bad, but why not 25?' He didn't push me but he did guide me. I thought he was an arsehole at times but now I love him for it.

Winning one Test cap – rather than, say, three or four – makes it that bit more special. Before the Test the chairman of selectors, Trevor Hohns, said: 'Make it hard for us to drop you.' And they didn't drop me because I was bad; they dropped me because Steve Waugh was fit again. I came in at 4 for 496, a real crisis. I only hit one four. I remember battling Muttiah Muralidaran and batting with Ricky Ponting, who was also making his debut. He was given lbw on 96 – it looked to be going well over. And then Mark Taylor called us in. Thanks, mate! As I was coming off, I felt: 'Yeah, you've done all right.' I knew I was on a hiding to nothing. But at least I had an opportunity. So many don't.

I was in and out of the Australian one-day side when somebody suggested county cricket would be a good place to learn how to play on different surfaces. It was over there that I met my wife. If I'd been a Test regular I probably wouldn't have come, I'd have rested. So you could say I owe my marriage to that. I always wanted to win at all costs. People hated me for that. I called things how I saw them, and that was probably my downfall. I didn't mean any harm. If it counted against me in terms of international cricket, I'm not bothered. I think that's the attitude you need. If it's about shaking hands with the opposition, that's not me.

Playing for Queensland was my Test cricket. They've just given me life membership, which isn't bad for a 35-year-old; Bill Brown had to wait until he was 80. I can go to my grave a very proud man. I'm trying not to think about the possibility of playing against Australia, but once I'm a naturalised Englishman the temptation will be there. Deep down, the Aussie in me thinks: 'Don't be stupid, you can't play for the Poms.' The other side of me thinks I've only had one opportunity to play Test cricket, and I've matured later than most, so I like to think I can still mix it with the youngsters. It'd be weird to go on to the field in a blue cap to face Ponting and the others. When the papers raised the idea of me playing for England in an Ashes series, I thought: 'I can't, I can't.' But stranger things have happened.**"**

Stuart Law was talking to Rob Steen.

To concentrate on Law's approach to captaincy, however, is to give a false, unfinished impression of the man as a player. Even towards the fag end of his career in Australia he remained a fine-looking stylist with the bat and cut an admirably, even enviably, youthful figure on the field. In his elegant stance and technique he recalled Greg Chappell – another long-time toiler in the service of Queensland. His air of diffident ease against the most difficult attacks was comparable to Mark Waugh at his best.

Indeed if Law can look askance at any one countryman, it must be the junior Waugh. True believers north of the Tweed River will forever shake their heads that Mark was so often indulged by selectors and Law so often ignored. He played but one Test for his country, batting a couple of hours and chalking up a creditable 54 not out. He probably regrets it now. He doesn't even have the cold comfort of a decent-looking Test average.

The scorecard for that match, against Sri Lanka at the WACA in 1995-96, offers a clue as to why he was seen so little at international level. Michael Slater hit 219, Mark Waugh 111 and Ricky Ponting, also making his Test debut, picked up 96. As Law would later remark: "I came up against world champions, not just guys who could play the game." A fitting analogy might be that of a giant fated to walk amongst gods, a destiny which can induce either bitterness or philosophy. Law seemed to favour the latter. "In another era," he mused on his retirement, "it could have been different. But you can't go through life with ifs and whats and could-bes or you end up a very disappointed person."

There were consolations. He played with the greatest talents of the modern era in the some of the hardest competitions, including the World Cup. Like his contemporary Michael Bevan, he was fated to deploy his skills with much greater regularity in the horribly constrained arena of limited-overs cricket. His naturally aggressive demeanour often translated into a punishing assault on opposition bowlers, while his proletarian medium-pacers were a useful bonus.

Yet even here he seemed jinxed. A member of the side which painfully lost the 1996 World Cup final to Sri Lanka, Law was dropped on the eve of Australia's soothingly triumphant 1999 campaign. One last example of his arguably wasted talents was the violent grace of his 69-ball hundred against Tasmania at Bellerive Oval last summer, an effort Law dedicated to another arguably wasted talent in David Hookes, who had died a week earlier.

He continues to turn out for Lancashire on the English county circuit, where he has hit a stack of his 67 first-class hundreds. He still trails his old nemesis Mark Waugh (81) on that score and may eventually finished second among Australian century-makers to Don Bradman (119). He may even one day pad up for England, where he has settled with his wife, Debbie-Lee, and taken out citizenship. There remains just a glimmer of hope that Law might yet thrill at the game's very pinnacle.

John Birmingham grew up in Ipswich, Queensland. His books include He Died with a Felafel in his Hand, Leviathan *and* Weapons of Choice.

Opposite SIT AND DELIVER: Michael Slater slays England's bowlers at Adelaide Oval, back in his carefree heyday of 1998-99.
Picture by Graham Chadwick, Getty Images.

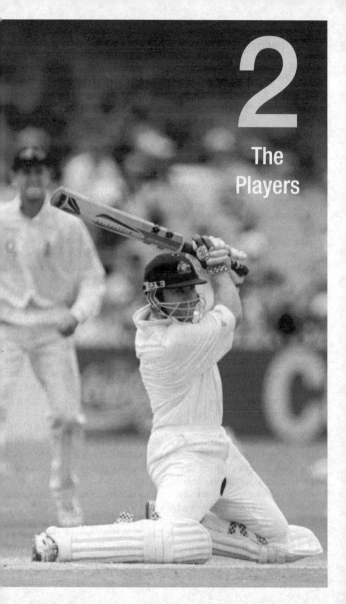

2

The
Players

WISDEN AUSTRALIA CRICKETER OF THE YEAR

Darren Lehmann

by CHRISTIAN RYAN

On a drizzly day in Cairns a Sri Lankan tailender cuffs the ball into the off side and hares away. There's a lazy single to be had but his partner is flat on his feet and slow to start running. The man at deepish mid-off jumps into action like he's been shot at, throwing down the stumps at the faraway batsman's end with one almighty pick-up-and-hurl. It is not so much the fielding that stands out, for fielding has come a long way since the days when pick-up-and-hurl was something Australian cricketers did during a long and productive night on the town. Rather, it is the fieldsman. His thick lips and droopy eyes look strangely familiar. His cap is pulled down tight, his shirt tucked in snug round his belly. Stranger still.

But it couldn't be. There must be some mistake. Surely that wasn't Darren Lehmann?

We should not have been so surprised. For 2004, after all, was the defining year of Lehmann's cricketing reincarnation, the year Homer Simpson turned into Buzz Lightyear, the year 'Boof' went bang. He ferreted runs, hugged catches and pinched wickets with left-arm off-breaks that seldom broke. As the months wore on he looked increasingly part of the Australian cricket team furniture: a comfy leather recliner next to Damien Martyn's stainless steel bar stool.

"To be perfectly honest," he told journalists, "I'm probably the last of that bunch who played a little bit overweight and enjoyed a beer and a cigarette." His confession came the weekend before that Sri Lankan series. Three days later Ricky Ponting was summoned away by a death in the family, Adam Gilchrist inherited the captaincy and Lehmann was named his deputy. The last Australian cricketer to refuse to give up his vices was now vice-captain.

This was no clearcut appointment. The vice-captain is normally the veteran pro, yet only Simon Katich in this particular Australian XI had played fewer Tests than Lehmann. It reflected a certain something he brings to the teams he plays in. It is not dazzling intuition,

Hotch-potch of hyperactivity: Darren Lehmann and the baggy green that is finally his.

nor some Brearleyesque grasp of tactics; while a worthy skipper of South Australia, Lehmann's idea of outsmarting opponents usually amounts to stationing an extra slip or offering the spinner the last over before lunch. Perhaps it's to do with his likeness to the un-air-brushed cricketers of old. Perhaps it's his unfailing zest, as if everything is new, as if cricket is still a game to him and not a job.

Whatever it is, you can see it in Ponting's eyes. He adores Boof. The night Lehmann bellowed "black cunts" after being run out against Sri Lanka in 2003; last summer's Achilles twinge that became a tear and took several yonks to heal: these were but irksome distractions. Ponting, you suspect, would happily cut out Lehmann's tongue and roll him on to the field in a wheelchair if necessary.

When Ponting faced up to the fraught business of succeeding Steve Waugh, more a monolith than a predecessor, Lehmann was his right-hand man. When Lehmann asked Ponting to return the favour, by penning a few introductory niceties to his autobiography, Ponting did more than offer the usual well-meaning foreword prod. It reads more like a rhapsodic slog-sweep: "What he brings to the team is a commonsense, no-nonsense approach ... a fine cricket brain ... he is always there to provide me with sound advice ... he is never short of a quick one-liner ... every team could do with Boof in its line-up."

We associate modern batting genius with Sachin Tendulkar, who is a study in stillness. Lehmann is more a hotchpotch of hyperactivity. Sometimes as the bowler is steaming in he will be bouncing gently on the tips of his toes. By the time of delivery stride he is invariably on the move, goosestepping across the crease, laying vacant his leg stump and often middle too. It seems untextbook until you realise that his head never moves, his hands stay soft, his eyes cradle the ball every last inch of its journey on to the bat. He is not so much rewriting as re-interpreting the textbook. At first, you cannot quite work out whether he is graceful or grotesque. At length, you cannot tear your eyes off him.

We associate modern batting beauty with Brian Lara, who unfurls swashbuckling cuts and drives and hooks. If Lehmann gets a bouncer at his throat, he is less likely to hook it than to scuttle away like a crab and deftly flick it over gully. Instead of lashing a half-volley outside off stump through the covers, he might bend down on his haunches and squirt it through a gap in the slips; maybe, once his eye is in, he will sidestep around that same delivery and thwack it behind square leg with a stiff-arm punch.

"He seems to have about four shots for any particular ball," Jamie Cox, the former Tasmanian captain, once observed. Over at Queensland, Andy Bichel would find himself wondering where on earth to aim: "He can put it on the off side and then the on side at will, even if it's the very same ball that's just been bowled." Paul Reiffel, during his days as Victoria's skipper, found that Lehmann would rapidly wrest the job out of his own hands. "As a captain you tend to be one step behind when he's playing well because he's working the ball where he wants to, and therefore almost setting the field where he wants it for himself too."

Last summer, better late than never, the Lehmann way left the world's best bowler in its thrall. Had you been asked to choose the batsman most likely to get the better of Muttiah Muralidaran, chances are you would not have plumped for a bloke variously written off as too fat, too skittish, a flat-track bully, a hometown glutton and dodgy against the short ball. Yet although Tendulkar and Lara have each had their moments against Murali, neither has demystified him so matter-of-factly as Lehmann did in March.

Reading the doosra was a doozey, perhaps because he watches the ball so intently. He charged and chipped over the top. He took guard outside leg, and occasionally outside off, wriggling and contorting his body into such extravagant positions that he seemed able to thump the ball to whichever corner of the field he wished. Murali, like Bichel years before, was left perplexed as to where to bowl. All that endangered Lehmann's wicket was his own lack of puff; realising this, his team-mates carried a chair, umbrella and towel out to him during the drinks breaks of the First Test in Galle.

And so Ponting's first series as Test captain, a potentially perilous one, was clean-swept 3–0. Lehmann's assured handling of Murali soon caught on among the rest of the top order if not a hypnotised tail, and his blazing knocks of 63 and 129 in that opening Test were the turning point. Several of his runs came from contemptuous lofts over mid-wicket, a shot Lehmann consciously added to his school-boy repertoire after seeing David Hookes play it. Nowadays Lehmann would much prefer to watch the Adelaide Crows than a game of cricket. But back then he caught the train from Gawler to Adelaide Oval just to watch Hookesy bat.

The pay-TV subscribers following the series back home knew Lehmann was shaken by the muddled, wasteful death of the 48-year-old Hookes. They had seen the tears cascading down his cheeks on Allan Border Medal night. What they did not realise, nearly two months on, was that he often sat alone in his hotel room on that tour crying. It was as if Hookes was sitting next to him, he writes: "I didn't 'speak' to him or have some out-of-body experience; I simply got this warm feeling that he was with me. So when I brought up the century in the second innings and looked up in thanks, it was as though he looked down and said in his typical manner: 'You're right now, mate, you don't need me any more, off you go, get on with it.'"

David looms as a Goliath over the life of Lehmann. Upon saun-tering into the kitchen to tell Mum he had been picked for South Australia, her first words were: "What, to play with David Hookes?" It was Hookes who advised him that attending the new-fangled Academy, run by some bloke called Potter whom Lehmann had never heard of, was a waste of time. Hookes was his initial first-class captain. Hookes was staring bug-eyed from the non-striker's end when Lehmann hit his maiden hundred: a scintillating 228 against Geoff Lawson, Mike Whitney, Wayne Holdsworth and Greg Matthews. It was his tenth first-class game, he was only 19 and Phil Wilkins, watching from the press box that day, dubbed Lehmann "the most improbable Galahad ... a short, bulbous, unathletic phenomenon".

Hookes seemed the man most disappointed when Lehmann spent three generally glum seasons with Victoria in the early 1990s. He was lured east at a meeting with John Elliott, the swaggering entre-preneur and Carlton football nut, who had a finger in more pies than a workaholic pastry-maker. Elliott asked him how much he wanted. A car, a house, a pile of money and jobs for me and the missus, Lehmann replied, testing his luck. "Right," Elliott shot back. "You ready to sign?" Hookes was eventually made a meaty enough offer and shifted to Victoria himself, as coach. He was in a St Kilda pub with Lehmann, among others, on the night he died.

Perhaps the eeriest parallel is their career trajectories. Both were gifted, freewheeling left-handers, fattened on the short square boundaries of Adelaide Oval. Both were pounced on by national selectors at precocious ages, then largely snubbed for a decade. At 19, Lehmann was named 12th man against Pakistan at the SCG, enough of a taste for him to decide that coach Bob Simpson's fielding routines were pointless and overblown. Eight years went by before he finally made his Test debut, in Bangalore, shortly after the Simpson reign had passed its use-by date. Coincidence? Lehmann is still not sure – "but we didn't get on … and I didn't get a look in".

Back in the 1940s Lindsay Hassett, his career disrupted by war, had to wait nine years between his maiden first-class and Test hundreds. Lehmann, his progress thwarted by a couple of Waughs, waited 13 years, five months and seven days – the longest gap of any Australian Test centurion. For most of those 13 years he was the new David Hookes, brilliant but jinxed. That he broke the jinx within weeks of Hookes's death added weight, resonance and romance to his achievement.

If there is a black mark, so to speak, it is his ruminations on the aftermath of that run-out at the Gabba on the night of January 15, 2003. Lehmann has said he does not know why he bellowed "black cunts" within earshot of the neighbouring Sri Lankan dressing room. He has said sorry, adding that there is "no excuse for those words ever being said". At the same time he appears equally aggrieved by the possibility that black cricketers might occasionally call someone a white so-and-so. And he seems positively furious about being hung out to dry by Cricket Australia, the ICC and the media. To most fair-minded people a ban of five one-day games was darn lenient. It appears he understands *that* he was wrong but not *why*, which is perhaps the more important bit.

Lehmann's selection as *Wisden Australia's* Cricketer of the Year will probably be seen by some as a whimsical choice. He had two good Test series, both against mid-table Sri Lanka. Ponting and Matthew Hayden had four each. Four beats two every time, as any self-respecting fat book with loads of microscopic numbers in it should realise.

This misses the point. The runs scored by Ponting and Hayden, though many and merry, had an inevitability about them. The only thing that has ever seemed remotely inevitable about Lehmann's cricketing life is that it would wind up unfulfilled. The plot had been determined, the epitaphs written and filed away on floppy disks. Only the precise dates and numbers remained to be filled in.

This was the year Lehmann rewrote his own story and became the best player of spin on the planet. From the new David Hookes to the new Neil Harvey. By midsummer the wheel had turned full circle.

A kid called Cosgrove, another lefty, kinda chubby but brazenly aggressive, was getting intimate with those same short square boundaries of Adelaide Oval. And the local paper asked the question: "Is Mark Cosgrove the New Darren Lehmann?"

Cosgrove might want to check exactly which Darren Lehmann they are talking about.

WISDEN AUSTRALIA CRICKETER OF THE YEAR

1998	Belinda Clark
1999	Glenn McGrath
2000-01	Steve Waugh
2001-02	Glenn McGrath
2002-03	Adam Gilchrist
2003-04	Ricky Ponting
2004-05	Darren Lehmann

WISDEN AUSTRALIA PURA CUP CRICKETER OF THE YEAR

1998	Colin Miller (Tas)
1999	Simon Katich (WAust)
2000-01	Paul Reiffel (Vic)
2001-02	Jamie Cox (Tas)
2002-03	Jimmy Maher (Qld)
2003-04	Wade Seccombe (Qld)
2004-05	Matthew Elliott (Vic)

Matthew Elliott

by PETER HANLON

Matthew Elliott's mind often surprises people. In his final year of secondary school he studied PE, the jock's staple, but only after concluding he would score a little heavier there than in physics. He teamed it with English, chemistry, two strains of mathematics and achieved his Higher School Certificate with a score of 346. The cut-off for medicine at Melbourne University was 352.

Elliott abandoned a physiotherapy degree after deciding it didn't suit him. He has been a professional cricketer ever since. He remains a career student.

Last season, when Victoria's captain Darren Berry challenged each of his players to give a presentation on one of the 799 men to wear the navy blue cap, Elliott chose Jack Ryder. As a graduate of Collingwood Cricket Club, he had seen Ryder's name on honour boards and his face staring out of pictures on clubroom walls. But he knew little else of the man, so loitered round his local library until he did. The result was an entertaining account of Ryder's life and cricket, worthy of newspaper publication.

He reads, but hates fiction. Biographies and historical tomes dominate his haul at birthday and Christmas times. He scans the compulsory cricket tour reading – *FHM* and *Ralph* magazines, for the articles of course – but only in between Einstein's life story or an account of the Kursk disaster.

When his dicky knee forced him to cut back on running he had Neil Buszard, a Collingwood mentor, introduce him to the Victorian Institute of Sport's road cycling coach. He did not just want to ride a bike, but to ride it properly. Another time, it was a sports science physical conditioner trained in the police force. Their purposes served, Elliott moved on to learn something else.

What really pushes his button, he says, is fishing. His former team-mate and sometime opening partner, Matthew Mott, thinks his skill with rod and reel has been somewhat overblown. "He can talk the talk," says Mott, "but I've been out with him and we didn't catch a thing all day." Mott thinks Elliott has "more theories than Nostradamus". Upon flying south from Queensland and getting to know him, Mott was shocked to discover that his new team-mate had such a dry sense of humour. "I'd looked at him and thought, he can't be a funny bloke. That seriousness. That slightly unfortunate look ..."

When Elliott led the Bushrangers' victory song after the Pura Cup final in March, with a space left in the circle for their late coach David Hookes, it was a moving end to a draining time for all. His wife Megan thinks he is basically a shy person. But the dressing room has brought out the inner Elliott, prompting hilarious dissertations on the performance of each of his peers in the wake of victories past. He is observant, a great mimic, and he has taken meticulous notes throughout his career.

In a general IQ test some years ago, Elliott was marked as an 86 percentile who works best when free to focus on one thing at a time. He remembered this in 2002-03 when he gave up the Victorian captaincy after one game. His resignation stoked whispers that he was mentally fragile, the same whispers he had heard throughout his struggles with injury. Looked at less cynically it was confirmation that, in cricket, Elliott has found something that really does suit him: a pursuit in which a common team purpose cannot mask the reality that an individual's survival depends on his own performance. For a batsman this is especially true. He lives or dies by his Gray Nicolls sword.

Elliott knows he is hard work. Most cricketers enjoy a simpler intellectual existence, and so in difficult times are less cluttered by self-analysis and the endless search for discovery. Elliott knows he has sometimes failed to come to terms with his lot, most destructively on the 1998-99 West Indies tour, when his international journey stalled on 20 Tests. He fought failure alone on that trip, spending too much time brooding in his hotel room and too little enjoying where his job had taken him.

Introspective behaviour never sat well in Steve Waugh's teams. The tale of Elliott's banishment was underpinned by gossip that Waugh told him he would never play for his country again. Elliott says that conversation never occurred, but concedes Waugh did tell him he was too "up and down". He thinks it a fair statement at the time.

Publicly at least, he wavered in the ensuing years, unsure how best to put forward his case for a return. One season's dawn would bring a declaration of renewed baggy-green intent; the next a drive for a World Cup spot; another the desire only to score runs and enjoy himself with Victoria. That last vow came at the start of his most recent, most golden summer. He has always been too dogmatic to have given up the chase entirely.

If Elliott's whirring brain does complicate a game already littered with mental potholes, there were no signs of unrest from October 2003 through March 2004. Clear-headed and calm, he batted as if the ball was suspended in a stocking on a Kyabram clothesline. His output increased steadily, at times alarmingly, and a seventh century in his 11th match won the Pura Cup final for Victoria and took him past Graham Yallop's long-standing season aggregate record. He finished the Bushrangers' spectacular campaign with 1,381 runs.

The foundation of Elliott's batting, his to-die-for technique, was so solid during 2003-04 that his highlights reel could double as a coaching manual. When the planets align for him, the thinker does not need to waste a thought on his work at the crease, so naturally does batting come. The gurus at Collingwood noted this long ago, snaring him from Melbourne Cricket Club's Dowling Shield side when he was still a stripling country teen, then pushing him up through the grades. They looked beyond his early failures. They knew he was simply too good not to one day be great.

Coaching the young Elliott was a thankless task; as much as he views his batting as a work in progress, his gifts were god-given. "I would never take the credit for his technique," says one coach. "Bloody hell, it was outstanding." The bits that weren't so good he took care of himself. He arrived in Victoria's Sheffield Shield side in 1992-93 as a wonderfully correct but not yet overly punishing batsman. Realising that attack must be met by counterattack, he soon taught himself to play the pull shot.

"He certainly didn't have it before," says another long-time watcher. "He'd play it off a shocking ball, but in Shield cricket you've got to pull off just short of a length. He taught himself to tighten his back elbow to minimise the swing width, like Allan Border. Blokes who hit them up in the air have got a full arc. It was a fantastic effort to teach himself that."

In England in 1997, his maiden Test hundred came on a difficult Lord's wicket after the hosts had been skittled for 77. Two Tests later at Headingley, team-mates and opponents flailed and floundered amid snorts of another Leeds minefield. Elliott made 199, sharing a stand of 268 with Ricky Ponting after they came together at 4 for 50. His conviction was as strong then as it was flimsy two years later in the Caribbean. He would lurch forward against Courtney Walsh and Curtly Ambrose and his back foot, his anchor at the crease, would drag across the turf behind him.

Exactly how Elliott has rooted his game again is difficult to pinpoint. It is cricket's charm and curse that the same preparation to play the same shot to the same ball can bring bouquets one day and brickbats the next. Stability in his life away from the game has certainly been a factor. He has grown as a person and is making a good living from his toil, a consideration that has always been important to him. And he is happy. "Megan's had to put up with heaps – me grizzling and unhappy all the time," he once said. "It's been tough on her. They [his family] have been a breath of fresh air. They stop you thinking about yourself."

If Steve Waugh's "up and down" critique resonates for some, then Elliott's experience in June 2004 might prove his most sinister test of all. He had planned a mid-season return from county duties with Glamorgan to be back home in Melbourne for the birth of their third child. He was with his family when Zac and Samuel were joined by baby William. Days later, Megan's brother Darren lost a long battle with cancer, leaving behind a young family and a story that would break your heart.

Elliott's bags were packed to return to Wales when Ponting suffered his own family bereavement, withdrawing from the First Test against Sri Lanka in Darwin. Suddenly Australia needed a No. 3. For the first time in more than five years the selectors turned to Elliott. In conditions tailored for swing bowling, he was twice undone by Chaminda Vaas in little more than a day.

Ponting returned, Elliott drifted out of sight again. Back in Glamorgan, he must have reflected on how he had flown halfway round the world and back in three weeks, experiencing along the way a birth, a death, the resurrection of his career and a failure that might mean the end of it. For if his surprise, abrupt recall against Sri Lanka had never happened he would have started the new summer with a cleanish slate, an Australian contract in his pocket and little reason to doubt his prospects of a return.

Yet as he made 1 and 0 in Darwin, the decision makers would have been more interested in Elliott's reaction to his emotional whirlpool than the placement of his head, hands and feet against the moving ball. Few of us face such an intense examination of our capacity to cope with life at its rawest. Elliott made all the right noises. It had been terrific just to be back in the fold, he said. The experience had spurred him on to prove it was where he belonged. "It definitely feels more like a beginning than an end."

Out of sight, but not out of mind.

Peter Hanlon is Saturday sports editor of The Age.

Farewells

Mark Waugh
Right-hand batsman, right-arm medium/off-spinner, superslip

Mark Waugh announced his arrival with a perfectly timed straight drive against England on the first day of the Fourth Test in January 1991. On any ground other than the elongated Adelaide Oval, Waugh's first shot would have earned four runs. As it was, he ran three.

In a way that very first drive – the ball dispatched with a speed impossible to reconcile with Waugh's liquid, slow-motion swing – summarises his Test career; falling, as it did, slightly short of numeric expectations. But Waugh belongs to that category of cricketers impossible, or inappropriate, to analyse by numbers alone. An average of 41.82 doesn't speak to the reasons why Waugh was able to draw non-cricket followers to watch him bat.

Actually "bat" is too blunt a term for it. Even as a limited-overs opener, Waugh worked within borders more artistic than barbaric. He subverted the one-day game, presenting precise minimalism to an audience primed for furious medieval assault. A straight six during a one-day match against West Indies in 1994-95 smashed a commentary box window, yet Waugh's apparent effort in achieving this feat would not have disturbed a royal funeral. He may as well have been quietly leafing through a Bible.

Like England's David Gower, Waugh had the unusual quality of appearing equally elegant whether scoring or being dismissed. Unlike Gower, whose appearance at the crease invariably required a second gully, Waugh had no clear technical weaknesses, apart from those which arose from his bemusement at the threat posed by off-spinners. Waugh simply didn't believe they could get him out. They did, more often than was acceptable.

These lapses mostly took place towards the end of Waugh's career, when the onset of summer was annually signified by newspaper articles calling for his sacking. At his mid-1990s peak, Waugh had refined his technique – minimal footwork, minimal backlift, minimal swing – to the point where he was a mere cypher, a transitional episode, between the ball leaving a bowler's hand and striking the fence. Compare Waugh with Brian Lara, whose extravagance can sometimes seem vulgar. Waugh was somehow able to invest less drama in a deliberate slice over the slips – a method he employed to glorious effect against West Indies – than Lara displays during a routine forward-defensive. The reactions of batsmen caught by Waugh, possibly Australia's finest slip fielder, were generally more animated than anything involved in the catch itself.

Waugh's retirement, calmly announced from Test cricket in October 2002, and from all first-class matches at the end of last summer, was as graceful as any of his 8,029 Test runs. Cricket followers are only now realising how much we miss him. –TIM BLAIR

For Australia: 128 Tests, 8,029 runs @ 41.82, hs153*, 20x100s, 47x50s; 59 wkts @ 41.17, bb5-40, sr82.25, 1x5wi; 181ct. 244 ODIs, 8,500 runs @ 39.35, hs173, sr76.54, 18x100s, 50x50s; 85 wkts @ 34.56, bb5-24, sr43.38, rpo4.78, 1x5wi; 108ct.

First-class: 368 matches, 26,855 runs @ 52.04, hs229*, 81x100s, 133x50s; 208 wkts @ 40.99, bb6-68, sr75.99, 3x5wi; 452ct.

Darren Berry *Wicket-keeper, right-hand batsman*

The distinguishing quality of a great wicket-keeper is not that he reliably takes all the chances made for him by bowlers fast and slow, off and leg, standing up and standing back, but that he conjures up wickets that are all his own doing. Darren Berry's record haul for Victoria comprised hundreds of regulation edges and stumpings, plus a clutch of dismissals – especially while hovering over the stumps – that were like rabbits pulled from a magician's hat.

Fast bowlers didn't like to see him come to the stumps, for it made them look slow. But none complained about the wickets that ensued. I saw Berry make wickets this way for Reiffel, Hughes, Fleming, Saker and Harvey. The dismissal he cherished most was a blink-of-the-eye leg-side stumping of David Boon from Paul Reiffel's bowling one day at the MCG. To a keeper, Berry always said, a leg-side stumping was like making a hundred.

Berry did not need to see the ball in all its possible drifts, dives, deviations and deflections to know where it would end up. The key, he said, was that he did not move until the last split second, even to a ball pitched outside leg stump, and that he concentrated on the length rather than the line, so that he took it in a kind of sweeping action. For catches standing up, his method was to train himself not to snatch at the ball but to leave his palms open for as long as he dared, giving the ball every chance of lodging in his gloves. Like Ian Healy on his best days, Berry turned cricket's most prosaic discipline into a spectacle.

He came as a precocious talent from a big family in country Wonthaggi. He began in the Fitzroy firsts, keeping artfully for the Academy, the Australian Under-19s, South Australia and, immediately upon his return, Victoria. But a keeper occupies a perverse place in the game's culture, for he needs not just lucky breaks but whim and fancy on his side too. Arguably Berry was once Australia's best keeper. In another era he might have been first picked for the national side; in ours he did not play so much as one Australia A game. All he asked was all a keeper ever asks, a half-chance, for that was all he needed as a gloveman. But, save a half-tour replacing the injured Adam Gilchrist in England in 1997, it did not come.

It is possible both to eulogise Berry and damn him with the same idea, that he was an old-fashioned keeper who put a premium on his keeping skills. It was no state secret that Berry's ambitions were thwarted by his batting. Berry could not bat like Gilchrist, but it was scarcely to his shame that he batted like Berry; his three centuries for Victoria were all against ancient rivals New South Wales. If some players are called "franchise", Berry could have been called "heartbeat". If Healy was the drummer in the Australian band, Berry was the pulse in the Victorian body. He thought of Victoria the way he thought of the bush teams of his upbringing, not as a selection of 11 individuals but as a club. It was why he was so devastated when he was dropped once, in 1995-96, and why the move, far from improving the team, tore it apart. It was why he stayed until Victoria at last won a Pura Cup.

Berry was talkative in the best traditions of his craft. He was warm, gregarious, inquisitive, good-humoured and media-savvy. He held many catches but no grudges. He made many friends and few enemies, and they soon became friends anyway. In all ways, Darren Berry stood up. —GREG BAUM

First-class: 153 matches, 4,273 runs @ 21.58, hs166*, 4x100s, 11x50s; 552ct, 51st.

Michael Slater *Right-hand batsman*

Michael Slater chose the hardest career there is, that of an aggressive opening batsman, and for what seems now a six-year honeymoon he excelled at it. His footwork was astonishing, and the phlegmatic, supportive Mark Taylor was for long years an ideal comrade at the battlefront. Slater made 14 Test centuries: one in only his second Test at Lord's; another after upper-cutting Phil De-Freitas's first ball of an Ashes series for four; two more in Rawalpindi, amid the dust and grit. All 14 times, upon reaching three figures, he kissed the Australian coat-of-arms on his helmet.

Slats came from Wagga and married Stephanie, the girl next door. He bought a good house in Bondi Junction, and then a more sumptuous residence nearby, just when his career began to unravel, and the mortgage hurt his marriage and possibly his concentration. He got out with a silly swipe against India, second ball of the second innings, in Delhi in 1996. He was blamed for the lost match and dropped from the side. Quickly back again – and a vibrant, vital cog in the Waugh team that won 16 straight Tests – he was frowned upon again for abusing Rahul Dravid over a disputed catch in March 2001, dropped from the side in August, and dropped by New South Wales the following January.

Sideburns, arthritis and hectic nightclubbing overseas contributed to his foreshortening. Steve Waugh and the coach, John Buchanan, told him sideburns were not what the Australian cricket team was all about, and when he kept them he was dropped. Like a fast bowler, an opening batsman must walk a fine line, in his life and his craft, between applied fury and cold discipline. Ian Botham, David Hookes, Ted Dexter, Keith Miller, Steve Waugh; like Slats they all overstepped the line sometimes, the way you almost always do.

But his punishment after Delhi and after his outburst seems excessive. If only the Indian weather had been less sticky that afternoon. If only the steadying Taylor, his gentle father figure for so long, had not in his bad patch left him at last unmentored. If only the Australian press had been less assiduous and prurient . . .

But those were the breaks, and for a good half-decade he was magnificent. Had he not been an opener Slater's average, 42.84, would have been over fifty. Waugh, batting at numbers five or six, made sure he was not out a good few times, and his average was thereby wondrously embellished. Slater won Tests and admirers. He hit nine nineties. He wrote a good book, *Slats Opens Up*, in mid-career, a sometimes unwise thing to do. His momentum dried up after that. His old foe arthritis, or more precisely ankylosing spondylitis, enforced his retirement last June.

His story reads like one of unfinished business, poisoned potential and sheer bad luck, and he will be sorely missed. –BOB ELLIS

For Australia: 74 Tests, 5,312 runs @ 42.84, hs219, 14x100s, 21x50s; 1 wkt @ 10.00, bb1-4, sr25.00; 33ct. 42 ODIs, 987 runs @ 24.07, hs73, sr60.22, 9x50s; 9ct.

First-class: 216 matches, 14,912 runs @ 40.85, hs221, 36x100s, 69x50s; 3 wkts @ 37.67, bb1-4, sr44.33; 117ct.

Jo Angel *Right-arm fast bowler*

Since the rise of Graham McKenzie then Dennis Lillee, Perth's pacy pitch and howling winds have been legendarily conducive to the nurturing of fast bowlers. In the 1990s, however, it was more often visitors who enjoyed the conditions. Surfaces varied in quality. Inexperience and injuries took a heavy toll. Only one bowler, Jo Angel, kept the lineage alive, becoming a kind of tradition of his own.

Western Australia's go-to guy for more than a decade did not share McKenzie's circus strongman physique and never imitated Lillee's histrionics. He was as lumbering as 203 cm and size-14 boots imply. He looked, as he was, an unselfconsciously amiable man; team-mate Brendon Julian thought him "the most liked first-class cricketer in Australia". Only in the presence of a ball, a batsman and a task did Angel's nature change: he jarred gloves, handles and splices perhaps as much as any Australian bowler of the period. He always appeared a little weary – until you realised that he looked exactly the same after 10 overs as one, and was as committed in his third spell as in his first.

Angel came from a sporting family in the hills east of Perth: father Ken and brother Robert played Australian Rules football for Swan Districts. He stumbled into the Sheffield Shield in November 1991 when Bruce Reid and Peter Capes pulled out on the morning of a match against New South Wales, taking an unexpected call at work and "shaking like a leaf" when he arrived. At once, he did what came naturally and simply, and his 31 wickets at 25 that season were instrumental in his state's Shield win. Rushed into the Test side on his home ground the following summer, he would have had a wicket in his first over had Craig McDermott caught a Desmond Haynes mis-hook.

Angel played only three more Tests, Glenn McGrath casting a long narrow shadow over his career. He became almost a victim of his success at home – his 283 first-class wickets at the WACA cost less than 23 runs each; his 202 everywhere else almost 28 – and

Raw and roaring: Jo Angel appeals in Karachi, on his way to a Test-best 3 for 54.

Shaun Botterill/Getty Images

there was always some doubt about his effectiveness away. But he was never chagrined, and West Australians were happy to have him. Only Clarrie Grimmett has taken more wickets in domestic cricket – and he got around a bit. Angel was earthbound, and Perthbound, with the greatest of pleasure. –GIDEON HAIGH

For Australia: 4 Tests, 10 wkts @ 46.30, bb3-54, sr74.80. 3 ODIs, 4 wkts @ 28.25, bb2-47, sr40.50, rpo4.18.

First-class: 121 matches, 485 wickets @ 25.11, bb6-35, sr52.47, 16x5wi, 1x10wm.

Adam Dale *Right-arm medium-pacer*

Australian cricketers have a reputation for hell-raising and beer-swilling, but this is merely a stereotype. When his team-mates headed for a bar or nightclub, Adam Dale was more likely to be found alone in a cafe, reading a book. For 10 years he bowled little seamers and swingers for Queensland and Australia with a similar lack of commotion. And by the end, though you would never know it from his gentle trot and easy action, he was a world-class performer.

Dale played his early cricket for Northcote in his native Melbourne before moving, quite infamously, to Queensland in the early 1990s. Victoria were often criticised for letting him go. Dale, gentle soul that he is, always maintained there were others ahead of him in the queue: Hughes, Dodemaide, Fleming, Reiffel, O'Donnell. At Queensland, meanwhile, what they needed was an into-the-wind bowler. Dale was the man.

He heeded the advice of John Buchanan, Queensland's coach at the time, who counselled him to keep things simple. He bowled stump-to-stump, extracted what lateral movement was available and awaited the batsman's mistake. In the 1996-97 Sheffield Shield final in Perth he took 6 for 38 versus Western Australia; in stifling heat in Cairns, against Alec Stewart's Englishmen, he took 7 for 33. His two Tests were equally memorable. On debut, in Bangalore in 1997-98, Australia beat India and Dale bowled Sachin Tendulkar – even if he had already made 177. "I remember thinking 'what an opportunity'," said Dale, "to witness Tendulkar versus Warne. I got to wear the baggy green. We won. I got to sing the song, with Ian Healy leading it. They're things I'll never forget."

A year later, in Antigua, he ran headlong into a rampant Brian Lara. Australia retained the Frank Worrell Trophy but Dale's contribution was muted, for he had contracted pneumonia. It would turn out to be his last Test. He played 30 one-dayers, invariably tight and probing, but missed out on Australia's glorious 1999 World Cup triumph when he was dropped midway through the tournament.

And then, eventually, his life turned full circle. Persistent shoulder problems forced Dale into first-class retirement in 2003 and he came home, accepting a job as Reebok's state sales manager. He played one season with North Melbourne, took 61 wickets at 12 apiece and shared the Jack Ryder Medal. This summer, in Melbourne suburban ranks, he has taken up a coaching position; and therein his future may lie. "I've retired, and I need to move to the next page. I'd love to still be playing but I'd love to win Tattslotto as well. The time's right for me." –MARTIN BLAKE

For Australia: 2 Tests, 6 wkts @ 31.17, bb3-71, sr58.00. 30 ODIs, 32 wkts @ 30.59, bb3-18, sr49.87, rpo3.68.

First-class: 59 matches, 245 wkts @ 20.76, bb7-24, sr58.64, 13x5wi, 1x10wm.

Paul Wilson *Right-arm fast bowler*

Paul Wilson had a footballer's build and an action that resembled a lunatic tearing off a straitjacket. As a raw-boned 19-year-old, he left his hometown of Newcastle and a trainee accountancy job, bound for the Cricket Academy in Adelaide. The fact he had not been invited mattered little. Heart and hard work were the only qualifications he needed.

Once at the Academy, Wilson was a carthorse among thoroughbreds. Yet nobody doubted his natural ability or resolve. Picked for South Australia in 1995-96, he forged a strong on-and-off-field bond with Jason Gillespie, another New South Wales-born speedster on the up and up. When pavilion shadows lengthened into late afternoon, and an 11th-hour wicket was needed to sustain a weary team, few bent their backs more for the cause than 'Blocker'.

Bowling a tight line on or just outside off stump, Wilson sweated for his every wicket. He cut the ball both ways and, when his tail was up and every fibre of his 6ft 6in frame was firing, he could extract disarming bounce too. Huffing and puffing, scowling and growling, he came at batsmen like a bull at a cape. These attributes saw him included in an injury-ravaged Australian side against India in 1997-98. Alas, it was a desultory debut. Taking the new ball with Michael Kasprowicz, he toiled valiantly on a benign Eden Gardens pitch before breaking down with sore ribs, wicketless after 12 overs. He watched forlornly from the sidelines as India racked up 5 for 633; his sole Test foray went down as a thumping innings-and-219-run defeat.

That same summer Wilson spearheaded Australia's one-day attack in the Carlton & United Series, finishing level with Shane Warne on 12 wickets to be his country's best. He went on to tour New Zealand, before injuries kept him away from the frontline ever after. Even a stellar domestic haul of 44 wickets at 24 in 1999-00 was not enough, and it was with heavy heart but typical gusto that he ventured west for two last summers with the Warriors.

His final season began with him breaking his jaw and being fined half his match fee for using abusive language against his old team; it climaxed with a starring performance in Western Australia's miraculous ING Cup triumph. Told his contract would not be renewed, he called it quits in March, respected and admired by thousands. Within three months he had taken over as coach of the Western Fury women's team – a gig the local paper described as the "toughest job in Australian cricket". If persistence counts for anything, he should make a hell of a fist of it. –ANGUS FONTAINE

For Australia: 1 Test, 0 wkts for 50. 11 ODIs, 13 wkts @ 34.62, bb3-39, sr43.23, rpo4.80.

First-class 51 matches, 151 wkts @ 30.77, bb6-76, sr73.47, 4x5wi.

Brad Young *Left-arm spinner, right-hand batsman*

When Brad Young was first picked for South Australia, the coach Jeff Hammond told him he would need to bowl quicker to survive at Sheffield Shield level. I intervened; he did not need to bowl faster, I said, just smarter. For a while he operated with a shorter delivery stride, spent more time on his front foot and extracted a lot more spin. But he finished his first-class career with only five five-wicket hauls in six seasons. He retired from West Torrens last summer at 31, his potential never fully realised.

Young's career hit an early hurdle during his days as a lawnmowing contractor. He had turned the mower off but the blades were still spinning when he slipped his right hand under the machine, suffering severe ligament damage and nearly severing one finger. He was an exciting talent, though, and won state selection soon afterwards. A left-arm orthodox spinner, his extraordinarily long delivery stride meant he struggled to stay on his front foot and therefore put fewer revolutions on the ball than he might have. He mixed up his pace skilfully, if sometimes none-too-subtly. Good players found his variations easy to detect early and punish heavily.

An outstanding athlete and brilliant fieldsman, Young was a resilient character who bounced back from various finger and knee injuries. He might have made a better fist of first-class cricket as a specialist bat and part-time spinner, in the vein of Michael Clarke. The innings I remember best was his unbeaten 91 in Adelaide in 1996-97 when he belted hell out of the NSW attack, savagely driving Wayne Holdsworth and slog-sweeping the chinaman bowler David Freedman. I later quizzed Greg Matthews about why he kept Freedman on: "I just wanted little Freddy to get a wicket. I love that little bloke."

Young was a different kind of bowler, frequently used to tie up one end while the leg-spinner Peter McIntyre persevered from the other. McIntyre possessed an eventual career strike-rate of 78.7; Young snared a wicket every 92.4 balls. It added up to a hard, long road for South Australian spinners of that era. –ASHLEY MALLETT

For Australia: 6 ODIs, 31 runs @ 15.50, hs18, sr65.96; 1 wkt @ 251.00, bb1-26, sr234.0, rpo6.43.

First-class: 54 matches, 2,119 runs @ 28.64, hs122, 3x100s, 8x50s; 141 wkts @ 44.72, bb6-85, sr92.46, 5x5wi.

Mark Harrity *Left-arm fast bowler*

In the late 1980s word got around about this 15-year-old at Taperoo High, lightning fast and frighteningly tall, who was scaring the wits out of Adelaide schoolboys. He hadn't been playing long but was already sending them down at around 130 kph. Port Adelaide invited him to join their B-grade team, then A-grade, and then the Academy said they fancied having a look at him too. By the early 1990s he had gatecrashed the state scene, with straggly hair and a goatee and a long angular run-up. He looked like someone who was not to be messed with.

Mark Harrity was actually a quiet and engaging bloke when he wasn't bowling. Rod Marsh called him "a left-handed Jeff Thomson". He might have slung the ball a bit like Thommo but he didn't put that same acute sense of fear in a batsman. Which is why, perhaps, he never ended up taking that next step and playing for his country.

He possessed genuine pace and his ability to angle the ball across a batsman ensured some early success. His inability to do much else with it was the problem. Endless back and shoulder troubles didn't help either. An early mentor was Jeff Hammond, his South Australian coach, who reinvented himself as an opening batsman after chronic back problems terminated his own international career. Harrity, a rabbit with the bat and worse in the field, never showed such adaptability.

Still, he made his Sheffield Shield debut in 1993-94 and took 22 wickets in his second season. In 1995-96 he was given a shot at the big time, picked in an Australian XI for a three-day game against Richie Richardson's West Indians. He bowled five overs, his back played up, and that was it. The years wore on and he kept rejigging his action, shortening his run-up, trying to stay fit. He'd spearhead the attack for a while and then fade away. The moment had passed. He has an English mum and earlier this year, still only 29, he decided his future lies with Worcestershire.

In 62 Pura Cup/Sheffield Shield games Harrity gathered two five-wicket hauls – seven years apart – and 166 wickets. Perhaps his lack of junior experience, which teaches players to cope with vagaries in performance, counted against him. At his worst he battled for a place in a mediocre SA team. At his best he could be lethal. You wonder what he might have achieved had he started playing earlier. –BARRY NICHOLLS

First-class: 84 matches, 216 wkts @ 39.31, bb5-65, sr71.38, 2x5wi.

Chris Davies *Right-hand batsman*

The Chris Davies story begins in 1993, which is when local newspapers started telling of a precociously talented 15-year-old cricket and soccer player who was overcoming great obstacles. He had already played a few matches for Southern Districts, a new club that had recently joined the Adelaide A-grade competition to accommodate that city's southern urban sprawl. They were a young team who endured some tough times in those formative seasons.

Davies, though, had to contend with a more imposing challenge still, for he suffered from cystic fibrosis, with its underlying threat of reduced life expectancy. We soon learned of his long periods of hospitalisation, especially before taking part in major junior competitions. As he moved up in the game, his successes at each new level seemed all the more remarkable.

He himself rarely used his affliction as a crutch. His batting was characterised by upright and powerful strokes; it suggested confidence and authority. He was picked for the Australian Under-19s and hit 109 against Pakistan. At 19, in the summer of 1997-98, he made his first-class debut for South Australia. A month before his 20th birthday he reeled off a magnificent 125 against Western Australia in a one-day match. He switched clubs to Adelaide and was instrumental in their 1998-99 premiership win, hitting 121 in the semis and a decisive 87 in a low-scoring final.

A couple of patchy seasons ensued. In 2001-02 he exploded with 233 not out for the state's 2nd XI, followed by his maiden first-class century: an unbeaten 119 at the Gabba. There was one more hundred a summer later, at the WACA this time, but injuries were becoming a frequent nuisance. In quick succession Davies suffered damage to his shoulder, knee, hamstring and elbow. When, for a fourth time, surgery was required on his left shoulder, he concluded that the joint would not recover to the level required of a first-class cricketer. In March, at the age of 25, he announced his retirement from the SA team.

And so he went back to his Adelaide club side for the 2003-04 A-grade final against Tea Tree Gully. His commanding century, laced with thunderous sweeps and drives, was a pleasant surprise. Cricket might yet get a little more enjoyment from Chris Davies's skills. –GEOFF SANDO

First-class: 25 matches, 1,266 runs @ 28.13, hs125, 2x100s, 7x50s.

Greg Rowell *Right-arm fast bowler*

If it was not already taken, *My Left Foot* might be an appropriate title for any retrospective on the cricketing life of Greg Rowell. He broke it four times, requiring two separate operations. In his darkest days he was once told to forget about bowling again and simply be happy that he could still walk on it.

It was his injured left foot that forced him out of the 1994-95 Sheffield Shield final, when the natural order was turned upside down and Queensland reached their holy grail. Rowell, a rangy fast bowler who had stints with New South Wales, Queensland and eventually Tasmania, looks back on that season with a mix of regret and wonderment.

Until the final, it had been as good as it gets. That year's World Series Cup saw the introduction, never to be repeated, of an Australia A side. Rowell was their spearhead. The tourists fell by the wayside and the first shootout of an all-Aussie finals series went down to the wire. Steve Waugh and Ian Healy needed three runs off the last over.

Rowell was the bowler. "It was what I dreamed of as a kid – playing for Australia in front of a big crowd with all of them behind you. The fact that we were also playing against Australia didn't matter. I remember pausing at the end of my mark each ball in that over, just to feel the crowd."

Bowling with bounce and pace and variety, he kept the batsmen to two runs in five balls. With the scores tied, Healy squirted the last ball through gully for four. Still, a possible Shield final, a county contract with Hampshire and maybe even an Australian tour of the West Indies all beckoned for Rowell. And then he broke his foot.

Matthew Hayden tells of a trip to New York City where Rowell was constantly rehearsing his run-up and delivery set-up, using the display windows of Fifth Avenue stores to check his progress. "I was really wrapped up in cricket, always in search of the perfect bowling action," says Rowell. In 1995-96 he broke his foot again, got the all-clear, weathered an umpire's report questioning his action, then found himself back on the sidelines a couple of years later. "It forced me to look at my life."

At 31 he embarked on a law degree in Tasmania, where he opened the bowling for a season. He returned to Brisbane and, if rumours are to be believed, went desperately close to earning a Pura Cup call-up at 35. When his club side Western Suburbs lost a heart-breaking Brisbane first-grade final last season he announced his retirement, making life hard for batsmen until the day he stopped.
–STEPHEN GRAY

First-class: 46 matches, 147 wkts @ 30.99, bb7-46, sr65.46, 4x5wi, 1x10wm.

Craig Howard *Right-arm leg-spinner*

Eleven years ago Craig Howard might have been asked to bowl leg-breaks for Australia. Two years ago he went close to an invitation to bowl off-breaks for Victoria. At the end of last summer he retired from Melbourne grade cricket, citing family and business reasons. He was only 30, an age at which bowlers of either variety have barely begun to mature.

It was as a tall, slim 17-year-old that he emerged in 1991-92, taking 5 for 38 for Ringwood on his first-grade debut. The following season he broke into Victoria's Sheffield Shield side for the last four games; the summer after that he was bowling them to victory with 5 for 42 against the touring South Africans. Astute judges like Terry Jenner and Rod Marsh liked what they saw. He had a dangerous wrong'un and a high action, which helped him generate bounce and turn. There was a bit of Warne in him. In his next game he took 5 for 112 at Bellerive Oval, and suddenly Peter Roebuck was urging the selectors to pick him for the Third Test against South Africa in Adelaide.

Howard went to the Gabba feeling like he was bowling for a Test spot. He was still only 19. He went for five an over and finished with 1 for 152. Three games later he didn't even have his Victorian spot.

Sadly, it soon became clear that his light frame could not withstand the physical demands of bowling long spells of leg-breaks. He suffered injuries to his shoulder, wrist, knees and shins, until a damaged spinning finger effectively meant he couldn't bowl leg-spin at all. He played three fruitless seasons with Ringwood, another at Richmond, then switched to sub-district club Balwyn. Which is where his reinvention began.

Quickly picking up the skills of bowling off-spin, which imposed fewer strains on his body, he captured 33 cheap wickets. His fitness and confidence restored, he returned to Ringwood. "I always thought when I was bowling leg-breaks that anyone could bowl off-breaks," he told *The Age*. "Now I'm finding it's easier to do, but harder to do well. You need to be a lot more patient. I've never had a lot of patience."

Howard took 35 wickets for Ringwood in 2001-02 and the state selectors, their interest pricked, sent him to the Academy over the winter. He took another 33 wickets the next summer but the call never came. Heading Ringwood's wicket-takers yet again in 2003-04, he retired on a high. He signed off with 235 first-grade scalps – 114 at 29.39 as a leggie, 121 at 24.62 as an offie – and a remarkable story to tell. –KEN WILLIAMS

First-class: 16 matches, 42 wkts @ 40.14, bb5-42, sr73.17, 2x5wi.

Ken Vowles *Right-hand batsman*

Certain stereotypes tend to fester about cricketers and their intellect. Off-spinners lack the imagination to bowl leg-spin. Fast bowlers aren't bright enough to captain teams. Aborigines are too thick to be anything other than fast bowlers. The latter is a scrap of racist buffoonery that selectors, administrators and talent scouts have been shamefully eager to embrace; if you discount Queensland's Daniel Payne (part-Japanese-Javanese-Dutch-Aboriginal) the last Aboriginal batsman to play first-class cricket was Johnny Mullagh in 1879. And Mullagh, in his one and only match, was sent in by Victoria at No. 9.

Ultimately Ken Vowles did not end up playing first-class cricket either. But he had more riding against him than the average right-hander. He took up cricket at 13, adapted instantly to Darwin's steamy humidity and goosebumped matting wickets, and was soon playing A-grade for a rural club of ramshackle misfits called Southern Districts. At 16 he left home, as all ambitious Darwin cricketers must, and debuted for Port Adelaide. "Before I even took guard I'd been branded a blackfella and a coon," he recalled last year. "I'm not going to name names but I lost a bit of respect for a few big cricketers, both first-class and Test players."

His strategy was simple: he fought bile with fire. "When we walk off," he'd say, "I'll still be the same colour and you'll still be a wanker." It served him well through a long and adventurous career. He went to the Academy, toured England and New Zealand with the Australian Under-19s, played a few games for the South Australian 2nd XI, captain-coached assorted Northern Territory sides.

In every team he played for, in every unwatched cranny of the Australian cricketing wilderness, Vowles was always the swash-buckler, ferocious on the pull and drive. Once he launched one of the most frenetic fusillades never seen, a 58-ball hundred at the MCG, against a Young England attack led by Darren Gough and Dominic Cork. The year was 1990 and Vowles was 18, his only instinct to butcher anything and everything. Visiting southern pros, drawn to Darwin by the beer and barra, would see him rifle a straight-drive and ask who the hell that was.

He retired from representative cricket last year, unmourned and unnoticed, aged 31. His farewell match was for a Northern Territory Chief Minister's XI against Bangladesh. He signed off with 20 and 34, outscoring Michael Clarke – no slowcoach himself – along the way. Vowles did not so much break with tradition as smash the cover off it. –CHRISTIAN RYAN

Stuart Law *Right-hand batsman*

See essay on page 87.

For Australia: 1 Test, 54 runs, hs54*, 1x50s; 54 ODIs, 1,237 runs @ 26.89, hs110, sr75.28, 1x100s, 7x50s.

First-class: 304 matches, 22,871 runs @ 51.28, hs263, 67x100s, 107x50s; 82 wkts @ 50.79, bb5-39, s101.67, 1x5wi; 340ct.

Steve Waugh *Right-hand batsman, right-arm medium-pacer, master captain*

See essays on pages 39, 45, 52.

For Australia: 168 Tests, 10,927 runs@ 51.06, hs200, 32x100s, 50x50s; 92 wkts@ 37.45, bb5-28, sr84.83, 3x5wi; 325 ODIs, 7,569 runs @ 32.91, hs120*, sr75.81, 3x100s, 45x50s; 195 wkts @ 34.67, bb4-33, sr45.55, rpo4.56

First-class: 356 matches, 24,051 runs @ 51.95, hs216*, 79x100s, 97x50s; 249 wkts @ 32.75, bb6-51, s69.99, 5x5wi; 273ct.

Player Profiles

The players in this section appeared in first-class or limited-overs matches during 2003-04, or are scheduled to feature in the 2004-05 Australian season. Statistics are accurate to August 1, 2004.

Player profiles written by:
Geoff Lawson (New South Wales)
Stephen Gray (Queensland)
Nabila Ahmed (Victoria)
Daniel Brettig (South Australia)
Ric Finlay (Tasmania)
Ken Casellas (Western Australia)

JASON ARNBERGER *Right-hand batsman* Victoria

Ushered into the Victorian side for last summer's Pura Cup final, Arnberger staged a display so uncharacteristic that even his team-mates were bemused. He smashed two half-centuries, having made only one all summer, and pummelled the off-spinner Nathan Hauritz for three consecutive sixes in a 24-run over. Those three mighty blows doused rumours that he was contemplating retirement. Hampered by injuries for much of the season, he had missed the previous four matches and was picked largely because of Matthew Mott's inability to convert solid starts into substantial scores. Arnberger suffered a similar problem. A veteran at 31, he continues his constant and very public battles with his fitness. For all his untypical dash in the final, only an injury-free and productive summer will save his spot.

	M	I	NO	Runs	HS	100s	50s	Avge	Ct	St	W	Avge	BB
First-class	72	135	10	4,689	214	8	26	37.51	53	0	0	–	–
Domestic first-class	68	129	10	4,539	214	8	25	38.14	49	0	0	–	–
Dom. limited-overs	27	26	1	541	79	0	4	21.64	0	0	0	–	–

GEORGE BAILEY *Right-hand batsman* Tasmania

A direct descendant of George Herbert Bailey, an 1878 Australian tourist to England, this 22-year-old has pedigree on his side. An exciting and natural strokemaker, he appeared in six ING Cup matches last summer and produced two innings of significant merit. He demonstrated both flair and poise against WA on a sporting wicket in Launceston, holding the lower order together and finishing with 36 off 39 balls. His unbeaten 52 at a cauldron-like MCG was even more impressive. He defied dehydration and an in-form Victorian attack to lead Tasmania to their only one-day victory of the season. A former Australian Under-19 player, Bailey is still prone to the occasional soft dismissal. He must show more steel if he is to at last win a first-class spot this summer.

	M	I	NO	Runs	HS	100s	50s	Avge	Ct	St	W	Avge	BB
Dom. limited-overs	13	12	3	238	57*	0	2	26.44	3	0	0	–	–

MICHAEL BEVAN *Left-hand batsman* NSW, Tasmania and Australia

This was the year that the man who has salvaged many a lost cause for Australia fell into freefall himself. After a dazzling tournament in India, followed by a workmanlike VB Series, Bevan endured a middling series in Sri Lanka and found himself out of contract. Suddenly, in the same week that he had been judged one of worldwide *Wisden*'s 40 best players on the planet, he did not rank among Australia's top 25. His sluggish strike-rate seemed the main cause – along with the head selector Trevor Hohns's observation that Bevan's "contribution to the one-day side has decreased … we thought it was the right time to move forward". Disillusioned, he went briefly into hibernation before moving forward himself, signing a two-year contract with Tasmania as player and assistant coach. And it is little wonder Tasmania sold the Tasman Bridge and half of Boonie's landholdings to lure him south; in three Pura Cup games for NSW last season he averaged 101. The national selectors wasted Bevan's prodigious talent, batting him at No. 7 in Test matches and dropping him from the one-day side at least 12 months too early. On the Bellerive belter, his new home, he might yet make 2,000 runs this summer.

	M	I	NO	Runs	HS	100s	50s	Avge	Ct	St	W	Avge	BB
First-class	214	356	63	16,922	216	59	74	57.75	115	0	115	45.06	6-82
Domestic first-class	99	175	33	8,512	216	33	35	59.94	44	0	21	64.95	3-40
Test	18	30	3	785	91	0	6	29.07	8	0	29	24.24	6-82
Int'l limited-overs	232	196	67	6,912	108*	6	46	53.58	69	0	36	45.97	3-36
Dom. limited-overs	60	60	20	2478	135*	1	22	61.95	14	0	5	38.80	2-24

ANDY BICHEL *Right-arm fast bowler* **Queensland and Australia**

The surprise hero of Australia's 2003 World Cup triumph fell from grace with indecent haste last summer. Bichel's version of cricketing snakes and ladders saw him dropped from the Test side after taking 4 for 118 against India in Adelaide, axed from a winning one-day side and then overlooked altogether for a national contract. Hard-boiled judges might point to a drop-off in bowling returns – certainly he found wickets hard to come by at Worcestershire recently – and the desire to infuse younger blood into the national line-up. Bichel, whose winning grin and floppy blond fringe make him a favourite of Australian crowds, accepted his fate stoically and threw himself into Queensland's campaign. He bowled with considerable bite in his 6 for 61 against SA, then peeled off his second first-class century at the SCG. An optimistic soul, he will no doubt back himself to construct a strong case for a Test recall in 2004-05. And those on the scout for some likely cricketing talent should look no further than the Bichel clan, which includes Tazelaars and Noffkes in their extended family. Among the 2004 birth notices was one Hayden Bichel: a youngster with some outstanding role models to look up to.

	M	I	NO	Runs	HS	100s	50s	Avge	Ct	St	W	Avge	BB
First-class	127	162	13	3,312	112	3	13	22.23	70	0	508	25.96	9-93
Domestic first-class	56	75	5	1,529	112	2	5	21.84	31	0	274	22.31	6-45
Test	19	22	1	355	71	0	1	16.90	16	0	58	32.24	5-60
Int'l limited-overs	67	36	13	471	64	0	1	20.48	19	0	78	31.59	7-20
Dom. limited-overs	46	26	10	438	59*	0	1	27.38	14	0	47	36.38	4-45

AARON BIRD *Right-arm fast bowler* **NSW**

If dedication counts for anything, Bird is bound for bigger things. Lean and not so lanky, he terrorised batsmen last summer in both the state 2nd XI and Sydney first-grade competitions, where he took more wickets than anyone else and cracked several bones for good measure. Born in Taree, in northern NSW, he was named Man of the Match in the 2001-02 Under-19 World Cup final and is perhaps best known for smashing Michael Slater in the face during a club game. Apart from bowling fast, he bats a bit too. Now 21, he has worked hard to allay concerns held in some quarters about the legitimacy of his action. He went within an inch of playing for the Blues last season and, with any luck, should finally don the baggy blue in 2004-05.
No major cricket played to date.

TRAVIS BIRT *Left-hand batsman*   **Tasmania**

Poor shot selection was Birt's biggest obstacle in his maiden summer of interstate cricket. A 22-year-old opener, born in the Victorian town of Sale, he forced his way into Tasmania's ING Cup side on the back of some hefty run-making at club level. He played four matches and twice reached double figures before giving his wicket away. Ultimately he lost his spot in the side, but further opportunities beckon this summer. Tasmanian authorities, keen to build on his potential, have awarded him a rookie contract for 2004-05, and he also toured India in August with a young Australian development squad. His biggest challenge now is to learn how to temper his natural aggression.

	M	I	NO	Runs	HS	100s	50s	Avge	Ct	St	W	Avge	BB
Dom. limited-overs	4	4	0	50	28	0	0	12.50	1	0	0	–	–

GREG BLEWETT *Right-hand batsman*   **SA**

After being the Swiss watch of South Australia's batting every year since the end of his international days, Blewett finally endured a summer that did not match up to his usual high standards. It was not that he stopped making neat starts; it was his inability to convert them into hundreds that proved most hurtful to his team. His 171 in Hobart in the first week of November was his only century all summer, as the eagerly anticipated big partnerships with Andy Flower never materialised. His drop-off in productivity could be explained at least partly by back and hand injuries, which prevented him playing every game and curbed his inventive bowling. For the first time in a long time Blewett, at 32, enters the new summer with something to prove.

	M	I	NO	Runs	HS	100s	50s	Avge	Ct	St	W	Avge	BB
First-class	215	386	26	16,464	268	43	81	45.73	168	0	135	42.11	5-29
Domestic first-class	100	190	10	8,794	268	23	43	48.86	60	0	85	39.87	4-39
Test	46	79	4	2,552	214	4	15	34.03	45	0	14	51.43	2-9
Int'l limited-overs	32	30	3	551	57*	0	2	20.41	7	0	14	46.14	2-6
Dom. limited-overs	79	77	7	2,740	109*	3	17	39.14	26	0	51	34.96	4-33

ANDY BLIGNAUT *Right-arm fast bowler, left-hand batsman*   **Tasmania**

The disintegration of Zimbabwean cricket has brought Blignaut, a slippery fast bowler and hard-hitting lower-order batsman, to Tasmania. One of Zimbabwe's 15 rebel white players, he has been touted as a partial replacement for Shane Watson, although the 26-year-old Blignaut's stronger suit is his bowling. His 51 wickets in 15 Tests are highly respectable figures, given the load he carried in an undermanned Zimbabwe attack. His likely new-ball partnership with Damien Wright will keep opening batsmen from the mainland on their toes. As a batsman, Blignaut possesses sufficient might to have thrashed the Australians for a memorable 54 off 28 balls in the 2003 World Cup. His one-day international strike-rate stands at an imposing 105.54, suggesting he might help trigger a long-overdue revival in Tasmania's ING Cup form.

	M	I	NO	Runs	HS	100s	50s	Avge	Ct	St	W	Avge	BB
First-class	42	64	4	1,712	194	2	7	28.53	26	0	114	34.22	5-73
Test	15	28	2	638	92	0	3	24.54	11	0	51	32.63	5-73
Int'l limited-overs	47	36	8	533	63*	0	4	19.04	10	0	41	43.39	4-43

DOUG BOLLINGER *Left-arm fast bowler*   **NSW**

It has been a frustrating time for a man with boundless enthusiasm and a deep love for the game. Bollinger's 2003-04 summer was interrupted from the start by lower back problems, the bane of many an energetic quick. The lesson it taught him was to train harder. He eventually made it back on the park, along with a restructured bowling action, for one Pura and ING Cup appearance. The wicket cupboard, not surprisingly, was as bare as his noggin. But with another pre-season of strengthening behind him, and with greater experience of managing his body, he could well prove a force in the coming summer. Left-arm quicks, after all, are few and far between in Australia. If he stays healthy, Bollinger might yet pose a question or two for the national selectors.

	M	I	NO	Runs	HS	100s	50s	Avge	Ct	St	W	Avge	BB
First-class	9	10	4	19	7	0	0	3.17	5	0	14	61.07	4-50
Domestic first-class	8	9	4	12	3	0	0	2.40	4	0	13	57.15	4-50
Dom. limited-overs	7	1	0	5	5	0	0	5.00	2	0	6	42.50	2-26

NATHAN BRACKEN *Left-arm fast bowler* **NSW and Australia**

It has been a fascinating year in the life of Bracken. At Test level, he made his debut against India but was employed in the questionable tactic of bowling well outside off-stump, rather than in-swinging at the castle. At one-day level, he was clearly Australia's man of the series during the TVS Cup in India – bowling tightly and taking 14 wickets in six matches – only to be promptly ignored by the selectors for the next ten months. It seems more than curious. His ING Cup form was only passable but his four Pura Cup appearances were particularly encouraging, as he discovered the need for toughness, persistence and hard work in the longer form of the game. With Steve Waugh retired and new captains in control, and with his first taste of international cricket behind him, Bracken can be expected to blossom at international level in 2004-05. First, if he is to impress Trevor Hohns and Co, he must do the hard work at state level.

	M	I	NO	Runs	HS	100s	50s	Avge	Ct	St	W	Avge	BB
First-class	36	49	20	428	38*	0	0	14.76	10	0	107	30.32	5-22
Domestic first-class	32	44	17	409	38*	0	0	15.15	8	0	96	29.50	5-22
Test	3	3	1	9	6*	0	0	4.50	1	0	6	58.50	2-12
Int'l limited-overs	17	1	1	7	7*	0	0	–	5	0	28	19.71	4-29
Dom. limited-overs	38	14	5	69	16*	0	0	7.67	5	0	52	27.15	5-38

SHAWN BRADSTREET *Right-arm medium-pacer, right hand batsman* **NSW**

For a man often labelled as "just a one-day player", Bradstreet offers much in leadership and grit. He is the ultimate team man and one of the most cerebral cricketers in the country. The tool-box that is his medium-pace bowling gains a new tool every season. Yet 2003-04 was his season of discontent and frustration. He played two ING Cup games, failed to trouble the scorers with either a run or a wicket, and didn't figure out thanks to a blown knee. He spent the rest of the season in rehabilitation, hanging round the physio's office trying to look cheerful. 'Winger' Bradstreet's presence around the rooms and on the practice field will be de rigueur in the coming summer if the Blues are to threaten any title.

	M	I	NO	Runs	HS	100s	50s	Avge	Ct	St	W	Avge	BB
First-class	9	17	4	296	60	0	1	22.77	6	0	12	62.00	2-32
Domestic first-class	8	16	4	281	60	0	1	23.42	6	0	11	52.18	2-32
Dom. limited-overs	41	31	13	457	75*	0	1	25.39	13	0	36	32.81	4-23

SCOTT BRANT *Left-arm fast bowler* **Queensland**

A genuine swing bowler with a jaunty approach, the blond-haired Brant can be a dangerous new-ball option in the right conditions. His slower-than-expected recovery from a knee injury removed him from Queensland's initial considerations last season, and he found it difficult to force his way back once fully fit. He did not play a first-class game but fared slightly brighter in the one-day arena, contributing handily in three ING Cup matches as the Bulls charged towards the final. His second stint with Essex in 2004 mirrored his Queensland experience: he was preferred for limited-overs matches rather than first-class. This apparent predilection for colours over whites extends to his career away from cricket. He works in the retail fashion industry, where he intrigues many of his older team-mates with his choices of social attire.

	M	I	NO	Runs	HS	100s	50s	Avge	Ct	St	W	Avge	BB
First-class	22	24	9	92	23	0	0	6.13	7	0	60	32.22	6-45
Domestic first-class	5	4	2	35	19*	0	0	17.50	4	0	11	20.45	3-23
Dom. limited-overs	13	2	1	1	1*	0	0	1.00	4	0	16	27.75	3-33

LUKE BUTTERWORTH *Left-hand batsman, right-arm medium-pacer* **Tasmania**

A 20-year-old all-rounder with an attacking, refreshing attitude, Butterworth made an immediate impact upon being picked for Tasmania's ING Cup team midway through last summer. With the ball, he picked up 3 for 33 at the MCG; with the bat, he hit a rapid 23 on debut against Queensland and was promoted to No. 3 for his last two games. He showed enough promise to be offered a state contract for 2004-05 and seems likely to figure even more prominently this summer. A tall but slender character, he needs to work at developing more zip and penetration in his bowling, something that should come with increased gym-work.

	M	I	NO	Runs	HS	100s	50s	Avge	Ct	St	W	Avge	BB
Dom. limited-overs	4	4	0	65	23	0	0	16.25	0	0	4	24.50	3-33

BEN CAMERON *Right-hand batsman* **SA**

Ignored at the selection table until late in the season, Ben Cameron immediately showed he has the application and stroke range of a ready-made first-class batsman. Sent in as opener on debut at the MCG, he fashioned two capable half-centuries. He followed up with 66 against NSW in his first ING Cup match. A pair at the SCG was a more sobering experience, but he fought back in his third and final first-class game against WA. Sporting a black eye after being clobbered in the head while fielding in close, he clattered 81 with a string of electrifying backfoot drives. At 22, Cameron has made no secret of his desire to help take SA's batting beyond its long-term reliance on Greg Blewett and Darren Lehmann. It is a heartening ambition.

	M	I	NO	Runs	HS	100s	50s	Avge	Ct	St	W	Avge	BB
First-class	3	6	1	199	81	0	3	39.80	0	0	0	–	–
Domestic first-class	3	6	1	199	81	0	3	39.80	0	0	0	–	–
Dom. limited-overs	2	2	0	78	66	0	1	39.00	1	0	0	–	–

MARK CAMERON *Right-arm fast bowler* **NSW**

It has been a year of net practice for the Newcastle scud as he endeavoured to regain the form, rhythm and technique that propelled him into a first-class debut two summers ago. It wasn't for a lack of trying that he failed to crack the NSW team; his effort could never be doubted. Injuries to ankles and knees didn't help his cause, and he joined the ever-growing list of contemporary fast men who spend more time with the physio than on the practice ground. Tall and lean, Cameron's wicketless hometown debut against WA in 2002-03 remains his only first-class appearance to date. He lost his state contract for this coming summer but at 22 he is young enough – and motivated enough – to make it back.

	M	I	NO	Runs	HS	100s	50s	Avge	Ct	St	W	Avge	BB
First-class	1	1	0	6	6	0	0	6.00	1	0	0	–	–
Domestic first-class	1	1	0	6	6	0	0	6.00	1	0	0	–	–

RYAN CAMPBELL *Right-hand batsman, wicket-keeper* **WA**
Gone was the pressure, much of it self-imposed, which hounded Campbell under Mike Veletta's reign. With Wayne Clark back in the Western Australian coaching job, he seemed genial and relaxed, a man transformed. He developed into an important team leader too, quickly overcoming the disappointment of being dropped – rather unfairly – in favour of Luke Ronchi for the last game of 2002-03. Campbell was fitter than he has been in a while, having recovered from knee injuries and undergone successful elbow surgery, and it showed. Unorthodox, entertaining and effective, he batted with tremendous flair and consistency – 664 Pura Cup runs at 39 – in all forms of the game. He kept splendidly to both the fast and slow men. For all that, he fell behind Brad Haddin in the national pecking order as Adam Gilchrist's understudy.

	M	I	NO	Runs	HS	100s	50s	Avge	Ct	St	W	Avge	BB
First-class	81	142	5	5,035	203	9	32	36.75	207	12	0	–	–
Domestic first-class	71	125	4	4,496	203	8	30	37.16	174	8	0	–	–
Int'l limited-overs	2	2	0	54	38	0	0	27.00	4	1	0	–	–
Dom. limited-overs	69	67	1	1,464	108	1	6	22.18	89	6	0	–	–

LEE CARSELDINE *Left-hand batsman, left-arm medium-pacer* **Queensland**
Informed touring teams to Australia might wish to check the whereabouts and bona fides of Carseldine as part of their future pre-tour planning. Three years ago he slaughtered an unbeaten 200 against New Zealand (and Glen Sulzberger has never been the same bowler since). He followed up two years ago with a PM's XI Man of the Match performance against England and a 92 against Bangladesh. Last summer it was India's turn to have their build-up disrupted, Carseldine stroking a century in each innings for a Queensland Academy side. This time his performance proved misleading. After his standout summer of 2002-03, he managed only four one-day and two first-class matches – averaging 9.50 – thanks to a steadily worsening back condition. He later scored 114 for the 2nd XI but question marks over his fitness lingered. Off-season rehabilitation failed to fix the problem, with surgery a possibility.

	M	I	NO	Runs	HS	100s	50s	Avge	Ct	St	W	Avge	BB
First-class	24	37	6	1,009	124*	1	5	32.55	23	0	8	35.63	3-25
Domestic first-class	23	36	6	958	124*	1	4	31.93	23	0	7	38.71	3-25
Dom. limited-overs	29	27	3	442	59	0	1	18.42	11	0	9	20.00	4-6

BEAU CASSON *Left-arm chinaman bowler* **WA**
It was a summer of mixed fortunes for this delightful 21-year-old. He dismissed Steve Waugh for a duck at the SCG, a rare achievement, then seized eight wickets and the Man of the Match award against Queensland in January. A week later, in the dying stages of an ING Cup contest, he dived forward at long-off in a valiant attempt to catch the NSW left-hander Aaron O'Brien. He fractured a finger in his bowling hand and missed the rest of the season, after capturing 17 wickets at 34 in his first four Pura Cup matches. Born with a congenital heart disease that requires constant monitoring, Casson's role model is his chinaman-bowling team-mate Brad Hogg. He boasts a couple of wrong'uns already and is working assiduously to develop new deliveries and greater variety in his action.

	M	I	NO	Runs	HS	100s	50s	Avge	Ct	St	W	Avge	BB
First-class	11	20	5	254	35	0	0	16.93	4	0	35	38.31	6-64
Domestic first-class	10	19	4	247	35	0	0	16.47	4	0	34	36.74	6-64
Dom. limited-overs	9	2	0	7	6	0	0	3.50	3	0	4	46.75	4-31

MICHAEL CLARK *Left-arm fast bowler* **WA**
Tall and graceful, Clark unveiled a new action last summer. His right arm now goes straight up and down instead of across his body, which had previously caused him to fall across, open up and place too much stress on his back. A late beginner, he describes his bowling as "pretty unnatural" and believes his body will to take time to adjust. So it proved in 2003-04. He appeared in only two ING Cup games, promptly breaking down in the second of those in Launceston. Scans revealed a minor crack in his vertebrae, and a screw was inserted into a spinal disc in a bid to relieve the pain. His WA predecessors Peter Capes, Bruce Reid and Brendon Julian all underwent similar surgery, and all came up roses. Clark's promising AFL career was terminated by a knee and two shoulder reconstructions. He is not about to let his cricket career end the same way.

	M	I	NO	Runs	HS	100s	50s	Avge	Ct	St	W	Avge	BB
First-class	16	22	10	138	26	0	0	11.50	10	0	48	27.35	5-47
Domestic first-class	15	20	9	134	26	0	0	12.18	10	0	45	26.73	5-47
Dom. limited-overs	7	3	1	44	27	0	0	22.00	5	0	12	24.08	3-34

STUART CLARK *Right-arm fast bowler* **NSW**
After a pre-season interrupted by hernia surgery, 'Sarfraz' Clark slowly worked his way back into reasonable form last summer, without ever quite producing the national selector-prodding stuff of two years ago. His 23 wickets in eight Pura Cup outings were fair enough but his average – 38.26 – was higher than he would have liked. Mind you, the pitches around Australia did bowlers few favours. Only Matt Nicholson bowled more overs for the Blues, and only Nicholson and Stuart MacGill took more wickets. Clark was more impressive in the one-day arena, playing all 10 ING Cup games and securing 16 scalps at a reasonable economy rate. NSW will again be counting on him to be a mainstay of their attack. His recent marriage and a settled lifestyle bode well for his prospects.

	M	I	NO	Runs	HS	100s	50s	Avge	Ct	St	W	Avge	BB
First-class	38	56	16	488	35	0	0	12.20	11	0	118	34.48	6-84
Domestic first-class	36	54	16	487	35	0	0	12.82	10	0	112	33.85	6-84
Dom. limited-overs	53	13	3	54	14	0	0	5.40	9	0	65	28.83	4-26

MICHAEL CLARKE *Right-hand batsman* **NSW and Australia**
Quicksilver on his feet like Michael Slater, and with wrists that flash late à la Steve Waugh, Michael Clarke has long been identified as Australian batting's next big thing. Unfortunately the national selectors have posted him as a one-day player and are not allowing him the first-class innings that will lead to a permanent Test spot. Last summer he played only two Pura Cup games, averaging 18.50, while trooping around India and Sri Lanka belting the white aspro. Rarely has there been a batsman so strong through backward point off both the front and back foot. Rarely has there been a player with such extravagant hairdressing bills. Whether platinum-blond or moggy-mottled, it matters little. His left-arm sliders are proving increasingly handy, and his 4 for 42 in Mumbai last November – including Tendulkar, Dravid and Yuvraj Singh – was top-drawer stuff. Add in his bullet arm and he is a phenom', as the Yanks might say. And he is still only 23. It is up to the selectors to get him in the Test team before he turns 29.

	M	I	NO	Runs	HS	100s	50s	Avge	Ct	St	W	Avge	BB
First-class	45	82	5	2,915	140	10	11	37.86	42	0	5	75.60	2-25
Domestic first-class	31	57	2	2,020	134	7	8	36.73	28	0	5	48.20	2-25
Int'l limited-overs	28	26	8	784	105*	1	4	43.56	12	0	17	29.18	5-35
Dom. limited-overs	28	26	5	806	101*	1	5	38.38	7	0	7	25.57	3-57

MARK CLEARY *Right-arm fast bowler, left-hand batsman* **SA**
Consistent line, subtle movement and a deceptively simple action are Cleary's big assets. Selected for Australia A against Zimbabwe last summer, he took three inexpensive

wickets in two matches to outperform his flashier SA team-mate Shaun Tait. His zippy pace made him an ideal third prong in the Redbacks attack behind Paul Rofe, naggingly accurate, and Tait, blindingly fast. Being part of a strong pace line-up perhaps robbed Cleary of bigger hauls. But his 30 Pura Cup wickets in nine matches represented a fine return in only his second first-class season. His batting flourished early and was instrumental in victories over WA and NSW. His subsequent decline after Christmas probably had something to do with the fact that he was playing with a broken finger for much of *that* time.

	M	I	NO	Runs	HS	100s	50s	Avge	Ct	St	W	Avge	BB
First-class	21	32	8	428	58	0	1	17.83	11	0	69	29.51	7-80
Domestic first-class	13	20	0	301	58	0	1	15.05	8	0	46	27.02	5-102
Dom. limited-overs	15	15	6	139	70	0	1	15.44	5	0	16	39.06	4-55

SEAN CLINGELEFFER *Wicket-keeper, left-hand batsman* **Tasmania**
A series of unobtrusive yet competent keeping displays, plus a return to something like his best batting form, enhanced Clingeleffer's reputation during 2003-04. Talented and affable, he is now – at 23 – a senior member of the Tasmanian team. He was one of the more obvious beneficiaries of a better wicket at Bellerive. A serious malfunction in his run production in 2002-03 had critics calling for his sacking, and the arrival of David Dawson – a young wicket-keeping tyro from Canberra – put Clingeleffer on his mettle right from the start. He responded admirably, accumulating three Pura Cup half-centuries and averaging 31 for the summer. His seven first-innings catches in Perth equalled the Tasmanian record, set by Joe Holyman 12 years earlier, and were only a thin edge away from a national one.

	M	I	NO	Runs	HS	100s	50s	Avge	Ct	St	W	Avge	BB
First-class	41	62	8	1,403	141*	2	6	25.98	119	8	0	–	–
Domestic first-class	41	62	8	1,403	141*	2	6	25.98	119	8	0	–	–
Dom. limited-overs	40	32	16	362	48	0	0	22.63	39	3	0	–	–

MARK COSGROVE *Left-hand batsman* **SA**
Known already as 'Junior Boof', Cosgrove's fearless, free-swinging technique radiates the confidence of a young man who knows he is good enough to attack the best bowlers. And, like Darren Lehmann, Cosgrove fields – and bowls – better than his rotund physique should allow. With 639 runs at 45.64, he earned the distinction of topping SA's aggregates in his first full season. His tally was the lowest to do so since Barry Causby's 642 in the first season of World Series Cricket, though that is more a reflection of his team-mates' failings than a criticism of the 19-year-old himself. There were a few untimely dismissals and some airy swings at wide deliveries. But his 118 in 147 balls to set up victory over NSW in Adelaide was sheer punchy perfection. It may not be long before he is pushing for a place in the Australian side.

	M	I	NO	Runs	HS	100s	50s	Avge	Ct	St	W	Avge	BB
First-class	11	19	1	727	144	2	3	40.39	14	0	3	23.67	1-0
Domestic first-class	11	19	1	727	144	2	3	40.39	14	0	3	23.67	1-0
Dom. limited-overs	14	14	0	270	55	0	2	19.29	2	0	0	–	–

JAMIE COX *Right-hand batsman* **Tasmania**
At 35, Cox is surely in the twilight of his illustrious career. He has averaged only 25 in each of the past two seasons. Last year, his Pura Cup career average dipped below 40. He can still bat beautifully when the mood takes him, as he proved with his elegant 119 against SA in his first innings of the summer. But he did not pass 50 again until his last, four long months and 16 innings later. Although largely excluded from Tasmania's ING Cup mix, no obvious opening candidates are pushing for his first-class spot; and Cox, with all his experience, brings more to the team than runs. Besides, there are records to be broken. This season he should overtake John Inverarity's 159 Sheffield Shield/Pura

Cup matches and Jamie Siddons's run tally. Then only Darren Lehmann will stand ahead of him.

	M	I	NO	Runs	HS	100s	50s	Avge	Ct	St	W	Avge	BB
First-class	253	448	30	17,970	245	50	78	42.99	116	0	5	90.00	3-46
Domestic first-class	153	279	17	10,459	245	30	44	39.92	72	0	1	182.00	1-44
Dom. limited-overs	75	73	4	1,879	99	0	14	27.23	19	0	0	–	–

DAN CULLEN *Right-arm off-spinner*   SA

The 20-year-old Cullen looks poised to compete with John Davison this summer for the spinner's berth in a pace-oriented Redbacks attack. He was deservedly named among SA's senior contracted players for 2004-05 after some startling grade returns with Adelaide (41 wickets at 20.98) and solid performances with the state 2nd XI (17 wickets at 29.82). Picked to tour India with an Australian youth development squad in August, a 1st XI spot may be just around the corner.
No major cricket played to date.

JOHN DAVISON *Right-arm off-spinner, right-hand batsman*   SA

Davison's 17 for 137 for Canada against the USA last May – the best first-class return since Jim Laker at Old Trafford in 1956 – could hardly have come at a better time. Figures of 8 for 61 and 9 for 76 in Fort Lauderdale, scene of their Intercontinental Cup match, were the perfect confidence-booster for a player whose morale took a battering last summer. Trumped as SA's all-round action man after the 2003 World Cup, he started promisingly with 59 and 5 for 26 to win an ING Cup match against Tasmania almost single-handedly. Ironically, though, he soon found himself in the very dilemma he left behind in Victoria – bowling the gap overs while a strong pace attack rested – and his figures suffered. Davison's low-percentage, attack-at-all-costs approach to opening the batting was also exposed. Fielding sides, far from cowering, simply waited for him to self-destruct. He usually did.

	M	I	NO	Runs	HS	100s	50s	Avge	Ct	St	W	Avge	BB
First-class	47	71	7	861	84	0	3	13.45	20	0	100	47.49	9-76
Domestic first-class	45	67	7	732	84	0	2	12.20	19	0	81	55.01	5-81
Int'l limited-overs	6	6	0	226	111	1	1	37.67	1	0	10	18.70	3-15
Dom. limited-overs	17	15	3	310	59	0	2	25.83	6	0	13	36.54	5-26

JOE DAWES *Right-arm fast bowler*   Queensland

Dawes is one of those rare selfless types, providing the quiet background direction any team needs to be successful. He is also, at 35, capable of bowling 20-odd overs into the wind at brisk pace. Despite failing to secure a five-for last summer, he led Queensland's wicket tally with 30 Pura Cup scalps at 36.03. He should eclipse 200 career wickets sometime this season, an impressive achievement for someone who came to first-class cricket late in life. Dawes has previously been a plainclothes policeman with the drug squad and a media adviser to the federal parliamentarian Peter Dutton. Now he has bought a newsagency and is going into partnership with team-mate Ashley Noffke. The advent of Fast Bowlers United – offering training apparel and cricket boot studding – both fills a niche and reinforces the perception that fast bowlers are a little different.

	M	I	NO	Runs	HS	100s	50s	Avge	Ct	St	W	Avge	BB
First-class	64	77	29	495	32*	0	0	10.31	12	0	239	25.69	7-67
Domestic first-class	52	62	23	386	29	0	0	9.90	9	0	192	25.21	7-67
Dom. limited-overs	13	1	1	1	1*	0	0	–	2	0	16	29.13	3-26

SHANE DEITZ *Left-hand batsman, wicket-keeper*   SA

After several summers playing musical wicket-keepers with Graham Manou, Deitz appeared exclusively as an opening batsman in 2003-04 and was promptly named

Bradman medallist in Adelaide's A-grade competition. In the light of all that his first-class performances were rather less satisfactory as, for the third summer in a row, he averaged below 30. Often he looked compact and fluent at the crease. Just as often, and in common with several of his team-mates, he was unable to turn solid starts into significant totals. His best score in nine Pura Cup matches was his 74 at the Gabba. It was a new-look Deitz last summer, freer and more aggressive in his approach. But at 29 he is too old to be hitting handsome 30s and 40s. The talent is there. Where is the application?

	M	I	NO	Runs	HS	100s	50s	Avge	Ct	St	W	Avge	BB
First-class	36	71	2	1,978	114	2	13	28.67	48	1	2	46.50	2-17
Domestic first-class	35	69	2	1,966	114	2	13	29.34	46	1	2	46.50	2-17
Dom. limited-overs	14	14	0	412	60	0	2	29.43	4	0	0	–	–

GERARD DENTON *Right-arm fast bowler* **Tasmania and Victoria**

In nine previous summers Denton, lively but injury-prone, had only once managed to play more than three games. Last summer he played eight, all in a row, and for the first time took 30 wickets. To protect this valuable new commodity, he was limited to one ING Cup game all year. Unfortunately for Denton, his re-emergence coincided with the toning down of the Bellerive pitch. Twenty two of his wickets came interstate. He particularly savoured the bounce at the WACA and Gabba; even Adelaide, where he had match figures of 6 for 56 in 33 overs, was preferable to bowling at Bellerive. His decision to accept an offer from Victoria in 2004-05 was at least partly influenced by his perception that Melbourne might provide a more sympathetic environment for his deceptive pace.

	M	I	NO	Runs	HS	100s	50s	Avge	Ct	St	W	Avge	BB
First-class	32	44	19	179	34	0	0	7.16	6	0	85	37.79	5-40
Domestic first-class	30	43	18	177	34	0	0	7.08	6	0	80	38.66	5-40
Dom. limited-overs	11	1	1	2	2*	0	0	–	2	0	13	37.77	3-53

MICHAEL DIGHTON *Right-hand batsman* **Tasmania**

Using his height and reach to great advantage, and with ever-growing confidence, Dighton is in the form of his life. He enjoyed last summer's trustworthy Bellerive wicket more than most, piling up 944 Pura Cup runs at 55. His three centuries all came in the New Year, all at Bellerive. His unbeaten 127 against Queensland included 16 fours and three sixes; his 101 versus WA comprised 80 runs in boundaries. It all culminated in an astonishing assault on Victoria's bowlers, Dighton clubbing five sixes on his way to 152 while colleagues fell all round him. He had earlier rustled up an ING Cup hundred against SA in similar circumstances. Although his one-day performances dimmed a little, he was again used as an opener and given licence to launch the innings with a bang. Watching him in seasons to come should be fun.

	M	I	NO	Runs	HS	100s	50s	Avge	Ct	St	W	Avge	BB
First-class	41	70	4	2,610	182*	6	12	39.55	32	0	0	–	–
Domestic first-class	40	68	3	2,560	182*	6	12	39.38	30	0	0	–	–
Dom. limited-overs	31	30	1	833	113	1	6	28.72	11	0	0	–	–

MICHAEL DI VENUTO *Left-hand batsman* **Tasmania**

When the mood takes him, Di Venuto continues to be one of the most powerful hookers and pullers in Australia. And his high ratio of fifties to hundreds continues to astound; he has now assembled more scores between 50 and 100 than anyone in Sheffield Shield/Pura Cup history. Typically, he hit four fifties and only one century in 2003-04, but it was a century to remember: a wonderful undefeated 174 against NSW, bringing Tasmania a famous victory on the last day after they had been outplayed for the first three. His early-season form indicated he was at the peak of his considerable powers, but untimely injury halted his momentum before Christmas and took the edge off his performances thereafter. He skipped the recent English county season – good news for Tasmania – and remains a safe catcher anywhere in the field.

	M	I	NO	Runs	HS	100s	50s	Avge	Ct	St	W	Avge	BB
First-class	189	331	16	13,331	230	28	84	42.32	208	0	5	96.00	1-0
Domestic first-class	104	182	7	7,043	189	11	52	40.25	101	0	2	122.00	1-0
Int'l limited-overs	9	9	0	241	89	0	2	26.78	1	0	0	–	–
Dom. limited-overs	75	73	7	2,020	129*	3	9	30.61	35	0	3	37.00	1-10

XAVIER DOHERTY *Left-arm spinner* **Tasmania**

The past year was an important one in the development of Doherty. He grew much more secure about his place in the team and provided effective relief when required for Tasmania's three-pronged pace attack. Still only 21, he added eight Pura Cup matches to the five he had played over the previous two seasons, missing out only on the quicker pitches of the Gabba and the WACA. His figures were unspectacular – 22 wickets at 51.45 – but his support role was crucial. There were two highlights: his 6 for 149 at the MCG when he spared the blushes of more senior bowlers against a relentless Victorian batting line-up; and his 1 for 28 from 10 overs in Adelaide when he encountered, and contained, Darren Lehmann in full flight.

	M	I	NO	Runs	HS	100s	50s	Avge	Ct	St	W	Avge	BB
First-class	13	17	5	151	52	0	1	12.58	3	0	35	47.51	6-149
Domestic first-class	13	17	5	151	52	0	1	12.58	3	0	35	47.51	6-149
Dom. limited-overs	15	10	2	79	37	0	0	9.88	5	0	10	43.00	4-49

ANDREW DOWNTON *Left-arm fast bowler* **Tasmania**

An underrated and tireless performer, Downton has dramatically improved his work ethic after a couple of drifting seasons. He bulked up in the gym last summer and maintained peak fitness throughout, taking 37 Pura Cup wickets to finish only two shy of NSW's Matthew Nicholson. He extracted considerable movement and was more aggressive in his approach, striking at least once in 17 of the 20 innings in which he bowled. Even benign Bellerive failed to dent his value to the side. He took 21 wickets at 36.62 on his home pitch, where the overall bowling average was 48, and his figures there were identical to his much-vaunted team-mate Damien Wright. Downton's batting ambition usually exceeds his output, which remains strangely negligible despite his considerable achievements at lower levels.

	M	I	NO	Runs	HS	100s	50s	Avge	Ct	St	W	Avge	BB
First-class	29	35	5	247	45	0	0	8.23	7	0	92	33.53	6-56
Domestic first-class	27	34	4	246	45	0	0	8.20	7	0	84	35.02	6-56
Dom. limited-overs	4	2	1	15	9	0	0	15.00	0	0	3	40.67	1-26

CHRIS DUVAL *Right-arm fast bowler* **SA**

Despite capturing 31 A-grade wickets and winning the Darren Lehmann medal for best player at Northern Districts, Duval's most noteworthy achievement of 2003-04 occurred in another sport. In a twist to the tradition of bowlers being kicked out of cricket for throwing, the 20-year-old Duval was touted as a possible baseball pitcher after an impressive tryout before an LA Dodgers talent scout at the Adelaide Oval in February. He would probably prefer to have grabbed the attention of the state selectors. He was retained on a rookie contract for 2004-05 despite spending all last year on the sidelines, along with Trent Kelly and Andrew Staunton, thanks to the consistency – and consistent availability – of SA's first-choice fast men. Powerfully built, Duval's pitches were timed at 137 kph. His bowling is similarly swift.
No major cricket played to date.

BEN EDMONDSON *Right-arm fast bowler* **WA**

Here is one of cricket's most remarkable journeys. In the winter of 2003 Edmondson, a lively fast bowler with a smooth rhythmic approach, was playing and coaching juniors in a district north of Copenhagen. He even played an international limited-overs match, for Denmark against Wales. He had already represented Queensland at Under-15, 17, 19 and 2nd XI levels. Then last summer, at age 25, he found himself struggling to get so much as a look-in at the Bulls. When the WA seconds played a Queensland academy side in November, he wasn't considered good enough even for that team. But when Damien McKenzie was called away on the second day, it was Edmondson who stepped in. He was Queensland's ninth bowler used. He bowled four overs and took four wickets: three bowled, one lbw. WA's coach, Doug Harris, was impressed. An approach was made, a gamble taken and Edmondson went west. Within a day he was playing club cricket for South Perth. Within five days he was pitchforked into Pura Cup action against Tasmania. His senior debut came about in bizarre circumstances; he was a final-day replacement for Brad Williams, who left the field just before tea to fly to Adelaide for a Test match. The history books will tell that Edmondson took three wickets in that last session, his first, and denied Tasmania victory. He became at once a permanent fixture in the WA side. The journey ahead might yet prove just as fascinating.

	M	I	NO	Runs	HS	100s	50s	Avge	Ct	St	W	Avge	BB
First-class	7	7	3	12	4*	0	0	3.00	2	0	28	31.61	5-90
Domestic first-class	7	7	3	12	4*	0	0	3.00	2	0	28	31.61	5-90
Dom. limited-overs	2	1	1	2	2*	0	0	–	1	0	2	64.50	1-57

MATTHEW ELLIOTT *Left-hand batsman* **Victoria and Australia**

Doubting he would ever represent Australia again, and having gained a new perspective on life with his brother-in-law's terminal illness and his wife's third pregnancy, Elliott sought to simplify his approach and just enjoy cricket for a change. Tired of worrying about the batsmen ahead of him, he began the summer by declaring he was "past it". The concession turned out to be his emancipation. A visibly more relaxed and settled Elliott finished the summer with 1381 Pura Cup runs – more than any man in history. His signature elegance shone through seven centuries, another record, in 11 matches. He won back his Australian contact and, briefly, the Test recall he dared not think about came too. Ricky Ponting withdrew at short notice because of a death in the family and Elliott went in at No. 3 against Sri Lanka. He was out for 1 and 0 on a tough Darwin pitch, walking away from the experience defeated but not dejected. Previously renowned for his aloofness, Elliott was not only named Victoria's player of the year but best clubman too.

	M	I	NO	Runs	HS	100s	50s	Avge	Ct	St	W	Avge	BB
First-class	167	308	25	14,301	203	45	63	50.53	190	0	10	65.00	1-3
Domestic first-class	93	178	16	8,885	203	31	38	54.85	120	0	7	50.86	1-3
Test	21	36	1	1,172	199	3	4	33.49	14	0	0	–	–
Int'l limited-overs	1	1	0	1	1	0	0	1.00	0	0	0	–	–
Dom. limited-overs	68	66	6	2,247	118*	6	12	37.45	28	0	0	–	–

SEAN ERVINE *Right-arm medium-pacer, left-hand batsman* **WA**

An international veteran at 21, Ervine will this summer become WA's first overseas import since the English off-spinner Vic Marks in 1986-87. He signed a two-year contract with WA after leaving his home in Zimbabwe in protest at that country's race-based selection policy. One of 15 white players sacked for supporting the deposed captain Heath Streak, Ervine's decision to move to Perth was made easier by the fact that it enabled him to be with his girlfriend Melissa Marsh, daughter of the former Test opener Geoff Marsh. A talented all-rounder with a whirling action, he impressed Perth fans with his lively bowling at the WACA while touring with Zimbabwe last summer. His batting is on the rise too; he has hit half-centuries in his last three Test innings.

	M	I	NO	Runs	HS	100s	50s	Avge	Ct	St	W	Avge	BB
First-class	27	45	6	1,460	126	4	8	37.44	31	0	46	44.39	6-82
Test	5	8	0	261	86	0	3	32.63	7	0	9	43.11	4-146
Int'l limited-overs	42	34	7	698	100	1	2	25.85	5	0	41	38.05	3-29

STEVEN FARRELL *Right-hand batsman* **Queensland**

Likened to Andrew Symonds for his ability to send the ball into and over pickets, Farrell's jump from grade to first-class cricket represented something of a punt by the Queensland selectors. He had little opportunity to demonstrate his hitting power in two Pura Cup games and a single one-dayer. But he hinted at what he could do with a cracking 49 off 40 balls in the second innings against Tasmania in November – his last innings of the summer and, to date, his career. He was dropped from Queensland's squad at season's end and will need to blend consistency with his robust strokeplay if he is to make it back. Farrell grew up in Townsville, where his father Joe has been a stalwart of the local association and served as grounds director at Endeavour Park.

	M	I	NO	Runs	HS	100s	50s	Avge	Ct	St	W	Avge	BB
First-class	2	4	0	91	49	0	0	22.75	0	0	0	–	–
Domestic first-class	2	4	0	91	49	0	0	22.75	0	0	0	–	–
Dom. limited-overs	1	1	0	8	8	0	0	8.00	0	0	0	–	–

CALLUM FERGUSON *Right-hand batsman* **SA**

One of a trio of SA batsmen to hit the $50,000 ING sign in 2003-04, Ferguson's blow – a sweet on-drive off Allan Wise's bowling – was certainly the most impressive. It was in keeping with the handsome, correct technique this slightly built 19-year-old possesses, and was part of a breakout innings of 58 that made observers sit up and take notice. Ferguson's three previous one-day knocks had produced only 13 runs. The innings was his last before travelling to Bangladesh with the Australian Under-19 World Cup squad. He promptly ruptured his anterior cruciate ligament in training for the tournament, a serious and infuriatingly timed mishap, and missed the rest of the season. His comeback to the state side will provide an exacting test of character for one so young.

	M	I	NO	Runs	HS	100s	50s	Avge	Ct	St	W	Avge	BB
Dom. limited-overs	4	4	0	71	58	0	1	17.75	1	0	0	–	–

DAVID FITZGERALD *Right-hand batsman* **SA**

An effective if slightly ungainly batsman, in the Geoff Marsh mould, Fitzgerald will approach this summer with trepidation after SA chose not to renew his contract. Apart from a grafting double-century in Hobart, his biggest first-class innings, his 2003-04 season was primarily one of single-digit scores. It may also turn out to be his last. At 31 he has time enough to make it back, but that will be no simple task in a team compelled to move towards youth. An opening batsman with an affection for long innings, Fitzgerald's favourite cut and cover-drive are ideal shots for Adelaide's short square boundaries. He can, however, become bogged down when deprived of scoring chances outside off, and several of his innings last season were halting, stifled affairs. But he fared no worse than several team-mates and his catching at first slip was dependable.

	M	I	NO	Runs	HS	100s	50s	Avge	Ct	St	W	Avge	BB
First-class	67	127	5	4,221	202*	13	14	34.60	47	0	0	–	–
Domestic first-class	65	123	4	4,053	202*	12	13	34.06	46	0	0	–	–
Dom. limited-overs	41	41	1	1,192	114	2	7	29.80	16	0	0	–	–

ANDY FLOWER *Left-hand batsman, wicket-keeper* **SA**

The failure of Flower, South Australia's new import and Zimbabwe's greatest ever batsman, was one of the big disappointments of 2003-04. He began well enough, clipping a tidy hundred in his first grade game and pocketing $50,000 for hitting the ING sign during his maiden innings at Adelaide Oval. A duck on his Pura Cup debut proved more indicative of things to come. A broken finger ruled him out of seven games either side of Christmas but, that apart, his run of low scores was hard to decipher. He averaged only 24 in the Pura Cup, with a best of 82. Most mystifying of all was his handling of the spinners; the man who had driven India's best to distraction was frequently out scooping gentle off-breaks to cover or gully. With the off-season came news that Flower had decided not to see out the rest of his three-year contract. Although he cited family reasons, there were whispers Essex had offered him an extra incentive to stay in the UK over winter.

	M	I	NO	Runs	HS	100s	50s	Avge	Ct	St	W	Avge	BB
First-class	184	309	56	13,049	232*	35	65	51.58	324	21	6	41.67	1-1
Domestic first-class	7	14	0	342	82	0	2	24.43	3	0	0	–	–
Test	63	112	19	4,794	232*	12	27	51.55	151	9	0	–	–
Int'l limited-overs	213	208	16	6,786	145	4	55	35.34	140	32	0	–	–
Dom. limited-overs	6	6	0	152	74	0	1	25.33	2	0	0	–	–

BRETT GEEVES *Right-arm fast bowler* **Tasmania**

A wholehearted trier, Geeves is still young enough at 22 to develop the guile and variety he needs to succeed in first-class cricket. He played the first five ING Cup matches last summer but was not sighted after the New Year, with injuries keeping him on the sidelines. His best performance was a tight 1 for 31 from 10 overs at the Gabba. He was encouraged by the offer of a state contract for 2004-05, a season which marks the fourth anniversary of his one-day debut. His long wait for a maiden first-class appearance goes on.

	M	I	NO	Runs	HS	100s	50s	Avge	Ct	St	W	Avge	BB
Dom. limited-overs	19	7	3	18	5	0	0	4.50	2	0	17	38.59	3-40

ADAM GILCHRIST *Left-hand batsman, wicket-keeper* **WA and Australia**

Arguably the greatest matchwinner in the world today, this wonderful entertainer continues to build a reputation as the finest batsman-keeper of all time. As a batsman, his technique is far from perfect but he makes up for it with natural flair. As a keeper, he became the fastest man in history last summer to reach 200 Test dismissals. In catching Tatenda Taibu, cutting at a Brad Hogg wrong'un, Gilchrist achieved the milestone in his 47th Test – five fewer than Mark Boucher. If he was slightly quieter than usual at Test level, averaging only 16 against India, he still provided his share of fireworks. Playing second fiddle to Matthew Hayden's 380, he raised his own blazing century against Zimbabwe in a session and 84 balls. When Ricky Ponting hurt his back in Kandy, Gilchrist volunteered to bat at No. 3 and struck an invaluable 144, putting forward his case for permanent promotion. He filled in for Ponting as captain too, against Sri Lanka in Darwin, his second victory in three Tests as stand-in skipper. Crowned one-day player of the year, the highlight was his breathtaking 172 versus Zimbabwe, when he looked on course for 200 until he was bowled attempting a huge hit. Gilchrist had earlier hinted that he might retire from one-dayers in the not-too-distant future and focus on Tests. Several million grateful spectators are hoping he reconsiders.

	M	I	NO	Runs	HS	100s	50s	Avge	Ct	St	W	Avge	BB
First-class	145	216	39	8,052	204*	23	33	45.49	580	42	0	–	–
Domestic first-class	60	95	13	3,196	203*	8	12	38.98	260	8	0	–	–
Test	56	80	14	3,485	204*	10	17	52.80	217	24	0	–	–
Int'l limited-overs	193	187	6	6,468	172	10	37	35.73	283	39	0	–	–
Dom. limited-overs	38	35	3	996	115	1	7	31.13	64	6	0	–	–

JASON GILLESPIE *Right-arm fast bowler*   **SA and Australia**

Sometimes injured, generally successful, invariably unlucky. Thus went the past 12 months for Gillespie, who managed only two four-fors and not a single five-wicket haul in nine Tests. The statistics do not tell of the countless plays-and-misses he elicited, nor of the way he manfully led Australia's attack in Glenn McGrath's absence, bowling long spells in often testing conditions, probing away relentlessly outside off stump. He persisted with little fortune or support against the fearfully straight bats of the Indians, jumping out of the blocks with a lionhearted 4 for 65 at the Gabba – including Dravid for 1 and Tendulkar for 0 – but fading a little thereafter. Always, though, Gillespie remained the one man the Indians were intent on seeing off safely. He shook up the Sri Lankan top order with some vigorous spells at key moments, setting the stage for Shane Warne's remarkable comeback. His domestic appearances were few and far between, as always, although one telling spell of reverse swing was instrumental in SA's victory over NSW. His ever-growing shaggy mullet was one of the summer's fringe fascinations. The trend even caught on with a couple of his team-mates.

	M	I	NO	Runs	HS	100s	50s	Avge	Ct	St	W	Avge	BB
First-class	101	131	33	1,412	58	0	3	14.41	37	0	375	24.69	8-50
Domestic first-class	26	43	6	504	58	0	2	13.62	13	0	107	22.96	8-50
Test	54	69	22	685	48*	0	0	14.57	16	0	206	25.72	7-37
Int'l limited-overs	72	31	14	223	33*	0	0	13.12	5	0	111	24.22	5-22
Dom. limited-overs	23	15	7	66	19	0	0	8.25	2	0	38	22.84	4-46

MURRAY GOODWIN *Right-hand batsman*   **WA**

A compact right-hander with an unconventional approach, Goodwin is at the peak of his powers. As a general rule he no longer bats in the nets against bowlers, particularly on the eve of a match. Instead he receives plenty of throw-downs and practises against a mechanical bowling machine, working on his weight transference forward and back. This special preparation has ironed out a couple of weaknesses and set him up for an exceptional season in 2003-04. He amassed four Pura Cup hundreds and 1,183 runs, beating Simon Katich's old WA record of 1,145. He started the recent English summer quietly but enjoyed a glorious 2003, helping Sussex end their 164-year County Championship drought. It makes you wonder what might have been at international level; it is now four years since Goodwin carved a brilliant unbeaten 148 against England in his 19th and last Test for Zimbabwe. At the start of last season he said his old country had a race-based selection policy; Cricket Australia reprimanded him, sadly, for speaking truthfully and honestly.

	M	I	NO	Runs	HS	100s	50s	Avge	Ct	St	W	Avge	BB
First-class	142	249	19	10,733	335*	32	44	46.67	88	0	7	50.71	2-23
Domestic first-class	46	84	6	3,173	201*	8	13	40.68	32	0	0	–	–
Test	19	37	4	1,414	166*	3	8	42.85	10	0	0	–	–
Int'l limited-overs	71	70	3	1,818	112*	2	8	27.13	20	0	4	52.50	1-12
Dom. limited-overs	40	36	7	1,251	167	1	9	43.14	13	0	0	–	–

ADAM GRIFFITH *Right-arm fast bowler*   **Tasmania**

It is not unusual for young players to struggle in their second season. Griffith's fortunes fell more sharply than most. An automatic pick at the start of 2003-04, he managed only nine wickets at 71.22 in five Pura Cup games and was dropped for the rest of the summer. In nine ING Cup matches he leaked 5.7 runs an over. The selectors, encouraged by his promising efforts of the season before, picked him for Australia A in two one-day matches against Zimbabwe. But he struggled with his line and length – one of the hallmarks of his maiden season – and strayed too often beyond the corridor of uncertainty. A tall bowler, capable of jagging the ball both ways, Tasmania ferociously beat off WA's attempts to lure Griffith to Perth. Last summer's downturn, they believe, was a temporary eclipse.

	M	I	NO	Runs	HS	100s	50s	Avge	Ct	St	W	Avge	BB
First-class	11	17	7	135	21	0	0	13.50	0	0	29	40.21	5-46
Domestic first-class	11	17	7	135	21	0	0	13.50	0	0	29	40.21	5-46
Dom. limited-overs	19	8	4	9	4*	0	0	2.25	0	0	25	31.16	3-14

BRAD HADDIN *Right-hand batsman, wicket-keeper* **NSW and Australia**

Under the tutelage of Steve Rixon, Haddin's glovework has gone ahead in leaps and bounds. It culminated in his selection ahead of Ryan Campbell – who was busy disappointing the WA selectors – in the Australia A team against Zimbabwe. Weeks later he made a fleeting appearance in the big show, twice filling in for Adam Gilchrist during the VB Series before going to Sri Lanka as the back-up one-day keeper. His summer was interrupted by a broken thumb, and his attempts to come back early didn't quite work out. He is aiming for greater consistency this season, after averaging 39 in first-class cricket but only 12 in the ING Cup while sliding all over the order. His other big challenge, with Trevor Bayliss succeeding Rixon as Blues coach, will be to continue refining his glovework without Rixon's eagle gaze.

	M	I	NO	Runs	HS	100s	50s	Avge	Ct	St	W	Avge	BB
First-class	48	84	9	2,435	117	2	16	32.47	125	13	0	–	–
Domestic first-class	43	78	8	2,263	117	2	15	32.33	113	11	0	–	–
Int'l limited-overs	4	4	0	68	32	0	0	17.00	1	2	0	–	–
Dom. limited-overs	53	52	1	1,399	133	2	10	27.43	73	19	0	–	–

RYAN HARRIS *Right-arm medium-pacer, right-hand batsman* **SA**

An aggressive batsman, swinging bowler and eyecatching fieldsman, injuries are the main reason why this talented 24-year-old has played only eight first-class matches in three seasons. Last summer he played just one, SA's crushing defeat at the Gabba, and found himself stuck in a queue behind fellow all-rounder Mick Miller and the state's handful of quality pacemen. He faces another battle to break into the 1st XI this summer. Harris was more successful at one-day level, chipping in with useful wickets in his four ING Cup matches. He has yet to exhibit his batting flair at interstate level, something he will be keen to rectify if he gets the chance.

	M	I	NO	Runs	HS	100s	50s	Avge	Ct	St	W	Avge	BB
First-class	8	13	1	98	27	0	0	8.17	7	0	13	44.62	3-64
Domestic first-class	8	13	1	98	27	0	0	8.17	7	0	13	44.62	3-64
Dom. limited-overs	17	10	6	72	31*	0	0	18.00	11	0	19	32.21	4-43

BRETT HARROP *Right-arm fast bowler* **Victoria**

Though he is no longer so rapid as was in his teenage tearaway years, Harrop remains decidedly quick. His challenge, at 24, is to develop the variation and subtlety to go with it. He broke through for his first-class debut last summer, impressing a scratchy Indian batting line-up with his pace and accuracy and claiming the wickets of Akash Chopra and Virender Sehwag. He shone in his three 2nd XI matches too, taking 12 wickets at 14.41. He hits hard in the lower order and was selected as a specialist batsman for his district team Melbourne University while recovering from injury. A physiotherapist by profession, Harrop has been examining the biomechanics of his action and making discreet adjustments in an attempt to defeat persistent back problems.

	M	I	NO	Runs	HS	100s	50s	Avge	Ct	St	W	Avge	BB
First-class	1	1	1	0	0*	0	0	–	2	0	2	44.50	1-34
Dom. limited-overs	1	0	0	0	–	0	0	–	0	0	0	–	–

CHRIS HARTLEY *Wicket-keeper, left-hand batsman*   **Queensland**

A blue-chip investment for Queensland, and potentially Australia, the pocket-sized Hartley rocketed to prominence in 2003-04. At 21, making his first-class debut, he held four catches and hit 103 against South Australia at the Gabba. On his one-day debut, the ING Cup final against WA, he snapped up two eyecatching stumpings. His brief but impressive resumé also incorporates an unbeaten 45 for the Prime Minister's XI, John Howard's boys almost snatching an exciting win over India. Hartley will need to be patient; Wade Seccombe, whose temporary absence gave him his chance, remains at the peak of his game. But the Queensland keeping lineage has always rewarded those who wait, and it was Ian Healy who reminded Hartley of that fact when presenting him with his maroon cap. Off the field, he is completing a marketing degree and is a player representative to the Australian Cricketers' Association. A talented AFL junior, he focused on cricket after being told at an interstate carnival that he was too small for football. Their loss is cricket's gain.

	M	I	NO	Runs	HS	100s	50s	Avge	Ct	St	W	Avge	BB
First-class	3	4	1	134	103	1	0	44.67	9	2	0	–	–
Domestic first-class	3	4	1	134	103	1	0	44.67	9	2	0	–	–
Dom. limited-overs	1	1	0	14	14	0	0	14.00	2	0	0	–	–

IAN HARVEY *Right-arm medium-pacer, right-hand batsman* **Victoria and Australia**

Harvey finally made the leap from fringe player to semi-permanent fixture in Australia's one-day side, but with Shane Watson fit and firing he will need to excel to keep it that way. As always, his bag of often indecipherable slower deliveries was his magic weapon. The highlight was his devastating, matchwinning spell of 4 for 21 in the TVS Cup final, where he cleaned up the Indian tail and silenced a deafening crowd at Eden Gardens. It earned him a spot in the VB Series, where he endured an indifferent tournament before peaking in the finals, followed by tours to Zimbabwe and Sri Lanka. Again he failed to live up to his batting potential. His innings against New Zealand in Guwahati was typical; he was invited to open, uncoiled some dreamy cover-drives on his way to 25 in 18 balls, then spooned an easy catch to cover. He seemed largely uninterested at times in state cricket, pulling out of Victoria's penultimate match against Tasmania at the last minute before making amends with 62 and a couple of wickets in the Pura Cup final.

	M	I	NO	Runs	HS	100s	50s	Avge	Ct	St	W	Avge	BB
First-class	125	208	18	6,175	136	9	36	32.50	91	0	350	27.13	8-101
Domestic first-class	69	118	11	3,631	136	4	26	33.93	49	0	161	33.38	7-44
Int'l limited-overs	73	51	11	715	48*	0	0	17.88	17	0	85	30.32	4-16
Dom. limited-overs	61	56	4	1,061	72	0	6	20.40	19	0	70	27.27	5-34

KADE HARVEY *Right-hand batsman, right-arm medium-pacer*   **WA**

With his skidding medium-pacers and capable middle-order batsmanship, the chunky Harvey enjoyed a highly successful summer in 2003-04. He was overlooked early and encountered further problems with his troublesome knee before shining in the second half of the season. He hit his maiden first-class hundred in Hobart and was easily his team's best one-day bowler, nailing 17 wickets in nine matches. The highlight was his heroic role in WA's triumphant ING Cup final at the Gabba: first he took 4 for 28, then he revived his side's batting with a brilliant and wonderfully composed 53 not out. Off the field, Harvey excelled in a leadership role and became one of the senior players. He won the Excalibur award for the player most responsible for upholding the spirit of the Warriors.

	M	I	NO	Runs	HS	100s	50s	Avge	Ct	St	W	Avge	BB
First-class	23	33	9	693	100*	1	2	28.88	13	0	49	36.51	4-43
Domestic first-class	19	29	8	598	100*	1	1	28.48	11	0	44	34.86	4-43
Dom. limited-overs	70	46	18	677	53*	0	2	24.18	12	0	87	27.45	4-8

SHANE HARWOOD *Right-arm fast bowler*   Victoria

For all his aggression, Harwood is seen in some quarters as a fragile bowler – and he did little to dispel the knockers last summer. He broke down with a hip injury in Victoria's opening Pura Cup game then struggled upon his return, taking seven wickets at 46. It was a depressing follow-up to his explosive debut season. There is a school of thought within the team that Harwood is often cotton-woolled. The coaches say his background in park cricket – he was an elderly 28 when he made his first-class debut – simply does not allow him to carry the same load as other bowlers. But his lack of hardiness is a concern and attempts were made to set up a meeting with Michael Voss, the Brisbane footballer famed for his ability to play with injuries. Due to a clash of schedules, it never eventuated.

	M	I	NO	Runs	HS	100s	50s	Avge	Ct	St	W	Avge	BB
First-class	11	14	4	155	32	0	0	15.50	4	0	36	31.17	5-54
Domestic first-class	10	12	2	144	32	0	0	14.40	4	0	35	30.49	5-54
Dom. limited-overs	14	7	1	17	10*	0	0	2.83	4	0	11	35.91	3-22

NATHAN HAURITZ *Right-arm off-spinner*   Queensland

Hauritz continues to make significant strides as a limited-overs bowler, despite losing both his Australian contract and his place in the one-day side. For Queensland he was a potent weapon, collecting 18 wickets at 23.05 in the ING Cup. The highlight was his 4 for 39 against SA, a showcase of skill and control, which bowled the Bulls into the final and impressed no less an authority than Richie Benaud. His first-class form – 16 wickets at 63.93 – was less inspiring, aside from his 94 at the WACA. Only a crook lbw decision robbed him of a maiden ton. Hauritz resisted an off-season approach from SA and triggered one of the media shocks of the year after a trip home to Hervey Bay; days later a newspaper revealed he had been crowned Champion Worm Digger during his days at Torquay State School.

	M	I	NO	Runs	HS	100s	50s	Avge	Ct	St	W	Avge	BB
First-class	24	31	5	407	94	0	1	15.65	13	0	47	43.62	4-95
Domestic first-class	20	27	3	333	94	0	1	15.14	9	0	40	44.70	4-95
Int'l limited-overs	8	4	3	35	20*	0	0	35.00	2	0	9	34.22	4-39
Dom. limited-overs	34	15	4	124	39*	0	0	11.27	10	0	54	21.93	4-39

MATTHEW HAYDEN *Left-hand batsman*   Queensland and Australia

The Matthew Hayden Story delivers more thrills per chapter than the average Matthew Reilly bestseller. Reilly delivers big blockbusters with plenty of exclamation marks, a sensation that sat well with watching Hayden bat last summer. Once again, he ruled the crease by intimidating, unorthodox means; no ball was too full to pull, and none too short to drive. The standout innings, perhaps of his life, was his exhilarating 380 against Zimbabwe in Perth. It gave him the world record for all of six months, Brian Lara topping it with 400 not out against England. Hayden, undaunted, continued on his merry marauding way. His joyous 136 in Melbourne was instrumental in Australia's only victory over India. His 130 in Galle helped salvage a lost cause. In Cairns, he pummelled Sri Lanka for a century in each innings, becoming only the eighth man in history to do so twice. From the start of the Zimbabwe series to the end of that Sri Lankan one, he plundered 1,523 runs at a breathtaking clip and an average of 80.15. For all that, one of his biggest thrills involved heading out for a surf off Stradbroke Island only to encounter Mark Occhilupo and a host of other pro surfers enjoying the waves. Rather than bounding into print with the de rigueur biography, Hayden's first publishing foray will be a cookbook due out in time for Christmas.

	M	I	NO	Runs	HS	100s	50s	Avge	Ct	St	W	Avge	BB
First-class	236	408	41	20,180	380	68	80	54.99	219	0	17	39.47	3-10
Domestic first-class	83	150	17	7,332	234	24	30	55.13	75	0	3	31.00	2-17
Test	55	95	8	5,059	380	20	15	58.15	67	0	0	–	–
Int'l limited-overs	95	91	11	3,366	146	4	22	42.08	34	0	0	–	–
Dom. limited-overs	51	51	9	2,231	152*	8	11	53.11	16	0	3	10.67	2-16

AARON HEAL *Left-arm orthodox spinner*   **WA**

He has a lot to learn, and he is the first to admit it, but the 21-year-old Heal showed considerable promise in his debut season. Tall and willowy, he made an immediate impact in his first ING Cup match in Launceston. He had Michael Di Venuto caught at long-on with his sixth ball, then deceived and bowled Dan Marsh, finishing with 2 for 34 off his 10 overs. He played in WA's final four one-day matches plus two Pura Cup games, deserving far better than his return of 2 for 243. He also scored a defiant 33 in his maiden first-class innings in Adelaide. As a teenager, Heal spent two winters in England playing club cricket in Devon and Hampshire. A stint with the Academy during 2004 should further refine his game.

	M	I	NO	Runs	HS	100s	50s	Avge	Ct	St	W	Avge	BB
First-class	2	2	0	42	33	0	0	21.00	0	0	2	121.50	1-19
Domestic first-class	2	2	0	42	33	0	0	21.00	0	0	2	121.50	1-19
Dom. limited-overs	4	2	1	19	17*	0	0	19.00	1	0	4	48.25	2-34

IAN HEWETT *Left-arm fast bowler, left-hand batsman*   **Victoria**

A tall, athletic and hard-hitting all-rounder, Hewitt's development continues to be stifled by a string of injuries. After playing only two ING Cup games in 2002-03 he was restricted to just three last summer. He did play an important role in the Bushrangers' nailbiting victory over SA at the MCG, picking up two wickets – including that of Darren Lehmann – in the last four minutes. He had endured a forgettable day until then, however, dropping two straightforward catches and being involved in a mid-pitch collision. Hewett's eyecatching beginning to elite-level cricket has perhaps proved more of a burden than an asset, with the Victorian selectors waiting patiently for him to fulfil his potential. The summer ahead looms as a critical one.

	M	I	NO	Runs	HS	100s	50s	Avge	Ct	St	W	Avge	BB
First-class	3	3	2	41	34*	0	0	41.00	1	0	6	51.83	3-63
Domestic first-class	3	3	2	41	34*	0	0	41.00	1	0	6	51.83	3-63
Dom. limited-overs	22	17	5	102	29*	0	0	8.50	4	0	29	26.31	4-22

MARK HIGGS *Left-hand batsman, left-arm spinner*   **SA**

There are few more enjoyable sights than watching this aggressive left-hander at his best. Unfortunately it has become an increasingly rare sight of late. Higgs seemed perpetually out of form last summer, with bowlers all too often finding a yawning gap between bat and pad. Even his longer innings were streaky, as he cobbled together 290 Pura Cup runs at 20.71. Just as disappointing was his bowling. He has the ability to generate exceptional turn but showed little imagination, and has largely given up on his wrist-spin variations. Higgs had been a revelation upon moving across from NSW the previous year, slamming a run-a-ball hundred on debut. A bountiful career at Adelaide Oval beckoned. His talent was let down last summer by a lack of focus and attention to detail, something that shouldn't be too difficult to put right.

	M	I	NO	Runs	HS	100s	50s	Avge	Ct	St	W	Avge	BB
First-class	38	66	7	1915	181*	3	9	32.46	21	0	31	56.16	4-25
Domestic first-class	37	65	7	1892	181*	3	9	32.62	20	0	29	56.38	4-25
Dom. limited-overs	50	46	5	984	77	0	0	24.00	20	0	31	31.32	4-15

BRAD HODGE *Right-hand batsman* **Victoria**

Stung by the disappointment of being overlooked for Victoria's one-day captaincy, Hodge began last summer with a point to prove. He did not let himself down, clattering four hundreds and 984 runs in the Pura Cup, plus three more centuries at one-day level. His reward after an eventful summer, during which he married his long-time girlfriend Megan, was his first national contract and the knowledge that he is closer than ever to winkling an Australian spot. Stints in England have helped channel Hodge's raw aggression, making him a more discerning batsman. He seemed as confident as ever too, twice predicting before matches that he would score centuries: he delivered in Adelaide but missed out in the Pura Cup final runfest. Hodge also fancies himself as a spinner. At one memorable training session he was overheard telling Cameron White, the man who did land the one-day captaincy, to "watch and learn".

	M	I	NO	Runs	HS	100s	50s	Avge	Ct	St	W	Avge	BB
First-class	139	251	23	10,400	302*	32	37	45.61	77	0	51	44.29	4-17
Domestic first-class	98	180	18	6,544	183	18	29	40.40	53	0	29	52.76	4-92
Dom. limited-overs	75	73	8	2,643	118*	6	16	40.66	30	0	8	46.13	2-25

BRAD HOGG *Left-arm chinaman bowler, left-hand batsman* **WA and Australia**
Few players in world cricket are as energetic or enthusiastic as Hogg, his dervish-like qualities in the field constantly helping to invigorate his team-mates. At 33, in what is surely the twilight of his career, he continues to make every post a winner. A surprise star of Australia's 2003 World Cup win, he appeared only intermittently in last summer's VB Series before firming up his one-day spot in Sri Lanka. Hogg consistently befuddled the Sri Lankan batsmen, despite their reputation as highly proficient players of spin, taking three wickets in four balls to finish with 5 for 41 in Dambulla. He formed part of a bizarre dual chinaman attack with Simon Katich in his only Test of the summer, against Zimbabwe at the SCG. Hogg was the tighter of the pair, taking 3 for 119 in 54 overs, but it was Katich who stole the wickets and ultimately Hogg's position. International duties restricted him to only three Pura Cup games but he leapt at the chance to make his county debut, joining Warwickshire under coach John Inverarity. Within a month he smashed a career-best 158 off 163 balls against Surrey.

	M	I	NO	Runs	HS	100s	50s	Avge	Ct	St	W	Avge	BB
First-class	83	121	26	3,193	158	3	21	33.61	48	0	125	44.69	5-53
Domestic first-class	59	92	19	2,250	111*	1	15	30.82	39	0	78	45.56	5-53
Test	4	5	1	38	17*	0	0	9.50	0	0	9	50.22	2-40
Int'l limited-overs	48	29	13	334	71*	0	2	20.88	13	0	53	31.13	5-41
Dom. limited-overs	59	47	19	847	59	0	2	30.25	27	0	43	27.14	4-50

JAMES HOPES *Right-hand batsman, right-arm medium-pacer* **Queensland**
A clean hitter and sharpish medium-pacer, Hopes progressed steadily last summer without quite answering the elusive question: is he good enough to hold his spot as either batsman or bowler? Essentially a one-day specialist in the past, he finally made his mark at first-class level, hitting 97 against Victoria and his maiden hundred against Tasmania. His season haul – 510 runs at 30, 12 wickets at 71 – suggested he still has some way to go. Hopes has a tidy technique and works assiduously in the gym. He was again a consistent ING Cup contributor, especially with the ball, and has moved rapidly into third spot – behind Mike Kasprowicz and Scott Prestwidge – on Queensland's all-time wicket-taking list. He played alongside Allan Border during the off-season for a combined Queensland Universities team that toured the subcontinent.

	M	I	NO	Runs	HS	100s	50s	Avge	Ct	St	W	Avge	BB
First-class	18	30	0	668	111	1	2	22.27	9	0	23	62.65	4-63
Domestic first-class	18	30	0	668	111	1	2	22.27	9	0	23	62.65	4-63
Dom. limited-overs	37	27	3	489	52*	0	1	20.38	10	0	55	24.53	5-29

DAVID HUSSEY *Right-hand batsman* **Victoria**
An exuberant batsman who sometimes walks a fine line between the audacious and the absurd, Hussey made his name with perhaps the innings of the season. His unbeaten 212 in Newcastle, breathtaking in its daring, spearheaded Victoria's successful chase of 455 to beat NSW. Steve Waugh commented afterwards that he must be in contention for national selection. Hussey had earlier crafted a lightning-fast 106 in Victoria's drought-

breaking win at the Gabba, eventually finishing the summer with four hundreds and 857 Pura Cup runs at 61. Increasingly, though, he succumbed to some inexplicable shots that looked better suited to a tennis court. He may need to harness some of his natural aggression or bowlers will prey on his inability to resist temptation. A brilliant fielder, he enjoyed a prodigious winter with Nottinghamshire while setting a new record for the player with the most speeding tickets.

	M	I	NO	Runs	HS	100s	50s	Avge	Ct	St	W	Avge	BB
First-class	26	36	5	1,842	212*	8	5	59.42	34	0	3	70.00	1-6
Domestic first-class	14	20	2	945	212*	4	3	52.50	11	0	2	34.00	1-6
Dom. limited-overs	13	11	3	331	113	1	0	41.38	7	0	1	91.00	1-37

MIKE HUSSEY *Left-hand batsman*   WA and Australia

After becoming a father for the first time, and wisely deciding against the grind of another full English county season, Hussey is knocking hard at the door of Australia's one-day side. He finally got his big break last summer, standing in for Michael Bevan on his home ground and hitting an accomplished 17 not out against India. He regained his Australian contract on the back of a consistent season with WA. In nine ING Cup games he averaged 60, rattled along at 90 runs per 100 balls, and was rewarded with the Australia A captaincy. His Pura Cup form was more solid than sensational – his one century was his first in two years – but he led the team splendidly in Justin Langer's frequent absences. For Northamptonshire in 2003, Hussey completed the remarkable feat of scoring an unbeaten triple-century in three successive English summers. He narrowly failed to join Don Bradman as the only Australian hit six hundreds in a row, stringing together tallies of 100, 331 not out, 115, 187, 147 and 50.

	M	I	NO	Runs	HS	100s	50s	Avge	Ct	St	W	Avge	BB
First-class	148	265	18	12,776	331*	32	57	51.72	156	0	9	49.44	2-21
Domestic first-class	91	166	8	6,471	187	13	33	40.96	86	0	5	56.60	2-21
Int'l limited-overs	1	1	1	17	17*	0	0	–	1	0	0	–	–
Dom. limited-overs	65	64	10	2,220	106	3	17	43.53	40	0	10	28.70	3-52

MATHEW INNESS *Left-arm fast bowler*   Victoria

Anointed as the leader of Victoria's bowling group at the start of the season, Inness soon found himself on the outer when he was sidelined by glandular fever. He made a concerted effort to improve his limited-overs reputation but failed to impress in four ING Cup matches. His Pura Cup output – 20 wickets at 28.90 – was consistent enough but he was disappointed to be made 12th man in Newcastle when he believed he was over his illness. He was then devastated to be left out of the Pura Cup final; his unhappiness was compounded when first-year bowler Allan Wise broke down with a foot injury after 10 overs. When Gerard Denton was announced as Victoria's new recruit Inness, fearing the worst, sought opportunities elsewhere. But despite offers from three states Victoria refused to release him.

	M	I	NO	Runs	HS	100s	50s	Avge	Ct	St	W	Avge	BB
First-class	61	63	25	208	27	0	0	5.47	22	0	215	24.90	7-19
Domestic first-class	53	58	24	139	27	0	0	4.09	16	0	185	24.59	7-19
Dom. limited-overs	21	2	1	1	1*	0	0	1.00	3	0	13	54.00	3-33

PHIL JAQUES *Left-hand batsman*   NSW

A solid and occasionally brilliant lefty, Jaques has the game and mental approach to be a major influence. His numbers in his first full Pura Cup summer – 636 runs at 31.80 – hinted at inconsistency. At times, though, he was devastating: his 146 in 147 balls at the Gabba turned a match; his 85 in 60 balls against Tasmania nearly pulled off a seemingly impossible run-chase. In eight ING Cup games his strike-rate was 107. He carries an English passport and his spectacular stints in 2003 with Northamptonshire, for whom he appeared as a local, and in 2004 with Yorkshire, where he was an import, have improved his skills and confidence. With the Waughs and Michaels, Slater and Bevan, gone he can become a senior contributor and will be shooting for 1000 runs. The Blues require nothing less.

	M	I	NO	Runs	HS	100s	50s	Avge	Ct	St	W	Avge	BB
First-class	34	59	1	2,793	243	8	12	48.16	27	0	0	–	–
Domestic first-class	12	24	0	722	146	1	4	30.08	8	0	0	–	–
Dom. limited-overs	10	10	0	364	75	0	2	36.40	0	0	0	–	–

NICK JEWELL *Right-hand batsman, left-arm medium-pacer* Victoria

A powerful striker of the ball, with a sound if unorthodox technique, Jewell managed only a single one-dayer for Victoria last summer. His biggest moments came in the 2nd XI: he hit a century in Shane Warne's famous comeback match at the Junction Oval and a gritty 43 on a moist pitch in Glenn McGrath's less-publicised comeback game. It proved he can do more than hit the ball hard. The son of Tony Jewell, the outspoken former Richmond football captain, he received his grounding in Australian Rules and is viewed as "young" in cricket years. Now 27, he hit his first district hundred only three seasons ago. His 794 runs at 41, together with 14 handy wickets, helped inspire St Kilda to back-to-back premierships last summer.

	M	I	NO	Runs	HS	100s	50s	Avge	Ct	St	W	Avge	BB
First-class	4	7	0	96	30	0	0	13.71	0	0	0	–	–
Domestic first-class	4	7	0	96	30	0	0	13.71	0	0	0	–	–
Dom. limited-overs	14	14	0	384	60	0	2	27.43	1	0	0	–	–

BEN JOHNSON *Left-hand batsman, right-arm medium-pacer* SA

A fine shotmaker and inventive medium-pacer, Johnson is slipping slowly off the selection radar and may struggle to come back. He was dropped from the Redbacks squad for 2004-05 after being kept out of the team last summer by a battery of fellow left-handers: Lehmann, Flower, Higgs, Cosgrove, Miller. In five ING Cup games, his only appearances all season, he averaged 17 with the bat and contributed four expensive wickets. Johnson has known seasons both bad and good before, of course; only once has he averaged 40-plus in successive years. For all his talent, he has produced neither the reliability nor consistency for which SA have long been waiting. At 31, he must focus his energies on having a bountiful grade season. Whether it will win him a first-class recall is another matter.

	M	I	NO	Runs	HS	100s	50s	Avge	Ct	St	W	Avge	BB
First-class	69	130	14	4,038	168	9	17	34.81	40	0	53	39.75	3-4
Domestic first-class	65	123	14	3,884	168	9	16	35.63	40	0	51	39.22	3-4
Dom. limited-overs	58	57	7	1,117	83	0	3	22.34	21	0	24	33.46	3-46

MITCHELL JOHNSON *Left-arm fast bowler* Queensland

Johnson tantalised briefly as he flashed once more across the first-class scene like a comet. Unlike those celestial phenomena, however, Johnson's orbit is decidedly trickier to predict. Richly talented and genuinely swift, he seemed to have beaten the back problems that have bedevilled him. He was picked for the one-day side, captured 4 for 37 against Tasmania on debut, then took two more wickets in the opening Pura Cup game. But a side-strain, followed by a recurrence of his back troubles associated with stress fractures, ended his season. The selectors opted not to renew his contract for 2004-05, gambling that no other state would snare him. He remains, at 23, that rarest of species: a genuinely fast left-armer. Physically, working for a plumbing supplies company is toughening him. But his tattooed and pierced front hides an affable interior.

	M	I	NO	Runs	HS	100s	50s	Avge	Ct	St	W	Avge	BB
First-class	3	4	2	44	15	0	0	22.00	0	0	8	34.38	2-59
Domestic first-class	2	3	1	38	15	0	0	19.00	0	0	5	33.80	2-59
Dom. limited-overs	2	0	0	0	–	0	0	–	0	0	4	21.75	4-37

BRENDAN JOSELAND *Right-hand batsman* **Victoria**
Joseland finally broke into first-class ranks last summer at the age of 26, cracking a composed 51 in 50 balls at Bellerive Oval in the last home-and-away round. He is a fluid batsman, athletic fielder and full-time engineer. He was not included in Victoria's squad yet still won selection for the opening ING Cup match, on the back of his renowned dedication to training and some strong performances in the state's 2nd XI. He batted twice in the one-dayers, hitting 23 in Bowral and 15 at the WACA. Opportunities should be more frequent this summer, following his promotion to the Victorian squad.

	M	I	NO	Runs	HS	100s	50s	Avge	Ct	St	W	Avge	BB
First-class	1	2	0	57	51	0	1	28.50	2	0	1	19.00	1-19
Domestic first-class	1	2	0	57	51	0	1	28.50	2	0	1	19.00	1-19
Dom. limited-overs	7	5	0	65	23	0	0	13.00	2	0	1	95.00	1-24

SHANE JURGENSEN *Right-arm fast bowler* **Queensland**
He has taken the long way home, but Jurgensen finally realised a boyhood dream last season when he turned out for Queensland at the Gabba. Tall and energetic, he left his home state in 1996 to escape the queue of quicks in front of him. He debuted for WA then found his niche in Tasmania, taking 91 wickets in the 2001-02 Pura Cup final. Back home at last, he gave Queensland an experienced hand to call on early when injury and representative demands took their toll. He captured 13 wickets at 23.15 in his three Pura Cup games, including match figures of 7 for 112 against Tasmania in his last. He played a leading role in Sandgate–Redcliffe's first-grade premiership, proving the ideal foil for his younger new-ball partner Nathan Rimmington.

	M	I	NO	Runs	HS	100s	50s	Avge	Ct	St	W	Avge	BB
First-class	22	30	9	250	56	0	1	11.90	3	0	69	30.07	6-65
Domestic first-class	21	29	8	237	56	0	1	11.29	0	0	68	29.22	6-65
Dom. limited-overs	9	1	1	3	3*	0	0	–	1	0	5	67.60	2-31

MICHAEL KASPROWICZ *Right-arm fast bowler* **Queensland and Australia**
In one of sport's cruel ironies, the door that was slammed on Andy Bichel swung back to admit his great mate Kasprowicz, whose own international career had seemed destined to be truncated well before its time. He resurrected it spectacularly, bowling with genuine pace, bounce and zest at almost every opportunity. It was Kasprowicz's reputation as an uncomplaining tourist and adaptable performer that initially convinced the selectors to take a fresh look. He was called to arms for the TVS Cup in India, where a strained buttock proved a minor setback, before continuing his resurgence in Sri Lanka. After a three-year Test absence he played all three matches and took 12 wickets, securing important breakthroughs every time he bowled. But his finest moment came in Darwin, his 7 for 39 on a responsive wicket spurring Australia to a Test victory over Sri Lanka. He became a father for the first time, played his 100th first-class match for Queensland and supplanted the great Carl Rackemann as the state's all-time leading first-class (445) and Sheffield Shield/Pura Cup (387) wicket-taker. Kasprowicz has not forgotten where he came from either. He lends his image to Queensland Cricket's volunteer recognition program, where cricket's grassroots workers toil under the banner of Kaspa's Crew.

	M	I	NO	Runs	HS	100s	50s	Avge	Ct	St	W	Avge	BB
First-class	207	279	60	3,964	92	0	11	18.10	83	0	842	26.07	9-36
Domestic first-class	89	114	20	1,393	52*	0	2	14.82	34	0	387	24.31	6-47
Test	22	33	8	282	25	0	0	11.28	10	0	67	33.46	7-36
Int'l limited-overs	24	10	7	62	28*	0	0	20.67	4	0	37	25.73	5-45
Dom. limited-overs	66	32	15	232	34	0	0	13.65	14	0	80	29.33	4-19

SIMON KATICH *Left-hand batsman, left-arm chinaman bowler* **NSW and Australia**
A free-flowing batsman against speed or spin, and a handy left-arm wrist spinner himself, Katich cannot be far away from commanding a permanent Test spot. After

seemingly consolidating his position with a glorious double of 125 and 77 not out against India, thus saving Steve Waugh's farewell Test from ending in defeat, he was promptly sent to Galle and left to carry the rehydration liquids. It must have been extraordinarily frustrating. Andrew Symonds was preferred for the first two Sri Lankan Tests because of his bits-and-pieces bowling; perhaps the selectors had forgotten Katich's own matchwinning haul of 6 for 65 in the second innings against Zimbabwe in Sydney. He was brought back for the final Test in Colombo, crafting a patient but crucial 86, but was less fluent in the return series back home. Katich's ability to play spin, as well as pace, is a new skill he has learned in his two summers at the SCG since being recruited from WA. His 182 against his old state last summer was a sweet-tasting gem. He was a significant factor whenever he donned the baggy blue, batting with grace and ferocity, fielding with style, and bowling with erratic menace. What were the Warriors thinking in letting him go?

	M	I	NO	Runs	HS	100s	50s	Avge	Ct	St	W	Avge	BB
First-class	115	201	30	8,847	228*	26	45	51.74	117	0	73	37.38	7-130
Domestic first-class	63	113	14	5,013	228*	14	26	50.64	56	0	36	32.00	7-130
Test	9	15	2	546	125	1	4	42.00	6	0	11	31.73	6-65
Int'l limited-overs	6	4	2	44	18*	0	0	22.00	1	0	0	–	–
Dom. limited-overs	55	53	7	1,851	136*	4	10	40.24	19	0	5	47.00	3-43

TRENT KELLY *Right-arm fast bowler* **SA**
It seems strange and distant now but Kelly, a skiddy 19-year-old tearaway, actually beat Shaun Tait in their race to see who would be first to break into the state side. That was way back in 2002-03 when Kelly was blooded in two ING Cup games. He was picked for only one more last summer – going for 38 runs in eight wicketless overs against WA – and was left languishing in the wake of Tait's rapid impact. Along with Chris Duval and Andrew Staunton, he now forms the youthful second line behind SA's first-choice pace attack. He took only 14 grade wickets at a disappointing 34.29 for West Torrens last season. An eyecatching start is required this summer if he is to have any chance of breaking into SA's 1st XI.

	M	I	NO	Runs	HS	100s	50s	Avge	Ct	St	W	Avge	BB
Dom. limited-overs	3	1	0	1	1	0	0	1.00	2	0	1	104.00	1-30

BRAD KNOWLES *Right-arm fast bowler* **Victoria**
Earmarked as an exciting prospect, Knowles is highly rated by Victoria's selectors for his brisk pace and handy lower-order batting. He bowled impressively on debut in a must-win ING Cup match against WA at the MCG, securing the cheap, crucial wicket of their captain Justin Langer. At 23 he has yet to play a first-class game, and was denied a more prominent role last summer by the dreaded osteitis pubis. Originally from Gippsland, he plays first-grade for Camberwell and was selected in the competition's premier team of the season in 2002-03.

	M	I	NO	Runs	HS	100s	50s	Avge	Ct	St	W	Avge	BB
Dom. limited-overs	1	1	1	0	0*	0	0	–	0	0	2	21.00	2-42

SCOTT KREMERSKOTHEN *Left-hand batsman, right-arm medium-pacer* **Tasmania**
Tidy as they are, Kremerskothen's medium-pacers are never going to blast sides out; this summer he must prove his worth and consistency as a batsman. A semi-regular player in previous years, he was given only one Pura Cup match last season – and that was as a stand-in opener for the injured Jamie Cox. He suffered a terrible run with the bat, normally his forte, and struggled to carve out 53 runs in seven ING Cup hits. No longer can he consider himself an entrenched member of Tasmania's one-day side. His bowling

was acceptably economical but it became clear as the season wore on that the selectors were beginning to look elsewhere for their all-round talent. Players such as the 20-year-old Luke Butterworth are jostling for attention.

	M	I	NO	Runs	HS	100s	50s	Avge	Ct	St	W	Avge	BB
First-class	34	50	9	1,146	82*	0	4	27.95	22	0	33	40.70	3-53
Domestic first-class	33	49	8	1,145	82*	0	4	27.93	21	0	31	40.94	3-53
Dom. limited-overs	38	31	5	495	64	0	1	19.04	14	0	24	34.63	3-33

NICHOLAS KRUGER *Left-hand batsman, right-arm medium-pacer* **Queensland**

A promising opener, the 21-year-old Kruger slipped down the Queensland pecking order as two bouts of shoulder surgery ruled him out of the entire season. After breaking through in 2002-03, he had looked set to capitalise on his potential with opening spots up for grabs in Matthew Hayden and Jimmy Maher's absence. Instead his shoulder injury meant a brief stint with the Academy and many months of recovery and rehabilitation. His planned grade comeback in January did not eventuate, and with a question mark over his return date he was dropped back to a rookie contract as the likes of Aaron Nye and Craig Philipson moved past him. The one positive from his enforced break was that it allowed him to further his studies as a PE teacher.

	M	I	NO	Runs	HS	100s	50s	Avge	Ct	St	W	Avge	BB
First-class	1	2	0	36	34	0	0	18.00	0	0	0	–	–
Domestic first-class	1	2	0	36	34	0	0	18.00	0	0	0	–	–
Dom. limited-overs	2	2	0	47	41	0	0	23.50	0	0	0	–	–

GRANT LAMBERT *Right-hand batsman, right-arm fast bowler* **NSW**

Bullocking and bespectacled, Lambert has had few chances to impress of late. Despite making only two fairly anonymous Pura and ING Cup appearances apiece last summer, he never lacked effort at either Blues training or with his club side Fairfield. He finished the year on an unfortunate note. Attempting to take a catch in a grade match, he managed to dislocate and break the middle finger of both hands – which makes it very hard to scratch anywhere vaguely remote. He was plastered and splinted into immobility. Still, he was awarded a state contract for 2004-05. In a young squad he should get the opportunity to make his mark as a genuine all-rounder.

	M	I	NO	Runs	HS	100s	50s	Avge	Ct	St	W	Avge	BB
First-class	5	8	1	160	45*	0	0	22.86	1	0	7	70.57	3-86
Domestic first-class	5	8	1	160	45*	0	0	22.86	1	0	7	70.57	3-86
Dom. limited-overs	4	4	2	13	7	0	0	6.50	1	0	6	30.00	2-33

JUSTIN LANGER *Left-hand batsman* **WA and Australia**

Few cricketers are as passionate as Langer. He thrives on hard work, self-discipline and believes physical fitness is a key to mental toughness. His pre-season entails running hundreds of consecutive singles, facing thousands of deliveries in the nets, sprinting up sandhills, going on 75 km bike rides and enduring countless boxing, karate, yoga and weight sessions. It paid off handsomely in 2003-04, he and Matthew Hayden honing their reputation as one of history's most prolific opening pairs. Cutting and pulling audaciously from the early overs, Langer again proved his reputation for stodginess is well past its use-by date. Despite suffering occasional flat periods, once set he invariably carried on to big hundreds. Troubled by Ajit Agarkar's swing, he bookended an otherwise mediocre series against India with thumping centuries in the first and last Tests. When runs were deserting him in Sri Lanka he produced a feisty, matchwinning 166. He was engulfed in controversy too, replays showing him flicking off a bail as he passed Hashan Tillakaratne's end; Langer said he didn't realise he had done it and the match referee accepted his word. At other times he was a spokesman for fair play: "If I think I am out, or I know I am out, I will walk." Appointed WA captain, he revealed a heart-warming desire to develop young players. He aims to run a marathon once he retires.

	M	I	NO	Runs	HS	100s	50s	Avge	Ct	St	W	Avge	BB
First-class	253	442	42	20,235	274*	64	76	50.59	211	0	5	40.80	2-17
Domestic first-class	83	150	12	7,353	274*	22	26	53.28	69	0	0	–	–
Test	76	128	6	5,488	250	19	20	44.98	50	0	0	–	–
Int'l limited-overs	8	7	2	160	36	0	0	32.00	2	1	0	–	–
Dom. limited-overs	78	74	6	2,815	146	6	19	41.40	34	0	0	–	–

BRETT LEE *Right-arm fast bowler* NSW and Australia

Truly fast bowlers are susceptible to periods of injury and of lost line and length. Last summer, Lee was afflicted by both. The least productive year of his dramatic sporting life ended with him hobbling off the field, and out of the Sri Lankan tour, with a broken foot. Laid low by ankle surgery, he subsequently spent time at the pace factory in India, where his good looks and sizzling speed make him a teenage idol. He is learning Hindi to make himself even more marketable and desirable in that part of the world. On the field, the only highlights were to be found in his hair. At one-day level he lacked his trademark white-ball menace; his 10 overs against India at the Gabba were garrotted for 83. At five-day level he was brought back too soon from injury, and wildly out of rhythm, for the last two Tests against India. He bowled 24 no-balls at the SCG and recorded the surreal match figures of 4 for 276 in 51.5 overs, becoming the first Australian fast bowler to give away a double-century in a single Test innings. Lee reckoned a phone call to Dennis Lillee was the cure – but it would help if the Australian coaching staff had some idea what to do.

	M	I	NO	Runs	HS	100s	50s	Avge	Ct	St	W	Avge	BB
First-class	68	75	13	1,079	79	0	4	17.40	19	0	283	26.76	7-114
Domestic first-class	18	25	4	306	74*	0	1	14.57	8	0	87	24.28	7-114
Test	37	36	6	593	62*	0	2	19.77	9	0	139	31.68	5-47
Int'l limited-overs	84	35	11	347	51*	0	1	14.46	22	0	151	22.15	5-27
Dom. limited-overs	14	6	3	74	44*	0	0	24.67	3	0	19	29.84	3-41

DARREN LEHMANN *Left-hand batsman* SA and Australia

His resolve had been stretched before – by umpteen instances of non-selection, by one regrettable racial outburst – but Lehmann had never fought his way through a more testing time than the summer of 2003-04. He began it as a seemingly entrenched component of both the Test and one-day sides. Then along came injury, initially thought to be a minor Achilles problem and later revealed to be a serious tear. He was consigned to a plastic "moon boot" for so long that he began publicly questioning his chances of ever being reselected. Back at the crease in the New Year, he then lived through the nightmare of watching his mentor and good friend David Hookes die before his eyes. For the second time in one summer, an unforeseen event had Lehmann considering his future. Not surprisingly, he struggled for a while. His form and enthusiasm returned during the course of one trademark ferocious innings – a blistering 237 for the Redbacks at the SCG. It sewed up his place in the squad for Sri Lanka. The rest is history. He took handy wickets with left-arm tweakers that barely deviated and even engineered the odd athletic run-out. More importantly, he became Australia's middle-order mainstay, punishing Muttiah Muralidaran's hand grenades with rare contempt. After his trials of the past six months, picking the doosra must have felt reassuringly straightforward.

	M	I	NO	Runs	HS	100s	50s	Avge	Ct	St	W	Avge	BB
First-class	238	405	28	21,506	255	69	97	57.05	125	0	92	34.53	4-35
Domestic first-class	125	227	14	11,467	255	38	44	53.84	78	0	24	48.25	3-42
Test	20	32	2	1,549	177	5	8	51.63	9	0	13	22.08	3-42
Int'l limited-overs	102	89	19	2,780	119	4	15	39.71	22	0	42	25.71	4-7
Dom. limited-overs	75	74	10	3,095	142*	6	22	48.36	24	0	18	30.33	3-16

MICK LEWIS *Right-arm fast bowler*　**Victoria**
An old-fashioned fast bowler who counts the fire in his belly among his major weapons, Lewis stepped up to lead Victoria's attack all through their triumphant summer. The 30-year-old overcame early injury to take 34 wickets, two more than in his breakthrough season of 2002-03, at 27.85. His Australia A selection of the previous summer, however, was not repeated. Lewis's standout performance came in the Pura Cup final, a game dominated by batsmen on a docile MCG pitch, where he took 6 for 59 in the second innings. He spoke afterwards of his quiet early-morning "conversation" with David Hookes, the late Victorian coach, on the morning of his six-for. Lewis had been out drinking with his friend and mentor the night he died; it was the memory of Hookes, he said, which spurred him on.

	M	I	NO	Runs	HS	100s	50s	Avge	Ct	St	W	Avge	BB
First-class	38	51	15	363	54*	0	1	10.08	22	0	124	30.68	6-59
Domestic first-class	37	50	14	357	54*	0	1	9.92	21	0	120	30.67	6-59
Dom. limited-overs	37	11	5	65	19	0	0	10.83	10	0	46	29.17	4-41

MARTIN LOVE *Right-hand batsman*　**Queensland and Australia**
Love scaled the highest of peaks, for Queenslanders anyway, when his 300 not out on a friendly Junction Oval wicket eclipsed Peter Burge's 40-year record for the highest score by a Queenslander (283) in Pura Cup history. The laid-back Love was well aware of the milestone, seeking out Peter's widow Joan for a quiet chat to pay his respects. It was the slowest triple ton in Australian domestic annals, clocking in at 610 minutes and surpassing the 561-minute effort of Jack Badcock in 1935-36. But it was enough to keep his inspirational aspirations alive, despite the No Vacancy sign flashing in the Australian batting line-up. He finished the summer with 893 Pura Cup runs, including one more century, at 59.53. Away from the field, he lent his profile to a public education campaign on behalf of the Queensland citrus industry during the citrus canker outbreak. His last Test innings, to date, was 100 not out against Bangladesh.

	M	I	NO	Runs	HS	100s	50s	Avge	Ct	St	W	Avge	BB
First-class	159	275	26	12,586	300*	29	60	50.55	190	0	1	11.00	1-5
Domestic first-class	102	176	16	7,668	300*	18	33	47.93	117	0	1	11.00	1-5
Test	5	8	3	233	100*	1	1	46.60	7	0	0	–	–
Dom. limited-overs	78	75	10	2,315	127*	4	9	35.62	28	0	0	–	–

STUART MacGILL *Right-arm leg-spinner*　**NSW and Australia**
MacGill's most telling contribution was the political wrong'un he floated down to cricket administrators, pulling out of the Zimbabwe tour because of moral concerns. No other player followed suit, confirming MacGill's reputation as the thinking man's Australian cricketer. He admirably declined to say he felt vindicated when the Test series was farcically aborted at the last nanosecond. On the field his strength, as always, was his big-spinning leg-break; his weakness was his inability to consistently land it on line. He played all four Tests against India as Shane Warne sat out his drugs ban, starting with 4 for 86 at the Gabba but growing less menacing as the series wore on. He still got through more overs (194.4) and wickets (14) than any other Australian. Perhaps distracted by the international stage, he often seemed on a different page to his NSW team-mates. His record in seven ING Cup matches was typically erratic: he took a wicket every 18 balls, a Spofforthesque strike-rate, while conceding 5.12 runs an over. He played the first two Tests in Sri Lanka, bowling in tandem with Warne as the selectors broke their rule of never playing two leg-spinners together. In Galle, Warne took 10 wickets and MacGill five; in Kandy, Warne added another 10 and MacGill

went wicketless. How often the experiment is repeated remains one of Australian cricket's ongoing fascinations.

	M	I	NO	Runs	HS	100s	50s	Avge	Ct	St	W	Avge	BB
First-class	130	161	41	1,153	53	0	1	9.61	62	0	557	29.94	8-111
Domestic first-class	56	77	22	530	53	0	1	9.64	27	0	206	34.83	6-64
Test	32	37	6	263	43	0	0	8.48	16	0	152	29.22	7-50
Int'l limited-overs	3	2	1	1	1	0	0	1.00	2	0	6	17.50	4-19
Dom. limited-overs	46	17	9	77	18	0	0	9.63	10	0	93	21.58	5-40

DAMIEN MacKENZIE *Right-arm fast bowler*   **Queensland**

MacKenzie remains a gunslinger in the wings after injuries and a lack of opportunities minimised his impact last season. Eight first-class and two ING scalps were not the summer haul he hoped for, although his Pura Cup wickets came at a tidy average of 15.87. Raw-boned, and one of Queensland's quickest on his day, MacKenzie has a knack of achieving breakthroughs when batsmen are well set. But he is fast approaching his season of reason. He was courted by Tasmania and WA during the off-season, although the Tigers dropped out of the running when his good mate Shane Watson returned to the Sunshine State. He has a passion for rugby league's Canberra Raiders, and works as a part-time producer of an evening sports show on Brisbane radio station 4BC.

	M	I	NO	Runs	HS	100s	50s	Avge	Ct	St	W	Avge	BB
First-class	5	6	1	67	30	0	0	13.40	1	0	14	23.71	4-43
Domestic first-class	4	5	0	64	30	0	0	12.80	1	0	14	19.29	4-43
Dom. limited-overs	10	5	3	42	23*	0	0	21.00	1	0	11	24.00	3-20

ANDREW McDONALD *Right-hand batsman, right-arm fast bowler*   **Victoria**

Tipped as Victoria's next big thing, McDonald seemed to confirm those expectations with a cool-headed 45 not out in the opening Pura Cup game as the Bushrangers broke their Gabba hoodoo. He struggled thereafter, dropping from No. 4 to No. 8 and looking increasingly uncomfortable as he went. His bowling, though, was a revelation. He makes good use of his height and subtle variations, and ripped apart WA's middle order with a devastating 4 for 2 in 14 balls at the Junction Oval. He cleaned up the same opponents a month later with 6 for 67, finishing the summer with 32 wickets in 10 matches. He looked likely to be edged out by the returning Ian Harvey for the Pura Cup final, only to belatedly strike form with the bat in the last round. In the end both played.

	M	I	NO	Runs	HS	100s	50s	Avge	Ct	St	W	Avge	BB
First-class	15	24	6	350	51*	0	1	19.44	11	0	36	27.03	6-67
Domestic first-class	14	23	6	349	51*	0	1	20.53	10	0	35	26.57	6-67
Dom. limited-overs	19	16	3	295	55*	0	2	22.69	4	0	12	49.92	2-24

BRYCE McGAIN *Right-arm leg-spinner*   **Victoria**

A journeyman of grade cricket with a ripping leg-break, McGain's first-class prospects have long seemed out of his hands. After labouring under Shane Warne's shadow, he now finds himself in a queue behind the boy wonder Cameron White. He broke through for only one game last summer, on a docile Junction Oval wicket, taking 0 for 109 as Queensland piled up 605. The 32-year-old McGain is a big turner of the ball but, not uncommonly for a leggie, he tends to average one loose delivery an over. That, coupled with his below-par batting and fielding, has curtailed his opportunities. He is highly regarded at Prahran, however, where he is both captain and the official face of the club, involved in their recruiting and marketing.

	M	I	NO	Runs	HS	100s	50s	Avge	Ct	St	W	Avge	BB
First-class	3	3	1	12	9*	0	0	6.00	2	0	6	51.83	3-46
Domestic first-class	3	3	1	12	9*	0	0	6.00	2	0	6	51.83	3-46

GLENN McGRATH *Right-arm fast bowler*   **NSW and Australia**

'Pigeon' sightings were more plentiful in the orthopaedic surgeon's waiting room than on cricket fields during 2003-04. McGrath's ankle injury and subsequent surgery kept him reclining until February, at which point he struggled through a handful of club, 2nd XI and state games. His efforts during Australia's ill-fated Zimbabwe tour proved more a concern than a comfort for Trevor Hohns, the chairman of selectors, who quite publicly put McGrath on notice. In hindsight, perhaps Hohns and Co could have been more patient; he had bowled only 110 overs since returning from injury ahead of that tour. The worry is that McGrath is now 34 – and at that age, no matter how hard you train and practise, it is a long way back after a year away from the bowling crease. In McGrath's case, 450-odd Test wickets at least give you a few extra cards to play with. The rust appeared to be shifting against Sri Lanka, admittedly on a helpful Darwin pitch, and his technique was generally back to its old robotic predictability. His pace remained a tad down. The jury, at the time of writing, is still on a coffee break.

	M	I	NO	Runs	HS	100s	50s	Avge	Ct	St	W	Avge	BB
First-class	158	159	54	758	55	0	1	7.22	43	0	695	20.74	8-38
Domestic first-class	22	22	8	113	26	0	0	8.07	3	0	83	26.82	5-36
Test	97	107	38	450	39	0	0	6.52	29	0	440	21.61	8-38
Int'l limited-overs	188	50	27	94	11	0	0	4.09	26	0	285	22.61	7-15
Dom. limited-overs	19	0	0	0	–	0	0	–	5	0	22	26.77	4-17

STEVE MAGOFFIN *Right-arm fast bowler*   **WA**

When he bowls, Magoffin tries to imitate the great West Indian Curtly Ambrose by banging the ball in hard. A tall man, he has headed west this summer in an attempt to break into first-class ranks and bolster WA's flagging fast-bowling stocks. He represented Queensland Colts for three seasons and was the Queensland Academy of Sport's best bowler, taking 21 wickets at 16.14, when they won the ACB Cup in 2002-03. But he found himself unable to break into the state's 1st XI last summer. Still, he took six wickets against a WA 2nd XI – including the talented opener Scott Meuleman in each innings – which was enough to make an impression on coaching staff in the west.

No major cricket played to date.

JIMMY MAHER *Left-hand batsman, wicket-keeper*   **Queensland and Australia**

After his international cameos of recent times, Maher put aside the keeping gloves to concentrate on what he does best: scoring lots of runs fast. In one extraordinary Black Friday afternoon at the Gabba, he galloped to an Australian one-day record of 187 in 129 balls as the Bulls amassed 4 for 405. It was an innings of typical élan from Maher, who starts this summer a nose ahead of Darren Lehmann as the all-time leading runscorer in domestic one-dayers. He made only one appearance in the green-and-gold, standing in for Adam Gilchrist in India, with Brad Haddin later preferred as deputy keeper. But Maher again produced some telling domestic performances, averaging 61 in the ING Cup with a strike-rate of 96. His captaincy continues to develop and he admits to learning a lot from Queensland's two finals defeats. His curious decision to bowl first in the Pura Cup final quickly backfired, but he clawed back some respect for copping the resulting criticism on the chin.

	M	I	NO	Runs	HS	100s	50s	Avge	Ct	St	W	Avge	BB
First-class	138	243	27	9,165	217	19	45	42.43	140	2	10	50.40	3-11
Domestic first-class	101	179	20	6,430	209	11	33	40.44	110	0	10	30.20	3-11
Int'l limited-overs	26	20	3	438	95	0	1	25.76	18	0	0	–	–
Dom. limited-overs	73	73	9	3,137	187	7	17	49.02	36	0	2	43.50	2-43

GREG MAIL *Right-hand batsman, right-arm medium-pacer* **NSW**

An old-fashioned sheet-anchor opening batsman, laying a foundation for the strokemakers to follow, Mail took significant strides forward in 2003-04. His centuries in each innings against SA at the SCG exhibited almost McCosker-like discipline and patience. He played all 10 Pura Cup matches, building on his breakthrough season of 2002-03, and finished the summer with 754 runs at 47. His jaunty medium-pacers – a surprise new string to his bow that emerged the previous season – were far less successful this time around, and he managed only two wickets in 39 expensive overs. Mail was not required at all in the ING Cup, though that should change in 2004-05. He may also like to add a few kilograms to his spindly frame, just so that the crowds can see him side-on.

	M	I	NO	Runs	HS	100s	50s	Avge	Ct	St	W	Avge	BB
First-class	39	72	4	2,536	176	5	14	37.29	33	0	11	29.64	4-18
Domestic first-class	37	68	4	2,382	176	5	12	37.22	33	0	10	31.00	4-18
Dom. limited-overs	3	2	1	29	19*	0	0	29.00	2	1	0	–	–

GRAHAM MANOU *Wicket-keeper, right-hand batsman* **SA**

Thirty-one catches and a maiden first-class hundred added up to the best summer of Manou's career. It culminated in his appointment as Darren Lehmann's vice-captain; barring personal disasters for Lehmann, the 25-year-old Manou will be a keeper-captain for most of the summer. He excelled with the gloves last season, though mostly standing back, and the decision to promote him to opener resulted in a polished, long overdue hundred at the SCG. His batting was otherwise disappointing. As a pure ball-striker he sometimes resembles a right-handed Adam Gilchrist; at other times his fluency is interspersed with runs of underwhelming scores. A batting average of 18 does not seem right – 28 would be more fitting – but first he must add steel to his technique. One of his prime tasks as de facto skipper will be to teach his tail how to hang around.

	M	I	NO	Runs	HS	100s	50s	Avge	Ct	St	W	Avge	BB
First-class	45	76	9	1,210	130	1	4	18.06	136	12	0	–	–
Domestic first-class	41	69	7	1,114	130	1	4	17.97	126	12	0	–	–
Dom. limited-overs	45	39	13	591	63	0	2	22.73	59	3	0	–	–

PAUL MARAZIOTIS *Right-hand batsman* **NSW**

After two years on the Blues staff, Maraziotis, prolific at club and 2nd XI level, has failed to convince the selectors he is worth another try in 2004-05. The affable Penrith man, who was induced to play at Bankstown, cannot be faulted for his dedication or perennial good humour. Now 30, his challenge – as with any player considered unworthy of full-time professionalism – is to get back to his club and make quality runs against the best bowlers in whatever conditions are served up at that level.
No major cricket played to date.

DAN MARSH *Right-hand batsman, left-arm orthodox spinner* **Tasmania**

Two cool-headed, early-season, brilliantly crafted centuries against NSW and WA might almost have excited the interest of the national selectors. On each occasion Tasmania trailed on the first innings and were left with a mammoth fourth-innings run-chase; each time Marsh paced the innings to perfection. He was effectively captain for the first time last summer in Ricky Ponting's absence, and his undemonstrative but thoughtful leadership style took Tasmania to the brink of the Pura Cup final. The extra responsibility did not impede his strokeplay: he amassed 751 runs at 57.76. He was less prodigious in the ING Cup, with a best score of 46, as Tasmania's poor performance mirrored his own unhappy experience. His left-arm spin has less impact than it used to, with Marsh content to assume the role of partnership-breaker.

	M	I	NO	Runs	HS	100s	50s	Avge	Ct	St	W	Avge	BB
First-class	97	161	28	5,209	157	10	27	39.17	104	0	140	44.03	7-57
Domestic first-class	85	141	24	4,295	134	7	22	36.71	90	0	129	43.88	7-57
Dom. limited-overs	72	65	14	1,574	101*	2	6	30.86	32	0	40	44.98	3-33

SHAUN MARSH *Left-hand batsman*   WA

There is no doubting Marsh's unlimited potential. Equally certain is the fact that he has failed to make the most of his opportunities. A clean striker and brilliant gap-finder, he had Steve Waugh raving enthusiastically after hitting his maiden first-class century in Newcastle. Almost two years on, he is still waiting to hit his second. A Lancashire League stint in 2004 should help his overall development. He was dropped by WA for the second half of last season after producing only 135 Pura Cup runs at 16.87. The son of Geoff Marsh, he identified poor concentration – ironically – as his biggest problem. Fate played its part too: it was unfortunate that he was dropped from WA's one-day side only a couple of days after hammering a stylish 57 in 58 balls for Australia A against Zimbabwe.

	M	I	NO	Runs	HS	100s	50s	Avge	Ct	St	W	Avge	BB
First-class	11	20	3	447	119	1	0	26.29	7	0	2	26.00	2-20
Domestic first-class	10	18	2	436	119	1	0	27.25	7	0	2	26.00	2-20
Dom. limited-overs	11	9	0	182	42	0	0	20.22	2	0	1	14.00	1-14

DAMIEN MARTYN *Right-hand batsman*   WA and Australia

Once the enfant terrible of Australian cricket, a playboy and committed partygoer, Martyn has turned his career around with a strict diet and fitness regime. He now shows signs of greater maturity, on and off the field, than ever. After going more than two years without a Test hundred, he scored two in a week against Sri Lanka in March. His 110 in Galle rescued his Test place as Australia turned probable defeat into emphatic victory. His 161 in Kandy, helping his team out of another tight spot, occupied 534 minutes and was the fourth slowest hundred by an Australian. If such vigilance illustrated a new side of Martyn, he showed he can still sizzle with a couple of gorgeous knocks against the same opponents in Cairns. He had earlier endured an underwhelming home summer, reaching 30 in eight out of nine Test innings but only once passing 50. It developed into a terrible slump with successive scores of 0, 1, 0 and 2 against India during the VB Series. His frustrations bubbled over and he gave a one-fingered salute to the TV cameras in Melbourne – a temporary departure from his new mature ways – earning himself a censure from Ricky Ponting. He soon regained his composure, and enters the new season with his position secure and his reputation as one of the game's sweetest timers intact.

	M	I	NO	Runs	HS	100s	50s	Avge	Ct	St	W	Avge	BB
First-class	175	295	40	12,669	238	37	65	49.68	141	2	36	42.64	4-30
Domestic first-class	93	163	16	6,705	203*	20	33	45.61	89	1	32	38.69	4-30
Test	44	71	10	2,875	161	7	17	47.13	21	0	2	84.00	1-0
Int'l limited-overs	151	130	40	3,713	144*	5	22	41.26	50	0	12	58.67	2-21
Dom. limited-overs	53	50	7	1,880	140	3	13	43.72	16	0	18	16.33	3-3

SCOTT MASON *Left-hand batsman*   Tasmania

With Jamie Cox, Mason forms one half of the least productive opening combination in the land. His summer of 2003-04 was almost a repeat of 2002-03: he played one substantial innings but otherwise failed to pass 60. His 126 against WA in February, part of an ultimately unsuccessful fourth-innings run-chase, was a masterpiece reminiscent of his astonishing 174 against Victoria the season before. As a whole, though, his was a moderate summer: he played all 10 Pura Cup games but averaged only 28. He was dismissed cheaply lbw (though never bowled) on six occasions, suggesting he needs to make some technical adjustments early on. Mason is an enthusiastic motivator in the field, adding value to his overall contribution. And as with Cox, there are no standout challengers for his position.

	M	I	NO	Runs	HS	100s	50s	Avge	Ct	St	W	Avge	BB
First-class	28	48	2	1,252	174	2	5	27.22	15	0	0	–	–
Domestic first-class	27	46	2	1,213	174	2	5	27.57	15	0	0	–	–
Dom. limited-overs	8	7	0	66	16	0	0	9.43	3	0	0	–	–

SCOTT MEULEMAN *Right-hand batsman* WA

It takes character and application to fight back after a truly horrific season – 58 runs at 7.25 in 2002-03 – and the stylish Meuleman showed he is made of the right stuff. He spent time at the Academy working diligently on his technique, overcoming his tendency to play too far away from his body. By the fifth Pura Cup game, with several WA batsmen on international duty, he regained his spot against Victoria. The Warriors were slaughtered inside three days but Meuleman top-scored twice with 53 and 106. The big names returned and Meuleman bowed out, before returning in style. Chosen for the ING Cup final he crafted a superb 71, while batsmen tumbled all round him, in his only one-day knock all summer. A brilliant fieldsman, he has declined an offer from Tasmania and will continue his bid to become a first-class regular in WA.

	M	I	NO	Runs	HS	100s	50s	Avge	Ct	St	W	Avge	BB
First-class	18	32	0	719	109	2	3	22.47	8	0	2	49.00	1-38
Domestic first-class	15	28	0	541	106	1	3	19.32	8	0	2	49.00	1-38
Dom. limited-overs	9	8	0	310	71	0	1	38.75	1	0	0		

MICK MILLER *Left-hand batsman, right-arm fast bowler* SA

Some consistent batting and the odd handy bowling spell have helped Miller strengthen his hold on the SA all-rounder's position without quite grabbing it outright. His ability to swing the new ball was curtailed last summer by having to wait long periods – behind Tait, Rofe and Cleary – before it was thrown to him. He chipped in occasionally and bowled thriftily enough in the one-dayers. If he rarely got the chance to bowl with a newish ball, the shortcomings of SA's top order ensured he regularly batted against one. He made plenty of starts without carrying on; among three half-centuries his best was an 84 at the MCG, bailing SA out of a tight spot. His record is remarkably similar to another Redbacks all-rounder from recent vintage, Mike Smith, whose failure to nail down a regular spot should be a cautionary tale for Miller.

	M	I	NO	Runs	HS	100s	50s	Avge	Ct	St	W	Avge	BB
First-class	18	32	2	745	112	1	4	24.83	15	0	28	39.50	7-55
Domestic first-class	18	32	2	745	112	1	4	24.83	15	0	28	39.50	7-55
Dom. limited-overs	20	20	5	304	82*	0	2	20.27	7	0	13	54.38	3-27

JONATHAN MOSS *Right-hand batsman, right-arm medium-pacer* Victoria

A proven partnership-breaker and increasingly commanding batsman, Moss underlined his gifts with one extraordinary game at the WACA. Standing in for Darren Berry and Cameron White as captain, he led from the front with an effervescent 172 not out as the Bushrangers triumphed by an innings and 158 runs. He later nominated the game as his career highlight, though things continued to look up as the season progressed. After his player-of-the-year exploits in 2002-03, Moss took further leaps forward as a cricketer. His ability to exert pressure on bowlers grew more pronounced, with his cutting and driving a delight. He collected seven half-centuries and 930 Pura Cup runs at 66. His lively mediums accounted for 19 wickets, keeping things tight and seizing important breakthroughs at opportune moments.

	M	I	NO	Runs	HS	100s	50s	Avge	Ct	St	W	Avge	BB
First-class	34	54	5	2,220	172*	4	15	45.31	17	0	53	29.32	4-50
Domestic first-class	27	43	4	1,833	172*	3	13	47.00	11	0	46	29.50	4-50
Dom. limited-overs	30	25	2	507	64*	0	4	22.04	7	0	25	29.88	5-47

MATTHEW MOTT *Left-hand batsman*   **Victoria**

Mott's long and winding career enters a new phase this summer following his decision to accept a job at NSW, his third state, as assistant coach. He has not been offered a playing contract with the Blues but is considered a rough chance of breaking into their 1st XI. Despite scoring a mountain of district runs, he never quite fulfilled his potential in six years at Victoria. He was painting a mate's house when he received a call-up last summer, Jason Arnberger withdrawing to attend the birth of his second child. Mott went on to play six Pura Cup games in 2003-04, with a best of 78 at the WACA, but was on the outer again come finals time. His cautious, restrictive strokeplay makes a striking contrast to his fun-loving, cheeky personality. The Victorian dressing room will be a quieter place.

	M	I	NO	Runs	HS	100s	50s	Avge	Ct	St	W	Avge	BB
First-class	66	116	6	3,723	216	7	20	33.85	55	0	7	65.00	3-35
Domestic first-class	62	110	6	3,557	216	7	18	34.20	50	0	7	62.57	3-35
Dom. limited-overs	18	16	1	275	55*	0	2	18.33	7	0	4	27.50	2-2

BRENDAN NASH *Left-hand batsman*   **Queensland**

In hindsight, Nash will look back on last summer as either his nadir or the moment he began the climb back to the top. Runs in grade cricket and at 2nd XI level looked increasingly elusive, as the slump that ended his 2002-03 season carried into the next. Two grade hundreds after Christmas won him selection as 13th man for the Pura Cup final, his chirpy demeanour enlivening a sometimes sombre Bulls dressing room. But it was not enough for Nash, so impressive in 2001-02, to retain his state contract for 2004-05. Rather than stew over the disappointment with his housemate Mitchell Johnson, who was also left out, Nash set about obtaining a pro contract in the English leagues. Interestingly, his best seasons for Queensland have come after a UK stint. There is still hope.

	M	I	NO	Runs	HS	100s	50s	Avge	Ct	St	W	Avge	BB
First-class	21	39	4	976	176	2	3	27.89	11	0	1	32.00	1-22
Domestic first-class	20	38	4	958	176	2	3	28.18	11	0	1	32.00	1-22
Dom. limited-overs	20	14	3	279	63	0	1	25.36	8	0	0	–	–

DON NASH *Right-arm fast bowler*   **NSW**

Nash has been working harder than ever at trimming down and topping up his fitness, instead of the cheese on the pizzas. The pity is that he rarely made it on to the park in 2003-04, a foot injury restricting him to three Pura and ING Cup appearances. The frustration for fans, selectors and fellow players is that his enormous potential is not being realised – and at 26, time is running short. His best figures last summer were 2 for 70 against WA, and it is almost five years since his bustling approach first attracted flickers of interest from the national selectors. As a batsman, his ferocious hitting has never quite lived up to its potential. We wait with baited picnic baskets to see if 2004-05 will be the year Nash makes a significant impact in both departments.

	M	I	NO	Runs	HS	100s	50s	Avge	Ct	St	W	Avge	BB
First-class	37	62	4	756	50	0	1	13.03	7	0	99	31.06	7-54
Domestic first-class	34	59	4	726	50	0	1	13.20	7	0	92	30.18	7-54
Dom. limited-overs	19	12	3	175	61*	0	1	19.44	1	0	21	30.71	4-26

MATTHEW NICHOLSON *Right-arm fast bowler, right-hand batsman*   **NSW**

Gone were the yips and the bickering, as Nicholson's hometown return from WA proved one of the success stories of 2003-04. He bowled with excellent pace and consistency, proving reliable in a crisis and leading the Pura Cup wickets table with 39 victims at 30.35. In the ING Cup he was second only to Stuart MacGill. He carried his form into the Australia A game against India, making observers sit up and take notice with 4 for 25 from 21.5 overs. If anything disappointed it was his spluttering run production, for he has the potential to be a genuine bowling all-rounder. Certainly communication was never a problem; it was getting him to stop talking that his team-mates battled with. It is six years since the lanky Nicholson played his one and only Test, an Ashes thriller at the MCG, and he was rumoured last summer to be close again. The selectors could do worse.

	M	I	NO	Runs	HS	100s	50s	Avge	Ct	St	W	Avge	BB
First-class	52	78	15	1,363	101*	1	3	21.63	25	0	189	29.30	7-77
Domestic first-class	44	69	13	1,103	59*	0	1	19.70	23	0	154	31.40	6-76
Test	1	2	0	14	9	0	0	7.00	0	0	4	28.75	3-56
Dom. limited-overs	19	12	3	112	25	0	0	12.44	7	0	22	32.95	3-34

ASHLEY NOFFKE *Right-arm fast bowler, right-hand batsman* **Queensland**
Noffke slid into a cricketing black hole, his menace and penetration vanishing without trace. Bubbling on the fringes of the Australian side at the start of the season, he ended it without a national contract. He did hang on to his place in the Bulls line-up, although his haul of eight one-day scalps and 15 Pura Cup wickets at 51.33 was light years away from previous summers. It was suspected that his off-season stint with Middlesex, which ended in injury, might have taken a greater toll than first thought. Not all was doom and gloom, though. Noffke's maiden first-class hundred against SA improved his bona fides as a bowling all-rounder, and he became a key stakeholder among a group of keen fishermen in the Queensland squad – by virtue of his 5.5 metre boat *Bilgaree*.

	M	I	NO	Runs	HS	100s	50s	Avge	Ct	St	W	Avge	BB
First-class	55	63	13	1,293	114*	1	4	25.86	19	0	191	30.21	8-24
Domestic first-class	31	39	10	817	114*	1	3	28.17	11	0	111	28.80	6-24
Dom. limited-overs	34	12	3	126	24	0	0	14.00	10	0	36	38.61	4-32

MARCUS NORTH *Left-hand basmant, right-arm off-spinner* **WA**
For many years North, a sturdy left-hander, lived contentedly in the comfort zone. He had the potential but was vulnerable early. He was a bit lazy and couldn't be bothered switching on. Then the realisation came: he did not want to be remembered as a player who didn't make full use of his talent. And so at last, in 2003-04, he adopted a disciplined, determined approach and watched the runs flow. There were 984 of them, including three hundreds, in the Pura Cup alone; there were another 387, at 96.75, in the ING Cup. Picked for Australia A against Zimbabwe, he opened the batting – not his normal forte – and blasted 115 in 108 deliveries. He got married, recovered from shoulder problems and added another string to his bow with some increasingly handy off-breaks.

	M	I	NO	Runs	HS	100s	50s	Avge	Ct	St	W	Avge	BB
First-class	52	90	6	3,341	219	9	16	39.77	37	0	28	41.71	4-16
Domestic first-class	35	61	3	2,243	200*	7	9	38.67	28	0	20	48.70	3-23
Dom. limited-overs	20	17	6	460	84*	0	4	41.82	6	0	4	54.00	2-17

AARON NYE *Right-hand batsman, right-arm off-spinner* **Queensland**
A late bloomer, Nye looks sure to pressure for a Queensland middle-order spot after his spectacular entry to first-class cricket. Picked at the age of 25, in the last home-and-away round, Nye hit an accomplished NSW attack for 102 in 231 balls. It remains his only first-class innings; a week later he was named 12th man in the Pura Cup final. An athletic right-hander, Nye has benefited from the captaincy opportunities afforded him at grade and 2nd XI level. He was a regular in Queensland under-age teams but had struggled to emerge from the pack, before switching clubs from Norths to Wests two summers ago. He amassed 918 grade runs in 2002-03 and

hasn't looked back. He is an excellent fieldsmen, useful off-spinner and close friend of the rising golfer Adam Scott. His older brother Dean played Under-17s and 19s for Queensland.

	M	I	NO	Runs	HS	100s	50s	Avge	Ct	St	W	Avge	BB
First-class	1	1	0	102	102	1	0	102.00	0	0	1	15.00	1-15
Domestic first-class	1	1	0	102	102	1	0	102.00	0	0	1	15.00	1-15

AARON O'BRIEN *Left-arm orthodox spinner, left-hand batsman*   NSW

Spinners take time to learn, gather experience and blossom, and O'Brien looks poised to make a significant impact in state cricket before too long. The cousin of WA's Chris Rogers, he made significant advances with his bowling last summer and broke into the NSW side for the first time in two years. It was his capable batting that won him a spot but, as with his left-arm predecessor Murray Bennett in the early 1980s, this is a vehicle that allows his bowling to develop. He bowled only 20 Pura Cup overs but shone with the bat in seven ING Cup matches; he was dismissed twice and averaged 75. He has changed clubs this season and may find the surf at Bondi more enticing than the Blue Gum Hotel at Waitara.

	M	I	NO	Runs	HS	100s	50s	Avge	Ct	St	W	Avge	BB
First-class	2	3	0	13	7	0	0	4.33	1	0	2	114.50	1-54
Domestic first-class	2	3	0	13	7	0	0	4.33	1	0	2	114.50	1-54
Dom. limited-overs	8	6	3	150	62*	0	1	50.00	2	0	3	71.00	2-14

DANIEL PAYNE *Right-hand batsman, right-arm off-spinner*   Queensland

As a budding real estate agent and keen student of the turf, Payne should know better than most the cycles of boom and bust. With his cricket in a downturn he will be hoping for an upswell in 2004-05. He was given a chance at the top of the order last season but struggled to impress, averaging only 12.40 in three Pura Cup matches. A free-flowing 52 against Victoria in the ING Cup hinted at his gifts but he was consigned to the also-rans for the second half of the summer. He was not offered a contract for the coming season and briefly considered a transfer, before opting to remain in Brisbane. He enjoyed his first summer as captain of the Redlands Tigers, showing some promise as a part-time off-spinner.

	M	I	NO	Runs	HS	100s	50s	Avge	Ct	St	W	Avge	BB
First-class	10	19	1	256	55	0	1	14.22	7	0	1	6.00	1-6
Domestic first-class	10	19	1	256	55	0	1	14.22	7	0	1	6.00	1-6
Dom. limited-overs	9	9	1	241	52	0	1	30.13	1	0	0	–	–

CLINTON PERREN *Right-hand batsman*   Queensland

A slow starter who has the knack of accelerating his scoring rate without noticeably changing gear, Perren is blossoming into an integral part of the Bulls' line-up. After being named Pura Cup player of the year in 2002-03, he followed up with a highly respectable 721 runs at 37 last summer. The highlight was his 141 against WA, sharing a second-wicket stand of 369 with his mentor Stuart Law, playing his last first-class innings at the Gabba. Perren had another productive one-day season too, clattering five half-centuries and averaging 64. A peach of a batsman, he copped the rough end of the pineapple when called on to bowl the last over of the ING Cup final after cramps had laid low Andy Bichel and James Hopes. The Warriors needed eight to win – and got them with time to kill.

	M	I	NO	Runs	HS	100s	50s	Avge	Ct	St	W	Avge	BB
First-class	41	69	6	2,195	224	5	7	34.84	36	0	1	129.00	1-15
Domestic first-class	38	64	5	2,066	224	5	7	35.02	33	0	0	–	–
Dom. limited-overs	47	41	10	1,391	96	0	12	44.87	16	0	4	49.00	1-10

MATTHEW PHELPS *Right-hand batsman* **NSW**

A beefy opener, Phelps wore the leather off the practice balls at one stage last season after spending most of his waking hours in the nets against a bowling machine. His change of club from Manly to Sydney Uni may have brought academic benefits but his batting suffered. He returned for only one Pura Cup game in February, making 39 and 62 at first-drop against SA. His two ING Cup matches included a run-a-ball 136, laced with 11 fours and three sixes, at suburban Drummoyne Oval. It was enough for the selectors to persevere with him again this summer. Michael Slater's retirement provides him with an opening – perhaps at No. 3 behind Greg Mail and Phil Jaques.

	M	I	NO	Runs	HS	100s	50s	Avge	Ct	St	W	Avge	BB
First-class	17	31	1	1,068	192	2	6	35.60	8	0	0	–	–
Domestic first-class	17	31	1	1,068	192	2	6	35.60	8	0	0	–	–
Dom. limited-overs	9	9	0	235	136	1	0	26.11	2	0	0	–	–

CRAIG PHILIPSON *Right-hand batsman* **Queensland**

Philipson boasts a keen eye and no-fuss approach, qualities he demonstrated to exquisite effect during his 110 on debut at Bellerive Oval. His one-day introduction was equally smooth, a vital 48 in Adelaide earning him a berth in Queensland's vanquished ING Cup final side. Aged 21, Philipson's stocky build belies a surprising nimbleness at the crease, and he has deftly trod a conventional path to first-class honours. A former Queensland Under-19 captain, he has looked comfortable at each new level he has ascended. A mature 85 for the Queensland academy against India last summer told the selectors he was ready to make the next jump. Sport runs in the Philipson blood, with his younger brother Michael selected in an Australian Under-17 development squad. With Stuart Law's No. 4 spot up for grabs, Philipson looks well placed to build on his early promise.

	M	I	NO	Runs	HS	100s	50s	Avge	Ct	St	W	Avge	BB
First-class	3	5	1	198	101*	1	1	49.50	2	0	0	–	–
Domestic first-class	3	5	1	198	101*	1	1	49.50	2	0	0	–	–
Dom. limited-overs	5	5	1	80	48	0	0	20.00	2	0	1	12.00	1-2

NATHAN PILON *Right-hand batsman, wicket-keeper* **NSW and Victoria**

A ferocious batsman and outstanding gloveman, Pilon has moved to Victoria this summer in a bid to win a regular spot in first-class cricket. He kept immaculately last season while Brad Haddin was nursing a broken thumb, but did not grasp his fellow keeper's misfortune strongly enough to make the change permanent. He never quite ignited with the bat the way he can at club level, averaging 28 in four Pura Cup games with a best of 78 against WA. Poor shot selection was usually the root cause of his dismissal, an aspect of his game that the former coach Steve Rixon has worked closely on. A fine player and popular squad member, Pilon will be missed in NSW.

	M	I	NO	Runs	HS	100s	50s	Avge	Ct	St	W	Avge	BB
First-class	7	13	1	234	78	0	2	19.50	28	1	0	–	–
Domestic first-class	7	13	1	234	78	0	2	19.50	28	1	0	–	–
Dom. limited-overs	4	2	0	31	28	0	0	15.50	6	3	0	–	–

RICKY PONTING *Right-hand batsman* **Tasmania and Australia**

For the second year in a row, Ponting confirmed his status as a super-player on the world stage. As a batsman, there was barely a dull moment: he brazenly thrashed the Zimbaweans, Indians and Sri Lankans alike. As a leader, he succeeded Steve Waugh as Australia's 42nd Test skipper and commenced his own tenure with four consecutive victories – the first Australian since Warwick Armstrong to kick off his captaincy career so emphatically. The Launceston lad has come a long way. In six home Tests last summer he plundered 965 runs at 107, studded with domineering double-centuries in consecutive Tests against a testing Indian attack. It was not just the quantity but the quality that took the breath away. Previously considered a vulnerable starter, he invariably hit hard and ran harder, moving his feet and hands into position with more assurance than ever. He pouched yet another swaggering VB Series triumph, and led Australia to 19 victories in 22 one-dayers prior to the Champions Trophy, collecting a hundred and eight fifties along the way. At state level his Tasmanian links became more tenuous than ever; he lived on the mainland, played only one ING Cup game and skipped a Pura Cup match to attend his wife Rianna's university graduation ceremony. But Ponting has always proclaimed the importance of Tasmanian cricket to his being. He was deservedly named worldwide *Wisden*'s inaugural Leading Cricketer in the World.

	M	I	NO	Runs	HS	100s	50s	Avge	Ct	St	W	Avge	BB
First-class	169	282	38	14,034	257	51	54	57.52	167	0	13	55.08	2-10
Domestic first-class	48	89	13	4,756	233	20	14	62.58	32	0	5	74.00	1-7
Test	79	127	15	6,086	257	20	22	54.34	91	0	4	47.50	1-0
Int'l limited-overs	201	196	25	7,255	145	15	41	42.43	82	0	3	34.67	1-12
Dom. limited-overs	32	32	4	942	102	1	6	33.64	13	0	5	28.60	3-34

PETER ROACH *Right-hand batsman, wicket-keeper*   **Victoria**

Darren Berry's retirement puts an end to an uncomfortable rivalry and means Roach will start a summer, for the first time in his life, as Victoria's No. 1 keeper. He filled in for a month last season while Berry was sidelined with a broken finger. Relishing the opportunity, Roach again proved his effectiveness with the bat and his competence – if not Berry's accomplishment – with the gloves. He was admonished by the selectors, however, after publicly venting his frustrations with Berry, who had joked about his stand-in dropping a catch during the opening game against Queensland. Roach's keeping might lack finesse but it is determined and competitive, and his main rival, the 20-year-old Adam Crosthwaite, has not advanced as quickly as hoped. The keeping job looks all his for now, something which can only relax his approach and benefit his game.

	M	I	NO	Runs	HS	100s	50s	Avge	Ct	St	W	Avge	BB
First-class	18	29	10	707	108*	1	4	37.21	57	1	0	–	–
Domestic first-class	15	24	8	563	108*	1	3	35.19	52	0	0	–	–
Dom. limited-overs	9	6	1	64	26	0	0	12.80	8	0	0	–	–

PAUL ROFE *Right-arm fast bowler*   **SA**

Rofe is tall, relentlessly accurate and possesses a plain, unspectacular action; the similarities with a young Glenn McGrath are considerable. Rofe is marginally slower, which would appear to be the main thing holding him back from wider recognition. His ongoing success was an encouraging subplot of SA's season. He took 35 Pura Cup wickets, five more than his highly acclaimed opening partner Shaun Tait, at a slightly superior average of 27. He bowled the Redbacks to their first-up victory in Perth and later scuttled Victoria's batsmen with 7 for 66, the competition's best figures all season. He can swing the ball around and his straightness will always be an asset on last-day Adelaide wickets. Regrettably, his most uncanny similarity with McGrath is with the bat – the only part of Rofe's game that appears to be regressing.

	M	I	NO	Runs	HS	100s	50s	Avge	Ct	St	W	Avge	BB
First-class	33	50	16	205	18	0	0	6.03	9	0	108	28.98	7-52
Domestic first-class	31	48	15	200	18	0	0	6.06	8	0	107	28.40	7-52
Dom. limited-overs	28	12	7	14	6*	0	0	2.80	2	0	23	43.22	3-33

CHRIS ROGERS *Left-hand batsman*   **WA**

There are no frills about Rogers, a gritty left-hander who strikes a certain resemblance to Allan Border. He is a watch-the-ball, hit-the-ball type of player; he is gutsy, works hard on his game and enjoyed another fruitful summer in 2003-04. Consistency was his watchword. After a moderate start he scored four Pura Cup centuries and averaged 57. He also recorded his maiden one-day hundred, opening and batting through the innings for an unbeaten 117 against Queensland. Again rewarded with Australia A selection, he opened the batting against India in Hobart and made 70 and 2. A budding journalist, Rogers shocked WA officials with the revelation that he is short-sighted and colour-blind, a heredity disorder that sometimes makes it difficult to pick up the red ball when it blends into the background.

	M	I	NO	Runs	HS	100s	50s	Avge	Ct	St	W	Avge	BB
First-class	40	72	6	2,908	194	9	14	44.06	36	0	0	–	–
Domestic first-class	28	50	4	2,139	194	8	9	46.50	28	0	0	–	–
Dom. limited-overs	25	24	4	718	117*	1	4	35.90	8	0	0	–	–

LUKE RONCHI *Wicket-keeper, right-hand batsman*   WA

Ronchi finds himself in one of the game's most frustrating positions: that of heir apparent keeper. He replaced an out-of-favour Ryan Campbell two summers ago in WA's last game of the season, top-scoring in each innings with 67 and 61 at the MCG. It mattered naught. Campbell was back fully fit and committed in 2003-04, and Ronchi was out in the cold. His one opportunity was an ING Cup game in Launceston when Campbell suffered a groin strain. He took two catches but didn't bat, a deluge flooding the ground. All he could do was bide his time fruitfully with grade side Perth, hitting two centuries in his 659 runs at 43.93. For now, Campbell remains a flamboyant keeper and punishing batsman. Ronchi, at 23, looms as an important part of WA's future.

	M	I	NO	Runs	HS	100s	50s	Avge	Ct	St	W	Avge	BB
First-class	4	7	0	275	90	0	3	39.29	5	1	0	–	–
Domestic first-class	4	7	0	275	90	0	3	39.29	5	1	0	–	–
Dom. limited-overs	2	1	0	0	0	0	0	0.00	3	0	0	–	–

GRAEME RUMMANS *Left-hand batsman*   Victoria

A classy left-hander, Rummans struggled to find a niche for himself among Victoria's new-found batting riches last summer. He played six ING Cup games, hitting polished half-centuries against NSW and SA, but the closest he got to a first-class appearance was 12th man. He had played eight Pura Cup games the previous summer, his first since moving south from NSW, but refused to be downcast. Gracious and grateful, he said he was happy just to be given a chance in his adopted state. Rummans had a prolific year at grade level, scoring 719 runs at 44.93 with St Kilda. He won the John Scholes Medal, awarded to the player of the final, for the second year in a row.

	M	I	NO	Runs	HS	100s	50s	Avge	Ct	St	W	Avge	BB
First-class	29	47	6	1,185	119	1	7	28.90	14	0	5	28.00	3-24
Domestic first-class	27	45	6	988	69*	0	6	25.33	12	0	2	57.00	2-71
Dom. limited-overs	38	35	6	938	75	0	7	32.34	9	0	0	–	–

WADE SECCOMBE *Wicket-keeper, right-hand batsman*   Queensland

With the retirement of Darren Berry, Seccombe can now comfortably be described as the best pure gloveman in Australia. It is a title, many would argue, that was already his. He picked up another 42 dismissals last summer while racking up his 100th first-class game for Queensland. The selectors tossed an Australia A cap his way and chose him as their insurance policy for Sri Lanka, where he played one tour match. His batting will never be stylish but remains highly effective. Another century when the Bulls needed it – this time to set up an outright win in Adelaide – and a brazen 67 not out to beat Tasmania in the ING Cup demonstrated his importance to the lower order. He took his family to Amsterdam in the off-season, coaching and playing for the Excelsior club and researching his hobby of home brewery. The wheel is now turning full circle for

Seccombe, just as it did for Ian Healy, with a classy keeper in Chris Hartley waiting in the wings. But like Healy before him, Seccombe will take some shifting.

	M	I	NO	Runs	HS	100s	50s	Avge	Ct	St	W	Avge	BB
First-class	107	159	28	3,304	151	4	10	25.22	478	19	0	–	–
Domestic first-class	93	139	25	2,952	151	4	9	25.89	436	12	0	–	–
Dom. limited-overs	69	51	15	731	67*	0	3	20.31	92	20	0	–	–

CRAIG SIMMONS *Left-hand batsman* WA

A beefy 21-year-old opener, Simmons's first-class debut against a rampant Victorian side at the WACA offered a steep learning curve. Standing in for Mike Hussey and Chris Rogers, who were opening for Australia A in Hobart, he stroked Ian Harvey through mid-wicket for three and square-drove Shane Harwood for four. He departed for 7 in the fourth over, driving at Harvey and edging to second slip, then for 1 in the second innings, driving at a Harvey in-swinger and missing it. The lesson learned was that he must tighten his technique and understand that bowlers serve up far greater pressure – and far fewer scoring opportunities – at first-class level. After solid seasons with Rockingham–Mandurah and the WA 2nd XI, he was picked to tour India in August with an Australian development squad.

	M	I	NO	Runs	HS	100s	50s	Avge	Ct	St	W	Avge	BB
First-class	1	2	0	8	7	0	0	4.00	0	0	0	–	–
Domestic first-class	1	2	0	8	7	0	0	4.00	0	0	0	–	–

CHRIS SIMPSON *Right-hand batsman, right-arm off-spinner* Queensland

A muscular all-rounder, Simpson is a clean hitter who gives his brisk off-breaks a vigorous rip. He flirted with his admirers last summer, producing a handful of cameos without revealing his full wares. He hit two half-centuries in the Pura Cup: a slashing 83 against Victoria, including nine fours and five sixes, from No. 8; and a more cautious 75 against NSW as opener. His other nine innings produced only 48 runs. Simpson's bowling was equally hit-or-miss. His 3 for 8 at the SCG helped bowl the Bulls to victory but his remaining four wickets cost 99 apiece. The coaching staff believe he is too young, at 22, to be pigeonholed, so he will probably continue to move up and down the order in a floating role. A keen musician and surfer, his choice of favourite song is appropriate: Billy Bragg's "Waiting for the Great Leap Forward".

	M	I	NO	Runs	HS	100s	50s	Avge	Ct	St	W	Avge	BB
First-class	7	13	0	223	83	0	2	17.15	8	0	7	61.14	3-8
Domestic first-class	7	13	0	223	83	0	2	17.15	8	0	7	61.14	3-8
Dom. limited-overs	5	4	1	38	15	0	0	12.67	1	0	5	30.00	3-45

JACK SMITH *Right-hand batsman* SA

Smith returns to the South Australian squad this summer at the age of 27, earmarked as much for his leadership skills as his batting. A former Canberra Comet, he was dropped off SA's list of contracted players in 2003-04 but enjoyed a prosperous grade season. He captained Adelaide to the A-grade flag while collecting 739 runs at 49.27. The departure of Andy Flower and the expected absence of Darren Lehmann on international business leaves a considerable gap in leadership skills among a young Redbacks side. The challenge for Smith will be to back his tactical skills with enough runs to earn a spot as a batsman. *No major cricket played to date.*

ANDREW STAUNTON *Right-arm fast bowler* SA

After moving across from NSW to further his cricket career, Staunton's bustling action and taste for wickets soon made a sizeable impression in Adelaide grade circles. He was a surprise selection for SA's pre-Christmas Pura Cup trip to Queensland after Shaun Tait and Paul Rofe were snapped up by Australia A. He managed one wicket – that of Andrew Symonds – in 24 overs. Not the youngest rookie at 25, Staunton could do worse than look to the example of another bustling type, Paul 'Blocker' Wilson, who similarly moved to Adelaide from NSW, and who eventually earned a Test cap.

	M	I	NO	Runs	HS	100s	50s	Avge	Ct	St	W	Avge	BB
First-class	1	2	2	4	3*	0	0	–	0	0	1	92.00	1-92
Domestic first-class	1	2	2	4	3*	0	0	–	0	0	1	92.00	1-92

ANDREW SYMONDS *Right-hand batsman, right-arm medium/off-spinner* **Qld, Aust.**
Symonds finally received the baggy green cap that had been at the core of his decision to eschew the chance to play for the country of his birth, England, in favour of his adopted home. Selected as a quasi-all-rounder for the Sri Lankan tour, his ability to bowl either medium-pace or off-spin, combined with 119 not out against the Sri Lankan President's XI, gained him selection in the first two Tests. While the results were not spectacular, Symonds at least earned his spot in trivia challenge folklore, taking the catch that gave Shane Warne his 500th Test victim. He married his high-school sweetheart Brooke Marshall before jetting off to Kent in the 2004 winter. While his first-class work was rock-solid, and featured his captaincy debut, the combination of Symonds and the hyperkinetic atmosphere of the Twenty20 Cup produced a display for the ages. Opening for Kent against Middlesex, he blasted 100 in 34 balls – including 16 fours and three sixes – and finished with 112 from 43. Built like a rugby union flanker, his growing maturity bodes well for the future. Typically, his love of the outdoors saw him embark on various expeditions throughout outback Queensland and its coastline. He is one of the few if not the only Test cricketers in the world to regularly embark on feral pig hunting expeditions, armed with just his dog and a knife. By all accounts his strike-rate there is high as well.

	M	I	NO	Runs	HS	100s	50s	Avge	Ct	St	W	Avge	BB
First-class	173	290	28	11,130	254*	33	45	42.48	120	0	170	36.93	6-105
Domestic first-class	70	113	9	3,771	163	10	13	36.26	40	0	82	30.13	4-39
Test	2	4	0	53	24	0	0	13.25	4	0	1	85.00	1-68
Int'l limited-overs	96	72	15	2,064	143*	1	10	36.21	42	0	72	35.99	4-11
Dom. limited-overs	55	51	6	1,152	91	0	5	25.60	26	0	27	33.30	3-32

SHAUN TAIT *Right-arm fast bowler* **SA and Australia**
Awesome speed, swing and plenty of menace landed Shaun Tait in Australia's Test squad by the autumn of 2004. In only his second first-class season, his pace in particular was the source of considerable excitement among team-mates, spectators and selectors. Batsmen unlucky enough to face both Tait and Jason Gillespie in the one state side must have pined for the early 1990s, when SA's bowling mainstay was the off-spinner Tim May. Although his 33 wickets at 29 were a more than acceptable first-class return, Tait's most fearsome moments came in the ING Cup. His tendency to lose control was compensated for by his explosiveness. Against NSW, on a fresh pitch, his 10-over spell of 2 for 12 earned verbal applause from Steve Waugh. Figures of 8 for 43 against Tasmania, the best in the competition's history, tell their own story. At the end of that performance Tait said he'd barely swung the ball all day, a subtle hint that the five batsmen bowled or lbw were beaten by pure speed. He was called up as a reserve in Sri Lanka and made Australia's 13-man squad for the return series back home. One of this summer's tantalising prospects is the possibility that Tait, if picked, will finally be tested by the speed gun.

	M	I	NO	Runs	HS	100s	50s	Avge	Ct	St	W	Avge	BB
First-class	14	21	10	58	12	0	0	5.27	3	0	53	26.57	5-68
Domestic first-class	13	21	10	58	12	0	0	5.27	3	0	50	26.02	5-68
Dom. limited-overs	10	4	1	6	4*	0	0	2.00	2	0	18	22.44	8-43

JOHN TAYLOR *Right-arm fast bowler* **WA and Victoria**
Feisty and talented, direction proved to be Taylor's biggest hurdle during his debut first-class season. He captured handy wickets but was too expensive – leaking 4.52 runs an over in his six Pura Cup games – and frequently tended to bowl both sides of the wicket. He returned home to Melbourne at summer's end and hopes to win a place in the well-stocked Victorian side. He has undoubted potential but must learn to become more consistent, to mount greater pressure on the batsmen. His best efforts for WA came against the Victorians: 4 for 70 in a Pura Cup match at the Junction Oval, and 3 for 27 off 10 overs in the ING Cup. He also proved his worth as a clean, hard-hitting batsman, smacking 50 off 51 balls against NSW.

	M	I	NO	Runs	HS	100s	50s	Avge	Ct	St	W	Avge	BB
First-class	6	9	2	132	50	0	1	18.86	3	0	12	51.25	4-70
Domestic first-class	6	9	2	132	50	0	1	18.86	3	0	12	51.25	4-70
Dom. limited-overs	7	4	1	34	34	0	0	11.33	0	0	11	22.45	3-27

MICHAEL THISTLE *Right-arm fast bowler* **WA**
Thistle hails from Bayswater–Morley – the Perth club that produced Test fast men Bob Massie, Wayne Clark and Bruce Reid – but must learn to come back strongly in his second and third spells if he is to follow in their footsteps. A tall right-armer, he does have the ability to swing the ball away from the right-handers. He made an impressive one-day debut against South Australia, picking 3 for 32 in 8.1 overs. His maiden first-class appearance was more daunting; against a Victorian batting line-up that amassed 3 for 613 at the WACA, Thistle went for just under five an over. But he had a good first-grade season, capturing 40 wickets at 24.42, and should receive further opportunities at senior level this summer.

	M	I	NO	Runs	HS	100s	50s	Avge	Ct	St	W	Avge	BB
First-class	1	2	0	14	14	0	0	7.00	0	0	0	–	–
Domestic first-class	1	2	0	14	14	0	0	7.00	0	0	0	–	–
Dom. limited-overs	2	0	0	0	–	0	0	–	0	0	4	21.50	3-32

DOMINIC THORNELY *Right-hand batsman, right-arm medium-pacer* **NSW**
The man who Rod Marsh declared should be in the state team at 17 finally got an extended shot in the big time eight years later. It was Thornely's fielding that burned in the memory. His infield catching was brilliant and may have been the principal factor that won him selection in two Australia A games against Zimbabwe. He began the season as a one-day specialist whose lack of pace makes him hard to get away. But he also broke through at first-class level. He was given more responsibility than the average debutant, with expectations high based on his one-day performances, and he responded accordingly. He took 3 for 52 on debut at the MCG and, despite being shuffled up and down the order, hit a fluent 143 against Victoria in Newcastle.

	M	I	NO	Runs	HS	100s	50s	Avge	Ct	St	W	Avge	BB
First-class	6	12	0	343	143	1	2	28.58	4	0	7	39.86	3-52
Domestic first-class	6	12	0	343	143	1	2	28.58	4	0	7	39.86	3-52
Dom. limited-overs	24	21	2	514	78	0	3	27.05	12	0	15	35.80	3-32

CALLUM THORP *Right-arm fast bowler* **WA**
An old-fashioned swing bowler capable of moving the ball both ways, Thorp must develop greater variety if he is to win a regular spot. He overcame stress fractures in his spine to be available from the start of last season but failed to grasp his opportunities.

He bowled too many full balls for a bowler of his modest pace and his line was inconsistent. He played the first three ING Cup games, taking one wicket while conceding five runs an over, and picked up seven wickets in three Pura Cup matches. Then the selectors looked elsewhere. A window cleaner and electrician by trade, Thorp triggered embarrassed "Window cleaner wrecks England" headlines on Fleet Street two years ago after knocking over England's top order in a warm-up game. He has failed to mop up since.

	M	I	NO	Runs	HS	100s	50s	Avge	Ct	St	W	Avge	BB
First-class	6	8	0	66	26	0	0	8.25	2	0	10	53.10	3-59
Domestic first-class	6	8	0	66	26	0	0	8.25	2	0	10	53.10	3-59
Dom. limited-overs	10	3	2	16	12	0	0	16.00	2	0	14	30.14	4-46

SHANNON TUBB *Left-arm chinaman bowler, right-hand batsman* **Tasmania**
A left-arm wrist-spinner who generated considerable excitement as a schoolboy prodigy almost a decade ago, Tubb has reinvented himself as more of a batsman in recent times. He took 0 for 130 across six ING Cup games last summer and bowled 12 expensive, wicketless overs in his only Pura Cup match in Adelaide. He looked a more adept contributor with the bat, averaging 27 in the one-dayers. He launched a superb counterattack against Queensland at Bellerive, arriving at the wicket with the score 4 for 33 and clubbing 79 in 75 balls, including 10 fours and a six. Now 24, Tubb underlined his new focus with a stunning 342 for Clarence against New Town in last summer's Tasmanian first-grade semi-finals.

	M	I	NO	Runs	HS	100s	50s	Avge	Ct	St	W	Avge	BB
First-class	8	13	0	151	42	0	0	11.62	2	0	8	50.88	3-57
Domestic first-class	8	13	0	151	42	0	0	11.62	2	0	8	50.88	3-57
Dom. limited-overs	7	7	0	178	79	0	1	25.43	0	0	–	–	–

ADRIAN TUCKER *Right-arm leg-spinner* **NSW**
Adrian who? Ten years and 103 games on from his last first-class match, Tucker set an Australian record for the longest gap between appearances when he was brought back for the Waugh brothers' final game against Queensland. His efforts for Eastern Suburbs had convinced the selectors that, with Stuart MacGill away, the 34-year-old Tucker was the man for the job at the SCG – and the romantics weren't about to argue. He bowled 27 overs, took 1 for 105 and was not offered a state contract for 2004-05. During his 10-year hiatus he spent time in London and Hong Kong, progressing the corporate ladder – at BZW, ABN Amro and Citigroup – and playing cricket for fun. How different that is to today's young men, who aspire to be professional cricketers and don't bother with other qualifications. It seems only yesterday that Tucker was twice dismissing Allan Border in a Sheffield Shield final at the SCG. It was 1990.

	M	I	NO	Runs	HS	100s	50s	Avge	Ct	St	W	Avge	BB
First-class	17	22	8	314	48*	0	0	22.43	13	0	45	40.13	5-38
Domestic first-class	15	20	7	266	46*	0	0	20.46	8	0	37	42.59	5-38

ADAM VOGES *Right-hand batsman* **WA**
Highly competent and elegant, Voges was starved of senior opportunities last summer by WA's strong and settled batting line-up. He performed solidly at all other levels, averaging 30 for the 2nd XI and 66 for Melville. He was the leading runscorer in Perth's first-grade competition and captained the side to victory over Bayswater–Morley in the final. Now 25, Voges played four Pura Cup matches in his debut season of 2002-03 and has the ability to force his way back. He spent time at the new-look Centre of Excellence in Brisbane this year and was named captain of a 13-man development squad that toured India in August, a sure vote of confidence in his future.

	M	I	NO	Runs	HS	100s	50s	Avge	Ct	St	W	Avge	BB
First-class	4	7	0	119	38	0	0	17.00	4	0	2	24.00	2-34
Domestic first-class	4	7	0	119	38	0	0	17.00	4	0	2	24.00	2-34

SHANE WARNE *Right-arm leg-spinner*   **Victoria and Australia**

Warne bounced back from his year-long drugs exile looking fitter and hungrier than
ever. And, as Warne repeatedly insisted, he seemed better too: a better bowler, more
mature man, nicer husband and kinder father. In his comeback Test in Galle, the man
who revived the ancient art of leg-spin became the first slow bowler to reach 500 Test
wickets. Spinning a dipping, curling, spitting web round the Sri Lankans, he swept up
26 wickets in three Tests and thoroughly outbowled his great rival Muttiah Muralidaran.
If the shine had faded from his flipper and wrong'un, his deadly accuracy and
competitive spirit remained intact. A month earlier, Warne returned to competitive
cricket in the humble surrounds of the Junction Oval, the ground he called home as a
young district cricketer. It was only a state 2nd XI game but he drew 10 times as big a
crowd as were watching the 1st XI down the road at the MCG; his penchant for drama
had not vanished either. The Shane Warne soap opera returned to the airwaves with a
vengeance, this time in the form of a sex saga starring a mobile phone and an exotic
dancer, among others. When Murali chose not to tour Australia, Warne was left needing
11 wickets in Darwin and Cairns to break the world record. He managed 10, they were
fleetingly tied on 527-all, and Warne promptly said Murali's wickets were worth less
because he whipped through tail-end batsmen on friendly pitches. And so the melodrama
continued ...

	M	I	NO	Runs	HS	100s	50s	Avge	Ct	St	W	Avge	BB
First-class	213	288	36	4,350	99	0	15	17.26	171	0	914	25.96	8-71
Domestic first-class	36	47	7	638	69	0	2	15.95	26	0	124	35.28	6-42
Test	112	156	13	2,326	99	0	8	16.27	93	0	527	25.47	8-71
Int'l limited-overs	193	106	28	1,016	55	0	1	13.03	80	0	291	25.82	5-33
Dom. limited-overs	25	20	1	208	32	0	0	10.95	10	0	38	25.89	5-35

DARREN WATES *Right-hand batsman, right-arm fast bowler*   **WA**

Wates returned for his first Pura Cup match in almost four years after pre-season surgery
cured a groin injury. He was picked for the opening game against SA, took a wicket,
aggravated a side-strain and was unable to bowl for the rest of the match. To make
matters worse he was struck on the foot by a Shaun Tait yorker during his second-
innings 48, the resultant fracture keeping him out of action for several weeks. A
practising lawyer, he later returned but his swing bowling was not as damaging as the
coaching staff had hoped for. He did enjoy a couple of special moments with the bat. He
scored 99 in Adelaide before running himself out attempting a second run to complete
a maiden first-class century, then hit a six and a four in the 50th over to clinch WA's ING
Cup final victory.

	M	I	NO	Runs	HS	100s	50s	Avge	Ct	St	W	Avge	BB
First-class	8	10	2	298	99	0	2	37.25	5	0	18	41.50	4-77
Domestic first-class	7	10	2	298	99	0	2	37.25	4	0	14	42.64	4-77
Dom. limited-overs	22	12	5	99	29*	0	0	14.14	5	0	22	38.23	3-32

SHANE WATSON *Right-hand batsman, right-arm medium-pacer*   **Tas., Qld, Aust.**

Long earmarked as Australia's next great all-rounder, Watson took care of one half of
the equation by confirming his arrival as a batsman of genuine class. Unable to bowl
because of the serious back injury that kept him out of the 2003 World Cup, he played
all summer for Tasmania as a specialist No. 3. He began with a majestic 103 against SA,
the first of four technically imposing hundreds that radiated a maturity far beyond his
23 years. Eventually he started bowling again too, initially in short spells, as his fitness
advisers nursed him back to full strength. He was rushed into Australia's one-day squad,
went on the farcical one-day tour of Zimbabwe, and played his one international match
of the summer in Harare; he hit 18 not out and got through eight overs unscathed. Watson

has followed the sun home to his native Queensland for 2004-05, largely for weather and lifestyle reasons, but Tasmania will happily take the credit for launching this talented cricketer on his international journey. He signed off with an almighty bang, hitting 300 not out and taking 7 for 29 in his farewell game for his club side Lindisfarne.

	M	I	NO	Runs	HS	100s	50s	Avge	Ct	St	W	Avge	BB
First-class	28	49	6	2,038	157	7	10	47.40	13	0	53	28.06	6-32
Domestic first-class	26	46	4	1,802	157	5	10	42.90	13	0	50	27.98	6-32
Int'l limited-overs	24	16	8	306	77*	0	1	38.25	7	0	18	37.22	3-27
Dom. limited-overs	30	29	2	803	96	0	7	29.74	6	0	19	39.21	3-42

CAMERON WHITE *Right-arm leg-spinner, right-hand batsman* **Victoria**

The man who models himself unashamedly on Shane Warne, from his distinctive walk-up to the way his tongue pokes out the side of his mouth at the point of delivery, moved one step closer to joining his mentor in the Australian side. Stuart MacGill's withdrawal from the Zimbabwe tour on moral grounds opened the door for White, only for that door to be slammed in his face when the Tests were scrapped. White lacks Warne's turn and loop, relying more on subtle changes of pace, and his batting has hitherto proved more effective: he averaged 40 with the bat and 37 with the ball in last summer's Pura Cup. But it was his captaincy that overshadowed everything. At 20, he became Victoria's youngest skipper, leading them to a third-place finish in the ING Cup and deputising with spectacular success in the Pura Cup. He will captain the Bushrangers in both codes this summer and has been described by Brian Freedman, Australia's Under-19 manager, as the most mature young captain since a youthful Steve Waugh.

	M	I	NO	Runs	HS	100s	50s	Avge	Ct	St	W	Avge	BB
First-class	28	42	5	978	91	0	7	26.43	36	0	69	34.01	6-66
Domestic first-class	26	39	5	919	91	0	7	27.03	35	0	65	34.23	6-66
Dom. limited-overs	21	15	2	154	42	0	0	11.85	4	0	15	45.87	3-25

BRAD WILLIAMS *Right-arm fast bowler* **WA and Australia**

Last summer was a memorable time for Williams for reasons good and bad. With Australia's pace frontline out of action, he took four wickets against Zimbabwe in his long-awaited Test debut at the SCG. He was then angered by his omission from the next Test, against India, and grew unhappier still when he discovered his replacement was the left-armer Nathan Bracken. "Apparently I just bowl with the wrong arm," he declared. Williams was reprimanded by Cricket Australia and underwent counselling. He regretted his outburst and apologised to both Trevor Hohns, chairman of selectors, and the captain Steve Waugh. The controversy camouflaged a breakthrough summer for Williams, who had been on Test standby five times before finally getting the nod. He bowled with commendable aggression and growing self-belief. He returned against India for the second and third Tests, straining ligaments in his left shoulder while diving in the Adelaide outfield, but roaring back with a vital 4 for 53 in the second innings in Melbourne. He sizzled during the TVS Cup in India and was Australia's most devastating bowler in last summer's VB Series, his 15 wickets including 5 for 22 against Zimbabwe. Just when things looked to be going swimmingly, a back injury forced him out of the Sri Lankan series in Darwin and Cairns.

	M	I	NO	Runs	HS	100s	50s	Avge	Ct	St	W	Avge	BB
First-class	57	73	21	719	41*	0	0	13.83	22	0	197	30.99	6-74
Domestic first-class	41	55	16	548	41*	0	0	14.05	13	0	155	30.15	6-74
Test	4	6	3	23	10*	0	0	7.67	4	0	9	45.11	4-53
Int'l limited-overs	25	6	4	27	13*	0	0	13.50	4	0	35	23.26	5-22
Dom. limited-overs	33	8	4	48	23	0	0	12.00	6	0	49	24.92	4-29

ALLAN WISE *Left-arm fast bowler* **Victoria**

Nicknamed 'Mule' for his habit of kicking up his left heel at the top of his run-up, Wise was one of last summer's surprise success stories. After a largely uneventful club career he made his first-class debut against Queensland, thanks partly to injuries and partly to his own eyecatching form in the 2nd XI. A towering left-armer, he picked up three wickets on debut and was a permanent fixture all season, capturing 33 wickets at 24.27. He wrecked SA's batting with 5 for 47 in the second innings in Adelaide, an emotional encounter played in the wake of David Hookes's funeral. His only disappointment was the Pura Cup final, where he bowled 10 overs before breaking down with stress fractures of the foot. A product of Richmond, Wise has previously complemented his cricket with stints of country football.

	M	I	NO	Runs	HS	100s	50s	Avge	Ct	St	W	Avge	BB
First-class	10	8	6	19	7	0	0	9.50	5	0	33	24.27	5-47
Domestic first-class	10	8	6	19	7	0	0	9.50	5	0	33	24.27	5-47
Dom. limited-overs	8	2	1	0	0*	0	0	0.00	0	0	10	28.70	2-31

PETER WORTHINGTON *Right-hand batsman, right-arm medium-pacer* **WA**

A glorious summer seemed to beckon when Worthington doubled up with nine wickets and a second-innings fifty in WA's opening Pura Cup match against SA. From there, his second season in the big time went quickly downhill. His form deteriorated and he played only three more games, managing three wickets and 47 runs from six innings. A psychiatric nurse, Worthington is tall, athletic and always works hard. He proved more successful at one-day level in 2003-04, taking 12 wickets in seven games and blazing away with a strike-rate of 114 with the bat. Restricted to the first-class sidelines he enjoyed a sound grade season with Midland–Guildford, scoring 530 runs at 48.18 and taking 19 wickets at 20.31.

	M	I	NO	Runs	HS	100s	50s	Avge	Ct	St	W	Avge	BB
First-class	6	12	1	177	50	0	1	16.09	6	0	12	39.25	6-59
Domestic first-class	5	10	0	102	50	0	1	10.20	5	0	12	34.58	6-59
Dom. limited-overs	10	6	4	112	49*	0	0	56.00	2	0	12	32.67	3-45

DAMIEN WRIGHT *Right-arm fast bowler* **Tasmania**

This was the year that hard work and honest endeavour paid off. Bowling with consistent hostility, stinginess and an ever-reliable line, Wright finished the summer with 37 Pura Cup wickets at 26.48, a tally bettered only by NSW's Matthew Nicholson. He took just one five-for, against SA in Adelaide, but was seldom left wicketless. His reward was Australia A selection for the match against India in Hobart, where he gave little away and sent Sachin Tendulkar on his way. Blond-haired and wholehearted, Wright's clean striking and stout resistance with the bat continued to provide spine to the Tasmanian lower order. Injury prevented him from fulfilling a county contract with Derbyshire but he again promises to be an integral part of Tasmania's attack.

	M	I	NO	Runs	HS	100s	50s	Avge	Ct	St	W	Avge	BB
First-class	52	75	15	1,272	65	0	6	21.20	23	0	154	32.80	6-39
Domestic first-class	47	71	14	1,188	65	0	6	20.84	20	0	136	33.75	6-39
Dom. limited-overs	42	31	11	296	40	0	0	14.80	8	0	51	27.31	4-23

LIAM ZAMMIT *Right-arm leg-spinner* **NSW**

Zammit is a tall sliding leggie, more in the style of Kerry O'Keeffe than Shane Warne, who will benefit from his 85 overs in the big league. He took three wickets on debut against WA and played twice more in Stuart MacGill's absence, before Adrian Tucker – 12 years his senior – was preferred late in the season. At 23, he is one in a long line of well-performed under-age spinners in NSW who need time at club and 2nd XI level for their skills to mature. Too much expectation has been placed on the likes of Zammit, Jason Krezja (reinstated with a rookie contract), Aaron O'Brien and Peter Wooden. History tells us there are good reasons why spinners develop slowly. Zammit has a state contract this summer and Tucker does not. But who will play in the games that matter?

	M	I	NO	Runs	HS	100s	50s	Avge	Ct	St	W	Avge	BB
First-class	3	4	0	32	15	0	0	8.00	4	0	5	69.80	2-71
Domestic first-class	3	4	0	32	15	0	0	8.00	4	0	5	69.80	2-71
Dom. limited-overs	1	0	0	0	–	0	0	–	0	0	0	–	–

Births and Deaths of Cricketers

The following list details information on the 3,187 players to have represented an Australian first-class cricket team.

STATE REPRESENTATION
New South Wales   694
Queensland   450
South Australia   570
Tasmania   500
Victoria   797
Western Australia   384
Other Teams   32

The compiler of this section welcomes any information from readers regarding the details contained therein.

Key to abbreviations

Australian states and territories: ACT – Australian Capital Territory, NSW – New South Wales, NT – Northern Territory, Qld – Queensland, SAust – South Australia, Tas – Tasmania, Vic – Victoria, WAust – Western Australia.

*Denotes Test player.

**Denotes Test player for two countries.

There is a full list of Australian Test players from page 246.

a'Beckett, Edward Clive (Vic) b Jan. 18, 1940 East Melbourne (Vic)

a'Beckett, Edward Fitzhayley (Vic) b April 16, 1836 Holborn, London, (England) d March 25, 1922 Upper Beaconsfield (Vic)

* a'Beckett, Edward Lambert (Vic) b Aug. 11, 1907 East St Kilda (Vic) d June 2, 1989 Terang (Vic)

a'Beckett, Malwyn (Vic) b Sept. 26, 1834 London, Middlesex (England) d June 25, 1906 Sale (Vic)

Abell, William (Qld) b April 16, 1874 Leeds, Yorkshire (England) d June 10, 1960 Herston (Qld)

Achurch, Claude Septimus (NSW) b Aug. 16, 1896 Dubbo (NSW) d Aug. 15, 1979 Nambour (Qld)

Adams, Edward William (NSW) b July 10, 1896 Bathurst (NSW) d May 25, 1977 Bexley (NSW)

Adams, Francis (NSW) b Feb. 12, 1835 Doohat, County Fermanagh (Ireland) d Feb. 10, 1911 North Sydney (NSW)

Adams, James William (Qld) b Feb. 22, 1904 Toowong (Qld) d Jan. 8, 1988 Willoughby (NSW)

Adamson, Charles Young (Qld) b April 18, 1875 Neville's Cross, Durham (England) d Sept. 17, 1918 Salonica (Greece)

Adcock, Nathan Tennyson (SAust) b April 22, 1978 Campbelltown (SAust)

Addison, Alexander Gollan (Tas) b Sept. 29, 1877 Adelaide (SAust) d Oct. 12, 1935 Double Bay (NSW)

Ainslie, James (Vic) b June 9, 1880 Elsternwick (Vic) d Dec. 31, 1953 St Kilda (Vic)

Albury, William Douglas (Qld) b Feb. 9, 1947 Herston (Qld)

* Alderman, Terence Michael (WAust) b June 12, 1956 Subiaco (WAust)

Aldridge, Keith John (Tas) b March 13, 1935 Evesham, Worcestershire (England)

Alexander, Francis James (WAust) b April 15, 1911 Perth (WAust)

* Alexander, George (Vic) b April 22, 1851 Oxfordshire (England) d Nov. 6, 1930 East Melbourne (Vic)

* Alexander, Henrry Houston (Vic) b June 9, 1905 Ascot Vale (Vic) d April 15, 1993 East Melbourne (Vic)

Alexander, Leonard James (Tas) b Sept. 1, 1922 Hobart (Tas)

Alexander, William Colin (SAust) b Sept. 14, 1907 Gawler (SAust) d Feb. 8, 1993 Melbourne (Vic)

* Allan, Francis Erskine (Vic) b Dec. 2, 1849 Allansford (Vic) d Feb. 9, 1917 East Melbourne (Vic)

Allan, George Harold (Tas) b Feb. 18, 1887 Albury (NSW) d Nov. 2, 1932 Adelaide (SAust)

Allan, Henry Alexander (NSW) b Jan. 6, 1846 Westminster, London, Middlesex (England) d Apr. 26, 1926 East Melbourne (Vic)

* Allan, Peter John (Qld) b Dec. 31, 1935 Coorparoo (Qld)

Allanby, Nicholas John (Tas) b Aug. 24, 1957 Hobart (Tas)

Allanby, Richard Andrew (Tas) b July 26, 1971 Hobart (Tas)

Allanson, Noel Laurence (Vic) b Dec. 25, 1925 North Carlton (Vic)

Allardice, Geoffrey John (Vic) b May 7, 1967 Melbourne (Vic)

Allee, Charles George (Vic) b Feb. 10, 1848 Melbourne (Vic) d June 7, 1896 East Melbourne (Vic)

Allen, Donald John (Qld) b Feb. 26, 1947 Lismore (NSW)

Allen, Donald Radford (Vic) b Dec. 13, 1926 East St Kilda (Vic)

Allen, Harold Eric (Tas) b Oct. 13, 1886 Invercargill (New Zealand) d July 9, 1939 West Hobart (Tas)

Allen, Harold Hedley (Tas) b Nov. 15, 1940 Latrobe (Tas)

Allen, Jeremy Michael (WAust) b June 11, 1971 Subiaco (WAust)

Allen, Leslie Graham (Tas) b Sept. 13, 1954 Wynyard (Tas)

* Allen, Reginald Charles (NSW) b July 2, 1858 Glebe (NSW) d May 2, 1952 Sydney (NSW)

Allen, Ross Thomas (Qld) b Aug. 12, 1939 Toowoomba (Qld)

Allen, Thomas (Qld) b Sept. 5, 1912 Toowoomba (Qld) d March 18, 1954 Cambooya (Qld)

Allen, Thorpe (Qld) b March 7, 1870 Oxley (Qld) d Jan. 25, 1950 East Brisbane (Qld)

Allen, William Miller (Vic) b July 7, 1889 Ballarat (Vic) d Nov. 13, 1948 Ringwood (Vic)

Alley, Phillip John Sydney (SAust & NSW) b July 26, 1970 Orange (NSW)

Alley, William Edward (NSW) b Feb. 3, 1919 Hornsby (NSW)

Alleyne, John Placid (NSW) b Aug. 1, 1908 Glebe (NSW) d June 24, 1980 Glebe (NSW)

Allison, Henry (Tas) b July 14, 1828 Campbell Town (Tas) d May 12, 1881 Coupeville Island, Washington (USA)

Allsopp, Arthur Henry (NSW & Vic) b March 1, 1908 Lithgow (NSW) d Feb. 6, 1993 Chadstone (Vic)

Alsop, Charles James (Vic) b Nov. 24, 1868 Moonee Ponds (Vic) d Sept. 17, 1948 Melbourne (Vic)

Amalfi, Anthony John (Vic) b Jan. 19, 1967 East Melbourne (Vic)

Ambler, Albert Mark (SAust) b Sept. 27, 1892 Murray Bridge (SAust) d Nov. 27, 1970 Prospect (SAust)

Amos, Gordon Stanley (NSW & Qld) b April 4, 1905 Newtown (NSW) d April 7, 1995 Labrador (Qld)

Amos, William (SAust) b April 20, 1860 Glen Osmond (SAust) d May 14, 1935 North Adelaide (SAust)

Anderson, Allan David (NSW) b April 22, 1949 Greenwich (NSW)

Anderson, Dale Thomas (Tas) b June 10, 1931 Latrobe (Tas)

Anderson, David John (Vic) b Jan. 26, 1940 Warrnambool (Vic)

Anderson, James William Falconer (Qld) b Feb. 25, 1889 birth place unknown (Qld) d Dec. 8, 1951 Bellevue Hill (NSW)

Anderson, John Gregory (Vic) b Feb. 15, 1955 East Melbourne (Vic)

Anderson, John Theodore (WAust) b Aug. 10, 1878 Warrnambool (Vic) d Aug. 29, 1926 South Yarra (Vic)

Anderson, Matthew Allan (Qld) b Nov. 30, 1976 Darwin (NT)

Anderson, Peter Gordon (NSW) b Oct. 4, 1933 Hawthorn (Vic)

Anderson, Peter McKenzie (Vic) b Sept. 17, 1968 Geelong (Vic)

Anderson, Peter William (Qld & SAust) b May 22, 1961 South Brisbane (Qld)

Andrew-Street, Alfred Gordon (Vic) b April 8, 1914 Bondi (NSW) d Dec. 13, 1984 Concord (NSW)

* Andrews, Thomas James Edwin (NSW) b Aug. 26, 1890 Newtown (NSW) d Jan. 28, 1970 Croydon (NSW)

Andrews, Wayne Stewart (WAust) b Nov. 19, 1958 Melbourne (Vic)

Andrews, William Charles (NSW & Qld) b July 14, 1908 West Maitland (NSW) d June 9, 1962 Bombay (India)

* Angel, Jo (WAust) b April 22, 1968 Mt Lawley (WAust)

Antill, Thomas Wills (Vic) b Nov. 20, 1830 Jarvisfield (NSW) d May 11, 1865 Nelson (New Zealand)

Appleton, Leslie Joseph Francis (Tas) b Sept. 28, 1947 Hobart (Tas)

Archer, Daniel John Lancelot (Tas) b June 17, 1939 Launceston (Tas)

* Archer, Kenneth Alan (Qld) b Jan. 17, 1928 Yeerongpilly (Qld)

* Archer, Ronald Graham (Qld) b Oct. 25, 1933 Highgate Hill (Qld)

Armstrong, Edward Killeen (Qld) b Feb. 15, 1881 Milton (Qld) d April 29, 1963 Brisbane (Qld)

Armstrong, George Gort (Qld) b Dec. 29, 1882 Milton (Qld) d Jan. 12, 1956 Brisbane (Qld)

Armstrong, Glenarvon Huntley (SAust) b Nov. 17, 1969 Hobart (Tas)

Armstrong, Thomas Goldsmith (Vic) b Oct. 31, 1889 Caulfield (Vic) d April 15, 1963 Bairnsdale (Vic)

* Armstrong, Warwick Windridge (Vic) b May 22, 1879 Kyneton (Vic) d July 13, 1947 Darling Point (NSW)

Armstrong, William Anthony (Qld) b May 2, 1886 Milton (Qld) d May 29, 1955 Brisbane (Qld)

Arnberger, Jason Lee (NSW & Vic) b Nov. 18, 1972 Penrith (NSW)

Arnold, Colin Robert (Tas) b Aug. 19, 1957 Devonport (Tas)

Arnold, Evan Matthew Campbell (SAust) b Aug. 20, 1974 North Adelaide (SAust)

Arnold, Weller (Tas) b Sept. 23, 1882 North Hobart (Tas) d Oct. 28, 1957 Hobart (Tas)

Arnott, Percival Sinclair (NSW) b July 9, 1889 Newcastle (NSW) d Dec. 23, 1950 Camperdown (NSW)

Arthur, Charles (Tas) b Feb. 5, 1808 Plymouth, Devon (England) d July 29, 1884 Longford (Tas)

Arthur, George Henry (Tas) b March 10, 1849 Longford (Tas) d Oct. 13, 1932 Longford (Tas)

Arthur, Gerald Charles (WAust) b July 25, 1913 Yarloop (WAust)

Arthur, John Lake Allen (Tas) b April 7, 1847 Longford (Tas) d April 26, 1877 Longford (Tas)

Asher, Oswald Philip (NSW) b May 21, 1891 Paddington (NSW) d July 16, 1970 Waverton (NSW)

Ashley, Nathan William (Cricket Academy) b Oct. 3, 1973 St Leonard's (NSW)

Astley, Graeme Patrick (Tas) b March 31, 1957 Sydney (NSW)

Atkins, Arthur Alfred (Qld & NSW) b April 22, 1874 (NSW) death details unknown

Atkinson, James Archibald (Vic & Tas) b April 4, 1896 North Fitzroy (Vic) d June 11, 1956 Beaconsfield (Tas)

Atkinson, Mark Neville (Tas) b Feb. 11, 1969 Sydney (NSW)

Atkinson, Mark Peter (WAust) b Nov. 27, 1970 Bentley (WAust)

Attenborough, Geoffrey Robert (SAust) b Jan. 17, 1951 Mile End (SAust)

Austen, Ernest Thomas (Vic) b Sept. 23, 1900 Hawthorn (Vic) d June 21, 1983 Donvale (Vic)

Austen, Victor Cecil (SAust) b Nov. 30, 1918 Kew (Vic)

Austin, Harold MacPherson (Vic) b March 8, 1903 Skipton (Vic) d July 31, 1981 Timboon (Vic)

Austin, Sydney Walter (NSW & Qld) b Nov. 16, 1866 Sydney (NSW) d Sept. 11, 1932 Randwick (NSW)

Auty, Clinton (WAust) b Oct. 29, 1969 Auckland (New Zealand)

Aylett, Allen James (Vic) b April 24, 1934 Melbourne (Vic)

Ayres, Ryall Sydney (Qld) b Sept. 1, 1931 Clayfield (Qld) d Nov. 24, 1991 Sydney (NSW)

Ayres, Sydney William (Qld) b Aug. 7, 1889 Enmore (NSW) d Aug. 7, 1974 Castle Hill (NSW)

Ayres, Warren Geoffrey (Vic) b Oct. 25, 1965 Moorabbin (Vic)

Back, William (WAust) b c. 1856 Rottnest Island (WAust) d Feb. 15, 1911 Perth (WAust)

Backman, Charles James (SAust) b April 11, 1884 Adelaide (SAust) d April 25, 1915 Gallipoli (Turkey)

* Badcock, Clayvel Lindsay (Tas & SAust) b April 10, 1914 Exton (Tas) d Dec. 13, 1982 Exton (Tas)

Badcock, Kevin Bruce (Tas) b March 24, 1951 Launceston (Tas)

Bagshaw, Kenneth James (SAust) b Oct. 22, 1920 Kadina (SAust) d Oct. 8, 1985 Watson (ACT)

Bailey, Alfred John Thomas Slater (SAust) b March 3, 1932 North Adelaide (SAust)

Bailey, Bertram Theodore (SAust) b Dec. 5, 1874 Adelaide (SAust) d Oct. 3, 1964 Payneham (SAust)

Bailey, Ernest Albert (SAust) b Nov. 15, 1881 Adelaide (SAust) d Aug. 16, 1966 Northfield (SAust)

Bailey, George Herbert (Tas) b Oct. 29, 1853 Colombo (Ceylon) d Oct. 10, 1926 Hobart (Tas)

Bailey, George Keith Brooke (Tas) b Jan. 3, 1882 Hobart (Tas) d June 17, 1964 Hobart (Tas)

Bailey, Peter George (Vic) b Aug. 16, 1939 Glenhuntly (Vic)

Bailey, Rowland Herbert (Vic) b Oct. 5, 1876 Melbourne (Vic) d March 24, 1950 Ivanhoe (Vic)

Bailey, William Henry (Vic) b July 20, 1898 Condoblin (NSW) d Feb. 27, 1983 Geelong (Vic)

Baird, James George (Vic) b Nov. 9, 1920 Parkville (Vic) d Nov. 4, 2003 Sandringham (Vic)

Baird, Keith Hugh (WAust) b Dec. 27, 1911 Perth (WAust) d July 18, 1965 Peppermint Grove (WAust)

Baker, Charles Michael (Vic) b June 18, 1880 Ballarat East (Vic) d May 4, 1962 Ballarat (Vic)

Baker, Charles Ronald (NSW) b March 24, 1939 Islington (NSW)

Baker, Dennis James (WAust & Tas) b Dec. 29, 1947 Norseman (WAust)

Baker, Everard Audley (Vic) b July 28, 1913 Cohuna (Vic) d March 30, 1987 Melbourne (Vic)

Baker, Frederick (Vic) b Aug. 5, 1851 (England) d Sept. 14, 1939 Perth (WAust)

Baker, Glen George (Qld) b Aug. 9, 1915 Townsville (Qld) d Dec. 15, 1943 Buna (Papua New Guinea) on active service

Baker, Leigh James (Vic) b Sept. 20, 1951 Oakleigh (Vic)

Baker, Robert Michael (WAust) b July 24, 1975 Osborne Park (WAust)

Bakker, Jason Richard (Vic) b Nov. 12, 1967 Geelong (Vic)

Balcam, Leonard Frank (Qld & Vic) b Aug. 20, 1957 Footscray (Vic)

Baldock, Darrel John (Tas) b Sept. 29, 1938 Devonport (Tas)

Baldry, Robert John (Vic) b Nov. 30, 1950 Warragul (Vic)

Ball, Thomas Edward (Qld) b Dec. 3, 1921 Atherton (Qld) d Jan. 13, 2002 Cairns (Qld)

Ballans, David Murray (SAust) b June 30, 1868 at sea d June 26, 1957 Goodwood Park (SAust)

Bandy, Lawrence Henry (WAust) b Sept. 3, 1911 Perth (WAust) d July 18, 1984 Scarborough (WAust)

Banks, Albert James (WAust) b Dec. 10, 1883 Maryborough (Vic) d July 5, 1930 Toodyay (WAust)

* Bannerman, Alexander Chalmers (NSW) b March 21, 1854 Paddington (NSW) d Sept. 19, 1924 Paddington (NSW)

* Bannerman, Charles (NSW) b July 23, 1851 Woolwich, Kent (England) d Aug. 20, 1930 Surry Hills (NSW)

Barbour, Eric Pitty (NSW) b Jan. 27, 1891 Ashfield (NSW) d Dec. 7, 1934 Darlinghurst (NSW)

Barbour, Robert Roy (Qld) b March 29, 1899 Ashfield (NSW) d Dec. 29, 1994 Berwick (Vic)

Bardsley, Raymond (NSW) b Jan. 19, 1894 Glebe Point (NSW) d June 25, 1983 Rose Bay (NSW)

* Bardsley, Warren (NSW) b Dec. 6, 1882 Nevertire (NSW) d Jan. 20, 1954 Collaroy (NSW)

Baring, Frederick Albert (Vic) b Dec. 15, 1890 Hotham East (Vic) d Dec. 10, 1961 Doncaster (Vic)

Baring, Hugh Thomas (Vic) b Aug. 17, 1906 East Melbourne (Vic) d July 9, 1968 Fitzroy (Vic)

Barnard, Francis George Allman (Vic) b Dec. 26, 1857 Kew (Vic) d June 1, 1932 Melbourne (Vic)

Barnes, James Charles (NSW) b Oct. 16, 1882 Alexandria (NSW) death details unknown

Barnes, Jeffrey Robert (SAust) b Jan. 9, 1948 Glenelg (SAust)

Barnes, John Francis (Qld) b Sept. 27, 1916 Rockhampton (Qld)

Barnes, John Robert (Vic) b May 20, 1905 Williamstown (Vic) d Oct. 6, 1999 Williamstown (Vic)

Barnes, Richard (Tas) b 1849 (Ireland) d April 30, 1902 Heidelberg (Vic)

* Barnes, Sydney George (NSW) b June 5, 1916 Annandale (NSW) d Dec. 16, 1973 Collaroy (NSW)

* Barnett, Benjamin Arthur (Vic) b March 23, 1908 Auburn (Vic) d June 27, 1979 Newcastle (NSW)

Barras, Alexander Edward Owen (WAust) b Jan. 26, 1914 Auburn (Vic) d Aug. 15, 1986 Mt Lawley (WAust)

Barrett, Edgar Alfred (Vic) b June 26, 1869 Emerald Hill (Vic) d April 29, 1959 Kew (Vic)

Barrett, Henry (Tas) b Aug. 19, 1837 Launceston (Tas) d Sept. 10, 1910 Westbury (Tas)

* Barrett, John Edward (Vic) b Oct. 15, 1866 Emerald Hill (Vic) d Feb. 6, 1916 Peak Hill (WAust)

Barsby, Trevor John (Qld) b Jan. 16, 1964 Herston (Qld)

Barstow, Charles Banks (Qld) b March 13, 1883 Brisbane (Qld) d July 12, 1935 Eagle Junction (Qld)

Bartlett, Albert James (SAust) b April 23, 1900 Parkside (SAust) d Oct. 6, 1968 Woodville South (SAust)

Bartlett, Robert Andrew (Vic) b Jan. 2, 1972 Melbourne (Vic)

Bassano, Christopher Warwick Godfrey (Tas) b Sept. 11, 1975 East London (South Africa)

Bateman, William Augustus (WAust) b Sept. 11, 1866 Fremantle (WAust) d July 27, 1935 South Perth (WAust)

Bates, Barry (NSW) b July 1, 1939 Mayfield (NSW)

Bayles, Robert Charles Alfred Vivian (Tas) b July 7, 1892 Ross (Tas) d May 16, 1959 Launceston (Tas)

Bayles, William Headlam (Tas) b Jan. 8, 1896 Ross (Tas) d Dec. 17, 1960 Launceston (Tas)

Bayliss, Trevor Harley (NSW) b Dec. 21, 1962 Goulburn (NSW)

Bayly, Henry Vincent (Tas) b Nov. 19, 1850 Dulcot (Tas) d Jan. 7, 1903 New Town (Tas)

Beacham, George (Vic) b Oct. 27, 1867 (Qld) d Jan. 11, 1925 South Fitzroy (Vic)

Beagley, John William (SAust) b March 23, 1933 Adelaide (SAust)

Beal, Charles William (Australians) b June 24, 1855 Sydney (NSW) d Feb. 5, 1921 Randwick (NSW)

Beal, James Charles (NSW) b May 26, 1830 Sydney (NSW) d Aug. 24, 1904 Milton (Qld)

Beames, Percy James (Vic) b July 27, 1911 Ballarat (Vic) d April 28, 2004 Kew (Vic)

Bean, Ernest Edward (Vic) b April 17, 1866 Miner's Rest, near Ballarat (Vic) d March 22, 1939 Hampton (Vic)

Beard, Barry Allan (Tas) b Dec. 21, 1941 Bothwell (Tas) d June 9, 2001 Ulverstone (Tas)

* Beard, Graeme Robert (NSW) b Aug. 19, 1950 Auburn (NSW)

Beath, Neville Ray James (NSW) b Nov. 12, 1921 Goolagong (NSW) d Nov. 22, 1987 Richmond (NSW)

Beattie, Simon Guy (Qld) b Dec. 10, 1958 Junee (NSW)

Beatty, Christopher (NSW) b Oct. 21, 1952 Newcastle (NSW)

Beatty, Reginald George (NSW) b Dec. 24, 1913 Wickham (NSW) d May 27, 1957 Waratah (NSW)

Becker, Gordon Charles (WAust) b March 14, 1935 Katanning (WAust)

Bedford, Albert Austen (SAust) b Sept. 12, 1932 Rose Park (SAust) d March 25, 2001 Noarlunga (SAust)

Bedford, Peter Lawrence Anthony (Vic) b April 11, 1947 Melbourne (Vic)

Bednall, Philip Malcolm (SAust) b Jan. 27, 1931 Burra (SAust)

Beeston, John Lievesley (NSW) b Jan. 17, 1831 Bingley Locks, Yorkshire (England) d June 1, 1873 Newcastle (NSW)

Beeston, Norman Charles (Qld) b Sept. 29, 1900 Brisbane (Qld) d Feb. 4, 1985 Brisbane (Qld)

Belcher, Samuel Harborne (NSW) b Nov. 1, 1834 (England) d Aug. 22, 1920 Garroorigang (NSW)

Bell, John Clifford (Qld) b Jan. 18, 1949 Ipswich (Qld)

* Benaud, John (NSW) b May 11, 1944 Auburn (NSW)

* Benaud, Richard (NSW) b Oct. 6, 1930 Penrith (NSW)

Benbow, Ernest Aldred (Qld) b March 14, 1888 Mt Walker (Qld) d Dec. 28, 1940 Springsure (Qld)

Bendixen, Hilton Fewtrell (Qld) b Feb. 21, 1910 Nambour (Qld) d April 15, 1962 Nambour (Qld)

Benjamin, Emmanuel (Tas) b Feb. 2, 1955 Jullundur City (India)

Bennett, Albert (NSW) b May 21, 1910 St Helens, Lancashire (England) d c. 1985 full death details unknown

Bennett, Floyd Chester (SAust & WAust) b April 12, 1919 North Perth (WAust) d Nov. 26, 1997 Stirling (SAust)

Bennett, George Henry (NSW) b Aug. 16, 1906 Brookvale (NSW) d c. 1984 full death details unknown

Bennett, Harry Francis (WAust) b June 22, 1859 Prahran (Vic) d Oct. 4, 1898 Guildford (WAust)

Bennett, Joseph (Vic) birth and death details unknown

* Bennett, Murray John (NSW) b Oct. 6, 1956 Brisbane (Qld)

Bennett, Rex Leland (SAust & Tas) b June 25, 1896 Snowtown (SAust) d Dec. 14, 1963 Collaroy (NSW)

Bennett, Richard John (Tas) b June 5, 1965 Launceston (Tas)

Bennett, Thomas (SAust) b Oct. 11, 1866 Littlehampton (SAust) d Dec. 26, 1942 Northfield (SAust)

Bennetts, Gordon Kissack (Vic) b March 26, 1909 Wellington (NSW) d April 4, 1987 Geelong (Vic)

Benneworth, Anthony John (Tas) b Dec. 12, 1949 Launceston (Tas)

Bennison, James Ernest (Tas) b Feb. 16, 1854 Hobart (Tas) d Nov. 14, 1916 Hobart (Tas)

Bensley, Gary Robert (NSW) b Oct. 17, 1958 Inverell (NSW)

Bensted, Eric Charles (Qld) b Feb. 11, 1901 Killarney (Qld) d March 24, 1980 Brisbane (Qld)

Benton, Jeffrey John (SAust) b Oct. 9, 1953 Mildura (Vic)

Bernard, Stephen Russell (NSW) b Dec. 28, 1949 Orange (NSW)

Berrie, Edward Bruce (NSW) b April 8, 1884 Tomenbil, near Forbes (NSW) d Dec. 8, 1963 Tamworth (NSW)

Berry, Darren Shane (Vic & SAust) b Dec. 10, 1969 Melbourne (Vic)

Berry, Walter Lyall (NSW) b April 9, 1893 Woolwich (NSW) d April 20, 1970 Ettalong Beach (NSW)

Bessen, Mervyn Oscar (WAust) b Aug. 29, 1913 Tambellup (WAust) d July 13, 2002 Mandurah (WAust)

Best, Leslie (NSW) b Nov. 20, 1893 Seven Hills (NSW) d Aug. 27, 1925 Sydney (NSW)

Bettington, Brindley Cecil John (NSW) b Sept. 2, 1898 Parramatta (NSW) d Aug. 26, 1931 Merriwa (NSW)

Bettington, Reginald Henshall Brindley (NSW) b Feb. 24, 1900 Parramatta (NSW) d June 24, 1969 Gisborne (New Zealand)

Betts, Arthur John (Tas) b Feb. 26, 1880 Launceston (Tas) d Aug. 4, 1948 Belgrave (Vic)

Bevan, Hubert George (WAust) b Dec. 21, 1932 Perth (WAust)

Bevan, John Lawrence (SAust) b May 10, 1846 Swansea, Glamorgan (Wales) d March 31, 1918 Portland Estate (SAust)

* Bevan, Michael Gwyl (SAust & NSW) b May 8, 1970 Belconnen (ACT)

Beven, Ian Robert (Tas) b Nov. 27, 1958 Hobart (Tas)

* Bichel, Andrew John (Qld) b Aug. 27, 1970 Laidley (Qld)

Bichel, Donald Alan (Qld) b May 4, 1935 Lowood (Qld)

Bidstrup, Trevor Allan (WAust) b Dec. 29, 1937 Midland (WAust)

Biffin, Raymond Leo (Tas) b May 6, 1949 Launceston (Tas)

Biggs, Malcolm (Qld) b July 7, 1904 Caboolture (Qld) d Aug. 1, 1972 Ipswich (Qld)

Bill, Oscar Wendell (NSW) b April 8, 1909 Waverley (NSW) d May 10, 1988 Sydney (NSW)

Bingham, John Edmund (Tas) b July 15, 1864 Forcett (Tas) d July 23, 1946 Hobart (Tas)

Binney, Edgar James (Vic) b May 31, 1885 Port Tremayne (SAust) d Sept. 9, 1978 Brighton (Vic)

Birch, William Thomas (Tas) b Oct. 26, 1849 Hobart (Tas) d Aug. 18, 1897 Hobart (Tas)

Birchall, James Thomas Wardlaw (SAust) b Nov. 23, 1962 North Adelaide (SAust)

Bird, Thomas Robert (Vic) b Aug. 31, 1904 Collingwood (Vic) d April 12, 1979 Thornbury (Vic)

Bishop, Edward George (WAust) b Aug. 4, 1872 birthplace unknown d Feb. 16, 1943 Nedlands (WAust)

Bishop, Glenn Andrew (SAust) b Feb. 25, 1960 North Adelaide (SAust)

Bishop, Henry Symons (Vic) b Dec. 15, 1849 Torrington, Devon (England) d July 18, 1891 Prahran (Vic)

Bitmead, Robert Clyde (Vic) b July 17, 1942 Fitzroy (Vic)

Bizzell, Graham Maurice (Qld) b Nov. 19, 1941 Beenleigh (Qld)

Black, Alfred A. (Vic) birth details unknown d c. 1859

Black, George Gordon (NSW) b Jan. 19, 1885 Darling Point (NSW) d Dec. 6, 1954 Orange (NSW)

Black, Graham Ash (SAust) b May 14, 1924 Unley (SAust)

* Blackham, John McCarthy (Vic) b May 11, 1854 North Fitzroy (Vic) d Dec. 28, 1932 Melbourne (Vic)

* Blackie, Donald Dearness (Vic) b April 5, 1882 Bendigo (Vic) d April 18, 1955 South Melbourne (Vic)

Blackman, Oswald Colin (NSW) b March 9, 1942 Griffith (NSW)

Blackstock, John MacDonald (Qld) b Jan. 16, 1871 Drum, Thornhill, Edinburgh (Scotland) d post-1945 Sydney (NSW)

Blair, Dennis John (Tas) b Sept. 27, 1934 Bulawayo (Southern Rhodesia)

Blair, Gregory David (Tas & Vic) b Dec. 15, 1947 Launceston (Tas)

Blanchard, Charles Joseph (Surrey) details unknowndetails unknown

Blaxland, Marcus Herbert (NSW & Qld) b April 29, 1884 Callan Park (NSW) d July 31, 1958 Clayfield (Qld)

* Blewett, Gregory Scott (SAust) b Oct. 29, 1971 North Adelaide (SAust)

Blewett, Robert Kevin (SAust) b March 30, 1943 Prospect (SAust)

Blinman, Harry (SAust) b Dec. 30, 1861 Adelaide (SAust) d July 23, 1950 Adelaide (SAust)

Blizzard, Phillip Ashley (Tas & NSW) b Feb. 6, 1958 Burnie (Tas)

Bloomfield, George Thomas (SAust) b Feb. 5, 1882 Bowden (SAust) d Nov. 1, 1958 Adelaide (SAust)

Blundell, George Robert (WAust) b April 19, 1896 Perth (WAust) d Feb. 11, 1940 West Perth (WAust)

Blundell, Norman Charles (Vic) b Sept. 2, 1917 North Carlton (Vic)

Blundell, Rex Pole (SAust) b May 8, 1942 Adelaide (SAust)

Blundell, William Walter (Vic) b Dec. 30, 1866 Majorca (Vic) d Feb. 28, 1946 Kensington (Vic)

Boag, Kenneth John (Qld) b Sept. 6, 1914 Toowoomba (Qld) d July 10, 1984 Port Kembla (NSW)

Boddam, Edmund Tudor (Tas) b Nov. 23, 1879 Hobart (Tas) d Sept. 9, 1959 New Town (Tas)

Bogle, James (NSW) b Jan. 4, 1893 Mossgiel (NSW) d Oct. 19, 1963 Southport (Qld)

Bollinger, Douglas (NSW) b July 24, 1981 Baulkham Hills (NSW)

Bolton, John Turner (Qld) b Oct. 3, 1888 Riverstone (NSW)

* Bonnor, George John (Vic & NSW) b Feb. 25, 1855 Bathurst (NSW) d June 27, 1912 East Orange (NSW)

* Boon, David Clarence (Tas) b Dec. 29, 1960 Launceston (Tas)

* Booth, Brian Charles (NSW) b Oct. 19, 1933 Perthville (NSW)

Booth, Ernest Brian Nelson (Tas) b Sept. 30, 1924 Scottsdale (Tas)

* Border, Allan Robert (NSW & Qld) b July 27, 1955 Cremorne (NSW)

Borgas, Cameron James (SAust) b Sept. 1, 1983 Flinders (SAust)

Bosley, Marcus Williams (NSW) b Aug. 10, 1897 Liverpool (NSW) d June 12, 1982 Ashfield (NSW)

* Botham, Ian Terence (Qld) b Nov. 24, 1955 Heswall, Cheshire (England)

Botham, Leslie John (Vic) b May 5, 1930 Hawthorn (Vic) d April 17, 1999 Melbourne (Vic)

Bott, Leonidas Cecil (WAust) b July 14, 1889 Adelaide (SAust) d Aug. 21, 1968 Perth (WAust)

Botten, Robert Dyas (SAust) b Oct. 11, 1853 Lewisham, Kent (England) d April 26, 1935 Medindie (SAust)

Boulter, Edward Samuel (Vic) b March 23, 1886 North Fitzroy (Vic) d June 10, 1968 North Balwyn (Vic)

Bourne, Gordon Alister (Qld) b April 21, 1913 Tintenbar (NSW) d Sept. 13, 1993 Goomeri (Qld)

Bovell, Henry Edward Joseph (WAust) b March 15, 1936 East Fremantle (WAust)

Bowden, Albert John (NSW) b Sept. 28, 1874 Sydney (NSW) d Aug. 8, 1943 Northwood (NSW)

Bowden, Samuel Hedskis (Qld) b Sept. 29, 1867 Sydney (NSW) d Aug. 25, 1945 Manly (NSW)

Bowe, Ronald Doig (WAust) b Dec. 10, 1939 Beaconsfield (WAust)

Bower, Rodney John (NSW) b Nov. 30, 1959 Bankstown (NSW)

Bower, Timothy Donald (Tas) b Sept. 10, 1968 Devonport (Tas)

Bowler, Peter Duncan (Tas) b July 30, 1963 Plymouth, Devon (England)

Bowley, Bruce Leonard (SAust) b Jan. 1, 1922 Clare (SAust)

Bowley, Edwin Leonard (SAust) b Feb. 27, 1888 Clare (SAust) d April 22, 1963 Woodville (SAust)

Bowman, Alcon Ninus Ascot (Vic) b May 10, 1862 Ascot Vale (Vic) d June 30, 1938 Surrey Hills (Vic)

Box, Henry (Vic) b c. Sept. 1837 Walshall, London, Middlesex (England) death details unknown

Boyce, Raymond Charles Manning (NSW) b June 28, 1891 Taree (NSW) d Jan. 20, 1941 Northwood (NSW)

Boyd, David Laurence (WAust) b Nov. 21, 1955 Kalgoorlie (WAust)

Boyd, Trevor Joseph (NSW) b Oct. 22, 1944 Nyngan (NSW)

* Boyle, Henry Frederick (Vic) b Dec. 10, 1847 Sydney (NSW) d Nov. 21, 1907 Bendigo (Vic)

Brabon, George William (Qld) b Aug. 2, 1957 Ayr (Qld)

Bracher, Herbert Henry Gladstone (Vic) b Aug. 28, 1886 Footscray (Vic) d Feb. 25, 1974 Donvale (Vic)

* Bracken, Nathan Wade (NSW) b Sept. 12, 1977 Penrith (NSW)

Bradbridge, John Sidney (NSW) b Dec. 1, 1831 Sydney (NSW) d July 14, 1905 Dulwich Hill (NSW)

Bradley, Craig Edwin (SAust & Vic) b Oct. 23, 1964 Ashford (SAust)

Bradley, William Francis (Qld) b Oct. 8, 1867 Brisbane (Qld) d Sept. 7, 1948 Ipswich (Qld)

* Bradman, Donald George (NSW & SAust) b Aug. 27, 1908 Cootamundra (NSW) d Feb. 25, 2001 Kensington Park (SAust)

Bradridge, John Sidney (NSW) b Dec. 1, 1831 Sydney (NSW) d July 14, 1905 Dulwich Hill (NSW)

Bradshaw, Keith (Tas) b Oct. 2, 1963 Hobart (Tas)

Bradstreet, Shawn David (NSW) b Feb. 28, 1972 Wollongong (NSW)

Braid, Rupert Lee (Vic) b March 3, 1888 Talbot (Vic) d Nov. 11, 1963 Upper Ferntree Gully (Vic)

Brain, Desmond Morrah (Tas) b Dec. 16, 1909 Hobart (Tas) d March 1, 1990 Tumut (NSW)

Brain, John Heather (Tas) b Feb. 9, 1905 Hobart (Tas) d June 21, 1961 Hobart (Tas)

Brain, Roy Albert (Tas) b Sept. 2, 1926 Hobart (Tas)

Braithwaite, Arthur (Tas) b Sept. 2, 1880 Rushworth (Vic) d Dec. 19, 1953 Cheltenham (Vic)

Brakey, Gary Leslie (Combined XI) b Oct. 8, 1942 Wynyard (Tas) d Feb. 3, 1987 Killarney Heights (NSW)

Brant, Scott Andrew (Qld) b Jan. 26, 1983 Harare (Zimbabwe)

Braslin, Leon Anthony (Tas) b May 12, 1938 New Norfolk (Tas)

Bratchford, James Douglas (Qld) b Feb. 2, 1929 Cleveland (Qld) d Oct. 5, 1997 on flight from USA to Australia

Braybrook, Clive (SAust) b Sept. 27, 1901 Goodwood (SAust) d July 16, 1985 Swan Hill (Vic)

Brayshaw, Ian James (WAust) b Jan. 14, 1942 South Perth (WAust)

Brayshaw, James Antony (WAust & SAust) b May 11, 1967 Subiaco (WAust)

Breman, Todd George (WAust) b Oct. 28, 1965 Subiaco (WAust)

Bremner, Colin David (Services) b Jan. 29, 1920 Hawthorn (Vic) d June 13, 2002 Canberra (ACT)

Brew, Francis Malcolm (Qld) b Jan. 5, 1903 Petrie Terrace (Qld) d Jan. 13, 1974 Sandgate (Qld)

Brewster, Robert Colin (NSW) b Aug. 17, 1867 Sydney (NSW) d Nov. 8, 1962 Killara (NSW)

Briant, George William (Tas) b c. 1828 Hackney, London, Middlesex (England) d May 10, 1914 Hobart (Tas)

Brideson, John Holmes (SAust) b July 9, 1856 Rushworth (Vic) d Feb. 1, 1898 Belair (SAust)

Bridgman, Hugh Hossick Mackay (SAust) b Feb. 1, 1890 Findon (SAust) d Dec. 3, 1953 Torrensville (SAust)

Bridson, John (SAust) b Feb. 2, 1863 Fitzroy (Vic) d Feb. 1, 1898 Belair (SAust)

Briggs, Ronald Edward (NSW) b Sept. 22, 1929 Belmore (NSW) d Oct. 10, 2003 Katoomba (NSW)

* Bright, Raymond James (Vic) b July 13, 1954 Footscray (Vic)

Britt, Harold James (Vic) b May 6, 1911 Doncaster (Vic) d Sept. 20, 1988 Healesville (Vic)

Broad, David John (Vic) b Sept. 25, 1953 Kew (Vic)

Broad, Wayne Ronald (Qld) b June 20, 1956 Herston (Qld)

Broadby, Christopher Laurence (Tas) b March 17, 1959 Hobart (Tas)

Brodie, James Chalmers (Vic) b Sept. 28, 1820 Perth, Perthshire (Scotland) d Feb. 19, 1912 Balwyn (Vic)

Brodie, Richard Sinclair (Vic) b Sept. 9, 1813 County Caithness (Scotland) d Jan. 18, 1872 Bulla Bulla (Vic)

* Bromley, Ernest Harvey (WAust & Vic) b Sept. 3, 1912 Fremantle (WAust) d Feb. 1, 1967 Clayton (Vic)

Brooks, Gordon Victor (SAust) b May 30, 1938 Ceduna (SAust) d Jan. 31, 2004 Chermside (Qld)

Brooks, Thomas Francis (NSW) b March 28, 1919 Paddington (NSW)

Broomby, Reginald Arthur (Tas) b Jan. 6, 1905 Launceston (Tas) d May 10, 1984 Southport (Qld)

Broster, Paul Alexander (Vic) b Jan. 31, 1973 Wangaratta (Vic)

Broughton, Donald Ean (Tas) b Feb. 4, 1931 Hobart (Tas) d Dec. 11, 1987 Hobart (Tas)

Brown, Albert Ernest (Vic) b Dec. 22, 1890 Clifton Hill (Vic) d Nov. 17, 1954 Northcote (Vic)

Brown, Anthony Norman (Qld) b March 30, 1961 Herston (Qld)

Brown, Craig Franklin Archer (Tas) b Jan. 25, 1954 Hobart (Tas)

Brown, Edward (NSW) b c. Jan. 1837 Uppingham, Rutland (England) d full death details unknown

Brown, Edward Keith Faulkner (NSW) b March 7, 1891 Newcastle (NSW) d March 12, 1949 Bowenfels (NSW)

Brown, Graham Campbell (Vic) b May 9, 1944 Burwood (Vic)

Brown, Guy Archibald Loeman (Qld) b July 31, 1884 Dalby (Qld) d March 21, 1958 New Farm (Qld)

Brown, John (Qld) b May 13, 1943 Mt Morgan (Qld)

Brown, Kevin Ronald (Tas) b July 1, 1941 Devonport (Tas)

Brown, Norman Eric (Vic) b April 1, 1889 North Fitzroy (Vic) d July 7, 1962 Carrum (Vic)

Brown, Raymond Kinnear (Tas) b Nov. 3, 1950 New Norfolk (Tas)

Brown, Roger Leedham (Tas) b Aug. 9, 1959 Launceston (Tas)

Brown, Vallancey Kennedy (Vic) b Dec. 7, 1912 Ashfield (NSW) d Oct. 24, 1987 Melbourne (Vic)

Brown, Walter Graham Fairfax (NSW) b April 12, 1899 Summer Hill (NSW) d May 21, 1931 Mosman (NSW)

Brown, Wilfred Martin (Qld) b March 21, 1930 Warwick (Qld)

Brown, William (Tas) b c. 1807 (England) d Aug. 28, 1859 Hobart (Tas)

* Brown, William Alfred (NSW & Qld) b July 31, 1912 Toowoomba (Qld)

Browne, William Creighton (Qld) b Nov. 6, 1898 Toowoomba (Qld) d Oct. 25, 1980 Southport (Qld)

Browning, George Richard (Vic) b Dec. 12, 1858 Hepburn (Vic) d Oct. 9, 1900 North Carlton (Vic)

Brownlow, Bertie (Tas) b May 22, 1920 Portland (Vic)

* Bruce, William (Vic) b May 22, 1864 South Yarra (Vic) d Aug. 3, 1925 Elwood (Vic)

Bryant, Francis Joseph (WAust) b Nov. 7, 1907 Perth (WAust) d March 11, 1984 Glendalough (WAust)

Bryant, James Mark (Vic) b 1826 birth day and month unknown Caterham, Surrey (England) d Dec. 10, 1881 Sale (Vic)

Bryant, Richard (NSW) b c. 1847 Maitland (NSW) d Oct. 27, 1931 Stockton (NSW)

Bryant, Richard John (WAust) b May 8, 1904 Perth (WAust) d Aug. 17, 1989 Mt Lawley (WAust)

Bryant, William James (WAust) b Jan. 15, 1906 Perth (WAust) d Jan. 1, 1995 Perth (WAust)

Bryce, William Cecil James (Qld) b Aug. 18, 1911 Maryborough (Qld) d Feb. 8, 1986 Spring Hill (Qld)

Bubb, Ernest Reinhard (NSW) b Dec. 6, 1884 Summer Hill (NSW) d Nov. 26, 1946 Neutral Bay (NSW)

Bubb, Roy Alfred Reinhard (NSW) b June 23, 1900 Darlinghurst (NSW) d April 4, 1965 Hamilton (NSW)

Buchanan, John Marshall (Qld) b April 5, 1953 Ipswich (Qld)

Buckingham, Danny James (Tas) b Dec. 2, 1964 Burnie (Tas)

Buckle, Frank (NSW) b Nov. 11, 1891 Pyrmont (NSW) d June 4, 1982 Sydney (NSW)

Buckle, William Harvey (Qld) b June 3, 1943 Wooloowin (Qld)

Buggins, Bruce Leonard (WAust) b Jan. 29, 1935 Perth (WAust)

Bull, Desmond Frederick Earl (Qld) b Aug. 13, 1935 South Brisbane (Qld)

Bull, Eric Alister (NSW) b Sept. 28, 1886 Bourke (NSW) d May 14, 1954 Mt Kuring-Gai (NSW)

Bullough, Walter (SAust) b Oct. 21, 1855 Hunslet, Yorkshire (England) d Sept. 17, 1888 Hindmarsh (SAust)

Burchett, Alfred (Vic) b May 22, 1831 London, Middlesex (England) d Nov. 12, 1888 St Kilda (Vic)

Burchett, Frederick (Vic) b April 27, 1824 London, Middlesex (England) d July 16, 1861 Melbourne (Vic)

* Burge, Peter John Parnell (Qld) b May 17, 1932 Kangaroo Point (Qld) d Oct. 5, 2001 Main Beach (Qld)

* Burke, James Wallace (NSW) b June 12, 1930 Mosman (NSW) d Feb. 2, 1979 Manly (NSW)

* Burn, Edwin James Kenneth (Tas) b Sept. 17, 1862 Richmond (Tas) d July 20, 1956 Hobart (Tas)

Burn, James Henry (Tas) b July 31, 1849 Hobart (Tas), death details unknown

Burns, Harold Vincent (Qld) b May 20, 1908 Ebagoolah (Qld) d June 6, 1944 Cairns (Qld)

Burrows, Arthur Owen (Tas) b Oct. 17, 1903 Hobart (Tas) d Jan. 4, 1984 Sandy Bay (Tas)

Burrows, Ian Donald (Combined XI) b Nov. 20, 1944 Hobart (Tas)

Burrows, J. (NSW) birth and death details unknown

Burt, Selby John Wright (NSW) b Dec. 12, 1903 Hillgrove (NSW) d Feb. 14, 1959 Camperdown (NSW)

* Burton, Frederick John (NSW & Vic) b Nov. 2, 1865 Collingwood (Vic) d Aug. 25, 1929 Wanganui (New Zealand)

Burton, Garth (SAust) b Jan. 21, 1913 Black Forest (SAust) d Sept. 6, 1993 South Brighton (SAust)

Burton, Jack Richard (SAust) b Nov. 3, 1923 Cleve (SAust) d Oct. 30, 2001 Elizabeth Vale (SAust)

Bush, Giles Edmund Wreford (WAust) b Sept. 9, 1956 Subiaco (WAust)

* Butcher, Roland Orlando (Tas) b Oct. 14, 1953 East Point, St Philip (Barbados)

Butler, Charles William (Tas) b Sept. 18, 1854 Battery Point (Tas) d June 10, 1937 Sandy Bay (Tas)

Butler, Edward Henry (Tas & Vic) b March 15, 1851 Battery Point (Tas) d Jan. 5, 1928 Lower Sandy Bay (Tas)

Butler, Edward Lionel Austin (Tas) b April 10, 1883 Hobart (Tas) d Aug. 23, 1916 Puchevillers (France)

Butler, Frank (Tas) b Nov. 13, 1889 Brighton (Vic) d May 8, 1965 Kew (Vic)

Butler, Walter John (WAust) b May 30, 1882 Port Adelaide (SAust) d March 12, 1966 Bruce Rock (WAust)

Butterworth, Benjamin (Vic) b 1832 birth day and month unknown Rochdale, Lancashire (England) d Jan. 6, 1879 Chiswick, Middlesex (England)

Butterworth, Thomas (Vic) b Dec. 17, 1828 Rochdale, Lancashire (England) d July 15, 1877 Kensington, London (England)

Buttsworth, Frederick James (WAust) b May 29, 1927 North Perth (WAust)

Buttsworth, Frederick Richard (WAust) b April 28, 1880 Wilberforce (NSW) d Feb. 26, 1974 Perth (WAust)

Buttsworth, Wallace Francis (WAust) b Jan. 21, 1917 North Perth (WAust) d May 22, 2002 Milton (NSW)

Byfield, Arnold Stanley (WAust) b Nov. 1, 1923 Northam (WAust)

Byrne, Thomas (Qld) b July 11, 1868 Paterson (NSW) d Dec. 19, 1951 Herston (Qld)

Caban, Timothy Kenneth (Qld) b Feb. 15, 1952 Cessnock (NSW)

Caffyn, William (NSW) b Feb. 2, 1828 Reigate, Surrey (England) d Aug. 28, 1919 Reigate, Surrey (England)

Cahill, Keyran William Jack (Tas) b Dec. 3, 1911 Hobart (Tas) d March 7, 1966 Launceston (Tas)

Cain, William (Qld) b Dec. 17, 1899 Paddington (Qld) d Dec. 24, 1981 Sherwood (Qld)

Calder, Henry (WAust) b July 3, 1906 Guildford (WAust) d Aug. 27, 1970 South Perth (WAust)

Caldwell, Tim Charles John (NSW) b Oct. 29, 1913 Clayfield (Qld) d June 17, 1994 Orange (NSW)

Callachor, John Joseph Casimir (NSW) b Nov. 10, 1857 Woolloomooloo (NSW) d Feb. 20, 1924 Lane Cove (NSW)

Callaway, Norman Frank (NSW) b April 5, 1896 Hay (NSW) d May 3, 1917 Bullecourt (France)

* Callaway, Sydney Thomas (NSW) b Feb. 6, 1868 Redfern (NSW) d Nov. 25, 1923 Christchurch (New Zealand)

* Callen, Ian Wayne (Vic) b May 2, 1955 Alexandra (Vic)

Calvert, Derreck (Tas) b Dec. 22, 1919 South Arm (Tas) d Dec. 25, 2003 Hobart (Tas)

Cameron, Benjamin Peter (SAust) b Feb. 21, 1981 Hobart (Tas)

Cameron, Mark Alan (NSW) b Jan. 31, 1981 Waratah (NSW)

Cameron, Robert Alastair (SAust) b Sept. 6, 1938 North Adelaide (SAust)

Cameron, Verney Lovett (Vic) b c. 1842 Sorrento (Vic) d May 27, 1881 Richmond (Vic)

Campbell, Blair Maismore (Vic & Tas) b Aug. 20, 1946 Kew (Vic)

Campbell, Colin Mansfield (Tas) b Aug. 13, 1872 Cressy (Tas) d April 3, 1907 Winlaton, Northumberland (Eng)

Campbell, Donald (Vic) b Sept. 18, 1851 Loddon Plains (Vic) d Sept. 14, 1887 South Yarra (Vic)

Campbell, Francis Beresford (Tas) b April 20, 1867 Hobart (Tas) d May 14, 1929 Gladesville (NSW)

Campbell, Gordon Cathcart (SAust) b June 4, 1885 Myrtle Bank (SAust) d Aug. 13, 1961 Woodville South (SAust)

* Campbell, Gregory Dale (Tas) b March 10, 1964 Launceston (Tas)

Campbell, Ivan James (WAust) b Oct. 29, 1908 Perth (WAust) d Jan. 22, 1962 Hollywood (WAust)

Campbell, James Norval (NSW) b Sept. 21, 1908 Chatswood (NSW) d Sept. 11, 1973 St Ives (NSW)

Campbell, Leslie Percy (NSW) b Oct. 14, 1902 Marrickville (NSW) d Aug. 19, 1970 Southport (Qld)

Campbell, Malcolm MacDonald (Qld) b Jan. 7, 1881 Ipswich (Qld) d Dec. 14, 1967 Ipswich (Qld)

Campbell, Ryan John (WAust) b Feb. 7, 1972 Osborne Park (WAust)

Campbell, Stoddart William Grylls (Vic) b Sept. 19, 1846 Melbourne (Vic) d Sept. 2, 1903 East Melbourne (Vic)

Camphin, William Joseph (NSW) b Nov. 13, 1867 Sydney (NSW) d Sept. 11, 1942 Quirindi (NSW)

Campling, Campbell Roy (NSW) b April 3, 1892 Burwood (NSW) d April 21, 1977 Greenwich (NSW)

Canning, Tamahau Karangatukituki (Cricket Academy) b April 7, 1977 Adelaide (SAust)

Cannon, William Henry (Vic) b Sept. 11, 1871 Eaglehawk (Vic) d April 29, 1933 North Fitzroy (Vic)

Cantrell, Peter Edward (Qld) b Oct. 28, 1962 Gunnedah (NSW)

Cantwell, Hubert Richard (WAust) b Oct. 24, 1905 Warbleton, Sussex (England) d April 22, 1956 Esperance (WAust)

Capes, Peter Andrew (WAust) b Feb. 26, 1962 East Fremantle (WAust)

Carew, James (Qld) b Jan. 23, 1872 Pine Mountain (Qld) d Sept. 4, 1950 Kelvin Grove (Qld)

Carew, Patrick (Qld) b Sept. 8, 1875 Pine Mountain (Qld) d March 31, 1942 Queanbeyan (NSW)

Carew, Paul John (Qld & SAust) b July 9, 1967 South Brisbane (Qld)

* Carkeek, William (Vic) b Oct. 17, 1878 Walhalla (Vic) d Feb. 20, 1937 Prahran (Vic)

* Carlson, Phillip Henry (Qld) b Aug. 8, 1951 Nundah (Qld)

Carlson, Victor Charles (WAust) b July 16, 1893 Adelaide (SAust) d Feb. 23, 1974 Perth (WAust)

Carlton, Alfred Robert (Vic) b Nov. 13, 1867 Bacchus Marsh (Vic) d Sept. 10, 1941 Camberwell (Vic)

Carlton, John (Vic & Qld) b July 6, 1866 Bacchus Marsh (Vic) d Aug. 13, 1945 Parkville (Vic)

Carlton, Thomas Andrew (Vic & SAust) b Dec. 8, 1890 Footscray (Vic) d Dec. 17, 1973 Brunswick (Vic)

Carlton, William (Vic) b May 22, 1876 Fitzroy (Vic) d Dec. 23, 1959 Parkville (Vic)

Carlyon, Norman Murdoch (Vic) b May 5, 1938 East Melbourne (Vic)

Carmichael, Ian Robert (SAust) b Dec. 17, 1960 Hull, Yorkshire (England)

Carmody, Douglas Keith (NSW & WAust) b Feb. 16, 1919 Mosman (NSW) d Oct. 21, 1977 Concord (NSW)

Carney, Brian William (Tas) b June 2, 1931 Launceston (Tas)

Carr, Charles Seymour (Vic) b Nov. 22, 1849 (Jamaica) d March 30, 1921 East Melbourne (Vic)

Carr, William Niall (Vic) b June 1, 1976 Box Hill (Vic)

Carracher, Arthur James (SAust) b July 7, 1867 Heywood (Vic) d Oct. 15, 1935 North Adelaide (SAust)

Carragher, Edward John (SAust) b June 1, 1891 Broken Hill (NSW) d Nov. 28, 1977 Broken Hill (NSW)

Carrigan, Aubrey Herbert (Qld) b Aug. 26, 1917 Zillmere (Qld)

Carroll, Edmund Louis (Vic) b Oct. 22, 1886 Albert Park (Vic) d June 6, 1959 Ormond (Vic)

Carroll, Eugene Vincent (Vic) b Jan. 17, 1885 South Melbourne (Vic) d Sept. 18, 1965 Elsternwick (Vic)

Carroll, Sidney Joseph (NSW) b Nov. 28, 1922 Willoughby (NSW) d Oct. 12, 1984 Willoughby (NSW)

Carroll, Thomas Davis (Tas) b Feb. 26, 1884 Hobart (Tas) d June 3, 1957 Hobart (Tas)

Carseldine, Lee Andrew (Qld) b Nov. 17, 1975 Nambour (Qld)

Carter, Alfred Snowden (Vic) b March 1, 1869 Kew (Vic) d June 7, 1920 Camberwell (Vic)

Carter, Edmund Sardinson (Vic) b Feb. 3, 1845 Malton, Yorkshire (England) d May 23, 1923 Scarborough, Yorkshire (England)

Carter, Edwin Lewis (Vic) b May 2, 1925 Caulfield (Vic)

* Carter, Hanson (NSW) b March 15, 1878 Halifax, Yorkshire (England) d June 8, 1948 Bellevue Hill (NSW)

Carter, Reginald Clarence (WAust) b March 1, 1888 Brunswick East (Vic) d July 16, 1970 Subiaco (WAust)

Carter, William Jack Sydney (NSW) b Dec. 7, 1907 Randwick (NSW) d Aug. 19, 1995 Penshurst (NSW)

Cartledge, Brian Lewis (Tas) b March 3, 1941 Smithton (Tas)

Cary, Sean Ross (WAust) b March 10, 1971 Subiaco (WAust)

Cass, George Rodney (Tas) b April 23, 1940 Overton, Yorkshire (Eng)

Cassell, Jerry Lee (Qld) b Jan. 12, 1975 Mona Vale (NSW)

Cassell, Robert James (Vic) b April 28, 1983 Melbourne (Vic)

Casson, Beau (WAust) b Dec. 7, 1982 Subiaco (WAust)

Castle, David James (Tas) b May 25, 1972 Launceston (Tas)

Catchlove, Walter Evered (SAust) b Feb. 24, 1907 North Adelaide (SAust) d April 12, 1997 Glen Osmond (SAust)

Caterer, Thomas Ainslie (SAust) b May 16, 1858 Woodville (SAust) d Aug. 25, 1924 Walkerville (SAust)

Causby, Barry Leon (SAust) b Sept. 11, 1948 Adelaide (SAust)

Causby, John Phillip (SAust) b Oct. 27, 1942 Hindmarsh (SAust)

Cavenagh, George (Vic) b June 16, 1836 Sydney (NSW) d Nov. 23, 1922 Albert Park (Vic)

Chadwick, Derek (WAust) b March 21, 1941 Busselton (WAust)

Chamberlain, Cornelius Thomas (SAust) b c. 1882 (Ireland) d Nov. 14, 1943 Rose Park (SAust)

Chamberlain, John Aloysius (WAust) b Aug. 29, 1884 Glanville (SAust) d April 1, 1941 Leabrook (SAust)

Chamberlain, William Leonard (SAust) b Jan. 15, 1889 Port Adelaide (SAust) d March 21, 1956 Darlinghurst (NSW)

Chambers, John Lindsay (Vic) b Oct. 14, 1930 Geelong (Vic)

Chancellor, Frederick Edgar (Tas) b Aug. 28, 1878 Hobart (Tas) d June 16, 1939 Hobart (Tas)

Chapman, Frederick Douglas (Vic) b March 21, 1901 Clifton Hill (Vic) d June 27, 1964 Northcote (Vic)

Chapman, George Arthur Northcote (NSW) b April 21, 1904 Chatswood (NSW) d May 22, 1986 Sydney (NSW)

Chapman, Henry William (Qld) b Jan. 7, 1866 Tredegar, Monmouthshire (Wales) d May 5, 1942 Herston (Qld)

Chapman, Lawrence Gordon (Qld) b June 25, 1928 Tingalpa (Qld)

Chapman, Ross Albert (NSW) b Oct. 22, 1952 New Lambton (NSW)

* Chappell, Gregory Stephen (SAust & Qld) b Aug. 7, 1948 Unley (SAust)

* Chappell, Ian Michael (SAust) b Sept. 26, 1943 Unley (SAust)

* Chappell, Trevor Martin (SAust, WAust & NSW) b Oct. 12, 1952 Glenelg (SAust)

Chardon, David Michael (NSW) b Dec. 8, 1951 Newtown (NSW)

Charlesworth, Lester (WAust) b Oct. 11, 1916 Kanowna (WAust) d Jan. 15, 1980 Perth (WAust)

Charlesworth, Richard Ian (WAust) b Dec. 6, 1952 Subiaco (WAust)

* Charlton, Percie Chater (NSW) b April 9, 1867 Surry Hills (NSW) d Sept. 30, 1954 Pymble (NSW)

Chee Quee, Richard (NSW) b Jan. 4, 1971 Camperdown (NSW)

Cheetham, Albert George (NSW) b Dec. 7, 1915 Ryde (NSW) d May 23, 1997 Sandringham (Vic)

Chegwyn, John William (NSW) b March 18, 1909 Botany (NSW) d May 26, 1992 Sydney (NSW)

Chillingworth, Garry Andrew (SAust) b Jan. 23, 1970 Sutherland (NSW)

Chilvers, Hugh Cecil (NSW) b Oct. 26, 1902 Sawbridgeworth, Hertfordshire (England) d Dec. 1, 1994 Sydney (NSW)

Chinner, Hubert George Williams (SAust) b Aug. 30, 1870 Brighton (SAust) d June 12, 1953 Unley Park (SAust)

* Chipperfield, Arthur Gordon (NSW) b Nov. 17, 1905 Ashfield (NSW) d July 29, 1987 Ryde (NSW)

Chittleborough, Henry Carew (SAust) b April 14, 1861 Wallaroo (SAust) d June 25, 1925 Malvern (SAust)

Chivers, Alfred Percy (Vic) b Aug. 15, 1908 Templestowe (Vic) d July 11, 1997 Templestowe (Vic)

Christ, Charles Percival (Qld) b June 10, 1911 Paddington (Qld) d Jan. 22, 1998 Redcliffe (Qld)

Christensen, Robert Thomas (SAust) b Oct. 31, 1959 Hindmarsh (SAust)

Christian, Arthur Hugh (Vic & WAust) b Jan. 22, 1877 Richmond (Vic) d Sept. 8, 1950 Claremont (WAust)

Christy, Frederick Collier (Surrey) b Sept. 9, 1822 Asperfield, Kent (England) d Jan. 17, 1909 South Yarra (Vic)

* Christy, James Alexander Joseph (Qld) b Dec. 12, 1904 Pretoria (South Africa) d Feb. 1, 1971 Durban (South Africa)

Chyer, Darren Scott (SAust) b July 28, 1966 Glenelg (SAust)

Clark, Anthony Michael (NSW) b March 23, 1977 St Leonard's (NSW)

Clark, Donald Jack (Tas) b Jan. 19, 1914 Hobart (Tas) d Aug. 16, 1994 Hobart (Tas)

Clark, Henry Judge (WAust) b April 23, 1892 Sydney (NSW) d Feb. 8, 1973 Perth (WAust)

Clark, James Patrick (Qld) b March 14, 1871 (Qld) d June 6, 1941 Coolangatta (Qld)

Clark, John Lawrence (Qld & NSW) b Oct. 14, 1928 Paddington (NSW)

Clark, Michael Wayne (WAust) b March 31, 1978 Perth (WAust)

Clark, Stuart Rupert (NSW) b Sept. 28, 1975 Caringbah (NSW)

* Clark, Wayne Maxwell (WAust) b Sept. 19, 1953 Perth (WAust)

Clarke, Alfred Edward (NSW) b April 6, 1868 Surry Hills (NSW) d Sept. 16, 1940 Wellington (New Zealand)

Clarke, David Alexander (SAust) b Jan. 25, 1970 Adelaide (SAust)

Clarke, Gerard John (Vic) b Dec. 31, 1966 Malvern (Vic)

Clarke, Gother Robert Carlisle (NSW) b April 27, 1875 North Sydney (NSW) d Oct. 12, 1917 Zonnebeke (Belgium)

Clarke, Graham Cornelius (SAust) b July 10, 1939 Laura (SAust)

Clarke, John (NSW) birth and death details unknown

Clarke, Michael John (NSW) b April 2, 1981 Liverpool (NSW)

Claxton, Norman (SAust) b Nov. 2, 1877 North Adelaide (SAust) d Dec. 5, 1951 North Adelaide (SAust)

Claxton, William David Hambridge (SAust) b June 2, 1857 Kensington (SAust) d March 12, 1937 Glenelg (SAust)

Clay, Ivor Thomas (Tas) b May 7, 1915 Bendigo (Vic) d Aug. 12, 1958 Essendon (Vic)

Clayton, Nicholas George (Tas) b March 11, 1826 Norfolk Plains (Tas) d April 23, 1867 Auckland (New Zealand)

Cleary, Edward Joseph (Vic) b April 18, 1913 Benalla (Vic) d April 6, 1985 Benalla (Vic)

Cleary, Mark Francis (SAust) b July 19, 1980 Moorabbin (Vic)

Cleeve, James Oatley (NSW) b Feb. 14, 1864 Sydney (NSW) d Feb. 8, 1909 Moree (NSW)

Clem, Gordon Rex (Qld) b July 5, 1909 Milora (Qld) d March 3, 1970 Melbourne (Vic)

Clements, Peter John (SAust) b Jan. 23, 1953 Glenelg (SAust)

Clements, Shane Clifton (WAust) b June 28, 1958 Middle Swan (WAust) d April 22, 2001 Inglewood (WAust)

Clews, Mark Lindsay (NSW) b Jan. 13, 1952 Grange (SAust)

Clifford, Peter Stanley (NSW & Qld) b Nov. 4, 1959 Bellingen (NSW)

Clingeleffer, Sean Geoffrey (Tas) b May 9, 1980 Hobart (Tas)

Clingly, Michael Thomas (SAust) b April 18, 1932 Prospect (SAust)

Clough, Peter Michael (Tas & WAust) b Aug. 17, 1956 Sydney (NSW)

Clutterbuck, Stanley Herwin (SAust) b May 27, 1888 Kapunda (SAust) d Jan. 24, 1972 Adelaide (SAust)

Coates, Joseph (NSW) b Nov. 13, 1844 Huddersfield, Yorkshire (England) d Sept. 9, 1896 Sydney (NSW)

Coats, James (Qld) b Feb. 26, 1914 Annerley (Qld) d June 8, 2002 Wynnum West (Qld)

Cobcroft, Leslie Thomas (NSW) b Feb. 12, 1867 Muswellbrook (NSW) d March 9, 1938 Wellington (New Zealand)

Cockburn, James Sydney David (Qld) b May 20, 1916 Maryborough (Qld) d Nov. 13, 1990 Herston (Qld)

Cockburn, William Frederick (Vic) b Nov. 28, 1916 Richmond (Vic)

Cody, Leslie Alwyn (NSW & Vic) b Oct. 11, 1889 Paddington (NSW) d Aug. 10, 1969 Toorak (Vic)

Cohen, Bertram Louis (Vic) b Sept. 25, 1892 London (England) d June 30, 1955 North Caulfield (Vic)

Cohen, Morton Barnett (NSW) b Sept. 19, 1913 Paddington (NSW) d Jan. 14, 1968 Vaucluse (NSW)

Colegrave, Mark David (Tas) b July 1, 1970 Hobart (Tas)

Colgan, Gregory (WAust) b Nov. 5, 1953 Subiaco (WAust)

* Colley, David John (NSW) b March 15, 1947 Mosman (NSW)

Colley, Timothy Peter Michael (SAust) b July 10, 1935 Sydney (NSW)

Collins, Frank Henry Kenneth (SAust) b Dec. 16, 1910 Queenstown (SAust) d Jan 24, 2001 Penola (SAust)

Collins, Frederick Bisset (Vic) b Feb. 25, 1881 Richmond (Vic) d Oct. 4, 1917 Ypres (Belgium)

* Collins, Herbert Leslie (NSW) b Jan. 21, 1888 Randwick (NSW) d May 28, 1959 Little Bay (NSW)

Collins, Ross Phillip (NSW) b Dec. 9, 1945 Paddington (NSW)

Collins, Vincent Aloysius (NSW) b Sept. 23, 1917 Newtown (NSW) d Oct. 30, 1989 Sunnybank (Qld)

Collins, William Anthony (Tas) b Dec. 9, 1837 Launceston (Tas) d Jan. 12, 1876 Launceston (Tas)

Colreavy, Bernard Xavier (NSW) b June 30, 1871 Dripstone (NSW) d Nov. 30, 1946 Dubbo (NSW)

Combes, Geoffrey Arthur (Tas) b May 19, 1913 Greymouth (New Zealand) d Feb. 4, 1997 Woodstock near Huonville (Tas)

Combes, Maxwell James (Tas) b July 29, 1911 Greymouth (New Zealand) d March 10, 1983 Longley (Tas)

* Coningham, Arthur (NSW & Qld) b July 14, 1863 South Melbourne (Vic) d June 13, 1939 Gladesville (NSW)

Connell, Thomas William (NSW) b March 4, 1869 Invercargill (New Zealand) death details unknown

* Connolly, Alan Norman (Vic) b June 29, 1939 Skipton (Vic)

Connor, Gerald O'Grady (WAust & Tas) b Sept. 15, 1932 Perth (WAust) d Sept. 5, 1993 Perth (WAust)

Considine, Bernard Thomas (Vic & Tas) b April 8, 1925 Ararat (Vic) d June 4, 1989 (Qld)

Conway, John (Vic) b Feb. 3, 1842 Fyansford (Vic) d Aug. 22, 1909 Frankston (Vic)

Cook, Bernard William (Qld) b March 15, 1879 Torquay, Devon (England) d March 15, 1944 Sherwood (Qld)

Cook, Bruce (NSW) b Oct. 24, 1914 Orange (NSW) d Jan. 2, 1981 Balgowlah (NSW)

Cook, Geoffrey Glover (Qld) b June 29, 1910 Chelmer (Qld) d Sept. 12, 1982 Chelmer (Qld)

Cook, Russell Frederick (Vic) b Sept. 23, 1947 South Melbourne (Vic)

* Cook, Simon Hewitt (Vic & NSW) b Jan. 29, 1972 Hastings (Vic)

Cooke, Colin John (Qld) b Nov. 21, 1947 Harrisville (Qld)

Cooley, Troy James (Tas) b Dec. 9, 1965 Launceston (Tas)

Coombe, Ephraim Henry (SAust) b Aug. 26, 1858 Gawler (SAust) d April 5, 1917 Semaphore (SAust)

Coombe, Percy Howard (SAust) b Jan. 7, 1880 Brompton (SAust) d July 28, 1947 Prospect (SAust)

Coombe, Thomas Melrose (WAust) b Dec. 3, 1873 Gladstone (SAust) d July 22, 1959 London (England)

Cooper, Allan Ferguson (NSW) b March 18, 1916 Sydney (NSW) d Sept. 7, 1970 Concord (NSW)

* Cooper, Bransby Beauchamp (Vic) b March 15, 1844 Dacca (India) d Aug. 7, 1914 Geelong (Vic)

Cooper, Bryce Arnot (NSW) b Dec. 19, 1905 Lewisham (NSW) d May 19, 1995 Gordon (NSW)

Cooper, Duncan Elphinstone (Vic) b c. 1813 (India) d Nov. 22, 1904 Paddington, London (England)

Cooper, George Henry (Qld) b Feb. 15, 1907 Gympie (Qld) d Jan. 3, 2000 Mudgeeraba (Qld)

Cooper, John Richard (Qld) b July 11, 1922 Lilydale (Vic)

Cooper, Lewis Dale (Qld) b May 14, 1937 Mackay (Qld)

* Cooper, William Henry (Vic) b Sept. 11, 1849 Maidstone, Kent (England) d April 5, 1939 Malvern (Vic)

Cooper, William Osborne (SAust) b Feb. 13, 1891 North Adelaide (SAust) d June 28, 1930 Glenelg (SAust)

Corbett, Troy Frederick (Vic) b Oct. 11, 1972 Ouyen (Vic)

Cordner, John Pruen (Vic) b March 20, 1929 Diamond Creek (Vic)

Cordner, Laurence Osmaston (Vic) b Feb. 7, 1911 Warrnambool (Vic) d July 11, 1992 Penshurst (Vic)

* Corling, Grahame Edward (NSW) b July 13, 1941 Newcastle (NSW)

Cormack, Geoffrey Fairhurst (Vic) b Feb. 26, 1929 Camberwell (Vic)

Cornelius, William John (Vic) b Feb. 17, 1915 Port Melbourne (Vic)

Corstorphin, Colin James (Vic) b July 20, 1954 Bairnsdale (Vic) d Sept. 4, 1998 Melbourne (Victoria)

Cosgrave, Bryan (Vic) b March 23, 1903 Clifton Hill (Vic) d Nov. 22, 1992 Melbourne (Vic)

Cosgrave, James (Vic) b March 16, 1932 Parkville (Vic)

Cosgrove, Mark James (SAust) b June 14, 1984 Elizabeth (SAust)

* Cosier, Gary John (Vic, SAust & Qld) b April 25, 1953 Richmond (Vic)

Cossart, Charles Edward (Qld) b Sept. 2, 1885 Rosewood (Qld) d June 6, 1963 Boonah (Qld)

Cosstick, Samuel (Vic & NSW) b Jan. 1, 1836 Croydon, Surrey (England) d April 8, 1896 West Maitland (NSW)

Cottam, John Thomas (NSW) b Sept. 5, 1867 Strawberry Hills (NSW) d Jan. 30, 1897 Coolgardie (WAust)

* Cotter, Albert (NSW) b Dec. 3, 1884 Sydney (NSW) d Oct. 31, 1917 Beersheba (Palestine)

Cotter, Denis Francis (Vic) b c. 1862 Fitzroy (Vic) d Nov. 18, 1905 North Fitzroy (Vic)

Cotton, Edward Kenneth (NSW) b Aug. 8, 1927 Paddington (NSW) d March 26, 2002 Kogarah (NSW)

Cotton, Harold Norman Jack (SAust) b Dec. 3, 1914 Prospect (SAust) d April 6, 1966 Malvern (SAust)

Coulson, Craig Edward (WAust) b June 13, 1967 South Perth (WAust)

Coulstock, Richard (Vic) b c. 1823 Surrey (England) d Dec. 15, 1870 South Melbourne (Vic)

* Coulthard, George (Vic) b Aug. 1, 1856 Boroondara (Vic) d Oct. 22, 1883 Carlton (Vic)

Courtice, Brian Andrew (Qld) b March 30, 1961 South Brisbane (Qld)

Courtney, Nicholas Charles Palliser (Tas) b July 18, 1967 Launceston (Tas)

Coverdale, Miles Colquhoun (Tas) b Aug. 4, 1846 Richmond (Tas) d April 3, 1898 Hobart (Tas)

Cowan, Robert Francis (SAust) b May 3, 1880 Angaston (SAust) d Nov. 11, 1962 Neutral Bay (NSW)

Cowley, Ian Arthur (Tas) b March 20, 1937 Launceston (Tas)

Cowley, Owen William (NSW & Qld) b Dec. 14, 1868 Port Louis (Mauritius) d Feb. 27, 1922 Brisbane (Qld)

Cowley, Terence John (Tas) b July 17, 1928 Evandale (Tas)

Cowmeadow, Garry John (Tas) b Aug. 21, 1954 Huonville (Tas)

Cowper, David Raymond (Vic) b Jan. 25, 1939 Kew (Vic)

Cowper, George (NSW) b c. 1858 full birth and death details unknown

* Cowper, Robert Maskew (Vic & WAust) b Oct. 5, 1940 Kew (Vic)

Cox, Douglas Edward (Qld) b July 9, 1919 West End (Qld) d Jan. 9, 1982 Dakabin (Qld)

Cox, Jamie b Oct. 15, 1969 Burnie (Tas)

Cox, John (Tas & Vic) b 1823 birth day and month unknown Norfolk Plains (Tas) full birth and death details unknown

Cox, Michael John (WAust) b April 26, 1957 Newcastle (NSW)

Cox, Peter John (Vic) b Jan. 13, 1954 Mildura (Vic)

Cox, Richard (Tas) b April 21, 1830 Hobart (Tas) d March 27, 1865 Fingal (Tas)

Coyle, Timothy Charles (Tas) b July 27, 1960 Launceston (Tas)

Coyne, Thomas Harold (WAust) b Oct. 12, 1873 Tornagullah (Vic) d April 8, 1955 Christchurch (New Zealand)

* Craig, Ian David (NSW) b June 12, 1935 Yass (NSW)

Craig, Reginald Jack (SAust) b Aug. 3, 1916 North Adelaide (SAust) d April 17, 1985 Walker Flat (SAust)

Craig, Shawn Andrew Jacob (Vic) b June 23, 1973 Carlton (Vic)

Craigie, John Edwin (SAust) b Aug. 25, 1866 Adelaide (SAust) d Sept. 11, 1948 Gilberton (SAust)

Crane, Frederick Robert (Qld) b July 10, 1942 Mullumbimby (NSW)

Cranney, Harold (NSW) b Oct. 23, 1886 Parramatta (NSW) d Jan. 29, 1971 North Rocks (NSW)

* Crawford, John Neville (SAust) b Dec. 1, 1886 Cane Hill, Surrey (England) d May 2, 1963 Epsom, Surrey (England)

* Crawford, William Patrick Anthony (NSW) b Aug. 3, 1933 Dubbo (NSW)

Creevey, Brendan Neville (Qld) b Feb. 18, 1970 Charleville (Qld)

Cresswick, Ernest Albert (Qld) b Oct. 16, 1867 Newcastle (NSW) d Sept. 23, 1939 Waverley (NSW)

Creswick, Henry (Vic) b April 13, 1824 Sheffield, Yorkshire (England) d Oct. 24, 1892 Hawthorn (Vic)

Crippin, Ronald James (NSW) b April 23, 1947 Darlinghurst (NSW)

Cripps, Alan Edward (WAust) b Aug. 11, 1930 Lakemba (NSW)

Cristofani, Desmond Robert (NSW) b Nov. 14, 1920 Waverley (NSW) d Aug. 22, 2002 Fleet, Hampshire (England)

Crompton, Colin Neil (Vic) b Aug. 16, 1937 Dandenong (Vic) d Dec. 11, 2003 Malvern (Vic)

Crook, Andrew Richard (SAust) b Oct. 14, 1980 Modbury (SAust)

Crossan, Ernest Eric (NSW) b Nov. 3, 1914 Footscray (Vic)

Crouch, Edward Robert (Qld) b Jan. 11, 1873 Holborn, London, (England) d Aug. 8, 1962 South Brisbane (Qld)

Crouch, George Stanton (Qld) b Aug. 20, 1878 Strand, London, Middlesex (England) d Aug. 21, 1952 Indooroopilly (Qld)

Crow, Thomas Leslie (Vic) b Aug. 23, 1931 Hawthorn (Vic)

Crowden, Ian Bruce (Tas) b Feb. 22, 1933 Deloraine (Tas)

Crowder, Arthur Beaumont (Tas) b July 4, 1892 Sorell (Tas) d Feb. 16, 1964 Hobart (Tas)

* Crowe, Jeffrey John (SAust) b Sept. 14, 1958 Cornwall Park, Auckland (New Zealand)

Cruse, Bruce Andrew (Tas) b April 26, 1967 Launceston (Tas)

Cuff, Alan Gordon (Tas) b June 7, 1908 Launceston (Tas) d April 23, 1995 Launceston (Tas)

Cuff, Leonard Albert (Tas) b March 28, 1866 Christchurch (New Zealand) d Oct. 9, 1954 Launceston (Tas)

Cuffe, John Alexander (NSW) b June 26, 1880 Dubbo (NSW) d May 16, 1931 Burton-on-Trent, Staffordshire (England)

Cullen, Daniel Robert (NSW) b April 27, 1889 Balmain (NSW) d July 21, 1971 Concord (NSW)

Cullen, Geoff Ian (WAust) b March 16, 1977 Claremont (WAust)

Cullen, William (NSW) b c. 1887 Wellington (New Zealand) d May 7, 1945 Double Bay (NSW)

Cullinan, Thomas (WAust) b (SAust) full birth details unknown d July 31, 1907 Fremantle (WAust)

Cumberland, Charles Brownlow (Vic) b c. 1801 d Nov. 27, 1882 Leamington, Warwickshire (England)

Cumming, Kenneth Roy (WAust) b April 12, 1916 East Coolgardie (WAust) d Oct. 11, 1988 Perth (WAust)

Cummins, Frank Septimus (NSW) b Aug. 8, 1906 West Maitland (NSW) d April 27, 1966 North Sydney (NSW)

Cunningham, Graeme Timothy (Tas) b Jan. 25, 1975 Goulburn (NSW)

Cunningham, Kenneth George (SAust) b July 26, 1939 Adelaide (SAust)

Currie, Ernest William (Qld) b April 9, 1873 Dunedin (New Zealand) d Oct. 23, 1932 Randwick (NSW)

Curtin, Barry George (SAust) b June 30, 1951 Rose Park (SAust)

Curtin, Paul (SAust) b May 10, 1954 Rose Park (SAust)

Curtin, Pearce William Edward (WAust) b Sept. 27, 1907 Boulder (WAust) d May 17, 1997 Canberra (ACT)

Curtin, Peter Donald (SAust) b Sept. 22, 1949 Rose Park (SAust)

Curtis, George Thomas (NSW) b Aug. 17, 1837 Sydney (NSW) d April 2, 1885 Darlinghurst (NSW)

Curtis, Louis David (SAust) b Aug. 5, 1928 Loxton (SAust)

Cush, Norman Lloyd (NSW) b Oct. 4, 1911 Glebe Point (NSW) d Jan. 22, 1983 Maroubra (NSW)

Cuthbert, Daniel Charles (Tas) b Feb. 2, 1846 Franklin (Tas) d July 6, 1912 Hobart (Tas)

* Dale, Adam Craig (Qld) b Dec. 30, 1968 Greensborough (Vic)

Daly, Anthony John (Tas) b July 25, 1969 Newcastle (NSW)

Daly, Thomas (Tas) b c. 1847 d Sept. 23, 1887 Inveresk (Tas)

Daniel, Jack (Vic) b Dec. 9, 1923 Leeds, Yorkshire (England) d Oct. 12, 2002 Tugan (Qld)

* Daniel, Wayne Wendell (WAust) b Jan. 16, 1956 Brereton Village, St Philip (Barbados)

Dansie, Hampton Neil (SAust) b July 2, 1928 Nuriootpa (SAust)

D'Arcy, D (NSW) birth and death details unknown

Darke, William Floyd (Vic) b July 24, 1846 Sydney (NSW) d Jan. 24, 1925 Elsternwick (Vic)

* Darling, Joseph (SAust) b Nov. 21, 1870 Glen Osmond (SAust) d Jan. 2, 1946 Hobart (Tas)

* Darling, Leonard Stuart (Vic) b Aug. 14, 1909 South Yarra (Vic) d June 24, 1992 Daw Park (SAust)

* Darling, Warrick Maxwell (SAust) b May 1, 1957 Waikerie (SAust)

Davey, John Richard (SAust) b Aug. 26, 1957 Bournemouth, Hampshire (England)

Davey, John Ryan (SAust) b Sept. 20, 1913 Broken Hill (NSW) d Sept. 6, 1992 Unley (SAust)

Davidson, Alan Andrew (Vic) b July 14, 1897 Brunswick (Vic) d Aug. 1, 1962 Ringwood (Vic)

* Davidson, Alan Keith (NSW) b June 14, 1929 Lisarow (NSW)

Davidson, Hugh Lavery (NSW) b May 17, 1907 South Yarra (Vic) d April 22, 1960 Wamberal (NSW)

Davidson, Thomas Rex (Tas) b July 30, 1927 Campbell Town (Tas)

Davie, Bert Joseph James (Tas & Vic) b May 2, 1899 Hobart (Tas) d June 3, 1979 Melbourne (Vic)

Davies, Christopher James (SAust) b Nov. 15, 1978 Bedford Park (SAust)

Davies, George Arthur (Vic) b March 19, 1892 Maindample (Vic) d Nov. 27, 1957 Essendon (Vic)

Davies, Geoffrey Robert (NSW) b July 22, 1946 Randwick (NSW)

Davies, Gerald Stanley (Tas) b Jan. 29, 1949 Cinderford, Gloucestershire (England)

Davies, John George (Tas) b Feb. 17, 1846 Melbourne (Vic) d Nov. 12, 1913 New Town (Tas)

Davies, Peter John (Vic) b Aug. 18, 1957 Melbourne (Vic)

Davis, Arthur Hugh (Tas) b Nov. 6, 1898 Launceston (Tas) d March 5, 1943 Camberwell (Vic)

Davis, Frank Alexander (Tas) b May 29, 1904 Launceston (Tas) d Sept. 12, 1973 Launceston (Tas)

Davis, Horace Hyman (NSW) b Feb. 1, 1889 Darlinghurst (NSW) d Feb. 4, 1960 Sydney (NSW)

* Davis, Ian Charles (NSW & Qld) b June 25, 1953 North Sydney (NSW)

Davis, Jonas J. (NSW) b May 12, 1859 Goulburn (NSW) d May 18, 1911 Waverley (NSW)

Davis, Neil Wilton (Tas) b Aug. 1, 1900 Launceston (Tas) d April 25, 1974 Evans Head (NSW)

Davis, Reginald Augur (Tas) b Oct. 22, 1892 Invermay (Tas) d July 11, 1957 Launceston (Tas)

* Davis, Simon Peter (Vic) b Nov. 8, 1959 Brighton (Vic)

* Davis, Winston Walter (Tas) b Sept. 18, 1958 Sion Hill, Kingstown (St Vincent)

Davison, Brian Fettes (Tas) b Dec. 21, 1946 Bulawayo (Southern Rhodesia)

Davison, John Michael (Vic & SAust) b May 9, 1970 Campbell River, Vancouver Island, British Columbia (Canada)

Davison, Lindsay John (Vic) b Oct. 11, 1941 Malvern (Vic)

Davison, Rodney John (NSW) b June 26, 1969 Kogarah (NSW)

Dawes, Joseph Henry (Qld) b Aug. 29, 1970 Herston (Qld)

Day, Arthur Charles (Vic) b Aug. 8, 1933 Sunshine (Vic)

Day, Herbert John (SAust) b April 1, 1868 Bowden (SAust) d Oct. 14, 1947 Hindmarsh (SAust)

* De Courcy, James Harry (NSW) b April 18, 1927 Newcastle (NSW) d June 20, 2000 Newcastle (NSW)

De Gruchy, Henry William (Vic) b May 15, 1898 Sydney (NSW) d May 2, 1952 Parkville (Vic)

De Jong, Howard Keith (Qld) b Feb. 12, 1956 Mt Lavinia, Colombo (Ceylon)

De Winter, Allister John (Tas) b March 12, 1968 Launceston (Tas)

Dean, Archibald Herbert (Vic) b Oct. 3, 1885 Hawthorn (Vic) d Sept. 3, 1939 Norfolk Island (NSW)

Dean, Arthur Edgar (Vic) b July 23, 1931 Williamstown (Vic)

Dean, Oscar Hessel (NSW) b April 30, 1886 Windsor (NSW) d May 11, 1962 Windsor (NSW)

Deane, Norman Younger (NSW) b Aug. 29, 1875 Neutral Bay (NSW) d Sept. 30, 1950 Lindfield (NSW)

Deane, Sydney Leslie (NSW) b March 1, 1863 Sydney (NSW) d March 20, 1934 Brooklyn, New York (United States of America)

Deely, Patrick Joseph (Vic) b Feb. 18, 1864 North Melbourne (Vic) d Feb. 28, 1925 Brighton (Vic)

Deitz, Shane Alan (SAust) b May 4, 1975 Bankstown (NSW)

Delaney, William (SAust) b Jan. 17, 1866 Kapunda (SAust) d Dec. 16, 1921 Port Augusta (SAust)

* Dell, Anthony Ross (Qld) b Aug. 6, 1945 Lymington, Hampshire (England)

Dell, Christopher Ronald (Tas) b Oct. 27, 1960 Devonport (Tas)

Delves, Thomas Frederick (Vic) b Aug. 23, 1876 Carlton (Vic) d July 28, 1944 Heidelberg (Vic)

Delves, Walter Frederick (Vic) b Feb. 17, 1891 Brunswick (Vic) d May 27, 1955 Canterbury (Vic)

Dempsey, Darren Michael (SAust) b Oct. 17, 1975 Mount Gambier (SAust)

Dempster, Robert Alexander (Vic) b March 11, 1915 Hotham West (Vic) d April 2, 1974 Fitzroy (Vic)

Denton, Gerard John (Tas) b Aug. 7, 1975 Mt Isa (Qld)

Desmazeures, Pitre Cesar (Vic & SAust) b Aug. 17, 1880 Collingwood (Vic) d Oct. 7, 1942 New Norfolk (Tas)

Deveney, Frank Barclay (Vic) b Aug. 16, 1910 Berwick (Vic) d Oct. 30, 1998 Melbourne (Vic)

Devenish-Meares, Frank (WAust & NSW) b April 25, 1873 Surry Hills (NSW) d July 4, 1952 Petersham (NSW)

Deverson, Charles Sydney (SAust) b Nov. 2, 1905 Alberton (SAust) d Feb. 2, 1945 Port Adelaide (SAust)

Di Venuto, Michael James (Tas) b Dec. 12, 1973 Hobart (Tas)

Diamond, Austin (NSW) b July 10, 1874 Huddersfield, Yorkshire (England) d Aug. 5, 1966 Concord (NSW)

Dick, Alexander Williamson (WAust) b Nov. 30, 1922 Boulder (WAust)

Dick, Andrew M. (Vic) birth and death details unknown

Dick, Ian Robinson (WAust) b Aug. 30, 1926 Boulder (WAust)

Dick, William Allan (Vic) b Nov. 10, 1922 Newcastle (NSW) d March 27, 2004 Melbourne (Vic)

Dickson, George D. (NSW) birth and death details unknown

Dighton, Michael Gray (WAust & Tas) b July 24, 1976 Toowoomba (Qld)

Dillon, Marshall (Vic) b July 22, 1925 Ballarat (Vic) d Oct. 11, 1979 Beaumaris (Vic)

Dimattina, Michael Gerard David (Vic) b May 11, 1965 Malvern (Vic)

Diprose, Noel Vertigan (Tas) b March 5, 1922 Glenorchy (Tas)

Ditchburn, Albert James (WAust) b Aug. 24, 1908 Boulder (WAust) d March 7, 1964 Perth (WAust)

Dive, Percy William (NSW) b July 10, 1881 Paddington (NSW) d Sept. 17, 1965 Roseville (NSW)

Dixon, Joseph Black (Tas) b Sept. 26, 1836 Hobart (Tas) d March 6, 1882 Battery Point (Tas)

Dixon, Patrick Leslie (Qld) b Jan. 13, 1916 Eagle Junction (Qld) d Nov. 5, 1996 Goulburn (NSW)

Dixon, Troy James (Qld) b Dec. 22, 1969 Geelong (Vic)

Doble, Alan William (Vic) b Dec. 27, 1942 Glenhuntly (Vic)

Docker, Arthur Robert (NSW) b June 3, 1848 Thornthwaite (NSW) d April 8, 1929 Enfield, Middlesex (England)

Docker, Cyril Talbot (NSW) b March 3, 1884 Ryde (NSW) d March 26, 1975 Double Bay (NSW)

Docker, Ernest Brougham (NSW) b April 1, 1842 Thornthwaite (NSW) d Aug. 12, 1923 Elizabeth Bay (NSW)

Docker, Keith Brougham (NSW) b Sept. 1, 1888 Ryde (NSW) d May 16, 1977 Ashfield (NSW)

Docker, Phillip Wybergh (NSW) b April 8, 1886 Ryde (NSW) d Oct. 29, 1978 Concord (NSW)

Docking, Trevor William (Tas) b Dec. 22, 1952 Burnie (Tas)

Dodds, Norman (Tas) b Aug. 30, 1876 Hobart (Tas) d Dec. 15, 1916 Hobart (Tas)

* Dodemaide, Anthony Ian Christopher (Vic) b Oct. 5, 1963 Williamstown (Vic)

Doherty, Xavier John (Tas) b Nov. 22, 1982 Scottsdale (Tas)

Doig, Ronald Oldham (WAust) b July 10, 1909 Fremantle (WAust) d Sept. 17, 1932 Beaconsfield (WAust)

Dollery, Keith Robert (Qld & Tas) b Dec. 9, 1924 Cooroy (Qld)

Dolling, Charles Edward (SAust) b Sept. 4, 1886 Wokurna (SAust) d June 11, 1936 Adelaide (SAust)

Dolman, Michael Charles (SAust) b June 14, 1960 North Adelaide (SAust)

Donahoo, Sydney John (Vic & Qld) b April 14, 1871 St Kilda (Vic) d Jan. 14, 1946 St Kilda (Vic)

Donaldson, John Stuart (SAust) b April 14, 1950 Adelaide (SAust)

Donaldson, William Peter James (NSW) b Oct. 26, 1923 Lilyfield (NSW) d Aug. 8, 1999 Sydney (NSW)

Done, Richard Phillip (NSW) b Aug. 5, 1955 Ryde (NSW)

* Donnan, Henry (NSW) b Nov. 12, 1864 Liverpool (NSW) d Aug. 13, 1956 Bexley (NSW)

Donnelly, James Louis (NSW) b June 24, 1906 Merimbula (NSW) d March 2, 1978 Koorawatha (NSW)

Doolan, Bruce Richard (Tas) b Sept. 9, 1947 Launceston (Tas)

* Dooland, Bruce (SAust) b Nov. 1, 1923 Cowandilla (SAust) d Sept. 8, 1980 Bedford Park (SAust)

Douglas, Adye (Tas) b May 31, 1815 Thorpe-next-Norwich (England) d April 10, 1906 Hobart (Tas)

Douglas, Alfred Jamieson (Tas) b Feb. 4, 1872 Newstead (Tas) d June 9, 1938 Malvern (Vic)

Douglas, John Raymond (Vic) b Oct. 24, 1951 East Brunswick (Vic)

Douglas, Osborne Henry (Tas) b March 14, 1880 Launceston (Tas) d April 24, 1918 Dernancourt, near Albert (France)

Dowling, Gerard Patrick (Vic) b Nov. 10, 1964 Preston (Vic)

Down, Granville James Stuart (SAust) b May 24, 1883 Dubbo (NSW) d May 14, 1970 St Kilda (Vic)

Downes, Francis (NSW) b June 11, 1864 Redfern (NSW) d May 20, 1916 Little Bay (NSW)

Downey, Donnell Raymond (SAust) b April 12, 1907 Parkside (SAust) d Jan. 23, 1966 Adelaide (SAust)

Downey, Joseph Aloysius (Qld) b Feb. 4, 1895 (Qld) d April 18, 1934 Kangaroo Point (Qld)

Downton, Andrew Graham (Tas) b July 17, 1977 Auburn (NSW)

Dowsley, Harcourt (Vic) b July 15, 1919 Essendon (Vic)

Doyle, Bryan Bernard John (Vic) b Oct. 20, 1968 Carlton (Vic)

Draney, John Davis Rodney (Qld) b May 10, 1927 Indooroopilly (Qld)

Drape, Isaac Selby (Vic & Qld) b May 13, 1864 Hotham (Vic) d Feb. 7, 1916 St Kilda (Vic)

Drennan, John (SAust) b Nov. 13, 1932 West Croydon (SAust)

Drew, Albert David (WAust) b Oct. 30, 1906 West Leederville (WAust) d Feb. 20, 1984 Shenton Park (WAust)

Drew, Charles Francis (SAust) b April 24, 1888 Kooringa, now Burra (SAust) d Feb. 19, 1960 Adelaide (SAust)

Drew, James Leggat (Vic) b Jan. 20, 1872 Williamstown (Vic) d Jan. 22, 1944 Maryborough (Vic)

Drew, Richard (Vic) b Jan. 20, 1871 Creswick (Vic) death details unknown

Drew, Thomas Mitchell (SAust) b June 9, 1875 Kooringa, now Burra (SAust) d Jan. 9, 1928 Toowoomba (Qld)

Drewer, Richard Harris (SAust) b June 12, 1946 Parkside (SAust)

Drinnen, Peter John (Qld) b Oct. 5, 1967 Bundaberg (Qld)

Driscoll, Clarence Rheuben (Tas) b Sept. 4, 1895 Glebe (Tas) d May 1, 1948 Hobart (Tas)

Driscoll, Vernon Reginald (Tas) b April 11, 1891 Glebe (Tas) d March 19, 1967 Bellerive (Tas)

Driver, Richard (NSW) b Sept. 16, 1829 Cabramatta (NSW) d July 8, 1880 Moore Park (NSW)

Driver, Walter George (Vic & WAust) b Sept. 25, 1922 Glenhuntly (Vic) d Jan. 11, 1994 Mooloolooba (Qld)

Druery, William Lance (Qld) b May 14, 1927 Townsville (Qld) d Aug. 10, 1993 Carina (Qld)

Drysdale, John (Vic) b Aug. 1, 1862 Castlemaine (Vic) d Feb. 15, 1922 Kew (Vic)

Du Croz, Gervase Bedford (Tas & Vic) b c. 1830 (England) d Feb. 19, 1855 Launceston (Tas)

Ducker, John Robert (SAust) b June 12, 1934 Prospect (SAust)

Dudgeon, Keith Edward (Qld) b Sept. 5, 1946 Cairns (Qld)

Dudley, Walter John (Vic) b May 29, 1918 Carlton North (Vic) d April 5, 1978 Northcote (Vic)

* Duff, Reginald Alexander (NSW) b Aug. 17, 1878 Sydney (NSW) d Dec. 13, 1911 North Sydney (NSW)

Duff, Walter Scott (NSW) b April 22, 1876 Sydney (NSW) d Nov. 11, 1921 Sydney (NSW)

Duffy, Joseph Thomas (Vic) b c. 1860 Ballarat (Vic) d May 30, 1936 Ballarat (Vic)

Duffy, William Vincent (WAust) b July 8, 1866 Doutta Galla (Vic) d June 13, 1959 Subiaco (WAust)

Dufty, Ross (Tas) b Aug. 13, 1927 Bingara (NSW)

Dugan, Roger Wayne (SAust) b Aug. 10, 1959 Broken Hill (NSW)

Duldig, Lance Desmond (SAust) b Feb. 21, 1922 Eudunda (SAust) d Sept. 14, 1998 Beaumont (SA)

Dulling, Philip (Tas) b May 5, 1909 Launceston (Tas) d Sept. 1, 1974 Launceston (Tas)

Dumaresq, Henry Rowland Gascoigne (Tas) b Feb. 28, 1839 Longford (Tas) d Oct. 31, 1924 Ulverstone (Tas)

Dummett, Arthur William (Vic) b Nov. 18, 1900 Clifton Hill (Vic) d June 4, 1968 Ivanhoe (Vic)

Dummett, William (NSW) b July 18, 1840 Sydney (NSW) d May 3, 1900 (NSW)

* Duncan, John Ross Frederick (Qld & Vic) b March 25, 1944 Herston (Qld)

Duncan, William (Qld) b Oct. 19, 1912 Brisbane (Qld) d July 27, 1943 South Brisbane (Qld)

Dunn, Martin Matthew Francis (Qld) b May 10, 1884 Maryborough (Qld) d Dec. 31, 1942 Woollahra (NSW)

Dunn, Wallace Peter (WAust) b Aug. 8, 1921 Westonia (WAust)

Dunstan, William John (WAust) b Dec. 4, 1878 Glen Osmond (SAust) d April 11, 1955 Perth (WAust)

Dupain, Francois Henri (NSW) b Aug. 19, 1889 Ashfield (NSW) d Sept. 29, 1959 Burradoo (NSW)

Duperouzel, Bruce (WAust) b April 21, 1950 Northam (WAust)

Dwyer, Christopher (Vic) b c. 1879 Albury (NSW) d July 21, 1961 Kew (Vic)

Dwyer, Edmund Alfred (NSW) b Oct. 19, 1894 Mosman (NSW) d Sept. 10, 1975 Mosman (NSW)

Dwyer, Eric William (Tas) b June 15, 1917 St Helen's (Tas) d May 15, 1997 Canberra (ACT)

* Dyer, Gregory Charles (NSW) b March 16, 1959 Parramatta (NSW)

Dyer, Robert Henry (SAust) b c. 1860 (England) d Aug. 31, 1950 Nailsworth (SAust)

Dykes, James Andrew (Tas) b Nov. 15, 1971 Hobart (Tas)

* Dymock, Geoffrey (Qld) b July 21, 1945 Maryborough (Qld)

* Dyson, John (NSW) b June 11, 1954 Kogarah (NSW)

* Eady, Charles John (Tas) b Oct. 29, 1870 Hobart (Tas) d Dec. 20, 1945 Hobart (Tas)

Easton, Frank Alexander (NSW) b Feb. 19, 1910 Waterloo (NSW) d May 5, 1989 Sydney (NSW)

Easton, Robert Peter (Qld) b Oct. 21, 1936 Windsor (Qld)

* Eastwood, Kenneth Humphrey (Vic) b Nov. 23, 1935 Chatswood (NSW)

Eaton, Anthony Mark (SAust) b June 11, 1953 Prospect (SAust)

Eaton, George Melville (Vic) b Oct. 23, 1904 Durban (South Africa) d May 28, 1938 East Melbourne (Vic)

Eaton, Harry Ronald (NSW) b c. 1909 St Leonard's (NSW) d May 13, 1960 Castlecrag (NSW)

* Ebeling, Hans Irvine (Vic) b Jan. 1, 1905 Avoca (Vic) d Jan. 12, 1980 East Bentleigh (Vic)

Ebsworth, Norman (NSW) b Jan. 2, 1878 Sydney (NSW) d Nov. 19, 1949 Kirribilli (NSW)

Edmondson, Ben Matthew (WAust) b Sept. 28, 1978 Southport (Qld)

Edmondson, Henry Pudsey Dawson (WAust) b Nov. 25, 1872 Hobart (Tas) d Aug. 18, 1946 Perth (WAust)

Edwards, Alan Robert (WAust) b Dec. 24, 1921 Perth (WAust)

Edwards, Allen Crisp (SAust) b Nov. 18, 1868 Brighton (SAust) d Jan. 1, 1961 Adelaide (SAust)

Edwards, Edmund Keane (WAust) b Jan. 6, 1910 Cottesloe (WAust) d Aug. 18, 1990 Cottesloe (WAust)

Edwards, Frederick Raymond (SAust) b Feb. 28, 1908 Sydney (NSW) d April 27, 1982 St Leonards (NSW)

* Edwards, John Dunlop (Vic) b June 12, 1860 Prahran (Vic) d July 31, 1911 Hawksburn (Vic)

Edwards, John Neild (Vic) b Aug. 16, 1928 Ormond (Vic) d Dec. 29, 2002 Malvern (Vic)

* Edwards, Ross (WAust & NSW) b Dec. 1, 1942 Cottesloe (WAust)

* Edwards, Walter John (WAust) b Dec. 23, 1949 Subiaco (WAust)

Egan, Grahame Maxwell (Qld) b June 8, 1941 Armidale (NSW)

Egan, Thomas Charles Wills (NSW) b Oct. 5, 1906 Warren (NSW) d Nov. 29, 1979 Double Bay (NSW)

Egglestone, John Waterhouse (Vic) b July 7, 1847 Hobart (Tas) d Oct. 17, 1912 Malvern (Vic)

Eime, Andrew Barry (SAust) b July 3, 1971 North Adelaide (SAust)

Elliott, Edward Hudspith (Vic) b April 19, 1851 Sunderland, Durham (England) d March 19, 1885 North Carlton (Vic)

Elliott, Gideon (Vic) b April 17, 1828 Merstham, Surrey (England) d Feb. 15, 1869 Richmond (Vic)

* Elliott, Matthew Thomas Gray (Vic) b Sept. 28, 1971 Chelsea (Vic)

Elliott, Raymond Allister (Tas) b Jan. 1, 1918 New Norfolk (Tas) d Sept. 8, 1997 New Town (Tas)

Elliott, Thomas Henry (Tas) b March 22, 1879 Hobart (Tas) d Oct. 21, 1939 Launceston (Tas)

Ellis, David Leigh (Qld) b Jan. 2, 1951 Herston (Qld)

Ellis, Donald George (Tas) b Oct. 5, 1917 Launceston (Tas) d Sept. 4, 2001 Launceston (Tas)

Ellis, John Albert (Qld) b June 10, 1914 Spring Hill (Qld) d Oct. 17, 1994 Greenslopes (Qld)

Ellis, John Leslie (Vic) b May 9, 1890 Malvern (Vic) d July 26, 1974 Glen Iris (Vic)

Ellis, Leslie George (NSW) b March 2, 1936 New Lambton (NSW)

Ellis, Matthew (Vic) b Feb. 3, 1870 Melbourne (Vic) d Nov. 19, 1940 Fitzroy (Vic)

Ellis, Percy Arthur (Vic) b May 10, 1906 Abbotsford (Vic) d April 25, 1992 Lilydale (Vic)

Ellis, Reginald Newnham (Vic) b Feb. 22, 1891 Randwick (NSW) d May 26, 1959 Cheltenham (Vic)

Ellis, Reginald Sidney (SAust) b Nov. 26, 1917 Angaston (SAust)

* Ellison, Richard Mark (Tas) b Sept. 21, 1959 Willesborough, Kent (England)

Eltham, William Keith (Tas) b Oct. 10, 1886 Hobart (Tas) d Dec. 31, 1916 Lesboeufs (France)

Emerson, David Alan (Vic) b March 10, 1961 Malvern (Vic)

Emerson, Norman Leonard (Vic) b Oct. 26, 1939 Ararat (Vic)

* Emery, Philip Allen (NSW) b June 25, 1964 St Ives (NSW)

* Emery, Sidney Hand (NSW) b Oct. 16, 1885 Macdonaldtown (NSW) d Jan. 7, 1967 Petersham (NSW)

Emery, Victor Rupert (NSW) b Dec. 20, 1920 Redfern (NSW)

Eneberg, Alfred (SAust) b Nov. 30, 1928 Birkenhead (SAust)

England, Ernest James (WAust & SAust) b May 26, 1927 Bunbury (WAust)

Englefield, William (SAust) b Oct. 6, 1917 Leichhardt (NSW) d June 3, 1988 Ryde (NSW)

Epstein, Jan (WAust) b Oct. 1, 1918 West Perth (WAust) d March 24, 1988 Melbourne (Vic)

Evan, Laurence William (SAust) b Oct. 27, 1864 Adelaide (SAust) d Aug. 12, 1894 North Adelaide (SAust)

Evans, Arthur Ernest (SAust) b July 12, 1871 East Adelaide (SAust) d March 26, 1950 Bordertown (SAust)

Evans, Charles F (Tas) birth and death details unknown

* Evans, Edwin (NSW) b March 26, 1849 Emu Plains (NSW) d July 2, 1921 Walgett (NSW)

Evans, George Nicholas (WAust) b Dec. 24, 1915 Boulder (WAust) d April 11, 1965 Hollywood (WAust)

Evans, Henry (Tas) b Aug. 6, 1846 Launceston (Tas) death details unknown

Evans, Richard (SAust) b Sept. 9, 1867 Hindmarsh (SAust) d Nov. 1, 1939 Hindmarsh (SAust)

Evans, Royston Macauley (WAust) b Jan. 13, 1884 Semaphore (SAust) d March 12, 1977 Perth (WAust)

Evans, Walter Allan (WAust) b Sept. 29, 1897 Gympie (Qld) d Jan. 15, 1955 Hollywood (WAust)

Evans, William Thomas (Qld) b April 9, 1876 Indooroopilly (Qld) d July 19, 1964 Woolloongabba (Qld)

Everett, Charles Samuel (NSW) b June 17, 1901 Marrickville (NSW) d Oct. 10, 1970 Concord (NSW)

Everett, Dudley Tabor (WAust) b March 9, 1912 Perth (WAust) d May 3, 1943 Ontario (Canada) on active service

Everett, James Seabrook (WAust) b July 20, 1884 Toodyay (WAust) d June 19, 1968 Nedlands (WAust)

Evers, Harold Albert (NSW & WAust) b Feb. 28, 1876 Newcastle (NSW) d Feb. 6, 1937 Perth (WAust)

Eyres, Gordon (WAust) b Dec. 20, 1912 Kalgoorlie (WAust)

Facy, Ashley Cooper (Tas & Vic) b Jan. 26, 1886 Bellerive (Tas) d Dec. 2, 1954 Hobart (Tas)

Fagan, Arthur Mervyn (NSW) b April 24, 1931 birthplace unknown

Fairbairn, Clive Lindsay (Vic) b Aug. 25, 1919 Geelong (Vic)

* Fairfax, Alan George (NSW) b June 16, 1906 Summer Hill (NSW) d May 17, 1955 Kensington, London (England)

Fairweather, Robert John (NSW) b July 24, 1845 Pyrmont (NSW) d May 31, 1925 Waverley (NSW)

Faithfull, Henry Montague (NSW) b June 16, 1847 Springfield (NSW) d Oct. 22, 1908 Elizabeth Bay (NSW)

Fallowfield, Leslie John (NSW) b March 12, 1914 North Sydney (NSW) d May 29, 1999 North Ryde (NSW)

Fanning, Edward (Vic) b March 16, 1848 Sydney (NSW) d Nov. 30, 1917 St Kilda (Vic)

Farnsworth, Andrew William (NSW) b Jan. 14, 1887 Sydney (NSW) d Oct. 30, 1966 Waterfall (NSW)

Farquhar, Barclay Wallace (NSW) b Feb. 22, 1875 West Maitland (NSW) d Jan. 23, 1961 Queanbeyan (NSW)

Farquhar, John Kennedy (Qld) b Jan. 30, 1887 Home Hill (Qld) d July 31, 1977 Chermside (Qld)

Farrar, Frank Martindale (NSW) b March 29, 1893 Rylstone (NSW) d May 30, 1973 Waverley (NSW)

Farrell, Graeme Ian (Tas) b Nov. 2, 1947 Launceston (Tas)

Farrell, Graeme Stanley (SAust) b Feb. 4, 1943 Norwood (SAust)

Farrell, Michael Graeme (Tas) b Sept. 24, 1968 Melbourne (Vic)

Farrell, Steven James (Qld) b Feb. 6, 1980 Townsville (Qld)

Faulkner, Peter Ian (Tas) b April 18, 1960 Launceston (Tas)

Faull, Martin Peter (SAust) b May 10, 1968 Darwin (NT)

Faunce, Thomas Bowman (Qld) b March 19, 1883 (Qld) d May 27, 1968 Greenslopes (Qld)

Favell, Alan Leslie (SAust) b June 6, 1960 North Adelaide (SAust)

* Favell, Leslie Ernest (SAust) b Oct. 6, 1929 Rockdale (NSW) d June 14, 1987 Magill (SAust)

Fennelly, Sidney James (Qld) b March 22, 1887 Sydney (NSW) d Aug. 25, 1964 Brighton (Qld)

Fenton, Arthur (Vic) b Feb. 27, 1870 Tarnagulla (Vic) d May 20, 1950 Melbourne (Vic)

Ferguson, James Alexander (Tas) b Feb. 19, 1848 Launceston (Tas) d May 10, 1913 Brisbane (Qld)

Ferguson, Leslie Drummond (Vic) b Dec. 8, 1892 North Brighton (Vic) d Jan. 30, 1957 East Melbourne (Vic)

Ferrall, Raymond Alfred (Tas) b May 27, 1906 Launceston (Tas) d June 1, 2000 Launceston (Tas)

Ferries, Kenneth Ian (WAust) b May 7, 1936 Wyalkatchem (WAust)

* Ferris, John James (NSW & SAust) b May 21, 1867 Sydney (NSW) d Nov. 17, 1900 Durban (South Africa)

Fett, Frederick (Qld) b May 2, 1886 Toowoomba (Qld) d Aug. 27, 1979 Woolloongabba (Qld)

Fewin, Henry (Qld) b Jan. 25, 1896 Townsville (Qld) d Aug. 25, 1980 Bongaree (Qld)

Fidock, Harold Edward (WAust) b Aug. 24, 1902 Adelaide (SAust) d Feb. 9, 1986 Nedlands (WAust)

Field, William (Tas) b March 17, 1816 Port Dalrymple (Tas) d June 22, 1890 Bishopsbourne (Tas)

Fielke, Noel Robert (SAust) b Dec. 23, 1966 Blackwood (SAust)

Findlay, Algernon Percy (Tas) b March 17, 1892 Launceston (Tas) d Jan. 9, 1956 Launceston (Tas)

* Fingleton, John Henry Webb (NSW) b April 28, 1908 Waverley (NSW) d Nov. 22, 1981 St Leonards (NSW)

Fisher, Alexander (Qld) b March 14, 1908 Gatton (Qld) d Oct. 6, 1968 Maryborough (Qld)

Fisher, Arthur Donnelly Wentworth (NSW) b Dec. 14, 1882 Lavender Bay (NSW) d July 9, 1968 Neutral Bay (NSW)

Fisher, Barry (Qld) b Jan. 20, 1934 Brisbane (Qld) d April 6, 1980 Inverell (NSW)

Fisher, Harry Medcalf (SAust) b May 28, 1899 North Adelaide (SAust) d Oct. 14, 1982 South Launceston (Tas)

Fisher, William Thornton (Qld) b Aug. 31, 1865 Brisbane (Qld) d June 1, 1945 Herston (Qld)

Fitchett, Michael King (Vic) b Nov. 30, 1927 Hawthorn (Vic)

Fitness, Gavin Arthur James (Qld) b June 4, 1968 Maryborough (Qld)

Fitzgerald, David Andrew (WAust & SAust) b Nov. 30, 1972 Osborne Park (WAust)

Fitzgerald, James (Qld) b Feb. 19, 1874 Surry Hills (NSW) d Aug. 20, 1950 Graceville (Qld)

Fitzmaurice, Desmond Michael John (Vic) b Oct. 16, 1917 Carlton (Vic) d Jan. 19, 1981 Prahran (Vic)

Fitzmaurice, Dudley James Anthony (Vic) b May 21, 1913 Carlton (Vic) d June 28, 2001 Frankston (Vic)

Fitzpatrick, Jack Herbert (NSW) b Sept. 18, 1911 Bankstown (NSW) d Jan. 23, 1999 Bankstown (NSW)

Fitzpatrick, John Milling (Vic) b June 26, 1889 Waverley (NSW) d Aug. 16, 1952 Coogee (NSW)

Fleay, Clarence William Edward James (WAust) b Dec. 27, 1886 Gilgering (WAust) d Aug. 6, 1955 Katanning (WAust)

* Fleetwood-Smith, Leslie O'Brien (Vic) b March 30, 1908 Stawell (Vic) d March 16, 1971 Fitzroy (Vic)

Flegler, Shawn Leonard (Qld) b March 23, 1972 Darwin (NT)

* Fleming, Damien William (Vic & SAust) b April 24, 1970 Bentley (WAust)

Fletcher, John Henry (Qld) b Oct. 27, 1893 Brisbane (Qld)

Fletcher, John William (Qld) b Jan. 25, 1884 Woollahra (NSW) d March 13, 1965 South Brisbane (Qld)

Flint, Kerry Royce (Tas) b Sept. 17, 1946 Smithton (Tas)

Flockton, Raymond George (NSW) b March 14, 1930 Paddington (NSW)

* Flower, Andrew (SAust) b April 28, 1968 Cape Town (South Africa)

Flynn, Brian James (Qld) b June 7, 1929 Darlinghurst (NSW) d Aug. 3, 1986 Vesty's Beach, Darwin (NT)

Flynn, John Paul (NSW) b June 29, 1890 Paddington (NSW) d May 28, 1952 Chatswood (NSW)

Foley, Geoffrey Ian (Qld) b Oct. 11, 1967 Jandowae (Qld)

Foley, Maurice Hinton (WAust) b Feb. 4, 1930 Perth (WAust)

Folkard, Bernard James (NSW) b May 17, 1878 Ryde (NSW) d Jan. 31, 1937 Leichhardt (NSW)

Fontaine, Frederick Ernest (Vic) b Dec. 14, 1912 Northcote (Vic) d Oct. 24, 1982 Greensborough (Vic)

Foot, Charles Francis (Vic) b Aug. 14, 1855 Brighton (Vic) d July 2, 1926 East Melbourne (Vic)

Foot, Henry Boorn (Vic) b Nov. 21, 1805 Romsey, Hampshire (England) d May 14, 1857 Brighton (Vic)

Ford, Douglas Allan (NSW) b Dec. 16, 1928 Maryville (NSW)

Forsaith, Geoffrey Milner (WAust) b Jan. 5, 1931 Perth (WAust)

Forssberg, Edward Ernest Brackley (NSW) b Dec. 10, 1894 Sydney (NSW) d May 23, 1953 Bondi (NSW)

Forster, William Robert (Tas) b March 1, 1884 Gateshead-on-Tyne, Durham (England) d Feb. 7, 1930 Richmond (Tas)

Foster, Michael Robert (Vic) b March 5, 1973 East Melbourne (Vic)

Foster, Norman Kelk (Qld) b Jan. 19, 1878 Brisbane (Qld) d March 15, 1960 Clayfield (Qld)

Foster, Thomas Henry (NSW) b Sept. 30, 1883 Glebe (NSW) d June 27, 1947 Leichhardt (NSW)

Fothergill, Desmond Hugh (Vic) b July 15, 1920 Northcote (Vic) d March 16, 1996 Melbourne (Vic)

Fowler, Edwin (Vic) b c. 1841 London (England) d May 31, 1909 St Kilda (Vic)

Fox, Albert Henry Newnham (Vic) b April 20, 1867 Battery Point (Tas) d Dec. 24, 1946 Brighton (Vic)

Fox, Norman Henry (NSW) b July 29, 1904 Longueville (NSW) d May 7, 1972 Castle Cove (NSW)

* Francis, Bruce Colin (NSW) b Feb. 18, 1948 Sydney (NSW)

Francis, Craig Lawrence (SAust) b Nov. 25, 1966 North Adelaide (SAust)

Francis, John Charles (Vic) b June 22, 1908 Hawthorn (Vic) d July 6, 2001 Camberwell (Vic)

Francis, Keith Raymond (NSW) b Nov. 14, 1933 Arncliffe (NSW)

Francis, Stanley George (WAust) b April 14, 1906 Geelong (Vic) d Jan. 25, 1994 Nedlands (WAust)

Francke, Fredrick Malcolm (Qld) b March 21, 1939 Mt Lavinia, Colombo (Ceylon)

Frankish, Ronald Richard (WAust) b Oct. 6, 1925 Perth (WAust)

Fraser, Neville Graham (Qld) b Sept. 28, 1930 Cleveland (Qld)

Fraser, Robert Alexander (SAust) b Feb. 13, 1954 Parkside (SAust)

Frazer, Ian Douglas (Vic) b Sept. 7, 1966 Lilydale (Vic)

Frederick, John (Vic) b Dec. 18, 1910 Armadale (Vic)

Free, Ernest Peardon (Tas) b Sept. 7, 1867 Rokeby (Tas) d July 5, 1946 Hobart (Tas)

Freedman, David Andrew (NSW) b June 19, 1964 Darlinghurst (NSW)

Freeman, Edward John (Tas) b Nov. 7, 1848 Hobart (Tas) d Aug. 11, 1905 Hobart (Tas)

* Freeman, Eric Walter (SAust) b July 13, 1944 Largs Bay (SAust)

Freeman, Harry Septimus (Vic & Qld) b June 11, 1860 Carlton (Vic) d Nov. 7, 1933 Brunswick (Vic)

Freeman, John Edward (Qld) b June 28, 1935 Nundah (Qld)

Freeman, Thomas Daniel (Tas) b June 13, 1894 Hobart (Tas) d June 19, 1965 Heidelberg (Vic)

Freemantle, Leslie Francis (Vic & WAust) b May 11, 1898 Canterbury (Vic) d June 6, 1963 Kew (Vic)

* Freer, Frederick Alfred William (Vic) b Dec. 4, 1915 North Carlton (Vic) d Nov. 2, 1998 Frankston (Vic)

Frei, Harald (Qld) b May 1, 1951 Nuremberg (Germany)

Frick, John (SAust) b March 24, 1957 Medindie (SAust)

Friend, Raymond Grattan (Tas) b April 11, 1898 Prahran (Vic) death details unknown

Frost, Albert Edgar (Tas) b March 19, 1878 Launceston (Tas) d Oct. 25, 1951 Launceston (Tas)

Frost, Allan Russell (SAust) b Dec. 2, 1942 Adelaide (SAust)

Frost, Sydney Robert (Tas) b Jan. 21, 1881 Launceston (Tas) d Dec. 19, 1952 Middle Park (Vic)

Fry, Herbert James (Vic) b Oct. 28, 1870 Morphett Vale (SAust) d Jan. 19, 1953 Hawthorn (Vic)

Furlong, Ronald William (Vic) b May 16, 1936 Ballarat (Vic)

Furness, Arthur John (NSW) b Jan. 11, 1873 Sydney (NSW) d Oct. 31, 1948 Strathfield (NSW)

Gaggin, William Wakeham (Vic) b Nov. 23, 1847 County Cork (Ireland) d July 5, 1925 Elsternwick (Vic)

Gallagher, Ian Noel (Qld) b Nov. 20, 1950 Greenslopes (Qld)

Gallash, Ian (WAust) b June 17, 1936 Perth (WAust)

Galloway, Paul Warren (SAust) b Sept. 14, 1943 North Sydney (NSW) d Aug. 20, 1996 Loxton (SAust)

Gamble, Herbert Spencer (Vic & Qld) b March 2, 1903 Sunbury (Vic) d June 15, 1962 Shorncliffe (Qld)

Gandy, Michael George (Tas) b Aug. 28, 1944 Hobart (Tas)

* Gannon, John Bryant (WAust) b Feb. 8, 1947 Subiaco (WAust)

Gardiner, George Alan (WAust) b Nov. 27, 1914 Perth (WAust) d Oct. 17, 1989 Melbourne (Vic)

Gardiner, Grant Bruce (Vic) b Feb. 26, 1965 Melbourne (Vic)

Gardiner, Jack (Tas) b May 20, 1913 Hobart (Tas) d Sept. 11, 1976 Hobart (Tas)

Gardner, Charles Allan (Vic) b Oct. 28, 1908 Brighton East (Vic) d Dec. 9, 2001 Frankston (Vic)

Gardner, Roy (Vic) b Jan. 18, 1914 Hotham West (Vic) d April 2, 2004 Mount Eliza (Vic)

Garland, John George Morton (Vic) b Aug. 22, 1875 Hotham (Vic) d Feb. 23, 1938 Hawthorn (Vic)

Garlick, Paul Anthony (Vic) b Sept. 21, 1968 Sandringham (Vic)

Garnaut, Matthew Stuart (WAust) b Nov. 7, 1973 Subiaco (WAust)

* Garner, Joel (SAust) b Dec. 16, 1952 Enterprise, Christ Church (Barbados)

Garnsey, George Leonard (NSW) b Feb. 10, 1881 Sydney (NSW) d April 18, 1951 Canberra (ACT)

* Garrett, Thomas William (NSW) b July 26, 1858 Wollongong (NSW) d Aug. 6, 1943 Warrawee (NSW)

Gartrell, Kevin Boyd (WAust) b March 4, 1936 Midland (WAust)

Gartrell, Robert Boyd (WAust & Tas) b March 9, 1962 Middle Swan (WAust)

Garwood, Rex Elvyn (Tas) b May 15, 1930 Hobart (Tas)

Gaskell, Mark Andrew (Qld) b Oct. 17, 1956 Herston (Qld)

Gatehouse, George Henry (Tas) b June 20, 1864 Sorell (Tas) d Jan. 25, 1947 Toorak (Vic)

Gatenby, David John (Tas) b Feb. 12, 1952 Launceston (Tas)

Gatenby, Lawrence Frank (Tas) b April 10, 1889 Epping Forest (Tas) d Jan. 14, 1917 Armentieres (France)

Gatenby, Peter Robert (Tas) b May 26, 1949 Launceston (Tas)

* Gaunt, Ronald Arthur (WAust & Vic) b Feb. 26, 1934 Yarloop (WAust)

Geary, Alfred (NSW) b Aug. 8, 1849 birthplace unknown d Oct. 14, 1911 Brisbane (Qld)

Gee, Daniel Albert (NSW) b Sept. 30, 1875 Sydney (NSW) d Jan. 16, 1947 Adelaide (SAust)

Gehan, Rodney Arthur Howard (SAust) b Nov. 12, 1942 Werribee (Vic) d Feb. 8, 2001 Hope Island (Qld)

* Gehrs, Donald Raeburn Algernon (SAust) b Nov. 29, 1880 Port Victor (SAust) d June 25, 1953 Kings Park (SAust)

Geise, Gregory Gordon (NSW) b April 3, 1960 Wallsend (NSW)

Gentle, Steven Robert (SAust) b May 30, 1955 Rose Park (SAust)

George, Shane Peter (SAust) b Oct. 20, 1970 Adelaide (SAust)

Germaine, Lewis (Vic & WAust) b March 1, 1935 Glenhuntly (Vic) d April 8, 1992 Melbourne (Vic)

Geyer, Kevin James (NSW) b Oct. 11, 1973 Bathurst (NSW)

Gibaud, Henry Peter (Vic) b May 1, 1892 Carlton (Vic) d July 29, 1964 Fitzroy (Vic)

Gibbs, Charles H. (SAust) b c. 1841 full birth and death details unknown

* Gibbs, Lancelot Richard (SAust) b Sept. 29, 1934 Georgetown (British Guiana)

Giblin, Vincent Wanostrocht (Tas) b Nov. 13, 1817 Kingston upon Thames, Surrey (England) d May 15, 1884 Milsons Point (NSW)

Gibson, George (Tas) b 1827 birth day and month unknown Norfolk Plains (Tas) d Oct. 8, 1873 Sandy Bay (Tas)

Gibson, George Watson Hogg (Vic) b Jan. 16, 1828 Thakambau (Jamaica) d Sept. 5, 1910 Carlton (Vic)

Gibson, Gordon Galloway (Tas) b Nov. 1, 1908 Hobart (Tas) d July 7, 1967 Melbourne (Vic)

Gibson, Vincent Roy (SAust) b May 14, 1916 Rose Park (SAust) d Nov. 28, 1983 Neutral Bay (NSW)

* Giffen, George (SAust) b March 27, 1859 Adelaide (SAust) d Nov. 29, 1927 Parkside (SAust)

* Giffen, Walter Frank (SAust) b Sept. 21, 1861 Adelaide (SAust) d June 28, 1949 North Unley (SAust)

Gilbert, Ashley Stephen (Vic) b Nov. 26, 1971 Melbourne (Vic)

* Gilbert, David Robert (NSW & Tas) b Dec. 19, 1960 Darlinghurst (NSW)

Gilbert, Eddie (Qld) b 1904 birth day and month unknown Woodford (Qld) d Jan. 9, 1978 Wacol (Qld)

Gilbert, George Henry Bailey (NSW) b Sept. 2, 1829 Cheltenham, Gloucestershire (England) d June 16, 1906 Summer Hill (NSW)

Gilbourne, Robert James (SAust) b July 16, 1943 Adelaide (SAust)

* Gilchrist, Adam Craig (NSW & WAust) b Nov. 14, 1971 Bellingen (NSW)

Giles, Leonard George (SAust) b June 17, 1921 Yorketown (SAust) d Aug. 23, 1994 Glandore (SAust)

Gill, Lynwood Laurence (Tas & Qld) b Nov. 19, 1891 Macquarie Plains (Tas) d Dec. 4, 1986 Pullenvale (Qld)

Giller, James Frederick (Vic) b May 1, 1870 Melbourne (Vic) d June 13, 1947 Albert Park (Vic)

* Gillespie, Jason Neil (SAust) b April 19, 1975 Darlinghurst (NSW)

Gilmore, Francis Patrick John (NSW) b Sept. 12, 1909 Yass (NSW) d April 26, 1955 Camperdown (NSW)

* Gilmour, Gary John (NSW) b June 26, 1951 Waratah (NSW)

Gladigau, Peter Wayne (SAust) b May 23, 1965 Whyalla (SAust)

Glassock, Craig Anthony (NSW) b Nov. 29, 1973 Mona Vale (NSW)

* Gleeson, John William (NSW) b March 14, 1938 Kyogle (NSW)

Glew, Steven Adam (Cricket Academy) b March 11, 1977 Perth (WAust)

Glynn, William Thomas (Tas) b c. 1846 d June 18, 1895 Fitzroy (Vic)

Goddard, Henry (NSW) b Nov. 16, 1885 Sydney (NSW) d May 13, 1925 Maroubra (NSW)

Godfrey, Charles George (SAust) b Nov. 17, 1860 Adelaide (SAust) d March 27, 1940 Rose Park (SAust)

Goffet, Gordon (NSW) b March 4, 1941 Speers Point (NSW) d July 29, 2004 Waratah (NSW)

Goggin, Peter John Thomas (Qld) b Oct. 30, 1965 Roma (Qld)

Gogler, Keith Geoffrey (SAust) b May 1, 1923 Port Augusta (SAust) d Aug. 24, 1983 Glenelg (SAust)

Goldman, Albert Edward Arms (Qld) b Oct. 4, 1868 Wee Waa (NSW) d Jan. 30, 1937 Sydney (NSW)

Goldsmith, Louis (Vic) b Sept. 14, 1846 Melbourne (Vic) d Sept. 15, 1911 East Melbourne (Vic)

Gonnella, Peter (WAust) b Jan. 14, 1963 Canberra (ACT)

Good, Robert Norman Scott (WAust) b March 29, 1885 East Melbourne (Vic) d June 16, 1962 Camberwell (Vic)

Goode, Benjamin Ryall (SAust) b Jan. 23, 1924 Port Lincoln (SAust)

Gooden, Henry Alfred (SAust) b Jan. 12, 1858 Adelaide (SAust) d March 30, 1904 North Fitzroy (Vic)

Gooden, James Edward (SAust) b Dec. 23, 1845 Brentford, Middlesex (England) d July 17, 1913 Norwood (SAust)

Gooden, Norman Leslie (SAust) b Dec. 27, 1889 Norwood (SAust) d July 5, 1966 Unley Park (SAust)

Goodfellow, James Edward (SAust) b Aug. 21, 1850 Surrey (England) d July 22, 1924 Malvern (SAust)

Goodman, Gary Weech (Tas & SAust) b Dec. 6, 1953 Sydney (NSW)

Goodrick, Garnet Gordon (Tas) b Feb. 19, 1895 Franklin (Tas) d Jan. 26, 1929 South Melbourne (Vic)

Goodwin, Charles Geoffrey (Tas) b Feb. 12, 1923 Hobart (Tas) d Sept. 20, 1981 Fitzroy (Vic)

* Goodwin, Murray William (WAust) b Dec. 11, 1972 Salisbury (Southern Rhodesia)

Goodwin, Victor Henry Vallance (Qld) b Oct. 26, 1906 Newtown (NSW) d Sept. 22, 1957 Leichhardt (NSW)

Gooma, George Arlington (Qld) b June 25, 1918 Fortitude Valley (Qld) d Oct. 1, 1985 Greenslopes (Qld)

Gooneseena, Gamini (NSW) b Feb. 16, 1931 Mt Lavinia, Colombo (Ceylon)

Gordon, Charles Steward (Vic) b Sept. 8, 1849 Oakleaze, Gloucestershire (England) d March 24, 1930 Nottington, Dorset (England)

Gordon, Evan Shawn (NSW) b Sept. 26, 1960 Pinelands, Cape Town (South Africa)

Gordon, George Birnie (Vic) b Aug. 12, 1860 South Melbourne (Vic) d March 5, 1946 Rose Bay (NSW)

Gordon, George Hollinworth (NSW) b Sept. 20, 1846 New England District (NSW) d May 18, 1923 Darling Point (NSW)

Gordon, Trevor Fairburn (Tas) b Feb. 18, 1915 Hobart (Tas)

Gorman, Frederick Owen (NSW) b Feb. 15, 1843 Sydney (NSW) death details unknown

Gorringe, Harrison Reginald (WAust) b March 7, 1928 Carlisle (WAust)

Gorry, Charles Richard (NSW) b Sept. 18, 1878 Auckland (New Zealand) d Sept. 13, 1950 Petersham (NSW)

Goss, Edward Alfred (Vic) b Nov. 28, 1875 Richmond (Vic) d Sept. 1, 1955 Camberwell (Vic)

Gostelow, Reginald Edwin Potter (NSW) b July 26, 1900 Darlinghurst (NSW) d Aug. 2, 1984 Darling Point (NSW)

Gott, Douglas Lawrence (Vic) b June 30, 1950 Melbourne (Vic)

Gough, Francis Joseph (Qld) b July 26, 1898 Sandgate (Qld) d Jan. 30, 1980 Sandgate (Qld)

Gould, Fred Keen (SAust) b Sept. 18, 1891 Hindmarsh (SAust) d Feb. 15, 1954 Kingswood (SAust)

Gould, John William (NSW) b Oct. 1, 1868 Sydney (NSW) d Dec. 4, 1908 Lewisham (NSW)

Gouly, Lionel (WAust) b Feb. 12, 1873 Woolloomooloo (NSW) d April 15, 1911 Perth (WAust)

Gourlay, Kenneth Garrett (Tas) b June 27, 1914 Hobart (Tas) d Jan. 28, 1999 Lenah Valley (Tas)

Govan, John Macmillan (Qld) b Dec. 30, 1914 Coorparoo (Qld) d July 20, 1996 South Brisbane (Qld)

Gow, Frederick Kingswood (NSW) b Dec. 18, 1882 Richmond (NSW) d Oct. 11, 1961 Randwick (NSW)

Grace, Brian James David (Qld) b Dec. 30, 1945 Herston (Qld)

Graf, Shaun Francis (Vic & WAust) b May 19, 1957 Somerville (Vic)

* Graham, Henry (Vic) b Nov. 22, 1870 Carlton (Vic) d Feb. 7, 1911 Dunedin (New Zealand)

Grangel, Horace Henry Eric (Vic) b Nov. 23, 1908 Burwood (NSW)

Grant, Bartholomew (Vic) b Aug. 13, 1876 St Kilda (Vic) death details unknown

Grant, Colin Spicer (SAust) b June 22, 1927 Alberton (SAust) d Sept. 3, 1998 Clare (SAust)

Grant, John William (Vic) b Feb. 9, 1941 Essendon (Vic)

Grant, Norman Frederic (Qld) b Jan. 15, 1891 Sydney (NSW) d Sept. 17, 1966 Coorparoo (Qld)

Grant, Thomas Christopher (Vic) b Dec. 20, 1878 St Kilda (Vic) d c. 1934 Kurri Kurri (NSW))

* Graveney, Thomas William (Qld) b June 16, 1927 Riding Mill, Northumberland (England)

Gray, Arthur Thomas (NSW) b June 12, 1892 Glebe (NSW) d July 19, 1977 Glebe (NSW)

Gray, Cecil Douglas (SAust) b April 28, 1902 Henley Beach (SAust) d c. 1976

Gray, Geoffrey Thomas (Qld) b Aug. 27, 1943 Ipswich (Qld)

Greaves, William Henry (Vic) b c. 1830 (England) d Aug. 6, 1869 Warrnambool (Vic)

Green, Albert (SAust) b Jan. 28, 1874 Medindie (SAust) d c. 1913

Green, Braddon Clive (Vic) b Jan. 18, 1958 Benalla (Vic)

Green, Donald William (Vic) b Nov. 22, 1933 Canterbury (Vic) d Nov. 7, 1994 Sydney (NSW)

Green, Douglas Carling (Tas) b May 19, 1902 Hobart (Tas) d Nov. 28, 1990 Hobart (Tas)

Green, Jack Godfrey (Vic) b Oct. 4, 1921 Brighton (Vic)

Green, Randal James (NSW) b July 15, 1961 Hawthorn (Vic)

Gregg, Donald Malcolm (SAust) b Sept. 17, 1924 Tumby Bay (SAust)

Gregg, Norman McAlister (NSW) b March 7, 1892 Burwood (NSW) d July 27, 1966 Woollahra (NSW)

Gregory, Arthur Herbert (NSW) b July 7, 1861 Sydney (NSW) d Aug. 17, 1929 Chatswood (NSW)

Gregory, Charles Smith (NSW) b June 5, 1847 Wollongong (NSW) d April 5, 1935 Chatswood (NSW)

Gregory, Charles William (NSW) b Sept. 30, 1878 Randwick (NSW) d Nov. 14, 1910 Darlinghurst (NSW)

* Gregory, David William (NSW) b April 15, 1845 Fairy Meadow (NSW) d Aug. 4, 1919 Turramurra (NSW)

* Gregory, Edward James (NSW) b May 29, 1839 Waverley (NSW) d April 22, 1899 Randwick (NSW)

* Gregory, Edward Sydney (NSW) b April 14, 1870 Randwick (NSW) d Aug. 1, 1929 Randwick (NSW)

* Gregory, Jack Morrison (NSW) b Aug. 14, 1895 North Sydney (NSW) d Aug. 7, 1973 Bega (NSW)

* Gregory, Ross Gerald (Vic) b Feb. 28, 1916 Malvern (Vic) d June 10, 1942 in action over Ghafargon, Assam (India)

Grew, Ernest Sadler (Qld) b Aug. 11, 1867 Birmingham, Warwickshire (England) d Sept. 3, 1954 Brisbane (Qld)

Grieves, Kenneth John (NSW) b Aug. 27, 1925 Burwood (NSW) d Jan. 3, 1992 Rawtenstall, Lancashire (England)

Griffith, Adam Richard (Tas) b Feb. 11, 1978 Launceston (Tas)

Griffith, Harold Bickerton (Qld) b Oct. 10, 1879 Manly (NSW) d May 30, 1947 Herston (Qld)

Griffiths, Charles Samuel (Qld) b May 28, 1889 Townsville (Qld) d May 12, 1928 Rockhampton (Qld)

Griffiths, George Edward (NSW & SAust) b
April 19, 1938 Glebe (NSW)

Grigg, Henry Tattersall (WAust) b May 24,
1906 Fremantle (WAust) d July 9, 1991
Inglewood (WAust)

* Grimmett, Clarence Victor (Vic & SAust) b
Dec. 25, 1891 Caversham, Dunedin (New
Zealand) d May 2, 1980 Kensington (SAust)

Grinrod, Barton (Vic) b April 25, 1834
Liverpool, Lancashire (England) d May 23,
1895 Great Crosby, Lancashire (England)

Grosser, John William (NSW) b Aug. 29, 1942
Gunnedah (NSW)

Groube, Thomas Underwood (Vic) b Sept. 2,
1857 New Plymounth, Taranaki (New
Zealand) d Aug. 5, 1927 Hawthorn (Vic)

Grounds, William Thomas (NSW) b Jan. 14,
1878 Surry Hills (NSW) d July 21, 1950
Mortdale (NSW)

* Grout, Arthur Theodore Wallace (Qld) b
March 30, 1927 Mackay (Qld) d Nov. 9,
1968 Spring Hill (Qld)

Grove, Percival Brian (SAust) b Feb. 23, 1921
Adelaide (SAust)

* Guest, Colin Ernest John (Vic & WAust) b
Oct. 7, 1937 Melbourne (Vic)

Gulliver, Kenneth Charles (NSW) b Aug. 14,
1913 East Maitland (NSW) d June 11, 2001
Collaroy (NSW)

Gumley, William Dudgeon (Qld) b June 28,
1923 Bangalow (NSW) d Aug. 14, 1988
Redcliffe (Qld)

Gun, Lancelot Townsend (SAust) b April 13,
1903 Port Adelaide (SAust) d May 25, 1958
North Adelaide (SAust)

Gunston, Edward Claude (Vic) b May 7, 1913
Brunswick (Vic) d Feb. 28, 1991 Melbourne
(Vic)

Gunthorpe, Gilbert Dudley (Qld) b Aug. 9,
1910 Mt Morgan (Qld) d June 3, 1998
Casino (NSW)

Gurr, Gordon Caleb (SAust) b Dec. 22, 1881
Hyde Park (SAust) d Aug. 11, 1960 Loxton
(SAust)

Guthrie, Herbert France (Vic) b Sept. 29, 1902
Brisbane (Qld) d Jan. 26, 1951 Bellevue Hill
(NSW)

Guttormsen, Maurice Stewart (Qld) b July 29,
1916 Coorpooroo (Qld) d Aug. 8, 1998
Redcliffe (Qld)

Guy, Richard Henry (NSW) b April 4, 1937 St
Leonard's (NSW)

Gwynne, Leslie William (NSW) b Jan. 26,
1893 Sydney (NSW) d Oct. 25, 1962 Keith
(SAust)

Hack, Alfred Thomas (SAust) b June 12, 1905
Glenelg (SAust) d Feb. 4, 1933 Adelaide
(SAust)

Hack, Frederick Theodore (SAust) b Aug. 24,
1877 Aldinga (SAust) d April 10, 1939
Brisbane (Qld)

Hack, Norman Reginald (SAust) b Feb. 25,
1907 Glenelg (SAust) d Oct. 13, 1971 Keith
(SAust)

Hackett, James Victor (Qld) b Oct. 8, 1917
Perth (WAust)

Haddin, Bradley James (NSW) b Oct. 23, 1977
Cowra (NSW)

Haddrick, Alfred Page (Vic) b July 14, 1868
Adelaide (SAust) d Feb. 15, 1939 Brisbane
(Qld)

Haddrick, Ronald Norman (SAust) b April 9,
1929 Glenelg (SAust)

* Hadlee, Richard John (Tas) b July 3, 1951 St
Albans, Christchurch (New Zealand)

Hagdorn, Kim John (WAust) b April 8, 1955
Subiaco (WAust)

Halbert, John Arno (SAust) b Sept. 5, 1937
Hyde Park (SAust)

Halcombe, Ronald Andrewes (SAust &
WAust) b March 19, 1906 Petersburg
(SAust) d Aug. 1, 1993 Geelong (Vic)

Haldane, Harry (SAust) b July 13, 1865 Kent
Town (SAust) d Aug. 12, 1951 Ararat (Vic)

Hale, David John (Qld) b Nov. 11, 1941
Ashgrove (Qld)

Hale, Harold (Tas) b March 27, 1867 Perth
(WAust) d Aug. 2, 1947 Melbourne (Vic)

Hall, Melmoth (Vic) b April 26, 1811
Horringer, Suffolk (England) d Oct. 4, 1885
Ashfield (NSW)

Hall, Richard (NSW) birth and death details
unknown

* Hall, Wesley Winfield (Qld) b Sept. 12, 1937
Glebe Land, Station Hill, St Michael
(Barbados)

Hallebone, Jeffrey (Vic) b Aug. 3, 1929 East
Coburg (Vic)

* Hamence, Ronald Arthur (SAust) b Nov. 25,
1915 Hindmarsh (SAust)

Hamilton, James (Tas) b May 16, 1843
birthplace unknown d July 28, 1881
Launceston (Tas)

Hamilton, Thomas Ferrier (Vic) b March 31,
1821 Cairnhill, Aberdeenshire (Scotland) d
Aug. 7, 1905 St Kilda (Vic)

Hammelmann, Andrew John (Qld) b May 9,
1966 Corinda (Qld)

Hammersley, William Josiah Sumner (Vic) b
Sept. 26, 1828 Ash, Surrey (England) d
Nov. 15, 1886 Fitzroy (Vic)

Hammond, Ashley James (SAust) b Sept. 27,
1969 Burnside (SAust)

Hammond, Charles Pitt (Tas) b Aug. 31, 1868
Hobart (Tas) d Sept. 25, 1955 Hollywood,
California (United States of America)

* Hammond, Jeffrey Roy (SAust) b April 19,
1950 North Adelaide (SAust)

* Hampshire, John Harry (Tas) b Feb. 10, 1941
Thurnscoe, Yorkshire (England)

Hand, Walter Charles (NSW) b July 22, 1847
Richmond, Surrey (England) death details
unknown

Handrickan, Anthony John (SAust) b Jan. 6, 1959 Largs Bay (SAust)

Hanify, Cecil Page (Qld) b Aug. 1, 1887 Brisbane (Qld) d Oct. 28, 1964 Manly (Qld)

Hanlin, David Walter (NSW) b Dec. 8, 1928 Chester (England) d June 6, 2001 Chester (England)

Hanna, Brian Leslie (WAust) b Oct. 7, 1946 Katanning (WAust)

Hansen, Christopher Desmond Petrie (Qld) b May 20, 1912 Childers (Qld)

Hanson, Frederick James (Tas) b April 7, 1872 Hobart (Tas) d Sept. 24, 1917 Moonah (Tas)

Hanson, Leopole Harry (SAust) b Sept. 27, 1883 Woodville (SAust) d April 27, 1952 Kingscote (SAust)

Hantke, Theodore Charles Muncaster (WAust) b Aug. 1, 1875 Blinman (SAust) d May 22, 1931 South Perth (WAust)

Harburn, Colin Malcolm (WAust) b Sept. 3, 1938 Subiaco (WAust)

Hardcastle, Gilbert William (Qld) b Feb. 26, 1910 Bowen Hills (Qld) d Feb. 14, 2000 Currimundi (Qld)

Hardie, Archibald Edward (WAust) b April 14, 1892 Warrnambool (Vic) d March 31, 1976 Nedlands (WAust)

Hardie, J. (Australians) birth and death details unknown

Hargrave, Christopher George (Tas) b Aug. 31, 1951 Kiverton, Yorkshire (England)

Harms, Christopher Louis (SAust) b April 21, 1956 Albury (NSW)

Harper, Barry James (Tas) b Oct. 30, 1938 Launceston (Tas) d April 28, 2003 Launceston (Tas)

Harper, Charles Walter (WAust) b Jan. 27, 1880 Guildford (WAust) d July 1, 1956 South Perth (WAust)

Harper, Laurence Damien (Vic) b Dec. 10, 1970 Deniliquin (NSW)

Harper, Peter Quinton (Vic) b Dec. 11, 1977 Burwood (Vic)

Harris, Daniel Joseph (SAust) b Dec. 31, 1979 Adelaide (SAust)

Harris, David (SAust) b Dec. 19, 1930 Alberton (SAust)

Harris, David Andrew (Vic) b March 17, 1966 Newtown (Vic)

Harris, Douglas James (WAust) b Dec. 20, 1962 Subiaco (WAust)

Harris, Errol John (Tas) b May 2, 1963 Cairns (Qld)

Harris, Gordon William (SAust) b Dec. 11, 1897 Alberton (SAust) d June 30, 1974 Kensington Park (SAust)

Harris, Henry Vere Poulett (Tas & WAust) b April 22, 1865 Hobart (Tas) d March 7, 1933 Perth (WAust)

Harris, Kim Phillip (SAust) b Jan. 24, 1952 North Adelaide (SAust)

Harris, Ryan James (SAust) b Oct. 11, 1979 Nowra (NSW)

Harrison, Colin William (SAust) b May 10, 1928 West Croydon (SAust)

Harrison, Ernest Weedon (Tas) b July 22, 1874 Campbell Town (Tas) d Nov. 14, 1968 New Norfolk (Tas)

Harrity, Mark Andrew (SAust) b March 9, 1974 Semaphore (SAust)

Harrold, Hubert Walton (WAust) b March 9, 1898 East Perth (WAust) d April 14, 1968 Hollywood (WAust)

Harrop, Brett David (Vic) b Dec. 11, 1979 Frankston (Vic)

* Harry, John (Vic) b Aug. 1, 1857 Ballarat (Vic) d Oct. 27, 1919 Surrey Hills (Vic)

Harry, Rex Alexander (Vic) b Oct. 19, 1936 Melbourne (Vic)

Hart, Harold William (Vic) b Jan. 4, 1889 Fitzroy South (Vic) d Jan. 2, 1953 Yarraville (Vic)

Hart, Trevor Herbert (Vic) b Nov. 18, 1935 Morwell (Vic)

Harten, James Thomas (Qld) b Nov. 11, 1924 Brisbane (Qld) d Sept. 11, 2001 Everton Hills (Qld)

* Hartigan, Michael Joseph (NSW & Qld) b Dec. 12, 1879 Chatswood (NSW) d June 7, 1958 Brisbane (Qld)

Hartigan, Thomas Joseph (NSW) b Dec. 8, 1877 Chatswood (NSW) d May 2, 1963 Mosman (NSW)

* Hartkopf, Albert Ernest Victor (Vic) b Dec. 28, 1889 South Fitzroy (Vic) d May 20, 1968 Kew (Vic)

Hartley, Christopher Desmond (Qld) b May 24, 1982 Nambour (Qld)

Harvey, Clarence Edgar (Vic & Qld) b March 17, 1921 Newcastle (NSW)

Harvey, Ernest (WAust) b Dec. 14, 1880 Redfern (NSW) d Oct. 19, 1923 Perth (WAust)

Harvey, George Graham (NSW) b May 7, 1885 Mudgee (NSW) death details unknown

Harvey, Ian Joseph (Vic) b April 10, 1972 Wonthaggi (Vic)

Harvey, Kade Murray (WAust) b Oct. 7, 1975 Subiaco (WAust)

* Harvey, Mervyn Roye (Vic) b April 29, 1918 Broken Hill (NSW) d March 18, 1995 Footscray (Vic)

Harvey, Raymond (Vic) b Jan. 3, 1926 Sydney (NSW)

* Harvey, Robert Neil (Vic & NSW) b Oct. 8, 1928 Fitzroy (Vic)

Harvey, Ronald Mason (NSW) b Oct. 26, 1933 Newcastle (NSW)

Harwood, Shane Michael (Vic) b March 1, 1974 Ballarat (Vic)

* Hassett, Arthur Lindsay (Vic) b Aug. 28, 1913 Geelong (Vic) d June 16, 1993 Batehaven (NSW)

Hassett, Richard Joseph (Vic) b Sept. 7, 1909 Geelong (Vic)

Hastings, Edward Percival (Vic) b June 16, 1849 (England) d May 31, 1905 Brighton East (Vic)

Hastings, Thomas James (Vic) b Jan. 16, 1865 Melbourne (Vic) d June 14, 1938 North Brighton (Vic)

Hatton, Mark Aaron (Tas) b Jan. 24, 1974 Waverley (NSW)

Hauritz, Nathan Michael (Qld) b Oct. 18, 1981 Wondai (Qld)

* Hawke, Neil James Napier (WAust, SAust & Tas) b June 27, 1939 Cheltenham (SAust) d Dec. 25, 2000 Adelaide (SAust)

Hawkins, George William (Vic) b Dec. 7, 1865 Brunswick (Vic) d July 20, 1979 Chiltern (Vic)

Hawson, Edgar Stanley (Tas) b July 25, 1878 Hobart (Tas) d Sept. 29, 1946 Hobart (Tas)

Hawson, Reginald James (Tas) b Sept. 2, 1880 Hobart (Tas) d Feb. 20, 1928 Hobart (Tas)

Hay, Henry (SAust) b March 30, 1874 Adelaide (SAust) d May 16, 1960 Adelaide (SAust)

* Hayden, Matthew Lawrence (Qld) b Oct. 29, 1971 Kingaroy (Qld)

Hayes, William Bede (Qld) b Oct. 16, 1883 Surry Hills (NSW) d Nov. 5, 1926 Corinda (Qld)

Haymes, Frederick George (Tas) b April 5, 1849 Launceston (Tas) d March 12, 1928 Lakes Entrance (Vic)

Hayne, Greg John (NSW) b Oct. 2, 1971 Moree (NSW)

Haysman, Michael Donald (SAust) b April 22, 1961 North Adelaide (SAust)

Hayward, Charles Waterfield (SAust) b June 6, 1867 Norwood (SAust) d Feb. 2, 1934 North Adelaide (SAust)

Haywood, Martin Thomas (NSW) b Oct. 7, 1969 Tamworth (NSW)

* Hazlitt, Gervys Rignold (Vic & NSW) b Sept. 4, 1888 Enfield (NSW) d Oct. 30, 1915 Parramatta (NSW)

Head, Lindsay Hudson (SAust) b Sept. 16, 1935 North Adelaide (SAust)

Headlam, Eustace Slade (Tas) b May 20, 1892 Bothwell (Tas) d May 25, 1958 Launceston (Tas)

Headlam, Felix Emerson (Tas) b June 20, 1897 Bothwell (Tas) d Oct. 5, 1965 Bowral (NSW)

Heairfield, Herbert Venters (SAust) b Feb. 28, 1907 Adelaide (SAust)

Heal, Aaron Keith (WAust) b March 13, 1983 Armadale (WAust)

Healy, Edwin Francis (Vic) b Sept. 26, 1909 Hawthorn (Vic) d June 14, 1995 Camberwell (Vic)

Healy, Eric Nicholas (WAust) b Nov. 5, 1888 Elizabeth Bay (NSW) d Oct. 9, 1954 Cottesloe (WAust)

Healy, Gerald Edward James (Vic) b March 26, 1885 Prahran (Vic) d July 12, 1946 Armadale (Vic)

* Healy, Ian Andrew (Qld) b April 30, 1964 Spring Hill (Qld)

Healy, John Joseph (Vic) b June 23, 1851 Burra (SAust) d May 17, 1916 East Melbourne (Vic)

Healy, Kenneth James (Qld) b Oct. 15, 1967 South Brisbane (Qld)

Heath, Henry Francis Trafford (SAust) b Dec. 19, 1885 Kadina (SAust) d July 9, 1967 Edinburgh (Scotland)

Heath, Jamie Matthew (NSW) b April 25, 1977 Belmont (NSW)

Heather, Edward Drinkall (Vic) b Oct. 6, 1848 Marylebone, London (England) d July 10, 1935 South Melbourne (Vic)

Heather, Percival Jackson (Vic) b Oct. 6, 1882 Emerald Hill (Vic) d June 29, 1956 Melbourne (Vic)

Hefferan, Francis Urban (Qld) b May 25, 1901 Bowen (Qld) d Sept. 21, 1974 Tweed Heads (NSW)

Heffernan, Ray Leslie (Tas) b Oct. 13, 1935 Hobart (Tas)

Heindrichs, Adolphos Heinrich Julius Carl (WAust) b April 28, 1883 (Germany) d June 24, 1967 Adelaide (SAust)

Henderson, Frank (NSW) b June 1, 1908 Wickham (NSW) d Dec. 6, 1954 Heidelberg (Vic)

Hendricks, Michael (NSW & SAust) b Dec. 12, 1942 Corrimal (NSW)

Hendrie, Charles Richard (Vic) b July 5, 1886 Richmond (Vic) death details unknown

* Hendry, Hunter Scott Thomas Laurie (NSW & Vic) b May 24, 1895 Woollahra (NSW) d Dec. 16, 1988 Rose Bay (NSW)

Hennah, Walter Henry (WAust) b March 16, 1880 Ballarat (Vic) d Aug. 13, 1946 Perth (WAust)

Henri, Harry James Tepapa (Tas) b July 27, 1865 Tauranga (New Zealand) d Feb. 5, 1947 Lindisfarne (Tas)

Henry, Albert (Qld) b c. 1880 Boonah (Qld) d March 13, 1909 Yarrabah (Qld)

Henry, Donald McKenzie (SAust) b June 24, 1885 Parkside (SAust) d July 31, 1973 Felixstow (SAust)

Henschell, Allan Brett (Qld) b June 6, 1961 Dalby (Qld)

Henty, Philip Guy (Tas) b Feb. 4, 1883 Pakenham (Vic) d Oct. 21, 1949 Hobart (Tas)

Henty, William (Tas) b Sept. 23, 1808 West Tarring, Sussex (England) d July 11, 1881 Hove, Sussex (England)

Hepburn, Thomas Robert (Vic) b Dec. 20, 1839 Collingwood (Vic) d April 22, 1921 St Kilda (Vic)

Herbert, Henry James (WAust) b April 24, 1895 Fremantle (WAust) d Nov. 21, 1957 Claremont (WAust)

Herbert, Morgan Uriah (WAust) b Aug. 4, 1918 Albany (WAust) d June 15, 2000 Duncraig (WAust)

Herbert, Peter Jeffrey (SAust) b Jan. 8, 1947 Adelaide (SAust)

Herman, Richard John (Vic) b July 31, 1967 Melbourne (Vic)

Herring, Llewellyn Lloyd (WAust) b April 3, 1871 Clunes (Vic) d Aug. 5, 1922 Fremantle (WAust)

Herring, Robert Wolseley (Vic) b June 8, 1898 Maryborough (Vic) d Oct. 8, 1964 Melbourne (Vic)

Hervey, Matthew (Vic) b Jan. 27, 1820 Glasgow, Lanarkshire (Scotland) d Dec. 1, 1874 Turnbull Plains (Vic)

Herzberg, Steven (WAust & Tas) b May 25, 1967 Carshalton, Surrey (England)

Hetherington, Henry Francisco (Vic) b Sept. 3, 1874 West Melbourne (Vic) d July 11, 1950 Malvern (Vic)

Hewer, William Albert (SAust) b May 7, 1877 Goodwood (SAust) d June 2, 1948 Wayville (SAust)

Hewett, Ian Stephen Louis (Vic) b Jan. 24, 1976 East Melbourne (Vic)

Hewitt, Albert Hedley Vickers (Qld) b Jan. 21, 1866 Nowra (NSW) d July 11, 1947 Brisbane (Qld)

Hewitt, Richard Child (NSW) b Feb. 13, 1844 Beverley, Yorkshire (England) d March 21, 1920 Granville (NSW)

Hewson, Robert Henry (WAust) b Aug. 4, 1893 Carlton (Vic) d Oct. 21, 1972 Melbourne (Vic)

* Hibbert, Paul Anthony (Vic) b July 23, 1952 Brunswick (Vic)

* Hick, Graeme Ashley (Qld) b May 23, 1966 Salisbury (Rhodesia)

Hickey, Denis Jon (Vic & SAust) b Dec. 31, 1964 Mooroopna (Vic)

Hickson, Robert Newburgh (NSW) b May 2, 1884 Newcastle (NSW) d June 21, 1963 Armidale (NSW)

Hiddleston, Hugh Charles Stewart (NSW) b c. 1855 full birth details unknown d May 14, 1934 Coolgardie (WAust)

Hide, Jesse Bollard (SAust) b March 12, 1857 Eastbourne, Sussex (England) d March 19, 1924 Edinburgh (Scotland)

Hiern, Barry Neil (SAust) b Aug. 8, 1951 North Adelaide (SAust)

Hiern, Ross Noel (SAust) b Aug. 2, 1922 Parkside (SAust) d Aug. 21, 1999 Morphettville (SAust)

Higgins, Benjamin Hugh (SAust) b March 8, 1972 Rose Park (SAust)

Higgins, Henry James Roy (Qld) b Jan. 27, 1900 Rosalie (Qld) d Feb. 24, 1990 Chermside (Qld)

Higgins, James (Qld) b Nov. 14, 1874 Ormiston (Qld) d Nov. 24, 1957 Sandgate (Qld)

* Higgs, James Donald (Vic) b July 11, 1950 Kyabram (Vic)

Higgs, Mark Anthony (NSW & SAust) b June 30, 1976 Queanbeyan (NSW)

* Hilditch, Andrew Mark Jefferson (NSW & SAust) b May 20, 1956 North Adelaide (SAust)

Hill, Arthur (SAust) b May 28, 1871 Adelaide (SAust) d June 22, 1936 Glenelg (SAust)

* Hill, Clement (SAust) b March 18, 1877 Hindmarsh (SAust) d Sept. 5, 1945 Parkville (Vic)

Hill, Clement John (NSW) b July 2, 1904 Beryl (NSW) d May 21, 1988 Belmont (NSW)

Hill, Henry John (SAust) b July 7, 1878 Adelaide (SAust) d Oct. 30, 1906 Kensington Park (SAust)

* Hill, John Charles (Vic) b June 25, 1923 Murrumbeena (Vic) d Aug. 11, 1974 Caulfield (Vic)

Hill, John Gerard (Qld) b Nov. 11, 1956 Waratah (NSW)

Hill, Kenneth Michael (NSW) b Jan. 26, 1945 Merewether (NSW)

Hill, Leon Trevor (SAust & Qld) b Feb. 28, 1936 West Croydon (SAust)

Hill, Leslie Roy (SAust) b April 27, 1884 Adelaide (SAust) d Dec. 15, 1952 North Adelaide (SAust)

Hill, Mark Anthony (Tas) b July 27, 1964 Perth (WAust)

Hill, Percy (SAust) b July 4, 1868 Kent Town (SAust) d July 24, 1950 Adelaide (SAust)

Hill, Peter Distin (SAust) b Jan. 28, 1923 North Adelaide (SAust) d Oct. 3, 2002 Adelaide (SAust)

Hill, Roland James (SAust) b Oct. 18, 1868 Parkside (SAust) d Jan. 10, 1929 Glenelg (SAust)

Hill, Stanley (SAust & NSW) b Aug. 22, 1885 Adelaide (SAust) d May 10, 1970 Englefield Green, Surrey (England)

Hill, Wayne Douglas (WAust) b Dec. 5, 1953 Subiaco (WAust)

Hill-Smith, Wyndham (WAust) b Feb. 16, 1909 Angaston (SAust) d Oct. 25, 1990 Angaston (SAust)

Hilliard, Henry (NSW) b Nov. 7, 1826 Sydney (NSW) d March 19, 1914 Willoughby (NSW)

Hills, Dene Fleetwood (Tas) b Aug. 27, 1970 Wynyard (Tas)

Hird, Sydney Francis (NSW) b Jan. 7, 1910 Balmain (NSW) d Dec. 20, 1980 Bloemfontein (South Africa)

Hird, William (Tas) b Sept. 23, 1921 Stanley, Durham (England)

Hiscock, Ernest John (SAust) b April 9, 1868 Penrice (SAust) d Dec. 16, 1894 Alberton (SAust)

Hitchcock, Oswould Charles (Qld) b Sept. 9, 1859 Greenhill, Shoalhaven (NSW) d July 13, 1948 Brisbane (Qld)

Hitchcock, Robert Alan (SAust) b May 14, 1938 North Adelaide (SAust)

* Hoare, Desmond Edward (WAust) b Oct. 19, 1934 Perth (WAust)

Hoare, William (Qld) b Oct. 23, 1868 Brisbane (Qld) d Dec. 16, 1954 Salt Lake City, Utah (USA)

Hodge, Bradley John (Vic) b Dec. 29, 1974 Sandringham (Vic)

Hodge, Malcolm Gordon Fergurson (SAust) b Aug. 28, 1934 Adelaide (SAust)

* Hodges, John Robart (Vic) b Aug. 11, 1855 Knightsbridge (London) death details unknown

Hodgetts, Bruce Frederick (Tas) b Jan. 25, 1947 Burnie (Tas)

Hodgkinson, John Ernest (NSW) b Feb. 7, 1873 Surry Hills (NSW) d Nov. 19, 1939 Burwood (NSW)

Hodgson, Robert William (Tas) b Feb. 22, 1973 Launceston (Tas)

* Hogan, Tom George (WAust) b Sept. 23, 1956 Merredin (WAust)

Hogg, Geoffrey Charles Huxtable (NSW) b Sept. 28, 1909 Goulburn (NSW) d Aug. 14, 1959 Coorparoo (Qld)

* Hogg, George Bradley (WAust) b Feb. 6, 1971 Narrogin (WAust)

Hogg, James Edgar Phipps (NSW & Qld) b Oct. 16, 1906 Goulburn (NSW) d Dec. 2, 1975 West Ryde (NSW)

* Hogg, Rodney Malcolm (SAust & Vic) b March 5, 1951 Richmond (Vic)

Hogg, Thomas (Combined XIII) b March 12, 1845 Hobart (Tas) d July 13, 1890 Trevallyn (Tas)

Hogue, Thomas Herbert (NSW & WAust) b Oct. 5, 1877 Wickham (NSW) d May 6, 1956 Nedlands (WAust)

Hogue, Wallace White (WAust) b Dec. 9, 1879 Wickham (NSW) d June 1, 1946 Cook's Hill (NSW)

* Hohns, Trevor Victor (Qld) b Jan. 23, 1954 Nundah (Qld)

* Holding, Michael Anthony (Tas) b Feb. 16, 1954 Half Way Tree, Kingston (Jamaica)

Holdsworth, Wayne John (NSW) b Oct. 5, 1968 Paddington (NSW)

* Hole, Graeme Blake (NSW & SAust) b Jan. 6, 1931 Concord West (NSW) d Feb. 14, 1990 Kensington Gardens (SAust)

* Holland, Robert George (NSW) b Oct. 19, 1946 Camperdown (NSW)

Holman, Raymond Sidney (SAust) b Sept. 17, 1919 Largs Bay (SAust) d Sept. 19, 1989 Woodville South (SAust)

Holten, Charles Valentine (Vic) b Sept. 15, 1927 Brighton (Vic)

Holton, Leslie George (SAust) b March 13, 1903 Carlton (Vic) d Feb. 1, 1956 Hawthorn (Vic)

Holyman, Josef Michael (Tas) b June 10, 1970 Launceston (Tas)

Homburg, Robert Otto (SAust) b Jan. 31, 1876 Norwood (SAust) d Oct. 21, 1948 Medindie (SAust)

Hone, Brian William (SAust) b July 1, 1907 Semaphore (SAust) d May 28, 1978 Paris (France)

Hone, Garton Maxwell (SAust) b Feb. 21, 1901 Morphett Vale (SAust) d May 28, 1991 Myrtle Bank (SAust)

Honeybone, George Alfred (Vic) b April 2, 1875 London (England) d Nov. 1, 1956 Ashburton (Vic)

Honour, Victor Gerald (Qld) b Oct. 25, 1910 Bierton, Buckinghamshire (England) d Jan. 3, 2001 Brookfield (Qld)

Hook, Benjamin James (SAust) b March 5, 1973 Kingswood (SAust)

Hooker, John Edward Halford (NSW) b March 6, 1898 Summer Hill (NSW) d Feb. 12, 1982 Winmalee (NSW)

* Hookes, David William (SAust) b May 3, 1955 Mile End (SAust) d Jan. 19, 2004 Prahran (Vic)

Hookey, Scott Gregory (NSW & Tas) b Feb. 10, 1967 Sydney (NSW)

Hooper, Kerry (Tas) b June 9, 1942 Launceston (Tas)

Hooper, Victor Leonard (Tas) b April 23, 1905 Mt Stuart (Tas) d Sept. 3, 1990 New Town (Tas)

Hope, Adam (Vic) b c. 1834 (England) d Oct. 9, 1916 East Melbourne (Vic)

Hopes, James Redfern (Qld) b Oct. 24, 1978 Townsville (Qld)

* Hopkins, Albert John Young (NSW) b May 3, 1874 Young (NSW) d April 25, 1931 North Sydney (NSW)

Hopkins, Isaac (Vic) b Nov. 9, 1870 Collingwood (Vic) d Oct. 25, 1913 Richmond (Vic)

Hopkinson, Samuel Good (Vic) b Oct. 1, 1825 Thorne, Yorkshire (England) d June 26, 1887 South Melbourne (Vic)

Horan, James Francis (Vic) b June 8, 1880 Fitzroy (Vic) d Nov. 1, 1945 Malvern (Vic)

Horan, Thomas Ignatius Bernard (Vic) b April 7, 1886 Fitzroy (Vic) d May 26, 1952 East Camberwell (Vic)

* Horan, Thomas Patrick (Vic) b March 8, 1854 Midleton, County Cork (Ireland) d April 16, 1916 Malvern (Vic)

* Hordern, Herbert Vivian (NSW) b Feb. 10, 1883 North Sydney (NSW) d June 17, 1938 Darlinghurst (NSW)

Horley, John Rasalle (SAust) b Jan. 23, 1936 Medindie (SAust)

* Hornibrook, Percival Mitchell (Qld) b July 27, 1899 Obi Obi (Qld) d Aug. 25, 1976 Spring Hill (Qld)

Horrocks, William John (WAust) b June 18, 1905 Warrington, Lancashire (England) d Nov. 15, 1985 Parkdale (Vic)

Horsell, Jack Aymat James (SAust) b July 12, 1914 Stepney (SAust) d April 20, 1985 Sydney (NSW)

Horsfield, Gordon Cameron (NSW) b March 24, 1913 Balmain (NSW) d Aug. 25, 1982 Mosman (NSW)

Horsley, Daniel, Anthony (NSW) b July 20, 1972 Sydney (NSW)

Horsnell, Kenneth George (SAust) b Sept. 3, 1933 Joslin (SAust)

Horton, Arnell Stanley (Tas) b Sept. 21, 1892 Burnie (Tas) d Sept. 15, 1987 Newstead (Tas)

Hosie, Robert (Vic) b Sept. 8, 1858 Collingwood (Vic) d Sept. 29, 1932 Richmond (Vic)

Hosking, Peter Mowat (Vic) b Sept. 30, 1932 Fairfield (Vic)

Hoskings, Arthur G. W. (WAust) b c. 1872 d Sept. 2, 1919 Dunella, New Jersey (United States of America)

Hotchin, Mortimer Douglas (Vic) b May 20, 1889 Prahran (Vic) d June 21, 1958 East Melbourne (Vic)

Hotham, Augustus Thomas (Vic) b c. 1817 (christened Jan. 25) Dennington, Suffolk (England) d Dec. 24, 1896 Tunbridge Wells, Kent (England)

Hourn, David William (NSW) b Sept. 9, 1949 Bondi (NSW)

House, Graham Warwick Charles (WAust & SAust) b Sept. 4, 1950 Busselton (WAust)

Houston, Richard Shinnock (Vic) b June 30, 1863 Brighton (Vic) d Nov. 27, 1921 Williamstown (Vic)

Howard, Craig (Vic) b April 8, 1974 Lilydale (Vic)

Howard, Harry Cecil (WAust) b June 30, 1885 Adelaide (SAust) d Sept. 18, 1960 Perth (WAust)

Howard, Leonard Easther (SAust) b April 18, 1886 Adelaide (SAust) d Aug. 14, 1945 Prospect (SAust)

Howard, Roy (Vic) b Nov. 15, 1922 Terang (Vic)

Howard, Stephen John (Tas) b Feb. 7, 1949 Launceston (Tas)

Howard, Thomas Harris (NSW) b May 2, 1877 Sydney (NSW) d Oct. 6, 1965 Randwick (NSW)

Howe, John Sidney (Tas) b Dec. 27, 1868 Kotree (India) d July 29, 1939 Neutral Bay (NSW)

Howell, George (NSW) b June 9, 1822 Sydney (NSW) d Nov. 18, 1890 Sydney (NSW)

Howell, William Hunter (NSW) b Jan. 12, 1902 Penrith (NSW) d Jan. 23, 1987 Penrith (NSW)

* Howell, William Peter (NSW) b Dec. 29, 1869 Penrith (NSW) d July 14, 1940 Castlereagh (NSW)

Howlett, John Thomas (Vic) b April 8, 1868 North Melbourne (Vic) d June 15, 1931 East Melbourne (Vic)

Howson, Herbert (Vic) b Aug. 11, 1872 Newstead (Vic) d May 8, 1948 Murrumbeena (Vic)

Hubbard, Edward Francis (Qld) b June 27, 1906 Brisbane (Qld) d Oct. 1, 1969 Herston (Qld)

Hubble, James Merrick (WAust) b Aug. 12, 1942 Beaconsfield (WAust)

Huddleston, John (Vic) b Nov. 25, 1837 Nottingham, Nottinghamshire (England) d July 29, 1904 Brunswick (Vic)

Hudson, Graeme Charles (Tas) b June 16, 1930 Wynyard (Tas) d Sept. 23, 1974 Launceston (Tas)

Hudson, John Lambert (Tas) b July 23, 1882 Launceston (Tas) d March 16, 1961 Hobart (Tas)

Hughes, David Paul (Tas) b April 13, 1947 Newton-le-Willows, Lancashire (England)

Hughes, Glenn Arthur (Tas) b Nov. 23, 1959 Goomalling (WAust)

Hughes, Graeme Christopher (NSW) b Dec. 6, 1955 Stanmore (NSW)

* Hughes, Kimberley John (WAust) b Jan. 26, 1954 Margaret River (WAust)

* Hughes, Mervyn Gregory (Vic) b Nov. 23, 1961 Euroa (Vic)

Hughes, Walter Cecil (WAust) b Aug. 13, 1882 Adelaide (SAust) d Aug. 16, 1917 Perth (WAust)

Hughson, Desmond George (Qld) b May 27, 1941 Herston (Qld)

Hugo, Victor (SAust) b Nov. 25, 1877 Adelaide (SAust) d April 8, 1930 Malvern (SAust)

Hume, Andrew Ernest (West) b Feb. 5, 1869 Redfern (NSW) d June 22, 1912 London (England)

Humphreys, Anthony John Rolph (Tas) b June 9, 1971 Launceston (Tas)

Humphreys, John (NSW) birth and death details unknown

Hunt, Horace Charles (Vic) b July 15, 1907 Stawell (Vic) d Oct. 15, 1984 Melbourne (Vic)

* Hunt, William Alfred (NSW) b Aug. 26, 1908 Balmain (NSW) d Dec. 30, 1983 Balmain (NSW)

Huntington, Ian Ross (Vic) b Oct. 18, 1931 Coburg (Vic)

Hurburgh, Clifton Maurice (Tas) b Jan. 15, 1917 Hobart (Tas)

Hurn, Brian Morgan (SAust) b March 4, 1939 Angaston (SAust)

* Hurst, Alan George (Vic) b July 15, 1950 Altona (Vic)

* Hurwood, Alexander (Qld) b June 17, 1902 Kangaroo Point (Qld) d Sept. 26, 1982 Coffs Harbour (NSW)

Hussey, David John (Vic) b July 15, 1977 Morley (WAust)

Hussey, Michael Edward Killeen (WAust) b May 27, 1975 Mt Lawley (WAust)

Hussey, Percival Leitch (WAust) b June 23, 1869 Perth (WAust) d May 13, 1944 Adelaide (SAust)

Hutcheon, Ernest Henry (Qld) b June 17, 1889 Toowoomba (Qld) d June 9, 1937 Brisbane (Qld)

Hutcheon, John Silvester (Qld) b April 5, 1882 Warwick (Qld) d June 18, 1957 Albion Heights (Qld)

Hutchison, Paul James (SAust & Tas) b Feb. 17, 1968 Glen Innes (NSW)

Hutton, Ernest Hamilton (Vic & Qld) b March 29, 1867 Mt Rouse (Vic) d July 12, 1929 Ascot (Qld)

Hutton, Henry George (SAust) b Aug. 26, 1878 Masterton (New Zealand) d Aug. 13, 1968 Norwood (SAust)

Hutton, Maurice Percy (SAust) b March 21, 1903 Parkside (SAust) d Feb. 20, 1940 Ararat (Vic)

Hutton, Mervyn Douglas (SAust) b Aug. 24, 1911 Port Augusta (SAust) d Sept. 28, 1988 Melbourne (Vic)

Hutton, Norman Harvey (SAust) b Aug. 10, 1911 Unley (SAust) d Aug. 27, 1965 Fullarton (SAust)

Hutton, William Frederick Percy (SAust) b Oct. 2, 1876 Mintaro (SAust) d Oct. 1, 1951 Millswood (SAust)

Hyatt, Roland Shane (Tas) b Dec. 30, 1961 Hobart (Tas)

Hyde, Phillip Andrew (Vic) b Oct. 22, 1958 Melbourne (Vic)

Hyett, Francis William (Vic) b Feb. 9, 1882 Bolwarra (Vic) d April 25, 1919 Fitzroy (Vic)

Hyland, Byron John (Tas) b Jan. 14, 1930 New Norfolk (Tas)

Hynes, Lincoln Carruthers (NSW) b April 12, 1912 Balmain (NSW) d Aug. 7, 1977 Killara (NSW)

Hyslop, Hector Henry (Australians) b Dec. 13, 1840 Southampton, Hampshire (England) d Sept. 11, 1920 Cosham, Hampshire (England)

* Ibadulla, Khalid (Tas) b Dec. 20, 1935 Lahore (Pakistan)

Iceton, Thomas Henry (NSW) b Oct. 12, 1849 Sydney (NSW) d May 19, 1908 Ashfield (NSW)

Illingworth, Edward Philip (Vic) b Nov. 27, 1938 Fairfield (Vic)

Illman, Brian Kevin (SAust) b Oct. 23, 1937 Unley Park (SAust)

* Imran Khan (NSW) b Nov. 25, 1952 Lahore (Pakistan)

Ingleton, Walter George (Vic) b Feb. 16, 1867 Collingwood (Vic) d Feb. 4, 1923 East Melbourne (Vic)

Inkster, Gordon Bradford (SAust) b June 30, 1893 Portland Estate (SAust) d March 22, 1957 Darlinghurst (NSW)

Inness, Mathew William Hunter (Vic) b Jan. 13, 1978 East Melbourne (Vic)

Inverarity, Mervyn (WAust) b Oct. 25, 1907 Claremont (WAust) d March 17, 1979 Cottesloe (WAust)

* Inverarity, Robert John (WAust & SAust) b Jan. 31, 1944 Subiaco (WAust)

Inwood, Bradley Phillip (Qld) b July 23, 1963 Gladstone (Qld)

* Iredale, Francis Adams (NSW) b June 19, 1867 Surry Hills (NSW) d April 15, 1926 Crows Nest (NSW)

Ireland, Gary John (WAust) b Oct. 3, 1961 Collie (WAust)

* Ironmonger, Herbert (Qld & Vic) b April 7, 1882 Pine Mountain (Qld) d June 1, 1971 St Kilda (Vic)

Irvine, John Taylor (WAust) b April 13, 1944 Subiaco (WAust)

* Iverson, John Bryan (Vic) b July 27, 1915 Melbourne (Vic) d Oct. 23, 1973 Brighton (Vic)

Ives, William Francis (NSW) b Nov. 14, 1896 Glebe (NSW) d March 23, 1975 Newport Beach (NSW)

Ivory, Wilfred Charles (Rest of Australia) b Sept. 12, 1888 South Yarra (Vic) d Oct. 13, 1975 North Brighton (Vic)

Jack, Keith Mayall (Qld) b April 25, 1927 Tambo (Qld) d Nov. 22, 1982 Buderim (Qld)

Jackman, Darrell (Tas) b May 31, 1921 Hobart (Tas) d April 5, 1991 Cheltenham (Vic)

* Jackson, Archibald (NSW) b Sept. 5, 1909 Rutherglen, Lanarkshire (Scotland) d Feb. 16, 1933 Clayfield (Qld)

Jackson, Arthur Enderby (WAust) b Jan. 6, 1872 Kapunda (SAust) d June 29, 1935 Cottesloe (WAust)

Jackson, Paul William (Vic & Qld) b Nov. 1, 1961 East Melbourne (Vic)

Jackson, Victor Edward (NSW) b Oct. 25, 1916 Woollahra (NSW) d Jan. 30, 1965 Manildra (NSW)

Jacobson, Alan Melville (Tas) b Nov. 12, 1942 Sydney (NSW)

Jacomb, John Newton (Vic) b 1841 Hobart (Tas) d Nov. 5, 1891 Walhalla (Vic)

Jakins, James Albert (Tas) b Oct. 1, 1886 Hawthorn (Vic) d Dec. 12, 1948 Wivenhoe (Tas)

James, Alec Pearce (SAust) b May 22, 1889 Neath, Glamorgan (Wales) d Aug. 14, 1961 Torquay, Devon (England)

James, Eric Lisle (Tas) b Oct. 21, 1881 Low Head (Tas) d Aug. 28, 1948 Malvern (Vic)

James, Eric Pearse (WAust) b Feb. 27, 1923 Albany (WAust) d March 28, 1999 Albany (WAust)

James, Gerald Thomas Henry (Tas) b March 22, 1908 New Norfolk (Tas) b Dec. 24, 1967 Hobart (Tas)

James, Ronald Victor (NSW & SAust) b May 23, 1920 Paddington (NSW) d April 28, 1983 Auburn (NSW)

James, Sidney Victor Austin (Tas) b Oct. 26, 1895 Adelaide (SAust) d Aug. 3, 1966 Canterbury (Vic)

Jamieson, Dudley Garfield (SAust) b July 4, 1912 Redruth (SAust) d Jan. 14, 1979 Burnside (SAust)

Jamieson, Walter Angus Bethune (Tas) b 1828 birth day and month unknown Plenty (Tas) d Dec. 28, 1881 Plenty (Tas)

Jansan, Ernest William (NSW) b Aug. 26, 1874 Gulgong (NSW) d May 31, 1945 Leichhardt (NSW)

Jaques, Philip Anthony (NSW) b May 3, 1979 Wollongong (NSW)

* Jarman, Barrington Noel (SAust) b Feb. 17, 1936 Hindmarsh (SAust)

Jarvis, Alfred (SAust) b Feb. 15, 1868 Hindmarsh (SAust) d Aug. 12, 1938 Semaphore (SAust)

* Jarvis, Arthur Harwood (SAust) b Oct. 19, 1860 Hindmarsh (SAust) d Nov. 15, 1933 Hindmarsh (SAust)

Jarvis, Carlisle Melrose Byron (WAust) b Dec. 10, 1906 East Fremantle (WAust) d Nov. 6, 1979 Mt Lawley (WAust)

Jarvis, Harwood Samuel Coombe (SAust) b Aug. 30, 1884 Brompton (SAust) d Oct. 10, 1936 Port Pirie (SAust)

Jeffrey, Clifton Linley (Tas) b Jan. 10, 1913 Hobart (Tas) d Feb. 11, 1987 Launceston (Tas)

Jeffrey, Robert Frederick (NSW & Tas) b Sept. 19, 1953 Goulburn (NSW)

Jeffreys, Arthur Frederick (NSW) b April 7, 1848 London (England) d Feb. 4, 1906 Lasham, Hampshire (England)

Jeffreys, John Alan (WAust) b April 17, 1913 Fremantle (WAust) d Nov. 3, 1943 Shipham, Somerset (England)

Jeffreys, Keith Stanley (WAust) b Jan. 18, 1921 Bridgetown (WAust) d May 16, 2000 Mandurah (WAust)

Jelich, Neville (Qld & Tas) b March 11, 1962 Orasje, near Belgrade (Yugoslavia)

* Jenner, Terrence James (WAust & SAust) b Sept. 8, 1944 Mt Lawley (WAust)

* Jennings, Claude Burrows (SAust & Qld) b June 5, 1884 East St Kilda (Vic) d June 20, 1950 Adelaide (SAust)

Jennings, Henry John (Vic) b April 9, 1849 Launceston (Tas) d June 6, 1925 St Kilda (Vic)

Jewell, Nicholas (Vic) b Aug. 27, 1977 East Melbourne (Vic)

Jinks, Allan (Vic) b Dec. 29, 1913 Carlton North (Vic) d Nov. 7, 1997 Melbourne (Vic)

Jinks, Frederick (Vic) b May 6, 1909 Eaglehawk (Vic) d Aug. 16, 1996 Pakenham (Vic)

John, Bruce Duncanson (Tas) b July 20, 1937 Launceston (Tas)

Johns, Alfred Edward (Vic) b Jan. 22, 1868 Hawthorn (Vic) d Feb. 13, 1934 Melbourne (Vic)

Johnson, Benjamin Andrew (SAust) b Aug. 1, 1973 Naracoorte (SAust)

Johnson, Eric Alfred (SAust) b July 11, 1902 North Norwood (SAust) d Jan. 10, 1976 Adelaide (SAust)

Johnson, Francis Barry (NSW) b May 21, 1882 Redfern (NSW) d May 28, 1951 Longueville (NSW)

* Johnson, Ian William Geddes (Vic) b Dec. 8, 1917 Hotham West (Vic) d Oct. 9, 1998 Malvern (Vic)

Johnson, James William (Vic) b Sept. 22, 1884 Footscray (Vic) d Aug. 14, 1941 Middle Park (Vic)

* Johnson, Leonard Joseph (Qld) b March 18, 1919 Ipswich (Qld) d April 20, 1977 Silkstone (Qld)

Johnson, Mitchell Guy (Qld) b Nov. 2, 1981 Townsville (Qld)

Johnston, Aubrey Edmund (NSW) b Sept. 7, 1882 Canterbury (NSW) d June 16, 1960 Manly (NSW)

Johnston, Clive William (NSW) b Aug. 4, 1925 Petersham (NSW) d May 11, 1991 Petersham (NSW)

Johnston, David Alexander Hughes (NSW) b July 10, 1955 Maitland (NSW)

Johnston, David Allan (SAust) b Dec. 4, 1954 Melbourne (Vic)

Johnston, David Trent (NSW) b April 29, 1974 Wollongong (NSW)

Johnston, Frederick Bourke (NSW) b Sept. 10, 1915 Sydney (NSW) d Sept. 6, 1977 Hillsdale (NSW)

* Johnston, William Arras (Vic) b Feb. 26, 1922 Beeac (Vic)

Johnstone, Richard Gordon (Vic) b Feb. 9, 1885 Malvern (Vic) d Nov. 9, 1961 Geelong (Vic)

Jolly, Harvey Bruce (SAust) b Aug. 1, 1960 Naracoorte (SAust)

Jones, Alan (WAust) b Nov. 4, 1938 Velindre, Glamorgan (Wales)

Jones, Alan Robert (Qld) b June 11, 1948 Greenslopes (Qld)

Jones, Arthur Harold (Qld) b Dec. 17, 1874 Brisbane (Qld) d Dec. 2, 1917 Salisbury Plain, Wiltshire (England)

Jones, Charles Frederick (Vic) b Feb. 9, 1870 Williamstown (Vic) d March 25, 1957 Williamstown (Vic)

* Jones, Dean Mervyn (Vic) b March 24, 1961 Coburg (Vic)

* Jones, Ernest (SAust & WAust) b Sept. 30, 1869 East Auburn (SAust) d Nov. 23, 1943 Norwood (SAust)

Jones, John Raymond (WAust) b May 10, 1899 Clunes (Vic) d March 14, 1991 Hamilton Hill (WAust)

Jones, Neil Richard (NSW) b July 12, 1966 Stourport-on-Severn, Worcestershire (England)

Jones, Ronald Andrew (NSW) b March 28, 1964 Dubbo (NSW)

* Jones, Samuel Percy (NSW & Qld) b Aug. 1, 1861 Sydney (NSW) d July 14, 1951 Auckland (New Zealand)

Jones, Sidney (NSW) birth and death details unknown

Jones, Stephen Alexander (WAust) b July 1, 1949 Sydney (NSW)

Jones, Victor Clarence (WAust) b May 11, 1881 Ballarat (Vic) d July 20, 1923 Mt Lawley (WAust)

Jones, William George (SAust) b May 13, 1864 Hindmarsh (SAust) d July 16, 1924 Adelaide (SAust)

Jordan, Frank Slater (NSW) b Sept. 19, 1905 Darlington (NSW) d Oct. 22, 1995 Vaucluse (NSW)

Jordan, Grant Leigh (Vic) b March 18, 1965 Ivanhoe (Vic)

Jordon, Raymond Clarence (Vic) b Feb. 17, 1936 Melbourne (Vic)

Jose, Anthony Douglas (SAust) b Feb. 17, 1929 Knoxville (SAust) d Feb. 3, 1972 Los Angeles, California (United States of America)

Jose, Gilbert Edgar (SAust) b Nov. 1, 1898 Taichow (China) d March 27, 1942 Changi POW Camp (Singapore)

Joseland, Brendan Richard (Vic) b April 2, 1976 Upper Ferntree Gully (Vic)

Joseph, Joel P. (NSW) b c. 1867 d c. 1942 Canterbury (NSW)

* Joslin, Leslie Ronald (Vic) b Dec. 13, 1947 Yarraville (Vic)

Joyce, Robert Eric (Qld) b Dec. 11, 1947 Auchenflower (Qld)

Joynt, Hartley Kelly (WAust) b June 14, 1938 Subiaco (WAust)

* Julian, Brendon Paul (WAust) b Aug. 10, 1970 Hamilton (New Zealand)

Junor, John Leonard (Vic) b April 27, 1914 Thornbury (Vic)

Junor, Robert Johnston (Vic) b Jan. 10, 1888 Marcus Hill (Vic) d July 26, 1957 Heidelberg (Vic)

Jurgensen, Shane John (WAust, Tas & Qld) b April 28, 1976 Redcliffe (Qld)

Kahler, Lance Warren (Qld) b June 27, 1977 Crows Nest (Qld)

* Kallicharran, Alvin Isaac (Qld) b March 21, 1949 Paidama (British Guiana)

* Kanhai, Rohan Bholal (WAust & Tas) b Dec. 26, 1935 Port Mourant, Berbice (British Guiana)

Karppinen, Stuart James (WAust) b June 13, 1973 Townsville (Qld)

* Kasprowicz, Michael Scott (Qld) b Feb. 10, 1972 South Brisbane (Qld)

* Katich, Simon Matthew (WAust & NSW) b Aug. 21, 1975 Middle Swan (WAust)

Kay, William Malcolm (Qld) b May 4, 1893 Gympie (Qld) d July 7, 1973 Taringa (Qld)

Keating, James Leslie (Vic) b Oct. 1, 1891 Brunswick East (Vic) d March 13, 1962 Fitzroy (Vic)

Kekwick, Edwin Huntley (SAust) b March 5, 1875 Port MacDonell (SAust) d Aug. 29, 1950 Adelaide (SAust)

* Kelleway, Charles (NSW) b April 25, 1886 Lismore (NSW) d Nov. 16, 1944 Lindfield (NSW)

Kellick, Charles Moore (NSW) b Nov. 21, 1842 Sydney (NSW) d March 27, 1918 Strathfield (NSW)

Kellick, James (NSW) b Aug. 24, 1840 Sydney (NSW) d Aug. 8, 1926 Sydney (NSW)

Kelly, David John (SAust) b Jan. 28, 1959 North Adelaide (SAust)

Kelly, Ian Donald Cameron (Qld) b May 5, 1959 Herston (Qld)

* Kelly, James Joseph (NSW) b May 10, 1867 Sandridge (Vic) d Aug. 14, 1938 Bellevue Hill (NSW)

Kelly, Otto Harvey (WAust) b May 15, 1880 Sandridge (Vic) d July 30, 1946 Mt Lawley (WAust)

Kelly, Peter Charles (NSW & WAust) b April 28, 1942 Mosman (NSW)

Kelly, Richard Terence Bonynge (Vic) b March 21, 1870 Ballan (Vic) d Dec. 27, 1941 St Kilda (Vic)

Kelly, Robert Charles (WAust) b May 18, 1969 Subiaco (WAust)

* Kelly, Thomas Joseph Dart (Vic) b May 3, 1844 County Waterford (Ireland) d July 20, 1893 Hawthorn (Vic)

Kelly, Trent Peter (SAust) b March 24, 1984 Henley Beach (SAust)

Kelly, William Harvey (WAust) b March 24, 1883 St Kilda (Vic) d July 30, 1944 Croydon (Vic)

Kelly, William Lucius Usna (Vic) b Jan. 20, 1875 Rosedale (Vic) d Dec. 27, 1968 Bulla (Vic)

Kelton, Matthew David (SAust) b April 9, 1974 Woodville South (SAust)

Kemp, Benjamin Charles Ernest (SAust & Vic) b Jan. 30, 1864 Plymouth, Devon (England) d Dec. 3, 1940 Albert Park (Vic)

Kemp, Leonard Denton (Vic) b June 6, 1909 Malvern (Vic)

Kendall, Keith Harold Dudley (Vic) b March 16, 1929 South Melbourne (Vic)

* Kendall, Thomas Kingston (Vic & Tas) b Aug. 24, 1851 Bedford, Bedfordshire (England) d Aug. 17, 1924 Hobart (Tas)

Kenneally, Cornelius James (SAust) b July 28, 1926 Edwardstown (Vic) d Jan. 18, 1995 Ashford (SAust)

Kenny, Arthur (Vic) b Aug. 9, 1878 Emerald Hill (Vic) d Aug. 2, 1934 South Melbourne (Vic)

Kenny, Justin Dean (NSW) b Sept. 24, 1966 Camperdown (NSW)

* Kent, Martin Francis (Qld) b Nov. 23, 1953 Mossman (Qld)

Keogh, Ernest John (WAust) b 1869 South Melbourne (Vic) d c. 1951 South Yarra (Vic)

Kermode, Alexander (NSW) b May 15, 1876 Sydney (NSW) d July 17, 1934 Balmain (NSW)

Kerr, Eric Alan David (Vic) b June 28, 1923 Auburn (Vic) d Feb. 16, 1989 Melbourne (Vic)

* Kerr, Robert Byers (Qld) b June 16, 1961 Herston (Qld)

Kershler, Anthony John (NSW) b July 6, 1968 St Leonard's (NSW)

Kessey, Gwilym Taf (WAust) b Jan. 13, 1919 Meekatharra (WAust) d June 25, 1986 Perth (WAust)

Kettle, John Louis (NSW) b Dec. 3, 1830 Sydney (NSW) d Oct. 30, 1891 Newtown (NSW)

Kiernan, Christopher (Vic) b March 23, 1878 Fitzroy (Vic) d Dec. 2, 1925 North Fitzroy (Vic)

Kierse, John Michael (SAust) b Jan. 11, 1918 Nhill (Vic)

Kildey, Edward Keith (Tas) b April 30, 1919 Leeton (NSW)

Killen, Christopher Michael (SAust) b Sept. 23, 1967 Dubbo (NSW)

Kimber, Adam Patrick (SAust) b Sept. 30, 1969 North Adelaide (SAust)

Kimpton, Robert Webb (WAust) b Jan. 5, 1914 Essendon (Vic)

King, Darryl James (Qld) b June 6, 1942 East Brisbane (Qld) d March 3, 2002 Buderim (Qld)

King, Ian Harold (Qld) b June 1, 1943 Herston (Qld)

King, James Francis (SAust) b May 23, 1851 Hindmarsh (SAust) d June 28, 1921 Hindmarsh (SAust)

King, Norman Reginald (SAust) b April 9, 1915 Mile End (SAust) d April 25, 1973 Linden Park (SAust)

King, Percy Macgregor (NSW) b Sept. 2, 1889 Richmond (Vic) d Dec. 9, 1967 Rose Bay (NSW)

King, Peter Denis (Vic) b May 24, 1959 Melbourne (Vic)

King, Stuart Patrick (Vic) b April 22, 1906 Ararat (Vic) d Feb. 28, 1943 in action on the Coral Sea

Kingdon, Darren Robert (Qld) b Sept. 24, 1969 Dubbo (NSW)

Kington, Philip Oliphant (Vic) b Dec. 17, 1832 Clifton, Gloucestershire (England) d July 2, 1892 Dachet, Buckinghamshire (England)

Kinloch, John (NSW) b c. 1833 Dublin (Ireland) d April 9, 1897 Camperdown (NSW)

Kinnear, Joseph David (Vic) b Feb. 12, 1912 West Brunswick (Vic) d Dec. 14, 1981 Moreland (Vic)

Kinnear, William George (Vic) b Aug. 19, 1914 West Brunswick (Vic) d Dec. 7, 1982 West Brunswick (Vic)

* Kippax, Alan Falconer (NSW) b May 25, 1897 Sydney (NSW) d Sept. 5, 1972 Bellevue Hill (NSW)

Kirby, Keith William (Vic) b Oct. 1, 1939 Essendon (Vic)

Kirby, Richard George (Tas) b Jan. 28, 1861 Hobart (Tas) d Aug. 26, 1947 Hobart (Tas)

Kirkman, William Stanley (Tas) b Feb. 14, 1961 Launceston (Tas)

Kirkwood, Harold Peter (SAust) b Sept. 15, 1882 Orroroo (SAust) d May 19, 1943 Unley (SAust)

Kissell, Ronald Keith (NSW) b Aug. 9, 1928 Camperdown (NSW)

Kitson, Eugene Henry (SAust) b Nov. 28, 1889 Adelaide (SAust) d Aug. 4, 1962 Heidelberg (Vic)

* Kline, Lindsay Francis (Vic) b Sept. 29, 1934 Camberwell (Vic)

Klinger, Michael (Vic) b July 4, 1980 Kew (Vic)

Klose, Tom Elliott (SAust) b Jan. 21, 1918 North Adelaide (SAust) d June 13, 1986 Nailsworth (SAust)

* Knight, David Jeffrey (Vic) b Aug. 21, 1956 Coburg (Vic)

Knight, Gary William (Combined XI) b July 20, 1950 Launceston (Tas)

Knight, Robert Leonard (Tas) b Nov. 20, 1957 Launceston (Tas)

Knill, William (SAust) b Jan. 28, 1859 Prospect Village (SAust) d July 8, 1940 North Adelaide (SAust)

* Knott, Alan Philip Eric (Tas) b April 9, 1946 Belvedere, Kent (England)

Knowles, Eric Charles (Qld) b March 9, 1896 Toowoomba (Qld) d Sept. 15, 1978 Southport (Qld)

Kortlang, Henry Frederick Lorenz (Vic) b March 12, 1880 Carlton (Vic) d Feb. 15, 1961 Cottesloe (WAust)

Kowalick, Jeffrey Peter (SAust) b July 22, 1946 Maylands (SAust)

Kremerskothen, Scott Paul (Tas) b Jan. 5, 1979 Launceston (Tas)

Kroger, Henry Jack (Vic) b June 27, 1906 Caulfield (Vic) d July 16, 1987 Malvern (Vic)

Kruger, Nicholas James (Qld) b Aug. 14, 1983 Paddington (NSW)

Kyle, James Henderson (Vic) b May 29, 1880 Bacchus Marsh (Vic) d Jan. 11, 1919 Albert Park (Vic)

La Frantz, Errold Campbell (Qld) b May 25, 1919 Wooloowin (Qld)

* Laird, Bruce Malcolm (WAust) b Nov. 21, 1950 Mt Lawley (WAust)

Lambert, Daryl John (SAust) b Oct. 8, 1946 Prospect (SAust)

Lambert, Grant Michael (NSW) b Aug. 5, 1977 Parramatta (NSW)

Lambert, Henry Francis (Vic) b July 8, 1918 Bairnsdale (Vic) d June 19, 1995 Grange (SAust)

Lambert, Oswald (NSW) b Aug. 23, 1926 New Lambton (NSW)

Lampard, Albert Wallis (Vic) b July 3, 1885 Richmond (Vic) d Jan. 11, 1984 Armadale (Vic)

Lampe, William Henry Warwick (NSW) b Aug. 29, 1902 Albert Park (Vic) d Dec. 22, 1987 Wagga Wagga (NSW)

Lane, John Bayley (NSW) b Jan. 7, 1886 Petersham (NSW) d Aug. 30, 1937 Manly (NSW)

Lang, Harold King (WAust) b Aug. 23, 1905 Banyena (Vic) d April 23, 1991 Nedlands (WAust)

Langdon, Christopher Walter (WAust) b July 4, 1922 Boulder (WAust) d May 2, 2004 Nedlands (WAust)

* Langer, Justin Lee (WAust) b Nov. 21, 1970 Subiaco (WAust)

Langer, Robert Samuel (WAust) b Oct. 3, 1948 Subiaco (WAust)

Langford, Ian Frederick (Vic) b June 2, 1936 Kew (Vic)

* Langley, Gilbert Roche Andrews (SAust) b Sept. 14, 1919 North Adelaide (SAust) d May 14, 2001 Fullarton (SAust)

Langley, Jeffrey Noel (SAust & Qld) b Oct. 28, 1948 Adelaide (SAust)

Lanigan, Emmet Robert (Vic) b Sept. 6, 1909 Maffra (Vic)

Lanigan, Joseph Patrick (WAust) b July 8, 1891 Mogumber (WAust) d Sept. 30, 1972 Glendalough (WAust)

Lansdown, Albert Joseph Walter (Vic) b March 10, 1897 Fitzroy South (Vic) d Jan. 7, 1979 Frankston (Vic)

Lansdown, Harold Charles (Vic) b Feb. 18, 1900 North Fitzroy (Vic) d April 18, 1957 Ivanhoe (Vic)

Larkin, Rohan Patrick (Vic) b Oct. 19, 1969 Seymour (Vic)

* Laughlin, Trevor John (Vic) b Jan. 30, 1951 Nyah West (Vic)

Lavender, Mark Philip (WAust) b Aug. 28, 1967 Madras (India)

* Laver, Frank (Vic) b Dec. 7, 1869 Castlemaine (Vic) d Sept. 24, 1919 East Melbourne (Vic)

Laver, John Francis Lee (Tas) b March 9, 1917 Malvern (Vic)

Law, Ian Kennon (Vic) b Sept. 27, 1938 Richmond (Vic)

Law, Rupert William (Qld) b Feb. 24, 1890 Sydney (NSW) d May 5, 1942 Randwick (NSW)

* Law, Stuart Grant (Qld) b Oct. 18, 1968 Herston (Qld)

Lawes, Charles Henry Wickham (NSW) b Dec. 9, 1899 Cobar (NSW) d Oct. 23, 1980 (NSW)

Lawlor, John (Vic) b Jan. 25, 1864 Castleisland, County Kerry (Ireland) d Jan. 29, 1908 Melbourne (Vic)

Lawrence, Charles (NSW) b Dec. 16, 1828 Hoxton, London (England) d Dec. 20, 1916 Canterbury (Vic)

Lawrence, Rodney John (Qld) b Aug. 8, 1954 Herston (Qld)

* Lawry, William Morris (Vic) b Feb. 11, 1937 Thornbury (Vic)

* Lawson, Geoffrey Francis (NSW) b Dec. 7, 1957 Wagga Wagga (NSW)

Lawson, Robert James (Vic) b March 23, 1901 South Melbourne (Vic) d Nov. 28, 1974 West Brunswick (Vic)

Laycock, Henry (SAust) b Oct. 31, 1901 Edwardstown (SAust) d Aug. 6, 1983 Port Noarlunga (SAust)

Le Couteur, Philip Ridgeway (Vic) b June 26, 1885 Kyneton (Vic) d June 30, 1958 Gunnedah (NSW)

Leabeater, Leonard Raymond (NSW) b July 10, 1906 Parramatta (NSW) d June 1, 1996 Port Macquarie (NSW)

Leak, Brian Headley (SAust) b May 5, 1917 Hawthorn (SAust)

Leak, Ernest Howard (SAust) b Oct. 28, 1872 Finniss Vale (SAust) d Aug. 22, 1945 Adelaide (SAust)

Leak, Stanley Garfield (SAust) b March 12, 1886 Goodwood (SAust) d Jan. 10, 1963 Millswood (SAust)

Leary, John Denis (Qld) b c. 1862 Picton (NSW) d Jan. 16, 1940 Herston (Qld)

Leather, Thomas William (Vic) b June 2, 1910 Rutherglen, Lanarkshire (Scotland) d May 10, 1991 Prahran (Vic)

Ledger, Scott Norman (Qld) b Sept. 1, 1952 Nambour (Qld)

Ledward, John Allan (Vic) b April 22, 1909 East Melbourne (Vic) d July 22, 1997 Box Hill (Vic)

* Lee, Brett (NSW) b Nov. 8, 1976 Wollongong (NSW)

Lee, Clarence Leslie (Tas) b Dec. 28, 1890 Cressy (Tas) d Feb. 5, 1959 Invermay (Tas)

Lee, Ian Somerville (Vic) b March 24, 1914 Brunswick North (Vic) d April 14, 1976 Port Melbourne (Vic)

* Lee, Philip Keith (SAust) b Sept. 15, 1904 Gladstone (SAust) d Aug. 8, 1980 Woodville South (SAust)

Lee, Robert William (SAust) b Jan. 31, 1927 Hindmarsh (SAust) d June 9, 2001 Adelaide (SAust)

Lee, Shane (NSW) b Aug. 8, 1973 Wollongong (NSW)

Lee, Terence Henderson (NSW) b Aug. 31, 1940 Manly (NSW)

Leedham, Michael John (Tas) b Feb. 22, 1950 Campbell Town (Tas)

Leehane, John Francis (Vic) b Dec. 11, 1950 Coburg (Vic)

Leehane, John Thomas (Vic) b Oct. 20, 1921 Brunswick (Vic) d July 22, 1991 Caulfield (Vic)

Leeson, Henry Follie (Qld) b July 20, 1908 Mount Morgan (Qld) d May 24, 1950 Logan River (Qld)

Lehmann, Charles Albert (WAust) b Sept. 16, 1878 Caltowie (SAust) d April 27, 1940 Melbourne (Vic)

* Lehmann, Darren Scott (SAust & Vic) b Feb. 5, 1970 Gawler (SAust)

Leslie, Peter Glen (NSW) b Feb. 24, 1947 Bexley (NSW)

Letcher, Charles (Vic) b Dec. 22, 1868 Collingwood (Vic) d Nov. 30, 1916 Perth (WAust)

Lethborg, Gordon John (Tas) b Nov. 23, 1907 Scottsdale (Tas) d Aug. 31, 1989 Launceston (Tas)

Lette, Henry Elms (Tas) b 1829 birth day and month unknown Curramore (Tas) d Aug. 15, 1892 Launceston (Tas)

* Lever, Peter (Tas) b Sept. 17, 1940 Todmorden, Yorkshire (England)

Levingston, Raydon Charles (Qld) b Jan. 17, 1946 Toowoomba (Qld)

Levy, Graham Bruce (SAust) b Feb. 10, 1938 North Adelaide (SAust)

Levy, Roy Mark (Qld) b April 20, 1906 Waverley (NSW) d Dec. 12, 1965 Clayfield (Qld)

Lewis, Arthur (Vic) b c. 1830 full birth details unknown d June 1, 1907 Alexandra (Vic)

Lewis, John William (Qld) b Nov. 21, 1867 St George (Qld) d Sept. 19, 1939 Brisbane (Qld)

Lewis, Keith (SAust) b Feb. 4, 1923 Prospect (SAust)

Lewis, Kevin John (SAust) b Nov. 27, 1947 Hindmarsh (SAust)

Lewis, Laurence Robert (SAust) b May 24, 1889 Cherry Gardens (SAust) d Sept. 2, 1947 Prospect (SAust)

Lewis, Michael Llewellyn (Vic) b June 29, 1974 Greensborough (Vic)

Lewis, Oswald Hoddle (NSW) b Feb. 28, 1833 Sydney (NSW) d April 28, 1895 Darlinghurst (NSW)

Lewis, Percy Markham (Vic) b March 13, 1864 Hamilton (Vic) d Nov. 24, 1922 St Kilda (Vic)

Lewis, Thomas Harvie (NSW) b c. 1828 London (England) d June 19, 1901 Darlinghurst (NSW)

Liddicut, Arthur Edward (Vic) b Oct. 17, 1891 Fitzroy (Vic) d April 8, 1983 Parkdale (Vic)

Lihou, Jack (Qld) b Sept. 9, 1930 Sandgate (Qld)

Lill, John Charles (SAust) b Dec. 7, 1933 Maylands (SAust)

* Lillee, Dennis Keith (WAust & Tas) b July 18, 1949 Subiaco (WAust)

Lillie, Dennis John (Qld) b Oct. 28, 1945 Auchenflower (Qld)

Lilly, Kenneth Edward (WAust) b Dec. 25, 1959 Perth (WAust)

Limb, Allen (Tas) b Sept. 29, 1886 Gawler (SAust) d July 1, 1975 Battery Point (Tas)

* Lindwall, Raymond Russell (NSW & Qld) b Oct. 3, 1921 Mascot (NSW) d June 22, 1996 Greenslopes (Qld)

Linney, George Frederick (Tas) b Nov. 18, 1869 Guildford, Surrey (England) d Nov. 5, 1927 Weston-super-Mare, Somerset (England)

Lister, Charles (Vic) b Nov. 7, 1811 Armitage Park, Staffordshire (England) d Aug. 18, 1873 Laverstock Asylum, Alderbury, Wiltshire (England)

Liston, George Grieve (SAust) b April 29, 1860 Tanunda (SAust) d June 6, 1929 Kent Town (SAust)

Litster, John Lewis (Qld) b Feb. 2, 1904 Townsville (Qld) d March 11, 1982 Railway Estate, Townsville (Qld)

Little, Raymond Cecil James (NSW) b Oct. 7, 1914 Armidale (NSW) d April 28, 1995 Burwood (NSW)

Living, Gary Francis (Vic) b Oct. 1, 1952 Dandenong (Vic)

Livingston, Bruce Arthur Lionel (NSW) b May 11, 1927 Marrickville (NSW)

Livingston, Leonard (NSW) b May 3, 1920 Hurlstone Park (NSW) d Jan. 16, 1998 Hurlstone Park (NSW)

Lloyd, Robert Grantley (SAust) b Oct. 24, 1940 Gladstone (SAust)

* Loader, Peter James (WAust) b Oct. 25, 1929 Wellington, Surrey (England)

Lochner, Augustus Meyer (Tas) b Oct. 1, 1827 Enfield, Middlesex (England) d Feb. 20, 1865 Plumstead Common, Kent (England)

* Lock, Graham Anthony Richard (WAust) b July 5, 1929 Limpsfield, Surrey (England) d March 29, 1995 Beechboro (WAust)

Lockie, George William (Qld) b Feb. 18, 1910 Mt Morgan (Qld) d Nov. 2, 1971 Northgate (Qld)

Lockwood, William Thomas (WAust) b June 26, 1868 Geelong (Vic) d Aug. 29, 1953 Tuart Hill (WAust)

Lodding, Brent Andrew (Vic) b March 20, 1973 Upper Ferntree Gully (Vic)

Loder, Robert Roy (NSW) b Dec. 17, 1896 East Maitland (NSW) d Feb. 13, 1964 French's Forest (NSW)

Lodge, Arthur Oliver (WAust) b April 7, 1933 Guildford (WAust)

Logan, William (Vic) birth and death details unknown

Lonergan, Albert Roy (SAust & NSW) b Dec. 6, 1909 Maylands (WAust) d Oct. 22, 1956 Adelaide (SAust)

Loney, Geoffrey Souter (Tas) b March 31, 1894 Campbelltown (NSW) d April 7, 1985 Hobart (Tas)

Long, Edmund James (NSW) b March 28, 1883 Darlinghurst (NSW) d Dec. 8, 1947 Leichhardt (NSW)

Long, Gordon Hillhouse (Combined XI) b May 6, 1934 Hobart (Tas)

Long, Thomas Tasman Thompson (Qld) b Sept. 11, 1875 at sea d Oct. 20, 1926 Spring Hill (Qld)

Longney, Geoffrey Wallace (Vic) b May 25, 1935 Oakleigh (Vic)

Lord, John Carr (Tas) b Aug. 17, 1844 Hobart (Tas) d May 25, 1911 Antill Ponds (Tas)

Lord, Sidney (Tas) b Oct. 20, 1886 birthplace and death details unknown

Loton, Cecil Vernon (WAust) b Jan. 5, 1906 Upper Swan (WAust) d June 8, 1986 Pinjarra (WAust)

Loton, Morris William (WAust) b March 18, 1905 Springhill (WAust) d March 2, 1976 Northam (WAust)

Lough, William David (NSW) b Oct. 31, 1886 Bourke (NSW) d c. 1939 Newtown (NSW)

Loughnan, Austin Robert (Vic) b June 15, 1851 Hobart (Tas) d Oct. 9, 1926 Cheltenham (Vic)

* Love, Hampden Stanley Bray (NSW & Vic) b Aug. 10, 1895 Lilyfield (NSW) d July 22, 1969 Sydney (NSW)

* Love, Martin Lloyd (Qld) b March 30, 1974 Mundubbera (Qld)

Lovell, David Cameron (SAust) b Feb. 17, 1955 North Adelaide (SAust)

Lovelock, Oswald Ifould (WAust) b Aug. 28, 1911 Highgate (WAust) d Aug. 1, 1981 Subiaco (WAust)

Loveridge, Eustace Alfred (SAust) b April 14, 1891 Yongala (SAust) d July 29, 1959 Adelaide (SAust)

Loveridge, Walter David (NSW) b Sept. 13, 1867 Redfern (NSW) d Jan. 6, 1940 East Brisbane (Qld)

Lovett, Arthur Frederick (Tas & WAust) b June 1, 1920 St Kilda (Vic) d July 1, 1990 Coffs Harbour (NSW)

Lovett, Henry Charles (Tas) b March 3, 1856 Battery Point (Tas) d May 20, 1937 Hobart (Tas)

Lowe, Frederick (Vic) b Sept. 7, 1827 Holme Pierrepont, Nottinghamshire (England) d Oct. 15, 1887 Ararat (Vic)

Lowry, Jack Brown (Vic) b Nov. 25, 1916 Lambton (NSW)

Loxton, Colin Cameron (Qld) b Jan. 1, 1914 Beecroft (NSW) d Sept. 2, 2000 Greenslopes (Qld)

Loxton, John Frederick Cameron (Qld) b Nov. 26, 1945 Ashgrove (Qld)

* Loxton, Samuel John Everett (Vic) b March 29, 1921 Albert Park (Vic)

Lucas, Clyde Edward (Tas) b Aug. 11, 1898 Kingston (Tas) d Jan. 12, 1988 Palm Beach (Qld)

Lucas, Edward (Tas) b June 16, 1848 Kingston (Tas) d April 19, 1916 Kingston (Tas)

Lucas, Frank Russell (SAust) b Nov. 9, 1888 Port Pirie (SAust) d Aug. 31, 1941 Adelaide (SAust)

Lucas, Michael John (Qld) b April 14, 1944 Ashgrove (Qld)

Lucas, Thomas Turland (SAust) b Feb. 18, 1852 Eyres Flat (SAust) d March 13, 1945 Norwood (SAust)

Lugton, Frank Leslie (Vic) b Nov. 4, 1893 Northcote (Vic) d July 29, 1916 near Villers-Bretonneux (France)

Lukeman, Eric William (NSW) b March 11, 1923 Drummoyne (NSW) d April 18, 1993 Palm Beach (Qld)

Lush, John Grantley (NSW) b Oct. 14, 1913 Prahran (Vic) d Aug. 23, 1985 Sydney (NSW)

* Lyons, John James (SAust) b May 21, 1863 Gawler (SAust) d July 21, 1927 Magill (SAust)

Lyons, Rodney Bernard (Qld) b April 24, 1924 Cairns (Qld)

* McAlister, Peter Alexander (Vic) b July 11, 1869 Williamstown (Vic) d May 10, 1938 Richmond (Vic)

McAllen, Charles (Tas) b July 2, 1860 Hobart (Tas) d Jan. 15, 1924 Hobart (Tas)

McAllister, Donald Ernest (SAust) b Nov. 19, 1935 Hindmarsh (SAust)

McAndrew, John William (Qld) b Nov. 4, 1889 Berrima (NSW) d April 10, 1960 Ipswich (Qld)

McArdle, Brendan Joseph (Vic) b March 2, 1952 Preston (Vic)

* Macartney, Charles George (NSW) b June 27, 1886 West Maitland (NSW) d Sept. 9, 1958 Little Bay (NSW)

McAulay, Kenneth James (WAust) b Sept. 29, 1949 Subiaco (WAust)

McBeath, Arthur (NSW & SAust) b June 17, 1876 Mudgee (NSW) d March 17, 1945 Surry Hills (NSW)

* McCabe, Stanley Joseph (NSW) b July 16, 1910 Grenfell (NSW) d Aug. 25, 1968 Beauty Point (NSW)

McCaffrey, Michael Francis (Qld) b Feb. 18, 1878 Rockhampton (Qld) d March 17, 1949 Brisbane (Qld)

McCaffrey, Victor William (NSW) b Aug. 11, 1918 Goulburn (NSW)

* McCague, Martin John (WAust) b May 24, 1969 Larne (Northern Ireland)

McCarthy, John Edward (Qld) b Feb. 22, 1917 Maryborough (Qld) d Feb. 18, 1998 Southport (Qld)

McCarthy, Kevin Joseph (SAust) b Oct. 11, 1945 Rose Park (SAust)

McCarthy, Patrick Covell Derrick (WAust) b Oct. 24, 1919 (Ceylon)

McCarthy, Richard Charles Arthur Marum (Vic) b Dec. 21, 1961 Geelong (Vic)

McCauley, Bede Vincent (NSW) b June 11, 1909 Coogee (NSW) d Oct. 14, 1994 Sydney (NSW)

McCloy, William Stanley Swain (Qld & NSW) b Nov. 10, 1886 Paddington (NSW) d Nov. 10, 1975 Young (NSW)

McCooke, Steven Milne (Vic) b Jan. 31, 1960 South Caulfield (Vic)

* McCool, Colin Leslie (NSW & Qld) b Dec. 9, 1916 Paddington (NSW) d April 5, 1986 Concord (NSW)

McCoombe, Clarence Arthur (Qld) b Feb. 23, 1904 Cooktown (Qld) d Sept. 6, 1955 Sydney (NSW)

McCormack, William Henry (Vic) b May 5, 1877 St Kilda (Vic) d April 26, 1946 Stawell (Vic)

* McCormick, Ernest Leslie (Vic) b May 16, 1906 North Carlton (Vic) d June 28, 1991 Tweed Heads (NSW)

McCormick, Raymond Vincent (SAust) b Jan. 30, 1931 Mile End (SAust)

* McCosker, Richard Bede (NSW) b Dec. 11, 1946 Inverell (NSW)

McCoy, Bernard Leslie (NSW) b March 26, 1896 Kangaroo Valley (NSW) d June 11, 1970 Sydney (NSW)

McCurdy, Rodney John (Tas, Vic & SAust) b Dec. 30, 1959 Melbourne (Vic)

* McDermott, Craig John (Qld) b April 14, 1965 Ipswich (Qld)

McDonald, Andrew Barry (Vic) b June 5, 1981 Wodonga (Vic)

* McDonald, Colin Campbell (Vic) b Nov. 17, 1928 Glen Iris (Vic)

* McDonald, Edgar Arthur (Tas & Vic) b Jan. 6, 1891 Launceston (Tas) d July 22, 1937 Blackrod, near Bolton, Lancashire (England)

McDonald, Ian Hamilton (Vic) b July 28, 1923 Windsor (Vic)

Macdonald, Kenneth Locke (Tas) b Jan. 3, 1934 Premaydena (Tas) d July 1, 1999 Hobart (Tas)

Macdonald, Robert (Qld) b Feb. 14, 1870 Clunes (Vic) d March 7, 1946 Victoria, British Columbia (Canada)

McDonald, Walter Hugh (Vic, Qld & Tas) b March 24, 1884 Shepparton (Vic) d March 22, 1955 Kew (Vic)

* McDonnell, Percy Stanislaus (Vic, NSW & Qld) b Nov. 13, 1858 Kennington, Kent (England) d Sept. 24, 1896 South Brisbane (Qld)

McDowall, Robert Murray (Tas) b Nov. 21, 1821 Edinburgh (Scotland) d Nov. 5, 1894 (New Zealand)

Mace, Christopher (Vic) b Dec. 24, 1830 Bedale, Yorkshire (England) d Nov. 23, 1907 Sydenham (New Zealand)

Mace, John (Vic) b Dec. 28, 1828 Bedale, Yorkshire (England) d April 30, 1905 Te Aroha (New Zealand)

Mace, John Cruttenden (Tas) b May 7, 1839 Sydney (NSW) d April 18, 1906 Hawley-with-Minley, Hampshire (England)

McElhone, Frank Eric (NSW) b June 27, 1887 Waverley (NSW) d July 21, 1981 Darlinghurst (NSW)

McEvoy, Daniel Michael (WAust) b Aug. 19, 1946 Mount Lawley (WAust)

McEvoy, Frederick Aloysius (Vic) b July 4, 1856 Gundagai (NSW) d Nov. 5, 1913 Brighton (Vic)

McEvoy, William Joseph (Vic) b c. 1845 Sydney (NSW) d July 14, 1930 (England)

McEwan, Kenneth Scott (WAust) b July 16, 1952 Bedford, Cape Province (South Africa)

McEwan, W. (Tas) b 1815 birth day and month unknown Perth, Perthshire (Scotland) d c. 1862 (Vic)

McFarland, Robert (Vic) b July 9, 1847 Coleraine (Vic) d July 4, 1876 Carlton (Vic)

McFarlane, Clement Basil Patrick (Qld) b Aug. 20, 1900 New Farm (Qld) d March 2, 1946 Grange (Qld)

McFarlane, Robert Donald (WAust) b Feb. 7, 1955 Corrigin (WAust)

McGain, Bryce Edward (Vic) b March 25, 1972 Mornington (Vic)

McGan, Bryan (Vic) b March 19, 1847 Melbourne (Vic) d July 9, 1894 South Melbourne (Vic)

McGhee, Robert William (Qld) b March 24, 1963 Richmond (Qld)

MacGill, Charles William Terry (WAust) b June 16, 1916 Perth (WAust) d Oct. 31, 1999 Perth (WAust)

* MacGill, Stuart Charles Glyndwr (WAust & NSW) b Feb. 25, 1971 Mt Lawley (WAust)

MacGill, Terry Mornington David (WAust) b Dec. 22, 1945 Moreland (Vic)

McGilvray, Alan David (NSW) b Dec. 6, 1909 Paddington (NSW) d July 17, 1996 Darlinghurst (NSW)

McGinn, Albert Howard (Qld) b Nov. 11, 1913 Upper Kedron (Qld)

McGinty, Adam David (Vic) b March 24, 1971 Melbourne (Vic)

McGlinchy, William Walter (NSW & Qld) b Jan. 31, 1864 Newcastle (NSW) d July 1, 1946 Sydney (NSW)

* McGrath, Glenn Donald (NSW) b Feb. 9, 1970 Dubbo (NSW)

McGregor, William (Australians) b Feb. 23, 1888 St Kilda (Vic) d Oct. 5, 1980 Benalla (Vic)

McGuire, David Victor (Tas) b Nov. 13, 1931 Hobart (Tas)

McGuirk, Harold Vincent (NSW) b Oct. 17, 1906 Crookwell (NSW) death details unknown

McGuire, Leo Daniel (NSW) b May 3, 1908 Crookwell (NSW) d June 15, 1974 Sydney (NSW)

* McIlwraith, John (Vic) b Sept. 7, 1857 Collingwood (Vic) d July 5, 1938 Camberwell (Vic)

McInnes, Alan Roderick (Vic) b May 29, 1907 Kensington (Vic) d Sept. 16, 1991 Dandenong (Vic)

McInnes, Mark William (Cricket Academy) b April 16, 1977 Wagga Wagga (NSW)

McIntyre, Ernest John (Vic) b April 19, 1921 Albert Park (Vic) d April 10, 2003 Melbourne (Vic)

* McIntyre, Peter Edward (Vic & SAust) b April 27, 1966 Gisborne (Vic)

McIntyre, William Robert (NSW) b April 10, 1877 Forbes (NSW) d c. 1943 Drummoyne (NSW)

Mack, Christopher David (WAust) b June 30, 1970 Subiaco (WAust)

McKay, Douglas Gordon (SAust) b July 2, 1904 North Adelaide (SAust) d April 9, 1994 North Adelaide (SAust)

Mackay, George (Vic) b July 6, 1860 Castlemaine (Vic) d May 22, 1948 Bendigo (Vic)

McKay, Henry James (SAust) b Jan. 1, 1883 Goodwood (SAust) d Feb. 12, 1926 Hawthorn (SAust)

Mackay, James Rainey Munro (NSW) b Sept. 9, 1880 Armidale (NSW) d June 13, 1953 Walcha (NSW)

Mackay, John Robert Edward (Qld) b Nov. 24, 1937 Rockhampton (Qld)

* Mackay, Kenneth Donald (Qld) b Oct. 24, 1925 Windsor (Qld) d June 13, 1982 Point Lookout, Stradbroke Island (Qld)

Mackay, Kerry (NSW) b May 7, 1949 Brighton-Le-Sands (NSW)

MacKenzie, Alexander Cecil Knox (NSW) b Aug. 7, 1870 Sydney (NSW) d April 11, 1947 Epping (NSW)

McKenzie, Colin (Vic) b Dec. 12, 1880 Trawool (Vic) d Aug. 31, 1930 Avenel (Vic)

MacKenzie, Damien Robert (Qld) b July 21, 1980 Herston (Qld)

McKenzie, Douglas Charles (WAust) b March 15, 1906 Kew (Vic) d July 1, 1979 Perth (WAust)

McKenzie, Eric Norman (WAust) b Dec. 9, 1910 Kalgoorlie (WAust) d April 28, 1994 Cottesloe (WAust)

* McKenzie, Graham Douglas (WAust) b June 24, 1941 Cottesloe (WAust)

McKenzie, John (SAust) b Oct. 11, 1862 Aldinga (SAust) d June 3, 1944 Hazelwood Park (SAust)

McKenzie, Matthew Stanley (Tas) b May 17, 1890 Launceston (Tas) d Dec. 8, 1915 Alexandria (Egypt)

McKew, Cecil George (NSW) b Aug. 12, 1887 Leichhardt (NSW) d Oct. 12, 1974 Lilli Pilli (NSW)

* McKibbin, Thomas Robert (NSW) b Dec. 10, 1870 Raglan (NSW) d Dec. 15, 1939 Bathurst (NSW)

McKone, John James (NSW) b Oct. 3, 1835 Sydney (NSW) d Aug. 7, 1882 Sydney (NSW)

McLachlan, Ian Murray (SAust) b Oct. 2, 1936 North Adelaide (SAust)

* McLaren, John William (Qld) b Dec. 22, 1886 Toowong (Qld) d Nov. 17, 1921 Highgate Hill (Qld)

McLaughlin, John Joseph (Qld) b Feb. 18, 1930 Corinda (Qld)

McLay, Gregory Francis (NSW) b May 7, 1969 Wagga Wagga (NSW)

McLean, Allan Robert Charles (SAust) b Feb. 1, 1914 Mile End (SAust) d Nov. 9, 1989 Christies Beach (SAust)

McLean, Hugh (Vic) b Nov. 26, 1864 Woodford (Vic) d Feb. 19, 1915 East Melbourne (Vic)

McLean, Ian Robert (SAust) b Jan. 30, 1954 Semaphore (SAust)

* Maclean, John Alexander (Qld) b April 27, 1946 Herston (Qld)

MacLeay, Kenneth Hervey (WAust) b April 2, 1959 Bedford-on-Avon, Wiltshire (England)

McLellan, Ross Malcolm (SAust) b Feb. 20, 1955 Glenhuntly (Vic)

* McLeod, Charles Edward (Vic) b Oct. 24, 1869 Sandridge (Vic) d Nov. 26, 1918 Armadale (Vic)

McLeod, Daniel Hutton (Vic) b March 29, 1872 Sandridge (Vic) d Nov. 25, 1901 Port Melbourne (Vic)

* McLeod, Robert William (Vic) b Jan. 19, 1868 Sandridge (Vic) d June 14, 1907 Middle Park (Vic)

McMahon, John Terrence (Qld) b May 18, 1932 Five Dock (NSW)

McMahon, Vincent Gerald (Qld) b Jan. 18, 1918 Chinchilla (Qld) d Jan. 23, 1988 Greenslopes (Qld)

McMichael, Samuel Albert (Vic) b July 18, 1869 Collingwood (Vic) d July 21, 1923 Elsternwick (Vic)

McNamara, Bradley Edward (NSW) b Dec. 30, 1965 Sydney (NSW)

McNamee, Raymond Leonard Alphonsus (NSW) b Aug. 26, 1895 Orange (NSW) d Sept. 18, 1949 Little Bay (NSW)

McNaughton, John Leonard (Vic) b Jan. 15, 1884 Richmond (Vic) d Dec. 26, 1970 Lower Kingswood, Surrey (England)

MacNish, William George (NSW) b Oct. 29, 1842 Paddington (NSW) d Nov. 29, 1873 Bundaberg (Qld)

McPetrie, William Martin (Vic) b Feb. 15, 1880 Emerald Hill (Vic) d June 30, 1951 Hawthorn (Vic)

McPhee, Mark William (WAust) b Jan. 25, 1964 Katanning (WAust) d Aug. 15, 1999 Gingin (WAust)

McPhee, Peter Thomas (Tas) b July 29, 1963 South Brisbane (Qld)

MacPherson, Herbert James Keele (NSW) b Feb. 20, 1869 Mudgee (NSW) d Nov. 12, 1953 Mudgee (NSW)

McPherson, James Philip (Vic) b Nov. 20, 1842 Moonee Ponds (Vic) d Aug. 23, 1891 Melbourne (Vic)

McPhillamy, Keith (NSW) b June 20, 1882 Bathurst (NSW) d May 3, 1937 Bowral (NSW)

McRae, Donald (SAust) b June 13, 1873 Aldinga (SAust) d Oct. 22, 1940 Prospect (SAust)

McRae, William Alexander (WAust) b June 18, 1904 Geelong (Vic) d July 25, 1973 Subiaco (WAust)

MacRow, William Reginald Fairbairn (Vic) b July 7, 1889 Kew (Vic) d May 19, 1970 Heidelberg (Vic)

* McShane, Patrick George (Vic) b April 18, 1858 Keilor (Vic) d Dec. 11, 1903 Kew (Vic)

Mace, Christopher (Vic) b Dec. 24, 1830 Bedale, Yorkshire (England) d Nov. 23, 1907 Sydenham (New Zealand)

Madden, Robert Harold (NSW) b Dec. 12, 1928 Camperdown (NSW)

Maddern, James Gregory (Qld) b March 22, 1914 Crows Nest (Qld) d March 27, 1987 Nambour (Qld)

Madders, Garry James (Qld) b Jan. 21, 1953 Maryborough (Qld)

Maddock, Charles Edward Rokeby (Qld) b Aug. 14, 1887 (Qld) d Feb. 14, 1957 Herston (Qld)

Maddocks, Ian Leonard (Vic) b April 12, 1951 Ashburton (Vic)

* Maddocks, Leonard Victor (Vic & Tas) b May 24, 1926 Beaconsfield (Vic)

Maddocks, Richard Ivor (Vic) b July 30, 1928 Carnegie (Vic) d Sept. 10, 1968 Blackburn (Vic)

Maddox, George (Tas) b c. 1811 (Ireland) d July 7, 1867 Melbourne (Vic)

Maddox, John Montgomery (Tas) b Dec. 30, 1930 St Mary's (Tas)

Magarey, William Ashley (SAust) b Jan. 30, 1868 North Adelaide (SAust) d Oct. 18, 1929 North Adelaide (SAust)

* Maguire, John Norman (Qld) b Sept. 15, 1956 Murwillumbah (NSW)

Maher, James Patrick (Qld) b Feb. 27, 1974 Innisfail (Qld)

Mahoney, Hector James Henry (Qld) b Sept. 8, 1913 Maryborough (Qld) d Sept. 25, 1991 Maryborough (Qld)

Mail, Gregory John (NSW) b April 29, 1978 Penrith (NSW)

Mailer, David (Vic) b Aug. 18, 1874 Coburg (Vic) d Dec. 21, 1937 Shepparton (Vic)

* Mailey, Arthur Alfred (NSW) b Jan. 3, 1886 Zetland (NSW) d Dec. 31, 1967 Kirrawee (NSW)

Mainhardt, Michael Shane (Qld) b Jan. 6, 1960 Clermont (Qld)

Mair, Frederick (NSW) b April 15, 1901 Balmain (NSW) d Dec. 25, 1959 Sydney (NSW)

Majewski, Neil John (Tas) b May 27, 1954 Footscray (Vic)

* Majid Jahangir Khan (Qld) b Sept. 28, 1946 Ludhiana (India)

Major, Albert George (Vic) b March 20, 1851 Langport, Somerset (England) d Oct. 16, 1921 Caulfield (Vic)

Makin, James Charles (Vic) b Feb. 11, 1904 Collingwood (Vic) d Jan. 15, 1973 Heidelberg (Vic)

Makin, William (NSW) birth details unknown d Jan. 11, 1962 West Kogarah (NSW)

Makinson, Charles (Vic) b c. 1831 Salford, Lancashire (England) d June 12, 1895 Rugeley, Staffordshire (England)

* Mallett, Ashley Alexander (SAust) b July 13, 1945 Chatswood (NSW)

* Malone, Michael Francis (WAust) b Oct. 9, 1950 Perth (WAust)

Maloney, Peter Ivan (NSW) b Nov. 5, 1950 Ballina (NSW)

Mancell, Peter John (Tas) b March 15, 1958 Goulburn (NSW)

* Mann, Anthony Longford (WAust) b Nov. 8, 1945 Middle Swan (WAust)

Mann, John Lewis (SAust) b April 26, 1919 Strathalbyn (SAust) d Sept. 24, 1969 Lockleys (SAust)

Manning, John Stephen (SAust) b June 11, 1923 Ethelton (SAust) d May 31, 1988 Belair (SAust)

Manou, Graham Allan (SAust) b April 23, 1979 Modbury (SAust)

Mansfield, Graeme Edward (Tas) b Dec. 27, 1942 Hobart (Tas)

Mansfield, J. (Tas) birth and death details unknown

Maplestone, Henry Carman (Vic) b Jan. 11, 1870 Parkville (Vic) d Dec. 10, 1949 Moonee Ponds (Vic)

Maranta, Michael Gerard (Qld) b March 20, 1961 South Brisbane (Qld)

Marjoribanks, Hugh Lynch (NSW) b Aug. 12, 1933 Mackay (Qld)

Marks, Alexander Edward (NSW) b Dec. 9, 1910 Toowong (Qld) d July 28, 1983 Wahroonga (NSW)

Marks, Lynn Alexander (NSW & SAust) b Aug. 15, 1942 Randwick (NSW) d Dec. 7, 1997 Mona Vale (NSW)

Marks, Neil Graham (NSW) b Sept. 13, 1938 Randwick (NSW)

Marks, Phillip Henry (NSW) b April 30, 1961 Salisbury (Southern Rhodesia)

* Marks, Victor James (WAust) b June 25, 1955 Middle Chinnock, Somerset (England)

Marquet, Joshua Phillip (Tas) b Dec. 3, 1968 Melbourne (Vic)

* Marr, Alfred Percy (NSW) b March 28, 1862 Pyrmont (NSW) d March 15, 1940 Arncliffe (NSW)

Marriott, Arthur John (Tas) b c. 1821 (England) d March 31, 1866 Nice (France)

Marsden, Albert John (Qld) b June 13, 1887 Maryborough (Qld) d Dec. 17, 1971 Kallista (Vic)

Marsden, Frederick William (Vic) b c. 1819 Lewisham, London (England) d March 20, 1870 Fitzroy (Vic)

Marsh, Daniel James (SAust & Tas) b June 14, 1973 Subiaco (WAust)

* Marsh, Geoffrey Robert (WAust) b Dec. 31, 1958 Northam (WAust)

Marsh, Jack (NSW) b c. 1874 Yugilbar (NSW) d May 25, 1916 Orange (NSW)

* Marsh, Rodney William (WAust) b Nov. 4, 1947 Armadale (WAust)

Marsh, Shaun Edwards (WAust) b July 9, 1983 Narrogin (WAust)

Marshal, Alan (Qld) b June 12, 1883 Warwick (Qld) d July 23, 1915 Imtarfa Military Hospital (Malta)

Marshall, Angus Neil (Qld) b Jan. 7, 1906 Essequibo (British Guiana) d Aug. 29, 1969 Nundah (Qld)

Marshall, George (Tas) b 1832 birth day and month unknown Sorell (Tas) d July 13, 1905 Sorell (Tas)

Marshall, George (Vic) b Dec. 20, 1829 Nottingham, Nottinghamshire (England) d March 6, 1868 Melbourne (Vic)

Marshall, John (Tas) b c. 1796 (England) d Sept. 7, 1876 New Town (Tas)

Martin, Charles (Qld) b May 15, 1867 Ipswich (Qld) d c. 1942 Sydney (NSW)

Martin, Charles Albert (SAust) b March 29, 1863 Adelaide (SAust) d May 14, 1955 St Georges (SAust)

Martin, Charles William Beresford (Tas) b Oct. 6, 1888 Launceston (Tas) d Oct. 30, 1951 Camberwell (Vic)

Martin, Edmund John (WAust) b Sept. 26, 1902 Eaglehawk (Vic) d June 9, 2004 Perth (WAust)

Martin, Geoffrey Bernard (Tas) b July 16, 1927 Launceston (Tas)

Martin, Geoffrey William (Tas) b March 7, 1896 Launceston (Tas) d March 7, 1968 Launceston (Tas)

Martin, Gordon Francis (Qld) b Jan. 14, 1885 Clunes (Vic) d Aug. 19, 1974 Canberra (ACT)

Martin, Hugh (NSW) b Aug. 3, 1947 Enkeldoorn (Southern Rhodesia)

Martin, James Macfie (sp) b Feb. 25, 1851 Launceston (Tas) d Oct. 22, 1930 Launceston (Tas)

Martin, John Frank (NSW) b May 8, 1942 Alton, Hampshire (England)

* Martin, John Wesley (NSW & SAust) b July 28, 1931 Wingham (NSW) d July 15, 1992 Burrell Creek (NSW)

Martin, William (Tas) b June 21, 1856 Westbury (Tas) d July 10, 1938 Launceston (Tas)

* Martyn, Damien Richard (WAust) b Oct. 21, 1971 Darwin (NT)

Mason, Matthew Sean (WAust) b March 20, 1974 Claremont (WAust)

Mason, Scott Robert (Tas) b July 27, 1976 George Town (Tas)

Massey, Richard Eric Charles (SAust) b June 5, 1961 Tamworth (NSW)

* Massie, Hugh Hamon (NSW) b April 11, 1854 near Belfast (Vic) d Oct. 12, 1938 Point Piper (NSW)

* Massie, Robert Arnold Lockyer (WAust) b April 14, 1947 Subiaco (WAust)

Massie, Robert John Allwright (NSW) b July 8, 1890 North Sydney (NSW) d Feb. 14, 1966 Mosman (NSW)

Mateljan, Tony (WAust) b Feb. 18, 1934 Middle Swan (WAust)

Mather, Adam (NSW) b Nov. 26, 1860 Paterson (NSW) d Aug. 31, 1917 Singleton (NSW)

Mather, John Henry (Vic) b Nov. 19, 1822 Everton, Lancashire (England) d Aug. 4, 1870 Iquique (Chile)

Mathers, James (Vic) b June 30, 1894 Minmi (NSW) d March 28, 1977 Eastwood (NSW)

Mathieson, Donald Kenneth (Vic) b April 24, 1931 Nhill (Vic)

Matson, George (Tas) b Dec. 5, 1817 Rochester, Kent (England) d July 22, 1898 Brighton, Sussex (England)

* Matthews, Christopher Darrell (WAust & Tas) b Sept. 22, 1962 Cunderdin (WAust)

* Matthews, Gregory Richard John (NSW) b Dec. 15, 1959 Newcastle (NSW)

Matthews, James George Facey (SAust) b Sept. 27, 1876 Roseworthy (SAust) d Oct. 8, 1963 Prospect (SAust)

Matthews, Robert Graham (Vic) b April 17, 1953 Camberwell (Vic)

Matthews, Thomas Harold (Tas) b Feb. 9, 1905 Longley (Tas) d May 11, 1990 Longley (Tas)

* Matthews, Thomas James (Vic) b April 3, 1884 Mt Gambier (SAust) d Oct. 14, 1943 Caulfield (Vic)

Maxwell, Eustace (Tas) b Jan. 20, 1864 Hobart (Tas) d May 18, 1939 Hobart (Tas)

Maxwell, Neil Donald (Vic & NSW) b June 12, 1967 Lautoka (Fiji)

* May, Timothy Brian Alexander (SAust) b Jan. 26, 1962 North Adelaide (SAust)

Mayes, Alexander Dunbar Aitken (NSW & Qld) b July 24, 1901 Toowoomba (Qld) d Feb. 8, 1983 Spring Hill (Qld)

* Mayne, Lawrence Charles (WAust) b Jan. 23, 1942 Westonia (WAust)

* Mayne, Richard Edgar (SAust & Vic) b July 2, 1882 Jamestown (SAust) d Oct. 26, 1961 Richmond (Vic)

* Meckiff, Ian (Vic) b Jan. 6, 1935 Mentone (Vic)

Meech, James Robert (Tas) b Dec. 16, 1884 Hobart (Tas) d Oct. 31, 1955 Hobart (Tas)

Meek, Andrew Bonar (WAust) b Dec. 7, 1889 Gulgong (NSW) d Feb. 13, 1957 Perth (WAust)

Meikle, George Stanley (Vic) b Oct. 22, 1916 Footscray (Vic) d July 25, 1991 Brighton (Vic)

Melville, Paul (Vic) b Dec. 27, 1956 South Shields, Durham (England) d Nov. 21, 1978 Vermont South (Vic)

Menegon, Lyndon John (Tas) b Feb. 11, 1948 Burnie (Tas)

Mengel, Douglas Charles (Qld) b March 2, 1933 Brisbane (Qld)

Metcalfe, Evelyn James (Qld) b Sept. 29, 1865 Kennington, Kent (England) d June 14, 1951 Cambridge, Cambridgeshire (England)

* Meuleman, Kenneth Douglas (Vic & WAust) b Sept. 5, 1923 Melbourne (Vic)

Meuleman, Robert Douglas (WAust) b Sept. 6, 1949 Melbourne (Vic)

Meuleman, Scott William (WAust) b July 17, 1980 Subiaco (WAust)

Michael, Constantine Anthony (WAust) b Jan. 12, 1953 Victoria Park (WAust)

Michael, Leonard (SAust) b June 3, 1921 Medindie (SAust) d March 16, 1996 Adelaide (SAust)

Middleton, Frederick Stewart (NSW) b May 28, 1883 Burrowa (now Booroowa) (NSW) d July 21, 1956 Auckland (New Zealand)

Middleton, Roy Foster (SAust) b Sept. 18, 1889 Kent Town (SAust) d March 19, 1975 Adelaide (SAust)

** Midwinter, William Evans (Vic) b June 19, 1851 St Briavel's, Gloucestershire (England) d Dec. 3, 1890 Kew Asylum (Vic)

Mihell, Robert William (Qld) b Jan. 8, 1937 Lismore (NSW)

* Milburn, Colin (WAust) b Oct. 23, 1941 Burnopfield, Durham (England) d Feb. 28, 1990 Newton Aycliffe, Durham (England)

Miles, Geoffrey John (Vic) b Aug. 7, 1957 Kew (Vic)

Millar, Geoffrey Alan (WAust) b Nov. 22, 1955 Subiaco (WAust)

Millar, Keith James (Vic) b Aug. 15, 1906 Richmond (Vic) d July 13, 1971 Camberwell (Vic)

* Miller, Colin Reid (Vic, SAust & Tas) b Feb. 6, 1964 Footscray (Vic)

Miller, David Lawson (NSW & Qld) b Jan. 30, 1870 Holytown, Lanarkshire (Scotland) d April 12, 1943 Clayfield (Qld)

Miller, Graeme Geoffrey (Combined XI) b Sept. 24, 1940 Launceston (Tas)

Miller, Ivan Derness (Vic) b Dec. 30, 1913 Ivanhoe (Vic) d May 6, 1966 Heidelberg (Vic)

* Miller, Keith Ross (Vic & NSW) b Nov. 28, 1919 Sunshine (Vic)

Miller, Kevin Roy (Tas) b Oct. 12, 1936 Launceston (Tas)

Miller, Leslie Percy Robert (Vic) b June 16, 1880 St Kilda (Vic) d July 2, 1963 death place unknown

Miller, Michael Christian (Qld & SAust) b May 30, 1979 Toowoomba (Qld)

Miller, Noel Keith (NSW) b July 1, 1913 Wyong (NSW)

Miller, William Edward (WAust) b March 9, 1905 East Perth (WAust) d July 24, 1974 Perth (WAust)

Milliken, Geoffrey Scott (NSW) b May 6, 1964 Hay (NSW)

Millns, David James (Tas) b Feb. 27, 1965 Clipstone, Nottinghamshire (England)

Mills, John (NSW) b June 3, 1836 Botley, Hampshire (England) d Feb. 24, 1899 Bisterne, Hampshire (England)

Mills, Rowland Leslie (WAust) b July 14, 1914 Leederville (WAust) d Feb. 27, 2000 Perth (WAust)

Milosz, Stephen Joseph (WAust & Tas) b Dec. 26, 1955 Northam (WAust)

Minagall, Matthew John Peter (SAust) b Nov. 13, 1971 Woodville (SAust)

Minchin, James Melbourne (Vic) b Aug. 15, 1859 Emerald Hill (Vic) d Feb. 13, 1919 Cheltenham (Vic)

Minnett, Leslie Alma (NSW) b May 19, 1883 St Leonard's (NSW) d Aug. 8, 1934 Collaroy (NSW)

* Minnett, Roy Baldwin (NSW) b June 13, 1886 St Leonard's (NSW) d Oct. 21, 1955 Manly (NSW)

Minnett, Rupert Villiers (NSW) b Sept. 2, 1884 St Leonard's (NSW) d June 24, 1974 Cremorne (NSW)

Minter, Eric James (NSW) b Sept. 13, 1917 Kempsey (NSW) d July 1, 1985 Vincentia (NSW)

* Misson, Francis Michael (NSW) b Nov. 19, 1938 Darlinghurst (NSW)

Mitchell, Brian Gordon (SAust) b March 15, 1959 Glenelg (SAust)

Mitchell, Norman Frederick (Vic) b Feb. 19, 1900 Collingwood (Vic) d March 8, 1973 Melbourne (Vic)

Mitchell, Robert (Vic) b April 11, 1863 Campbellfield (Vic) d Sept. 17, 1926 West Preston (Vic)

Moffat, William (SAust) b July 22, 1858 Byethorne (SAust) d July 30, 1922 Jamestown (SAust)

Moffatt, Alfred Augustine (WAust) b March 15, 1870 Perth (WAust) d Dec. 8, 1956 Perth (WAust)

Moir, Bruce Graeme (Vic) b Nov. 10, 1960 Melbourne (Vic)

Monfries, John Elliott (Vic) b Dec. 25, 1873 Gumeracha (SAust) d Sept. 2, 1954 Hobart (Tas)

Monohan, Vincent Clifford (Vic) b April 22, 1896 Collingwood (Vic) d July 9, 1974 Linden Park (SAust)

Monty, Stephen (Qld) b March 3, 1963 Glenelg (SAust)

* Moody, Thomas Masson (WAust) b Oct. 2, 1965 Adelaide (SAust)

Moore, David John Arthur (NSW) b Oct. 16, 1964 Sydney (NSW)

Moore, George (NSW) b April 18, 1820 Ampthill, Bedfordshire (England) d Sept. 29, 1916 West Maitland (NSW)

Moore, George Stanley (NSW & Qld) b April 18, 1886 North Sydney (NSW) d March 22, 1948 Bundaberg (Qld)

Moore, Henry Thomas (SAust) b c. 1860 Plomesgate (England) death details unknown

Moore, James (NSW) b c. 1839 Ampthill, Bedfordshire (England) d April 19, 1890 West Maitland (NSW)

Moore, Leonard David (NSW) b Feb. 8, 1871 West Maitland (NSW) d Sept. 11, 1934 Maitland (NSW)

Moore, William Henry (NSW & WAust) b Oct. 16, 1863 West Maitland (NSW) d Feb. 25, 1956 Lane Cove (NSW)

Morcom, Samuel (Combined XIII) b c.1847 full birth details unknown d Jan. 15, 1888 Adelaide (SAust)

Morgan, Charles Edward (Vic) b Aug. 10, 1900 Collingwood (Vic) d Dec. 8, 1965 Preston (Vic)

Morgan, Charles William (Qld) b Jan. 10, 1877 Hotham (Vic) d April 15, 1937 death place unknown

Morgan, George (NSW) b July 7, 1844 Bathurst (NSW) d July 17, 1896 Sydney (NSW)

Morgan, John Gordon (NSW) b March 6, 1893 Camperdown (NSW) d May 7, 1967 Concord (NSW)

Morgan, Oliver John (Qld) b June 7, 1945 Herston (Qld)

Morgan, Walter Millard (Vic) b Nov. 1, 1871 Ballarat (Vic) d July 10, 1941 Ballarat (Vic)

Morgan, Wayne Geoffrey (Qld) b July 10, 1955 Greenslopes (Qld)

* Moroney, John (NSW) b July 24, 1917 Macksville (NSW) d July 1, 1999 Orange (NSW)

Moroney, Robert (SAust) b Jan. 23, 1885 Upper Sturt (SAust) d Aug. 4, 1958 Parkside (SAust)

Morres, Thomas Furley (Vic) b Sept. 12, 1829 Wokingham, Berkshire (England) d Sept. 28, 1884 East Melbourne (Vic)

* Morris, Arthur Robert (NSW) b Jan. 19, 1922 Bondi (NSW)

Morris, John Humphrey (NSW) b June 5, 1831 Sydney (NSW) d Dec. 9, 1921 Glebe Point (NSW)

Morris, Maesmore Alfred (Vic) b April 30, 1868 Northcote (Vic) d Aug. 31, 1917 Heidelberg (Vic)

Morris, Norman O'Neil (NSW) b May 9, 1907 Camperdown (NSW) d July 15, 1982 Leichhardt (NSW)

* Morris, Samuel (Vic) b June 22, 1855 Hobart (Tas) d Sept. 20, 1931 South Melbourne (Vic)

Morris, William Wallace (Qld) b March 6, 1918 Thornleigh (NSW)

Morrisby, Ronald Orlando George (Tas) b Jan. 12, 1915 Hobart (Tas) d June 12, 1995 Hobart (Tas)

Morrissey, Charles Vincent (NSW) b April 26, 1903 Corowa (NSW) d Feb. 20, 1938 Quirindi (NSW)

Morse, Eric George Arnold (Tas) b Aug. 26, 1918 Sheffield (Tas)

Morton, Francis Lonsdale (SAust & Vic) b Dec. 21, 1901 Fullarton (SAust) d Oct. 14, 1971 Caulfield (Vic)

Morton, Hugh Gilbert Stuart (Qld) b Oct. 14, 1881 Maryborough (Qld) d Jan. 28, 1936 Herston (Qld)

* Moses, Henry (NSW) b Feb. 13, 1858 Windsor (NSW) d Dec. 7, 1938 Strathfield (NSW)

* Moss, Jeffrey Kenneth (Vic) b June 29, 1947 Melbourne (Vic)

Moss, Jonathan (Vic) b May 4, 1975 Manly (NSW)

Moss, Ronald Barbar (NSW) b June 13, 1922 Alexandria (NSW)

Mossop, Kenneth Leonard Mario (Qld) b Aug. 15, 1909 New Farm (Qld) d Sept. 18, 1975 Surfers Paradise (Qld)

Mott, Matthew Peter (Qld & Vic) b Oct. 3, 1973 Charleville (Qld)

* Moule, William Henry (Vic) b Jan. 31, 1858 Brighton (Vic) d Aug. 24, 1939 St Kilda (Vic)

Moyes, Alban George (SAust & Vic) b Jan. 2, 1893 Gladstone (SAust) d Jan. 18, 1963 Chatswood (NSW)

Moyle, Charles Rule (SAust) b April 16, 1884 Adelaide (SAust) d Aug. 2, 1952 Adelaide (SAust)

Moyle, Edward James Ross (SAust) b Oct. 15, 1913 Moonta Mines (SAust) d Oct. 24, 1942 Cairo (Egypt) on active service

Moysey, George Bickford (WAust) b May 14, 1874 Battery Point (Tas) d May 18, 1932 Canterbury (Vic)

Muddle, Donald Gordon (Qld) b July 26, 1937 The Grange (Qld)

Mudge, Harold (NSW) b Feb. 14, 1914 Stanmore (NSW)

Mueller, Mervyn Edward Christopher Edgar (SAust) b Oct. 3, 1914 Yatala (SAust) d July 22, 1984 South Plympton (SAust)

Muggleton, Mervyn Brian (WAust) b Sept. 4, 1941 Unley (SAust)

Muhl, Arthur Henry (Qld) b Feb. 12, 1913 South Brisbane (Qld) d April 17, 1994 South Brisbane (Qld)

Muir, William Frederick (Vic) b Feb. 8, 1907 Prahran (Vic) d Nov. 27, 1964 Box Hill (Vic)

Mulder, Brett (WAust) b Feb. 6, 1964 Subiaco (WAust)

Mulherin, Wayne Michael (NSW) b June 17, 1957 Canterbury (NSW)

Mullagh, Johnny (Unaarrimin) (Vic) b Aug. 13, 1841 Harrow (Vic) d Aug. 14, 1891 Pine Hills Station (Vic)

* Mullally, Alan David (WAust) b July 12, 1969 Southend-on-Sea, Essex (England)

Mullarkey, Desmond Antony (NSW) b Sept. 19, 1899 Rockdale (NSW) d Sept. 1, 1975 death place unknown

* Muller, Scott Andrew (Qld) b July 11, 1971 Herston (Qld)

Mullett, David Anthony (Tas) b Aug. 18, 1958 Burnie (Tas)

Mullett, Leonard Thomas (Vic) b Nov. 27, 1894 Moonee Ponds (Vic) d April 22, 1944 Toorak (Vic)

Mullooly, Thomas Cade (WAust) b Jan. 30, 1954 Mt Lawley (WAust)

Mundy, David Lloyd (SAust) b June 30, 1947 Enfield (SAust)

Munn, Arthur Reginald (NSW) b Feb. 22, 1888 Paddington (NSW) d Sept. 15, 1975 Sydney (NSW)

Munro, Charles (WAust) b March 21, 1871 Wallan (Vic) d Feb. 7, 1969 North Fremantle (WAust)

Munro, John Knox Ewing (WAust) b Dec. 27, 1928 Perth (WAust)

Munro, William (Qld) b Aug. 7, 1862 Ardwick, Lancashire (England) d Feb. 18, 1896 Stanthorpe (Qld)

Murch, Stewart Nigel Clifford (Vic) b June 27, 1944 Warrnambool (Vic)

**Murdoch, William Lloyd (Vic) b Oct. 18, 1854 Sandhurst (Vic) d Feb. 18, 1911 Melbourne (Vic)

Murfett, Julian Ivor (Tas) b July 2, 1915 Dunorlan (Tas) d April 27, 1982 Hobart (Tas)

Murphy, James Joseph (NSW) b Sept. 29, 1911 Bega (NSW) d May 7, 1984 Glenfield (NSW)

Murphy, Michael Augustus (Vic) b June 12, 1854 Sydney (NSW) d Sept. 2, 1890 Richmond (Vic)

Murray, Alfred Wynyatt (Vic) b Feb. 4, 1868 Long Gully (Vic) d July 29, 1936 Regent (Vic)

Murray, George Ian (WAust) b Nov. 6, 1940 South Perth (WAust)

Murray, John Tinline (SAust) b Dec. 1, 1892 Norwood (SAust) d Sept. 19, 1974 Stirling (SAust)

Murray, Norman Eric (Tas) b Nov. 2, 1908 Perth (WAust) d Aug. 21, 1967 Manly (NSW)

Murray, Richard (NSW) b c. 1831 Sydney (NSW) d Nov. 21, 1861 Manly (NSW)

Murray, William Walter Bruce (Vic) b Sept. 4, 1929 Red Cliffs (Vic)

* Musgrove, Henry Alfred (Vic) b Nov. 27, 1860 Surbiton, Surrey (England) d Nov. 2, 1931 Darlinghurst (NSW)

Musgrove, John (SAust) b July 28, 1861 Adelaide (SAust) d June 9, 1940 death place unknown

Mutton, Howard James Charles (SAust) b Oct. 21, 1924 Angaston (SAust) d Nov. 20, 1992 Adelaide (SAust)

Myers, Hubert (Tas) b Jan. 2, 1875 Yeadon, Yorkshire (England) d June 12, 1944 Hobart (Tas)

* Nagel, Lisle Ernest (Vic) b March 26, 1905 Bendigo (Vic) d Nov. 23, 1971 Mornington (Vic)

Nagel, Vernon George (Vic) b March 26, 1905 Bendigo (Vic) d April 27, 1974 Sandringham (Vic)

Nash, Brendan Paul (Qld) b Dec. 14, 1977 Bentley (WAust)

Nash, Don Anthony (NSW) b March 29, 1978 Dubbo (NSW)

Nash, John Eric (SAust) b April 16, 1950 North Adelaide (SAust)

* Nash, Laurence John (Tas & Vic) b May 2, 1910 Fitzroy (Vic) d July 24, 1986 Heidelberg (Vic)

Neill, Bruce William (Tas) b Feb. 23, 1949 Cabramatta (NSW)

Nettelton, Robert Glanville (Vic) b Sept. 16, 1909 Newport (Vic) d April 6, 1972 Newport (Vic)

Neville, Kevin John (Vic) b March 24, 1968 Numurkah (Vic)

Neville, Warwick John (Qld) b Dec. 31, 1948 Melbourne (Vic)

Newcombe, Henry Charles Edwin (NSW) b c. 1835 Sydney (NSW) d Oct. 26, 1908 Randwick (NSW)

Newell, Andrew Livingstone (NSW) b Nov. 13, 1865 Dungog (NSW) death details unknown

Newland, Philip Mesmer (SAust) b Feb. 2, 1875 Kensington (SAust) d Aug. 11, 1916 Knightsbridge (SAust)

Newman, Charles Frederick (WAust) b Nov. 7, 1909 Fremantle (WAust) d March 28, 1977 Fremantle (WAust)

Newman, Henry Albert (WAust) b March 13, 1907 Fremantle (WAust) d April 23, 1988 Riverton (WAust)

Newman, Richard Nelson (Tas) b Aug. 9, 1924 Brunswick (Vic)

Newstead, George Holt (Vic) b Aug. 11, 1910 Brighton (Vic) d July 21, 2000 Deepdene (Vic)

Newton, Alan Colin (Tas) b April 6, 1894 Longford (Tas) d March 27, 1979 Narrabeen (NSW)

Newton, Percy Allen (NSW) b Dec. 21, 1880 Newtown (NSW) d April 25, 1946 Rose Bay (NSW)

Nichols, Arthur Joseph (NSW) b Sept. 3, 1881 Sydney (NSW) d Nov. 19, 1937 North Sydney (NSW)

Nicholls, Charles Omer (NSW) b Dec. 5, 1901 Freeman's Reach (NSW) d Jan. 14, 1983 Freeman's Reach (NSW)

Nicholls, Paul Allen (WAust) b Nov. 10, 1946 East Fremantle (WAust)

Nicholls, Ronald Charles (Vic) b Sept. 1, 1951 Footscray (Vic)

Nicholson, Matthew James (WAust & NSW) b Oct. 2, 1974 St Leonard's (NSW)

Nicolson, John Norman Walter (Tas) b April 14, 1917 Campbell Town (Tas) d Oct. 7, 1992 Launceston (Tas)

Niehuus, Richard Dudley (SAust) b July 6, 1917 St Peters (SAust)

Nielsen, Timothy John (SAust) b May 5, 1968 Forest Gate, London (England)

Nikitaras, Steven (NSW & WAust) b Aug. 31, 1970 Port Kembla (NSW)

* Nitschke, Holmesdale Carl (SAust) b April 14, 1905 Adelaide (SAust) d Sept. 29, 1982 North Adelaide (SAust)

Nobes, Paul Christopher (Vic & SAust) b April 20, 1964 West Heidelberg (Vic)

Noble, Edward George (NSW) b Jan. 16, 1865 Brickfield Hill (NSW) d May 4, 1941 Balmain (NSW)

* Noble, Montague Alfred (NSW) b Jan. 28, 1873 Sydney (NSW) d June 22, 1940 Randwick (NSW)

* Noblet, Geffery (SAust) b Sept. 14, 1916 Evandale (SAust)

Noel, John (SAust) b March 28, 1856 Hindmarsh (SAust) d Jan. 9, 1938 Largs Bay (SAust)

Noffke, Ashley Allan (Cricket Academy) b April 30, 1977 Nambour (Qld)

Nolan, Francis Edward (Qld) b June 27, 1920 Manly (Qld)

Noonan, Daniel Francis (Vic) b May 11, 1873 North Melbourne (Vic) d May 30, 1910 North Melbourne (Vic)

Noonan, David James (NSW) b Jan. 8, 1876 Newtown (NSW) d March 10, 1929 Sydney (NSW)

Norman, Michael John (Tas) b Aug. 17, 1952 Launceston (Tas)

Norman, Hercules Rex Clive (NSW) b Aug. 8, 1891 North Annandale (NSW) d Dec. 30, 1961 Parramatta (NSW)

North, Frederic Dudley (WAust) b Nov. 9, 1866 Kensington, London, Middlesex (England) d Aug. 22, 1921 Cottesloe (WAust)

North, Marcus James (WAust) b July 28, 1979 Melbourne (Vic)

* Nothling, Otto Ernest (NSW & Qld) b Aug. 1, 1900 Teutoburg (Qld) d Sept. 26, 1965 Chelmer (Qld)

Noyes, Alfred William Finch (Vic) b c. 1835 Torquay, Devon (England) d Sept. 30, 1902 Deniliquin (NSW)

Noyes, Harold David (Qld) b Aug. 12, 1892 Warwick (Qld) d July 14, 1968 Brisbane (Qld)

Numa, Herbert Leslie (Vic) b June 22, 1925 Carlton (Vic) d April 17, 1984 Heidelberg (Vic)

Nunn, Thomas (NSW) b Jan. 21, 1846 Penshurst, Kent (England) d May 31, 1889 Bexley (NSW)

Nutt, Richard Nathaniel (NSW) b June 25, 1911 Balmain (NSW) d Feb. 5, 1985 Gladesville (NSW)

Nye, Aaron James (Qld) b Nov. 9, 1978 Herston (Qld)

Oakes, Cecil James Grellis (Tas) b March 1, 1915 Hobart (Tas) d Oct. 10, 1994 Canberra (ACT)

Oakley, Hector Herbert (Vic) b Jan. 10, 1909 North Fitzroy (Vic) d Dec. 19, 1998 Sandringham (Vic)

Oatley, James Napoleon (NSW) b Aug. 12, 1845 Newtown (NSW) d Dec. 17, 1925 Cremorne (NSW)

O'Brien, Aaron Warren (NSW) b Oct. 2, 1981 St Leonard's (NSW)

O'Brien, Charles Joseph (NSW) b May 19, 1921 d Dec. 15, 1980 Coal Point (NSW)

O'Brien, Ernest Francis (NSW) b Aug. 26, 1900 Paddington (NSW) d Nov. 2, 1935 Newcastle (NSW)

* O'Brien, Leo Patrick Joseph (Vic) b July 2, 1907 West Melbourne (Vic) d March 13, 1997 Mentone (Vic)

O'Brien, Leslie John (NSW) b c. 1968 full birth and death details unknown

O'Brien, Matthew Evanson (Anderson's XI) details unknown

O'Brien, Robert (Qld) b July 16, 1869 Redfern (NSW) d Oct. 2, 1922 Brisbane (Qld)

O'Connell, Thomas Reginald (SAust) b March 10, 1916 Parkside (SAust)

O'Connor, Brian Redmond Devereaux (Qld) b July 5, 1913 South Brisbane (Qld) d Dec. 20, 1963 Red Hill (Qld)

O'Connor, Donald Frederick Gregory (SAust & Tas) b July 20, 1958 Gilgandra (NSW)

* O'Connor, John Denis Alphonsus (NSW & SAust) b Sept. 9, 1875 Booroowa (NSW) d Aug. 23, 1941 Lewisham (NSW)

O'Connor, John William (Vic) b Aug. 19, 1868 Geelong (Vic) d Feb. 2, 1952 Windsor (Vic)

O'Connor, Leo Patrick Devereaux (Qld) b April 11, 1890 Murtoa (Vic) d Jan. 16, 1985 Melbourne (Vic)

* O'Donnell, Simon Patrick (Vic) b Jan. 26, 1963 Deniliquin (NSW)

O'Dwyer, Thomas Edmund (WAust) b Nov. 5, 1919 Bridgetown (WAust)

* Ogilvie, Alan David (Qld) b June 3, 1951 Southport (Qld)

Ogilvy, David Skene (NSW) b June 7, 1859 Wollongong (NSW) d Aug. 6, 1917 Liverpool (NSW)

O'Halloran, Dale Francis (Tas) b Feb. 15, 1955 Smithton (Tas)

O'Halloran, James Patrick (Vic) b Jan. 12, 1872 Richmond (Vic) d April 28, 1943 East Melbourne (Vic)

O'Halloran, William Matthew (Vic) b June 18, 1934 Corowa (NSW) d Dec. 13, 1994 East Melbourne (Vic)

O'Hanlon, William James (NSW) b March 10, 1863 Carlton (Vic) d June 23, 1940 Randwick (NSW)

Ohlstrom, Patrick Andreas Paul (SAust) b Dec. 16, 1890 Warooka (SAust) d June 10, 1940 Adelaide (SAust)

O'Keeffe, Francis Aloysius (NSW & Vic) b May 11, 1896 Waverley (NSW) d March 26, 1924 Hampstead, London (England)

* O'Keeffe, Kerry James (NSW) b Nov. 25, 1949 Hurstville (NSW)

O'Leary, Scott James (Qld) b Dec. 17, 1977 South Brisbane (Qld)

* Oldfield, William Albert Stanley (NSW) b Sept. 9, 1894 Alexandria (NSW) d Aug. 10, 1976 Killara (NSW)

Oldroyd, Bradley John (WAust) b Nov. 5, 1973 Bentley (WAust)

Oliver, Benjamin Carl (Vic & Tas) b Oct. 24, 1979 Castlemaine (Vic)

Oliver, Charles Nicholson Jewel (NSW) b April 24, 1848 Hobart (Tas) d June 14, 1920 Manly (NSW)

Oliver, Stuart Bradley (Tas) b March 20, 1972 Launceston (Tas)

O'Meara, Phillip Anthony (WAust) b June 13, 1951 Kellerberrin (WAust)

O'Mullane, George Jeremiah Patrick (Vic) b Dec. 3, 1842 Melbourne (Vic) d Dec. 20, 1866 East Melbourne (Vic)

O'Neill, Kevin Ignatius (SAust) b Aug. 16, 1919 Hectorville (SAust)

O'Neill, Mark Dorian (WAust & NSW) b March 5, 1959 Sutherland (NSW)

* O'Neill, Norman Clifford (NSW) b Feb. 19, 1937 Carlton (NSW)

Onyons, Basil Austin (Vic) b March 14, 1887 Prahran (Vic) d May 31, 1967 Glen Iris (Vic)

O'Regan, James Bernard (Vic) b April 23, 1938 Ashfield (NSW) d May 15, 1998 Randwick (NSW)

O'Reilly, John William (NSW) b Nov. 16, 1930 Mosman (NSW)

* O'Reilly, William Joseph (NSW) b Dec. 20, 1905 White Cliffs (NSW) d Oct. 6, 1992 Sutherland (NSW)

Orr, Herbert Richard (WAust) b Feb. 3, 1865 Kensington, London (England) d May 22, 1940 Sevenoaks, Kent (England)

Osborn, Francis James (SAust) b Feb. 13, 1935 Alberton (SAust)

Osborne, Mark (Vic) b Oct. 8, 1961 Kogarah (NSW)

Osborne, Noton Michael (Vic) b c. 1844 (England) d Dec. 10, 1878 Hobart (Tas)

Osborne, Robert Henry (NSW) b Feb. 4, 1897 Redfern (NSW) d Feb. 21, 1975 Long Jetty (NSW)

Osborne, Robert Moorhead (Vic) b Sept. 29, 1881 St Kilda (Vic) d Nov. 19, 1927 Melbourne (Vic)

O'Shannassy, Robert Martin (SAust) b March 7, 1949 Hindmarsh (SAust)

O'Shaughnessy, Barney (WAust) b Feb. 28, 1912 Wiluna (WAust)

Oswald, Norman Hamilton (SAust) b Oct. 31, 1916 Prospect (SAust) d June 22, 1970 Adelaide (SAust)

Outridge, Thomas Michael (WAust) b Sept. 8, 1927 Perth (WAust) d July 21, 2003 Bunbury (WAust)

Over, Willie (Vic) b Jan. 20, 1862 Richmond (Vic) d Nov. 10, 1910 Krugersdorp, Transvaal (South Africa)

Owen, Christopher John (SAust) b Dec. 21, 1963 Henley Beach (SAust)

Owen, Kerry Alfred (NSW) b June 23, 1943 Bondi Beach (NSW)

Oxenford, Bruce Nicholas James (Qld) b March 5, 1960 Southport (Qld)

Oxenford, Ian Bruce (Qld) b Sept. 3, 1932 South Brisbane (Qld)

Oxenham, Lionel Emmanuel (Qld) b Jan. 27, 1888 Nundah (Qld) d Jan. 10, 1970 Clayfield (Qld)

* Oxenham, Ronald Keven (Qld) b July 28, 1891 Nundah (Qld) d Aug. 16, 1939 Nundah (Qld)

Packham, Leonard (WAust) b Sept. 15, 1891 Norwood (SAust) d Oct. 4, 1958 Swanbourne (WAust)

Page, Clive Basil (Qld) b May 25, 1894 Rockhampton (Qld) d July 1, 1967 Greenslopes (Qld)

Palfreyman, Brent Avis Hardcastle (Tas) b Jan. 20, 1945 Hobart (Tas)

* Palmer, George Eugene (Vic & Tas) b Feb. 22, 1859 Mulwala (NSW) d Aug. 22, 1910 Benalla (Vic)

Palmer, George Hamilton (SAust) b Aug. 2, 1903 Eastwood (SAust) d Aug. 24, 1986 Woodville South (SAust)

Palmer, Jack Stirling (SAust) b Oct. 20, 1903 East Adelaide (SAust) d Dec. 11, 1979 Glenelg (SAust)

Panitzki, Robert James (Tas) b April 29, 1948 Hobart (Tas)

Park, Alfred Leath (NSW) b April 15, 1840 Oatlands (Tas) d Jan. 16, 1924 Liverpool (NSW)

* Park, Roy Lindsay (Vic) b July 30, 1892 Charlton (Vic) d Jan. 23, 1947 Middle Park (Vic)

Parker, Alec David (Qld) b June 12, 1955 Dalby (Qld)

Parker, Ernest Frederick (WAust) b Nov. 5, 1883 Perth (WAust) d May 2, 1918 Caestre (France)

Parker, Geoffrey Ross (Vic & SAust) b March 31, 1968 Malvern (Vic)

Parker, John Francis (WAust) b March 13, 1936 South Perth (WAust)

Parker, Robert Ernest (Qld) b Sept. 18, 1942 Toowoomba (Qld)

Parker, Ronald Arthur (SAust) b Feb. 23, 1916 Goodwood (SAust) d Aug. 27, 1993 San Francisco, California (United States of America)

Parker, Russell John (SAust) b Aug. 3, 1952 Sudbury, Middlesex (England)

Parkin, George Thomas (SAust) b Oct. 11, 1864 Adelaide (SAust) d Aug. 6, 1933 Adelaide (SAust)

Parkinson, Henry (Tas) b June 10, 1882 Port Arthur (Tas) d c. 1962 death place unknown

Parkinson, Samuel David Haslam (SAust) b July 8, 1960 Adelaide (SAust)

Parry, Cyril Norman (SAust & Tas) b Oct. 14, 1900 Queenstown (Tas) d July 6, 1984 Kew (Vic)

Parsonage, Thomas Griffiths (NSW) b Nov. 13, 1910 Chatswood (NSW) d Feb. 3, 1951 Manly (NSW)

Parsons, Herbert Fulton (Vic) b May 21, 1875 Hawthorn (Vic) d Dec. 20, 1937 Canterbury (Vic)

* Pascoe, Len Stephen (NSW) b Feb. 13, 1950 Bridgetown (WAust)

Pascoe, Matthew David (Qld) b Jan. 10, 1977 Camperdown (NSW)

Pateman, Robert (Vic) b Aug. 28, 1856 Magpie (Vic) death details unknown

Patfield, Alfred Samuel (WAust) b Sept. 6, 1884 Paterson (NSW) d Nov. 9, 1961 Perth (WAust)

Paton, George Douglas (Tas) b March 1, 1879 Hobart (Tas) d Oct. 5, 1950 Hobart (Tas)

Patrick, Charles Wright (NSW & Qld) b Jan. 13, 1866 Sydney (NSW) d Nov. 29, 1919 Coogee (NSW)

* Patterson, Balfour Patrick (Tas) b Sept. 15, 1961 Portland (Jamaica)

Patterson, Brian Clifford (Tas) b June 28, 1937 Hobart (Tas)

Patterson, Mark Winston (NSW) b Nov. 15, 1966 Dubbo (NSW)

Patterson, Thomas Francis (Tas) b Sept. 16, 1839 Hobart (Tas)

Paulsen, Robert George (Qld & WAust) b Oct. 18, 1947 Herston (Qld)

Pavy, Leonard (WAust) b Aug. 21, 1936 Boulder (WAust)

Pawley, Michael Bernard (NSW) b March 10, 1944 Glen Innes (NSW)

Payne, Charles Percy (Tas) b July 31, 1876 Hobart (Tas) d Jan. 28, 1938 Lower Sandy Bay (Tas)

Payne, Daniel Martin (Qld) b Oct. 27, 1978 Herston (Qld)

Peachey, Mark (Qld) b Oct. 31, 1900 Tannymorel (Qld) d Nov. 23, 1987 Ipswich (Qld)

Peake, Clinton John (Vic) b March 25, 1977 Geelong (Vic)

Pearce, Donald Rex (Tas) b Feb. 21, 1941 Ulverstone (Tas) d Feb. 13, 1999 Burnie (Tas)

Pearce, Kevin Dudley (Tas) b Feb. 29, 1960 Devonport (Tas)

Pearce, Reginald Manus (NSW) b April 20, 1918 Tumbarumba (NSW) d June 19, 1995 Sydney (NSW)

Pearsall, Alan Louden (Tas) b May 24, 1915 Hobart (Tas) d March 8, 1941 in action in English Channel

Pearson, Trevor John (SAust) b Oct. 13, 1943 Goodwood (SAust)

Pearson, William Ernest (Vic) b Nov. 10, 1912 Kerang (Vic) d Sept. 11, 1987 Melbourne (Vic)

Pegg, Harry Robert Edgar (Qld) b March 19, 1916 Moorooka (Qld)

Pellew, Arthur Howard (SAust) b Jan. 20, 1878 Riverton (SAust) d Aug. 21, 1948 Rose Park (SAust)

* Pellew, Clarence Everard (SAust) b Sept. 21, 1893 Port Pirie (SAust) d May 9, 1981 Adelaide (SAust)

Pellew, John Harold (SAust) b July 17, 1882 Truro (SAust) d Oct. 17, 1946 Unley (SAust)

Pellew, Lancelot Vivian (SAust) b Dec. 15, 1899 Port Elliott (SAust) d Dec. 8, 1970 Adelaide (SAust)

Penman, Arthur Percival (NSW) b Jan. 23, 1885 Ultimo (NSW) d Sept. 11, 1944 Rockley (NSW)

Pennefather, George Shirley (Tas) b Sept. 28, 1864 Launceston (Tas) d Oct. 16, 1945 Launceston (Tas)

Pennycuick, Rupert James (Tas) b April 11, 1893 Jericho (Tas) d Jan. 17, 1963 Concord (NSW)

Penter, Colin Edward (WAust) b July 20, 1955 Albany (WAust)

Pepper, Cecil George (NSW) b Sept. 15, 1916 Forbes (NSW) d March 24, 1993 Littleborough, Lancashire (England)

Perraton, Jack Oldfield (Vic) b Feb. 26, 1909 Prahran (Vic) d Oct. 1, 1950 Kings Cross (NSW)

Perraton, William Thomas Crooke (Vic) b Aug. 27, 1867 Collingwood (Vic) d Sept. 23, 1952 Elsternwick (Vic)

Perren, Clinton Terrence (Qld) b Feb. 22, 1975 Herston (Qld)

Perrin, Thomas Henry (Vic) b Oct. 27, 1928 Prahran (Vic)

Perrins, Keith Robinson (Qld) b Jan. 17, 1931 Rockhampton (Qld)

Perry, Cecil Thomas Henry (Tas) b March 3, 1846 Battery Point (Tas) d Aug. 4, 1917 Timaru (New Zealand)

Perryman, Charles Henry (Vic) b Jan. 20, 1872 Richmond (Vic) d Aug. 30, 1950 St Kilda (Vic)

Peters, Arthur Ernest (SAust) b March 8, 1872 Adelaide (SAust) d Sept. 24, 1903 Henley Beach (SAust)

Pettiford, Jack (NSW) b Nov. 29, 1919 Freshwater (NSW) d Oct. 11, 1964 North Sydney (NSW)

Pettinger, Aldam Murr (SAust) b July 30, 1859 Kent Town (SAust) d Aug. 18, 1950 Lower Mitcham (SAust)

Phelps, Leslie Roy (Tas) details unknown

Phelps, Matthew James (Tas) b Sept. 1, 1972 Lismore (NSW)

Philipson, Craig Andrew (Qld) b Nov. 18, 1982 Herston (Qld)

Phillips, Edward George (SAust) b March 1, 1851 Port Adelaide (SAust) d Feb. 8, 1933 North Adelaide (SAust)

Phillips, Edward Lauriston (SAust) b Sept. 2, 1892 North Adelaide (SAust) d Jan. 8, 1971 Adelaide (SAust)

Phillips, James (Vic) b Sept. 1, 1860 Pleasant Creek (Vic) d April 21, 1930 Burnaby, Vancouver, British Columbia (Canada)

Phillips, Joseph (Vic) b April 22, 1840 Parramatta (NSW) d May 7, 1901 Heidelberg (Vic)

Phillips, Norbert Eugene (NSW) b July 9, 1896 Cowra (NSW) d Oct. 3, 1961 Sydney (NSW)

Phillips, Raymond Berry (NSW & Qld) b May 23, 1954 Paddington (NSW)

* Phillips, Wayne Bentley (SAust) b March 1, 1958 Adelaide (SAust)

* Phillips, Wayne Norman (Vic) b Nov. 7, 1962 Geelong (Vic)

Philpott, Albert John William (Vic) b March 14, 1873 Gaffneys Creek (Vic) d Nov. 25, 1950 Kew (Vic)

* Philpott, Peter Ian (NSW) b Nov. 21, 1934 Manly (NSW)

Philpott, Richard (Vic) b Feb. 7, 1813 West Farleigh, Kent (England) d June 8, 1888 Brenchley, Kent (England)

Philpott, William (Vic) b Jan. 24, 1819 West Farleigh, Kent (England) d Nov. 4, 1891 Linton, Kent (England)

Pickering, George Thomas (Vic) b c. 1832 Sydney (NSW) d Dec. 1, 1858 Sandridge (Vic)

Pickering, Kelby Sinclair (SAust) b Jan. 3, 1973 Lameroo (SAust)

Pickett, Alfred William (Tas) b c. 1871 Ulverstone (Tas) d March 19, 1953 Ulverstone (Tas)

Pickett, Edward Arthur (Tas) b April 2, 1909 Ulverstone (Tas)

Pictet, Francis Stewart (Tas) b June 4, 1866 Bath, Somerset (England) death details unknown

Pierce, Michael (NSW & Qld) b Sept. 3, 1869 Paddington (NSW) d Feb. 4, 1913 Sydney (NSW)

Pilon, Nathan Steven (NSW) b Oct. 27, 1976 Dubbo (NSW)

Pinch, Colin John (NSW & SAust) b June 23, 1921 Brownsville (NSW)

Pinkus, Harold William (Tas) b Sept. 27, 1934 Smithton (Tas)

Pinnington, Todd Andrew (Tas) b March 21, 1971 Hobart (Tas)

Pitcher, Franklyn Joseph (Vic) b June 24, 1879 Collingwood (Vic) d Jan. 23, 1921 Northcote (Vic)

Pite, Walter Edward (NSW) b Sept. 24, 1876 Sydney (NSW) d May 7, 1955 Waverley (NSW)

Pittman, Brian Harold (SAust) b June 17, 1930 Rose Park (SAust)

Plant, Hugh Joseph (Vic) b Oct. 12, 1907 Narrandera (NSW) d Aug. 30, 1993 Geelong (Vic)

* Playle, William Rodger (WAust) b Dec. 1, 1938 Palmerston North (New Zealand)

Plummer, Neil Robert (SAust) b July 6, 1955 Lobethal (SAust)

Pocock, William Johnstone (NSW) b c. 1848 Clifton, Gloucestershire (England) d Sept. 27, 1928 East Brighton (Vic)

Poeppel, George Augustus (Qld) b Nov. 6, 1893 Bundaberg (Qld) d Feb. 2, 1917 Hermies (France)

Poidevin, Leslie Oswald Sheridan (NSW) b Nov. 5, 1876 Merrilla (NSW) d Nov. 19, 1931 Waverley (NSW)

Polkinghorne, Adam William (Tas) b Aug. 23, 1975 Karoonda (SAust)

Polzin, Michael Allan (Qld) b June 23, 1964 Wondai (Qld)

* Ponsford, William Harold (Vic) b Oct. 19, 1900 North Fitzroy (Vic) d April 6, 1991 Kyneton (Vic)

* Ponting, Ricky Thomas (Tas) b Dec. 19, 1974 Launceston (Tas)

Poon, Hunter Robert George (Qld) b May 14, 1894 Pimlico (NSW) d Jan. 25, 1980 Greenslopes (Qld)

* Pope, Roland James (NSW) b Feb. 18, 1864 Ashfield (NSW) d July 27, 1952 Manly (NSW)

Porter, Brian Clifford (Vic) b Dec. 20, 1942 Carlton (Vic)

Porter, Graham David (WAust) b March 18, 1955 Middle Swan (WAust)

Potter, Jack (Vic) b April 13, 1938 Melbourne (Vic)

Powell, George (NSW) b April 12, 1918 Newtown (NSW) d April 11, 1994 Clovelly (NSW)

Powell, Ronald Hartley (Tas) b Sept. 27, 1883 New Norfolk (Tas) d Aug. 22, 1922 (Qld)

Powell, Theodore (NSW) b July 10, 1852 Berrima (NSW) d Sept. 3, 1913 Sydney (NSW)

Power, John Francis (Vic) b March 23, 1932 Port Melbourne (Vic)

Power, Laurence James (SAust) b July 31, 1898 Ovingham (SAust) d March 20, 1963 Glenelg (SAust)

Power, Louis Bertrand (SAust) b Oct. 10, 1905 Ovingham (SAust) d Sept. 30, 1988 Bedford Park (SAust)

Power, Robert (Vic) b c. 1833 Galway (Ireland) d Nov. 4, 1914 Toorak (Vic)

Powlett, Frederick Armand (Vic) b Jan. 6, 1811 Shrewsbury, Shropshire (England) d June 9, 1865 Kyneton (Vic)

Pratten, Herbert Graham (NSW) b April 22, 1892 Ashfield (NSW) d Sept. 11, 1979 Neutral Bay (NSW)

Preen, Alan Thomas (WAust) b July 4, 1935 Fremantle (WAust)

Prentice, Warden Selby (NSW) b July 30, 1886 Homebush (NSW) d Feb. 26, 1969 Rosebery (NSW)

Prescott, Shaun St Aubyn (Vic) b Sept. 7, 1966 Melbourne (Vic)

Prestwidge, Scott Arthur (Qld) b May 15, 1968 Bankstown (NSW)

Pretty, Alfred Henry (SAust) b Jan. 29, 1874 Willunga (SAust) d June 21, 1929 Mile End (SAust)

Price, Charles Frederick Thomas (Services) b Feb. 17, 1917 Sydney (NSW) d Jan. 19, 1997 Avalon (NSW)

Price, Henry Alexander (Qld) b March 31, 1913 Spring Hill (Qld) d May 3, 1999 Wavell Heights (Qld)

Price, Reuben Henry (WAust) b April 27, 1923 London (England) d Feb. 26, 1991 Perth (WAust)

Price, Walter Davies (SAust) b March 24, 1886 Hawthorn (Vic) d July 29, 1944 Adelaide (SAust)

Prindiville, Kevin Joseph (WAust) b Sept. 18, 1949 Subiaco (WAust)

Prindiville, Terence John (WAust) b Nov. 20, 1942 Subiaco (WAust)

Prior, Wayne (SAust) b Sept. 30, 1952 Salisbury (SAust)

Pritchard, David Edward (SAust) b Jan. 5, 1893 Queenstown (SAust) d July 4, 1983 Myrtle Bank (SAust)

Prout, James Alexander (Qld) b Aug. 12, 1889 Flemington (Vic) d Feb. 18, 1952 Double Bay (NSW)

Pryor, David Godfrey (NSW) b Feb. 3, 1870 Maitland (NSW) d Jan. 3, 1937 Gosford (NSW)

Puckett, Charles William (WAust) b Feb. 21, 1911 Beddington Corner, Surrey (England) d Jan. 22, 2002 Morphett Vale (SAust)

Puckett, Maxwell Charles (SAust) b June 3, 1935 Unley Park (SAust) d Aug. 25, 1991 North Adelaide (SAust)

Punch, Austin Thomas Eugene (NSW & Tas) b Aug. 16, 1894 North Sydney (NSW) d Aug. 25, 1985 Cremorne (NSW)

Punch, Keith Francis (WAust) b Oct. 19, 1940 Subiaco (WAust)

Putman, Sydney William Leslie (Tas) b March 25, 1912 Hobart (Tas) d Sept. 20, 1947 Hobart (Tas)

Pye, Leslie Walter (NSW) b July 6, 1871 Windsor (NSW) d March 9, 1949 Parramatta (NSW)

Pyke, James Kendrick (SAust) b June 7, 1966 Cottesloe (WAust)

Pyke, Richard Dimond (Qld) b Aug. 15, 1877 Collingwood (Vic) d Dec. 4, 1914 Gympie (Qld)

Pynor, Ernest Ivan (SAust) b April 23, 1920 Essendon (Vic) d Oct. 23, 1999 East Doncaster (Vic)

Quelch, Leslie Norman (Qld) b Feb. 26, 1918 Maryborough (Qld) d April 13, 1987 Paddington (Qld)

Quick, Ian William (Vic) b Nov. 5, 1933 Geelong (Vic)

Quigley, Brian Maxwell (SAust) b Dec. 27, 1935 Henley Beach (SAust)

Quilty, John (SAust) b c. 1860 Adelaide (SAust) d May 9, 1942 Kent Town (SAust)

Quin, Stanley Oldfield (Vic) b April 17, 1908 Caulfield (Vic) d Nov. 27, 1967 Brighton (Vic)

Quinlan, Francis Patrick (WAust) b March 17, 1891 Perth (WAust) d Aug. 15, 1935 Perth (WAust)

Quinn, Michael Brian (Vic) b July 2, 1962 Adelaide (SAust)

Quist, Karl Hugo (NSW, WAust & SAust) b Aug. 18, 1875 Milson's Point (NSW) d March 31, 1957 Plympton (SAust)

* Rackemann, Carl Gray (Qld) b June 3, 1960 Wondai (Qld)

Rahmann, Herbert William (Qld) b Aug. 23, 1886 Maryborough (Qld) d Oct. 12, 1957 Nundah (Qld)

Rainey, Leslie Newburn (Vic) b Jan. 10, 1881 South Yarra (Vic) d Aug. 27, 1962 Melbourne (Vic)

Ramsay, John (Tas) b Dec. 26, 1872 Glasgow, Lanarkshire (Scotland) d Feb. 6, 1944 Launceston (Tas)

Ramsay, Marmaduke Francis (Qld) b Dec. 8, 1860 Cheltenham, Gloucestershire (England) d Dec. 31, 1947 Lee, Canterbury, Kent (England)

Ramshaw, Darrin Joseph (WAust & Vic) b Nov. 29, 1965 Subiaco (WAust)

Randell, Alfred Charles (WAust) b May 10, 1884 Perth (WAust) d Sept. 13, 1958 Sydney (NSW)

Randell, Ernest Arthur (WAust) b Jan. 25, 1873 Perth (WAust) d May 12, 1938 Perth (WAust)

Randell, James Arthur (NSW) b Aug. 4, 1880 Gulgong (NSW) d Dec. 7, 1952 Balgowlah (NSW)

* Ransford, Vernon Seymour (Vic) b March 20, 1885 South Yarra (Vic) d March 19, 1958 Brighton (Vic)

Ratcliffe, Andrew Thomas (NSW) b April 3, 1891 Leichhardt (NSW) d Aug. 31, 1974 Banksia (NSW)

Rathie, David Stewart (Qld) b May 29, 1951 Roma (Qld)

Rawle, Keith Trevillian (Vic) b Oct. 29, 1924 Essendon (Vic)

Ray, Mark (NSW & Tas) b Oct. 2, 1952 Surry Hills (NSW)

Raymer, Vincent Norman (Qld) b May 4, 1918 Toowoomba (Qld)

Raymond, Ralph Cossart (Qld) b Nov. 28, 1912 Boonah (Qld) d Oct. 11, 1982 Murgon (Qld)

Rayson, Maxwell William (Vic) b Aug. 26, 1912 Kew (Vic) d May 11, 1993 Heidelberg (Vic)

Rayson, Roger William (Vic) b Feb. 17, 1942 Windsor (Vic)

Rayson, William Jones (Vic) b Dec. 18, 1889 Malmsbury (Vic) d Sept. 8, 1957 Parkdale (Vic)

Read, Arthur Edwin (WAust) b May 26, 1908 Unley (SAust) d March 1, 2001 Bentley (WAust)

Rebbeck, Phillip Douglas (SAust) b July 31, 1948 North Adelaide (SAust)

Reddrop, Walter William (Vic) b Sept. 9, 1901 Kyneton (Vic) d March 31, 1983 Parkville (Vic)

Redfearn, James (Vic) b c. 1836 Yorkshire (England) d March 10, 1916 Glenhuntly (Vic)

Redgrave, John Sidney (NSW & Qld) b Aug. 5, 1878 North Sydney (NSW) d Aug. 3, 1958 West End (Qld)

* Redpath, Ian Ritchie (Vic) b May 11, 1941 Geelong (Vic)

* Reedman, John Cole (SAust) b Oct. 9, 1865 Taminda (SAust) d March 25, 1924 Gilberton (SAust)

Rees, John Newman Stace (SAust) b Sept. 2, 1880 Hindmarsh (SAust) d Jan. 17, 1959 St Peters (SAust)

Rees, Robert Blackie Colston (SAust) b April 15, 1882 Hindmarsh (SAust) d Sept. 20, 1966 Bowmans Green, Hertfordshire (England)

Rees, William Gilbert (NSW) b April 6, 1827 St Issell's, Pembrokeshire (Wales) d Oct. 31, 1898 Marlborough (New Zealand)

Rees, William Lee (Vic) b Dec. 16, 1836 Bristol, Gloucestershire (England) d May 13, 1912 Gisborne (New Zealand)

Reeves, Damion Albert (SAust) b July 12, 1971 Darwin (NT)

Reeves, William Henry (Vic) b Aug. 11, 1881 Fitzroy (Vic) d Sept. 13, 1962 Kew (Vic)

Regeling, Donald Carl (Qld) b Aug. 13, 1955 Boonah (Qld)

Reid, Alan Walter (Qld) b June 30, 1931 Maryborough (Qld)

Reid, Basil Stanley (Tas) b May 17, 1924 Launceston (Tas) d July 16, 2000 Launceston (Tas)

* Reid, Bruce Anthony (WAust) b March 14, 1963 Osborne Park (WAust)

Reid, Curtis Alexander (Vic) b July 16, 1836 Inverary Park (NSW) d July 1, 1886 Hawthorn (Vic)

Reid, Douglas Clement (NSW) b Sept. 23, 1886 St Peters (NSW) d Aug. 21, 1959 Wahroonga (NSW)

Reid, Stanley John (Tas) b May 5, 1955 St Helen's (Tas)

Reid, William (Tas) details unknown

Reid, William (SAust) b c. 1871 North Adelaide (SAust) full birth and death details unknown

* Reiffel, Paul Ronald (Vic) b April 19, 1966 Box Hill (Vic)

Renfrey, Leslie Cotswold (WAust) b Feb. 15, 1893 Wallaroo Mines (SAust) d Sept. 23, 1958 Mt Lawley (WAust)

* Renneberg, David Alexander (NSW) b Sept. 23, 1942 Rozelle (NSW)

Reynolds, George Raymond (Qld) b Aug. 24, 1936 Bundaberg (Qld)

Rhodes, Brian Leslie (NSW) b March 7, 1951 Paddington (NSW)

Ricci, Brendan Paul (Vic) b April 24, 1965 East Melbourne (Vic)

* Richards, Barry Anderson (SAust) b July 21, 1945 Morningside, Durban, Natal (South Africa)

Richards, Corey John (NSW) b Aug. 25, 1975 Camden (NSW)

Richards, Frank Hitchen (Vic) d Fremantle (WAust) full birth and death details unknown

* Richards, Isaac Vivian Alexander (Qld) b March 7, 1952 St John's (Antigua)

Richards, Thomas Oliver (SAust) b July 5, 1855 Norwood (SAust) d Dec. 14, 1923 Cottonville (Qld)

* Richardson, Arthur John (SAust & WAust) b July 24, 1888 Sevenhills (SAust) d Dec. 23, 1973 Semaphore (SAust)

Richardson, Brian Douglas (Tas) b May 15, 1932 Hobart (Tas)

Richardson, Charles Augustus (NSW) b Feb. 22, 1864 Sydney (NSW) d Aug. 17, 1949 Waipara, Canterbury (New Zealand)

Richardson, Colin George (Tas) b June 6, 1920 Hobart (Tas) d Dec. 22, 1993 Hobart (Tas)

Richardson, Edward Noel (Tas) b Dec. 8, 1929 Hobart (Tas)

Richardson, Frederick William (Tas) b March 29, 1878 Campbell Town (Tas) d March 7, 1955 Campbell Town (Tas)

Richardson, Geoffrey William (Vic) b Dec. 7, 1956 Koo Wee Rup (Vic)

Richardson, George Biggs (NSW) b May 28, 1834 Bathurst (NSW) d May 1, 1911 Dandaloo (NSW)

Richardson, Howard James (Vic) b Oct. 29, 1894 Berwick (Vic) d Dec. 21, 1959 Richmond (Vic)

Richardson, Joseph (SAust) b Feb. 28, 1878 Kooringa (SAust) d June 13, 1951 Glenelg (SAust)

Richardson, Leonard Martin (NSW & Qld) b May 5, 1950 Paddington (NSW)

Richardson, Leslie Lambert (Tas) b Jan. 9, 1887 Ralph's Bay (Tas) d Nov. 15, 1962 Hobart (Tas)

Richardson, Leslie Walter (Tas) b Sept. 5, 1911 New Town (Tas) d Nov. 1, 1981 Hobart (Tas)

Richardson, Reginald Maxwell (Tas) b Oct. 6, 1922 Hobart (Tas) d June 2, 2003 Lenah Valley (Tas)

* Richardson, Victor York (SAust) b Sept. 7, 1894 Parkside (SAust) d Oct. 29, 1969 Fullarton (SAust)

Richardson, Walter Barrett (Tas) b Oct. 24, 1876 Ralph's Bay (Tas) d May 30, 1962 Hobart (Tas)

Richardson, William Alfred (NSW) b Aug. 22, 1866 Sydney (NSW) d Jan. 3, 1930 Mosman (NSW)

Richter, Arthur Frederick (SAust) b Sept. 1, 1908 Telowie (SAust) d Aug. 16, 1936 Adelaide (SAust)

Rickman, Wilfred (Vic) b c. 1856 South Yarra (Vic) d June 6, 1911 Frankston (Vic)

Ridge, Frank Macquarie (NSW) b Jan. 10, 1873 Dubbo (NSW) d May 25, 1959 Manly (NSW)

Ridgway, Mark William (Vic) b May 21, 1960 Warragul (Vic)

Ridings, Kenneth Lovett (SAust) b Feb. 7, 1920 Malvern (SAust) d May 17, 1943 in action over Bay of Biscay, France

Ridings, Phillip Lovett (SAust) b Oct. 2, 1917 Malvern (SAust) d Sept. 13, 1998 Adelaide (SAust)

Rigaud, Stephen (SAust) b Nov. 25, 1856 Kenton Valley, Talunga (SAust) d Nov. 13, 1922 Claremont (WAust)

Rigby, Albert (WAust) b c.1901 Lancashire (England) d Oct. 10, 1963 Hollywood (WAust)

Rigg, Basil Augustus (WAust) b Aug. 12, 1926 Highgate (WAust)

Rigg, Herbert William Hardy (WAust) b Aug. 18, 1923 Highgate (WAust)

* Rigg, Keith Edward (Vic) b May 21, 1906 Malvern (Vic) d Feb. 28, 1995 Malvern (Vic)

Riley, William Norman (SAust) b April 9, 1894 Hyde Park (SAust) d Oct. 2, 1960 North Adelaide (SAust)

Rimington, Stanley Garnet (Vic) b Jan. 22, 1892 Kew (Vic) d Nov. 23, 1991 Kew (Vic)

* Ring, Douglas Thomas (Vic) b Oct. 14, 1918 Hobart (Tas) d June 23, 2003 Melbourne (Vic)

* Ritchie, Gregory Michael (Qld) b Jan. 23, 1960 Stanthorpe (Qld)

Ritossa, David John (SAust) b Jan. 22, 1971 Rose Park (SAust)

* Rixon, Stephen John (NSW) b Feb. 25, 1954 Albury (NSW)

Roach, Peter John (Vic) b May 19, 1975 Kew (Vic)

Roach, William Alexander (WAust) b Dec. 12, 1914 South Fremantle (WAust) d June 8, 1944 in action over Friesian Islands (Netherlands)

* Roberts, Anderson Montgomery Everton (NSW) b Jan. 29, 1951 Urlings Village (Antigua)

Roberts, Kevin Joseph (NSW) b July 2, 1972 North Sydney (NSW)

Roberts, Peter Gerald (Tas) b Feb. 16, 1952 Hobart (Tas)

Roberts, William (NSW) birth and death details unknown

Roberts, William Maurice (SAust) b Aug. 26, 1916 Wallaroo Mines (SAust) d Jan. 21, 1989 Adelaide (SAust)

Robertson, Ashley Peter Scott (Vic) b March 9, 1972 Footscray (Vic)

Robertson, David Alexander (SAust) b March 4, 1959 North Adelaide (SAust)

* Robertson, Gavin Ron (NSW & Tas) b May 28, 1966 St Leonard's (NSW)

Robertson, George Pringle (Vic) b Aug. 22, 1842 Hobart (Tas) d June 23, 1895 East Melbourne (Vic)

Robertson, Trevor John (SAust) b Nov. 20, 1947 Rose Park (SAust)

* Robertson, William Roderick (Vic) b Oct. 6, 1861 Deniliquin (NSW) d June 24, 1938 Brighton (Vic)

Robins, Donnell (SAust) b March 7, 1934 Blackwood (SAust)

Robinson, Alexander (WAust) b Aug. 19, 1886 Brighton (Vic) d Oct. 4, 1967 Perth (WAust)

Robinson, Alexander William (WAust) b Aug. 14, 1924 Boulder (WAust)

Robinson, Brian Anthony (Tas) b Nov. 22, 1967 Devonport (Tas)

Robinson, Charles Henry (Tas & WAust) b Feb. 18, 1879 Dubbo (NSW) d Sept. 23, 1951 Ashfield (NSW)

Robinson, David Brian (Tas & Vic) b March 20, 1958 Devonport (Tas)

Robinson, George David (WAust) b Jan. 21, 1921 Boulder (WAust) d March 12, 1999 Kew (Vic)

Robinson, Henry Joseph Wickham (NSW) b March 11, 1864 Watsons Bay (NSW) d March 24, 1931 Mascot (NSW)

* Robinson, Rayford Harold (NSW & SAust) b March 26, 1914 Stockton (NSW) d Aug. 10, 1965 Stockton (NSW)

* Robinson, Richard Daryl (Vic) b June 8, 1946 East Melbourne (Vic)

Robison, William Carr (NSW) b Dec. 14, 1874 Camden (NSW) d July 5, 1916 Darlinghurst (NSW)

Robran, Barrie Charles (SAust) b Sept. 25, 1947 Whyalla (SAust)

Roche, William (Vic) b July 20, 1871 Brunswick (Vic) d Jan. 2, 1950 East Brunswick (Vic)

Rocher, Thomas Walter (Tas) b June 17, 1930 Scottsdale (Tas)

Rock, Claude William (Tas) b June 9, 1863 Deloraine (Tas) d July 27, 1950 Longford (Tas)

Rock, Harry Owen (NSW) b Oct. 18, 1896 Scone (NSW) d March 9, 1978 Manly (NSW)

Rock, Norman Vosper (Tas) b Aug. 30, 1864 Deloraine (Tas) d Feb. 7, 1945 Brighton (Vic)

Rockliffe, Thornton Francis Edward (Tas) b July 5, 1887 Sassafras (Tas) d March 18, 1961 East Devonport (Tas)

Rodwell, Edwin Emerson (Tas) b April 12, 1921 Hobart (Tas)

Roe, Richard (WAust) b Jan. 22, 1913 Geraldton (WAust)

Rofe, Paul Cameron (SAust) b Jan. 16, 1981 Adelaide (SAust)

Rogers, Christopher John Llewellyn (WAust) b Aug. 31, 1977 Kogarah (NSW)

Rogers, John Edward (Vic) b Feb. 8, 1858 Botany (NSW) d July 8, 1935 South Melbourne (Vic)

Rogers, Noel Thomas (Qld) b Dec. 28, 1923 Spring Hill (Qld) d May 27, 1982 Annerley (Qld)

Rogers, Rex Ernest (Qld) b Aug. 24, 1916 Cairns (Qld) d May 22, 1996 Coorparoo (Qld)

Rogers, William John (NSW) b May 7, 1943 Gosford (NSW)

Rolfe, Douglas John (Vic & SAust) b Feb. 26, 1953 Wheelers Hill (Vic)

Ronchi, Luke (WAust) b April 23, 1981 Dannevirke (New Zealand)

Roper, Arthur William (NSW) b Feb. 20, 1917 Petersham (NSW) d Sept. 4, 1972 Woy Woy (NSW)

* Rorke, Gordon Frederick (NSW) b June 27, 1938 Neutral Bay (NSW)

Rose, Robert Peter (Vic) b Feb. 6, 1952 Eastern Hill (Vic) d May 12, 1999 Heidelberg (Vic)

Rosen, Marshall Frederick (NSW) b Sept. 17, 1948 Paddington (NSW)

Rosman, Arthur Victor (SAust) b Nov. 26, 1870 Barossa Goldfields (SAust) d Feb. 10, 1948 Kent Town (SAust)

Ross, Charles Howard (Vic) b May 10, 1863 St Kilda (Vic) d Feb. 5, 1935 Sydney (NSW)

Ross, Graeme Thomson (Vic) b Feb. 5, 1955 Geelong (Vic)

Ross, William A. (Vic) birth and death details unknown

Rosser, John (Vic) b April 22, 1862 Fremantle (WAust) d Dec. 25, 1925 Toowoomba (Qld)

Rothwell, Barry Alan (NSW) b Aug. 18, 1939 Ryde (NSW)

Rothwell, John Wilson (Tas) b Oct. 1, 1913 Hobart (Tas)

Rowan, Robert Keith (Vic) b Sept. 14, 1947 Coburg (Vic)

Rowe, Raymond Curtis (NSW) b Dec. 9, 1913 Harris Park (NSW) d May 14, 1995 Parramatta (NSW)

Rowe, Samuel Harold Drew (WAust) b Nov. 5, 1883 Perth (WAust) d Oct. 29, 1968 Perth (WAust)

Rowe, William Denis (Qld) b Jan. 10, 1892 East Brisbane (Qld) d Sept. 3, 1972 South Brisbane (Qld)

Rowell, Gregory John (NSW, Qld & Tas) b Sept. 1, 1966 Lindfield (NSW)

Rowland, Frank Walter (NSW) b March 1, 1893 Inverell (NSW) d Feb. 25, 1957 Mosman (NSW)

Rowlands, Edward Richard (Vic) b c. 1826 Claines, Worcestershire (England) d c. 1860

Rowlands, William Trevor (WAust) b May 7, 1904 Echuca (Vic) d May 18, 1984 Subiaco (WAust)

Rowley, Francis (NSW) b Sept. 27, 1835 Burwood (NSW) d June 23, 1862 Woolloomooloo (NSW)

Roxby, Robert Charles (NSW & SAust) b March 16, 1926 Newcastle (NSW)

Rummans, Graeme Clifford (NSW & Vic) b Dec. 13, 1976 Camperdown (NSW)

Rundell, Joshua Upcott (SAust) b May 6, 1858 Sandhurst (Vic) d Jan. 7, 1922 Alberton (SAust)

Rundell, Percy Davies (SAust) b Nov. 20, 1890 Alberton (SAust) d March 24, 1979 North Adelaide (SAust)

Rush, Edward Reynolds (Vic) b March 29, 1868 Flemington (Vic) d May 6, 1936 Malvern (Vic)

Rush, John (Vic) b April 5, 1910 Malvern (Vic) d Jan. 13, 1982 Adelaide (SAust)

Rush, Thomas Reynolds (Vic) b Dec. 7, 1874 Collingwood (Vic) d Oct. 29, 1926 Malvern (Vic)

Rushbrook, Roy Francis Kerr (Qld) b Sept. 29, 1911 Spring Hill (Qld) d March 31, 1987 Mackay (Qld)

Rushforth, Alfred William (Tas) b April 23, 1898 Hobart (Tas) d Dec. 30, 1985 Taroona (Tas)

Russell, Bernard (NSW) b Aug. 1, 1891 Leichhardt (NSW) d July 13, 1961 Belmore (NSW)

Russell, Richard Stevan (WAust) b Jan. 22, 1968 Helensville (New Zealand)

Russen, Charles Gordon (Tas) b May 9, 1886 Launceston (Tas) d Dec. 16, 1969 Newstead (Tas)

* Rutherford, John Walter (WAust) b Sept. 25, 1929 Bungulluping (WAust)

Ryan, Alfred James (SAust) b April 27, 1904 Adelaide (SAust) d July 10, 1990 Semaphore (SAust)

Ryan, Gregory William (NSW) b March 13, 1913 Wallsend (NSW) d May 10, 1986 Randwick (NSW)

Ryan, Peter Andrew (Qld) b Feb. 18, 1951 East Melbourne (Vic)

Ryan, Roderick Thomas (WAust) b Nov. 15, 1909 Cannington (WAust) d Oct. 23, 1979 Toronto, Ontario (Canada)

Ryan, Thomas Patrick (Tas) b May 4, 1865 Hobart (Tas) d April 20, 1921 Hobart (Tas)

* Ryder, John (Vic) b Aug. 8, 1889 Collingwood (Vic) d April 3, 1977 Fitzroy (Vic)

Rymill, Jack Westall (SAust) b March 20, 1901 North Adelaide (SAust) d Feb. 11, 1976 Adelaide (SAust)

Saballus, Andrew William (Tas) b June 1, 1969 Hobart (Tas)

Sacristani, Peter Geoffrey (Vic) b Sept. 5, 1957 Melbourne (Vic)

Saddler, Edward (NSW) d Oct. 28, 1874 full birth and death details unknown

* Sadiq Mohammad (Tas) b May 5, 1945 Junagadh (India)

* Saggers, Ronald Arthur (NSW) b May 15, 1917 Sydenham (NSW) d March 17, 1987 Harbord (NSW)

Sainsbury, Andrew John (NSW) b May 11, 1974 Gosford (NSW)

Saint, John Michael (Tas) b Jan. 31, 1969 Auburn (NSW)

Saker, David James (Vic & Tas) b May 29, 1966 Oakleigh (Vic)

Salmon, Benjamin Melville (NSW) b Jan. 9, 1906 Footscray (Vic) d Jan. 24, 1979 Mosman (NSW)

Salmon, John Lionel (Vic) b March 31, 1934 Canterbury (Vic)

Salvado, John Frederick (Vic) b Nov. 11, 1939 Carlton (Vic)

Salvana, Louis Charles (Vic) b Jan. 20, 1897 Hawthorn (Vic) d Dec. 8, 1974 Mitcham (Vic)

Sams, Louis Robert (Tas) b Sept. 26, 1863 Westbury (Tas) d July 6, 1941 Redcliffe (Qld)

Sams, Richard Horace (Tas) b c. 1864 Westbury (Tas) d March 5, 1933 Roseville (NSW)

Samuels, Edward (NSW) b May 25, 1833 Sydney (NSW)

Sanders, Leyland Arthur (Qld) b Oct. 17, 1927 Sandgate (Qld)

Sandford, Horace Charles Augustus (Vic) b Oct. 14, 1891 St Leonard's (NSW) d Aug. 16, 1967 Heidelberg (Vic)

Sands, Ronald Francis (WAust) b Sept. 16, 1921 Perth (WAust) d Sept. 5, 1995 Nedlands (WAust)

Sangster, Christopher Bagot (SAust) b May 1, 1908 Kooringa (SAust) d Feb. 27, 1995 North Adelaide (SAust)

Sangster, John Fraser (SAust) b Jan. 21, 1942 Adelaide (SAust)

Sankey, Clarence Joseph (Tas) b Oct. 27, 1913 Northtown (Tas) d March 12, 1996 Launceston (Tas)

Sargent, Murray Alfred James (SAust) b Aug. 23, 1928 Adelaide (SAust)

Sarovich, Theodor Keith (Vic) b May 20, 1915 Port Melbourne (Vic) d Nov. 23, 1987 Atherton (Qld)

Sarre, Ronald Basil (WAust) b Jan. 20, 1932 Midland (WAust)

Sartori, Ronald Joseph (WAust) b March 23, 1915 Fremantle (WAust) d July 1, 1991 Perth (WAust)

* Saunders, John Victor (Vic) b March 21, 1876 Melbourne (Vic) d Dec. 21, 1927 Toorak (Vic)

Saunders, Stuart Lucas (Tas) b June 27, 1960 Hobart (Tas)

Saunders, Warren Joseph (NSW) b July 18, 1934 Arncliffe (NSW)

Savage, Harry Milton (NSW) b July 1, 1887 Ermington (NSW) d Nov. 14, 1964 (NSW)

Savage, Keith Douglas (Qld) b Sept. 19, 1926 Brisbane (Qld) d Jan. 18, 1979 Mt Morgan (Qld)

Savigny, John Horatio (Tas) b Aug. 25, 1867 Bathurst (NSW) d Feb. 11, 1923 Carrick (Tas)

Savigny, William Henry (Tas) b Feb. 17, 1864 Sydney (NSW) d Aug. 6, 1922 Burwood (NSW)

Sawle, Lawrence Michael (WAust) b Aug. 19, 1925 East Fremantle (WAust)

Sayers, Dean Keith (SAust) b June 11, 1954 Hindmarsh (SAust)

Sayers, Mervyn Gerald (WAust) b March 5, 1958 Subiaco (WAust)

Scaife, John Willie (Vic) b Nov. 14, 1908 Haslingden, Lancashire (England) d Oct. 27, 1995 Melbourne (Vic)

Scanes, Albert Edward (NSW) b Aug. 6, 1900 Erskineville (NSW) d Nov. 1, 1969 death place unknown

Scanlan, Edmund (NSW) b c. 1848 Newcastle on Tyne, Northumberland (England) d Jan. 9, 1916 Erskineville (NSW)

Scannell, Timothy Francis (Vic) b Nov. 12, 1882 Hotham (Vic) d July 9, 1939 Royal Park (Vic)

Scarff, Clark Steven (WAust) b Nov. 19, 1948 Subiaco (WAust)

Schade, Matias Anderson (Vic) b March 25, 1887 Huntly (Vic) d June 9, 1959 Williamstown (Vic)

Schenscher, Peter Malcolm (SAust) b May 4, 1962 Murray Bridge (SAust)

Schmidt, Keith Ernest (Tas) b Dec. 19, 1921 Hobart (Tas)

Schneider, Karl Joseph (Vic & SAust) b Aug. 15, 1905 Hawthorn (Vic) d Sept. 5, 1928 Kensington Park (SAust)

Scholes, Mark Bradley (Tas) b July 1, 1957 Carlton (Vic)

Scholes, Walter John (Vic) b Jan. 5, 1950 East Brunswick (Vic) d July 14, 2003 North Eltham (Vic)

Schrader, Heinrich Christian (Vic) b Dec. 5, 1893 East Prahran (Vic) d June 10, 1980 Kew (Vic)

Schreiber, Sidney Arthur (Qld) b April 7, 1873 birth and death details unknown

Schuller, Denis Clemenceau (Qld) b May 5, 1948 Herston (Qld)

Schultz, Bruce (SAust) b March 13, 1913 Royston Park (SAust) d Jan. 11, 1980 Modbury (SAust)

Schultz, Julius William Eugene (SAust) b Sept. 25, 1888 Summer Town (SAust) d Aug. 8, 1966 Berri (SAust)

Scott, Darryl Bryan (SAust) b March 9, 1961 Glenelg (SAust)

* Scott, Henry James Herbert (Vic) b Dec. 26, 1858 Prahran (Vic) d Sept. 23, 1910 Scone (NSW)

Scott, Jack A. (SAust) b Jan. 14, 1910 Sydney (NSW) d May 22, 1980 Collaroy Beach (NSW)

Scott, John Drake (NSW & SAust) b Jan. 31, 1888 Petersham (NSW) d April 7, 1964 Springbank (SAust)

Scott, Robert Barrington (Vic & NSW) b Oct. 9, 1916 South Melbourne (Vic) d April 6, 1984 Melbourne (Vic)

Scott, Walter Aubrey (Vic) b Feb. 19, 1907 Camberwell (Vic) d Oct. 23, 1989 death place unknown

Scott, William John (Vic) b June 14, 1882 Hotham (Vic) d Sept. 30, 1965 Ferntree Gully (Vic)

Scrymgour, Bernard Vincent (SAust) b July 31, 1864 Adelaide (SAust) d April 16, 1943 Medindie (SAust)

Scuderi, Joseph Charles (SAust) b Dec. 24, 1968 Ingham (Qld)

Seabrook, Wayne John Stephen (NSW) b Sept. 6, 1961 Ryde (NSW)

Seale, Joseph (NSW) b April 18, 1855 Grafton (NSW) d Aug. 19, 1941 Waratah (NSW)

Searle, James (NSW) b Aug. 8, 1861 Surry Hills (NSW) d Dec. 28, 1936 Manly (NSW)

Searle, Richard Henry (Qld) b Jan. 16, 1934 Red Hill (Qld)

Seccombe, Donald Harry (Qld) b April 3, 1942 Goomeri (Qld)

Seccombe, Wade Anthony (Qld) b Oct. 30, 1971 Murgon (Qld)

Seddon, Cecil Dudley (NSW) b July 3, 1902 Campbelltown (NSW) d April 18, 1978 Dulwich Hill (NSW)

Seib, Ian Martin (Qld) b Sept. 15, 1946 Herston (Qld)

Seitz, John Arnold (Vic) b Sept. 19, 1883 Carlton (Vic) d May 1, 1963 St Kilda (Vic)

Selk, Rudolph Albert (WAust) b Oct. 6, 1871 Omeo (Vic) d Jan. 31, 1940 Pickering Brook (WAust)

Sellers, Michael John (Tas) b July 5, 1952 Launceston (Tas)

* Sellers, Reginald Hugh Durning (SAust) b Aug. 20, 1940 Bulsar (India)

Selth, Victor Poole (SAust) b June 1, 1895 Parkside (SAust) d Sept. 2, 1967 Daw Park (SAust)

* Serjeant, Craig Stanton (WAust) b Nov. 1, 1951 Nedlands (WAust)

Serjeant, David Maurice (Vic) b Jan. 18, 1830 Ramsey, Huntingdonshire (England) d Jan. 12, 1929 Camberwell, London (England)

Sewart, William Isaac (Qld & Vic) b Nov. 12, 1881 Allendale East (SAust) d Dec. 13, 1928 Caulfield (Vic)

Shade, Eric (Vic) b Aug. 27, 1943 Brighton (Vic)

Sharman, Baden Eric (Tas) b Aug. 11, 1939 Beulah (Tas)

* Sharpe, Duncan Albert (SAust) b Aug. 3, 1937 Rawalpindi (India)

Shaw, John Hilary (Vic) b Oct. 18, 1932 Geelong (Vic)

Shaw, Noel Clyde (Vic) b May 10, 1937 Euroa (Vic)

Shawe, Patrick Henry Villiers Washington (Tas) b Bangalore (India) d Sept. 24, 1945 East Melbourne (Vic)

Shea, John Adrian (WAust) b May 8, 1913 Boulder (WAust) d Feb. 7, 1986 Claremont (WAust)

Shea, Morris (NSW) b c. 1869 Campbelltown (NSW) death details unknown

Shea, Patrick Augustus (Vic) b March 17, 1886 Clunes (Vic) d May 29, 1954 Northbridge (NSW)

* Sheahan, Andrew Paul (Vic) b Sept. 30, 1948 Werribee (Vic)

Sheen, Brian Lawrence (Tas) b Dec. 30, 1938 Hobart (Tas)

Shelton, Herbert John (Tas) b Jan. 21, 1924 Launceston (Tas)

Shepard, David John (Vic) b Dec. 30, 1970 Berwick (Vic)

Shephard, Athol Lennard (Tas) b Aug. 16, 1920 Burnie (Tas)

Shepherd, Alan Gordon (SAust) b Sept. 29, 1912 Kilkenny (SAust) d Oct. 9, 1998 Marion (SAust)

* Shepherd, Barry Kenneth (WAust) b April 23, 1937 Donnybrook (WAust) d Sept. 17, 2001 Fremantle (WAust)

Shepherd, David Stanmore (Vic) b Aug. 3, 1956 Melbourne (Vic)

Shepherd, James (NSW) b May 24, 1856 Steiglitz (Vic) death details unknown

Shepherdson, Hartley Robert (SAust) b Sept. 4, 1913 Mt Gambier (SAust) d Aug. 19, 1992 Fitzroy (Vic)

Shepley, Herbert Neil (SAust) b Oct. 7, 1899 Knightsbridge (SAust) d Nov. 14, 1953 Tranmere (SAust)

Sheppard, Benjamin Joseph (Vic) b June 23, 1892 Fitzroy (Vic) d Sept. 9, 1931 Fitzroy (Vic)

Sheppard, James Francis (Qld) b Jan. 16, 1888 Brisbane (Qld) d Dec. 10, 1944 Hendra (Qld)

Sheridan, Edward Orwell (NSW) b Jan. 3, 1842 Sydney (NSW) d Nov. 30, 1923 West End (Qld)

Sherriff, Rowan James (Tas) b July 7, 1951 Sheffield (Tas)

Shewan, Leslie James (Qld) b June 12, 1892 Rushworth (Vic) d Sept. 25, 1977 Windsor (Vic)

Shiell, Alan Bruce (SAust) b April 25, 1945 St Peters (SAust)

Shillinglaw, Harold Arthur Edward (Vic) b Dec. 2, 1927 Fitzroy (Vic)

Shipperd, Gregory (WAust & Tas) b Nov. 13, 1956 Subiaco (WAust)

Short, Henry William (SAust) b March 31, 1874 Morphett Vale (SAust) d May 11, 1916 Lower Mitcham (SAust)

Shortland, Herbert (NSW) b April 7, 1881 Sydney (NSW) d July 17, 1946 death place unknown

Shugg, Albert William (Tas) b July 5, 1894 Hawthorn (Vic) d July 20, 1941 Hobart (Tas)

Siddons, James Darren (Vic & SAust) b April 25, 1964 Robinvale (Vic)

Sidebottom, William Lemuel (Tas) b Sept. 24, 1862 Evandale (Tas) d April 11, 1948 Launceston (Tas)

Sides, Francis William (Qld & Vic) b Dec. 15, 1913 Mackay (Qld) d Aug. 25, 1943 Kunai Spur, Salamaua (Papua New Guinea) in action

Sieler, Alan John (Vic) b July 17, 1948 Arncliffe (NSW)

* Sievers, Morris William (Vic) b April 13, 1912 Powlett River (Vic) d May 10, 1968 Parkville (Vic)

Siggs, Douglas (Qld) b Aug. 11, 1920 Fortitude Valley (Qld)

Sim, Charles Wallace (Qld) b March 30, 1895 Brisbane (Qld) d July 3, 1971 Woodville South (SAust)

Simmonds, William (Anderson's XI) details unknown

Simmons, Arthur Harry (NSW) b Nov. 13, 1909 Croydon (NSW) d Feb. 28, 1990 Mirrabooka (NSW)

Simmons, Craig Joseph (WAust) b Dec. 1, 1982 Paddington (NSW)

Simmons, Jack (Tas) b March 28, 1941 Clayton-le-Moors, Lancashire (England)

Simpson, Charles Edward (Qld & NSW) b March 27, 1882 Parramatta (NSW) d June 26, 1956 Sydney (NSW)

Simpson, Christopher Patrick (Qld) b Jan. 9, 1982 South Brisbane (Qld)

* Simpson, Robert Baddeley (NSW & WAust) b Feb. 3, 1936 Marrickville (NSW)

Sims, Alfred Edward (Qld) b Nov. 8, 1875 birthplace and death details unknown

Sims, Arthur (Australians) b July 27, 1877 Spridlington, Lincolnshire (England) d April 27, 1969 East Hoathly, Sussex (England)

Simunsen, Robert Francis (SAust) b June 7, 1941 Adelaide (SAust)

Sinclair, Arthur (NSW) birth details unknown d Nov. 29, 1869 Sydney (NSW)

Sincock, Andrew Thomas (SAust) b June 7, 1951 Adelaide (SAust)

* Sincock, David John (SAust) b Feb. 1, 1942 North Adelaide (SAust)

Sincock, Harrold Keith (SAust) b Dec. 10, 1907 Eastwood (SAust) d Feb. 2, 1982 Plympton (SAust)

Sincock, Peter Damien (SAust) b July 8, 1948 North Adelaide (SAust)

Sincock, Russell John (Vic) b Dec. 28, 1947 Kew (Vic)

Sindrey, Clive Alexander Hazell (Vic) b Aug. 10, 1903 Richmond (Vic) d June 26, 1981 Vermont (Vic)

Single, Clive Vallack (NSW) b Sept. 17, 1888 Penrith (NSW) d July 10, 1931 Woollahra (NSW)

Sismey, Stanley George (NSW) b July 15, 1916 Junee (NSW)

Skilbeck, Andrew John (NSW) b July 21, 1958 St Leonard's (NSW)

Skuse, Alan Raymond (Qld) b March 28, 1942 Herston (Qld)

Sladen, Charles (Vic) b Aug. 28, 1816 Walmer, Kent (England) d Feb. 22, 1884 Geelong (Vic)

* Slater, Keith Nichol (WAust) b March 12, 1935 Midland (WAust)

* Slater, Michael Jonathon (NSW) b Feb. 21, 1970 Wagga Wagga (NSW)

* Sleep, Peter Raymond (SAust) b May 4, 1957 Penola (SAust)

Slight, Alexander Frank (SAust) b March 13, 1861 Emerald Hill (Vic) d July 5, 1930 Maylands (SAust)

* Slight, James (Vic) b Oct. 20, 1855 Ashby, Geelong (Vic) d Dec. 9, 1930 Elsternwick (Vic)

Slight, William (Vic & SAust) b Sept. 19, 1858 Emerald Hill (Vic) d Dec. 22, 1941 Toorak Gardens (SAust)

Small, Gladstone Cleophas (SAust) b Oct. 18, 1961 Brighton, St George (Barbados)

Small, Stephen Mark (NSW & Tas) b March 2, 1955 Canterbury (NSW)

Smart, Christopher Boddington (Qld) b Oct. 17, 1958 Port Moresby (Papua New Guinea)

Smart, Hadyn Warren Gavin (SAust) b Nov. 26, 1958 Hobart (Tas)

Smart, Lawrence Maxwell (SAust) b Feb. 16, 1928 Narridy (SAust)

Smith, Adam Matthew (Vic) b April 6, 1976 Greensborough (Vic)

Smith, Alfred Edward Charles (WAust) b Oct. 4, 1908 Prahran (WAust) d Jan. 17, 1989 Fremantle (WAust)

Smith, Andrew (SAust) b Sept. 1, 1889 Port Adelaide (SAust) d May 18, 1983 Adelaide (SAust)

Smith, Carey Kenneth (Vic) b Oct. 16, 1960 Moreland (Vic)

Smith, Cyril Robert (Qld) b Nov. 1, 1926 South Brisbane (Qld)

Smith, Darryl Donald (WAust) b June 8, 1960 Adelaide (SAust)

Smith, David Anthony (Tas) b Sept. 1, 1957 Launceston (Tas)

* Smith, David Betram Miller (Vic) b Sept. 14, 1884 Richmond (Vic) d July 29, 1963 Hawthorn (Vic)

Smith, Douglas Roy (Tas) b Oct. 9, 1880 Fingal (Tas) d Feb. 27, 1933 Port Fairy (Vic)

Smith, Edward Henry (Tas) b July 30, 1911 Nook (Tas) d Dec. 26, 1999 Launceston (Tas)

Smith, George Elms (Vic) b July 22, 1855 Emerald Hill (Vic) d April 7, 1897 St Kilda (Vic)

Smith, Harry Oxley (Tas & Vic) b Oct. 27, 1887 Launceston (Tas) d Aug. 24, 1916 Pinewood, London (England)

Smith, Herbert George (Vic) b March 21, 1914 Richmond (Vic) d Feb. 23, 1997 Caulfield (Vic)

Smith, Horace Clitheroe (Tas) b Oct. 31, 1892 Sandy Bay (Tas) d April 6, 1977 Hobart (Tas)

Smith, Hubert George Selwyn (Qld) b Oct. 9, 1891 Beaudesert (Qld) d June 7, 1917 Messines (France)

Smith, James Halliburton (NSW) b March 20, 1880 Parramatta (NSW) d June 18, 1958 Killara (NSW)

Smith, John Phillips (Vic) b March 6, 1936 Ballarat (Vic)

Smith, Lavington Albert (SAust) b Oct. 9, 1904 Medindie (SAust) d May 9, 1953 Adelaide (SAust)

Smith, Leonard Angus (Vic) b Oct. 25, 1882 Hotham (Vic) d July 29, 1943 Heidelberg (Vic)

Smith, Lloyd Harold James (Tas) b Aug. 5, 1928 Hobart (Tas)

Smith, Michael John (SAust) b July 17, 1973 Rose Park (SAust)

Smith, Peter Julian (Vic) b Feb. 8, 1968 Greensborough (Vic)

Smith, Robert Thomas (Vic) b May 27, 1868 Harrow (Vic) d Aug. 21, 1927 East Melbourne (Vic)

Smith, Stanley Arthur John (Vic) b Jan. 8, 1910 Footscray (Vic) d c. 1984 Ryde (NSW)

* Smith, Stephen Barry (NSW) b Oct. 18, 1961 Sydney (NSW)

Smith, Struan McKinley (Rest of Australia) b June 4, 1907 St Leonard's (NSW)

Smith, Thomas Henry (Qld) b Sept. 19, 1898 Talgai (Qld) d March 6, 1926 Warwick (Qld)

Smith, Warren Robert (WAust) b Dec. 29, 1941 Guildford (WAust)

Smyth, Neil Weston (Vic) b June 6, 1928 South Yarra (Vic)

* Sobers, Garfield St Aubrun (SAust) b July 28, 1936 Chelsea Road, Bay Land, Bridgetown (Barbados)

Solomon, Cyril Moss (NSW) b March 11, 1911 Cootamundra (NSW) d July 15, 1995 Manly (NSW)

Soule, Richard Eric (Tas) b Sept. 5, 1966 Launceston (Tas)

Souter, Vernon John (Vic) b Feb. 26, 1894 Uranquinty (NSW) d July 17, 1915 Elsternwick (Vic)

Spalding, Earl George (WAust) b March 13, 1965 South Perth (WAust)

Speirs, Norman Lennox (Vic) b May 31, 1886 Caulfield (Vic) d Aug. 1, 1960 Noosa Heads (Qld)

Spencer, Duncan John (WAust) b April 5, 1972 Burnley, Lancashire (England)

Spencer, Ernest Lott (Vic) b May 1, 1888 Hotham West (Vic) d Nov. 4, 1953 Essendon (Vic)

* Spofforth, Frederick Robert (NSW & Vic) b Sept. 9, 1853 Balmain (NSW) d June 4, 1926 Ditton Hill, Surrey (England)

Spring, Graham Allan (NSW) b April 20, 1961 Sydney (NSW)

Spry, Richard (Qld) b July 18, 1862 Melbourne (Vic) d Nov. 10, 1920 Linville (Qld)

Squires, Philip Horley (SAust) b June 18, 1939 Marden (SAust)

Stacey, Bradley John (Vic) b June 11, 1972 Geelong (Vic)

Stack, George Bagot (NSW) b March 12, 1846 West Maitland (NSW) d Oct. 7, 1930 Orange (NSW)

Stack, Walter Jaques (NSW) b Oct. 31, 1884 Croydon (NSW) d March 26, 1972 Bathurst (NSW)

* Stackpole, Keith Raymond (Vic) b July 10, 1940 Collingwood (Vic)

Stackpole, Keith William (Vic) b July 31, 1916 Melbourne (Vic) d Sept. 19, 1992 Heidelberg (Vic)

Stackpoole, John (Qld) b Nov. 23, 1916 Jundah (Qld)

Stalker, Walter (Vic) b Oct. 29, 1909 Elaine (Vic) d Jan. 13, 1977 Ballarat (Vic)

Stanes, John Gladstone (Vic) b Dec. 15, 1910 South Melbourne (Vic) d Sept. 2, 1997 Narrabeen (NSW)

Stanford, Graham Edwin (SAust) b April 25, 1948 Adelaide (SAust)

Stanford, Ross Milton (SAust) b Sept. 25, 1917 Fulham (SAust)

Stapleton, Harold Vincent (NSW) b Jan. 7, 1915 Kyogle (NSW)

Starr, Cecil Leonard Berry (SAust) b July 20, 1907 Quorn (SAust)

Staunton, Andrew Michael (SAust) b May 18, 1979 Canterbury (SAust)

Steele, Donald Macdonald (SAust) b Aug. 17, 1892 East Adelaide (SAust) d July 13, 1962 Adelaide (SAust)

Steele, Harry Cornwall (NSW) b April 22, 1901 East Sydney (NSW) d Nov. 9, 1985 Sydney (NSW)

Steele, John Anthony (NSW) b Nov. 13, 1942 Waverley (NSW)

Steele, Kenneth Nagent (SAust) b Dec. 17, 1889 East Adelaide (SAust) d Dec. 19, 1956 North Adelaide (SAust)

Stephens, Jack Lawson (Vic) b Aug. 31, 1913 Majorca (Vic) d Sept. 2, 1967 Daylesford (Vic)

Stephens, John Raymond (Vic) b Sept. 15, 1950 East Melbourne (Vic)

Stephens, Reginald Stanley (Vic) b April 16, 1883 Creswick (Vic) d Sept. 7, 1965 Malvern (Vic)

Stephenson, Franklyn Dacosta (Tas) b April 8, 1959 Halls, St James (Barbados)

Stepto, Paul Douglas (NSW) b Dec. 23, 1966 Sydney (NSW)

* Stevens, Gavin Byron (SAust) b Feb. 29, 1932 Glenelg (SAust)

Stevens, John Grenfell (NSW) b Feb. 22, 1948 Muswellbrook (NSW)

Stevens, John Whitehall (Vic) birth and death details unknown

Stevens, Robert Barry (Vic) b Nov. 5, 1929 Melbourne (Vic)

Stewart, Barry James (Tas) b May 6, 1940 Wynyard (Tas) d July 23, 1975 Wynyard (Tas)

Stewart, Gordon Lionel (NSW) b June 16, 1906 Petersham (NSW) d Oct. 21, 1984 Katoomba (NSW)

Stewart, James (WAust & NSW) b Aug. 22, 1970 East Fremantle (WAust)

Stewart, James C. (Vic) birth and death details unknown

Stewart, Trevor George (Qld) b March 15, 1940 Mt Isa (Qld)

Stewart, William (Vic) b c. 1844 full birth and death details unknown

Stibe, Colin George Reinzi (Qld) b April 22, 1916 Bundaberg (Qld) d Jan. 6, 1970 Sydney (NSW)

Still, Robert Stuart (Tas) b March 15, 1822 Bathurst (NSW) d July 5, 1907 Launceston (Tas)

Still, William Cathcart (NSW) b c. 1820 (England) d July 5, 1910 Sydney (NSW)

Stillman, William Leslie (Vic & SAust) b Oct. 5, 1949 Alexandra (Vic)

Stirling, William Stuart (SAust) b March 19, 1891 Jamestown (SAust) d July 18, 1971 Adelaide (SAust)

Stobo, Richard Montagu (NSW) b June 20, 1965 Toowoomba (Qld)

Stokes, George William (Vic) b Dec. 11, 1857 South Yarra (Vic) d Aug. 16, 1929 Brighton (Vic)

Stokes, Raymond Gordon (Tas) b May 21, 1924 Longford (Tas)

Stokes, William (WAust) b July 28, 1886 Geraldton (WAust) d Oct. 4, 1954 Perth (WAust)

Storey, Stephen Craig (Qld) b Nov. 23, 1964 Mona Vale (NSW)

Stratford, H. E. (Vic) birth and death details unknown

Strauss, Raymond Bernard (WAust) b Nov. 4, 1927 Perth (WAust)

Strudwick, David Charles (SAust) b Jan. 11, 1934 Adelaide (SAust)

Stuart, Anthony Mark (NSW) b Jan. 2, 1970 Waratah (NSW)

Stuart, William Percy (SAust) b March 7, 1871 Goolwa (SAust) d Aug. 20, 1956 Unley Park (SAust)

Stubbs, John Robert Marshall (WAust) b Oct. 15, 1931 Collie (WAust)

Stuckey, George (Vic) b July 6, 1871 Walhalla (Vic) d March 15, 1932 North Melbourne (Vic)

Stuckey, John Henry (Vic) b July 3, 1869 Walhalla (Vic) d Aug. 10, 1952 Cheltenham (Vic)

Such, Bruce Vincent (Qld) b c. 1907 Sydney (NSW) d April 14, 1933 Townsville (Qld)

Sullivan, Alfred Ernest (NSW) b Dec. 10, 1872 Balmain (NSW) d Sept. 25, 1942 Balmain (NSW)

Sullivan, William (Qld) b Aug. 19, 1877 Hotham (Vic) d Aug. 29, 1924 Albury (NSW)

Suppel, James Thomas (NSW) b Oct. 19, 1914 Warren (NSW) d March 9, 1994 Lidcombe (NSW)

* Surti, Rusi Framroz (Qld) b May 25, 1936 Surat (India)

Sutherland, David (Vic) b June 4, 1873 Boroondara (Vic) d Oct. 6, 1971 Hawthorn (Vic)

Sutherland, Donald John (SAust) b Nov. 28, 1949 Adelaide (SAust)

Sutherland, James Alexander (Vic) b July 14, 1965 East Melbourne (Vic)

Swain, Brett Andrew (SAust) b Feb. 14, 1974 Stirling (SAust)

Swan, Gavin Graham (WAust) b Oct. 30, 1970 Subiaco (WAust)

Swanson, John David (Vic) b April 5, 1910 Brunswick (Vic)

Swendsen, Robert Charles (Qld) b Oct. 18, 1929 Charters Towers (Qld)

Swift, John Sheddon (Vic) b Feb. 3, 1852 birthplace unknown d Feb. 28, 1926 Kew (Vic)

* Symonds, Andrew (Qld) b June 9, 1975 Birmingham, West Midlands (England)

Symonds, Crawford (SAust) b Feb. 15, 1915 North Adelaide (SAust) d uly 20, 2000 Bedford Park (SAust)

Taaffe, Frederick Herbert (WAust) b Jan. 7, 1899 Deolali (India) d April 2, 1964 Ulladulla (NSW)

Tabart, John Lewis Benjamin (Tas) b Nov. 30, 1827 St Pancras, London (England) d Sept. 9, 1894 Launceston (Tas)

Tabart, Thomas Alfred (Tas) b Aug. 10, 1877 Campbell Town (Tas) d Aug. 29, 1950 East Melbourne (Vic)

* Taber, Hedley Brian (NSW) b April 29, 1940 Wagga Wagga (NSW)

Tait, Alan Houston (Qld) b Feb. 17, 1908 Toowoomba (Qld) d July 27, 1988 Indooroopilly (Qld)

Tait, George (Parr's XI) b April 12, 1844 Parramatta (NSW) d Dec. 21, 1934 East Malvern (Vic)

Tait, Shaun William (SAust) b Feb. 22, 1983 Bedford Park (SAust)

* Tallon, Donald (Qld) b Feb. 17, 1916 Bundaberg (Qld) d Sept. 7, 1984 Bundaberg (Qld)

Tallon, Leslie William Thomas (Qld) b July 9, 1914 Bundaberg (Qld) d Sept. 18, 1972 Coopers Plains (Qld)

Tamblyn, Geoffrey Leonard (Vic) b April 8, 1949 Melbourne (Vic)

Tamblyn, Gordon Erle (Vic) b April 23, 1918 Wallaroo Mines (SAust) d Dec. 31, 2001 Melbourne (Vic)

Tame, Michael Philip (Tas) b Jan. 6, 1956 Hobart (Tas)

Tardif, Joseph Henry (SAust) b May 17, 1860 Gawler (SAust) d June 14, 1920 Prospect (SAust)

Targett, Benjamin Stuart (Tas) b Dec. 27, 1972 Paddington (NSW)

Tarrant, Francis Alfred (Vic) b Dec. 11, 1880 Fitzroy (Vic) d Jan. 29, 1951 Upper Hawthorn (Vic)

Tarrant, William Ambrose (Vic) b Sept. 22, 1866 Fitzroy (Vic) d Nov. 1, 1938 North Fitzroy (Vic)

Tatchell, Thomas (Vic) b June 13, 1867 Inglewood (Vic) d Oct. 18, 1936 East Melbourne (Vic)

Taylor, Bruce William (Qld) b June 14, 1924 Brisbane (Qld) d Oct. 16, 1984 New Farm (Qld)

Taylor, David (NSW) b May 2, 1881 Sydney (NSW) death details unknown

Taylor, John James (WAust) b April 3, 1979 Essendon (Vic)

* Taylor, John Morris (NSW) b Oct. 10, 1895 Stanmore (NSW) d May 12, 1971 Turramurra (NSW)

Taylor, Joseph Stanley (NSW) b Nov. 1, 1887 Leichhardt (NSW) d Sept. 3, 1954 Waratah (NSW)

* Taylor, Mark Anthony (NSW) b Oct. 27, 1964 Leeton (NSW)

Taylor, Michael David (Vic & Tas) b June 9, 1955 Chelsea (Vic)

* Taylor, Peter Laurence (NSW & Qld) b Aug. 22, 1956 North Sydney (NSW)

Taylor, Ross Simeon (NSW) b May 8, 1938 Mudgee (NSW) d Dec. 7, 1996 Tamworth (NSW)

Taylor, Stuart Gifford (Tas) b April 13, 1900 Prahran (Vic) d Feb. 2, 1978 Mosman Park (WAust)

Tazelaar, Dirk (Qld) b Jan. 13, 1963 Ipswich (Qld)

Teagle, Reginald Crump (SAust) b Feb. 27, 1909 Parkside (SAust) d June 8, 1987 Adelaide (SAust)

Teece, Richard (Combined XIII) b April 29, 1847 Paihia (New Zealand) d Dec. 13, 1928 Point Piper (NSW)

Teisseire, Francis Lawrence (SAust) b July 8, 1917 Rose Park (SAust) d Nov. 23, 1998 Glenelg (SAust)

Templeton, Robert Ian (Vic) b March 15, 1957 Hamilton (Vic)

Tennent, Hector Norman (Australians) b April 6, 1843 Hobart (Tas) d April 16, 1904 Westminster, London (England)

Tennent, John Pattison (Vic) b July 31, 1846 Hobart (Tas) d Oct. 31, 1893 Clifton Hill (Vic)

Terry, Richard Benjamin (Vic) birth and death details unknown

Thamm, Carl Friedrich Wilhelm (SAust) b Nov. 1, 1874 Nuriootpa (SAust) d July 4, 1944 Subiaco (WAust)

Thatcher, Allen Norman (NSW) b April 17, 1899 Sydney (NSW) d Feb. 12, 1932 Dulwich Hill (NSW)

Theak, Henry John Thomas (NSW) b March 19, 1909 Pyrmont (NSW) d Sept. 14, 1979 Narwee (NSW)

Thistle, Michael James (WAust) b Aug. 5, 1980 Perth (WAust)

Thollar, Douglas Hugh (Tas) b Feb. 13, 1919 George Town (Tas)

Thomas, Arthur Churchill (SAust) b May 4, 1869 Unley (SAust) d April 28, 1934 Unley (SAust)

Thomas, Brad John (Tas) b Jan. 18, 1972 Hobart (Tas)

Thomas, George Alexander (NSW) b April 22, 1881 Sydney (NSW)

* Thomas, Grahame (NSW) b March 21, 1938 Croydon Park (NSW)

Thomas, Jeffrey Mark (Qld) b Oct. 19, 1971 Toowoomba (Qld)

Thomas, John Oliver (Tas) b April 12, 1852 Merthyr Tydfil (Wales) d May 29, 1915 Carlton (Vic)

Thomas, Josiah (Vic) b Aug. 27, 1910 Golden Square, Bendigo (Vic) d May 28, 1960 Essendon (Vic)

Thomas, Kenneth Bruce (Vic) b Oct. 5, 1942 East Melbourne (Vic)

Thomas, Llewellyn (Tas) b April 1, 1883 Fitzroy (Vic) d Nov. 2, 1962 Evandale (Tas)

Thomas, Maxwell Raymond (Tas) b June 28, 1921 Launceston (Tas) d May 20, 2001 Lenah Valley (Tas)

Thomas, Ramon Cedric (SAust) b Nov. 18, 1932 Mile End (SAust)

Thomas, Ronald Vivian (Tas) b Sept. 21, 1915 Longford (Tas) d May 28, 1987 Launceston (Tas)

Thomlinson, Arthur (Tas) b c. 1887 full birth and death details unknown

Thompson, C.D. (NSW) birth and death details unknown

Thompson, Francis Cecil (Qld) b Aug. 17, 1890 Stanwell (Qld) d Sept. 24, 1963 Southport (Qld)

Thompson, Horace Malcolm (SAust) b Nov. 29, 1913 Malvern (SAust) d March 19, 1936 Kalgoorlie (WAust)

Thompson, James Bogne (Vic) b c. 1829 Yorkshire (England) d July 18, 1877 Melbourne (Vic)

Thompson, Kerry William (NSW) b Dec. 12, 1949 Wallsend (NSW)

Thompson, Scott Michael (NSW) b May 4, 1972 Bankstown (NSW)

Thompson, William James (Qld) b Jan. 2, 1891 (Qld)

* Thoms, George Ronald (Vic) b March 22, 1927 Footscray (Vic) d Aug. 29, 2003 Melbourne (Vic)

Thomsett, Harold King (Qld) b Oct. 23, 1913 Yarraman (Qld) d April 12, 1991 Spring Hill (Qld)

* Thomson, Alan Lloyd (Vic) b Dec. 2, 1945 Reservoir (Vic)

Thomson, Alan Ogilvie (Vic) b Sept. 1, 1899 Tibooburra (NSW) d c. 1938 Tibooburra (NSW)

Thomson, Alfred Taddy (Vic) b 1818 birth day and month unknown Paddington, London, Middlesex (England) d Oct. 12, 1895 London (England)

Thomson, Geoffrey David (WAust) b April 21, 1959 Subiaco (WAust)

* Thomson, Jeffrey Robert (NSW & Qld) b Aug. 16, 1950 Greenacre (NSW)

Thomson, Joseph (Qld) b May 27, 1877 South Brisbane (Qld) d July 5, 1953 (Qld)

Thomson, Kenneth Stephen (Tas) b Jan. 5, 1947 Hobart (Tas)

* Thomson, Nathaniel Frampton Davis (NSW) b May 29, 1839 Surry Hills (NSW) d Sept. 2, 1896 Burwood (NSW)

Thorn, Frank Leslie Oliver (Vic) b Aug. 16, 1912 St Arnaud (Vic) d Feb. 11, 1942 Gasmata (New Britain) in action

Thornely, Dominic John (NSW) b Oct. 1, 1978 Albury (NSW)

Thornton, Barry Thomas (WAust) b June 3, 1941 South Perth (WAust)

Thornton, John (Vic) b Jan. 16, 1835 Huddersfield, Yorkshire (England) d Dec. 15, 1919 Camperdown (Vic)

Thorp, Callum David (WAust) b Feb. 11, 1975 Mount Lawley (WAust)

Thorpe, Henry (Combined XI) b June 15, 1862 Parramatta (NSW) d April 18, 1937 Artarmon (NSW)

Thorpe, Linsley James (Qld) b Feb. 15, 1923 Alpha (Qld)

Thurgarland, Wilfred John (SAust) b March 11, 1892 Queenstown (SAust) d July 12, 1974 Campbelltown (SAust)

* Thurlow, Hugh Morley (Qld) b Jan. 10, 1903 Townsville (Qld) d Dec. 3, 1975 Rosalie (Qld)

Thwaites, Colin Geoffrey (Vic) b Jan. 23, 1955 Lang Lang (Vic)

Thwaites, Thomas Edwin (Qld) b July 1, 1910 Nindooinbah (Qld) d May 24, 2000 Beaudesert (Qld)

Tilyard, Gregory Almeria Sydney (Tas) b March 19, 1932 Sandford (Tas)

Timbury, Fredrick Richard Vaughan (Qld) b July 12, 1885 Gladstone (Qld) d April 14, 1945 Sydney (NSW)

Tindall, Edwin (NSW) b March 31, 1851 Liverpool (NSW) d Jan. 16, 1926 Marrickville (NSW)

Tobin, Bertrandt Joseph (SAust) b Nov. 11, 1910 North Adelaide (SAust) d Oct. 19, 1969 Adelaide (SAust)

Tobin, William Andrew (Vic) b June 7, 1859 Kensington, London, Middlesex (England) d Feb. 17, 1904 South Melbourne (Vic)

Toby, Frederick James (NSW) b Dec. 9, 1888 Redfern (NSW) d c. 1963 death details unknown

Tolhurst, Edward Keith (Vic) b Oct. 29, 1895 St Kilda (Vic) d May 24, 1982 East Prahran (Vic)

Tooher, John Andrew (NSW) b Nov. 18, 1846 Sydney (NSW) d May 23, 1941 Neutral Bay (NSW)

* Toohey, Peter Michael (NSW) b April 20, 1954 Blayney (NSW)

Tooley, Mark Victor (Qld) b April 29, 1965 Toowoomba (Qld)

Toovey, Ernest Albert (Qld) b May 16, 1922 Warwick (Qld)

* Toshack, Ernest Raymond Herbert (NSW) b Dec. 8, 1914 Cobar (NSW) d May 11, 2003 Bobbin Head (NSW)

Tovey, Edward Richard (Qld) b Dec. 25, 1930 Kings Cross (NSW) d May 31, 2002 St Leonard's (NSW)

Townley, Reginald Colin (Tas) b April 15, 1904 Hobart (Tas) d May 3, 1982 Hobart (Tas)

Townsend, Richard James Bruce (SAust) b Aug. 12, 1886 Mt Torrens (SAust) d Jan. 17, 1960 Waikerie (SAust)

Tozer, Claude John (NSW) b Sept. 27, 1890 Sydney (NSW) d Dec. 21, 1920 Lindfield (NSW)

Tozer, George Bruce (Vic) b June 27, 1926 Hopetoun (Vic)

Trapp, Vincent Burney (Vic) b Jan. 26, 1861 Prahran (Vic) d Oct. 21, 1929 Armadale (Vic)

* Travers, Joseph Patrick Francis (SAust) b Jan. 10, 1871 Adelaide (SAust) d Sept. 15, 1942 Adelaide (SAust)

Traves, Roger Norman (Qld) b Oct. 15, 1961 Cairns (Qld)

Treanor, John Cassimar (NSW) b Aug. 17, 1922 Darlinghurst (NSW) d Nov. 7, 1993 East Ballina (NSW)

Trebilcock, Arthur Joseph (Tas) b Dec. 13, 1907 Zeehan (Tas) d May 2, 1972 Hobart (Tas)

Tregoning, Jack (SAust) b June 13, 1919 West Adelaide (SAust) d June 26, 1989 North Adelaide (SAust)

Trembath, Thomas James (Vic) b Jan. 16, 1912 Moonta (SAust) d April 2, 1978 West Brunswick (Vic)

Trenerry, Edwin (NSW) b Feb. 24, 1897 Queanbeyan (NSW) d July 8, 1983 Woollahra (NSW)

Trenerry, William Leo (NSW) b Nov. 29, 1892 Queanbeyan (NSW) d Sept. 4, 1975 Mosman (NSW)

Trethewey, Peter Grant (SAust & Qld) b May 12, 1935 Croydon (SAust)

* Tribe, George Edward (Vic) b Oct. 4, 1920 Footscray (Vic)

Triffitt, Arthur James (Tas) b March 17, 1914 Branxholm (Tas) d March 12, 1973 Cuckoo (Tas)

Trimble, Glenn Samuel (Qld) b Jan. 1, 1963 Herston (Qld)

Trimble, Samuel Christy (Qld) b Aug. 16, 1934 Lismore (NSW)

Tringrove, James (Tas) b Nov. 25, 1907 Blackmans Bay (Tas) d Sept. 11, 1979 Blackmans Bay (Tas)

Trinnick, James (Vic) b Dec. 13, 1853 Kingsbridge, Devon (England) d July 12, 1928 Northcote (Vic)

**Trott, Albert Edwin (Vic) b Feb. 6, 1873 Collingwood (Vic) d July 30, 1914 Willesden Green, London (England)

* Trott, George Henry Stephens (Vic) b Aug. 5, 1866 Collingwood (Vic) d Nov. 10, 1917 South Melbourne (Vic)

Trowse, Dean Frederick (SAust) b Oct. 18, 1931 Rose Park (SAust)

Trueman, Geoffrey Stanley (NSW) b Jan. 7, 1926 Double Bay (NSW) d June 28, 1981 Sydney (NSW)

Truman, Frederick George (Vic) b Dec. 6, 1886 Carlton (Vic) d June 17, 1955 Brighton (Vic)

* Trumble, Hugh (Vic) b May 12, 1867 Abbotsford (Vic) d Aug. 14, 1938 Hawthorn (Vic)

* Trumble, John William (Vic) b Sept. 16, 1863 Collingwood (Vic) d Aug. 17, 1944 Brighton (Vic)

Trumper, Victor (NSW) b Oct. 7, 1913 Chatswood (NSW) d Aug. 31, 1981 Sydney (NSW)

* Trumper, Victor Thomas (NSW) b Nov. 2, 1877 Sydney (NSW) d June 28, 1915 Darlinghurst (NSW)

Truscott, William John (WAust) b Oct. 9, 1886 Lithgow (NSW) d June 20, 1966 Bayswater (WAust)

Tubb, Shannon Benjamin (Tas) b May 11, 1980 Bracknell (Tas)

Tucker, Adrian Edward (NSW) b Sept. 19, 1969 Ryde (NSW)

Tucker, Rodney James (NSW & Tas) b Aug. 28, 1964 Auburn (NSW)

Tuckwell, Bertie Joseph (Vic) b Oct. 6, 1882 Carlton (Vic) d Jan. 2, 1943 Wellington (New Zealand)

Tumilty, Leonard Ross (Tas) b June 12, 1884 Launceston (Tas) d March 27, 1962 Launceston (Tas)

Tunks, William (NSW) b April 8, 1816 Castlereagh (NSW) d April 12, 1883 St Leonards (NSW)

* Turner, Alan (NSW) b July 23, 1950 Camperdown (NSW)

* Turner, Charles Thomas Byass (NSW) b Nov. 16, 1862 Bathurst (NSW) d Jan. 1, 1944 Manly (NSW)

Turner, Dale Andrew (NSW) b Jan. 30, 1974 Bankstown (NSW)

Turner, Edward (Vic) b Aug. 8, 1858 Northcote (Vic) d Jan. 26, 1893 Prahran (Vic)

Turner, J. B. (Vic) birth and death details unknown

Turner, Thomas (SAust & Vic) b March 7, 1865 Nuriootpa (SAust) d Oct. 27, 1936 Prospect (SAust)

Turner, Wilfred Herbert (Vic) b July 6, 1921 Woodvale near Bendigo (Vic) d Feb. 24, 2002 Bendigo (Vic)

Tuttle, Roy Thomas (Vic) b Sept. 11, 1920 Carlton (Vic) d c. 1997 Canberra (ACT)

Tweeddale, Ernest Richard (NSW) b Aug. 23, 1895 Newtown (NSW) d April 28, 1956 Dover Heights (NSW)

Twible, Paul William (Qld) b Dec. 14, 1957 Herston (Qld)

Twopenny (Murrumgunarriman) (NSW) b c. 1845 Bathurst (NSW) d March 12, 1883 West Maitland (NSW)

Van Deinsen, Brett Paul (NSW) b Dec. 28, 1977 Bankstown (NSW)

Varis, Leslie (WAust) b May 13, 1947 Kalgoorlie (WAust)

Vaughan, Frederick (Vic) b Nov. 8, 1876 Croydon, Surrey (England) d Sept. 30, 1926 Elsternwick (Vic)

Vaughan, Jeffrey Mark (SAust) b March 26, 1974 Blacktown (NSW)

Vaughan, Leonard J. (NSW) b March 16, 1908 Waverley (NSW) d c. 1960 full death details unknown

Vaughan, Robert (NSW) b c. 1834 d July 12, 1865 at sea between Australia and New Zealand

Vaughton, Roland William (SAust) b May 5, 1914 Ardrossan (SAust) d Jan. 5, 1979 Adelaide (SAust)

Vautin, Charles Edwin (Tas) b June 24, 1867 Sorell (Tas) d Dec. 11, 1942 Moonah (Tas)

Vautin, Douglas Maynard (Tas) b July 26, 1896 Hobart (Tas) d Jan. 11, 1976 Mt Martha (Vic)

Vautin, George James Phillips (Tas & Vic) b April 23, 1869 Orielton (Tas) d Jan. 9, 1949 West Preston (Vic)

Vawser, Bruce Forbes (Vic) b June 17, 1929 Mitcham (Vic) d May 1, 2004 Melbourne (Vic)

* Veivers, Thomas Robert (Qld) b April 6, 1937 Beenleigh (Qld)

* Veletta, Michael Robert John (WAust) b Oct. 30, 1963 Subiaco (WAust)

Vernon, Edward Henry George (Vic) b Oct. 11, 1911 Northcote (Vic) d May 8, 1968 Kew (Vic)

Vernon, Leslie Phillip (Vic) b May 29, 1880 Melbourne (Vic) d May 11, 1957 Ashwood (Vic)

Vernon, Murray Trevor (WAust) b Feb. 9, 1937 Kondinin (WAust)

Vidler, Robert Trevor (NSW) b Feb. 5, 1957 Cronulla (NSW)

Vimpani, Graeme Ronald (Vic) b Jan. 27, 1972 Herston (Qld)

Vincent, Brian Alfred (SAust) b Feb. 16, 1960 Unley (SAust)

Vincent, Norman Hill (Tas) b Nov. 10, 1883 Sunderland, Durham (England) d Feb. 12, 1958 Prahran (Vic)

Vincent, Russell George (SAust) b March 25, 1954 Jamestown (SAust)

Vint, William (Vic) b June 30, 1851 Belfast (Ireland) d March 28, 1897 Helens Bay (Ireland)

Voges, Adam Charles (WAust) b Oct. 4, 1979 Perth (WAust)

Waddy, Edgar Lloyd (NSW) b Dec. 3, 1879 Morpeth (NSW) d Aug. 2, 1963 Collaroy (NSW)

Waddy, Ernest Frederick (NSW) b Oct. 5, 1880 Morpeth (NSW) d Sept. 23, 1958 Evesham, Worcestershire (England)

Wade, Frank Hainsworth (NSW) b Sept. 1, 1871 Farsley, Yorkshire (England) d Oct. 4, 1940 Lindfield (NSW)

Wainwright, Edmund George Chalwin (SAust) b May 18, 1903 North Adelaide (SAust) d Aug. 8, 1995 North Geelong (Vic)

* Waite, Mervyn George (SAust) b Jan. 7, 1911 Kent Town (SAust) d Dec. 16, 1985 Georgetown (SAust)

Waldron, Alfred Edward (SAust) b Feb. 26, 1857 Moorooduc (Vic) d June 7, 1929 Adelaide (SAust)

Wales, Isaac (NSW) b Jan. 31, 1865 Auckland Park, near Bishop Auckland, Durham (England) d Jan. 11, 1949 death place unknown

Walford, Sydney Rundle (NSW) b Nov. 19, 1857 Darlinghurst (NSW) d July 2, 1949 Woollahra (NSW)

Walker, Alan Keith (NSW) b Oct. 4, 1925 Manly (NSW)

Walker, Charles William (SAust) b Feb. 19, 1909 Brompton Park (SAust) d Dec. 18, 1942 in action over Soltau (Germany)

Walker, Darren Kenneth (Vic) b June 8, 1966 Bendigo (Vic)

Walker, Jeffrey Milton (Qld) b Sept. 11, 1960 Beaudesert (Qld)

Walker, Kenneth Victor John (Vic) b June 25, 1941 Melbourne (Vic)

* Walker, Maxwell Henry Norman (Vic) b Sept. 12, 1948 West Hobart (Tas)

Walker, Ronald Radford (Vic) b Jan. 1, 1926 Collingwood (Vic)

Walker, William Holden (Tas) b Dec. 16, 1835 Islington, London (England) d June 14, 1886 Hobart (Tas)

Walkerden, Henry Ernest (WAust) b Nov. 20, 1885 Brunswick (Vic) d May 16, 1966 Richmond (Vic)

Walkley, Edwin (SAust) b May 10, 1876 Wallaroo (SAust) d April 18, 1950 Randwick (NSW)

Wall, John Craik Lyall Sydney (NSW) b Oct. 25, 1891 Balmain (NSW) d June 9, 1969 West Pymble (NSW)

* Wall, Thomas Welbourn (SAust) b May 13, 1904 Semaphore (SAust) d March 26, 1981 Adelaide (SAust)

Wallace, Percival Henry (Vic) b Oct. 6, 1891 Bendigo (Vic) d Oct. 3, 1959 Glen Iris (Vic)

Wallace, Richard Miscamble (Tas) b March 22, 1934 Melbourne (Vic)

Walmsley, Walter Thomas (NSW, Tas & Qld) b March 16, 1916 Homebush (NSW) d Feb. 25, 1978 Hamilton (New Zealand)

Walsh, James Michael (Tas) b May 28, 1913 Launceston (Tas) d July 5, 1986 Launceston (Tas)

Walsh, John Edward (NSW) b Dec. 4, 1912 Walcha (NSW) d May 20, 1980 Wallsend (NSW)

Walsh, Lawrence Stanley (SAust) b Feb. 8, 1902 North Adelaide (SAust) d Jan. 12, 1976 St Georges (SAust)

Walsh, Mark Jason (WAust) b April 28, 1972 Townsville (Qld)

Walsh, Norman Arthur (SAust) b Feb. 8, 1902 North Adelaide (SAust) d Dec. 7, 1969 Adelaide (SAust)

Walshe, John Hamilton (Tas) b c. 1841 (England) d April 17, 1893 Sandy Bay (Tas)

* Walters, Francis Henry (Vic & NSW) b Feb. 9, 1860 Richmond (Vic) d June 1, 1922 at sea near Bombay

* Walters, Kevin Douglas (NSW) b Dec. 21, 1945 Dungog (NSW)

Walters, Maxwell John (Qld) b July 28, 1953 Bundaberg (Qld)

Walton, Douglas John (Tas) b April 9, 1927 New Norfolk (Tas) d Feb. 18, 2001 Glenorchy (Tas)

Ward, Edward Wolstenholme (NSW) b Aug. 17, 1823 Calcutta (India) d Feb. 5, 1890 Cannes (France)

* Ward, Francis Anthony (SAust) b Feb. 23, 1906 Leichhardt (NSW) d May 25, 1974 Brooklyn (NSW)

Ward, Harry Alexander (Tas) b Dec. 8, 1924 Hobart (Tas) d Dec. 8, 1993 Sandy Bay (Tas)

Ward, John Charles (Vic) b Nov. 15, 1946 Melbourne (Vic)

Ward, Leonard Keith (Tas) b Feb. 17, 1879 South Kingston (SAust) d Sept. 30, 1964 Heathpool (SAust)

Ward, Maxwell John (NSW) b Feb. 3, 1907 Randwick (NSW) d Oct. 24, 1983 New Lambton Heights (NSW)

Ward, Ronald Egbert (Tas) b May 7, 1905 Adelaide (SAust) d Nov. 8, 2000 Launceston (Tas)

Ward, William George (Tas) b May 15, 1863 West Hobart (Tas) d June 22, 1948 East Malvern (Vic)

Warden, Lester Griffith (Qld) b April 14, 1940 Wooloowin (Qld) d April 3, 1989 Greenslopes (Qld)

Wardill, Benjamin Johnson (Vic) b Oct. 15, 1842 Everton, Lancashire (England) d Oct. 15, 1917 Sandringham (Vic)

Wardill, Richard Wilson (Vic) b Nov. 3, 1840 Everton, Lancashire (England) d Aug. 17, 1873 Melbourne (Vic)

Wardlaw, Douglas McLaren Searl (Tas) b July 19, 1904 Hobart (Tas) d May 20, 1968 St Marys (Tas)

Wardlaw, Robert Bruce Searl (Tas) b Jan. 9, 1914 Hobart (Tas) d Sept. 12, 1986 Launceston (Tas)

Ware, Joseph Maitland (Tas) b Sept. 8, 1822 London (England) d Sept. 21, 1868 Lausanne (Switzerland)

Warne, Frank Belmont (Vic) b Oct. 3, 1906 North Carlton (Vic) d May 29, 1994 Edenvale (South Africa)

* Warne, Shane Keith (Vic) b Sept. 13, 1969 Ferntree Gully (Vic)

Warne, Tom Summerhayes (Vic) b Jan. 13, 1870 North Melbourne (Vic) d July 7, 1944 Carlton (Vic)

Warr, Gerald Gerrard (Qld) b May 17, 1939 Casino (NSW)

Warren, Peter Charles (Tas) b May 13, 1953 Launceston (Tas)

Wasley, Mark Andrew (WAust & Tas) b Oct. 6, 1965 Subiaco (WAust)

Waterman, Leonard William (Qld) b Feb. 18, 1892 Brisbane (Qld) d Jan. 1, 1952 Kangaroo Point (Qld)

Waters, Glen Wayne (Tas) b May 3, 1943 Launceston (Tas)

Waters, Robert William (SAust) b April 29, 1874 Gravesend, Kent (England) d Feb. 20, 1912 Woodville (SAust)

Wates, Darren Jude (WAust) b July 2, 1977 Subiaco (WAust)

* Watkins, John Russell (NSW) b April 16, 1943 Hamilton (NSW)

Watling, Walter Herbert (SAust) b March 13, 1864 Unley (SAust) d Dec. 19, 1928 Randfontein (South Africa)

Watmuff, Frederick John (Vic) b Sept. 16, 1915 St Kilda (Vic) d Aug. 10, 1972 Castlemaine (Vic)

Watsford, Goulburn (SAust) b July 1, 1859 Goulburn (NSW) d May 16, 1951 Melbourne (Vic)

Watson, Alfred Edward (Tas) b Aug. 31, 1888 Carlton (Vic) d May 6, 1957 South Melbourne (Vic)

Watson, Andrew Simon (SAust) b Oct. 14, 1955 Woomera (SAust)

Watson, Bertie Francis (NSW) b March 13, 1898 Maclean (NSW) d Nov. 18, 1987 Canberra (ACT)

* Watson, Graeme Donald (Vic, WAust & NSW) b March 8, 1945 Kew (Vic)

Watson, Gregory George (NSW & WAust) b Jan. 29, 1955 Gulgong (NSW)

Watson, John Wentworth (Tas) b 1828 birth day and month unknown Sorell (Tas) d June 26, 1920 Scottsdale (Tas)

Watson, Roy Clarence William (WAust) b June 21, 1933 Fremantle (WAust)

Watson, Shane Robert (Tas) b June 17, 1981 Ipswich (Qld)

Watson, William (NSW) b Nov. 10, 1881 Lambton (NSW) d Feb. 12, 1926 North Sydney (NSW)

* Watson, William James (NSW) b Jan. 31, 1931 Randwick (NSW)

Watt, Arthur David (WAust) b Nov. 24, 1913 Edinburgh (Scotland)

Watt, Arthur Kenneth Elwyn (Tas) b Dec. 12, 1891 Hobart (Tas) d Oct. 8, 1973 Hobart (Tas)

Watt, Donald (Qld) b March 15, 1920 Southport (Qld)

Watt, John (Tas) b Feb. 16, 1858 Hobart (Tas) d Nov. 14, 1918 Glebe (Tas)

Watt, John Charles (Tas) b July 6, 1884 Hobart (Tas) d Aug. 4, 1961 Hobart (Tas)

Watters, John Charles (Vic) b Oct. 6, 1924 Footscray (Vic)

Watts, Colin Arthur (SAust) b Jan. 9, 1921 St Peters (SAust)

Watts, Gary Maxwell (Vic) b Oct. 22, 1958 Dunolly (Vic)

Waugh, Dean Parma (NSW) b Feb. 3, 1969 Campsie (NSW)

* Waugh, Mark Edward (NSW) b June 2, 1965 Canterbury (NSW)

Waugh, Russell Frederick (NSW & WAust) b Sept. 29, 1941 Sydney (NSW)

* Waugh, Stephen Rodger (NSW) b June 2, 1965 Canterbury (NSW)

Waye, Libby Sibly (SAust) b Jan. 14, 1885 Willunga (SAust) d June 10, 1951 Frewville (SAust)

Wearne, William Stewart (NSW) b Jan. 18, 1857 Campbelltown (NSW) d Jan. 28, 1929 Kalk Bay (South Africa)

Webb, Berrowes Littleton (Qld) b April 15, 1915 Brisbane (Qld) d Feb. 7, 1983 Greenslopes (Qld)

Webb, Colin Ralph (SAust) b Jan. 20, 1926 North Adelaide (SAust)

Webb, Kenneth Norman (SAust) b Feb. 27, 1921 Unley (SAust) d March 7, 1994 Daw Park (SAust)

Webber, Darren Scott (SAust) b Aug. 18, 1971 Burnside (SAust)

Webster, Alexander Miles Clifton (WAust) b Nov. 25, 1908 East Fremantle (WAust) d March 28, 1964 Shenton Park (WAust)

Webster, Harold Wynne (SAust) b Feb. 17, 1887 Randwick (NSW) d Oct. 7, 1949 Randwick (NSW)

Webster, Stuart Edward (NSW) b June 11, 1946 Orange (NSW)

Wedgwood, Walter Bernard (Vic) b Oct. 23, 1912 Clifton Hill (Vic) d Dec. 2, 1977 Mornington (Vic)

Weekley, Leonard Rex (SAust) b July 21, 1922 Port Wakefield (SAust)

Weeks, Albert Edmund (SAust) b July 23, 1864 Bowden (SAust) d April 21, 1948 Hollywood (WAust)

Weir, Alexander John (SAust) b March 5, 1921 Largs Bay (SAust)

Weir, Harold Stanley (Qld) b April 23, 1904 Croydon Junction (Qld) d June 11, 2002 Maryborough (Qld)

Welch, Charles William (Vic) b June 9, 1907 birthplace unknown d April 11, 1983 Melbourne (Vic)

* Wellham, Dirk Macdonald (NSW, Tas & Qld) b March 13, 1959 Marrickville (NSW)

Wellham, Walter Arthur (NSW) b Sept. 17, 1932 Belmont (NSW)

Wellington, Clement Wellesley (WAust) b Aug. 17, 1880 Yongala (SAust) d July 26, 1956 Underdale (SAust)

Wellington, Stephen Leslie (Tas) b July 4, 1899 Beaconsfield (Tas) d June 11, 1974 Scotts Head (NSW)

Wells, Arthur Phillip (NSW) b Sept. 4, 1900 Paddington (NSW) d Dec. 27, 1964 South Coogee (NSW)

**Wessels, Kepler Christoffel (Qld) b Sept. 14, 1957 Bloemfontein, Orange Free State (South Africa)

West, Neville Leonard (Vic) b Nov. 9, 1933 Marysville (Vic) d Aug. 8, 1987 Belrose (NSW)

Westaway, Colin Edward (Qld) b Aug. 27, 1936 Indooroopilly (Qld)

Westbrook, Keith Raymond (Tas) b May 28, 1887 Scottsdale (Tas) d Jan. 20, 1982 Burnie (Tas)

Westbrook, Norman Russell (Tas) b June 25, 1868 Launceston (Tas) d May 29, 1931 Launceston (Tas)

Westbrook, Roy Austin (Tas) b Jan. 3, 1889 Ringarooma (Tas) d Aug. 7, 1961 Wellington (New Zealand)

Westbrook, Thomas (Tas) b 1827 birth day and month unknown Hobart (Tas) d Sept. 13, 1911 Sandy Bay (Tas)

Westbrook, Walter Horatio (Tas) b Nov. 21, 1827 Hobart (Tas) d Jan. 3, 1897 Launceston (Tas)

Whalley, John (Qld) b Nov. 27, 1872 Spring Hill (Qld) d Oct. 29, 1925 Brisbane (Qld)

* Whatmore, Davenell Frederick (Vic) b March 16, 1954 Colombo (Ceylon)

Whiddon, Henry (NSW) b Nov. 20, 1878 Sydney (NSW) d Dec. 19, 1935 Manly (NSW)

White, Alfred Becher Stewart (NSW) b Oct. 4, 1879 Mudgee (NSW) d Dec. 15, 1962 Karuah (NSW)

White, Alfred Henry Ebsworth (NSW) b Oct. 18, 1901 Scone (NSW) d March 6, 1964 Darling Point (NSW)

White, Cameron Leon (Vic) b Aug. 18, 1983 Bairnsdale (Vic)

* White, Craig (Vic) b Dec. 16, 1969 Morley, Yorkshire (England)

White, Edward Clive Stewart (NSW) b April 17, 1913 Mosman (NSW) d Oct. 10, 1999 Hornsby (NSW)

Whiteside, Warren Gregory (Vic) b Nov. 1, 1961 Box Hill (Vic)

Whitesides, Thomas (Tas) b 1836 birth day and month unknown Hobart (Tas) d Sept. 24, 1919 Hobart (Tas)

Whitfield, Henry Edward (SAust) b Feb. 25, 1903 Kent Town (SAust) d Jan. 14, 1937 Royston Park (SAust)

Whitfield, Stephen Bourke John (NSW) b Nov. 21, 1950 Ryde (NSW)

Whitford, Graham Sydney (Vic) b July 25, 1938 Ascot Vale (Vic)

Whiting, Albert William Harley (NSW) b May 31, 1866 Darlinghurst (NSW) death details unknown

Whitington, Richard Smallpeice (SAust) b June 30, 1912 Unley Park (SAust) d March 13, 1984 Sydney (NSW)

Whitlow, Edward Hardmond (Vic) b c. 1832 Manchester, Lancashire (England) d Nov. 29, 1870 South Melbourne (Vic)

Whitney, Gary Reginald (Tas) b March 19, 1951 Campbell Town (Tas)

* Whitney, Michael Roy (NSW) b Feb. 24, 1959 Surry Hills (NSW)

Whitting, William Charles (NSW) b July 9, 1884 Drummoyne (NSW) d Oct. 26, 1936 Bellevue Hill (NSW)

* Whitty, William James (NSW & SAust) b Aug. 15, 1886 Sydney (NSW) d Jan. 30, 1974 Tantanoola (SAust)

Whyte, Graham Keith (Qld) b March 29, 1952 Herston (Qld)

* Wiener, Julien Mark (Vic) b May 1, 1955 Melbourne (Vic)

Wigley, Robert Strangways (SAust) b March 15, 1864 Windsor (Vic) d April 20, 1926 Glenelg (SAust)

Wigney, Bradley Neil (SAust) b June 30, 1965 Leongatha (Vic)

Wilberforce, Robert James (WAust) b July 31, 1910 Subiaco (WAust) d Oct. 10, 1987 Woodlands (WAust)

Wildsmith, Andrew (Vic) b Jan. 9, 1958 East Melbourne (Vic)

Wildsmith, John (Vic) b July 1, 1939 Fitzroy (Vic)

Wilkes, Alfred Ernest (Tas) b Nov. 15, 1922 Launceston (Tas) d Aug. 27, 1998 Evandale (Tas)

Wilkie, Daniel (Vic) b Dec. 1, 1843 Melbourne (Vic) d May 11, 1917 St Kilda (Vic)

Wilkin, John Winstanley Symons (SAust) b April 28, 1924 North Adelaide (SAust)

Wilkins, Roy (Tas) b April 18, 1892 North Hobart (Tas) d July 17, 1965 Hobart (Tas)

Wilkinson, Alfred (SAust) b Jan. 2, 1863 Kooringa (SAust) d Jan. 22, 1922 Lower Mitcham (SAust)

Wilkinson, James Scott (Tas) b Dec. 4, 1951 Hobart (Tas)

Wilkinson, Robert B. (Vic) birth and death details unknown

Wilkinson, William Archer (Vic) b Sept. 1, 1899 Clifton Hill (Vic) d May 5, 1974 Mildura (Vic)

Willcocks, Robert James (Qld) b Dec. 23, 1891 Brisbane (Qld) d March 21, 1965 Toowoomba (Qld)

* Williams, Bradley Andrew (Vic & WAust) b Nov. 20, 1974 Frankston (Vic)

Williams, Brett Douglas (SAust) b Dec. 15, 1967 Camden (NSW)

Williams, Douglas Samuel Thomas (WAust) b July 3, 1919 Elwood (Vic)

Williams, Edward Alexander (Vic) b Sept. 18, 1915 North Fitzroy (Vic)

Williams, Luke (SAust) b Dec. 24, 1979 Henley Beach (SAust)

* Williams, Neil Fitzgerald (Tas) b July 2, 1962 Hope Well (St Vincent)

Williams, Norman Leonard (SAust) b Sept. 23, 1899 Exeter (SAust) d May 31, 1947 Semaphore (SAust)

Williams, Owen Charles (Vic) b June 20, 1847 Impression Bay (Tas) d Nov. 18, 1917 Kandy (Ceylon)

Williams, Peter David (Vic) b Feb. 9, 1942 Brighton (Vic)

Williams, Robert Graham (SAust) b April 4, 1911 St Peters (SAust) d Aug. 31, 1978 Medindie (SAust)

Williams, Scott Bradley (Qld) b Feb. 1, 1971 Herston (Qld)

Williams, Vaughan Morgan (NSW) b Dec. 19, 1977 Blaxland (NSW)

Williamson, Cameron John (SAust) b March 26, 1970 Ryde (NSW)

Willis, Carl Bleackley (Vic) b March 23, 1893 Daylesford (Vic) d May 12, 1930 Berrigan (NSW)

Wills, Thomas Wentworth (Vic) b Dec. 19, 1835 Molonglo Plains (NSW) d May 2, 1880 Heidelberg (Vic)

Willsmore, Hurtle Binks (SAust) b Dec. 26, 1889 Beverley (SAust) d Sept. 17, 1985 Kings Park (SAust)

Wilson, Charles Geldart (Vic) b Jan. 9, 1869 Carngham (Vic) d June 28, 1952 Rosenerth (New Zealand)

Wilson, George Lindsay (Vic) b April 27, 1868 Collingwood (Vic) d March 9, 1920 St Kilda (Vic)

Wilson, Gregory James (Tas) b Jan. 4, 1958 Launceston (Tas)

Wilson, Henry (Tas) b March 31, 1865 Westbury (Tas) d Aug. 18, 1914 Sydney (NSW)

Wilson, Horace (WAust) b June 28, 1864 Kadina (SAust) d May 15, 1923 West Perth (WAust)

Wilson, John Thomas (Tas) b Nov. 27, 1868 Westbury (Tas) d July 24, 1906 Launceston (Tas)

Wilson, John Warwick (NSW) b Sept. 1, 1947 Paddington (NSW)

* Wilson, John William (Vic & SAust) b Aug. 20, 1921 Albert Park (Vic) d Oct. 13, 1985 Bayswater (Vic)

Wilson, Joseph Cameron (NSW) b Feb. 11, 1869 Braidwood (NSW) d Aug. 26, 1938 Wollongong (NSW)

* Wilson, Paul (SAust & WAust) b Jan. 12, 1972 Newcastle (NSW)

Wilson, Richard (Qld) b Jan. 14, 1869 Paddington (NSW) d Oct. 8, 1937 Parramatta (NSW)

Wilson, Stanley Vincent (WAust & SAust) b Sept. 23, 1948 Midland (WAust)

Wilson, William John (Vic) b c. 1912 Mildura (Vic)

Wilson, William Young (Vic) b Dec. 13, 1909 Essendon (Vic) d Sept. 30, 1976 Ascot Vale (Vic)

Windsor, Edward Arthur Cartwright (Tas) b March 9, 1869 Launceston (Tas) d Dec. 23, 1953 Launceston (Tas)

Wingrove, Francis William (Combined XI) b April 20, 1863 Eltham (Vic) d May 27, 1892 Rupanyup (Vic)

Winning, Charles Samuel (AIF) b July 17, 1889 Paddington (NSW) d April 20, 1967 Newport (NSW)

Winser, Cyril Legh (SAust) b Nov. 27, 1884 High Legh, Staffordshire (England) d Dec. 20, 1983 Barwon Heads (Vic)

Winter, Graham John (SAust) b Nov. 6, 1955 Medindie (SAust)

Wise, Allan Brett (Vic) b Feb. 24, 1979 Melbourne (Vic)

Wishart, Peter William (WAust) b June 18, 1937 Perth (WAust)

Wishart, Warren Keith (WAust) b Feb. 17, 1971 Subiaco (WAust)

Wolfe, Malcolm Frederick (WAust) b July 28, 1952 Gnowangerup (WAust)

Wood, Cecil Clunas (Tas) b April 8, 1896 Erin Bay (Tas) death details unknown

* Wood, Graeme Malcolm (WAust) b Nov. 6, 1956 East Fremantle (WAust)

Wood, Hartley Lionel (SAust) b April 5, 1930 Flinders Park (SAust) d Dec. 16, 1988 Elizabeth Vale (SAust)

Wood, John Robert (NSW) b April 11, 1865 Newcastle (NSW) d Feb. 14, 1928 Putney, London (England)

Wood, Percy Barnes (WAust) b Dec. 22, 1901 Wellington (New Zealand) d June 9, 1941 Litani River (Syria) in action

* Wood, Reginald (Vic) b March 7, 1860 Woodchurch, Cheshire (England) d Jan. 6, 1915 Manly (NSW)

Wood, William (NSW) b Nov. 11, 1849 Forglen, Banffshire (Scotland) d April 12, 1924 Marrickville (NSW)

Woodbury, William Joseph George (Vic) b Dec. 6, 1892 Balmain (NSW) d Aug. 31, 1983 Moe (Vic)

* Woodcock, Ashley James (SAust) b Feb. 27, 1947 Adelaide (SAust)

Woodford, John Robert Herbert (Vic & SAust) b June 23, 1881 Camberwell (Vic) d May 1, 1949 North Fitzroy (Vic)

* Woodfull, William Maldon (Vic) b Aug. 22, 1897 Maldon (Vic) d Aug. 11, 1965 Tweed Heads (NSW)

Woodhead, Derek John (WAust) b Sept. 7, 1934 Subiaco (WAust)

Woods, Julian Augustus (Tas) b Sept. 4, 1887 Oatlands (Tas) d Oct. 11, 1975 Lindisfarne (Tas)

**Woods, Samuel Moses James (Australia) b April 13, 1867 Ashfield (NSW) d April 30, 1931 Taunton, Somerset (England)

Woolcock, Arthur Henry (SAust) b June 10, 1887 Port Pirie (SAust) d June 29, 1975 Adelaide (SAust)

Woolf, Louis Sydney (Vic) b July 28, 1855 Collingwood (Vic) d July 6, 1942 Richmond (Vic)

Woolley, Hastings Talbot (Tas) b June 6, 1884 Melbourne (Vic) d Feb. 3, 1946 Sydney (NSW)

* Woolley, Roger Douglas (Tas) b Sept. 16, 1954 Hobart (Tas)

Woolmer, Gordon Rae (NSW) b Feb. 24, 1917 Hamilton (NSW) d July 31, 1999 Fairfield (NSW)

Wootton, John Richard (Vic) b Jan. 18, 1906 Rushworth (Vic) d July 18, 1986 death place unknown

Wootton, Stanley Eli (Vic) b April 28, 1895 South Yarra (Vic) d March 20, 1962 Heidelberg (Vic)

Wordsworth, Charles William (NSW) b Sept. 9, 1877 Rotherham, Yorkshire (England) d June 10, 1960 Redfern (NSW)

Workman, James Allen (Services) b March 17, 1917 Peterhead (SAust) d Dec. 23, 1970 Westminster, London (England)

* Worrall, John (Vic) b June 21, 1861 Chinamans Flat, Maryborough (Vic) d Nov. 17, 1937 Fairfield Park (Vic)

Worthington, Peter Colin (WAust) b July 12, 1979 Middle Swan (WAust)

Wray, Thomas Fawcett (Vic) b c. 1827 Cleasby, Yorkshire (England) d Sept. 6, 1877 Melbourne (Vic)

Wrigglesworth, Ian Alastair (Vic) b Nov. 29, 1967 Sale (Vic)

Wright, Albert William (SAust) b Sept. 24, 1875 Norwood (SAust) d Dec. 23, 1938 North Adelaide (SAust)

Wright, Bert Harold (Vic) b Dec. 2, 1926 Wonthaggi (Vic) d Nov. 20, 1994 Beaumaris (Vic)

Wright, Damien Geoffrey (Tas) b July 25, 1975 Casino (NSW)

Wright, Francis John (Vic) b March 13, 1874 Ballarat East (Vic) d Oct. 10, 1899 Ballarat East (Vic)

Wright, Gary John (SAust) b Nov. 9, 1970 Henley Beach (SAust)

Wright, Herbert Lovegrove (Vic) b April 13, 1870 Ballarat West (Vic) d March 19, 1950 West Melbourne (Vic)

* Wright, Kevin John (SAust & WAust) b Dec. 27, 1953 North Fremantle (WAust)

Wright, Robert Raymond (SAust) b Nov. 11, 1914 Marryatville (SAust) d Jan. 20, 1965 Springfield (SAust)

Wundke, Stephen Christopher (SAust) b July 2, 1961 North Adelaide (SAust)

Wyatt, Alan Edward (NSW) b April 4, 1935 Annandale (NSW)

Wyeth, Ezra Robert Harding (Qld) b March 13, 1910 Toowoomba (Qld) d Oct. 15, 1992 Northbridge, California (United States of America)

Wynne, Lester Alan (Vic) b Oct. 7, 1908 Carlton (Vic) d Nov. 29, 1980 Melbourne (Vic)

Yagmich, Dennis Brian (WAust & SAust) b Aug. 23, 1948 Victoria Park (WAust)

* Yallop, Graham Neil (Vic) b Oct. 7, 1952 Balwyn (Vic)

* Yardley, Bruce (WAust) b Sept. 5, 1947 Midland (WAust)

Yeates, George Walter Carrington (NSW) b May 5, 1918 Erskineville (NSW) d April 8, 1967 Kogarah Bay (NSW)

Yeates, Sydney Fergus Macrae (Qld) b Aug. 20, 1912 Toowoomba (Qld) d March 19, 1992 Auchenflower (Qld)

Yeomans, Frederick Caleb (Vic) b Nov. 11, 1888 Northcote (Vic) d Jan. 16, 1965 Brighton (Vic)

Youill, George Joseph (NSW) b Oct. 2, 1871 Sydney (NSW) d Dec. 21, 1936 Glebe (NSW)

Young, Allan Stanley (Qld) b July 7, 1920 Ipswich (Qld) d Dec. 23, 1974 Albion (Qld)

Young, Bradley Evan (SAust) b Feb. 23, 1973 Semaphore (SAust)

Young, Claye Michael (Tas) b Dec. 31, 1964 Hobart (Tas)

Young, George Albert (WAust) b Feb. 3, 1949 Caulfield (Vic)

Young, Jason Carl (NSW) b Feb. 17, 1971 Wagga Wagga (NSW)

Young, Peter William (Vic) b Dec. 31, 1961 Geelong (Vic)

* Young, Shaun (Tas) b June 13, 1970 Burnie (Tas)

* Younis Mohammad Ahmed (SAust) b Oct. 20, 1947 Jullundur (India)

Zachariah, Harry (Vic) b June 4, 1911 Stirling (SAust)

Zadow, Robert John (SAust) b Jan. 17, 1954 Mannun (SAust)

Zammit, Liam Aaron (NSW) b Jan. 27, 1981 Camden (NSW)

Zesers, Andris Karlis (SAust) b March 11, 1967 Medindie (SAust)

Ziebell, Keith Percy (Qld) b July 26, 1942 Rosewood (Qld)

Zimbulis, Anthony George (WAust) b Feb. 11, 1918 Perth (WAust) d May 17, 1963 Palm Beach (WAust)

* Zoehrer, Timothy Joseph (WAust) b Sept. 25, 1961 Armadale (WAust)

Zschorn, Paul William (SAust) b July 16, 1886 North Unley (SAust) d June 13, 1953 Glen Iris (Vic)

Births and Deaths of Other Cricketing Notables

The following list shows the births and deaths of people who have made a significant contribution to cricket in Australia but did not play first-class cricket for an Australian team. It includes umpires, administrators, curators, writers, coaches, managers and many more besides.

Abbott, Roy William *WACA curator 1951-81* b Nov. 14, 1915 d Sept. 25, 1993

Alcott, Errol Laurence *Physiotherapist* b Dec. 2, 1955

Allen, Joseph *ACB chairman 1913-18* b *c.* 1861 d Nov. 5, 1932

Argall, Philip *Test umpire* b Feb. 27, 1855 d April 3, 1912

Armstrong, Henry James *Test umpire* b not known d Mar. 23, 1945

Bailhache, Robin Carl *Test umpire* b May 4, 1937

Barbour, George Pitty *ACB chairman 1907-08* b Jan. 27, 1867 d Sept. 7, 1951

Barlow, Andrew Nicholas *Test umpire* b July 3, 1899 d July 13, 1961

Barnes, Alan Robert *ACB secretary 1960-81; NSWCA secretary 1950-76* b Sept. 16, 1916 d Mar. 14, 1989

Barton, Edmund *Cricket-loving prime minister, first-class umpire* b Jan. 18, 1849 d Jan. 7, 1920

Battersby, Dr Arthur Cameron "Cam" *QCA chairman 1993-2000* b Jan. 21, 1935.

Bennett, Frederick William Cecil *ACB chairman 1983-86* b Sept. 5, 1915 d Jan. 26, 1995

Borwick, George Eric *Test umpire* b Apr. 2, 1896 d Aug. 1, 1981

Bowden, Percy Kelly *NSWCA secretary 1894-1914* b Dec. 11, 1861 d Feb. 23, 1922

Brereton, Henry Evan *VCA secretary 1925-50* b June 13, 1887 d Dec. 31, 1950

Buggy, Edward Hugh *Journalist; coined the word "Bodyline"* b June 9, 1896 d June 17, 1974

Bunning, Charles Robert *WACA president 1963-80* b Mar. 1, 1905 d June 3, 1994

Burdett, Les Underwood *Adelaide Oval curator 1980-* b Jan. 11, 1951

Burge, Thomas John *Test team manager* b Sept. 23, 1903 d Jan. 7, 1957

Bushby, Charles Harold *ACB chairman 1919, 1925-26; NTCA chairman 1924-74; Test team manager* b Dec. 3, 1887 d Oct. 3, 1975

Butler, Keith *Journalist* b *c.* 1912 d May 29, 1990.

Callaway, Richard *Test umpire* b Aug. 2, 1860 d Mar. 19, 1935

Cameron, John Daniel "Jack" *Scorer* b Aug. 24, 1923

Cameron, John Laurence *Scorer* b Aug. 2, 1893 d Jan. 4, 1980

Casellas, Kenneth Francis John *Journalist* b Nov. 8, 1936.

Charlton, John Michael *Radio commentator* b May 1, 1927

Creswell, John *SACA secretary 1883-1909* b Dec. 8, 1858 d Mar. 24, 1909

Coady, P. *Test umpire* b not known d not known

Cocks, Arthur F. *Test umpire* b not known d not known

Cohen, Victor *Test team manager* b Aug. 5, 1851 d not known

Cole, Nicholas "Tom" *Test umpire* b July 12, 1844 d Jan. 27, 1924

Collins, John Richard *Test umpire* b Aug. 1, 1932

Cooper, George Stephen *Test umpire* b Mar. 1, 1907 d Dec. 29, 1980

Copeland, William John *Test umpire* b Aug. 16, 1929

Coward, Michael John *Journalist* b Aug. 2, 1946

Crafter, Anthony Ronald *Test umpire* b Dec. 5, 1940

Crockett, Robert Maxwell *Test umpire* b 1863 d Dec. 11, 1935

Crompton, Alan Barons *ACB chairman 1992-95; Test team manager* b Feb. 28, 1941

Cronin, Peter Michael *Test umpire* b Feb. 21, 1947

Curran, William Gregory *Test umpire* b not known d Dec. 21, 1921

Cush, Frank Maitland *ACB chairman 1955-57* b Aug. 10, 1893 d Nov. 1985

Davis, John Corbett *Journalist* b Apr. 11, 1868 d Feb. 16, 1941

Davis, Stephen James *Test umpire* b Apr. 9, 1952

Deare, Michael John *SACA chief executive 1996-* b Feb. 14, 1947

Dixon, Graham *Queensland Cricket chief executive 1997-* b Nov. 15, 1952

Dowling, William Joseph *ACB chairman 1957-60; VCA president 1963-73; Test team manager* b Sept. 23, 1904 d Aug. 24, 1973

Downs, George Edward *Test umpire* b July 25, 1856 d Apr. 2, 1936

Drysdale, George Russell *Painter of "The Cricketers"* b Feb. 7, 1912 d June 29, 1981

Dundas, Ross Lloyd *Statistician* b Sept. 7, 1953

Edwards, John Ernest "Jack" *VCA president 1992-97; Test team manager* b Aug. 29, 1930

Egan, Jack *Film researcher* b Jan. 28, 1941

Egar, Colin John *Test umpire; ACB chairman 1989-92; Test team manager* b Mar. 30, 1928

Elder, David Alexander *Test umpire* b Apr. 29, 1865 d Apr. 20, 1954

Elphinston, Herbert Alfred Rhys *Test umpire* b Feb. 25, 1905 d July 8, 1966

Enright, Peter Robert *Test umpire* b Jan. 18, 1925

Evan, Griffith Mostyn *ACB chairman 1910-11; SACA president 1920-24* b 1861 d Dec. 25, 1924

Evans, Richard James "Ric" *Test umpire* b Nov. 20, 1942

Evatt, Dr Herbert Vere "Doc" *ALP leader, cricket enthusiast* b Apr. 30, 1894 d Nov. 2, 1965

Ferguson, William Henry *Scorer, baggageman* b June 6, 1880 d Sept. 22, 1957

Fisher, Isaac Alfred *Test umpire* b Apr. 12, 1851 d June 19, 1944

Flynn, Thomas *Test umpire* b 1869 d Apr. 21, 1931

Foster, Daryl Hugh *Coach* b Dec. 9, 1938

Foxton, Justin Fox Greenlaw *ACB chairman 1908-10; QCA president 1902-16* b Sept. 24, 1849 d June 23, 1916

French, Richard Allan "Dick" *Test umpire* b Aug. 7, 1938

French, Walter G. *Test umpire* b not known d 1961

Frith, David Edward John *Author, editor* b Mar. 16, 1937

Garing, Clement *Test umpire* b Dec. 17, 1873 d 1951

Gibbs, Barry Montgomery *SACA secretary 1960-66* b Mar. 11, 1933

Goodman, Thomas Lyall *Journalist, author* b c. 1902 d Sept. 28, 1989

Gray, Malcolm Alexander *ACB chairman 1986-89* b May 30, 1940

Gregory, Henry *ACB chairman 1919-20, 1922-23, 1926-27* b Mar 15, 1860 d Nov. 15, 1940

Greig, Anthony William *TV commentator* b Oct. 6, 1946

Grose, James Robert *SACA president 1987-99* b Aug. 21, 1930

Haigh, Gideon Clifford Jeffrey Davidson *Journalist, author* b Dec. 29, 1965

Hair, Darrell Bruce *Test umpire* b Sept. 30, 1952

Halbish, Graham Wilfred *ACB chief executive 1993-97* b Dec. 31, 1948

Hannah, William *Test umpire* b 1867 d Oct. 18, 1942

Harburg, Clive Henry *Radio commentator* b July 13, 1912 d July 21, 2002

Harmer, John *Coach* b June 2, 1942

Harper, Daryl John *Test umpire* b Oct. 23, 1951

Hedley, Harry Wharton *Journalist* b Jan. 7, 1848 d Nov. 20, 1911

Hele, George Alfred *Test umpire* b July 16, 1892 d Aug. 28, 1982

Heydon, Harold *NSWCA secretary 1926-50* b Oct. 9, 1893 d Dec. 14, 1967

Hiley, Thomas Alfred *QCA president 1965-69* b Nov. 25, 1905 d Nov. 6, 1990

Hodges, George James *Test umpire* b not known d not known

Holroyd, Henry North (Lord Sheffield) *Founded the Sheffield Shield* b Jan. 18, 1832 d Apr. 21, 1909

Hoy, Colin *Test umpire* b May 9, 1922 d Mar. 24, 1999

Hughes, Canon Ernest Selwyn *VCA president 1932-42* b May 12, 1860 d June 16, 1942

Ingamells, Christopher Robert *TCC chairman* b Aug. 9, 1914 d Oct. 27, 1986

Ironside, Frederick James *Invented matting wickets* b Mar. 3, 1836 d Dec. 24, 1912

Isherwood, Raymond Charles *Test umpire* b Jan. 20, 1938

Jacobs, Kenneth William *VCA secretary/chief exec 1980-* b July 6, 1952

Jacobs, William Lawson *Test team manager* b Jan. 5, 1918

James, Arthur Edward *Masseur* b not known d Sept. 1974

James, John Charles Horsey *WACA president 1885-97* b Jan. 30, 1841 d Feb. 3, 1899

Jeanes, William Henry *ACB secretary 1927-54; SACA secretary 1926-55; Test team manager* b May 19, 1883 d Sept. 1, 1958

Jenkins, Arthur George *Test umpire* b c. 1886 d May 19, 1963

Jillett, Maxwell John *TCA chairman 1967-79* b Sept. 15, 1915 d Feb. 27, 1999

Johnson, Melville William *Test umpire* b May 17, 1942

Jones, Alfred Charles *Test umpire* b June 6, 1859 d Feb. 10, 1949

King, Bennett Alfred *Academy coach* b Dec. 19, 1964

King, Leonard John *Test umpire* b July 31, 1941

Laing, James *Test umpire* b Apr. 21, 1833 d Sept. 11, 1913

Lance, Arthur Alfred *Adelaide Oval curator 1953-80* b Dec. 9, 1913 d Sept. 11, 1999

Lane, Timothy Paul *Radio commentator* b Sept. 18, 1951

Ledwidge, Reginald Ross *Test umpire* b *c.* 1922 d Dec. 10, 1977

Leroy, Peter *SCG curator 1983-* b Nov. 16, 1949

Lillywhite, Jas jnr *Test umpire* b Feb. 23, 1842 d Oct. 25, 1929

Luttrell, Albert John Wesley "Bert"*MCG curator 1920-46* b 1875 d July 29, 1951

McAlpine, Walter *MCG curator 1880-88* b 1826 d Apr. 7, 1888

McConnell, Peter John *Test umpire* b Nov. 11, 1944

McElhone, William Percy *ACB chairman/ secretary 1911-12* b Dec. 22, 1870 d Apr. 21, 1932

McFarline, Peter Muir *Journalist* b Mar. 27, 1945 d Apr. 7, 2002

McInnes, Melville James *Test umpire* b June 30, 1915 d July 23, 1996

McKenzie, John Reginald *Helped found Country Championships* b Dec. 23, 1918 d Mar. 20, 1985

Mackinnon, Hon. Donald *VCA president 1906-32* b Sept. 29, 1859 d Apr. 25, 1932

Mackley, Allan E. *Test umpire* b 1913 d 1982

Maley, John Kennedy *Curator who pioneered drop-in pitches* b May 2, 1947

McMahon, Norman Thomas *QCA chairman 1967-87* b Feb. 21, 1922 d Dec. 21, 1991

Macmillan, Ewart Gladstone *ACB chairman 1963-66* b July 31, 1898 d Nov. 26, 1970

McQuillan, Anthony John *Test umpire* b Mar. 19, 1951

Martin, Bruce Edward *Test umpire* b June 11, 1942

Maxwell, James Edward *Radio commentator* b July 28, 1950

Menzies, Sir Robert Gordon *Cricket-loving prime minister, patron* b Dec. 20, 1894 d May 15, 1978

Merriman, Robert Frederick *CA chairman 2001-; VCA president 1997-; Test team manager* b Aug. 22, 1935

Mitchell, Kevin Michael *Gabba curator 1991-* b Sept.2, 1959

Mitchell, Kevin Vincent *Gabba curator 1982-91* b June 11, 1935

Moody, Clarence Percival *Journalist* b Aug. 11, 1867 d Nov. 28, 1937

Morton, Dr Reginald Lonsdale *VCA president 1942-47* b 1878 d May 26, 1947

Mullins, Joseph *Collector* b Jan 12, 1923 d Sept. 7, 2002

Mulvaney, Richaed *Bradman Museum curator* b Mar 8, 1957

Norton, John Edward "Jack" *Test team manager* b 1910 d Jan. 28, 1992

O'Connell, Maxwell George *Test umpire* b Apr. 4, 1936

O'Reilly, Charles Bernard *Journalist* b Nov. 2, 1871 d Oct. 30, 1960

Orr, James Patrick *Test umpire* b July 18, 1868 d Dec. 26, 1940

Oxlade, Robert Aubrey *ACB chairman 1927-30, 1933-36, 1945-48, 1951-52* b 1886 d Sept. 13, 1955

Packer, Kerry Francis Bullmore *Creator of World Series Cricket* b Dec. 17, 1937

Page, Roger *Bookseller* b June 25, 1936

Parish, Robert James *ACB chairman 1966-69, 1975-80; VCA vice-pres 1970-1992; Test team manager* b May 7, 1916

Parker, Peter Douglas *Test umpire* b July 20, 1959

Payne, John William *Test umpire* b 1844 d May 12, 1928

Pettigrew, Alan Charles *QCA chairman 1988-93* b Dec. 12, 1935 d Dec. 16, 1993

Piesse, Kendrick Bruce *Author* b Aug. 7, 1955

Pollard, Jack Ernest *Journalist, author* b Jul. 31, 1926 d May 25, 2002

Prue, Terry Arthur *Test umpire* b Dec. 11, 1948

Pyke, Dr Frank Sherman *Sports scientist* b Dec. 1, 1941.

Radford, Robert Michael *NSWCA secretary/ chief exec 1976-95* b Nov. 18, 1943 d Feb. 28, 2004

Randell, Stephen Grant *Test umpire* b Feb. 19, 1956

Rawlinson, Elisha Barker *Test umpire* b Apr. 10, 1837 d Feb. 17, 1892

Richards, David Lyle *ACB chief exec 1981-93; VCA secretary 1973-80* b July 28, 1946

Richards, Joseph *Test umpire* b not known d not known

Robertson, Dr Allen William David *ACB chairman 1930-33, 1936-45, 1948-51* b 1867 d 1954

Robinson, Raymond John *Journalist, author* b July 8, 1905 d July 6, 1982

Roebuck, Peter Michael *Journalist* b Mar. 6, 1956

Rogers, Denis Walsh *ACB chairman 1995-2001; TCA chairman 1986-2004* b June 20, 1940

Rowan, Louis Patrick *Test umpire* b May 2, 1925

Rush, Henry Reynolds *ACB chairman 1920-22* b 1865 d Sept. 28, 1928

Searcy, George Henry Graff *Test umpire* b Jan. 15, 1855 d Jan. 6, 1927

Sheahan, William Peter *Test umpire* b Jan. 12, 1953

Sheridan, Philip *SCG Trust secretary 1877-1910* b Feb. 17, 1834 d Jan. 15, 1910

Sherwood, David Knox Patrick *Scorer* b *c.* 1911 d Mar. 12, 1985

Smeaton, John Henry *Test umpire* b Aug. 31 1948

Smith, Edwin Thomas *SACA president 1897-1919* b Apr. 6, 1830 d 237Dec. 25, 1919

Smith, Sydney *ACB sec 1911-27; NSWCA president 1936-66; Test team manager* b Mar. 1, 1880 d Apr. 11, 1972

Smyth, William Joseph *Test umpire* b July 8, 1916

Speed, Malcolm Walter *ACB chief exec 1997-2001* b Sept. 14, 1948

Steele, Raymond Charles *VCA president 1973-1992; Test team manager* b May 19, 1917 d Nov. 22, 1993

Swift, James *Test umpire* b Jan. 5, 1848 d June 27, 1910

Taufel, Simon James Arthur *Test umpire* b Jan. 21, 1971

Timmins, Colin Douglas *Test umpire* b Apr. 2, 1947

Townsend, Leslie Hyde *Test umpire* b Oct. 4, 1914 d Jan. 30, 1986

Townsend, Norman E. *Test umpire* b Oct. 24, 1924

Tresidder, Phillip Lyle *Journalist* b Sept. 20, 1928 d Oct. 19, 2003

Truman, Leslie Ernest *WACA secretary 1947-73* b Oct. 11, 1919 d Jan. 13, 1973

Tyson, Frank Holmes *Author, coach* b June 6, 1930

Ware, Anthony *MCG curator 1990-* b Dec. 25, 1957

Watkins, Athol George *SCG curator 1958-84* b Apr. 11, 1919 d Apr. 9, 2001

Watson, George Albert *Test umpire* b not known d 237not known

Watt, William Brockbank *SCG curator 1951-57; MCG curator 1958-78* b Aug. 3, 1918

Webb, Sydney George *Test team manager* b Jan. 31, 1900 d Aug. 5, 1976

Webster, Raymond Merryn *Statistician* b Apr. 22, 1941

Weser, Donald Gordon *Test umpire* b Feb. 8, 1937

Whitehead, Rex Vernon *Test umpire* b Oct. 26, 1948

Whitridge, William Oswald *Test umpire; SACA adminstrator* b Aug. 14, 1853 d Feb. 12, 1919

Wilkins, Philip Laurence *Journalist* b June 26, 1939.

Williams, Alfred Percy *Test umpire* b not known d 237May 22, 1933

Winning, Clifford McGregor *Librarian* b Dec. 8, 1909 d 237Aug. 1, 2002

Wright, Ronald James John *Test umpire* b 1913 d June 14, 1968

Wyeth, Arthur Edwin *Test umpire* b July 3, 1887 d Oct. 18, 1971

Wykes, Edgar Frederick "Ted" *Test umpire* b Apr. 28, 1921

"Yabba" (Gascoigne, Stephen Harold) *Barracker* b Mar. 19, 1878 d Jan. 8, 1942

Yeomans, Ernest Charles *Test team manager* b May 3, 1883 d Oct. 28, 1955

Young, W. A. *Test umpire* b not known d not known

3

Records

Records

Compiled by ROSS DUNDAS

Records are accurate to: Tests, October 1, 2004; Limited-overs and first-class to August 1, 2004.

* Denotes not out or an unbroken partnership.

Key to abbreviations

Australian States: NSW – New South Wales, Qld – Queensland, SAust – South Australia, Tas – Tasmania, Vic – Victoria, WAust – Western Australia.

Countries: Aust – Australia, Ban – Bangladesh, Can – Canada, Eng – England, HK – Hong Kong, Ind – India, Ire – Ireland, Kya – Kenya, NAmer – North America, Nam – Namibia, Net – Netherlands, NZ – New Zealand, Pak – Pakistan, SAf – South Africa, Sco – Scotland, SL – Sri Lanka, UAE – United Arab Emirates, WI – West Indies, Zim – Zimbabwe.

Australian Grounds: Bel – Bellerive Oval, DS Docklands Stadium, Ex – Exhibition Ground, LRG – Lower Railway Ground, TCA – Tasmanian Cricket Association Ground.

Other Grounds: BS Bradbourne Stadium (Mumbai), Chepauk – M. A. Chidambaram Stadium (Chennai), Corp – Corporation Stadium (Chennai), EP – Ellis Park (Johannesburg), OW – Old Wanderers (Johannesburg), PIS – R. Premadasa (Khettarama) International Stadium (Colombo), PSS – P.Saravanamuttu Stadium (Colombo), SSC – Sinhalese Sports Club Ground (Colombo), WS – Wanderers Stadium (Johannesburg), Wankhede Stadium (Bombay/Mumbai).

CONTENTS

AUSTRALIAN TEST MATCH RECORDS

BOWLING

ALL-ROUNDERS

WICKET-KEEPING

FIELDING

TEAM

APPEARANCES

UMPIRES

CAPTAINCY

AUSTRALIAN TEST CRICKET

AUSTRALIAN LIMITED-OVERS INTERNATIONAL RECORDS

BATTING

BOWLING

ALL-ROUNDERS

BOWLING

ALL-ROUNDERS

WICKET-KEEPING

FIELDING

TEAM

MISCELLANEOUS

Australian Test Match Records

AUSTRALIAN TEST PLAYERS IN ORDER OF APPEARANCE

Player	Career	M	I	NO	R	HS	Avge	100s	50s	Ct	St	Balls	Mdns	R	W	Avge	S-R	RPO	BB	5	10
1 C. Bannerman	1876-77 to 1878-79	3	6	2	239	165+	59.75	1	–	1	–	–	–	–	–	–	–	–	–	–	–
2 J.M. Blackham	1876-77 to 1894-95	35	62	11	800	74	15.69	–	4	37	24	–	–	–	–	–	–	–	–	–	–
3 B.B. Cooper	1876-77	1	2	–	18	15	9.00	–	–	2	–	–	–	–	–	–	–	–	–	–	–
4 T.W. Garrett	1876-77 to 1887-88	19	33	6	339	51*	12.56	–	1	7	–	2,728	297	970	36	26.94	75.78	2.13	6-78	2	–
5 D.W. Gregory	1876-77 to 1878-79	3	5	2	60	43	20.00	–	–	2	–	20	1	9	0	–	–	2.70	–	–	–
6 E.J. Gregory	1876-77	1	2	–	11	11	5.50	–	–	1	–	–	–	–	–	–	–	–	–	–	–
7 J.R. Hodges †‡	1876-77	2	4	1	10	8	3.33	–	–	1	–	136	9	84	6	14.00	22.67	3.71	2-7	–	–
8 T.P. Horan	1876-77 to 1884-85	15	27	2	471	124	18.84	1	6	6	–	373	45	143	11	13.00	33.91	2.30	6-40	–	–
9 T.K. Kendall ††	1876-77	2	4	1	39	17*	13.00	–	–	1	–	563	56	215	14	15.36	40.21	2.29	7-55	1	–
10 W.E. Midwinter	1876-77 to 1886-87	8	14	1	174	37	13.38	–	1	5	–	949	104	333	14	23.79	67.79	2.11	5-78	1	–
11 N.F.D. Thomson	1876-77	2	4	–	67	41	16.75	–	–	3	–	112	16	31	1	31.00	112.00	1.66	1-14	–	–
12 T.J.D. Kelly	1876-77 to 1878-79	2	3	–	64	35	21.33	–	–	1	–	–	–	–	–	–	–	–	–	–	–
13 W.L. Murdoch	1876-77 to 1890	18	33	5	896	211	32.00	2	–	14	–	–	–	–	–	–	–	–	–	–	–
14 F.R. Spofforth	1876-77 to 1886-87	18	29	6	217	50	9.43	–	1	11	–	4,185	416	1,731	94	18.41	44.52	2.48	7-44	7	4
15 F.E. Allan ††	1878-79	1	1	–	5	5	5.00	–	–	–	–	180	15	80	4	20.00	45.00	2.67	2-30	–	–
16 A.C. Bannerman	1878-79 to 1893	28	50	2	1,108	94	23.08	–	8	21	–	292	17	163	4	40.75	73.00	3.35	3-111	–	–
17 H.F. Boyle	1878-79 to 1884-85	12	16	4	153	36*	12.75	–	–	10	–	1,744	175	641	32	20.03	54.50	2.21	6-42	1	–
18 G. Alexander	1880 to 1884-85	2	4	–	52	33	13.00	–	–	2	–	168	13	93	2	46.50	84.00	3.32	2-69	–	–
19 G.J. Bonnor	1880 to 1888	17	30	–	512	128	17.07	1	2	16	–	164	16	84	2	42.00	82.00	3.07	1-5	–	–
20 T.U. Groube	1880	1	2	–	11	11	5.50	–	–	–	–	–	–	–	–	–	–	–	–	–	–
21 P.S. McDonnell	1880 to 1888	19	34	1	955	147	28.94	3	2	6	–	52	–	53	0	–	–	6.12	–	–	–
22 W.H. Moule	1880	1	2	–	40	34	20.00	–	–	1	–	51	4	23	3	7.67	17.00	2.71	3-23	–	–
23 G.E. Palmer	1880 to 1886	17	25	4	296	48	14.10	–	–	13	–	4,517	452	1,678	78	21.51	57.91	2.23	7-65	6	2
24 J. Slight	1880	1	2	–	11	11	5.50	–	–	–	–	–	–	–	–	–	–	–	–	–	–
25 W.H. Cooper	1881-82 to 1884-85	2	3	1	13	7	6.50	–	–	1	–	466	31	226	9	25.11	51.78	2.91	6-120	1	–
26 E. Evans	1881-82 to 1886	6	10	2	82	33	10.25	–	–	5	–	1,247	166	332	7	47.43	178.14	1.60	3-64	–	–

No.	Player	Career	M	I	NO	Runs	HS	Avge	100	50	Ct	St	Balls	Mdns	Runs	Wkts	Avge	SR	Econ	Best	5wi	10wm
27	G. Giffen	1881-82 to 1896	31	53	–	1,238	161	23.36	1	6	24	–	6,391	434	2,791	103	27.10	62.05	2.62	7-117	7	1
28	H.H. Massie	1881-82 to 1884-85	9	16	–	249	55	15.56	–	1	5	–	–	–	–	–	–	–	–	–	–	–
29	G. Coulthard	1881-82	1	1	1	6	6*	–	–	–	–	–	–	–	–	–	–	–	–	–	–	–
30	S.P. Jones	1881-82 to 1887-88	12	24	4	428	87	21.40	–	1	12	–	262	26	112	6	18.67	43.67	2.56	4-47	–	–
31	H.J.H. Scott	1884 to 1886	8	14	1	359	102	27.62	1	1	8	–	28	1	26	0	–	–	5.57	–	–	–
32	W. Bruce †‡	1884-85 to 1894-95	14	26	2	702	80	29.25	–	2	12	–	988	72	440	12	36.67	82.33	2.67	3-88	–	–
33	A.H. Jarvis	1884-85 to 1894-95	11	21	3	303	82	16.83	–	1	9	–	–	–	–	–	–	–	–	–	–	–
34	A.P. Marr	1884-85	1	2	–	5	5	2.50	–	–	–	–	48	6	14	0	–	–	1.75	–	–	–
35	S. Morris	1884-85	1	2	1	14	10*	14.00	–	–	–	–	136	14	73	2	36.50	68.00	3.22	2-73	–	–
36	H.A. Musgrove	1884-85	1	2	–	13	9	6.50	–	–	–	–	–	–	–	–	–	–	–	–	–	–
37	R.J. Pope	1884-85	1	2	–	3	3	1.50	–	–	–	–	–	–	–	–	–	–	–	–	–	–
38	W.R. Robertson	1884-85	1	2	–	2	2	1.00	–	–	–	–	–	–	–	–	–	–	–	–	–	–
39	J.W. Trumble	1884-85 to 1886	7	13	1	243	59	20.25	–	1	3	–	600	59	222	10	22.20	60.00	2.22	3-29	–	–
40	J. Worrall	1884-85 to 1899	11	22	3	478	76	25.16	–	3	13	–	255	29	127	1	127.00	255.00	2.99	1-97	–	–
41	P.G. McShane †‡	1884-85 to 1887-88	3	6	1	26	12*	5.20	–	–	2	–	108	9	48	1	48.00	108.00	2.67	1-39	–	–
42	F.H. Walters	1884-85	1	2	–	12	7	6.00	–	–	1	–	–	–	–	–	–	–	–	–	–	–
43	J. McIlwraith	1886	1	2	–	9	7	4.50	–	–	–	–	–	–	–	–	–	–	–	–	–	–
44	J.J. Ferris †‡	1886-87 to 1890	9	16	4	98	20*	8.17	–	–	4	–	2,030	224	684	48	14.25	42.29	2.02	5-26	4	–
45	H. Moses †	1886-87 to 1894-95	6	10	–	198	33	19.80	–	–	–	–	–	–	–	–	–	–	–	–	–	–
46	C.T.B. Turner	1886-87 to 1894-95	17	32	4	323	29	11.54	–	–	8	–	5,179	457	1,670	101	16.53	51.28	1.93	7-43	11	2
47	R.C. Allen	1886-87	1	2	–	44	30	22.00	–	–	2	–	–	–	–	–	–	–	–	–	–	–
48	F.J. Burton	1886-87 to 1887-88	2	4	2	4	2*	2.00	–	–	2	1	–	–	–	–	–	–	–	–	–	–
49	J.T. Cottam	1886-87	1	2	–	4	3	2.00	–	–	–	–	–	–	–	–	–	–	–	–	–	–
50	W.F. Giffen	1886-87 to 1891-92	3	6	–	11	3	1.83	–	–	2	–	–	–	–	–	–	–	–	–	–	–
51	J.J. Lyons	1886-87 to 1897-98	14	27	–	731	134	27.07	1	4	3	–	316	17	149	6	24.83	52.67	2.83	5-30	1	–
52	J.D. Edwards	1888	3	6	1	48	26	9.60	–	–	3	–	–	–	–	–	–	–	–	–	–	–
53	G.H.S. Trott	1888 to 1897-98	24	42	–	921	143	21.93	1	4	21	–	1,891	48	1,019	29	35.14	65.21	3.23	4-71	–	–
54	S.M.J. Woods	1888	3	6	–	32	18	5.33	–	–	1	–	217	18	121	5	24.20	43.40	3.35	2-35	–	–
55	J.E. Barrett †	1890	2	4	1	80	67*	26.67	–	1	2	–	–	–	–	–	–	–	–	–	–	–
56	E.J.K. Burn	1890	2	4	–	41	19	10.25	–	–	–	–	–	–	–	–	–	–	–	–	–	–
57	P.C. Charlton	1890	2	4	–	29	11	7.25	–	–	2	–	45	1	24	3	8.00	15.00	3.20	3-18	–	–
58	S.E. Gregory	1890 to 1912	58	100	7	2,282	201	24.54	4	8	25	–	30	0	33	0	–	–	6.60	–	–	–
59	H. Trumble	1890 to 1903-04	32	57	14	851	70	19.79	–	4	45	–	8,099	452	3,072	141	21.79	57.44	2.28	8-65	9	3
60	S.T. Callaway	1891-92 to 1894-95	3	6	1	87	41	17.40	–	–	2	–	471	33	142	6	23.67	78.50	1.81	5-37	1	–
61	H. Donnan	1891-92 to 1896	5	10	1	75	15	8.33	–	–	–	–	54	2	22	0	–	–	2.44	–	–	–
62	R.W. McLeod †	1891-92 to 1893	6	11	–	146	31	13.27	–	–	3	–	1,089	67	382	12	31.83	90.75	2.10	5-53	1	–
63	H. Graham	1893 to 1896	6	10	–	301	107	30.10	2	–	3	–	–	–	–	–	–	–	–	–	–	–

Player	Period	M	I	NO	R	HS	Avge	100s	50s	Ct	St	Balls	Mdns	R	W	Avge	S-R	RPO	BB	5	10
64 J. Darling †	1894-95 to 1905	34	60	2	1,657	178	28.57	3	8	27	—	12	1	—	—	—	—	1.50	—	—	—
65 F. A. Iredale	1894-95 to 1899	14	23	2	807	140	36.68	2	4	16	—	—	—	—	—	—	—	—	—	—	—
66 E. Jones	1894-95 to 1902-03	19	26	6	126	20	5.04	—	—	21	—	3,754	161	1,857	64	29.02	58.66	2.97	7-88	3	1
67 C. E. McLeod	1894-95 to 1905	17	29	5	573	112	23.88	1	4	9	—	3,374	171	1,325	33	40.15	102.24	2.36	5-65	2	—
68 J. C. Reedman	1894-95	1	2	0	21	17	10.50	—	—	1	—	57	2	24	1	24.00	57.00	2.53	1-12	—	—
69 A. Coningham ‡‡	1894-95	1	2	0	13	10	6.50	—	—	1	—	186	9	76	2	38.00	93.00	2.45	2-17	—	—
70 J. Harry	1894-95	1	2	0	8	6	4.00	—	—	1	—	—	—	—	—	—	—	—	—	—	—
71 A. E. Trott	1894-95	3	5	3	205	85*	102.50	—	2	4	—	474	17	192	9	21.33	52.67	2.43	8-43	1	—
72 T. R. McKibbin	1894-95 to 1897-98	5	8	2	88	28*	14.67	—	—	4	—	1,032	41	496	17	29.18	60.71	2.88	3-35	—	—
73 C. J. Eady	1896 to 1901-02	2	4	1	20	10*	6.67	—	—	2	—	223	14	112	7	16.00	31.86	3.01	3-30	—	—
74 C. Hill †	1896 to 1911-12	49	89	2	3,412	191	39.22	7	19	33	—	—	—	—	—	—	—	—	—	—	—
75 J. J. Kelly	1896 to 1905	36	56	17	664	46*	17.03	—	—	43	20	—	—	—	—	—	—	—	—	—	—
76 M. A. Noble	1897-98 to 1909	42	73	7	1,997	133	30.26	1	16	26	—	7,159	361	3,025	121	25.00	59.17	2.54	7-17	9	2
77 W. P. Howell †	1897-98 to 1903-04	18	27	6	158	35	7.52	—	—	12	—	3,892	245	1,407	49	28.71	79.43	2.17	5-81	1	—
78 F. Laver	1899 to 1909	15	23	6	196	45	11.53	—	—	8	—	2,361	121	964	37	26.05	63.81	2.45	8-31	2	—
79 V. T. Trumper	1899 to 1911-12	48	89	8	3,163	214*	39.05	8	13	31	—	546	20	317	8	39.63	68.25	3.48	3-60	—	—
80 W. W. Armstrong	1901-02 to 1921	50	84	10	2,863	159*	38.69	6	8	44	—	8,022	407	2,923	87	33.60	92.21	2.19	6-35	3	—
81 R. A. Duff	1901-02 to 1905	22	40	3	1,317	146	35.59	2	6	14	—	180	8	85	4	21.25	45.00	2.83	2-43	—	—
82 A. J. Y. Hopkins	1901-02 to 1909	20	33	2	509	43	16.42	—	—	11	—	1,327	49	696	26	26.77	51.04	3.15	4-81	—	—
83 J. V. Saunders ‡	1901-02 to 1907-08	14	23	6	39	11*	2.29	—	—	5	—	3,565	116	1,796	79	22.73	45.13	3.02	7-34	6	—
84 J. P. F. Travers ††	1901-02	1	2	0	10	9	5.00	—	—	1	—	48	2	14	1	14.00	48.00	1.75	1-14	—	—
85 A. Cotter	1903-04 to 1911-12	21	37	2	457	45	13.06	—	—	8	—	4,639	86	2,549	89	28.64	52.12	3.30	7-148	7	—
86 P. A. McAlister	1903-04 to 1909	8	16	1	252	41	16.80	—	—	10	—	—	—	—	—	—	—	—	—	—	—
87 D. R. A. Gehrs	1903-04 to 1910-11	6	11	0	221	67	20.09	—	1	6	—	6	—	4	0	—	—	4.00	—	—	—
88 H. Carter	1907-08 to 1921-22	28	47	9	873	72	22.97	—	4	44	21	—	—	—	—	—	—	—	—	—	—
89 G. R. Hazlitt	1907-08 to 1912	9	12	4	89	34*	11.13	—	—	9	—	1,563	74	623	23	27.09	67.96	2.39	7-25	1	—
90 C. G. Macartney ‡	1907-08 to 1926	35	55	4	2,131	170	41.78	7	9	17	—	3,561	177	1,240	45	27.56	79.13	2.09	7-58	2	1
91 V. S. Ransford ††	1907-08 to 1911-12	20	38	6	1,211	143*	37.84	1	7	10	—	43	3	28	1	28.00	43.00	3.91	1-9	—	—
92 M. J. Hartigan	1907-08	2	4	0	170	116	42.50	1	—	1	—	12	—	7	0	—	—	3.50	—	—	—
93 J. D. A. O'Connor †	1907-08 to 1909	4	8	1	86	20	12.29	—	—	3	—	692	24	340	13	26.15	53.23	2.95	5-40	1	—
94 W. Bardsley ‡	1907-08 to 1926	41	66	5	2,469	193*	40.48	6	14	12	—	—	—	—	—	—	—	—	—	—	—
95 W. J. Whitty ‡	1909 to 1912	14	19	7	161	39*	13.42	—	—	3	—	3,357	163	1,373	65	21.12	51.65	2.45	6-17	3	—
96 C. Kelleway	1910-11 to 1928-29	26	42	4	1,422	147	37.42	3	6	24	—	4,363	146	1,683	52	32.37	83.90	2.31	5-33	1	—
97 H. V. Hordern	1910-11 to 1911-12	7	13	2	254	50	23.09	—	1	6	—	2,148	49	1,075	46	23.37	46.70	3.00	7-90	5	2
98 R. B. Minnett	1911-12 to 1912	9	15	0	391	90	26.07	—	3	7	—	589	26	290	11	26.36	53.55	2.95	4-34	—	—
99 T. J. Matthews	1911-12	8	10	1	153	53	17.00	—	1	7	—	1,081	46	419	16	26.19	67.56	2.33	4-29	—	—

#	Player	Career	M	I	NO	HS	Runs	Avg	100	50	0	Ct	St	Balls	Mdns	Runs	Wkts	Avg	SR	Econ	BB	5	10
100	J. W. McLaren	1911-12	1	2	2	0*	0	0.00	–	–	–	–	–	144	3	70	1	70.00	144.00	2.92	1-23	–	–
101	W. Carkeek †	1912	6	5	2	6*	16	5.33	–	–	–	6	2	–	–	–	–	–	–	–	–	–	–
102	S. H. Emery	1912	4	2	–	5	6	3.00	–	–	–	2	–	462	13	249	5	49.80	92.40	3.23	2-46	–	–
103	C. B. Jennings	1912	6	8	2	32	107	17.83	–	–	–	5	–	–	–	–	–	–	–	–	–	–	–
104	D. B. M. Smith	1912	2	3	1	24*	30	15.00	–	–	–	–	–	–	–	–	–	–	–	–	–	–	–
105	R. E. Mayne	1912 to 1921-22	4	4	1	25*	64	21.33	–	–	–	2	–	6	–	1	0	–	–	1.00	–	–	–
106	H. L. Collins ‡	1920-21 to 1926	19	31	1	203	1,352	45.07	4	6	–	13	–	654	31	252	4	63.00	163.50	2.31	2-47	–	–
107	J. M. Gregory †	1920-21 to 1928-29	24	34	3	119	1,146	36.97	2	7	–	37	–	5,582	138	2,648	85	31.15	65.67	2.85	7-69	4	–
108	A. A. Mailey	1920-21 to 1926	21	29	9	46*	222	11.10	–	–	4	14	–	6,119	115	3,358	99	33.92	61.81	3.29	9-121	6	2
109	W. A. S. Oldfield	1920-21 to 1936-37	54	80	17	65*	1,427	22.65	–	4	–	78	52	–	–	–	–	–	–	–	–	–	–
110	C. E. Pellew	1920-21 to 1921-22	10	14	1	116	484	37.23	2	1	–	4	–	78	1	34	0	–	–	2.62	–	–	–
111	J. Ryder	1920-21 to 1928-29	20	32	5	201*	1,394	51.63	3	9	1	17	–	1,897	71	743	17	43.71	111.59	2.35	2-20	–	–
112	J. M. Taylor	1920-21 to 1926	20	28	–	108	997	35.61	1	8	1	11	–	114	5	45	1	45.00	114.00	2.37	1-25	–	–
113	R. L. Park	1920-21	1	1	–	0	0	0.00	–	–	1	–	–	6	0	9	0	–	–	9.00	–	–	–
114	E. A. McDonald	1920-21	11	12	5	36	116	16.57	–	–	–	3	–	2,885	90	1,431	43	33.28	67.09	2.98	5-32	2	–
115	T. J. E. Andrews	1921 to 1926	16	23	1	94	592	26.91	–	4	–	12	–	156	3	116	1	116.00	156.00	4.46	1-23	–	–
116	H. S. T. L. Hendry	1921 to 1928-29	11	18	2	112	335	20.94	–	2	–	10	–	1,706	73	640	16	40.00	106.63	2.25	3-36	–	–
117	W. H. Ponsford	1924-25 to 1934	29	48	–	266	2,122	48.23	7	6	–	21	–	–	–	–	–	–	–	–	–	–	–
118	A. J. Richardson	1924-25 to 1926	9	13	1	100	403	31.00	1	–	1	6	–	1,812	91	521	12	43.42	151.00	1.73	2-20	–	–
119	V. Y. Richardson	1924-25 to 1935-36	19	30	–	138	706	23.53	1	4	–	24	–	–	–	–	–	–	–	–	–	–	–
120	A. E. V. Hartkopf	1924-25	1	2	–	80	80	40.00	–	1	–	–	–	240	2	134	1	134.00	240.00	3.35	1-120	–	–
121	C. V. Grimmett	1924-25 to 1935-36	37	50	10	50	557	13.93	–	1	8	17	–	14,513	736	5,231	216	24.22	67.19	2.16	7-40	21	7
122	A. F. Kippax	1924-25 to 1934	22	34	2	146	1,192	36.12	2	8	2	13	–	72	5	19	0	–	–	1.58	–	–	–
123	W. M. Woodfull	1926 to 1934	35	54	4	161	2,300	46.00	7	13	–	7	–	–	–	–	–	–	–	–	–	–	–
124	D. G. Bradman	1928-29 to 1948	52	80	10	334	6,996	99.94	29	13	7	32	–	160	3	72	2	36.00	80.00	2.70	1-8	–	–
125	H. Ironmonger ‡‡	1928-29 to 1932-33	14	21	5	12	42	2.63	–	–	4	3	–	4,695	328	1,330	74	17.97	63.45	1.70	7-23	4	2
126	D. D. Blackie †	1928-29 to 1928-29	3	6	3	11*	24	8.00	–	–	–	2	–	1,260	51	444	14	31.71	90.00	2.11	6-94	1	–
127	O. E. Nothling	1928-29	1	2	–	44	52	26.00	–	–	–	–	–	276	15	72	0	–	–	1.57	–	–	–
128	E. L. A'Beckett	1928-29 to 1931-32	4	7	2	41	143	20.43	–	–	–	4	–	1,062	47	317	3	105.67	354.00	1.79	1-41	–	–
129	R. K. Oxenham	1928-29 to 1931-32	7	10	–	48	151	15.10	–	–	–	4	–	1,802	112	522	14	37.29	128.71	1.74	4-39	–	–
130	A. Jackson	1928-29 to 1930-31	8	11	–	164	474	47.40	1	2	–	7	–	–	–	–	–	–	–	–	–	–	–
131	A. G. Fairfax	1928-29 to 1930-31	10	12	1	65	410	51.25	–	2	–	15	–	1,520	54	645	21	30.71	72.38	2.55	4-31	1	–
132	P. M. Hornibrook ‡‡	1928-29 to 1930	6	7	1	26	60	10.00	–	–	–	7	–	1,579	63	664	17	39.06	92.88	2.52	7-92	1	–
133	T. W. Wall	1928-29 to 1934	18	24	5	20	121	6.37	–	–	7	11	–	4,812	154	2,010	56	35.89	85.93	2.51	5-14	3	–
134	S. J. McCabe	1930 to 1938	39	62	5	232	2,748	48.21	6	13	–	41	–	3,746	127	1,543	36	42.86	104.06	2.47	4-13	–	–
135	A. Hurwood	1930-31 to 1930-31	2	2	–	5	5	2.50	–	–	–	1	–	517	28	170	11	15.45	47.00	1.97	4-22	–	–
136	K. E. Rigg	1930-31 to 1936-37	8	12	1	127	401	33.42	1	2	1	5	–	–	–	–	–	–	–	–	–	–	–

#	Name	Years	M	I	NO	R	HS	Avge	100s	50s	0s	Ct	St	Balls	Mdns	R	W	Avge	S-R	RPO	BB	5	10
137	H.C. Nitschke †	1931-32	2	2	–	53	47	26.50	–	–	–	3	–									–	–
138	P.K. Lee ‡	1931-32 to 1932-33	2	3	–	57	42	19.00	–	–	–	–	–	436	19	212	5	42.40	87.20	2.92	4-111	–	–
139	W.A. Hunt ‡	1931-32	1	1	–	0	0	0.00	–	–	1	–	–	96	2	39	0			2.44		–	–
140	W.J. O'Reilly	1931-32 to 1945-46	27	39	7	410	56*	12.81	–	1	7	7	–	10,024	585	3,254	144	22.60	69.61	1.95	7-54	11	3
141	H.M. Thurlow	1931-32	1	–	–	–	–	–	–	–	–	–	–	234	7	86	0			2.21		–	–
142	J.H.W. Fingleton	1931-32 to 1938	18	29	1	1,189	136	42.46	5	3	1	13	–									–	–
143	L.J. Nash	1931-32 to 1936-37	2	2	–	30	17	15.00	–	–	–	6	–	311	12	126	10	12.60	31.10	2.43	4-18	–	–
144	L.E. Nagel	1932-33	1	2	1	21	21*	21.00	–	–	–	–	–	262	9	110	2	55.00	131.00	2.52	2-110	–	–
145	L.P.J. O'Brien †	1932-33 to 1936-37	5	8	–	211	61	26.38	–	2	–	3	–									–	–
146	E.H. Bromley ††	1932-33 to 1934	2	4	–	38	26	9.50	–	–	–	2	–	60	4	19	0			1.90		–	–
147	L.S. Darling †	1932-33 to 1936-37	12	18	–	474	85	27.88	–	3	–	8	–	162	7	65	0			2.41		–	–
148	H.S.B. Love	1932-33	1	2	–	8	5	4.00	–	–	–	3	–									–	–
149	H.H. Alexander	1932-33	1	2	1	17	17*	17.00	–	–	–	–	–	276	3	154	1	154.00	276.00	3.35	1-129	–	–
150	W.A. Brown	1934 to 1948	22	35	1	1,592	206*	46.82	4	9	1	14	–									–	–
151	A.G. Chipperfield	1934 to 1938	14	20	3	552	109	32.47	1	3	1	15	–	924	28	437	5	87.40	184.80	2.84	3-91	–	–
152	H.I. Ebeling	1934	1	2	–	43	41	21.50	–	–	–	–	–	186	9	89	3	29.67	62.00	2.87	3-74	–	–
153	L.O. Fleetwood-Smith †	1935-36 to 1938	10	11	5	54	16*	9.00	–	–	2	–	–	3,093	78	1,570	42	37.38	73.64	3.05	6-110	2	1
154	E.L. McCormick	1935-36 to 1938	12	14	5	54	17*	6.00	–	–	–	8	–	2,107	50	1,079	36	29.97	58.53	3.07	4-101	–	–
155	F.C. Badcock	1936-37 to 1938	7	12	1	160	118	14.55	1	–	2	3	–									–	–
156	R.H. Robinson	1936-37	1	2	–	5	3	2.50	–	–	–	–	–									–	–
157	M.W. Sievers	1936-37	3	6	1	67	25*	13.40	–	–	1	4	–	602	25	161	9	17.89	66.89	1.60	5-21	1	–
158	F.A. Ward	1936-37 to 1938	4	8	4	36	18	6.00	–	–	2	1	–	1,268	30	574	11	52.18	115.27	2.72	6-102	1	–
159	R.G. Gregory	1936-37	2	3	–	153	80	51.00	–	2	–	1	–	24	0	14	0			3.50		–	–
160	B.A. Barnett †	1938	4	8	1	195	57	27.86	–	1	–	3	2									–	–
161	A.L. Hassett	1938 to 1953	43	69	3	3,073	198*	46.56	10	11	3	30	–	111	2	78	0			4.22		–	–
162	M.G. Waite	1938	2	3	–	11	8	3.67	–	–	–	1	–	552	23	190	1	190.00	552.00	2.07	1-150	–	–
163	S.G. Barnes	1938 to 1948	13	19	2	1,072	234	63.06	3	5	1	14	–	594	11	218	4	54.50	148.50	2.20	2-25	–	–
164	I.W.G. Johnson	1945-46 to 1956-57	45	66	13	1,000	77	18.52	–	2	5	30	–	8,780	330	3,182	109	29.19	80.55	2.17	7-44	3	–
165	R.R. Lindwall	1945-46 to 1959-60	61	84	13	1,502	118	21.15	2	5	26	26	–	13,650	419	5,251	228	23.03	59.87	2.31	7-38	12	–
166	C.L. McCool	1945-46 to 1949-50	14	17	4	459	104*	35.31	1	–	1	14	–	2,504	44	958	36	26.61	69.56	2.30	5-41	2	–
167	K.D. Meuleman	1945-46	1	1	–	0	0	0.00	–	–	1	–	–									–	–
168	K.R. Miller	1945-46 to 1956-57	55	87	7	2,958	147	36.98	7	13	3	38	–	10,389	337	3,906	170	22.98	61.11	2.26	7-60	7	1
169	D. Tallon	1945-46 to 1953	21	26	3	394	92	17.13	–	2	2	50	8									–	–
170	E.R.H. Toshack ‡	1945-46 to 1948	12	11	6	73	20*	14.60	–	–	4	4	–	3,140	155	989	47	21.04	66.81	1.89	6-29	4	1
171	A.R. Morris ††	1946-47 to 1954-55	46	79	3	3,533	206	46.49	12	12	15	15	–	111	1	50	2	25.00	55.50	2.70	1-5	–	–
172	G.E. Tribe ††	1946-47 to 1946-47	3	3	–	35	25*	17.50	–	–	–	–	–	760	9	330	2	165.00	380.00	2.61	2-48	–	–

No.	Player	Career	M	I	NO	Runs	HS	Avge	100	50	0	Ct	St	Balls	Runs	Wkts	Avge	SR	Econ	BB	5	10
173	F. W. Freer	1946-47	1	1	1	28	28*	–	–	–	–	–	–	160	74	3	24.67	53.33	2.78	2-49	–	–
174	B. Dooland	1946-47 to 1947-48	3	5	1	76	29	19.00	–	–	–	–	–	880	419	9	46.56	97.78	2.86	4-69	–	–
175	M. R. Harvey	1946-47	1	2	–	43	31	21.50	–	–	–	1	–	–	–	–	–	–	–	–	–	–
176	R. A. Hamence	1946-47 to 1947-48	3	4	1	81	30*	27.00	–	–	–	–	–	–	–	–	–	–	–	–	–	–
177	W. A. Johnston †‡	1947-48 to 1954-55	40	49	25	273	29	11.38	–	–	8	16	–	11,048	3,826	160	23.91	69.05	2.08	6-44	7	–
178	R. N. Harvey †	1947-48 to 1962-63	79	137	10	6,149	205	48.42	21	24	–	64	–	414	120	3	40.00	138.00	1.74	1-8	–	–
179	L. J. Johnson	1947-48	1	1	1	25	25*	–	–	–	–	–	–	282	74	6	12.33	47.00	1.57	3-8	–	–
180	S. J. E. Loxton	1947-48 to 1950-51	12	15	–	554	101	36.93	1	3	1	7	–	906	349	8	43.63	113.25	2.31	3-55	–	–
181	D. T. Ring	1947-48 to 1953	13	21	2	426	67	22.42	–	1	1	5	–	3,024	1,305	35	37.29	86.40	2.59	6-72	2	–
182	R. A. Saggers	1948 to 1949-50	6	5	2	30	14	10.00	–	–	–	16	8	–	–	–	–	–	–	–	–	–
183	J. Moroney	1949-50 to 1951-52	7	12	1	383	118	34.82	2	1	–	–	–	–	–	–	–	–	–	–	–	–
184	G. Noblet	1949-50 to 1952-53	3	4	1	22	13*	7.33	–	–	–	–	–	774	183	7	26.14	110.57	1.42	3-21	–	–
185	J. B. Iverson	1950-51	5	7	3	3	1*	0.75	–	–	3	–	–	1,108	320	21	15.24	52.76	1.73	6-27	1	–
186	K. A. Archer	1950-51 to 1951-52	5	9	–	234	48	26.00	–	2	–	1	–	–	–	–	–	–	–	–	–	–
187	J. W. Burke	1950-51 to 1958-59	24	44	7	1,280	189	34.59	3	5	2	18	–	814	230	8	28.75	101.75	1.70	4-37	–	–
188	G. B. Hole	1950-51 to 1954-55	18	33	2	789	66	25.45	–	6	3	21	–	398	126	3	42.00	132.67	1.90	1-9	–	–
189	G. R. A. Langley	1951-52 to 1956-57	26	37	12	374	53	14.96	–	1	–	83	15	–	–	–	–	–	–	–	–	–
190	R. Benaud	1951-52 to 1963-64	63	97	7	2,201	122	24.46	3	9	–	65	–	19,108	6,704	248	27.03	77.05	2.11	7-72	16	1
191	C. C. McDonald	1951-52 to 1961	47	83	4	3,107	170	39.33	5	17	–	14	–	–	–	–	–	–	–	–	–	–
192	G. R. Thoms	1951-52	1	2	–	44	28	22.00	–	–	–	–	–	–	–	–	–	–	–	–	–	–
193	R. G. Archer	1952-53 to 1956-57	19	30	1	713	128	24.59	1	5	2	20	–	3,576	1,318	48	27.46	74.50	2.21	5-53	1	–
194	I. D. Craig	1952-53 to 1957-58	11	18	–	358	53	19.89	–	2	2	2	–	–	–	–	–	–	–	–	–	–
195	A. K. Davidson †‡	1953 to 1962-63	44	61	7	1,328	80	24.59	–	5	5	42	–	11,587	3,819	186	20.53	62.30	1.98	7-93	14	2
196	J. C. Hill	1953 to 1954-55	3	6	3	21	8*	7.00	–	–	2	3	–	606	273	8	34.13	75.75	2.70	3-35	–	–
197	J. H. de Courcy	1953	3	6	1	81	41	16.20	–	–	1	3	–	–	–	–	–	–	–	–	–	–
198	L. E. Favell	1954-55 to 1960-61	19	31	3	757	101	27.04	1	5	1	9	–	–	–	–	–	–	–	–	–	–
199	L. V. Maddocks	1954-55 to 1956-57	7	12	2	177	69	17.70	–	1	–	18	1	–	–	–	–	–	–	–	–	–
200	P. J. P. Burge	1954-55 to 1965-66	42	68	8	2,290	181	38.17	4	12	4	23	–	6	5	0	–	–	5.00	–	–	–
201	W. J. Watson	1954-55	4	7	1	106	30	17.67	–	–	–	–	–	–	–	–	–	–	–	–	–	–
202	W. P. A. Crawford	1956	4	5	2	53	34	17.67	–	–	–	–	–	437	107	7	15.29	62.43	1.47	3-28	–	–
203	K. D. Mackay †	1956 to 1962-63	37	52	7	1,507	89	33.49	–	13	3	16	–	5,792	1,721	50	34.42	115.84	1.78	6-42	2	–
204	J. W. Rutherford	1956-57	1	1	–	30	30	30.00	–	–	–	–	–	36	15	1	15.00	36.00	2.50	1-11	–	–
205	J. W. Wilson ‡	1956-57	1	–	–	–	–	–	–	–	–	–	–	216	64	1	64.00	216.00	1.78	1-25	–	–
206	A. T. W. Grout	1957-58 to 1965-66	51	67	8	890	74	15.08	–	3	5	163	24	–	–	–	–	–	–	–	–	–
207	L. F. Kline †‡	1957-58 to 1960-61	13	16	9	58	15*	8.29	–	–	–	9	–	2,373	776	34	22.82	69.79	1.96	7-75	2	–
208	I. Meckiff ‡	1957-58 to 1963-64	18	20	7	154	45*	11.85	–	–	–	9	–	3,734	1,423	45	31.62	82.98	2.38	6-38	2	–
209	R. B. Simpson	1957-58 to 1977-78	62	111	7	4,869	311	46.82	10	27	9	110	–	6,881	3,001	71	42.27	96.92	2.62	5-57	2	–

No.	Player	Career	M	I	NO	R	HS	Avge	100s	50s	Ct	St	Balls	Mdns	R	W	Avge	S-R	RPO	BB	5	10
210	R. A. Gaunt †	1957-58 to 1963-64	3	4	1	6	3	3.00	–	–	1	–	716	14	310	7	44.29	102.29	2.60	3-53	–	–
211	N. C. O'Neill	1958-59 to 1964-65	42	69	8	2,779	181	45.56	6	15	21	–	1,392	48	667	17	39.24	81.88	2.88	4-41	–	–
212	K. N. Slater	1958-59	1	–	–	–	–	–	–	–	–	–	256	9	101	2	50.50	128.00	2.37	2-40	–	–
213	G. F. Rorke †	1958-59	4	4	2	9	7	4.50	–	–	1	–	703	26	203	10	20.30	70.30	1.73	3-23	–	–
214	G. B. Stevens	1959-60	4	7	–	112	28	16.00	–	–	1	–	–	–	–	–	–	–	–	–	–	–
215	B. N. Jarman	1959-60 to 1968-69	19	30	3	400	78	14.81	–	2	50	4	–	–	–	–	–	–	–	–	–	–
216	J. W. Martin ‡‡	1960-61 to 1966-67	8	13	1	214	55	17.83	–	1	5	–	1,846	57	832	17	48.94	108.59	2.70	3-56	–	–
217	F. M. Misson	1960-61 to 1961	5	5	3	38	25*	19.00	–	–	6	–	1,197	30	616	16	38.50	74.81	3.03	4-58	–	–
218	D. E. Hoare	1960-61	1	2	–	35	35	17.50	–	–	2	–	232	–	156	2	78.00	116.00	4.03	2-68	–	–
219	W. M. Lawry †	1961 to 1970-71	68	123	12	5,234	210	47.15	13	27	30	–	14	–	6	0	–	–	2.57	–	–	–
220	G. D. McKenzie	1961 to 1970-71	61	89	12	945	76	12.27	–	2	34	–	17,684	547	7,328	246	29.79	71.89	2.49	8-71	16	3
221	B. C. Booth	1961 to 1965-66	29	48	6	1,773	169	42.21	5	10	17	–	436	27	146	3	48.67	145.33	2.01	2-33	–	–
222	C. E. J. Guest	1962-63	1	1	–	11	11	11.00	–	–	–	–	144	–	59	0	–	–	2.46	–	–	–
223	B. K. Shepherd †	1962-63 to 1964-65	9	14	2	502	96	41.83	–	5	2	–	–	–	–	–	–	–	2.08	–	–	–
224	N. J. N. Hawke	1962-63 to 1968	27	37	15	365	45*	16.59	–	1	9	–	6,974	238	2,677	91	29.42	76.64	2.30	7-105	6	1
225	A. N. Connolly	1963-64 to 1970-71	29	37	12	260	37	10.40	–	–	17	–	7,818	289	2,981	102	29.23	76.65	2.29	6-47	4	–
226	T. R. Veivers †	1963-64 to 1966-67	21	30	4	813	88	31.27	–	7	7	–	4,191	195	1,375	33	41.67	127.00	1.97	4-68	–	–
227	I. R. Redpath	1963-64 to 1975-76	66	120	11	4,737	171	43.46	8	31	83	–	64	2	41	0	–	–	3.84	–	–	–
228	G. E. Corling	1964	5	4	2	3	3	1.67	–	–	1	–	1,159	50	447	12	37.25	96.58	2.31	4-60	–	–
229	R. M. Cowper †	1964 to 1968	27	46	2	2,061	307	46.84	5	10	21	–	3,005	138	1,139	36	31.64	83.47	2.27	4-48	–	–
230	R. H. D. Sellers †	1964-65	1	1	–	0	0	0.00	–	–	–	–	30	–	17	0	–	–	3.40	–	–	–
231	I. M. Chappell	1964-65 to 1979-80	76	136	10	5,345	196	42.42	14	26	105	–	2,873	87	1,316	20	65.80	143.65	2.75	2-21	–	–
232	D. J. Sincock ‡	1964-65 to 1965-66	3	4	1	80	29	26.67	–	–	2	–	724	7	410	8	51.25	90.50	3.40	3-67	–	–
233	L. C. Mayne †	1964-65 to 1969-70	6	11	3	76	13	9.50	–	–	2	–	1,251	37	628	19	33.05	65.84	3.01	4-43	–	–
234	P. I. Philpott	1964-65 to 1965-66	8	10	1	93	22	10.33	–	–	5	–	2,262	67	1,000	26	38.46	87.00	2.65	5-90	1	–
235	G. Thomas	1964-65 to 1965-66	8	12	1	325	61	29.55	–	3	5	–	–	–	–	–	–	–	–	–	–	–
236	P. J. Allan	1965-66	1	–	–	–	–	–	–	–	–	–	192	6	83	2	41.50	96.00	2.59	2-58	–	–
237	K. D. Walters	1965-66 to 1980-81	75	125	14	5,357	250	48.26	15	33	43	–	3,295	79	1,425	49	29.08	67.24	2.59	5-66	1	–
238	K. R. Stackpole	1965-66 to 1973-74	44	80	5	2,807	207	37.43	7	14	47	–	2,321	86	1,001	15	66.73	154.73	2.59	2-33	–	–
239	D. A. Renneberg	1966-67 to 1967-68	8	13	7	22	9	3.67	–	–	2	–	1,598	42	830	23	36.09	69.48	3.12	5-39	1	–
240	H. B. Taber	1966-67 to 1969-70	16	27	5	353	48	16.05	–	–	56	4	–	–	–	–	–	–	–	–	–	–
241	G. D. Watson	1966-67 to 1972	5	9	–	97	50	10.78	–	1	1	–	552	23	254	6	42.33	92.00	2.76	2-67	–	–
242	J. W. Gleeson	1967-68 to 1972	30	46	8	395	45	10.39	–	–	17	–	8,857	378	3,367	93	36.20	95.24	2.28	5-61	3	–
243	A. P. Sheahan	1967-68 to 1973-74	31	53	6	1,594	127	33.91	2	7	17	–	–	–	–	–	–	–	–	–	–	–
244	E. W. Freeman ‡‡	1967-68 to 1969-70	11	18	–	345	76	19.17	–	2	5	–	2,183	58	1,128	34	33.18	64.21	3.10	4-52	–	–
245	L. R. Joslin ‡‡	1967-68	1	2	–	9	7	4.50	–	–	–	–	–	–	–	–	–	–	–	–	–	–

No.	Player	From	To	M	I	NO	Runs	HS	Avge	100	50	Ct	St	Balls	Mdns	Runs	Wkts	Avge	SR	Econ	BB	5wi	10wm
246	R.J. Inverarity ‡	1968	1972	6	11	1	174	56	17.40	—	1	4	—	372	26	93	4	23.25	93.00	1.50	3-26	—	—
247	A.A. Mallett †	1968	1980	38	50	13	430	43*	11.62	—	—	30	—	9,990	419	3,940	132	29.85	75.68	2.37	8-59	6	1
248	T.J. Jenner	1970-71	1975-76	9	14	5	208	74	23.11	—	1	5	—	1,881	62	749	24	31.21	78.38	2.39	5-90	1	—
249	R.W. Marsh †	1970-71	1983-84	96	150	13	3,633	132	26.52	3	16	343	12	72	—	54	—	—	—	4.50	—	—	—
250	A.L. Thomson	1970-71	1970-71	4	5	4	22	12*	22.00	—	—	—	—	1,519	33	654	12	54.50	126.58	2.58	3-79	—	—
251	G.S. Chappell	1970-71	1983-84	87	151	19	7,110	247*	53.86	24	31	122	—	5,327	208	1,913	47	40.70	113.34	2.15	5-61	1	—
252	J.R.F. Duncan	1970-71	1970-71	3	3	2	3	3	3.00	—	—	1	—	112	4	30	—	—	—	1.61	—	—	—
253	K.J. O'Keeffe	1970-71	1977	24	34	9	644	85	25.76	—	3	15	—	5,384	189	2,018	53	38.08	101.58	2.25	5-101	1	—
254	D.K. Lillee	1970-71	1983-84	70	90	24	905	73*	13.71	—	1	23	—	18,467	652	8,493	355	23.92	52.02	2.75	7-83	23	7
255	A.R. Dell ‡	1970-71	1973-74	2	2	2	6	3*	—	—	—	1	—	559	18	160	6	26.67	93.17	1.72	3-65	—	—
256	K.H. Eastwood ††	1970-71	1970-71	1	2	—	5	5	2.50	—	—	—	—	40	1	21	1	21.00	40.00	3.15	1-21	—	—
257	D.J. Colley	1972	1972	3	5	1	84	54	21.00	—	1	1	—	729	20	312	6	52.00	121.50	2.57	3-83	—	—
258	B.C. Francis	1972	1972	3	5	—	52	27	10.40	—	—	1	—	—	—	—	—	—	—	—	—	—	—
259	R. Edwards	1972	1975	20	32	3	1,171	170*	40.38	2	9	7	—	12	—	20	—	—	—	10.00	—	—	—
260	R.A.L. Massie †	1972	1972-73	6	8	1	78	42	11.14	—	—	1	—	1,739	74	647	31	20.87	56.10	2.23	8-53	2	1
261	J. Benaud	1972-73	1972-73	3	5	—	223	142	44.60	1	1	—	—	24	1	12	2	6.00	12.00	3.00	2-12	—	—
262	J.R. Thomson	1972-73	1985	51	73	20	679	49	12.81	—	—	20	—	10,535	300	5,602	200	28.01	52.68	3.19	6-46	8	—
263	M.H.N. Walker	1972-73	1977	34	43	13	586	78*	19.53	—	1	12	—	10,094	380	3,792	138	27.48	73.14	2.25	8-143	6	—
264	J.R. Watkins	1972-73	1972-73	1	2	1	39	36	39.00	—	—	—	—	48	1	21	—	—	—	2.62	—	—	—
265	J.R. Hammond	1972-73	1972-73	5	5	2	28	19	9.33	—	—	2	—	1,031	47	488	15	32.53	68.73	2.84	4-38	—	—
266	I.C. Davis	1973-74	1977	15	27	1	692	105	26.62	1	4	9	—	—	—	—	—	—	—	—	—	—	—
267	G.J. Gilmour ††	1973-74	1976-77	15	22	1	483	101	23.00	1	3	8	—	2,661	51	1,406	54	26.04	49.28	3.17	6-85	3	—
268	G. Dymock ††	1973-74	1979-80	21	32	7	236	31*	9.44	—	—	1	—	5,545	179	2,116	78	27.13	71.09	2.29	7-67	5	1
269	A.G. Hurst	1973-74	1979-80	12	20	3	102	26	6.00	—	—	3	—	3,054	74	1,200	43	27.91	71.02	2.36	5-28	2	—
270	A.J. Woodcock	1973-74	1973-74	1	1	—	27	27	27.00	—	—	—	—	—	—	—	—	—	—	—	—	—	—
271	W.J. Edwards †	1974-75	1974-75	3	6	—	68	30	11.33	—	—	—	—	—	—	—	—	—	—	—	—	—	—
272	R.B. McCosker	1974-75	1979-80	25	46	5	1,622	127	39.56	4	9	21	—	—	—	—	—	—	—	—	—	—	—
273	A. Turner †	1975	1976-77	14	27	1	768	136	29.54	—	3	15	—	—	—	—	—	—	—	—	—	—	—
274	G.J. Cosier †	1975-76	1978-79	18	32	1	897	168	28.94	2	3	14	—	899	30	341	5	68.20	179.80	2.28	2-26	—	—
275	G.N. Yallop ††	1975-76	1984-85	39	70	3	2,756	268	41.13	8	9	23	—	192	5	116	1	116.00	192.00	3.63	1-21	—	—
276	D.W. Hookes ††	1976-77	1985-86	23	41	3	1,306	143*	34.37	1	8	12	—	96	4	41	1	41.00	96.00	2.56	1-4	—	—
277	L.S. Pascoe	1976-77	1981-82	14	19	9	106	30*	10.60	—	—	2	—	3,403	112	1,668	64	26.06	53.17	2.94	5-59	1	—
278	R.D. Robinson	1977	1977	3	6	—	100	34	16.67	—	—	4	—	—	—	—	—	—	—	—	—	—	—
279	C.S. Serjeant	1977	1977-78	12	23	1	522	124	23.73	1	2	13	—	—	—	—	—	—	—	—	—	—	—
280	R.J. Bright ‡	1977	1986-87	25	39	8	445	33	14.35	—	1	13	—	5,541	298	2,180	53	41.13	104.55	2.36	7-87	4	—
281	K.J. Hughes	1977	1984-85	70	124	6	4,415	213	37.42	9	22	50	—	85	2	28	—	—	—	1.98	—	—	—
282	M.F. Malone	1977	1977	1	1	—	46	46	46.00	—	—	1	—	342	24	77	6	12.83	57.00	1.35	5-63	1	—

Player	Span	M	I	NO	R	HS	Avge	100s	50s	Ct	St	Balls	Mdns	R	W	Avge	S-R	RPO	BB	5	10
283 W. M. Clark	1977-78 to 1978-79	10	19	2	98	33	5.76	–	–	6	–	2,793	63	1,264	44	28.73	63.48	2.72	4-46	–	–
284 P. A. Hibbert †‡	1977-78	1	2	–	15	13	7.50	–	–	1	–	–	–	–	–	–	–	–	–	–	–
285 A. L. Mann †	1977-78	4	8	–	189	105	23.63	1	–	2	–	552	4	316	4	79.00	138.00	3.43	3-12	–	–
286 A. D. Ogilvie	1977-78	5	10	–	178	47	17.80	–	–	5	–	–	–	–	–	–	–	–	–	–	–
287 S. J. Rixon	1977-78 to 1984-85	13	24	3	394	54	18.76	–	1	42	5	–	–	–	–	–	–	–	–	–	–
288 P. M. Toohey	1977-78 to 1979-80	15	29	1	893	122	31.89	1	7	9	–	2	–	4	0	–	–	12.00	–	–	–
289 J. Dyson	1977-78 to 1984-85	30	58	5	1,359	127*	26.65	2	5	10	–	2	–	–	–	–	–	–	–	–	–
290 J. B. Gannon ‡	1977-78	3	5	4	3	3*	3.00	–	–	1	–	726	13	361	11	32.82	66.00	2.98	4-77	–	–
291 I. W. Callen †	1977-78	1	2	2	26	22*	–	–	–	–	–	440	5	191	6	31.83	73.33	2.60	3-83	–	–
292 W. M. Darling	1977-78 to 1979-80	14	27	1	697	91	26.81	–	5	3	–	–	–	–	–	–	–	–	–	–	–
293 G. M. Wood †	1977-78 to 1988-89	59	112	6	3,374	172	31.83	9	13	41	–	–	–	–	–	–	–	–	–	–	–
294 B. Yardley	1977-78 to 1982-83	33	54	4	978	74	19.56	–	4	31	–	8,909	379	3,986	126	31.63	70.71	2.68	7-98	6	1
295 J. D. Higgs	1977-78 to 1980-81	22	36	16	111	16	5.55	–	–	3	–	4,752	176	2,057	66	31.17	72.00	2.60	7-143	2	1
296 T. J. Laughlin †	1977-78 to 1978-79	3	5	–	87	35	17.40	–	–	3	–	516	16	262	6	43.67	86.00	3.05	5-101	1	–
297 R. M. Hogg	1978-79 to 1984-85	38	48	13	439	52	9.76	–	1	7	–	7,633	230	3,503	123	28.48	62.06	2.75	6-74	6	2
298 J. A. Maclean	1978-79	4	8	1	79	33*	11.29	–	–	18	–	–	–	–	–	–	–	–	–	–	–
299 A. R. Border †‡	1978-79 to 1993-94	156	265	44	11,174	205	50.56	27	63	156	–	4,009	199	1,525	39	39.10	102.79	2.28	7-46	2	1
300 P. H. Carlson	1978-79	2	4	–	23	21	5.75	–	–	2	–	368	10	99	2	49.50	184.00	1.61	2-41	–	–
301 K. J. Wright	1978-79 to 1979-80	10	18	5	219	55*	16.85	–	1	31	4	–	–	–	–	–	–	–	–	–	–
302 A. M. J. Hilditch	1978-79 to 1985-86	18	34	1	1,073	119	31.56	2	6	13	–	–	–	–	–	–	–	–	–	–	–
303 P. R. Sleep	1978-79 to 1989-90	14	21	1	483	90	24.15	–	4	4	–	2,982	132	1,397	31	45.06	96.19	2.81	5-72	1	–
304 D. F. Whatmore	1978-79	7	13	–	293	77	22.54	–	2	13	–	30	2	11	0	–	–	2.20	–	–	–
305 I. K. Moss †	1978-79	1	2	1	60	38*	60.00	–	–	1	–	–	–	–	–	–	–	–	–	–	–
306 B. M. Laird	1979-80 to 1982-83	21	40	2	1,341	92	35.29	–	11	16	–	18	1	12	0	–	–	4.00	–	–	–
307 J. M. Wiener	1979-80	6	11	–	281	93	25.55	–	2	4	–	78	4	41	0	–	–	3.15	–	–	–
308 G. R. Beard	1979-80	3	6	1	114	49	22.80	–	–	2	–	259	17	109	1	109.00	259.00	2.53	1-26	–	–
309 G. F. Lawson	1980-81 to 1989-90	46	68	12	894	74	15.96	–	4	10	–	11,118	386	5,501	180	30.56	61.77	2.97	8-112	11	2
310 T. M. Alderman	1981 to 1990-91	41	53	22	203	26*	6.55	–	–	27	–	10,181	432	4,616	170	27.15	59.89	2.72	6-47	14	1
311 T. M. Chappell	1981	3	6	1	79	27	15.80	–	–	2	–	–	–	–	–	–	–	–	–	–	–
312 M. F. Kent	1981	3	6	–	171	54	28.50	–	2	6	–	–	–	–	–	–	–	–	–	–	–
313 M. R. Whitney ‡	1981 to 1992-93	12	19	8	68	13	6.18	–	–	2	–	2,672	90	1,325	39	33.97	68.51	2.98	7-27	2	–
314 D. M. Wellham	1981 to 1986-87	6	11	1	257	103	23.36	1	1	7	–	6	–	10	0	–	–	10.00	–	–	–
315 G. M. Ritchie	1982-83 to 1986-87	30	53	5	1,690	146	35.21	3	7	14	–	–	–	–	–	–	–	–	–	–	–
316 C. G. Rackemann	1982-83 to 1990-91	12	14	4	53	15*	5.30	–	–	3	–	2,719	132	1,137	39	29.15	69.72	2.51	6-86	3	1
317 K. C. Wessels †	1982-83 to 1985-86	24	42	1	1,761	179	42.95	4	9	18	–	90	3	42	0	–	–	2.80	–	–	–
318 T. G. Hogan ‡	1982-83 to 1983-84	7	12	1	205	42*	18.64	–	–	2	–	1,436	54	706	15	47.07	95.73	2.95	5-66	1	–

No.	Player	Career	M	I	NO	Runs	HS	Avg	100	50	Ct	St	Balls	Runs	W	Avg	SR	BB	5w	10w	Econ
319	R.D. Woolley	1982-83 to 1983-84	2	2	—	21	13	10.50	—	—	7	—	—	—	—	—	—	—	—	—	—
320	W.B. Phillips †	1983-84 to 1985-86	27	48	2	1,485	159	32.28	2	7	52	—	—	—	—	—	—	—	—	—	—
321	J.N. Maguire	1983-84	3	5	1	28	15*	7.00	—	—	—	—	616	323	10	32.30	61.60	4-57	—	—	3.15
322	G.R.J. Matthews	1983-84 to 1992-93	33	53	8	1,849	130	41.09	4	12	17	—	6,271	2,942	61	48.23	102.80	5-103	2	1	2.81
323	S.B. Smith	1983-84	3	5	—	41	12	8.20	—	—	—	—	—	—	—	—	—	—	—	—	—
324	D.M. Jones	1983-84 to 1992-93	52	89	11	3,631	216	46.55	11	14	34	—	198	64	—	—	—	—	—	—	1.94
325	D.C. Boon	1984-85 to 1995-96	107	190	20	7,422	200	43.66	21	32	99	—	36	14	—	—	—	—	—	—	2.33
326	R.G. Holland	1984-85 to 1985-86	11	15	6	35	10	3.18	—	—	5	—	2,889	1,352	34	39.76	84.97	6-54	1	—	2.81
327	M.J. Bennett	1984-85 to 1985	3	5	2	71	23	23.67	—	—	4	—	665	325	6	54.17	110.83	3-79	—	—	2.93
328	C.J. McDermott	1984-85 to 1995-96	71	90	13	940	42*	12.21	—	—	19	—	16,586	8,332	291	28.63	57.00	8-97	14	2	3.01
329	S.P. O'Donnell	1985 to 1985-86	6	10	3	206	48	29.43	—	—	—	—	940	504	6	84.00	156.67	3-37	—	—	3.22
330	D.R. Gilbert	1985 to 1986-87	9	12	4	57	15	7.13	—	—	—	—	1,647	843	16	52.69	102.94	3-48	—	—	3.07
331	R.B. Kerr	1985-86	2	4	—	31	17	7.75	—	—	—	—	—	—	—	—	—	—	—	—	—
332	M.G. Hughes	1985-86 to 1993-94	53	70	8	1,032	72*	16.65	—	2	23	—	12,285	6,017	212	28.38	57.95	8-87	7	1	2.94
333	G.R. Marsh	1985-86 to 1991-92	50	93	7	2,854	138	33.19	4	15	38	—	—	—	—	—	—	—	—	—	—
334	B.A. Reid ††	1985-86 to 1992-93	27	34	14	93	13	4.65	—	—	5	—	6,244	2,784	113	24.64	55.26	7-51	5	2	2.68
335	S.R. Waugh	1985-86 to 2003-04	168	260	46	10,927	200	51.06	32	50	112	—	7,805	3,445	92	37.45	84.84	5-28	3	—	2.65
336	S.P. Davis	1985-86	1	1	—	0	0	0.00	—	—	—	—	150	70	—	—	—	—	—	—	2.80
337	T.J. Zoehrer	1985-86 to 1986-87	10	14	2	246	52*	20.50	—	1	18	1	—	—	—	—	—	—	—	—	—
338	C.D. Matthews ‡‡	1986-87 to 1988-89	3	5	—	54	32	10.80	—	—	—	—	570	313	6	52.17	95.00	3-95	—	—	3.29
339	G.C. Dyer	1986-87 to 1987-88	6	6	—	131	60	21.83	—	1	22	2	—	—	—	—	—	—	—	—	—
340	P.L. Taylor	1986-87 to 1991-92	13	19	3	431	87	26.94	—	2	10	—	2,227	1,068	27	39.56	82.48	6-78	1	—	2.88
341	M.R.J. Veletta	1987-88 to 1989-90	8	11	—	207	39	18.82	—	—	12	—	—	—	—	—	—	—	—	—	—
342	T.B.A. May	1987-88 to 1994-95	24	28	12	225	42*	14.06	—	—	6	—	6,577	2,606	75	34.75	87.69	5-9	3	—	2.38
343	A.I.C. Dodemaide	1987-88 to 1992-93	10	15	6	202	50	22.44	—	1	6	—	2,184	953	34	28.03	64.24	6-58	1	—	2.62
344	I.A. Healy	1988-89 to 1999-00	119	182	23	4,356	161*	27.40	4	22	366	29	—	—	—	—	—	—	—	—	—
345	T.V. Hohns †	1988-89 to 1989	7	7	—	136	40	19.43	—	—	7	—	1,528	580	17	34.12	89.88	3-59	—	—	2.28
346	M.A. Taylor †	1988-89 to 1998-99	104	186	13	7,525	334*	43.50	19	40	157	—	42	26	1	26.00	42.00	1-11	—	—	3.71
347	G.D. Campbell	1989 to 1989-90	4	6	2	10	6	2.50	—	—	—	—	951	503	13	38.69	73.15	3-79	—	—	3.17
348	T.M. Moody	1989-90 to 1992-93	8	14	—	456	106	32.57	2	—	9	—	432	147	2	73.50	216.00	1-17	—	—	2.04
349	M.E. Waugh	1990-91 to 2002-03	128	209	17	8,029	153*	41.82	20	47	181	—	4,853	2,429	59	41.17	82.25	5-40	1	—	3.00
350	S.K. Warne	1991-92 to 2004-05	117	156	13	2,326	99	16.27	—	11	93	—	31,489	13,425	527	25.47	59.75	8-71	27	8	2.56
351	W.N. Phillips	1991-92	1	2	—	22	14	11.00	—	—	—	—	—	—	—	—	—	—	—	—	—
352	P.R. Reiffel	1991-92 to 1997-98	35	50	14	955	79*	26.53	—	6	15	—	6,403	2,804	104	26.96	61.57	6-71	5	—	2.63
353	D.R. Martyn	1992-93 to 2004-05	44	71	10	2,875	161	47.13	7	14	16	—	348	168	2	84.00	174.00	1-0	—	—	2.90
354	J.L. Langer †	1992-93 to 2004-05	76	128	6	5,488	250	44.98	16	18	50	—	6	3	—	—	—	—	—	—	3.00
355	J. Angel †	1992-93 to 1994-95	4	7	1	35	11	5.83	—	—	—	—	748	463	10	46.30	74.80	3-54	—	—	3.71

Player	Span	M	I	NO	R	HS	Avge	100s	50s	Ct	St	Balls	Mdns	R	W	Avge	S-R	RPO	BB	5	10
356 B.P. Julian ‡	1993 to 1995-96	7	9	1	128	56*	16.00	—	1	4	—	1,098	43	599	15	39.93	73.20	3.27	4-36	—	—
357 M.J. Slater ‡	1993 to 2001	74	131	7	5,312	219	42.84	14	21	33	—	25	1	10	1	10.00	25.00	2.40	1-4	—	—
358 G.D. McGrath	1993-94 to 2004-05	97	107	38	450	39	6.52	—	—	29	—	22,860	1146	9,509	440	21.61	51.95	2.50	8-38	24	3
359 M.L. Hayden †	1994-95 to 2004-05	95	95	8	5,059	380	58.15	20	15	67	—	54	—	40	0	—	—	4.44	—	—	—
360 M.G. Bevan ††	1994-95 to 1997-98	18	30	3	785	91	29.07	—	6	8	—	1,285	30	703	29	24.24	44.31	3.28	6-82	1	—
361 D.W. Fleming	1994-95 to 2000-01	20	19	3	305	71*	19.06	—	2	9	—	4,129	153	1,942	75	25.89	55.05	2.82	5-30	1	—
362 P.A. Emery †	1994-95	1	1	1	8	8*	—	—	—	—	2	—	—	—	—	—	—	—	—	—	—
363 G.S. Blewett	1994-95 to 1999-00	46	79	4	2,552	214	34.03	4	15	45	—	1,436	60	720	14	51.43	102.57	3.01	2-9	—	—
364 P.E. McIntyre	1994-95 to 1996-97	2	4	1	22	16	7.33	—	—	1	—	393	10	194	5	38.80	78.60	2.96	3-103	—	—
365 S.G. Law	1995-96	1	1	1	54	54*	—	—	1	—	—	18	1	9	0	—	—	3.00	—	—	—
366 R.T. Ponting	1995-96 to 2004-05	79	127	15	6,086	257	54.34	20	22	91	—	437	18	190	4	47.50	109.25	2.61	1-0	—	—
367 G.B. Hogg ††	1996-97 to 2003-04	7	5	1	38	17*	9.50	—	—	3	—	774	26	452	9	50.22	86.00	3.50	2-40	—	—
368 M.T.G. Elliott ††	1996-97 to 2004-05	21	36	1	1,172	199	33.49	3	4	14	—	12	—	4	0	—	—	2.00	—	—	—
369 M.S. Kasprowicz	1996-97 to 2004-05	23	33	8	282	25	11.28	—	—	16	—	4,391	153	2,242	67	33.46	65.54	3.06	7-36	3	—
370 J.N. Gillespie	1996-97 to 2004-05	54	69	22	685	48*	14.57	—	—	16	—	11,143	509	5,298	206	25.72	54.09	2.85	7-37	7	—
371 A.J. Bichel	1996-97 to 2003-04	11	22	4	355	71	19.72	—	1	16	—	3,337	112	1,870	58	32.24	57.53	3.36	5-39	1	—
372 S. Young †	1997	1	2	1	4	4*	4.00	—	—	1	—	48	—	13	0	—	—	1.63	—	—	—
373 S.H. Cook †	1997-98	2	2	—	3	3	1.50	—	—	—	—	224	10	142	7	20.29	32.00	3.80	3-39	—	—
374 S.C.G. MacGill	1997-98 to 2003-04	32	37	6	263	43	8.48	—	—	16	—	8,447	291	4,441	152	29.22	55.57	3.15	7-50	9	2
375 G.R. Robertson	1997-98	4	7	—	140	57	20.00	—	1	2	—	898	20	515	13	39.62	69.08	3.44	4-72	—	—
376 P. Wilson	1997-98	1	2	2	0	0*	—	—	—	—	—	72	2	50	0	—	—	4.17	—	—	—
377 A.C. Dale †	1997-98 to 1998-99	2	2	—	5	5	2.00	—	—	1	—	348	19	187	6	31.17	58.00	3.22	3-71	—	—
378 D.S. Lehmann ††	1997-98 to 2004-05	20	32	2	1,549	177	51.63	5	8	9	—	740	29	289	13	22.08	56.92	2.33	3-42	—	—
379 C.R. Miller	1998-99 to 2000-01	18	24	3	174	43	8.29	—	—	6	—	4,091	163	1,805	69	26.16	59.29	2.65	5-32	3	1
380 M.J. Nicholson	1998-99	1	2	—	14	9	7.00	—	—	1	—	150	4	115	4	28.75	37.50	4.60	3-56	—	—
381 A.C. Gilchrist †	1999-00 to 2004-05	56	80	14	3,485	204*	52.80	10	17	217	24	—	—	—	—	—	—	—	—	—	—
382 S.A. Muller	1999-00	2	2	1	6	6*	6.00	—	—	—	—	348	8	258	7	36.86	49.71	4.45	3-68	—	—
383 B. Lee	1999-00 to 2003-04	37	36	6	593	62*	19.77	—	2	7	—	7,380	256	4,403	139	31.68	53.10	3.58	5-47	4	—
384 S.M. Katich ††	2001 to 2004-05	9	15	2	546	125	42.00	1	2	6	—	575	11	349	11	31.73	52.27	3.64	6-65	1	—
385 M.L. Love	2002-03 to 2003-04	5	8	3	233	100*	46.60	1	1	7	—	—	—	—	—	—	—	—	—	—	—
386 B.A. Williams	2003-04	4	6	3	23	10*	7.67	—	—	1	—	852	43	406	9	45.11	94.67	2.86	4-53	—	—
387 N.W. Bracken ‡	2003-04	2	4	2	9	6*	4.50	—	—	2	—	768	38	351	6	58.50	128.00	2.74	2-12	—	—
388 A. Symonds ‡	2003-04	2	4	—	53	24	13.25	—	—	4	—	144	4	85	1	85.00	144.00	3.54	1-68	—	—

† denotes left-hand batsman; ‡ denotes left-arm bowler; + denotes retired hurt.

BATTING RECORDS

HIGHEST INDIVIDUAL INNINGS

380	M. L. Hayden	v Zimbabwe at Perth	2003-04
334	D. G. Bradman	v England at Leeds	1930
334*	M. A. Taylor	v Pakistan at Peshawar	1998-99
311	R. B. Simpson	v England at Manchester	1964
307	R. M. Cowper	v England at Melbourne	1965-66
304	D. G. Bradman	v England at Leeds	1934
299*	D. G. Bradman	v South Africa at Adelaide	1931-32
270	D. G. Bradman	v England at Melbourne	1936-37
268	G. N. Yallop	v Pakistan at Melbourne	1983-84
266	W. H. Ponsford	v England at The Oval	1934
257	R. T. Ponting	v India at Melbourne	2003-04
254	D. G. Bradman	v England at Lord's	1930
250	K. D. Walters	v New Zealand at Christchurch	1976-77
250	J. L. Langer	v England at Melbourne	2002-03
247*	G. S. Chappell	v New Zealand at Wellington	1973-74
244	D. G. Bradman	v England at The Oval	1934
242	K. D. Walters	v West Indies at Sydney	1968-69
242	R. T. Ponting	v India at Adelaide	2003-04
235	G. S. Chappell	v Pakistan at Faisalabad	1979-80
234	D. G. Bradman	v England at Sydney	1946-47
234	S. G. Barnes	v England at Sydney	1946-47
232	D. G. Bradman	v England at The Oval	1930
232	S. J. McCabe	v England at Nottingham	1938
226	D. G. Bradman	v South Africa at Brisbane	1931-32
225	R. B. Simpson	v England at Adelaide	1965-66
223	D. G. Bradman	v West Indies at Brisbane (Ex)	1930-31
223	J. L. Langer	v India at Sydney	1999-00
219	M. A. Taylor	v England at Nottingham	1989
219	M. J. Slater	v Sri Lanka at Perth	1995-96
216	D. M. Jones	v West Indies at Adelaide	1988-89
214*	V. T. Trumper	v South Africa at Adelaide	1910-11
214	G. S. Blewett	v South Africa at Johannesburg (WS)	1996-97
213	K. J. Hughes	v India at Adelaide	1980-81
212	D. G. Bradman	v England at Melbourne	1936-37
211	W. L. Murdoch	v England at The Oval	1884
210	W. M. Lawry	v West Indies at Bridgetown	1964-65
210	D. M. Jones	v India at Chennai (Chepauk)	1986-87
207	K. R. Stackpole	v England at Brisbane	1970-71
206*	W. A. Brown	v England at Lord's	1938
206	A. R. Morris	v England at Adelaide	1950-51
206	R. T. Ponting	v West Indies at Port-of-Spain	2002-03
205	R. N. Harvey	v West Indies at Melbourne	1952-53
205	W. M. Lawry	v West Indies at Melbourne	1968-69
205	A. R. Border	v New Zealand at Adelaide	1987-88
204	R. N. Harvey	v West Indies at Kingston	1954-55
204	G. S. Chappell	v India at Sydney	1980-81
204*	A. C. Gilchrist	v South Africa at Johannesburg (WS)	2001-02
203	H. L. Collins	v South Africa at Johannesburg (OW)	1921-22
203	M. L. Hayden	v India at Chennai	2000-01
201	S. E. Gregory	v England at Sydney	1894-95
201*	J. Ryder	v England at Adelaide	1924-25
201	D. G. Bradman	v India at Adelaide	1947-48
201	R. B. Simpson	v West Indies at Bridgetown	1964-65
201	G. S. Chappell	v Pakistan at Brisbane	1981-82
200	D. C. Boon	v New Zealand at Perth	1989-90
200*	A. R. Border	v England at Leeds	1993
200	S. R. Waugh	v West Indies at Kingston	1994-95

HIGHEST INDIVIDUAL INNINGS AGAINST AUSTRALIA

281	L. Hutton	for England at The Oval	1938
287	R. E. Foster	for England at Sydney	1903-04
281	V. V. S. Laxman	for India at Kolkata	2000-01
277	B. C. Lara	for West Indies at Sydney	1992-93
274	R. G. Pollock	for South Africa at Durban (Kingsmead)	1969-70

HUNDRED ON DEBUT

†C. Bannerman (165*)	v England at Melbourne	1876-77
H. Graham (107)	v England at Lord's	1893
R. A. Duff (104)	v England at Melbourne	1901-02
M. J. Hartigan (116)	v England at Adelaide	1907-08
H. L. Collins (104)	v England at Sydney	1920-21
W. H. Ponsford (110)	v England at Sydney	1924-25
A. Jackson (164)	v England at Adelaide	1928-29
J. W. Burke (101*)	v England at Adelaide	1950-51
K. D. Walters (155)	v England at Brisbane	1965-66
G. S. Chappell (108)	v England at Perth	1970-71
G. J. Cosier (109)	v West Indies at Melbourne	1975-76
D. M. Wellham (103)	v England at The Oval	1981
K. C. Wessels (162)	v England at Brisbane	1982-83
W. B. Phillips (159)	v Pakistan at Perth	1983-84
M. E. Waugh (138)	v England at Adelaide	1990-91
G. S. Blewett (102*)	v England at Adelaide	1994-95

† Retired hurt

HUNDRED IN EACH INNINGS OF A MATCH

	1st	2nd		
W. Bardsley	136	130	v England at The Oval	1909
A. R. Morris	122	124*	v England at Adelaide	1946-47
D. G. Bradman	132	127*	v India at Melbourne	1947-48
J. Moroney	118	101*	v South Africa at Johannesburg (EP)	1949-50
R. B. Simpson	153	115	v Pakistan at Karachi	1964-65
K. D. Walters	242	103	v West Indies at Sydney	1968-69
I. M. Chappell	145	121	v New Zealand at Wellington	1973-74
G. S. Chappell	247*	133	v New Zealand at Wellington	1973-74
G. S. Chappell	123	109*	v West Indies at Brisbane	1975-76
A. R. Border	150*	153	v Pakistan at Lahore	1979-80
A. R. Border	140	114*	v New Zealand at Christchurch	1985-86
D. M. Jones	116	121*	v Pakistan at Adelaide	1989-90
S. R. Waugh	108	116	v England at Manchester	1997
M. L. Hayden	197	103	v England at Brisbane	2002-03
M. L. Hayden	117	132	v Sri Lanka at Cairns	2004-05

MOST HUNDREDS

	100s	Eng	SAf	WI	NZ	Ind	Pak	SL	Zim	Ban
S. R. Waugh	32	10	2	7	2	2	3	3	1	2
D. G. Bradman	29	19	4	2	0	4	0	0	0	0
A. R. Border	27	8	0	3	5	4	6	1	0	0
G. S. Chappell	24	9	0	5	3	1	6	0	0	0
R. N. Harvey	21	6	8	3	0	4	0	0	0	0
D. C. Boon	21	7	0	3	3	6	1	1	0	0
M. E. Waugh	20	6	4	4	1	1	3	1	0	0
R. T. Ponting	20	4	2	4	1	4	3	1	1	0
M. L. Hayden	20	3	4	3	1	3	1	3	2	0
M. A. Taylor	19	6	2	1	2	2	4	2	0	0
J. L. Langer	19	3	2	3	3	3	2	0	0	0
K. D. Walters	15	4	0	6	3	1	1	0	0	0

	100s	Eng	SAf	WI	NZ	Ind	Pak	SL	Zim	Ban
I. M. Chappell	14	4	0	5	2	2	1	0	0	0
M. J. Slater	14	7	0	1	2	0	3	1	0	0
W. M. Lawry	13	7	1	4	0	1	0	0	0	0
A. R. Morris	12	8	2	1	0	1	0	0	0	0
D. M. Jones	11	3	0	1	0	2	2	3	0	0
A. L. Hassett	10	4	3	2	0	1	0	0	0	0
R. B. Simpson	10	2	1	1	0	4	2	0	0	0
A. C. Gilchrist	10	2	2	1	1	1	1	1	1	0

MOST HUNDREDS AGAINST AUSTRALIA

	100s	In Australia	Elsewhere
J. B. Hobbs (England)	12	9	3
W. R. Hammond (England)	9	7	2
D. I. Gower (England)	9	5	4
R. B. Richardson (West Indies)	8	4	4
H. Sutcliffe (England)	8	6	2
S. M. Gavaskar (India)	8	5	3
B. C. Lara (West Indies)	8	3	5

MOST DOUBLE-HUNDREDS

	200s	Eng	SAf	WI	NZ	Ind	Pak	SL	Zim	Ban
D. G. Bradman	12	8	2	1	0	1	0	0	0	0
G. S. Chappell	4	0	0	0	1	1	2	0	0	0
R. B. Simpson	3	2	0	1	0	0	0	0	0	0
R. T. Ponting	3	0	0	1	0	2	0	0	0	0

CARRYING BAT THROUGH AN INNINGS

(Figures in brackets show side's total)

J. E. Barrett	67*	(176)	v England at Lord's	1890
W. W. Armstrong	159*	(309)	v South Africa at Johannesburg (OW)	1902-03
W. Bardsley	193*	(383)	v England at Lord's	1926
W. M. Woodfull	30*	(66)†	v England at Brisbane (Ex)	1928-29
W. M. Woodfull	73*	(193)†	v England at Adelaide	1932-33
W. A. Brown	206*	(422)	v England at Lord's	1938
W. M. Lawry	49*	(107)	v India at Delhi	1969-70
W. M. Lawry	60*	(116)†	v England at Sydney	1970-71
I. R. Redpath	159*	(346)	v New Zealand at Auckland	1973-74
D. C. Boon	58*	(103)	v New Zealand at Auckland	1985-86
M. A. Taylor	169*	(350)	v South Africa at Adelaide	1997-98

† *Denotes one or more batsmen absent or retired.*

MOST RUNS IN A SERIES

	M	I	NO	R	HS	100s	Avge	Series
D. G. Bradman ...	5	7	0	974	334	4	139.14	1930 v England in England
M. A. Taylor	6	11	1	839	219	2	83.90	1989 v England in England
R. N. Harvey	5	9	0	834	205	4	92.66	1952-53 v South Africa in Australia
D. G. Bradman ...	5	9	0	810	270	3	90.00	1936-37 v England in Australia
D. G. Bradman ...	5	5	1	806	299*	4	201.50	1931-32 v South Africa in Australia
D. G. Bradman ...	5	8	0	758	304	2	94.75	1934 v England in England
D. G. Bradman ...	5	6	2	715	201	4	178.75	1947-48 v India in Australia
R. T. Ponting	4	8	1	706	257	2	100.86	2002-03 v West Indies in West Indies
G. S. Chappell ...	6	11	5	702	182*	3	117.00	1975-76 v West Indies in Australia
K. D. Walters	4	6	0	699	242	4	116.50	1968-69 v West Indies in Australia
A. R. Morris	5	9	1	696	196	3	87.00	1948 v England in England

	M	I	NO	R	HS	100s	Avge	Series
D. G. Bradman ...	5	8	1	680	234	2	97.14	1946-47 v England in Australia
W. M. Lawry	5	8	0	667	205	3	83.38	1968-69 v West Indies in Australia
V. T. Trumper ...	5	9	2	661	214*	2	94.43	1910-11 v South Africa in Australia
R. N. Harvey	5	8	3	660	178	4	132.00	1949-50 v South Africa in S. Africa
R. N. Harvey	5	7	1	650	204	3	108.33	1954-55 v West Indies in West Indies
K. R. Stackpole ..	7	12	0	627	207	2	52.25	1970-71 v England in Australia
M. J. Slater	5	10	0	623	176	3	62.30	1994-95 v England in Australia
G. S. Chappell ...	6	11	0	608	144	2	55.27	1974-75 v England in Australia
A. R. Border	6	11	2	597	196	2	66.33	1985 v England in England
K. J. Hughes	6	12	2	594	100	1	59.40	1979-80 v India in India
W. M. Lawry	5	7	0	592	166	3	84.57	1965-66 v England in Australia
I. R. Redpath	6	11	0	575	103	3	52.27	1975-76 v West Indies in Australia
V. T. Trumper ...	5	10	1	574	185*	2	63.77	1903-04 v England in Australia
W. Bardsley	5	9	0	573	132	1	63.67	1910-11 v South Africa in Australia
W. H. Ponsford ..	4	7	1	569	266	2	94.83	1934 v England in England
D. M. Jones	6	9	1	566	157	2	70.75	1989 v England in England
H. L. Collins	5	9	0	557	162	2	61.89	1920-21 v England in Australia
D. C. Boon	5	9	2	556	135	3	79.43	1991-92 v India in Australia
M. T. G. Elliott ..	6	10	0	556	199	2	55.60	1997 v England in England
D. C. Boon	6	10	2	555	164*	3	69.38	1993 v England in England
G. N. Yallop	5	6	0	554	268	2	92.33	1983-84 v Pakistan in Australia
M. E. Waugh	6	10	1	550	137	1	61.11	1993 v England in England

Most runs in a series against opponents not mentioned above:

	M	I	NO	R	HS	100s	Avge	Series
D. S. Lehmann ...	3	6	0	375	153	2	62.50	2003-04 v Sri Lanka in Sri Lanka
G. S. Chappell ...	3	6	1	449	247*	2	89.30	1973-74 v New Zealand in NZ
M. L. Hayden	2	3	1	501	380	2	250.50	2003-04 v Zimbabwe in Australia
D. S. Lehmann ...	2	2	0	287	177	2	143.50	2003-04 v Bangladesh in Australia

MOST RUNS IN A SERIES AGAINST AUSTRALIA

	M	I	NO	R	HS	100s	Avge	Series
W. R. Hammond .	5	9	1	905	251	4	113.13	1928-29 for England in Australia
C. L. Walcott ...	5	10	0	827	155	5	82.70	1954-55 for West Indies in West Indies
H. Sutcliffe	5	9	0	734	176	4	81.56	1924-25 for England in Australia
G. A. Faulkner ...	5	10	0	732	204	2	73.20	1910-11 for South Africa in Australia
D. I. Gower	6	9	0	732	215	3	81.33	1985 for England in England

MOST RUNS IN A THREE-TEST SERIES

	M	I	NO	R	HS	100s	Avge	Series
M. L. Hayden	3	6	1	549	203	2	109.80	2000-01 v India in India
M. A. Taylor	3	5	1	513	334*	1	128.25	1998-99 v Pakistan in Pakistan
A. C. Gilchrist ...	3	5	2	473	204*	2	157.67	2001-02 v SAf in South Africa
G. S. Chappell ...	3	6	1	449	247*	2	89.80	1973-74 v NZ in New Zealand
M. L. Hayden	3	6	2	429	138	2	107.25	2001-02 v South Africa in Australia

Note: M. L. Hayden scored 501 runs in a two-Test series against Zimbabwe in Australia in 2003-04.

MOST RUNS IN A CALENDAR YEAR

	M	I	NO	R	HS	100s	Avge	Year
R. T. Ponting	11	18	3	1,503	257	4	100.20	2003
M. L. Hayden	14	25	3	1,391	203	5	63.23	2001
R. B. Simpson	14	26	3	1,381	311	3	60.04	1964
M. L. Hayden	12	21	4	1,312	380	5	77.17	2003
D. C. Boon	16	25	5	1,241	164*	4	62.05	1993
M. A. Taylor	11	20	1	1,219	219	4	64.16	1989
K. J. Hughes	15	28	4	1,163	130*	2	48.45	1979
M. L. Hayden	11	17	1	1,160	197	6	72.50	2002

	M	I	NO	R	HS	100s	Avge	Year
M. A. Taylor	12	22	3	1,112	334*	3	58.53	1998
M.A. Taylor	15	23	2	1,106	170	4	52.67	1993
A.R. Border	11	20	3	1,099	196	4	64.65	1985
D.M. Jones	11	18	3	1,099	216	4	73.27	1989
A.R. Border	14	27	3	1,073	162	3	44.70	1979
G.S. Blewett	15	25	0	1,067	214	2	42.68	1997
R.T. Ponting	11	16	1	1,064	154	5	70.93	2002
C. Hill	12	21	2	1,060	142	2	55.79	1902
W.M. Lawry	14	27	2	1,056	157	2	42.24	1964
M.J. Slater	14	25	2	1,051	169	3	45.70	1999
M.E. Waugh	12	22	6	1,034	153	4	64.63	1998
D.G. Bradman	8	13	4	1,025	201	5	113.89	1948
A.R. Border	11	19	3	1,000	140	5	62.50	1986

MOST RUNS IN A CAREER

		M	I	NO	R	HS	100s	Avge
1	A.R. Border	156	265	44	11,174	205	27	50.56
2	S.R. Waugh	168	260	46	10,927	200	32	51.06
3	M.E. Waugh	128	209	17	8,029	153*	20	41.82
4	M.A. Taylor	104	186	13	7,525	334*	19	43.50
5	D.C. Boon	107	190	20	7,422	200	21	43.66
6	G.S. Chappell	88	151	19	7,110	247*	24	53.86
7	D.G. Bradman	52	80	10	6,996	334	29	99.94
8	R.N. Harvey	79	137	10	6,149	205	21	48.42
9	R.T. Ponting	79	127	15	6,086	257	22	54.34
10	J.L. Langer	76	128	6	5,488	250	19	44.98
11	K.D. Walters	75	125	14	5,357	250	15	48.26
12	I.M. Chappell	76	136	10	5,345	196	14	42.42
13	M.J. Slater	74	131	7	5,312	219	14	42.84
14	M.L. Hayden	95	85	8	5,059	380	20	58.15
15	W.M. Lawry	68	123	12	5,234	210	13	47.15
16	R.B. Simpson	62	111	7	4,869	311	10	46.82
17	I.R. Redpath	67	120	11	4,737	171	8	43.46
18	K.J. Hughes	70	124	6	4,415	213	9	37.42
19	I.A. Healy	119	182	23	4,356	161*	4	27.40
20	R.W. Marsh	97	150	13	3,633	132	3	26.52
21	D.M. Jones	52	89	11	3,631	216	11	46.55
22	A.R. Morris	46	79	3	3,533	206	12	46.49
23	A.C. Gilchrist	56	80	14	3,485	204*	10	52.80
24	C. Hill	49	89	2	3,412	191	7	39.22
25	G.M. Wood	59	112	6	3,374	172	9	31.83
26	V.T. Trumper	48	89	8	3,163	214*	8	39.05
27	C.C. McDonald	47	83	4	3,107	170	5	39.33
28	A.L. Hassett	43	69	3	3,073	198*	10	46.56
29	K.R. Miller	55	87	7	2,958	147	7	36.98
30	D.R. Martyn	44	71	10	2,875	161	7	47.13

MOST RUNS AGAINST OPPONENT

	M	I	NO	R	HS	100s	Avge
v England							
D.G. Bradman	37	63	7	5,028	334	19	89.79
A.R. Border	47	82	19	3,548	200*	8	56.32
S.R. Waugh	46	73	18	3,200	177*	10	58.18
v South Africa							
R.N. Harvey	14	23	3	1,625	205	8	81.25
S.R. Waugh	16	25	2	1,147	164	2	49.87
M.E. Waugh	18	29	2	1,135	116	4	42.04

	M	I	NO	R	HS	100s	Avge
v West Indies							
S. R. Waugh	32	51	7	2,192	200	7	49.82
A. R. Border	31	59	7	2,052	126	3	39.46
M. E. Waugh	28	48	3	1,858	139*	4	41.29
v New Zealand							
A. R. Border	23	32	3	1,500	205	5	51.72
D. C. Boon	17	27	2	1,187	200	3	47.48
S. R. Waugh	23	34	5	1,117	151*	2	38.52
v India							
A. R. Border	20	35	5	1,567	163	4	52.23
R. T. Ponting	14	25	3	1,230	257	4	55.91
D. C. Boon	11	20	3	1,204	135	6	70.82
v Pakistan							
A. R. Border	22	36	8	1,666	153	6	59.50
G. S. Chappell	17	27	2	1,581	235	6	63.24
M. A. Taylor	12	20	3	1,347	334*	4	79.24
v Sri Lanka							
R. T. Ponting	10	16	1	711	105*	1	47.40
S. R. Waugh	8	11	3	701	170	3	87.63
M. A. Taylor	8	15	1	611	164	2	43.64
v Zimbabwe							
M. L. Hayden	2	3	1	501	380	2	250.50
R. T. Ponting	3	4	1	290	169	1	96.67
S. R. Waugh	3	3	1	290	151*	1	145.00
v Bangladesh							
D. S. Lehmann	2	2	0	287	177	2	143.50
S. R. Waugh	2	2	2	256	156*	2	–
M. L. Love	2	2	1	100	100*	1	100.00

MOST RUNS AGAINST AUSTRALIA

	M	I	NO	R	HS	100s	Avge
for England							
J. B. Hobbs	41	71	4	3,636	187	12	54.27
D. I. Gower	42	77	4	3,269	215	9	44.78
G. Boycott	39	71	9	2,945	191	7	47.50
for South Africa							
R. G. Pollock	14	23	2	1,453	274	5	69.19
E. J. Barlow	14	26	2	1,149	201	5	47.88
G. Kirsten	18	34	1	1,134	153	2	34.36
for West Indies							
B. C. Lara	27	50	2	2,470	277	8	51.46
I. V. A. Richards	34	54	3	2,266	208	5	44.43
D. L. Haynes	33	59	6	2,233	145	5	42.13
for New Zealand							
J. G. Wright	19	36	3	1,277	141	2	38.70
M. D. Crowe	17	29	3	1,255	188	3	48.27
C. L. Cairns	14	26	1	863	109	1	34.52
for India							
S. R. Tendulkar	19	35	4	1,789	241*	7	57.71
S. M. Gavaskar	20	31	1	1,550	172	8	51.67
G. R. Viswanath	18	31	2	1,538	161*	4	53.03
for Pakistan							
Javed Miandad	25	40	2	1,797	211	6	47.29
Zaheer Abbas	20	34	2	1,411	126	2	44.09
Salim Malik	15	26	2	1,106	237	2	46.08
for Sri Lanka							
P. A. de Silva	12	19	2	803	167	1	47.24
A. Ranatunga	12	19	3	673	127	1	42.06
S. T. Jayasuriya	11	20	2	592	131	2	32.89

	M	I	NO	R	HS	100s	Avge
for Zimbabwe							
T. R. Gripper	3	6	0	179	60	0	29.83
M. A. Vermeulen	2	4	0	166	63	0	41.50
S. V. Carlisle	2	4	0	160	118	1	40.00
for Bangladesh							
Hannan Sarkar	2	4	0	166	76	0	41.50
Habibul Bashar	2	4	0	141	54	0	35.25
Khaled Mashud	2	4	0	75	44	0	18.75

MOST RUNS AT EACH AUSTRALIAN VENUE

	M	I	NO	R	HS	100s	Avge
Melbourne Cricket Ground (Melbourne)							
D. G. Bradman	11	17	4	1,671	270	9	128.54
S. R. Waugh	17	30	6	1,284	131*	3	53.30
A. R. Border	20	36	3	1,272	163	4	38.55
Most by non-Australian							
J. B. Hobbs (Eng)	10	18	1	1,178	178	5	69.29
Sydney Cricket Ground (Sydney)							
A. R. Border	17	29	8	1,177	89	0	56.05
G. S. Chappell	12	22	4	1,150	204	4	63.89
D. C. Boon	11	21	3	1,127	184*	4	62.61
Most by non-Australian							
W. R. Hammond (Eng) .	5	7	2	808	251	4	161.60
Adelaide Oval (Adelaide)							
A. R. Border	16	29	5	1,415	205	4	58.96
S. R. Waugh	15	26	2	1,056	170	3	44.00
D. G. Bradman	7	11	3	970	299*	3	107.78
Most by non-Australian							
J. B. Hobbs (Eng)	5	10	1	601	187	3	66.78
Brisbane Exhibition Ground (Brisbane)							
D. G. Bradman	2	3	0	242	223	1	80.67
E. H. Hendren (Eng) ..	1	2	0	214	169	1	107.00
G. A. Headley (WI) ...	1	2	1	130	102*	1	130.00
Brisbane Cricket Ground (Brisbane)							
G. S. Chappell	7	11	2	1,006	201	5	111.78
S. R. Waugh	17	26	4	915	147*	3	41.59
M. A. Taylor	10	18	2	912	164	2	57.00
Most by non-Australian							
R. B. Richardson (WI) .	3	6	1	314	138	1	62.80
WACA Ground (Perth)							
A. R. Border	16	26	3	931	125	2	40.48
D. C. Boon	11	19	2	846	200	2	49.76
S. R. Waugh	15	21	2	843	99*	0	44.37
Most by non-Australian							
D. I. Gower (Eng)	5	10	1	471	136	2	52.33
Bellerive Oval (Hobart)							
M. A. Taylor	4	7	1	405	123	2	67.50
M. J. Slater	3	5	0	365	168	1	73.00
J. L. Langer	2	3	0	309	127	2	103.00
M. E. Waugh	5	8	0	309	111	1	38.63
Most by non-Australian							
Inzamam-ul-Haq (Pak) .	2	4	0	197	149*	1	49.25
Marrara Cricket Ground (Darwin)							
D. S. Lehmann	2	3	0	218	110	1	72.67
A. C. Gilchrist	2	3	0	123	80	0	41.00
J. L. Langer	2	3	0	111	71	0	37.00
Most by non-Australian							
Habibul Bashar (Ban). .	1	2	0	70	54	0	35.00

	M	I	NO	R	HS	100s	Avge
Cazaly's Stadium (Cairns)							
M. L. Hayden	2	3	0	299	132	2	99.67
D. S. Lehmann	2	3	0	248	177	1	82.67
J. L. Langer	2	3	0	171	162	1	57.00
Most by non-Australian							
M. S. Atapattu (SL) . . .	1	2	0	142	133	1	71.00

HIGHEST CAREER AVERAGE

(Qualification: 1,000 runs)

	M	I	NO	R	HS	100s	Avge
D. G. Bradman	52	80	10	6,996	334	29	99.94
S. G. Barnes	13	19	2	1,072	234	3	63.06
M. L. Hayden	**55**	**95**	**8**	**5,059**	**380**	**20**	**58.15**
R. T. Ponting	**79**	**127**	**15**	**6,086**	**257**	**20**	**54.34**
G. S. Chappell	88	151	19	7,110	247*	24	53.86
A. C. Gilchrist	**56**	**80**	**14**	**3,485**	**204***	**10**	**52.80**
D. S. Lehmann	**20**	**32**	**2**	**1,549**	**177**	**5**	**51.63**
J. Ryder	20	32	5	1,394	201*	3	51.63
S. R. Waugh	**168**	**260**	**46**	**10,927**	**200**	**32**	**51.06**
A. R. Border	156	265	44	11,174	205	27	50.56
R. N. Harvey	79	137	10	6,149	205	21	48.42
K. D. Walters	75	125	14	5,357	250	15	48.26
W. H. Ponsford	29	48	4	2,122	266	7	48.23
S. J. McCabe	39	62	5	2,748	232	6	48.21
W. M. Lawry	68	123	12	5,234	210	13	47.15

FASTEST FIFTIES

Minutes

22	V. T. Trumper	v South Africa at Johannesburg (OW)	1902-03
31	W. J. O'Reilly	v South Africa at Johannesburg (OW)	1935-36
35	C. G. Macartney	v South Africa at Sydney	1910-11
38	R. Benaud	v West Indies at Kingston	1954-55
40	J. Darling	v England at Sydney	1897-98
40	S. J. McCabe	v South Africa at Johannesburg (OW)	1935-36

Balls

42	J. L. Langer	v New Zealand at Hamilton	1999-00
43	J. M. Gregory	v South Africa at Johannesburg (OW)	1921-22
43	D. R. Martyn	v England at The Oval	2001
45	W. J. O'Reilly	v South Africa at Johannesburg (OW)	1935-36
46	A. C. Gilchrist	v Pakistan at Brisbane	1999-00

FASTEST HUNDREDS

Minutes

70	J. M. Gregory	v South Africa at Johannesburg (OW)	1921-22
78	R. Benaud	v West Indies at Kingston	1954-55
91	J. Darling	v England at Sydney	1897-98
91	S. J. McCabe	v South Africa at Johannesburg (OW)	1935-36
94	V. T. Trumper	v England at Sydney	1903-04

Balls

67	J. M. Gregory	v South Africa at Johannesburg (OW)	1921-22
84	A. C. Gilchrist	v India at Mumbai	2000-01
84	A. C. Gilchrist	v Zimbabwe at Perth	2003-04
84	M. L. Hayden	v Zimbabwe at Sydney	2003-04
88	R. R. Lindwall	v England at Melbourne	1946-47

FASTEST DOUBLE-HUNDREDS

Minutes

214	D. G. Bradman	v England at Leeds	1930
223	S. J. McCabe	v England at Nottingham	1938
226	V. T. Trumper	v South Africa at Adelaide	1910-11
234	D. G. Bradman	v England at Lord's	1930
241	S. E. Gregory	v England at Sydney	1894-95

Balls

212	A. C. Gilchrist	v South Africa at Johannesburg (WS)	2001-02
242	D. G. Bradman	v England at The Oval	1934
258	S. J. McCabe	v England at Nottingham	1938
259	D. G. Bradman	v England at Leeds	1930
266	D. G. Bradman	v England at Lord's	1934

FASTEST TRIPLE-HUNDREDS

Minutes

336	D. G. Bradman	v England at Leeds	1930
425	D. G. Bradman	v England at Leeds	1934
529	M. L. Hayden	v Zimbabwe at Perth	2003-04
681	M. A. Taylor	v Pakistan at Peshawar	1998-99
693	R. W. Cowper	v England at Melbourne	1965-66
752	R. B. Simpson	v England at Manchester	1964

Balls

362	M. L. Hayden	v Zimbabwe at Perth	2003-04
410	D. G. Bradman	v England at Leeds	1930
458	D. G. Bradman	v England at Leeds	1934
520	M. A. Taylor	v Pakistan at Peshawar	1998-99
580	R. W. Cowper	v England at Melbourne	1965-66
737	R. B. Simpson	v England at Manchester	1964

Note: Cowper's 580 balls are approximate based on his innings details.

MOST RUNS OFF AN OVER

Eight Balls

21	V. Y. Richardson	off J. W. H. T Douglas v England at Melbourne	1924-25
21	R. N. Harvey and C. L. McCool	off J. C. Watkins v South Africa at Cape Town	1949-50
21	K. R. Miller and R. R. Lindwall	off S. Ramadhin v West Indies at Brisbane	1951-52
21	I. M. Chappell	off Intikhab Alam v Pakistan at Adelaide	1972-73
21	G. J. Cosier and G. S. Chappell	off Saleem Altaf v Pakistan at Melbourne	1976-77
21	J. R. Thomson and A. G. Hurst	off Madan Lal v India at Brisbane	1977-78

Six Balls

22	A. C. Gilchrist	off M. A. Butcher v England at Birmingham	2001
21	D. G. Bradman and S. G. Barnes	off J. C. Laker v England at Lord's	1948
21	R. T. Ponting and M. L. Hayden	off A. M. Blignaut v Zimbabwe at Sydney	2003-04
20	A. K. Davidson	off D. A. Allen v England at Manchester	1961
20	S. K. Warne and I. A. Healy	off C. E. L. Ambrose v West Indies at Perth	1996-97
20	A. C. Gilchrist	off Mushtaq Ahmed v Pakistan at Brisbane	1999-00
20	A. C. Gilchrist	off P. R. Adams v South Africa at Cape Town	2001-02
20	S. R. Waugh	off Danish Kaneria v Pakistan at Sharjah	2002-03
20	J. L. Langer	off A. R. Kumble v India at Adelaide	2003-04

MOST RUNS IN A DAY'S PLAY

309	D. G. Bradman	v England at Leeds	1930
271	D. G. Bradman	v England at Leeds	1934
244	D. G. Bradman	v England at The Oval	1934
223	D. G. Bradman	v West Indies at Brisbane (Ex)	1930-31
222	M. A. Taylor	v Pakistan at Peshawar	1998-99
213	S. J. McCabe	v England at Nottingham	1938
208	V. T. Trumper	v South Africa at Adelaide	1910-11
205	W. H. Ponsford	v England at The Oval	1934
203	H. L. Collins	v South Africa at Johannesburg (OW)	1921-22
201	D. G. Bradman	v India at Adelaide	1947-48
200	D. G. Bradman	v South Africa at Brisbane	1931-32

LONGEST TO GET OFF THE MARK

Minutes

72	C. G. Rackemann	v England at Sydney	1990-91
70	W. L. Murdoch	v England at Sydney	1882-83
69	R. M. Hogg	v West Indies at Adelaide	1984-85
62	M. A. Taylor	v England at Sydney	1994-95

SLOWEST FIFTIES

Minutes

310	A. R. Border	v West Indies at Sydney	1988-89
304	P. L. Taylor	v Pakistan at Karachi	1988-89
275	W. M. Lawry	v England at Melbourne	1962-63

SLOWEST HUNDREDS

Minutes

388	J. L. Langer	v Pakistan at Hobart	1999-00
385	D. M. Jones	v India at Chennai (Chepauk)	1986-87
384	M. A. Taylor	v India at Adelaide	1991-92
378	D. R. Martyn	v Sri Lanka at Kandy	2003-04

MOST CAREER DUCKS

	Total	Eng	SAf	WI	NZ	Ind	Pak	SL	Zim	Ban
S. K. Warne	29	8	3	4	0	5	4	5	0	0
G. D. McGrath	27	8	4	6	1	1	5	2	0	0
S. R. Waugh	22	6	2	3	3	3	5	0	0	0
M. E. Waugh	19	0	1	4	1	4	4	5	0	0
I. A. Healy	18	3	1	10	2	0	1	1	0	0
D. C. Boon	16	5	0	3	3	0	2	3	0	0
G. D. McKenzie	15	7	3	1	0	4	0	0	0	0

HIGHEST PARTNERSHIPS FOR EACH WICKET

First Wicket
382 W.M. Lawry (210) and R.B. Simpson (201)   v West Indies at Bridgetown . . . 1964-65
329 G.R. Marsh (138) and M.A. Taylor (219)   v England at Nottingham 1989
269 M.J. Slater (169) and G.S. Blewett (89)   v Pakistan at Brisbane 1999-00
260 M.A. Taylor (111) and M.J. Slater (152)   v England at Lord's 1993
255 J.L. Langer (162) and M.L. Hayden (117)   v Sri Lanka at Cairns 2004-05

Second Wicket
451 W.H. Ponsford (266) and D.G. Bradman (244)   v England at The Oval 1934
301 A.R. Morris (182) and D.G. Bradman (173*)   v England at Leeds 1948
298 W.M. Lawry (205) and I.M. Chappell (165)   v West Indies at Melbourne . . 1968-69
279 M.A. Taylor (334*) and J.L. Langer (116)   v Pakistan at Peshawar 1998-99
277 R.B. McCosker (127) and I.M. Chappell (192)   v England at The Oval 1975

Third Wicket
315 R.T. Ponting (206) and D.S. Lehmann (160)   v West Indies at Port-of-Spain . 2002-03
295 C.C. McDonald (172) and R.N. Harvey (204)   v West Indies at Kingston . . 1954-55
276 D.G. Bradman (187) and A.L. Hassett (128)   v England at Brisbane 1946-47
264 I.M. Chappell (145) and G.S. Chappell (247*)   v New Zealand at Wellington . . 1973-74
249 D.G. Bradman (169) and S.J. McCabe (112)   v England at Melbourne 1936-37

Fourth Wicket
388 W.H. Ponsford (181) and D.G. Bradman (304)   v England at Leeds 1934
336 W.M. Lawry (151) and K.D. Walters (242)   v West Indies at Sydney 1968-69
251 G.M. Wood (126) and C.S. Serjeant (124)   v West Indies at Georgetown . . 1977-78
250 D.S. Lehmann (177) and S.R. Waugh (156*)   v Bangladesh at Cairns 2003-04
243 D.G. Bradman (232) and A. Jackson (73)   v England at The Oval 1930

Fifth Wicket
405 S.G. Barnes (234) and D.G. Bradman (234)   v England at Sydney 1946-47
385 S.R. Waugh (160) and G.S. Blewett (214*)   v SAf at Johannesburg (WS) . . 1996-97
332*A.R. Border (200*) and S.R. Waugh (157*)   v England at Leeds 1993
327 J.L. Langer (144) and R.T. Ponting (197)   v Pakistan at Perth 1999-00
281 S.R. Waugh (199) and R.T. Ponting (104)   v West Indies at Bridgetown . . . 1998-99

Sixth Wicket
346 J.H.W. Fingleton (136) and D.G. Bradman (270)   v England at Melbourne 1936-37
317 D.R. Martyn (133) and A.C. Gilchrist (204*)   v SAf at Johannesburg (WS) . . 2001-02
260*D.M. Jones (118*) and S.R. Waugh (134*)   v Sri Lanka at Hobart 1989-90
238 J.L. Langer (127) and A.C. Gilchrist (149*)   v Pakistan at Hobart 1999-00
233 M.L. Hayden (380) and A.C. Gilchrist (113*)   v Zimbabwe at Perth 2003-04

Seventh Wicket
217 K.D. Walters (250) and G.J. Gilmour (101)   v New Zealand at Christchurch 1976-77
185 G.N. Yallop (268) and G.R.J. Matthews (75)   v Pakistan at Melbourne 1983-84
168 W.M. Marsh (132) and K.J. O'Keeffe (85)   v New Zealand at Adelaide . . . 1973-74
165 C. Hill (188) and H. Trumble (46)   v England at Melbourne 1897-98
160 R. Benaud (90) and G.D. McKenzie (76)   v South Africa at Sydney 1963-64

Eighth Wicket
243 M.J. Hartigan (116) and C. Hill (160)   v England at Adelaide 1907-08
173 C.E. Pellew (116) and J.M. Gregory (100)   v England at Melbourne 1920-21
154 G.J. Bonnor (128) and S.P. Jones (40)   v England at Sydney 1884-85
154 D. Tallon (92) and R.R. Lindwall (100)   v England at Melbourne 1946-47
137 R. Benaud (128) and I.W.G. Johnson (27*)   v West Indies at Kingston . . . 1954-55

Ninth Wicket
154 S.E. Gregory (201) and J.M. Blackham (74)   v England at Sydney 1894-95
133 S.R. Waugh (110) and J.N. Gillespie (46)   v India at Kolkata 2000-01
130 S.R. Waugh (152*) and G.F. Lawson (74)   v England at Lord's 1989
114 D.M. Jones (216) and M.G. Hughes (72*)   v West Indies at Adelaide . . . 1988-89
108 J. Ryder (201*) and W.A.S. Oldfield (47)   v England at Adelaide 1924-25

Tenth Wicket
127 J.M. Taylor (108) and A.A. Mailey (46*)   v England at Sydney 1924-25
120 R.A. Duff (104) and W.W. Armstrong (45*)   v England at Melbourne 1901-02
98 A.K. Davidson (77*) and G.D. McKenzie (32)   v England at Manchester 1961
97 T.G. Hogan (52) and R.M. Hogg (42*)   v West Indies at Georgetown . . 1983-84
88 W.L. Murdoch (153*) and W.H. Moule (34)   v England at The Oval 1880

BOWLING RECORDS

MOST WICKETS IN AN INNINGS

9-121	A. A. Mailey	v England at Melbourne	1920-21
8-31	F. Laver	v England at Manchester	1909
8-38	G. D. McGrath	v England at Lord's	1997
8-43	A. E. Trott	v England at Adelaide	1894-95
8-53	R. A. L. Massie	v England at Lord's	1972
8-59	A. A. Mallett	v Pakistan at Adelaide	1972-73
8-65	H. Trumble	v England at The Oval	1902
8-71	G. D. McKenzie	v West Indies at Melbourne	1968-69
8-71	S. K. Warne	v England at Brisbane	1994-95
8-84	R. A. L. Massie	v England at Lord's	1972
8-87	M. G. Hughes	v West Indies at Perth	1988-89
8-97	C. J. McDermott	v England at Perth	1990-91
8-112	G. F. Lawson	v West Indies at Adelaide	1984-85
8-141	C. J. McDermott	v England at Manchester	1985
8-143	M. H. N. Walker	v England at Melbourne	1974-75

MOST WICKETS IN AN INNINGS AGAINST AUSTRALIA

9-37	J. C. Laker	for England at Manchester	1956
9-52	R. J. Hadlee	for New Zealand at Brisbane	1985-86
9-69	J. M. Patel	for India at Kanpur	1959-60
9-86	Sarfraz Nawaz	for Pakistan at Melbourne	1978-79
8-35	G. A. Lohmann	for England at Sydney	1886-87

MOST WICKETS IN A MATCH

16-137	R. A. L. Massie	v England at Lord's	1972
14-90	F. R. Spofforth	v England at The Oval	1882
14-199	C. V. Grimmett	v South Africa at Adelaide	1931-32
13-77	M. A. Noble	v England at Melbourne	1901-02
13-110	F. R. Spofforth	v England at Melbourne	1878-79
13-148	B. A. Reid	v England at Melbourne	1990-91
13-173	C. V. Grimmett	v South Africa at Durban (Kingsmead)	1935-36
13-217	M. G. Hughes	v West Indies at Perth	1988-89
13-236	A. A. Mailey	v England at Melbourne	1920-21
12-87	C. T. B. Turner	v England at Sydney	1887-88
12-89	H. Trumble	v England at The Oval	1896
12-107	S. C. G. MacGill	v England at Sydney	1998-99
12-124	A. K. Davidson	v India at Kanpur	1959-60
12-126	B. A. Reid	v India at Melbourne	1991-92
12-128	S. K. Warne	v South Africa at Sydney	1993-94
12-166	G. Dymock	v India at Kanpur	1979-80
12-173	H. Trumble	v England at The Oval	1902
12-175	H. V. Hordern	v England at Sydney	1911-12

MOST WICKETS IN A MATCH AGAINST AUSTRALIA

19-90	J. C. Laker	for England at Manchester	1956
15-104	H. Verity	for England at Lord's	1934
15-123	R. J. Hadlee	for New Zealand at Brisbane	1985-86
15-124	W. Rhodes	for England at Melbourne	1903-04
15-217	Harbhajan Singh	for India at Chennai (Chepauk)	2000-01

MOST WICKETS IN AN INNINGS ON DEBUT

8-43	A. E. Trott	v England at Adelaide	1894-95
8-53	R. A. L. Massie	v England at Lord's (2nd innings)	1972
8-84	R. A. L. Massie	v England at Lord's (1st innings)	1972
7-55	T. K. Kendall	v England at Melbourne	1876-77
6-15	C. T. B. Turner	v England at Sydney	1886-87
6-37	C. V. Grimmett	v England at Sydney	1924-25
6-49	M. A. Noble	v England at Melbourne	1897-98
6-58	A. I. C. Dodemaide	v New Zealand at Melbourne	1987-88
6-74	R. M. Hogg	v England at Brisbane	1978-79
6-78	P. L. Taylor	v England at Sydney	1986-87
6-102	F. A. Ward	v England at Brisbane	1936-37
6-120	W. H. Cooper	v England at Melbourne	1881-82

Note: I. W. G. Johnson (6-42 v Eng at Sydney, 1946-47) and S. M. Katich (6-65 v Zim at Sydney, 2003-04) took six wickets in their first match at the crease but not on debut.

MOST WICKETS IN A MATCH ON DEBUT

16-137	R. A. L. Massie	v England at Lord's	1972
11-82	C. V. Grimmett	v England at Sydney	1924-25
9-103	J. J. Ferris	v England at Sydney	1886-87
9-130	T. M. Alderman	v England at Nottingham	1981
9-162	J. V. Saunders	v England at Sydney	1901-02
9-200	W. H. Cooper	v England at Melbourne	1881-82
8-52	A. E. Trott	v England at Adelaide	1894-95
8-68	C. T. B. Turner	v England at Sydney	1886-87
8-99	L. C. Mayne	v West Indies at Kingston	1964-65
8-105	H. V. Hordern	v South Africa at Melbourne	1910-11
8-109	T. K. Kendall	v England at Melbourne	1876-77
8-147	W. M. Clark	v India at Brisbane	1977-78
8-150	J. D. A. O'Connor	v England at Adelaide	1907-08
8-154	P. L. Taylor	v England at Sydney	1986-87
8-177	I. Meckiff	v South Africa at Johannesburg (WS)	1957-58
8-189	T. W. Wall	v England at Melbourne	1928-29
8-240	F. A. Ward	v England at Brisbane	1936-37

HAT-TRICKS

F. R. Spofforth	v England at Melbourne	1878-79
H. Trumble	v England at Melbourne	1901-02
H. Trumble	v England at Melbourne	1903-04
T. J. Matthews (1st Inns)	v South Africa at Manchester	1912
T. J. Matthews (2nd Inns)	v South Africa at Manchester	1912
L. F. Kline	v South Africa at Cape Town	1957-58
M. G. Hughes	v West Indies at Perth	1988-89
D. W. Fleming	v Pakistan at Rawalpindi	1994-95
S. K. Warne	v England at Melbourne	1994-95
G. D. McGrath	v West Indies at Perth	2000-01

MOST WICKETS IN A SERIES

	M	O	Mdns	R	W	BB	5 W/i	10 W/m	Avge	
C. V. Grimmett	5	346.1	140	642	44	7-40	5	3	14.59	1935-36 v SAf in South Africa
T. M. Alderman	6	325	76	893	42	6-135	4	0	21.26	1981 v England in England
R. M. Hogg	6	217.4	60	527	41	6-74	5	2	12.85	1978-79 v England in Australia
T. M. Alderman	6	269.2	68	712	41	6-128	6	1	17.37	1989 v England in England
D. K. Lillee	6	311.4	81	870	39	7-89	2	1	22.31	1981 v England in England
W. J. Whitty	5	232.3	55	632	37	6-17	2	0	17.08	1910-11 v SAf in Australia

	M	O	Mdns	R	W	BB	5 W/i	10 W/m	Avge	
A. A. Mailey	5	244.1	27	946	36	9-121	4	2	26.28	1920-21 v England in Australia
G. D. McGrath	6	249.5	67	701	36	8-38	2	0	19.47	1997 v England in England
G. Giffen	5	343.2	111	820	34	6-155	3	0	24.12	1894-95 v England in Australia
G. F. Lawson	5	230.4	51	687	34	6-47	4	1	20.21	1982-83 v England in Australia
S. K. Warne	6	439.5	178	877	34	5-82	1	0	25.79	1993 v England in England
C. V. Grimmett	5	239.2	61	593	33	7-87	2	1	17.97	1930-31 v WI in Australia
C. V. Grimmett	5	306	108	557	33	7-83	3	1	16.88	1931-32 v SAf in Australia
A. K. Davidson	4	173.7	25	612	33	6-53	5	1	18.55	1960-61 v WI in Australia
J. R. Thomson	5	175.1	34	592	33	6-46	2	0	17.94	1974-75 v England in Australia
M. A. Noble	5	230	68	608	32	7-17	4	1	19.00	1901-02 v England in Australia
H. V. Hordern	5	277.3	43	780	32	7-90	4	2	24.38	1911-12 v England in Australia
C. J. McDermott	5	232.5	56	675	32	6-38	4	0	21.09	1994-95 v England in Australia
G. D. McGrath	5	194.2	56	542	32	7-76	4	0	16.94	2001 v England in England
J. V. Saunders	5	267.1	52	716	31	5-28	3	0	23.10	1907-08 v England in Australia
H. Ironmonger	4	221.5	112	296	31	6-18	3	1	9.55	1931-32 v SAf in Australia
R. Benaud	5	233.2	65	584	31	5-83	2	0	18.84	1958-59 v England in Australia
D. K. Lillee	5	249.5	83	548	31	6-66	3	1	17.68	1972 v England in England
C. J. McDermott	5	264.2	75	670	31	5-54	3	1	21.61	1991-92 v India in Australia
M. G. Hughes	6	296.2	78	845	31	5-92	1	0	27.26	1993 v England in England
S. K. Warne	5	195.2	41	580	31	7-165	3	1	18.71	2001 v England in England
R. Benaud	5	242.1	56	658	30	5-49	4	0	21.93	1957-58 v SAf in South Africa
G. D. McKenzie	5	206.1	27	758	30	8-71	1	1	25.27	1968-69 v WI in Australia
C. J. McDermott	6	234.2	21	901	30	8-141	2	0	30.03	1985 v England in England
G. D. McGrath	4	199.4	59	508	30	5-28	4	1	16.93	1998-99 v WI in West Indies

Most wickets in a series against opponents not mentioned above:

	M	O	Mdns	R	W	BB	5 W/i	10 W/m	Avge	
S. K. Warne	3	124	29	342	27	7-94	2	1	12.67	2002-03 v Pak in SL/UAE
S. K. Warne	3	169	37	521	26	5-43	4	2	59.03	2003-04 v SL in Sri Lanka
S. K. Warne	3	170.4	36	476	19	5-88	1	0	25.05	1997-98 v NZ in Australia
A. J. Bichel	2	92.4	29	255	10	4-63	0	0	55.60	2003-04 v Zim in Australia
S. C. G. MacGill	2	70.1	17	219	17	5-56	3	1	24.76	2003-04 v Ban in Australia

MOST WICKETS IN A SERIES AGAINST AUSTRALIA

	M	O	Mdns	R	W	BB	5 W/i	10 W/m	Avge	
J. C. Laker	5	283.5	127	442	46	10-53	4	2	9.61	1956 for England in England
A. V. Bedser	5	265.1	58	682	39	7-44	5	1	17.49	1953 for England in England
M. W. Tate	5	421.2	62	881	38	6-99	5	1	23.18	1924-25 for Eng in Australia
S. F. Barnes	5	297	64	778	34	5-44	3	0	22.88	1911-12 for Eng in Australia
I. T. Botham	6	272.3	81	700	34	6-95	3	1	20.59	1981 for England in England

MOST WICKETS IN A THREE-TEST SERIES

	M	O	Mdns	R	W	BB	5 W/i	10 W/m	Avge	
S. K. Warne	3	124	29	342	27	7-94	2	1	12.67	2002-03 v Pakistan in SL/UAE
S. K. Warne	3	168	37	521	26	5-43	4	2	20.04	2003-04 v SL in Sri Lanka
R. Benaud	3	169.5	52	388	23	7-72	3	1	16.87	1956-57 v India in India
D. K. Lillee	3	155.1	41	388	23	6-60	2	1	16.87	1979-80 v England in Australia
C. T. B. Turner	3	109.2	62	261	21	6-112	4	1	12.43	1888 v England in England
D. K. Lillee	3	173.4	16	540	21	6-82	2	1	25.71	1976-77 v Pakistan in Australia
D. K. Lillee	3	148.3	33	452	21	4-65	0	0	21.52	1980-81 v India in Australia
G. D. McGrath	3	154.5	35	438	21	5-40	1	0	20.86	1995-96 v SL in Australia

MOST WICKETS IN A CALENDAR YEAR

	M	Balls	Mdns	R	W	BB	5W/i	10W/m	Avge	Year
D. K. Lillee	13	3,710	162	1,781	85	7-83	5	2	20.95	1981
S. K. Warne	16	5,054	316	1,697	72	6-31	2	0	23.56	1993
G. D. McKenzie	14	4,106	119	1,737	71	7-153	4	1	24.46	1964
S. K. Warne	10	3,773	217	1,274	70	8-71	6	2	18.20	1994
G. D. McGrath	14	3,508	196	1,473	68	7-78	4	0	21.68	2001
S. K. Warne	15	4,091	194	1,661	68	6-48	2	0	24.42	1997
S. K. Warne	10	2,874	109	1,310	67	7-94	3	1	19.55	2002
G. D. McGrath	14	3,364	169	1,425	67	5-28	4	1	21.26	1999
G. D. McGrath	13	3,113	151	1,347	63	8-38	4	0	21.38	1997
S. K. Warne	13	3,501	113	1,809	58	7-165	4	1	31.19	2001
M. G. Hughes	12	3,033	127	1,448	57	5-64	2	0	25.40	1993
S. C. G. MacGill	11	3,148	107	1,688	57	5-56	4	1	29.61	2003
C. J. McDermott	9	2,416	84	1,188	56	8-97	4	1	21.21	1991
R. Benaud	9	3,248	177	1,031	55	5-76	4	0	18.74	1959
A. A. Mailey	10	2,849	63	1,567	55	9-121	4	2	28.49	1921
T. M. Alderman	9	2,672	105	1,222	54	6-135	4	0	22.62	1981
H. Trumble	8	2,520	140	994	53	8-65	4	2	18.75	1902
G. D. McGrath	10	2,319	92	1,138	52	6-47	4	0	21.88	1995
S. K. Warne	12	3,051	156	1,254	52	7-23	1	1	24.11	1995
M. A. Noble	12	2,208	100	989	51	7-17	6	2	19.39	1902
J. M. Gregory	12	2,702	84	1,292	51	7-69	3	0	25.33	1921
T. M. Alderman	10	2,414	106	1,019	50	6-128	6	1	20.38	1989
S. K. Warne	8	3,099	174	1,084	50	7-56	4	1	21.68	1994

MOST WICKETS IN A CAREER

		M	Balls	Mdns	R	W	BB	5W/i	10W/m	Avge
1	S. K. Warne	112	31,489	1,479	13,425	527	8-71	27	8	25.47
2	G. D. McGrath	97	22,860	1,146	9,509	440	8-38	24	3	21.61
3	D. K. Lillee	70	18,467	652	8,493	355	7-83	23	7	23.92
4	C. J. McDermott	71	16,586	581	8,332	291	8-97	14	2	28.63
5	R. Benaud	63	19,108	805	6,704	248	7-72	16	1	27.03
6	G. D. McKenzie	61	17,684	547	7,328	246	8-71	16	3	29.79
7	R. R. Lindwall	61	13,650	419	5,251	228	7-38	12	0	23.03
8	C. V. Grimmett	37	14,513	736	5,231	216	7-40	21	7	24.22
9	M. G. Hughes	53	12,285	499	6,017	212	8-87	7	1	28.38
10	J. N. Gillespie	54	11,143	509	5,298	206	7-37	7	0	25.72
11	J. R. Thomson	51	10,535	300	5,602	200	6-46	8	0	28.01
12	A. K. Davidson	44	11,587	431	3,819	186	7-93	14	2	20.53
13	G. F. Lawson	46	11,118	386	5,501	180	8-112	11	2	30.56
14	K. R. Miller	55	10,389	337	3,906	170	7-60	7	1	22.98
	T. M. Alderman	41	10,181	432	4,616	170	6-47	14	1	27.15
16	W. A. Johnston	40	11,048	372	3,826	160	6-44	7	0	23.91
17	S. C. G. MacGill	32	8,447	291	4,441	152	7-50	9	2	29.22
18	W. J. O'Reilly	27	10,024	585	3,254	144	7-54	11	3	22.60
19	H. Trumble	32	8,099	452	3,072	141	8-65	9	3	21.79
20	B. Lee	37	7,380	256	4,403	139	5-47	4	0	31.68

MOST WICKETS AGAINST OPPONENTS

	M	Balls	Mdns	R	W	BB	5W/i	10W/m	Avge
v England									
D. K. Lillee	29	8,516	361	3,507	167	7-89	11	4	21.00
H. Trumble	31	7,895	448	2,945	141	8-65	9	3	20.89
S. K. Warne	26	7,792	408	3,040	132	8-71	7	2	23.03

	M	Balls	Mdns	R	W	BB	5W/i	10W/m	Avge
v South Africa									
S.K. Warne	18	6,130	303	2,257	101	7-56	6	2	22.35
C.V. Grimmett	10	3,913	248	1,199	77	7-40	8	4	15.57
R. Benaud	13	4,136	116	1,413	52	5-49	5	0	27.17
v West Indies									
G.D. McGrath	20	4,701	248	1,847	97	6-17	8	2	19.04
J.R. Thomson	14	2,774	56	1,818	62	6-50	3	0	29.32
C.J. McDermott	14	3,036	84	1,703	59	5-80	1	0	28.86
v New Zealand									
S.K. Warne	15	4,409	210	1,881	75	6-31	2	0	25.08
C.J. McDermott	13	3,214	130	1,460	48	5-97	1	0	30.42
D.K. Lillee	8	1,770	63	740	38	6-53	4	1	19.47
v India									
R. Benaud	8	2,953	198	956	52	7-72	5	1	18.38
G.D. McKenzie	10	2,563	106	967	47	7-66	4	2	20.57
G.D. McGrath	7	1,712	106	595	37	5-48	2	1	16.08
v Pakistan									
S.K. Warne	12	3,303	168	1,414	76	7-23	6	2	18.61
D.K. Lillee	17	4,433	127	2,161	71	6-82	5	1	30.44
G.D. McGrath	14	3,193	139	1,476	62	5-61	2	0	23.81
v Sri Lanka									
S.K. Warne	13	3,167	133	1,507	59	5-43	5	2	25.54
G.D. McGrath	8	1,828	84	823	37	5-37	2	0	22.24
C.J. McDermott	7	1,534	60	735	27	4-53	0	0	27.22
v Zimbabwe									
A.J. Bichel	2	556	29	255	10	4-63	0	0	25.50
S.M. Katich	1	197	3	90	6	6-65	1	0	15.00
G.D. McGrath	1	324	19	90	6	3-44	0	0	15.00
B. Lee	2	438	17	222	6	3-48	0	0	37.00
v Bangladesh									
S.C.G. MacGill	2	421	17	219	17	5-56	3	1	12.88
J.N. Gillespie	2	370	14	170	11	4-38	0	0	15.45
B. Lee	2	296	10	190	6	3-23	0	0	31.67

MOST WICKETS AGAINST AUSTRALIA

	M	Balls	Mdns	R	W	BB	5W/i	10W/m	Avge
for England									
I.T. Botham	36	8,479	297	4,093	148	6-78	9	2	27.66
R.G.D. Willis	36	7,294	200	3,346	128	8-43	7	0	26.14
W. Rhodes	41	5,790	234	2,616	109	8-68	6	1	24.00
for South Africa									
H.J. Tayfield	15	6,027	179	2,208	64	7-23	4	1	34.50
T.L. Goddard	18	5,089	259	1,462	53	6-53	2	0	27.58
A.A. Donald	14	3,266	115	1,647	53	6-59	2	0	31.08
for West Indies									
C.A. Walsh	38	8,560	286	3,872	135	6-54	4	0	28.68
C.E.L. Ambrose	27	6,696	279	2,718	128	7-25	8	1	21.23
L.R. Gibbs	24	9,358	361	3,222	103	6-29	6	0	31.28
for New Zealand									
R.J. Hadlee	23	6,099	213	2,674	130	9-52	14	3	20.57
C.L. Cairns	14	2,623	88	1,636	39	5-146	1	0	41.95
J.G. Bracewell	11	2,697	125	1,004	38	6-32	2	1	26.42
for India									
Kapil Dev	20	4,746	198	2,003	79	8-106	7	0	25.35
A.R. Kumble	10	3,651	119	1,706	61	8-141	6	1	27.97
E.A.S. Prasanna	13	4,331	173	1,637	57	6-74	5	1	28.72
for Pakistan									
Imran Khan	18	3,994	140	1,598	64	6-63	4	1	24.97
Iqbal Qasim	13	3,957	206	1,490	57	7-49	2	1	26.14
Sarfraz Nawaz	15	4,520	151	1,828	52	9-86	1	1	35.15

	M	Balls	Mdns	R	W	BB	5W/i	10W/m	Avge
for Sri Lanka									
M. Muralidaran	10	3,093	83	1,571	50	6-59	5	1	31.42
W. P. U. J. C. Vaas	11	2,425	87	1,127	37	5-31	1	0	30.46
C. P. H. Ramanayake	6	1,384	35	744	21	5-82	1	0	35.43
for Zimbabwe									
H. H. Streak	3	540	18	353	7	5-93	1	0	50.43
R. W. Price	2	538	11	371	6	6-121	1	0	61.83
S. M. Ervine	1	186	4	146	4	4-146	0	0	36.50
for Bangladesh									
Mashrafe Bin Mortaza ...	2	288	14	134	4	3-74	0	0	33.50
Sanwar Hossain	1	180	2	128	2	2-128	0	0	64.00
Tapash Baisya	2	287	9	165	2	1-69	0	0	82.50

MOST WICKETS AT EACH AUSTRALIAN VENUE

	M	Balls	Mdns	R	W	BB	5W/i	10W/m	Avge
Melbourne Cricket Ground (Melbourne)									
D. K. Lillee	14	3,833	105	1,798	82	7-83	7	4	21.93
H. Trumble	7	1,708	71	646	46	7-28	3	0	14.04
G. D. McKenzie	8	2,370	35	1,019	45	8-71	3	2	22.64
Most by non-Australian									
S. F. Barnes (Eng)	5	1,723	83	632	35	7-121	5	1	18.06
Sydney Cricket Ground (Sydney)									
S. K. Warne	10	3,120	143	1,291	49	7-56	4	2	26.35
C. T. B. Turner	6	2,106	209	602	45	7-43	4	1	13.38
D. K. Lillee	8	2,191	61	1,036	43	4-40	0	0	24.09
Most by non-Australian									
G. A. Lohmann (Eng)	4	1,219	114	331	35	8-35	3	2	9.46
Adelaide Oval (Adelaide)									
D. K. Lillee	9	2,479	63	1,206	45	6-171	4	0	26.80
C. J. McDermott	8	2,325	98	1,162	42	5-76	3	1	27.67
S. K. Warne	10	2,908	134	1,188	41	5-113	1	0	28.98
Most by non-Australian									
Kapil Dev (Ind)	3	984	38	439	19	8-106	2	0	23.11
Brisbane Exhibition Ground (Brisbane)									
C. V. Grimmett	2	841	24	442	18	6-131	2	0	24.56
H. Larwood (Eng)	1	130	4	62	8	6-32	1	0	7.75
H. Ironmonger	2	813	61	236	7	2-43	0	0	33.71
Brisbane Cricket Ground (Brisbane)									
G. D. McGrath	10	2,577	127	1,131	51	6-17	0	0	22.18
S. K. Warne	8	2,643	139	1,071	51	8-71	2	2	21.00
C. J. McDermott	8	1,887	69	905	40	6-53	2	0	22.63
Most by non-Australian									
R. J. Hadlee (NZ)	3	807	29	343	21	9-52	2	1	16.33
WACA Ground (Perth)									
M. G. Hughes	6	1,618	63	752	39	8-87	3	1	19.28
C. J. McDermott	8	1,781	67	847	38	8-97	2	1	22.29
G. D. McGrath	9	2,256	105	977	38	4-49	0	0	25.71
Most by non-Australian									
C. E. L. Ambrose (WI) ...	3	639	28	310	24	7-25	3	0	12.91
Bellerive Oval (Hobart)									
S. K. Warne	5	1,073	44	461	24	6-31	3	0	19.21
G. D. McGrath	3	693	39	274	13	5-61	1	0	21.08
P. R. Reiffel	3	449	21	195	11	4-38	0	0	17.73
Most by non-Australian									
Mushtaq Ahmed (Pak) ...	1	408	13	198	9	5-115	1	0	22.00

	M	Balls	Mdns	R	W	BB	5W/i	10W/m	Avge
Marrara Cricket Ground (Darwin)									
G. D. McGrath	2	324	19	106	11	5-37	1	0	9.64
S. C. G. MacGill	1	157	5	86	7	5-65	1	0	12.29
M. S. Kasprowicz	1	148	4	54	7	7-39	1	0	7.71
Most by non-Australian									
W. P. U. J. C. Vaas (SL) . . .	1	195	10	82	7	5-31	1	0	11.71
Cazaly's Stadium (Cairns)									
J. N. Gillespie	2	560	22	250	12	4-38	0	0	20.82
S. C. G. MacGill	1	264	12	133	10	5-56	2	1	13.30
U. D. U. Chandana (SL) . .	1	268	3	210	10	5-101	2	1	21.00

LOWEST CAREER AVERAGE

(Qualification: 20 wickets)

	M	Balls	Mdns	R	W	BB	5W/i	10W/m	Avge
J. J. Ferris	8	2,030	224	684	48	5-26	4	0	14.25
J. B. Iverson	5	1,108	29	320	21	6-27	1	0	15.24
C. T. B. Turner	17	5,179	457	1,670	101	7-43	11	2	16.53
H. Ironmonger	14	4,695	328	1330	74	7-23	4	2	17.97
F. R. Spofforth	18	4,185	416	1,731	94	7-44	7	4	18.41
H. F. Boyle	12	1,743	175	641	32	6-42	1	0	20.03
A. K. Davidson	44	11,587	431	3,819	186	7-93	14	2	20.53
R. A. L. Massie	6	1,739	74	647	31	8-53	2	1	20.87
E. R. H. Toshack	12	3,140	155	989	47	6-29	4	1	21.04
W. J. Whitty	14	3,357	163	1,373	65	6-17	3	0	21.12

MOST ECONOMICAL

(Qualification: 20 wickets, and calculated on six-ball overs)

	Wkts	RPO	Eng	SAf	WI	NZ	Ind	Pak	SL	Zim	Ban
H. Ironmonger . .	74	1.70	1.74	1.33	2.11	–	–	–	–	–	–
J. B. Iverson	21	1.73	1.73	–	–	–	–	–	–	–	–
K. D. Mackay . . .	50	1.78	1.86	1.54	2.28	–	1.55	1.47	–	–	–
E. R. H. Toshack .	47	1.89	1.95	–	0.62	2.04	–	–	–	–	–
C. T. B. Turner . .	101	1.93	1.93	–	–	–	–	–	–	–	–
W. J. O'Reilly . .	144	1.95	1.97	1.86	–	1.74	–	–	–	–	–
L. F. Kline	34	1.96	–	1.62	3.05	–	1.72	1.61	–	–	–
T. R. Veivers . . .	33	1.97	2.19	1.95	–	–	1.64	1.77	–	–	–
A. K. Davidson .	186	1.98	2.00	1.58	2.64	–	1.77	1.91	–	–	–
J. J. Ferris	48	2.02	2.02	–	–	–	–	–	–	–	–

MOST WICKETS PER MATCH

(Qualification: 20 wickets)

	Wkts	WPM	Eng	SAf	WI	NZ	Ind	Pak	SL	Zim	Ban
H. V. Hordern . .	46	6.57	6.40	7.00	–	–	–	–	–	–	–
J. J. Ferris	48	6.00	6.00	–	–	–	–	–	–	–	–
C. T. B. Turner . .	101	5.94	5.94	–	–	–	–	–	–	–	–
C. V. Grimmett . .	216	5.84	4.82	7.70	6.60	–	–	–	–	–	–
J. V. Saunders . .	79	5.64	5.33	7.50	–	–	–	–	–	–	–
W. J. O'Reilly . .	144	5.33	5.37	4.86	–	8.00	–	–	–	–	–
H. Ironmonger . .	74	5.29	3.50	7.75	5.50	–	–	–	–	–	–
F. R. Spofforth . .	94	5.22	5.22	–	–	–	–	–	–	–	–
R. A. L. Massie .	31	5.17	5.75	–	–	–	–	4.00	–	–	–
D. K. Lillee	355	5.07	5.76	–	4.58	4.75	7.00	4.18	3.00	–	–

MOST MAIDENS

	Mdns	Eng	SAf	WI	NZ	Ind	Pak	SL	Zim	Ban
S. K. Warne	1,479	408	303	132	210	112	168	133	13	–
G. D. McGrath	1,146	245	174	248	115	106	138	84	19	17
R. Benaud	805	289	116	103	–	198	99	–	–	–
C. V. Grimmett	736	427	248	61	–	–	–	–	–	–
D. K. Lillee	652	361	–	62	63	33	127	6	–	–

MOST BALLS IN A CAREER

	Balls	Eng	SAf	WI	NZ	Ind	Pak	SL	Zim	Ban
S. K. Warne	31,489	7,792	6,130	3,284	4,409	3,085	3,303	3,167	319	–
G. D. McGrath	22,860	5,221	3,284	4,701	2,266	1,712	3,193	1,828	324	331
R. Benaud	19,108	7,284	4,136	3,289	–	2,953	1,446	–	–	–
D. K. Lillee	18,467	8,516	–	2,677	1,770	891	4,433	180	–	–
G. D. McKenzie	17,684	7,489	3,745	3,185	–	2,563	702	–	–	–

MOST BALLS IN A MATCH

708	G. Giffen	v England at Sydney	1894-95
672	W. A. Johnston	v South Africa at Melbourne	1952-53
656	C. V. Grimmett	v England at The Oval	1930
656	F. A. Ward	v England at Brisbane	1936-37
654	H. Trumble	v England at Adelaide	1901-02
654	C. V. Grimmett	v South Africa at Melbourne	1931-32

ALL-ROUNDERS

HUNDRED AND FIVE WICKETS IN AN INNINGS

C. Kelleway	114	5-33	v South Africa at Manchester	1912
J. M. Gregory	100	7-69	v England at Melbourne	1920-21
K. R. Miller	109	6-107	v West Indies at Kingston	1954-55
R. Benaud	100	5-84	v South Africa at Johannesburg (WS)	1957-58

HUNDRED RUNS AND TEN WICKETS IN A MATCH

A. K. Davidson	44	5-135	v West Indies at Brisbane	1960-61
	and 80	and 6-87		

1,000 RUNS AND 100 WICKETS IN A CAREER

	M	R	W	Tests for Double
R. Benaud	63	2,201	248	32
A. K. Davidson	44	1,328	186	34
G. Giffen	31	1,238	103	30
M. G. Hughes	53	1,032	212	52
I. W. G. Johnson	45	1,000	109	45
R. R. Lindwall	61	1,502	228	38
K. R. Miller	55	2,958	170	33
M. A. Noble	42	1,997	121	27
S. K. Warne	112	2,326	525	58

WICKET-KEEPING RECORDS

MOST DISMISSALS IN AN INNINGS

6	(all ct)	A. T. W. Grout	v South Africa at Johannesburg (WS)	1957-58
6	(all ct)	R. W. Marsh	v England at Brisbane	1982-83
6	(all ct)	I. A. Healy	v England at Birmingham	1997

Note: There are 43 instances of five dismissals in an innings.

MOST DISMISSALS IN A MATCH

10	(all ct)	A. C. Gilchrist	v New Zealand at Hamilton	1999-00
9	(8ct, 1st)	G. R. A. Langley	v England at Lord's	1956
9	(all ct)	R. W. Marsh	v England at Brisbane	1982-83
9	(all ct)	I. A. Healy	v England at Brisbane	1994-95

Note: There are 14 instances of eight dismissals in a match.

MOST DISMISSALS IN A SERIES

28	(all ct)	R. W. Marsh	v England in Australia	1982-83
27	(25ct, 2st)	I. A. Healy	v England in England	1997
26	(all ct)	R. W. Marsh	v West Indies in Australia	1975-76
26	(21ct, 5st)	I. A. Healy	v England in England	1993
26	(24ct, 2st)	A. C. Gilchrist	v England in England	2001
25	(23ct, 2st)	I. A. Healy	v England in Australia	1994-95
25	(23ct, 2st)	A. C. Gilchrist	v England in Australia	2002-03
24	(all ct)	I. A. Healy	v England in Australia	1990-91
23	(20ct, 3st)	A. T. W. Grout	v West Indies in Australia	1960-61
23	(21ct, 2st)	R. W. Marsh	v England in England	1972
23	(all ct)	R. W. Marsh	v England in England	1981
23	(19ct, 4st)	I. A. Healy	v West Indies in Australia	1992-93
22	(all ct)	S. J. Rixon	v India in Australia	1977-78
21	(13ct, 8st)	R. A. Saggers	v South Africa in South Africa	1949-50
21	(16ct, 5st)	G. R. A. Langley	v West Indies in Australia	1951-52
21	(20ct, 1st)	A. T. W. Grout	v England in England	1961
21	(all ct)	R. W. Marsh	v Pakistan in Australia	1983-84
21	(19ct, 2st)	A. C. Gilchrist	v West Indies in Australia	2000-01
20	(16ct, 4st)	D. Tallon	v England in Australia	1946-47
20	(16ct, 4st)	G. R. A. Langley	v West Indies in West Indies	1954-55
20	(17ct, 3st)	A. T. W. Grout	v England in Australia	1958-59
20	(19ct, 1st)	H. B. Taber	v South Africa in South Africa	1966-67

MOST DISMISSALS IN A THREE-TEST SERIES

19	(17ct, 2st)	I. A. Healy	v Sri Lanka in Australia	1995-96
18	(17ct, 1st)	A. C. Gilchrist	v New Zealand in New Zealand	1999-00
17	(16ct, 1st)	R. W. Marsh	v New Zealand in Australia	1973-74
16	(all ct)	R. W. Marsh	v Pakistan in Australia	1972-73
16	(15ct, 1st)	R. W. Marsh	v India in Australia	1980-81

MOST DISMISSALS IN A CAREER

		M	Ct	St	Total
1	I. A. Healy	119	366	29	395
2	R. W. Marsh	97	343	12	355
3	A. C. Gilchrist	56	217	24	241
4	A. T. W. Grout	51	163	24	187
5	W. A. S. Oldfield	54	78	52	130
6	G. R. A. Langley	26	83	15	98

		M	Ct	St	Total
7	H. Carter	28	44	21	65
8	J. J. Kelly	36	43	20	63
9 {	J. M. Blackham	35	36	24	60
	H. B. Taber	16	56	4	60
11	D. Tallon	21	50	8	58
12	B. N. Jarman	19	50	4	54
13	S. J. Rixon	13	42	5	47
14	W. B. Phillips	27	43	0	43
15	K. J. Wright	10	31	4	35
16 {	R. A. Saggers	6	16	8	24
	G. C. Dyer	6	22	2	24
18 {	T. J. Zoehrer	10	18	1	19
	L. V. Maddocks	7	18	1	19
20	J. A. Maclean	4	18	0	18
21	A. H. Jarvis	11	8	9	17
22	R. D. Woolley	2	7	0	7
23 {	W. Carkeek	6	6	0	6
	P. A. Emery	1	5	1	6
25	B. A. Barnett	4	3	2	5
26	H. S. B. Love	1	3	0	3
27 {	W. L. Murdoch	1	2	0	2
	F. J. Burton	2	1	1	2

MOST DISMISSALS AGAINST OPPONENTS

		M	Ct	St	Dismissals
v England	R. W. Marsh	43	141	7	148
v South Africa	H. B. Taber	9	35	3	38
v West Indies	I. A. Healy	28	72	6	78
v New Zealand	R. W. Marsh	14	57	1	58
v India	A. C. Gilchrist	10	32	2	34
v Pakistan	R. W. Marsh	20	66	2	68
v Sri Lanka	I. A. Healy	11	32	2	34
v Zimbabwe	A. C. Gilchrist	2	9	2	11
v Bangladesh	A. C. Gilchrist	2	9	0	9

MOST DISMISSALS AGAINST AUSTRALIA

		M	Ct	St	Dismissals
for England	A. P. E. Knott	35	97	8	105
for South Africa	D. J. Richardson	12	39	1	40
for West Indies	P. J. L. Dujon	21	83	1	84
for New Zealand	I. D. S. Smith	15	34	5	39
for India	S. M. H. Kirmani	17	29	12	41
for Pakistan	Wasim Bari	19	56	10	66
for Sri Lanka	R. S. Kaluwitharana	9	15	6	21
for Zimbabwe	A. Flower	1	3	0	3

MOST DISMISSALS IN A CALENDAR YEAR

	M	Ct	St	Dismissals	Year
I. A. Healy	16	58	9	67	1993
I. A. Healy	15	55	4	59	1997
A. C. Gilchrist	14	52	5	57	2001
R. W. Marsh	13	52	1	53	1981
A. C. Gilchrist	12	43	7	50	2003

MOST DISMISSALS PER MATCH

	D/M	Eng	SAf	WI	NZ	Ind	Pak	SL	Zim	Ban
P. A. Emery	6.00	–	–	–	–	–	6.00	–	–	–
J. A. Maclean	4.50	4.50	–	–	–	–	–	–	–	–
A. C. Gilchrist	4.30	5.10	4.00	4.00	4.17	3.40	4.00	5.40	5.50	4.50
R. A. Saggers	4.00	3.00	4.20	–	–	–	–	–	–	–
G. C. Dyer	4.00	2.50	–	–	4.33	–	–	6.00	–	–

MOST STUMPINGS IN A MATCH

4	J. M. Blackham	v England at Lord's	1888
4	A. H. Jarvis	v England at Sydney	1894-95
4	W. A. S. Oldfield	v England at Melbourne	1924-25
4	W. A. S. Oldfield	v England at Sydney	1924-25
4	W. A. S. Oldfield	v West Indies at Adelaide	1930-31
4	R. A. Saggers	v South Africa at Port Elizabeth	1949-50
4	G. R. A. Langley	v West Indies at Brisbane	1951-52

BEST KEEPER–BOWLER COMBINATIONS

Dismissals
95 ...... R. W. Marsh – D. K. Lillee
58 .... I. A. Healy – G. D. McGrath
56 .... A. C. Gilchrist – G. D. McGrath
55 .... I. A. Healy – C. J. McDermott

Dismissals
49 ...... I. A. Healy – S. K. Warne
47 ..... A. C. Gilchrist – J. N. Gillespie
46 ..... I. A. Healy – M. G. Hughes
45 ..... A. T. W. Grout – A. K. Davidson

FIELDING RECORDS

MOST CATCHES IN AN INNINGS

5	V. Y. Richardson	v South Africa at Durban (Kingsmead)	1935-36

Note: There are 19 instances of four catches in an innings.

MOST CATCHES IN A MATCH

7	G. S. Chappell	v England at Perth	1974-75
7	M. L. Hayden	v Sri Lanka at Galle	2003-04
7	J. M. Gregory	v England at Sydney	1920-21
6	V. Y. Richardson	v South Africa at Durban (Kingsmead)	1935-36
6	R. N. Harvey	v England at Sydney	1962-63
6	I. M. Chappell	v New Zealand at Adelaide	1973-74
6	D. F. Whatmore	v India at Kanpur	1979-80
6	M. E. Waugh	v India at Chennai (Chepauk)	2000-01

Note: There are 12 instances of five catches in a match.

MOST CATCHES IN A SERIES

15	J. M. Gregory	v England in Australia	1920-21
14	G. S. Chappell	v England in Australia	1974-75
13	R. B. Simpson	v South Africa in South Africa	1957-58
13	R. B. Simpson	v West Indies in Australia	1960-61
12	D. F. Whatmore	v India in India	1979-80
12	A. R. Border	v England in England	1981

11	R. B. Simpson	v West Indies in West Indies	1964-65
11	I. M. Chappell	v England in Australia	1974-75
11	I. R. Redpath	v England in Australia	1974-75
11	A. R. Border	v England in England	1985
11	M. A. Taylor	v England in England	1993
11	M. E. Waugh	v India in India	2000-01
11	R. T. Ponting	v South Africa in Australia	2001-02

Note: There are 14 instances of 10 catches in a series.

MOST CATCHES IN A CAREER

1	M. E. Waugh	181 in 128 matches
2	M. A. Taylor	157 in 104 matches
3	A. R. Border	156 in 156 matches
4	G. S. Chappell	122 in 88 matches
5	R. B. Simpson	110 in 62 matches
5	S. R. Waugh	112 in 168 matches
6	R. B. Simpson	110 in 62 matches
7	I. M. Chappell	105 in 76 matches
8	D. C. Boon	99 in 107 matches
9	S. K. Warne	93 in 112 matches
10	R. T. Ponting	91 in 79 matches

MOST CATCHES AGAINST OPPONENTS

v England	G. S. Chappell	61 in 36 matches
v South Africa	R. B. Simpson	27 in 15 matches
v West Indies	M. E. Waugh	45 in 28 matches
v New Zealand	A. R. Border	31 in 23 matches
v India	M. E. Waugh	29 in 14 matches
v Pakistan	M. E. Waugh	23 in 15 matches
v Sri Lanka	S. K. Warne	15 in 13 matches
v Zimbabwe	M. E. Waugh	5 in 1 match
v Bangladesh	J. L. Langer	3 in 2 matches

MOST CATCHES AGAINST AUSTRALIA

for England	I. T. Botham	57 in 36 matches
for South Africa	T. L. Goddard	21 in 18 matches
for West Indies	C. L. Hooper	38 in 25 matches
for New Zealand	J. V. Coney	24 in 15 matches
for India	S. M. Gavaskar	19 in 20 matches
	R. S. Dravid	19 in 14 matches
for Pakistan	Mudassar Nazar	16 in 19 matches
for Sri Lanka	S. T. Jayasuriya	11 in 11 matches
for Zimbabwe	S. V. Carlisle	3 in 2 matches
	N. C. Johnson	3 in 1 match
for Bangladesh	Javed Omar	3 in 2 matches

MOST CATCHES IN A CALENDAR YEAR

J. M. Gregory	27 in 12 matches	1921
M. A. Taylor	27 in 15 matches	1997
R. B. Simpson	26 in 14 matches	1964
M. E. Waugh	26 in 14 matches	1999
R. T. Ponting	25 in 14 matches	2001
M. A. Taylor	25 in 15 matches	1993

BEST FIELDER–BOWLER COMBINATION

Catches

		Catches	
51	M. A. Taylor – S. K. Warne	23	R. T. Ponting – S. K. Warne
39	M. E. Waugh – S. K. Warne	22	G. S. Chappell – D. K. Lillee
34	M. E. Waugh – G. D. McGrath	22	R. T. Ponting – G. D. McGrath

TEAM

HIGHEST INNINGS TOTALS

8-758 dec.	v West Indies at Kingston	1954-55
6-735 dec.	v Zimbabwe at Perth	2003-04
6-729 dec.	v England at Lord's	1930
701	v England at The Oval	1934
695	v England at The Oval	1930
674	v India at Adelaide	1947-48
668	v West Indies at Bridgetown	1954-55
8-659 dec.	v England at Sydney	1946-47
8-656 dec.	v England at Manchester	1964
4-653 dec.	v England at Leeds	1993
7-652 dec.	v South Africa at Johannesburg (WS)	2001-02
6-650 dec.	v West Indies at Bridgetown	1964-65
645	v England at Brisbane	1946-47
7-641 dec.	v England at The Oval	2001
4-632 dec.	v England at Lord's	1993
8-628 dec.	v South Africa at Johannesburg (WS)	1996-97
619	v West Indies at Sydney	1968-69
617	v Pakistan at Faisalabad	1979-80
5-617 dec.	v Sri Lanka at Perth	1995-96
6-607 dec.	v New Zealand at Brisbane	1993-94
9-605 dec.	v West Indies at Bridgetown	2002-03
604	v England at Melbourne	1936-37
6-602 dec.	v England at Nottingham	1989
8-601 dec.	v England at Brisbane	1954-55
7-601 dec.	v England at Leeds	1989
600	v England at Melbourne	1924-25
9-600 dec.	v West Indies at Port-of-Spain	1954-55

HIGHEST INNINGS TOTALS AGAINST AUSTRALIA

7-903 dec.	for England at The Oval	1938
7-705 dec.	for India at Sydney	2003-04
8-658 dec.	for England at Nottingham	1938
7-657 dec.	for India at Kolkata	2000-01
636	for England at Sydney	1928-29

HIGHEST FOURTH-INNINGS TOTALS

3-404 v England (won) at Leeds	1948
402 v England (set 505) at Manchester	1981
7-381 v New Zealand (set 439) at Perth	2001-02
6-369 v Pakistan (won) at Hobart (Bel)	1999-00
7-362 v West Indies (won) at Georgetown	1977-78
7-344 v England (set 448) at Sydney	1994-95
8-342 v India (won) at Perth	1977-78

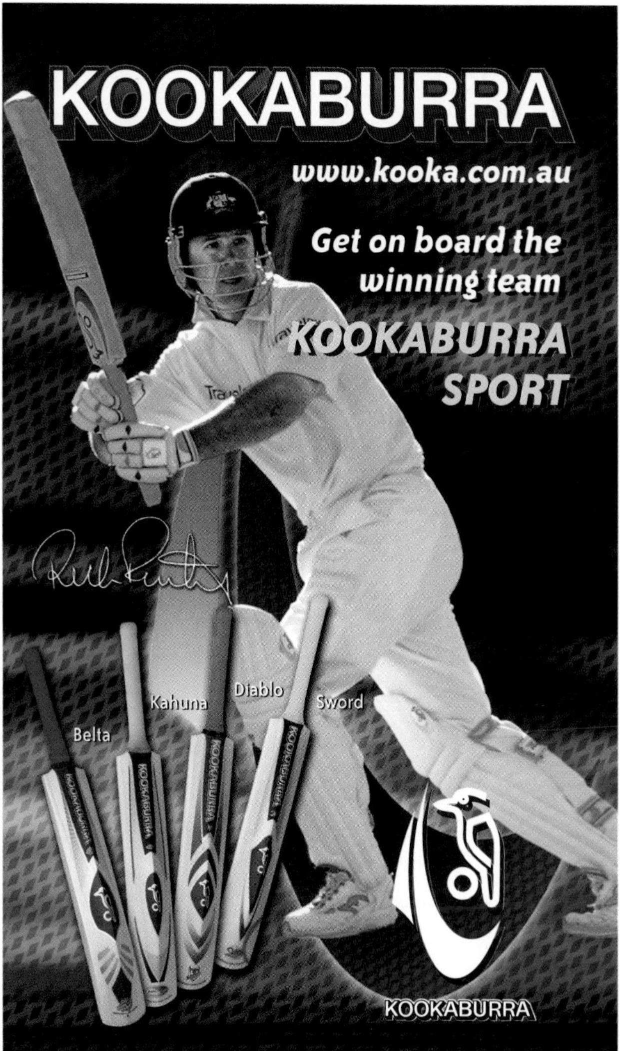
KOOKABURRA
www.kooka.com.au
Get on board the
winning team
KOOKABURRA
SPORT
Kahuna
Diablo
Sword
Belta
KOOKABURRA

ALBION
GD

All Albion helmets conform to AS/NZS4499 Parts 1 and 3 Protective headgear for cricket

CRICKET
AUSTRALIA
Official Supplier of Cricket Headwear to Cricket Australia.

Classic Debut

Test Series Club Edition

Centurion Kevlar®2004

Test Series Elite Edition

Cricket Australia's got the heads, Albion's got the helmets

www.albionsports.com.au

9-339 v West Indies (set 359) at Adelaide	....	1968-69
339 v South Africa (set 377) at Adelaide	....	1910-11
336 v England (set 348) at Adelaide	....	1928-29
5-336 v South Africa (won) at Durban (Kingsmead)	....	1949-50
335 v England (set 428) at Nottingham	....	1930
333 v England (set 427) at Melbourne	....	1894-95
3-329 v England (set 483) at Lord's	....	1975
3-328 v England (set 468) at Adelaide	....	1970-71

LOWEST COMPLETED INNINGS TOTALS

36	v England at Birmingham	1902
42	v England at Sydney	1887-88
44	v England at The Oval	1896
53	v England at Lord's	1896
58	v England at Brisbane	1936-37
60	v England at Lord's	1888
63	v England at The Oval	1882
65	v England at The Oval	1912
66	v England at Brisbane	1928-29
68	v England at The Oval	1886
70	v England at Manchester	1888
74	v England at Birmingham	1909
75	v South Africa at Durban (Kingsmead)	1949-50
76	v West Indies at Perth	1984-85
78	v England at Lord's	1968
80	v England at The Oval	1888
80	v England at Sydney	1936-37
80	v Pakistan at Karachi	1956-57
81	v England at Manchester	1888
82	v England at Sydney	1887-88
82	v West Indies at Adelaide	1951-52
83	v England at Sydney	1882-83
83	v India at Melbourne	1980-81
84	v England at Sydney	1886-87
84	v England at Manchester	1956

Lowest completed innings totals for opponents not mentioned above:

103	v New Zealand at Auckland	1985-86
120	v Sri Lanka at Kandy	2003-04
403	v Zimbabwe at Sydney	2003-04
7d-407	v Bangladesh at Cairns	2003-04

LOWEST COMPLETED INNINGS TOTALS AGAINST AUSTRALIA

36	for South Africa at Melbourne	1931-32
42	for New Zealand at Wellington	1945-46
45	for England at Sydney	1886-87
45	for South Africa at Melbourne	1931-32
51	for West Indies at Port-of-Spain	1998-99

MOST RUNS IN A DAY'S PLAY

6-494	1st day	v South Africa at Sydney	1910-11
2-475	1st day	v England at The Oval	1934
3-458	1st day	v England at Leeds	1930
1-455	2nd day	v England at Leeds	1934
450	1st day	v South Africa at Johannesburg (OW)	1921-22

HIGHEST MATCH AGGREGATE

1,028-20	v England at The Oval	1934
1,013-18	v West Indies at Sydney	1968-69
971-14	v New Zealand at Wellington	1973-74
936-20	v England at Adelaide	1920-21
917-20	v West Indies at Bridgetown	1954-55

LOWEST COMPLETED MATCH AGGREGATE

124-20	v England at Sydney	1887-88
151-20	v England at Manchester	1888
163-20	v England at The Oval	1896
176-20	v England at Lord's	1888
176-20	v England at The Oval	1912

LARGEST VICTORIES

By Innings and Runs Margin

Innings and 360	v South Africa at Johannesburg (WS)	2001-02
Innings and 332	v England at Brisbane	1946-47
Innings and 259	v South Africa at Port Elizabeth	1949-50
Innings and 226	v India at Brisbane	1947-48
Innings and 222	v New Zealand at Hobart	1993-94
Innings and 217	v West Indies at Brisbane (Ex)	1930-31
Innings and 200	v England at Melbourne	1936-37

By Runs Margin

562 runs	v England at The Oval	1934
530 runs	v South Africa at Melbourne	1910-11
409 runs	v England at Lord's	1948
384 runs	v England at Brisbane	2002-03
382 runs	v England at Adelaide	1894-95
382 runs	v West Indies at Sydney	1968-69
377 runs	v England at Sydney	1920-21
365 runs	v England at Melbourne	1936-37
352 runs	v West Indies at Melbourne	2000-01
348 runs	v Pakistan at Melbourne	1976-77

NARROWEST VICTORIES

By One Wicket

v West Indies at Melbourne (*Last Wkt:* 38 – D. T. Ring 32* and W. A. Johnston 7*) 1951-52

By 20 Runs or Less

3	v England at Manchester	1902
6	v England at Sydney	1884-85
7	v England at The Oval	1882
11	v England at Adelaide	1924-25
16	v India at Brisbane	1977-78
16	v Sri Lanka at Colombo (SSC)	1992-93

HEAVIEST DEFEATS

By Innings and Runs Margin

Innings and 579	by England at The Oval	1938
Innings and 230	by England at Adelaide	1891-92
Innings and 225	by England at Melbourne	1911-12
Innings and 219	by India at Calcutta	1997-98
Innings and 217	by England at The Oval	1886

By Runs Margin

675 runs	by England at Brisbane (Ex)	1928-29
408 runs	by West Indies at Adelaide	1979-80
343 runs	by West Indies at Bridgetown	1990-91
338 runs	by England at Adelaide	1932-33
323 runs	by South Africa at Port Elizabeth	1969-70
322 runs	by England at Brisbane	1936-37
307 runs	by South Africa at Johannesburg (WS)	1969-70

NARROWEST DEFEATS

By One Wicket

v England at The Oval (*Last Wkt:* 15 – G. H. Hirst 58* and W. Rhodes 6*) 1902
v England at Melbourne (*Last Wkt:* 39 – S. F. Barnes 38* and A. Fielder 18*) 1907-08
v Pakistan at Karachi (*Last Wkt:* 57 – Inzamam-ul-Haq 58* and Mushtaq Ahmed 20*) . . . 1994-95
v West Indies at Bridgetown (*Last Wkt:* 9 – B. C. Lara 153* and C. A. Walsh 0*) 1998-99

By 20 Runs or Less

1	by West Indies at Adelaide	1992-93
3	by England at Melbourne	1982-83
5	by South Africa at Sydney	1993-94
10	by England at Sydney	1894-95
12	by England at Adelaide	1928-29
12	by England at Melbourne	1998-99
13	by England at Sydney	1886-87
18	by England at Leeds	1981
19	by England at The Oval	1997

TIED TESTS

Australia (505 and 232) tied with West Indies (453 and 284) at Brisbane 1960-61
India (397 and 347) tied with Australia (7d-574 and 5d-170) at Chennai (Chepauk) 1986-87

APPEARANCE RECORDS

MOST TEST APPEARANCES

	M	Eng	SAf	WI	NZ	Ind	Pak	SL	Zim	Ban
S. R. Waugh	168	46	16	32	23	18	20	8	3	2
A. R. Border	156	47	6	31	23	20	22	7	0	0
M. E. Waugh	128	29	18	28	14	14	15	9	1	0
I. A. Healy	119	33	12	28	11	9	14	11	1	0
S. K. Warne	112	26	18	16	15	11	12	13	1	0
D. C. Boon	107	31	6	22	17	11	11	9	0	0
M. A. Taylor	104	33	11	20	11	9	12	8	0	0
R. W. Marsh	97	43	0	17	14	3	20	0	0	0
G. D. McGrath	97	22	14	20	9	7	14	8	1	2
G. S. Chappell	88	36	0	17	14	3	17	1	0	0

MOST TEST APPEARANCES AGAINST AUSTRALIA

M. C. Cowdrey (England)	44
G. A. Gooch (England)	42
D. I. Gower (England)	42
J. B. Hobbs (England)	41
W. Rhodes (England)	41
G. Boycott (England)	39
C. A. Walsh (West Indies)	38
I. T. Botham (England)	36
R. G. D. Willis (England)	36
A. C. MacLaren (England)	35

YOUNGEST AUSTRALIAN PLAYERS ON DEBUT

Years	Days			
17	239	I. D. Craig	v South Africa at Sydney	1952-53
18	232	T. W. Garrett	v England at Melbourne	1876-77
19	54	A. Cotter	v England at Sydney	1903-04
19	96	C. Hill	v England at Lord's	1896
19	100	G. R. Hazlitt	v England at Sydney	1907-08
19	104	R. G. Archer	v South Africa at Melbourne	1952-53
19	107	R. N. Harvey	v India at Adelaide	1947-48
19	149	A. Jackson	v England at Adelaide	1928-29
19	173	J. T. Cottam	v England at Sydney	1886-87
19	252	J. J. Ferris	v England at Sydney	1886-87
19	252	C. J. McDermott	v West Indies at Melbourne	1984-85
19	331	S. J. McCabe	v England at Nottingham	1930
19	354	K. D. Walters	v England at Brisbane	1965-66
19	363	G. D. McKenzie	v England at Lord's	1961

OLDEST AUSTRALIAN PLAYERS ON DEBUT

Years	Days			
46	253	D. D. Blackie	v England at Sydney	1928-29
46	237	H. Ironmonger	v England at Brisbane (Ex)	1928-29
38	328	N. F. D. Thomson	v England at Melbourne	1876-77
38	35	R. G. Holland	v West Indies at Brisbane	1984-85
37	290	E. J. Gregory	v England at Melbourne	1876-77
37	184	H. S. B. Love	v England at Brisbane	1932-33
37	163	J. Harry	v England at Adelaide	1894-95
37	154	R. K. Oxenham	v England at Melbourne	1928-29
36	148	A. J. Richardson	v England at Sydney	1924-25
35	127	J. B. Iverson	v England at Brisbane	1950-51
35	81	K. H. Eastwood	v England at Sydney	1970-71
35	67	J. W. Wilson	v India at Bombay	1956-57
35	4	A. E. V. Hartkopf	v England at Melbourne	1924-25
35	3	T. V. Hohns	v West Indies at Sydney	1988-89

OLDEST AUSTRALIAN PLAYERS

Years	Days			
50	327	H. Ironmonger	v England at Sydney	1932-33
46	309	D. D. Blackie	v England at Adelaide	1928-29
44	69	C. V. Grimmett	v South Africa at Durban (Kingsmead)	1935-36
43	259	H. Carter	v South Africa at Cape Town	1921-22
43	255	W. Bardsley	v England at The Oval	1926
42	224	C. Kelleway	v England at Brisbane (Ex)	1928-29
42	130	S. E. Gregory	v England at The Oval	1912
42	86	W. W. Armstrong	v England at The Oval	1921
42	74	W. A. S. Oldfield	v England at Melbourne	1936-37

Years	Days			
41	178	V. Y. Richardson . . . . . v South Africa at Durban (Kingsmead)	1935-36
40	227	A. A. Mailey . . . . v England at The Oval	1926
40	223	J. M. Blackham . . . . . . v England at Sydney	1894-95
40	127	R. K. Oxenham . . . . . . v South Africa at Brisbane	1931-32
40	100	W. J. O'Reilly . . . . v New Zealand at Wellington	1945-46
40	52	C. G. Macartney . . . . . v England at The Oval	1926

UMPIRES

MOST APPEARANCES BY AUSTRALIAN UMPIRES

D. B. Hair	55	1995-96	to	2004
D. J. Harper	42	1998-99	to	2004
S. G. Randell	36	1990-91	to	1997-98
A. R. Crafter	33	1978-79	to	1981-82
R. M. Crockett	32	1903-04	to	1907-08
J. Phillips	29	1895-96	to	1905-06
C. J. Egar	29	1962-63	to	1968-69
R. C. Bailhache	27	1974-75	to	1988-89
L. P. Rowan	26	1962-63	to	1968-69
T. F. Brooks	24	1970-71	to	1975-76

CAPTAINCY

THE CAPTAINS

		M	W	L	D	T
1	D. W. Gregory	3	2	1	0	0
2	W. L. Murdoch	16	5	7	4	0
3	T. P. Horan	2	0	2	0	0
4	H. H. Massie	1	1	0	0	0
5	J. M. Blackham	8	3	3	2	0
6	H. J. H. Scott	3	0	3	0	0
7	P. S. McDonnell	6	1	5	0	0
8	G. Giffen	4	2	2	0	0
9	G. H. S. Trott	8	5	3	0	0
10	J. Darling	21	7	4	10	0
11	H. Trumble	2	2	0	0	0
12	M. A. Noble	15	8	5	2	0
13	C. Hill	10	5	5	0	0
14	S. E. Gregory	6	2	1	3	0
15	W. W. Armstrong	10	8	0	2	0
16	H. L. Collins	11	5	2	4	0
17	W. Bardsley	2	0	0	2	0
18	J. Ryder	5	1	4	0	0
19	W. M. Woodfull	25	14	7	4	0
20	V. Y. Richardson	5	4	0	1	0
21	D. G. Bradman	24	15	3	6	0
22	W. A. Brown	1	1	0	0	0
23	A. L. Hassett	24	14	4	6	0
24	A. R. Morris	2	0	2	0	0
25	I. W. G. Johnson	17	7	5	5	0
26	R. R. Lindwall	1	0	0	1	0
27	I. D. Craig	5	3	0	2	0
28	R. Benaud	28	12	4	11	1
29	R. N. Harvey	1	1	0	0	0
30	R. B. Simpson	39	12	12	15	0
		M	*W*	*L*	*D*	*T*

		M	W	L	D	T
31	B. C. Booth	2	0	1	1	0
32	W. M. Lawry	26	9	8	9	0
33	B. N. Jarman	1	0	0	1	0
34	I. M. Chappell	30	15	5	10	0
35	G. S. Chappell	48	21	13	14	0
36	G. N. Yallop	7	1	6	0	0
37	K. J. Hughes	28	4	13	11	0
38	A. R. Border	93	32	22	38	1
39	M. A. Taylor	50	26	13	11	0
40	S. R. Waugh	57	41	9	7	0
41	A. C. Gilchrist	3	2	1	0	0
42	R. T. Ponting	4	3	0	1	0

MOST SUCCESSFUL CAPTAINS
(Qualification: 10 Tests)

	M	W	L	D	T	% Won
W. W. Armstrong	10	8	0	2	0	80.00
S. R. Waugh	57	41	9	7	0	71.93
D. G. Bradman	24	15	3	6	0	62.50
A. L. Hassett	24	14	4	6	0	58.33
W. M. Woodfull	25	14	7	4	0	56.00
M. A. Noble	15	8	5	2	0	53.33
M. A. Taylor	50	26	13	11	0	52.00
C. Hill	10	5	5	0	0	50.00
I. M. Chappell	31	15	5	11	0	48.38
H. L. Collins	11	5	2	4	0	45.45

SUMMARY OF AUSTRALIAN TEST CRICKET

Note: The Third Test at the Melbourne Cricket Ground from December 31, 1970, to January 5, 1971, has been sanctioned by Cricket Australia as an official Test match. In consultation with the MCC tour management, the Test was declared a 'DRAW'. This decision was determined as the two teams had been officially announced, including the 12th men, and the toss had been made. The umpires were walking out to the ground when rain began to fall, thus preventing any further play in the match.

Opponent	Date of First Test	Tests	Won	Lost	Drawn	Tied
England	Mar 15, 1877	307	125	95	87	0
South Africa	Oct 11, 1902	71	39	15	17	0
West Indies	Dec 12, 1930	99	45	32	21	1
New Zealand	Mar 29, 1946	41	18	7	16	0
India	Nov 28, 1947	64	30	14	19	1
Pakistan	Oct 11, 1956	49	21	11	17	0
Sri Lanka	Apr 22, 1983	18	11	1	6	0
Zimbabwe	Oct 14, 1999	3	3	0	0	0
Bangladesh	July 18, 2003	2	2	0	0	0
Total		654	294	175	183	2

TEST MATCHES

Venue	Opponent	Result for Australia	Captain	Test/Opp
1876-77 in Australia				
Melbourne	England	Won by 45 runs	D. W. Gregory	1/1
Melbourne	England	Lost by four wickets	D. W. Gregory	2/2
1878-79 in Australia				
Melbourne	England	Won by 10 wickets	D. W. Gregory	3/3

Venue	Opponent	Result for Australia	Captain	Test/Opp
1880 in England				
The Oval	England	Lost by five wickets	W. L. Murdoch	4/4
1881-82 in Australia				
Melbourne	England	Drawn	W. L. Murdoch	5/5
Sydney	England	Won by five wickets	W. L. Murdoch	6/6
Sydney	England	Won by six wickets	W. L. Murdoch	7/7
Melbourne	England	Drawn	W. L. Murdoch	8/8
1882 in England				
The Oval	England	Won by seven runs	W. L. Murdoch	9/9
1882-83 in Australia				
Melbourne	England	Won by nine wickets	W. L. Murdoch	10/10
Melbourne	England	Lost by an innings and 27 runs	W. L. Murdoch	11/11
Sydney	England	Lost by 69 runs	W. L. Murdoch	12/12
Sydney	England	Won by four wickets	W. L. Murdoch	13/13
1884 in England				
Manchester	England	Drawn	W. L. Murdoch	14/14
Lord's	England	Lost by an innings and five runs	W. L. Murdoch	15/15
The Oval	England	Drawn	W. L. Murdoch	16/16
1884-85 in Australia				
Adelaide	England	Lost by eight wickets	W. L. Murdoch	17/17
Melbourne	England	Lost by 10 wickets	T. P. Horan	18/18
Sydney	England	Won by six runs	H. H. Massie	19/19
Sydney	England	Won by eight wickets	J. M. Blackham	20/20
Melbourne	England	Lost by an innings and 98 runs	T. P. Horan	21/21
1886 in England				
Manchester	England	Lost by four wickets	H. J. H. Scott	22/22
Lord's	England	Lost by an innings and 106 runs	H. J. H. Scott	23/23
The Oval	England	Lost by an innings and 217 runs	H. J. H. Scott	24/24
1886-87 in Australia				
Sydney	England	Lost by 13 runs	P. S. McDonnell	25/25
Sydney	England	Lost by 71 runs	P. S. McDonnell	26/26
1887-88 in Australia				
Sydney	England	Lost by 126 runs	P. S. McDonnell	27/27
1888 in England				
Lord's	England	Won by 61 runs	P. S. McDonnell	28/28
The Oval	England	Lost by an innings and 137 runs	P. S. McDonnell	29/29
Manchester	England	Lost by an innings and 21 runs	P. S. McDonnell	30/30
1890 in England				
Lord's	England	Lost by seven wickets	W. L. Murdoch	31/31
The Oval	England	Lost by two wickets	W. L. Murdoch	32/32
1891-92 in Australia				
Melbourne	England	Won by 54 runs	J. M. Blackham	33/33
Sydney	England	Won by 72 runs	J. M. Blackham	34/34
Adelaide	England	Lost by an innings and 230 runs	J. M. Blackham	35/35
1893 in England				
Lord's	England	Drawn	J. M. Blackham	36/36
The Oval	England	Lost by an innings and 43 runs	J. M. Blackham	37/37
Manchester	England	Drawn	J. M. Blackham	38/38
1894-95 in Australia				
Sydney	England	Lost by 10 runs	J. M. Blackham	39/39
Melbourne	England	Lost by 94 runs	G. Giffen	40/40
Adelaide	England	Won by 382 runs	G. Giffen	41/41
Sydney	England	Won by an innings and 147 runs	G. Giffen	42/42
Melbourne	England	Lost by six wickets	G. Giffen	43/43

Venue	Opponent	Result for Australia	Captain	Test/Opp
1896 in England				
Lord's	England	Lost by six wickets	G. H. S. Trott	44/44
Manchester	England	Won by three wickets	G. H. S. Trott	45/45
The Oval	England	Lost by 66 runs	G. H. S. Trott	46/46
1897-98 in Australia				
Sydney	England	Lost by nine wickets	G. H. S. Trott	47/47
Melbourne	England	Won by an innings and 55 runs	G. H. S. Trott	48/48
Adelaide	England	Won by an innings and 13 runs	G. H. S. Trott	49/49
Melbourne	England	Won by eight wickets	G. H. S. Trott	50/50
Sydney	England	Won by six wickets	G. H. S. Trott	51/51
1899 in England				
Nottingham	England	Drawn	J. Darling	52/52
Lord's	England	Won by 10 wickets	J. Darling	53/53
Leeds	England	Drawn	J. Darling	54/54
Manchester	England	Drawn	J. Darling	55/55
The Oval	England	Drawn	J. Darling	56/56
1901-02 in Australia				
Sydney	England	Lost by an innings and 124 runs	J. Darling	57/57
Melbourne	England	Won by 229 runs	J. Darling	58/58
Adelaide	England	Won by four wickets	J. Darling	59/59
Sydney	England	Won by seven wickets	H. Trumble	60/60
Melbourne	England	Won by 32 runs	H. Trumble	61/61
1902 in England				
Birmingham	England	Drawn	J. Darling	62/62
Lord's	England	Drawn	J. Darling	63/63
Sheffield	England	Won by 143 runs	J. Darling	64/64
Manchester	England	Won by three runs	J. Darling	65/65
The Oval	England	Lost by one wicket	J. Darling	66/66
1902-03 in South Africa				
Johannesburg (OW)	South Africa	Drawn	J. Darling	67/1
Johannesburg (OW)	South Africa	Won by 159 runs	J. Darling	68/2
Cape Town	South Africa	Won by 10 wickets	J. Darling	69/3
1903-04 in Australia				
Sydney	England	Lost by five wickets	M. A. Noble	70/67
Melbourne	England	Lost by 185 runs	M. A. Noble	71/68
Adelaide	England	Won by 216 runs	M. A. Noble	72/69
Sydney	England	Lost by 157 runs	M. A. Noble	73/70
Melbourne	England	Won by 218 runs	M. A. Noble	74/71
1905 in England				
Nottingham	England	Lost by 213 runs	J. Darling	75/72
Lord's	England	Drawn	J. Darling	76/73
Leeds	England	Drawn	J. Darling	77/74
Manchester	England	Lost by an innings and 80 runs	J. Darling	78/75
The Oval	England	Drawn	J. Darling	79/76
1907-08 in Australia				
Sydney	England	Won by two wickets	M. A. Noble	80/77
Melbourne	England	Lost by one wicket	M. A. Noble	81/78
Adelaide	England	Won by 245 runs	M. A. Noble	82/79
Melbourne	England	Won by 308 runs	M. A. Noble	83/80
Sydney	England	Won by 49 runs	M. A. Noble	84/81
1909 in England				
Birmingham	England	Lost by 10 wickets	M. A. Noble	85/82
Lord's	England	Won by nine wickets	M. A. Noble	86/83
Leeds	England	Won by 126 runs	M. A. Noble	87/84
Manchester	England	Drawn	M. A. Noble	88/85
The Oval	England	Drawn	M. A. Noble	89/86

Venue	Opponent	Result for Australia	Captain	Test/Opp
1910-11 in Australia				
Sydney	South Africa	Won by an innings and 114 runs	C. Hill	90/4
Melbourne	South Africa	Won by 89 runs	C. Hill	91/5
Adelaide	South Africa	Lost by 38 runs	C. Hill	92/6
Melbourne	South Africa	Won by 530 runs	C. Hill	93/7
Sydney	South Africa	Won by seven wickets	C. Hill	94/8
1911-12 in Australia				
Sydney	England	Won by 146 runs	C. Hill	95/87
Melbourne	England	Lost by eight wickets	C. Hill	96/88
Adelaide	England	Lost by seven wickets	C. Hill	97/89
Melbourne	England	Lost by an innings and 225 runs	C. Hill	98/90
Sydney	England	Lost by 70 runs	C. Hill	99/91
1912 in England				
Manchester	South Africa	Won by an innings and 88 runs	S. E. Gregory	100/9
Lord's	England	Drawn	S. E. Gregory	101/92
Lord's	South Africa	Won by 10 wickets	S. E. Gregory	102/10
Manchester	England	Drawn	S. E. Gregory	103/93
Nottingham	South Africa	Drawn	S. E. Gregory	104/11
The Oval	England	Lost by 244 runs	S. E. Gregory	105/94
1920-21 in Australia				
Sydney	England	Won by 377 runs	W. W. Armstrong	106/95
Melbourne	England	Won by an innings and 91 runs	W. W. Armstrong	107/96
Adelaide	England	Won by 119 runs	W. W. Armstrong	108/97
Melbourne	England	Won by eight wickets	W. W. Armstrong	109/98
Sydney	England	Won by nine wickets	W. W. Armstrong	110/99
1921 in England				
Nottingham	England	Won by 10 wickets	W. W. Armstrong	111/100
Lord's	England	Won by eight wickets	W. W. Armstrong	112/101
Leeds	England	Won by 219 runs	W. W. Armstrong	113/102
Manchester	England	Drawn	W. W. Armstrong	114/103
The Oval	England	Drawn	W. W. Armstrong	115/104
1921-22 in South Africa				
Durban (Lord's)	South Africa	Drawn	H. L. Collins	116/12
Johannesburg (OW)	South Africa	Drawn	H. L. Collins	117/13
Cape Town	South Africa	Won by 10 wickets	H. L. Collins	118/14
1924-25 in Australia				
Sydney	England	Won by 193 runs	H. L. Collins	119/105
Melbourne	England	Won by 81 runs	H. L. Collins	120/106
Adelaide	England	Won by 11 runs	H. L. Collins	121/107
Melbourne	England	Lost by an innings and 29 runs	H. L. Collins	122/108
Sydney	England	Won by 307 runs	H. L. Collins	123/109
1926 in England				
Nottingham	England	Drawn	H. L. Collins	124/110
Lord's	England	Drawn	H. L. Collins	125/111
Leeds	England	Drawn	W. Bardsley	126/112
Manchester	England	Drawn	W. Bardsley	127/113
The Oval	England	Lost by 289 runs	H. L. Collins	128/114
1928-29 in Australia				
Brisbane (Ex)	England	Lost by 675 runs	J. Ryder	129/115
Sydney	England	Lost by eight wickets	J. Ryder	130/116
Melbourne	England	Lost by three wickets	J. Ryder	131/117
Adelaide	England	Lost by 12 runs	J. Ryder	132/118
Melbourne	England	Won by five wickets	J. Ryder	133/119

Venue	Opponent	Result for Australia	Captain	Test/Opp
1930 in England				
Nottingham	England	Lost by 93 runs	W. M. Woodfull	134/120
Lord's	England	Won by seven wickets	W. M. Woodfull	135/121
Leeds	England	Drawn	W. M. Woodfull	136/122
Manchester	England	Drawn	W. M. Woodfull	137/123
The Oval	England	Won by an innings and 39 runs	W. M. Woodfull	138/124
1930-31 in Australia				
Adelaide	West Indies	Won by 10 wickets	W. M. Woodfull	139/1
Sydney	West Indies	Won by an innings and 172 runs	W. M. Woodfull	140/2
Brisbane (Ex)	West Indies	Won by an innings and 217 runs	W. M. Woodfull	141/3
Melbourne	West Indies	Won by an innings and 122 runs	W. M. Woodfull	142/4
Sydney	West Indies	Lost by 30 runs	W. M. Woodfull	143/5
1931-32 in Australia				
Brisbane	South Africa	Won by an innings and 163 runs	W. M. Woodfull	144/15
Sydney	South Africa	Won by an innings and 155 runs	W. M. Woodfull	145/16
Melbourne	South Africa	Won by 169 runs	W. M. Woodfull	146/17
Adelaide	South Africa	Won by 10 wickets	W. M. Woodfull	147/18
Melbourne	South Africa	Won by an innings and 72 runs	W. M. Woodfull	148/19
1932-33 in Australia				
Sydney	England	Lost by 10 wickets	W. M. Woodfull	149/125
Melbourne	England	Won by 111 runs	W. M. Woodfull	150/126
Adelaide	England	Lost by 338 runs	W. M. Woodfull	151/127
Brisbane	England	Lost by six wickets	W. M. Woodfull	152/128
Sydney	England	Lost by eight wickets	W. M. Woodfull	153/129
1934 in England				
Nottingham	England	Won by 238 runs	W. M. Woodfull	154/130
Lord's	England	Lost by an innings and 38 runs	W. M. Woodfull	155/131
Manchester	England	Drawn	W. M. Woodfull	156/132
Leeds	England	Drawn	W. M. Woodfull	157/133
The Oval	England	Won by 562 runs	W. M. Woodfull	158/134
1935-36 in South Africa				
Durban (Kingsmead)	South Africa	Won by nine wickets	V. Y. Richardson	159/20
Johannesburg (OW)	South Africa	Drawn	V. Y. Richardson	160/21
Cape Town	South Africa	Won by an innings and 78 runs	V. Y. Richardson	161/22
Johannesburg (OW)	South Africa	Won by an innings and 184 runs	V. Y. Richardson	162/23
Durban (Kingsmead)	South Africa	Won by an innings and six runs	V. Y. Richardson	163/24
1936-37 in Australia				
Brisbane	England	Lost by 322 runs	D. G. Bradman	164/135
Sydney	England	Lost by an innings and 22 runs	D. G. Bradman	165/136
Melbourne	England	Won by 365 runs	D. G. Bradman	166/137
Adelaide	England	Won by 148 runs	D. G. Bradman	167/138
Melbourne	England	Won by an innings and 200 runs	D. G. Bradman	168/139
1938 in England				
Nottingham	England	Drawn	D. G. Bradman	169/140
Lord's	England	Drawn	D. G. Bradman	170/141
Leeds	England	Won by five wickets	D. G. Bradman	171/142
The Oval	England	Lost by an innings and 579 runs	D. G. Bradman	172/143
1945-46 in New Zealand				
Wellington	New Zealand	Won by an innings and 103 runs	W. A. Brown	173/1
1946-47 in Australia				
Brisbane	England	Won by an innings and 332 runs	D. G. Bradman	174/144
Sydney	England	Won by an innings and 33 runs	D. G. Bradman	175/145
Melbourne	England	Drawn	D. G. Bradman	176/146
Adelaide	England	Drawn	D. G. Bradman	177/147
Sydney	England	Won by five wickets	D. G. Bradman	178/148

Venue	Opponent	Result for Australia	Captain	Test/Opp
1947-48 in Australia				
Brisbane	India	Won by an innings and 226 runs	D. G. Bradman	179/1
Sydney	India	Drawn	D. G. Bradman	180/2
Melbourne	India	Won by 233 runs	D. G. Bradman	181/3
Adelaide	India	Won by an innings and 16 runs	D. G. Bradman	182/4
Melbourne	India	Won by an innings and 177 runs	D. G. Bradman	183/5
1948 in England				
Nottingham	England	Won by eight wickets	D. G. Bradman	184/149
Lord's	England	Won by 409 runs	D. G. Bradman	185/150
Manchester	England	Drawn	D. G. Bradman	186/151
Leeds	England	Won by seven wickets	D. G. Bradman	187/152
The Oval	England	Won by an innings and 149 runs	D. G. Bradman	188/153
1949-50 in South Africa				
Johannesburg (EP)	South Africa	Won by an innings and 85 runs	A. L. Hassett	189/25
Cape Town	South Africa	Won by eight wickets	A. L. Hassett	190/26
Durban (Kingsmead)	South Africa	Won by five wickets	A. L. Hassett	191/27
Johannesburg (EP)	South Africa	Drawn	A. L. Hassett	192/28
Port Elizabeth	South Africa	Won by an innings and 259 runs	A. L. Hassett	193/29
1950-51 in Australia				
Brisbane	England	Won by 70 runs	A. L. Hassett	194/154
Melbourne	England	Won by 28 runs	A. L. Hassett	195/155
Sydney	England	Won by an innings and 13 runs	A. L. Hassett	196/156
Adelaide	England	Won by 274 runs	A. L. Hassett	197/157
Melbourne	England	Lost by eight wickets	A. L. Hassett	198/158
1951-52 in Australia				
Brisbane	West Indies	Won by three wickets	A. L. Hassett	199/6
Sydney	West Indies	Won by seven wickets	A. L. Hassett	200/7
Adelaide	West Indies	Lost by six wickets	A. R. Morris	201/8
Melbourne	West Indies	Won by one wicket	A. L. Hassett	202/9
Sydney	West Indies	Won by 202 runs	A. L. Hassett	203/10
1952-53 in Australia				
Brisbane	South Africa	Won by 96 runs	A. L. Hassett	204/30
Melbourne	South Africa	Lost by 82 runs	A. L. Hassett	205/31
Sydney	South Africa	Won by an innings and 38 runs	A. L. Hassett	206/32
Adelaide	South Africa	Drawn	A. L. Hassett	207/33
Melbourne	South Africa	Lost by six wickets	A. L. Hassett	208/34
1953 in England				
Nottingham	England	Drawn	A. L. Hassett	209/159
Lord's	England	Drawn	A. L. Hassett	210/160
Manchester	England	Drawn	A. L. Hassett	211/161
Leeds	England	Drawn	A. L. Hassett	212/162
The Oval	England	Lost by eight wickets	A. L. Hassett	213/163
1954-55 in Australia				
Brisbane	England	Won by an innings and 154 runs	I. W. G. Johnson	214/164
Sydney	England	Lost by 38 runs	A. R. Morris	215/165
Melbourne	England	Lost by 128 runs	I. W. G. Johnson	216/166
Adelaide	England	Lost by five wickets	I. W. G. Johnson	217/167
Sydney	England	Drawn	I. W. G. Johnson	218/168
1954-55 in West Indies				
Kingston	West Indies	Won by nine wickets	I. W. G. Johnson	219/11
Port-of-Spain	West Indies	Drawn	I. W. G. Johnson	220/12
Georgetown	West Indies	Won by eight wickets	I. W. G. Johnson	221/13
Bridgetown	West Indies	Drawn	I. W. G. Johnson	222/14
Kingston	West Indies	Won by an innings and 82 runs	I. W. G. Johnson	223/15

Venue	Opponent	Result for Australia	Captain	Test/Opp
1956 in England				
Nottingham	England	Drawn	I. W. G. Johnson	224/169
Lord's	England	Won by 185 runs	I. W. G. Johnson	225/170
Leeds	England	Lost by an innings and 42 runs	I. W. G. Johnson	226/171
Manchester	England	Lost by an innings and 170 runs	I. W. G. Johnson	227/172
The Oval	England	Drawn	I. W. G. Johnson	228/173
1956-57 in Pakistan				
Karachi	Pakistan	Lost by nine wickets	I. W. G. Johnson	229/1
1956-57 in India				
Madras (Corp)	India	Won by an innings and five runs	I. W. G. Johnson	230/6
Bombay (BS)	India	Drawn	R. R. Lindwall	231/7
Calcutta	India	Won by 94 runs	I. W. G. Johnson	232/8
1957-58 in South Africa				
Johannesburg (WS)	South Africa	Drawn	I. D. Craig	233/35
Cape Town	South Africa	Won by an innings and 141 runs	I. D. Craig	234/36
Durban (Kingsmead)	South Africa	Drawn	I. D. Craig	235/37
Johannesburg (WS)	South Africa	Won by 10 wickets	I. D. Craig	236/38
Port Elizabeth	South Africa	Won by eight wickets	I. D. Craig	237/39
1958-59 in Australia				
Brisbane	England	Won by eight wickets	R. Benaud	238/174
Melbourne	England	Won by eight wickets	R. Benaud	239/175
Sydney	England	Drawn	R. Benaud	240/176
Adelaide	England	Won by 10 wickets	R. Benaud	241/177
Melbourne	England	Won by nine wickets	R. Benaud	242/178
1959-60 in Pakistan				
Dacca	Pakistan	Won by eight wickets	R. Benaud	243/2
Lahore	Pakistan	Won by seven wickets	R. Benaud	244/3
Karachi	Pakistan	Drawn	R. Benaud	245/4
1959-60 in India				
Delhi	India	Won by an innings and 127 runs	R. Benaud	246/9
Kanpur	India	Lost by 119 runs	R. Benaud	247/10
Bombay (BS)	India	Drawn	R. Benaud	248/11
Madras (Corp)	India	Won by an innings and 55 runs	R. Benaud	249/12
Calcutta	India	Drawn	R. Benaud	250/13
1960-61 in Australia				
Brisbane	West Indies	Tied	R. Benaud	251/16
Melbourne	West Indies	Won by seven wickets	R. Benaud	252/17
Sydney	West Indies	Lost by 222 runs	R. Benaud	253/18
Adelaide	West Indies	Drawn	R. Benaud	254/19
Melbourne	West Indies	Won by two wickets	R. Benaud	255/20
1961 in England				
Birmingham	England	Drawn	R. Benaud	256/179
Lord's	England	Won by five wickets	R. N. Harvey	257/180
Leeds	England	Lost by eight wickets	R. Benaud	258/181
Manchester	England	Won by 54 runs	R. Benaud	259/182
The Oval	England	Drawn	R. Benaud	260/183
1962-63 in Australia				
Brisbane	England	Drawn	R. Benaud	261/184
Melbourne	England	Lost by seven wickets	R. Benaud	262/185
Sydney	England	Won by eight wickets	R. Benaud	263/186
Adelaide	England	Drawn	R. Benaud	264/187
Sydney	England	Drawn	R. Benaud	265/188

Venue	Opponent	Result for Australia	Captain	Test/Opp
1963-64 in Australia				
Brisbane	South Africa	Drawn	R. Benaud	266/40
Melbourne	South Africa	Won by eight wickets	R. B. Simpson	267/41
Sydney	South Africa	Drawn	R. B. Simpson	268/42
Adelaide	South Africa	Lost by 10 wickets	R. B. Simpson	269/43
Sydney	South Africa	Drawn	R. B. Simpson	270/44
1964 in England				
Nottingham	England	Drawn	R. B. Simpson	271/189
Lord's	England	Drawn	R. B. Simpson	272/190
Leeds	England	Won by seven wickets	R. B. Simpson	273/191
Manchester	England	Drawn	R. B. Simpson	274/192
The Oval	England	Drawn	R. B. Simpson	275/193
1964-65 in India				
Madras (Corp)	India	Won by 139 runs	R. B. Simpson	276/14
Bombay (BS)	India	Lost by two wickets	R. B. Simpson	277/15
Calcutta	India	Drawn	R. B. Simpson	278/16
1964-65 in Pakistan				
Karachi	Pakistan	Drawn	R. B. Simpson	279/5
1964-65 in Australia				
Melbourne	Pakistan	Drawn	R. B. Simpson	280/6
1964-65 in West Indies				
Kingston	West Indies	Lost by 179 runs	R. B. Simpson	281/21
Port-of-Spain	West Indies	Drawn	R. B. Simpson	282/22
Georgetown	West Indies	Lost by 212 runs	R. B. Simpson	283/23
Bridgetown	West Indies	Drawn	R. B. Simpson	284/24
Port-of-Spain	West Indies	Won by 10 wickets	R. B. Simpson	285/25
1965-66 in Australia				
Brisbane	England	Drawn	B. C. Booth	286/194
Melbourne	England	Drawn	R. B. Simpson	287/195
Sydney	England	Lost by an innings and 93 runs	B. C. Booth	288/196
Adelaide	England	Won by an innings and nine runs	R. B. Simpson	289/197
Melbourne	England	Drawn	R. B. Simpson	290/198
1966-67 in South Africa				
Johannesburg (WS)	South Africa	Lost by 233 runs	R. B. Simpson	291/45
Cape Town	South Africa	Won by six wickets	R. B. Simpson	292/46
Durban (Kingsmead)	South Africa	Lost by eight wickets	R. B. Simpson	293/47
Johannesburg (WS)	South Africa	Drawn	R. B. Simpson	294/48
Port Elizabeth	South Africa	Lost by seven wickets	R. B. Simpson	295/49
1967-68 in Australia				
Adelaide	India	Won by 146 runs	R. B. Simpson	296/17
Melbourne	India	Won by an innings and four runs	R. B. Simpson	297/18
Brisbane	India	Won by 39 runs	W. M. Lawry	298/19
Sydney	India	Won by 144 runs	W. M. Lawry	299/20
1968 in England				
Manchester	England	Won by 159 runs	W. M. Lawry	300/199
Lord's	England	Drawn	W. M. Lawry	301/200
Birmingham	England	Drawn	W. M. Lawry	302/201
Leeds	England	Drawn	B. N. Jarman	303/202
The Oval	England	Lost by 226 runs	W. M. Lawry	304/203
1968-69 in Australia				
Brisbane	West Indies	Lost by 125 runs	W. M. Lawry	305/26
Melbourne	West Indies	Won by an innings and 30 runs	W. M. Lawry	306/27
Sydney	West Indies	Won by 10 wickets	W. M. Lawry	307/28
Adelaide	West Indies	Drawn	W. M. Lawry	308/29
Sydney	West Indies	Won by 382 runs	W. M. Lawry	309/30

Venue	Opponent	Result for Australia	Captain	Test/Opp
1969-70 in India				
Bombay (BS)	India	Won by eight wickets	W. M. Lawry	310/21
Kanpur	India	Drawn	W. M. Lawry	311/22
Delhi	India	Lost by seven wickets	W. M. Lawry	312/23
Calcutta	India	Won by 10 wickets	W. M. Lawry	313/24
Madras (Chepauk)	India	Won by 77 runs	W. M. Lawry	314/25
1969-70 in South Africa				
Cape Town	South Africa	Lost by 170 runs	W. M. Lawry	315/50
Durban (Kingsmead)	South Africa	Lost by an innings and 129 runs	W. M. Lawry	316/51
Johannesburg (WS)	South Africa	Lost by 307 runs	W. M. Lawry	317/52
Port Elizabeth	South Africa	Lost by 323 runs	W. M. Lawry	318/53
1970-71 in Australia				
Brisbane	England	Drawn	W. M. Lawry	319/204
Perth	England	Drawn	W. M. Lawry	320/205
Melbourne	England	Drawn	W. M. Lawry	321/206
Sydney	England	Lost by 299 runs	W. M. Lawry	322/207
Melbourne	England	Drawn	W. M. Lawry	323/208
Adelaide	England	Drawn	W. M. Lawry	324/209
Sydney	England	Lost by 62 runs	I. M. Chappell	325/210
1972 in England				
Manchester	England	Lost by 89 runs	I. M. Chappell	326/211
Lord's	England	Won by eight wickets	I. M. Chappell	327/212
Nottingham	England	Drawn	I. M. Chappell	328/213
Leeds	England	Lost by nine wickets	I. M. Chappell	329/214
The Oval	England	Won by five wickets	I. M. Chappell	330/215
1972-73 in Australia				
Adelaide	Pakistan	Won by an innings and 114 runs	I. M. Chappell	331/7
Melbourne	Pakistan	Won by 92 runs	I. M. Chappell	332/8
Sydney	Pakistan	Won by 52 runs	I. M. Chappell	333/9
1972-73 in West Indies				
Kingston	West Indies	Drawn	I. M. Chappell	334/31
Bridgetown	West Indies	Drawn	I. M. Chappell	335/32
Port-of-Spain	West Indies	Won by 44 runs	I. M. Chappell	336/33
Georgetown	West Indies	Won by 10 wickets	I. M. Chappell	337/34
Port-of-Spain	West Indies	Drawn	I. M. Chappell	338/35
1973-74 in Australia				
Melbourne	New Zealand	Won by an innings and 25 runs	I. M. Chappell	339/2
Sydney	New Zealand	Drawn	I. M. Chappell	340/3
Adelaide	New Zealand	Won by an innings and 57 runs	I. M. Chappell	341/4
1973-74 in New Zealand				
Wellington	New Zealand	Drawn	I. M. Chappell	342/5
Christchurch	New Zealand	Lost by five wickets	I. M. Chappell	343/6
Auckland	New Zealand	Won by 297 runs	I. M. Chappell	344/7
1974-75 in Australia				
Brisbane	England	Won by 166 runs	I. M. Chappell	345/216
Perth	England	Won by nine wickets	I. M. Chappell	346/217
Melbourne	England	Drawn	I. M. Chappell	347/218
Sydney	England	Won by 171 runs	I. M. Chappell	348/219
Adelaide	England	Won by 163 runs	I. M. Chappell	349/220
Melbourne	England	Lost by an innings and four runs	I. M. Chappell	350/221
1975 in England				
Birmingham	England	Won by an innings and 85 runs	I. M. Chappell	351/222
Lord's	England	Drawn	I. M. Chappell	352/223
Leeds	England	Drawn	I. M. Chappell	353/224
The Oval	England	Drawn	I. M. Chappell	354/225

Venue	Opponent	Result for Australia	Captain	Test/Opp
1975-76 in Australia				
Brisbane	West Indies	Won by eight wickets	G. S. Chappell	355/36
Perth	West Indies	Lost by an innings and 87 runs	G. S. Chappell	356/37
Melbourne	West Indies	Won by eight wickets	G. S. Chappell	357/38
Sydney	West Indies	Won by seven wickets	G. S. Chappell	358/39
Adelaide	West Indies	Won by 190 runs	G. S. Chappell	359/40
Melbourne	West Indies	Won by 165 runs	G. S. Chappell	360/41
1976-77 in Australia				
Adelaide	Pakistan	Drawn	G. S. Chappell	361/10
Melbourne	Pakistan	Won by 348 runs	G. S. Chappell	362/11
Sydney	Pakistan	Lost by eight wickets	G. S. Chappell	363/12
1976-77 in New Zealand				
Christchurch	New Zealand	Drawn	G. S. Chappell	364/8
Auckland	New Zealand	Won by 10 wickets	G. S. Chappell	365/9
1976-77 in Australia				
Melbourne	England	Won by 45 runs	G. S. Chappell	366/226
1977 in England				
Lord's	England	Drawn	G. S. Chappell	367/227
Manchester	England	Lost by nine wickets	G. S. Chappell	368/228
Nottingham	England	Lost by seven wickets	G. S. Chappell	369/229
Leeds	England	Lost by an innings and 85 runs	G. S. Chappell	370/230
The Oval	England	Drawn	G. S. Chappell	371/231
1977-78 in Australia				
Brisbane	India	Won by 16 runs	R. B. Simpson	372/26
Perth	India	Won by two wickets	R. B. Simpson	373/27
Melbourne	India	Lost by 222 runs	R. B. Simpson	374/28
Sydney	India	Lost by an innings and two runs	R. B. Simpson	375/29
Adelaide	India	Won by 47 runs	R. B. Simpson	376/30
1977-78 in West Indies				
Port-of-Spain	West Indies	Lost by an innings and 106 runs	R. B. Simpson	377/42
Bridgetown	West Indies	Lost by nine wickets	R. B. Simpson	378/43
Georgetown	West Indies	Won by three wickets	R. B. Simpson	379/44
Port-of-Spain	West Indies	Lost by 198 runs	R. B. Simpson	380/45
Kingston	West Indies	Drawn	R. B. Simpson	381/46
1978-79 in Australia				
Brisbane	England	Lost by seven wickets	G. N. Yallop	382/232
Perth	England	Lost by 166 runs	G. N. Yallop	383/233
Melbourne	England	Won by 103 runs	G. N. Yallop	384/234
Sydney	England	Lost by 93 runs	G. N. Yallop	385/235
Adelaide	England	Lost by 205 runs	G. N. Yallop	386/236
Sydney	England	Lost by nine wickets	G. N. Yallop	387/237
Melbourne	Pakistan	Lost by 71 runs	G. N. Yallop	388/13
Perth	Pakistan	Won by seven wickets	K. J. Hughes	389/14
1979-80 in India				
Madras (Chepauk)	India	Drawn	K. J. Hughes	390/31
Bangalore	India	Drawn	K. J. Hughes	391/32
Kanpur	India	Lost by 153 runs	K. J. Hughes	392/33
Delhi	India	Drawn	K. J. Hughes	393/34
Calcutta	India	Drawn	K. J. Hughes	394/35
Bombay (WS)	India	Lost by an innings and 100 runs	K. J. Hughes	395/36

Venue	Opponent	Result for Australia	Captain	Test/Opp
1979-80 in Australia				
Brisbane	West Indies	Drawn	G. S. Chappell	396/47
Perth	England	Won by 138 runs	G. S. Chappell	397/238
Melbourne	West Indies	Lost by 10 wickets	G. S. Chappell	398/48
Sydney	England	Won by six wickets	G. S. Chappell	399/239
Adelaide	West Indies	Lost by 408 runs	G. S. Chappell	400/49
Melbourne	England	Won by eight wickets	G. S. Chappell	401/240
1979-80 in Pakistan				
Karachi	Pakistan	Lost by seven wickets	G. S. Chappell	402/15
Faisalabad	Pakistan	Drawn	G. S. Chappell	403/16
Lahore	Pakistan	Drawn	G. S. Chappell	404/17
1980 in England				
Lord's	England	Drawn	G. S. Chappell	405/241
1980-81 in Australia				
Brisbane	New Zealand	Won by 10 wickets	G. S. Chappell	406/10
Perth	New Zealand	Won by eight wickets	G. S. Chappell	407/11
Melbourne	New Zealand	Drawn	G. S. Chappell	408/12
Sydney	India	Won by an innings and four runs	G. S. Chappell	409/37
Adelaide	India	Drawn	G. S. Chappell	410/38
Melbourne	India	Lost by 59 runs	G. S. Chappell	411/39
1981 in England				
Nottingham	England	Won by four wickets	K. J. Hughes	412/242
Lord's	England	Drawn	K. J. Hughes	413/243
Leeds	England	Lost by 18 runs	K. J. Hughes	414/244
Birmingham	England	Lost by 29 runs	K. J. Hughes	415/245
Manchester	England	Lost by 103 runs	K. J. Hughes	416/246
The Oval	England	Drawn	K. J. Hughes	417/247
1981-82 in Australia				
Perth	Pakistan	Won by 286 runs	G. S. Chappell	418/18
Brisbane	Pakistan	Won by 10 wickets	G. S. Chappell	419/19
Melbourne	Pakistan	Lost by an innings and 82 runs	G. S. Chappell	420/20
Melbourne	West Indies	Won by 58 runs	G. S. Chappell	421/50
Sydney	West Indies	Drawn	G. S. Chappell	422/51
Adelaide	West Indies	Lost by five wickets	G. S. Chappell	423/52
1981-82 in New Zealand				
Wellington	New Zealand	Drawn	G. S. Chappell	424/13
Auckland	New Zealand	Lost by five wickets	G. S. Chappell	425/14
Christchurch	New Zealand	Won by eight wickets	G. S. Chappell	426/15
1982-83 in Pakistan				
Karachi	Pakistan	Lost by nine wickets	K. J. Hughes	427/21
Faisalabad	Pakistan	Lost by an innings and three runs	K. J. Hughes	428/22
Lahore	Pakistan	Lost by nine wickets	K. J. Hughes	429/23
1982-83 in Australia				
Perth	England	Drawn	G. S. Chappell	430/248
Brisbane	England	Won by seven wickets	G. S. Chappell	431/249
Adelaide	England	Won by eight wickets	G. S. Chappell	432/250
Melbourne	England	Lost by three runs	G. S. Chappell	433/251
Sydney	England	Drawn	G. S. Chappell	434/252
1982-83 in Sri Lanka				
Kandy	Sri Lanka	Won by an innings and 38 runs	G. S. Chappell	435/1
1983-84 in Australia				
Perth	Pakistan	Won by an innings and nine runs	K. J. Hughes	436/24
Brisbane	Pakistan	Drawn	K. J. Hughes	437/25
Adelaide	Pakistan	Drawn	K. J. Hughes	438/26
Melbourne	Pakistan	Drawn	K. J. Hughes	439/27
Sydney	Pakistan	Won by 10 wickets	K. J. Hughes	440/28

Venue	Opponent	Result for Australia	Captain	Test/Opp
1983-84 in West Indies				
Georgetown	West Indies	Drawn	K. J. Hughes	441/53
Port-of-Spain	West Indies	Drawn	K. J. Hughes	442/54
Bridgetown	West Indies	Lost by 10 wickets	K. J. Hughes	443/55
St John's	West Indies	Lost by an innings and 36 runs	K. J. Hughes	444/56
Kingston	West Indies	Lost by 10 wickets	K. J. Hughes	445/57
1984-85 in Australia				
Perth	West Indies	Lost by an innings and 112 runs	K. J. Hughes	446/58
Brisbane	West Indies	Lost by eight wickets	K. J. Hughes	447/59
Adelaide	West Indies	Lost by 191 runs	A. R. Border	448/60
Melbourne	West Indies	Drawn	A. R. Border	449/61
Sydney	West Indies	Won by an innings and 55 runs	A. R. Border	450/62
1985 in England				
Leeds	England	Lost by five wickets	A. R. Border	451/253
Lord's	England	Won by four wickets	A. R. Border	452/254
Nottingham	England	Drawn	A. R. Border	453/255
Manchester	England	Drawn	A. R. Border	454/256
Birmingham	England	Lost by an innings and 118 runs	A. R. Border	455/257
The Oval	England	Lost by an innings and 94 runs	A. R. Border	456/258
1985-86 in Australia				
Brisbane	New Zealand	Lost by an innings and 41 runs	A. R. Border	457/16
Sydney	New Zealand	Won by four wickets	A. R. Border	458/17
Perth	New Zealand	Lost by six wickets	A. R. Border	459/18
Adelaide	India	Drawn	A. R. Border	460/40
Melbourne	India	Drawn	A. R. Border	461/41
Sydney	India	Drawn	A. R. Border	462/42
1985-86 in New Zealand				
Wellington	New Zealand	Drawn	A. R. Border	463/19
Christchurch	New Zealand	Drawn	A. R. Border	464/20
Auckland	New Zealand	Lost by eight wickets	A. R. Border	465/21
1986-87 in India				
Madras (Chepauk)	India	Tied	A. R. Border	466/43
Delhi	India	Drawn	A. R. Border	467/44
Bombay (WS)	India	Drawn	A. R. Border	468/45
1986-87 in Australia				
Brisbane	England	Lost by seven wickets	A. R. Border	469/259
Perth	England	Drawn	A. R. Border	470/260
Adelaide	England	Drawn	A. R. Border	471/261
Melbourne	England	Lost by an innings and 14 runs	A. R. Border	472/262
Sydney	England	Won by 55 runs	A. R. Border	473/263
1987-88 in Australia				
Brisbane	New Zealand	Won by nine wickets	A. R. Border	474/22
Adelaide	New Zealand	Drawn	A. R. Border	475/23
Melbourne	New Zealand	Drawn	A. R. Border	476/24
Sydney	England	Drawn	A. R. Border	477/264
Perth	Sri Lanka	Won by an innings and 108 runs	A. R. Border	478/2
1988-89 in Pakistan				
Karachi	Pakistan	Lost by an innings and 188 runs	A. R. Border	479/29
Faisalabad	Pakistan	Drawn	A. R. Border	480/30
Lahore	Pakistan	Drawn	A. R. Border	481/31
1988-89 in Australia				
Brisbane	West Indies	Lost by eight wickets	A. R. Border	482/63
Perth	West Indies	Lost by 169 runs	A. R. Border	483/64
Melbourne	West Indies	Lost by 285 runs	A. R. Border	484/65
Sydney	West Indies	Won by seven wickets	A. R. Border	485/66
Adelaide	West Indies	Drawn	A. R. Border	486/67

Venue	Opponent	Result for Australia	Captain	Test/Opp
1989 in England				
Leeds	England	Won by 210 runs	A. R. Border	487/265
Lord's	England	Won by six wickets	A. R. Border	488/266
Birmingham	England	Drawn	A. R. Border	489/267
Manchester	England	Won by nine wickets	A. R. Border	490/268
Nottingham	England	Won by an innings and 180 runs	A. R. Border	491/269
The Oval	England	Drawn	A. R. Border	492/270
1989-90 in Australia				
Perth	New Zealand	Drawn	A. R. Border	493/25
Brisbane	Sri Lanka	Drawn	A. R. Border	494/3
Hobart	Sri Lanka	Won by 173 runs	A. R. Border	495/4
Melbourne	Pakistan	Won by 92 runs	A. R. Border	496/32
Adelaide	Pakistan	Drawn	A. R. Border	497/33
Sydney	Pakistan	Drawn	A. R. Border	498/34
1989-90 in New Zealand				
Wellington	New Zealand	Lost by nine wickets	A. R. Border	499/26
1990-91 in Australia				
Brisbane	England	Won by 10 wickets	A. R. Border	500/271
Melbourne	England	Won by eight wickets	A. R. Border	501/272
Sydney	England	Drawn	A. R. Border	502/273
Adelaide	England	Drawn	A. R. Border	503/274
Perth	England	Won by nine wickets	A. R. Border	504/275
1990-91 in West Indies				
Kingston	West Indies	Drawn	A. R. Border	505/68
Georgetown	West Indies	Lost by 10 wickets	A. R. Border	506/69
Port-of-Spain	West Indies	Drawn	A. R. Border	507/70
Bridgetown	West Indies	Lost by 343 runs	A. R. Border	508/71
St John's	West Indies	Won by 157 runs	A. R. Border	509/72
1991-92 in Australia				
Brisbane	India	Won by 10 wickets	A. R. Border	510/46
Melbourne	India	Won by eight wickets	A. R. Border	511/47
Sydney	India	Drawn	A. R. Border	512/48
Adelaide	India	Won by 38 runs	A. R. Border	513/49
Perth	India	Won by 300 runs	A. R. Border	514/50
1992-93 in Sri Lanka				
Colombo (SSC)	Sri Lanka	Won by 16 runs	A. R. Border	515/5
Colombo (PIS)	Sri Lanka	Drawn	A. R. Border	516/6
Moratuwa	Sri Lanka	Drawn	A. R. Border	517/7
1992-93 in Australia				
Brisbane	West Indies	Drawn	A. R. Border	518/73
Melbourne	West Indies	Won by 139 runs	A. R. Border	519/74
Sydney	West Indies	Drawn	A. R. Border	520/75
Adelaide	West Indies	Lost by one run	A. R. Border	521/76
Perth	West Indies	Lost by an innings and 25 runs	A. R. Border	522/77
1992-93 in New Zealand				
Christchurch	New Zealand	Won by an innings and 60 runs	A. R. Border	523/27
Wellington	New Zealand	Drawn	A. R. Border	524/28
Auckland	New Zealand	Lost by five wickets	A. R. Border	525/29
1993 in England				
Manchester	England	Won by 179 runs	A. R. Border	526/276
Lord's	England	Won by an innings and 62 runs	A. R. Border	527/277
Nottingham	England	Drawn	A. R. Border	528/278
Leeds	England	Won by an innings and 148 runs	A. R. Border	529/279
Birmingham	England	Won by eight wickets	A. R. Border	530/280
The Oval	England	Lost by 161 runs	A. R. Border	531/281

Venue	Opponent	Result for Australia	Captain	Test/Opp
1993-94 in Australia				
Perth	New Zealand	Drawn	A. R. Border	532/30
Hobart	New Zealand	Won by an innings and 222 runs	A. R. Border	533/31
Brisbane	New Zealand	Won by an innings and 96 runs	A. R. Border	534/32
Melbourne	South Africa	Drawn	A. R. Border	535/54
Sydney	South Africa	Lost by five runs	A. R. Border	536/55
Adelaide	South Africa	Won by 191 runs	A. R. Border	537/56
1993-94 in South Africa				
Johannesburg (WS)	South Africa	Lost by 197 runs	A. R. Border	538/57
Cape Town	South Africa	Won by nine wickets	A. R. Border	539/58
Durban (Kingsmead)	South Africa	Drawn	A. R. Border	540/59
1994-95 in Pakistan				
Karachi	Pakistan	Lost by one wicket	M. A. Taylor	541/35
Rawalpindi	Pakistan	Drawn	M. A. Taylor	542/36
Lahore	Pakistan	Drawn	M. A. Taylor	543/37
1994-95 in Australia				
Brisbane	England	Won by 184 runs	M. A. Taylor	544/282
Melbourne	England	Won by 295 runs	M. A. Taylor	545/283
Sydney	England	Drawn	M. A. Taylor	546/284
Adelaide	England	Lost by 106 runs	M. A. Taylor	547/285
Perth	England	Won by 329 runs	M. A. Taylor	548/286
1994-95 in West Indies				
Bridgetown	West Indies	Won by 10 wickets	M. A. Taylor	549/78
St John's	West Indies	Drawn	M. A. Taylor	550/79
Port-of-Spain	West Indies	Lost by nine wickets	M. A. Taylor	551/80
Kingston	West Indies	Won by an innings and 53 runs	M. A. Taylor	552/81
1995-96 in Australia				
Brisbane	Pakistan	Won by an innings and 126 runs	M. A. Taylor	553/38
Hobart	Pakistan	Won by 155 runs	M. A. Taylor	554/39
Sydney	Pakistan	Lost by 74 runs	M. A. Taylor	555/40
Perth	Sri Lanka	Won by an innings and 36 runs	M. A. Taylor	556/8
Melbourne	Sri Lanka	Won by 10 wickets	M. A. Taylor	557/9
Adelaide	Sri Lanka	Won by 148 runs	M. A. Taylor	558/10
1996-97 in India				
Delhi	India	Lost by seven wickets	M. A. Taylor	559/51
1996-97 in Australia				
Brisbane	West Indies	Won by 123 runs	M. A. Taylor	560/82
Sydney	West Indies	Won by 124 runs	M. A. Taylor	561/83
Melbourne	West Indies	Lost by six wickets	M. A. Taylor	562/84
Adelaide	West Indies	Won by an innings and 183 runs	M. A. Taylor	563/85
Perth	West Indies	Lost by 10 wickets	M. A. Taylor	564/86
1996-97 in South Africa				
Johannesburg (WS)	South Africa	Won by an innings and 196 runs	M. A. Taylor	565/60
Port Elizabeth	South Africa	Won by two wickets	M. A. Taylor	566/61
Centurion	South Africa	Lost by eight wickets	M. A. Taylor	567/62
1997 in England				
Birmingham	England	Lost by nine wickets	M. A. Taylor	568/287
Lord's	England	Drawn	M. A. Taylor	569/288
Manchester	England	Won by 268 runs	M. A. Taylor	570/289
Leeds	England	Won by an innings and 61 runs	M. A. Taylor	571/290
Nottingham	England	Won by 264 runs	M. A. Taylor	572/291
The Oval	England	Lost by 19 runs	M. A. Taylor	573/292

Venue	Opponent	Result for Australia	Captain	Test/Opp
1997-98 in Australia				
Brisbane	New Zealand	Won by 186 runs	M. A. Taylor	574/33
Perth	New Zealand	Won by an innings and 70 runs	M. A. Taylor	575/34
Hobart	New Zealand	Drawn	M. A. Taylor	576/35
Melbourne	South Africa	Drawn	M. A. Taylor	577/63
Sydney	South Africa	Won by an innings and 21 runs	M. A. Taylor	578/64
Adelaide	South Africa	Drawn	M. A. Taylor	579/65
1997-98 in India				
Chennai (Chepauk)	India	Lost by 179 runs	M. A. Taylor	580/52
Calcutta	India	Lost by an innings and 219 runs	M. A. Taylor	581/53
Bangalore	India	Won by eight wickets	M. A. Taylor	582/54
1998-99 in Pakistan				
Rawalpindi	Pakistan	Won by an innings and 99 runs	M. A. Taylor	583/40
Peshawar	Pakistan	Drawn	M. A. Taylor	584/41
Karachi	Pakistan	Drawn	M. A. Taylor	585/42
1998-99 in Australia				
Brisbane	England	Drawn	M. A. Taylor	586/293
Perth	England	Won by seven wickets	M. A. Taylor	587/294
Adelaide	England	Won by 205 runs	M. A. Taylor	588/295
Melbourne	England	Lost by 12 runs	M. A. Taylor	589/296
Sydney	England	Won by 98 runs	M. A. Taylor	590/297
1998-99 in West Indies				
Port-of-Spain	West Indies	Won by 312 runs	S. R. Waugh	591/87
Kingston	West Indies	Lost by 10 wickets	S. R. Waugh	592/88
Bridgetown	West Indies	Lost by one wicket	S. R. Waugh	593/89
St John's	West Indies	Won by 176 runs	S. R. Waugh	594/90
1999-2000 in Sri Lanka				
Kandy	Sri Lanka	Lost by six wickets	S. R. Waugh	595/11
Galle	Sri Lanka	Drawn	S. R. Waugh	596/12
Colombo (SSC)	Sri Lanka	Drawn	S. R. Waugh	597/13
1999-2000 in Zimbabwe				
Harare	Zimbabwe	Won by 10 wickets	S. R. Waugh	598/1
1999-2000 in Australia				
Brisbane	Pakistan	Won by 10 wickets	S. R. Waugh	599/44
Hobart (Bel)	Pakistan	Won by four wickets	S. R. Waugh	600/45
Perth	Pakistan	Won by an innings and 20 runs	S. R. Waugh	601/46
Adelaide	India	Won by 285 runs	S. R. Waugh	602/55
Melbourne	India	Won by 180 runs	S. R. Waugh	603/56
Sydney	India	Won by an innings and 141 runs	S. R. Waugh	604/57
1999-2000 in New Zealand				
Auckland	New Zealand	Won by 62 runs	S. R. Waugh	605/36
Wellington	New Zealand	Won by six wickets	S. R. Waugh	606/37
Hamilton	New Zealand	Won by six wickets	S. R. Waugh	607/38
2000-01 in Australia				
Brisbane	West Indies	Won by an innings and 126 runs	S. R. Waugh	608/91
Perth	West Indies	Won by an innings and 27 runs	S. R. Waugh	609/92
Adelaide	West Indies	Won by five wickets	A. C. Gilchrist	610/93
Melbourne	West Indies	Won by 352 runs	S. R. Waugh	611/94
Sydney	West Indies	Won by six wickets	S. R. Waugh	612/95
2000-01 in India				
Mumbai (WS)	India	Won by 10 wickets	S. R. Waugh	613/58
Kolkata	India	Lost by 171 runs	S. R. Waugh	614/59
Chennai (Chepauk)	India	Lost by two wickets	S. R. Waugh	615/60

Venue	Opponent	Result for Australia	Captain	Test/Opp
2001 in England				
Birmingham	England	Won by an innings and 126 runs	S. R. Waugh	616/298
Lord's	England	Won by eight wickets	S. R. Waugh	617/299
Nottingham	England	Won by seven wickets	S. R. Waugh	618/300
Leeds	England	Lost by six wickets	A. C. Gilchrist	619/301
The Oval	England	Won by an innings and 25 runs	S. R. Waugh	620/302
2001-02 in Australia				
Brisbane	New Zealand	Drawn	S. R. Waugh	621/39
Hobart (Bel)	New Zealand	Drawn	S. R. Waugh	622/40
Perth	New Zealand	Drawn	S. R. Waugh	623/41
Adelaide	South Africa	Won by 246 runs	S. R. Waugh	624/66
Melbourne	South Africa	Won by nine wickets	S. R. Waugh	625/67
Sydney	South Africa	Won by 10 wickets	S. R. Waugh	626/68
2001-02 in South Africa				
Johannesburg (WS)	South Africa	Won by an innings and 360 runs	S. R. Waugh	627/69
Cape Town	South Africa	Won by four wickets	S. R. Waugh	628/70
Durban (Kingsmead)	South Africa	Lost by five wickets	S. R. Waugh	629/71
2002-03 in Sri Lanka and United Arab Emirates				
Colombo	Pakistan	Won by 41 runs	S. R. Waugh	630/47
Sharjah	Pakistan	Won by an innings and 198 runs	S. R. Waugh	631/48
Sharjah	Pakistan	Won by an innings and 20 runs	S. R. Waugh	632/49
2002-03 in Australia				
Brisbane	England	Won by 384 runs	S. R. Waugh	633/303
Adelaide	England	Won by an innings and 51 runs	S. R. Waugh	634/304
Perth	England	Won by an innings and 48 runs	S. R. Waugh	635/305
Melbourne	England	Won by five wickets	S. R. Waugh	636/306
Sydney	England	Lost by 225 runs	S. R. Waugh	637/307
2002-03 in West Indies				
Georgetown	West Indies	Won by nine wickets	S. R. Waugh	638/96
Port-of-Spain	West Indies	Won by 118 runs	S. R. Waugh	639/97
Bridgetown	West Indies	Won by nine wickets	S. R. Waugh	640/98
St John's	West Indies	Lost by seven wickets	S. R. Waugh	641/99
2003-04 in Australia				
Darwin	Bangladesh	Won by an innings and 132 runs	S. R. Waugh	642/1
Cairns	Bangladesh	Won by an innings and 98 runs	S. R. Waugh	643/2
Perth	Zimbabwe	Won by an innings and 175 runs	S. R. Waugh	644/2
Sydney	Zimbabwe	Won by nine wickets	S. R. Waugh	645/3
Brisbane	India	Drawn	S. R. Waugh	646/61
Adelaide	India	Lost by four wickets	S. R. Waugh	647/62
Melbourne	India	Won by nine wickets	S. R. Waugh	648/63
Sydney	India	Drawn	S. R. Waugh	649/64
2003-04 in Sri Lanka				
Galle	Sri Lanka	Won by 197 runs	R. T. Ponting	650/14
Kandy	Sri Lanka	Won by 27 runs	R. T. Ponting	651/15
Colombo (SSC)	Sri Lanka	Won by 121 runs	R. T. Ponting	652/16
2004-05 in Australia				
Darwin	Sri Lanka	Won by 149 runs	A. C. Gilchrist	653/17
Cairns	Sri Lanka	Drawn	R. T. Ponting	654/18

Australian Limited-Overs International Records

AUSTRALIAN ONE-DAY PLAYERS IN ORDER OF APPEARANCE

Player	Span	M	I	NO	R	HS	Avge	S-R	100s	50s	Ct/St	Balls	Mdns	R	W	Avge	S-R	RPO	BB	5i
1 G. S. Chappell	1970-71 to 1982-83	74	72	14	2,331	138*	40.19	75.44	3	14	23	3,108	41	2,096	72	29.11	43.17	4.05	5-15	2
2 I. M. Chappell	1970-71 to 1979-80	16	16	2	673	86	48.07	77.00	–	8	5	42	1	23	2	11.50	21.00	3.29	2-14	–
3 A. N. Connolly	1970-71	1	–	–	–	–	–	–	–	–	–	64	–	62	0	–	–	5.81	–	–
4 W. M. Lawry †	1970-71	1	1	–	27	27	27.00	55.10	–	–	1	–	–	–	–	–	–	–	–	–
5 A. A. Mallett	1970-71 to 1975-76	9	3	1	14	8	7.00	38.89	–	–	4	502	7	341	11	31.00	45.64	4.08	3-34	–
6 R. W. Marsh †	1970-71 to 1983-84	92	76	15	1,225	66	20.08	80.28	–	4	120/4	–	–	–	–	–	–	–	–	–
7 G. D. McKenzie	1970-71	1	–	–	–	–	–	–	–	–	–	60	–	22	2	11.00	30.00	2.20	2-22	–
8 I. R. Redpath	1970-71 to 1975-76	5	5	1	46	24	9.20	68.66	–	–	2	–	–	–	–	–	–	–	–	–
9 K. R. Stackpole	1970-71 to 1973-74	6	6	–	224	61	37.33	57.88	–	3	1	77	–	54	3	18.00	25.67	4.21	3-40	–
10 A. L. Thomson	1970-71	1	–	–	–	–	–	–	–	–	–	64	2	22	1	22.00	64.00	2.06	1-22	–
11 K. D. Walters	1970-71 to 1980-81	28	24	6	513	59	28.50	70.18	–	2	10	314	–	273	4	68.25	78.50	5.22	2-24	–
12 R. Edwards	1972	9	8	1	255	80*	36.43	73.07	–	3	2	–	–	–	–	–	–	–	–	–
13 D. K. Lillee	1972 to 1983	63	34	8	240	42*	9.23	75.47	–	–	10	3,593	80	2,145	103	20.83	34.88	3.58	5-34	1
14 R. A. L. Massie †	1972	3	1	–	16	16*	–	66.67	–	–	1	183	5	129	3	43.00	61.00	4.23	2-35	–
15 A. P. Sheahan	1972	3	3	1	75	50*	25.00	60.48	–	1	–	–	–	–	–	–	–	–	–	–
16 G. D. Watson	1972	2	2	1	11	11*	11.00	68.75	–	–	–	48	1	28	0	–	–	3.50	–	–
17 D. J. Colley	1972	1	1	–	15	15*	–	53.57	–	–	–	66	4	72	0	–	–	6.55	–	–
18 J. R. Hammond	1972	1	1	–	19	19*	–	54.10	–	–	–	54	3	41	1	41.00	54.00	4.56	1-41	–
19 R. J. Bright ‡	1973-74 to 1985-86	11	8	4	66	19*	16.50	33.33	–	–	2	462	3	350	3	116.67	154.00	4.55	1-28	–
20 I. C. Davis	1973-74 to 1977	3	3	1	12	11*	6.00	42.68	–	–	1	–	–	–	–	–	–	–	–	–
21 G. Dymock ‡	1973-74 to 1980	15	7	4	35	14*	11.67	–	–	–	1	806	16	412	15	27.47	53.73	3.07	2-21	–
22 G. J. Gilmour †‡	1973-74 to 1975-76	5	2	1	42	28*	42.00	107.69	–	–	–	320	16	165	16	10.31	20.00	3.09	6-14	1
23 M. H. N. Walker	1973-74 to 1980-81	17	11	3	79	20	9.88	46.75	–	–	6	1,006	24	546	20	27.30	50.30	3.26	4-19	–
24 A. J. Woodcock	1973-74	1	1	–	53	53	53.00	79.10	–	1	–	–	–	–	–	–	–	–	–	–
25 W. J. Edwards †	1974-75	1	1	–	2	2	2.00	14.29	–	–	–	–	–	–	–	–	–	–	–	–
26 A. G. Hurst	1974-75 to 1979	8	4	4	7	3*	–	36.84	–	–	–	402	11	203	12	16.92	33.50	3.03	5-21	1

No.	Player	Career	M	I	NO	Runs	HS	Avge	100	50	Ct	St	Balls	Mdns	Runs	Wkts	Avge	SR	RpO	Best
27	T. J. Jenner	1974-75	1	1	–	12	12	12.00	–	–			64	1	28	0	–	–	2.63	–
28	J. R. Thomson	1974-75 to 1985	50	30	6	181	21	7.54	–	–	9		2,696	37	1,942	55	35.31	49.02	4.32	4-67
29	R. B. McCosker	1975 to 1981-82	14	14	–	320	95	22.86	–	2	5									
30	A. Turner †	1975	6	6	–	247	101	41.17	1	1	2									
31	G. J. Cosier	1975-76 to 1979	9	7	2	154	84	30.80	–	1	3		409	9	248	14	17.71	29.21	3.64	5-18
32	D. W. Hookes †‡	1977 to 1985-86	39	36	2	826	76	24.29	–	5	11		30		29	1	29.00		5.79	1-2
33	M. F. Malone	1977 to 1981-82	10	6	2	36	15*	9.00	–	–			612	16	315	11	28.64	55.64	3.09	2-9
34	K. J. O'Keeffe	1977	2	2	1	16	16*	16.00	–	–			132	3	79	2	39.50	66.00	3.59	1-36
35	L. S. Pascoe	1977 to 1981-82	29	11	7	39	15*	9.75	–	–			1,568	21	1,066	53	20.11	29.58	4.08	5-30
36	C. S. Serjeant	1977 to 1977-78	3	3	–	73	46	24.33	–	–										
37	K. J. Hughes	1977 to 1984-85	97	88	7	1,968	98	24.33	–	17										
38	R. D. Robinson	1977	2	2	–	82	70	41.00	–	1	3	1								
39	I. W. Callen †	1977-78 to 1982-83	5	2	1	6	3*	6.00	–	–			180	2	148	5	29.60	36.00	4.93	3-24
40	W. M. Clark	1977-78	2	–	–	–	–	–	–	–			100	3	61	3	20.33	33.33	3.66	2-39
41	W. M. Darling	1977-78 to 1981-82	18	18	1	363	74	21.35	–	2										
42	T. J. Laughlin †	1977-78 to 1979-80	6	5	1	105	74	26.25	–	1			308	8	224	8	28.00	38.50	4.36	3-54
43	S. J. Rixon	1977-78 to 1984-85	6	5	2	40	20*	13.33	–	–	9	2								
44	R. B. Simpson	1977-78	2	2	–	36	23	18.00	–	–	3		102		95	2	47.50	51.00	5.59	2-30
45	P. M. Toohey	1977-78 to 1978-79	5	4	2	105	54*	52.50	–	1										
46	G. M. Wood †	1977-78 to 1988-89	83	77	11	2,219	114*	33.62	3	11										
47	G. N. Yallop †‡	1977-78 to 1984-85	30	27	6	823	66*	39.19	–	4			138		119	3	39.67	46.00	5.17	2-28
48	B. Yardley	1977-78 to 1982-83	7	6	2	58	28	14.50	–	–			198		130	7	18.57	28.29	3.94	3-28
49	A. R. Border †‡	1978-79 to 1993-94	273	252	39	6,524	127*	30.63	3	39	127		2,661		2,071	73	28.37	36.45	4.67	3-20
50	P. H. Carlson	1978-79	4	4	2	11	11	5.50	–	–			168			2	84.00		2.50	1-21
51	J. A. Maclean	1978-79	2	2	1	11	11	11.00	–	–										
52	A. M. J. Hilditch	1978-79 to 1985	8	8	–	226	72	28.25	–	1										
53	R. M. Hogg	1978-79 to 1984-85	71	35	20	137	22	9.13	–	–			3,677	57	2,418	85	28.45	43.26	3.95	4-29
54	K. J. Wright	1978-79	5	2	–	29	23	14.50	–	–										
55	J. K. Moss †	1979	1	1	–	7	7	7.00	–	–										
56	G. D. Porter	1979	2	2	1	3	3	3.00	–	–			108	5	33	3	11.00	36.00	1.83	2-13
57	B. M. Laird	1979-80 to 1982-83	23	23	3	594	117*	29.70	1	3										
58	J. M. Wiener	1979-80	7	7	–	140	50	20.00	–	1										
59	D. F. Whatmore	1979-80	1	1	–	2	2	2.00	–	–			24		34	0	–	–	8.50	–
60	J. Dyson	1980 to 1982-83	29	27	4	755	79	32.83	–	5										
61	T. M. Chappell	1980-81 to 1983	20	13	–	229	110	17.62	1	1			736	19	538	14	38.74	52.57	4.39	3-31
62	S. F. Graf †	1980-81 to 1981-82	11	6	–	24	4	4.00	–	–			522		345	8	43.13	65.25	3.97	2-23
63	G. F. Lawson	1980-81 to 1989-90	79	52	18	378	33*	11.12	–	–	18		4,259	94	2,592	88	29.45	48.40	3.65	4-26

Player	Span	M	I	NO	R	HS	Avge	S-R	100	50	Ct/St	Balls	Md	R	W	Avge	S-R	RPO	BB	5i
64 M.F. Kent	1980-81 to 1981	5	5	1	78	33	19.50	58.65	–	–	4	112	3	70	4	17.50	28.00	3.75	2-20	–
65 G.R. Beard	1980-81	2	2	–	9	9*	–	–	–	–	–	–	–	–	–	–	–	–	–	–
66 T.M. Alderman	1981 to 1990-91	65	18	6	32	9*	2.67	32.99	–	–	8	3,371	75	2,056	88	23.36	38.31	3.66	5-17	2
67 D.M. Wellham	1981-82 to 1986-87	17	17	2	379	97	25.27	54.22	–	1	8	–	–	–	–	–	–	–	–	–
68 G.M. Ritchie	1982-83 to 1986-87	44	42	7	959	84	27.40	61.95	–	6	9	–	–	–	–	–	–	–	–	–
69 W.B. Phillips †	1982-83 to 1985-86	48	41	6	852	75*	24.34	85.80	–	6	42/7	–	–	–	–	–	–	–	–	–
70 C.G. Rackemann	1982-83 to 1990-91	52	18	6	34	14*	2.83	44.16	–	–	7	2,791	51	1,833	82	22.35	34.04	3.94	5-16	1
71 K.C. Wessels †	1982-83 to 1985	54	51	3	1,740	107	36.25	58.97	1	14	19	737	12	655	18	36.39	40.94	5.33	2-16	–
72 J.N. Maguire	1982-83 to 1984-85	23	11	5	42	14*	7.00	59.15	–	–	2	1,009	12	769	19	40.47	53.11	4.57	3-61	–
73 T.G. Hogan ‡	1982-83 to 1984-85	16	12	4	72	27	9.00	78.82	–	–	10	917	12	574	23	24.96	39.87	3.76	4-33	–
74 K.H. MacLeay	1982-83 to 1986-87	16	13	2	139	57	12.64	84.31	–	–	2	857	–	626	15	41.73	57.13	4.38	6-39	1
75 S.B. Smith	1982-83 to 1984-85	28	24	2	861	117	39.14	65.28	1	8	8	–	–	–	–	–	–	–	–	–
76 R.N. Whitney ‡	1982-83 to 1992-93	38	13	7	40	16	6.67	44.44	–	–	11	2,106	8	1,249	46	27.15	45.78	3.56	4-34	–
77 R.D. Woolley ‡	1982-83	4	3	2	31	16	31.00	81.58	–	–	1/1	–	–	–	–	–	–	–	–	–
78 G.R.J. Matthews †	1983-84 to 1992-93	59	50	13	619	54	16.73	63.42	–	1	23	2,808	21	1,999	57	35.07	49.26	4.27	3-27	–
79 D.M. Jones	1983-84 to 1993-94	164	161	25	6,068	145	44.62	72.49	7	46	54	106	–	81	3	27.00	35.33	4.58	2-34	–
80 D.C. Boon	1983-84 to 1994-95	181	177	16	5,964	122	37.04	65.12	5	37	45	82	–	86	4	21.50	20.50	6.29	2-27	–
81 M.J. Bennett	1984-85	8	3	–	6	6*	–	42.86	–	–	1	408	–	275	4	68.75	102.00	4.04	–	–
82 C.J. McDermott	1984-85 to 1995-96	138	78	17	432	37	7.08	77.80	–	–	27	7,460	99	5,020	203	24.73	36.75	4.04	5-44	1
83 S.P. O'Donnell	1984-85 to 1991-92	87	64	15	1,242	74*	25.35	80.54	–	3	22	4,350	49	3,102	108	28.72	40.28	4.28	5-13	1
84 R.G. Holland	1984-85	11	4	1	33	13*	11.00	46.48	–	–	–	126	–	99	2	49.50	63.00	4.71	2-49	–
85 R.J. McCurdy	1984-85	11	6	1	41	8	8.25	–	–	–	2	515	8	375	12	31.25	42.92	4.37	3-19	–
86 R.B. Kerr	1984-85	4	4	1	97	87	32.33	61.01	–	1	1	–	–	–	–	–	–	–	–	–
87 S.P. Davis	1985-86 to 1987-88	39	11	7	20	8	5.00	58.82	–	–	5	2,019	46	1,133	44	25.75	45.89	3.37	3-10	–
88 D.R. Gilbert	1985-86	6	5	–	39	8	7.80	38.24	–	–	3	684	4	552	18	30.67	38.00	4.84	5-46	1
89 B.A. Reid †‡	1985-86 to 1991-92	61	21	8	49	10	3.77	38.89	–	–	6	3,250	53	2,201	63	34.94	51.59	4.06	5-53	1
90 S.R. Waugh	1985-86 to 2001-02	325	288	58	7,569	120*	32.91	75.81	3	45	111	8,883	54	6,764	195	34.69	45.55	4.57	4-33	–
91 G.R. Marsh	1985-86 to 1991-92	117	115	6	4,357	126*	39.97	55.77	9	22	31	–	–	–	–	–	–	–	–	–
92 G.S. Trimble	1985-86	1	1	–	4	4	4.00	80.00	–	–	–	24	–	32	–	–	–	8.00	–	–
93 T.J. Zoehrer	1985-86 to 1993-94	22	15	3	130	50	10.83	71.04	–	–	21/2	–	–	–	–	–	–	–	–	–
94 G.C. Dyer	1986-87 to 1987-88	23	13	2	174	45*	15.82	76.99	–	–	24/4	–	–	–	–	–	–	–	–	–
95 G.A. Bishop	1986-87	2	2	–	13	8	6.50	29.55	–	–	–	–	–	–	–	–	–	–	–	–
96 P.L. Taylor	1986-87 to 1991-92	83	47	25	437	54*	19.86	75.87	–	1	34	3,937	32	2,740	97	28.25	40.59	4.18	4-38	–
97 M.R.J. Veletta	1986-87 to 1989	20	19	4	484	68*	32.27	75.39	–	2	8	–	–	–	–	–	–	–	–	–
98 T.M. Moody	1987-88 to 1999-00	76	64	12	1,211	89	23.29	69.00	–	10	21	2,797	31	2,014	52	38.73	53.79	4.32	3-25	–
99 T.B.A. May	1987-88 to 1994-95	47	12	8	39	15	9.75	75.00	–	–	3	2,504	16	1,772	39	45.44	64.21	4.25	3-19	–

No	Player	Span	M	I	NO	Runs	HS	Avg	S/R	100	50	Ct	St	Balls	Runs	Wkts	S/R	Avg	Best	5w	Econ
100	A.K. Zesers	1987-88	2	2	2	10	8*	–	–	–	–	–	–	90	74	1	90.00	74.00	1-37	–	4.93
101	A.I.C. Dodemaide	1987-88 to 1992-93	24	16	7	124	30	13.78	71.43	–	–	–	–	1,327	753	36	36.86	20.92	5-21	1	3.40
102	I.A. Healy †	1988-89 to 1997	168	120	36	1,764	56	21.00	77.99	–	4	194	39	–	–	–	–	–	–	–	–
103	J.D. Siddons	1988-89	1	1	–	32	32	32.00	83.64	–	–	–	–	–	–	–	–	–	–	–	–
104	M.G. Hughes	1988-89 to 1993	33	17	8	100	20	11.11	86.49	–	–	–	–	1,639	1,115	38	43.13	29.34	4-44	–	4.08
105	M.E. Waugh †	1988-89 to 2001-02	244	236	20	8,500	173	39.35	72.99	18	50	108	–	3,687	2,938	85	43.38	34.56	5-24	1	4.78
106	G.D. Campbell	1989-90	12	3	1	6	4*	3.00	76.54	–	–	–	–	613	404	18	34.06	22.44	3-17	–	3.95
107	M.A. Taylor †	1989-90 to 1997	113	110	1	3,514	105	32.24	59.42	1	28	56	–	–	–	–	–	–	–	–	–
108	P.R. Reiffel †	1991-92 to 1999	92	57	21	503	58	13.97	71.25	–	1	–	–	4,732	3,095	106	44.64	29.20	4-13	–	3.92
109	D.R. Martyn	1992-93 to 2003-04	151	130	40	3,713	146	41.26	79.22	5	–	–	–	794	704	12	66.17	58.67	5-32	2	5.32
110	S.K. Warne	1992-93 to 2002-03	193	106	28	1,016	55	13.03	71.75	–	1	80	–	10,600	7,514	291	36.43	25.82	5-33	1	4.25
111	M.L. Hayden †	1993 to 2003-04	95	91	11	3,366	146	42.08	77.93	7	22	34	–	6	18	–	–	–	–	–	18.00
112	B.P. Julian ‡	1993 to 1999	25	17	–	224	35	13.18	89.96	–	–	9	–	1,146	997	22	52.09	45.32	3-40	–	5.22
113	G.D. McGrath	1993-94 to 2003-04	188	50	27	94	11*	4.09	49.21	–	–	34	–	9,940	6,443	285	34.88	22.61	7-15	6	3.89
114	M.J. Slater	1993-94 to 1997	42	42	1	987	73	24.07	60.22	–	6	–	–	–	–	–	–	–	–	–	–
115	D.W. Fleming †	1993-94 to 2001	88	31	18	152	29	11.69	67.86	–	–	–	–	4,619	3,402	134	34.47	25.39	5-36	1	4.42
116	M.G. Bevan †‡	1993-94 to 2003-04	232	196	67	6,912	108*	53.58	73.96	6	36	69	–	1,966	1,655	36	54.61	45.97	3-36	–	5.05
117	J.L. Langer †	1993-94 to 1997	8	7	2	160	36	32.00	88.89	–	–	–	–	–	–	–	–	–	–	–	–
118	J. Angel †	1994-95 to 1994-95	5	4	–	0	0	0.00	–	–	–	–	–	162	113	4	40.50	28.25	2-47	–	4.19
119	G.R. Robertson	1994-95 to 1997-98	13	7	4	45	–	15.00	78.95	–	–	–	–	597	430	8	74.63	53.75	3-29	–	4.32
120	P.A. Emery †	1994-95	2	–	–	–	–	–	–	–	–	1	2	–	–	–	–	–	–	–	–
121	S.G. Law	1994-95 to 1998-99	54	51	5	1,237	110	26.89	74.74	–	7	–	–	807	635	12	67.25	52.92	2-22	–	4.72
122	G.S. Blewett	1994-95 to 1998-99	32	30	3	551	57*	20.41	61.63	–	2	–	–	749	646	14	53.50	46.14	2-6	–	5.17
123	R.T. Ponting	1994-95 to 2003-04	201	187	16	7,255	145	42.43	77.64	15	41	–	–	150	104	3	50.00	34.67	1-12	–	4.16
124	S. Lee	1995-96 to 2000-01	45	35	8	477	57	17.67	95.40	–	–	–	–	1,706	1,245	48	35.54	25.94	5-33	1	4.51
125	M.S. Kasprowicz	1995-96 to 2003-04	24	10	7	62	28*	20.67	80.52	–	–	–	–	1,267	952	37	34.24	25.73	5-45	1	4.33
126	G.B. Hogg †‡	1996-97 to 2003-04	48	29	13	334	71*	20.88	78.77	–	1	–	–	2,287	1,650	53	43.15	31.13	5-41	1	4.13
127	J.N. Gillespie †‡	1996-97 to 2003-04	72	31	14	223	33*	13.12	75.08	–	–	–	–	3,903	2,688	111	35.16	24.22	5-22	3	4.75
128	D.S. Lehmann †‡	1996-97 to 2003-04	102	89	19	2,780	119	39.71	82.32	4	15	–	–	1,364	1,080	42	32.48	25.71	4-7	–	4.70
129	A.C. Gilchrist †	1996-97 to 2003-04	193	187	6	6,468	172	35.73	94.11	10	37	283	59	–	–	–	–	–	–	–	–
130	A.J. Bichel	1996-97 to 2003-04	67	36	13	471	64	20.48	78.50	–	1	–	–	3,257	2,464	78	41.76	31.59	7-20	2	4.54
131	A.M. Stuart	1996-97	3	3	–	3	1	1.00	14.29	–	–	–	–	180	109	8	22.50	13.63	5-26	1	5.26
132	A.C. Dale †	1996-97 to 1999-00	30	12	8	78	15*	19.50	56.12	–	–	–	–	1,596	979	32	49.88	30.59	3-18	–	3.68
133	M.J. Di Venuto †	1996-97	9	9	–	241	89	26.78	84.86	–	2	–	–	–	–	–	–	–	–	–	–
134	M.T.G. Elliott †	1997	2	1	–	1	1	1.00	20.00	–	–	–	–	–	–	–	–	–	–	–	–
135	I.J. Harvey †	1997-98 to 2003-04	73	51	11	715	48*	17.88	88.05	–	–	–	–	3,279	2,577	85	38.58	30.32	4-16	–	4.72
136	P. Wilson	1997-98	11	5	2	4	4	1.33	33.33	–	–	–	–	562	450	13	43.23	34.62	3-39	–	4.80

	Player		M	I	NO	R	HS	Avge	S-R	100	50	Ct/St	Balls	Md	R	W	Avge	S-R	RPO	BB	5i
137	J.P. Maher †	1997-98 to 2003-04	26	20	3	438	95	25.76	64.89	–	–	18	–	–	–	–	–	–	–	–	–
138	B.E. Young ‡	1997-98 to 1998-99	6	3	1	31	18	15.50	65.96	–	–	2	234	–	251	1	251.00	234.00	6.44	1-26	–
139	A. Symonds	1998-99 to 2003-04	96	72	15	2,064	143*	36.21	89.23	1	10	42	3,157	14	2,591	72	35.99	43.85	4.92	4-11	–
140	B. Lee	1999-00 to 2003-04	84	35	11	347	51*	14.46	80.70	–	1	22	4,291	59	3,344	151	22.15	28.42	4.68	5-27	3
141	S.C.G. MacGill	1999-00	3	2	1	1	1	1.00	33.33	–	–	–	180	4	105	4	17.50	30.00	3.50	4-19	–
142	N.W. Bracken ‡	2000-01 to 2003-04	17	2	1	7	7*	7.00	70.00	–	–	5	852	18	552	28	19.71	30.43	3.89	4-29	–
143	S.M. Katich †	2000-01 to 2003-04	6	4	2	44	18*	22.00	73.33	–	–	1	–	–	–	–	–	–	–	–	–
144	B.J. Haddin	2000-01 to 2003-04	4	4	–	68	32	17.00	71.58	–	–	1/2	–	–	–	–	–	–	–	–	–
145	B.A. Williams	2001-02 to 2003-04	25	6	4	27	13*	13.50	58.70	–	–	4	1,203	19	814	35	23.26	34.37	4.06	5-22	2
146	R.J. Campbell	2001-02	2	2	–	54	38	27.00	77.14	–	–	4/1	–	–	–	–	–	–	–	–	–
147	N.M. Hauritz	2001-02 to 2002-03	8	2	1	35	20*	35.00	89.74	–	–	2	360	1	308	9	34.22	40.00	5.13	4-39	–
148	S.R. Watson	2001-02 to 2003-04	24	16	8	306	77*	38.25	66.96	–	1	7	869	8	670	18	37.22	48.28	4.63	3-27	–
149	M.J. Clarke ‡	2002-03 to 2003-04	28	26	8	784	105*	43.56	87.40	1	4	12	581	1	496	17	29.18	34.18	5.12	5-35	1
150	M.E.K. Hussey †	2003-04	1	1	1	17	17*	–	73.91	–	–	1	18	–	15	0	–	–	5.00	–	–

† denotes left-hand batsman; ‡ denotes left-arm bowler.

BATTING RECORDS

MOST RUNS IN A CAREER

	M	I	NO	R	HS	100s	Avge	S-R
M. E. Waugh	244	236	20	8,500	173	18	39.35	76.54
S. R. Waugh	325	288	58	7,569	120*	3	32.91	75.81
R. T. Ponting	201	196	25	7,255	145	15	42.43	77.64
M. G. Bevan	232	196	67	6,912	108*	6	53.58	73.96
A. R. Border	273	252	39	6,524	127*	3	30.63	71.22
A. C. Gilchrist	193	187	6	6,468	172	10	35.73	94.11
D. M. Jones	164	161	25	6,068	145	7	44.62	72.49
D. C. Boon	181	177	16	5,964	122	5	37.04	65.12
G. R. Marsh	117	115	6	4,357	126*	9	39.97	55.77
D. R. Martyn	151	130	40	3,713	144*	5	41.26	79.22
M. A. Taylor	113	110	1	3,514	105	1	32.24	59.42
M. L. Hayden	95	91	11	3,366	146	4	42.08	77.93
D. S. Lehmann	102	89	19	2,780	119	4	39.71	82.32
G. S. Chappell	74	72	14	2,331	138*	3	40.19	75.44
G. M. Wood	83	77	11	2,219	114*	3	33.62	59.43
A. Symonds	96	72	15	2,064	143*	1	36.21	89.23
K. J. Hughes	97	88	6	1,968	98	0	24.00	66.98
I. A. Healy	168	120	36	1,764	56	0	21.00	83.64
K. C. Wessels	54	51	3	1,740	107	1	36.25	58.97
S. P. O'Donnell	87	64	15	1,242	74*	0	25.35	80.54

HIGHEST CAREER STRIKE-RATE

(Qualification: 500 runs)

	M	I	NO	R	HS	100s	Avge	S-R
A. C. Gilchrist	193	187	6	6,468	172	10	35.73	94.11
A. Symonds	96	72	15	2,064	143*	1	36.21	89.23
I. J. Harvey	73	51	11	715	48*	0	17.88	88.05
M. J. Clarke	28	26	8	784	105*	1	43.56	87.40
W. B. Phillips	48	41	6	852	75*	0	24.34	85.80
I. A. Healy	168	120	36	1,764	56	0	21.00	83.64
D. S. Lehmann	102	89	19	2,780	119	4	39.71	82.32
S. P. O'Donnell	87	64	15	1,242	74*	0	25.35	80.54
R. W. Marsh	92	76	15	1,225	66	0	20.08	80.28
D. R. Martyn	151	130	40	3,713	144*	5	41.26	79.22

HIGHEST CAREER AVERAGE

(Qualification: 500 runs)

	M	I	NO	R	HS	100s	Avge	S-R
M. G. Bevan	232	196	67	6,912	108*	6	53.58	73.96
I. M. Chappell	16	16	2	673	86	0	48.07	77.00
D. M. Jones	164	161	25	6,068	145	7	44.62	72.49
M. J. Clarke	28	26	8	784	105*	1	43.56	87.40
R. T. Ponting	201	196	25	7,255	145	15	42.43	77.64
M. L. Hayden	95	91	11	3,366	146	4	42.08	77.93
D. R. Martyn	151	130	40	3,713	144*	5	41.26	79.22
G. S. Chappell	74	72	14	2,331	138*	3	40.19	75.44
G. R. Marsh	117	115	6	4,357	126*	9	39.97	55.77
D. S. Lehmann	102	89	19	2,780	119	4	39.71	82.32

CENTURY-MAKERS

M. G. Bevan (6)	103	v South Africa at Centurion	1996-97
	108*	v England at The Oval	1997
	101*	v India at Sharjah	1997-98
	107	v New Zealand at Napier	1999-00
	106	v South Africa at Melbourne (DS)	2000-01
	102*	v New Zealand at Melbourne	2001-02
D. C. Boon (5)	111	v India at Jaipur	1986-87
	122	v Sri Lanka at Adelaide	1987-88
	102*	v India at Hobart	1991-92
	100	v New Zealand at Auckland	1991-92
	100	v West Indies at Melbourne	1991-92
A. R. Border (3)	105*	v India at Sydney	1980-81
	118*	v Sri Lanka at Adelaide	1984-85
	127*	v West Indies at Sydney	1984-85
G. S. Chappell (3)	125*	v England at The Oval	1977
	138*	v New Zealand at Sydney	1980-81
	108	v New Zealand at Auckland	1981-82
T. M. Chappell	110	v India at Nottingham	1983
M. J. Clarke	105*	v Zimbabwe at Harare	2003-04
A. C. Gilchrist (10)	100	v South Africa at Sydney	1997-98
	118	v New Zealand at Christchurch	1997-98
	103	v Pakistan at Lahore	1998-99
	131	v Sri Lanka at Sydney	1998-99
	154	v Sri Lanka at Melbourne	1998-99
	128	v New Zealand at Christchurch	1999-00
	105	v South Africa at Durban	2001-02
	124	v England at Melbourne	2002-03
	111	v India at Bangalore	2003-04
	172	v Zimbabwe at Hobart	2003-04
D. M. Jones (7)	104	v England at Perth	1986-87
	121	v Pakistan at Perth	1986-87
	101	v England at Brisbane	1986-87
	107	v New Zealand at Christchurch	1989-90
	102*	v New Zealand at Auckland	1989-90
	117*	v Sri Lanka at Sharjah	1989-90
	145	v England at Brisbane	1990-91
M. L. Hayden (4)	111	v India at Visakhapatnam	2000-01
	146	v Pakistan at Nairobi	2002-03
	109	v India at Brisbane	2003-04
	126	v India at Sydney	2003-04
B. M. Laird	117*	v West Indies at Sydney	1981-82
S. G. Law	110	v Zimbabwe at Hobart	1994-95
D. S. Lehmann (4)	103*	v Pakistan at Karachi	1998-99
	110*	v West Indies at St George's	1998-99
	119	v Sri Lanka at Perth	2002-03
	107	v West Indies at St George's	2002-03
G. R. Marsh (9)	125	v India at Sydney	1985-86
	104	v India at Jaipur	1986-87
	110	v India at Chennai	1987-88
	126*	v New Zealand at Chandigarh	1987-88
	101	v New Zealand at Sydney	1987-88
	125*	v Pakistan at Melbourne	1988-89
	111*	v England at Lord's	1989
	113	v West Indies at Bridgetown	1990-91
	106*	v West Indies at Georgetown	1990-91
D. R. Martyn (5)	116*	v New Zealand at Auckland	1999-00
	144*	v Zimbabwe at Perth	2000-01
	104*	v South Africa at Brisbane	2001-02
	101*	v England at Hobart	2002-03

		100	v India at Mumbai	2003-04
R. T. Ponting (15)	...	123	v Sri Lanka at Melbourne	1995-96
		102	v West Indies at Jaipur	1995-96
		100	v New Zealand at Melbourne	1997-98
		145	v Zimbabwe at Delhi	1997-98
		124*	v Pakistan at Lahore	1998-99
		115	v India at Melbourne	1999-00
		101	v India at Visakhapatnam	2000-01
		102	v England at Bristol	2001
		129	v South Africa at Bloemfontein	2001-02
		119	v England at Melbourne	2002-03
		106*	v Sri Lanka at Melbourne	2002-03
		114	v Sri Lanka at Centurion	2002-03
		140*	v India at Johannesburg	2002-03
		101	v Bangladesh at Darwin	2003-04
		108*	v India at Bangalore	2003-04
S. B. Smith (2)	......	117	v New Zealand at Melbourne	1982-83
		106	v Pakistan at Sydney	1983-84
A. Symonds	....	143*	v Pakistan at Johannesburg	2002-03
M. A. Taylor	....	105	v India at Bangalore	1996-97
A. Turner	....	101	v Sri Lanka at The Oval	1975
M. E. Waugh (18)	...	108	v New Zealand at Hamilton	1992-93
		113	v England at Birmingham	1993
		107	v South Africa at Sydney	1993-94
		121*	v South Africa at Rawalpindi	1994-95
		130	v Sri Lanka at Perth	1995-96
		130	v Kenya at Vishakhapatnam	1995-96
		126	v India at Mumbai	1995-96
		110	v New Zealand at Chennai	1995-96
		102	v West Indies at Brisbane	1996-97
		115*	v South Africa at Port Elizabeth	1996-97
		104	v New Zealand at Adelaide	1996-97
		104	v Zimbabwe at Lord's	1999
		106	v Zimbabwe at Bulawayo	1999-00
		116	v India at Adelaide	1999-00
		112*	v West Indies at Brisbane	2000-01
		102*	v Zimbabwe at Hobart	2000-01
		173	v West Indies at Melbourne	2000-01
		133*	v India at Pune	2000-01
S. R. Waugh (3)	.....	102*	v Sri Lanka at Melbourne	1995-96
		120*	v South Africa at Leeds	1999
		114*	v South Africa at Melbourne (DS)	2000-01
K. C. Wessels	....	107	v India at New Delhi	1984-85
G. M. Wood (3)	.....	108	v England at Leeds	1981
		104*	v West Indies at Adelaide	1984-85
		114*	v England at Lord's	1985

FASTEST FIFTIES

Balls			
18	S. P. O'Donnell	v Sri Lanka at Sharjah	1989-90
22	D. R. Martyn	v Bangladesh at Cairns	2003-04
27	A. C. Gilchrist	v South Africa at Port Elizabeth	2001-02
28	T. M. Moody	v Bangladesh at Chester-le-Street	1999
28	A. C. Gilchrist	v India at Margoa	2000-01
28	A. C. Gilchrist	v Pakistan at Nottingham	2001

FASTEST HUNDREDS

Balls

78	A.R. Border	v Sri Lanka at Adelaide	1984-85
78	A.C. Gilchrist	v New Zealand at Christchurch	1999-00
82	G.S. Chappell	v New Zealand at Auckland	1981-82
85	A.C. Gilchrist	v Sri Lanka at Melbourne	1998-99
88	D.S. Lehmann	v West Indies at St George's	1998-99

MOST RUNS OFF AN OVER

28 (444646)	D.S. Lehmann	off R.J. Van Vuuren v Namibia at Potchefstroom	2002-03
27 (164646)	A.A. Donald	off A.A. Donald v South Africa at Perth	2001-02
	and B. Lee		
26 (64646.)	R.W. Marsh	off B.L. Cairns v New Zealand at Adelaide	1980-81
24 (66624x)	I.J. Harvey	off D.P. Viljoen v Zimbabwe at Perth	2000-01

SLOWEST FIFTIES

Balls

116	K.C. Wessels	v West Indies at Sydney	1984-85
111	G.R. Marsh	v West Indies at Sydney	1991-92
108	D.M. Jones	v India at Adelaide	1991-92
107	G.R. Marsh	v India at Hamilton	1989-90
106	B.M. Laird	v New Zealand at Dunedin	1981-82
106	G.R. Marsh	v India at Sydney	1991-92

SLOWEST HUNDREDS

Balls

166	D.C. Boon	v India at Hobart (Bel)	1991-92
156	G.R. Marsh	v England at Lord's	1989
150	G.R. Marsh	v West Indies at Georgetown	1990-91
146	G.R. Marsh	v New Zealand at Sydney	1987-88
146	D.C. Boon	v West Indies at Melbourne	1991-92

MOST CAREER DUCKS

16	M.E. Waugh
15	C.J. McDermott
15	S.R. Waugh
12	K.J. Hughes
12	R.T. Ponting

HIGHEST PARTNERSHIPS

212 for 1st	G.R. Marsh and D.C. Boon	v India at Jaipur	1986-87
225 for 2nd	A.C. Gilchrist and R.T. Ponting	v England at Melbourne	2002-03
234* for 3rd	R.T. Ponting and D.R. Martyn	v India at Johannesburg	2002-03
222 for 4th	M.G. Bevan and S.R. Waugh	v South Africa at Melbourne (DS)	2000
172 for 5th	D.L. Lehmann and M.G. Bevan	v West Indies at Kingston	1998-99
112 for 6th	M.E. Waugh and S.P. O'Donnell	v England at Sydney	1990-91
102* for 7th	S.R. Waugh and G.C. Dyer	v India at Delhi	1986-87
119 for 8th	S.K. Warne and P.R. Reiffel	v South Africa at Port Elizabeth	1993-94
77 for 9th	S.K. Warne and M.G. Bevan	v West Indies at Port-of-Spain	1998-99
63 for 10th	A.J. Bichel and S.R. Watson	v Sri Lanka at Sydney	2002-03

BOWLING RECORDS

MOST WICKETS IN A CAREER

	M	Balls	Mdns	R	W	BB	5W/i	Avge
S. K. Warne	193	10,600	109	7,514	291	5-33	1	25.82
G. D. McGrath	188	9,940	221	6,443	285	7-15	6	22.61
C. J. McDermott	138	7,460	99	5,020	203	5-44	1	24.73
S. R. Waugh	325	8,883	54	6,764	195	4-33	0	34.69
B. Lee	84	4,291	59	3,344	151	5-27	3	22.15
D. W. Fleming	88	4,619	62	3,402	134	5-36	1	25.39
J. N. Gillespie	72	3,903	68	2,688	111	5-22	3	24.22
S. P. O'Donnell	87	4,350	49	3,102	108	5-13	1	28.72
P. R. Reiffel	92	4,732	84	3,095	106	4-13	0	29.20
D. K. Lillee	63	3,593	80	2,145	103	5-34	1	20.83
P. L. Taylor	83	3,937	32	2,740	97	4-38	0	28.25
T. M. Alderman	65	3,371	75	2,056	88	5-17	2	23.36
G. F. Lawson	79	4,259	94	2,592	88	4-26	0	29.45
R. M. Hogg	71	3,677	57	2,418	85	4-29	0	28.45
M. E. Waugh	244	3,687	10	2,938	85	5-24	1	34.56
I. J. Harvey	73	3,279	29	2,577	85	4-16	0	30.32
C. G. Rackemann	52	2,791	51	1,833	82	5-16	1	22.35
A. J. Bichel	67	3,257	28	2,071	73	7-20	2	31.59
A. R. Border	273	2,661	11	2,071	73	3-20	0	28.37
G. S. Chappell	74	3,108	41	2,096	72	5-15	2	29.11
A. Symonds	96	3,157	14	2,591	72	4-11	0	35.99

BEST CAREER STRIKE-RATE

(Qualification: 25 wickets)

	M	Balls	Mdns	R	W	BB	5W/i	Avge	S-R
B. Lee	84	4,291	59	3,344	151	5-27	3	22.15	28.42
L. S. Pascoe	29	1,568	21	1,066	53	5-30	1	20.11	29.58
N. W. Bracken	17	852	18	552	28	4-29	0	19.71	30.43
D. S. Lehmann	102	1,364	2	1,080	42	4-7	0	25.71	32.48
C. G. Rackemann	52	2,791	51	1,833	82	5-16	1	22.35	34.04
M. S. Kasprowicz	24	1,267	14	952	37	5-45	1	25.73	34.24
B. A. Williams	25	1,203	19	814	35	5-22	2	23.26	34.37
D. W. Fleming	88	4,619	62	3,402	134	5-36	1	25.39	34.47
D. K. Lillee	63	3,593	80	2,145	103	5-34	1	20.83	34.88
G. D. McGrath	188	9,940	221	6,443	284	7-15	6	22.61	34.88

BEST CAREER ECONOMY-RATE

(Qualification: 25 wickets)

	M	Balls	Mdns	R	W	BB	5W/i	Avge	RPO
S. P. Davis	39	2,019	46	1,133	44	3-10	0	25.75	3.37
A. I. C. Dodemaide	24	1,327	30	753	36	5-21	1	20.92	3.40
M. R. Whitney	38	2,106	42	1,249	46	4-34	0	27.15	3.56
D. K. Lillee	63	3,593	80	2,145	103	5-34	1	20.83	3.58
G. F. Lawson	79	4,259	94	2,592	88	4-26	0	29.45	3.65
T. M. Alderman	65	3,371	75	2,056	88	5-17	2	23.36	3.66
A. C. Dale	30	1,596	34	979	32	3-18	0	30.59	3.68
G. D. McGrath	188	9,940	221	6,443	285	7-15	6	22.61	3.89
N. W. Bracken	17	852	18	552	28	4-29	0	19.71	3.89
P. R. Reiffel	92	4,732	84	3,095	106	4-13	0	29.20	3.92

BEST CAREER AVERAGE

(Qualification: 25 wickets)

	M	Balls	Mdns	R	W	BB	5W/i	Avge
N. W. Bracken	17	852	18	552	28	4-29	0	19.71
L. S. Pascoe	29	1,568	21	1,066	53	5-30	1	20.11
D. K. Lillee	63	3,593	80	2,145	103	5-34	1	20.83
A. I. C. Dodemaide	24	1,327	30	753	36	5-21	1	20.92
B. Lee	84	4,291	59	3,344	151	5-27	3	22.15
C. G. Rackemann	52	2,791	51	1,833	82	5-16	1	22.35
G. D. McGrath	188	9,940	221	6,443	285	7-15	6	22.61
B. A. Williams	25	1,203	19	814	35	5-22	2	23.26
T. M. Alderman	65	3,371	75	2,056	88	5-17	2	23.36
J. N. Gillespie	72	3,903	68	2,688	111	5-22	3	24.22

FIVE WICKETS IN AN INNINGS

T. M. Alderman (2)	5-17	v New Zealand at Wellington	1981-82
	5-32	v India at Christchurch	1989-90
A. J. Bichel (2)	5-19	v South Africa at Sydney	2001-02
	7-20	v England at Port Elizabeth	2002-03
G. S. Chappell (2)	5-20	v England at Birmingham	1977
	5-15	v India at Sydney	1980-81
M. J. Clarke	5-35	v Sri Lanka at Dambulla	2003-04
G. J. Cosier	5-18	v England at Birmingham	1977
A. I. C. Dodemaide	5-21	v Sri Lanka at Perth	1989-90
D. W. Fleming	5-36	v India at Mumbai	1995-96
D. R. Gilbert	5-46	v New Zealand at Sydney	1985-86
J. N. Gillespie (3)	5-22	v Pakistan at Nairobi	2002-03
	5-70	v Pakistan at Nairobi	2002-03
	5-32	v Zimbabwe at Harare	2003-04
G. J. Gilmour (2)	6-14	v England at Leeds	1975
	5-48	v West Indies at Lord's	1975
A. G. Hurst	5-21	v Canada at Birmingham	1979
G. B. Hogg	5-41	v Sri Lanka at Dambulla	2003-04
B. Lee (3)	5-27	v India at Adelaide	1999-00
	5-30	v England at Melbourne	2002-03
	5-42	v New Zealand at Port Elizabeth	2002-03
S. Lee	5-33	v Sri Lanka at Melbourne	1998-99
D. K. Lillee	5-34	v Pakistan at Leeds	1975
K. H. MacLeay	6-39	v India at Nottingham	1983
C. J. McDermott	5-44	v Pakistan at Lahore	1987-88
G. D. McGrath (6)	5-52	v Pakistan at Lahore	1994-95
	5-40	v Sri Lanka at Adelaide	1998-99
	5-14	v West Indies at Manchester	1999
	5-49	v Pakistan at Sydney	1999-00
	5-37	v New Zealand at Colombo	2002-03
	7-15	v Namibia at Potchefstroom	2002-03
S. P. O'Donnell	5-13	v New Zealand at Christchurch	1989-90
L. S. Pascoe	5-30	v New Zealand at Sydney	1980-81
C. G. Rackemann	5-16	v Pakistan at Adelaide	1983-84
B. A. Reid	5-53	v India at Adelaide	1985-86
A. M. Stuart	5-26	v Pakistan at Melbourne	1996-97
S. K. Warne	5-23	v West Indies at Sydney	1996-97
M. E. Waugh	5-24	v West Indies at Melbourne	1992-93
B. A. Williams (2)	5-53	v New Zealand at Pune	2003-04
	5-22	v Zimbabwe at Sydney	2003-04

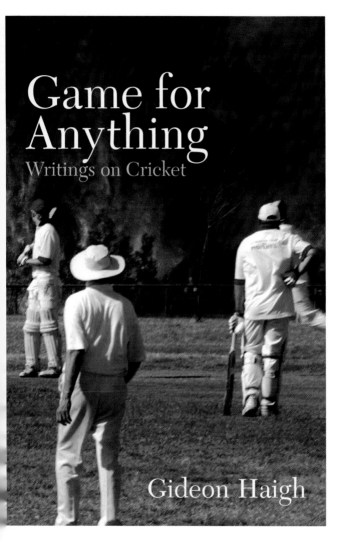

Game for Anything
Writings on Cricket

Gideon Haigh

Out Now • Black Inc. • $32

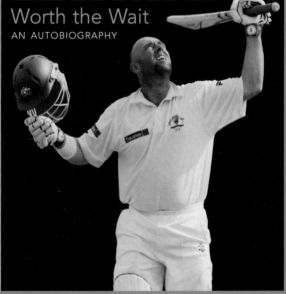

DARREN LEHMANN

Worth the Wait

AN AUTOBIOGRAPHY

Available at all good bookstores
$35

Hardie Grant Books

HAT-TRICKS

B. A. Reid	v New Zealand at Sydney	1985-86
A. M. Stuart	v Pakistan at Melbourne	1996-97
B. Lee	v Kenya at Durban	2002-03

ALL-ROUND RECORDS

FIFTY RUNS AND THREE WICKETS IN A MATCH

G. S. Chappell	90 and 3-43	v New Zealand at Melbourne	1980-81
G. R. J. Matthews	54 and 3-33	v New Zealand at Auckland	1985-86
S. R. Waugh	82 and 4-48	v Pakistan at Perth	1986-87
S. R. Waugh	54 and 3-57	v West Indies at Melbourne	1988-89
S. P. O'Donnell	57* and 4-36	v Sri Lanka at Melbourne	1989-90
M. E. Waugh	57 and 5-24	v West Indies at Melbourne	1992-93
M. G. Bevan	79* and 3-36	v Pakistan at Melbourne	1996-97
T. M. Moody	56* and 3-25	v Bangladesh at Chester-le-Street	1999
D. S. Lehmann	67 and 4-7	v Zimbabwe at Harare	2003-04

1,000 RUNS AND 50 WICKETS IN A CAREER

	Runs	Batting Average	Wickets	Bowling Average	Games for the Double
A. R. Border	6,524	30.63	73	28.37	199
G. S. Chappell	2,331	40.19	72	29.11	44
T. M. Moody	1,211	23.29	52	38.73	75
S. P. O'Donnell	1,242	25.35	108	28.72	40
A. Symonds	2,064	36.21	72	35.99	70
S. R. Waugh	7,569	32.91	195	34.69	46
M. E. Waugh	8,500	39.35	85	34.56	93
S. K. Warne	1,016	13.03	291	25.82	104

WICKET-KEEPING RECORDS

MOST DISMISSALS IN A CAREER

	M	Ct	St	Total
A. C. Gilchrist	322	283	39	322
I. A. Healy	168	194	39	233
R. W. Marsh	92	120	4	124
W. B. Phillips	42	42	7	49
G. C. Dyer	23	24	4	28
T. J. Zoehrer	22	21	2	23
S. J. Rixon	6	9	2	11
K. J. Wright	5	8	0	8
J. P. Maher	4	8	0	8
R. J. Campbell	2	4	1	5
R. D. Robinson	1	3	1	4
P. A. Emery	1	3	0	3
B. J. Haddin	3	1	2	3
R. D. Woolley	4	1	1	2
J. L. Langer	4	1	1	2
M. R. J. Veletta	1	1	0	1
J. A. Maclean	2	0	0	0
D. C. Boon	1	0	0	0

MOST DISMISSALS IN AN INNINGS

6	(all ct)	A.C. Gilchrist	v South Africa at Cape Town	1999-00
6	(5ct, 1st)	A.C. Gilchrist	v England at Sydney	2002-03
6	(all ct)	A.C. Gilchrist	v Namibia at Potchefstroom	2002-03
6	(all ct)	A.C. Gilchrist	v Sri Lanka at Colombo (PIS)	2003-04

MOST DISMISSALS PER MATCH

	M	Ct	St	Dismissals	Dismissals per Match
A.C. Gilchrist	188	283	39	322	1.71
I.A. Healy	168	194	39	233	1.39
R.W. Marsh	92	120	4	124	1.35
G.C. Dyer	23	24	4	28	1.22
W.B. Phillips	42	42	7	49	1.17
T.J. Zoehrer	22	21	2	23	1.05

FIELDING RECORDS

MOST CATCHES IN A CAREER

A.R. Border	127 in 273 matches	M.G. Bevan	69 in 232 matches
S.R. Waugh	111 in 325 matches	M.A. Taylor	56 in 113 matches
M.E. Waugh	108 in 244 matches	D.M. Jones	54 in 164 matches
R.T. Ponting	82 in 201 matches	D.R. Martyn	50 in 151 matches
S.K. Warne	80 in 193 matches	D.C. Boon	45 in 181 matches

MOST CATCHES IN AN INNINGS

| 4 | M.A. Taylor | v West Indies at Sydney | 1992-93 |
| 4 | M.J. Clarke | v India at Melbourne | 2003-04 |

Note: There are 23 instances of three catches in an innings.

TEAM RECORDS

HIGHEST INNINGS TOTALS

Batting first

2-359	v India at Johannesburg (WS)	2002-03
5-359	v India at Sydney	2003-04
6-349	v New Zealand at Christchurch	1999-00
2-347	v India at Bangalore	2003-04
7-344	v Zimbabwe at Hobart (Bel)	2003-04
6-338	v West Indies at Melbourne	2000-01
4-338	v India at Visakhapatnam	2000-01
7-337	v Pakistan at Sydney	1999-00
3-332	v Sri Lanka at Sharjah	1989-90
5-332	v Pakistan at Nairobi	2002-03

Batting Second

7-330	v South Africa at Port Elizabeth	2001-02
4-316	v Pakistan at Lahore	1998-99
4-289	v New Zealand at Chennai (Chepauk)	1995-96
5-287	v South Africa at Centurion	1996-97
284	v India at Chandigarh	1996-97
284	v India at Brisbane	2003-04
4-282	v Zimbabwe at Hobart (Bel)	2000-01
4-280	v England at Birmingham	1993

| 4-279 | v England at Lord's | 1989 |
| 6-275 | v England at Sydney | 1998-99 |

LOWEST COMPLETED INNINGS TOTAL

101	v England at Melbourne	1978-79
139	v India at Sharjah	1984-85
146	v West Indies at Melbourne	1981-82
147	v West Indies at Melbourne	1992-93
154	v South Africa at Durban	1993-94

LARGEST VICTORIES

By Runs

256	v Namibia at Potchefstroom	2002-03
232	v Sri Lanka at Adelaide	1984-85
224	v Pakistan at Nairobi	2002-03
208	v India at Sydney	2003-04
164	v New Zealand at Colombo	2002-03

By Wickets

| 10 | v West Indies at Adelaide | 2000-01 |
| 10 | v England at Sydney | 2002-03 |

Note: There are 17 instances of a victory by nine wickets.

NARROWEST VICTORIES

By Runs

1	v India at Chennai (Chepauk)	1987-88
1	v India at Brisbane	1991-92
1	v South Africa at Bloemfontein	1993-94
1	v Zimbabwe at Perth	2000-01
1	v New Zealand at Christchurch	1992-93
1	v West Indies at Sydney	1995-96

HEAVIEST DEFEATS

By Runs

206	by India at Adelaide	1980-81
164	by West Indies at Perth	1986-87
133	by West Indies at Port-of-Spain	1994-95
128	by West Indies at Melbourne	1981-82
118	by India at Chelmsford	1983
118	by India at Indore	2000-01
109	by South Africa at Bloemfontein	1996-97
107	by India at Perth	1991-92
101	by England at Birmingham	1977
101	by West Indies at Leeds	1983

By Wickets

| 9 | by South Africa at Sydney | 1991-92 |
| 9 | by Pakistan at Rawalpindi | 1994-95 |

NARROWEST DEFEATS

By Runs

1	by New Zealand at Sydney	1980-81
1	by New Zealand at Perth	1987-88
1	by West Indies at Sydney	1988-89
1	by New Zealand at Hobart (Bel)	1990-91
1	by Sri Lanka at Dambulla	2003-04

By Wickets

| 1 | by Pakistan at Perth | 1986-87 |

TIED MATCHES

Australia (9-222) tied West Indies (5-222) at Melbourne 1983-84
England (5-226) tied Australia (8-226) at Nottingham 1989
Australia (7-228) tied Pakistan (9-228) at Hobart (Bel) 1992-93
West Indies (5-173) tied Australia (7-173) at Georgetown 1998-99
Australia (213) tied South Africa (213) at Birmingham 1999
South Africa (8-226) tied Australia (9-226) at Melbourne (DS) 2000-01
South Africa (7-259) tied Australia (9-259) at Potchefstroom 2001-02

APPEARANCE RECORDS

MOST LIMITED-OVERS APPEARANCES

	M	Eng	NZ	Pak	SL	WI	Can	Ind	Zim	SAf	Ban	Kya	Sco	Net	Nam
S.R. Waugh	325	30	60	43	24	50	–	53	14	47	2	1	1	–	–
A.R. Border	273	43	52	34	23	61	1	38	5	15	1	–	–	–	–
M.E. Waugh	244	21	39	29	23	47	–	27	13	42	1	1	1	–	–
M.G. Bevan	232	18	28	28	30	29	–	35	18	35	5	3	1	1	1
R.T. Ponting	201	15	21	21	26	28	–	33	20	26	5	3	1	1	1
S.K. Warne	193	18	27	22	18	27	–	18	12	45	2	3	1	–	–
A.C. Gilchrist	193	19	24	21	18	20	–	32	15	34	5	3	1	–	1
G.D. McGrath	188	18	20	26	20	24	–	21	14	37	2	3	1	1	1
D.C. Boon	181	21	39	19	16	32	–	29	5	19	1	–	–	–	–
I.A. Healy	168	16	23	25	20	39	–	15	5	23	1	1	–	–	–

YOUNGEST PLAYERS ON DEBUT

Years	Days			
19	260	R.J. Bright	v New Zealand at Dunedin	1973-74
19	267	C.J. McDermott	v West Indies at Melbourne	1984-85
20	58	R.T. Ponting	v South Africa at Wellington	1994-95
20	155	N.M. Hauritz	v South Africa at Johannesburg (WS)	2002-03
20	221	S.R. Waugh	v New Zealand at Melbourne	1985-86
20	225	A.K. Zesers	v India at Delhi	1987-88
20	278	I.C. Davis	v New Zealand at Dunedin	1973-74
20	280	S.R. Watson	v South Africa at Centurion	2002-03
20	297	W.M. Darling	v West Indies at St John's	1977-78

OLDEST PLAYERS ON DEBUT

Years	Days			
42	20	R.B. Simpson	v West Indies at St John's	1977-78
38	88	R.G. Holland	v West Indies at Sydney	1984-85
33	328	W.M. Lawry	v England at Melbourne	1970-71
32	261	J.A. Maclean	v England at Sydney	1978-79
31	349	J.K. Moss	v Pakistan at Nottingham	1979
31	190	A.N. Connolly	v England at Melbourne	1970-71

OLDEST PLAYERS

Years	Days			
42	69	R.B. Simpson	v West Indies at Castries	1977-78
38	255	A.R. Border	v South Africa at Bloemfontein	1993-94
38	223	R.G. Holland	v England at Manchester	1985
36	246	S.R. Waugh	v South Africa at Perth	2001-02
36	246	M.E. Waugh	v South Africa at Perth	2001-02
36	110	I.M. Chappell	v England at Sydney	1979-80
36	100	R.W. Marsh	v West Indies at Melbourne	1983-84

CAPTAINCY

THE CAPTAINS

	M	W	L	NR	T
W. M. Lawry	1	1	0	0	0
I. M. Chappell	11	6	5	0	0
G. S. Chappell	49	21	25	3	0
R. B. Simpson	2	1	1	0	0
G. N. Yallop	4	2	1	1	0
K. J. Hughes	49	21	23	4	1
D. W. Hookes	1	0	1	0	0
A. R. Border	178	107	67	3	1
R. J. Bright	1	0	1	0	0
G. R. Marsh	4	3	1	0	0
M. A. Taylor	67	37	29	0	1
I. A. Healy	8	5	3	0	0
S. R. Waugh	106	67	35	1	3
S. K. Warne	11	10	1	0	0
A. C. Gilchrist	7	6	1	0	0
R. T. Ponting	70	56	11	2	1

MOST SUCCESSFUL CAPTAINS

(Qualification: 10 games)

	M	W	L	NR	T	% Won
S. K. Warne	11	10	1	0	0	90.91
R. T. Ponting	70	56	11	2	1	85.71
S. R. Waugh	106	67	35	1	3	63.21
A. R. Border	178	107	67	3	1	60.11
I. M. Chappell	11	6	5	0	0	54.44
M. A. Taylor	67	36	30	0	1	53.73
G. S. Chappell	49	21	25	3	0	42.86
K. J. Hughes	49	21	23	4	1	42.86

SUMMARY OF AUSTRALIAN LIMITED-OVERS INTERNATIONALS

	First Game	M	W	L	NR	T	% Won
England	1970-71	77	45	30	1	1	58.44
New Zealand	1973-74	89	61	25	3	–	68.53
Pakistan	1975	67	37	26	3	1	55.22
Sri Lanka	1975	55	36	17	2	–	65.45
West Indies	1975	105	47	55	1	2	44.76
Canada	1979	1	1	–	–	–	100.00
India	1980-81	79	49	27	3	–	62.02
Zimbabwe	1983	27	25	1	1	–	92.59
Bangladesh	1989-90	6	6	–	–	–	100.00
South Africa	1991-92	56	29	24	–	3	51.78
Kenya	1995-96	4	4	–	–	–	100.00
Scotland	1999	1	1	–	–	–	100.00
Netherlands	2002-03	1	1	–	–	–	100.00
Namibia	2002-03	1	1	–	–	–	100.00
Total		569	343	205	14	7	60.28

AUSTRALIAN LIMITED-OVERS INTERNATIONAL MATCHES

Date	Venue	Opponent	Result for Australia	Captain	Team/Opp
1970-71 in Australia					
Jan 5	Melbourne	England	Won by five wickets	W. M. Lawry	1/1
1972 in England					
Aug 24	Manchester	England	Lost by six wickets	I. M. Chappell	2/2
Aug 26	Lord's	England	Won by five wickets	I. M. Chappell	3/3
Aug 28	Birmingham	England	Lost by two wickets	I. M. Chappell	4/4
1973-74 in New Zealand					
Mar 30	Dunedin	New Zealand	Won by seven wickets	I. M. Chappell	5/1
Mar 31	Christchurch	New Zealand	Won by 31 runs	I. M. Chappell	6/2
1974-75 in Australia					
Jan 1	Melbourne	England	Lost by three wickets	I. M. Chappell	7/5
1975 World Cup in England					
Jun 7	Leeds	Pakistan	Won by 73 runs	I. M. Chappell	8/1
Jun 11	The Oval	Sri Lanka	Won by 52 runs	I. M. Chappell	9/1
Jun 14	The Oval	West Indies	Lost by seven wickets	I. M. Chappell	10/1
Jun 18	Leeds	England	Won by four wickets	I. M. Chappell	11/6
Jun 21	Lord's	West Indies	Lost by 17 runs	I. M. Chappell	12/2
1975-76 in Australia					
Dec 20	Adelaide	West Indies	Won by five wickets	G. S. Chappell	13/3
1977 in England					
Jun 2	Manchester	England	Lost by two wickets	G. S. Chappell	14/7
Jun 4	Birmingham	England	Lost by 99 runs	G. S. Chappell	15/8
Jun 6	The Oval	England	Won by two wickets	G. S. Chappell	16/9
1977-78 in West Indies					
Feb 22	St John's	West Indies	Lost on run-rate	R. B. Simpson	17/4
Apr 12	Castries	West Indies	Won by two wickets	R. B. Simpson	18/5
1978-79 in Australia					
Jan 13	Sydney	England	No result	G. N. Yallop	19/10
Jan 24	Melbourne	England	Lost by seven wickets	G. N. Yallop	20/11
Feb 4	Melbourne	England	Won by four wickets	G. N. Yallop	21/12
Feb 7	Melbourne	England	Won by six wickets	G. N. Yallop	22/13
1979 World Cup in England					
Jun 9	Lord's	England	Lost by six wickets	K. J. Hughes	23/14
Jun 13–14	Nottingham	Pakistan	Lost by 89 runs	K. J. Hughes	24/2
Jun 16	Birmingham	Canada	Won by seven wickets	K. J. Hughes	25/1
1979-80 World Series Cup in Australia					
Nov 27	Sydney	West Indies	Won by five wickets	G. S. Chappell	26/6
Dec 8	Melbourne	England	Lost by three wickets	G. S. Chappell	27/15
Dec 9	Melbourne	West Indies	Lost by 80 runs	G. S. Chappell	28/7
Dec 11	Sydney	England	Lost by 72 runs	G. S. Chappell	29/16
Dec 21	Sydney	West Indies	Won by seven runs	G. S. Chappell	30/8
Dec 26	Sydney	England	Lost by four wickets	G. S. Chappell	31/17
Jan 14	Sydney	England	Lost by two wickets	G. S. Chappell	32/18
Jan 18	Sydney	West Indies	Won by nine runs	G. S. Chappell	33/9
1980 in England					
Aug 20	The Oval	England	Lost by 23 runs	G. S. Chappell	34/19
Aug 22	Birmingham	England	Lost by 47 runs	G. S. Chappell	35/20

Date	Venue	Opponent	Result for Australia	Captain	Team/Opp
1980-81 World Series Cup in Australia					
Nov 23	Adelaide	New Zealand	Lost by three wickets	G. S. Chappell	36/3
Nov 25	Sydney	New Zealand	Won by 94 runs	G. S. Chappell	37/4
Dec 6	Melbourne	India	Lost by 66 runs	G. S. Chappell	38/1
Dec 7	Melbourne	New Zealand	Won by four wickets	G. S. Chappell	39/5
Dec 18	Sydney	India	Won by nine wickets	G. S. Chappell	40/2
Jan 8	Sydney	India	Won by nine wickets	G. S. Chappell	41/3
Jan 11	Melbourne	India	Won by seven wickets	G. S. Chappell	42/4
Jan 13	Sydney	New Zealand	Lost by one run	G. S. Chappell	43/6
Jan 15	Sydney	India	Won by 27 runs	G. S. Chappell	44/5
Jan 21	Sydney	New Zealand	No result	G. S. Chappell	45/7
Jan 29	Sydney	New Zealand	Lost by 78 runs	G. S. Chappell	46/8
Jan 31	Melbourne	New Zealand	Won by seven wickets	G. S. Chappell	47/9
Feb 1	Melbourne	New Zealand	Won by six runs	G. S. Chappell	48/10
Feb 3	Sydney	New Zealand	Won by six wickets	G. S. Chappell	49/11
1981 in England					
Jun 4	Lord's	England	Lost by six wickets	K. J. Hughes	50/21
Jun 6	Birmingham	England	Won by two runs	K. J. Hughes	51/22
Jun 8	Leeds	England	Won by 71 runs	K. J. Hughes	52/23
1981-82 World Series Cup in Australia					
Nov 21	Melbourne	Pakistan	Lost by four wickets	G. S. Chappell	53/3
Nov 24	Sydney	West Indies	Won by seven wickets	G. S. Chappell	54/10
Dec 6	Adelaide	Pakistan	Won by 38 runs	G. S. Chappell	55/4
Dec 17	Sydney	Pakistan	Lost by six wickets	G. S. Chappell	56/5
Dec 20	Perth	West Indies	Lost by eight wickets	G. S. Chappell	57/11
Jan 20	Melbourne	Pakistan	Lost by 25 runs	G. S. Chappell	58/6
Jan 10	Melbourne	West Indies	Lost by five wickets	G. S. Chappell	59/12
Jan 14	Sydney	Pakistan	Won by 76 runs	G. S. Chappell	60/7
Jan 17	Brisbane	West Indies	Lost by five wickets	G. S. Chappell	61/13
Jan 19	Sydney	West Indies	Won on run-rate	G. S. Chappell	62/14
Jan 23	Melbourne	West Indies	Lost by 86 runs	G. S. Chappell	63/15
Jan 24	Melbourne	West Indies	Lost by 128 runs	G. S. Chappell	64/16
Jan 26	Sydney	West Indies	Won by 46 runs	G. S. Chappell	65/17
Jan 27	Sydney	West Indies	Lost by 18 runs	G. S. Chappell	66/18
1981-82 in New Zealand					
Feb 13	Auckland	New Zealand	Lost by 46 runs	G. S. Chappell	67/12
Feb 17	Dunedin	New Zealand	Won by six wickets	G. S. Chappell	68/13
Feb 9	Wellington	New Zealand	Won by eight wickets	G. S. Chappell	69/14
1982-83 in Pakistan					
Sep 20	Hyderabad	Pakistan	Lost by 59 runs	K. J. Hughes	70/8
Oct 8	Lahore	Pakistan	Lost by 28 runs	K. J. Hughes	71/9
Oct 22	Karachi	Pakistan	No result	K. J. Hughes	72/10
1982-83 World Series Cup in Australia					
Jan 9	Melbourne	New Zealand	Won by eight wickets	K. J. Hughes	73/15
Jan 11	Sydney	England	Won by 31 runs	K. J. Hughes	74/24
Jan 16	Brisbane	England	Won by seven wickets	K. J. Hughes	75/25
Jan 18	Sydney	New Zealand	Lost by 47 runs	K. J. Hughes	76/16
Jan 22	Melbourne	New Zealand	Lost by 58 runs	K. J. Hughes	77/17
Jan 23	Melbourne	England	Won by five wickets	K. J. Hughes	78/26
Jan 26	Sydney	England	Lost by 98 runs	K. J. Hughes	79/27
Jan 30	Adelaide	England	Lost by 14 runs	K. J. Hughes	80/28
Jan 31	Adelaide	New Zealand	Lost by 46 runs	K. J. Hughes	81/18
Feb 6	Perth	New Zealand	Won by 27 runs	K. J. Hughes	82/19
Feb 9	Sydney	New Zealand	Won by six wickets	K. J. Hughes	83/20
Feb 13	Melbourne	New Zealand	Won by 149 runs	K. J. Hughes	84/21
1982-83 in Australia					
Mar 17	Sydney	New Zealand	Lost by 14 runs	K. J. Hughes	85/22

Date	Venue	Opponent	Result for Australia	Captain	Team/Opp
1982-83 in Sri Lanka					
Apr 13	Colombo (PSS)	Sri Lanka	Lost by two wickets	G. S. Chappell	86/2
Apr 16	Colombo (PSS)	Sri Lanka	Lost by four wickets	G. S. Chappell	87/3
Apr 20	Colombo (SSC)	Sri Lanka	No result	G. S. Chappell	88/4
Apr 30	Colombo (SSC)	Sri Lanka	No result	G. S. Chappell	89/5
1983 World Cup in England					
Jun 9	Nottingham	Zimbabwe	Lost by 13 runs	K. J. Hughes	90/1
Jun 11–12	Leeds	West Indies	Lost by 101 runs	K. J. Hughes	91/19
Jun 13	Nottingham	India	Won by 162 runs	K. J. Hughes	92/6
Jun 16	Southampton	Zimbabwe	Won by 32 runs	K. J. Hughes	93/2
Jun 18	Lord's	West Indies	Lost by seven wickets	K. J. Hughes	94/20
Jun 20	Chelmsford	India	Lost by 118 runs	D. W. Hookes	95/7
1983-84 World Series Cup in Australia					
Jan 8	Melbourne	West Indies	Lost by 27 runs	K. J. Hughes	96/21
Jan 10	Sydney	Pakistan	Won by 34 runs	K. J. Hughes	97/11
Jan 15	Brisbane	Pakistan	No result	K. J. Hughes	98/12
Jan 17	Sydney	West Indies	Lost by 28 runs	K. J. Hughes	99/22
Jan 21	Melbourne	Pakistan	Won by 45 runs	K. J. Hughes	100/13
Jan 22	Melbourne	West Indies	Lost by 26 runs	K. J. Hughes	101/23
Jan 25	Sydney	Pakistan	Won by 87 runs	K. J. Hughes	102/14
Jan 29	Adelaide	West Indies	Lost by six wickets	K. J. Hughes	103/24
Jan 30	Adelaide	Pakistan	Won by 70 runs	K. J. Hughes	104/15
Feb 5	Perth	West Indies	Won by 14 runs	K. J. Hughes	105/25
Feb 8	Sydney	West Indies	Lost by nine wickets	K. J. Hughes	106/26
Feb 11	Melbourne	West Indies	Tied	K. J. Hughes	107/27
Feb 12	Melbourne	West Indies	Lost by six wickets	K. J. Hughes	108/28
1983-84 in West Indies					
Feb 29	Berbice	West Indies	Lost by eight wickets	K. J. Hughes	109/29
Mar 14	Port-of-Spain	West Indies	Won by four wickets	K. J. Hughes	110/30
Apr 19	Castries	West Indies	Lost by seven wickets	K. J. Hughes	111/31
Apr 26	Kingston	West Indies	Lost by nine wickets	K. J. Hughes	112/32
1984-85 in India					
Sep 28	New Delhi	India	Won by 48 runs	K. J. Hughes	113/8
Oct 1	Trivandrum	India	No result	K. J. Hughes	114/9
Oct 3	Jamshedpur	India	No result	K. J. Hughes	115/10
Oct 5	Ahmedabad	India	Won by seven wickets	K. J. Hughes	116/11
Oct 6	Indore	India	Won by six wickets	K. J. Hughes	117/12
1984-85 World Series Cup in Australia					
Jan 6	Melbourne	West Indies	Lost by seven wickets	A. R. Border	118/33
Jan 8	Sydney	Sri Lanka	Won by six wickets	A. R. Border	119/6
Jan 13	Brisbane	West Indies	Lost by five wickets	A. R. Border	120/34
Jan 15	Sydney	West Indies	Lost by five wickets	A. R. Border	121/35
Jan 19	Melbourne	Sri Lanka	Lost by four wickets	A. R. Border	122/7
Jan 20	Melbourne	West Indies	Lost by 65 runs	A. R. Border	123/36
Jan 23	Sydney	Sri Lanka	Won by three wickets	A. R. Border	124/8
Jan 27	Adelaide	West Indies	Lost by six wickets	A. R. Border	125/37
Jan 28	Adelaide	Sri Lanka	Won by 232 runs	A. R. Border	126/9
Feb 3	Perth	Sri Lanka	Won by nine wickets	A. R. Border	127/10
Feb 6	Sydney	West Indies	Won by 26 runs	A. R. Border	128/38
Feb 10	Melbourne	West Indies	Lost by four wickets	A. R. Border	129/39
Feb 12	Sydney	West Indies	Lost by seven wickets	A. R. Border	130/40
1984-85 World Championship of Cricket in Australia					
Feb 17	Melbourne	England	Won by seven wickets	A. R. Border	131/29
Feb 24	Melbourne	Pakistan	Lost by 62 runs	A. R. Border	132/16
Mar 3	Melbourne	India	Lost by eight wickets	A. R. Border	133/13

Date	Venue	Opponent	Result for Australia	Captain	Team/Opp
1984-85 in United Arab Emirates					
Mar 24	Sharjah	England	Won by two wickets	A.R. Border	134/30
Mar 29	Sharjah	India	Lost by three wickets	A.R. Border	135/14
1985 in England					
May 30	Manchester	England	Won by three wickets	A.R. Border	136/31
Jun 1	Birmingham	England	Won by four wickets	A.R. Border	137/32
Jun 3	Lord's	England	Lost by eight wickets	A.R. Border	138/33
1985-86 World Series Cup in Australia					
Jan 9	Melbourne	New Zealand	No result	A.R. Border	139/23
Jan 12	Brisbane	India	Won by four wickets	A.R. Border	140/15
Jan 14	Sydney	New Zealand	Won by four wickets	A.R. Border	141/24
Jan 16	Melbourne	India	Lost by eight wickets	A.R. Border	142/16
Jan 19	Perth	New Zealand	Won by four wickets	A.R. Border	143/25
Jan 21	Sydney	India	Won by 100 runs	A.R. Border	144/17
Jan 26	Adelaide	India	Won by 36 runs	A.R. Border	145/18
Jan 27	Adelaide	New Zealand	Lost by 206 runs	A.R. Border	146/26
Jan 29	Sydney	New Zealand	Won by 99 runs	A.R. Border	147/27
Jan 31	Melbourne	India	Lost by six wickets	A.R. Border	148/19
Feb 5	Sydney	India	Won by 11 runs	A.R. Border	149/20
Feb 9	Melbourne	India	Won by seven wickets	A.R. Border	150/21
1985-86 in New Zealand					
Mar 19	Dunedin	New Zealand	Lost by 30 runs	A.R. Border	151/28
Mar 22	Christchurch	New Zealand	Lost by 53 runs	A.R. Border	152/29
Mar 26	Wellington	New Zealand	Won by three wickets	A.R. Border	153/30
Mar 29	Auckland	New Zealand	Won by 44 runs	A.R. Border	154/31
1985-86 in United Arab Emirates					
Apr 11	Sharjah	Pakistan	Lost by eight wickets	R.J. Bright	155/17
1986-87 in India					
Sep 7	Jaipur	India	Lost by seven wickets	A.R. Border	156/22
Sep 9	Srinagar	India	Won by three wickets	A.R. Border	157/23
Sep 24	Hyderabad	India	No result	A.R. Border	158/24
Oct 2	Delhi	India	Lost by three wickets	A.R. Border	159/25
Oct 5	Ahmedabad	India	Lost by 52 runs	A.R. Border	160/26
Oct 7	Rajkot	India	Won by seven wickets	A.R. Border	161/27
1986-87 World Challenge in Australia					
Jan 1	Perth	England	Lost by 37 runs	A.R. Border	162/34
Jan 2	Perth	Pakistan	Lost by one wicket	A.R. Border	163/18
Jan 4	Perth	West Indies	Lost by 164 runs	A.R. Border	164/41
1986-87 World Series Cup in Australia					
Jan 18	Brisbane	England	Won by 11 runs	A.R. Border	165/35
Jan 20	Melbourne	West Indies	Lost by seven wickets	A.R. Border	166/42
Jan 22	Sydney	England	Lost by three wickets	A.R. Border	167/36
Jan 25	Adelaide	West Indies	Lost by 16 runs	A.R. Border	168/43
Jan 26	Adelaide	England	Won by 33 runs	A.R. Border	169/37
Jan 28	Sydney	West Indies	Won by 36 runs	A.R. Border	170/44
Feb 1	Melbourne	England	Won by 109 runs	A.R. Border	171/38
Feb 6	Sydney	West Indies	Won by two wickets	A.R. Border	172/45
Feb 8	Melbourne	England	Lost by six wickets	A.R. Border	173/39
Feb 11	Sydney	England	Lost by eight runs	A.R. Border	174/40
1986-87 in United Arab Emirates					
Apr 3	Sharjah	Pakistan	Lost by six wickets	A.R. Border	175/19
Apr 6	Sharjah	India	Lost by seven wickets	G.R. Marsh	176/28
Apr 9	Sharjah	England	Lost by 11 runs	A.R. Border	177/41

Date	Venue	Opponent	Result for Australia	Captain	Team/Opp
1987-88 World Cup in India and Pakistan					
Oct 9	Chennai	India	Won by one run	A. R. Border	178/29
Oct 13	Chennai	Zimbabwe	Won by 96 runs	A. R. Border	179/3
Oct 19	Indore	New Zealand	Won by three runs	A. R. Border	180/32
Oct 22	New Delhi	India	Lost by 56 runs	A. R. Border	181/30
Oct 27	Chandigarh	New Zealand	Won by 17 runs	A. R. Border	182/33
Oct 30	Cuttack	Zimbabwe	Won by 70 runs	A. R. Border	183/4
Nov 4	Lahore	Pakistan	Won by 18 runs	A. R. Border	184/20
Nov 8	Calcutta	England	Won by seven runs	A. R. Border	185/42
1987-88 World Series Cup in Australia					
Jan 2	Perth	Sri Lanka	Won by 81 runs	A. R. Border	186/11
Jan 3	Perth	New Zealand	Lost by one run	A. R. Border	187/34
Jan 7	Melbourne	New Zealand	Won by six runs	A. R. Border	188/35
Jan 10	Adelaide	Sri Lanka	Won by 81 runs	A. R. Border	189/12
Jan 14	Melbourne	Sri Lanka	Won by 38 runs	A. R. Border	190/13
Jan 17	Brisbane	New Zealand	Won by five wickets	A. R. Border	191/36
Jan 19	Sydney	Sri Lanka	Won by three wickets	A. R. Border	192/14
Jan 20	Sydney	New Zealand	Won by 78 runs	A. R. Border	193/37
Jan 22	Melbourne	New Zealand	Won by eight wickets	A. R. Border	194/38
Jan 24	Sydney	New Zealand	Won by six wickets	A. R. Border	195/39
1987-88 in Australia					
Feb 4	Melbourne	England	Won by 22 runs	A. R. Border	196/43
1988-89 in Pakistan					
Oct 14	Lahore	Pakistan	Lost on fewer wickets	A. R. Border	197/21
1988-89 World Series Cup in Australia					
Dec 11	Adelaide	Pakistan	Won by nine wickets	A. R. Border	198/22
Dec 13	Sydney	West Indies	Lost by one run	A. R. Border	199/46
Dec 15	Melbourne	West Indies	Lost by 34 runs	A. R. Border	200/47
Jan 2	Perth	Pakistan	Lost by 38 runs	A. R. Border	201/23
Jan 5	Melbourne	West Indies	Won by eight runs	A. R. Border	202/48
Jan 8	Brisbane	Pakistan	Won by five wickets	A. R. Border	203/24
Jan 10	Melbourne	Pakistan	Won on run-rate	A. R. Border	204/25
Jan 12	Sydney	West Indies	Won by 61 runs	A. R. Border	205/49
Jan 14	Melbourne	West Indies	Won by two runs	A. R. Border	206/50
Jan 16	Sydney	West Indies	Lost by 92 runs	A. R. Border	207/51
Jan 18	Sydney	West Indies	Lost on run-rate	A. R. Border	208/52
1989 in England					
May 25	Manchester	England	Lost by 95 runs	A. R. Border	209/44
May 27	Nottingham	England	Tied	A. R. Border	210/45
May 29	Lord's	England	Won by six wickets	A. R. Border	211/46
1989-90 in India					
Oct 19	Hyderabad	England	Lost by seven wickets	A. R. Border	212/47
Oct 21	Chennai	West Indies	Won by 99 runs	A. R. Border	213/53
Oct 23	Bombay	Pakistan	Lost by 66 runs	A. R. Border	214/26
Oct 25	Goa	Sri Lanka	Won by 28 runs	A. R. Border	215/15
Oct 27	Bangalore	India	Lost by three wickets	A. R. Border	216/31
1989-90 World Series in Australia					
Dec 26	Melbourne	Sri Lanka	Won by 30 runs	A. R. Border	217/16
Dec 30	Perth	Sri Lanka	Won by nine wickets	A. R. Border	218/17
Jan 3	Melbourne	Pakistan	Won by seven wickets	A. R. Border	219/27
Jan 4	Melbourne	Sri Lanka	Won by 73 runs	A. R. Border	220/18
Feb 11	Brisbane	Pakistan	Won by 67 runs	A. R. Border	221/28
Feb 13	Sydney	Pakistan	Lost by five wickets	A. R. Border	222/29
Feb 18	Adelaide	Sri Lanka	Won by seven wickets	A. R. Border	223/19

Date	Venue	Opponent	Result for Australia	Captain	Team/Opp
Feb 20	Sydney	Pakistan	Lost by two runs	A. R. Border	224/30
Feb 23	Melbourne	Pakistan	Won by seven wickets	A. R. Border	225/31
Feb 25	Sydney	Pakistan	Won by 69 runs	A. R. Border	226/32

1989-90 in New Zealand

Mar 3	Christchurch	India	Won by 18 runs	A. R. Border	227/32
Mar 4	Christchurch	New Zealand	Won by 150 runs	A. R. Border	228/40
Mar 8	Hamilton	India	Won by seven wickets	A. R. Border	229/33
Mar 10	Auckland	New Zealand	Won on run-rate	G. R. Marsh	230/41
Mar 11	Auckland	New Zealand	Won by eight wickets	A. R. Border	231/42

1989-90 in United Arab Emirates

Apr 26	Sharjah	New Zealand	Won by 63 runs	A. R. Border	232/43
Apr 30	Sharjah	Bangladesh	Won by seven wickets	A. R. Border	233/1
May 2	Sharjah	Sri Lanka	Won by 114 runs	A. R. Border	234/20
May 4	Sharjah	Pakistan	Lost by 36 runs	A. R. Border	235/33

1990-91 World Series in Australia

Nov 29	Sydney	New Zealand	Won by 61 runs	A. R. Border	236/44
Dec 2	Adelaide	New Zealand	Won by six wickets	A. R. Border	237/45
Dec 9	Perth	England	Won by six wickets	A. R. Border	238/48
Dec 11	Melbourne	New Zealand	Won by 39 runs	A. R. Border	239/46
Dec 16	Brisbane	England	Won by 37 runs	A. R. Border	240/49
Dec 18	Hobart (Bel)	New Zealand	Lost by one run	A. R. Border	241/47
Jan 1	Sydney	England	Won by 68 runs	A. R. Border	242/50
Jan 10	Melbourne	England	Won by three runs	A. R. Border	243/51
Jan 13	Sydney	New Zealand	Won by six wickets	G. R. Marsh	244/48
Jan 15	Melbourne	New Zealand	Won by seven wickets	G. R. Marsh	245/49

1990-91 in West Indies

Feb 26	Kingston	West Indies	Won by 35 runs	A. R. Border	246/54
Mar 9	Port-of-Spain	West Indies	Won by 45 runs	A. R. Border	247/55
Mar 10	Port-of-Spain	West Indies	Lost on run-rate	A. R. Border	248/56
Mar 13	Bridgetown	West Indies	Won by 46 runs	A. R. Border	249/57
Mar 20	Georgetown	West Indies	Won by six wickets	A. R. Border	250/58

1991-92 World Series in Australia

Dec 8	Perth	India	Lost by 107 runs	A. R. Border	251/34
Dec 10	Hobart (Bel)	India	Won by eight wickets	A. R. Border	252/35
Dec 12	Melbourne	West Indies	Won by nine runs	A. R. Border	253/59
Dec 15	Adelaide	India	Won by six wickets	A. R. Border	254/36
Dec 18	Sydney	West Indies	Won by 51 runs	A. R. Border	255/60
Jan 9	Melbourne	West Indies	No result	A. R. Border	256/61
Jan 12	Brisbane	West Indies	Lost by 12 runs	A. R. Border	257/62
Jan 14	Sydney	India	Won by nine wickets	A. R. Border	258/37
Jan 18	Melbourne	India	Won by 88 runs	A. R. Border	259/38
Jan 20	Sydney	India	Won by six wickets	A. R. Border	260/39

1991-92 World Cup in Australia and New Zealand

Feb 22	Auckland	New Zealand	Lost by 37 runs	A. R. Border	261/50
Feb 26	Sydney	South Africa	Lost by nine wickets	A. R. Border	262/1
Mar 1	Brisbane	India	Won by one run	A. R. Border	263/40
Mar 5	Sydney	England	Lost by eight wickets	A. R. Border	264/52
Mar 7	Adelaide	Sri Lanka	Won by seven wickets	A. R. Border	265/21
Mar 11	Perth	Pakistan	Lost by 48 runs	A. R. Border	266/34
Mar 14	Hobart (Bel)	Zimbabwe	Won by 128 runs	A. R. Border	267/5
Mar 18	Melbourne	West Indies	Won by 57 runs	A. R. Border	268/63
Date	*Venue*	*Opponent*	*Result for Australia*	*Captain*	*Team/Opp*

1992-93 in Sri Lanka

Aug	15	Colombo (PSS)	Sri Lanka	Lost by four wickets	A. R. Border	269/22
Sep	4	Colombo (PIS)	Sri Lanka	Lost on run-rate	A. R. Border	270/23
Sep	5	Colombo (PIS)	Sri Lanka	Won by five wickets	A. R. Border	271/24

1992-93 World Series in Australia

Dec	6	Perth	West Indies	Lost by nine wickets	A. R. Border	272/64
Dec	8	Sydney	West Indies	Won by 14 runs	M. A. Taylor	273/65
Dec	10	Hobart (Bel)	Pakistan	Tied	M. A. Taylor	274/35
Dec	13	Adelaide	Pakistan	Won by eight wickets	M. A. Taylor	275/36
Dec	15	Melbourne	West Indies	Won by four runs	M. A. Taylor	276/66
Jan	10	Brisbane	West Indies	Lost by seven runs	A. R. Border	277/67
Jan	12	Melbourne	Pakistan	Won by 32 runs	A. R. Border	278/37
Jan	14	Sydney	Pakistan	Won by 23 runs	A. R. Border	279/38
Jan	16	Sydney	West Indies	Lost by 25 runs	A. R. Border	280/69
Jan	18	Melbourne	West Indies	Lost by four wickets	A. R. Border	281/69

1992-93 in New Zealand

Mar	19	Dunedin	New Zealand	Won by 129 runs	A. R. Border	282/51
Mar	21-22	Christchurch	New Zealand	Won by one wicket	M. A. Taylor	283/52
Mar	24	Wellington	New Zealand	Lost by 88 runs	A. R. Border	284/53
Mar	27	Hamilton	New Zealand	Lost by three wickets	M. A. Taylor	285/54
Mar	28	Auckland	New Zealand	Won by three runs	A. R. Border	286/55

1993 in England

May	19	Manchester	England	Won by four runs	A. R. Border	287/53
May	21	Birmingham	England	Won by six wickets	A. R. Border	288/54
May	23	Lord's	England	Won by 19 runs	M. A. Taylor	289/55

1993-94 World Series in Australia

Dec	9	Melbourne	South Africa	Lost by seven wickets	A. R. Border	290/2
Dec	12	Adelaide	New Zealand	Won by eight wickets	A. R. Border	291/56
Dec	14	Sydney	South Africa	Won by 103 runs	A. R. Border	292/3
Dec	16	Melbourne	New Zealand	Won by three runs	A. R. Border	293/57
Jan	9	Brisbane	South Africa	Won by 48 runs	A. R. Border	294/4
Jan	11	Sydney	New Zealand	Lost by 13 runs	A. R. Border	295/58
Jan	16	Perth	South Africa	Lost by 82 runs	M. A. Taylor	296/5
Jan	19	Melbourne	New Zealand	Won by 51 runs	A. R. Border	297/59
Jan	21	Melbourne	South Africa	Lost by 28 runs	A. R. Border	298/6
Jan	23	Sydney	South Africa	Won by 69 runs	A. R. Border	299/7
Jan	25	Sydney	South Africa	Won by 35 runs	A. R. Border	300/8

1993-94 in South Africa

Feb	19	Johannesburg	South Africa	Lost by five runs	A. R. Border	301/9
Feb	20	Pretoria	South Africa	Lost by 56 runs	A. R. Border	302/10
Feb	22	Port Elizabeth	South Africa	Won by 88 runs	A. R. Border	303/11
Feb	24	Durban	South Africa	Lost by seven wickets	A. R. Border	304/12
Apr	2	East London	South Africa	Won by seven wickets	A. R. Border	305/13
Apr	4	Port Elizabeth	South Africa	Lost by 26 runs	A. R. Border	306/14
Apr	6	Cape Town	South Africa	Won by 36 runs	A. R. Border	307/15
Apr	8	Bloemfontein	South Africa	Won by one run	A. R. Border	308/16

1993-94 in United Arab Emirates

Apr	14	Sharjah	Sri Lanka	Won by nine wickets	M. A. Taylor	309/25
Apr	16	Sharjah	New Zealand	Won by seven wickets	M. A. Taylor	310/60
Apr	19	Sharjah	India	Lost by seven wickets	M. A. Taylor	311/41

Date	Venue	Opponent	Result for Australia	Captain	Team/Opp
1994-95 in Sri Lanka					
Sep 7	Colombo (SSC)	Pakistan	Won by 28 runs	M. A. Taylor	312/39
Sep 9	Colombo (PIS)	India	Lost by 31 runs	M. A. Taylor	313/42
Sep 13	Colombo (SSC)	Sri Lanka	Lost on run-rate	M. A. Taylor	314/26
1994-95 in Pakistan					
Oct 12	Lahore	South Africa	Won by six wickets	M. A. Taylor	315/17
Oct 14	Multan	Pakistan	Won by seven wickets	M. A. Taylor	316/40
Oct 18	Faisalabad	South Africa	Won by 22 runs	M. A. Taylor	317/18
Oct 22	Rawalpindi	Pakistan	Lost by nine wickets	M. A. Taylor	318/41
Oct 24	Peshawar	South Africa	Won by three wickets	M. A. Taylor	319/19
Oct 30	Lahore	Pakistan	Won by 64 runs	M. A. Taylor	320/42
1994-95 World Series in Australia					
Dec 2	Perth	Zimbabwe	Won by two wickets	M. A. Taylor	321/6
Dec 6	Sydney	England	Won by 28 runs	M. A. Taylor	322/56
Dec 8	Hobart (Bel)	Zimbabwe	Won by 85 runs	M. A. Taylor	323/7
Jan 10	Melbourne	England	Lost by 37 runs	M. A. Taylor	324/57
1994-95 in New Zealand					
Feb 15	Wellington	South Africa	Won by three wickets	M. A. Taylor	325/20
Feb 19	Auckland	New Zealand	Won by 27 runs	M. A. Taylor	326/61
Feb 22	Dunedin	India	Lost by five wickets	M. A. Taylor	327/43
Feb 26	Auckland	New Zealand	Won by six wickets	M. A. Taylor	326/62
1994-95 in West Indies					
Mar 8	Bridgetown	West Indies	Lost by six runs	M. A. Taylor	329/70
Mar 11	Port-of-Spain	West Indies	Won by 26 runs	M. A. Taylor	330/71
Mar 12	Port-of-Spain	West Indies	Lost by 133 runs	M. A. Taylor	331/72
Mar 15	Kingstown	West Indies	Lost on run-rate	M. A. Taylor	332/73
Mar 18	Georgetown	West Indies	Lost by five wickets	M. A. Taylor	333/74
1995-96 World Series in Australia					
Dec 17	Adelaide	West Indies	Won by 121 runs	M. A. Taylor	334/75
Dec 19	Melbourne	West Indies	Won by 24 runs	M. A. Taylor	335/76
Dec 21	Sydney	Sri Lanka	Won by five wickets	M. A. Taylor	336/27
Jan 1	Sydney	West Indies	Won by one wicket	M. A. Taylor	337/77
Jan 7	Brisbane	West Indies	Lost by 14 runs	M. A. Taylor	338/78
Jan 9	Melbourne	Sri Lanka	Lost by three wickets	M. A. Taylor	339/28
Jan 12	Perth	Sri Lanka	Won by 83 runs	M. A. Taylor	340/29
Jan 16	Melbourne	Sri Lanka	Lost by three wickets	M. A. Taylor	341/30
Jan 18	Melbourne	Sri Lanka	Won by 18 runs	M. A. Taylor	342/31
Jan 20	Sydney	Sri Lanka	Won on run-rate	M. A. Taylor	343/32
1995-96 World Cup in India, Pakistan and Sri Lanka					
Feb 23	Vishakhapatnam	Kenya	Won by 97 runs	M. A. Taylor	344/1
Feb 27	Bombay	India	Won by 16 runs	M. A. Taylor	345/44
Mar 1	Nagpur	Zimbabwe	Won by eight wickets	M. A. Taylor	346/8
Mar 4	Jaipur	West Indies	Lost by four wickets	M. A. Taylor	347/79
Mar 11	Chennai	New Zealand	Won by six wickets	M. A. Taylor	348/63
Mar 14	Chandigarh	West Indies	Won by five runs	M. A. Taylor	349/80
Mar 17	Lahore	Sri Lanka	Lost by seven wickets	M. A. Taylor	350/33
1996-97 in Sri Lanka					
Aug 26	Colombo (PIS)	Zimbabwe	Won by 125 runs	I. A. Healy	351/9
Aug 30	Colombo (PIS)	Sri Lanka	Lost by four wickets	I. A. Healy	352/34
Sep 6	Colombo (SSC)	India	Won by three wickets	I. A. Healy	353/45
Sep 7	Colombo (SSC)	Sri Lanka	Lost by 50 runs	I. A. Healy	354/35
1996-97 in India					
Oct 19	Indore	South Africa	Lost by seven wickets	M. A. Taylor	355/21
Oct 21	Bangalore	India	Lost by two wickets	M. A. Taylor	356/46
Oct 25	Faridabad	South Africa	Lost by two wickets	M. A. Taylor	357/22

Date	Venue	Opponent	Result for Australia	Captain	Team/Opp
Nov 1	Guwahati	South Africa	Lost by eight wickets	M. A. Taylor	358/23
Nov 3	Chandigarh	India	Lost by five runs	M. A. Taylor	359/47

1996-97 Carlton & United Series in Australia

Dec 6	Melbourne	West Indies	Won by five wickets	M. A. Taylor	360/81
Dec 8	Sydney	West Indies	Won by eight wickets	M. A. Taylor	361/82
Dec 15	Adelaide	Pakistan	Lost by 12 runs	M. A. Taylor	362/43
Jan 1	Sydney	Pakistan	Lost by four wickets	M. A. Taylor	363/44
Jan 5	Brisbane	West Indies	Lost by seven wickets	M. A. Taylor	364/83
Jan 7	Hobart (Bel)	Pakistan	Lost by 29 runs	M. A. Taylor	365/45
Jan 12	Perth	West Indies	Lost by four wickets	M. A. Taylor	366/84
Jan 16	Melbourne	Pakistan	Won by three wickets	M. A. Taylor	367/46

1996-97 in South Africa

Mar 29	East London	South Africa	Lost by six wickets	M. A. Taylor	368/24
Mar 31	Port Elizabeth	South Africa	Won by seven wickets	M. A. Taylor	369/25
Apr 3	Cape Town	South Africa	Lost by 46 runs	I. A. Healy	370/26
Apr 5	Durban	South Africa	Won by 15 runs	I. A. Healy	371/27
Apr 8	Johannesburg	South Africa	Won by eight runs	I. A. Healy	372/28
Apr 10	Centurion	South Africa	Won by five wickets	I. A. Healy	373/29
Apr 13	Bloemfontein	South Africa	Lost by 109 runs	S. R. Waugh	374/30

1997 in England

May 22	Leeds	England	Lost by six wickets	M. A. Taylor	375/58
May 24	The Oval	England	Lost by six wickets	M. A. Taylor	376/59
May 25	Lord's	England	Lost by six wickets	S. R. Waugh	377/60

1997-98 Carlton & United Series in Australia

Dec 4	Sydney	South Africa	Lost by 67 runs	S. R. Waugh	378/31
Dec 7	Adelaide	New Zealand	Won by three wickets	S. R. Waugh	379/64
Dec 9	Melbourne	South Africa	Lost by 45 runs	S. R. Waugh	380/32
Dec 17	Melbourne	New Zealand	Won by six wickets	S. R. Waugh	381/65
Jan 11	Brisbane	South Africa	Lost by five wickets	S. R. Waugh	382/33
Jan 14	Sydney	New Zealand	Won by 131 runs	S. K. Warne	383/66
Jan 18	Perth	South Africa	Lost by seven wickets	S. R. Waugh	384/34
Jan 21	Melbourne	New Zealand	Lost by four wickets	S. R. Waugh	385/67
Jan 23	Melbourne	South Africa	Lost by six wickets	S. R. Waugh	386/35
Jan 26	Sydney	South Africa	Won by seven wickets	S. R. Waugh	387/36
Jan 27	Sydney	South Africa	Won by 14 runs	S. R. Waugh	388/37

1997-98 in New Zealand

Feb 8	Christchurch	New Zealand	Won by seven wickets	S. R. Waugh	389/68
Feb 10	Wellington	New Zealand	Won by 66 runs	S. R. Waugh	390/69
Feb 12	Napier	New Zealand	Lost by seven wickets	S. R. Waugh	391/70
Feb 14	Auckland	New Zealand	Lost by 30 runs	S. R. Waugh	392/71

1997-98 in India

Apr 1	Kochi	India	Lost by 41 runs	S. R. Waugh	393/48
Apr 3	Ahmedabad	Zimbabwe	Won by 13 runs	S. R. Waugh	394/10
Apr 7	Kanpur	India	Lost by six wickets	S. R. Waugh	395/49
Apr 11	Delhi	Zimbabwe	Won by 16 runs	S. R. Waugh	396/11
Apr 14	Delhi	India	Won by four wickets	S. R. Waugh	397/50

1997-98 in United Arab Emirates

Apr 18	Sharjah	New Zealand	Won by six wickets	S. R. Waugh	398/72
Apr 19	Sharjah	India	Won by 58 runs	S. R. Waugh	399/51
Apr 21	Sharjah	New Zealand	Won by five wickets	S. R. Waugh	400/73
Apr 22	Sharjah	India	Won on run-rate	S. R. Waugh	401/52
Apr 24	Sharjah	India	Lost by six wickets	S. R. Waugh	402/53

1998-99 in Bangladesh

| Oct 28 | Dhaka | India | Lost by 44 runs | S. R. Waugh | 403/54 |

Date	Venue	Opponent	Result for Australia	Captain	Team/Opp
1998-99 in Pakistan					
Nov 6	Karachi	Pakistan	Won by 86 runs	S. R. Waugh	404/47
Nov 8	Peshawar	Pakistan	Won by five wickets	S. R. Waugh	405/48
Nov 10	Lahore	Pakistan	Won by six wickets	S. R. Waugh	406/49
1998-99 Carlton & United Series in Australia					
Jan 10	Brisbane	England	Won on run-rate	S. K. Warne	407/61
Jan 13	Sydney	Sri Lanka	Won by eight wickets	S. K. Warne	408/36
Jan 15	Melbourne	England	Won by nine wickets	S. K. Warne	409/62
Jan 17	Sydney	England	Lost by seven runs	S. R. Waugh	410/63
Jan 21	Hobart (Bel)	Sri Lanka	Lost by three wickets	S. R. Waugh	411/37
Jan 24	Adelaide	Sri Lanka	Won by 80 runs	S. K. Warne	412/38
Jan 26	Adelaide	England	Won by 16 runs	S. K. Warne	413/64
Jan 31	Perth	Sri Lanka	Won by 45 runs	S. K. Warne	414/39
Feb 5	Sydney	England	Won by four wickets	S. K. Warne	415/65
Feb 7	Melbourne	Sri Lanka	Won by 43 runs	S. K. Warne	416/40
Feb 10	Sydney	England	Won by 10 runs	S. K. Warne	417/66
Feb 13	Melbourne	England	Won by 162 runs	S. K. Warne	418/67
1998-99 in West Indies					
Apr 11	Kingstown	West Indies	Lost by 44 runs	S. R. Waugh	419/85
Apr 14	St George's	West Indies	Won by 46 runs	S. R. Waugh	420/86
Apr 17	Port-of-Spain	West Indies	Lost by five wickets	S. R. Waugh	421/87
Apr 18	Port-of-Spain	West Indies	Won by 20 runs	S. R. Waugh	422/88
Apr 21	Georgetown	West Indies	Tied	S. R. Waugh	423/89
Apr 24	Bridgetown	West Indies	Won by four wickets	S. R. Waugh	424/90
Apr 25	Bridgetown	West Indies	Lost on run-rate	S. R. Waugh	425/91
1999 World Cup in England					
May 16	Worcester	Scotland	Won by six wickets	S. R. Waugh	426/1
May 20	Cardiff	New Zealand	Lost by five wickets	S. R. Waugh	427/74
May 23	Leeds	Pakistan	Lost by ten runs	S. R. Waugh	428/50
May 27	Chester-le-Street	Bangladesh	Won by seven wickets	S. R. Waugh	429/2
May 30	Manchester	West Indies	Won by six wickets	S. R. Waugh	430/92
Jun 4	The Oval	India	Won by 77 runs	S. R. Waugh	431/55
Jun 9	Lord's	Zimbabwe	Won by 44 runs	S. R. Waugh	432/12
Jun 13	Leeds	South Africa	Won by five wickets	S. R. Waugh	433/38
Jun 17	Birmingham	South Africa	Tied	S. R. Waugh	434/39
Jun 20	Lord's	Pakistan	Won by eight wickets	S. R. Waugh	435/51
1999-2000 in Sri Lanka					
Aug 22	Galle	Sri Lanka	Won on run-rate	S. R. Waugh	436/41
Aug 23	Galle	India	Won on run-rate	S. R. Waugh	437/56
Aug 26	Colombo (PIS)	Sri Lanka	Won by 27 runs	S. R. Waugh	438/42
Aug 28	Colombo (SSC)	India	Won by 41 runs	S. R. Waugh	439/57
Aug 31	Colombo (PIS)	Sri Lanka	Lost by eight wickets	S. R. Waugh	440/43
1999-2000 in Zimbabwe					
Oct 21	Bulawayo	Zimbabwe	Won by 83 runs	S. R. Waugh	441/13
Oct 23	Harare	Zimbabwe	Won by nine wickets	S. R. Waugh	442/14
Oct 24	Harare	Zimbabwe	Won by nine wickets	S. R. Waugh	443/15
1999-2000 Carlton & United Series in Australia					
Jan 9	Brisbane	Pakistan	Lost by 45 runs	S. R. Waugh	444/52
Jan 12	Melbourne	India	Won by 28 runs	S. R. Waugh	445/58
Jan 14	Sydney	India	Won by five wickets	S. R. Waugh	446/59
Jan 16	Melbourne	Pakistan	Won by six wickets	S. R. Waugh	447/53
Jan 19	Sydney	Pakistan	Won by 81 runs	S. R. Waugh	448/54
Jan 23	Melbourne	Pakistan	Won by 15 runs	S. R. Waugh	449/55
Jan 26	Adelaide	India	Won by 152 runs	S. R. Waugh	450/60
Jan 30	Perth	India	Won by four wickets	S. R. Waugh	451/61
Feb 2	Melbourne	Pakistan	Won by six wickets	S. R. Waugh	452/56
Feb 4	Sydney	Pakistan	Won by 152 runs	S. R. Waugh	453/57

Date	Venue	Opponent	Result for Australia	Captain	Team/Opp
1999-2000 in New Zealand					
Feb 17	Wellington	New Zealand	No result	S.R. Waugh	454/75
Feb 19	Auckland	New Zealand	Won by five wickets	S.R. Waugh	455/76
Feb 23	Dunedin	New Zealand	Won by 50 runs	S.R. Waugh	456/77
Feb 26	Christchurch	New Zealand	Won by 48 runs	S.R. Waugh	457/78
Mar 1	Napier	New Zealand	Won by five wickets	S.R. Waugh	458/79
Mar 3	Auckland	New Zealand	Lost by seven wickets	S.R. Waugh	459/80
1999-2000 in South Africa					
Apr 12	Durban	South Africa	Lost by six wickets	S.R. Waugh	460/40
Apr 14	Cape Town	South Africa	Won by five wickets	S.R. Waugh	461/41
Apr 16	Johannesburg	South Africa	Lost by four wickets	S.R. Waugh	462/42
2000-2001 in Australia					
Aug 12	Melbourne (DS)	South Africa	Won by 94 runs	S.R. Waugh	463/43
Aug 14	Melbourne (DS)	South Africa	Tied	S.R. Waugh	464/44
Aug 16	Melbourne (DS)	South Africa	Lost by eight runs	S.R. Waugh	465/45
2000-01 in Kenya					
Oct 7	Nairobi	India	Lost by 20 runs	S.R. Waugh	466/62
2000-01 Carlton Series in Australia					
Jan 11	Melbourne	West Indies	Won by 74 runs	S.R. Waugh	467/93
Jan 14	Brisbane	West Indies	Won by nine wickets	A.C. Gilchrist	468/94
Jan 17	Sydney	West Indies	Won on run-rate	A.C. Gilchrist	469/95
Jan 21	Melbourne	Zimbabwe	Won by eight wickets	A.C. Gilchrist	470/16
Jan 26	Adelaide	West Indies	Won by 10 wickets	S.R. Waugh	471/96
Jan 28	Sydney	Zimbabwe	Won by 86 runs	S.R. Waugh	472/17
Jan 30	Hobart (Bel)	Zimbabwe	Won by six wickets	S.R. Waugh	473/18
Feb 4	Perth	Zimbabwe	Won by one run	S.R. Waugh	474/19
Feb 7	Sydney	West Indies	Won by 134 runs	S.R. Waugh	475/97
Feb 9	Melbourne	West Indies	Won by 39 runs	S.R. Waugh	476/98
2000-01 in India					
Mar 23	Bangalore	India	Lost by 60 runs	S.R. Waugh	477/63
Mar 28	Pune	India	Won by eight wickets	S.R. Waugh	478/64
Mar 31	Indore	India	Lost by 118 runs	S.R. Waugh	479/65
Apr 3	Visakhapatnam	India	Won by 93 runs	S.R. Waugh	480/66
Apr 6	Goa	India	Won by four wickets	S.R. Waugh	481/67
2001 in England					
Jun 9	Cardiff	Pakistan	Won by seven wickets	S.R. Waugh	482/58
Jun 10	Bristol	England	Won by five wickets	S.R. Waugh	483/68
Jun 14	Manchester	England	Won on run-rate	S.R. Waugh	484/69
Jun 19	Nottingham	Pakistan	Lost by 36 runs	S.R. Waugh	485/59
Jun 21	The Oval	England	Won by eight wickets	S.R. Waugh	486/70
Jun 23	Lord's	Pakistan	Won by nine wickets	S.R. Waugh	487/60
2001-02 VB Series in Australia					
Jan 11	Melbourne	New Zealand	Lost by 23 runs	S.R. Waugh	488/81
Jan 13	Melbourne	South Africa	Lost by four wickets	S.R. Waugh	489/46
Jan 17	Sydney	New Zealand	Lost by 23 runs	S.R. Waugh	490/82
Jan 20	Brisbane	South Africa	Won by 27 runs	S.R. Waugh	491/47
Jan 22	Sydney	South Africa	Won by eight wickets	S.R. Waugh	492/48
Jan 26	Adelaide	New Zealand	Lost by 77 runs	S.R. Waugh	493/83
Jan 29	Melbourne	New Zealand	Won by two wickets	S.R. Waugh	494/84
Feb 3	Perth	South Africa	Lost by 33 runs	S.R. Waugh	495/49
2001-02 in South Africa					
Mar 23	Johannesburg	South Africa	Won by 19 runs	R.T. Ponting	496/50
Mar 24	Centurion	South Africa	Won by 45 runs	R.T. Ponting	497/51
Mar 27	Potchefstroom	South Africa	Tied	R.T. Ponting	498/52
Mar 30	Bloemfontein	South Africa	Won by 37 runs	R.T. Ponting	499/53

Date	Venue	Opponent	Result for Australia	Captain	Team/Opp
Apr 4	Durban	South Africa	Won by eight wickets	R. T. Ponting	500/54
Apr 6	Port Elizabeth	South Africa	Won by three wickets	R. T. Ponting	501/55
Apr 9	Cape Town	South Africa	Lost on run-rate	R. T. Ponting	502/56

2001-02 in Australia

Jun 12	Melbourne (DS)	Pakistan	Won by seven wickets	R. T. Ponting	503/61
Jun 15	Melbourne (DS)	Pakistan	Lost by two wickets	R. T. Ponting	504/62
Jun 19	Brisbane	Pakistan	Lost by 91 runs	R. T. Ponting	505/63

2002-03 in Kenya

Aug 30	Nairobi	Pakistan	Won by 224 runs	R. T. Ponting	506/64
Sep 2	Nairobi	Kenya	Won by eight wickets	R. T. Ponting	507/2
Sep 4	Nairobi	Pakistan	Won by nine wickets	R. T. Ponting	508/65
Sep 5	Nairobi	Kenya	Won by five wickets	A. C. Gilchrist	509/3
Sep 7	Nairobi	Pakistan	No result	R. T. Ponting	510/66

2002-03 in Sri Lanka

Sep 15	Colombo (SSC)	New Zealand	Won by 164 runs	R. T. Ponting	511/85
Sep 19	Colombo (SSC)	Bangladesh	Won by nine wickets	R. T. Ponting	512/3
Sep 27	Colombo (PIS)	Sri Lanka	Lost by seven wickets	R. T. Ponting	513/44

2002-03 VB Series in Australia

Dec 13	Sydney	England	Won by seven wickets	R. T. Ponting	514/71
Dec 15	Melbourne	England	Won by 89 runs	R. T. Ponting	515/72
Dec 22	Perth	Sri Lanka	Won by 142 runs	R. T. Ponting	516/45
Jan 9	Sydney	Sri Lanka	Lost by 79 runs	R. T. Ponting	517/46
Jan 11	Hobart (Bel)	England	Won by seven runs	R. T. Ponting	518/73
Jan 15	Brisbane	Sri Lanka	Won by four wickets	R. T. Ponting	519/47
Jan 19	Adelaide	England	Won by four wickets	A. C. Gilchrist	520/74
Jan 21	Melbourne	Sri Lanka	Won by nine wickets	R. T. Ponting	521/48
Jan 23	Sydney	England	Won by 10 wickets	R. T. Ponting	522/75
Jan 25	Melbourne	England	Won by five wickets	R. T. Ponting	523/76

2002-03 World Cup in South Africa and Zimbabwe

Feb 11	Johannesburg	Pakistan	Won by 82 runs	R. T. Ponting	524/67
Feb 15	Centurion	India	Won by nine wickets	R. T. Ponting	525/68
Feb 20	Potchefstroom	Netherlands	Won by 75 runs	R. T. Ponting	526/1
Feb 24	Bulawayo	Zimbabwe	Won by seven wickets	R. T. Ponting	527/20
Feb 27	Potchefstroom	Namibia	Won by 256 runs	R. T. Ponting	528/1
Mar 2	Port Elizabeth	England	Won by two wickets	R. T. Ponting	529/77
Mar 7	Centurion	Sri Lanka	Won by 96 runs	R. T. Ponting	530/49
Mar 11	Port Elizabeth	New Zealand	Won by 96 runs	R. T. Ponting	531/86
Mar 15	Durban	Kenya	Won by five wickets	R. T. Ponting	532/4
Mar 18	Port Elizabeth	Sri Lanka	Won by 48 runs	R. T. Ponting	533/50
Mar 23	Johannesburg	India	Won by 125 runs	R. T. Ponting	534/69

2002-03 in West Indies

May 17	Kingston	West Indies	Won by two runs	R. T. Ponting	535/99
May 18	Kingston	West Indies	Won by eight wickets	R. T. Ponting	536/100
May 21	St Lucia	West Indies	Won by 25 runs	R. T. Ponting	537/101
May 24	Port-of-Spain	West Indies	Won by 67 runs	R. T. Ponting	538/102
May 25	Port-of-Spain	West Indies	Won by 39 runs	R. T. Ponting	539/103
May 30	St George's	West Indies	Lost by three wickets	R. T. Ponting	540/104
Jun 1	St George's	West Indies	Lost by nine wickets	R. T. Ponting	541/105

2003-04 in Australia

Aug 2	Cairns	Bangladesh	Won by eight wickets	R. T. Ponting	542/4
Aug 3	Cairns	Bangladesh	Won by nine wickets	R. T. Ponting	543/5
Aug 6	Darwin	Bangladesh	Won by 112 runs	R. T. Ponting	544/6

Date	Venue	Opponent	Result for Australia	Captain	Team/Opp
2003-04 in India					
Oct 26	Gwalior	India	Lost by 37 runs	R. T. Ponting	545/70
Oct 29	Faridabad	New Zealand	Won by eight wickets	R. T. Ponting	546/87
Nov 1	Mumbai	India	Won by 77 runs	R. T. Ponting	547/71
Nov 3	Pune	New Zealand	Won by two wickets	R. T. Ponting	548/88
Nov 9	Guwahati	New Zealand	Won by 44 runs	R. T. Ponting	549/89
Nov 12	Bangalore	India	Won by 61 runs	R. T. Ponting	550/72
Nov 18	Kolkata	India	Won by 18 runs	R. T. Ponting	551/73
2003-04 VB Series					
Jan 9	Melbourne	India	Won by 18 runs	R. T. Ponting	552/74
Jan 11	Sydney	Zimbabwe	Won by 99 runs	R. T. Ponting	553/21
Jan 16	Hobart (Bel)	Zimbabwe	Won by 148 runs	R. T. Ponting	554/22
Jan 18	Brisbane	India	Lost by 19 runs	R. T. Ponting	555/75
Jan 22	Sydney	India	Won by two wickets	R. T. Ponting	556/76
Jan 26	Adelaide	Zimbabwe	Won by 13 runs	R. T. Ponting	557/23
Jan 29	Melbourne	Zimbabwe	No result	R. T. Ponting	558/24
Feb 1	Perth	India	Won by five wickets	A. C. Gilchrist	559/77
Feb 6	Melbourne	India	Won by seven wickets	R. T. Ponting	560/78
Feb 8	Sydney	India	Won by 208 runs	R. T. Ponting	561/79
2003-04 in Sri Lanka					
Feb 20	Dambulla	Sri Lanka	Won by 84 runs	R. T. Ponting	562/51
Feb 22	Dambulla	Sri Lanka	Lost by one run	R. T. Ponting	563/52
Feb 25	Colombo (PIS)	Sri Lanka	Won by five wickets	R. T. Ponting	564/53
Feb 27	Colombo (PIS)	Sri Lanka	Won by 40 runs	R. T. Ponting	565/54
Feb 29	Colombo (SSC)	Sri Lanka	Lost by three wickets	A. C. Gilchrist	566/55
2003-04 in Zimbabwe					
May 25	Harare	Zimbabwe	Won by seven wickets	R. T. Ponting	567/25
May 27	Harare	Zimbabwe	Won by 139 runs	R. T. Ponting	568/26
May 29	Harare	Zimbabwe	Won by eight wickets	R. T. Ponting	569/27

Australian First-Class Records

BATTING RECORDS

HIGHEST INDIVIDUAL SCORES

452*	D. G. Bradman	New South Wales v Queensland at Sydney	1929-30
437	W. H. Ponsford	Victoria v Queensland at Melbourne	1927-28
429	W. H. Ponsford	Victoria v Tasmania at Melbourne	1922-23
383	C. W. Gregory	New South Wales v Queensland at Brisbane	1906-07
380	M. L. Hayden	Australia v Zimbabwe at Perth	2003-04
369	D. G. Bradman	South Australia v Tasmania at Adelaide	1935-36
365*	C. Hill	South Australia v New South Wales at Adelaide	1900-01
364	L. Hutton	England v Australia at The Oval	1938
359	R. B. Simpson	New South Wales v Queensland at Brisbane	1963-64
357	D. G. Bradman	South Australia v Victoria at Melbourne	1935-36
356	B. A. Richards	South Australia v Western Australia at Perth	1970-71
355*	G. R. Marsh	Western Australia v South Australia at Perth	1989-90
352	W. H. Ponsford	Victoria v New South Wales at Melbourne	1926-27
345	C. G. Macartney	Australians v Nottinghamshire at Nottingham	1921
340*	D. G. Bradman	New South Wales v Victoria at Sydney	1928-29
336	W. H. Ponsford	Victoria v South Australia at Melbourne	1927-28
335*	M. W. Goodwin	Sussex v Leicestershire at Hove	2003
334	D. G. Bradman	Australia v England at Leeds	1930
334*	M. A. Taylor	Australia v Pakistan at Peshawar	1998-99
331*	M. E. K. Hussey	Northamptonshire v Somerset at Taunton	2003
329*	M. E. K. Hussey	Northamptonshire v Essex at Northampton	2001
325*	H. S. T. L. Hendry	Victoria v New Zealanders at Melbourne	1925-26
325	C. L. Badcock	South Australia v Victoria at Adelaide	1935-36
324*	D. M. Jones	Victoria v South Australia at Melbourne	1994-95
321	W. L. Murdoch	New South Wales v Victoria at Sydney	1881-82
315*	A. F. Kippax	New South Wales v Queensland at Sydney	1927-28
311	R. B. Simpson	Australia v England at Manchester	1964
310*	M. E. K. Hussey	Northamptonshire v Gloucestershire at Bristol	2002
307	M. C. Cowdrey	MCC v South Australia at Adelaide	1962-63
307	R. M. Cowper	Australia v England at Melbourne	1965-66
306*	D. W. Hookes	South Australia v Tasmania at Adelaide	1986-87
305*	F. E. Woolley	MCC v Tasmania at Hobart (TCA)	1911-12
304	D. G. Bradman	Australia v England at Leeds	1934
303*	W. W. Armstrong	Australians v Somerset at Bath	1905
302*	B. J. Hodge	Leicestershire v Nottinghamshire at Nottingham	2003
300*	V. T. Trumper	Australians v Sussex at Hove	1899
300*	M. L. Love	Queensland v Victoria at St Kilda	2003-04

HUNDRED ON FIRST-CLASS DEBUT
FOR AUSTRALIAN TEAMS

C. S. Gordon	121	Victoria v New South Wales at Melbourne	1869-70
J. P. O'Halloran	128*	Victoria v South Australia at Melbourne	1896-97
L. W. Pye	166	New South Wales v Queensland at Brisbane (Ex)	1896-97
H. G. S. Morton	135*	Queensland v Victoria at Melbourne	1904-05
W. M. McPetrie	123	Victoria v Tasmania at Melbourne	1904-05
A. G. Moyes	104	South Australia v Western Australia at Adelaide	1912-13
N. L. Gooden	102	South Australia v Western Australia at Adelaide	1912-13
F. W. Hyett	108*	Victoria v Tasmania at Melbourne	1914-15
N. F. Callaway	207	New South Wales v Queensland at Sydney	1914-15
J. Bogle	145	New South Wales v Victoria at Sydney	1918-19
E. E. B. Forssberg	143	New South Wales v Queensland at Sydney	1920-21
D. A. Mullarkey	130	New South Wales v Queensland at Brisbane (Ex)	1923-24
S. E. Wootton	105	Victoria v Tasmania at Hobart (TCA)	1923-24
H. O. Rock	127	New South Wales v South Australia at Sydney	1924-25
L. T. Gun	136*	South Australia v New South Wales at Adelaide	1924-25
D. G. Bradman	118	New South Wales v South Australia at Adelaide	1927-28
R. N. Ellis	100	Victoria v Tasmania at Hobart (TCA)	1927-28
B. W. Hone	137	South Australia v Victoria at Adelaide	1928-29
R. M. Levy	129	Queensland v Victoria at Brisbane (Ex)	1928-29
A. H. Allsopp	117	New South Wales v MCC at Sydney	1929-30
O. W. Bill	115	New South Wales v Tasmania at Sydney	1929-30
L. R. Leabeater	128	New South Wales v Tasmania at Sydney	1929-30
F. E. Fontaine	118	Victoria v Tasmania at Hobart (TCA)	1930-31
R. J. Lawson	119	Victoria v Tasmania at Hobart (TCA)	1930-31
R. N. Nutt	102	New South Wales v South Australia at Adelaide	1931-32
J. C. Francis	135	Victoria v Tasmania at Launceston	1932-33
H. H. E. Grangel	108	Victoria v Tasmania at Melbourne	1935-36
R. A. Hamence	121	South Australia v Tasmania at Adelaide	1935-36
K. R. Miller	181	Victoria v Tasmania at Melbourne	1937-38
A. E. O. Barras	113	Western Australia v Victoria at Perth	1938-39
A. R. Morris	148	New South Wales v Queensland at Sydney	1940-41
M. R. Thomas	164	Tasmania v Australian Services at Hobart (TCA)	1945-46
S. J. E. Loxton	232*	Victoria v Queensland at Melbourne	1946-47
E. W. Lukeman	118	New South Wales v South Australia at Adelaide	1946-47
E. A. D. Kerr	112	Victoria v Tasmania at Launceston	1946-47
J. L. Chambers	122	Victoria v Tasmania at Melbourne	1949-50
L. E. Favell	164	South Australia v New South Wales at Adelaide	1951-52
J. Hallebone	202	Victoria v Tasmania at Melbourne	1951-52
R. E. Briggs	121	New South Wales v Western Australia at Perth	1952-53
B. K. Shepherd	103*	Western Australia v Queensland at Perth	1955-56
R. B. Lyons	102	Queensland v Victoria at Brisbane	1955-56
H. W. Pinkus	102*	Tasmania v South Australia at Hobart (TCA)	1956-57
N. G. Marks	180*	New South Wales v South Australia at Sydney	1958-59
D. Chadwick	129	Western Australia v Queensland at Brisbane	1963-64
J. F. C. Loxton	100	Queensland v Western Australia at Perth	1966-67
M. J. Lucas	107	Queensland v New South Wales at Brisbane	1968-69
R. W. Marsh	104	Western Australia v West Indians at Perth	1968-69
G. J. Gilmour	122	New South Wales v South Australia at Sydney	1971-72
M. F. Kent	140	Queensland v New South Wales at Brisbane	1974-75
K. J. Hughes	119	Western Australia v New South Wales at Perth	1975-76
J. M. Wiener	106	Victoria v Queensland at Brisbane	1977-78
M. D. Taylor	107	Victoria v Queensland at Melbourne	1977-78
C. E. Penter	112	Western Australia v New South Wales at Sydney	1979-80
D. M. Wellham	100	New South Wales v Victoria at Melbourne	1980-81
M. D. Haysman	126	South Australia v Queensland at Adelaide	1982-83
S. P. O'Donnell	130	Victoria v South Australia at Melbourne	1983-84
W. J. S. Seabrook	165	New South Wales v Victoria at Melbourne	1984-85
E. J. Harris	118	Tasmania v South Australia at Adelaide	1985-86

W. N. Phillips	111	Victoria v West Indians at Melbourne	1988-89
M. G. Bevan	114	South Australia v Western Australia at Perth	1989-90
G. I. Foley	155	Queensland v Pakistanis at Brisbane	1989-90
M. P. Lavender	118	Western Australia v Victoria at St Kilda	1990-91
M. L. Hayden	149	Queensland v South Australia at Brisbane	1991-92
R. J. Davison	133*	New South Wales v Tasmania at Sydney	1993-94

Note: A. R. Morris scored a century (111) in the second innings of his debut match, thus becoming the first player in world cricket to achieve such a feat.

HUNDRED IN EACH INNINGS OF A MATCH FOR AUSTRALIAN TEAMS

C. J. Eady	116	112*	Tasmania v Victoria at Hobart (TCA)	1894-95
V. T. Trumper	109	119	Australians v Essex at Leyton	1902
J. R. M. Mackay	105	102*	New South Wales v South Australia at Sydney	1905-06
D. R. A. Gehrs	148*	100*	South Australia v Western Australia at Fremantle	1905-06
M. A. Noble	176	123	New South Wales v Victoria at Sydney	1907-08
V. S. Ransford	182	110	Victoria v New South Wales at Sydney	1908-09
W. Bardsley	136	130	Australia v England at The Oval	1909
A. Kenny	164	100*	Victoria v Queensland at Brisbane	1909-10
C. G. Macartney	119	126	New South Wales v South Africans at Sydney	1910-11
C. G. Macartney	142	121	Australians v Sussex at Hove	1912
R. S. Stephens	108	181	Victoria v Tasmania at Launceston	1913-14
J. M. Gregory	122	102	AIF Team v New South Wales at Sydney	1919-20
W. W. Armstrong	157*	245	Victoria v South Australia at Melbourne	1920-21
F. A. O'Keefe	177	141	The Rest v Australian XI at Sydney	1921-22
W. H. Ponsford	110	110*	Victoria v New South Wales at Sydney	1923-24
V. Y. Richardson	100	125	South Australia v New South Wales at Sydney	1924-25
A. F. Kippax	122	131	New South Wales v Queensland at Brisbane (Ex)	1926-27
L. P. D. O'Connor	103	143*	Queensland v New South Wales at Sydney	1926-27
A. Jackson	131	122	New South Wales v South Australia at Sydney	1927-28
D. G. Bradman	131	133*	New South Wales v Queensland at Brisbane (Ex)	1928-29
B. A. Onyons	105	127	Victoria v Queensland at Brisbane (Ex)	1928-29
D. G. Bradman	124	225	W. M. Woodfull's XI v J. Ryder's XI at Sydney	1929-30
A. F. Kippax	158	102*	Australians v Sussex at Hove	1930
S. J. McCabe	106	103*	New South Wales v Victoria at Sydney	1931-32
A. R. Lonergan	115	100	South Australia v Victoria at Melbourne	1933-34
K. E. Rigg	100	167*	Victoria v New South Wales at Melbourne	1936-37
D. G. Bradman	107	113	South Australia v Queensland at Brisbane	1937-38
A. L. Hassett	122	122	Victoria v New South Wales at Sydney	1939-40
C. L. Badcock	120	102	South Australia v Victoria at Melbourne	1940-41
R. A. Hamence	130	103*	South Australia v Victoria at Melbourne	1940-41
A. R. Morris	148	111	New South Wales v Queensland at Sydney	1940-41
A. L. Hassett	187	124*	Australian Services v Prince's XI at Delhi	1945-46
A. R. Morris	122	124*	Australia v England at Adelaide	1946-47
R. A. Hamence	132	101*	South Australia v New South Wales at Adelaide	1946-47
D. G. Bradman	132	127*	Australia v India at Melbourne	1947-48
J. Moroney	118	101*	Australia v South Africa at Johannesburg (EP)	1949-50
A. R. Edwards	103	105	Western Australia v Queensland at Perth	1950-51
K. R. Miller	100	101	A. L. Hassett's XI v A. R. Morris's XI at Melbourne	1953-54
J. W. Burke	138	125*	Australians v Somerset at Taunton	1956
L. E. Favell	112	114	South Australia v New South Wales at Sydney	1956-57
C. J. Pinch	110	100	South Australia v Western Australia at Perth	1956-57
C. J. Pinch	102	102	South Australia v Victoria at Melbourne	1957-58
G. B. Stevens	164	111	South Australia v New South Wales at Sydney	1957-58
L. E. Favell	104	145	South Australia v Western Australia at Adelaide	1958-59
S. C. Trimble	113	136*	Queensland v Victoria at Brisbane	1963-64
R. B. Simpson	153	115	Australia v Pakistan at Karachi	1964-65
R. B. Simpson	121	142*	New South Wales v South Australia at Sydney	1964-65
P. C. Kelly	119	108*	Western Australia v MCC at Perth	1965-66

K. G. Cunningham.	107	101* South Australia v Western Australia at Adelaide	1966-67
K. D. Walters	242	103 Australia v West Indies at Sydney	1968-69
G. S. Chappell	129	156* South Australia v Queensland at Brisbane	1969-70
I. M. Chappell	145	106 Australians v World XI at Brisbane	1971-72
A. J. Sieler	157	105 Victoria v Queensland at Brisbane	1973-74
G. S. Chappell	180	101 Queensland v Victoria at Brisbane	1973-74
I. M. Chappell	141*	130 South Australia v Victoria at Adelaide	1973-74
I. M. Chappell	145	121 Australia v New Zealand at Wellington	1973-74
G. S. Chappell	247*	133 Australia v New Zealand at Wellington	1973-74
R. B. McCosker	138	136* New South Wales v Western Australia at Sydney	1974-75
R. B. McCosker	111	115 Australians v Sussex at Hove	1975
G. S. Chappell	123	109* Australia v West Indies at Brisbane	1975-76
D. W. Hookes	185	105 South Australia v Queensland at Adelaide	1976-77
D. W. Hookes	135	156 South Australia v New South Wales at Adelaide	1976-77
G. N. Yallop	105	114* Victoria v New South Wales at Sydney	1977-78
A. R. Border	150*	153 Australia v Pakistan at Lahore	1979-80
R. B. McCosker	123*	118* New South Wales v Victoria at Sydney	1981-82
R. B. Kerr	158	101 Queensland v Western Australia at Perth	1981-82
D. W. Hookes	137	107 South Australia v Victoria at Adelaide	1982-83
G. N. Yallop	113	145* Victoria v Western Australia at Melbourne	1983-84
S. B. Smith	105	116 Australians v Guyana at Georgetown	1983-84
A. R. Border	140	114* Australia v New Zealand at Christchurch	1985-86
K. C. Wessels	135	105* Australians v South Africans at Port Elizabeth	1986-87
D. C. Boon	108	143 Tasmania v Queensland at Launceston	1987-88
M. A. Taylor	107	152* New South Wales v Western Australia at Perth	1988-89
T. M. Moody	162	159 Western Australia v South Australia at Perth	1988-89
D. M. Jones	116	121* Australia v Pakistan at Adelaide	1989-90
J. Cox	175	102 Tasmania v New South Wales at Hobart (Bel)	1989-90
M. A. Taylor	127	100 New South Wales v Queensland at Sydney	1989-90
S. M. Small	115	126 New South Wales v Wellington at North Sydney	1990-91
S. G. Law	142*	105 Queensland v Western Australia at Perth	1990-91
D. R. Martyn	132*	112 Western Australia v Queensland at Brisbane	1992-93
R. T. Ponting	107	100* Tasmania v Western Australia at Hobart (Bel)	1992-93
D. C. Boon	108	106 Australians v Worcestershire at Worcester	1993
M. L. Hayden	165	116 Queensland v South Australia at Adelaide	1993-94
P. C. Nobes	140	106 South Australia v Queensland at Adelaide	1993-94
M. L. Hayden	126	155 Queensland v Victoria at Brisbane	1993-94
D. M. Jones	145	152* Victoria v South Australia at Melbourne	1993-94
D. F. Hills	114	126 Tasmania v South Australia at Adelaide	1993-94
M. L. Love	187	116 Queensland v Tasmania at Brisbane	1994-95
S. G. Law	102	138 Queensland v Tasmania at Hobart (Bel)	1994-95
R. T. Ponting	118*	100* Tasmania v Queensland at Brisbane	1995-96
M. T. G. Elliott	104*	135 Victoria v Western Australia at Perth	1995-96
R. T. Ponting	126	145* Tasmania v Queensland at Hobart (Bel)	1996-97
J. Cox	143	125 Tasmania v New South Wales at Sydney	1996-97
S. R. Waugh	108	116 Australia v England at Manchester	1997
A. Symonds	163	100* Queensland v South Australia at Adelaide	1997-98
D. S. Lehmann	103	100† Australians v Rawalpindi Cricket Assn at Rawalpindi	1998-99
M. T. G. Elliott	108	103* Victoria v New South Wales at Melbourne	1998-99
G. S. Blewett	169*	213* Australian XI v England XI at Hobart (Bel)	1998-99
D. S. Lehmann	101*	113 South Australia v Tasmania at Hobart (Bel)	1999-00
J. Cox	106	128* Tasmania v New South Wales at Hobart (Bel)	2000-01
R. T. Ponting	102	102 Australians v BCCI President's XI at Delhi	2000-01
B. J. Hodge	140	110* Victoria v South Australia at Adelaide	2001-02
R. T. Ponting	126	154 Tasmania v New South Wales at Sydney	2001-02
C. J. L. Rogers	101*	102* Western Australia v South Australia at Perth	2001-02
J. L. Arnberger	172*	102 Victoria v Tasmania at Melbourne	2002-03
M. L. Hayden	197	103 Australia v England at Brisbane	2002-03
G. J. Mail	128	152* New South Wales v South Australia at Sydney	2003-04
M. T. G. Elliott	166	102* Victoria v Tasmania at Melbourne	2003-04
M. L. Hayden	117	132 Australia v Sri Lanka at Cairns	2003-04

† *Retired hurt.*

MOST HUNDREDS IN CONSECUTIVE INNINGS

Six	*1st*	*2nd*		
D. G. Bradman	118	dnb	D. G. Bradman's XI v K. E. Rigg's XI at Melbourne ...	1938-39
	143	dnb	South Australia v New South Wales at Adelaide	1938-39
	225	dnb	South Australia v Queensland at Adelaide	1938-39
	107	dnb	South Australia v Victoria at Melbourne	1938-39
	186	dnb	South Australia v Queensland at Brisbane	1938-39
	135*	dnb	South Australia v New South Wales at Sydney	1938-39
Five				
M. E. K. Hussey	100	dnb	Northamptonshire v Hampshire at Southampton	2003
	331*	dnb	Northamptonshire v Somerset at Taunton	2003
	115	dnb	Northamptonshire v Derbyshire at Derby	2003
	187	dnb	Northamptonshire v Durham at Northampton	2003
	147	dnb	Northamptonshire v Glamorgan at Cardiff	2003
Four				
C. G. Macartney	105	dnb	Australians v Hampshire at Southampton	1921
	193	dnb	Australians v Northamptonshire at Northampton	1921
	345	dnb	Australians v Nottinghamshire at Nottingham	1921
	115	30	Australia v England at Leeds	1921
D. G. Bradman	dnb	135	New South Wales v South Africans at Sydney	1931-32
	226	dnb	Australia v South Africa at Brisbane	1931-32
	219	dnb	New South Wales v South Africans at Sydney	1931-32
	112	dnb	Australia v South Africa at Sydney	1931-32
D. G. Bradman	150	dnb	Australians v Gentlemen of England at Lord's	1948
	143	dnb	Australians v South of England at Hastings	1948
	153	dnb	Australians v H. G. D. Leveson Gower's XI at Scarborough	1948
	123	10	D. G. Bradman's XI v A. L. Hassett's XI at Melbourne .	1948-49
D. W. Hookes	185	105	South Australia v Queensland at Adelaide	1976-77
	135	156	South Australia v New South Wales at Adelaide	1976-77
A. R. Border	106	dnb	Australians v Somerset at Taunton	1985
	135	dnb	Australians v Worcestershire at Worcester	1985
	125	dnb	Australians v MCC at Lord's	1985
	100	dnb	Australians v Derbyshire at Derby	1985
M. G. Bevan	20	104	New South Wales v South Australia at Adelaide	1990-91
	153*	dnb	New South Wales v Victoria at Sydney	1990-91
	121	dnb	New South Wales v Queensland at Sydney	1990-91
	136	3	New South Wales v Tasmania at Hobart (Bel)	1990-91
G. S. Blewett	158	dnb	South Australia v Victoria at Melbourne	1998-99
	152	dnb	South Australia v Tasmania at Hobart (Bel)	1998-99
	169*	213*	Australian XI v England XI at Hobart (Bel)	1998-99

MOST HUNDREDS IN A CAREER
(30 or more)

	100s	*I*	*400+*	*300+*	*200+*
D. G. Bradman	117	338	1	6	37
M. E. Waugh	81	591	0	0	5
S. R. Waugh	79	551	0	0	5
G. S. Chappell	74	542	0	0	4
A. R. Border	70	625	0	0	3
D. S. Lehmann	69	405	0	0	9
D. C. Boon	68	585	0	0	3
M. L. Hayden	68	408	0	1	5
R. N. Harvey	67	461	0	0	7
S. G. Law	67	502	0	0	5
K. C. Wessels	66	539	0	0	4
T. M. Moody	64	501	0	0	4
J. L. Langer	64	442	0	0	9

100s	*I*	*400+*	*300+*	*200+*	
R.B. Simpson	60	436	0	2	10
A.L. Hassett	59	322	0	0	8
I.M. Chappell	59	448	0	0	3
M.G. Bevan	59	359	0	0	4
D.M. Jones	55	415	0	1	8
W. Bardsley	53	376	0	0	7
W.H. Ponsford	51	282	2	2	9
R.T. Ponting	51	282	0	0	5
W.M. Lawry	50	417	0	0	4
J. Cox	50	448	0	0	3
C.G. Macartney	49	360	0	1	3
W.M. Woodfull	49	245	0	0	7
A.R. Morris	46	250	0	0	4
C. Hill	45	416	0	1	3
W.W. Armstrong	45	406	0	6	1
N.C. O'Neill	45	306	0	0	2
K.D. Walters	45	426	0	0	4
M.T.G. Elliott	45	310	0	0	2
A.F. Kippax	43	256	0	1	6
G.S. Blewett	43	386	0	0	5
V.T. Trumper	42	401	0	1	7
K.R. Miller	41	326	0	0	7
M.A. Taylor	41	435	0	1	1
W.A. Brown	39	284	0	0	5
P.J.P. Burge	38	354	0	0	5
M.A. Noble	37	377	0	0	7
D.R. Martyn	37	295	0	0	2
M.J. Slater	36	384	0	0	4
G.M. Wood	35	375	0	0	0
J.D. Siddons	35	280	0	0	3
L. Livingston	34	384	0	0	4
F.A. Tarrant	33	541	0	0	4
G.R. Marsh	33	323	0	1	2
A. Symonds	33	290	0	0	1
B.J. Hodge	33	252	0	1	4
H.L. Collins	32	258	0	0	3
I.R. Redpath	32	391	0	0	2
D.W. Hookes	32	304	0	0	1
M.W. Goodwin	32	249	0	1	3
M.E.K. Hussey	32	267	0	3	3
W.E. Alley	31	682	0	0	3
G.N. Yallop	30	283	0	0	3

MOST RUNS IN AN AUSTRALIAN SEASON

	Season	*M*	*I*	*NO*	*R*	*HS*	*100s*	*50s*	*Avge*
D.G. Bradman (New South Wales)	1928-29	13	24	6	1,690	340*	7	5	93.88
R.N. Harvey (Victoria)	1952-53	16	27	1	1,659	205	5	8	63.80
D.G. Bradman (New South Wales)	1929-30	11	16	2	1,586	452*	5	4	113.28
W.R. Hammond (MCC)	1928-29	13	18	1	1,553	251	7	1	91.35
D.G. Bradman (South Australia)	1936-37	12	19	1	1,552	270	6	2	86.22
G.S. Chappell (Queensland)	1975-76	15	26	8	1,547	182*	6	7	85.94
R.B. Simpson (Western Australia)	1960-61	15	26	2	1,541	221*	4	9	64.21
B.A. Richards (South Australia)	1970-71	10	16	2	1,538	356	6	3	109.85
G. Boycott (MCC)	1970-71	13	22	6	1,535	173	6	7	95.93
G.A. Faulkner (South Africans)	1910-11	14	27	1	1,534	204	3	13	59.00
R.B. Simpson (New South Wales)	1963-64	14	25	2	1,524	359	4	4	66.26
E.J. Barlow (South Africans)	1963-64	14	25	2	1,523	209	6	4	66.21
G.S. Chappell (Queensland)	1980-81	14	22	2	1,502	204	5	6	75.10

1,000 RUNS IN A SEASON

12 Times: D. G. Bradman 1928-29 (1,690), 1929-30 (1,586), 1930-31 (1,422), 1931-32 (1,403), 1932-33 (1,171), 1933-34 (1,192), 1935-36 (1,173), 1936-37 (1,552), 1937-38 (1,437), 1939-40 (1,475), 1946-47 (1,032), 1947-48 (1,296).

6 Times: I. M. Chappell 1965-66 (1,019), 1968-69 (1,476), 1970-71 (1,210), 1971-72 (1,140), 1973-74 (1,074), 1975-76 (1,310).

5 Times: G. S. Chappell 1973-74 (1,288), 1974-75 (1,484), 1975-76 (1,547), 1979-80 (1,066), 1980-81 (1,502); A. R. Border 1978-79 (1,220), 1982-83 (1,081), 1985-86 (1,247), 1986-87 (1,002), 1987-88 (1,164); D. S. Lehmann 1989-90 (1,142), 1993-94 (1,087), 1994-95 (1,104), 1995-96 (1,237), 1999-00 (1,142); G. S. Blewett 1993-94 (1,036), 1995-96 (1,173), 1998-99 (1,187), 2000-01 (1,162), 2001-02 (1,025); M. L. Hayden 1991-92 (1,028), 1992-93 (1,249), 1993-94 (1,136), 2001-02 (1,243), 2003-04 (1,022); M. T. G. Elliott 1994-95 (1,029), 1995-96 (1,233), 1998-99 (1,014), 1997-98 (1,108), 2001-02 (1,030).

4 Times: R. B. Simpson 1960-61 (1,541), 1962-63 (1,337), 1963-64 (1,524), 1967-68 (1,082); W. M. Lawry 1960-61 (1,042), 1963-64 (1,340), 1965-66 (1,445), 1968-69 (1,140); J. L. Langer 1993-94 (1,198), 1997-98 (1,075), 1999-00 (1,028), 2003-04 (1,030).

3 Times: A. R. Morris 1946-47 (1,234), 1948-49 (1,069), 1950-51 (1,332); D. W. Hookes 1982-83 (1,424), 1985-86 (1,001), 1987-88 (1,149); J. D. Siddons 1987-88 (1,077), 1990-91 (1,034), 1992-93 (1,190); M. L. Love 1994-95 (1,097), 2001-02 (1,189), 2002-03 (1,120); S. M. Katich 1998-99 (1,039), 2000-01 (1,282), 2003-04 (1,249).

MOST RUNS ON AN AUSTRALIAN OVERSEAS TOUR

		Season	M	I	NO	R	HS	100s	50s	Avge
D. G. Bradman.....	England	1930	27	36	6	2,960	334	10	5	98.66
V. T. Trumper	England	1902	36	53	0	2,570	128	11	11	48.49
D. G. Bradman.....	England	1938	20	26	5	2,429	278	13	5	115.66
D. G. Bradman.....	England	1948	23	31	4	2,428	187	11	8	89.92
W. Bardsley.......	England	1912	36	52	6	2,365	184*	8	9	51.41
C. G. Macartney....	England	1921	31	41	2	2,317	345	8	6	59.41
C. G. Macartney....	England	1912	33	49	1	2,187	208	6	8	45.56
S. J. McCabe	England	1934	26	37	7	2,078	240	8	7	69.26
W. Bardsley.......	England	1909	33	49	4	2,072	219	6	7	46.04
M. A. Noble........	England	1905	31	46	2	2,053	267	6	13	46.66
R. N. Harvey	England	1953	25	35	4	2,040	202*	10	5	65.80
D. G. Bradman.....	England	1934	22	27	3	2,020	304	7	6	84.16
W. M. Lawry	England	1961	23	39	6	2,019	165	9	7	61.18
W. Bardsley.......	England	1921	30	41	4	2,005	209	8	10	54.18

Most in countries other than England:

R. N. Harvey	South Africa	1949-50	19	25	5	1,526	178	8	4	76.30
A. R. Border	India	1979-80	15	28	3	1,423	178	5	4	56.92
G. S. Chappell ...	West Indies	1972-73	10	17	1	1,109	154	4	6	69.31
W. M. Woodfull ..	New Zealand	1927-28	6	9	3	781	284	3	2	130.16
A. R. Border	Pakistan	1979-80	5	9	3	674	178	3	1	112.33
W. Bardsley.....	North America	1913-14	5	6	2	437	142*	3	0	109.25
D. S. Lehmann.....	Sri Lanka	2003-04	4	7	0	509	153	3	1	72.71
S. R. Waugh	Zimbabwe	1999-00	2	3	1	339	161	2	0	169.50

LEADING BATSMEN IN EACH AUSTRALIAN SEASON
(Qualification for top of averages: 8 completed innings)

Season	Leading Scorer	Runs	Avge	Top of Averages	Runs	Avge
1850-51	T. F. Hamilton (Vic)	45	22.50	n/a		
1851-52	T. F. Hamilton (Vic)	84	42.00	n/a		
1853-54	G. Cavenagh (Vic)	45	22.50	n/a		
1854-55	no games played					
1855-56	{ J. J. McKone (NSW)	18	18.00	n/a		
	{ R. Driver (NSW)	18	9.00	n/a		
1856-57	G. H. B. Gilbert (NSW)	33	16.50	n/a		
1857-58	T. W. Wills (Vic)	94	23.50	n/a		
1858-59	O. W. Lewis (Vic)	53	26.50	n/a		
1859-60	T. W. Wills (Vic)	24	12.00	n/a		
1860-61	J. M. Bryant (Vic)	32	16.00	n/a		
1861-62	W. Caffyn (England)	88	88.00	n/a		
1862-63	D. D'Arcy (NSW)	51	51.00	n/a		
1863-64	T. Lockyer (England)	84	84.00	n/a		
1864-65	no games played					
1865-66	E. J. Gregory (NSW)	61	30.50	n/a		
1866-67	S. Cosstick (Vic)	29	14.50	n/a		
1867-68	R. W. Wardill (Vic)	155	155.00	n/a		
1868-69	J. Phillips (Vic)	133	44.33	n/a		
1869-70	C. S. Gordon (Vic)	143	71.50	n/a		
1870-71	A. R. Loughnan (Vic)	71	23.67	n/a		
1871-72	N. F. D. Thomson (NSW)	46	23.00	n/a		
1872-73	J. L. A. Arthur (Tas)	86	28.67	n/a		
1873-74	no games played					
1874-75	C. Bannerman (NSW)	113	113.00	n/a		
1875-76	D. W. Gregory (NSW)	116	38.67	n/a		
1876-77	C. Bannerman (NSW)	243	48.60	n/a		
1877-78	N. F. D. Thomson (NSW)	101	33.67	n/a		
1878-79	G. Ulyett (England)	306	34.00	G. Ulyett (England)	306	34.00
1879-80	A. C. Bannerman (NSW)	103	25.75	n/a		
1880-81	T. P. Horan (Vic)	318	35.33	H. H. Massie (NSW)	299	37.38
1881-82	W. L. Murdoch (NSW)	679	61.73	W. L. Murdoch (NSW)	679	61.73
1882-83	A. C. Bannerman (NSW)	434	54.25	A. C. Bannerman (NSW)	434	54.25
1883-84	W. L. Murdoch (NSW)	567	113.40	n/a		
1884-85	W. Barnes (England)	520	43.33	W. Barnes (England)	520	43.33
1885-86	J. McIlwraith (Vic)	315	78.75	n/a		
1886-87	A. Shrewsbury (England)	721	48.07	A. Shrewsbury (England)	721	48.07
1887-88	H. Moses (NSW)	815	62.69	H. Moses (NSW)	815	62.69
1888-89	G. H. S. Trott (Vic)	507	39.00	G. H. S. Trott (Vic)	507	39.00
1889-90	J. J. Lyons (SAust)	254	63.50	n/a		
1890-91	G. Giffen (SAust)	275	91.67	n/a		
1891-92	J. J. Lyons (SAust)	557	55.70	J. J. Lyons (SAust)	557	55.70
1892-93	G. Giffen (SAust)	468	58.50	G. Giffen (SAust)	468	58.50
1893-94	G. Giffen (SAust)	526	75.14	G. Giffen (SAust)	526	75.14
1894-95	A. Ward (England)	916	41.64	A. E. Stoddart (England)	870	51.18
1895-96	H. Donnan (NSW)	626	69.56	H. Donnan (NSW)	626	69.56
1896-97	J. J. Lyons (SAust)	404	57.71	G. H. S. Trott (Vic)	323	40.38
1897-98	C. Hill (SAust)	1,196	66.44	C. Hill (SAust)	1,196	66.44
1898-99	V. T. Trumper (NSW)	873	62.36	C. Hill (SAust)	841	64.69
1899-00	V. T. Trumper (NSW)	721	72.10	V. T. Trumper (NSW)	721	72.10
1900-01	C. Hill (SAust)	620	103.33	n/a		
1901-02	C. Hill (SAust)	1,035	51.75	A. C. MacLaren (England)	929	58.06
1902-03	R. A. Duff (NSW)	786	87.33	R. A. Duff (NSW)	786	87.33
1903-04	V. T. Trumper (NSW)	990	55.00	M. A. Noble (NSW)	961	56.33
1904-05	W. W. Armstrong (Vic)	460	57.50	W. W. Armstrong (Vic)	460	57.50
1905-06	J. R. M. Mackay (NSW)	902	112.75	J. R. M. Mackay (NSW)	902	112.75
1906-07	A. J. Y. Hopkins (NSW)	617	56.09	A. J. Y. Hopkins (NSW)	617	56.09

Season	Leading Scorer	Runs	Avge	Top of Averages	Runs	Avge
1907-08	J. Hardstaff sr (MCC)	1,360	52.30	F. A. Tarrant (Vic)	762	76.20
1908-09	V. S. Ransford (Vic)	825	103.13	V. S. Ransford (Vic)	825	103.13
1909-10	H. H. L. Kortlang (Vic)	656	131.20	C. McKenzie (Vic)	377	47.13
1910-11	G. A. Faulkner (SAf)	1,534	59.00	V. T. Trumper (NSW)	1,246	69.22
1911-12	W. Rhodes (MCC)	1,098	54.90	R. B. Minnett (NSW)	882	63.00
1912-13	V. T. Trumper (NSW)	843	84.30	V. T. Trumper (NSW)	843	84.30
1913-14	C. G. Macartney (NSW)	892	111.50	C. G. Macartney (NSW)	892	111.50
1914-15	J. Ryder (Vic)	445	74.17	C. E. Pellew (SAust)	287	35.88
1915-16	no games played					
1916-17	no games played					
1917-18	no games played					
1918-19	W. W. Armstrong (Vic)	249	83.00	n/a		
1919-20	R. L. Park (Vic)	648	72.00	R. L. Park (Vic)	648	72.00
1920-21	E. H. Hendren (MCC)	1,178	62.00	W. W. Armstrong (Vic)	1,069	89.08
1921-22	F. A. O'Keefe (Vic)	708	118.00	H. S. B. Love (NSW)	424	43.00
1922-23	A. P. F. Chapman (MCC)	782	65.17	A. J. Richardson (SAust)	758	75.80
1923-24	W. H. Ponsford (Vic)	777	111.00	F. C. Thompson (Qld)	397	49.63
1924-25	H. Sutcliffe (MCC)	1,250	69.44	A. F. Kippax (NSW)	853	77.55
1925-26	A. J. Richardson (SAust)	904	50.22	C. G. Macartney (NSW)	795	88.33
1926-27	W. H. Ponsford (Vic)	1,229	122.90	W. H. Ponsford (Vic)	1,229	122.90
1927-28	W. H. Ponsford (Vic)	1,217	152.12	W. H. Ponsford (Vic)	1,217	152.12
1928-29	D. G. Bradman (NSW)	1,690	93.88	D. G. Bradman (NSW)	1,690	93.88
1929-30	D. G. Bradman (NSW)	1,586	113.28	D. G. Bradman (NSW)	1,586	113.28
1930-31	D. G. Bradman (NSW)	1,422	79.00	D. G. Bradman (NSW)	1,422	79.00
1931-32	D. G. Bradman (NSW)	1,403	116.91	D. G. Bradman (NSW)	1,403	116.91
1932-33	H. Sutcliffe (MCC)	1,318	73.22	H. Sutcliffe (MCC)	1,318	73.22
1933-34	D. G. Bradman (NSW)	1,192	132.44	D. G. Bradman (NSW)	1,192	132.44
1934-35	J. H. W. Fingleton (NSW)	880	58.67	L. S. Darling (Vic)	634	70.44
1935-36	D. G. Bradman (SAust)	1,173	130.33	D. G. Bradman (SAust)	1,173	130.33
1936-37	D. G. Bradman (SAust)	1,552	86.22	D. G. Bradman (SAust)	1,552	86.22
1937-38	D. G. Bradman (SAust)	1,437	89.81	D. G. Bradman (SAust)	1,437	89.81
1938-39	W. A. Brown (Qld)	1,057	105.70	W. A. Brown (Qld)	1,057	105.70
1939-40	D. G. Bradman (SAust)	1,475	122.91	D. G. Bradman (SAust)	1,475	122.91
1940-41	S. G. Barnes (NSW)	1,050	75.00	S. G. Barnes (NSW)	1,050	75.00
1941-42	V. N. Raymer (Qld)	130	130.00	n/a		
1942-43	no games played					
1943-44	no games played					
1944-45	no games played					
1945-46	S. G. Barnes (NSW)	794	88.22	S. G. Barnes (NSW)	794	88.22
1946-47	D. C. S. Compton (MCC)	1,432	65.09	D. G. Bradman (SAust)	1,032	79.38
1947-48	D. G. Bradman (SAust)	1,296	129.60	D. G. Bradman (SAust)	1,296	129.60
1948-49	A. R. Morris (NSW)	1,069	66.81	J. Moroney (NSW)	897	81.55
1949-50	A. R. C. McLean (SAust)	660	50.77	A. R. C. McLean (SAust)	660	50.77
1950-51	A. L. Hassett (Vic)	1,423	64.68	K. R. Miller (NSW)	1,332	78.35
1951-52	A. L. Hassett (Vic)	855	61.07	A. L. Hassett (Vic)	855	61.07
1952-53	R. N. Harvey (Vic)	1,659	63.80	R. N. Harvey (Vic)	1,659	63.80
1953-54	C. C. McDonald (Vic)	857	57.13	K. D. Mackay (Qld)	723	72.30
1954-55	R. N. Harvey (Vic)	1,009	45.86	D. C. S. Compton (MCC)	799	57.07
1955-56	J. W. Burke (NSW)	979	61.19	K. R. Miller (NSW)	638	70.89
1956-57	C. J. Pinch (SAust)	840	52.50	R. N. Harvey (Vic)	836	104.50
1957-58	N. C. O'Neill (NSW)	1,005	83.75	N. C. O'Neill (NSW)	1,005	83.75
1958-59	P. B. H. May (MCC)	1,197	57.00	C. C. McDonald (Vic)	990	61.87
1959-60	R. B. Simpson (WAust)	902	300.66	R. G. Flockton (NSW)	617	77.12
1960-61	R. B. Simpson (WAust)	1,541	64.21	B. C. Booth (NSW)	981	65.40
1961-62	R. B. Simpson (NSW)	704	46.93	B. K. Shepherd (WAust)	808	62.15
1962-63	K. F. Barrington (MCC)	1,451	85.35	K. F. Barrington (MCC)	1,451	85.35
1963-64	R. B. Simpson (NSW)	1,524	66.26	B. C. Booth (NSW)	1,180	90.76
1964-65	S. C. Trimble (Qld)	984	57.87	W. M. Lawry (Vic)	848	84.80
1965-66	W. M. Lawry (Vic)	1,445	72.25	R. M. Cowper (Vic)	1,418	74.63
1966-67	L. E. Favell (SAust)	847	49.82	N. C. O'Neill (NSW)	815	67.91

Season	Leading Scorer	Runs	Avge	Top of Averages	Runs	Avge
1967-68	R. B. Simpson (NSW)	1,082	56.94	A. P. Sheahan (Vic)	973	64.86
1968-69	I. M. Chappell (SAust)	1,476	82.00	I. M. Chappell (SAust)	1,476	82.00
1969-70	G. S. Chappell (SAust)	856	65.84	J. A. Steele (NSW)	677	67.70
1970-71	B. A. Richards (SAust)	1,538	109.85	B. A. Richards (SAust)	1,538	109.85
1971-72	I. M. Chappell (SAust)	1,140	60.00	K. D. Walters (NSW)	895	68.84
1972-73	A. P. Sheahan (Vic)	1,002	83.50	A. P. Sheahan (Vic)	1,002	83.50
1973-74	G. S. Chappell (Qld)	1,288	85.86	G. S. Chappell (Qld)	1,288	85.86
1974-75	G. S. Chappell (Qld)	1,484	61.83	G. S. Chappell (Qld)	1,484	61.83
1975-76	G. S. Chappell (Qld)	1,547	85.94	G. S. Chappell (Qld)	1,547	85.94
1976-77	D. W. Hookes (SAust)	861	71.75	R. D. Robinson (Vic)	828	82.80
1977-78	A. D. Ogilvie (Qld)	1,215	50.62	G. M. Wood (WAust)	678	56.50
1978-79	A. R. Border (NSW)	1,220	55.45	J. K. Moss (Vic)	881	67.77
1979-80	G. S. Chappell (Qld)	1,066	71.06	G. S. Chappell (Qld)	1,066	71.06
1980-81	G. S. Chappell (Qld)	1,502	75.10	G. S. Chappell (Qld)	1,502	75.10
1981-82	K. C. Wessels (Qld)	1,094	60.77	H. A. Gomes (West Indians)	712	89.00
1982-83	D. W. Hookes (SAust)	1,424	64.72	G. N. Yallop (Vic)	1,418	67.52
1983-84	G. N. Yallop (Vic)	1,132	113.20	G. N. Yallop (Vic)	1,132	113.20
1984-85	K. C. Wessels (Qld)	1,020	53.68	G. Shipperd (WAust)	823	68.58
1985-86	A. R. Border (Qld)	1,247	73.35	A. R. Border (Qld)	1,247	73.35
1986-87	G. R. Marsh (WAust)	1,200	48.00	M. R. J. Veletta (WAust)	971	74.69
1987-88	D. C. Boon (Tas)	1,287	67.74	M. D. Crowe (NZ)	715	89.38
1988-89	M. A. Taylor (NSW)	1,241	49.64	I. V. A. Richards (WI)	683	68.30
1989-90	M. A. Taylor (NSW)	1,403	70.15	M. E. Waugh (NSW)	1,009	77.62
1990-91	S. G. Law (Qld)	1,204	75.25	S. G. Law (Qld)	1,204	75.25
1991-92	D. M. Jones (Vic)	1,248	96.00	D. M. Jones (Vic)	1,248	96.00
1992-93	M. L. Hayden (Qld)	1,249	52.04	J. D. Siddons (SAust)	1,190	66.11
1993-94	M. G. Bevan (NSW)	1,312	77.18	M. L. Hayden (Qld)	1,136	126.22
1994-95	D. M. Jones (Vic)	1,251	69.50	D. M. Jones (Vic)	1,251	69.50
1995-96	D. S. Lehmann (SAust)	1,237	56.22	M. T. G. Elliott (Vic)	1,233	68.50
1996-97	J. Cox (Tas)	1,349	67.45	J. L. Langer (WAust)	771	77.10
1997-98	D. F. Hills (Tas)	1,220	55.45	T. M. Moody (WAust)	702	78.00
1998-99	G. S. Blewett (SAust)	1,187	118.70	G. S. Blewett (SAust)	1,187	118.70
1999-00	D. S. Lehmann (SAust)	1,142	63.44	R. T. Ponting (Tas)	582	72.75
2000-01	S. M. Katich (WAust)	1,282	71.22	R. T. Ponting (Tas)	726	80.67
2001-02	M. L. Hayden (Qld)	1,243	82.87	N. J. Astle (New Zealanders)	554	110.80
2002-03	M. L. Love (Qld)	1,120	65.88	M. L. Love (Qld)	1,120	65.88
2003-04	M. T. G. Elliott (Vic)	1,429	79.39	R. S. Dravid (Indians)	620	103.33

HIGHEST AVERAGE IN AN AUSTRALIAN SEASON
(Qualification: 500 runs)

	Season	M	I	NO	R	HS	100s	50s	Avge
R. B. Simpson (Western Australia)	1959-60	5	6	3	902	236*	3	3	300.66
W. H. Ponsford (Victoria)	1922-23	3	4	0	616	429	2	1	154.00
D. G. Bradman (South Australia)	1938-39	7	7	1	919	225	6	0	153.17
C. Hill (South Australia)	1909-10	3	4	0	609	205	3	0	152.25
W. H. Ponsford (Victoria)	1927-28	6	8	0	1,217	437	4	1	152.13
D. G. Bradman (New South Wales)	1933-34	7	11	2	1,192	253	5	3	132.44
H. H. L. Kortlang (Victoria)	1909-10	5	9	4	656	197	2	3	131.20
D. G. Bradman (South Australia)	1935-36	8	9	0	1,173	369	4	1	130.33
D. G. Bradman (South Australia)	1947-48	9	12	2	1,296	201	8	1	129.60
W. M. Woodfull (Victoria)	1927-28	5	7	2	645	191*	2	3	129.00
M. L. Hayden (Queensland)	1993-94	6	12	3	1,136	173*	7	1	126.22
D. G. Bradman (South Australia)	1939-40	9	15	3	1,475	267	5	4	122.92
W. H. Ponsford (Victoria)	1926-27	6	10	0	1,229	352	6	2	122.90
G. S. Blewett (South Australia)	1998-99	7	12	2	1,187	213*	6	1	118.70
F. A. O'Keefe (Victoria)	1921-22	4	6	0	708	180	3	2	118.00
D. G. Bradman (New South Wales)	1931-32	10	13	1	1,403	299*	7	0	116.92
W. L. Murdoch (New South Wales)	1883-84	4	6	1	567	279*	2	1	113.40
D. G. Bradman (New South Wales)	1929-30	11	16	2	1,586	452*	5	4	113.29

	Season	M	I	NO	R	HS	100s	50s	Avge
G. N. Yallop (Victoria)	1983-84	8	11	1	1,132	268	5	2	113.20
J. R. M. Mackay (New South Wales)	1905-06	6	9	1	902	203	5	2	112.75
M. D. Crowe (New Zealanders)	1985-86	4	7	2	562	242*	2	1	112.40
C. G. Macartney (New South Wales)	1913-14	7	9	1	892	201	5	2	111.50
W. H. Ponsford (Victoria)	1923-24	5	8	1	777	248	4	1	111.00
B. A. Richards (South Australia)	1970-71	10	16	2	1,538	356	6	3	109.86
C. L. Badcock (South Australia)	1938-39	7	8	3	540	271*	2	1	108.00
C. G. Macartney (New South Wales)	1912-13	4	7	1	646	154	2	4	107.67
M. G. Bevan (New South Wales)	1998-99	6	10	4	636	202*	3	1	106.00
W. A. Brown (Queensland)	1938-39	7	11	1	1,057	215	3	6	105.70
R. N. Harvey (Victoria)	1956-57	6	10	2	836	209	4	3	104.50
C. Hill (South Australia)	1900-01	4	7	1	620	365*	1	2	103.33
V. S. Ransford (Victoria)	1908-09	6	10	2	825	182	4	2	103.13
J. Ryder (Victoria)	1921-22	4	8	2	609	242	1	4	101.50

AUSTRALIANS WITH 10,000 FIRST-CLASS RUNS

	Career	M	I	NO	R	HS	100s	50s	Avge
D. G. Bradman	1927-28 – 1948-49	234	338	43	28,067	452*	117	69	95.14
A. R. Border	1976-77 – 1995-96	385	625	97	27,131	205	70	142	51.38
M. E. Waugh	1985-86 – 2003-04	368	591	75	26,855	229*	81	133	52.04
K. C. Wessels	1973-74 – 1999-00	316	539	50	25,738	254	66	132	50.50
G. S. Chappell	1966-67 – 1983-84	322	542	72	24,535	247*	74	111	52.20
S. R. Waugh	1984-85 – 2003-04	356	551	88	24,051	216*	79	97	51.95
D. C. Boon	1978-79 – 1999	350	585	53	23,413	227	68	114	44.01
S. G. Law	1988-89 – 2004	304	502	56	22,871	263	67	107	51.28
K. J. Grieves	1945-46 – 1964	490	746	79	22,454	224	29	136	33.66
R. N. Harvey	1946-47 – 1962-63	306	461	35	21,699	231*	67	94	50.93
D. S. Lehmann	1987-88 – 2004	238	405	28	21,506	255	69	97	57.05
R. B. Simpson	1952-53 – 1977-78	257	436	62	21,029	359	60	100	56.22
T. M. Moody	1985-86 – 2000-01	300	501	47	21,001	272	64	94	46.26
J. L. Langer	1991-92 – 2004-05	253	442	42	20,235	274*	64	76	50.59
M. L. Hayden	1991-92 – 2004-05	236	408	41	20,180	380	68	80	54.99
I. M. Chappell	1961-62 – 1979-80	263	448	41	19,680	209	59	96	48.35
W. E. Alley	1945-46 – 1968	400	682	67	19,612	221*	31	92	31.88
D. M. Jones	1981-82 – 1997-98	245	415	45	19,188	324*	55	88	51.86
W. M. Lawry	1955-56 – 1971-72	250	417	49	18,734	266	50	100	50.90
J. Cox	1987-88 – 2003-04	253	448	30	17,970	245	50	78	42.99
F. A. Tarrant	1898-99 – 1936-37	329	541	48	17,952	250*	33	93	36.41
M. A. Taylor	1985-86 – 1998-99	253	435	20	17,415	334*	41	97	41.96
C. Hill	1892-93 – 1924-25	252	416	21	17,213	365*	45	82	43.57
W. Bardsley	1903-04 – 1926-27	250	376	35	17,025	264	53	74	49.92
M. G. Bevan	1989-90 – 2004	215	359	63	17,023	216	59	75	57.51
W. L. Murdoch	1875-76 – 1904	391	679	48	16,953	321	19	85	26.86
V. T. Trumper	1894-95 – 1913-14	255	401	21	16,939	300*	42	87	44.57
A. L. Hassett	1932-33 – 1953-54	216	322	32	16,890	232	59	76	58.24
G. S. Blewett	1991-92 – 2003-04	215	386	26	16,664	268	43	81	45.73
K. D. Walters	1962-63 – 1980-81	259	426	57	16,180	253	45	81	43.84
W. W. Armstrong	1898-99 – 1921-22	269	406	61	16,158	303*	45	57	46.83
V. E. Jackson	1936-37 – 1958	354	605	53	15,698	170	21	72	28.43
S. M. J. Woods	1886 – 1910	401	690	35	15,345	215	19	62	23.42
L. Livingston	1941-42 – 1964	236	384	45	15,269	210	34	78	45.04
S. E. Gregory	1889-90 – 1912	368	587	55	15,192	201	25	65	28.55
C. G. Macartney	1905-06 – 1935-36	249	360	32	15,019	345	49	53	45.78
I. R. Redpath	1961-62 – 1975-76	226	391	34	14,993	261	32	84	41.99
M. J. Slater	1991-92 – 2003-04	216	384	19	14,912	221	36	69	40.85
P. J. P. Burge	1952-53 – 1966-67	233	354	46	14,640	283	38	66	47.53
M. T. G. Elliott	1992-93 – 2004	168	310	26	14,432	203	45	65	50.82

	Career	M	I	NO	R	HS	100s	50s	Avge
K.R. Miller	1937-38 – 1959	226	326	36	14,183	281*	41	63	48.90
R.T. Ponting	1992-93 – 2004	169	282	38	14,034	257	51	54	57.52
M.A. Noble	1893-94 – 1919-20	248	377	34	13,975	284	37	65	40.74
N.C. O'Neill	1955-56 – 1967-68	188	306	34	13,859	284	45	64	50.95
W.A. Brown	1932-33 – 1949-50	189	284	15	13,838	265*	39	65	51.44
W.H. Ponsford	1920-21 – 1934-35	162	235	23	13,819	437	47	42	65.18
W.M. Woodfull	1921-22 – 1934-35	174	245	39	13,388	284	49	58	64.99
G.M. Wood	1976-77 – 1991-92	227	375	42	13,353	186*	25	61	40.09
M.J. Di Venuto	1991-92 – 2003-04	189	331	16	13,331	230	28	84	42.32
M.E.K. Hussey	1994-95 – 2004	149	267	19	12,844	331*	32	58	51.79
A.F. Kippax	1918-19 – 1935-36	175	256	33	12,762	315*	43	45	57.22
K.J. Hughes	1975-76 – 1990-91	216	368	20	12,711	213	26	69	36.52
D.W. Hookes	1975-76 – 1991-92	178	304	16	12,671	306*	32	65	43.39
D.R. Martyn	1990-91 – 2004-05	175	295	40	12,669	238	37	65	49.68
A.R. Morris	1940-41 – 1963-64	162	250	15	12,614	290	46	46	53.67
M.L. Love	1992-93 – 2003-04	159	275	26	12,586	300*	29	60	50.55
C.L. McCool	1939-40 – 1960	251	412	34	12,420	172	18	66	32.85
L.E. Favell	1951-52 – 1969-70	202	347	9	12,379	190	27	68	36.62
S.J. McCabe	1928-29 – 1941-42	182	262	20	11,951	240	29	68	49.38
R.J. Inverarity	1962-63 – 1984-85	223	377	49	11,777	187	26	60	35.90
G.R. Marsh	1977-78 – 1993-94	184	323	25	11,760	355*	33	46	39.46
G. Giffen	1877-78 – 1903-04	251	421	23	11,758	271	18	51	29.54
R. Benaud	1948-49 – 1967-68	259	365	44	11,719	187	23	61	36.50
G.N. Yallop	1972-73 – 1986-87	164	283	30	11,615	268	30	57	45.90
J.D. Siddons	1984-85 – 1999-00	160	280	22	11,587	245	35	53	44.91
C.C. McDonald	1947-48 – 1962-63	192	307	26	11,376	229	24	57	40.48
B.C. Booth	1954-55 – 1968-69	183	283	35	11,265	214*	26	60	45.42
R.W. Marsh	1968-69 – 1983-84	258	396	41	11,067	236	12	54	31.17
K.D. Mackay	1946-47 – 1962-63	201	294	46	10,823	223	23	58	43.64
M.W. Goodwin	1994-95 – 2004	142	249	19	10,733	335*	32	44	46.67
V.Y. Richardson	1918-19 – 1937-38	184	297	12	10,727	231	27	46	37.63
A.E. Trott	1892-93 – 1911	375	602	53	10,696	164	8	43	19.48
J. Darling	1893-94 – 1907-08	202	333	25	10,635	210	19	55	34.52
R.M. Cowper	1959-60 – 1969-70	147	228	31	10,595	307	26	58	53.78
J. Ryder	1912-13 – 1935-36	177	274	37	10,499	295	24	55	44.29
B.J. Hodge	1993-94 – 2004	140	252	23	10,662	302*	33	37	46.56
S.C. Trimble	1959-60 – 1975-76	144	262	16	10,282	252*	26	48	41.79
G.E. Tribe	1945-46 – 1959	308	454	82	10,177	136*	7	48	27.34
G.M. Ritchie	1980-81 – 1991-92	159	255	24	10,171	213*	24	54	44.03
K.R. Stackpole	1959-60 – 1973-74	167	279	22	10,100	207	22	50	39.29

HIGHEST CAREER AVERAGE

(Qualification: 500 runs)

	Career	M	I	NO	R	HS	100s	50s	Avge
D.G. Bradman	1927-28 – 1948-49	234	338	43	28,067	452*	117	69	95.14
H.O. Rock	1924-25 – 1925-26	6	9	1	758	235	3	2	94.75
F.A. O'Keeffe	1919-20 – 1921-22	9	13	0	926	180	3	4	71.23
W.H. Ponsford	1920-21 – 1934-35	162	235	23	13,819	437	47	42	65.18
W.M. Woodfull	1921-22 – 1934-35	174	245	39	13,388	284	49	58	64.99
B.A. Onyons	1918-19 – 1928-29	11	17	1	997	136	6	3	62.31
D.J. Hussey	2002-03 – 2004	27	37	5	1,958	212*	9	5	61.19
A.L. Hassett	1932-33 – 1953-54	216	322	32	16,890	232	59	76	58.24
R.T. Ponting	1992-93 – 2004	169	282	38	14,034	257	51	54	57.52
M.G. Bevan	1989-90 – 2004	215	359	63	17,023	216	59	75	57.51
A.F. Kippax	1918-19 – 1935-36	175	256	33	12,762	315*	43	45	57.22
D.S. Lehmann	1987-88 – 2004	238	405	28	21,506	255	69	97	57.05
R.B. Simpson	1952-53 – 1977-78	257	436	62	21,029	359	60	100	56.22
M.L. Hayden	1991-92 – 2004-05	236	408	41	20,180	380	68	80	54.99

	Career	M	I	NO	R	HS	100s	50s	Avge
S. G. Barnes	1936-37 – 1952-53	110	164	10	8,333	234	26	37	54.11
R. M. Cowper	1959-60 – 1969-70	147	228	31	10,595	307	26	58	53.78
A. R. Morris	1940-41 – 1963-64	162	250	15	12,614	290	46	46	53.67
J. R. Moroney	1945-46 – 1951-52	57	93	16	4,023	217	12	19	52.24
G. S. Chappell	1966-67 – 1983-84	322	542	72	24,535	247*	74	111	52.20
M. E. Waugh	1985-86 – 2003-04	368	591	75	26,855	229*	81	133	52.04
S. R. Waugh	1984-85 – 2003-04	356	551	88	24,051	216*	79	97	51.95
D. M. Jones	1981-82 – 1997-98	245	415	45	19,188	324*	55	88	51.86
M. E. K. Hussey	1994-95 – 2004	149	267	19	12,844	331*	32	58	51.79
S. M. Katich	1996-97 – 2004-05	115	201	30	8,847	228*	26	45	51.74
C. L. Badcock	1929-30 – 1940-41	97	159	16	7,371	325	26	21	51.54
W. A. Brown	1932-33 – 1949-50	189	284	15	13,838	265*	39	65	51.44
A. R. Border	1976-77 – 1995-96	385	625	97	27,131	205	70	142	51.38
J. R. M. Mackay	1902-03 – 1906-07	20	33	2	1,556	203	6	7	50.19
S. G. Law	1988-89 – 2004	304	502	56	22,871	263	67	107	51.28
N. C. O'Neill	1955-56 – 1967-68	188	306	34	13,859	284	45	64	50.95
R. N. Harvey	1946-47 – 1962-63	306	461	35	21,699	231*	67	94	50.93
W. M. Lawry	1955-56 – 1971-72	250	417	49	18,734	266	50	100	50.90
M. T. G. Elliott	1992-93 – 2004	168	310	26	14,432	203	45	65	50.82
J. L. Langer	1991-92 – 2004-05	253	442	42	20,235	274*	64	76	50.59
M. L. Love	1992-93 – 2003-04	159	275	26	12,586	300*	29	60	50.55
K. C. Wessels	1973-74 – 1999-00	316	539	50	25,738	254	66	132	50.50

FASTEST FIFTIES

Mins

11	T. M. Moody	Warwickshire v Glamorgan at Swansea	1990
14	S. J. Pegler	South Africans v Tasmania at Launceston	1910-11
15	D. J. Shepherd	Glamorgan v Australians at Swansea	1961
17	D. W. Hookes	South Australia v Victoria at Adelaide	1982-83
18	J. H. Sinclair	South Australians v Tasmania at Launceston	1910-11
18	A. Cotter	New South Wales v Victoria at Sydney	1911-12
18	A. Symonds	Gloucestershire v Durham at Bristol	1995

FASTEST HUNDREDS

Mins

26	T. M. Moody	Warwickshire v Glamorgan at Swansea	1990
43	R. N. S. Hobbs	Essex v Australians at Chelmsford	1975
43	D. W. Hookes	South Australia v Victoria at Adelaide	1982-83
50	D. R. A. Gehrs	South Australia v Western Australia at Adelaide	1912-13

Balls

34	D. W. Hookes	South Australia v Victoria at Adelaide	1982-83
36	T. M. Moody	Warwickshire v Glamorgan at Swansea	1990

FASTEST DOUBLE-HUNDREDS

Mins

131	V. T. Trumper	Australians v Canterbury at Christchurch	1913-14
135	S. M. J. Woods	Somerset v Susses at Hove	1895
143	C. G. Macartney	Australians v Nottinghamshire at Nottingham	1921
154	F. E. Woolley	MCC v Tasmania at Hobart (TCA)	1911-12
154	D. G. Bradman	South Australia v Western Australia at Perth	1939-40

FASTEST TRIPLE-HUNDREDS

Mins			
198	C. G. Macartney	Australians v Nottingham at Nottingham	1921
209	F. E. Woolley	MCC v Tasmania at Hobart (TCA)	1911-12
213	D. G. Bradman	South Australia v Tasmania at Adelaide	1935-36
285	W. H. Ponsford	Victoria v New South Wales at Melbourne	1926-27
288	D. G. Bradman	New South Wales v Queensland at Sydney	1929-30

MOST RUNS IN A DAY'S PLAY

Runs			
345	C. G. Macartney	Australians v Nottinghamshire at Nottingham	1921
334	W. H. Ponsford	Victoria v New South Wales at Melbourne	1926-27
325	B. A. Richards	South Australia v Western Australia at Perth	1970-71
318	C. W. Gregory	New South Wales v Queensland	1906-07
309	D. G. Bradman	Australia v England at Leeds	1930

LONGEST INNINGS

Mins			
797	L. Hutton	England v Australia at The Oval	1938
766	M. R. J. Veletta	Western Australia v Victoria at Perth	1986-87
762	R. B. Simpson	Australia v England at Manchester	1964
727	R. M. Cowper	Australia v England at Melbourne	1965-66
720	M. A. Taylor	Australia v Pakistan at Peshawar	1998-9

MOST RUNS SCORED OFF AN OVER

Eight Balls

32	(34166066)	D. K. Carmody and I. D. Craig	(off I. W. G. Johnson) A. R. Morris's XI v A. L. Hassett's XI at Melbourne	1953-54

Six Balls

32	(666644)	I. R. Redpath	(off N. Rosendorff) Australians v Orange Free State at Bloemfontein	1969-70
31	(166666)	M. H. Bowditch and M. J. Procter	(off A. A. Mallett) Western Province v Australians at Cape Town	1969-70
30	(466464)	D. G. Bradman	(off A. P. Freeman) Australians v England XI at Folkestone	1934
30	(644646)	T. M. Moody	(off A. E. Tucker) Western Australia v New South Wales at Sydney	1990-91

MOST SIXES IN AN INNINGS

16	A. Symonds	Gloucestershire v Glamorgan at Abergavenny	1995
12	D. M. Jones	Australians v Warwickshire at Birmingham	1989
11	R. Benaud	Australians v T. N. Pearce's XI at Scarborough	1953
11	M. L. Hayden	Australia v Zimbabwe at Perth	2003-04
10	D. W. Hookes	South Australia v New South Wales at Adelaide	1985-86

MOST SIXES IN A MATCH

20   A. Symonds   Gloucestershire v Glamorgan at Abergavenny 1995

SLOWEST FIFTIES

Mins
357   T. E. Bailey   England v Australia at Brisbane 1958-59
316   D. J. Ramshaw   Victoria v New South Wales at Sydney 1991-92
313   D. J. McGlew   South Africa v Australia at Johannesburg (WS) 1957-58
310   B. A. Edgar   New Zealand v Australia at Wellington 1981-82

SLOWEST HUNDREDS

Mins
545   D. J. McGlew   South Africa v Australia at Durban 1957-58
481   G. Shipperd   Tasmania v Victoria at Launceston 1989-90
462   M. J. Greatbatch New Zealand v Australia at Perth 1989-90
460   S. M. Katich   Western Australia v Queensland at Perth 2000-01
449   G. Shipperd   Tasmania v Western Australia at Perth 1989-90

LONGEST TO GET OFF THE MARK

Mins
97   T. G. Evans   England v Australia at Adelaide 1946-47
93   G. J. Denton   Tasmania v Queensland at Hobart (Bel) 1999-00
88   B. P. Nash   Queensland v Tasmania at Hobart (Bel) 2002-03
74   J. T. Murray   England v Australia at Sydney 1962-63
72   C. G. Rackemann   Australia v England at Sydney 1990-91

HIGHEST PARTNERSHIPS FOR EACH WICKET

First wicket

456   W. H. Ponsford and R. E. Mayne, Victoria v Queensland at Melbourne 1923-24
431   M. R. J. Veletta and G. R. Marsh, Western Australia v South Australia at Perth 1989-90
388   K. C. Wessels and R. B. Kerr, Queensland v Victoria at St Kilda 1982-83
382   W. M. Lawry and R. B. Simpson, Australia v West Indies at Bridgetown 1964-65
375   W. M. Woodfull and W. H. Ponsford, Victoria v New South Wales at Melbourne ... 1926-27
374   G. R. Marsh and M. R. J. Veletta, Western Australia v Tamil Nadu at Perth 1988-89
353   M. T. G. Elliott and J. L. Arnberger, Victoria v Tasmania at Richmond 1999-00
337   C. C. McDonald and K. D. Meuleman, Victoria v South Australia at Adelaide 1949-50
331   B. A. Courtice and R. B. Kerr, Queensland v Tasmania at Brisbane 1984-85
329   G. R. Marsh and M. A. Taylor, Australia v England at Nottingham 1989

Second wicket

451   W. H. Ponsford and D. G. Bradman, Australia v England at The Oval 1934
386   G. S. Blewett and D. S. Lehmann, South Australia v Tasmania at Hobart (Bel) 2001-02
382   L. Hutton and M. Leyland, England v Australia at The Oval 1938
378   L. A. Marks and K. D. Walters, New South Wales v South Australia at Adelaide 1964-65
374   R. B. Simpson and R. M. Cowper, Australians v N. E. Transvaal at Pretoria 1966-67
369   C. T. Perren and S. G. Law, Queensland v Western Australia at Brisbane 2003-04
368   W. Rhodes and C. A. G. Russell, MCC v South Australia at Adelaide 1920-21
368* M. L. Hayden and M. L. Love, Queensland v Tasmania at Hobart (Bel) 1995-96
365   M. L. Hayden and M. L. Love, Queensland v Tasmania at Brisbane 1995-96
358   C. McKenzie and H. H. L. Kortlang, Victoria v Western Australia at Perth 1909-10

Third wicket

390* J. M. Wiener and J. K. Moss, Victoria v Western Australia at St Kilda 1981-82
389 W. H. Ponsford and S. J. McCabe, Australians v MCC at Lord's 1934
363 D. G. Bradman and A. F. Kippax, New South Wales v Queensland at Sydney 1933-34
362 W. Bardsley and C. G. Macartney, Australians v Essex at Leyton 1912
356 D. G. Bradman and R. A. Hamence, South Australia v Tasmania at Adelaide 1935-36
355 W. Bardsley and V. S. Ransford, Australians v Essex at Leyton 1909
349 D. M. Jones and T. M. Moody, Australians v Warwickshire at Birmingham 1989
345 W. Bardsley and J. M. Taylor, New South Wales v South Australia at Adelaide 1920-21
341 E. J. Barlow and R. G. Pollock, South Africa v Australia at Adelaide 1963-64
330 G. M. Wood and G. R. Marsh, Western Australia v New South Wales at Sydney 1983-84

Fourth wicket

462* D. W. Hookes and W. B. Phillips, South Australia v Tasmania at Adelaide 1986-87
424 I. S. Lee and S. O. Quin, Victoria v Tasmania at Melbourne 1933-34
388 W. H. Ponsford and D. G. Bradman, Australia v England at Leeds 1934
377 K. R. Miller and J. H. de Courcy, Australians v Comb. Services at Kingston-on-Thames . . 1953
369 C. J. L. Rogers and M. J. North, Western Australia v New South Wales at Perth 2002-03
353 S. R. Tendulkar and V. V. S. Laxman, India v Australia at Sydney 2003-04
336 W. M. Lawry and K. D. Walters, Australia v West Indies at Sydney 1968-69
333 E. H. Hendren and W. R. Hammond, MCC v New South Wales at Sydney 1928-29
325 N. C. O'Neill and B. C. Booth, New South Wales v Victoria at Sydney 1957-58
321 D. R. Martyn and M. W. Goodwin, Western Australia v Tasmania at Perth 2001-02

Fifth wicket

464* M. E. Waugh and S. R. Waugh, New South Wales v Western Australia at Perth 1990-91
405 S. G. Barnes and D. G. Bradman, Australia v England at Sydney 1946-47
397 W. Bardsley and C. Kelleway, New South Wales v South Australia at Sydney 1920-21
385 S. R. Waugh and G. S. Blewett, Australia v South Africa at Johannesburg (WS) 1996-97
377* G. P. Thorpe and M. R. Ramprakash, England XI v South Australia at Adelaide 1998-99
376 V. V. S. Laxman and R. S. Dravid, India v Australia at Kolkata 2000-01
344 M. C. Cowdrey and T. W. Graveney, MCC v South Australia at Adelaide 1962-63
344 B. C. Lara, †P. T. Collins and J. C. Adams, West Indies v Australia at Kingston 1998-99
343 R. I. Maddocks and J. Hallebone, Victoria v Tasmania at Melbourne 1951-52
336 W. H. Ponsford and H. S. B. Love, Victoria v Tasmania at Melbourne 1922-23

Sixth wicket

428 M. A. Noble and W. W. Armstrong, Australians v Sussex at Hove 1902
365 R. D. Jacobs and B. C. Lara, West Indians v Australia A at Hobart (Bel) 2000-01
346 J. H. W. Fingleton and D. G. Bradman, Australia v England at Melbourne 1936-37
332 N. G. Marks and G. Thomas, New South Wales v South Australia at Sydney 1958-59
323 E. H. Hendren and J. W. H. T. Douglas, MCC v Victoria at Melbourne 1920-21
317 D. R. Martyn and A. C. Gilchrist, Australia v South Africa at Johannesburg (WS) . . . 2001-02
298* D. B. Vengsarkar and R. J. Shastri, India v Australia at Bombay 1986-87
290 M. T. G. Elliott and D. S. Berry, Victoria v New South Wales at Sydney 1996-97
289 I. S. Loxton and D. T. Ring, Victoria v Queensland at Melbourne 1946-47
279 A. L. Hassett and E. A. Williams, Australian Services v Prince's XI at Delhi 1945-46

Seventh wicket

347 D. S. Atkinson and C. C. Depeiza, West Indies v Australia at Bridgetown 1954-55
335 C. W. Andrews and E. C. Bensted, Queensland v New South Wales at Sydney 1934-35
273* W. W. Armstrong and J. Darling, Australians v Gentlemen of England at Lord's 1905
268 A. H. Kardar and Imtiaz Ahmed, North Zone v Australian Services at Lahore 1945-46
255 G. Thomas and R. Benaud, New South Wales v Victoria at Melbourne 1961-62
244 W. R. Patrick and C. F. W. Allcott, New Zealanders v South Australia at Sydney 1925-26
232 W. Bruce and H. Trumble, Australians v Oxford and Cambridge Univ. at Portsmouth . . 1893
229 K. J. Schneider and W. A. S. Oldfield, Australians v Canterbury at Christchurch 1927-28
222* N. Deonarine and C. S. Baugh, Carib Beer XI v Australians at Georgetown 2002-03
221 D. T. Lindsay and P. L. van der Merwe, South Africa v Australia at Johannesburg (WS) 1966-67

Eighth wicket

433 V.T. Trumper and A. Sims, Australians v Canterbury at Christchurch 1913-14
270 V.T. Trumper and E.P. Barbour, New South Wales v Victoria at Sydney 1912-13
253 N.J. Astle and A.C. Parore, New Zealand v Australia at Perth 2001-02
243 M.J. Hartigan and C. Hill, Australia v England at Adelaide 1907-08
242* T.J. Zoehrer and K.H. MacLeay, Western Australia v New South Wales at Perth 1990-91
236 R.A. Duff and A.J.Y. Hopkins, New South Wales v Lord Hawke's XI at Sydney . . . 1902-03
222 M.C. Miller and B.E. Young, South Australia v Queensland at Adelaide 2002-03
218 C.G. Macartney and J.D. Scott, New South Wales v Queensland at Sydney 1913-14
215 W.W. Armstrong and R.L. Park, Victoria v South Australia at Melbourne 1919-20
204 W.A.S. Oldfield and C.O. Nicholls, New South Wales v Victoria at Sydney 1927-28

Ninth wicket

232 C. Hill and E. Walkley, South Australia v New South Wales at Adelaide 1900-01
226 C. Kelleway and W.A.S. Oldfield, New South Wales v Victoria at Melbourne 1925-26
225 W.W. Armstrong and E.A.C. Windsor, Australian XI v The Rest at Sydney 1907-08
221 E.F. Waddy and W.P. Howell, New South Wales v South Australia at Adelaide 1904-05
201 E.E.B. Forssberg and H.S.B. Love, New South Wales v Queensland at Sydney 1920-21
172 R.G. Barlow and W. Flowers, Players v Australians at Nottingham 1886
171 D.P.B. Morkel and N.A. Quinn, South Africans v Western Australia at Perth 1931-32
170 T.W. Garrett and T.R. McKibbin, New South Wales v South Australia at Sydney . . . 1896-97
169 C.B. Willis and W.A.S. Oldfield, A.I.F. v Nottinghamshire at Nottingham 1919
168* K.H. MacLeay and V.J. Marks, Western Australia v New South Wales at Perth 1986-87

Tenth wicket

307 A.F. Kippax and J.E.H. Hooker, New South Wales v Victoria at Melbourne 1928-29
211 M. Ellis and T.J. Hastings, Victoria v South Australia at Melbourne 1902-03
169 R.B. Minnett and C.G. McKew, New South Wales v Victoria at Sydney 1911-12
154 F.R. Buttsworth and J.P. Lanigan, Western Australia v Victoria at Perth 1921-22
147 C.G. Macartney and S.C. Everett, Australian XI v Tasmania at Hobart (TCA) 1925-26
145 G.A. Rotherham and J.H. Naumann, Cambridge Univ. v AIF Team at Cambridge . . 1919
138* B.E. McNamara and P.J.S. Alley, New South Wales v Tasmania at Hobart (Bel) 1996-97
136 J.P. O'Halloran and A.E. Johns, Victoria v South Australia at Melbourne 1896-97
135 W.A.S. Oldfield and A.A. Mailey, New South Wales v South Australia at Adelaide . 1923-24
132 R.W. McLeod and C.H. Ross, Victoria v South Australia at Adelaide 1899-00

BOWLING RECORDS

TEN WICKETS IN AN INNINGS

10-43 E. Barratt   The Players v Australians at The Oval 1878
10-66 G. Giffen   Australian XI v The Rest at Sydney 1883-84
10-69 S.M.J. Woods   Cambridge University v C.I. Thornton's XI at Cambridge . . 1890
10-28 W.P. Howell   Australians v Surrey at The Oval 1899
10-42 A.E. Trott   Middlesex v Somerset at Taunton 1900
10-66 A.A. Mailey   Australians v Gloucestershire at Cheltenham 1921
10-37 C.V. Grimmett   Australians v Yorkshire at Sheffield 1930
10-36 T.W. Wall   South Australia v New South Wales at Sydney 1932-33
10-53 J.C. Laker   England v Australia at Manchester 1956
10-88 J.C. Laker   Surrey v Australians at The Oval 1956
10-61 P.J. Allan   Queensland v Victoria at Melbourne 1965-66
10-44 I.J. Brayshaw   Western Australia v Victoria at Perth 1967-68

BEST BOWLING IN AN INNINGS ON DEBUT

9-55	J. Quilty	South Australia v Victoria at Adelaide	1881-82
9-67	H. P. Hay	South Australia v Lord Hawke's XI at Unley	1902-03
8-31	W. Brown	Tasmania v Victoria at Hobart (LRG)	1857-58
8-35	R. Wilson	Queensland v Auckland at Auckland	1896-97
8-36	J. L. Bevan	South Australia v Tasmania at Adelaide	1877-78
8-81	H. V. Hordern	New South Wales v Queensland at Sydney	1905-06
8-111	M. Pierce	New South Wales v South Australia at Adelaide	1892-93

BEST BOWLING IN A MATCH ON DEBUT

15-73	W. Brown	Tasmania v Victoria at Hobart (LRG)	1857-58
14-59	J. L. Bevan	South Australia v Tasmania at Adelaide	1877-78
13-61	T. W. Antill	Victoria v Tasmania at Launceston	1850-51
13-265	M. Pierce	New South Wales v South Australia at Adelaide	1892-93
11-48	S. Cosstick	Victoria v New South Wales at Sydney	1860-61
11-80	J. E. Barrett	Victoria v South Australia at Melbourne	1884-85
11-97	R. Wilson	Queensland v Auckland at Auckland	1896-97
11-103	M. A. Polzin	Queensland v South Australia at Brisbane	1986-87
11-126	D. J. Noonan	New South Wales v Canterbury at Christchurch	1895-96
10-34	G. Elliott	Victoria v New South Wales at Melbourne	1855-56
10-36	J. J. McKone	New South Wales v Victoria at Melbourne	1855-56
10-46	F. D. Stephenson	Tasmania v Victoria at Melbourne	1981-82
10-97	J. Quilty	South Australia v Victoria at Adelaide	1881-82
10-141	R. B. C. Rees	South Australia v Victoria at Melbourne	1903-04
10-145	L. O. Fleetwood -Smith	Victoria v Tasmania at Hobart (TCA)	1931-32
10-226	A. C. Facy	Tasmania v Victoria at Hobart (TCA)	1908-09

MOST WICKETS IN A MATCH BY AUSTRALIANS

17-50	C. T. B. Turner, Australians v England XI at Hastings	1888
17-54	W. P. Howell, Australians v Western Province at Cape Town	1902-03
17-137	J. M. Davison, Canada v United States of America at Fort Lauderdale	2003-04
17-201	G. Giffen, South Australia v Victoria at Adelaide	1885-86
16-65	G. Giffen, Australians v Lancashire at Manchester	1886
16-69	F. A. Tarrant, England XII v Indian XII at Mumbai	1915-16
16-79	C. T. B. Turner, New South Wales v A. Shrewsbury's XI at Sydney	1887-88
16-83	B. Dooland, Nottinghamshire v Essex at Nottingham	1954
16-86	H. V. Hordern, Philadelphia v Jamaica at Kingston	1908-09
16-101	G. Giffen, Australians v Derbyshire at Derby	1886
16-137	R. A. L. Massie, Australia v England at Lord's	1972
16-166	G. Giffen, South Australia v Victoria at Adelaide	1891-92
16-176	F. A. Tarrant, Middlesex v Lancashire at Manchester	1914
16-186	G. Giffen, South Australia v New South Wales at Adelaide	1894-95
16-201	G. Giffen, Australians v Derbyshire at Derby	1886
16-225	J. E. Walsh, Leicestershire v Oxford University at Oxford	1953
16-289	C. V. Grimmett, South Australia v Queensland at Adelaide	1934-35

HAT-TRICKS FOR OR AGAINST AUSTRALIAN TEAMS

G. H. B. Gilbert	New South Wales v Victoria at Melbourne	1857-58
F. R. Spofforth	Australians v MCC at Lord's	1878
J. Robertson	Middlesex v Australians at Lord's	1878
F. R. Spofforth	Australians v Players of England at The Oval	1878
F. R. Spofforth	Australia v England at Melbourne	1878-79
G. Ulyett (4 in 4)	Lord Hawke's XI v New South Wales at Sydney	1878-79
W. A. Humphreys	Sussex v Australians at Hove	1880

G. E. Palmer	Australians v Sussex at Hove	1882
W. Bates	England v Australia at Melbourne	1882-83
W. A. Humphreys	Sussex v Australians at Hove	1884
G. Giffen	Australians v Lancashire at Manchester	1884
F. R. Spofforth	Australians v South of England at The Oval	1884
C. T. B. Turner	New South Wales v Victoria at Melbourne	1886-87
G. Giffen	South Australia v G. F. Vernon's XI at Adelaide	1887-88
J. Briggs	England v Australia at Sydney	1891-92
H. Trumble	Australians v Gloucestershire at Cheltenham	1896
G. Giffen	Australians v Wembley Park XI at Wembley Park	1896
A. D. Pougher	MCC v Australians at Lord's	1896
T. R. McKibbin	Australians v Lancashire at Liverpool	1896
M. A. Noble	New South Wales v Tasmania at Sydney	1898-99
J. T. Hearne	England v Australia at Leeds	1899
H. Trumble	Australia v England at Melbourne	1901-02
A. J. Y. Hopkins	Australians v Cambridge University at Cambridge	1902
W. P. Howell (4 in 5)	Australians v Western Province at Cape Town	1902-03
W. W. Armstrong	Victoria v New South Wales at Melbourne	1902-03
T. H. Howard (4 in 5)	New South Wales v Queensland at Sydney	1902-03
H. Hay	South Australia v Lord Hawke's XI at Unley	1902-03
A. J. Y. Hopkins	New South Wales v South Australia at Sydney	1903-04
H. Trumble	Australia v England at Melbourne	1903-04
W. P. Howell	Australians v New Zealand XI at Wellington	1904-05
G. A. Wilson	Worcestershire v Australians at Worcester	1905
T. J. Matthews	Victoria v Tasmania at Launceston	1908-09
J. A. Newman	Hampshire v Australians at Southampton	1909
T. J. Matthews (1st inns)	Australia v South Africa at Manchester	1912
T. J. Matthews (2nd inns)	Australia v South Africa at Manchester	1912
T. J. Matthews	Australians v Philadelphia at Philadelphia	1912-13
J. N. Crawford	South Australia v Western Australia at Adelaide	1912-13
C. Kelleway	New South Wales v Queensland at Brisbane	1913-14
J. Horsley	Derbyshire v AIF Team at Derby	1919
J. W. H. T. Douglas	MCC v New South Wales at Sydney	1920-21
A. P. Freeman	MCC v South Australia at Adelaide	1922-23
H. Ironmonger	Victoria v MCC at Melbourne	1924-25
H. I. Ebeling	Victoria v Queensland at Melbourne	1928-29
J. E. H. Hooker (4 in 4)	New South Wales v Victoria at Sydney	1928-29
C. V. Grimmett	South Australia v Queensland at Brisbane (Ex)	1928-29
F. L. Morton	Victoria v Tasmania at Melbourne	1931-32
H. J. Enthoven	Middlesex v Australians at Lord's	1934
R. K. Oxenham	Australians v All Ceylon at Colombo (PSS)	1935-36
M. G. Waite	South Australia v MCC at Adelaide	1935-36
B. Dooland	South Australia v Victoria at Melbourne	1945-46
C. R. Rangachari	Indians v Tasmania at Hobart (TCA)	1947-48
A. K. Walker	New South Wales v Queensland at Sydney	1948-49
H. J. Tayfield	South Africans v Victoria at Melbourne	1952-53
J. C. Treanor	New South Wales v Queensland at Brisbane	1954-55
L. F. Kline	Australia v South Africa at Cape Town	1957-58
G. F. Rorke	New South Wales v Queensland at Sydney	1958-59
L. R. Gibbs	West Indies v Australia at Adelaide	1960-61
A. K. Davidson	New South Wales v Western Australia at Perth	1962-63
D. Robins (4 in 4)	South Australia v New South Wales at Adelaide	1965-66
R. F. Surti	Queensland v Western Australia at Perth	1968-69
R. A. Woolmer	MCC v Australians at Lord's	1975
W. Prior	South Australia v New South Wales at Adelaide	1975-76
A. T. Sincock	South Australia v Indians at Adelaide	1977-78
L. S. Pascoe	New South Wales v South Australia at Adelaide	1980-81
P. M. Clough	Tasmania v New South Wales at Hobart (TCA)	1982-83
J. R. Thomson	Queensland v Western Australia at Brisbane	1984-85
D. R. Gilbert	New South Wales v Victoria at Sydney	1984-85
G. S. Le Roux	South Africans v Australian XI at Johannesburg (WS)	1985-86
C. E. B. Rice	South Africans v Australian XI at Johannesburg (WS)	1985-86

J. N. Maguire	Australians v Eastern Province at Port Elizabeth	1986-87
C. A. Walsh	West Indies v Australia at Brisbane	1988-89
M. G. Hughes	Australia v West Indies at Perth	1988-89
W. K. M. Benjamin	Leicestershire v Australians at Leicester	1989
W. J. Holdsworth	Australians v Derbyshire at Derby	1993
D. W. Fleming	Australia v Pakistan at Rawalpindi	1994-95
S. K. Warne	Australia v England at Melbourne	1994-95
S. C. G. MacGill	New South Wales v New Zealanders at Newcastle	1997-98
D. Gough	England v Australia at Sydney	1998-99
M. S. Kasprowicz	Queensland v Victoria at Brisbane	1998-99
M. W. H. Inness	Victoria v New South Wales at Melbourne	1999-00
G. D. McGrath	Australia v West Indies at Perth	2000-01
Harbhajan Singh	India v Australia at Kolkata	2000-01
I. J. Harvey	Victoria v South Australia at Adelaide	2001-02
S. J. Jurgensen	Tasmania v New South Wales at Hobart (Bel)	2001-02
S. M. Harwood	Victoria v Tasmania at Melbourne	2002-03
J. J. C. Lawson	West Indies v Australia at Bridgetown	2002-03

FOUR WICKETS IN FOUR BALLS

G. Ulyett	Lord Hawke's XI v New South Wales at Sydney	1878-79
J. E. H. Hooker	New South Wales v Victoria at Sydney	1928-29
D. Robins	South Australia v New South Wales at Adelaide	1965-66

FOUR WICKETS IN FIVE BALLS

F. S. Jackson	Yorkshire v Australians at Leeds	1902
W. P. Howell	Australians v Western Province at Cape Town	1902-03
T. H. Howard	New South Wales v Queensland at Sydney	1902-03
D. J. Hickey	South Australia v England XI at Adelaide	1990-9

MOST HAT-TRICKS

5 times: F. A. Tarrant
4 times: F. R. Spofforth, T. J. Matthews
3 times: G. Giffen, E. A. McDonald, H. Trumble

MOST WICKETS IN AN AUSTRALIAN SEASON

	Season	M	B	Mdns	R	W	BB	5Wi	10W/m	Avge
C. T. B Turner (NSW)	1887-88	12	4,267	473	1,441	106	8-39	13	5	13.59
G. Giffen (S Aust)	1894-95	11	4,787	196	2,097	93	8-77	12	4	22.54
C. V. Grimmett (S Aust)	1929-30	11	3,795	51	1,943	82	7-136	9	3	23.69
R. Benaud (NSW)	1958-59	13	4,467	142	1,579	82	7-32	6	1	19.25
A. A. Mailey (NSW)	1920-21	10	2,993	45	1,825	81	9-121	8	3	22.53
M. W. Tate (MCC)	1924-25	14	4,018	93	1,464	77	7-74	7	2	19.01
C. V. Grimmett (S Aust)	1931-32	12	4,096	166	1,535	77	7-83	7	1	19.93
E. Jones (S Aust)	1897-98	11	3,529	121	1,653	76	7-80	9	3	21.75
R. M. Hogg (S Aust)	1978-79	14	3,483	97	1,249	76	6-74	6	2	16.43
C. V. Grimmett (S Aust)	1930-31	11	3,524	99	1,417	74	7-87	7	1	19.14
C. V. Grimmett (S Aust)	1939-40	9	3,543	57	1,654	73	6-118	10	3	22.65
C. V. Grimmett (S Aust)	1928-29	10	5,152	135	2,432	71	6-109	5	0	34.25
C. T. B. Turner (NSW)	1886-87	7	2,145	273	538	70	8-32	8	3	7.68
W. J. Whitty (S Aust)	1910-11	11	2,957	109	1,419	70	6-17	4	0	20.27
H. J. Tayfield (SAf)	1952-53	14	4,836	123	1,954	70	7-71	5	1	27.91
D. K. Lillee (W Aust)	1976-77	11	2,832	59	1,368	70	6-26	8	4	19.54
C. R. Miller (Tas)	1997-98	12	3,896	172	1,749	70	7-49	5	2	24.99

50 WICKETS IN AN AUSTRALIAN SEASON

10 Times: C. V. Grimmett 59 (1924-25), 59 (1925-26), 71 (1928-29), 82 (1929-30), 74 (1930-31), 77 (1931-32), 55 (1932-33), 66 (1933-34), 58 (1934-35), 73 (1939-40).
6 Times: D. K. Lillee 56 (1972-73), 62 (1974-75), 62 (1975-76), 70 (1976-77), 69 (1980-81), 59 (1983-84).
5 Times: L. O. Fleetwood-Smith 50 (1932-33), 53 (1933-34), 63 (1934-35), 53 (1936-37), 64 (1937-38); A. A. Mallett 54 (1971-72), 62 (1972-73), 57 (1974-75), 56 (1975-76), 53 (1979-80); W. J. O'Reilly 62 (1932-33), 51 (1936-37), 64 (1937-38), 55 (1939-40), 55 (1940-41).
4 Times: C. J. McDermott 58 (1986-87), 54 (1989-90), 67 (1990-91), 60 (1991-92).
3 Times: G. D. McKenzie 51 (1962-63), 53 (1967-68), 60 (1968-69); A. A. Mailey 81 (1920-21), 55 (1922-23), 59 (1924-25); C. D. Matthews 57 (1986-87), 57 (1987-88), 53 (1991-92); J. R. Thomson 62 (1974-75), 62 (1975-76), 57 (1977-78); M. S. Kasprowicz 51 (1992-93), 64 (1995-96), 51 (2001-02); S. C. G. MacGill 50 (1997-98), 60 (2002-03), 58 (2003-04).

MOST WICKETS ON AN AUSTRALIAN OVERSEAS TOUR

			M	O	Mdns	R	W	BB	5W/i	10W/m	Avge
C. T. B. Turner	England	1888	36	2,427.2	1,127	3,307	283	9-15	31	12	11.69
F. R. Spofforth	England	1884	31	1,538.2	646	2,564	201	8-62	24	11	12.75
J. J. Ferris	England	1888	37	2,080.1	937	2,934	199	8-41	17	3	14.74
J. J. Ferris	England	1890	31	1,545.2	628	2,657	186	7-16	15	5	14.28
C. T. B. Turner	England	1890	31	1,500.1	652	2,526	178	7-23	16	4	14.19
F. R. Spofforth	England	1882	30	1,470	646	2,079	157	9-51	16	6	13.24
G. Giffen	England	1886	35	1,673.2	710	2,674	154	9-60	13	5	17.36
C. T. B. Turner	England	1893	26	1,079	413	2,018	148	8-95	16	5	13.64
H. Trumble	England	1896	30	1,140.1	380	2,340	148	7-67	11	5	15.81
C. V. Grimmett	England	1930	26	1,015.1	262	2,427	144	10-37	15	5	16.85
H. Trumble	England	1899	32	1,246.3	432	2,618	142	8-35	10	3	18.44
E. A. McDonald	England	1921	26	809.2	158	2,284	138	8-41	9	3	16.55
H. Trumble	England	1902	20	912	292	1,921	137	9-39	13	7	14.02
E. Jones	England	1899	28	1,163.2	331	2,849	135	7-31	10	4	21.10
A. A. Mailey	England	1921	28	800	103	2,595	133	10-66	7	1	19.51
G. E. Palmer	England	1884	30	1,214.3	446	2,099	130	7-74	13	5	16.14
A. A. Mailey	England	1926	27	816	162	2,437	126	9-86	12	4	19.34
H. F. Boyle	England	1882	27	1,101.2	488	1,523	125	7-32	13	3	12.18
T. W. Garrett	England	1886	34	1,654.1	778	2,221	123	6-22	5	1	18.06
J. V. Saunders	England	1902	25	710	160	2,085	123	6-9	10	3	16.95
W. W. Armstrong	England	1905	30	990.4	298	2,221	122	8-50	9	2	18.20
E. Jones	England	1896	29	868.3	282	1,940	121	8-39	7	1	16.03

Most in countries other than England:

			M	O	Mdns	R	W	BB	5W/i	10W/m	Avge
R. Benaud	SAf	1957-58	18	743.6	187	2,057	106	7-46	11	2	19.40
R. K. Oxenham	Ind	1935-36	11	303.3	89	555	75	7-13	8	4	7.40
W. W. Armstrong	NZ	1913-14	8	312.0	81	789	52	7-17	7	1	15.17
S. W. Austin	NZ	1893-94	7	1,747.0	85	612	52	8-14	6	1	11.77
P. I. Philpott	WI	1964-65	9	449.0	99	1,207	49	6-86	2	0	24.63
R. J. Bright	Pak	1979-80	5	230.2	72	558	29	7-87	4	2	19.24
J. N. Crawford	NAmer	1913-14	5	116.2	21	359	33	6-40	3	0	10.88
S. K. Warne	SL	2003-04	4	197.2	43	621	29	5-43	4	2	21.41
D. R. Gilbert	Zim	1985-86	2	68.0	14	215	15	7-43	2	1	14.33

LEADING BOWLERS IN EACH AUSTRALIAN SEASON

(Qualification for top of averages: 20 wickets)

Season	Leading Wicket-Taker	W	Avge	Top of Averages	W	Avge
1850-51	T. W. Antill (Vic)	13	4.00	n/a		
1851-52	W. Henty (Tas)	10	10.00	n/a		
1852-53	no games played					
1853-54	R. M. McDowall (Tas)	8	6.25	n/a		
1854-55	no games played					
1855-56	J. J. McKone (NSW)	10	3.60	n/a		
	G. Elliott (Vic)	10	3.20	n/a		
1856-57	T. W. Wills (Vic)	10	6.50	n/a		
1857-58	T. W. Wills (Vic)	26	5.03	T. W. Wills (Vic)	26	5.03
1858-59	T. W. Wills (Vic)	11	4.45	n/a		
1859-60	T. W. Wills (Vic)	9	4.33	n/a		
	G. B. Richardson (NSW)	9	6.00	n/a		
1860-61	S. Cosstick (Vic)	11	4.36	n/a		
1861-62	G. Bennett (The World)	14	8.21	n/a		
1862-63	C. Lawrence (NSW)	14	5.21	n/a		
1863-64	E. M. Grace (Anderson's XI)	9	7.67	n/a		
1864-65	no games played					
1865-66	S. Cosstick (NSW)	8	13.63	n/a		
	J. Conway (Vic)	8	15.25	n/a		
1866-67	D. W. Gregory (NSW)	7	9.57	n/a		
1867-68	T. W. Wills (Vic)	9	16.56	n/a		
1868-69	S. Cosstick (Vic)	23	5.42	S. Cosstick (Vic)	23	5.42
1869-70	S. Cosstick (Vic)	10	7.70	n/a		
1870-71	C. A. Reid (Vic)	16	9.50	n/a		
1871-72	F. E. Allan (Vic)	13	4.62	n/a		
1872-73	S. Cosstick (Vic)	23	6.52	S. Cosstick (Vic)	23	6.52
1873-74	no games played					
1874-75	J. Coates (NSW)	15	10.67	n/a		
1875-76	E. Evans (NSW)	21	5.62	E. Evans (NSW)	21	5.62
1876-77	A. Shaw (Lillywhite's XI)	17	11.76	n/a		
1877-78	E. Evans (NSW)	18	10.72	n/a		
1878-79	T. Emmett (Eng)	44	11.84	T. Emmett (Eng)	44	11.84
1879-80	W. H. Cooper (Vic)	12	10.75	n/a		
1880-81	E. Evans (NSW)	32	11.25	E. Evans (NSW)	32	11.25
1881-82	G. E. Palmer (Vic)	47	21.55	W. Bates (Eng)	30	17.33
1882-83	G. E. Palmer (Vic)	51	11.53	H. F. Boyle (Vic)	24	11.00
1883-84	G. E. Palmer (Vic)	29	17.51	G. E. Palmer (Vic)	29	17.51
1884-85	R. Peel (England)	35	19.22	W. Barnes (England)	26	13.23
1885-86	F. R. Spofforth (NSW)	18	15.22	n/a		
1886-87	C. T. B. Turner (NSW)	70	7.68	C. T. B. Turner (NSW)	70	7.68
1887-88	C. T. B. Turner (NSW)	106	13.59	W. Attewell (Eng)	55	10.72
1888-89	J. J. Ferris (NSW)	36	15.83	G. Giffen (SAust)	22	12.95
1889-90	H. Trumble (Vic)	29	14.21	H. Trumble (Vic)	29	14.21
1890-91	J. Phillips (Vic)	25	10.00	J. Phillips (Vic)	25	10.00
1891-92	G. Giffen (SAust)	50	17.30	W. Attewell (Eng)	44	13.02
1892-93	G. Giffen (SAust)	33	23.00	H. Trumble (Vic)	22	13.55
1893-94	C. T. B. Turner (NSW)	30	12.30	C. T. B. Turner (NSW)	30	12.30
1894-95	G. Giffen (SAust)	93	22.54	T. R. McKibbin (NSW)	44	16.66
1895-96	T. R. McKibbin (NSW)	46	23.87	E. Jones (SAust)	31	17.67
1896-97	T. R. McKibbin (NSW)	44	14.89	T. R. McKibbin (NSW)	44	14.89
1897-98	E. Jones (SAust)	76	21.75	W. Roche (Vic)	33	20.73
1898-99	E. Jones (SAust)	45	27.53	C. E. McLeod (Vic)	36	17.86
1899-00	M. A. Noble (NSW)	37	20.65	M. A. Noble (NSW)	37	20.65
1900-01	J. V. Saunders (Vic)	29	17.14	J. V. Saunders (Vic)	29	17.14
	J. P. F. Travers (SAust)	29	20.76			
1901-02	L. C. Braund (Eng)	62	28.69	S. F. Barnes (Eng)	41	16.49
1902-03	J. V. Saunders (Vic)	32	20.81	L. W. Pye (NSW)	23	19.30

Season	Leading Wicket-Taker	W	Avge	Top of Averages	W	Avge
1903-04	W. Rhodes (MCC)	65	16.23	A. Cotter (NSW)	30	13.47
1904-05	F.B. Collins (Vic)	27	23.37	F.B. Collins (Vic)	27	23.37
1905-06	G.L. Garnsey (NSW)	36	21.03	J.D.A. O'Connor (NSW)	33	21.70
1906-07	G.L. Garnsey (NSW)	32	21.94	M.A. Noble (NSW)	24	13.92
1907-08	J.V. Saunders (Vic)	66	24.04	S.F. Barnes (Eng)	54	21.94
	J.N. Crawford (MCC)	66	25.19			
1908-09	J.D.A. O'Connor (SAust)	40	23.00	A.H. Christian (WAust)	25	17.28
1909-10	J.V. Saunders (Vic)	49	17.33	J.D. Scott (NSW)	25	12.56
1910-11	W.J. Whitty (SAust)	70	20.27	H.V. Hordern (NSW)	58	14.83
1911-12	F.R. Foster (MCC)	62	20.19	F.R. Foster (MCC)	62	20.19
1912-13	R.J.A. Massie (NSW)	59	18.66	A.A. Mailey (NSW)	21	16.05
1913-14	C. Kelleway (NSW)	45	12.69	C. Kelleway (NSW)	45	12.69
1914-15	H. Ironmonger (Vic)	36	17.53	H. Ironmonger (Vic)	36	17.53
1915-16	no games played					
1916-17	no games played					
1917-18	no games played					
1918-19	E.A. McDonald (Vic)	25	15.72	E.A. McDonald (Vic)	25	15.72
1919-20	H.S.T.L. Hendry (NSW)	29	18.14	H.S.T.L. Hendry (NSW)	29	18.14
1920-21	A.A. Mailey (NSW)	81	22.53	J.M. Gregory (NSW)	43	22.37
1921-22	E.A. McDonald (Vic)	28	21.50	P.H. Wallace (Vic)	20	17.85
1922-23	A.A. Mailey (NSW)	55	21.64	A.E. Liddicut (Vic)	20	21.05
1923-24	A.E.V. Hartkopf (Vic)	26	24.58	A.E.V. Hartkopf (Vic)	26	24.58
	N.L. Williams (SAust)	26	26.88			
1924-25	M.W. Tate (MCC)	77	19.01	R.K. Oxenham (Qld)	22	14.50
1925-26	C.V. Grimmett (SAust)	59	30.41	C.G. Macartney (NSW)	24	18.88
1926-27	N.L. Williams (SAust)	35	32.03	D.D. Blackie (Vic)	33	24.64
1927-28	C.V. Grimmett (SAust)	42	27.40	D.D. Blackie (Vic)	31	22.23
1928-29	C.V. Grimmett (SAust)	71	34.25	J.C. White (MCC)	65	22.63
1929-30	C.V. Grimmett (SAust)	82	23.69	E.L. A'Beckett (Vic)	27	15.22
1930-31	C.V. Grimmett (SAust)	74	19.14	H. Ironmonger (Vic)	68	14.29
1931-32	C.V. Grimmett (SAust)	77	19.93	L.O. Fleetwood-Smith (Vic)	37	16.27
1932-33	W.J. O'Reilly (NSW)	62	19.95	C.J. Hill (NSW)	22	15.27
1933-34	C.V. Grimmett (SAust)	66	21.83	S.A.J. Smith (Vic)	20	17.90
1934-35	L.O. Fleetwood-Smith (Vic)	63	20.34	H.C. Chilvers (NSW)	46	18.63
1935-36	F.A. Ward (SAust)	50	20.94	T.W. Wall (SAust)	22	17.09
1936-37	L.O. Fleetwood-Smith (Vic)	53	20.25	J.G. Lush (NSW)	27	17.89
	F.A. Ward (SAust)	53	28.41			
1937-38	W.J. O'Reilly (NSW)	64	12.25	W.J. O'Reilly (NSW)	64	12.25
	L.O. Fleetwood-Smith (Vic)	64	22.43			
1938-39	L.O. Fleetwood-Smith (Vic)	30	39.73	C.V. Grimmett (SAust)	27	20.85
1939-40	C.V. Grimmett (SAust)	73	22.65	W.J. O'Reilly (NSW)	55	15.13
1940-41	W.J. O'Reilly (NSW)	55	12.43	W.J. O'Reilly (NSW)	55	12.43
1941-42	W.J. O'Reilly (NSW)	9	13.78	n/a		
1942-43	no games played					
1943-44	no games played					
1944-45	no games played					
1945-46	G.E. Tribe (Vic)	40	19.03	W.J. O'Reilly (NSW)	33	14.36
1946-47	D.V.P. Wright (MCC)	51	33.31	R.R. Lindwall (NSW)	39	22.08
1947-48	M.H. Mankad (Ind)	61	26.14	G. Noblet (SAust)	40	19.43
1948-49	I.W.G. Johnson (Vic)	43	24.12	A.K. Walker (NSW)	39	15.31
1949-50	J.B. Iverson (Vic)	46	16.52	J.B. Iverson (Vic)	46	16.52
1950-51	A.V. Bedser (MCC)	51	19.80	R.H. Price (WAust)	24	18.42
1951-52	W.A. Johnston (Vic)	54	20.63	R.R. Lindwall (NSW)	42	17.33
1952-53	H.J. Tayfield (SAf)	70	27.91	G. Noblet (SAust)	55	17.84
1953-54	I.W.G. Johnson (Vic)	45	22.76	R.R. Lindwall (Qld)	22	20.14
1954-55	F.H. Tyson (MCC)	51	19.64	W.P.A. Crawford (NSW)	34	16.03
1955-56	R. Benaud (NSW)	44	21.61	W.P.A. Crawford (NSW)	35	19.80
1956-57	L.F. Kline (Vic)	39	28.21	I. Meckiff (Vic)	27	23.67
1957-58	I.W. Quick (Vic)	32	27.25	N.C. O'Neill (NSW)	26	20.42
1958-59	R. Benaud (NSW)	82	19.25	J.C. Laker (MCC)	38	17.23

Season	Leading Wicket-Taker	W	Avge	Top of Averages	W	Avge
1959-60	J. W. Martin (NSW)	45	23.64	R. A. Gaunt (WAust)	24	16.75
1960-61	A. K. Davidson (NSW)	47	20.87	A. K. Davidson (NSW) . . .	47	20.87
1961-62	R. Benaud (NSW)	47	17.97	A. K. Davidson (NSW) . . .	42	13.61
1962-63	I. Meckiff (Vic)	58	19.86	I. Meckiff (Vic)	58	19.86
1963-64	R. H. D. Sellers (SAust)	54	26.57	P. I. Philpott (NSW)	30	25.73
1964-65	N. J. N. Hawke (SAust)	41	26.29	D. E. Hoare (WAust)	29	22.86
1965-66	N. J. N. Hawke (SAust)	49	25.73	O. J. Morgan (Qld)	25	19.20
1966-67	G. A. R. Lock (WAust)	51	21.29	R. C. Bitmead (Vic)	33	19.66
1967-68	A. N. Connolly (Vic)	60	20.18	L. C. Mayne (WAust)	20	15.10
1968-69	G. D. McKenzie (WAust)	60	27.66	P. J. Allan (Qld)	46	16.37
1969-70	A. L. Thomson (Vic)	55	18.74	A. L. Thomson (Vic)	55	18.74
1970-71	A. L. Thomson (Vic)	51	30.09	J. R. Hammond (SAust) . . .	34	20.26
1971-72	A. A. Mallett (SAust)	54	19.64	A. A. Mallett (SAust)	54	19.64
1972-73	A. A. Mallett (SAust)	62	19.09	G. D. Watson (WAust)	20	18.40
1973-74	G. Dymock (Qld)	51	19.88	R. J. Bright (Vic)	32	19.66
1974-75 {	J. R. Thomson (Qld)	62	19.37	J. R. Thomson (Qld)	62	19.37
	D. K. Lillee (WAust)	62	25.14			
1975-76 {	J. R. Thomson (Qld)	62	23.75	W. Prior (SAust)	43	19.67
	D. K. Lillee (WAust)	62	24.03			
1976-77	D. K. Lillee (WAust)	70	19.54	J. R. Thomson (Qld)	27	14.00
1977-78	J. R. Thomson (Qld)	57	21.86	I. J. Brayshaw (WAust) . . .	35	18.03
1978-79	R. M. Hogg (SAust)	76	16.43	P. H. Carlson (Qld)	31	15.90
1979-80	A. A. Mallett (SAust)	53	28.30	J. Garner (WI)	32	20.03
1980-81	D. K. Lillee (WAust)	69	21.18	L. S. Pascoe (NSW)	63	19.52
1981-82	B. Yardley (WAust)	49	22.55	J. Garner (WI)	23	16.17
1982-83	G. F. Lawson (NSW)	65	21.04	C. G. Rackemann (Qld) . . .	35	15.80
1983-84	D. K. Lillee (WAust)	58	25.64	C. G. Rackemann (Qld) . . .	28	18.68
1984-85	R. G. Holland (NSW)	59	25.80	Imran Khan (Pak)	28	19.14
1985-86	R. G. Holland (NSW)	48	32.40	R. J. Hadlee (NZ)	37	14.51
1986-87	C. J. McDermott (Qld)	58	22.34	G. C. Small (England)	33	18.97
1987-88	C. D. Matthews (WAust)	57	22.40	G. F. Lawson (NSW)	42	18.86
1988-89	M. R. Whitney (NSW)	58	23.62	T. M. Alderman (WAust) . . .	48	20.94
1989-90	C. G. Rackemann (Qld)	50	21.48	C. D. Matthews (WAust) . . .	42	19.19
1990-91	C. J. McDermott (Qld)	67	19.46	A. I. C. Dodemaide (Vic) . . .	20	12.25
1991-92	C. J. McDermott (Qld)	60	20.80	D. A. Freedman (NSW) . . .	22	18.59
1992-93	W. J. Holdsworth (NSW) . . .	53	25.96	C. E. L. Ambrose (WI)	38	18.13
1993-94	S. K. Warne (Vic)	63	19.92	S. K. Warne (Vic)	63	19.92
1994-95	C. G. Rackemann (Qld)	52	23.60	S. K. Warne (Vic)	40	20.35
1995-96	M. S. Kasprowicz (Qld)	64	20.47	A. M. Stuart (NSW)	25	13.40
1996-97	M. S. Kasprowicz (Qld)	48	25.54	J. C. Scuderi (SAust)	23	17.34
1997-98	C. R. Miller (Tas)	70	24.99	D. W. Fleming (Vic)	39	18.08
1998-99	D. J. Saker (Vic)	45	23.31	A. C. Dale (Qld)	31	17.10
1999-00	A. J. Bichel (Qld)	60	20.12	M. S. Kasprowicz (Qld) . . .	49	14.41
2000-01 {	A. J. Bichel (Qld)	49	23.35	J. H. Dawes (Qld)	49	20.47
	J. H. Dawes (Qld)	49	20.47			
2001-02	M. S. Kasprowicz (Qld)	51	24.29	M. W. H. Inness (Vic)	31	19.26
2002-03	S. C. G. MacGill (NSW)	60	29.57	D. A. Nash (NSW)	26	16.46
2003-04	S. C. G. MacGill (NSW)	58	35.95	J. N. Gillespie (SAust)	37	21.54

BEST AVERAGE IN AN AUSTRALIAN SEASON

(Qualification: 30 wickets)

		M	B	Mdns	R	W	BB	5Wi	10Wm	Avge
C. T. B. Turner (NSW)	1886-87	7	2,145	273	538	70	8-32	8	3	7.68
E. Attewell (England)	1887-88	9	3,086	425	590	54	7-15	4	2	10.92
E. Evans (NSW)	1880-81	7	1,749	251	360	32	5-34	5	1	11.25
G. E. Palmer (Vic)	1882-83	7	1,772	201	588	51	7-65	5	2	11.53
T. Emmett (England)	1878-79	5	1,933	255	521	44	8-47	6	2	11.84
G. A. Lohmann (England)	1887-88	8	2,667	364	755	63	7-43	7	2	11.98
W. J. O'Reilly (NSW)	1937-38	11	2,487	91	784	64	9-41	6	2	12.25
C. T. B. Turner (NSW)	1893-94	3	940	35	369	30	6-51	5	2	12.30
W. J. O'Reilly (NSW)	1940-41	8	1,838	48	684	55	6-60	5	0	12.43
C. Kelleway (NSW)	1913-14	7	1,498	76	571	45	7-35	3	1	12.69
W. Attewell (England)	1891-92	8	2,858	241	573	44	6-34	4	1	13.02
J. Briggs (England))	1891-92	8	1,212	71	420	32	6-49	4	1	13.13
A. Cotter (NSW)	1903-04	5	740	18	404	30	6-40	2	0	13.47
C. T. B. Turner (NSW)	1887-88	12	4,267	473	1,441	106	8-39	12	5	13.59
A. K. Davidson (NSW)	1961-62	9	1,696	52	572	42	7-31	2	0	13.61
H. Ironmonger (Vic)	1930-31	10	3,037	112	972	68	8-31	7	4	14.29
W. J. O'Reilly (NSW)	1945-46	6	1,257	20	474	33	6-43	1	0	14.36
M. S. Kasprowicz (Qld)	1999-00	8	1485	69	706	49	5-32	4	1	14.41
R. J. Hadlee (New Zealanders)	1985-86	5	1,449	65	537	37	9-52	5	2	14.51
J. Briggs (England)	1887-88	8	2,263	215	436	30	6-40	2	1	14.53
J. J. Ferris (NSW)	1886-87	7	1,967	224	689	47	5-28	3	0	14.66
H. V. Hordern (NSW)	1910-11	8	1,448	29	860	58	7-31	6	2	14.83
T. R. McKibbin (NSW)	1896-97	4	1,381	46	655	44	8-74	5	2	14.89

AUSTRALIANS WITH 400 FIRST-CLASS WICKETS

		M	R	W	BB	5Wi	10Wm	Avge
A. E. Trott	1892-93 – 1911	375	35,317	1,674	10-42	131	41	21.09
F. A. Tarrant	1898-99 – 1936-37	329	26,391	1,506	10-90	133	38	17.52
C. V. Grimmett	1911-12 – 1940-41	248	31,740	1,424	10-37	127	33	22.28
E. A. McDonald	1909-10 – 1935	281	28,966	1,395	8-41	119	31	20.76
G. E. Tribe	1945-46 – 1959	308	28,321	1,378	9-43	93	23	20.55
G. D. McKenzie	1959-60 – 1975	383	32,868	1,219	8-71	49	5	26.96
J. E. Walsh	1936-37 – 1956	296	29,226	1,190	9-101	98	26	24.56
S. M. J. Woods	1886 – 1910	401	21,653	1,040	10-69	77	21	20.82
G. Giffen	1877-78 – 1903-04	251	21,782	1,023	10-66	95	30	21.29
B. Dooland	1945-46 – 1957-58	214	22,332	1,016	8-20	84	23	21.98
C. T. B. Turner	1882-83 – 1909-10	155	14,147	993	9-15	102	35	14.24
V. E. Jackson	1936-37 – 1958	354	23,874	965	8-43	43	6	24.73
T. M. Alderman	1974-75 – 1992-93	245	22,701	956	8-46	53	8	23.74
R. Benaud	1948-49 – 1967-68	259	23,370	945	7-18	56	9	24.73
H. Trumble	1887-88 – 1903-04	344	17,134	929	9-39	69	25	18.44
S. K. Warne	1990-91 – 2004	214	23,872	923	8-71	46	8	25.86
D. K. Lillee	1969-70 – 1988	198	20,696	882	8-29	50	13	23.46
F. R. Spofforth	1874-75 – 1897	155	12,759	853	9-18	84	32	14.95
M. S. Kasprowicz	1989-90 – 2004	208	22,072	845	9-36	47	6	26.12
W. W. Armstrong	1898-99 – 1921-22	269	16,406	832	8-47	50	5	19.71
J. J. Ferris	1886-87 – 1897-98	198	14,260	813	8-41	63	11	17.53
R. R. Lindwall	1941-42 – 1961-62	228	16,956	794	7-20	34	2	21.35
A. A. Mailey	1912-13 – 1930-31	158	18,778	779	10-66	61	16	24.10
W. J. O'Reilly	1927-28 – 1945-46	135	12,850	774	9-38	63	17	16.60
W. E. Alley	1945-46 – 1968	400	17,421	768	8-65	30	1	22.68
J. A. Cuffe	1902-03 – 1914	221	18,798	738	9-38	33	7	25.47
G. D. McGrath	1992-93 – 20045	159	14,546	700	8-38	37	7	20.78
A. A. Mallett	1967-68 – 1980-81	183	18,208	693	8-59	33	5	26.27

		M	R	W	BB	5Wi	10Wm	Avge
C.J. McDermott	1983-84 – 1995-96	174	19,025	677	8-44	37	4	28.10
A.N. Connolly	1959-60 – 1970-71	201	17,974	676	9-67	25	4	26.58
J.R. Thomson	1972-73 – 1985-86	187	17,864	675	7-27	28	3	26.46
A.K. Davidson	1949-50 – 1962-63	193	14,048	672	7-31	33	2	20.90
G.F. Lawson	1977-78 – 1991-92	191	16,564	666	8-112	28	2	24.87
E. Jones	1892-93 – 1907-08	144	14,638	641	8-39	47	9	22.83
M.A. Noble	1893-94 – 1919-20	248	14,445	625	8-48	33	7	23.11
I.W.G. Johnson	1935-36 – 1956-57	189	14,423	619	7-42	27	4	23.30
C.G. Rackemann	1979-80 – 1995-96	167	16,629	616	8-84	22	3	26.99
C.L. McCool	1939-40 – 1960	251	16,542	602	8-74	34	2	27.47
L.O. Fleetwood-Smith	1931-32 – 1939-40	112	13,519	597	9-36	57	18	22.64
G.E. Palmer	1878-79 – 1896-97	133	10,520	594	8-48	54	16	17.71
M.G. Hughes	1981-82 – 1994-95	165	17,249	593	8-87	21	3	29.09
S.C.G. MacGill	1993-94 – 2004	131	16,910	567	8-111	34	6	29.82
W.A. Johnston	1945-46 – 1954-55	142	12,936	554	8-52	29	6	23.35
J.V. Saunders	1899-00 – 1913-14	107	12,064	553	8-106	48	9	21.81
P.R. Reiffel	1987-88 – 2001-02	167	14,392	545	6-57	16	2	26.41
A.I.C. Dodemaide	1983-84 – 1997-98	184	17,096	534	6-58	17	0	32.01
W.P. Howell	1894-95 – 1905-06	141	11,157	520	10-28	30	5	21.45
G.R.J. Matthews	1982-83 – 1997-98	190	16,413	516	8-52	22	5	31.81
J.S. Manning	1951-52 – 1960	146	11,662	513	8-43	25	4	22.73
A.J. Bichel	1992-93 – 2004	128	13,288	509	9-93	24	5	26.11
J.M. Gregory	1919 – 1928-29	129	10,580	504	9-32	33	8	20.99
M.H.N. Walker	1968-69 – 1981-82	135	13,209	499	8-143	21	0	26.47
K.R. Miller	1937-38 – 1959	226	11,087	497	7-12	16	1	22.30
W.J. Whitty	1907-08 – 1925-26	119	11,488	491	8-27	26	4	23.39
J. Angel	1991-92 – 2003-04	121	12,178	485	6-35	16	1	25.11
K.J. O'Keeffe	1968-69 – 1979-80	169	13,382	476	7-38	24	5	28.11
R.J. Bright	1972-73 – 1987-88	184	15,114	471	7-87	24	2	32.08
H. Ironmonger	1909-10 – 1935-36	96	9,980	464	8-31	36	10	21.50
N.J.N. Hawke	1959-60 – 1970-71	145	12,088	458	8-61	23	5	26.39
D.T. Ring	1938-39 – 1953	129	12,847	451	7-88	21	2	28.48
C.R. Miller	1985-86 – 2001-02	126	13,814	446	7-49	16	3	30.97
T.W. Garrett	1876-77 – 1897-98	160	8,353	445	7-38	29	5	18.77
J.W. Martin	1956-57 – 1967-68	135	13,872	444	8-97	17	1	31.17
A. Cotter	1901-02 – 1913-14	113	10,730	442	7-15	31	4	24.27
T.B.A. May	1984-85 – 1995-96	142	15,721	439	7-93	19	2	35.81
B.P. Julian	1989-90 – 2000-01	138	13,295	435	7-39	21	2	30.56
J.W. Gleeson	1966-67 – 1974-75	116	10,729	430	7-52	22	2	24.95
G. Dymock	1971-72 – 1981-82	126	11,438	425	7-67	13	1	26.91
W.E. Midwinter	1874-75 – 1886-87	160	7,298	419	7-27	27	3	17.41
C.G. Macartney	1905-06 – 1935-36	249	8,781	419	7-58	17	1	20.95
M.R. Whitney	1980-81 – 1994-95	118	11,023	412	7-27	19	1	26.75
F.J. Laver	1891-92 – 1913-14	163	9,989	404	8-31	19	5	24.72

BEST CAREER AVERAGE

(Qualification: 50 wickets)

		M	R	W	BB	5Wi	10Wm	Avge
S. Cosstick	1860-61 – 1875-76	18	998	106	9-61	11	5	9.41
T.W. Wills	1854 – 1875-76	32	1,217	121	7-44	15	3	10.06
J. Coates	1867-68 – 1879-80	15	885	76	7-39	5	1	11.64
S.W. Austin	1892-93 – 1894-95	10	709	60	8-14	6	1	11.81
F.E. Allan	1867-68 – 1882-83	31	1,638	123	8-20	11	2	13.32
C.T.B. Turner	1882-83 – 1909-10	155	14,147	993	9-15	102	35	14.24
F.R. Spofforth	1874-75 – 1897	155	12,760	853	9-18	84	32	14.95
H.F. Boyle	1871-72 – 1890	140	5,692	370	7-32	26	6	15.38
F.S. Middleton	1905-06 – 1921-22	14	911	56	7-36	5	2	16.26
W.J. O'Reilly	1927-28 – 1945-46	135	12,850	774	9-38	63	17	16.60

		M	*R*	*W*	*BB*	*5Wi*	*10Wm*	*Avge*
E. Evans............	1874-75 – 1887-88	65	3,356	201	7-16	18	4	16.69
H. V. Hordern	1905-06 – 1912-13	33	3,644	217	8-31	23	9	16.79
S. T. Callaway.......	1888-89 – 1906-07	62	5,460	320	8-33	33	12	17.06
W. E. Midwinter......	1874-75 – 1886-87	160	7,298	419	7-27	27	3	17.41
F. A. Tarrant	1898-99 – 1935-36	329	26,450	1,512	10-90	133	38	17.49
J. J. Ferris..........	1886-87 – 1897-98	198	14,260	813	8-41	63	11	17.53
G. E. Palmer........	1878-79 – 1896-97	133	10,520	594	8-48	54	16	17.71
R. J. A. Massie.......	1910-11 – 1913-14	16	1,280	99	7-110	7	4	18.38
H. Trumble.........	1887-88 – 1903-04	344	17,134	929	9-39	69	25	18.44
T. W. Garrett	1876-77 – 1897-98	160	8,353	445	7-38	29	5	18.77
W. W. McGlinchy	1885-86 – 1899-00	20	1,345	71	6-62	4	2	18.94
D. L. Miller	1892-93 – 1905-06	15	1,045	55	5-38	2	0	19.00
J. B. Iverson.........	1949-50 – 1953-54	34	3,019	157	7-77	9	1	19.23
G. Noblet..........	1945-46 – 1956	71	5,432	282	7-29	13	2	19.26
W. W. Armstrong	1898-99 – 1921-22	269	16,405	832	8-47	50	5	19.71
T. R. McKibbin	1894-95 – 1898-99	57	6,297	319	9-68	28	11	19.73
P. C. Charlton	1888-89 – 1897-98	40	1,937	97	7-44	6	1	19.96

MOST WICKETS PER MATCH

(Qualification: 50 wickets)

		M	*R*	*W*	*BB*	*5W*	*10W*	*Avge*	*Wkts/ Match*
H. V. Hordern	1905-06 – 1912-13	33	3,644	217	8-31	23	9	16.79	6.57
C. T. B. Turner......	1882-83 – 1909-10	155	14,147	993	9-15	102	35	14.24	6.40
S. W. Austin.........	1892-93 – 1894-95	10	709	60	8-14	6	1	11.81	6.00
R. J. A. Massie.......	1910-11 – 1913-14	16	1,280	99	7-110	7	4	18.38	6.18
S. Cosstick.........	1860-61 – 1875-76	18	998	106	9-61	11	5	9.41	5.88
C. V. Grimmett......	1911-12 – 1940-41	248	31,740	1,424	10-37	127	33	22.28	5.74
W. J. O'Reilly.......	1927-28 – 1945-46	135	12,850	774	9-38	63	17	16.60	5.73
T. R. McKibbin	1894-95 – 1898-99	57	6,297	319	9-68	28	11	19.73	5.59
F. R. Spofforth......	1874-75 – 1897	155	12,760	853	9-18	84	32	14.95	5.50
L. O. Fleetwood-Smith	1931-32 – 1939-40	112	13,519	597	9-36	57	18	22.64	5.33
S. T. Callaway.......	1888-89 – 1906-07	62	5,460	320	8-33	33	12	17.06	5.16
J. V. Saunders	1899-00 – 1913-14	107	12,064	553	8-106	48	9	21.81	5.16
J. Coates..........	1867-68 – 1879-80	15	885	76	7-39	5	1	11.64	5.06

MOST BALLS BOWLED IN AN INNINGS

Balls	*M*	*R*	*W*		
571	36	155	3	T. R. Veivers, Australia v England at Manchester	1964
522	12	309	5	G. Giffen, South Australia v A. E. Stoddart's XI at Adelaide ..	1894-95
522	11	298	1	L. O. Fleetwood-Smith, Australia v England at The Oval	1938
512	0	362	4	A. A. Mailey, New South Wales v Victoria at Melbourne	1926-27
510	26	178	5	W. J. O'Reilly, Australia v England at The Oval	1938
501	35	150	6	G. Giffen, South Australia v New South Wales at Adelaide ..	1890-91

MOST BALLS BOWLED IN A MATCH

Balls	*M*	*R*	*W*		
848	14	394	10	C. V. Grimmett, South Australia v New South Wales at Sydney ..	1925-26
749	37	256	13	J. C. White, England v Australia at Adelaide	1928-29
743	22	255	10	D. D. Blackie, Victoria v South Australia at Adelaide	1926-27
736	16	267	9	C. V. Grimmett, South Australia v Victoria at Adelaide	1924-25
725	58	152	11	R. W. McLeod, Victoria v New South Wales at Melbourne ..	1892-93
712	19	228	11	M. W. Tate, England v Australia at Sydney	1924-25
708	42	239	8	G. Giffen, Australia v England at Sydney	1894-95

MOST RUNS CONCEDED IN A MATCH

Runs

394	(4/192, 6/202)	C. V. Grimmett, South Australia v New South Wales at Sydney ... 1925-26
362	(4-362)	A. A. Mailey, New South Wales v Victoria at Melbourne 1926-27
345	(3-190, 0-155)	J. D. Scott, South Australia v New South Wales at Sydney 1925-26
326	(6-134, 5-192)	N. L. Williams, South Australia v Victoria at Adelaide 1928-29
322	(5-309, 0-13)	G. Giffen, South Australia v A. E. Stoddart's XI at Adelaide 1894-95
308	(4-129, 3-179)	A. A. Mailey, Australia v England at Sydney 1924-25
302	(5-160, 5-142)	A. A. Mailey, Australia v England at Adelaide 1920-21

ALL-ROUND RECORDS

100 RUNS IN AN INNINGS AND TEN WICKETS IN A MATCH

R. G. Barlow 101	10/48	North of England v Australians at Nottingham	1884
G. Giffen 166	14-125	South Australia v Victoria at Adelaide	1887-88
G. Giffen 135	13-159	South Australia v Victoria at Melbourne	1888-89
G. Giffen 237	12-192	South Australia v Victoria at Melbourne	1890-91
G. Giffen 271	16-165	South Australia v Victoria at Adelaide	1891-92
G. Giffen 120	12-150	South Australia v New South Wales at Sydney	1891-92
G. Giffen 181	11-235	South Australia v Victoria at Adelaide	1892-93
A. E. Trott 101*	11-140	Lord Hawke's XI v Transvaal at Johannesburg (OW)	1898-99
A. E. Trott 123	12-190	Middlesex v Sussex at Lord's	1899
A. E. Trott 112	11-138	Middlesex v Essex at Lord's	1901
W. W. Armstrong . 126*	10-52	Australians v New Zealanders at Christchurch	1904-05
F. A. Tarrant 152	12-149	Middlesex v Gloucestershire v Bristol	1908
F. A. Tarrant 101*	16-176	Middlesex v Lancashire at Manchester	1914
F. A. Tarrant 182*	11-112	Behar's XI v Willingdon's XI at Pune	1918-19
V. E. Jackson 108	10-99	Leicestershire v Kent at Gillingham	1954
B. Dooland 115*	10-102	Nottinghamshire v Sussex at Worthing	1957
P. H. Carlson 102*	10-73	Queensland v New South Wales at Brisbane	1978-79
J. C. Scuderi 110	10-165	South Australia v New South Wales at Adelaide	1991-92

500 RUNS AND 50 WICKETS IN AN AUSTRALIAN SEASON

		M	R	Avge	W	Avge
G. Giffen (S Aust)	1891-92	6	509	50.90	50	17.30
G. Giffen (S Aust)...........	1894-95	11	902	50.11	93	22.55
L. C. Braund (MCC)	1907-08	16	783	35.59	50	32.88
J. N. Crawford (MCC)	1907-08	16	610	26.52	66	25.20
F. R. Foster (MCC)	1911-12	13	641	35.61	62	20.19
M. H. Mankad (Indians)........	1947-48	13	889	38.65	61	26.15
G. S. Sobers (S Aust)	1962-63	10	1,001	52.68	51	26.56
G. S. Sobers (S Aust)	1963-64	9	1,128	80.57	51	28.25
G. R. J. Matthews (NSW).......	1991-92	12	603	40.20	52	21.46
G. R. J. Matthews (NSW).......	1992-93	13	625	36.76	51	28.92

10,000 RUNS AND 500 WICKETS IN A CAREER

	M	R	Avge	W	Avge
W. E. Alley	400	19,612	31.88	768	22.68
W. W. Armstrong	269	16,158	46.83	832	19.71
R. Benaud	259	11,719	36.50	945	23.74
G. Giffen	251	11,758	29.54	1,023	21.29
V. E. Jackson	354	15,698	28.43	965	24.73
C. L. McCool	251	12,420	32.85	602	27.47
M. A. Noble	248	13,975	40.74	625	23.11
F. A. Tarrant	326	17,857	36.37	1,489	17.66
G. E. Tribe	308	10,177	27.34	1,378	20.55
A. E. Trott	375	10,696	19.48	1,674	21.09

WICKET-KEEPING RECORDS

MOST DISMISSALS IN AN INNINGS

8	(all ct)	A. T. W. Grout, Queensland v Western Australia at Brisbane	1959-60
8	(6ct, 2st)	T. J. Zoehrer, Australians v Surrey at The Oval	1993
8	(7ct, 1st)	D. S. Berry, Victoria v South Australia at Melbourne	1996-97
7	(3ct, 4st)	D. Tallon, Queensland v Victoria at Brisbane	1938-39
7	(all ct)	R. A. Saggers, New South Wales v Combined XI at Brisbane	1940-41
7	(6ct, 1st)	H. B. Taber, New South Wales v South Australia at Adelaide	1968-69
7	(all ct)	J. A. Maclean, Queensland v Victoria at Melbourne	1977-78
7	(6ct, 1st)	R. B. Phillips, Queensland v New Zealanders at Brisbane	1982-83
7	(all ct)	J. M. Holyman, Tasmania v Western Australia at Hobart (Bel)	1990-91
7	(all ct)	A. C. Gilchrist, Western Australia v South Australia at Perth	1995-96
7	(all ct)	R. D. Jacobs, West Indies v Australia at Melbourne	2000-01
7	(all ct)	W. A. Seccombe, Queensland v New South Wales at Brisbane	2001-02

MOST DISMISSALS IN A MATCH

12	(9ct, 3st)	D. Tallon, Queensland v New South Wales at Sydney	1938-39
12	(9ct, 3st)	H. B. Taber, New South Wales v South Australia at Adelaide	1968-69
11	(all ct)	R. W. Marsh, Western Australia v Victoria at Perth	1975-76
11	(all ct)	T. J. Nielsen, South Australia v Western Australia at Perth	1990-91
11	(10ct, 1st)	I. A. Healy, Australians v N. Transvaal at Verwoerdburg	1993-94
11	(all ct)	D. S. Berry, Victoria v Pakistanis at Melbourne	1995-96
11	(10ct, 1st)	W. A. Seccombe, Queensland v Western Australia at Brisbane	1995-96
11	(10ct, 1st)	D. S. Berry, Victoria v South Australia at Melbourne	1996-97
10	(all ct)	A. C. Gilchrist, Australia v New Zealand at Hamilton	1999-00
10	(9ct, 1st)	R. A. Saggers, New South Wales v Combined XI at Brisbane	1940-41
10	(7ct, 3st)	B. N. Jarman, South Australia v New South Wales at Adelaide	1961-62
10	(9ct, 1st)	R. C. Jordon, Victoria v South Australia at Melbourne	1970-71
10	(all ct)	R. W. Marsh, Western Australia v South Australia at Perth	1976-77
10	(all ct)	S. J. Rixon, Australian XI v South Africa at Johannesburg (WS)	1985-86
10	(all ct)	S. J. Rixon, Australian XI v South Africa at Johannesburg (WS)	1986-87
10	(7ct, 3st)	A. C. Gilchrist, Young Australia v TCCB XI at Birmingham	1995
10	(all ct)	P. J. Roach, Victoria v South Australia at Melbourne	1995-96
10	(all ct)	A. C. Gilchrist, Western Australia v Victoria at Perth	1997-98
10	(all ct)	A. C. Gilchrist, Australia v New Zealand at Hamilton	1999-00

MOST DISMISSALS IN AN AUSTRALIAN SEASON

Total	Ct	St	M		
67	63	4	15	R. W. Marsh (Western Australia)	1975-76
67	64	3	13	W. A. Seccombe (Queensland)	1999-00
64	58	6	14	R. W. Marsh (Western Australia)	1974-75
62	58	4	12	A. C. Gilchrist (Western Australia)	1995-96
62	60	2	12	A. C. Gilchrist (Western Australia)	1996-97
61	59	2	14	R. W. Marsh (Western Australia)	1980-81
61	61	0	13	R. W. Marsh (Western Australia)	1982-83
59	54	5	13	R. W. Marsh (Western Australia)	1983-84
59	57	2	9	W. A. Seccombe (Queensland)	1995-96
58	57	1	11	W. A. Seccombe (Queensland)	2000-01
57	53	4	13	K. J. Wright (Western Australia)	1978-79
56	55	1	12	R. B. Phillips (Queensland)	1984-85
55	55	0	11	A. C. Gilchrist (Western Australia)	1994-95
54	52	2	13	P. A. Emery (New South Wales)	1992-93
54	52	2	11	D. S. Berry (Victoria)	1999-00
53	53	0	11	R. W. Marsh (Western Australia)	1976-77
52	43	6	11	W. A. Seccombe (Queensland)	2001-02

AUSTRALIANS WITH 300 FIRST-CLASS DISMISSALS

	Career	M	Ct	St	Total
R. W. Marsh	1968-69 – 1983-84	257	803	66	869
I. A. Healy	1986-87 – 1999-00	231	698	69	767
W. A. S. Oldfield	1919 – 1937-38	245	399	262	661
D. S. Berry	1989-90 – 2003-04	153	552	51	603
A. C. Gilchrist	1992-93 – 2004-05	145	580	42	602
A. T. W. Grout	1946-47 – 1965-55	183	473	114	587
B. N. Jarman	1955-56 – 1968-69	191	431	129	560
W. A. Seccombe	1992-93 – 2003-04	107	478	19	497
S. J. Rixon	1974-75 – 1987-88	151	394	66	460
T. J. Zoehrer	1980-81 – 1993-94	144	411	38	449
J. M. Blackham	1874-75 – 1894-95	250	259	181	440
D. Tallon	1933-34 – 1953-54	150	303	129	432
H. B. Taber	1964-65 – 1973-74	129	345	50	395
P. A. Emery	1987-88 – 1998-99	121	337	47	384
J. A. Maclean	1968-69 – 1978-79	108	353	31	384
G. R. A. Langley	1945-46 – 1956-57	120	292	77	369
B. A. Barnett	1929-30 – 1961	173	216	142	358
J. J. Kelly	1894-95 – 1906-07	180	243	112	355
R. D. Robinson	1971-72 – 1981-82	97	289	40	329
C. W. Walker	1928-29 – 1940-41	109	171	149	320
T. J. Nielsen	1990-91 – 1998-99	101	284	32	316

MOST DISMISSALS PER MATCH

(Qualification: 200 dismissals)

		M	Ct	St	Total	Per match
W. A. Seccombe	1992-93 – 2003-04	107	478	19	497	4.64
A. C. Gilchrist	1992-93 – 2004-05	145	580	42	602	4.14
D. S. Berry	1989-90 – 2003-04	153	552	51	603	3.94
J. A. Maclean	1968-69 – 1978-79	108	353	31	384	3.55
K. J. Wright	1974-75 – 1983-84	85	268	26	294	3.45
R. D. Robinson	1971-72 – 1981-82	97	289	40	329	3.39
R. W. Marsh	1968-69 – 1983-84	257	803	66	869	3.38
I. A. Healy	1986-87 – 1999-00	231	698	69	767	3.32
R. B. Phillips	1978-79 – 1985-86	89	271	15	286	3.21
A. T. W. Grout	1946-47 – 1965-55	183	473	114	587	3.20

FIELDING RECORDS

MOST CATCHES IN AN INNINGS

6	F. A. Tarrant	Middlesex v Essex at Leyton	1906
6	J. F. Sheppard	Queensland v New South Wales at Brisbane	1914-15
6	K. J. Grieves	Lancashire v Sussex at Manchester	1951

Note: There are 16 instances of five catches in an innings.

MOST CATCHES IN A MATCH

8	K. J. Grieves	Lancashire v Sussex at Manchester	1951
7	L. O. S. Poidevin	Lancashire v Yorkshire at Manchester	1906
7	F. A. Tarrant	Middlesex v Essex at Leyton	1906
7	M. E. K. Hussey	Northamptonshire v Oxford University at Oxford	2002
7	M. L. Hayden	Australia v Sri Lanka at Galle	2003-04

MOST CATCHES IN AN AUSTRALIAN SEASON

Ct	M		
27	14	I. M. Chappell (South Australia)	1968-69
26	13	G. B. Hole (South Australia)	1952-53
26	13	M. A. Taylor (New South Wales)	1997-98
25	16	L. C. Braund (MCC)	1907-08
25	14	M. A. Taylor (New South Wales)	1991-92
24	11	L. C. Braund (A. C. MacLaren's XI)	1901-02
24	12	J. M. Gregory (New South Wales)	1920-21
24	15	R. B. Simpson (Western Australia)	1960-61
24	11	R. B. Simpson (New South Wales)	1967-68
24	14	I. M. Chappell (South Australia)	1974-75
24	14	G. S. Chappell (Queensland)	1974-75
24	14	G. S. Chappell (Queensland)	1980-81
24	13	S. R. Waugh (New South Wales)	1986-87
24	13	M. R. J. Veletta (Western Australia)	1987-88
24	11	M. A. Taylor (New South Wales)	1995-96

AUSTRALIANS WITH 200 FIRST-CLASS CATCHES

	Career	M	Ct
K. J. Grieves	1945-46 – 1964	490	610
A. E. Trott	1892-93 – 1911	375	452
M. E. Waugh	1985-86 – 2003-04	368	452
R. B. Simpson	1952-53 – 1977-78	257	383
A. R. Border	1976-77 – 1995-96	385	379
G. S. Chappell	1966-67 – 1983-84	322	376
M. A. Taylor	1985-86 – 1998-99	253	350
S. G. Law	1988-89 – 2004	304	340
H. Trumble	1887-88 – 1903-04	213	328
I. M. Chappell	1961-62 – 1979-80	263	312
F. A. Tarrant	1898-99 – 1936-37	329	304
T. M. Moody	1985-86 – 2000-01	300	294
W. E. Alley	1945-46 – 1968	400	293
D. C. Boon	1978-79 – 1999	350	283
S. M. J. Woods	1886 – 1910	401	279
W. W. Armstrong	1898-99 – 1921-22	269	274
S. R. Waugh	1984-85 – 2003-04	356	273
K. C. Wessels	1973-74 – 1999-00	316	268
C. L. McCool	1939-40 – 1960	251	262
R. Benaud	1948-49 – 1967-68	259	255
V. E. Jackson	1936-37 – 1958	354	250
R. J. Inverarity	1962-63 – 1984-85	223	250
G. E. Tribe	1945-46 – 1959	308	242
R. N. Harvey	1946-47 – 1962-63	306	228
M. L. Hayden	1991-92 – 2004-05	236	219
V. Y. Richardson	1918-19 – 1937-38	184	213
I. R. Redpath	1961-62 – 1975-76	226	211
J. L. Langer	1991-92 – 2004-05	253	211
J. E. Walsh	1936-37 – 1956	296	209
M. J. Di Venuto	1991-92 – 2003-04	189	208
J. D. Siddons	1984-85 – 1999-00	160	206
G. D. McKenzie	1959-60 – 1975	383	201

TEAM RECORDS

HIGHEST INNINGS TOTALS

1,107	Victoria v New South Wales at Melbourne	1926-27
1,059	Victoria v Tasmania at Melbourne	1922-23
918	New South Wales v South Australia at Sydney	1900-01
7-903 dec.	England v Australia at The Oval	1938
843	Australians v Oxford and Cambridge Universities at Portsmouth	1893
839	New South Wales v Tasmania at Sydney	1898-99
7-821 dec.	South Australia v Queensland at Adelaide	1939-40
815	New South Wales v Victoria at Sydney	1908-09
807	New South Wales v South Australia at Adelaide	1899-00
805	New South Wales v Victoria at Melbourne	1905-06
803	Non Smokers v Smokers at East Melbourne	1886-87
802	New South Wales v South Australia at Sydney	1920-21
793	Victoria v Queensland at Melbourne	1927-28
786	New South Wales v South Australia at Adelaide	1922-23
775	New South Wales v Victoria at Sydney	1881-82
7-774 dec.	Australians v Gloucestershire at Bristol	1948
770	New South Wales v South Australia at Adelaide	1920-21
769	A. C. MacLaren's XI v New South Wales at Sydney	1901-02
763	New South Wales v Queensland at Brisbane	1906-07
8-761 dec.	New South Wales v Queensland at Sydney	1929-30
8-758 dec.	Australia v West Indies at Kingston	1954-55
8-752 dec.	New South Wales v Otago at Dunedin	1923-24
6-735 dec.	Australia v Zimbabwe at Perth	2003-04
7-734 dec.	MCC v New South Wales at Sydney	1928-29
6-729 dec.	Australia v England at Lord's	1930
724	Victoria v South Australia at Melbourne	1920-21
721	Australians v Essex at Southend	1948
713	New South Wales v South Australia at Adelaide	1908-09
6-713 dec.	New South Wales v Victoria at Sydney	1928-29
710	Victoria v Queensland at Melbourne	2003-04
5-708 dec.	Australians v Cambridge University at Cambridge	1921
7-708 dec.	Australians v Hampshire at Southampton	1938
708	New South Wales v Victoria at Sydney	1925-26
705	New South Wales v Victoria at Melbourne	1925-26
7-705 dec.	India v Australia at Sydney	2003-04
701	Australia v England at The Oval	1934

HIGHEST FOURTH-INNINGS TOTALS

572	New South Wales (set 593 to win) v South Australia at Sydney	1907-08
9-529	Combined XI (set 579 to win) v South Africans at Perth	1963-64
518	Victoria (set 753 to win) v Queensland at Brisbane (Ex)	1926-27
6-506	South Australia (won) v Queensland at Adelaide	1991-92
495	South Australia (set 521 to win) v New South Wales at Sydney	2003-04
472	New South Wales (set 552 to win) v Australian XI at Sydney	1905-06
466	New South Wales (set 466 to win) v West Indians at Sydney	1930-31
456	Queensland (set 507 to win) v Victoria at Melbourne	1928-29
7-455	Victoria (won) v New South Wales at Newcastle	2003-04
6-446	New South Wales (won) v South Australia at Adelaide	1926-27
445	India (set 493 to win) v Australia at Adelaide	1977-78
442	South Africans (set 487 to win) v New South Wales at Sydney	1910-11

HIGHEST MATCH AGGREGATES

R	W	Avge		
1,929	39	49.46	New South Wales v South Australia at Sydney	1925-26
1,911	34	56.20	New South Wales v Victoria at Sydney	1908-09
1,801	40	45.02	A. L. Hassett's XI v A. R. Morris's XI at Melbourne	1953-54
1,764	39	45.23	Australia v West Indies at Adelaide	1968-69
1,753	40	43.82	Australia v England at Adelaide	1920-21
1,752	34	51.52	New South Wales v Queensland at Sydney	1926-27
1,747	25	69.88	Australia v India at Sydney	2003-04
1,744	30	58.13	New South Wales v South Africans at Sydney	1910-11
1,739	40	43.47	New South Wales v A. E. Stoddart's XI at Sydney	1897-98
1,723	31	55.58	England v Australia at Leeds	1948
1,716	40	42.90	New South Wales v South Australia at Sydney	1907-08
1,704	39	43.69	J. Ryder's XI v W. M. Woodfull's XI at Sydney	1929-30

LOWEST COMPLETED INNINGS TOTALS

15	Victoria v MCC at Melbourne	1903-04
17	Gloucestershire v Australians at Cheltenham	1896
18	Tasmania v Victoria at Melbourne	1868-69
18	Australians v MCC at Lord's	1896
19	MCC v Australians at Lord's	1878
23	South Australia v Victoria at East Melbourne	1882-83
23	Australians v Yorkshire at Leeds	1902
25	Tasmania v Victoria at Hobart (LRG)	1857-58
26	England XI v Australians at Birmingham	1884
27	Lord Sheffield's XI v Australians at Sheffield Park	1890
27	South Australia v New South Wales at Sydney	1955-56
28	Victoria v New South Wales at Melbourne	1855-56
28	England XI v Australians at Stoke-on-Trent	1888
28	Lancashire v Australians at Liverpool	1896
28	Leicestershire v Australians at Leicester	1899

LOWEST COMPLETED MATCH AGGREGATE

R	W	Avge		
105	31	3.38	MCC v Australians at Lord's	1878

LARGEST VICTORIES

By Innings

Inns and 666	Victoria (1,059) v Tasmania at Melbourne	1922-23
Inns and 656	Victoria (1,107) v New South Wales at Melbourne	1926-27
Inns and 605	New South Wales (918) v South Australia at Sydney	1900-01
Inns and 579	England (7 dec 903) v Australia at The Oval	1938
Inns and 572	New South Wales (713) v South Australia at Adelaide	1908-09
Inns and 517	Australians (675) v Nottinghamshire at Nottingham	1921

By Runs

685 runs	New South Wales (235 and 8 dec 761) v Queensland at Sydney	1929-30
675 runs	England (521 and 8 dec 342) v Australia at Brisbane (Ex)	1928-29
638 runs	New South Wales (304 and 770) v South Australia at Adelaide	1920-21
571 runs	Victoria (309 and 649) v South Australia at Melbourne	1926-27
562 runs	Australia (701 and 327) v England at The Oval	1934
550 runs	Victoria (295 and 521) v Tasmania at Launceston	1913-14
541 runs	New South Wales (642 and 593) v South Australia at Sydney	1925-26
530 runs	Australia (328 and 578) v South Africa at Melbourne	1910-11

NARROWEST VICTORIES

Victory by One Wicket

New South Wales def Victoria at Sydney (*Last Wkt*: 16) 1877-78
Nottinghamshire def Australians at Nottingham (*Last Wkt*: 2) 1880
Canterbury def Tasmania at Christchurch (*Last Wkt*: 8) 1883-84
Australians def Liverpool and Districts at Liverpool (*Last Wkt*: 4) 1884
Australians def Middlesex at Lord's (*Last Wkt*: 8) 1886
Victoria def New South Wales at Sydney (*Last Wkt*: 10) 1900-01
England def Australia at The Oval (*Last Wkt*: 15) .... 1902.
Australians def England XI at Bournemouth (*Last Wkt*: 1) 1905
England def Australia at Melbourne (*Last Wkt*: 39) 1907-08
Australians def Sussex at Hove (*Last Wkt*: 22) 1909
AIF Team def Yorkshire at Sheffield (*Last Wkt*: 54) 1919
South Australia def New South Wales at Adelaide (*Last Wkt*: 5) 1927-28
Queensland def South Australia at Brisbane (Ex) (*Last Wkt*: 3) 1928-29
J. Ryder's XI def W. M. Woodfull's XI at Sydney (*Last Wkt*: 8) 1929-30
South Australia def West Indians at Adelaide (*Last Wkt*: 22) 1930-31
Tasmania def Victoria at Hobart (TCA) (*Last Wkt*: 11) 1935-36
Australians def Madras Presidency at Madras (*Last Wkt*: 77) 1935-36
New South Wales def Queensland at Brisbane (*Last Wkt*: 6) 1936-37
New South Wales def Queensland and Victorian XI at Brisbane (*Last Wkt*: 10) 1940-41
New South Wales def Queensland at Sydney (*Last Wkt*: 17) 1949-50
Western Australia def West Indians at Perth (*Last Wkt*: 48) 1951-52
Australia def West Indies at Melbourne (*Last Wkt*: 38) 1951-52
Western Australia def South Australia at Adelaide (*Last Wkt*: 36) 1961-62
Queensland def Victoria at Melbourne (*Last Wkt*: 11) 1968-69
Queensland def Western Australia at Perth (*Last Wkt*: 2) 1968-69
Victoria def New South Wales at Melbourne (*Last Wkt*: 4) 1969-70
South Australia def New South Wales at Sydney (*Last Wkt*: 51) 1971-72
South Australia def Victoria at Adelaide (*Last Wkt*: 12) 1977-78
Victoria def New South Wales at Melbourne (*Last Wkt*: 6) 1979-80
England XI def Western Australia at Perth (*Last Wkt*: 5) 1982-83
New South Wales def Queensland at Sydney (*Last Wkt*: 14) 1984-85
New South Wales def Victoria at Sydney (*Last Wkt*: 2) 1986-87
Victoria def New South Wales at Melbourne (*Last Wkt*: 2) 1993-94
Pakistan def Australia at Karachi (*Last Wkt*: 57) 1994-95
Victoria def Tasmania at Melbourne (*Last Wkt*: 17) 1996-97
Derbyshire def Australians at Derby (*Last Wkt*: 11) 1997
England XI def Queensland at Cairns (*Last Wkt*: 36) 1998-99
West Indies def Australia at Bridgetown (*Last Wkt*: 9) 1998-99

Victory by Five Runs or Less

1	West Indies def Australia at Adelaide	1992-93
2	New South Wales def Queensland at Sydney	1903-04
2	Tasmania def Victoria at Launceston	1911-12
2	Philadelphia def Australians at Mannheim	1912-13
2	Western Australia def Victoria at Perth	1998-99
2	South Australia def Western Australia at Adelaide	1999-00
3	Australia def England at Manchester	1902
3	England def Australia at Melbourne	1982-83
3	Victoria def Queensland at Melbourne	1993-94
5	Western Australia def New South Wales at Fremantle	1906-07
5	Surrey def Australians at The Oval	1909
5	South Africa def Australia at Sydney	1993-94

VICTORY AFTER FOLLOWING ON

A. Shaw's XI (146 and 198) def Victoria (251 and 75) at Melbourne 1881-82
A. Shaw's XI (201 and 264) def Australian XI (294 and 114) at Melbourne 1886-87
Victoria (137 and 178) def New South Wales (240 and 63) at Sydney 1888-89
South Australia (212 and 330) def New South Wales (337 and 148) at Adelaide 1892-93
Kent (127 and 198) def Australians (229 and 60) at Canterbury 1893
Australians (196 and 319) def Cambridge University (290 and 108) at Cambridge 1893
England (325 and 437) def Australia (586 and 166) at Sydney 1894-95
South Australia (304 and 454) def Lord Hawke's XI (553 and 108) at Unley 1902-03
New South Wales (108 and 450) def Queensland (307 and 224) at Brisbane 1965-66
England (174 and 356) def Australia (9 for 401 dec. and 111) at Leeds 1981
India (171 and 7 for 657 dec.) def Australia (445 and 212) at Kolkata 2000-01

TIED MATCHES

Gloucestershire tied with Australians at Bristol 1930
MCC tied with Victoria at Melbourne 1932-33
A.L. Hassett's XI tied with D.G. Bradman's XI at Melbourne 1948-49
Victoria tied with New South Wales at St Kilda 1956-57
West Indies tied with Australia at Brisbane 1960-61
South Australia tied with Queensland at Adelaide 1976-77
New Zealanders tied with Victoria at Melbourne 1982-83
Australia tied with India at Chennai 1986-87

MATCHES COMPLETED IN ONE DAY

Australians (41 and 1-12) def MCC (33 and 19) at Lord's .... May 27, 1878
Australia (76 and 6-33) def England XI (82 and 26) at Birmingham .... May 26, 1884
New South Wales (185 and 1-14) def Auckland (93 and 102) at Auckland .... Jan 20, 1894

MOST RUNS BY ONE SIDE IN A MATCH

R	W	Avge		
1,235	20	61.75	New South Wales v South Australia at Sydney	1925-26
1,107	10	110.70	Victoria v New South Wales at Melbourne	1926-27
1,074	20	53.70	New South Wales v South Australia at Adelaide	1920-21
1,059	10	105.90	Victoria v Tasmania at Melbourne	1922-23
1,034	20	51.70	Victoria v South Australia at Melbourne	1920-21
1,028	20	51.50	Australia v England at The Oval	1934
1,013	18	56.27	Australia v West Indies at Sydney	1968-69

LONGEST MATCHES

Eight days
Australia v England at Melbourne 1928-29
Seven days
Australia v England at Sydney 1911-12
Australia v England at Sydney 1924-25
Australia v England at Melbourne 1924-25
Australia v England at Adelaide 1924-25
Australia v England at Melbourne 1928-29
Australia v England at Adelaide 1928-29

MISCELLANEOUS

FIRST-CLASS TEAMS IN AUSTRALIA

	First Game	M	W	L	D	T
Tasmania	Feb 11 1851	425	66	187	172	0
Victoria	Feb 11 1851	995	386	294	312	3
New South Wales	Mar 26 1856	964	424	277	262	1
English Teams	Mar 1 1862	472	190	124	157	1
Combined Teams/Australian XIs	Dec 26 1872	147	41	44	62	0
Australia	Mar 15 1877	339	182	87	69	1
South Australia	Nov 10 1877	855	246	365	243	1
Western Australia	Mar 17 1893	600	182	186	232	0
Queensland	Apr 3 1893	734	195	275	263	1
New Zealanders	Feb 17 1899	81	11	33	36	1
South Africans	Nov 5 1910	81	20	27	34	0
West Indians	Nov 21 1930	133	43	51	38	1
Indians	Oct 17 1947	67	14	31	22	0
Pakistanis	Nov 27 1964	62	12	24	26	0
World XI	Nov 5 1971	12	5	2	5	0
Sri Lankans	Feb 10 1983	19	1	8	10	0
Zimbabweans	Dec 18 1994	5	0	3	2	0
Bangladeshi	Jly 18 2003	2	0	2	0	0
Others		46	14	14	16	2
Total		3,202				

TOURING TEAMS IN AUSTRALIA

			First-Class					All Matches				
		Captain	M	W	L	D	T	M	W	L	D	T
1861-62	H. H. Stephenson's Team	H. H. Stephenson	1	0	1	0	0	14	6	3	5	0
1863-64	G. Parr's Team	G. Parr	1	0	1	0	0	14	7	2	5	0
1873-74	W. G. Grace's Team	W. G. Grace	0	0	0	0	0	15	10	3	2	0
1876-77	J. Lillywhite's Team	J. Lillywhite	3	1	1	1	0	15	5	4	6	0
1878-79	Lord Harris's Team	Lord Harris	5	2	3	0	0	13	5	3	5	0
1881-82	A. Shaw's Team	A. Shaw	7	3	2	2	0	18	8	3	7	0
1882-83	Hon I.F.W. Bligh's Team	Hon I.F.W. Bligh	7	4	3	0	0	17	9	3	5	0
1884-85	A. Shaw's Team	A. Shrewsbury	8	6	2	0	0	33	16	2	15	0
1886-87	A. Shaw's Team	A. Shrewsbury	10	6	2	2	0	30	12	2	16	0
1887-88	G. F. Vernon's Team	G. F. Vernon	8	6	1	1	0	26	11	1	14	0
	A. Shrewsbury's Team	A. Shrewsbury	7	5	2	0	0	22	14	2	6	0
	Combined England	W. W. Read	1	1	0	0	0	1	1	0	0	0
1891-92	Lord Sheffield's Team	W. G. Grace	8	6	2	0	0	27	12	2	13	0
1894-95	A. E. Stoddart's Team	A. E. Stoddart	12	8	4	0	0	23	9	4	10	0
1897-98	A. E. Stoddart's Team	A. E. Stoddart	12	4	5	3	0	22	6	5	11	0
1898-99	New Zealanders	L. T. Cobcroft	2	0	2	0	0	4	1	2	1	0
1901-02	A. C. MacLaren's Team	A. C. MacLaren	11	5	6	0	0	22	8	6	8	0
1902-03	Lord Hawke's Team	P. F. Warner	3	0	2	1	0	3	0	2	1	0
1903-04	MCC	P. F. Warner	14	9	2	3	0	20	10	2	8	0
1907-08	MCC	A. O. Jones	18	7	4	7	0	19	7	4	8	0
1910-11	South Africans	P. W. Sherwell	15	6	7	2	0	22	12	7	3	0
1911-12	MCC	J. W. H. T. Douglas	14	11	1	2	0	18	12	1	5	0
1913-14	New Zealanders	D. Reese	4	1	2	1	0	9	5	2	2	0
1920-21	MCC	J. W. H. T. Douglas	13	5	6	2	0	22	9	6	7	0
1922-23	MCC	A. C. MacLaren	7	0	3	4	0	8	0	3	5	0
1924-25	MCC	A. E. R. Gilligan	17	7	6	4	0	23	8	6	9	0
1925-26	New Zealanders	W. R. Patrick	4	0	1	3	0	9	3	1	5	0
1927-28	New Zealanders	T. C. Lowry	1	0	1	0	0	1	0	1	0	0
1928-29	MCC	A. P. F. Chapman	17	8	1	8	0	24	10	1	13	0
1929-30	MCC	A. H. H. Gilligan	5	2	2	1	0	5	2	2	1	0
1930-31	West Indians	G. C. Grant	14	4	8	2	0	16	5	8	3	0

			First-Class					All Matches				
		Captain	M	W	L	D	T	M	W	L	D	T
1931-32	South Africans	H. B. Cameron	16	4	6	6	0	18	6	6	6	0
1932-33	MCC	D. R. Jardine	17	10	1	5	1	22	10	1	10	1
1935-36	MCC	E. R. T. Holmes	6	3	1	2	0	6	3	1	2	0
1936-37	MCC	G. O. B. Allen	17	5	5	7	0	25	7	5	13	0
1937-38	New Zealanders	M. L. Page	3	0	3	0	0	3	0	3	0	0
1946-47	MCC	W. R. Hammond	17	1	3	13	0	25	4	3	18	0
1947-48	Indians	L. Amarnath	14	2	7	5	0	20	5	7	8	0
1950-51	MCC	F. R. Brown	16	5	4	7	0	25	7	4	14	0
1951-52	West Indians	J. D. C. Goddard	13	4	8	1	0	15	5	8	2	0
1952-53	South Africans	J. E. Cheetham	16	4	3	9	0	23	7	3	13	0
1953-54	New Zealanders	B. Sutcliffe	3	2	0	1	0	3	2	0	1	0
1954-55	MCC	L. Hutton	17	8	2	7	0	23	13	2	8	0
1958-59	MCC	P. B. H. May	17	4	4	9	0	20	7	4	9	0
1960-61	West Indians	F. M. M. Worrell	14	4	5	4	1	22	10	5	5	2
1961-62	New Zealanders	J. R. Reid	3	0	2	1	0	3	0	2	1	0
1962-63	MCC	E. R. Dexter	15	4	3	8	0	26	12	3	11	0
1963-64	South Africans	T. L. Goddard	14	5	3	6	0	28	16	4	8	0
1964-65	Pakistanis	Hanif Mohammad	4	0	0	4	0	4	0	0	4	0
1965-66	MCC	M. J. K. Smith	15	5	2	8	0	23	13	2	8	0
1967-68	New Zealanders	B. W. Sinclair	4	0	2	2	0	7	2	2	3	0
	Indians	Nawab of Pataudi jr	9	0	6	3	0	15	4	6	5	0
1968-69	West Indians	G. S. Sobers	15	4	5	6	0	23	9	5	9	0
1969-70	New Zealanders	G. T. Dowling	3	0	0	3	0	8	3	0	5	0
1970-71	MCC	R. Illingworth	15	3	1	11	0	25	10	2	13	0
	New Zealanders	G. T. Dowling	1	0	0	1	0	2	0	1	1	0
1971-72	World XI	G. S. Sobers	12	5	2	5	0	16	5	3	8	0
	New Zealanders	G. T. Dowling	0	0	0	0	2	1	1	0	0	0
1972-73	Pakistanis	Intikhab Alam	8	2	5	1	0	13	5	6	2	0
	New Zealanders	B. E. Congdon	1	0	0	1	0	3	2	0	1	0
1973-74	New Zealanders	B. E. Congdon	9	2	5	2	0	13	5	6	2	0
1974-75	MCC	M. H. Denness	15	5	5	5	0	23	8	9	6	0
	New Zealanders	B. E. Congdon	0	0	0	0	0	3	3	0	0	0
1975-76	West Indians	C. H. Lloyd	13	3	6	4	0	21	8	7	6	0
1976-77	Pakistanis	Mushtaq Mohammad	5	1	2	2	0	5	1	2	2	0
	MCC	A. W. Greig	2	0	1	1	0	2	0	1	1	0
1977-78	Indians	B. S. Bedi	11	6	5	0	0	20	12	6	2	0
1978-79	England XI	J. M. Brearley	13	8	2	3	0	26	17	4	5	0
	Pakistanis	Mushtaq Mohammad	4	1	1	2	0	5	2	1	2	0
1979-80	England XI	J. M. Brearley	8	3	3	2	0	21	13	5	3	0
	West Indians	C. H. Lloyd	7	5	1	1	0	20	10	7	3	0
1980-81	New Zealanders	G. P. Howarth	7	1	2	4	0	29	14	9	6	0
	Indians	S. M. Gavaskar	8	2	2	4	0	25	8	11	6	0
1981-82	Pakistanis	Javed Miandad	8	2	2	4	0	21	8	8	5	0
	West Indians	C. H. Lloyd	7	4	1	2	0	24	16	5	3	0
1982-83	England XI	R. G. D. Willis	11	4	3	4	0	23	10	9	4	0
	New Zealanders	G. P. Howarth	2	0	0	1	1	22	13	7	1	1
	Sri Lankans	L. R. D. Mendis	2	0	0	2	0	5	1	1	3	0
1983-84	Pakistanis	Imran Khan	11	3	3	5	0	24	7	11	6	0
	West Indians	C. H. Lloyd	0	0	0	0	0	13	10	2	0	1
1984-85	West Indians	C. H. Lloyd	11	4	2	5	0	33	24	4	5	0
	Sri Lankans	L. R. D. Mendis	1	1	0	0	0	22	11	11	0	0
	England XI	D. I. Gower	0	0	0	0	0	3	0	3	0	0
	Indians	S. M. Gavaskar	0	0	0	0	0	5	5	0	0	0
	Pakistanis	Javed Miandad	0	0	0	0	0	5	3	2	0	0
	New Zealanders	G. P. Howarth	0	0	0	0	0	4	1	2	1	0
1985-86	New Zealanders	J. V. Coney	6	2	1	3	0	19	5	7	7	0
	Indians	Kapil Dev	5	1	0	4	0	19	8	7	4	0
1986-87	England XI	M. W. Gatting	11	5	3	3	0	30	19	7	4	0
	Pakistanis	Imran Khan	0	0	0	0	0	4	2	2	0	0
	West Indians	I. V. A. Richards	1	0	0	1	0	13	4	8	1	0

			First-Class					All Matches				
		Captain	M	W	L	D	T	M	W	L	D	T
1987-88	New Zealanders	J. J. Crowe	6	1	2	3	0	19	8	8	3	0
	Sri Lankans	R. S. Madugalle	3	0	1	2	0	18	6	9	3	0
	England XI	M. W. Gatting	1	0	0	1	0	2	0	1	1	0
1988-89	West Indians	I. V. A. Richards	11	4	2	5	0	23	11	7	5	0
	Tamil Nadu	S. Vasudevan	1	0	1	0	0	3	0	3	0	0
	Pakistanis	Imran Khan	1	0	0	1	0	14	6	7	1	0
	New Zealanders	J. G. Wright	0	0	0	0	0	1	0	1	0	0
	Worcestershire	P. A. Neale	0	0	0	0	0	2	0	2	0	0
1989-90	New Zealanders	J. G. Wright	3	0	0	3	0	4	0	1	3	0
	Sri Lankans	A. Ranatunga	6	0	2	4	0	17	5	9	3	0
	Pakistanis	Imran Khan	6	0	3	3	0	27	6	14	7	0
	Lancashire	D. P. Hughes	0	0	0	0	0	8	3	5	0	0
1990-91	England XI	G. A. Gooch	11	1	5	5	0	28	8	14	6	0
	Wellington	E. B. McSweeney	1	0	1	0	0	4	1	1	2	0
	New Zealanders	M. D. Crowe	0	0	0	0	0	11	4	7	0	0
	Lancashire	G. Fowler	0	0	0	0	0	6	4	2	0	0
1991-92	New Zealanders	M. D. Crowe	0	0	0	0	0	6	4	2	0	0
	Indians	M. Azharuddin	7	1	5	1	0	29	7	19	2	1
	West Indians	R. B. Richardson	1	0	0	1	0	22	12	8	1	1
	Pakistanis	Imran Khan	2	0	0	2	0	14	5	6	3	0
	South Africans	K. C. Wessels	0	0	0	0	0	12	7	3	2	0
	Zimbabweans	D. L. Houghton	0	0	0	0	0	6	1	5	0	0
	Sri Lankans	P. A. de Silva	0	0	0	0	0	7	2	4	1	0
	England XI	G. A. Gooch	0	0	0	0	0	9	6	2	1	0
1992-93	West Indians	R. B. Richardson	8	3	1	4	0	22	13	5	4	0
	Pakistanis	Javed Miandad	1	1	0	0	0	12	5	6	0	1
	England A	M. D. Moxon	4	0	2	2	0	11	4	4	3	0
1993-94	New Zealanders	M. D. Crowe	7	2	3	2	0	16	5	9	2	0
	South Africans	K. C. Wessels	5	1	2	2	0	17	6	9	2	0
	Indians	S. R. Tendulkar	0	0	0	0	0	3	0	3	0	0
1994-95	England XI	M. A. Atherton	11	3	4	4	0	24	9	11	4	0
	Zimbabweans	A. Flower	2	0	1	1	0	19	8	10	1	0
1995-96	Western Province	E. O. Simons	2	0	2	0	0	5	1	3	1	0
	Pakistanis	Rameez Raja	6	1	3	2	0	7	2	3	2	0
	Sri Lankans	A. Ranatunga	5	0	4	1	0	17	5	11	1	0
	West Indians	R. B. Richardson	2	0	0	2	0	14	4	8	2	0
1996-97	England A	A. J. Hollioake	3	2	0	1	0	6	3	1	2	0
	West Indians	C. A. Walsh	8	4	4	0	0	25	12	13	0	0
	Pakistanis	Wasim Akram	1	0	0	0	0	10	6	4	0	0
1997-98	Transvaal	K. R. Rutherford	0	0	0	0	0	7	1	6	0	0
	New Zealanders	S. P. Fleming	6	0	5	1	0	21	5	13	2	1
	South Africans	W. J. Cronje	6	0	1	5	0	20	11	4	5	0
1998-99	England XI	A. J. Stewart	10	2	4	4	0	27	10	13	4	0
	Sri Lankans	A. Ranatunga	0	0	0	0	0	15	5	10	0	0
1999-00	Pakistanis	Wasim Akram	5	1	4	0	0	21	6	15	0	0
	Indians	S. R. Tendulkar	6	1	4	1	0	15	2	12	1	0
2000	South Africans	S. M. Pollock	0	0	0	0	0	3	1	1	0	1
2000-01	South Africans	S. M. Pollock	0	0	0	0	0	3	1	1	0	1
	West Indians	J. C. Adams	8	0	7	1	0	18	2	14	2	0
	Zimbabweans	H. H. Streak	0	0	0	0	0	9	1	8	0	0
2001-02	New Zealanders	S. P. Fleming	5	0	1	4	0	18	6	8	4	0
	South Africans	S. M. Pollock	5	0	3	2	0	14	9	3	2	0
	Pakistanis	Waqar Younis	0	0	0	0	0	4	3	1	0	0
2002-03	England XI	N. Hussain	8	1	4	3	0	24	3	16	5	0
	Sri Lankans	S. T. Jayasuriya	0	0	0	0	0	13	4	9	0	0
	South Africa A	G. Dros	2	0	0	2	0	6	1	3	2	0
2003-04	Bangladeshi	Khaled Mahmud	2	0	2	0	0	8	3	5	0	0
	Zimbabweans	H. H. Streak	3	0	2	1	0	16	2	11	3	0
	Indians	S. C. Ganguly	5	1	1	3	0	18	7	6	5	0
2004-05	Sri Lankans	M. S. Atapattu	2	0	1	1	0	3	1	1	1	0

AUSTRALIANS ON TOUR

				First-Class					All Matches				
		Country	Captain	M	W	L	D	T	M	W	L	D	T
1868	Aboriginals	England	C. Lawrence	0	0	0	0	0	47	14	14	19	0
1877-78	Australians	New Zealand	D. W. Gregory	0	0	0	0	0	7	5	1	1	0
1878	Australians	England	D. W. Gregory	15	7	4	4	0	37	18	7	12	0
1878-79	Australians	North America	D. W. Gregory	1	0	0	1	0	6	4	0	2	0
1880	Australians	England	W. L. Murdoch	9	4	2	3	0	37	21	4	12	0
1880-81	Australians	New Zealand	W. L. Murdoch	0	0	0	0	0	10	6	1	3	0
1882	Australians	England	W. L. Murdoch	33	18	4	11	0	38	23	4	11	0
1882-83	Australians	North America	W. L. Murdoch	0	0	0	0	0	2	2	0	0	0
1883-84	Tasmania	New Zealand	J. G. Davies	4	0	3	1	0	7	2	3	2	0
1884	Australians	England	W. L. Murdoch	31	17	7	7	0	32	18	7	7	0
1886	Australians	England	H. J. H. Scott	37	9	7	21	0	39	9	8	22	0
1886-87	Australians	New Zealand	H. J. H. Scott	0	0	0	0	0	5	2	0	3	0
1888	Australians	England	P. S. McDonnell	37	17	13	7	0	40	19	14	7	0
1889-90	NSW	New Zealand	J. Davis	5	4	0	1	0	7	6	0	1	0
1890	Australians	England	W. L. Murdoch	34	10	16	8	0	38	13	16	9	0
1893	Australians	England	J. M. Blackham	31	14	10	7	0	36	18	10	8	0
1893-94	Australians	North America	J. M. Blackham	2	1	1	0	0	6	4	1	1	0
	NSW	New Zealand	J. Davis	7	4	1	2	0	8	4	1	3	0
1895-96	NSW	New Zealand	L. T. Cobcroft	5	3	1	1	0	5	3	1	1	0
1896	Australians	England	G. H. S. Trott	34	20	6	8	0	34	20	6	8	0
1896-97	Australians	North America	G. H. S. Trott	3	2	1	0	0	6	4	1	1	0
	Australians	New Zealand	G. H. S. Trott	0	0	0	0	0	5	3	0	2	0
	Queensland	New Zealand	O. C. Hitchcock	5	3	1	1	0	8	4	1	3	0
1899	Australians	England	J. Darling	35	16	3	16	0	35	16	3	16	0
1902	Australians	England	J. Darling	37	21	2	14	0	39	23	2	14	0
1902-03	Australians	South Africa	J. Darling	4	3	0	1	0	6	3	0	3	0
1904-05	Australians	New Zealand	M. A. Noble	4	3	0	1	0	6	4	0	2	0
1905	Australians	England	J. Darling	35	15	3	17	0	38	16	3	19	0
1909	Australians	England	M. A. Noble	37	11	4	22	0	39	13	4	22	0
1909-10	Australians	New Zealand	W. W. Armstrong	6	5	0	1	0	9	7	0	2	0
1912	Australians	England	E. S. Gregory	36	9	8	19	0	37	9	8	20	0
1912-13	Australians	North America	E. S. Gregory	2	1	1	0	0	7	5	1	1	0
1913-14	NSW	Ceylon	E. F. Waddy	0	0	0	0	0	9	8	1	0	0
	Australians	North America	A. Diamond	5	4	0	1	0	53	49	1	3	0
	Australians	New Zealand	A. Sims	8	6	0	2	0	16	8	0	8	0
1919	AIF Team	England	H. L. Collins	28	12	4	12	0	32	13	4	15	0
1919-20	AIF Team	South Africa	H. L. Collins	8	6	0	2	0	10	8	0	2	0
1920-21	Australians	New Zealand	V. S. Ransford	9	6	0	3	0	15	12	0	3	0
1921	Australians	England	W. W. Armstrong	34	21	2	11	0	39	23	2	14	0
1921-22	Australians	South Africa	H. L. Collins	6	4	0	2	0	6	4	0	2	0
1923-24	NSW	New Zealand	C. G. Macartney	6	5	0	1	0	12	8	0	4	0
1924-25	Victoria	New Zealand	R. E. Mayne	6	1	1	4	0	12	4	1	7	0
1926	Australians	England	H. L. Collins	33	9	1	23	0	40	12	1	27	0
1927-28	Australians	New Zealand	V. Y. Richardson	6	4	0	2	0	13	6	0	7	0
1930	Australians	England	W. M. Woodfull	31	11	1	18	0	33	12	1	19	1
1932-33	Australians	North America	V. Y. Richardson	0	0	0	0	0	51	46	1	4	0
1934	Australians	England	W. M. Woodfull	30	13	1	16	0	34	15	1	18	0
1935-36	Australians	Ceylon	J. Ryder	1	1	0	0	0	1	1	0	0	0
	Australians	India	J. Ryder	16	9	3	4	0	22	10	3	9	0
	Australians	South Africa	V. Y. Richardson	16	13	0	3	0	16	13	0	3	0
1938	Australians	England	D. G. Bradman	29	15	2	12	0	35	20	2	13	0
1945	Aus. Services	England	A. L. Hassett	6	3	2	1	0	48	24	9	15	0
1945-46	Australians	India	A. L. Hassett	8	1	2	5	0	9	1	2	6	0
	Australians	Ceylon	A. L. Hassett	1	1	0	0	0	1	1	0	0	0
	Australians	New Zealand	W. A. Brown	5	5	0	0	0	5	5	0	0	0
1948	Australians	England	D. G. Bradman	31	23	0	8	0	34	25	0	9	0
1949-50	Australians	South Africa	A. L. Hassett	21	14	0	7	0	25	18	0	7	0
	Australians	New Zealand	W. A. Brown	5	3	0	2	0	14	9	0	5	0
1953	Australians	England	A. L. Hassett	33	16	1	16	0	35	16	1	18	0

				First-Class					All Matches				
	Country	Captain	M	W	L	D	T	M	W	L	D	T
1954-55	Australians	West Indies	I. W. G. Johnson	9	5	0	4	0	11	5	0	6	0
1956	Australians	England	I. W. G. Johnson	31	9	3	19	0	35	12	3	20	0
1956-57	Australians	Pakistan	I. W. G. Johnson	1	0	1	0	0	1	0	1	0	0
	Australians	India	I. W. G. Johnson	3	2	0	1	0	3	2	0	1	0
	Australians	New Zealand	I. D. Craig	7	5	0	2	0	12	7	0	5	0
1957-58	Australians	South Africa	I. D. Craig	20	11	0	9	0	22	11	0	11	0
1959-60	Australians	Pakistan	R. Benaud	4	3	0	1	0	4	3	0	1	0
	Australians	India	R. Benaud	7	2	1	4	0	7	2	1	4	0
	Australians	New Zealand	I. D. Craig	6	2	0	4	0	9	4	0	5	0
1961	Australians	England	R. Benaud	32	13	1	18	0	37	14	2	21	0
1964	Australians	England	R. B. Simpson	30	11	3	16	0	36	14	4	18	0
1964-65	Australians	India	R. B. Simpson	3	1	1	1	0	3	1	1	1	0
	Australians	Pakistan	R. B. Simpson	1	0	0	1	0	1	0	0	1	0
	Australians	West Indies	R. B. Simpson	11	3	2	6	0	16	4	3	9	0
1966-67	Australians	South Africa	R. B. Simpson	17	7	5	5	0	24	11	6	7	0
	Australians	New Zealand	L. E. Favell	9	1	2	6	0	10	2	2	6	0
1968	Australians	England	W. M. Lawry	25	8	3	14	0	29	10	3	16	0
1969-70	Australians	Ceylon	W. M. Lawry	1	0	0	1	0	4	1	0	3	0
	Australians	India	W. M. Lawry	10	5	1	4	0	10	5	1	4	0
	Australians	South Africa	W. M. Lawry	12	4	4	4	0	12	4	4	4	0
	Australians	New Zealand	S. C. Trimble	8	2	0	6	0	8	2	0	6	0
1972	Australians	England	I. M. Chappell	26	11	5	10	0	37	14	10	13	0
1972-73	Australians	West Indies	I. M. Chappell	12	7	0	5	0	15	10	0	5	0
1973-74	Australians	New Zealand	I. M. Chappell	7	2	1	4	0	11	6	1	4	0
1974-75	Australians	North America	I. M. Chappell	0	0	0	0	0	5	2	1	2	0
1975	Australians	England	I. M. Chappell	15	8	2	5	0	21	12	4	5	0
1976-77	Australians	New Zealand	G. S. Chappell	6	5	0	1	0	8	5	2	1	0
1977	Australians	England	G. S. Chappell	22	5	4	13	0	31	8	8	15	0
1977-78	Australians	West Indies	R. B. Simpson	11	5	3	3	0	13	6	4	3	0
1979	Australians	England	K. J. Hughes	0	0	0	0	0	6	2	3	1	0
1979-80	Australians	India	K. J. Hughes	11	0	3	8	0	11	0	3	8	0
	Australians	Pakistan	G. S. Chappell	5	0	1	4	0	5	0	1	4	0
1980	Australians	England	G. S. Chappell	5	1	2	2	0	8	1	4	3	0
1980-81	Australians	Sri Lanka	K. J. Hughes	1	0	0	1	0	4	2	1	1	0
1981	Australians	England	K. J. Hughes	17	3	3	11	0	26	7	7	12	0
1981-82	Australians	New Zealand	G. S. Chappell	5	1	1	3	0	11	4	4	3	0
1982-83	Australians	Pakistan	K. J. Hughes	6	0	3	3	0	9	0	5	4	0
	Australians	Zimbabwe	D. M. Wellham	2	1	1	0	0	8	7	1	0	0
	Australians	Sri Lanka	G. S. Chappell	2	1	0	1	0	6	1	2	3	0
1983	Australians	England	K. J. Hughes	0	0	0	0	0	9	3	5	1	0
1983-84	Australians	West Indies	K. J. Hughes	10	1	3	6	0	15	2	6	7	0
1984-85	Australians	India	K. J. Hughes	0	0	0	0	0	6	4	0	2	0
	NSW	New Zealand	D. M. Wellham	0	0	0	0	0	1	1	0	0	0
	Australians	Sharjah, UAE	A. R. Border	0	0	0	0	0	2	1	1	0	0
1985	Australians	England	A. R. Border	20	4	3	13	0	29	9	5	15	0
1985-86	Australians	Zimbabwe	R. B. Kerr	2	1	0	1	0	9	3	5	1	0
	Australians	South Africa	K. J. Hughes	10	2	2	6	0	25	10	9	6	0
	Australians	New Zealand	A. R. Border	5	1	1	3	0	11	5	3	3	0
	Australians	Sharjah, UAE	R. J. Bright	0	0	0	0	0	1	0	1	0	0
1985-86	NSW	Zimbabwe	G. C. Dyer	2	1	0	1	0	8	5	2	1	0
1986-87	Australians	India	A. R. Border	7	0	0	6	1	13	2	3	7	1
	NSW	New Zealand	D. M. Wellham	0	0	0	0	0	2	1	1	0	0
	Australians	South Africa	K. J. Hughes	12	2	3	7	0	25	8	9	8	0
	SAust	New Zealand	D. W. Hookes	0	0	0	0	0	4	4	0	0	0
	Australians	Sharjah, UAE	A. R. Border	0	0	0	0	0	3	0	3	0	0
1987-88	NSW	Zimbabwe	D. M. Wellham	2	0	0	2	0	8	5	1	2	0
	Australians	India	A. R. Border	0	0	0	0	0	7	6	1	0	0
	Australians	Pakistan	A. R. Border	0	0	0	0	0	1	1	0	0	0
	Victoria	New Zealand	D. F. Whatmore	0	0	0	0	0	2	0	2	0	0
	Queensland	New Zealand	R. B. Kerr	0	0	0	0	0	3	3	0	0	0

			First-Class					All Matches				
		Country	Captain	M	W	L	D	T	M	W	L	D	T
1988	Aboriginals	England	J. McGuire	0	0	0	0	0	27	15	11	1	0
1988-89	Australians	Pakistan	A. R. Border	6	0	1	5	0	7	0	2	5	0
1989	Australians	England	A. R. Border	20	12	1	7	0	31	20	3	7	1
1989-90	W.Aust	India	G. M. Wood	1	0	0	1	0	4	1	2	1	0
	Australians	India	A. R. Border	0	0	0	0	0	5	2	3	0	0
	Australians	New Zealand	A. R. Border	1	0	1	0	0	6	5	0	1	0
	Australians	Sharjah, UAE	A. R. Border	0	0	0	0	0	4	3	1	0	0
1990-91	Australians	West Indies	A. R. Border	10	2	2	6	0	19	10	3	6	0
1991	Victoria	England	S. P. O'Donnell	1	0	0	1	0	4	1	1	2	0
1991-92	Australians	Zimbabwe	M. A. Taylor	2	2	0	0	0	6	5	1	0	0
	Australians	New Zealand	A. R. Border	0	0	0	0	0	2	1	1	0	0
1992-93	Australians	Sri Lanka	A. R. Border	5	1	0	4	0	8	2	2	4	0
	Australians	New Zealand	A. R. Border	4	2	1	1	0	10	5	4	1	0
1993	Australians	England	A. R. Border	21	10	2	9	0	30	18	3	9	0
1993-94	Australians	South Africa	A. R. Border	6	3	1	2	0	16	7	5	4	0
	NSW	New Zealand	P. A. Emery	0	0	0	0	0	1	1	0	0	0
	Australians	Sharjah, UAE	M. A. Taylor	0	0	0	0	0	3	2	1	0	0
1994-95	Australians	Sri Lanka	M. A. Taylor	0	0	0	0	0	3	1	2	0	0
	Australians	Pakistan	M. A. Taylor	4	0	1	3	0	10	5	2	3	0
	Australians Cricket Academy	New Zealand	M. A. Taylor	0	0	0	0	0	4	3	1	0	0
		New Zealand	N. W. Ashley	1	1	0	0	0	6	6	0	0	0
	Australians	West Indies	M. A. Taylor	7	3	1	3	0	16	8	5	3	0
1995	Young Australia	England	S. G. Law	8	5	1	2	0	16	11	3	2	0
	NSW	England	M. A. Taylor	1	0	0	1	0	2	1	0	1	0
1995-96	Tasmania	Zimbabwe	D. C. Boon	2	0	0	2	0	5	3	0	2	0
	Australians	India	M. A. Taylor	0	0	0	0	0	6	5	1	0	0
	Australians	Pakistan	M. A. Taylor	0	0	0	0	0	1	0	1	0	0
1996-97	Australians	Sri Lanka	I. A. Healy	0	0	0	0	0	6	4	2	0	0
	Australians	India	M. A. Taylor	2	0	1	1	0	7	0	6	1	0
	Australians	South Africa	M. A. Taylor	6	5	1	0	0	17	13	4	0	0
1997	Australians	England	M. A. Taylor	16	6	3	6	1	27	11	7	7	2
1997-98	Australians	New Zealand	S. R. Waugh	0	0	0	0	0	4	2	2	0	0
	Australians	India	M. A. Taylor	6	1	2	3	0	6	1	2	3	0
	Australians	Sharjah, UAE	S. R. Waugh	0	0	0	0	0	5	4	1	0	0
1998	Australians	Scotland	M. J. Di Venuto	2	0	0	2	0	5	2	0	3	0
	Australians	Ireland	M. J. Di Venuto	1	1	0	0	0	6	5	0	1	0
1998-99	Australians	Pakistan	M. A. Taylor	5	2	0	3	0	9	6	0	3	0
	Australians	Bangladesh	M. A. Taylor	0	0	0	0	0	1	0	1	0	0
	Australians Cricket Academy	West Indies	S. R. Waugh	7	4	2	1	0	14	7	5	1	1
		Zimbabwe	B. J. Hodge	2	2	0	0	0	7	5	2	0	0
1999	Australians	England	S. R. Waugh	0	0	0	0	0	10	7	2	0	1
1999-00	Australians	North America	A. C. Gilchrist	0	0	0	0	0	5	4	1	0	0
	Australians	Sri Lanka	S. R. Waugh	5	2	1	2	0	10	6	2	2	0
	Australians	Zimbabwe	S. R. Waugh	2	2	0	0	0	5	5	0	0	0
	Australians	New Zealand	S. R. Waugh	5	4	1	0	0	11	8	1	2	0
	Australians	South Africa	S. R. Waugh	0	0	0	0	0	3	2	1	0	0
2000-01	Australians	Kenya	S. R. Waugh	0	0	0	0	0	2	1	1	0	0
	Australians	India	S. R. Waugh	6	1	2	3	0	12	4	5	3	0
2001	Australians	England	S. R. Waugh	11	8	2	1	0	20	13	4	2	1
2001-02	Australians	South Africa	S. R. Waugh	6	3	2	1	0	13	8	2	2	1
2001-02	Australians	South Africa	S. R. Waugh	6	3	2	1	0	13	8	2	2	1
2002-03	Australians	Kenya	R. T. Ponting	0	0	0	0	0	5	4	0	1	0
	Australia A	South Africa	J. L. Langer	0	0	0	0	0	6	5	1	0	0
	Australians	Sri Lanka	R. T. Ponting	0	0	0	0	0	4	3	1	0	0
	Australians	Sri Lanka/Sh	R. T. Ponting	3	3	0	0	0	3	3	0	0	0
	Australians	South Africa	R. T. Ponting	0	0	0	0	0	11	11	0	0	0
	Australians	West Indies	S. R. Waugh	6	4	1	1	0	13	8	4	1	0

	Country	Captain	First-Class					All Matches				
			M	W	L	D	T	M	W	L	D	T
2003-04 Australians	India	R. T. Ponting	0	0	0	0	0	7	6	1	0	0
Australians	Sri Lanka	R. T. Ponting	4	4	0	0	0	9	7	2	0	0
Australians	Zimbabwe	R. T. Ponting	0	0	0	0	0	4	3	0	1	0

FIRST-CLASS GROUNDS

	First Game	Last Game	Games
NTCA Ground, Launceston, Tasmania	1850-51	1995-96	81
Emerald Hill Cricket Ground, Emerald Hill, Victoria	*1851-52		1
Melbourne Cricket Ground (MCG), Victoria	1855-56	2003-04	611
The Domain, Sydney, New South Wales	*1856-57	1868-69	6
Lower Domain Ground, Hobart, Tasmania	*1857-58		1
Albert Ground, Redfern, New South Wales	*1870-71	1876-77	5
Adelaide Oval, South Australia	1877-78	2003-04	542
Sydney Cricket Ground (SCG), New South Wales	1877-78	2003-04	615
East Melbourne Cricket Ground, Victoria	*1880-81		4
Tasmanian Cricket Association Ground, Hobart, Tasmania	1906-07	1986-87	86
Exhibition Ground, Brisbane, Queensland	**1892-93	1930-31	28
Brisbane Cricket Ground (The Gabba), Queensland	1897-98	2003-04	420
Western Australian Cricket Association Ground, Perth, Western Australia	1898-99	2003-04	381
Unley Oval, South Australia	1902-03		1
Fremantle Oval, Western Australia	**1905-06	1909-10	5
South Melbourne Cricket Ground (Lakeside Oval), Victoria	*1907-08	1931-32	2
Fitzroy Cricket Ground (Brunswick Street Oval), Victoria	*1925-26		1
Richmond Cricket Ground (Punt Road Oval), Victoria	1932-33	2001-02	6
Carlton Recreation Ground (Princes Park), Victoria	1945-46	1997-98	7
St Kilda Cricket Ground (Junction Oval), Victoria	1945-46	2003-04	31
Kardinia Park, Geelong, Victoria	**1961-62	1981-92	6
Sydney Cricket Ground No 2, New South Wales	*1966-67		1
Devonport Oval, Tasmania	1977-78	1997-98	27
Manuka Oval, Canberra, Australian Capital Territory	1978-79	1998-99	5
Oakes Oval, Lismore, New South Wales	1979-80	1991-92	2
No 1 Sports Ground, Newcastle, New South Wales	1981-82	2003-04	18
Salter Oval, Bundaberg, Queensland	1982-83		1
Showgrounds Oval, Wangaratta, Victoria	1986-87	1996-97	2
Endeavour Park, Townsville, Queensland	1986-87		1
Bellerive Oval, Tasmania	1987-88	2003-04	96
Sale Oval, Victoria	1989-90		1
Lavington Sports Ground, Albury, New South Wales	1989-90	1990-91	2
North Sydney Oval, New South Wales	1990-91	2000-01	3
Eastern Oval, Ballarat, Victoria	1990-91		1
Carrara Sports Ground, Queensland	**1990-91		1
Queen Elizabeth Oval, Bendigo, Victoria	1991-92	1994-95	2
Henzell Park, Caloundra, Queensland	1992-93		1
Southern Cross Reserve, Toowoomba, Queensland	1994-95		1
Newtown Oval, Maryborough, Queensland	1994-95		1
Hurstville Oval, New South Wales	1995-96		1
Harrup Park, Mackay, Queensland	1995-96		1
Bankstown Memorial Oval, New South Wales	1996-97		1
Cazaly's Australian Football Park, Cairns, Queensland	1997-98	2004-05	3
Allan Border Field, Albion, Queensland	1999-00	2002-03	7
Marrara Cricket Ground, Darwin	2002-03	2004-05	2

* Denotes the ground no longer exists; ** Denotes the ground is no longer used for cricket.

Opposite LITTLE MASTER OF SELF-DENIAL: Sachin
Tendulkar indulges in a rare cover drive during the SCG Test,
where 188 of his first-innings 241 came on the leg side.
Picture by Adam Pretty, Getty Images.

4

International Summer

India in Australia, 2003-04

by DILEEP PREMACHANDRAN

Fifty years from now, people who skim over the details of this series could be forgiven for concentrating their attention on one man, Stephen Rodger Waugh. His four-match farewell was the constant twisting subplot to a contest almost as epic as that staged between the teams led by Richie Benaud and Frank Worrell 43 years earlier. But it was just that: a subplot. When they look a little closer, they might come to appreciate just how good the Indians were, and how close they came to branding Waugh with the scar of defeat in his final outing.

That they didn't owed much to the pugnacity of the man. Chasing a chimera of a target in front of an emotional final-day crowd at the SCG, Waugh appeared to traipse back in time to his glory years. He chiselled out a frenetic 80, founded on the whiplash square-drives that had come to epitomise his batting. It momentarily deflected attention from the fact that Australia had been comprehensively outplayed, Sachin Tendulkar and V.V.S. Laxman producing marathon innings of contrasting character to render any thoughts of a victorious Waugh swansong obsolete.

Tendulkar's unconquered 241 was an exercise in self-denial, a testament to the determination of a genius who had been written off by immature critics. Laxman's 178 was created for the aesthete's pleasure, studded with the most gorgeous strokes. Glenn McGrath and Shane Warne were badly missed and Australia's attack, bravely led by a half-fit Jason Gillespie, was cruelly exposed.

Instead of surging to victory, Waugh was left to marshal one last rearguard action. He managed it too, warding off the threat of Anil Kumble, who proved the outstanding bowler of the summer with 24 wickets, enough to silence those who reckoned him useless when separated from Indian dustbowls. Waugh then departed to rapturous acclaim, a few thousand red-handkerchief waves and a 1–1 series draw.

It was never supposed to end this way. India had won only three Tests on Australian soil going back to 1947-48. Two of those were against Bobby Simpson's depleted team of 1977-78, when Australia's finest had taken the Packer coin, and the most recent dated back to February 1981. Having lost seven of their previous eight Tests in Australia, India were expected to go where every other visiting team had gone in the past decade – to the scrapheap, steamrollered by one of the greatest sides in the history of sport.

If you looked beneath the surface, though, the makings of an intriguing battle were always there. India flew into Australia with perhaps the most formidable batting line-up they had ever assembled. And while they had no genuinely great bowler to support Kumble, weighty contributions came not entirely surprisingly from the likes of Ajit Agarkar, Zaheer Khan and Irfan Pathan, reckoned by some to be the most exciting all-round talent the country has produced since Kapil Dev.

Skill levels aside, they possessed a tenacity that Waugh's Australians had seldom encountered. Unlike past Indian teams, there was no dissension in the camp. Well-prepared by their coach John Wright, the former New Zealand opener, and inspired by Sourav Ganguly's instinctive and courageous captaincy, they looked Australia in the eye without blinking.

In those eyes, Australian cricket glimpsed a future that may not be quite so golden as previously thought. McGrath and Warne proved irreplaceable, as many had long feared. Having had their way with most teams for so long, Australia lacked a Plan B when shock and awe failed to work. Accustomed to bludgeoning opponents into submission, they had few answers once on the rope themselves.

The crowds that thronged to the matches were entranced by the quality on offer, perhaps conscious that they were witnessing a series which would be talked about in reverential tones years from now. There were isolated incidents of beer-fuelled name-calling and racism in Adelaide. But there was also plenty of good-natured banter between two sets of supporters who recognised that they had ringside seats to a modern-day cricketing blockbuster.

It was Ganguly, Waugh's old adversary, who initially set about rewriting the script, in Brisbane of all places. For more than a decade the Gabba had been a coliseum where Australia's pride mauled all those who crossed their path. But in a rain-hit match with only psychological points to play for, Ganguly struck the most telling blows. He drove and slashed his way to a glorious century, and it meant much more to his men than simply a first-innings lead. Australia's batsmen, who suffered the worst of the conditions in the first innings, reasserted themselves in the second. But Ganguly and Laxman with the bat, and Zaheer Khan with the ball, had suggested that Waugh's valedictory march might yet have to cross some inhospitable terrain.

The manner of Waugh's dismissal was indicative of that. Pushed on to the back foot by Zaheer, who was targeting his body, Waugh inadvertently trod on his stumps. Minutes earlier he had been the guilty party in Damien Martyn's run-out. Australia departed Brisbane with honour intact, but whispers behind the scenes were already questioning the wisdom of allowing an individual such an extended public farewell.

After two days in Adelaide, where the weather veered from intolerably hot to cool and windy, the small strides that India had taken in Brisbane were seemingly cancelled out by a staggering Australian counterpunch. Having lost Harbhajan Singh to finger surgery and Zaheer to a hamstring twinge, an enfeebled India attack was taken apart by Ricky Ponting. His 242 was full of crisp shot-making and brio, as nonchalant as the kisses blown to his wife, Rianna, sitting in the stands.

But with India shipping water at 4 for 85 in response to Australia's mammoth 556, fate stepped in with one of those twists that have become an integral part of modern Test matches between these teams. As in Kolkata 33 months earlier, Laxman and Rahul Dravid were the central characters, putting on 303 with a panache and commonsense that left Waugh as helpless as he had been at Eden Gardens.

Laxman was all wristy elegance and wondrous timing, piercing the field almost at will, while Dravid knuckled down to play the sort of innings that defines a career. Laxman's 281 in Kolkata had been lauded for its quintessentially Indian qualities: style, artistry, amazing grace. Dravid's 233 in Adelaide was redolent of the outback pioneers, of hardy weather-beaten men panning for gold in a muddy river.

Although Australia led by 33, the momentum-shift over four sessions bordered on cataclysmic. But India still needed a bowling hero. She got one in the shape of Agarkar, famous previously only for the moniker of 'Bombay Duck', which he had earned after an inglorious run of seven innings without so much as a run in anger against Australia.

On that fourth afternoon in Adelaide, he generated a lively pace that belied his frail frame, moving the ball cleverly and using the bouncer judiciously. Australia imploded. India needed a modest

233 for victory but on an Adelaide pitch noted for its capriciousness towards fourth-innings targets, and against an Australian team smarting after their abysmal batting display, it might as well have been 400. Yet again it was Dravid, as unflustered and unhurried as Sunil Gavaskar at his peak, who saw India home. Yet again he was helped by Laxman, whose glittering cameo lifted the veil of tension that had shrouded the Indian dressing room.

Such was the magnificence of Dravid's match contribution – 305 runs, 835 minutes – that Waugh picked up the ball from the fence after the winning runs had been cut through point and presented it to him. It was a grand gesture in recognition of a virtuoso batting display.

Ten days later the two sides arrived in Melbourne. India had stopped off in Hobart along the way for the luxury of a match against Australia A, where they tried to cajole the likes of Tendulkar into the groove. Years from now, when they are old and grey, the players will look back to Boxing Day 2003 and wonder how they allowed Australia to recover after bludgeoning them into submission for the first five hours.

Before the team left India, Virender Sehwag's technical flaws had been the subject of lively debate, with many critics choosing to ignore the evidence of superb hundreds in Bloemfontein (on debut) and at Trent Bridge. Australia's bouncy pitches and fast bowlers, they said, would catch him out. They did eventually at the MCG, but only after he had swashbuckled his way to within five runs of one of the most exhilarating double-centuries the ground had seen. Disdainful of pace, despite being struck on the helmet, and contemptuous of Stuart MacGill's leg-spin, Sehwag's innings was a gentle reminder that flair and self-belief can take a man far further than any coaching manual ever could.

That India lost the match from there said much about the mental make-up of the two teams. Suddenly harbouring visions of a series victory in Australia, the Indians were blinded by the realisation. Waugh and his men, their aura of invincibility fast receding, dug deep and found the inspiration that had been lacking. The monolithic figure of Matthew Hayden provided the solidity and Ponting completed the edifice, combining his usual exuberance with tenacity. It was left to Brad Williams, playing Test cricket at his old home ground, to apply a glossy coat. Having somehow summoned the nerve to survive Sehwag's Boxing Day knockout, Australia journeyed to Sydney as favourites to win an engrossing series.

But there again, the script was shredded. And for once, nobody cared. Impromptu plays have a charm all their own. The final act, played out on an epic stage, was just the sort of curtain that one of the game's legends deserved, in a series that proved the words "bore" and "draw" are not necessarily soulmates.

INDIAN TOURING PARTY

S. C. Ganguly (*captain*), R. S. Dravid (*vice-captain*), A. B. Agarkar, A. Chopra, A. R. Kumble, A. Nehra, D. Dasgupta, Harbhajan Singh, I. K. Pathan, P. A. Patel, S. R. Tendulkar, S. Ramesh, V. Sehwag, V. V. S. Laxman, Zaheer Khan. *Coach:* J. G. Wright. *Bowling coach:* B. A. Reid. *Manager:* N. S. Yadav.

A. M. Salvi withdrew before the start of the tour and was replaced by L. Balaji. M. Kartik was added to the squad in mid-December.

VB SERIES PARTY

S. C. Ganguly (*captain*), R. S. Dravid (*vice-captain*), A. B. Agarkar, H. K. Badani, L. Balaji, S. B. Bangar, M. Kartik, A R Kumble, V V S Laxman, A. Nehra, P. A. Patel, I. K. Pathan, Yuvraj Singh, V. Sehwag, S. R. Tendulkar. M. Kaif withdrawn due to injurey early in the series and was replaced by R. S. Gavaskar. A. Bhandari added to the squad on January 10.

INDIAN TOUR RESULTS

Test matches – Played 4: Won 1, Lost 1, Drawn 1.
First-class matches – Played 6, Won 1, Lost 1, Drawn 4.
Wins – Australia.
Losses – Australia.
Draws – Australia (2), Victoria, Australia A.
International limited overs - Played 10: Won 5, Lost 5. *Wins* - Australia (1), Zimbabwe 4.
Other non first-class matches: Played 2: Won 1, Drawn 1. *Wins* – Prime Minister's XI; *Drawn* – Queensland Academy of Sport.

TEST BATTING AVERAGES

	M	I	NO	R	HS	100s	50s	Avge	Ct/St	S-R
R. S. Dravid (Ind)	4	8	3	619	233	1	3	123.80	4	51.45
R. T. Ponting (Aus) . . .	4	8	1	706	257	2	2	100.86	1	58.78
V. V. S. Laxman (Ind) .	4	7	1	494	178	2	1	82.33	5	54.47
S. R. Tendulkar (Ind) . .	4	7	2	383	241*	1	1	76.60	3	56.91
S. M. Katich (Aus) . . .	4	6	1	353	125	1	2	70.60	3	68.81
M. L. Hayden (Aus) . .	4	8	1	451	136	1	3	64.43	9	79.12
V. Sehwag (Ind)	4	8	0	464	195	1	1	58.00	8	79.32
S. C. Ganguly (Ind) . . .	4	6	0	284	144	1	1	47.33	1	66.98
J. L. Langer (Aus)	4	8	0	369	121	2	1	46.13	3	69.62
S. R. Waugh (Aus) . . .	4	7	1	267	80	0	2	44.50	0	51.05
D. R. Martyn (Aus) . . .	4	7	1	254	66*	0	1	42.33	3	51.00
J. N. Gillespie (Aus) . .	3	5	2	110	48*	0	0	36.67	2	52.88
P. A. Patel (Ind)	4	6	1	160	62	0	1	32.00	8/3	58.39
A. Chopra (Ind)	4	8	0	186	48	0	0	23.25	5	34.51

	M	I	NO	R	HS	100s	50s	Avge	Ct/St	S-R
A. C. Gilchrist (Aus)..	4	6	0	96	43	0	0	16.00	10/1	73.85
I. K. Pathan (Ind).....	2	2	1	14	13*	0	0	14.00	1	51.85
Zaheer Khan (Ind)....	2	3	1	28	27	0	0	14.00	0	50.91
B. A. Williams (Aus)..	2	3	2	14	10*	0	0	14.00	1	60.87
A. J. Bichel (Aus)	2	3	0	31	19	0	0	10.33	4	50.82
A. B. Agarkar (Ind) ...	4	6	1	26	12	0	0	5.20	1	36.06
A. R. Kumble (Ind) ...	3	3	0	15	12	0	0	5.00	1	25.86
N. W. Bracken (Aus)..	3	3	1	9	6*	0	0	4.50	1	34.62
B. Lee (Aus)	2	2	0	8	8	0	0	4.00	0	19.51
S. C. G. MacGill (Aus)	4	5	1	2	1	0	0	0.50	2	20.00
A. Nehra (Ind).......	3	4	1	0	0*	0	0	0.00	2	0.00
Harbhajan Singh (Ind)	1	1	1	19	19*	0	0	–	0	48.72
M. Kartik (Ind)	1	0	–	–	–	–	–	–	0	–

TEST BOWLING AVERAGES

	O	Mdns	R	W	BB	5W/i	10W/m	Avge	S-R
A. R. Kumble (Ind)	206.1	28	710	24	8-141	3	1	29.58	51.54
A. B. Agarkar (Ind)	154.5	23	596	16	6-41	1	0	37.25	58.06
J. N. Gillespie (Aus) ...	139.1	41	377	10	4-65	0	0	37.70	83.50
Zaheer Khan (Ind).....	51	6	213	5	5-95	1	0	42.60	61.20
S. M. Katich (Aus).....	51	5	215	5	2-22	0	0	43.00	61.20
B. A. Williams (Aus)...	79	24	225	5	4-53	0	0	45.00	94.80
S. R. Tendulkar (Ind)...	28	0	141	3	2-36	0	0	47.00	56.00
A. J. Bichel (Aus)	70.4	11	295	6	4-118	0	0	49.17	70.67
S. C. G. MacGill (Aus) .	194.4	29	711	14	4-86	0	0	50.79	83.43
N. W. Bracken (Aus)...	128	38	351	6	2-12	0	0	58.50	128.00
B. Lee (Aus)	100.5	17	476	8	4-201	0	0	59.50	75.63
I. K. Pathan (Ind)......	68	7	266	4	2-80	0	0	66.50	102.00
S. R. Waugh (Aus).....	31	5	82	1	1-35	0	0	82.00	186.00
A. Nehra (Ind)........	101	16	382	4	2-115	0	0	95.50	151.50
Harbhajan Singh (Ind)..	35	2	169	1	1-101	0	0	169.00	210.00
M. Kartik (Ind)	45	6	211	1	1-89	0	0	211.00	270.00
S. C. Ganguly (Ind)	2	1	8	0	–	0	0	–	–
D. R. Martyn (Aus)	9	1	27	0	–	0	0	–	–
R. T. Ponting (Aus)	1	0	4	0	–	0	0	–	–
V. Sehwag (Ind)	18	1	71	0	–	0	0	–	–

INDIAN FIRST-CLASS BATTING AVERAGES

	M	I	NO	R	HS	100s	50s	Avge	Ct/St	S-R
R. S. Dravid	5	10	4	620	233	1	3	103.33	7	50.45
V. V. S. Laxman......	4	7	1	494	178	2	1	82.33	5	54.47
S. R. Tendulkar	6	9	2	499	241*	1	2	71.29	4	60.19
V. Sehwag	6	11	0	537	195	1	1	48.82	9	79.91
P. A. Patel	6	9	3	261	62	0	2	43.50	10/3	55.06
D. Dasgupta.........	1	2	1	40	21	0	0	40.00	3	32.00
S. Ramesh	2	4	0	149	87	0	1	37.25	0	44.48
S. C. Ganguly........	6	8	0	291	144	1	0	36.38	6	67.05
A. Chopra...........	6	12	1	314	55*	0	1	28.55	7	34.66
M. Kartik	2	1	0	26	26	0	0	26.00	4	40.63
Harbhajan Singh	2	2	1	22	19*	0	0	22.00	0	42.31
I. K. Pathan	3	3	1	25	13*	0	0	12.50	1	43.10
Zaheer Khan	3	4	1	30	27	0	0	10.00	0	46.88
L. Balaji	2	2	0	12	8	0	0	6.00	0	46.15
A. B. Agarkar........	4	6	1	26	12	0	0	5.20	1	36.06
A. R. Kumble........	3	3	0	15	12	0	0	5.00	1	25.86
A. Nehra............	5	6	3	0	0*	0	0	0.00	2	0.00

INDIAN FIRST-CLASS BOWLING AVERAGES

	O	Mdns	R	W	BB	5W/i	10W/m	Avge	S-R
A.R. Kumble	206.1	28	710	24	8-141	3	1	29.58	51.54
A.B. Agarkar	154.5	23	596	16	6-41	1	0	37.25	58.06
Zaheer Khan	75	11	288	6	5-95	1	0	48.00	75.00
I.K. Pathan	104	14	383	7	2-40	0	0	54.71	89.14
S.R. Tendulkar	33	0	170	3	2-36	0	0	56.67	66.67
A. Nehra	155	24	555	9	2-33	0	0	61.67	103.33
S.C. Ganguly	14	2	68	1	1-38	0	0	68.00	84.00
L. Balaji	69	8	293	4	3-87	0	0	73.25	103.50
V. Sehwag	27	3	101	1	1-30	0	0	101.00	40.50
Harbhajan Singh	72	7	328	3	2-159	0	0	109.33	144.00
M. Kartik	72.4	11	328	3	1-53	0	0	109.33	145.33

Note: Matches in this section that were not first-class are signified by a dagger.

VICTORIA v INDIANS

At Melbourne Cricket Ground, Melbourne, November 25, 26, 27, 2003. Match drawn. *Toss:* Indians. *First-class debut:* B.D. Harrop.

Aside from confirmation of Sachin Tendulkar's greatness, the Indians took little out of a drawn game which appeared to herald the beginning of yet another listless jaunt down under. Tendulkar hooked and pulled with confidence once the wicket dried out, his sparkling 80 was speckled with 14 brilliantly struck fours, delighting a small but adoring crowd. Even the Victorians seemed mesmerised by his sweet timing, imploring each other at the drinks break to "get behind the bowlers a bit, rather than just enjoying watching him bat". The only other Indians worth watching were the gritty Sadagoppan Ramesh and their hobbit-like keeper Parthiv Patel, who showed impressive resolve. Things got worse for the tourists as Brad Hodge, watched by the Test selector David Boon, sought to further register his name on the cricketing consciousness. Despatching all bowlers to all points of the ground, he made the Indians appear amateurish at times. Often they didn't need his help, bowling too short, too full or too wide. Hodge was caught off a no-ball on 103 but otherwise batted flawlessly. He faced 380 deliveries, overtaking Justin Langer's 223 in 1999-00 as the highest score by an Australian against India. The match ended sourly, Victoria's coach David Hookes accusing Sourav Ganguly of treating the match as a net session and reneging on a pre-game agreement to play for a result.

Attendance: 6,519.

Close of play: First day, Indians (1) 9-265 (Patel 52, Nehra 0); Second day, Victoria (1) 5-348 (Hodge 153, Harvey 54).

Indians

A. Chopra c Roach b Harrop	2	– not out	55
V. Sehwag c Hodge b Inness	23	– lbw b Harrop	20
S. Ramesh c Harrop b White	87	– c Harrop b McDonald	36
R.S. Dravid c Moss b Inness	0	– not out	1
S.R. Tendulkar c Hussey b Inness	80		
*S.C. Ganguly c Arnberger b Inness	2		
†P.A. Patel not out	52		
Harbhajan Singh c Harvey b White	3		
L. Balaji c and b White	4		
Zaheer Khan c McDonald b White	2		
A. Nehra not out	0		
L-b 7, n-b 4	11	B 1, l-b 2, n-b 1	4

(90 overs, 353 mins) (9 wkts dec) 266   (42 overs, 159 mins) (2 wkts) 116
Fall: 8 41 45 173 175 220 232 241 249   Fall: 24 114

Bowling: *First Innings*—Inness 20–5–64–4; Harrop 16–2–55–1; Moss 18–10–31–0; Harvey 9–2–22–0; McDonald 9–4–28–0; White 18–1–59–4. *Second Innings*—Inness 10–3–27–0; Harrop 12–3–34–1; Moss 8–3–18–0; McDonald 6–2–15–1; Hussey 5–0–17–0; Roach 1–0–2–0.

Victoria

M. T. G. Elliott c Chopra b Harbhajan	48	*C. L. White c Patel b Zaheer Khan 39
J. L. Arnberger c Dravid b Nehra	8	†P. J. Roach not out 0
B. J. Hodge c Dravid b Sehwag	264	B. D. Harrop not out 0
J. Moss run out (Harbhajan)	42	B 1, l-b 8, w 1, n-b 14 24
D. J. Hussey c Dravid b Nehra	21	
A. B. McDonald lbw b Harbhajan	1	(134 overs, 556 mins) (8 wkts dec) 518
I. J. Harvey lbw b Balaji	71	Fall: 21 85 192 231 232 393 518 518

M. W. H. Inness did not bat.

Bowling: Zaheer Khan 24–5–75–1; Nehra 29–6–91–2; Balaji 29–4–122–1; Harbhajan Singh 37–5–159–2; Sehwag 9–2–30–1; Tendulkar 2–0–10–0; Ganguly 4–0–22–0.

Umpires: R. G. Patterson and J. D. Ward.

†QUEENSLAND ACADEMY OF SPORT v INDIANS

At Allan Border Field, Albion, November 29, 30, December 1, 2003. Match drawn. *Toss:* Queensland Academy of Sport.

Catches were dropped, overthrows conceded, bowlers slogged and batsmen humbled as the Indians were outplayed in their final warm-up game before the First Test. Of biggest concern were the openers, Virender Sehwag and Akash Chopra, whose double failures increased doubts about whether India's top order could adapt to the bouncier Australian wickets. Those worries were hardly allayed in the second innings, with Sadagoppan Ramesh struck between the shoulder-blades and Sourav Ganguly on the helmet. Ganguly did at least hang around for his first decent hit-out, while Rahul Dravid and V. V. S. Laxman showed tantalising glimpses. Anil Kumble was comfortably the most dangerous of the bowlers, although Lee Carseldine was largely untroubled in cruising to a century in each innings. It continued something of a trend for Carseldine, who has produced starring performances against touring New Zealand, English and Bangladeshi sides in recent years. The Indians were set 305 to win in 60 overs but showed not a flicker of interest, much to the surprise of the academy's captain Aaron Nye, who nonetheless issued a timely warning about the tourists' capabilities. "They're great players," he said. "You've got to feel they'll go up a peg for Thursday."

Attendance: There was no figures attendance figures for the Queensland Academy of Sport game – admittance was free.

Close of play: Day 1, Indians (1) 3-17 (Laxman 1, Ganguly 5); Day 2, Queensland Academy of Sport (2) 2-79 (Carseldine 31, Nye 2).

Queensland Academy of Sport

C. P. Simpson c and b Agarkar	43	– (2) lbw b Pathan	5
D. M. Payne lbw b Pathan	0	– (1) lbw b Sehwag	35
L. A. Carseldine c Dasgupta b Kumble	112	– not out	109
*A. J. Nye b Kumble	15	– lbw b Kumble	16
C. A. Philipson st Dasgupta b Kumble	85	– c Ramesh b Pathan	11
S. J. Farrell lbw b Kumble	9	– st Patel b Kumble	2
†C. D. Hartley not out	21	– c Sehwag b Balaji	8
R. N. Le Loux not out	5	– not out	12
B 4, l-b 1, w 2, n-b 7	14	B 4, l-b 1, n-b 5	10

(81 overs, 315 mins)	(6 wkts dec) 304	(52 overs, 205 mins)	(6 wkts dec) 208

Fall: 4 65 137 222 256 284   Fall: 6 73 121 142 156 194

S. J. Jurgensen, S. A. Brant, J. H. Dawes and S. J. Magoffin did not bat.

Bowling: *First Innings*—Agarkar 18-4-73-1; Pathan 17-2-70-1; Balaji 11-3-36-0; Ganguly 4-0-16-0; Kumble 26-4-74-4; Sehwag 5-0-30-0. *Second Innings*—Agarkar 10-0-30-0; Pathan 13-0-54-2; Balaji 9-1-47-1; Kumble 17-6-58-2; Sehwag 3-0-14-1.

Indians

A. Chopra c Carseldine b Brant	0	– c Carseldine b Magoffin	11
V. Sehwag c Hartley b Dawes	6	– lbw b Dawes	4
†D. Dasgupta b Brant	0	– b Jurgensen	8
V. V. S. Laxman b Simpson	74		
*S. C. Ganguly c Hartley b Dawes	6	– c Nye b Simpson	35
R. S. Dravid c Le Loux b Dawes	38	– not out	20
S. Ramesh run out (Nye)	21	– (4) not out	37
P. A. Patel c Le Loux b Magoffin	19		
A. B. Agarkar c Farrell b Magoffin	18		
A. R. Kumble not out	8		
I. K. Pathan not out	4		
L-b 11, w 1, n-b 2	14	L-b 6	6

(73 overs, 310 mins)	(9 wkts dec) 208	(52 overs, 199 mins)	(4 wkts dec) 121

Fall: 7 7 11 26 103 145 177 192 203   Fall: 13 28 32 88

L. Balaji did not bat.

Bowling: *First Innings*—Dawes 17-4-36-3; Brant 13-5-39-2; Jurgensen 12-5-20-0; Magoffin 12-4-28-2; Simpson 15-2-54-1; Le Loux 4-0-20-0. *Second Innings*—Dawes 7-5-10-1; Brant 7-2-11-0; Magoffin 9-2-13-1; Jurgensen 5-2-13-1; Simpson 14-4-22-1; Philipson 3-2-6-0; Le Loux 7-0-32-0.

Umpires: N. S. McNamara and J. F. Torpey.

AUSTRALIA v INDIA

First Test Match

by JOHN BIRMINGHAM

At Brisbane Cricket Ground, Brisbane, December 4, 5, 6, 7, 8, 2003. Match drawn. *Toss:* India. *Test debut:* N. W. Bracken.

It is a measure of Australia's recent dominance that there was a slightly fevered sense of hubris in the hot, damp, tropical air before the First Test in Brisbane. Even the absence of Glenn McGrath, Brett Lee and the serially embarrassed Shane Warne could not puncture the smug superiority around the home side's preparations. Much of the two days before the match were given over to spin-doctoring and sponsor commitments; a misallocation of scarce resources that the skipper Steve Waugh would later openly regret.

Indeed the accelerating hysteria generated by Waugh's retirement plans did almost as much to distract local minds from the challenge of Sourav Ganguly's Indians as did the visitors' own underwhelming form in the early tour matches. At times, if the media coverage could be even half-believed, it seemed India had flown in to provide nothing more than background vision for a succession of farewell bows and lingering encores by the Australian captain. It is possible that Waugh himself, a grim existentialist when confronted with fortune's dark sense of humour, was the only local to pay the threat any heed.

There were omens, for those so inclined. The weather, for one thing, was glowering and thunderous, despite a long drought that had baked most of the state into cracked saltpans and red dust. Change was about. The second-string Australian pace attack had to contend with a greasy ball, a challenge they seemed to have more trouble meeting than India's surprisingly zippy opening bowler Zaheer Khan. Andy Bichel, a barrel-chested local hero, must have wondered which gods of the Vedas he had offended to be punished with 1 for 130 in the first innings, while Zaheer treated himself to a five-wicket haul.

At first, however, all seemed as it should be. Ganguly repeated Nasser Hussain's Gabba blunder of England's last Ashes tour, winning the toss and inviting Australia to do their worst with the willow. Justin Langer and Matthew Hayden were only too happy to oblige. They strode out across the greenest stretch of grass in Queensland, and each in his own way soon had ragged Indian fielders haring about all over it.

Hayden was the bar-room brawler as always, standing his ground and clobbering the ball with a cheerfully barbaric lack of respect for the feelings of his victims. Langer was more the anonymous assassin, despatching his targets with quiet efficiency. His shots were a silenced 9 mm Parabellum to Hayden's long-barrelled elephant gun. The blunderbuss misfired first, a neat catch streaking off Hayden's edge into V. V. S. Laxman's lap at slip. The first wicket fell at 73 and the Australians went home to dinner with a total of 262 costing them just one more batsman, Ricky Ponting.

The Tasmanian, and heir apparent to Waugh's throne, would likely have felt conflicted about his half-century. It was a savage answer to the lone spinner Harbhajan Singh, who had bested him five times out of five on the subcontinent in 2001. Ponting showed how little he cared for their personal history by skipping down the pitch to reacquaint himself with the mysteries of Harbhajan's off-breaks, lifting one delivery into low-earth orbit for six. Having monstered the attack so thoroughly, however, Ponting then did the job for them, dollying up a catch behind with an inept swat across the line.

Perhaps it was another omen. The second day was nearly a total reversal of the first, with only 16 overs bowled, seemingly all of them injurious to the Australian cause. Play began late, stuttered to an early close in poor light, and was frequently interrupted by rain. While the batsmen's rhythm was knocked off kilter, the bowlers revelled in the sporadic tempo. Zaheer and Ajit Agarkar popped in and out of the dressing room looking more refreshed each time. They hit a perfect line and length and generated good pace in the thick air. The Aussies fell apart, losing all but one of their remaining wickets for a mere 61 runs.

The nadir was reached by Waugh who, oblivious to his partner Damien Martyn, charged down the pitch wanting a third run. Martyn, his back turned, suddenly found his captain at the same end as him, and jogged down the wicket in an act of sacrifice. Waugh compounded his sin by treading on his own wicket shortly after. Perhaps the gods were toying with him. They certainly did him no favours on the morrow. The Australian press hounded Waugh for his apparent selfishness, and the Australian innings breathed its last on the first ball of an abbreviated day. The Indians gathered 11 runs without loss from the 37 balls they faced. Otherwise they sat around awaiting the return of El Nino, the weather pattern which is supposed to guarantee decade-long droughts, not keep visiting cricketers peering out through sheets of dark rain for hours at a time.

The enforced rest was as much a boon for Ganguly's batsmen as it had been to his bowlers. The fourth day belonged to India, despite a couple of unfortunate incidents which saw Rahul Dravid and Sachin Tendulkar walk all the way to and from the wicket for a single run between them. Dravid was bamboozled by Jason Gillespie's swing and seam, edging a catch to Hayden at slip. A few balls later Gillespie had Tendulkar leg-before, shouldering arms to a steeply rising delivery. Close to a billion fans in India would swear the ball was destined to clear the stumps as easily as Ponting's six had cleared the boundary on day one.

Still, it was a measure of Ganguly's steel. Unlike so many previous touring Indian skippers, he did not let an arguable point distract him. With Laxman he set about surgically dismembering Waugh's B-grade attack. On the first truly sunny day of the match, the Australians worked up a lather, chasing the ball to all points. Between lunch and tea the locals were spread as far and wide as a mob of runaway cattle in the back-country, while Ganguly and Laxman lorded it over them like wealthy squatters.

A sweep off Stuart MacGill brought four runs for Ganguly's century, a landmark which called forth a considerable display of emotion at the wicket. Waugh has often spoken of the need to get the boot on the enemy's throat from the first days of a long series. Ganguly and Laxman took him at his word. When bad light put an end to the day Australia trailed by 39 runs, still looking for another four Indian wickets.

The final day's fortunes swung back and forth. The Indian tail fell limp. Hayden launched a ferocious counterattack, bludgeoning away the tourists' first-innings lead before succumbing to 99. Waugh bagged a half-century, Australia hitting the accelerator in a rush to set up some sort of contest. With 23 overs to play he declared, tempting Ganguly to have a dash at the victory target of 199. Nathan Bracken, the stand-in swing bowler, grabbed the two openers in two balls, but that was the only moment hearts might have fluttered. Dravid and Laxman refused the bait and interest trickled away, the match bound for a draw.

Man of the Match: S.C. Ganguly. *Attendance:* 52,905.

Close of play: First day, Australia (1) 2-262 (Langer 115, Martyn 36); Second day, Australia (1) 9-323 (Bracken 6, MacGill 1); Third day, India (1) 0-11 (Chopra 5, Sehwag 5); Fourth day, India (1) 6-362 (Patel 37, Agarkar 12).

Australia

	R	B	4/6			R	B	4/6
J.L. Langer lbw b Agarkar	121	194	17	– (2) c Patel b Agarkar		0	6	0
M.L. Hayden c Laxman b Zaheer	37	52	6	– (1) c Sehwag b Harbhajan		99	98	11 2
R.T. Ponting c Patel b Zaheer Khan	54	88	7 1	– c Sehwag b Nehra		50	75	5
D.R. Martyn run out (Harbhjan/Patel/Ganguly)	42	79	5	– not out		66	100	3 2
*S.R. Waugh hit wicket b Zaheer	0	4	0	– not out		56	102	7
S.M. Katich c Patel b Zaheer	16	25	4					
†A.C. Gilchrist c Laxman b Zaheer	0	4	0					
A.J. Bichel c Laxman b Agarkar	11	10	2					
J.N. Gillespie run out (Harbhajan/Agarkar)	8	11	0 1					
N.W. Bracken not out	6	13	0					
S.C.G. MacGill c Chopra b Agarkar	1	3	0					
B 4, l-b 7, w 2, n-b 14	27			B 4, n-b 9		13		

(78.1 overs, 391 mins)	323	(62 overs, 240 mins)(3-dec)	284
Fall: 73 162 268 275 275 276 302 310 317 323		Fall: 6 146 156	

Bowling: *First Innings*—Zaheer Khan 23-2-95-5; Nehra 15-4-51-0; Agarkar 25.1-5-90-3; Harbhajan Singh 14-1-68-0; Ganguly 1-0-8-0. *Second Innings*—Zaheer Khan 3-0-15-0; Agarkar 12-3-45-1; Nehra 19-1-89-1; Harbhajan Singh 21-1-101-1; Tendulkar 2-0-9-0; Sehwag 5-1-21-0.

India

	R	B	4/6		R	B	4/6
A. Chopra c Hayden b Gillespie	36	135	2	– c Langer b Bracken	4	7	1
V. Sehwag c Hayden b Bracken	45	51	5	– c Martyn b Bracken	0	1	0
R. S. Dravid c Hayden b Gillespie	1	11	0	– not out	43	47	6
S. R. Tendulkar lbw b Gillespie	0	3	0				
*S. C. Ganguly c Gillespie b MacGill	144	196	18				
V. V. S. Laxman c Katich b MacGill	75	113	11	– (4) not out	24	43	3
†P. A. Patel c Bichel b Gillespie	37	105	5				
A. B. Agarkar c Hayden b Bichel	12	26	1				
Harbhajan Singh not out	19	39	2				
Zaheer Khan b MacGill	27	46	3 1				
A. Nehra lbw b MacGill	0	2	0				
L-b 6, w 1, n-b 6	13			N-b 2	2		
(120.1 overs, 501 mins)	409			(16 overs, 72 mins) (2 wkts)	73		
Fall: 61 62 62 127 273 329 362 362 403 409				Fall: 4 4			

Bowling: *First Innings*—Gillespie 31–12–65–4; Bracken 26–5–90–1; Bichel 28–6–130–1; MacGill 26.1–4–86–4; Waugh 7–3–16–0; Katich 2–0–16–0. *Second Innings*—Gillespie 5–1–17–0; Bracken 4–1–12–2; MacGill 4–0–32–0; Bichel 3–0–12–0.

Umpires: S. A. Bucknor (West Indies) and R. E. Koertzen (South Africa).
TV Umpire: P. D. Parker.
Referee: M. J. Procter (South Africa).

AUSTRALIA v INDIA

Second Test Match

by ROHIT BRIJNATH

At Adelaide Oval, Adelaide, December 12, 13, 14, 15, 16, 2003. India won by four wickets. *Toss:* Australia. *Test debut:* I. K. Pathan.

In the beginning, both captains' faces resembled a map of grim lines. In the end, one would carry a smile so incandescent that it lit up the evening; the other would steel his facial muscles and attempt to avoid looking like a professional mourner. It would be a long five days.

When it began, Steve Waugh's batting was under scrutiny, his retirement decision under dissection, his run-out of Damien Martyn in Brisbane chewed on by critic and cynic. Sourav Ganguly was not throwing confetti around either. Harbhajan Singh's spinning finger was too sore to be cured by anti-inflammatories. Zaheer Khan's hamstring was misbehaving. An already thin bowling attack was looking anorexic. Rumour swirled that Murali Kartik, the left-arm spinner who had caused the Australians some discomfort in the recent one-dayers in India, was flying in, cape and all. But this was subterfuge. This Superman would carry the drinks.

India looked confused, and Australia flexed their muscles. The toss was won by Waugh and in the shadows of St Peter's Cathedral, on a strip of earth imported from batting heaven, the Australians produced a clinic of sorts. Friendly bowling and debatable captaincy – Ganguly's packed off-side field turned former captains apoplectic – hurt the Indians. Then Ricky Ponting made them bleed.

Ponting had struck 11 centuries in his previous 25 Tests. Now he hit the ball with the audacious cool of a blindfolded knife thrower. In full flow, even the seagulls stood by in admiring attention. Upon reaching his double-century on the second day he blew a kiss to his wife, Rianna, a moment of sweet unorthodoxy from a man whose innings was anything but.

Two other moments on the first day merited attention. First, when Waugh came to bat, Ganguly surrounded him with three slips, two gullies and a point; and later, too late, a short leg. He then ordered a short-pitched welcome that suggested here was a private battle within a larger war. The second moment came late in the day when Simon Katich, on 75, mis-hooked and watched Virender Sehwag engineer a daring, running, diving catch. The Indians had given up 400 runs on the day. But as the team ran to Sehwag, it was clear their spirit was not stripped away.

Australia were all out next day for 556, Jason Gillespie's 48 not easily forgotten because none of India's first four wickets – Sehwag, Akash Chopra, Sachin Tendulkar or Ganguly – could match it. Tendulkar, still carrying the label of world's best batsman, for none of his peers had produced such consistent excellence over an entire decade, was suffering from a rare flight of confidence. Low scores in his past few Tests had brought anxiety. His indiscreet exit – caught behind off a widish ball without moving his feet – triggered celebrations but disappointment too, for the crowds here have long held him in high esteem.

At 4 for 85, it was evident that if India wriggled out of this position Houdini would never be heard of again. But then, as escape artists go, none are more practised against Australia than V. V. S. Laxman and Rahul Dravid. Their partnership of 376 in Kolkata in 2001, while following on, found a dazzling echo in Adelaide. Laxman, who for all his new-found circumspection still resembled D'Artagnan, and Dravid, who batted as if he had taken some holy pledge, stayed together for 303 runs over 564 balls.

On the third night, stuck on an elegantly heroic 199 not out, a weary Dravid would say over dinner: "I don't have some of the gifts of a Tendulkar or Lara, but I have other things. I'd very much like to be respected as someone who is courageous and fights and does his best." His innings, punctuated by cover drives of some sophistication, made the point emphatically.

Of course, not all was deadly serious. Dravid's sly smile at day's end stemmed not just from his uncharacteristic hook for six to reach his century – imagine Mozart composing rap – but from his bemused realisation that he had scored more quickly than his fluent partner. "Not bad for a blocker," he would say later.

The Test turned ferociously on the fourth day. India finished on 523, at which point Waugh's Australians produced a batting performance succinctly described by their coach John Buchanan as "immature". Aggression is the Australians' signature, and for years they had subscribed to that plan with great reward. But extravagant shot-making was now their undoing. So intent were they on setting a target that it appeared to obscure the possibility they might lose.

Six batsmen fell under 20, none passed 50. Anil Kumble, who had persevered for 43 overs and five wickets in the first innings, tightened the noose. Tendulkar found his usual appreciable turn. But it was an unusual hero that emerged, Ajit Agarkar, whose run-up resembles a fellow bouncing amiably along on a trampoline. A shade quicker than his toothpick physique suggested possible, he bowled with discipline, put the ball in what captains are prone to call the "right places", and watched a collective harakiri unfold before him.

With Australia gone for 196, and with 230 to get in 10 overs and a day, Ganguly's men were in smelling distance of history. A first win in Australia since Sunil Gavaskar's side in 1980-81; the first time a team had gone ahead 1–0 in Australia since West Indies in 1988-89. It was not bad company to be in. The wicket still offered much to the batsmen, and Australia's undermanned attack lacked a penetrative edge. But this, also, was not simply the most gifted Indian batting side ever assembled. It was a team with undiminished belief in itself. Its time had come.

India hiccuped briefly. But Dravid, again, unconquered on 72, showed that adversity brings out the best in him. He would eventually construct the winning runs, with four wickets to spare, and Waugh would retrieve the ball from the gutters and hand it to him. Later, Ganguly's smile would not leave him. Waugh could not find one. The series was alive.

This one's for you: Ricky Ponting blows a kiss to his wife, Rianna, on reaching the first of his two double-hundreds.

Man of the Match: R. S. Dravid.   *Attendance:* 75,021.

Close of play: First day, Australia (1) 5-400 (Ponting 176, Gilchrist 9); Second day, India (1) 4-180 (Dravid 43, Laxman 55); Third day, India (1) 7-477 (Dravid 199, Kumble 1); Fourth day, India (2) 0-37 (Chopra 10, Sehwag 25).

Australia

	R	B	4/6		R	B	4/6
J. L. Langer c Sehwag b Kumble	58	72	7 2	– lbw b Agarkar	10	8	1
M. L. Hayden c Patel b Pathan	12	15	2	– c Sehwag b Nehra	17	32	0
R. T. Ponting c Dravid b Kumble	242	352	31	– c Chopra b Agarkar	0	17	0
D. R. Martyn c Laxman b Nehra	30	39	6	– c Dravid b Tendulkar	38	76	4
*S. R. Waugh b Nehra	30	53	5	– c Dravid b Tendulkar	42	64	8
S. M. Katich c Sehwag b Agarkar	75	109	9 1	– c Nehra b Agarkar	31	59	1
†A. C. Gilchrist c Sehwag b Agarkar	29	24	4	– b Kumble	43	45	4 2
A. J. Bichel c Chopra b Kumble	19	45	2	– b Agarkar	1	6	0
J. N. Gillespie not out	48	54	6	– c Patel b Agarkar	3	19	0
B. A. Williams b Kumble	0	3	0	– not out	4	9	0
S. C. G. MacGill lbw b Kumble	0	1	0	– b Agarkar	1	4	0
L-b 8, w 1, n-b 4	13			B 2, l-b 2, w 1, n-b 1	6		

(127 overs, 537 mins) 556   (56.2 overs, 248 mins) 196

Fall: 22 135 200 252 390 426 473 556 556 556

Fall: 10 18 44 109 112 183 184 188 192 196

Bowling: *First Innings*—Agarkar 26-1-119-2; Pathan 27-3-136-1; Nehra 25-3-115-2; Kumble 43-3-154-5; Sehwag 5-0-21-0; Tendulkar 1-0-3-0. *Second Innings*—Agarkar 16.2-2-41-6; Pathan 7-0-24-0; Nehra 7-2-21-1; Kumble 17-2-58-1; Tendulkar 6-0-36-2; Sehwag 3-0-12-0.

India

	R	B	4/6		R	B	4/6
A. Chopra c and b Bichel	27	44	3	– lbw b Gillespie	20	54	2
V. Sehwag c Hayden b Bichel	47	41	6	– st Gilchrist b MacGill	47	81	7
R. S. Dravid c Bichel b Gillespie	233	446	23 1	– not out	72	170	7
S. R. Tendulkar c Gilchrist b Bichel	1	6	0	– lbw b MacGill	37	59	5
*S. C. Ganguly run out (Williams/MacGill)	2	7	0	– c Katich b Bichel	12	22	1
V. V. S. Laxman c Gilchrist b Bichel	148	283	18	– c Bichel b Katich	32	34	6
†P. A. Patel c Ponting b Katich	31	52	6	– b Katich	3	16	0
A. B. Agarkar c MacGill b Katich	11	30	1	– not out	0	0	0
A. R. Kumble lbw b MacGill	12	44	1				
I. K. Pathan c and b MacGill	1	13	0				
A. Nehra not out	0	8	0				
B 4, l-b 2, w 2, n-b 2	10			B 3, l-b 6, w 1	10		

(161.5 overs, 647 mins) 523   (72.4 overs, 306 m)(6 wkts) 233

Fall: 66 81 83 85 388 447 469 510 518 523

Fall: 48 79 149 170 221 229

Bowling: *First Innings*—Gillespie 40.5-13-106-1; Williams 23-7-72-0; Bichel 28-3-118-4; MacGill 44-8-143-2; Katich 16-3-59-2; Waugh 9-2-15-0; Ponting 1-0-4-0. *Second Innings*—Gillespie 10.2-2-22-1; Williams 14-6-34-0; MacGill 24.4-3-101-2; Bichel 11.4-2-35-1; Katich 8-1-22-2; Waugh 4-0-10-0.

Umpires: R. E. Koertzen (South Africa) and D. R. Shepherd (England).
TV Umpire: S. J. Davis.
Referee: M. J. Procter (South Africa).

AUSTRALIA A v INDIANS

At Bellerive Oval, Hobart, December 19, 20, 21, 2003. Match drawn. *Toss:* Australia A.

Martin Love, Michael Clarke and Matthew Nicholson reminded selectors of their capabilities as the Indians conducted some fine-tuning ahead of the Boxing Day Test. Love's chanceless 94, laced with 12 fours and a six, lit up a first day played beneath overcast skies and on a pitch that had spent 48 hours under covers. He took a particular shine to the left-arm spinner Murali Kartik, flown in to replace the injured Harbhajan Singh. Mike Hussey and Chris Rogers repeatedly played and missed during a 119-run opening stand that was broken up minutes after lunch. Love, though, was never troubled by an Indian attack that intermingled wides and long hops with some perfectly pitched deliveries. India's reply fell 66 runs short, Sachin Tendulkar squandering a bright start and failing to silence claims he was in a form slump. He fell out of the world's top 10 batting rankings during the week but looked his old self here, unfurling cuts, pulls, cover drives and a couple of deft flicks off the toes, before hooking Damien Wright straight to backward square leg. Nicholson was the best bowler, giving up 25 runs in 21.5 choking overs. With a draw looming, Clarke cut and drove his way to 131 in 140 balls, showing the Indian bowlers scant respect. He brought up his century with a massive six – one of four – over square leg. In windy, wintry conditions, India showed no interest in chasing 308 to win, Akash Chopra taking 64 minutes and 44 balls to open his account.

Attendance: 2,963.

Close of play: First day, Indians (1) 1-37 (Chopra 12, Dasgupta 18); Second day, Australia A (2) 3-57 (Hodge 11, Clarke 22).

Australia A

*M. E. K. Hussey c Ganguly b Nehra	67	– (2) c Tendulkar b Pathan	7
C. J. L. Rogers c Dasgupta b Ganguly	70	– (1) c Chopra b Balaji	2
M. L. Love c Dasgupta b Pathan	94	– b Balaji	11
B. J. Hodge b Nehra	1	– b Pathan	33
M. J. Clarke not out	38	– not out	131
C. L. White b Kartik	15	– c Dasgupta b Nehra	5
†W. A. Seccombe not out	0	– c Sehwag b Kartik	27
M. J. Nicholson (did not bat)		– c Patel b Balaji	7
D. G. Wright (did not bat)		– not out	10
L-b 6, w 3, n-b 17	26	B 1, l-b 1, n-b 6	8

(74.4 overs, 319 mins)   (5 wkts dec) 311   (65 overs, 280 mins)   (7 wkts dec) 241

Fall: 119 204 207 279 302   Fall: 5 9 28 97 112 150 195

P. C. Rofe and S. W. Tait did not bat.

Bowling: *First Innings*—Pathan 22–6–77–1; Balaji 18–2–84–0; Nehra 10–2–33–2; Ganguly 8–1–38–1; Tendulkar 1–0–9–0; Kartik 15.4–2–64–1. *Second Innings*—Pathan 14–1–40–2; Balaji 22–2–87–3; Kartik 12–3–53–1; Nehra 15–0–49–1; Tendulkar 2–0–10–0.

Indians

A. Chopra run out (Hussey)	46	– c Seccombe b Rofe	25
S. Ramesh c Wright b Nicholson	4	– c Hussey b Wright	22
†D. Dasgupta lbw b Tait	21	– not out	19
S. R. Tendulkar c Rofe b Wright	36		
V. Sehwag c Seccombe b Tait	30		
*S. C. Ganguly c Hussey b Nicholson	5		
P. A. Patel c Love b Nicholson	49	– (4) not out	0
L. Balaji lbw b Tait	8		
M. Kartik run out (Rofe)	26		
I. K. Pathan c Wright b Nicholson	11		
A. Nehra not out	0		
L-b 4, n-b 5	9		

(82.5 overs, 345 mins)	245		(33 overs, 136 mins) (2 wkts)	66
Fall: 5 51 104 139 149 150 162 233 233 245			Fall: 22 66	

Bowling: *First Innings*—Nicholson 21.5–13–25–4; Wright 16–9–33–1; White 13–1–60–0; Tait 20–2–85–3; Rofe 12–3–38–0. *Second Innings*—Nicholson 8–5–19–0; Wright 8–4–17–1; Tait 5–1–22–0; Rofe 8–4–5–1; White 4–2–3–0.

Umpires: P. D. Parker and R. L. Parry.
TV Umpire: J. H. Smeaton.

AUSTRALIA v INDIA

Third Test Match

by GREG BAUM

At Melbourne Cricket Ground, Melbourne, December 26, 27, 28, 29, 30, 2003. Australia won by nine wickets. *Toss:* India.

There was a frisson in Melbourne this Boxing Day morning such as had not been felt for years. Unremitting success had spoiled the game for some Australians, even more than a long run of defeats, but India's startling victory in Adelaide had made Test cricket again the game of innumerable possibilities. Big crowds came every day to an MCG made gap-toothed by the demolition of the Members' Stand, and they were not let down. Nearly 30,000 turned up on the last day for barely an hour and a half of formalities.

Brett Lee and Zaheer Khan returned from injury, notionally to strengthen their respective teams, but the pitch was cut for batting. Virender Sehwag and Akash Chopra again weathered the early storm. Lee and the other Australian bowlers slavered to see early pace and bounce, repeatedly hitting the batsmen in the helmet but never in the scorebook. One full-pitched, well-aimed ball might have given this day a different complexion. There were only 24 runs in the first hour and no attacking shots in front of the wicket until the 17th over. The shackles eventually loosened, the openers running with urgency and Sehwag lofting Stuart MacGill's second ball for six. Australia were again unexpectedly fallible in the field, dropping two catches – Sehwag on 66, most crucially, by Simon Katich at point – and forgoing a certain run-out because of a stray throw.

The day was half-done before a wicket fell, and the impish and impudent Sehwag was by now in his irresistible stride. He proceeded to play an astonishing innings in which nobody was safe from his onslaught; not bowler, not fieldsman, not even partner, for he almost ran out one with a fierce drive, and struck another. The best that could be said of his footwork was that it did not get in the way of his shot-making. Steve Waugh was back to bowling angry bouncers and hoping for rain, as he was in his first Test, on this ground against this opponent 18 years previously.

But one of cricket's fascinations is that the next twist is only ever one ball away, and it does not have to be a good one. Suddenly Rahul Dravid clipped Waugh straight to mid-wicket. The luckless Sachin Tendulkar leg-glanced his first ball directly to the wicket-keeper. And Sehwag finally outdid himself, belting a Katich full toss for his fifth six before swiping the next ball, another full toss, directly to deep mid-wicket. He was on 195 but he was unrepentant, saying it was his duty to have a crack at such a ball. He had faced only 233 balls.

Next morning the pitch quickened, the bowlers sobered up and India lost 6 for 16 to settle on 366. Justin Langer was an early casualty but Matthew Hayden and Ricky Ponting, Australia's batting colossi, put on 234 to take charge of the match. Hayden was a commanding presence, hitting the ball so hard that bowlers sometimes skipped out of the way of drives, and cover fieldsmen hesitated in their duty to walk in with the bowler. He reached 100 by sweeping Anil Kumble for four, notwithstanding that the same shot against the same bowler had gotten him out for 99 in Brisbane. This was his third hundred in a row in Boxing Day Tests.

Ponting played mostly in that perfect place where timing, technique and confidence meet, departing from it every other hour or so to swish in an idiosyncratic way that said there was still some Sehwag in him. He batted nearly 10 hours, hitting his second double-century in two Tests and his third in this, the year of its consummation. He and Hayden sped along at four an over, Australia's statutory rate now. India's bowling was disciplined early but loosened through the day. Their ground fielding especially grew lax.

They were not necessarily shamed, for many carefully laid plans have been laid to waste by Australian batsmen in this mood. The bowlers grow tired, the ball old and despair sets in. Every rejected appeal and bad bounce becomes an injustice. Kumble persevered and in another time and place might have won more leg-befores. But all sense of an attack was lost; the bowlers were there to introduce the ball to play. Five runs were conceded near stumps when a ball hit a helmet on the ground behind the wicket-keeper. At least, this time, Sehwag's head was not in it.

Hayden departed and Adam Gilchrist's elevation to No. 4 did not come off. The third morning was memorable for another stutter in the Waugh swansong. He came in to a thundering ovation, but upon turning his back to the second ball he faced from Ajit Agarkar was hit on his left elbow, which immediately swelled up as if a golf ball had become embedded. Waugh retired hurt, prompting fears for his gala Sydney farewell. However, the damage proved to be not a broken bone but a burst blood vessel.

He returned more than two hours later wearing a guard and batted another 80 minutes. But without power in his left arm he dragged everything to leg, then was out leg-before to Kumble without offering. Cricket, unlike theatre, can be bent to the will of no man. Greg Chappell made a century in his last innings and Don Bradman a duck. The only certainty for Waugh was that there would be no certainties in Sydney.

India returned admirably to their task, restricting Australia to three an over this day despite another breakdown for Zaheer. Ponting was dashing as quickly between wickets in the 10th hour of his innings as the first, which used to be said of Bradman. With the tail in he began to lash out, in antithesis to the Waugh way, and fell trying to hit Kumble out of the ground. Kumble bowled 51 overs for his sixth wickets.

Trailing by 192, India lost both openers that night, Chopra unluckily, as happens when the momentum is against a team. Ganguly put himself in at No. 4, in long shadows, with menace all around, to spare Tendulkar, saying the little master had earned the right to protection. India toughed out most of the fourth day, the slowest but most absorbing of the match. Ganguly was struck nastily in the helmet by Brad Williams and retired hurt, returning to make a redoubtable half-century. Tendulkar sweated for 44, then fell when reaching for Williams outside off stump, whereupon he resolved in Sydney to eschew every ball there, and did so for days. Dravid made 92 and at 4 for 253, leading by 61, the game was in the balance.

Australia's bowling was like India's the previous day, constant but not menacing. Lee was 10 to 15 kph slower than his best, MacGill lacked penetration and the two likeliest were the least sung, Williams and Bracken, who at summer's end would lose his contract. The Indian batsmen talked constantly at the crease, imitating Australia's togetherness but failing to build one big partnership. The new ball sped up the day in all its elements, first yielding a flurry of boundaries, then a clatter of wickets. The coach John Wright's injunction on tailenders that they must make runs fell on deaf ears. India lost 6 for 33, and thereby the match.

A final drama was played on the fifth morning when the match referee Mike Procter discovered that the curator, Tony Ware, had replaced a lump of soil about the size of two 50-cent coins which had been displaced by sweeping the previous evening. The patch was on a good length for left-armers bowling to left-handers. Procter ordered the plug to be dug up but otherwise saw the incident as an innocent mistake. He took no further action, puzzling Ganguly. Langer went early again, trapped on the crease by Agarkar for the fifth time in the series, but Hayden and Ponting soothed Australia's palpitations.

The bumper last-day crowd – admitted free – had the best of all worlds: an Australian win, a chance to bow to Waugh and an idle afternoon in the sun. It is a great Test match when it can be said that the sense of anticipation on the last morning was as strong as on the first, and that it failed no one.

Man of the Match: R. T. Ponting.   *Attendance:* 179,662.

Close of play: First day, India (1) 4-329 (Ganguly 20, Laxman 6); Second day, Australia (1) 3-317 (Ponting 120, Martyn 7); Third day, India (2) 2-27 (Dravid 6, Ganguly 6); Fourth day, India all out 286.

India

	R	B	4/6		R	B	4/6
A. Chopra c Katich b MacGill	48	138	6	– c Gilchrist b Bracken	4	8	1
V. Sehwag c Bracken b Katich	195	233	25 5	– c Williams b Lee	11	13	2
R. S. Dravid c Martyn b Waugh	49	89	5	– c Gilchrist b Lee	92	244	13
S. R. Tendulkar c Gilchrist b Lee	0	1	0	– (5) c Gilchrist b Williams	44	79	5
*S. C. Ganguly c Langer b Lee	37	63	6	– (4) b Bracken	73	125	12
V. V. S. Laxman b Hayden b MacGill	19	86	2	– c Hayden b MacGill	18	50	3
†P. A. Patel c Gilchrist b Bracken	0	1	0	– not out	27	50	4
A. B. Agarkar run out (Williams)	0	1	0	– b Williams	1	10	0
A. R. Kumble c Langer b Williams	3	12	0	– lbw b Williams	0	2	0
Zaheer Khan not out	0	1	0	– c Hayden b Williams	1	8	0
A. Nehra c Gilchrist b MacGill	0	4	0	– c Hayden b MacGill	0	17	0
L-b 3, w 1, n-b 11	15			B 4, l-b 3, w 1, n-b 7	15		

(103 overs, 424 mins) 366   (99.5 overs, 410 mins) 286
Fall: 141 278 286 311 350 353 353   Fall: 5 19 126 160 253 258 271
         366 366 366   271 277 286

Bowling: *First Innings*—Lee 27–7–103–2; Bracken 28–6–71–1; Williams 20–6–66–1; MacGill 15–3–70–3; Katich 4–0–18–1; Waugh 9–0–35–1. *Second Innings*—Lee 22–3–97–2; Bracken 25–13–45–2; Williams 22–5–53–4; MacGill 26.5–5–68–2; Katich 4–0–16–0.

Demolition job: Nathan Bracken bowls to V.V.S. Laxman and the MCG Members Stand turns to rubble, Boxing Day 2003.

Australia

	R	B	4/6			R	B	4/6
J.L. Langer c Tendulkar b Agarkar	14	29	2	– lbw b Agarkar		2	14	0
M.L. Hayden lbw b Kumble	136	173	17 1	– not out		53	63	9
R.T. Ponting st Patel b Kumble	257	458	25	– not out		31	59	3
†A.C. Gilchrist c Nehra b Kumble	14	29	2					
D.R. Martyn c Patel b Agarkar	31	63	3					
*S.R. Waugh lbw b Kumble	19	69	1					
S.M. Katich c Chopra b Kumble	29	58	3					
B. Lee c Laxman b Kumble	8	29	0					
N.W. Bracken c and b Tendulkar	1	5	0					
B.A. Williams not out	10	11	0 1					
S.C.G. MacGill lbw b Agarkar	0	1						
B 4, l-b 8, w 5, n-b 17, pen 5	39			B 4, l-b 2, w 1, n-b 4		11		

(151.2 overs, 626 mins)	558		(22.2 overs, 95 mins)(1 wkt)	97
Fall: 30 264 295 373 437 502 535 542			Fall: 9	
555 558				

Bowling: *First Innings*—Agarkar 33.2–5–115–3; Zaheer Khan 25–4–103–0; Nehra 29–3–90–0; Kumble 51–8–176–6; Tendulkar 13–0–57–1. *Second Innings*—Agarkar 7–2–25–1; Nehra 6–3–16–0; Kumble 6.2–0–43–0; Sehwag 3–0–7–0.

Umpires: B.F. Bowden (New Zealand) and D.R. Shepherd (England).
TV Umpire: R.L. Parry.
Referee: M.J. Procter (South Africa).

AUSTRALIA v INDIA

Fourth Test

by DAVID FRITH

At Sydney Cricket Ground, Sydney, January 2, 3, 4, 5, 6, 2004. Match drawn. *Toss:* India.
    Not since Sydney's last electric tram rattled off to the breaker's yard in 1961 had the city been swept by such a strong wave of emotional farewell. Now, again, it was a Streetcar named Retire, for it was Steve Waugh's 168th and final Test. He was leading Australia for the 57th time, with an extraordinary 41 victories to date. It was therefore important that the adoring masses should see him and his team go out on a triumphant note. To that end, thousands came armed with red rags provided by a local newspaper. These tokens of Waugh's idiosyncratic face-mopper, as it turned out, were to be used mainly to wipe away tears of frustration. Australia lost an important toss and were batted out of the game by an Indian top six – or even seven – which probably compares with any in history.
    In a match of many new landmarks their 7 for 705 was India's highest Test total, the best by a visiting team in Australia and the best by any country in a Sydney Test. The spinal cord of the innings was a 353-run stand between Sachin Tendulkar and V.V.S. Laxman. Only one bigger partnership had been seen on this ground, when Don Bradman and Sid Barnes put on 405 against England in 1946-47. That Test attracted a record 195,253 spectators over its six days. Waugh's finale drew only 5,264 fewer – including 24,954 on the fifth day, which *was* a record.
    The opening session was India's, thanks to the indulgence of their hosts. Brett Lee had Akash Chopra caught behind off a no-ball - one of 18 he let fly this innings – missed chest-high by Simon Katich at gully, then edging just past Matthew Hayden. Virender Sehwag raced to fifty. He exploded a six over point and fours to long leg and cover in

one over, costing the rudderless Lee 18 runs. Jason Gillespie, nervously re-selected after injury, held the attack together. But Nathan Bracken and Stuart MacGill seemed innocuous, and a big Indian total inevitable.

Batting into a third day was still an unforeseen course, especially when both openers eventually departed. Chopra was bowled by a rare rocket of a yorker from Lee, who celebrated with his frenzied charade of a man trying to start his reluctant lawnmower. It came as something of a shock when Rahul Dravid, having eclipsed Gundappa Viswanath's series record of 518 runs for India against Australia, fell to a sharp off-cutter from Gillespie. Tendulkar and Laxman saw their side through to a late close, adding 90 just when Australia were hoping for a new-ball breakthrough.

Not until 5 p.m. next day was the stand broken by another Gillespie off-cutter. Moments earlier Laxman had been dropped by MacGill on 177, a fielding failure which uncorked booing and catcalls from a frustrated Saturday crowd, who had come to worship Australia's outgoing skipper, not two wristy and determined Indian master batsmen. Tendulkar's 32nd Test hundred was his first in 14 months. He eliminated the cover drive, after it had got him into some trouble in the early Tests, and made 188 of his 241 runs on the leg side. His touch was well and truly restored, his precise manipulation of the ball worthy of a table-tennis champion. Laxman was equally smooth and classical, composing his fourth enchanting hundred in eight matches against Australia. It could only be imagined how great was the appreciation of this mammoth stand as it beamed from a quarter of a billion TV sets across the subcontinent.

Waugh was left with little option but to close the game up with negative field placings. Sourav Ganguly played some contemptuous shots off Lee before that same bowler scuppered him with the third new ball. When Tendulkar, Don Bradman's "reincarnation", reached his third Test double-century in 534 minutes the deflated spectators could hardly forbear but to cheer. Parthiv Patel's delicious square-driven four off Lee was as good as anything seen on this day of 366 runs. With three days still to play, the Border-Gavaskar Trophy looked already to be in India's safe keeping.

And on they batted, into the third morning, Patel to his first Test fifty, clobbering the desperate Lee, who was glad of two late wickets to finish with 4 for 201. Among Australians, only 'Chuck' Fleetwood-Smith (1 for 298, The Oval, 1938) had ever conceded 200. Lee, still brisk but lacking the high pace of his early years, went for 34 fours and a six. To Pathan fell the honour of raising India's first 700, Ganguly declaring at the ninth-highest total in Test history. Tendulkar's unbeaten 241 was his highest first-class score, a gem which his true believers knew would come after the darkness of 2003.

Typically Australia's reply began at a gallop, as it needed to. Langer and Hayden posted their century stand in the 23rd over. Hayden was out driving across the line at Anil Kumble, but Langer launched into the slow left-armer Murali Kartik, reverse-sweeping him for his hundred. A skied slog ultimately did for Langer, and when Ricky Ponting was deceived by a flipper – "we had a plan for him," said Kumble – in came the captain at 3 for 229. This was the moment the audience had paid good money for. The shrieks from 40,000 throats shook the rafters of the Bradman Stand.

After settling, Waugh slapped consecutive balls from Ajit Agarkar to the cover boundary, a trademark manoeuvre. But he had lost Damien Martyn, who batted an hour for seven, Kumble passing Derek Underwood's Test record of 20 caught-and-bowleds. The milestones kept coming: 1,000 runs against India by Waugh, to further tumultuous applause; then 1,000 runs at the SCG. On 40, he edged a hesitant drive and strode off, holding his bat by the blade. The combined age of the Indians responsible for his dismissal was slightly less than his own.

The rest of the innings belonged to Katich, whose first Test hundred impressed with its calmness and poise, keeping hope alight. On a hot and humid fourth day, the tireless Kumble was the greatest threat on a wearing pitch. He soon had Lee but was obliged to wait for his sixth wicket, with Gillespie holding out stubbornly and the field spread for

Katich. After 165 minutes the left-handed Katich became a Test centurion. He survived a stumping chance on 116 before holing out at long-on after lunch, ending a 117-run stand. Gillespie narrowly missed his fifty, stumped after a video referral, and Kumble finished with 8 for 141, the fourth-best figures in a Sydney Test.

Ganguly could have enforced Australia's first follow-on since Karachi in 1988. But with his bowlers' freshness and the state of the pitch in mind, he batted again. It gave Australia further opportunity to display their incipient flaws; Sehwag was caught behind off another Lee no-ball then dropped by Ponting at second slip, Australia's 15th spillage of the series. An uncharacteristic straight six by Dravid off Bracken, and some more polished strokeplay by Tendulkar, carried India to a position of renewed impregnability. Dravid was not out 91, sustaining a cut on his right ear when Lee clanged a bouncer into his helmet.

MOST CAUGHT-AND-BOWLEDS

C&B		Wkts	C&B%
22	A. R. Kumble (India)	397	5.5
20	D. L. Underwood (England)	297	6.7
19	M. Muralidaran (Sri Lanka)	485	3.9
17	R. Benaud (Australia)	248	6.8
	S. K. Warne (Australia)	491	4.0
15	L. R. Gibbs (West Indies)	309	4.8
	H. Trumble (Australia)	141	10.6
12	H. J. Howarth (New Zealand)	86	13.9
11	C. V. Grimmett (Australia)	216	5.0
	H. J. Tayfield (South Africa)	170	6.4
10	P. R. Adams (South Africa)	134	7.4
	G. Giffen (Australia)	103	9.7
	A. W. Greig (England)	141	7.0
	R. J. Hadlee (New Zealand)	431	2.3

Australia's target, in just over a day, was 443. The finale brought a smaller crowd, grey skies and a 22-minute hold-up for rain. At lunch, on 2 for 117, the challenge was still faintly sustainable. After Martyn's meek dismissal at leg slip, Steve Waugh came in for indisputably the last time in a Test. There were plaintive cries of his name, but the Indian captain chose to give him three close fielders rather than three cheers. Many wondered what might be crossing Waugh's fireproof, resolute mind. Backed, perhaps, by the communal power of prayer, he was soon placing Kartik wide of mid-on and then to the rope again off the back foot.

Ponting played early at Irfan Pathan and was caught and bowled just before tea. With Waugh and Katich together, and the dangerous Adam Gilchrist to come, 239 off 35 overs was still not an impossible demand if the trophy was to be won and the skipper ushered into retirement with the result most characteristic of his era – victory. It became the most prolific SCG Test when 1,644 runs (Australia v West Indies, 1968-69) were exceeded. But the way Kumble made the ball jump established that liberties could not be taken.

When Waugh swept Sehwag to raise his 50th score between 50 and 99, the ferries on Sydney Harbour sounded their klaxons. But realistically now, the match could only be saved, and personal considerations began naturally to whisper themselves. Katich, missed by Agarkar at mid-off on 41, ceded Waugh the strike. With four overs remaining Waugh was 80, and the dream of a valedictory hundred was very much alive.

And then Waugh, having batted, we were told, for a couple of hours short of 500 and made 10,927 runs, was gone. He slog-swept Kumble to Tendulkar, fittingly, in front of the Brewongle Stand. The boos and groans gave way to cheering of a unique calibre as Waugh trudged from the Test field forever. The cheeky 18-year-old keeper Patel had suggested the slog-sweep, only to be put in his place by the batsman, who told him a little respect might be in order. After all, Patel was in nappies when Waugh first batted for Australia. That Waugh fell for the suggestion all the same gave an indication of his fevered state of mind.

Patel closed a poor batting series for Gilchrist by stumping him, giving the heroic Kumble his 12th wicket. Katich and Gillespie again held the fort, and soon the gloomy evening gave way to speeches and presentations, followed by a lap of farewell, with Steve Waugh on his team-mates' shoulders, a working-class emperor departing. Soon he was trying to convince a large media gathering, and himself, that: "It's only a game, after all."

SCG: SUPERSTARS CLAPPED GOODBYE

A selection of cricketers who played their last Test in Sydney

S. R. Waugh (Australia)	40 & 80	2003-04
A. R. Caddick (England)	3-121 & 7-94	2002-03
J. C. Adams (West Indies)	10 & 5	2000-01
M. A. Taylor (Australia)	2 & 2	1998-99
G. R. J. Matthews (Australia)	79, 2-169	1992-93
S. M. H. Kirmani (India)	dnb, 1ct/1st	1985-86
C. H. Lloyd (West Indies)	33 & 72	1984-85
G. S. Chappell (Australia)	182	1983-84
D. K. Lillee (Australia)	4-65 & 4-88	1983-84
R. W. Marsh (Australia)	15*, 6ct	1983-84
Wasim Bari (Pakistan)	7* & 20, 3ct	1983-84
G. D. McKenzie (Australia)	0-74 & 1-65	1970-71
A. N. Connolly (Australia)	1-43 & 0-38	1970-71
B. C. Booth (Australia)	8 & 27	1965-66
R. Benaud (Australia)	11 & 3, 4-118 & 0-25	1963-64
A. K. Davidson (Australia)	15, 3-43 & 3-80	1962-63
R. N. Harvey (Australia)	22 & 28	1962-63
H. Ironmonger (Australia)	0-64 & 2-34	1932-33
H. Larwood (England)	4-98 & 1-44	1932-33
V. T. Trumper (Australia)	5 & 50	1911-12
C. Hill (Australia)	20 & 8	1911-12
J. V. Saunders (Australia)	3-114 & 5-82	1907-08
G. H. S. Trott (Australia)	18, 2-56 & 0-12	1897-98
T. Richardson (England)	8-94 & 2-110	1897-98
J. M. Blackham (Australia)	74 & 2, 1ct/1st	1894-95
C. T. B. Turner (Australia)	3-18 & 4-33	1894-95
F. R. Spofforth (Australia)	1-17	1886-87

The long-running emotional bombora had flattened out at long last. But its aftershock bore an element of trepidation, a fear for what might lie ahead for Australian cricket, now that it no longer had this stoic man at the helm.

Man of the Match: S. R. Tendulkar. *Man of the Series:* R. S. Dravid. *Attendance:* 181,053.

Close of play: First day, India (1) 3-284 (Tendulkar 73, Laxman 29); Second day, India (1) 5-650 (Tendulkar 220, Patel 45); Third day, Australia (1) 6-342 (Katich 51, Lee 0); Fourth day, Australia (2) 0-10 (Langer 4, Hayden 1)

India

	R	B	4/6			R	B	4/6
A. Chopra b Lee	45	139	5	– c Martyn b Gillespie		2	14	0
V. Sehwag c Gilchrist b Gillespie	72	115	10 1	– c Gillespie b MacGill		47	50	8
R. S. Dravid lbw b Gillespie	38	82	7	– not out		91	114	11 1
S. R. Tendulkar not out	241	436	33	– not out		60	89	5
V. V. S. Laxman b Gillespie	178	298	30					
*S. C. Ganguly b Lee	16	11	3					
†P. A. Patel c Gilchrist b Lee	62	50	11					
A. B. Agarkar b Lee	2	5	0					
I. K. Pathan not out	13	14	2					
B 4, l-b 5, w 4, n-b 25	38			L-b 3, w 1, n-b 7	11			

(187.3 overs, 806 mins)   (7 wkts dec) 705   (43.2 overs, 185 m) (2-dec) 211
Fall: 123 128 194 547 570 671 678   Fall: 11 73

A. R. Kumble and M. Kartik did not bat.

Bowling: *First Innings*—Lee 39.3–5–201–4; Gillespie 45–11–135–3; Bracken 37–13–97–0; MacGill 38–5–146–0; Waugh 2–0–6–0; Katich 17–1–84–0; Martyn 9–1–27–0. *Second Innings*—Lee 12.2–2–75–0; Gillespie 7–2–32–1; MacGill 16–1–65–1; Bracken 8–0–36–0.

Australia

	R	B	4/6			R	B	4/6
J. L. Langer c Patel b Kumble	117	149	17 1	– c Sehwag b Kartik		47	58	8
M. L. Hayden c Ganguly b Kumble	67	88	12 1	– c Dravid b Kumble		30	49	2
R. T. Ponting lbw b Kumble	25	48	2	– c and b Pathan		47	104	7
D. R. Martyn c and b Kumble	7	45	1	– c (sub) Yuvraj b Kumble		40	96	4
*S. R. Waugh c Patel b Pathan	40	72	6	– c Tendulkar b Kumble		80	159	15
S. M. Katich c Sehwag b Kumble	125	166	17	– not out		77	96	9
†A. C. Gilchrist b Pathan	6	25	1	– st Patel b Kumble		4	3	1
B. Lee c Chopra b Kumble	0	12	0					
J. N. Gillespie st Patel b Kumble	47	113	10	– (8) not out		4	11	1
N. W. Bracken c Agarkar b Kumble	2	8	0					
S. C. G. MacGill not out	0	1	0					
B 6, l-b 9, w 3, n-b 20	38			B 6, l-b 7, w 2, n-b 13	28			

(117.5 overs, 502 mins)   474   (94 overs, 383 m) (6 wkts) 357
Fall: 147 214 229 261 311 341 350 467   Fall: 75 92 170 196 338 342
                                                           473 474

Bowling: *First Innings*—Agarkar 25–3–116–0; Pathan 26–3–80–2; Kumble 46.5–7–141–8; Kartik 19–1–122–0; Ganguly 1–1–0–0. *Second Innings*—Agarkar 10–2–45–0; Kumble 42–8–138–4; Pathan 8–1–26–1; Kartik 26–5–89–1; Tendulkar 6–0–36–0; Sehwag 2–0–10–0.

Umpires: B. F. Bowden (New Zealand) and S. A. Bucknor (West Indies).
TV Umpire: P. D. Parker.
Referee: M. J. Procter (South Africa).

Indian matches v Australia and Zimbabwe in the VB Series (January 9–February 8) may be found in that section.

†PRIME MINISTER'S XI v INDIANS

At Manuka Oval, Canberra, January 28, 2004. Indians won by one run. *Toss:* Indians.

A game billed as Steve Waugh's last international outing climaxed in suitably thrilling fashion, with the Indians snatching victory on the last ball of the day. Waugh, the oldest man in the team by more than a decade, made seven runs and took the wicket of Irfan Pathan with his first delivery. Between innings the prime minister, John Howard, presented Waugh with his Australian of the Year award, which had been announced three days earlier. The Indians wore blue and the PM's men white, adding to the carnival atmosphere. Hemang Badani faced 121 balls, hitting eight fours and two sixes, and looked to have underpinned a comfortable Indian victory. They reckoned without local grade player Cade Brown, uncapped at first-class level, who produced a 96-ball 80 when it was needed most. Four members of Don Bradman's 1948 Invincibles side were among the blue-chip audience: Bill Brown, Sam Loxton, Neil Harvey and Arthur Morris. Harvey and Loxton even gave India's resting captain Sourav Ganguly an impromptu coaching session, with an unimpressed Loxton reportedly telling him: "This is probably the first time you have played side-on in your career. You ain't going to get a hang of it immediately."

Man of the Match: H. K. Badani.   *Attendance:* 11,300.

Indians

S. B. Bangar c McDonald b Doherty	33	I. K. Pathan c Cleary b Waugh		1
†P. A. Patel c Wright b Cleary	19	M. Kartik not out		12
H. K. Badani b McDonald	100			
R. S. Gavaskar st Hartley b McDonald	26	L-b 6, w 20, n-b 1		27
Yuvraj Singh run out	16			
*R. S. Dravid c Waugh b Wright	15	(50 overs, 225 mins)	(8 wkts)	254
A. B. Agarkar c Brown b McDonald	5	Fall: 36 96 150 176 218 230 239 254		

A. Bhandari and A. Nehra did not bat.

Bowling: Tait 10–0–48–0; Wright 10–0–51–1; Cleary 10–1–32–1; McDonald 9–0–70–3; Doherty 10–0–42–1; Waugh 1–0–5–1.

Prime Minister's XI

M. S. Bradley c Kartik b Bhandari	12	A. B. McDonald c Pathan b Bhandari		8
M. J. North c Nehra b Bangar	74	M. F. Cleary not out		0
D. J. Hussey c Patel b Nehra	9	B 6, l-b 7, w 4, n-b 1		18
C. Brown c Agarkar b Nehra	80			
S. R. Waugh c Pathan b Kartik	7	(50 overs, 214 mins)	(6 wkts)	253
C. D. Hartley not out	45	Fall: 38 59 143 175 213 252		

D. G. Wright, X. J. Doherty and S. W. Tait did not bat.

Bowling: Nehra 10–2–41–2; Bhandari 9–0–58–2; Pathan 10–0–39–0; Bangar 10–0–50–1; Kartik 10–1–43–1; Badani 1–0–9–0.

Umpires: S. D. Fry and D. B. Harris.
TV Umpire: A. Shelley.

Zimbabwe in Australia, 2003-04

by DAVID FRITH

These two-Test "series" tend to be the outcast offspring of the International Cricket Council's master policy that all countries must play all others in a given period. They are usually too fleeting to secure any lasting place in the memory. Occasionally, though, a mini-series is rescued by something quite out of the ordinary. And cricket has little to offer that is as sensational as the breaking of the world record for an individual Test score.

Matthew Hayden's 380 in the Perth Test sent sunbeams radiating in all directions, except perhaps into the zone where live the mean-minded who moaned that the feat was devalued by the ordinariness of Zimbabwe's bowling. These sourpusses would do well to reflect on the fact that previous record-holders – Wally Hammond and Garry Sobers among them – have seized the crown by plundering weak and depleted bowling. Long-term survival at the crease, as in life itself, calls for determination, stamina, skill and a measure of luck.

The Zimbabwe squad which touched down for the country's inaugural Test tour of Australia was lacking in several of these qualities. They had lost both Tests in England earlier in the year, each in three days and by innings margins, and were welcomed to Australia by Steve Waugh's warning that physical pain awaited them on the traditionally fast, bouncy WACA pitch. Suspended from the Commonwealth because of the excesses of the country's government, they were a struggling Test nation battling the loss of several major players. Henry Olonga and Andy Flower, formerly the world's No. 1 batsman, were victims of the political imbroglio for their polite black-armband protests during the World Cup. Neil Johnson had defected to South Africa and Murray Goodwin to Western Australia and Sussex. Alistair Campbell was allegedly excluded for indulging in free speech. And Grant Flower, to make matters worse, missed the first-class section of the tour with a broken finger.

They gave a hint of their potential in an exciting drawn match against WA, the only first-class contest outside the Tests. Craig

Wishart hit a hundred and Trevor Gripper a half-century. Andy Blignaut, Mark Vermeulen and the captain Heath Streak all caught the eye. On the eve of the First Test they were given two further items of encouragement. Glenn McGrath was to undergo surgery on his left ankle, thus joining his suspended comrade Shane Warne on the sidelines; and the Australians, responding to ongoing condemnation of their on-field behaviour, had come up with a two-page manifesto which promised more virtuous conduct henceforth.

Of course, this did not preclude the kind of assault by cricket bat carried out by Hayden. There was an air of unreality about his 380. It was still early October, so cricket in Australia was only just waking up after its winter slumber. Also, the excitement on the second day at the WACA as the records were ticked off one by one was coupled with the surreal thrill of contemplating unprecedented statistics; not only the highest score by a batsman in Test history but the highest total by Australia – or any side – in 126 years of Test cricket on Australian soil. The Zimbabweans toiled manfully on, perhaps mesmerised by it all and oddly proud at being part of such lofty proceedings. Ray Price scowled throughout, and the even-tempered Streak did too. They bowled on and on until at last the ordeal was over.

Zimbabwe's batsmen were predictably swept away first time round, leaving them with an oppressive deficit of almost 500. Then life grew easier for them. Jason Gillespie and Stuart MacGill broke down early in the second innings. When Brett Lee also left the field, and when Andy Bichel's movements were restricted by injury, an opportunity to fight their way to an unlikely draw presented itself.

Having lost Vermeulen unluckily for 63 – given out caught off his upper arm – Zimbabwe mounted resistance against Australia's part-time bowlers and dragged the match into a fifth day. Sean Ervine made good runs to go with his impressive bowling. Streak hung around for more than three hours and was supported by Price, his obstinate No. 11. For a while it looked as if even the weather might save Zimbabwe. It was only right, and just, that the rain relented in time for the world champions to pick up the conclusive wicket, limping away from a remarkable Test match three days before the next one.

Australia's grotesque injury list left a slightly sinister aftertaste. Beyond the sounds of celebration could be heard solemn strains of warning from the Australian Cricketers' Association. Not only are

VIEW FROM THE RECEIVING END

Heath Streak on Matthew Hayden's 380

"He mistimed shots for six, he flat-batted the ball, he left his crease no matter who was bowling. The bowlers were literally concerned about getting hit. You see people like Blignaut, Gilchrist, Kallis, Gibbs and Flintoff sustain that sort of hitting for maybe four or five overs. But Hayden did it relatively comfortably for pretty much 100 overs. We tried everything to stop him. We set fields similar to the last 10 overs of a one-day game. We tried changing our pace, bringing back our length, bowling outside off stump, on the leg side, bowling to the other batsman instead – except that was Adam Gilchrist, and people forget he got a hundred too. Hayden was timing the ball so well that he was beating the fielders on the fence. There were a couple of close chances. Mark Vermeulen dropped a relatively easy catch in the deep after he had passed his triple-century, and we had an lbw shout in the first over before he'd got off the mark. Between that we spent the whole time wondering how to get him out."

the schedules too heavy, they feared, but "cold-start" Tests like this one, while presumably fine for the likes of Hayden, can be perilous for bowlers. Then came news that Darren Lehmann was sidelined with an Achilles tendon problem, probably brought on by excessive preparatory training. Cricket has always thrived on irony.

Stuart Carlisle brought cheer to Zimbabwe with a neat, painstaking maiden Test century that spanned almost the whole of the opening day in Sydney. Any support from his partners came strictly in the form of time spent at the crease, not in any solid run contribution. Streak, for example, batted 117 minutes for his 14. They were four down before the hundred came up against a below-strength Australian attack, who had the ball swinging and swerving for most of the day.

Carlisle's hundred was the first by a Zimbabwean since the last time they played Bangladesh in Chittagong, a full 23 months and 10 Tests ago. Unfortunately his achievement came in front of gapingly empty terraces. An attendance of 5,455 was thought to be the lowest ever for the first day of a Test at the SCG, and only 18,363 watched the entire match. We shall never know in what numbers the fans would have responded if the October visitors had been England or West Indies. Meanwhile a torn stomach muscle ruled Lee out of the attack. This latest injury was blamed on the physical stress of back-to-back Tests. Within only eight days Australia had bowled to Zimbabwe through three consecutive innings.

After Blignaut's two promising early strikes Waugh's men were soon piling up the runs again. Ricky Ponting dominated with a characteristic century, and Waugh and Simon Katich made half-centuries that lifted Australia to a handy but not conclusive lead. This time Price's steady left-arm slows were richly rewarded with six wickets, giving him immense pleasure. "It's quite hard bowling to those guys," he said. "You can forget they're actually human."

Zimbabwe then failed to summon the uncompromising resistance that was needed. Dion Ebrahim failed again, and the ease with which so many of the tourists surrendered their wickets brought intense frustration to the normally serene features of their coach Geoff Marsh, the former Australian opening batsman. Katich's left-arm wrist-spin was a revelation. He also ran out Streak, who took a needless risk while batting with his impressive young vice-captain Tatenda Taibu. Had they mustered another 75 or so, Zimbabwe might just have pushed Australia. As it was, Hayden and Ponting's second-wicket stand of 151 in under two hours raced Australia irresistibly home on the fourth evening. After some thunderous stroke-play, Hayden managed to fit in his 16th Test hundred and stretch his series average beyond 250.

A few months earlier, a ghoulish commentator had envisaged Australia making a thousand runs against Bangladesh before declaring with no wickets lost. By those lights, Hayden's headline feats against Zimbabwe may be viewed as a fairly average performance.

ZIMBABWE TOURING PARTY

H. H. Streak (*captain*), T. Taibu (*vice-captain*), A. M. Blignaut, G. B. Brent, S. V. Carlisle, D. D. Ebrahim, S. M. Ervine, C. N. Evans, G. M. Ewing, T. R. Gripper, D. T. Hondo, S. Matsikenyeri, R. W. Price, M. A. Vermeulen, N. B. Mahwire, C. B. Wishart. *Coach:* G. R. Marsh. *Bowling coach:* B. A. Reid. *Manager:* B. Meman. *Media manager:* M. Harrison.

ZIMBABWE TOUR RESULTS

Test matches – Played 2: Lost 2.
First-class matches – Played 3, Lost 2, Drawn 1.
Losses – Australia (2)
Draws – Western Australia.
International limited overs – Played 8: Lost 7, No Result 1. *Losses* – Australia (3), India (4); *No result* – Australia.
Other non first-class matches: Played 5: Won 2, Lost 2, Drawn 1. *Wins* – Cricket Australia's Chairman's XI, Australia A; *Losses* – Australia A, Western Australia. *Drawn* – Rockingham-Mandurah Invitational XI.

TEST BATTING AVERAGES

	M	I	NO	R	HS	100s	50s	Avge	Ct/St	S-R
M. L. Hayden (Aus) ...	2	3	1	501	380	2	0	250.50	4	89.15
A. C. Gilchrist (Aus) ..	2	2	1	133	113*	1	0	133.00	9/2	110.83
R. T. Ponting (Aus) ...	2	3	1	259	169	1	1	129.50	2	67.27
S. M. Katich (Aus)	1	1	0	52	52	0	1	52.00	1	60.47
D. R. Martyn (Aus)	2	2	0	85	53	0	1	42.50	1	68.00
M. A. Vermeulen (Zim)	2	4	0	166	63	0	1	41.50	0	52.53
S. V. Carlisle (Zim) ...	2	4	0	160	118	1	0	40.00	3	45.07
H. H. Streak (Zim)	2	4	1	119	71*	0	1	39.67	1	30.28
A. M. Blignaut (Zim) ..	2	4	1	104	44	0	0	34.67	0	63.03
D. S. Lehmann (Aus) ..	1	1	0	30	30	0	0	30.00	1	62.50
S. M. Ervine (Zim)	1	2	0	59	53	0	1	29.50	2	53.64
T. R. Gripper (Zim) ...	2	4	0	115	53	0	1	28.75	0	44.92
T. Taibu (Zim)	2	4	0	80	35	0	0	20.00	1	28.07
R. W. Price (Zim).....	2	4	1	58	36	0	0	19.33	1	32.95
C. N. Evans (Zim)	1	2	0	27	22	0	0	13.50	0	33.75
G. B. Hogg (Aus)	1	1	0	13	13	0	0	13.00	0	33.33
J. L. Langer (Aus).....	2	3	0	36	26	0	0	12.00	1	55.38
D. D. Ebrahim (Zim) ..	2	4	0	42	29	0	0	10.50	1	40.38
N. B. Mahwire (Zim) ..	1	2	1	7	6	0	0	7.00	0	21.21
A. J. Bichel (Aus).....	2	1	0	5	5	0	0	5.00	0	33.33
G. M. Ewing (Zim).....	1	2	0	2	2	0	0	1.00	0	20.00
B. Lee (Aus).........	2	1	1	6	6*	0	0	–	0	35.29
J. N. Gillespie (Aus)..	1	0	–	–	–	–	–	–	0	–
S. C. G. MacGill (Aus).	1	0	–	–	–	–	–	–	0	–

TEST BOWLING AVERAGES

	O	Mdns	R	W	BB	5W/i	10W/m	Avge	S-R
J. N. Gillespie (Aus)..	28.3	9	58	5	3-52	0	0	11.60	34.20
S. M. Katich (Aus)......	32.5	3	90	6	6-65	1	0	15.00	32.83
D. S. Lehmann (Aus)....	33.2	16	64	3	3-61	0	0	21.33	66.67
A. J. Bichel (Aus)	92.4	29	255	10	4-63	0	0	25.50	55.60
S. C. G. MacGill (Aus) ..	24.4	5	64	2	2-54	0	0	32.00	74.00
S. M. Ervine (Zim)	31	4	146	4	4-146	0	0	36.50	93.00
B. Lee (Aus)	73	17	222	6	3-48	0	0	37.00	73.00
G. B. Hogg (Aus).......	54	17	119	3	2-49	0	0	39.67	108.00
R. W. Price (Zim)	89.4	11	371	6	6-121	1	0	61.83	89.67
T. R. Gripper (Zim)	26.3	0	144	2	2-142	0	0	72.00	79.50
A. M. Blignaut (Zim) ...	52	6	233	3	3-83	0	0	77.67	104.00
H. H. Streak (Zim)......	56	10	260	2	1-46	0	0	130.00	168.00
G. M. Ewing (Zim)	14	1	73	0	–	0	0	–	–
N. B. Mahwire (Zim)....	10	1	61	0	–	0	0	–	–
D. R. Martyn (Aus)	16	6	43	0	–	0	0	–	–
R. T. Ponting (Aus)	5	1	15	0	–	0	0	–	–

Note: Matches in this section that were not first-class are signified by a dagger.

†ROCKINGHAM–MANDURAH INVITATIONAL XI v ZIMBABWEANS

At Setters Hill, Baldivis, September 28, 29, 30, 2003. Match drawn. Zimbabweans 149 (S. M. Ervine 41; D. J. Wates 4-22, T. Gilbert 3-35, A. C. Voges 2-15) and 9 dec 255 (C. B. Wishart 116, S. M. Ervine 51; J. J. Taylor 3-34, A. K. Heal 3-53, A. C. Voges 2-42); Rockingham–Mandurah Invitational XI 123 (L. Ronchi 44; S. M. Ervine 5-37, R. W. Price 2-20) and 6 for 135 (L. Ronchi 47, C. J. Simmons 35; R. W. Price 4-55, S. M. Ervine 2-21).

†CRICKET AUSTRALIA CHAIRMAN'S XI v ZIMBABWEANS

At Lilac Hill Park, Caversham, October 1, 2003. Zimbabweans won by seven wickets. *Toss:* Cricket Australia Chairman's XI.

Never had pretty Lilac Hill witnessed such a brutal onslaught. Damien Martyn watched Adam Gilchrist fall to the fifth delivery of the match, then unleashed an amazing assault on Sean Ervine. Totally uninhibited, Martyn smashed three sixes and three fours to take 30 runs off the second over. He holed out a short while later, succumbing to his own adrenalin, his 31 coming of eight deliveries. Shaun Marsh departed for a first-ball duck, a lifter from Heath Streak clipping the shoulder of his bat and flying to third slip, thus denying Zimbabwe's coach Geoff Marsh the rare opportunity to bat with his son. Streak greeted Marsh, the former Australian opener, with a cordon of nine slips. He got an edge second ball but was dropped at second slip, and went on to play some punishing drives. Ryan Campbell provided some much-needed fireworks, clubbing three fours and three sixes, and the wonderfully competitive Streak finished with 4 for 32. After a shaky start, the Zimbabweans batted encouragingly. Mark Vermeulen stroked 61 at a run a ball, before an unbroken fourth-wicket partnership of 137 between Stuart Carlisle and Craig Wishart. The former Australian off-spinner Colin Miller was decidedly rusty, conceding 69 runs off nine overs.

Man of the Match: H. H. Streak.   *Attendance:* 7,000.

Cricket Australia's Chairman's XI

†A. C. Gilchrist b Streak	2	(6)	P. C. Worthington b Streak	12	(10)
D. R. Martyn c Evans b Blignaut	31	(8)	*J. Angel b Streak	2	(3)
J. L. Langer run out (Blignaut)	27	(77)	B. A. Williams not out	1	(1)
S. E. Marsh c Ebrahim b Streak	0	(1)			
G. R. Marsh c Wishart b Mahwire	27	(46)	L-b 2, w 11, n-b 2	15	
R. J. Campbell run out (Vermeulen/Taibu)	65	(82)			
G. B. Hogg c Taibu b Blignaut	38	(57)	(49.5 overs, 204 mins)	240	
M. E. K. Hussey c Taibu b Blignaut	20	(21)	Fall: 3 35 36 84 117 190 216 237 239 240		

C. R. Miller did not bat.

Bowling: Streak 9.5–0–32–4; Ervine 6–0–59–0; Blignaut 10–0–47–3; Mahwire 4–0–19–1; Price 10–1–21–0; Gripper 10–0–60–0.

Zimbabweans

D. D. Ebrahim c Gilchrist b Williams	6	(24)			
T. R. Gripper b Angel	2	(2)	L-b 5, w 13, n-b 2	20	
M. A. Vermeulen c Hogg b Worthington	61	(63)			
S. V. Carlisle not out	89	(95)	(41.2 overs, 174 mins) (3 wkts)	241	
C. B. Wishart not out	63	(76)	Fall: 5 26 104		

C. N. Evans, †T. Taibu, S. M. Ervine, *H. H. Streak, R. W. Price, A. M. Blignaut, N. B. Mahwire did not bat.

Bowling: Williams 9–1–33–1; Angel 7–0–45–1; Miller 9–0–69–0; Worthington 7–1–35–0; Hogg 7–1–31–0; S. E. Marsh 2–0–21–0; Hussey 0.2–0–2–0.

Umpires: J. K. Brookes and I. H. Lock.

WESTERN AUSTRALIA v ZIMBABWEANS

At WACA Ground, Perth, October 3, 4, 5, 2003. Match drawn. *Toss:* Western Australia.

In a glorified practice match that included two sporting declarations, Western Australia fell four runs short of an exciting victory. Set 270 to win in 38 overs, the home side took up the challenge and the fans were treated to some exhilarating strokeplay from Chris Rogers, Mike Hussey, Ryan Campbell and Marcus North. Peter Worthington, promoted to No. 4, slammed three fours and a six in his 27-ball 45. Had he lasted an over or two longer, WA might well have got up. Once again, Zimbabwe's top order looked fragile against a spirited opening attack led by the veteran Paul Wilson and Darren Wates, playing his first first-class match in four years. Craig Wishart's century, which included 18 fours and a six, was a promising sign ahead of the Test series.

Attendance: 3,108.

Close of play: First day, Zimbabweans (1) 7-254 (Wishart 93, Streak 45); Second day, WA (1) 6-207 (Worthington 30, Casson 7).

Zimbabweans

D. D. Ebrahim c Campbell b Wilson	8	– c Campbell b Wates	6
T. R. Gripper c Hussey b Wates	9	– c Campbell b Wilson	54
M. A. Vermeulen c Campbell b Wilson	38	– run out (Marsh/Angel)	30
S. V. Carlisle lbw b Angel	17	– c Campbell b Wilson	9
C. B. Wishart b Wilson	100	– (8) not out	11
C. N. Evans c Campbell b Wates	4	– (5) c Rogers b Wates	17
†T. Taibu c Worthington b Angel	21	– (6) b Wilson	0
S. M. Ervine c Wates b Hussey	6	– (7) not out	15
*H. H. Streak lbw b Wilson	45		
A. M. Blignaut st Campbell b Casson	57		
R. W. Price not out	8		
B 5, l-b 6, w 1, n-b 5	17	L-b 4	4

(124.3 overs, 473 mins) 330 (49.4 overs, 196 mins) (6 wkts dec) 146
Fall: 12 20 65 79 89 149 174 261 267 330
Fall: 21 78 98 105 111 124

Bowling: *First Innings*

Wilson 30–16–41–4; Wates 28–7–97–2; Angel 27–9–74–2; Worthington 16–6–35–0; Casson 11.3–1–60–1; Hussey 11–8–10–1; North 1–0–2–0. *Second Innings*—Wilson 14–6–26–3; Wates 10–1–53–2; Angel 8–4–10–0; Worthington 5–1–21–0; Casson 12.4–4–32–0.

Western Australia

*M. E. K. Hussey lbw b Streak	15	– (2) c Ervine b Gripper	79
C. J. L. Rogers c (sub) S. Matsikenyeri b Streak	20	– (1) c Vermeulen b Blignaut	26
M. J. North c Taibu b Blignaut	59	– (5) not out	31
S. E. Marsh c Blignaut b Streak	5	– (6) not out	6
S. W. Meuleman run out (Streak)	47		
†R. J. Campbell c Taibu b Blignaut	0	– (3) st Taibu b Gripper	59
P. C. Worthington not out	30	– (4) c Carlisle b Ervine	45
B. Casson not out	7		
B 4, l-b 3, w 6, n-b 11	24	B 3, l-b 8, n-b 9	20

(61 overs, 261 mins) (6 wkts dec) 207 (38 overs, 181 mins) (4 wkts) 266
Fall: 21 60 68 156 156 168
Fall: 32 160 211 240

D. J. Wates, P. Wilson and J. Angel did not bat.

Bowling: *First Innings*—Streak 14–4–35–3; Blignaut 12–1–63–2; Ervine 15–3–36–0; Evans 2–0–12–0; Price 1–0–12–0; Gripper 17–4–42–0. *Second Innings*—Streak 13–0–81–0; Blignaut 9–0–60–1; Ervine 9–0–57–1; Gripper 7–0–57–2.

Umpires: B. Bennett and I. H. Lock.

AUSTRALIA v ZIMBABWE

First Test Match

by KEN CASELLAS

At WACA Ground, Perth, October 9, 10, 11, 12, 13, 2003. Australia won by an innings and 175 runs. *Toss:* Zimbabwe.

Matthew Hayden had never enjoyed much success in Perth. He had scored first-class centuries on 25 different grounds around the globe and in every Australian state apart from Western Australia. In four Tests at the WACA he had managed a mere 203 runs at an average of 33.83. The first time he batted in a Perth Test he edged the third ball of the contest, from Curtly Ambrose, into the hands of Brian Lara at first slip. Another time he made a five-ball duck against New Zealand. His record in 11 first-class innings for Queensland at the WACA amounted to 353 runs at 35.30, with one half-century. So when back trouble flared during the couple of days leading into this Test, Hayden was not expecting a major turnaround in his Perth form.

His first stroke of luck came when Heath Streak won the toss and decided to bowl on an unusually hot spring day. After a cool, wet September the curator Richard Winter was convinced the pitch would lack its normal lively pace and bounce. Indeed the strip was one of the barest Test pitches seen at the ground. It was uncharacteristically dry, its docile appearance persuading the Australian selectors to opt for the leg-spinner Stuart MacGill instead of the fast bowler Brad Williams.

Streak had misread the pitch, which proved to be slow and unhelpful to the bowlers. Justin Langer cover-drove the second ball of the match (from Streak) to the boundary and raced to 26 off 38 deliveries, before getting a bottom edge on a ball from Sean Ervine and watching it bounce high and then drop, dislodging the off bail. Hayden, who survived a raucous leg-before appeal by Andy Blignaut before he had scored, was 31 at lunch. By tea he had chugged along to 76 off 154 deliveries, overshadowed by Langer, Ricky Ponting and a flamboyant Damien Martyn. Hayden brought up three figures with a sweep for a single from the off-spin of Trevor Gripper. His defence had been watertight, he had batted without flair, he had been selective in his shot-making. He was deliberately – and most unusually for Hayden – holding himself back.

Then, as though relieved of a massive burden, he cast off the shackles, lofting spinners Ray Price and Gripper over the long-off and long-on boundaries respectively. He had never hit a six in his previous 10 first-class appearances at the ground. Off Streak's first over with the new ball, Hayden scored 14: a back-foot punch through the covers, a vicious pull to the boundary and another mighty six over long-on. Zimbabwe, steady and competitive before tea, were now being overwhelmed. Hayden surged from 100 to 150 in 32 balls and added 107 in the final session. That evening he admitted that he had to fight hard to maintain focus on the slow pitch, and that his back ailment had helped him concentrate.

On the second morning Hayden dispensed with the heavy vest he had worn all through the first day to keep his back warm, as if signalling that now he really meant business. He soon relieved himself of his helmet too, replacing it with his baggy green cap. Resuming on 183, he lofted a succession of straight sixes off Streak, Ervine and Gripper to add 88 in the session, during which both Steve Waugh and Darren Lehmann spooned return catches to Ervine. Waugh received a standing ovation – his first of more than a dozen for the summer – as he walked out for what would later prove, though the crowd didn't know it yet, to be his last Test knock in Perth. He got an inside edge onto his boot and the ball ballooned back down the pitch, Ervine sprinting and diving to hold a brilliant catch.

Adam Gilchrist joined Hayden and the two left-handers scored almost at will, each hitting a century in the second session, a unique occurrence in Test cricket. Gilchrist was on fire, yet his 84-ball century drifted by almost unnoticed, as Hayden kept on breaking records. He passed Bob Cowper's mark (307) for the highest Test score in Australia. He drove Gripper to long-off for a single to move to 335, erasing Don Bradman and Mark Taylor's joint Australian Test record. The relief was palpable.

Hayden skied the next ball from Gripper to wide long-on where Mark Vermeulen dropped a comparative sitter. This was the first real chance he had offered. In the final over before tea, a straight drive for a single off Price took Hayden to 376, eclipsing the world record set by Brian Lara against England in 1993-94. He hugged Gilchrist, grinned broadly and touched the black armband strapped onto his right bicep, worn to commemorate the first anniversary of the deaths of 88 Australians in the terrorist attacks in Bali.

Waugh delayed his declaration to give Hayden the opportunity to reach 400 but, three balls after tea, he swept at Gripper and a tumbling Stuart Carlisle held a fine catch at deep backward square leg. Hayden's 11 sixes fell one short of Wasim Akram's world record and beat Gilchrist's Australian record of eight (against South Africa in Johannesburg in 2001-02). Hayden and Gilchrist's sixth-wicket partnership yielded 233 in 140 minutes from 34 overs. When Waugh declared, Australia had reached their highest total in a home Test. Each of the five Zimbabwean bowlers had conceded more than 100 runs, but the tireless Ervine fully deserved his four wickets. Months later, with Zimbabwe's cricket in ruin, Ervine would make Perth his home.

ANATOMY OF DESTRUCTION

Matthew Hayden's journey to 380

R	B	Mins	4s	6s
0-50	108	167	7	0
51-100	102	141	6	0
101-150	32	35	5	3
151-200	50	69	8	0
201-250	31	51	3	4
251-300	41	66	4	1
301-350	40	59	2	2
351-380	34	34	3	1
Total	438	622	38	11

Zimbabwe faced an impossible mission but made a spirited start on the second evening. Brett Lee bowled with considerable fire on the third day, softening up the defiant Gripper. He received a sickening blow on the right ear when he missed a hook, then gloved a defensive jab to another lifter and lobbed a catch to gully. Craig Evans was struck on the helmet by an Andy Bichel bouncer. All the Zimbabweans looked uncomfortable against the fast men.

Following on 496 behind, Zimbabwe's openers quickly fell to Jason Gillespie, Gripper playing back defensively and edging to the wicket-keeper and Dion Ebrahim getting an inside edge onto his stumps. But Gillespie left the field shortly afterwards with a torn muscle in his left side, and MacGill broke down with a torn right calf muscle. Vermeulen, Carlisle, Ervine, Streak, Blignaut and Price all revealed admirable fighting qualities against a depleted attack.

Price was wonderfully defiant, joining Streak at 9 for 247 and hanging on until rain ended play on the fourth day. After another rain delay on the final day, Australia clinched victory when Price drove Bichel to mid-off. Price had scored 36 off 110 deliveries in a last-wicket stand of 74. Streak underlined his leadership qualities, qualities that would become increasingly apparent during the troubled months ahead for Zimbabwe, with a defiant unbeaten 71.

Man of the Match: M. L. Hayden.   *Attendance:* 24,051.

Close of play: First day, Australia (1) 3-372 (Hayden 183, Waugh 61); Second day, Zimbabwe (1) 1-79 (Gripper 37, Vermeulen 9); Third day, Zimbabwe (2) 2-87 (Vermeulen 50, Carlisle 26); Fourth day, Zimbabwe (2) 9-272 (Streak 42, Price 17).

Australia

	R	B	4/6
J. L. Langer b Ervine	26	38	5
M. L. Hayden c Carlisle b Gripper	380	438	38 11
R. T. Ponting lbw b Ervine	37	65	6
D. R. Martyn c Wishart b Gripper	53	75	9
*S. R. Waugh c and b Ervine	78	124	10 1
D. S. Lehmann c and b Ervine	30	48	3 1
†A. C. Gilchrist not out	113	95	12 4
B 4, l-b 10, w 1, n-b 3	18		

(146.3 overs, 622 mins)   (6 wkts dec) 735
Fall: 43 102 199 406 502 735

A. J. Bichel, B. Lee, J. N. Gillespie and S. C. G. MacGill did not bat.

Bowling: Streak 26–6–131–0; Blignaut 28–4–115–0; Ervine 31–4–146–4; Price 36–5–187–0; Gripper 25.3–0–142–2.

Zimbabwe

	R	B	4/6		R	B	4/6
D. D. Ebrahim b Gillespie	29	62	5	– b Gillespie	4	26	0
T. R. Gripper c Lehmann b Lee	53	136	6	– c Gilchrist b Gillespie	0	1	0
M. A. Vermeulen c Hayden b MacGill	38	94	5	– c Gilchrist b Lee	63	120	9 1
S. V. Carlisle c Hayden b MacGill	2	17	0	– c Hayden b Lehmann	35	115	6
C. B. Wishart c Gilchrist b Bichel	46	78	6	– lbw b Bichel	8	13	1
C. N. Evans b Bichel	22	55	3	– b Lehmann	5	25	1
†T. Taibu lbw b Gillespie	15	46	1	– c Gilchrist b Bichel	3	19	0
*H. H. Streak b Lee	9	37	1	– (9) not out	71	217	10
S. M. Ervine c Waugh b Gillespie	6	12	1	– (8) b Bichel	53	98	7 1
A. M. Blignaut lbw b Lee	0	1	0	– st Gilchrist b Lehmann	22	29	5
R. W. Price not out	2	6	0	– c Waugh b Bichel	36	110	6
L-b 10, w 2, n-b 5	17			B 4, l-b 6, w 5, n-b 6	21		

(89.3 overs, 376 mins) 239   (127.2 overs, 488 mins) 321
Fall: 61 105 120 131 199 200 231 231   Fall: 2 11 110 112 118 126 126
    231 239   209 247 321

Bowling: *First Innings*—Lee 15–4–48–3; Gillespie 25.3–9–52–3; Bichel 21–2–62–2; MacGill 21–4–54–2; Lehmann 2–1–3–0; Waugh 5–1–10–0. *Second Innings*—Lee 35–8–96–1; Gillespie 3–0–6–2; MacGill 3.4–1–10–0; Bichel 28.2–15–63–4; Lehmann 31.2–15–61–3; Martyn 13–5–34–0; Waugh 8–2–26–0; Ponting 5–1–15–0.

Umpires: S. Venkataraghavan (India) and P. Willey (England).
TV Umpire: S. J. Davis.
Referee: G. R. Viswanath (India).

AUSTRALIA v ZIMBABWE

Second Test Match

by WARWICK FRANKS

At Sydney Cricket Ground, Sydney, October 17, 18, 19, 20, 2003. Australia won by nine wickets. *Toss:* Zimbabwe. *Test debut:* B. A. Williams and G. M. Ewing.

Zimbabwe recovered spiritedly from their drubbing in Perth, and had they shown greater batting resolve on the last day they might have stretched the home side's capabilities. Yet Sydney's crowds revealed themselves to be event junkies rather than sports connoisseurs; the match attendance figure was more than doubled on the Sunday night of the Test when 40,000 spectators turned out to see Ireland thrash Namibia in a meaningless Rugby World Cup match. The near-deserted cricket ground resembled the post-nuclear desolation of Neville Shute's novel *On the Beach*, particularly on the last day when Blessing Mahwire had to search alone for the ball in the empty vastness of the Bill O'Reilly Stand after Matthew Hayden hit a six. The aggregate attendance of 18,363 was the smallest for a completed Test in Sydney since the three Tests of 1886-87 and 1887-88.

Australia were forced to make three changes. Brad Williams made his Test debut at 28, replacing Jason Gillespie who had torn muscles in his side. Brad Hogg and Simon Katich played their first Tests on Australian soil, coming in for the injured Stuart MacGill and Darren Lehmann, who had suffered damage to an Achilles tendon. Zimbabwe replaced Sean Ervine, who had hurt himself playing soccer, with the debutant off-spinner Gavin Ewing, while the fast bowler Mahwire came in for Craig Evans.

Heath Streak won the toss on a still, overcast and humid morning, conditions which offered the bowlers some encouragement all day. Scorched by his decision in Perth to send the opposition in, Streak let his batsmen take their chances on a pitch whose preparation had been restricted to 12 days after the unexpected success of the Sydney Swans in reaching the Australian Football League finals. Nevertheless, the wicket played unremarkably throughout. Williams began his first over by kissing the ball and holding it aloft as a gesture to his late father, Clive. He generated lively pace, moving the ball both ways and gaining his first Test wicket when he captured Mark Vermeulen leg-before.

In general, though, the attack looked competent rather than menacing, and it was the frailty of Zimbabwe's batsmen which reduced the score to 4 for 95 just after lunch. It fell to Stuart Carlisle to produce an innings of character. A magpie chorus of Australian fieldsmen reminded him that he was playing his 31st Test yet had never passed the seventies. Their voices simply hardened his resolve. He mixed watchful defence with vigorous off-drives and pulls, profiting from an uncharacteristic spill at slip by Hayden off Brett Lee when he was 36.

Tatenda Taibu and Streak supported him in productive stands, but Carlisle's dismissal just before stumps underlined the visitors' tendency to lose wickets at crucial times. Next morning, Andy Blignaut and Ray Price added vital runs to stretch the total beyond a competitive 300. Hogg bowled with good control, he and Katich presenting the unique sight in Australian Test history of two left-arm wrist-spinners operating in concert. The morning added to the list of Australian injuries when Lee left the field with an abdominal strain.

After the rapid departure of the Australian openers, Ricky Ponting played an innings brimming with mature confidence, as evidenced by the power of his driving on both sides of the wicket and the sweetness of his timing off his pads. His century took only 113 balls, and soon after he passed 5,000 Test runs. He was assisted first by Damien Martyn and then by Steve Waugh in making Zimbabwe's prospects look as gloomy as the light which forced the players from the field at 4.54 p.m.

Play began half an hour early next morning. Price extracted some turn and bite from the rough outside leg stump, accounting for Waugh after a fourth-wicket partnership of 135 and then Ponting. From there, only Katich lingered, displaying an array of attractive shots combined with sure defence to reach his maiden Test fifty. Price bowled another long spell of intelligently probing orthodox left-arm spin. Unlike in Perth, his patience and skill were rewarded, Australia losing their last seven wickets for 120 to lead by only 95.

Zimbabwe's second innings was a case of unfulfilled promise. Five players reached 30 but none converted their starts into the century that might have set Australia a testing run-chase. Trevor Gripper and Vermeulen both reached the doorstep of 50 and then surrendered. On the fourth morning Zimbabwe led by 81, with six wickets in hand, when Craig Wishart undid his good work with a suicidal charge at Katich. Blignaut again showed finesse in the lower order, as Katich extracted plenty of turn without suffering the waywardness often associated with his type of bowling. At the other end Hogg maintained a good line. The sight of a long spell of the baroque skill of the chinaman bowlers was a delight to the eye of the cricket connoisseur.

Even so, Australia had to get 172, the sort of target which has occasionally produced outbreaks of the batting jitters for them in the past. Justin Langer departed quickly and Price, who was quickly into the attack, again looked potentially difficult. Hayden and Ponting, however, decided on a policy of uncompromising but controlled aggression, putting on 151 in only 24.2 overs. Hayden's innings took him past 4,000 Test runs as he resumed the assault that he had started in Perth, while Ponting was at his quicksilver best. As for the concept of staging Test cricket as early as October, the jury remained out. A paltry attendance of 1,312 on the final day prompted Waugh to comment dryly that he had considered taking his players around the ground to introduce them to each spectator.

Man of the Match: R. T. Ponting. *Man of the Series:* M. L. Hayden. *Attendance:* 18,363.

Close of play: First day, Zimbabwe (1) 8-256 (Blignaut 9, Price 7); Second day, Australia (2) 3-245 (Ponting 137, Waugh 43); Third day, Zimbabwe (2) 4-151 (Wishart 32, Taibu 13).

Zimbabwe

	R	B	4/6			R	B	4/6
D. D. Ebrahim b Lee	9	12	2	– c Katich b Williams		0	4	0
T. R. Gripper c Gilchrist b Bichel	15	32	1	– c Hayden b Katich		47	87	8
M. A. Vermeulen lbw b Williams	17	32	2	– c Waugh b Williams		48	70	8
S. V. Carlisle c Ponting b Bichel	118	213	15 2	– c Williams b Katich		5	10	1
C. B. Wishart c Gilchrist b Williams	14	62	1	– st Gilchrist b Katich		45	89	7
†T. Taibu c Gilchrist b Hogg	27	70	5	– c Ponting b Katich		35	150	4
*H. H. Streak lbw b Hogg	14	89	1	– run out (Katich/Gilchrist)		25	50	5
G. M. Ewing c Martyn b Lee	2	5	0	– c Gilchrist b Hogg		0	5	0
A. M. Blignaut not out	38	72	7	– c Williams b Katich		44	63	7 1
R. W. Price c Williams b Bichel	20	46	3	– lbw b Katich		0	14	0
N. B. Mahwire c Gilchrist b Bichel	6	20	1	– not out		1	13	0
B 4, l-b 12, w 3, n-b 9	28			B 6, l-b 5, w 1, n-b 4		16		

(107.2 overs, 441 mins)	308	(91.5 overs, 342 mins)	266

Fall: 15 45 47 95 151 218 222 243
296 308

Fall: 0 93 103 114 176 212 216
230 244 266

Bowling: *First Innings*—Lee 23–5–78–2; Williams 23–6–58–2; Bichel 24.2–7–66–4; Hogg 23–8–49–2; Waugh 4–0–7–0; Katich 7–0–25–0; Martyn 3–1–9–0. *Second Innings*—Williams 16–8–56–2; Bichel 19–5–64–0; Hogg 31–9–70–1; Katich 25.5–3–65–6.

Australia

	R	B	4/6		R	B	4/6
J.L. Langer c Streak b Blignaut	2	4	0	– c Taibu b Streak	8	23	0
M.L. Hayden c Carlisle b Blignaut	20	39	3	– not out	101	85	11 3
R.T. Ponting b Price	169	249	23 2	– not out	53	71	8
D.R. Martyn lbw b Price	32	50	3				
*S.R. Waugh c Carlisle b Price	61	98	9				
S.M. Katich b Price	52	86	8				
†A.C. Gilchrist b Streak	20	25	2 1				
G.B. Hogg c Ebrahim b Price	13	39	0				
A.J. Bichel b Wishart b Blignaut	5	15	1				
B. Lee not out	6	17	1				
B.A. Williams c and b Price	7	11	0				
L-b 2, w 1, n-b 13	16			B 3, l-b 3, n-b 4	10		

(103.3 overs, 448 mins)   403   (29.1 overs, 140 m) (1 wkt) 172
Fall: 7 51 148 283 306 347 375 384 394 403   Fall: 21

Bowling: *First Innings*—Streak 21–3–83–1; Blignaut 20–2–83–3; Mahwire 10–1–61–0; Price 41.3–6–121–6; Ewing 11–1–53–0. *Second Innings*—Streak 9–1–46–1; Blignaut 4–0–35–0; Price 12.1–0–63–0; Gripper 1–0–2–0; Ewing 3–0–20–0.

Umpires: B.F. Bowden (New Zealand) and S. Venkataraghavan (India).
TV Umpire: P.D. Parker.
Referee: G.R. Viswanath (India).

†AUSTRALIA A v ZIMBABWEANS

At WACA Ground, Perth, January 1, 2004. Day/night game. Zimbabweans won by eight runs. *Toss:* Zimbabweans.

Back in Australia again, after zipping home for two Tests and five one-day matches against West Indies, the Zimbabweans displayed familiar strengths and weaknesses. They looked to be in cruise control after Douglas Hondo and Andy Blignaut reduced the cream of Australia's young talent to 6 for 66 in the 23rd over. Then the gifted 20-year-old Shaun Marsh, enduring a miserable trot with Western Australia, engineered a trio of useful lower-order stands with Nathan Hauritz, Mark Cleary and Adam Griffith. The game looked to be up when Marsh was ninth man out, succumbing to a fine one-handed catch on the boundary by Blignaut. But Griffith and Shaun Tait scurried hard and found the gaps, adding 53 and bringing Australia A to within nine runs of victory with seven balls left. Stuart Carlisle finally settled Zimbabwe's jangling nerves, holding a catch at backward point to give Sean Ervine his fourth wicket. But for Carlisle, who carried his bat for 100 not out amid a regular clatter of wickets, the visitors would have struggled to post a competitive total. Only Mark Vermeulen and Grant Flower offered any top-order support. Both underestimated the vigorous fielding of the young Australians and were run out.

Man of the Match: S.V. Carlisle.   *Attendance*: 5,007.

Zimbabweans

V. Sibanda c Haddin b Cleary	3	(21)	A.M. Blignaut b Thornely	0	(2)
S.V. Carlisle not out	100	(129)	R.W. Price b Griffith	21	(37)
M.A. Vermeulen run out (Cleary/Haddin)	37	(26)	D.T. Hondo b Thornely	3	(9)
G.W. Flower run out (Watson/Haddin)	26	(38)	L-b 6, w 10, n-b 8	24	
S. Matsikenyeri c Cleary b Hauritz	0	(1)			
†T. Taibu st Haddin b Hauritz	4	(9)	(49.5 overs, 206 mins)	240	
*H.H. Streak b Tait	2	(12)	Fall: 10 68 129 129 135 142 174 174		
S.M. Ervine c Clarke b Thornely	20	(30)	226 240		

Bowling: Tait 9–0–41–1; Cleary 7–1–34–1; Griffith 10–0–49–1; Hauritz 10–0–46–2; Thornely 9.5–0–38–3; White 4–0–26–0.

Australia A

D. J. Thornely c Vermeulen b Hondo	1	(13)	M. F. Cleary c Sibanda b Price	29	(23)
†B. J. Haddin lbw b Ervine	25	(40)	A. R. Griffith c Carlisle b Ervine	33	(37)
*M. J. Clarke c Taibu b Hondo	8	(21)	S. W. Tait not out	22	(26)
S. R. Watson c Flower b Blignaut	5	(21)			
M. J. North c Flower b Blignaut	9	(24)	L-b 6, w 9, n-b 9	24	
S. E. Marsh c Blignaut b Ervine	57	(58)			
C. L. White c Taibu b Ervine	2	(11)	(49 overs, 230 mins)	232	
N. M. Hauritz c and b Price	17	(35)	Fall: 4 24 43 51 60 66 103 157 179 232		

Bowling: Streak 10–1–44–0; Hondo 10–1–34–2; Blignaut 8–2–27–2; Ervine 10–0–44–4; Price 8–0–53–2; Flower 3–0–24–0.

Umpires: B. N. J. Oxenford and R. L. Parry.
TV Umpire: I. H. Lock.

†WESTERN AUSTRALIA v ZIMBABWEANS

At WACA Ground, Perth, January 4, 2004. Day/night game. Western Australia won by 70 runs. *Toss:* Western Australia.

Zimbabwe's promising youngster Sean Ervine gave a taste of his undoubted ability with a splendid all-round performance. But his efforts with bat and ball were not enough to prevent the home side recording a comfortable victory. Scott Meuleman, Murray Goodwin and Brad Hogg provided the bulk of Western Australia's 9 for 286, which was lower than it might have been, given that they were cruising at 3 for 148 in the 27th over. The Zimbabweans kept pace with the required run-rate but bled wickets. Mark Vermeulen faced only 35 balls for his 55, thrashing 12 fours, but he was the only Zimbabwean to exceed 33. An injury to Craig Wishart's left knee was a major blow for the tourists.

Man of the Match: S. M. Ervine. *Attendance:* 3,993.

Western Australia

S. W. Meuleman b Flower	67	(82)	P. C. Worthington c Sibanda b Ervine	3	(5)
†R. J. Campbell c Taibu b Hondo	17	(15)	J. J. Taylor b Ervine	13	(11)
C. J. L. Rogers c Blignaut b Ervine	9	(22)	D. J. Wates not out	1	(1)
*M. E. K. Hussey retired hurt (Blignaut/Taibu)	21	(36)	L-b 3, w 7, n-b 13	23	
M. W. Goodwin c Flower b Blignaut	77	(85)			
M. J. North c Taibu b Ervine	7	(9)	(50 overs, 225 mins) (9 wkts)	286	
G. B. Hogg b Ervine	48	(54)	Fall: 31 55 111 148 161 256 263 281 286		

P. Wilson did not bat.

Bowling: Hondo 8–1–38–1; Mahwire 10–0–59–0; Ervine 10–0–56–5; Blignaut 8–0–56–1; Friend 4–0–26–0; Flower 10–0–48–1.

Zimbabweans

V. Sibanda c Campbell b Wilson	13	(24)	T. J. Friend c Worthington b North	12	(22)
S. V. Carlisle c North b Wilson	8	(17)	N. B. Mahwire c Hogg b North	6	(6)
M. A. Vermeulen c Campbell b Worthington	55	(35)	D. T. Hondo not out	2	(4)
G. W. Flower c Campbell b Wates	22	(36)	L-b 6, w 4	10	
C. B. Wishart retired hurt	13	(15)			
*†T. Taibu c Wilson b Wates	33	(28)	(44.1 overs, 187 mins) (9 wkts)	216	
S. M. Ervine c Goodwin b Worthington	31	(51)	Fall: 13 42 101 101 151 175 197		
A. M. Blignaut st Campbell b Hogg	11	(31)	204 216		

Bowling: Wilson 7–1–21–2; Taylor 6–0–43–0; Wates 10–0–51–2; Worthington 10–0–53–2; Hogg 10–1–37–1; North 1.1–0–5–2.

Umpires: B. Bennett and J. K. Brookes.

†AUSTRALIA A v ZIMBABWEANS

At Adelaide Oval, Adelaide, January 7, 2004. Australia A won by 119 runs. *Toss:* Australia A.

Four days before the start of the VB Series, Heath Streak's men received a foretaste of torrid times ahead when they were savaged by the buccaneering duo of Marcus North and Michael Clarke. North and Brad Haddin set the tone from the start, opening up with 75 in 67 balls. Zimbabwe's bowlers were wayward in the windy conditions; Streak took himself off after three overs and Andy Blignaut's opening two overs went for 34. Shane Watson maintained the tempo before Clarke, the 22-year-old captain, raised it another notch. He was at his brutally elegant best, thumping 11 fours and a six in his 71-ball stay. North smashed 14 fours and two sixes, including one off Douglas Hondo that sailed 20 metres over the mid-wicket boundary. It was the highest limited-overs total by an Australia A side, eclipsing the 4 for 321 against Zimbabwe in January 2001. Stuart Carlisle, the chief Zimbabwean scourge of Australian bowlers, was unable to bat after hurting his thumb. But they started brightly without him, Vusi Sibanda and Mark Vermeulen putting 51 on the board inside nine overs. The chase soon petered out, Grant Flower and Sean Ervine adding a sluggish 122 for the fourth wicket. The next best partnership after that was worth 11.

Man of the Match: M. J. North.   *Attendance:* 8,813.

Australia A

M. J. North c Price b Streak	.........115 (108)		D. J. Thornely b Streak	....	5	(5)
†B. J. Haddin c Taibu b Hondo	...... 45 (41)		N. M. Hauritz not out	....	3	(2)
S. R. Watson st Taibu b Price	.... 37 (53)		L-b 2, w 9, n-b 4	....	15	
*M. J. Clarke b Ervine	.... 93 (71)					
C. L. White c Price b Hondo	.... 9 (16)		(50 overs, 220 mins)	(6 wkts)	327	
M. J. Cosgrove not out	.... 5 (7)		Fall: 75 177 248 295 317 324			

M. F. Cleary, A. R. Griffith and S. W. Tait did not bat.

Bowling: Streak 10–1–55–2; Hondo 10–0–65–2; Ervine 5–0–37–1; Blignaut 4–0–49–0; Mahwire 6–0–33–0; Price 10–0–58–1; Flower 5–0–28–0.

Zimbabweans

V. Sibanda c Haddin b Cleary	.... 23 (27)		R. W. Price b White	....	3	(9)
M. A. Vermeulen c and b Cleary	..... 22 (34)		D. T. Hondo b White	....	0	(4)
G. W. Flower b Clarke	.... 67 (87)		N. B. Mahwire c Haddin b Tait	.....	0	(4)
†T. Taibu c Thornely b Griffith	...... 0 (5)		L-b 11, w 8, n-b 4	....	23	
S. M. Ervine run out (Thornely)	...... 51 (74)					
*H. H. Streak not out	.... 16 (18)		(44 overs, 181 mins)	(9 wkts)	208	
A. M. Blignaut st Haddin b Clarke	... 3 (7)		Fall: 51 56 57 179 185 193 204 204 208			

S. V. Carlisle did not bat.

Bowling: Tait 6–0–27–1; Griffith 10–1–36–1; Cleary 6–0–21–2; White 8–2–28–2; Thornely 7–0–42–0; Hauritz 4–0–27–0; Clarke 3–0–16–2.

Umpires: I. H. Lock and J. H. Smeaton.
TV Umpire: S. D. Fry.

Zimbabwe matches v Australia and India in the VB Series (January 9–February 8) may be found in that section on page 415.

VB Series, 2003-04

by ANDREW WEBSTER

Arthur Morris, the former Australian Test great and sharp-witted icon from another time, uses this adage to sum up his opinion of one-day cricket. "It's like All Bran," he grins. "It's good for the system but it produces a lot of rubbish." Last summer's triangular series involving Australia, India and Zimbabwe followed a reverse trend to the analogy Morris offers. It produced some marvellous cricket but, in the end, achieved little for the system. As the tournament wore on it became painfully clear that the present one-day format in Australia needs an enema.

Predictability is one of its problems. Australia and India were earmarked to make the finals long before the first match had been played, no matter how much Zimbabwe talked up their chances, which gave the 12 preliminary games an unshakeable air of inevitability. Once they were over, the best-of-three finals should have been a climactic high point of the summer. But as contests they, too, petered out into something unremarkable. Indian legs had grown weary after a never-ending season of Tests, exhibition matches and one-day games of no consequence. They were promptly thrashed.

The solution? No, not the re-introduction of an Australia A side – as was trialled and abandoned in 1994-95 – but a revamped format: fewer preliminary games and a longer finals series. That way, sides wouldn't have to contest so many meaningless matches. The finals wouldn't be over just as everybody's excitement levels are rising. Adam Gilchrist is among those who have mooted the idea. It is something Cricket Australia should take on board.

To its credit, it is belatedly starting to do so. In 2004-05, New Zealand are coming out for a new three-match series – the Chappell–Hadlee Trophy – and the number of VB qualifying games have been trimmed from 12 to nine. The board seems reluctant to budge much further. It has contractual obligations to television and sponsors, and if you listen carefully enough you can still hear the turnstiles around Australia *ka-chinging* all through January and February.

But Cricket Australia would do well to keep one eye on the bigger picture. Too many mismatches and too much inevitability cannot be healthy; sooner or later, relevancy becomes an issue. Twenty-six years ago the one-day game brought about a much-needed revolution that enabled cricket to move with the times. Now one-day cricket requires its own revolution for the same reasons.

For all that, the 2003-04 VB Series provided several healthy reminders of why one-day cricket remains compulsive viewing, even for the purist. It showed that a unique kind of intensity is required to compete at the level reached by Ricky Ponting's side in the last two years. Scoring at a clip of a run per ball is now considered standard, not brilliant, something Ponting, Matthew Hayden, Michael Clarke and Andrew Symonds regularly illustrated. For Gilchrist, even a run a ball was too tardy; he required only 126 deliveries to belt 172 against Zimbabwe in Hobart, and finished the tournament with a strike-rate of 122.

Among the Indians, V. V. S. Laxman hit three hundreds – matching the feat of David Gower in 1982-83, Graeme Hick in 1998-99 and Mark Waugh in 2000-01. Rahul Dravid, Virender Sehwag and Laxman demonstrated that their classical styles in the Test arena are transferable to the one-day game. Yuvraj Singh signalled himself as the man most likely to join them.

Bowlers were again the forgotten men as monolithic totals were tallied. Brad Williams outshone Jason Gillespie as Australia's spearhead. India's Irfan Pathan arrived as a fast bowler not to be crossed, even if his aggression did hurt his back pocket in the second final at the SCG when he was thwacked for 75 runs in 10 overs.

In the first final Brett Lee showed that, despite the modern fixation with economy-rates, there is still a place for raw speed. He bowled Sachin Tendulkar all ends up with a shuddering off-cutter, then rattled Laxman's helmet with a 145 kph rocket. Earlier in the competition Lee had provided one of the batting highlights, clobbering a match-winning six over cover at the death as India lost a heartbreaker at the SCG by two wickets. They were never the same team again.

And what of Zimbabwe? Nobody could have forecast (or maybe they could?) the dramatic off-field events that would follow months after Heath Streak and his side returned to their homeland. What did become abundantly clear was that Zimbabwe's on-field struggles would have been far worse if not for their captain's spirited efforts. In what seems likely to have been one of his last acts as an international cricketer, Streak topped his country's bowling and batting averages while carrying himself and his team with dignity, even when they were being hammered.

Nobody begrudged Zimbabwe's presence. Indeed, one of the positive things to have come out of Australia's triangular one-day series is the opportunity it has given cricket's minnow powers to grow. But let's be realistic: Zimbabwe have now won three out of 25 one-day matches in Australia, two of them against England. Their presence does devalue the overall quality of the series. A happy compromise between what is best for them, the game and the fans needs to be struck. And soon.

VB SERIES RUN SCORERS, 2003-04

	M	I	NO	R	HS	100s	50s	Avge	Ct/St	S-R
A. C. Gilchrist (Aus)	8	8	0	498	172	1	2	62.25	16/1	121.46
V. V. S. Laxman (Ind)	10	10	3	443	131	3	0	63.29	12	82.34
M. L. Hayden (Aus) .	9	9	0	425	126	2	2	47.22	5	81.89
A. Symonds (Aus) ..	9	9	1	349	88	0	3	43.63	4	93.82
R. T. Ponting (Aus) .	9	9	0	315	88	0	3	35.00	4	82.68
Yuvraj Singh (Ind) ..	8	9	0	314	139	1	1	39.25	4	92.63
R. S. Dravid (Ind) ...	10	9	0	277	84	0	3	30.78	5	74.86
S. M. Ervine (Zim) ..	8	7	1	265	100	1	0	44.17	2	100.00
M. J. Clarke (Aus) ..	10	9	1	248	63	0	1	31.00	4	89.86
S. R. Tendulkar (Ind)	7	7	0	236	86	0	2	33.71	2	78.15
S. V. Carlisle (Zim) .	7	6	0	223	109	1	0	37.17	2	65.78
H. H. Streak (Zim) ..	8	7	3	211	64*	0	2	52.75	2	68.73
D. R. Martyn (Aus)..	10	10	2	209	67	0	1	26.13	0	89.70
V. Sehwag (Ind)	6	6	0	195	90	0	1	32.50	3	83.33
M. G. Bevan (Aus)..	7	7	1	195	75	0	2	32.50	0	83.33
G. W. Flower (Zim) .	7	6	0	195	94	0	1	32.50	3	67.01
S. C. Ganguly (Ind) .	9	9	1	177	82	0	1	22.13	5	75.32
H. K. Badani (Ind) ..	6	6	3	133	60*	0	1	44.33	3	68.21
T. Taibu (Zim)	8	6	0	113	44	0	0	18.83	5	47.88
R. S. Gavaskar (Ind).	6	6	2	90	54	0	1	22.50	4	83.33
I. J. Harvey (Aus)...	7	5	0	87	28	0	0	17.40	1	89.69
I. K. Pathan (Ind) ...	10	7	3	85	30	0	0	21.25	2	80.19
D. D. Ebrahim (Zim)	6	5	1	80	39	0	0	20.00	3	72.73
A. B. Agarkar (Ind) .	6	4	1	75	53	0	1	25.00	1	65.22
M. Kartik (Ind)......	4	2	1	55	32*	0	0	55.00	2	82.09
S. Matsikenyeri (Zim)	5	5	1	51	36	0	0	12.75	2	68.92
A. M. Blignaut (Zim)	8	5	1	50	31*	0	0	12.50	3	94.34
P. A. Patel (Ind)	3	3	0	47	28	0	0	15.67	4	67.14
B. J. Haddin (Aus) ..	2	2	0	46	32	0	0	23.00	1/1	73.02
A. J. Bichel (Aus)...	8	5	3	37	23*	0	0	18.50	2	88.10
V. Sibanda (Zim)	6	5	0	32	12	0	0	6.40	2	37.65
R. W. Price (Zim)....	8	4	2	31	18*	0	0	15.50	0	88.57
S. M. Katich (Aus) ..	4	3	2	31	18*	0	0	31.00	0	68.89
B. Lee (Aus).........	8	4	2	27	12*	0	0	13.50	6	93.10
M. A. Vermeulen (Zim)	4	4	1	22	14*	0	0	7.33	1	36.07
M. E. K. Hussey (Aus)	1	1	1	17	17*	0	0	–	1	73.91
T. J. Friend (Zim) ...	4	4	0	16	8	0	0	4.00	2	34.78
J. N. Gillespie (Aus).	8	3	2	15	8*	0	0	15.00	0	71.43
L. Balaji (Ind)......	10	4	1	15	11	0	0	5.00	6	34.01

	M	I	NO	R	HS	100s	50s	Avge	Ct/St	S-R
A. Nehra (Ind)	4	1	1	14	14*	0	0	–	0	350.00
N. B. Mahwire (Zim)	2	1	1	8	8*	0	0	–	1	29.63
G. B. Hogg (Aus) ...	3	3	2	7	6*	0	0	7.00	0	100.00
A. R. Kumble (Ind)..	5	2	0	7	5	0	0	3.50	2	100.00
S. B. Bangar (Ind)...	2	2	0	3	3	0	0	1.50	0	33.33
D. T. Hondo (Zim) ..	7	2	1	1	1*	0	0	1.00	3	33.33
B. A. Williams (Aus)	9	3	1	0	0*	0	0	0.00	3	0.00
A. Bhandari (Ind) ...	1	0	–	–	–	–	–	–	0	–

* Denotes not out.

WICKET-TAKERS, 2003-04

	M	O	Mdns	R	W	BB	5Wfi	Avge	RPO
I. K. Pathan (Ind)	10	89.4	4	497	16	4-24	0	31.06	5.54
B. A. Williams (Aus)..	9	64.5	7	250	15	5-22	1	16.67	3.86
H. H. Streak (Zim).....	8	72	7	338	15	3-45	0	22.53	4.69
L. Balaji (Ind)	10	90	6	441	13	4-48	0	33.92	4.90
B. Lee (Aus)	8	66	4	285	12	3-22	0	23.75	4.32
S. M. Ervine (Zim) ...	8	63.3	2	361	12	3-47	0	30.08	5.69
A. B. Agarkar (Ind)	6	52.4	4	281	11	6-42	1	25.55	5.34
J. N. Gillespie (Aus) ...	8	77	4	343	10	2-21	0	34.30	4.45
A. Symonds (Aus).....	9	68	2	350	10	2-24	0	35.00	5.15
I. J. Harvey (Aus)	7	49	3	265	8	3-52	0	33.13	5.41
A. M. Blignaut (Zim) ..	8	53	2	301	6	2-21	0	50.17	5.68
S. C. Ganguly (Ind)	9	30	0	189	6	3-41	0	31.50	6.30
A. Nehra (Ind)	4	36	2	199	5	2-63	0	39.80	5.53
D. T. Hondo (Zim).....	7	45	1	293	5	2-59	0	58.60	6.51
R. W. Price (Zim)	8	70	0	324	4	1-38	0	81.00	4.63
M. J. Clarke (Aus)	10	33	0	186	4	1-14	0	46.50	5.64
A. Bhandari (Ind)	1	7.4	0	31	3	3-31	0	10.33	4.04
V. Sehwag (Ind)	6	22	1	107	3	2-40	0	35.67	4.86
G. W. Flower (Zim).....	7	52.4	0	256	3	2-42	0	85.33	4.86
A. J. Bichel (Aus)	6	37	2	197	3	1-31	0	65.67	5.32
G. B. Hogg (Aus)......	3	20	0	76	2	1-36	0	38.00	3.80
A. R. Kumble (Ind)	5	47	2	227	2	1-38	0	113.50	4.83
H. K. Badani (Ind).....	8	7	0	31	1	1-31	0	31.00	4.43
S. B. Bangar (Ind)	2	11	0	61	1	1-42	0	61.00	5.55
N. B. Mahwire (Zim)...	2	6	1	35	1	1-35	0	35.00	5.83
R. S. Gavaskar (Ind) ...	6	9	0	56	1	1-56	0	56.00	6.22
M. Kartik (Ind)	4	26	0	178	1	1-39	0	178.00	6.85
S. R. Tendulkar (Ind)...	7	8	0	60	1	1-60	0	60.00	7.50
T. J. Friend (Ind)	4	5	0	24	0	–	0	–	4.80
M. E. K. Hussey (Aus)..	1	3	0	15	0	–	0	–	5.00
S. Matsikenyeri (Zim)..	5	1	0	17	0	–	0	–	17.00

AUSTRALIA v INDIA

At Melbourne Cricket Ground, Melbourne, January 9, 2004. Day/night game. Australia won by 18 runs. *Toss:* Australia. Australia 5 pts, India 1 pt. *Limited-overs international debut:* I. K. Pathan.

Police trawled the regular haunts outside the MCG before the opening game, sniffing out potential hooligans. They had every right to enter the arena later that night and arrest the Australian team for escaping from jail – repeatedly. The ascendancy swung ceaselessly from one team to the other in this schizoid match. Ajit Agarkar, producing the best figures of his career, stifled Australia to 4 for 89 at one stage before Andrew Symonds and Michael Clarke guided them to a hefty 288. Symonds pummelled five fours and three sixes along the way. But the real twists came later when India appeared headed for certain victory. It had been a fumblefest for the Australians in the Tests but on this night catching was their saviour. First Ricky Ponting pulled down a one-handed screamer at mid-wicket to remove Sachin Tendulkar. Then Clarke lunged to dismiss Yuvraj Singh. Next ball Sanjay Bangar fended a short one from Ian Harvey, took a couple of steps down the wicket and left Sourav Ganguly in no-man's land. Harvey pounced, threw down the stumps and India were on their way to losing six wickets for 13 in 19 balls. Australia won. Exactly how was anyone's guess.

Man of the Match: A. Symonds.   *Attendance:* 63,271.

Australia

†A. C. Gilchrist c Pathan b Agarkar	.. 34	(34)	
M. L. Hayden c Yuvraj Singh b Agarkar	20	(22)	
*R. T. Ponting c and b Balaji	 18	(19)	
D. R. Martyn c Balaji b Agarkar	 0	(1)	
A. Symonds c Kumble b Agarkar	 88	(102)	
M. J. Clarke c Laxman b Kumble	 63	(66)	
M. G. Bevan c Ganguly b Sehwag	 1	(8)	
I. J. Harvey c Tendulkar b Agarkar	... 28	(24)	

A. J. Bichel run out (Balaji) 1 (7)
J. N. Gillespie not out 8 (10)
B. A. Williams c Yuvraj Singh b Agarkar 0 (1)

L-b 10, w 14, n-b 3 27

(48.3 overs, 212 mins) 288

Fall: 59 70 70 89 232 233 258 272 287 288

Bowling: Agarkar 9.3–1–42–6; Pathan 10–0–61–0; Balaji 9–0–52–1; Kumble 10–0–56–1; Bangar 3–0–19–0; Ganguly 5–0–40–0; Sehwag 2–1–8–1.

India

V. Sehwag b Harvey	 35	(59)	
S. R. Tendulkar c Ponting b Symonds	. 63	(69)	
*S. C. Ganguly run out (Harvey)	 82	(83)	
V. V. S. Laxman c Clarke b Symonds	.. 16	(22)	
†R. S. Dravid c Harvey b Clarke	 16	(19)	
Yuvraj Singh c Clarke b Harvey	 25	(24)	
S. B. Bangar c Ponting b Harvey	 3	(5)	
A. B. Agarkar c Clarke b Gillespie	... 1	(4)	

I. K. Pathan c Hayden b Williams ... 3 (6)
A. R. Kumble c Clarke b Williams .. 5 (4)
L. Balaji not out 0 (0)

B 1, l-b 8, w 11, n-b 1 21

(49 overs, 224 mins) 270

Fall: 103 134 168 195 257 257 260
263 266 270

Bowling: Gillespie 10–1–50–1; Williams 9–0–52–2; Bichel 6–0–38–0; Harvey 10–1–52–3; Symonds 10–0–47–2; Clarke 4–0–22–1.

Umpires: S. A. Bucknor (West Indies) and S. J. A. Taufel.
TV Umpire: R. L. Parry.
Referee: C. H. Lloyd (West Indies).

AUSTRALIA v ZIMBABWE

At Sydney Cricket Ground, Sydney, January 11, 2004. Day/night game. Australia won by 99 runs. *Toss:* Australia. Australia 6 pts.

"We're going to be out to win every game," Zimbabwe's captain Heath Streak declared ahead of his side's opening match. "We're not here to make up the numbers." It became clear soon after his men were bundled out for 126 that he possessed the optimism of a Vegas desperado. The most worrying aspect for Streak was that the Australians barely seemed interested in this match at the SCG, the ground where they had farewelled Steve Waugh five days earlier. Australia's top order contemptuously lashed and cross-batted at anything dished up by the Zimbabwe bowlers, and it was again left to Andrew Symonds and Michael Clarke to ensure a defendable target was set. When the visitors crumbled to 5 for 17 in the eighth over, the gulf between a disinterested Australia and a revved-up Zimbabwe was plain to see. Apart from the six points, the only tangible gain for Australia was the form of the livewire fast bowler Brad Williams, a belated addition to the squad. He jagged the ball about at a lively speed, nailing four wickets in his first 27 balls and finishing with career-best figures of 5 for 22.

Man of the Match: B. A. Williams.   *Attendance:* 19,494.

Australia

†A. C. Gilchrist c Taibu b Blignaut	34 (44)	I. J. Harvey c and b Ervine	22 (17)
M. L. Hayden b Streak	14 (36)	A. J. Bichel not out	11 (13)
*R. T. Ponting c Carlisle b Blignaut	21 (31)	J. N. Gillespie not out	1 (2)
D. R. Martyn c and b Flower	21 (17)	L-b 4, w 6, n-b 6	16
A. Symonds c Hondo b Ervine	42 (82)		
M. G. Bevan c and b Flower	3 (7)	(50 overs)	(8 wkts) 225
M. J. Clarke c Sibanda b Ervine	40 (57)	Fall: 42 73 77 112 118 184 192 222	

B. A. Williams did not bat.

Bowling: Streak 10–2–36–1; Hondo 5–1–35–0; Ervine 10–0–53–3; Blignaut 5–0–21–2; Price 10–0–34–0; Flower 10–0–42–2.

Zimbabwe

V. Sibanda c Williams b Gillespie	7 (16)	A. M. Blignaut c Ponting b Williams	4 (10)
S. V. Carlisle c Hayden b Williams	1 (6)	R. W. Price b Gillespie	0 (7)
M. A. Vermeulen b Williams	5 (12)	D. T. Hondo not out	1 (2)
G. W. Flower lbw b Williams	0 (1)		
S. Matsikenyeri c Gilchrist b Williams	0 (3)	B 1, l-b 6, w 12	19
†T. Taibu c Gilchrist b Symonds	29 (59)		
*H. H. Streak st Gilchrist b Clarke	46 (92)	(37.3 overs)	126
S. M. Ervine c Ponting b Symonds	14 (17)	Fall: 2 13 13 14 17 90 119 122 124 126	

Bowling: Gillespie 8–0–21–2; Williams 8.3–2–22–5; Bichel 6–2–24–0; Harvey 4–0–14–0; Symonds 6–1–24–2; Clarke 5–0–14–1.

Umpires: R. E. Koertzen (South Africa) and S. J. A. Taufel.
TV Umpire: R. L. Parry.
Referee: C. H. Lloyd (West Indies).

INDIA v ZIMBABWE

At Bellerive Oval, Hobart, January 14, 2003. India won by seven wickets. *Toss:* Zimbabwe. India 6 pts.

Zimbabwe's chance of winning this match effectively ended when the covers were rolled back, so flat was the pitch that had been prepared. A cautious, horribly out-of-sorts top order crawled to 5 for 83 in the 29th over. Irfan Pathan swung the ball and bowled tightly, continuing to justify the gut instincts of the Indian selectors. A couple of vital unbeaten knocks from Heath Streak and Sean Ervine, who piled up 93 in the last 12 overs, eventually lifted Zimbabwe to something approaching respectability. Ervine, watched by a small Hobart crowd, crashed three sixes in his 33-ball rampage. But that was merely a foretaste of even greater carnage to come, India's guns blazing away to reach the target with 12.2 overs to spare. Virender Sehwag, dropped on 27, thumped five fours and five sixes in his 90. But for Streak, who troubled Sehwag and Sachin Tendulkar during the early moments of India's run-chase, the covers would have been back on far sooner than five o'clock.

Man of the Match: V. Sehwag.   *Attendance:* 3,109.

Zimbabwe

V. Sibanda run out (Yuvraj Singh)	... 12	(19)	*H. H. Streak not out	59	(68)
S. V. Carlisle lbw b Sehwag	36	(71)	S. M. Ervine not out	48	(33)
S. Matsikenyeri c Badani b Pathan	... 9	(18)	L-b 4, w 6, n-b 1	11	
M. A. Vermeulen b Kumble	2	(24)		—	
G. W. Flower c and b Sehwag	15	(32)	(50 overs, 190 mins)	(6 wkts) 208	
†T. Taibu b Badani	16	(36)	Fall: 14 36 48 78 83 115		

A. M. Blignaut, R. W. Price and D. T. Hondo did not bat.

Bowling: Agarkar 8–2–39–0; Pathan 8–0–30–1; Balaji 7–2–26–0; Kumble 10–1–38–1; Sehwag 10–0–40–2; Badani 7–0–31–1.

India

V. Sehwag c Flower b Price	90	(102)			
S. R. Tendulkar b Ervine	44	(59)	L-b 4, w 7, n-b 6	17	
H. K. Badani c Taibu b Hondo	15	(20)		—	
V. V. S. Laxman not out	13	(24)	(37.4 overs, 167 mins)	(3 wkts) 211	
*S. C. Ganguly not out	32	(26)	Fall: 130 158 172		

Yuvraj Singh, †R. S. Dravid, A. B. Agarkar, I. K. Pathan, L. Balaji and A. R. Kumble did not bat.

Bowling: Streak 5–2–23–0; Hondo 8–0–39–1; Ervine 8–0–42–1; Blignaut 5–0–28–0; Price 10–0–67–1; Flower 1.4–0–8–0.

Umpires: S. A. Bucknor (West Indies) and P. D. Parker.
TV Umpire: S. J. Davis.
Referee: C. H. Lloyd (West Indies).

AUSTRALIA v ZIMBABWE

At Bellerive Oval, Hobart, January 16, 2004. Australia won by 148 runs. *Toss:* Australia. Australia 6 pts.

You have to feel for the Tasmanians. The good TV shows are shown long after they have already aired on the mainland. The AFL won't give them their own team. And Cricket Australia continues to hand them dud one-dayers. That's the price you pay for not having as many seats as the MCG. Maybe giving the punters bang for their buck was on Adam Gilchrist's mind when he made his way to the centre. By the time he was out – heaving at and missing a straight ball from Sean Ervine – Australia had set a monstrous total and Gilchrist had fallen one run short of Mark Waugh's highest one-day total by an Australian. He scooted to his first fifty in 44 balls, his second in 45 and his third in only 25, facing 126 deliveries in all. But numbers are deceiving: though he bludgeoned 13 fours and three sixes, most of Gilchrist's runs came in ones and twos. Australia's imposing 7 for 344 was their highest limited-overs score on home soil, and miles too many for Zimbabwe after another top-order tumble. Brett Lee bowled tightly on his return to the team. Streak, with bat and ball, again made the scorebook look merely dreadful instead of downright embarrassing.

Man of the Match: A. C. Gilchrist. *Attendance:* 12,715.

Australia

†A. C. Gilchrist b Ervine ....172(126)	M. J. Clarke c Vermeulen b Streak .. 0 (1)
M. L. Hayden c Sibanda b Streak 63 (75)	A. J. Bichel b Streak 0 (1)
*R. T. Ponting c Matsikenyeri b Flower 37 (46)	G. B. Hogg not out 6 (4)
D. R. Martyn not out 47 (39)	B 1, l-b 5, w 4, n-b 2 12
A. Symonds run out	
(Matsikenyeri/Ervine) ... 0 (1)	(50 overs, 225 mins) (7 wkts) 344
M. G. Bevan c Streak b Ervine 7 (9)	Fall: 140 246 310 310 326 332 333

B. Lee and B. A. Williams did not bat.

Bowling: Streak 10–1–50–3; Hondo 6–0–41–0; Blignaut 8–0–66–0; Ervine 9–0–65–2; Price 10–0–59–0; Flower 6–0–40–0; Matsikenyeri 1–0–17–0.

Zimbabwe

D. D. Ebrahim c Gilchrist b Symonds . 21 (43)	†T. Taibu c Hayden b Bichel 44 (72)
V. Sibanda c Gilchrist b Lee 1 (10)	S. Matsikenyeri not out 1 (2)
M. A. Vermeulen c Gilchrist b Williams 1 (7)	L-b 11, w 5 16
G. W. Flower run out (Hogg/Symonds) 40 (74)	
S. M. Ervine c Bichel b Hogg 8 (10)	(50 overs, 195 mins) (6 wkts) 196
*H. H. Streak not out 64 (82)	Fall: 15 19 36 52 93 195

A. M. Blignaut, R. W. Price and D. T. Hondo did not bat.

Bowling: Lee 10–1–29–1; Williams 8–0–25–1; Bichel 9–0–31–1; Symonds 10–0–48–1; Hogg 10–0–36–1; Clarke 3–0–16–0.

Umpires: R. E. Koertzen (South Africa) and S. J. Davis.
TV Umpire: P. D. Parker.
Referee: C. H. Lloyd (West Indies).

AUSTRALIA v INDIA

At Brisbane Cricket Ground, Brisbane, January 18, 2004. Day/night game. India won by 19 runs. *Toss:* India. India 5 pts, Australia 1 pt. *Limited-overs international debut:* R. S. Gavaskar.

At last came relief and a timely reminder of why they invented the abbreviated version of the game. Two strong-armed centuries, almost 600 runs, demonic bowling and a close finish; this was the injection of excitement the series desperately required. Australia were searching for their own antidote afterwards, one designed to get rid of V. V. S. Laxman. He had inexplicably missed out on a spot in India's World Cup squad, apparently because he does not score his runs quickly or agriculturally enough. But in this innings, comprising only eight fours, he proved that masterful strokeplay does have a place in one-day cricket. He also showed for a flair for the dramatic; off the last ball of India's innings, with the Australians close in to cut off the single, Laxman went from 99 to 103 by thumping Ian Harvey to the mid-on fence. Brett Lee's 10 overs were the costliest in the 33-year history of limited-overs internationals in Australia. But to Australia's credit they took the game almost to the wire. The key wicket was that of Matthew Hayden, fifth man out, tempted outside off by Irfan Pathan. Until then, he had clumped 12 fours in between ducking and weaving the fiery Pathan's short deliveries. When Pathan then dismissed Michael Clarke, swinging lustily and edging a wide delivery, some typical heroics at the death were needed from Michael Bevan. But the Indians held their nerve and Bevan watched helplessly from the non-striker's end as Australia lost their tail.

Man of the Match: V. V. S. Laxman.   *Attendance:* 35,052.

India

*S. C. Ganguly c and b Williams 18 (24)	R. S. Gavaskar not out 2 (3)
S. R. Tendulkar c and b Symonds 86 (95)	B 4, l-b 2, w 6, n-b 3 15
V. V. S. Laxman not out ....103(113)	
†R. S. Dravid c Williams b Harvey .. 74 (64)	(50 overs, 219 mins) (4 wkts) 303
Yuvraj Singh b Lee 5 (4)	Fall: 37 147 280 295

H. K. Badani, I. K. Pathan, A. R. Kumble, L. Balaji and A. Nehra did not bat.

Bowling: Gillespie 10–0–40–0; Williams 8–0–40–1; Lee 10–0–83–1; Harvey 10–0–61–1; Symonds 8–0–47–1; Clarke 4–0–26–0.

Australia

†A. C. Gilchrist c Balaji b Pathan 21 (15)	B. Lee c Kumble b Balaji 6 (12)
M. L. Hayden c Dravid b Pathan .....109(107)	J. N. Gillespie c Pathan b Balaji 6 (9)
*R. T. Ponting c Laxman b Balaji 7 (13)	B. A. Williams run out (Dravid) 0 (3)
D. R. Martyn c Yuvraj Singh b Balaji . 1 (6)	B 1, l-b 3, w 12, n-b 2 18
A. Symonds c and b Gavaskar 20 (28)	
M. J. Clarke c Dravid b Pathan 42 (45)	(49.4 overs, 230 mins) 284
M. G. Bevan not out 41 (43)	Fall: 46 86 94 141 204 224 249 266
I. J. Harvey c Gavaskar b Nehra 13 (19)	282 284

Bowling: Nehra 10–0–53–1; Pathan 9.4–0–64–3; Balaji 10–0–48–4; Kumble 10–0–53–0; Gavaskar 9–0–56–1; Ganguly 1–0–6–0.

Umpires: S. A. Bucknor (West Indies) and P. D. Parker.
TV Umpire: S. J. Davis.
Referee: C. H. Lloyd (West Indies)

INDIA v ZIMBABWE

At Brisbane Cricket Ground, Brisbane, January 20, 2004. Day/night game. India won by 24 runs. *Toss:* India. India 5 pts, Zimbabwe 1 pt.

No match screams "mismatch" more than when the pre-game hype whirs around a surname. Granted, the Gavaskar surname is worth whirring about; and Rohan Gavaskar, son of Sunil, did play a useful role in only his second one-dayer, plundering 22 in the slog overs. But two genuine talking points emerged from this game – Zimbabwe almost caused the boilover of the series and Rahul Dravid was fined for ball-tampering. Dravid, previously an unblemished character, was docked half his match fee after TV replays showed him rubbing an energy lozenge on the shiny side of the ball. John Wright, India's coach, maintained it was an "innocent mistake" and that fragments of the lolly had accidentally got stuck on his fingers; Clive Lloyd, the match referee, insisted the video evidence was conclusive. Dravid's acquisitive 114-run stand with Yuvraj Singh – they hit only six fours between them – was the cornerstone of India's innings. But with Grant Flower promoted to opener, Zimbabwe finally cobbled together a legitimate run-chase. Some lower-order hitting from Sean Ervine and Dion Ebrahim dragged them to within 25 runs of victory, but the innings ended in a hurry. Mark Vermeulen had earlier trudged off with a deep cut above his right eye thanks to an Irfan Pathan fireball; it was later revealed to be a hairline fracture. His absence proved crucial.

Man of the Match: Yuvraj Singh.   *Attendance:* 9,638.

India

†P. A. Patel b Streak	19	(29)		H. K. Badani not out	1	(1)
*S. C. Ganguly c Hondo b Ervine	33	(43)		I. K. Pathan not out	5	(3)
V. V. S. Laxman c Taibu b Ervine	12	(21)		l-b 3, w 6, n-b 1	10	
R. S. Dravid c Streak b Ervine	84	(106)				
Yuvraj Singh b Price	69	(76)		(50 overs, 204 mins) (6 wkts)	255	
R. S. Gavaskar b Streak	22	(22)		Fall: 41 67 74 188 249 249		

A. Nehra, A. R. Kumble and L. Balaji did not bat.

Bowling: Streak 10–1–48–2; Blignaut 7–1–44–0; Hondo 6–0–39–0; Ervine 10–0–47–3; Price 10–0–43–1; Flower 7–0–31–0.

Zimbabwe

M. A. Vermeulen retired hurt	14	(18)		D. D. Ebrahim c Ganguly b Pathan	39	(30)
G. W. Flower c Laxman b Nehra	36	(64)		R. W. Price not out	18	(12)
T. J. Friend run out (Ganguly)	7	(19)		D. T. Hondo run out (Kumble/Ganguly)	0	(1)
S. V. Carlisle c Patel b Ganguly	34	(61)				
A. M. Blignaut c Yuvraj Singh b Balaji	1	(3)		L-b 11, w 13, n-b 1	25	
*H. H. Streak b Ganguly	3	(13)				
†T. Taibu c Laxman b Ganguly	15	(36)		(47.1 overs, 217 mins) (9 wkts)	231	
S. M. Ervine c Ganguly b Balaji	39	(27)		Fall: 66 70 73 81 128 148 197 231 231		

Bowling: Nehra 9–1–44–1; Pathan 9–2–40–1; Balaji 9.1–0–37–2; Kumble 10–1–44–0; Ganguly 10–0–55–3.

Umpires: R. E. Koertzen (South Africa) and S. J. Davis.
TV Umpire: P. D. Parker.
Referee: C. H. Lloyd (West Indies).

AUSTRALIA v INDIA

At Sydney Cricket Ground, Sydney, January 22, 2004. Day/night game. Australia won by two wickets (D/L method). *Toss:* India. Australia 5 pts, India 1 pt.

Australia won the battle but Yuvraj Singh won Indian hearts and minds with a sparkling century. If not for a two-hour lightning storm and a last-over six from Brett Lee, the reward might have been victory. Instead Australia chased down 225 off 34 overs with two wickets and a ball to spare. The revised target seemed less imposing than the original 297, of which Yuvraj contributed 139. He and V. V. S. Laxman were a contrast in styles. They added 213 in 206 balls, a fourth-wicket record for India against Australia, with Laxman's unbeaten 106 containing only five fours. Rain, India's bowlers and Adam Gilchrist – who bashed 14 fours and a six – kept Australia in the hunt. Gilchrist, who had earlier hung on to his 300th career dismissal, thrashed Ajit Agarkar and Lakshmipathy Balaji early on. But then came the minor, almost mandatory, collapse. It fell to Lee and Andy Bichel to finish the job. Needing 11 runs from the last over, they nudged runs wherever they could. A monster hit was required and on the fourth delivery Lee, who had been wearing criticism all summer for his no-balls and waywardness, obliged. He sailed one over the extra-cover rope, later dedicating the stroke to David Hookes, who had died three days earlier: "There was a bit of luck with us and he was watching down and helping us out, I think." Australia won on a misfield off the penultimate ball and India left the field with their heads on their chests. Yuvraj, however, had every right to hold his high.

Man of the Match: Yuvraj Singh.　　*Attendance:* 37,731.

India

*S. C. Ganguly c Gilchrist b Lee	1	(8)	R. S. Gavaskar not out	2	(2)

*S. C. Ganguly c Gilchrist b Lee 1 (8)
†P. A. Patel c Gilchrist b Gillespie ... 28 (33)
V. V. S. Laxman not out ....106(130)
R. S. Dravid c Gilchrist b Bichel 12 (7)
Yuvraj Singh lbw b Lee ....139(122)

R. S. Gavaskar not out 2 (2)
l-b 1, w 5, n-b 2 8
—
(50 overs, 227 mins)   (4 wkts) 296
Fall: 1 63 80 293

H. K. Badani, A. B. Agarkar, M. Kartik, I. K. Pathan and L. Balaji did not bat.

Bowling: Gillespie 10–0–50–1; Lee 9–0–46–2; Bichel 9–0–60–1; Harvey 10–0–68–0; Symonds 7–0–42–0; Clarke 5–0–29–0.

Australia

†A. C. Gilchrist c and b Kartik 95 (72)
S. M. Katich c Ganguly b Pathan ... 2 (7)
*R. T. Ponting c Patel b Pathan 42 (54)
D. R. Martyn c Patel b Pathan 0 (1)
A. Symonds c Agarkar b Ganguly ... 16 (16)
M. G. Bevan b Ganguly 12 (20)
M. J. Clarke c Badani b Ganguly 21 (20)

I. J. Harvey run out (Agarkar/Ganguly) 1 (2)
A. J. Bichel not out 2 (2)
B. Lee not out 12 (9)
B 7, w 15 22
—
(33.5 overs, 172 mins)   (8 wkts) 225
Fall: 24 150 150 154 176 195 202 210

J. N. Gillespie did not bat.

Bowling: Agarkar 7–1–47–0; Pathan 7–1–51–3; Balaji 5.5–0–40–0; Ganguly 7–0–41–3; Kartik 7–0–39–1.

Umpires: S. A. Bucknor (West Indies) and D. J. Harper.
TV Umpire: S. J. A. Taufel.
Referee: C. H. Lloyd (West Indies).

INDIA v ZIMBABWE

At Adelaide Oval, Adelaide, January 24, 2004. Day/night game. India won by three runs. *Toss:* India. India 5 pts, Zimbabwe 1 pt.

Just as the last match belonged to Yuvraj Singh, this one belonged to V. V. S. Laxman. This time it yielded a win but, once again, there was only a fingernail in it. Fittingly it was Laxman's fingernail, after he raced from deep mid-wicket to catch Andy Blignaut with the Zimbabweans needing seven runs from the final four balls. Sanjay Bangar, beginning the final over with Zimbabwe nine runs short, kept them to five. Until Laxman's intervention, Zimbabwe looked headed for a watershed victory. Stuart Carlisle and Sean Ervine put on 202 runs, the highest one-day partnership in the fledgling cricket nation's history. You sensed, after the rubbishing their top order had copped, that they had simply had enough. India, conversely, got off to the worst start in their own, far longer, one-day history, slumping to 3 for 4 in the fourth over. From that moment on it was V. V. V. S.: Vintage V. V. S. He finessed his way to his third hundred in four innings, reeling off 13 fours and a six, and sharing century stands with Rahul Dravid and Rohan Gavaskar. Zimbabwe deserved better out of this match. If not for Laxman, they probably would have got it.

Man of the Match: V. V. S. Laxman.   *Attendance:* 8,680.

India

S. B. Bangar c Carlisle b Streak	0	(4)	A. B. Agarkar not out		12	(8)
†P. A. Patel c Taibu b Streak	0	(8)	I. K. Pathan not out		5	(4)
V. V. S. Laxman c Friend b Hondo	131	(138)				
*S. C. Ganguly c Ebrahim b Blignaut	1	(5)	L-b 4, w 8, n-b 4		16	
R. S. Dravid c Blignaut b Price	56	(72)				
R. S. Gavaskar c Blignaut b Hondo	54	(62)	(50 overs, 213 mins)	(7 wkts)	280	
H. K. Badani b Streak	5	(3)	Fall: 0 3 4 137 255 261 271			

M. Kartik and L. Balaji did not bat.

Bowling: Streak 10–1–53–3; Blignaut 5–0–25–1; Ervine 6–0–48–0; Hondo 10–0–59–2; Price 10–0–43–1; Flower 9–0–48–0.

Zimbabwe

V. Sibanda c and b Balaji	12	(36)	*H. H. Streak not out		5	(5)
G. W. Flower c Patel b Agarkar	10	(14)	D. D. Ebrahim not out		2	(1)
T. J. Friend c Laxman b Agarkar	0	(3)	B 3, l-b 12, w 12		27	
S. V. Carlisle c Kartik b Agarkar	109	(128)				
S. M. Ervine run out (Ganguly)	100	(100)	(50 overs, 277 mins)	(6 wkts)	277	
A. M. Blignaut c Laxman b Bangar	12	(13)	Fall: 14 25 46 248 261 274			

†T. Taibu, R. W. Price and D. T. Hondo did not bat.

Bowling: Agarkar 10–0–39–3; Pathan 10–0–47–0; Balaji 10–1–52–1; Bangar 8–0–42–1; Kartik 7–0–49–0; Ganguly 5–0–33–0.

Umpires: R. E. Koertzen (South Africa) and D. J. Harper.
TV Umpire: S. J. Davis.
Referee: C. H. Lloyd (West Indies).

AUSTRALIA v ZIMBABWE

At Adelaide Oval, Adelaide, January 26, 2004. Day/night game. Australia won by 13 runs. *Toss:* Australia. Australia 5 pts, Zimbabwe 1 pt.

It is a sign of greatness when a team can win the toss, underestimate the pitch then miscue, mistime and mis-hit – yet still post a decent total. Australia are one such side. Promoted to the top of the order in a bid to discover some form, Damien Martyn struggled to get the ball off the square. Matthew Hayden gambled and got away with it for a while, before departing for 20. If not for timely contributions from Ricky Ponting and Michael Bevan, Australia might never have got near a total as daunting as 279. But that's the point; they did, and they invariably do. Zimbabwe know no such guarantees. Grant Flower rode his luck for a while, feathering several fours past the outstretched gloves of the stand-in keeper Brad Haddin, while team-mates came and went. Eventually Flower settled in and eliminated any risks, punching Brad Williams through cover whenever the opportunity presented itself. But calculated batting does not always keep a run-rate ticking over; in Flower and Zimbabwe's case, it merely prolonged the inevitable. Andy Blignaut and Ray Price, the ninth-wicket pair, ended proceedings by smashing 37 runs in 25 balls, as if to underline the opportunity that had been wasted.

Man of the Match: G. W. Flower. *Attendance:* 27,612.

Australia

M. L. Hayden c Ebrahim b Blignaut	.. 20	(27)
D. R. Martyn c Ebrahim b Streak	9	(13)
*R. T. Ponting run out (Blignaut/Taibu)	63	(71)
M. G. Bevan c Ervine b Hondo	75	(91)
M. J. Clarke run out (Flower/Taibu)	.. 36	(49)
A. Symonds c Hondo b Streak	34	(30)
†B. J. Haddin lbw b Streak	14	(17)

G. B. Hogg not out	1	(1)
B. Lee not out	6	(3)

B 1, l-b 9, w 9, n-b 2 21

(50 overs, 225 mins)   (7 wkts) 279
Fall: 25 84 128 205 230 271 272

J. N. Gillespie and B. A. Williams did not bat.

Bowling: Streak 10–0–45–3; Blignaut 9–0–53–1; Ervine 5–0–41–0; Hondo 6–0–45–1; Price 10–0–40–0; Flower 10–0–45–0.

Zimbabwe

G. W. Flower c Haddin b Gillespie	... 94	(106)
†T. Taibu b Williams	9	(32)
T. J. Friend b Lee	8	(14)
S. V. Carlisle c (sub) I. J. Harvey		
b Williams	... 15	(23)
S. M. Ervine c Lee b Hogg	33	(43)
*H. H. Streak c and b Symonds	28	(34)
D. D. Ebrahim st Haddin b Symonds	.. 11	(13)

S. Matsikenyeri b Clarke	5	(3)
A. M. Blignaut not out	31	(22)
R. W. Price not out	13	(12)

B 11, l-b 1, w 5, n-b 2 19

(50 overs)   (8 wkts) 266
Fall: 29 55 90 159 169 191 206 229

D. T. Hondo did not bat.

Bowling: Gillespie 10–2–40–1; Lee 8–0–32–1; Williams 8–1–38–2; Hogg 10–0–40–1; Clarke 7–0–57–1; Symonds 7–0–47–2.

Umpires: S. A. Bucknor (West Indies) and S. J. Davis.
TV Umpire: D. J. Harper.
Referee: C. H. Lloyd (West Indies).

AUSTRALIA v ZIMBABWE

At Melbourne Cricket Ground, Melbourne, January 29, 2004. Day/night game. No result. *Toss:* Zimbabwe. Australia 3 pts, Zimbabwe 3 pts. *Limited-overs international debut:* N. B. Mahwire.

Heath Streak finally won a toss – only his second in seven matches – and must have been salivating at the prospect of batting first for a change. Instead he led with the head, not the heart, and sent Australia in under cloudy skies. Despite the helpful conditions, it was a brave move given his lack of bowling strike-power, but one for which he was never punished thanks to the gods. The rain held off long enough for Damien Martyn to hit eight crisp fours and enjoy some overdue time in the middle, and for Michael Bevan to endure intense pain. Struck by a net bowler a few days earlier, Bevan's initial discomfort turned increasingly to agony as his innings wore on. X-rays revealed a cracked rib.

Man of the Match: No award.   *Attendance:* 15,218.

Australia

M. L. Hayden b Hondo	23	(34)	A. J. Bichel not out	23	(19)
D. R. Martyn lbw b Streak	42	(40)	B. Lee c Blignaut b Ervine	3	(5)
*R. T. Ponting c Mahwire b Price	35	(58)	B. A. Williams not out	0	(0)
M. J. Clarke b Mahwire	11	(9)			
I. J. Harvey run out (Blignaut/Taibu)	23	(35)	l-b 7, w 4, n-b 4	15	
M. G. Bevan run out (Blignaut/Taibu)	56	(56)			
†B. J. Haddin b Streak	32	(46)	(50 overs, 216 mins) (9 wkts)	263	
G. B. Hogg run out (Streak)	0	(2)	Fall: 59 69 97 139 155 213 214 252 257		

Bowling: Streak 10–0–47–2; Blignaut 4–1–23–0; Hondo 4–0–35–1; Mahwire 6–1–35–1; Ervine 7–0–36–1; Flower 9–0–42–0; Price 10–0–38–1.

Zimbabwe

G. W. Flower, V. Sibanda, S. V. Carlisle, S. M. Ervine, †T. Taibu, *H. H. Streak, D. D. Ebrahim, A. M. Blignaut, R. W. Price, D. T. Hondo, N. B. Mahwire.

Umpires: R. E. Koertzen (South Africa) and P. D. Parker.
TV Umpire: R. L. Parry.
Referee: C. H. Lloyd (West Indies).

AUSTRALIA v INDIA

At WACA Ground, Perth, February 1, 2004. Day/night game. Australia won by five wickets. *Toss:* India. Australia 6 pts. *Limited-overs international debut:* M. E. K. Hussey.

Various mini-controversies bubbled ahead of a game that was supposed to be a sneak preview of the finals. The out-of-sorts Damien Martyn was reprimanded for flipping his middle finger at a TV camera crew; India officially complained about the antics of umpire Steve Bucknor, who had joked to Rahul Dravid about the Great Lozenge Scandal; and Mike Hussey was making his hometown debut in place of a resting Ricky Ponting. The hype proved short-lived as Brett Lee, Adam Gilchrist and Andrew Symonds steamrolled the Indians to a timid defeat. Lee loves nothing more than bowling 150 kph widow-makers on a bouncy WACA deck. On this day, for the first time in a long time, he uncoiled them with accuracy, shooting out Sachin Tendulkar and V. V. S. Laxman in his opening three overs. India never recovered. When Australia staggered to 3 for 37 the commonsense strategy may have been to eke out a win. Instead Gilchrist and Symonds belted 22 fours and three sixes between them. Simon Katich hit the winning single, capping a day in which he had been heckled endlessly by unforgiving Perth fans for defecting to New South Wales. With the exception of Lakshmipathy Balaji, India's bowlers were cannon fodder. The half-volleys they served up were indeed a sneak preview, the first hint of something that was about to become blindingly obvious: these tired Indians were dead on their feet.

Man of the Match: A. C. Gilchrist. *Attendance:* 18,901.

India

V. Sehwag c Lee b Gillespie	32	(35)	I. K. Pathan c Bichel b Symonds	20	(25)
S. R. Tendulkar c Hayden b Lee	5	(7)	M. Kartik not out	32	(42)
V. V. S. Laxman c Gilchrist b Lee	1	(8)	L. Balaji run out (Martyn/Gilchrist)	11	(27)
†R. S. Dravid c Hussey b Williams	13	(37)			
*S. C. Ganguly c Gilchrist b Bichel	1	(10)	L-b 7, w 16, n-b 3	26	
Yuvraj Singh c Gilchrist b Symonds	47	(68)			
R. S. Gavaskar b Lee	6	(8)	(49 overs, 213 mins)	203	
A. B. Agarkar run out (Katich/Hussey)	9	(41)	Fall: 20 32 50 57 79 101 129 142 172 203		

Bowling: Gillespie 10–0–51–1; Lee 10–2–22–3; Williams 7–2–23–1; Bichel 7–0–44–1; Symonds 10–0–37–2; Hussey 3–0–15–0; Clarke 2–0–4–0.

Australia

*†A. C. Gilchrist c Balaji b Pathan	...	75	(67)	M. E. K. Hussey not out	 17	(23)
M. L. Hayden c Gavaskar b Agarkar	..	0	(5)			
D. R. Martyn c Laxman b Agarkar	...	2	(3)	B 1, l-b 2, w 14	 17	
M. J. Clarke c Sehwag b Balaji	......	2	(9)			
A. Symonds c Laxman b Pathan	.....	73	(59)	(32 overs, 145 mins)	(5 wkts)	204
S. M. Katich not out	....	18	(34)	Fall: 14 16 37 159 165		

B. Lee, J. N. Gillespie, B. A. Williams and A. J. Bichel did not bat.

Bowling: Agarkar 9–0–56–2; Pathan 8–0–69–2; Balaji 10–1–37–1; Kartik 5–0–39–0.

Umpires: S. A. Bucknor (West Indies) and D. J. Harper.

TV Umpire: S. J. A. Taufel.

Referee: C. H. Lloyd (West Indies).

INDIA v ZIMBABWE

At WACA Ground, Perth, February 3, 2004. Day/night game. India won by four wickets.
Toss: Zimbabwe. India 6 pts.

In 40-degree heat and in front of a small crowd, India played this the same way Australia tend to treat dead rubbers in a Test series: with minimal enthusiasm. They started well enough, Zimbabwe's fragile top order disintegrating in the 19-year-old hands of Irfan Pathan, who had uprooted both openers by the end of his first over. His meteoric rise again gave the TV commentators something to discuss as Zimbabwe were routed in less than three hours, forcing India to face six overs before the interval. When Heath Streak hit Sachin Tendulkar on the shoulder and then had him caught behind, and when Virender Sehwag slashed Andy Blignaut to deep third man, the commentators suddenly had a game to call. There was more drama after the break. Rahul Dravid chopped Blignaut onto his stumps. Yuvraj Singh hoicked lazily at Sean Ervine and he too holed out at third man. India were 4 for 73; and for Zimbabwe, finally, it was game on. Regrettably, it didn't last long. The Zimbabweans grassed two chances and Hemang Badani heaved his side across the line.

Man of the Match: I. K. Pathan.   *Attendance:* 4,135.

Zimbabwe

V. Sibanda c Laxman b Pathan	......	0	(4)	A. M. Blignaut c Sehwag b Nehra	... 2	(5)
†T. Taibu lbw b Pathan	....	0	(1)	R. W. Price c Laxman b Pathan	 0	(4)
D. D. Ebrahim c Laxman b Pathan	...	7	(23)	N. B. Mahwire not out	 8	(27)
S. V. Carlisle run out (Yuvraj Singh)	..	28	(50)			
S. M. Ervine c (sub) M. Kartik b Bhandari		23	(35)	L-b 9, w 15	 24	
*H. H. Streak c Laxman b Balaji	.....	6	(13)			
S. Matsikenyeri c Dravid b Bhandari	.	36	(48)	(34.4 overs, 170 mins)	135	
T. J. Friend c Gavaskar b Bhandari	...	1	(10)	Fall: 0 1 11 74 79 85 103 114 115 135		

Bowling: Pathan 10–1–24–4; Balaji 10–1–32–1; Nehra 7–1–39–1; Bhandari 7.4–0–31–3.

India

V. Sehwag c Matsikenyeri b Blignaut	23	(23)
S. R. Tendulkar c Taibu b Streak	3	(10)
V. V. S. Laxman b Ervine	32	(50)
*†R. S. Dravid b Blignaut	10	(25)
Yuvraj Singh c Friend b Ervine	4	(9)
H. K. Badani not out	34	(63)

R. S. Gavaskar run out (Matsikenyeri)	4	(11)
I. K. Pathan not out	3	(8)
L-b 6, w 15, n-b 2	23	
	—	
(30.3 overs, 157 mins) (6 wkts)	136	
Fall: 28 34 61 73 105 115		

L. Balaji, A. Bhandari and A. Nehra did not bat.

Bowling: Streak 7–0–36–1; Blignaut 10–0–41–2; Ervine 8.3–2–29–2; Friend 5–0–24–0.

Umpires: R. E. Koertzen (South Africa) and S. J. A. Taufel.
TV Umpire: D. J. Harper.
Referee: C. H. Lloyd (West Indies).

QUALIFYING TABLE

	Played	Won	Lost	No Result	Bonus Points	Points	Net Run-Rate
Australia	8	6	1	1	4	37	1.0999
India	8	5	3	0	4	29	0.2816
Zimbabwe	8	0	7	1	3	6	–1.3260

Net run-rate was calculated by subtracting runs conceded per over from runs scored per over.

FIRST FINAL

AUSTRALIA v INDIA

At Melbourne Cricket Ground, Melbourne, February 6, 2004. Day/night game. Australia won by seven wickets. *Toss:* India.

With the drab preliminaries over, this first final failed to dish up the classic contest everyone was anticipating. Some rousing cricket was played but nearly all of it came from the Australians. With India all out for 222, Ricky Ponting batted with an identical mindset – as if he had something to prove – to the one he displayed during his swaggering unbeaten 140 against these same opponents in the 2003 World Cup final. But what was going on in Ponting's mind seemed almost incidental. He danced like Michael Jackson and swung like he was wielding a Big Bertha rather than his trusty Kookaburra. Seven fours and two towering sixes off Anil Kumble left a smallish MCG crowd sitting back and marvelling. Adam Gilchrist enjoyed himself too, plundering three fours off Lakshmipathy Balaji's first over. Matthew Hayden found himself in unfamiliar territory, anchoring the innings while his counterparts exploded. Earlier it was Australia's bowlers who pitched the ball up, tossed down the odd nastily directed short one and forced India's imposing top order onto the back foot. Brett Lee, back to his fast and furious finest, cleaned up a gobsmacked Sachin Tendulkar with a gloriously late off-cutter, then thudded V. V. S. Laxman on the helmet. When the field switched round after 15 overs, India were down and almost out at 4 for 52. Hemang Badani was also struck on the helmet, this time by Brad Williams, before settling down with Ajit Agarkar. The pair carried on for a record seventh-wicket stand at the MCG, preventing a walkover but not the sneaking suspicion that Australia had a psychological edge over these opponents in the big one-day games.

Man of the Match: R. T. Ponting.   *Attendance:* 44,835.

India

V. Sehwag c Gilchrist b Gillespie	....	3	(8)	I. K. Pathan run out (Clarke/Gilchrist)	19	(19)
S. R. Tendulkar b Lee	....	8	(22)	A. R. Kumble run out (Clarke/Gilchrist)	2	(3)
V. V. S. Laxman c Symonds b Williams		24	(25)	L. Balaji b Gillespie	2	(7)
†R. S. Dravid c Hayden b Harvey	....	12	(29)			
*S. C. Ganguly c Gilchrist b Harvey	.	6	(21)	L-b 6, w 2, n-b 4	12	
Yuvraj Singh c Gilchrist b Lee	......	21	(21)			
H. K. Badani not out	....	60	(81)	(49 overs, 219 mins)	222	
A. B. Agarkar c Lee b Clarke	....	53	(62)	Fall: 6 14 48 48 75 75 177 209 217 222		

Bowling: Gillespie 10–0–39–2; Lee 9–0–34–2; Williams 10–1–38–1; Harvey 10–0–40–2; Symonds 7–0–47–0; Clarke 3–0–18–1.

Australia

†A. C. Gilchrist c Tendulkar b Balaji	.	38	(20)		
M. L. Hayden c and b Balaji	....	50	(91)	B 6, l-b 2, w 8, n-b 2	18
*R. T. Ponting c Dravid b Balaji	.....	88	(80)		
D. R. Martyn not out	....	20	(37)	(40.1 overs, 171 mins) (3 wkts)	224
A. Symonds not out	....	10	(15)	Fall: 48 187 193	

M. J. Clarke, S. M. Katich, I. J. Harvey, B. Lee, J. N. Gillespie, and B. A. Williams did not bat.

Bowling: Agarkar 9.1–0–58–0; Balaji 10–1–52–3; Pathan 8–0–36–0; Kumble 7–0–36–0; Sehwag 5–0–29–0; Ganguly 1–0–5–0.

Umpires: S. A. Bucknor (West Indies) and S. J. A. Taufel.
TV Umpire: D. J. Harper.
Referee: C. H. Lloyd (West Indies).

SECOND FINAL

AUSTRALIA v INDIA

At Sydney Cricket Ground, Sydney, February 8, 2004. Day/night game. Australia won by 208 runs. *Toss:* India.

Australia's demolition of India was eerily reminiscent of the hatchet job applied in the World Cup final in Johannesburg. There was an identical score – 359, no less – after winning the toss and batting on a flat pitch. There was a belligerent century and a classic cameo, followed by a lusty slash-and-burn from the all-rounders during the slog overs that elevated the innings into the stratosphere. The only difference this time is that Matthew Hayden, not Ricky Ponting, was daubing the masterstrokes. Hayden's defiance was best summed up when he glared down Lakshmipathy Balaji during the early stages of his rampage. Next delivery, Balaji bounced and Hayden swatted over mid-off for six. It was one of three sixes, together with 11 fours, in his 122-ball exhibition. After Gilchrist and Ponting came, belted and went, Damien Martyn found himself riding Hayden's back into form, just as he did in the World Cup final alongside Ponting. Sourav Ganguly brought the spinners on to stop the haemorrhaging but it worked only fleetingly. Andrew Symonds, in a mere 52 minutes at the crease, slaughtered three sixes and seven fours before hazarding one reverse-sweep too many. When India came out to bat, the question on everyone's lips wasn't whether they could win but by how much they might lose. Fourteen overs later their famed top five were back in the room. Jason Gillespie had both openers caught – Virender Sehwag spectacularly, Sachin Tendulkar nonchalantly – by Brett Lee at leg-gully. Australia's four quicks divided the spoils equally, India sinking to the second-worst defeat in their one-day history. It was an inglorious end to a glorious tour.

Man of Match: M. L. Hayden. *Man of the Series:* A. C. Gilchrist. *Attendance:* 38,182.

Australia

†A.C. Gilchrist c Ganguly b Nehra	29	(32)	S.M. Katich not out	11	(4)
M.L. Hayden b Tendulkar	126	(122)			
*R.T. Ponting c Dravid b Pathan	4	(9)	L-b 6, w 15, n-b 2	23	
D.R. Martyn c Badani b Pathan	67	(76)			
A. Symonds b Nehra	66	(39)	(50 overs, 217 mins) (5 wkts)	359	
M.J. Clarke not out	33	(20)	Fall: 62 73 230 248 347		

I.J. Harvey, B. Lee, J.N. Gillespie and B.A. Williams did not bat.

Bowling: Pathan 10–0–75–2; Balaji 9–0–65–0; Nehra 10–0–63–2; Kartik 7–0–51–0; Sehwag 5–0–30–0; Ganguly 1–0–9–0; Tendulkar 8–0–60–1.

India

V. Sehwag c Lee b Gillespie	12	(7)	M. Kartik c Gilchrist b Williams	23	(25)
S.R. Tendulkar c Lee b Gillespie	27	(40)	L. Balaji b Williams	2	(10)
V.V.S. Laxman c and b Lee	5	(7)	A. Nehra not out	14	(4)
*S.C. Ganguly c Symonds b Harvey	3	(15)			
†R.S. Dravid run out (Martyn)	0	(11)	L-b 7, w 4, n-b 2	13	
Yuvraj Singh c Gilchrist b Harvey	4	(15)			
H.K. Badani run out (Gilchrist/Symonds)	18	(27)	(33.2 overs, 155 mins)	151	
I.K. Pathan b Lee	30	(41)	Fall: 22 49 49 52 56 59 99 123 136 151		

Bowling: Gillespie 9–1–52–2; Lee 10–1–39–2; Williams 6.2–1–12–2; Harvey 5–2–30–2; Symonds 3–1–11–0.

Umpires: R.E. Koertzen (South Africa) and D.J. Harper.
TV Umpire: S.J.A. Taufel.
Referee: C.H. Lloyd (West Indies).

VB/World Series Records

TOURNAMENT RESULTS

Benson & Hedges World Series Cup

Season	Winner	Runner-Up	Third Team	Fourth Team
1979-80	West Indies	England	Australia	–
1980-81	Australia	New Zealand	India	–
1981-82	West Indies	Australia	Pakistan	–
1982-83	Australia	New Zealand	England	–
1983-84	West Indies	Australia	Pakistan	–
1984-85	West Indies	Australia	Sri Lanka	–
1985-86	Australia	India	New Zealand	–
1986-87	England	Australia	West Indies	–
1987-88	Australia	New Zealand	Sri Lanka	–
1988-89	West Indies	Australia	Pakistan	–

Benson & Hedges World Series

Season	Winner	Runner-Up	Third Team	Fourth Team
1989-90	Australia	Pakistan	Sri Lanka	–
1990-91	Australia	New Zealand	England	–
1991-92	Australia	India	West Indies	–
1992-93	West Indies	Australia	Pakistan	–
1993-94	Australia	South Africa	New Zealand	–
1994-95	Australia	Australia A	England	Zimbabwe
1995-96	Australia	Sri Lanka	West Indies	–

Carlton & United Series

Season	Winner	Runner-Up	Third Team	Fourth Team
1996-97	Pakistan	West Indies	Australia	–
1997-98	Australia	South Africa	New Zealand	–
1998-99	Australia	England	Sri Lanka	–
1999-00	Australia	Pakistan	India	–

Carlton Series

Season	Winner	Runner-Up	Third Team	Fourth Team
2000-01	Australia	West Indies	Zimbabwe	–

VB Series

Season	Winner	Runner-Up	Third Team	Fourth Team
2001-02	South Africa	New Zealand	Australia	–
2002-03	Australia	England	Sri Lanka	–
2003-04	Australia	India	Zimbabwe	–

TEAM RESULTS

	Debut	M	W	L	NR	T
Australia	Nov 27, 1979	265	170	88	5	2
West Indies	Nov 27, 1979	114	67	44	1	2
England	Nov 28, 1979	65	27	38	0	0
New Zealand	Nov 23, 1980	81	31	48	2	0
India	Dec 6, 1980	50	17	32	0	1
Pakistan	Nov 21, 1981	66	23	41	1	1
Sri Lanka	Jan 8, 1985	54	12	42	0	0
South Africa	Jan 9, 1993	31	18	13	0	0
Zimbabwe	Dec 2, 1994	22	2	19	1	0
Australia A	Dec 4, 1994	8	3	5	0	0
Total		378				

HIGHEST INDIVIDUAL SCORES

173	M.E. Waugh	Australia v West Indies at Melbourne	2000-01
172	A.C. Gilchrist	Australia v Zimbabwe at Hobart (Bellerive)	2003-04
158	D.I. Gower	England v New Zealand at Brisbane	1982-83
154	A.C. Gilchrist	Australia v Sri Lanka at Melbourne	1998-99
153*	I.V.A. Richards	West Indies v Australia at Melbourne	1979-80
145	D.M. Jones	Australia v England at Brisbane	1990-91
144*	D.R. Martyn	Australia v Zimbabwe at Perth	2000-01
141	S.C. Ganguly	India v Pakistan at Adelaide	1999-00
139	Yuvraj Singh	India v Australia at Sydney	2003-04
138*	G.S. Chappell	Australia v New Zealand at Sydney	1980-81

MOST RUNS

	M	I	NO	R	HS	100s	50s	Avge	S-R
A.R. Border (Aust)	160	148	22	3,899	127*	3	23	30.94	69.67
M.E. Waugh (Aust)	116	110	9	3,730	173	8	22	36.93	73.56
D.M. Jones (Aust)	93	90	16	3,456	145	2	28	46.70	70.26
R.T. Ponting (AustA/Aust)	84	83	7	3,026	123	5	19	39.82	78.23
D.C. Boon (Aust)	94	91	9	3,016	122	2	20	36.78	63.31
S.R. Waugh (Aust)	142	126	31	2,801	102*	1	14	29.48	70.77
M.G. Bevan (Aust/AustA)	89	78	28	2,785	105	2	19	55.70	73.19
D.L. Haynes (WI)	83	83	8	2,782	123*	4	21	37.09	59.42
I.V.A. Richards (WI)	65	60	5	2,563	153*	3	22	46.60	85.26
A.C. Gilchrist (Aust)	65	62	3	2,282	172	5	9	38.68	96.12

HIGHEST PARTNERSHIPS FOR EACH WICKET

237	for 1st	S.T. Jayasuriya and M.S. Atapattu	Sri Lanka v Australia at Sydney	2002-03
225	for 2nd	A.C. Gilchrist and R.T. Ponting	Australia v England at Melbourne	2002-03
224*	for 3rd	D.M. Jones and A.R. Border	Australia v Sri Lanka at Adelaide	1984-85
213	for 4th	V.V.S. Laxman and Yuvraj Singh	India v Australia at Sydney	2003-04
159	for 5th	R.T. Ponting and M.G. Bevan	Australia v Sri Lanka at Melbourne	1995-96
124	for 6th	C.D. McMillan and C.Z. Harris	New Zealand v South Africa at Adelaide	1997-98
110	for 7th	P.D. Collingwood and C. White	England v Sri Lanka at Perth	2002-03
88*	for 8th	D.S. Lehmann and B. Lee	Australia v South Africa at Perth	2001-02
63	for 9th	R.J. Hadlee and G.B. Troup	New Zealand v England at Brisbane	1982-83
		M.D. Marshall and J. Garner	West Indies v Australia at Sydney	1984-85
63	for 10th	S.R. Watson and A.J. Bichel	Australia v Sri Lanka at Sydney	2002-03

* Denotes unbroken partnership.

HIGHEST INNINGS TOTALS

Batting first

5-359 Australia defeated India at Sydney	2003-04
7-344 Australia defeated Zimbabwe at Hobart (Bellerive)	2003-04
5-343 Sri Lanka defeated Australia at Sydney	2002-03
6-338 Australia defeated West Indies at Melbourne	2000-01
7-337 Australia defeated Pakistan at Sydney	1999-00
329 Australia defeated India at Adelaide	1999-00
2-323 Australia defeated Sri Lanka at Adelaide	1984-85
6-318 Australia defeated England at Melbourne	2002-03
3-315 Pakistan defeated Sri Lanka at Adelaide	1989-90
8-310 Australia defeated Sri Lanka at Melbourne	1998-99

Batting second

9-303	Sri Lanka defeated England at Adelaide	1998-99
6-301	Zimbabwe lost to Australia at Perth	2000-01
299	West Indies lost to Australia at Melbourne	2000-01
9-298	New Zealand lost to South Africa at Brisbane	1997-98
6-297	New Zealand defeated England at Adelaide	1982-83
8-288	Sri Lanka lost to Pakistan at Adelaide	1989-90
3-284	West Indies defeated Australia at Brisbane	1996-97
284	Australia v India at Brisbane	2003-04
4-282	Australia defeated Zimbabwe at Hobart	2000-01
6-275	Australia defeated England at Sydney	1998-99

LOWEST INNINGS TOTALS

Batting first

63	India lost to Australia at Sydney	1980-81
71	Pakistan lost to West Indies at Brisbane	1992-93
100	India lost to Australia at Sydney	1999-00
102	Sri Lanka lost to West Indies at Brisbane	1995-96
106	South Africa lost to Australia at Sydney	2001-02

Batting second

69	South Africa lost to Australia at Sydney	1993-94
70	Australia lost to New Zealand at Adelaide	1985-86
81	Pakistan lost to West Indies at Sydney	1992-93
87	West Indies lost to Australia at Sydney	1992-93
91	Sri Lanka lost to Australia at Adelaide	1984-85
91	West Indies lost to Zimbabwe at Sydney	2000-01

BEST BOWLING FIGURES

6-42	A.B. Agarkar	India v Australia at Melbourne	2003-04
5-15	G.S. Chappell	Australia v India at Sydney	1980-81
5-15	R.J. Shastri	India v Australia at Perth	1991-92
5-16	C.G. Rackemann	Australia v Pakistan at Adelaide	1983-84
5-17	C.E.L. Ambrose	West Indies v Australia at Melbourne	1988-89
5-19	A.J. Bichel	Australia v South Africa at Sydney	2001-02
5-21	A.I.C. Dodemaide	Australia v Sri Lanka at Perth	1987-88
5-22	A.M.E. Roberts	West Indies v England at Adelaide	1979-80
5-22	B.A. Williams	Australia v Zimbabwe at Sydney	2003-04
5-24	M.E. Waugh	Australia v West Indies at Melbourne	1992-93
5-24	L. Klusener	South Africa v Australia at Melbourne	1997-98

MOST WICKETS

	M	O	Mdns	R	W	BB	5W/i	Avge	RPO
S.K. Warne (Aust)	81	754.5	40	3,183	132	5-33	1	24.11	4.22
G.D. McGrath (Aust) ..	72	650.4	80	2,514	128	5-40	2	19.64	3.86
C.J. McDermott (Aust).	82	728	67	2,805	122	4-25	0	22.99	3.85
S.R. Waugh (Aust)	142	648.5	27	2,775	86	4-33	0	32.27	4.28
M.A. Holding (WI)....	49	459.4	44	1,602	74	5-26	1	21.65	3.49
P.L Taylor (Aust)	54	465.1	23	1,878	71	4-38	0	26.45	4.04
J. Garner (WI)	48	435.5	62	1,381	70	5-31	1	19.73	3.17
M.D. Marshall (WI) ...	56	497	50	1,748	69	4-18	0	25.33	3.52
S.P. O'Donnell (Aust) .	52	432	26	1,826	69	4-19	0	26.46	4.23
D.K. Lillee (Aust).....	40	358.2	55	1,248	68	4-12	0	18.35	3.48

MOST CATCHES

A. R. Border (Aust) . . . 83 in 160 matches
S. R. Waugh (Aust) . . . 55 in 142 matches
M. E. Waugh (Aust) . . 48 in 116 matches
S. K. Warne (Aust) . . . 41 in 81 matches
M. G. Bevan (Aust) . . . 35 in 89 matches

M. A. Taylor (Aust) . . 32 in 53 matches
D. R. Martyn (Aust) . . 31 in 70 matches
D. M. Jones (Aust) . . . 29 in 93 matches
P. L. Taylor (Aust) . . . 28 in 54 matches
I. V. A. Richards (WI) 28 in 65 matches

MOST DISMISSALS

I. A. Healy (Aust) 124 (108ct, 16st)
A. C. Gilchrist (Aust) . 124 (109ct, 15st)
R. W. Marsh (Aust) . . . 79 (78ct, 1st)
P. J. L. Dujon (WI) . . . 69 (60ct, 9st)
Moin Khan (Pak) 31 (24ct, 7st)
A. J. Stewart (Eng) . . . 31 (30ct. 1st)

D. J. Richardson (SAf) 30 (27ct, 3st)
W. B. Phillips (Aust) 29 (26ct, 3st)
J. R. Murray (WI) 25 (21ct, 4st)
R. S. Kaluwitharana (SL) . . 25 (19ct, 6st)
A. C. Parore (NZ) 25 (23ct, 2st)
C. O. Browne (WI) 19 (16ct, 3st)

MOST APPEARANCES

	M	Aust	Aust A	Eng	Ind	NZ	Pak	SAf	SL	WI	Zim
A. R. Border (Aust) . .	160	–	–	19	18	35	22	13	6	47	–
S. R. Waugh (Aust) . .	142	–	3	12	17	27	23	16	14	27	3
M. E. Waugh (Aust) . .	116	–	4	13	7	17	16	16	11	27	5
D. C. Boon (Aust)	94	–	4	6	13	21	9	10	7	22	2
D. M. Jones (Aust) . . .	93	–	–	10	8	15	14	11	5	30	–
M. G. Bevan (Aust) . .	89	3	1	13	7	8	10	10	14	14	9
I. A. Healy (Aust)	86	–	3	6	6	10	18	10	6	25	2
R. T Ponting (Aust) . .	84	4	–	13	9	7	7	10	13	11	10
D. L. Haynes (WI) . .	83	49	–	8	4	–	18	–	4	–	–
C. J. McDermott (Aust)	82	–	4	1	13	13	8	11	6	25	1
S. K. Warne (Aust) . . .	81	–	3	13	1	12	7	16	1	13	5

Bangladesh in Australia, 2003-04

By MALCOLM CONN

Cricket's international debut in Australia's tropical north was a celebration of the game. Steve Waugh's world champion Australians were treated like rock stars and mobbed by autograph hunters from the moment they arrived at Darwin airport to the spontaneous cheers of passengers. Rarely can an Australian cricket team have had a more relaxing working holiday. Many of the players, escaping a cold and wet southern winter, were delighted to find cloudless skies and constant 31-degree days. They soon blended in with the many tanned tourists who flood the Northern Territory and far north Queensland every dry season.

The experiment of staging midwinter Tests in Darwin and Cairns was a direct result of the International Cricket Council's exhausting everybody-plays-everybody schedule. Forced to find alternative dates and venues away from the cluttered southern summer to fulfil their commitments, Cricket Australia enthusiastically embraced the new locations. The board lost about $1 million on the two Tests and three limited-overs matches but considered it an investment in the future, not a drain on the present.

In a winter of firsts, it was also the inaugural Test visit by Bangladesh. They were never expected to provide much of a contest and nor did they; they lost both Tests by an innings – ensuring ample spare time for the Australians to go fishing for barramundi – and all three one-dayers at a canter. But they were a more accomplished unit than a track record of 18 defeats in their previous 19 Tests suggested. They appeared most comfortable, and unfailingly positive apart from a nervous opening morning, in the Tests. Indeed at one point in Cairns, careering along at 1 for 155 after being sent in on a greenish pitch, they fleetingly had Australia on the ropes.

The young opener Hannan Sarkar looked a star of the future, wristy and authoritative and blessed with a rich repertoire of strokes. His confidence blossomed with every innings. Habibul

Bashar, ever adventurous, unfurled a couple of charming knocks. Bangladesh's bowlers made less of an impression, collecting only 11 wickets for 963 in 257 overs. The seamers Mashrafe Bin Mortaza and Tapash Baisya showed flickers of promise but lacked support. The jovial captain Khaled Mahmud, repeatedly overbowling himself, returned home with a career Test average of 406 and never looked like improving on it.

For the Australians, there was much to savour. Steve Waugh's pair of centuries, rock-solid and virtually error-free, lifted his Test average back above 50. His 100 not out in Darwin gave him a Test hundred against every other nation; in Cairns he upped it to 150 against all-comers. Darren Lehmann made the most of batting at No. 4 in place of an injured Damien Martyn, and Stuart MacGill deputised skilfully and enthusiastically for a banned Shane Warne. MacGill upstaged the highly rated pace trio of Jason Gillespie, Glenn McGrath and Brett Lee to claim 17 wickets and be named Man of the Series. Martin Love recovered from a duck in the First Test to make his maiden hundred in the second – in what, to date, remains his last Test innings.

If the cricket had a humdrum inevitability about it at times, the debutant venues at least gave the contest a sense of occasion. During the first 126 years of Test cricket in Australia, the 330 matches had been shared between seven venues. Only two new Test grounds, the WACA in Perth and Bellerive Oval in Hobart, had emerged in the past 71 years. Suddenly there were two more.

Staging cricket in the deep north was a considerable logistical undertaking. Tony Ware, the MCG curator, was flown up to lay two drop-in pitches which had been growing locally. A total of 33 tonnes of equipment made the week-long truck journey from Melbourne to Darwin. When Australia's batsmen took guard at Marrara Oval, they peered into the same sightscreens as Don Bradman and a galaxy of other famous names who had graced the MCG in the past century. The Northern Territory government had poured a further $2.5 million into upgrading Marrara during the previous year, making it a suitable venue for international cricket and AFL football.

The enthusiasm among the locals was palpable. A massive B-52 bomber was the backdrop for the official Test match dinner at Darwin's aviation museum. It was there, in front of more than 400 people, that Cricket Australia's chairman Bob Merriman returned the world championship mace – which had briefly been held by South

Africa courtesy of a bizarre mathematical quirk – to Steve Waugh. The mace, the World Cup, the Frank Worrell Trophy and the ICC's one-day championship trophy were each carried into the dinner by sailors from HMAS *Coonawarra* amid considerable fanfare.

The total number of people who watched eight-and-a-bit days of international cricket in Darwin and Cairns over the three-week period came to more than 51,000. Television ratings held up well and merchandising was over budget. While many a turbulent day-nighter at the MCG has dragged in more spectators, the combined populations of Darwin (90,000) and Cairns (130,000) means that in rough figures almost a quarter of those two cities' populations attended a day at the cricket.

BANGLADESH TOURING PARTY

Khaled Mahmud (*captain*), Al Sahariar Rokon, Alok Kapali, Anwar Hossain Monir, Habibul Bashar, Hannan Sarkar, Javed Omar, Khaled Mashud, Manjural Islam, Mashrafe Bin Mortaza, Mohammad Ashraful, Mohammad Rafiq, Sanwar Hossain, Tapash Baisya, Tareq Aziz. *Coach:* D. F. Whatmore.

Hasibul Hussain and Tushar Imran joined the tour party for the limited-overs internationals.

BANGLADESH TOUR RESULTS

Test matches – Played 2, Lost 2.
First-class matches – Played 2, Lost 2.
Losses – Australia (2).
International limited overs – Played 3, Lost 3. *Losses* – Australia (3).
Other non-first-class matches – Played 3: Won 3. *Wins* – Australian Cricket
   Academy, Northern Territory Chief Minister's XI, Queensland Academy of Sport.

TEST BATTING AVERAGES

	M	I	NO	R	HS	100s	50s	Avge	Ct/St	S-R
D. S. Lehmann (Aus)	2	2	0	287	177	2	0	143.50	0	66.74
M. L. Love (Aus)	2	2	1	100	100*	1	0	100.00	2	64.52
A. C. Gilchrist (Aus)	2	1	0	43	43	0	0	43.00	9	91.49
Hannan Sarkar (Ban)	2	4	0	166	76	0	2	41.50	0	51.88
J. L. Langer (Aus)	2	2	0	72	71	0	1	36.00	3	33.03
Habibul Bashar (Ban)	2	4	0	141	54	0	1	35.25	0	54.44
R. T. Ponting (Aus)	2	2	0	69	59	0	1	34.50	2	64.49
Sanwar Hossain (Ban)	1	2	0	62	46	0	0	31.00	0	42.47
M. L. Hayden (Aus)	2	2	0	61	50	0	1	30.50	1	54.46
B. Lee (Aus)	2	1	0	23	23	0	0	23.00	2	58.97
Khaled Mashud (Ban)	2	4	0	75	44	0	0	18.75	0	32.61
Al Sahariar Rokon (Ban)	1	2	0	36	36	0	0	18.00	0	60.00
Javed Omar (Ban)	2	4	0	44	26	0	0	11.00	3	36.07
Khaled Mahmud (Ban)	2	4	0	43	21	0	0	10.75	0	57.33
Tapash Baisya (Ban)	2	4	1	31	25	0	0	10.33	0	47.69

	M	I	NO	R	HS	100s	50s	Avge	Ct/St	S-R
Mashrafe Bin Mortaza (Ban)	2	4	1	29	15	0	0	9.67	0	107.41
Mohammad Ashraful (Ban)	2	4	0	30	23	0	0	7.50	2	29.70
Alok Kapali (Ban)	2	4	0	22	17	0	0	5.50	0	33.85
Anwar Hossain Monir (Ban)	1	2	1	4	4	0	0	4.00	0	44.44
Manjural Islam (Ban)	1	2	1	1	1	0	0	1.00	0	20.00
J.N. Gillespie (Aus).	2	1	1	16	16*	0	0	–	1	106.67
S.R. Waugh (Aus) ..	2	2	2	256	156*	2	0	–	0	60.38
S.C.G. MacGill (Aus)	2	0	–	–	–	–	–	–	2	–
G.D. McGrath (Aus)	2	0	–	–	–	–	–	–	0	–

TEST BOWLING AVERAGES

	O	Mdns	R	W	BB	5W/i	10W/m	Avge	S-R
S.C.G. MacGill (Aus) .	70.1	17	219	17	5-56	3	1	12.88	24.76
J.N. Gillespie (Aus) ...	61.4	14	170	11	4-38	0	0	15.45	33.63
G.D. McGrath (Aus)...	55.1	17	124	5	3-20	0	0	24.80	66.20
B. Lee (Aus)	49.2	10	190	6	3-23	0	0	31.67	49.33
Mashrafe Bin Mortaza (Ban)	48	14	134	4	3-74	0	0	33.50	72.00
Sanwar Hossain (Ban)..	30	2	128	2	2-128	0	0	64.00	90.00
Manjural Islam (Ban) ..	24	4	78	1	1-78	0	0	78.00	144.00
Tapash Baisya (Ban)...	47.5	9	165	2	1-69	0	0	69.00	143.50
Alok Kapali (Ban).....	32.2	2	134	1	1-65	0	0	65.00	194.00
Khaled Mahmud (Ban) .	47	5	173	0	–	0	0	–	–
Mohammad Ashraful (Ban)	6	0	31	0	–	0	0	–	–
Habibul Bashar (Ban) ..	1	0	1	0	–	0	0	–	–
Anwar Hossain Monir (Ban)	21	4	95	0	–	0	0	–	–
S.R. Waugh (Aus).....	5	3	4	0	–	0	0	–	–
D.S. Lehmann (Aus)...	3	1	4	0	–	0	0	–	–

Note: Matches in this section that were not first-class are signified by a dagger.

†QUEENSLAND ACADEMY OF SPORT INVITATION XI v BANGLADESHIS

At Allan Border Field, Albion, June 27, 28, 29, 2003. Queensland Academy of Sport Invitation XI won by 29 runs. *Toss:* Queensland Academy of Sport Invitation XI.

Bangladesh's first day of cricket in Australia could hardly have gone more swimmingly. It began when they won the toss and knocked a young Queensland academy side over cheaply; it ended with Mohammad Ashraful thumping the last two balls of the day for four and six. Alok Kapali top-scored next morning with a punchy 55, containing six fours and a six, before whipping out the home side's top order with his leg-breaks. Needing 175 to win however, the Bangladeshis stumbled badly. Javed Omar completed a particularly unconvincing pair, following up his 37-ball duck in the first innings with a three-ball effort in the second. Habibul Bashar and Hannan Sarkar put them back on course for victory, only for the last nine wickets to capitulate for 103 runs and leave them 29 short. They were lucky to get that close, the Queenslanders dropping a string of catches on the last day. It was Bangladesh's first match under their upbeat new coach Dav Whatmore, who immediately identified erratic shot selection as the side's biggest problem.

Queensland Academy of Sport Invitation 201 (L. A. Carseldine 92, J. R. Hopes 53; Tapash Baisya 3-33, Khaled Mahmud 2-34) and 176 (D. M. Payne 52, L. A. Carseldine 31*; Manjural Islam 2-37, Alok Kapali 4-27, Anwar Hossain Monir 3-37); Bangladeshis 9 dec 203 (Mohammad Ashraful 39, Alok Kapali 55, Khaled Mashud 38; D. R. MacKenzie 2-37, J. R. Hopes 4-35) and 145 (Hannan Sarkar 33, Habibul Bashar 33; J. R. Hopes 2-25, D. R. MacKenzie 3-28, C. P. Simpson 2-15).

†AUSTRALIAN CRICKET ACADEMY v BANGLADESHIS

At Allan Border Field, Albion, July 3, 4, 5, 2003. Bangladeshis won by two wickets. *Toss:* Australian Cricket Academy.

The Bangladeshis recorded their first victory on Australian soil, thanks chiefly to two generous declarations from the opposition captain Aaron Nye. But it was the young academy side, boasting only a handful of players with first-class experience, who controlled the game's trajectory from the moment Victoria's Matthew Innes and New South Wales' Rhett Lockyear came together on the first morning. Innes, not to be confused with his fast-bowling near-namesake, faced 200 balls and hit 17 fours and two sixes. The only bright news for Bangladesh on the first two days was a 146-run stand between Javed Omar and Habibul Bashar, who was bowled one run short of becoming the country's first centurion in Australia. Their confidence was lifted immeasurably on a thrilling last day. Most of the batsmen made starts, Mohammad Ashraful clobbering eight fours and two sixes in an aggressive 61, as Bangladesh skated home with six minutes and an over to spare. It was their captain Khaled Mahmud, appropriately, who hit Peter Worthington over mid-on for the winning boundary.

Australian Cricket Academy 3 dec 258 (M. L. Innes 128*, R. J. G. Lockyear 90) and 4 dec 203 (A. J. Nye 89*, C. J. Ferguson 48*; Mashrafe Bin Mortaza 2-31); Bangladeshis 7 dec 232 (Javed Omar 59, Habibul Bashar 99; A. J. Nye 2-40, C. J. Ferguson 2-5) and 8 for 232 (Mohammad Ashraful 61, Alok Kapali 44; M. F. Cleary 2-45, P. C. Worthington 3-31).

†NORTHERN TERRITORY CHIEF MINISTER'S XI v BANGLADESHIS

At Marrara Cricket Ground, Darwin, July 10, 11, 12, 13, 2003. Bangladeshis won by two wickets. *Toss:* Northern Territory Chief Minister's XI.

International cricket arrived for the first time at Darwin's lush, modern and well-appointed Marrara Cricket Ground, normally an Australian Rules football oval. It provided the attractive backdrop for Michael Clarke's captaincy debut at senior level, as he led a team of 10 local players plus himself and Nathan Hauritz. Clarke promptly produced a vintage captain's knock, displaying uncharacteristic patience during his 79 off 152 balls. On a sluggish drop-in pitch – adjacent to the following week's Test strip – no other batsman in the match reached 50. None of the Territory players distinguished themselves with the bat, although the Alice Springs fast bowler Adrian McAdam showed impressive zip with the ball. The Bangladeshis crawled along at under two runs an over in the first innings. Batting a second time, and again showing more commonsense than fluency, they narrowly achieved a tight run-chase in a low-scoring contest for the second game in a row. But it was their seamers, particularly Mashrafe Bin Mortaza and Tapash Baisya, who gave them the greater cause for cautious optimism with the Test series only days away.

Northern Territory Chief Minister's XI 189 (M. J. Clarke 79; Manjural Islam 2-23, Khaled Mahmud 3-43, Mashrafe Bin Mortaza 3-28) and 136 (K. E. Vowles 34; Manjural Islam 2-23, Tapash Baisya 3-19, Mohammad Ashraful 2-21); Bangladeshis 139 (Hannan Sarkar 34; B. J. Hatton 2-20, N. M. Hauritz 2-37) and 8 for 187 (Javed Omar 44, Al Sahariar Rokon 41; A. McAdam 2-30, N. M. Hauritz 2-48).

AUSTRALIA v BANGLADESH

First Test Match

At Marrara Cricket Ground, Darwin, July 18, 19, 20, 2003. Australia won by an innings and 132 runs. *Toss:* Australia.

Darwin was the unlikely but grateful location, and Bangladesh the hapless opponent, as Steve Waugh chalked up two of captaincy's most lustrous milestones. Leading his side in the first Australian Test ever played outside a state capital city, Waugh followed in the steps of his predecessors Allan Border and Mark Taylor by becoming only the third Australian to command his country 50 times. Three wonderfully warm days of cricket were watched by a disappointing crowd of 13,862, about half the number expected. But by the end they were on their feet applauding as Waugh, the most capped player in Test history, became the game's most successful captain. His 37th win eclipsed the former West Indian captain Clive Lloyd's record of 36 victories from 74 matches.

Not that the result of this Test was ever in doubt. One of the strongest teams of all time easily beat one of the weakest. By stumps on the first day Australia had opened up a first-innings lead and Glenn McGrath and Jason Gillespie had already partaken in one of this match's many slices of history. The tall, lean, probing pair secured five wickets between them as Bangladesh tumbled for 97, stretching their combined wicket total in matches where they have shared the new ball to 247 in 30 Tests. This overtook the record of Ray Lindwall and Keith Miller, who took 245 wickets in 33 matches leading the attack together, long before the country of Bangladesh even existed.

Not for the first time Steve Waugh won the toss and bowled in the quest for early psychological supremacy. Bangladesh responded with the fourth sub-100 total of their 20-Test lifetime. This, though, was nothing to be particularly ashamed of. It was the fifth time teams led by Waugh had dismissed their Test opponents for under 100, and only eight months since Nasser Hussain's England side had collapsed for 79 at the Gabba. The 18-year-old Mohammad Ashraful and wicket-keeper Khaled Mashud were the only batsmen to linger longer than an hour, although reckless shot selection – rather than the unfamiliar Australian bounce – was primarily to blame.

On a slow pitch and sluggish outfield, the Australian innings proceeded at a moderate pace. Mashrafe Bin Mortaza, only 19, bowled at a brisk speed and made the Australians toil hard for their runs. When Waugh came to the wicket the total had reached only 3 for 184 after 71 overs. Thereafter the scoring accelerated. Darren Lehmann completed a fine first Test century in Darwin before falling victim to a second brilliant catch by Javed Omar. Waugh was quicker still, though entirely methodical, in compiling his 31st hundred. He declared the moment he reached three figures, joining South Africa's Gary Kirsten as the only men to hit Test centuries against all nine possible opponents.

Bangladesh made an enterprising start to their second innings, speeding to 1 for 70 off 15 overs by stumps on the second day. The spin of Stuart MacGill was too much for them next morning. Habibul Bashar continued his exciting form of the previous evening before utterly misreading a gaping MacGill wrong'un. Al Sahariar batted sensibly and fluently but the rest had little idea of how to combat MacGill's hard-spun leg-breaks. By 12.41 p.m. on the third day – minutes short of the scheduled halfway point – the match was over.

Still Bangladesh, in reaching 178, had almost doubled their first-innings effort. Their single pre-Test ambition, as stated by their bushily moustachioed coach Dav Whatmore, was to improve. Nobody could take that away from them.

Man of the Match: S. R. Waugh.   *Attendance:* 13,862.

Close of play: First day, Australia (1) 2-121 (Langer 40, Lehmann 51); Second day, Bangladesh (2) 1-70 (Hannan Sarkar 29, Habibul Bashar 26).

Bangladesh

	R	B	4/6		R	B	4/6
Hannan Sarkar lbw b McGrath	0	13	0	– c Gilchrist b Gillespie	35	69	2
Javed Omar c Gilchrist b Gillespie	5	37	0	– lbw b McGrath	5	11	1
Habibul Bashar b Lee	16	28	1	– b MacGill	54	91	4
Mohammad Ashraful c Gillespie b McGrath	23	52	1	– c Gilchrist b Lee	7	41	1
Al Sahariar Rokon b Lee	0	9	0	– c and b MacGill	36	51	3 1
Alok Kapali lbw b MacGill	0	2	0	– lbw b MacGill	0	4	0
†Khaled Mashud lbw b McGrath	11	63	1	– c Gilchrist b MacGill	6	11	1
*Khaled Mahmud c Gilchrist b MacGill	21	39	3	– b Gillespie	5	17	0
Mashrafe Bin Mortaza c Gilchrist b Gillespie	3	5	0	– (10) run out (Lehmann)	15	6	1 1
Tapash Baisya not out	2	6	0	– (9) lbw b MacGill	4	7	0
Manjural Islam c Langer b Lee	1	3	0	– not out	0	2	0
B 1, l-b 5, w 6, n-b 3	15			L-b 6, w 2, n-b 3	11		
	97				178		

(42.2 overs, 171 mins)   97
Fall: 4 26 36 39 40 60 87 91
      94 97

(51.1 overs, 217 mins)   178
Fall: 8 89 112 112 112 122 143
      152 171 178

Bowling: *First Innings*—McGrath 13–6–20–3; Gillespie 8–1–27–2; Lee 8.2–2–23–3; MacGill 13–4–21–2. *Second Innings*—McGrath 10–0–25–1; Gillespie 16–3–48–2; Lee 12–5–34–1; MacGill 13.1–1–65–5.

Australia

	R	B	4/6
J. L. Langer lbw b Kapali	71	201	7
M. L. Hayden b Mortaza	11	23	2
R. T. Ponting c Omar b Baisya	10	28	1
D. S. Lehmann c Omar b Mortaza	110	223	10 1
*S. R. Waugh not out	100	133	10 1
M. L. Love b Mortaza	0	1	0
†A. C. Gilchrist b Manjural	43	47	7
B. Lee run out (Baisya)	23	39	1 1
J. N. Gillespie not out	16	15	3
B 5, l-b 8, w 7, n-b 3	23		

(117.5 overs, 483 mins)   (7 wkts dec) 407
Fall: 13 43 184 243 244 313 377

S. C. G. MacGill and G. D. McGrath did not bat.

Bowling: Manjural Islam 24–4–78–1; Mashrafe Bin Mortaza 23–7–74–3; Tapash Baisya 21.5–4–69–1; Khaled Mahmud 28–2–98–0; Alok Kapali 18–2–65–1; Mohammad Ashraful 2–0–9–0; Habibul Bashar 1–0–1–0.

Umpires: R. E. Koertzen (South Africa) and D. R. Shepherd (England).
TV Umpire: S. J. A. Taufel.
Referee: M. J. Procter (South Africa).

AUSTRALIA v BANGLADESH

Second Test Match

At Cazaly's Stadium, Cairns, July 25, 26, 27, 28, 2003. Australia won by an innings and 98 runs. *Toss:* Australia. *Test debut:* Anwar Hossain Monir.

At Test cricket's 90th venue, Stuart MacGill upstaged Australia's prized pace bowlers – and Bangladesh's supposed fear of them – for the second time in a week. Again Steve Waugh sent the visitors in to bat and again Australia won by an innings inside four days, clean-sweeping this first series between the two countries 2-0. But this was a more spirited performance from Bangladesh. They stretched the game into a fourth day and for the first session and a half, to widespread amazement, cricket's whipping boys actually got the better of the world champions.

All the pre-match gossip suggested that the pitch would be a seam bowler's delight. But from the outset the Bangladesh batsmen played with confidence and surety on a wicket that was moist underneath and tinged green on top. They left the ball judiciously and attacked with purpose, surviving and ultimately thriving after what must have been one of their most searching examinations. Despite the fast pitch, Hannan Sarkar and Habibul Bashar picked off anything full or short – and there was more than the usual amount on offer. Jason Gillespie and Brett Lee strayed too short while Glenn McGrath seemed to be lacking in zest. He missed the subsequent one-day series for an operation on his ankle, and this was to prove his last Test for almost a year.

BEGINNING WITH A BANG

Number of first-class matches played at each Australian venue
before hosting their first Test:

0	Marrara Oval, Darwin	First Test 2003-04
2	Cazaly's Australian Football Park, Cairns	First Test 2003-04
4	Adelaide Oval	First Test 1884-85
6	Bellerive Oval, Hobart	First Test 1989-90
8	Sydney Cricket Ground	First Test 1881-82
15	Melbourne Cricket Ground	First Test 1876-77
19	Exhibition Ground, Brisbane	First Test 1928-29
42	Brisbane Cricket Ground	First Test 1931-32
146	WACA Ground, Perth	First Test 1970-71

At the first lunch break Bangladesh were dreamily placed at 1 for 103. MacGill had conceded 35 runs off six overs, Sarkar hitting 14 off one over with wristy, elegant strokes. The end of the 108-run partnership between Sarkar and Bashar disrupted Bangladesh's momentum, triggering a mini-clatter of four wickets for 15 runs. But the emboldened Bangladeshis would not be intimidated. Sanwar Hossain, a diminutive right-hander, was struck a fierce blow on the left shoulder by Lee early in his innings. He then despatched the same bowler three times in one over to the backward point fence. The final two wickets were wrapped up 13 balls into the second morning. But Bangladesh had made commendable progress in batting throughout the first day. Few local observers had thought them capable of it.

Sadly for the visitors, the match followed a more predictable script for the remaining three days. Australia rattled up a big total, Matthew Hayden and Ricky Ponting showing more flair than they had in Darwin. Darren Lehmann had another field day, smashing 105 in the final 32-over session of the second afternoon. He batted for 260 minutes in all, mixing exquisite late cuts with thumping pulls. Waugh further embellished his career statistics, batting seven hours and remaining undismissed in the series. He built on the milestone he established in Darwin by now racking up 150 or more against every other Test-playing country.

It was Waugh's 32nd Test century, moving him ahead of Sachin Tendulkar and into second place on the all-time list behind Sunil Gavaskar. Along the way, he helped guide Martin Love to his first, giving him plenty of the strike as the declaration beckoned. Love batted with his characteristic unhurried elegance, although he survived several leg-before appeals. He reached his hundred, accepted the cheers of his home state, and Waugh declared. Only Sanwar Hossain, the off-spinner, took multiple wickets; and any happiness on his part dimmed when his action was reported to the ICC as dubious.

Facing a deficit of 261, Bangladesh were hopeful of making Australia bat again. But after another bright start from Sarkar and Bashar they lost their last nine wickets for 76. Gillespie bowled with accuracy and purpose but MacGill was the chief danger man. He had narrowly missed out on a hat-trick in the first innings, dismissing Sanwar, Khaled Mahmud and having a confident leg-before appeal against Tapash Baisya rejected. Now, with the mountain ranges as a picturesque distant backdrop, he worked his way through the middle order for the second 10-wicket haul of his Test career. Shane Warne, five months into his one-year drugs ban and watching on from the Channel Nine commentary box, could not have spun the ball more – or more menacingly – had he been out there himself.

Man of the Match: S. C. G. MacGill. *Man of the Series:* S. C. G. MacGill. *Attendance:* 13,279.

Close of play: First day, Bangladesh (1) 8-289 (Tapash Baisya 21, Mashrafe Bin Mortaza 7); Second day, Australia (1) 3-351 (Lehmann 156, Waugh 74); Third day, Bangladesh (2) 4-106 (Sanwar Hossain 6, Alok Kapali 10).

Bangladesh

	R	B	4/6		R	B	4/6
Hannan Sarkar lbw b MacGill	76	134	9	– c Hayden b MacGill	55	104	8
Javed Omar c Gilchrist b Lee	26	58	3	– lbw b Gillespie	8	16	1
Habibul Bashar c and b MacGill	46	81	6	– c Langer b Lee	25	59	1
Mohammad Ashraful c Gilchrist b Gillespie	0	5	0	– c Ponting b MacGill	0	3	0
Sanwar Hossain b MacGill	46	90	8	– c Ponting b MacGill	16	56	2
Alok Kapali c Love b MacGill	5	14	0	– c Langer b MacGill	17	45	2
†Khaled Mashud c Love b Gillespie	44	114	7	– lbw b Gillespie	14	42	1
*Khaled Mahmud lbw b MacGill	0	1	0	– c Lee b MacGill	17	18	3
Tapash Baisya c Gilchrist b McGrath	25	50	2	– lbw b Gillespie	0	2	0
Mashrafe Bin Mortaza c Lee b Gillespie	8	13	1	– not out	3	3	0
Anwar Hossain Monir not out	0	3	0	– b Gillespie	4	6	1
L-b 8, n-b 11	19			L-b 2, n-b 2	4		

(92.1 overs, 378 mins) 295   (58.4 overs, 240 mins) 163
Fall: 47 155 156 156 170 230 230 281 .   Fall: 12 87 90 90 123 136 156
   295 295   156 156 163

Bowling: *First Innings* – McGrath 17.1–2–57–1; Gillespie 25–7–57–3; Lee 18–1–88–1; MacGill 24–9–77–5; Waugh 5–3–4–0; Lehmann 3–1–4–0.*Second Innings* – McGrath 15–9–22–0; Gillespie 12.4–3–38–4; MacGill 20–3–56–5; Lee 11–2–45–1.

Australia

	R	B	4/6
J. L. Langer c Omar b Mortaza	1	17	0
M. L. Hayden b Sanwar	50	89	8
R. T. Ponting c Ashraful b Sanwar	59	79	10 1
D. S. Lehmann c Ashraful b Baisya	177	207	22
*S. R. Waugh not out	156	291	17
M. L. Love not out	100	154	7
L-b 11, w 1, n-b 1	13		

(139.2 overs, 566 mins)   (4 wkts dec) 556
Fall: 14 105 132 382

†A. C. Gilchrist, B. Lee, J. N. Gillespie, S. C. G. MacGill and G. D. McGrath did not bat.

Bowling: Mashrafe Bin Mortaza 25–7–60–1; Tapash Baisya 26–5–96–1; Anwar Hossain Monir 21–4–95–0; Khaled Mahmud 19–3–75–0; Sanwar Hossain 30–2–128–2; Alok Kapali 14.2–0–69–0; Mohammad Ashraful 4–0–22–0.

Umpires: R. E. Koertzen (South Africa) and D. R. Shepherd (England).
TV Umpire: S. J. Davis.
Referee: M. J. Procter (South Africa).

AUSTRALIA v BANGLADESH
ONE-DAY SERIES

BATTING AVERAGES

	M	I	NO	R	HS	100s	50s	Avge	Ct	S-R
M. G. Bevan (Aus)	3	2	1	97	57	0	1	97.00	2	78.86
D. R. Martyn (Aus)	3	3	2	93	92*	0	1	93.00	2	163.16
M. L. Hayden (Aus)	3	2	1	88	46*	0	0	88.00	1	67.69
R. T. Ponting (Aus)	3	2	0	130	101	1	0	65.00	4	73.03
Alok Kapali (Ban)	3	3	0	83	49	0	0	27.67	0	70.34
A. C. Gilchrist (Aus)	3	2	0	49	31	0	0	24.50	6	90.74
Khaled Mahmud (Ban)	3	3	1	41	25*	0	0	20.50	2	51.90
Khaled Mashud (Ban)	1	1	0	18	18	0	0	18.00	0	42.86
Javed Omar (Ban)	2	2	0	27	16	0	0	13.50	0	25.00
Sanwar Hossain (Ban)	3	3	0	37	27	0	0	12.33	1	48.68
Habibul Bashar (Ban)	3	3	0	33	31	0	0	11.00	0	42.86
Tushar Imran (Ban)	3	3	0	31	28	0	0	10.33	1	68.89
Mohammad Rafiq (Ban)	3	3	1	17	8*	0	0	8.50	2	39.53
Al Sahariar Rokon (Ban)	2	2	0	16	8	0	0	8.00	0	38.10
Hannan Sarkar (Ban)	3	3	0	21	19	0	0	7.00	2	31.82
Tapash Baisya (Ban)	2	2	0	13	11	0	0	6.50	0	41.94
Hasibul Hussain (Ban)	2	2	1	6	6	0	0	6.00	0	28.57
I. J. Harvey (Aus)	2	1	0	5	5	0	0	5.00	0	71.43
Mohammad Ashraful (Ban)	1	1	0	4	4	0	0	4.00	0	50.00
A. Symonds (Aus)	3	2	0	7	7	0	0	3.50	2	36.84
Mashrafe Bin Mortaza (Ban)	2	2	0	2	2	0	0	1.00	0	22.22
G. B. Hogg (Aus)	3	1	1	4	4*	0	0	–	2	133.33
A. J. Bichel (Aus)	3	0	–	–	–	–	–	–	1	–
J. N. Gillespie (Aus)	2	0	–	–	–	–	–	–	0	–
B. Lee (Aus)	2	0	–	–	–	–	–	–	0	–
D. S. Lehmann (Aus)	2	0	–	–	–	–	–	–	0	–
B. A. Williams (Aus)	1	0	–	–	–	–	–	–	0	–

BOWLING AVERAGES

	M	O	Mdns	R	W	BB	5W/i	Avge	RPO
D. S. Lehmann (Aus)...	*	4.1	0	16	3	3-16	0	5.33	3.84
I. J. Harvey (Aus)	*	13.3	1	37	5	4-16	0	7.40	2.74
J. N. Gillespie (Aus) ...	*	20	9	39	4	3-23	0	9.75	1.95
B. Lee (Aus)	*	17	3	49	4	4-25	0	12.25	2.88
G. B. Hogg (Aus)......	*	30	0	90	5	3-31	0	18.00	3.00
A. J. Bichel (Aus)	*	25	1	88	4	2-24	0	22.00	3.52
Mohammad Rafiq (Ban)	*	19	2	67	3	2-31	0	22.33	3.53
Mashrafe Bin Mortaza (Ban)	*	17	2	81	3	2-41	0	27.00	4.76
A. Symonds (Aus).....	*	7	1	29	1	1-24	0	29.00	4.14
Alok Kapali (Ban).....	*	10	1	43	1	1-43	0	43.00	4.30
Hasibul Hussain (Ban) .	*	11	0	68	1	1-37	0	68.00	6.18
Tapash Baisya (Ban)...	*	15	0	94	1	1-63	0	94.00	6.27
B. A. Williams (Aus)...	*	10	2	32	0	–	0	–	3.20
Sanwar Hossain (Ban)..	*	4.2	0	29	0	–	0	–	6.69
Khaled Mahmud (Ban) .	*	6.3	0	120	0	–	0	–	7.27

†QUEENSLAND ACADEMY OF SPORT v BANGLADESHIS

At Technical and Further Education Ground, Innisfail, July 31, 2003. Bangladeshis won by four wickets. Queensland Academy of Sport 7 for 175 (C. A. Philipson 67, C. D. Hartley 41*; Hasibul Hussain 3-39, Khaled Mahmud 2-33); Bangladeshis 6 for 176 (Hannan Sarkar 35, Alok Kapali 36, Khaled Mashud 37*; C. P. Simpson 2-28).

†AUSTRALIA v BANGLADESH

First Limited-Overs International

At Cazaly's Stadium, Cairns, August 2, 2003. Australia won by eight wickets. *Toss:* Australia.

Brett Lee continues to confound. A disappointment at Test level ever since the 2001 Ashes tour, he has become an increasingly lethal weapon in the one-day arena where conservatism – not his standard modus operandi – is usually king. He bounced back from another flat Test series to reduce Bangladesh, sent in to bat, to 5 for 33 in the 12th over. Hannan Sarkar was run out in the second over and Lee took the next four wickets, later breaking the wicket-keeper Khaled Mashud's thumb for good measure. Sarkar stood in behind the stumps for the rest of the series. Jason Gillespie and Andy Bichel cleaned up the rest as Bangladesh subsided in 34 overs. Only the probing left-arm spin of Mohammad Rafiq, who was left out of the Tests, delayed an easy Australian victory. It was Bangladesh's 35th straight defeat in one-day internationals. Ricky Ponting was booed after winning the toss and electing to bowl, with the spectators at Cairns' first ever one-day international anticipating they were about to be short-changed.

Man of the Match: B. Lee. *Attendance:* 8,308.

Bangladesh

Hannan Sarkar run out (Martyn/Hogg)	1	(5)	Mohammad Rafiq c Symonds b Gillespie	3	(6)
Al Sahariar Rokon c Hayden b Lee ...	8	(17)	Hasibul Hussain c Gilchrist b Bichel	6	(16)
Habibul Bashar c Gilchrist b Lee	0	(9)	Mashrafe Bin Mortaza c Gilchrist		
Alok Kapali b Lee..................	0	(9)	b Bichel..	0	(2)
Sanwar Hossain c Gilchrist b Lee	7	(14)	L-b 1, w 5, n-b 3	9	
Tushar Imran c Ponting b Gillespie ...	28	(33)			
†Khaled Mashud lbw b Gillespie	18	(42)	(34 overs, 156 mins)	105	
*Khaled Mahmud not out	25	(54)	Fall: 2 9 14 19 33 66 76 80 105 105		

Bowling: Gillespie 10–3–23–3; Lee 8–1–25–4; Bichel 5–0–24–2; Hogg 10–0–27–0; Symonds 1–0–5–0.

Australia

†A. C. Gilchrist c Sarkar b Mortaza ...	18	(19)	W 6, n-b 8	14	
M. L. Hayden not out	46	(58)			
*R. T. Ponting b Rafiq	29	(65)	(22.3 overs, 107 mins) (2 wkts)	107	
D. R. Martyn not out	0	(1)	Fall: 29 107		

D. S. Lehmann, M. G. Bevan, A. Symonds, G. B. Hogg, B. Lee, J. N. Gillespie and A. J. Bichel did not bat.

Bowling: Mashrafe Bin Mortaza 7–0–40–1; Hasib–ul–Hassan 5–0–31–0; Khaled Mahmud 5.3–0–29–0; Mohammad Rafiq 5–2–7–1.

Umpires: D. R. Shepherd (England) and S. J. A. Taufel.
TV Umpire: P. D. Parker.
Referee: G. R. Viswanath (India).

†AUSTRALIA v BANGLADESH

Second Limited-Overs International

At Cazaly's Stadium, Cairns, August 3, 2003. Australia won by nine wickets. *Toss:* Bangladesh.

Damien Martyn announced his return to international cricket with a spectacular display of power hitting. He blazed 92 not out from 51 balls, sprinting to his half-century in only 22 deliveries and crashing 15 fours and a six. It was Martyn's first lengthy innings since the 2003 World Cup final, when he batted with a broken finger throughout a 234-run stand with Ricky Ponting. He was not at the crease nearly so long this time, Australia cantering to victory at more than seven runs an over. Only the smallness of Australia's target and some late runs from Michael Bevan denied Martyn the chance to beat Allan Border and Adam Gilchrist's record – 78 balls – for the fastest one-day hundred by an Australian. Martyn confessed afterwards that he "wouldn't have had a clue" about the potential milestone and did not discuss it with Bevan. Bangladesh's batsmen again showed little aptitude for one-day cricket, this time dollying up simple catches off the left-arm spin of Brad Hogg and Darren Lehmann, who was playing his 100th limited-overs game for Australia.

Man of the Match: D. R. Martyn.   *Attendance:* 7,654.

Bangladesh

†Hannan Sarkar c Gilchrist b Harvey	19	(44)	
Javed Omar c Gilchrist b Bichel	11	(52)	
Habibul Bashar c and b Symonds	31	(56)	
Sanwar Hossain c Ponting b Hogg	3	(11)	
Al Sahariar Rokon c Martyn b Hogg	8	(25)	
Tushar Imran c Bichel b Hogg	2	(11)	
Alok Kapali c Martyn b Lehmann	34	(44)	
*Khaled Mahmud run out (Lehmann)	11	(12)	

Tapash Baisya c Bevan b Lehmann	2	(7)
Mohammad Rafiq c Bevan b Lehmann	6	(6)
Hasibul Hussain not out	0	(5)
L-b 2, w 16, n-b 2	20	
(45.1 overs, 188 mins)	147	

Fall: 37 46 52 84 86 101 121 133 144 147

Bowling: Lee 9–2–24–0; Bichel 10–0–29–1; Harvey 7–1–21–1; Hogg 10–0–31–3; Symonds 5–0–24–1; Lehmann 4.1–0–16–3.

Australia

A. Symonds c Sanwar b Hasibul Hussain	7	(14)
M. G. Bevan not out	40	(62)
D. R. Martyn not out	92	(51)
W 4, n-b 5	9	
(20.2 overs, 90 mins) (1 wkt)	148	

Fall: 17

*R. T. Ponting, D. S. Lehmann, M. L. Hayden, †A. C. Gilchrist, G. B. Hogg, I. J. Harvey, B. Lee and A. J. Bichel did not bat.

Bowling: Tapash Baisya 5–0–31–0; Hasib–ul–Hassan 6–0–37–1; Khaled Mahmud 3–0–34–0; Mohammad Rafiq 4–0–29–0; Sanwar Hossain 2.2–0–17–0.

Umpires: D. R. Shepherd (England) and S. J. Davis.
TV Umpire: P. D. Parker.
Referee: G. R. Viswanath (India)

†AUSTRALIA v BANGLADESH

Third Limited-Overs International

At Marrara Cricket Ground, Darwin, August 6, 2003. Australia won by 112 runs. *Toss:* Australia.

Bangladesh lost by more than 100 runs for the 16th time in 74 matches after Ricky Ponting won the toss and batted, thus guaranteeing a longer game. On a less responsive Darwin drop-in wicket, strokeplay was more difficult than it had been on the true bounce and pace of Cairns. The promising Bangladeshi speedster Mashrafe Bin Mortaza conceded only 11 runs in his six-over opening spell, although he was later trumped by Jason Gillespie – who gave away just two singles in his first seven overs – and Ian Harvey, who cut off the Bangladeshi run supply with his discreet pace variations. Mohammad Rafiq was again impressive, dismissing both openers and restricting the Australians to 31 off his 10 overs. Ponting was named man of the match and series, hitting four sixes and only two fours in his 101 from 113 balls. It was his 12th hundred for Australia in 12 months. Sweaty, tanned and smiling, he later made no secret of his preference for winter cricket in the tropical north rather than the chilly experiments of previous years, when Australia played South Africa and Pakistan indoors in Melbourne during the football season.

Man of the Match: R. T. Ponting.   *Man of the Series:* R. T. Ponting.
Attendance: 8,398.

Australia

†A. C. Gilchrist c Hannan b Rafiq	31	(35)	I. J. Harvey c Rafiq b Mortaza	5	(7)
M. L. Hayden c and b Rafiq	42	(72)	G. B. Hogg not out	4	(3)
*R. T. Ponting c Imran b Baisya	101	(113)	L-b 7, w 5, n-b 1	13	
D. R. Martyn b Kapali	1	(5)			
A. Symonds run out (Sanwar/Sarkar)	0	(5)	(50 overs, 207 mins) (7 wkts)	254	
M. G. Bevan b Mortaza	57	(61)	Fall: 54 112 113 114 241 247 254		

A. J. Bichel, J. N. Gillespie, B. A. Williams did not bat.

Bowling: Mashrafe Bin Mortaza 10–2–41–2; Tapash Baisya 10–0–63–1; Khaled Mahmud 8–0–57–0; Mohammad Rafiq 10–0–31–2; Alok Kapali 10–1–43–1; Sanwar Hossain 2–0–12–0.

Bangladesh

†Hannan Sarkar lbw b Gillespie	1	(17)	Tapash Baisya c Ponting b Harvey	11	(24)
Javed Omar lbw b Harvey	16	(56)	Mohammad Rafiq not out	8	(31)
Habibul Bashar c Ponting b Bichel	2	(12)	Mashrafe Bin Mortaza b Harvey	2	(7)
Sanwar Hossain c and b Hogg	27	(51)	L-b 11, w 5	16	
Tushar Imran run out (Hogg/Gillchrist)	1	(1)			
Mohammad Ashraful b Harvey	4	(8)	(47.3 overs, 190 mins)	142	
Alok Kapali c and b Hogg	49	(65)			
Khaled Mahmud run out (Williams/Hogg)	5	(13)	Fall: 4 24 27 30 36 102 119 119 136 142		

Bowling: Gillespie 10–6–16–1; Williams 10–2–32–0; Bichel 10–1–35–1; Harvey 6.3–0–16–4; Hogg 10–0–32–2; Symonds 1–1–0–0.

Umpires: D. R. Shepherd (England) and S. J. A. Taufel.
TV Umpire: S. J. Davis.
Referee: G. R. Viswanath (India).

Sri Lanka in Australia, 2004-05

by KERRY O'KEEFFE

This contest, the second staged in Australia's north, offered as much drama, action and entertainment as a two-Test series can. The climax came in its dying minutes, in fading light in Cairns, when Shane Warne spun a leg-break past Upul Chandana to claim a record-equalling 527th Test wicket. Warne had started the series on 517 and never quite seemed in his full pomp; there were no flippers and barely a teaspoon of wrong'uns, as he focused on subtle variations of his leg-break. Instead he crept up stealthily, tantalisingly, towards the world record. The only thing missing was the man with whom he drew level.

Muttiah Muralidaran withdrew from this series a fortnight before it began for personal reasons. Ricky Ponting, due to captain Australia for the first time in a home Test series, also pulled out of the opening match because of the death of his aunt. Ponting won widespread sympathy but many in Australia thought Murali a little too precious. Beating the world champions in their own backyard, they said, should have been incentive enough for him to put aside any lingering resentment of the rudeness which heckling Australian crowds display towards him. His decision to remain in the trenches did not sit entirely happily with some within Sri Lankan cricket either.

Minus Murali, the Sri Lankans showed admirable fighting qualities but failed to win the important moments. They lost the first Test, drew the second and again showed signs of a negative psyche against the Australians. They seemed too easily bullied. The captain, Marvan Atapattu, twice won the toss and sent Australia in, a particularly peculiar decision on a perfect pitch in Cairns. With such classy batsmen as Kumar Sangakkara and Atapattu himself, technically the best front-foot cover driver in the world, the Sri Lankans have the ability to dictate a game. Instead they prefer to play from behind in the hope of punishing their opponent's mistakes.

Despite the history and entertainment on offer, Cricket Australia again lost money by taking Test cricket to the tropics. Attendances were generally disappointing and doubts linger about the sustainability of staging matches in July. The Northern Territory has a strong Australian Rules culture, which consumes Darwinians and jeopardises cricket's advance, while Cairns is principally a tourist destination with a heavy accent on Asian holiday-makers. Cricket Australia should be commended for its enterprise but may eventually see the Top End Tour, as it was christened, as a worthwhile exercise rather than a regular event.

The First Test was a low-scoring affair. Only Darren Lehmann, a considerable force on slower pitches, came to terms with the swing of Chaminda Vaas in Australia's first innings. He slapped the ball past point and over the slips, or muscled it wide of mid-off. Matthew Elliott, replacing Ponting at No. 3, was twice caught lunging hesitantly and edging to the slips cordon. But his talent is too grand for the Pura Cup and Elliott's time should come again; his Test record, like Matthew Hayden's, might well improve dramatically with prolonged exposure.

Standing in for Ponting as captain was Adam Gilchrist, unlucky not to be named Man of the Match for his eight catches and devastating 80 in the second innings. With Australia lurching to 5 for 77 – a lead of only 187 – Gilchrist strode out and reeled off nine blistering boundaries, putting the match at once beyond Sri Lanka.

Pipping him for the award was Glenn McGrath, who rediscovered his best form with 5 for 37 in the first innings. He came into the Test, his first in 11 months after ankle surgery, under intense scrutiny. Despite his early success, jurors remain divided on whether he has entered the dimming twilight. As is McGrath's wont, he bowled countless spectacular unspectacular deliveries. But his pace looks diminished and he too often chose width as the platform on which to build his strategy. Michael Kasprowicz, Queensland's favourite son, moved the ball away from the right-handers at pace to capture seven wickets in the second innings. He benefited from the techniques of the Sri Lankan batsmen, who showed less of the bat-face than was required to avoid snicking the ball on a seaming wicket.

Indeed Tony Ware's drop-in pitch was the main topic of post-match discussion in Darwin. The batsmen said it meant their job was more about survival than strokeplay. Hard-headed fast bowlers reckoned this was an over-reaction, and said it was good for batsmen's souls to be presented with something other than a road. The 9.30 a.m. start, apparently dictated by TV coverage, ensured that conditions were nobody's idea of ideal, with the ball swinging and moving dramatically off the seam in the heavy atmosphere.

In Cairns, Atapattu opted to bowl – why does he even bother with the coin ritual? – on a pitch guaranteed to last a fortnight. His motives were understandable, for 11 of Sri Lanka's previous 15 victories had come batting second, but it backfired again. Justin Langer and Hayden, known to team-mates as 'Romeo' and 'Juliet' because of their public affection for each other at the crease, were in honeymoon mode. Their 255-run opening stand was a brilliant display of "tag batting": Langer was deliberate off his legs and prolific through cover point; Hayden, more circumspect, issued his signature heaves over long-on and whips through mid-wicket.

The real star was Damien Martyn, who made only 97 but bolted down the No. 4 position with his combination of rapier-like leg-side flicks and wristy slaps through the off side. Chandana, so lean he could sleep in a bat cover, wheeled his leg-breaks and top-spinners into a stiff wind, finishing with 5 for 109 in 26 character-filled overs. Atapattu led Sri Lanka's reply, delighting the purists with a brilliant 133 as the Australian attack was made to work extremely hard. Hayden had serious carnage on his mind in the second innings, intimidating then crushing the Sri Lankans with a torrid 132 as Ponting pondered an appropriate declaration.

Set 355 to win at around four runs an over, Atapattu's men appeared only briefly interested in victory. Once Sanath Jayasuriya fell to Warne, a draw was their priority. The Australians, normally so clinical during the big points, dropped crucial catches in the final session. Ponting, a culprit himself, missed out on a 2-0 clean sweep.

Chandana had earlier taken 5 for 101 in Australia's second innings, his first 10-wicket haul, suggesting that he and Murali will be a dangerous spin cocktail in the coming years. But this was Warne's match, and series. Pressing on relentlessly against a resolute Sri Lankan tail, he grabbed his share of history and showed he still has the competitive juices of a predator. He will keep Murali honest for a season or two yet.

SRI LANKAN TOURING PARTY

*M. S. Atapattu (*captain*), R. P. Arnold, U. D. U. Chandana, T. M. Dilshan, C. R. D. Fernando, H. M. R. K. B. Herath, S. T. Jayasuriya, D. P. M. D. Jayawardene, R. S. Kaluwitharana, M. F. Maharoof, S. L. Malinga, T. T. Samaraweera, K. C. Sangakkara, W. P. U. J. C. Vaas, D. N. T. Zoysa.

M. Muralidaran withdrew on June 15.

Manager: A. Jayasekera. *Coach:* J. Dyson. *Media manager:* R. Illangakoon.

SRI LANKAN TOUR RESULTS

Test matches – Played 2, Lost 2.
Other non first-class matches: Played 1: Won 1. *Wins* – Northern Territory Chief Minister's XI.

TEST BATTING AVERAGES

	M	I	NO	R	HS	100s	50s	Avge	Ct/St	S-R
M. L. Hayden (Aus)	2	4	0	288	132	2	0	72.00	2	64.72
J. L. Langer (Aus)	2	4	0	210	162	1	0	52.50	1	55.85
D. R. Martyn (Aus)	2	4	0	203	97	0	2	50.75	0	68.12
D. S. Lehmann (Aus) ...	2	4	0	179	57	0	3	44.75	1	70.75
M. S. Atapattu (SL).....	2	4	0	156	133	1	0	39.00	1/1	45.88
K. C. Sangakkara (SL) ..	2	4	0	142	74	0	2	35.50	7	46.10
R. T. Ponting (Aus)......	1	2	0	67	45	0	0	33.50	2	49.26
T. M. Dilshan (SL)	2	4	1	87	35	0	0	29.00	2	40.47
A. C. Gilchrist (Aus)...	2	4	0	115	80	0	1	28.75	11/2	71.43
D. P. M. Jayawardene (SL)	2	4	0	107	44	0	0	26.75	2	35.31
T. T. Samaraweera (SL)	2	4	0	103	70	0	1	25.75	4	33.44
R. S. Kaluwitharana (SL)	1	2	0	48	34	0	0	24.00	4/2	58.54
U. D. U. Chandana (SL) .	2	4	0	64	19	0	0	16.00	1	36.16
S. T. Jayasuriya (SL)....	2	4	0	59	22	0	0	14.75	3	47.97
M. S. Kasprowicz (Aus) .	2	4	2	29	15	0	0	14.50	2	49.15
W. P. U. J. C. Vaas (SL) .	2	4	2	28	11*	0	0	14.00	0	36.36
R. P. Arnold (SL)	1	2	0	17	11	0	0	8.50	2	44.74
D. N. T. Zoysa (SL).....	2	4	2	16	12	0	0	8.00	0	21.05
S. M. Katich (Aus)	2	4	0	26	15	0	0	6.50	0	20.63
J. N. Gillespie (Aus)	2	4	2	22	16	0	0	5.50	2	30.99
S. K. Warne (Aus).......	2	4	0	9	4	0	0	2.25	4	27.27
M. T. G. Elliott (Aus) ...	1	2	0	1	1	0	0	0.50	1	9.09
S. L. Malinga (SL).......	2	3	0	0	0	0	0	0.00	1	0.00
G. D. McGrath (Aus) ...	2	3	2	0	0*	0	0	0.00	0	0.00

* Denotes not out.

TEST BOWLING AVERAGES

	O	Mdns	R	W	BB	5W/i	10W/m	Avge	S-R
T. M. Dilshan (SL)	2	0	4	2	2-4	0	0	2.00	6.00
G. D. McGrath (Aus)...	81	30	171	10	5-37	1	0	17.10	48.60
U. D. U. Chandana (SL)	61.4	4	270	12	5-101	2	1	22.50	30.83
M. S. Kasprowicz (Aus)	67.4	13	201	8	7-39	1	0	25.13	50.75
S. L. Malinga (SL).....	63.3	8	264	10	4-42	0	0	26.40	38.10
S. K. Warne (Aus)	100.5	24	280	10	4-70	0	0	28.00	60.50
J. N. Gillespie (Aus) ...	81.4	18	210	7	3-116	0	0	30.00	70.00
W. P. U. J. C. Vaas (SL).	72.3	15	236	7	5-31	1	0	33.71	62.14
S. T. Jayasuriya (SL)...	26	7	58	1	1-21	0	0	58.00	156.00
D. N. T. Zoysa (SL)....	62	18	187	3	2-34	0	0	62.33	124.00
T. T. Samaraweera (SL)	37	3	148	2	1-43	0	0	74.00	111.00
R. P. Arnold (SL)......	1	0	9	0	–	0	0	–	–
D. S. Lehmann (Aus)...	6	2	6	0	–	0	0	–	–

Note: Matches in this section that were not first-class are signified by a dagger.

†NORTHERN TERRITORY CHIEF MINISTER'S XI
v SRI LANKANS

At Marrara Cricket Ground, Darwin, June 24, 25, 26, 27, 2004. Sri Lankans won by five wickets. *Toss:* Northern Territory Chief Minister's XI.

Sri Lanka's only warm-up match, a 12-a-side affair, proved a mixed experience for Justin Langer. He made 151 in the first innings, a golden duck in the second and was taken to hospital before the game after being yorked on the left foot by Terry Bayly, a local fast bowler. "I was just trying to leave an impression," said the 21-year-old Bayly, born in Papua New Guinea. "As it's turned out it might be the wrong one." Once play started, it was Kumar Sangakkara and the young tearaway Lasith Malinga who left the biggest impression, keeping the tourists in the match while the NT side piled up 419. Sangakkara faced 306 balls, hitting 21 fours and a six. Much attention centred on the out-of-sorts Glenn McGrath, who bowled tightly on a slow pitch and proclaimed his best form was not far away. With the bat he was unusually buccaneering, smashing Upul Chandana for a four and a six in consecutive balls. The Australians sent for footage of Malinga's slinging action at the end of the game.

NT Chief Minister's XI 419 (J. L. Langer 151, R. Bowden 75, M. M. Brown 45, D. L. Treumer 65, G. D. McGrath 31*; M. F. Maharoof 2-73, S. L. Malinga 6-90, U. D. U. Chandana 2-118) and 9 for 145 dec (H. M. R. K. B. Herath 4-45, U. D. U. Chandana 2-29); Sri Lankans 7 for 378 dec (S. T. Jayasuriya 64, K. C. Sangakkara 203*; A. C. Dent 2-51) and 5 for 187 (T. T. Samaraweera 32, T. M. Dilshan 66*, R. P. Arnold 34; I. Redpath 2-22).

AUSTRALIA v SRI LANKA

First Test Match

by CHRISTIAN RYAN

At Marrara Cricket Ground, Darwin, July 1, 2, 3, 2004. Australia won by 149 runs. *Toss:* Sri Lanka. *Test debut:* S. L. Malinga.

Australian batsmen, so the legend goes, are a rugged happy-go-lucky lot, ready for anything. It is a product of their upbringing, which invariably takes place on gruesome roughly mown backyard pitches, with a Hills Hoist at mid-off and a taped-up tennis ball for an enemy. In this match they seemed genuinely spooked by a vaguely mottled drop-in strip, one that was fractionally slow and popped a bit. Twenty years ago it might have been pronounced a good cricket wicket. In 2004 the players and papers called it "unpredictable", "abnormal" and "treacherous", a more sinister adjective with every passing hour. The game was won in three days – the norm, it seems, for a Darwin Test – but the national stereotype took a tumble.

Batting became an immeasurably less taxing exercise from the moment Muttiah Muralidaran declared himself unavailable. He had long been reluctant to revisit Australia because of scrutiny of his doosra, the ball that looks like an off-break but spins like a leg-break, and the tendency of intoxicated spectators to extend one arm horizontally and bellow "no-ball" just as he is about to let it go. Murali's resolve appeared to harden when John Howard, the prime minister, told a Liberal Party luncheon that he too reckoned Murali was a chucker. "I thought of coming to Australia," was Murali's response, "but now I will think three times before I come."

Marvan Atapattu might have thought four or five times himself before inviting the Australians to bat. They were without their captain, Ricky Ponting, who had flown home to Launceston for his aunt's funeral. The Australians took the field in black armbands, Ponting's aunt thus superseding Brett's Lee grandma (SCG, 2003-04) as the most far-removed recipient of the black-armband treatment. Recalled to the side was Matthew Elliott, in form and in the country at a time when potential rivals were gorging themselves on the English county circuit. When told by Trevor Hohns, chairman of selectors, that he could dust off his baggy green – it was at the bottom of the wardrobe – Elliott put the phone down and screamed with joy.

There was no yelling, only an emu-like jab of his head, when the comeback that took five years to arrive was terminated after seven minutes. Elliott shaped too loosely to drive at Chaminda Vaas and edged to second slip. It was a rare spot of bother in the first two sessions. Matthew Hayden, shaking off the midwinter rust, was uncharacteristically stern in defence and typically scornful of anything short. Damien Martyn, batting for the first time in the town of his birth, got marooned in his teens before erupting with five crisp fours in 15 minutes. Darren Lehmann, with sure feet and soft hands, alternately nudged and heaved Sri Lanka's part-time spinners. The pitch looked sluggish, the kind of wicket where you had to loiter a while to adjust to the pace, but not half as scary as what you might find in the average Australian backyard.

A TEST OF PATIENCE

Longest gap between appearances by Australian cricketers

	Tests missed	Time on sidelines	Period
G. B. Hogg	78	6 years, 179 days	1996–2003
R. B. Simpson	72	9 years, 305 days	1968–1977
D. R. Martyn	68	6 years, 65 days	1994–2000
S. J. Rixon	66	6 years, 218 days	1978–1984
M. T. G. Elliott	**59**	**5 years, 92 days**	**1999–2004**

A masterful exhibition of old-style swing bowling from Vaas helped wipe out the last six wickets for 18 runs. Curling the ball away from the left-handers – and there were six of them in Australia's top seven, which was surely unprecedented – he joined Wasim Akram as the second left-arm quick in Test history to scale 250 wickets. Ironically Wasim, months earlier, had warned that the modern preoccupation with the speed gun was killing swing bowling. All eyes turned to the speedometer in mid-afternoon when Lasith Malinga, the 20-year-old debutant, found his momentum. His slingshot action sparked excited comparisons with Jeff Thomson but was perhaps more reminiscent of his bowling coach Rumesh Ratnayake. If Thomson was a human catapult, as the critics dubbed him, then Malinga is a human windmill, a flurry of arms, bowling from close to the stumps at a good 15 klicks slower than Thommo. Still, that is invariably swift enough. Lehmann was cuffed on the shoulder then gormlessly spooned another – a no-ball at his throat – to gully. Seemingly unnerved, Lehmann tiptoed extravagantly across his crease (a curious habit that works better against the spinners than the quicks) and was leg-before. Three balls later Adam Gilchrist – half-hooking, half-evading – paddled a wild inswinging bouncer through to the keeper.

Sri Lanka, all out five minutes before lunch on day two, imploded via more conventional means: the Glenn McGrath back-of-a-lengther, pitching just outside off and wobbling a whisker this way or that. It was a reassuring sight. This was his first Test back since ankle surgery, and 'Pigeon' had looked listless and old as a pterodactyl during the one-dayers in Zimbabwe. Here he was a different bowler, higher and more aggressive in his action, following through with intent. Thilan Samaraweera feathered a gorgeous fizzing leg-cutter. Russel Arnold was shaken up by a fast bouncer then sucked in by a slow floater, edging to third slip. Neither could blame you-know-what. "The wicket has played well," said Tony Ware, the MCG curator who prepared it. "I can't explain why Sri Lanka were bowled out for 97."

Ware might have been equally perplexed when Australia folded again for 201. Langer, Hayden and Elliott all fenced at gentle out-dippers. Only Lehmann, again inconvenienced by Malinga, and Gilchrist, the stand-in skipper, dug in. They flashed inventively, moved their feet decisively and accounted for 46% of Australia's runs in this game. Gilchrist was in particularly deft touch, unfurling a couple of loose-armed hooks and one trademark flick over Kumar Sangakkara's head, dominating stands of 37 with Simon Katich, 27 with Jason Gillespie and 47 with Michael Kasprowicz.

At various times on the third morning, Sri Lanka's pursuit of 312 did not seem remotely far-fetched. Atapattu and Sanath Jayasuriya looked at home until 45 minutes of earnest discipline was undone by half an hour's reckless sacrifice. Atapattu stabbed tentatively at Kasprowicz. Sangakkara, the white zinc cream still sticky on his face, was wastefully run out when Jayasuriya dabbed and darted for an imaginary single. Jayasuriya promptly compounded his error, struck beneath the knee roll by a harmless McGrath full-toss.

Mahela Jayawardene and Samaraweera batted with charm and commonsense for Sri Lanka's first half-century stand. Gillespie was heartily hooked when he dropped short and McGrath wristily driven when he overpitched. Then Samaraweera wafted at Kasprowicz, was pouched by Gilchrist – his first of five – and the rest followed meekly. Kasprowicz, generating robust pace, kept banging the ball in outside off and the batsmen kept nicking it. He finished with 7 for 39; he might bowl better some day and take none.

The crowds were disappointing, not so much for their size (smallish) as their colour (overwhelmingly white). In a corner of Australia where a quarter of the population is Aboriginal, there was hardly a black face to be seen. The other quibble was the 9.30 a.m. start. Cricket Australia's travelling press officer, a touch sheepishly, admitted that the sole logic was to let Channel Nine lead into its six o'clock news on the eastern seaboard with *The Price Is Right*. But the time was wrong. It disrupted Test cricket's time-honoured rhythms. There was little time for reflection, or for anticipation to ferment through the morning; there was scarcely time for breakfast.

Besides, the early-morning dew and humidity offered the fast men an unnecessary edge – though most preferred to blame the pitch. A rare dissenting voice came from a bloke who watched the first two days on telly. Ricky Ponting lamented "spoilt" modern batsmen and described the proliferation of identikit flat brown pitches as "a huge concern". "You'll end up having grounds that don't have any character. The grounds in Australia will be exactly the same." He still hadn't led his country in a home Test. But already you sensed that, with Ponting as a captain, Australian cricket was on a good wicket.

Man of the Match: G. D. McGrath.   *Attendance:* 13,355.

Close of play: First day, Sri Lanka (1) 3-43 (Jayawardene 12, Zoysa 8); Second day, Australia (2) 201 all out.

Australia

	R	B	4/6		R	B	4/6
J.L. Langer c Chandana b Samaraweera	30	70	4	– c Sangakkara b Vaas	10	12	1
M.L. Hayden c Jayasuriya b Vaas	37	83	4	– c Sangakkara b Zoysa	2	6	0
M.T.G. Elliott c Arnold b Vaas	1	8	0	– c Dilshan b Vaas	0	3	0
D.R. Martyn c Arnold b Jayasuriya	47	83	5	– c Sangakkara b Malinga	7	31	1
D.S. Lehmann lbw b Malinga	57	108	7	– c Sangakkara b Malinga	51	59	8
S.M. Katich c Sangakkara b Vaas	9	43	0	– c Dilshan b Chandana	15	56	2
*†A.C. Gilchrist c Sangakkara b Malinga	0	3	0	– run out (Jayawardene/Sangakkara)	80	123	10
S.K. Warne run out (Arnold/Sangakkara)	2	18	0	– lbw b Malinga	1	5	0
J.N. Gillespie lbw b Vaas	4	13	0	– c Samaraweera b Chandana	16	45	4
M.S. Kasprowicz not out	2	7	0	– c and b Malinga	15	39	1 1
G.D. McGrath c Samaraweera b Vaas	0	1	0	– not out	0	2	0
B 2, l-b 6, w 2, n-b 8	18			L-b 3, n-b 1	4		

(71.3 overs, 311 mins)	207	
Fall: 72 73 80 177 189 189 201		
202 207 207		

(63.1 overs, 292 mins)	201	
Fall: 12 12 14 64 77 114 127		
154 201 201		

Bowling: *First Innings*—Vaas 18.3–6–31–5; Malinga 14–3–50–2; Zoysa 13.4–4–24–0; Samaraweera 9–1–43–1; Chandana 6–0–30–0; Jayasuriya 11–4–21–1. *Second Innings*—Vaas 14–4–51–2; Zoysa 16–3–57–1; Malinga 15.1–3–42–4; Jayasuriya 6–3–9–0; Chandana 11–1–30–2; Arnold 1–0–9–0.

Sri Lanka

	R	B	4/6		R	B	4/6
*M. S. Atapattu b McGrath	4	9	0	– c Warne b Kasprowicz	10	39	0
S. T. Jayasuriya lbw b McGrath	8	25	1	– lbw b McGrath	16	46	2
†K. C. Sangakkara lbw b Gillespie	2	17	0	– run out (Martyn)	0	4	0
D. P. M. Jayawardene c Langer b Gillespie	14	43	2	– b McGrath	44	113	2
D. N. T. Zoysa c Gilchrist b McGrath	12	27	2	– (10) c Gilchrist b Kasprowicz	1	9	0
T. T. Samaraweera c Gilchrist b McGrath	1	9	0	– (5) c Gilchrist b Kasprowicz	32	82	2
T. M. Dilshan not out	17	59	1	– (6) c Gilchrist b Kasprowicz	14	44	0
R. P. Arnold c Elliott b McGrath	6	15	1	– (7) c Gilchrist b Kasprowicz	11	23	1
U. D. U. Chandana c Gilchrist b Warne	14	36	1 [1]	– (8) b Kasprowicz	17	22	3
W. P. U. J. C. Vaas c Hayden b Warne	5	12	1	– (9) not out	10	15	1
S. L. Malinga c Gillespie b Warne	0	6	0	– c Gilchrist b Kasprowicz	0	1	0
L-b 7, n-b 7	14			L-b 1, w 2, n-b 4	7		
(41.5 overs, 186 mins)	97			(65.4 overs, 278 mins)	162		

Fall: 10 20 33 47 50 51 59 85
  91 97

Fall: 23 23 30 109 113 132 141
  152 162 162

Bowling: _First Innings_—McGrath 15–4–37–5; Gillespie 13–4–18–2; Kasprowicz 7–1–15–0; Warne 6.5–1–20–3. _Second Innings_—McGrath 16–9–24–2; Gillespie 13–2–37–0; Kasprowicz 17.4–3–39–7; Warne 19–2–61–0.

Umpires: Aleem Dar (Pakistan) and B. F. Bowden (New Zealand).
TV Umpire: S. J. A. Taufel.
Referee: B. C. Broad (England).

AUSTRALIA v SRI LANKA

Second Test Match

by CHLOE SALTAU

At Cazaly's Stadium, Cairns, July 9, 10, 11, 12, 13, 2004. Match drawn. _Toss:_ Sri Lanka.

This was the first drawn Test in Australia's tropics, securing a one-nil series victory for the home side, but it was much more than that. Matthew Hayden's thunderous twin centuries were a bold footnote. Marvan Atapattu's exquisite 133 was a charming subplot, the story of an earnest man whose first six Test innings yielded a solitary run but who had now given his country a fighting chance. An unassuming leg-spinner, Upul Chandana, captured his maiden 10-wicket haul.

Everything was overshadowed by the seven history-making wickets conjured by another leg-spinner, blond-haired and rather better known. Shane Warne, on a thankless slow-turning pitch, had menace in his glare and magic in his fingers. Chaminda Vaas and Nuwan Zoysa will be remembered in the years to come not for thwarting Australia's victory push, but for denying Warne individual ownership of the world wicket-taking record. Chandana's 10 wickets will be forgotten too. He will be remembered mostly for the moment late on the fifth afternoon when Warne slid a ball past him, his back foot searched for the crease, Adam Gilchrist flicked off the bails and he became the 527th Test victim of the greatest leg-spinner in history.

Warne and Muttiah Muralidaran each defined this Top End series in his own way, the Australian by his record pursuit and the Sri Lankan by his absence. Magnetic and controversial figures both, they have seldom seen eye to eye, their public bickering intimating a fractured off-field relationship. But by the end of 37 consecutive Warne overs – mostly breathtaking, occasionally luckless and stretching well into the Cairns twilight – the two spin kings stood top of the world with 527 Test wickets each. The whirl of international cricket meant they would be disentangled soon enough. But for now, the great rivals were statistical equals.

Warne caught Murali by stealth. He needed eight wickets in the match to go past him, then five in the second innings. He finished with 3 for 129 and 4 for 70, enough to ensure a share of history only five months after his return from a 12-month drug ban. He became the first Australian to hold the world bowling record since Dennis Lillee snaffled his 310th Test victim, the West Indian Larry Gomes, in December 1981.

It was not enough, though, for Australia to win a Test they had controlled from the moment Hayden and Justin Langer stepped out to bat. Ricky Ponting came back for Matthew Elliott, while Sri Lanka called up the wicket-keeper Romesh Kaluwitharana for his first Test in more than a year, replacing the out-of-sorts Russel Arnold. Atapattu stumbled into a classic tourist's trap when he elected to bowl first on a pitch rumoured to be fast and bouncy, but which was deceptively friendly to batsmen. He could not have imagined Australia's formidable openers would punish him so mercilessly.

Langer and Hayden embraced at every milestone: Langer's 19th Test hundred, their sixth double-century opening partnership (two more than any other pair in history), Hayden's 19th hundred. Fast-forward a few hours and Australia's answer to Gordon Greenidge and Desmond Haynes were sitting beside each other in the depths of the Cazaly's grandstand. Their easy chemistry, the closeness of the partnership that bowlers around the world find so difficult to break, was obvious as they fielded questions from journalists.

What about Hayden's wild swipe, off a rank wide ball from the part-timer Thilan Samaraweera, which scuppered their chance of a 300-run stand? "Threw it away, didn't I?" said Hayden. "Good ball that got you out, though," needled Langer. "See, this is what I have to put up with for five hours, eh," moaned Hayden.

HAYDEN v BRADMAN

Duration:	Matthew Hayden's last 31 Tests December 2001 – July 2004	Don Bradman's last 31 Tests February 1933 – August 1948
Runs	3,443	4,124
Highest score	380	304
Hundreds	16	16
Fifties	8	10
Average	71.72	95.90

And what of the fact that Langer had for once outpaced his monstrous partner? "Like you saw today, Haydos likes to block 'em and see off the new ball and I tend to smack 'em around. And I think that's the key to it; I'm the aggressor and he's the blocker." Smiles all round. Sri Lanka could be forgiven for not sharing the love that emanated from the Australian dressing room.

No sooner had they seen the back of Langer and Hayden's 255-run stand than Damien Martyn found his range. He was at his most silky and sublime until getting bogged down by Zoysa in the nineties, eventually prodding forward to Chandana and being trapped leg-before. Darren Lehmann produced yet another swashbuckling half-century, Gilchrist yet another cavalier cameo and Australia lost their last eight wickets for 125.

Atapattu needed to make amends for his tactical errors of the first day and did so. He is not an exuberant character, but he played with firm resolve and caressed cover drive after cover drive to raise his 15th hundred in Tests. He and Mahela Jayawardene, previously cool-headed, self-destructed in the first two overs after lunch on day three, a day when gloomy light and blustery rain terminated play 21 overs early. A destructive fourth-morning assault from Glenn McGrath and Jason Gillespie disintegrated Sri Lanka's tail, and they trailed by 62.

Hayden, after his comparatively dour first innings, was typically explosive in the second. His 64 runs on the final morning, as Australia set up a declaration, arrived in only 45 balls. Along the way he became the eighth man in history to twice hit two hundreds in a Test; his 20th hundred in his 95th innings gave him a ratio better than one every five hits. Ponting laboured over his declaration, eventually setting Sri Lanka an implausible 355 to win in 85 overs. His caution proved costly, for Australia and Warne.

Sri Lanka's innings revolved around their classy No. 3 Kumar Sangakkara, at last unburdened of the keeping responsibilities, who crafted a wonderful 66. More importantly, he frustrated the Australians by occupying the crease for more than four hours. One ball from Warne spat up from the rough outside off stump and broke Gilchrist's nose. Another caught the edge of Sangakkara's bat and Hayden misjudged the chance at slip. Kaluwitharana defended gamely in the face of Warne's oohs and aahs, before finally pushing forward and being snapped up at short leg. Warne had wicket No. 525.

His 526th, finally dislodging Sangakkara, was a leg-break reminiscent of some of his most vicious, for it drifted and pitched outside the left-hander's off stump, jagging back in to hit middle. Then, as if to extend the already protracted drama, the Chandana stumping went to the third umpire, who ruled him out by a toenail. Dusk descended and the Australian fielders crowded the bat. One more wicket and the No. 11 Lasith Malinga, yet to score a Test run, would be exposed. But Zoysa and Vaas survived a nerve-jangling 31 minutes and 57 balls.

Ponting, having drawn his first Test on Australian soil as captain, would later lament dropping Zoysa off Gillespie, a relatively simple chance at second slip that might have swung things Australia's way. But the result seemed almost incidental. Warne seized a stump with which to remember his record-equalling achievement as 1,684 people at this delightful ground – including mum Brigitte and dad Keith – stood and applauded him from the field.

Man of the Match: M. L. Hayden. *Man of the Series:* S. K. Warne. *Attendance:* 20,102.

Close of play: First day, Australia (1) 2-370 (Langer 159, Martyn 56); Second day, Sri Lanka (1) 2-184 (Atapattu 75, Jayawardene 9); Third day, Sri Lanka (1) 5-411 (Samaraweera 53, Kaluwitharana 30); Fourth day, Australia (2) 2-194 (Hayden 68, Martyn 52).

Australia

	R	B	4/6			R	B	4/6
J. L. Langer c Jayawardene b Malinga	162	284	22	– c Kaluwitharana b Zoysa		8	10	2
M. L. Hayden c Jayasuriya								
b Samaraweera	117	185	14[2]	– b Chandana		132	171	10[1]
*R. T. Ponting c Atapattu b Malinga	22	27	3	– c Jayasuriya b Zoysa		45	109	3[1]
D. R. Martyn lbw b Chandana	97	123	13	– st Kaluwitharana b Chandana	52	61	8[1]
D. S. Lehmann c Sangakkara b Chandana	50	56	9	– c Jayawardene b Chandana	21	30	1
S. M. Katich b Chandana	1	20	0	– st Kaluwitharana b Dilshan	1	7	0
†A. C. Gilchrist c Kaluwitharana b Malinga	35	33	2[2]	– b Dilshan	0	2	0
S. K. Warne c Samaraweera b Chandana	2	7	0	– c Samaraweera b Chandana	4	3	1
J. N. Gillespie c Kaluwitharana b Malinga	1	5	0	– st Atapattu b Chandana	1	8	0
M. S. Kasprowicz c Kaluwitharana								
b Chandana	9	10	2	– not out		3	3	0
G. D. McGrath not out	0	3	0					
B 7, l-b 3, w 4, n-b 7	21			L-b 20, w 1, n-b 4		25		
	—					—		
(124.2 overs, 539 mins)	517			(66.4 overs, 288 m) (9-dec)		292		

Fall: 255 291 392 454 462 469 474
476 485 517

Fall: 288 288 292

Bowling: *First Innings*—Vaas 27–2–102–0; Zoysa 19–5–72–0; Samaraweera 17–2–55–1; Malinga 29.2–2–149–4; Chandana 26–2–109–5; Jayasuriya 6–0–20–0. *Second Innings*—Vaas 13–3–52–0; Zoysa 14–6–34–2; Malinga 5–0–23–0; Samaraweera 11–0–50–0; Chandana 18.4–1–101–5; Jayasuriya 3–0–8–0; Dilshan 2–0–4–2.

Sri Lanka

	R	B	4/6			R	B	4/6
*M. S. Atapattu c Hayden b McGrath	133	268	19	– c Warne b Gillespie		9	24	2
S. T. Jayasuriya c Gilchrist b Gillespie	13	9	3	– c Gilchrist b Warne		22	43	3
K. C. Sangakkara c Gillespie b Warne	74	114	8	– b Warne		66	173	8
D. P. M. Jayawardene c and b Kasprowicz	43	118	7	– c Gilchrist b McGrath		6	29	1
T. T. Samaraweera c Ponting b Gillespie	70	199	6	– run out (Martyn)		0	18	0
T. M. Dilshan c Kasprowicz b Warne	35	61	5	– c Warne b Gillespie		21	51	4
†R. S. Kaluwitharana c Warne b McGrath	34	46	3	– c Lehmann b Warne		14	36	1
U. D. U. Chandana st Gilchrist b Warne	19	49	0[1]	– st Gilchrist b Warne		14	70	1
W. P. U. J. C. Vaas c Ponting b Gillespie	2	6	0	– not out		11	44	0
D. N. T. Zoysa not out	0	9	0	– not out		3	31	0
S. L. Malinga run out (Lehmann)	0	5	0					
B 3, l-b 10, w 2, n-b 17	32			B 5, l-b 3, n-b 9		17		
	—					—		
(144.4 overs, 610 mins)	455			(85 overs, 345 m) (8 wkts)		183		

Fall: 18 156 280 280 345 420 445 455
455 455

Fall: 15 49 58 64 107 136
159 174

Bowling: *First Innings*—McGrath 34–10–79–2; Gillespie 37.4–6–116–3; Kasprowicz 32–5–113–1; Warne 38–7–129–3; Lehmann 3–0–5–0. *Second Innings*—McGrath 16–7–31–1; Gillespie 18–6–39–2; Warne 37–14–70–4; Kasprowicz 11–4–34–0; Lehmann 3–2–1–0.

Umpires: Aleem Dar (Pakistan) and B. F. Bowden (New Zealand).
TV Umpire: R. L. Parry.
Referee: B. C. Broad (England).

A BAGGY GREEN FOR A FEW BEERS

Who was the last Irishman to wear a baggy green? Thomas Patrick Horan was born in Middleton, Ireland, on March 8, 1854 to be sure. He played for Australia in the first Test in March 1877 and captained his adopted country in 1884-85. But, then, Horan never wore a green cap because neither did Australia's cricketers until 1899. And they weren't baggy at all.

Bill O'Reilly played 27 Tests for Australia from 1932 to 1946, wearing the baggy green with distinction while taking 144 wickets. He exhibited many of the traits of fiery Irishmen and boasted a rich Irish ancestry. However, his place of birth was no closer to the Emerald Isle than White Cliffs, New South Wales. In fact, it was about as far away as you can get.

So how about Perry Montgomery? Who?

Perry Montgomery was an 18-year-old Campbell College schoolboy when he was named 12th man for Ireland against the 1961 Australians at the Ormeau Ground, Belfast, on September 15 and 16. It was the first visit by an Australian team to Ireland since 1938. Perry was chosen because he was captain of the Irish schoolboys team and it was customary to select the captain of such a team to be drinks waiter, giving him the feel of top-level cricket.

Picture Perry's excitement at the prospect of mixing with the cream of Australian cricket: a side led by Richie Benaud and including Bob Simpson, Colin McDonald, Neil Harvey, Norm O'Neill, Alan Davidson, Wally Grout, Barry Jarman, Ron Gaunt, Graham McKenzie and Lindsay Kline. *Wisden* records the game as a "light-hearted exhibition", O'Neill appropriately top-scoring with 85 out of 209 in the first innings. Anomalies abound in the scorecard. Australia played both their wicket-keepers, with Grout opening and the regular opener Colin McDonald appearing at No. 11. There is no record of the performance of the drinks waiter. But was anything amiss?

Picture Perry's bewilderment when after the Australian innings ended his kit was removed from the Irish dressing-rooms to that of the tourists. Picture the puzzlement of Perry's school pals when Ireland batted and he arrived on the ground wearing an Australian jumper, with a baggy green cap perched on his head. Several of the Australians figured they had better things to do than field in a second-class game at the end of a long tour, preferring to knock the froth of a Guinness or a McArdle's ale. Perry was decked out as an Australian to field substitute while different players rotated their absence. *Wisden* shows Benaud kept wickets and rested his key bowlers in the second innings. Opening with the leg-spin of Simpson and gentle off-spin of Harvey, he gave a further nine overs to the reserve keeper Jarman, who took two wickets with his lofted leg-breaks. The game was drawn.

Perry's favourite memory was of fielding alongside Harvey in the covers, and of something special which happened at the end of the day – and which has remained special down the years. Perry had to return his Aussie jumper but was allowed to keep the baggy green. These days, baggy greens fetch thousands of dollars at the world's leading auction houses and are possibly the object of too much veneration. It is lovely to think that, not all that long ago, you could get one in exchange for a few beers.

– BERNARD WHIMPRESS

Opposite RED-HOT REDBACK: Shaun Tait lets fly at Tasmania's batsmen on his way to figures of 8 for 43, the best return in domestic one-day history. *Picture by Tom Lewis, Getty Images.*

5

The Domestic Scene

First-Class Season

FEATURES OF 2003-04

(Season runs from July 1 to June 30.)

Highest Individual Scores

380	M.L. Hayden	Australia v Zimbabwe at Perth.
300*	M.L. Love	Queensland v Victoria at St Kilda.
264	B.J. Hodge	Victoria v Indians at Melbourne.
257	R.T. Ponting	Australia v India at Adelaide.
242	R.T. Ponting	Australia v India at Melbourne.
241*	S.R. Tendulkar	India v Australia at Sydney.
247	D.S. Lehmann	South Australia v New South Wales at Sydney.
233	R.S. Dravid	India v Australia at Adelaide.
216	M.G. Bevan	New South Wales v Tasmania at Sydney.
212*	D.J. Hussey	Victoria v New South Wales at Newcastle.

Leading Run-Makers

	M	I	NO	R	HS	100s	50s	Avge
1. M.T.G. Elliott (Vic)	12	21	3	1,429	182	7	3	79.39
2. S.M. Katich (NSW/Aust)	11	19	4	1,301	182*	4	8	86.73
3. B.J. Hodge (Vic/Aust A)	12	22	3	1,282	264	5	4	67.47
4. S.R. Waugh (NSW/Aust)	16	26	4	1,222	157	4	6	55.55
5. M.W. Goodwin (W Aust)	10	20	2	1,183	201*	4	5	65.72
6. J.L. Langer (W Aust/Aust)	14	24	1	1,099	163*	3	6	47.78
7. M.L. Love (Qld/Aust/Aust A)	13	22	4	1,098	300*	3	6	61.00
8. M.J. North (W Aust)	11	21	2	1,074	130*	3	6	56.53
9. S.G. Law (Qld)	11	20	4	1,053	203	2	6	65.81
10. R.T. Ponting (Tas/Aust)	8	13	2	1,034	257	3	4	94.00

Leading Batting Averages

(Qualification: 500 runs)

	M	I	NO	R	HS	100s	50s	Avge
1. R.S. Dravid (Indians)	5	10	4	620	233	1	3	103.33
2. M.G. Bevan (NSW)	3	6	1	507	216	2	2	101.40
3. R.T. Ponting (Tas/Aust)	8	13	2	1,034	257	3	4	94.00
4. S.M. Katich (NSW/Aust)	11	19	4	1,301	182*	4	8	86.73
5. M.L. Hayden (Qld/Aust)	9	14	2	1,022	380	3	4	85.17
6. M.T.G. Elliott (Vic)	12	21	3	1,429	182	7	3	79.39
7. D.S. Lehmann (S Aust/Aust)	7	11	1	689	237	3	–	68.90
8. B.J. Hodge (Vic/Aust A)	12	22	3	1,282	264	5	4	67.47
9. S.G. Law (Qld)	11	20	4	1,053	203	2	6	65.81
10. M.W. Goodwin (W Aust)	10	20	2	1,183	201*	4	5	65.72
11. J. Moss (Vic)	12	18	3	972	172*	1	7	64.80
12. M.L. Love (Qld/Aust/Aust A)	13	22	4	1,098	300*	3	6	61.00
13. D.J. Hussey (Vic)	12	17	2	878	212*	4	2	58.53
14. D.J. Marsh (Tas)	10	18	5	751	111*	2	4	57.77

	M	I	NO	R	HS	100s	50s	Avge
15. M. J. North (W Aust)	11	21	2	1,074	130*	3	6	56.53
16. S. R. Waugh (NSW/Aust)	16	26	4	1,222	157	4	6	55.55
17. M. G. Dighton (Tas)	10	18	1	944	152	3	5	55.53
18. S. R. Watson (Tas)	10	19	1	983	157	4	3	54.61
19. C. J. L. Rogers (W Aust/Aust A)	10	20	1	982	142	4	4	51.68
20. V. Sehwag (Indians)	6	11	–	537	195	1	1	48.82

Notable Partnerships

First Wicket
165   M. T. G. Elliott/J. L. Arnberger, Victoria v Queensland at Melbourne.
157   J. L. Langer/M. E. K. Hussey, Western Australia v New South Wales at Perth.
147   J. L. Langer/M. L. Hayden, Australia v India at Sydney.
141   A. Chopra/V. Sehwag, India v Australia at Melbourne.
134   J. L. Langer/M. E. K. Hussey, Western Australia v New South Wales at Sydney.

Second Wicket
369   C. T. Perren/S. G. Law, Queensland v Western Australia at Brisbane.
281   D. A. Fitzgerald/G. S. Blewett, South Australia v Tasmania at Hobart (Bel).
251   M. T. G. Elliott/B. J. Hodge, Victoria v Tasmania at Melbourne.
234   M. L. Hayden/R. T. Ponting, Australia v India at Melbourne.
213   J. Cox/S. R. Watson, Tasmania v South Australia at Hobart (Bel).

Third Wicket
270   S. M. Katich/S. R. Waugh, New South Wales v Tasmania at Hobart (Bel).
234   C. J. L. Rogers/M. W. Goodwin, Western Australia v Queensland at Brisbane.
210   G. A. Manou/D. S. Lehmann, South Australia v New South Wales at Sydney.
198   S. M. Katich/D. J. Thornely, New South Wales v Victoria at Newcastle.
190   M. L. Love/S. G. Law, Queensland v Tasmania at Hobart (Bel).

Fourth Wicket
353   S. R. Tendulkar/V. V. S. Laxman, India v Australia at Sydney.
309*   J. Moss/D. J. Hussey, Victoria v Western Australia at Perth.
250   D. S. Lehmann/S. R. Waugh, Australia v Bangladesh at Cairns.
207   M. L. Hayden/S. R. Waugh, Australia v Zimbabwe at Perth.
194   S. R. Watson/M. G. Dighton, Tasmania v Western Australia at Hobart (Bel).

Fifth Wicket
303   R. S. Dravid/V. V. S. Laxman, India v Australia at Adelaide.
236   M. L. Love/J. R. Hopes, Queensland v Victoria at St Kilda.
220*   M. J. Di Venuto/D. J. Marsh, Tasmania v New South Wales at Hobart (Bel).
185   C. A. Philipson/J. R. Hopes, Queensland v Tasmania at Hobart (Bel).
174*   S. R. Waugh/M. L. Love, Australia v Bangladesh at Cairns.

Sixth Wicket
233   M. L. Hayden/A. C. Gilchrist, Australia v Zimbabwe at Perth.
189   R. J. Campbell/K. M. Harvey, Western Australia v Tasmania at Hobart (Bel).
163   M. G. Dighton/S. G. Clingeleffer, Tasmania v Victoria at Hobart (Bel).
161   B. J. Hodge/I. J. Harvey, Victoria v New South Wales at Sydney.
158   S. M. Katich/N. S. Pilon, New South Wales v Western Australia at Sydney.

Seventh Wicket
218   C. D. Hartley/A. A. Noffke, Queensland v South Australia at Brisbane.
189   A. J. Nye/A. J. Bichel, Queensland v New South Wales at Sydney.
181   M. J. Cosgrove/J. M. Davison, South Australia v New South Wales at Adelaide.
125   B. J. Hodge/C. L. White, Victoria v Indians at Melbourne.
118   M. E. Waugh/M. J. Nicholson, New South Wales v Queensland at Brisbane.

Eighth Wicket
134   A. A. Noffke/N. M. Hauritz, Queensland v Western Australia at Perth.
119   G. B. Hogg/D. J. Wates, Western Australia v South Australia at Adelaide.
117   S. M. Katich/J. N. Gillespie, Australia v India at Sydney.
100   P. C. Worthington/D. J. Wates, Western Australia v South Australia at Perth.
89   D. J. Hussey/P. J. Roach, Victoria v New South Wales at Melbourne.

Ninth Wicket

76	M. J. North/A. K. Heal, Western Australia v South Australia at Adelaide.
62	M. W. Goodwin/C. D. Thorp, Western Australia v New South Wales at Sydney.
61	S. G. Clingeleffer/A. R. Griffith, Tasmania v New South Wales at Sydney.
59	S. G. Clingeleffer/A. R. Downton, Tasmania v Western Australia at Perth.
58*	N. M. Hauritz/M. S. Kasprowicz, Queensland v Tasmania at Hobart (Bel).

Tenth Wicket

74	H. H. Streak/R. W. Price, Zimbabwe v Australia at Perth.
65	C. P. Simpson/J. H. Dawes, Queensland v Victoria at Brisbane.
63	H. H. Streak/A.M. Blignaut, Zimbabweans v Western Australia at Perth.
58	W. A. Seccombe/M. S. Kasprowicz, Queensland v South Australia at Adelaide.
55	X. J. Doherty/G. J. Denton, Tasmania v Victoria at Hobart (Bel).

* Denotes not out or unfinished partnership

Highest Innings Totals

6-735 dec	Australia v Zimbabwe at Perth.
710	Victoria v Queensland at Melbourne.
7-705 dec	India v Australia at Sydney.
3-613 dec	Victoria v Western Australia at Perth.
7-605	Queensland v Victoria at St Kilda.
6-562 dec	Western Australia v Tasmania at Hobart (Bel).
558	Australia v India at Melbourne.
4-556 dec	Australia v Bangladesh at Cairns.
556	Australia v India at Adelaide.
523	India v Australia at Adelaide.
523	Western Australia v Queensland at Brisbane.

Highest Fourth-Innings Totals

495	South Australia (set 521) v New South Wales at Sydney.
7-455	Victoria (won) v New South Wales at Newcastle.
9-396	Tasmania (set 449) v Western Australia at Hobart.
4-386	Tasmania (set 386) v New South Wales at Hobart.
7-386	Tasmania (set 387) v Western Australia at Perth.
6-357	Australia (set 443) v India at Sydney
314	Western Australia (set 371) v South Australia at Perth.
5-303	New South Wales (won) v Western Australia at Sydney.
3-287	Western Australia (won) v Queensland at Brisbane.
8-277	New South Wales (set 327) v Queensland at Brisbane.

Lowest Innings Totals

97	Bangladesh v Australia at Darwin.
104	Queensland v Tasmania at Brisbane.
112	South Australia v Tasmania at Adelaide.
129	South Australia v New South Wales at Sydney.
151	Western Australia v Victoria at Perth.
156	South Australia v Queensland at Brisbane.
156	South Australia v Victoria at Adelaide.
163	Bangladesh v Australia at Cairns.
168	Queensland v Tasmania at Brisbane.
178	Bangladesh v Australia at Darwin.

Best Innings Analyses

8-141	A.R. Kumble	India v Australia at Sydney.
7-66	P.C. Rofe	South Australia v Victoria at Adelaide.
6-41	A.B. Agarkar	India v Australia at Adelaide.
6-59	P.C. Worthington	Western Australia v South Australia at Perth.
6-59	M.L. Lewis	Victoria v Queensland at Melbourne.
6-61	A.J. Bichel	Queensland v South Australia at Adelaide.
6-65	S.M. Katich	Australia v Zimbabwe at Sydney.
6-67	A.B. McDonald	Victoria v Western Australia at Perth.
6-76	M.J. Nicholson	New South Wales v South Australia at Adelaide.
6-121	R.W. Price	Zimbabwe v Australia at Sydney.

Leading Wicket-Takers

		M	O	Mdns	R	W	BB	5W/i	10W/m	Avge
1.	S.C.G. MacGill (NSW/Aust)	13	545.2	93	2,085	58	5-56	5	1	35.95
2.	M.J. Nicholson (NSW/Aust A)	10	372.5	82	1,228	43	6-76	2	0	28.56
3.	D.G. Wright (Tas/Aust A)	10	386.5	114	1,030	39	5-43	1	0	26.41
4.	A.J. Bichel (Qld/Aust)	8	313.2	63	1,158	37	6-61	1	1	31.30
5.	A.G. Downton (Tas)	10	373.5	76	1,353	37	5-71	1	0	36.57
6.	J.N. Gillespie (S Aust/Aust)	8	315.2	85	797	37	5-54	1	0	21.54
7.	P.C. Rofe (S Aust/Aust A)	10	328.5	83	989	36	7-66	2	0	27.47
8.	M.L. Lewis (Vic)	9	312.3	74	947	34	6-59	2	0	27.85
9.	A.B. Wise (Vic)	10	284	88	801	33	5-47	2	0	24.27

Leading Bowling Averages

(Qualification: 20 wickets)

		M	O	Mdns	R	W	BB	5W/i	10W/m	Avge
1.	J.N. Gillespie (S Aust/Aust)	8	315.2	85	797	37	5-54	1	0	21.54
2.	M.S. Kasprowicz (Qld)	5	196.1	54	559	24	5-84	1	0	23.29
3.	A.B. Wise (Vic)	10	284	88	801	33	5-47	2	0	24.27
4.	D.G. Wright (Tas/Aust A)	10	386.5	114	1,030	39	5-43	1	0	26.41
5.	A.B. McDonald (Vic)	11	270.1	67	889	33	6-67	1	0	26.94
6.	P.C. Rofe (S Aust/Aust A)	10	328.5	83	989	36	7-66	2	0	27.47
7.	M.L. Lewis (Vic)	9	312.3	74	947	34	6-59	2	0	27.85
8.	M.W.H. Inness (Vic)	8	229.4	69	669	24	4-26	0	0	27.88
9.	M.J. Nicholson (NSW/Aust A)	10	372.5	82	1,228	43	6-76	2	0	28.56
10.	S.W. Tait (S Aust/Aust A)	9	256	40	957	33	5-85	1	0	29.00
11.	A.R. Kumble (Indians)	3	206.1	28	710	24	8-141	3	1	29.58
12.	M.F. Cleary (S Aust)	9	261.1	45	893	30	5-102	1	0	29.77
13.	A.J. Bichel (Qld/Aust)	8	313.2	63	1,158	37	6-61	1	1	31.30
14.	B.M. Edmondson (W Aust)	7	212.2	24	885	28	5-90	1	0	31.61
15.	G.J. Denton (Tas)	8	276.3	60	994	30	4-60	0	0	33.13
16.	N.W. Bracken (NSW/Aust)	7	290	98	747	22	5-38	1	0	33.95
17.	S.C.G. MacGill (NSW/Aust)	13	545.2	93	2,085	58	5-56	5	1	35.95
18.	J.H. Dawes (Qld)	10	364.2	94	1,081	30	4-89	0	0	36.03
19.	A.G. Downton (Tas)	10	373.5	76	1,353	37	5-71	1	0	36.57
20.	C.L. White (Vic/Aust A)	12	294.1	39	1,105	30	4-27	0	0	36.83

Most Catches in an Innings – Fielders

4	C. L. White	Victoria v New South Wales at Melbourne.
4	V. V. S. Laxman	India v Australia at Brisbane.
4	M. L. Hayden	Australia v India at Brisbane.
3*	C. L. White	Victoria v Queensland at Brisbane.
3†	C. L. White	Victoria v Queensland at Brisbane.
3	S. M. Katich	New South Wales v Western Australia at Sydney.
3	S. R. Mason	Tasmania v Queensland at Brisbane.
3	R. S. Dravid	Indians v Victoria at Melbourne.
3	S. A. Deitz	South Australia v Queensland at Adelaide.
3	V. Sehwag	India v Australia at Adelaide.
3	M. L. Hayden	Australia v India at Melbourne.
3	M. L. Lewis	Victoria v New South Wales at Newcastle.
3	J. P. Maher	Queensland v New South Wales at Brisbane.
3	M. J. Di Venuto	Tasmania v Victoria at Melbourne.

* First Innings; † Second Innings.

Most Catches in a Match – Fielders

6	C. L. White	Victoria v Queensland at Brisbane.
6	C. L. White	Victoria v New South Wales at Melbourne.
4	S. A. Deitz	South Australia v Queensland at Adelaide.
4	M. L. Hayden	Australia v India at Brisbane.
4	V. Sehwag	India v Australia at Adelaide.
4	M. L. Hayden	Australia v India at Melbourne.
4	M. L. Lewis	Victoria v New South Wales at Newcastle.
4	D. S. Lehmann	South Australia v Victoria at Adelaide.
4	G. B. Hogg	Western Australia v South Australia at Adelaide.

Most Dismissals in an Innings

7	(7ct)	S. G. Clingeleffer	Tasmania v Western Australia at Perth.
5*	(5ct)	W. A. Seccombe	Queensland v Victoria at Brisbane.
5†	(5ct)	W. A. Seccombe	Queensland v Tasmania at Brisbane.
5	(5ct)	W. A. Seccombe	Queensland v South Australia at Adelaide.
5	(5ct)	G. A. Manou	South Australia v Victoria at Adelaide

* First Innings; † Second Innings.

Most Dismissals in a Match

10	(10ct)	W. A. Seccombe	Queensland v Tasmania at Brisbane.
8	(8ct)	S. G. Clingeleffer	Tasmania v Western Australia at Perth.
7	(7ct)	R. J. Campbell	Western Australia v Zimbabweans.
7	(7ct)	G. A. Manou	South Australia v Tasmania at Adelaide.
7	(7ct)	W. A. Seccombe	Queensland v South Australia at Adelaide.
7	(7ct)	D. S. Berry	Victoria v South Australia at Adelaide.

FIRST-CLASS AVERAGES, 2003-04

BATTING

* Denotes not out. † Denotes left-handed batsman.

	M	I	NO	R	HS	100s	50s	Avge	Ct/St
A. B. Agarkar (Indians)	4	6	1	26	12	–	–	5.20	1
Al Sahariar Rokon (Bangladeshis) . .	1	2	–	36	36	–	–	18.00	–
Alok Kapali (Bangladeshis)	2	4	–	22	17	–	–	5.50	–
† J. Angel (W Aust)	5	6	2	20	12*	–	–	5.00	1
Anwar Hossain Monir (Bangladeshis)		1	2	1	1	4	4	–	4.00–
J. L. Arnberger (Vic)	7	12	–	427	90	–	3	35.58	4
L. Balaji (Indians)	2	2	–	12	8	–	–	6.00	–
D. S. Berry (Vic)	6	7	1	139	61	–	1	23.17	20/3
† M. G. Bevan (NSW)	3	6	1	507	216	2	2	101.40	–
A. J. Bichel (Qld/Aust)	8	10	–	244	112	1	–	24.40	6
G. S. Blewett (S Aust)	8	16	1	586	171	1	3	39.07	2
† A. M. Blignaut (Zimbabweans)	3	5	1	161	57	–	1	40.25	1
† D. Bollinger (NSW)	1	1	1	2	2*	–	–	–	–
N. W. Bracken (NSW/Aust)	7	7	2	52	27	–	–	10.40	2
B. P. Cameron (S Aust)	3	6	1	199	81	–	3	39.80	–
R. J. Campbell (W Aust)	11	21	2	723	134	1	6	38.05	29/8
S. V. Carlisle (Zimbabweans)	3	6	–	186	118	1	–	31.00	4
† L. A. Carseldine (Qld)	2	2	–	19	10	–	–	9.50	1
B. Casson (W Aust)	5	9	4	108	28*	–	–	21.60	2
A. Chopra (Indians)	6	12	1	314	55*	–	1	28.55	7
S. R. Clark (NSW)	8	10	5	75	20	–	–	15.00	2
M. J. Clarke (NSW/Aust A)	3	6	2	243	131*	1	–	60.75	3
† M. F. Cleary (S Aust)	9	15	–	252	58	–	1	16.80	6
S. G. Clingeleffer (Tas)	10	16	2	434	79	–	3	31.00	28/4
† M. J. Cosgrove (S Aust)	8	15	1	639	144	2	2	45.64	10
J. Cox (Tas)	9	17	1	415	119	1	1	25.94	5
D. Dasgupta (Indians)	1	2	1	40	21	–	–	40.00	3
C. J. Davies (S Aust)	1	2	–	20	12	–	–	10.00	–
J. M. Davison (S Aust)	9	16	2	253	84	–	1	18.07	4
J. H. Dawes (Qld)	10	15	5	85	21	–	–	17.00	2
† S. A. Deitz (S Aust)	9	18	–	473	74	–	3	26.28	10
G. J. Denton (Tas)	8	11	8	85	34	–	–	28.33	4
† M. J. Di Venuto (Tas)	9	15	1	649	174*	1	4	46.36	12
M. G. Dighton (Tas)	10	18	–	944	152	3	5	55.53	5
X. J. Doherty (Tas)	8	10	4	88	21*	–	–	14.67	2
A. G. Downton (Tas)	10	15	3	146	45	–	–	12.17	4
R. S. Dravid (Indians)	5	10	4	620	233	1	3	103.33	7
D. D. Ebrahim (Zimbabweans)	3	6	–	56	29	–	–	9.33	1
† B. M. Edmondson (W Aust)	7	7	3	12	4*	–	–	3.00	2
† M. T. G. Elliott (Vic)	12	21	3	1429	182	7	3	79.39	11
† S. M. Ervine (Zimbabweans)	2	4	1	80	53	–	1	26.67	3
C. N. Evans (Zimbabweans)	2	4	–	48	22	–	–	12.00	–
G. M. Ewing (Zimbabweans)	1	2	–	2	2	–	–	1.00	–
S. J. Farrell (Qld)	2	4	–	91	49	–	–	22.75	–
D. A. Fitzgerald (S Aust)	7	14	1	431	202*	1	–	33.15	9
† A. Flower (S Aust)	7	14	–	342	82	–	2	24.43	3
† S. C. Ganguly (Indians)	6	8	–	291	144	1	1	36.38	2
† A. C. Gilchrist (W Aust/Aust)	8	9	1	272	113*	1	–	34.00	28/3
J. N. Gillespie (S Aust)	8	10	4	184	48*	–	–	30.67	5
M. W. Goodwin (W Aust)	10	20	2	1183	201*	4	5	65.72	4
A. R. Griffith (Tas)	5	7	–	78	21	–	–	11.14	–
T. R. Gripper (Zimbabweans)	3	6	–	178	54	–	2	29.67	–
Habibul Bashar (Bangladeshis)	2	4	–	141	54	–	1	35.25	–

	M	I	NO	R	HS	100s	50s	Avge	Ct/St
B. J. Haddin (NSW)	6	11	2	351	76	–	3	39.00	18/4
Hannan Sarkar (Bangladeshis)	2	4	–	166	76	–	2	41.50	–
Harbhajan Singh (Indians)	2	2	1	22	19*	–	–	22.00	–
R. J. Harris (S Aust)	1	2	–	18	14	–	–	9.00	2
B. D. Harrop (Vic)	1	1	1	0	0*	–	–	–	2
† C. D. Hartley (Qld)	3	4	1	134	103	1	–	44.67	9/2
I. J. Harvey (Vic)	4	4	–	133	71	–	2	33.25	4
K. M. Harvey (W Aust)	5	9	4	219	100*	1	–	43.80	1
S. M. Harwood (Vic)	3	3	1	43	22	–	–	21.50	1
N. M. Hauritz (Qld)	8	10	3	196	94	–	1	28.00	3
† M. L. Hayden (Qld/Aust)	9	14	2	1022	380	3	4	85.17	14
† A. K. Heal (W Aust)	2	2	–	42	33	–	–	21.00	–
† M. A. Higgs (S Aust)	7	14	–	290	71	–	2	20.71	5
B. J. Hodge (Vic/Aust A)	12	22	3	1282	264	5	4	67.47	5
† G. B. Hogg (W Aust/Aust)	4	7	1	148	75	–	1	24.67	5
J. R. Hopes (Qld)	10	17	–	510	111	1	2	30.00	7
D. J. Hussey (Vic)	12	17	2	878	212*	4	2	58.53	10
† M. E. K. Hussey (W Aust/Aust A)	11	22	–	920	138	1	8	41.82	17
† M. W. H. Inness (Vic)	8	6	3	28	10*	–	–	9.33	3
† P. A. Jaques (NSW)	10	20	–	636	146	1	4	31.80	6
Javed Omar (Bangladeshis)	2	4	–	44	26	–	–	11.00	3
† M. G. Johnson (Qld)	1	2	–	26	15	–	–	13.00	–
B. R. Joseland (Vic)	1	2	–	57	51	–	1	28.50	2
S. J. Jurgensen (Qld)	3	4	1	6	5	–	–	2.00	1
† M. Kartik (Indians)	2	1	–	26	26	–	–	26.00	1
M. S. Kasprowicz (Qld)	5	5	1	96	47	–	–	24.00	3
† S. M. Katich (NSW/Aust)	11	19	4	1301	182*	4	8	86.73	10
Khaled Mahmud (Bangladeshis)	2	4	–	43	21	–	–	10.75	–
Khaled Mashud (Bangladeshis)	2	4	–	75	44	–	–	18.75	–
† S. P. Kremerskothen (Tas)	1	2	–	29	24	–	–	14.50	1
A. R. Kumble (Indians)	3	3	–	15	12	–	–	5.00	1
G. M. Lambert (NSW)	2	3	–	72	38	–	–	24.00	1
† J. L. Langer (W Aust/Aust)	14	24	1	1099	163*	3	6	47.78	10
S. G. Law (Qld)	11	20	4	1053	203	2	6	65.81	9
V. V. S. Laxman (Indians)	4	7	1	494	178	2	1	82.33	5
B. Lee (NSW/Aust)	8	7	2	151	74*	–	1	30.20	1
† D. S. Lehmann (S Aust/Aust)	7	11	1	689	237	3	–	68.90	5
M. L. Lewis (Vic)	9	10	1	65	16	–	–	7.22	9
M. L. Love (Qld/Aust/Aust A)	13	22	4	1098	300*	3	6	61.00	13
S. C. G. MacGill (NSW/Aust)	13	10	4	38	13*	–	–	6.33	9
D. R. MacKenzie (Qld)	2	3	–	43	30	–	–	14.33	–
† J. P. Maher (Qld)	7	12	–	532	116	1	4	44.33	5
N. B. Mahwire (Zimbabweans)	1	2	1	7	6	–	–	7.00	–
G. J. Mail (NSW)	10	18	2	754	152*	3	2	47.13	6
† Manjural Islam (Bangladeshis)	1	2	1	1	1	–	–	1.00	–
G. A. Manou (S Aust)	10	18	–	331	130	1	1	18.39	31
D. J. Marsh (Tas)	10	18	5	751	111*	2	4	57.77	11
† S. E. Marsh (W Aust)	5	10	1	146	47	–	–	16.22	3
D. R. Martyn (W Aust/Aust)	6	9	1	339	66*	–	2	42.38	4
Mashrafe Bin Mortaza (Bangladeshis)	2	4	1	29	15	–	–	9.67	–
† S. R. Mason (Tas)	10	19	–	548	126	1	3	28.84	8
A. B. McDonald (Vic)	11	16	5	226	51*	–	1	20.55	8
B. E. McGain (Vic)	1	1	1	9	9*	–	–	–	–
G. D. McGrath (NSW/Aust)	3	1	–	2	2	–	–	2.00	–
S. W. Meuleman (W Aust)	4	7	–	277	106	1	2	39.57	2
† M. C. Miller (Vic)	7	13	2	341	84	–	3	31.00	6
Mohammad Ashraful (Bangladeshis)	2	4	–	30	23	–	–	7.50	2

	M	I	NO	R	HS	100s	50s	Avge	Ct/St
J. Moss (Vic)	12	18	3	972	172*	1	7	64.80	6
† M. P. Mott (Vic)	6	10	1	218	78	–	2	24.22	6
D. A. Nash (NSW)	3	6	–	96	46	–	–	16.00	1
A. Nehra (Indians)	5	6	3	0	0*	–	–	0.00	2
M. J. Nicholson (NSW/Aust A)	10	15	3	184	42	–	–	15.33	5
A. A. Noffke (Qld)	8	12	4	326	114*	1	1	40.75	–
† M. J. North (W Aust)	11	21	2	1074	130*	3	6	56.53	8
A. J. Nye (Qld)	1	1	–	102	102	1	–	102.00	–
† A. W. O'Brien (NSW)	1	2	–	7	7	–	–	3.50	1
† P. A. Patel (Indians)	6	9	3	261	62	–	2	43.50	10/3
† I. K. Pathan (Indians)	3	3	1	25	13*	–	–	12.50	1
D. M. Payne (Qld)	3	5	–	62	35	–	–	12.40	1
C. T. Perren (Qld)	11	20	1	721	141	1	4	37.95	5
M. J. Phelps (NSW)	1	2	–	101	62	–	1	50.50	–
C. A. Philipson (Qld)	3	5	1	198	101*	1	1	49.50	2
N. S. Pilon (NSW)	4	8	1	197	78	–	2	28.14	12
R. T. Ponting (Tas/Aust)	8	13	2	1034	257	3	4	94.00	5
R. W. Price (Zimbabweans)	3	5	2	66	36	–	–	22.00	1
† S. Ramesh (Indians)	2	4	–	149	87	–	1	37.25	–
P. J. Roach (Vic)	6	7	1	128	47	–	–	21.33	18
P. C. Rofe (S Aust/Aust A)	10	15	3	43	15	–	–	3.58	4
† C. J. L. Rogers (W Aust/Aust A)	10	20	1	982	142	4	4	51.68	9
Sanwar Hossain (Bangladeshis)	1	2	–	62	46	–	–	31.00	–
W. A. Seccombe (Qld/Aust A)	9	16	3	409	115	1	2	31.46	43/1
V. Sehwag (Indians)	6	11	–	537	195	1	1	48.82	9
† C. J. Simmons (W Aust)	1	2	–	8	7	–	–	4.00	–
C. P. Simpson (Qld)	6	11	–	206	83	–	2	18.73	6
M. J. Slater (NSW)	3	6	–	106	45	–	–	17.67	1
A. M. Staunton (NSW)	1	2	2	4	3*	–	–	–	–
H. H. Streak (Zimbabweans)	3	5	1	164	71*	–	1	41.00	1
A. Symonds (Qld)	2	3	–	112	102	1	–	37.33	–
T. Taibu (Zimbabweans)	3	6	–	101	35	–	–	16.83	3/1
S. W. Tait (S Aust/Aust A)	9	14	8	37	9*	–	–	6.17	2
Tapash Baisya (Bangladeshis)	2	4	1	31	25	–	–	10.33	–
J. J. Taylor (W Aust)	6	9	2	132	50	–	1	18.86	3
S. R. Tendulkar (Indians)	6	9	2	499	241*	1	2	71.29	4
M. J. Thistle (W Aust)	1	2	–	14	14	–	–	7.00	–
D. J. Thornely (NSW)	6	12	–	343	143	1	2	28.58	4
C. D. Thorp (W Aust)	3	4	–	31	18	–	–	7.75	1
S. B. Tubb (Tas)	1	2	–	25	21	–	–	12.50	–
A. E. Tucker (NSW)	1	1	–	12	12	–	–	12.00	–
M. A. Vermeulen (Zimbabweans)	3	6	–	234	63	–	1	39.00	1
S. K. Warne (Vic)	1	1	–	18	18	–	–	18.00	1
D. J. Wates (W Aust)	6	6	1	194	99	–	1	38.80	4
S. R. Watson (Tas)	10	19	1	983	157	4	3	54.61	9
M. E. Waugh (NSW)	10	18	2	598	90	–	3	37.38	10
S. R. Waugh (NSW/Aust)	16	26	4	1222	157	4	6	55.55	6
C. L. White (Vic/Aust A)	12	18	2	581	78	–	5	36.31	21
B. A. Williams (W Aust/Aust)	4	5	2	30	10*	–	–	10.00	1
P. Wilson (W Aust)	6	7	4	18	7*	–	–	6.00	2
A. B. Wise (Vic)	10	8	6	19	7	–	–	9.50	5
C. B. Wishart (Zimbabweans)	3	6	1	224	100	1	–	44.80	2
P. C. Worthington (W Aust)	5	10	1	173	50	–	1	19.22	4
D. G. Wright (Tas/Aust A)	10	14	2	270	65	–	2	22.50	4
Zaheer Khan (Indians)	3	4	1	30	27	–	–	10.00	–
L. A. Zammit (NSW)	3	4	–	32	15	–	–	8.00	–

BOWLING

† Denotes left-arm bowler.

	M	O	Mdns	R	W	BB	5W/i	10W/m	Avge
A. B. Agarkar (Indians)	4	154.5	23	596	16	6-41	1	–	37.25
Alok Kapali (Bangladeshis) ...	2	32.2	2	134	1	1-65	–	–	134.00
J. Angel (W Aust)	5	168.4	47	512	14	3-48	–	–	36.57
Anwar Hossain Monir (Bang.) .	1	21	4	95	–	–	–	–	–
L. Balaji (Indians)	2	69	8	293	4	3-87	–	–	73.25
A. J. Bichel (Qld/Aust)	8	313.2	63	1158	37	6-61	1	1	31.30
G. S. Blewett (S Aust)	8	76	16	205	5	2-29	–	–	41.00
A. M. Blignaut (Zimbabweans)	3	73	7	356	6	3-83	–	–	59.33
† D. Bollinger (NSW)	1	23	5	87	1	1-87	–	–	87.00
† N. W. Bracken (NSW/Aust) ...	7	290	98	747	22	5-38	1	–	33.95
† B. Casson (W Aust)	5	174.1	21	672	18	5-109	1	–	37.33
S. R. Clark (NSW)	8	289.2	57	880	23	4-52	–	–	38.26
† M. J. Clarke (NSW/Aust A) ...	3	18	5	63	1	1-47	–	–	63.00
M. F. Cleary (S Aust)	9	261.1	45	893	30	5-102	1	–	29.77
M. J. Cosgrove (S Aust)	8	17	5	62	3	1-0	–	–	20.67
J. Cox (Tas)	9	30	7	104	1	1-44	–	–	104.00
J. M. Davison (S Aust)	9	251.3	36	823	16	4-72	–	–	51.44
J. H. Dawes (Qld)	10	364.2	94	1081	30	4-89	–	–	36.03
G. J. Denton (Tas)	8	276.3	60	994	30	4-60	–	–	33.13
M. J. Di Venuto (Tas)	9	6	–	50	–	–	–	–	–
M. G. Dighton (Tas)	10	3	–	31	–	–	–	–	–
† X. J. Doherty (Tas)	8	306.2	41	1132	22	6-149	1	–	51.45
† A. G. Downton (Tas)	10	373.5	76	1353	37	5-71	1	–	36.57
B. M. Edmondson (W Aust) ...	7	212.2	24	885	28	5-90	1	–	31.61
S. M. Ervine (Zimbabweans) ..	2	55	7	239	5	4-146	–	–	47.80
C. N. Evans (Zimbabweans) ...	2	2	–	12	–	–	–	–	–
G. M. Ewing (Zimbabweans) ..	1	14	1	73	–	–	–	–	–
S. C. Ganguly (Indians)	6	14	2	68	1	1-38	–	–	68.00
J. N. Gillespie (S Aust/Aust) ...	8	315.2	85	797	37	5-54	1	–	21.54
A. R. Griffith (Tas)	5	171	38	641	9	2-26	–	–	71.22
T. R. Gripper (Zimbabweans) .	3	50.3	4	243	4	2-57	–	–	60.75
Habibul Bashar (Bangladeshis) .	2	1	–	1	–	–	–	–	–
Harbhajan Singh (Indians)	2	72	7	328	3	2-159	–	–	109.33
R. J. Harris (S Aust)	1	30	4	97	1	1-97	–	–	97.00
B. D. Harrop (Vic)	1	28	5	89	2	1-34	–	–	44.50
I. J. Harvey (Vic)	4	83.1	17	229	9	3-57	–	–	25.44
K. M. Harvey (W Aust)	5	143.1	22	573	14	3-40	–	–	40.93
S. M. Harwood (Vic)	3	82.1	13	327	7	3-93	–	–	46.71
N. M. Hauritz (Qld)	8	274.1	60	1023	16	4-95	–	–	63.94
† A. K. Heal (W Aust)	2	63	9	243	2	1-19	–	–	121.50
† M. A. Higgs (S Aust)	7	125.3	21	424	7	3-36	–	–	60.57
B. J. Hodge (Vic/Aust A)	12	17	1	74	–	–	–	–	–
† G. B. Hogg (W Aust/Aust) ...	4	149.5	31	490	9	3-66	–	–	54.44
J. R. Hopes (Qld)	10	271	71	853	12	4-63	–	–	71.08
D. J. Hussey (Vic)	12	17	1	79	1	1-45	–	–	79.00
M. E. K. Hussey (W A/Aust A) .	11	44	15	124	3	1-10	–	–	41.33
† M. W. H. Inness (Vic)	8	229.4	69	669	24	4-26	–	–	27.88
P. A. Jaques (NSW)	10	2	–	10	–	–	–	–	–
† M. G. Johnson (Qld)	1	15	1	59	2	2-59	–	–	29.50
B. R. Joseland (Vic)	1	6	1	19	1	1-19	–	–	19.00
S. J. Jurgensen (Qld)	3	122.2	35	301	13	4-52	–	–	23.15
† M. Kartik (Indians)	2	72.4	11	328	3	1-53	–	–	109.33
M. S. Kasprowicz (Qld)	5	196.1	54	559	24	5-84	1	–	23.29
† S. M. Katich (NSW/Aust)	11	143.4	11	549	17	6-65	1	–	32.29
Khaled Mahmud (Bangladeshis)	2	47	5	173	–	–	–	–	–
S. P. Kremerskothen (Tas)	1	13	1	42	–	–	–	–	–
A. R. Kumble (Indians)	3	206.1	28	710	24	8-141	3	1	29.58
G. M. Lambert (NSW)	2	64.5	22	212	3	2-55	–	–	70.67

	M	O	Mdns	R	W	BB	5Wi	10W/m	Avge
J. L. Langer (W Aust/Aust)	14	0.2	–	5	–	–	–	–	–
S. G. Law (Qld)	11	15.5	2	57	–	–	–	–	–
B. Lee (NSW/Aust)	8	318.1	58	1231	30	5-124	1	–	41.03
† D. S. Lehmann (S Aust/Aust) ..	7	65.2	22	154	6	3-61	–	–	25.67
M. L. Lewis (Vic)	9	312.3	74	947	34	6-59	2	–	27.85
M. L. Love (Qld/Aust/Aust A) .	13	4	–	6	–	–	–	–	–
S. C. G. MacGill (NSW/Aust) .	13	545.2	93	2085	58	5-56	5	1	35.95
D. R. MacKenzie (Qld)	2	37	5	127	8	4-43	–	–	15.88
N. B. Mahwire (Zimbabweans)	1	10	1	61	–	–	–	–	–
G. J. Mail (NSW)	10	39	8	177	2	2-57	–	–	88.50
† Manjural Islam (Bangladeshis)	1	24	4	78	1	1-78	–	–	78.00
† D. J. Marsh (Tas)	10	112	19	371	6	2-19	–	–	61.83
† S. E. Marsh (W Aust)	5	11	–	52	2	2-20	–	–	26.00
D. R. Martyn (W Aust/Aust) ...	6	25	7	70	–	–	–	–	–
Mashrafe Bin Mortaza (Bang.)	2	48	14	134	4	3-74	–	–	33.50
A. B. McDonald (Vic)	11	270.1	67	889	33	6-67	1	–	26.94
B. E. McGain (Vic)	1	31	4	109	–	–	–	–	–
G. D. McGrath (NSW/Aust) ...	3	82.3	31	184	7	3-20	–	–	26.29
S. W. Meuleman (W Aust)	4	19	2	97	2	1-38	–	–	48.50
M. C. Miller (S Aust)	7	156.5	39	467	11	2-25	–	–	42.45
Mohammad Ashraful (Bang.) .	2	6	–	31	–	–	–	–	–
J. Moss (Vic)	12	189	62	563	19	4-60	–	–	29.63
D. A. Nash (NSW)	3	79	22	265	5	2-70	–	–	53.00
† A. Nehra (Indians)	5	155	24	555	9	2-33	–	–	61.67
M. J. Nicholson (NSW/Aust A)	10	372.5	82	1228	43	6-76	2	–	28.56
A. A. Noffke (Qld)	8	241	50	770	15	4-48	–	–	51.33
M. J. North (W Aust)	11	113.3	17	421	8	2-17	–	–	52.63
A. J. Nye (Qld)	1	3	1	15	1	1-15	–	–	15.00
† A. W. O'Brien (NSW)	1	20	1	95	1	1-54	–	–	95.00
† I. K. Pathan (Indians)	3	104	14	383	7	2-40	–	–	54.71
D. M. Payne (Qld)	2	2	–	6	1	1-6	–	–	6.00
C. T. Perren (Qld)	11	22	6	75	–	–	–	–	–
C. A. Philipson (Qld)	3	2	1	5	–	–	–	–	–
N. S. Pilon (NSW)	4	1	1	0	–	–	–	–	–
R. T. Ponting (Tas/Aust)	8	6	1	19	–	–	–	–	–
† R. W. Price (Zimbabweans) ..	3	90.4	11	383	6	6-121	1	–	63.83
P. J. Roach (Vic)	6	1	–	2	–	–	–	–	–
P. C. Rofe (S Aust/Aust A)	10	328.5	83	989	36	7-66	2	–	27.47
C. J. L. Rogers (W Aust/Aust A)	10	3	–	12	–	–	–	–	–
Sanwar Hossain (Bangladeshis)	1	30	2	128	2	2-128	–	–	64.00
V. Sehwag (Indians)	6	27	3	101	1	1-30	–	–	101.00
† C. J. Simmons (W Aust)	1	1	–	4	–	–	–	–	–
C. P. Simpson (Qld)	6	124.1	28	407	7	3-8	–	–	58.14
M. J. Slater (NSW)	3	1	–	1	–	–	–	–	–
A. M. Staunton (S Aust)	1	24	4	92	1	1-92	–	–	92.00
H. H. Streak (Zimbabweans) ..	3	83	14	376	5	3-35	–	–	75.20
A. Symonds (Qld)	2	36	8	97	4	3-25	–	–	24.25
S. W. Tait (S Aust/Aust A)	9	256	40	957	33	5-85	1	–	29.00
Tapash Baisya (Bangladeshis) .	2	47.5	9	165	2	1-69	–	–	82.50
J. J. Taylor (W Aust)	6	136	18	615	12	4-70	–	–	51.25
S. R. Tendulkar (Indians)	6	33	–	170	3	2-36	–	–	56.67
M. J. Thistle (W Aust)	1	22	2	103	–	–	–	–	–
D. J. Thornely (NSW)	6	94	28	279	7	3-52	–	–	39.86
C. D. Thorp (W Aust)	3	92	15	344	7	3-59	–	–	49.14
† S. B. Tubb (Tas)	1	12	1	71	–	–	–	–	–
A. E. Tucker (NSW)	1	27	2	105	1	1-105	–	–	105.00
S. K. Warne (Vic)	1	36	11	100	6	4-51	–	–	16.67
D. J. Wates (W Aust)	6	167.4	33	647	16	4-77	–	–	40.44
S. R. Watson (Tas)	10	58	8	215	4	2-31	–	–	53.75
M. E. Waugh (NSW)	10	45	7	159	–	–	–	–	–
S. R. Waugh (NSW/Aust)	16	69	11	194	2	1-23	–	–	97.00

	M	O	Mdns	R	W	BB	5W/i	10W/m	Avge
C. L. White (Vic/Aust A)	12	294.1	39	1105	30	4-27	–	–	36.83
B. A. Williams (W Aust/Aust) .	4	156	42	494	15	4-53	–	–	32.93
P. Wilson (W Aust)	6	206	76	550	13	4-41	–	–	42.31
† A. B. Wise (Vic)	10	284	88	801	33	5-47	2	–	24.27
P. C. Worthington (W Aust) ...	5	114.4	27	395	12	6-59	1	–	32.92
D. G. Wright (Tas/Aust A)	10	386.5	114	1030	39	5-43	1	–	26.41
† Zaheer Khan (Indians)	3	75	11	288	6	5-95	1	–	48.00
L. A. Zammit (NSW)	3	85.2	10	349	5	2-71	–	–	69.80

INDIVIDUAL SCORES OF 100 AND OVER

There were 101 three-figure innings in 44 first-class matches in 2003-04, 30 more than in 2002-03 when the same number of matches were played. Of these, 13 were double-hundreds compared with eight in 2002-03. This list includes 76 hundreds hit in the Pura Cup, 27 more than in the 2002-03 season.

  * *Denotes not out*

M. T. G. Elliott (7)
106	Victoria v Queensland, St Kilda.
182	Victoria v Western Australia, Perth.
111	Victoria v South Australia, Adelaide.
154*	Victoria v South Australia, Melbourne.
166	Victoria v Tasmania, Melbourne.
102*	Victoria v Tasmania, Melbourne.
155	Victoria v Queensland, Melbourne.

B. J. Hodge (5)
125	Victoria v Queensland, St Kilda.
100	Victoria v Western Australia, St Kilda.
264	Victoria v Indians, Melbourne.
121	Victoria v Tasmania, Melbourne.
125	Victoria v Tasmania, Hobart (Bel).

M. W. Goodwin (4)
201*	Western Australia v New South Wales, Sydney.
104*	Western Australia v Tasmania, Perth.
156	Western Australia v Queensland, Perth.
119	Western Australia v Queensland, Brisbane.

D. J. Hussey (4)
106	Victoria v Queensland, Brisbane.
120	Victoria v New South Wales, Melbourne.
160*	Victoria v Western Australia, Perth.
212*	Victoria v New South Wales, Newcastle.

S. M. Katich (4)
182*	New South Wales v Western Australia, Sydney.
171	New South Wales v Tasmania, Hobart.
125	Australia v India, Sydney.
126	New South Wales v Victoria, Newcastle.

C. J. L. Rogers (4)
103	Western Australia v Victoria, St Kilda
120	Western Australia v Tasmania, Perth.
142	Western Australia v New South Wales, Perth.
119*	Western Australia v Queensland, Brisbane.

S. R. Watson (4)
103	Tasmania v South Australia, Hobart (Bel).
157	Tasmania v New South Wales, Sydney.
139	Tasmania v Western Australia, Hobart (Bel).
117	Tasmania v Victoria, Hobart (Bel).

S. R. Waugh (4)
100*	Australia v Bangladesh, Darwin.
156*	Australia v Bangladesh, Cairns.
117*	New South Wales v Western Australia, Sydney.
157	New South Wales v Tasmania, Hobart.

M. G. Dighton (3)
127*	Tasmania v Queensland, Hobart.
101	Tasmania v Western Australia, Hobart.
152	Tasmania v Victoria, Hobart.

M. L. Hayden (3)
380	Australia v Zimbabwe, Perth.
101*	Australia v Zimbabwe, Sydney.
136	Australia v India, Melbourne.

J. L. Langer (3)
163*	Western Australia v New South Wales, Sydney.
121	Australia v India, Brisbane.
117	Australia v India, Sydney.

D. S. Lehmann (3)
110	Australia v Bangladesh, Darwin.
177	Australia v Bangladesh, Cairns.
237	South Australia v New South Wales, Sydney.

M. L. Love (3)
100*	Australia v Bangladesh, Cairns.
300*	Queensland v Victoria, St Kilda.
100	Queensland v Tasmania, Hobart.

G. J. Mail (3)
107*	New South Wales v Tasmania, Hobart.
128	New South Wales v South Australia, Sydney.
152*	New South Wales v South Australia, Sydney.

M. J. North (3)
118   Western Australia v Tasmania, Hobart.
130   Western Australia v Queensland,
         Brisbane.
130* Western Australia v South Australia,
         Adelaide.

R. T. Ponting (3)
169   Australia v Zimbabwe, Sydney.
242   Australia v India, Adelaide.
257   Australia v India, Melbourne.

M. G. Bevan (2)
106   New South Wales v Victoria,
         Melbourne.
216   New South Wales v Tasmania, Sydney.

M. J. Cosgrove (2)
118   South Australia v New South Wales,
         Adelaide.
144   South Australia v Western Australia,
         Adelaide.

S. G. Law (2)
146* Queensland v New South Wales,
         Brisbane.
203   Queensland v Western Australia,
         Brisbane.

V. V. S. Laxman (2)
148   India v Australia, Adelaide.
178   India v Australia, Sydney.

D. J. Marsh (2)
107* Tasmania v New South Wales, Hobart.
111* Tasmania v Western Australia, Perth.

The following each played one three-figure innings:

A. J. Bichel 112, Queensland v New South Wales, Sydney; G. S. Blewett 171, South Australia v Tasmania, Hobart (Bel).

R. J. Campbell 134, Western Australia v Tasmania, Hobart (Bel); S. V. Carlisle 118, Zimbabwe v Australia, Sydney; M. J. Clarke 131*, Australians v Indians, Hobart (Bel); J. Cox 119, Tasmania v South Australia, Hobart (Bel).

M. J. Di Venuto 174*, Tasmania v New South Wales, Hobart (Bel); R. S. Dravid 233, India v Australia, Adelaide.

D. A. Fitzgerald 202*, South Australia v Tasmania, Hobart (Bel).

S. C. Ganguly 144, India v Australia, Brisbane; A. C. Gilchrist 113*, Australia v Zimbabwe, Perth.

C. D. Hartley 103, Queensland v South Australia, Brisbane; K. M. Harvey 100*, Western Australia v Tasmania, Hobart (Bel); J. R. Hopes 111, Queensland v Tasmania, Hobart (Bel); M. E. K. Hussey 138, Western Australia v Tasmania, Perth.

P. A. Jaques 146, New South Wales v Queensland, Brisbane.

J. P. Maher 116, Queensland v New South Wales, Brisbane; G. A. Manou 130, South Australia v New South Wales, Sydney; S. R. Mason 126, Tasmania v Western Australia, Hobart (Bel); S. W. Meuleman 106, Western Australia v Victoria, Perth; J. Moss 172*, Victoria v Western Australia, Perth.

A. A. Noffke 114*, Queensland v South Australia, Brisbane.

A. J. Nye 102, Queensland v New South Wales, Sydney.

C. T. Perren 141, Queensland v Western Australia, Brisbane; C. A. Philipson 101*, Queensland v Tasmania, Hobart (Bel).

W. A. Seccombe 115, Queensland v South Australia, Adelaide; V. Sehwag 195, India v Australia, Melbourne; A. Symonds 102, Queensland v South Australia, Brisbane.

S. R. Tendulkar 241*, India v Australia, Sydney; D. J. Thornely 143, New South Wales v Victoria, Newcastle.

C. B. Wishart 100, Zimbabweans v Western Australia, Perth.

TEN OR MORE WICKETS IN A MATCH

A. J. Bichel (1)
10-113 Queensland v South Australia,
Adelaide.

A. R. Kumble (1)
12-279 India v Australia, Sydney.

S. C. G. MacGill (1)
10-143 Australia v Bangladesh, Cairns.

FIVE OR MORE WICKETS IN AN INNINGS

S. C. G. MacGill (5)
5–65   Australia v Bangladesh, Darwin.
5–77   Australia v Bangladesh, Cairns.
5–66   Australia v Bangladesh, Cairns.
5–79   New South Wales v Tasmania, Hobart.
5–94   New South Wales v Victoria,
           Newcastle.

A. R. Kumble (3)
5–154 India v Australia, Adelaide.
6–176 India v Australia, Melbourne.
8–141 India v Australia, Sydney.

M. L. Lewis (2)
5–58   Victoria v Western Australia, St Kilda.
6–59   Victoria v Queensland, Melbourne.

M. J. Nicholson (2)
6–76   New South Wales v South Australia,
           Adelaide.
5–36   New South Wales v South Australia,
           Sydney.

P. C. Rofe (2)
5–89   South Australia v Western Australia,
           Perth.
7–66   South Australia v Victoria, Adelaide.

A. B. Wise (2)
5–59   Victoria v New South Wales,
           Melbourne.
5–47   Victoria v South Australia, Adelaide.

The following each took five wickets or more in an innings on one occasion:

A. B. Agarkar 6–41, India v Australia, Adelaide.

A. J. Bichel 6–61, Queensland v South Australia, Adelaide; N. W. Bracken 5–38, New South Wales v Western Australia, Perth.

B. Casson 5–109, Western Australia v Queensland, Perth; M. F. Cleary 5–102, South Australia v Tasmania, Hobart (Bel).

X. J. Doherty 6–149, Tasmania v Victoria, Melbourne; A. G. Downton 5–71, Tasmania v South Australia, Hobart (Bel).

B. M. Edmondson 5–90, Western Australia v South Australia, Adelaide.

J. N. Gillespie 5–54, South Australia v New South Wales, Adelaide.

M. S. Kasprowicz 5–84, Queensland v South Australia, Adelaide; S. M. Katich 6–65, Australia v Zimbabwe, Sydney.

B. Lee 5–124, New South Wales v Tasmania, Sydney.

A. B. McDonald 6–67, Victoria v Western Australia, Perth.

R. W. Price 6–121, Zimbabwe v Australia, Sydney.

S. W. Tait 5–85, South Australia v New South Wales, Sydney.

P. C. Worthington 6–59, Western Australia v South Australia, Perth; D. G. Wright 5–43, Tasmania v South Australia, Adelaide.

Zaheer Khan 5–95, India v Australia, Brisbane.

Pura Cup, 2003-04

by CHRISTIAN RYAN

From a batsman's perspective, seldom can motion and emotion have intertwined quite so neatly as they did in the summer of 2003-04.

Matthew Elliott pulled past Graham Yallop's all-time season run record, collected an unprecedented third player-of-the-year bauble, then confided to his team-mates: "You have helped me find a love of the game again." David Hookes's final swaggering act in first-class cricket was to urge his Victorian tyros, chasing 452 for victory in Newcastle, to think of it in terms of making 226 in 50 overs twice. They bolted it in. The man who got them there, David Hussey, reminded himself of his coach and mentor. "I guess I'm a bit like Hookesy in that I'm always trying to hit the ball to the fence. It certainly beats running." Three days later Hookes was dead.

Had Shakespeare scripted last season's Pura Cup he might have been criticised for being too morbid, for striving too hard for dramatic effect. Certainly his killing off of umpteen key cast members would have been thought unnecessarily distracting, if not downright far-fetched. Victoria's victorious captain Darren Berry waltzed into the sunset as the most successful wicket-keeper in Sheffield Shield/Pura Cup history. Gentle Joe Angel, the competition's most prolific fast bowler, hobbled off with a gammy knee and minimum of fuss. It was also the end of the road for Stuart Law, the pirate-like mastermind of Queensland's inaugural 1994-95 triumph and the last link to their bad old days, when the Banana Benders couldn't be relied on to pilfer a game before Christmas let alone the whole Shield. He signed off with a moving 203 against WA in his final first-class innings at his cherished Gabba.

If none of that brought the mist to your eyes, there was plenty more where it came from. The retiring Mark Waugh batted 18 times but was denied the farewell hundred he must have craved in his own nonchalant way. His twin brother and fellow retiree Steve was reminded, for the second time in two months, just how rare fairytale finishes are.

At least their admirers got to say goodbye. Michael Bevan, lured by a pot of gold and the assistant coaching position in Tasmania, discreetly fled New South Wales – for whom he had squirrelled nearly as many runs as Don Bradman and Victor Trumper put together – during the off-season. A week later Michael Slater quit the game at 34 because of his losing battle with ankylosing spondylitis, a form of arthritis. A batsman quick of foot and sharp of wit, so vivaciously young at heart, had conceded defeat to what is commonly reckoned an old-timer's disease.

Overhanging it all was Victoria's runaway conquest, ending a 13-year drought – the longest in the once-mighty state's history – since Simon O'Donnell last thrust the old blue shield skywards in 1990-91. Apart from being overdue, their victory radiated a shimmering sense of romance, of pre-destiny. On January 19, in high summer, their coach Hookes died at 48 in the most wrenching circumstances. Six months earlier John Scholes, one of the state's best-loved sons and another former Bushrangers coach, passed away at 53. In the year that the Ponsford, Members and Olympic Stands were turned to rubble – leaving the MCG looking, as the lyrical essayist Martin Flanagan put it, "like a face with the two front teeth missing" – a shadow of a different kind hung over the nation's grandest old coliseum.

Even if you monitored the Pura Cup from the most remote, abstract, unattached distance – is there anyone left who monitors it any other way? – you probably allowed yourself a quiet blubber at some point. Mostly, though, the tears were the bowlers'. A grand total of 76 hundreds, the highest in the competition's 111-year history, were struck in 2003-04. The bowler's equivalent of five wickets in an innings was managed only 25 times. By this calculation, the batsmen found the going three times as easy as the poor haggard blistered old footsloggers.

More amazing still was the fact that in 31 matches, with a potential 1,240 wickets up for grabs, there was just one 10-wicket haul: Andy Bichel's 6 for 61 and 4 for 52 for Queensland in Adelaide. Nineteen batsmen averaged fifty or more. Only Michael Kasprowicz, among those bowlers who took 14 or more wickets, averaged better than 24. Bat did not so much dominate as assassinate ball.

Two obvious explanations sprang to mind. First, the land is bloated with gifted strokemakers and bereft of emerging bowlers. It sounds crazy but there are more left-arm chinaman operators in

Australian domestic cricket – Beau Casson, Brad Hogg, Simon Katich, Shannon Tubb – than there are thrusting young quicks. Unique is a dangerous word. But this, surely, is not simply an Australian first but a world premiere, as those commercial TV networks who refuse to send their cameras within cooee of a Pura Cup game are fond of saying. Aside from South Australia's Shaun Tait, the up-and-coming pace larder looks empty.

The other factor is the pitches. These days, the main bounce at the once trampoline-like WACA comes off the advertising boards. The SCG still turns a little, but so slowly that the batsman's most likely mode of dismissal is keeling over with boredom. At the Gabba captains continue to bowl first sometimes, but this is down to dewy logic rather than any noticeable moisture in the wicket, and the tactic invariably backfires. The Bellerive and Adelaide Ovals are either batting featherbeds or bowlers' deathbeds, depending on your line of duty. Even the part-time wickets – Melbourne's Junction Oval, Newcastle's No. 1 Sports Ground – are not so much backstreets as roads.

Was it pure bad luck that Elliott, after clobbering 1,381 runs in the batsman's lair that is the Pura Cup, could eke out only 1 and 0 when confronted by a seaming Darwin wicket on his Test return? Or was it inevitable?

About the only batsman not to cash in was the Zimbabwean Andy Flower, whose highest score in seven matches for South Australia was 82. This made him the biggest imported flop since cuddly Roland Butcher failed to get past 53 in 10 matches for Tasmania back in 1982-83. Flower's summer-long struggle was disappointing for the connoisseurs but gave many Australians that peculiar sense of satisfaction which comes from knowing someone who averages 51 in Test cricket can't buy a run in our domestic comp.

If the wickets were flat, the cricket was anything but. At 20 years of age, Cameron White, his blond hair as spiky as Ray Bright's beard was bushy, became the first man since Bright to captain Victoria to a win at the Gabba. On a rollicking day's play in Sydney, Steve Waugh bulldozed a century, 511 runs were helter-skeltered in 89.2 overs, and NSW made 303 in the fourth innings to edge out WA. This was the domestic game at its most unmissable.

Except that virtually everyone missed it. When White led Victoria on their hoodoo-breaking Gabba rampage, only 166 diehards were there to see it. A mere 466 Sydneysiders witnessed the Blues' miraculous run-chase.

The funny thing about these two games was they took place in a November entirely free, for once, of international matches. Australia's elite players were in India that month for a one-day tournament. This anomaly presented Cricket Australia with a one-off, never-to-be-repeated chance to make the Pura Cup the hottest ticket in town. Quite the reverse happened. Those two momentous final days were scheduled on a Wednesday and Friday respectively, with the masses at work and school. People could not have gone even if they had wanted to.

All summer long crowds, to borrow the term loosely, often consisted of mums and wives and family friends. Radio coverage was minimal and TV interest non-existent; not a single match graced Australian screens. Even the big broadsheet newspapers have stopped sending a reporter along if the game is more than a 10-minute bus trip away from their offices.

This seems the most disturbing trend of all. It has long been claimed that the proportion of people who follow Australian domestic cricket is far bigger than the handful of desperados who actually go along to matches. How much longer this comforting cliché will ring true is questionable. Soon nobody may care. Yawning indifference will be the overriding emotion.

2003-04 POINTS TABLE

	Played	Won	Lost	Drawn	1st-inns Points	Points	Quotient
Victoria	10	6	0	4	4	40	1.457
Queensland	10	3	3	4	6	24	1.108
Tasmania	10	3	1	6	6	24	0.917
Western Australia	10	3	3	6	4	21	0.934
New South Wales	10	2	6	2	6	17	0.927
South Australia	10	2	6	2	0	12	0.802

Note: New South Wales penalised one point for slow over rates against Victoria at the MCG and Western Australia penalised one point for slow over rates against New South Wales at the WACA. Outright win 6 pts; lead on first innings in a drawn or lost game 2 pts. Quotient runs per wicket scored divided by runs per wicket conceded.

PURA CUP FINAL, 2003-04

VICTORIA v QUEENSLAND

At Melbourne Cricket Ground, Melbourne, March 12, 13, 14, 15, 16, 2004. Victoria won by 321 runs. *Toss:* Queensland.

As the Victorians prepared to sing their victory song, Matthew Elliott urged his team-mates to clear a space in the circle for a missing friend. One of David Hookes's final acts as coach had been to link arms with his side and belt out the words. His considerable presence, along with that of John Scholes, another former Bushrangers coach who passed away six months earlier, was felt throughout these five days. Queensland's captain Jimmy Maher said it was as if the Bulls were battling 13 players, not 11. Victoria, capping a season of sustained brilliance and bitter sorrow, fulfilled their destiny at 3.08 p.m. on the last day when their captain Darren Berry pouched the catch to dismiss Joe Dawes.

On a predictably bland MCG wicket, Maher shocked Berry by electing to field first. Victoria left out the fast bowler Matthew Inness, opting instead for Ian Harvey and a lengthy batting line-up. Matthew Elliott reeled off an effortless, irresistible hundred – his seventh of the summer – and became the highest runscorer in an Australian domestic season, eclipsing Graham Yallop's 1,254 runs in 1982-83. Andy Bichel was the only bowler to beat Elliott's bat during the entire first day, passing it once in the third over. It was Bichel who dropped the one chance Elliott offered, off Nathan Hauritz on 61, and it was Bichel who Elliott crunched for his 14th four to bring up his century. The wicket of Jason Arnberger, making a striking return to both the team and form, was the only one to fall on the first of five disheartening days. Seven batsmen had passed fifty by the time Victoria were finally dismissed shortly before lunch on day three. "We now know what it's like to literally be a Bull standing out in the grass for three days," said Maher. "The only thing we weren't doing was eating it."

Maher's mood was furthered dampened by the loss of six wickets before stumps and a serious sinus infection to Martin Love. Cameron White's accurate leg-spin claimed the important scalp of the retiring Stuart Law, one of his three victims in 35 balls after tea. Love, forced to stay in his hotel room until an hour and a half before the close, proved immovable. Helped by Dawes, an obstinate No. 11, he stretched Queensland's innings past the lunch break on day four. But still they trailed by a daunting 435 runs on the first innings. Berry chose not to enforce the follow-on and Elliott and Arnberger wasted no time in extending the lead. Arnberger blasted three consecutive sixes off Hauritz and Queensland were set an out-of-reach 576.

Moments after lecturing his men on the need to guard their wickets jealously and hang around as long as possible, Maher was dismissed first ball. White mopped up the rebound after Berry fumbled the chance. Love could linger only half an hour this time as the Queenslanders struggled to fight off a menacing and rampaging Mick Lewis, who seized a career-best 6 for 59 on the last day. Only Law, in his final first-class innings in Australia, reached fifty. The man who some Victorians believe single-handedly claimed them two Pura Cup titles in controversial circumstances, in 1999-2000 and 2000-01, was offered warm handshakes all round.

Berry, the single surviving member of Victoria's last champion side of 1990-91, held the final catch in his final game and pocketed the ball. He was mobbed by team-mates and presented with a piece of the pitch, covered in glad-wrap, by the curator Tony Ware. As the beer bottles were popped open and the celebrations began, Berry felt sure that in some distant dressing-room Hookes and Scholes were doing exactly the same thing. – NABILA AHMED

Man of the Match: M. T. G. Elliott.   *Attendance:* 25,644.

Close of play: First day, Victoria (1) 1-322 (Elliott 140, Hodge 85); Second day, Victoria (1) 6-592 (Harvey 34, McDonald 37); Third day, Queensland (1) 6-177 (Love 22, Bichel 2); Fourth day, Queensland (2) 2-56 (Perren 32, Law 8).

Victoria

M. T. G. Elliott c Hartley b Bichel	155	– (2) not out	55
J. L. Arnberger lbw b Hauritz	90	– (1) c and b Hauritz	72
B. J. Hodge c Hopes b Dawes	89	– not out	5
J. Moss c Law b Hauritz	98		
D. J. Hussey c Hartley b Noffke	16		
C. L. White c Hartley b Simpson	54		
I. J. Harvey b Noffke	62		
A. B. McDonald c (sub) Nye b Dawes	42		
*†D. S. Berry c Law b Hauritz	61		
M. L. Lewis lbw b Noffke	11		
A. B. Wise not out	1		
B 3, l-b 14, w 2, n-b 12	31	L-b 5, w 2, n-b 1	8

(212 overs, 834 mins) 710   (30 overs, 121 mins) (1 wkt dec) 140
Fall: 165 336 342 369 504 516 614 656 708 710   Fall: 119

Bowling: *First Innings*—Bichel 37–4–170–1; Dawes 38–9–97–2; Noffke 31–4–104–3; Hopes 24–5–80–0; Hauritz 50–13–145–3; Simpson 22–5–66–1; Law 9–2–26–0; Perren 1–0–5–0. *Second Innings*—Dawes 7–2–22–0; Bichel 6–0–22–0; Hopes 9–2–37–0; Hauritz 8–0–54–1.

Queensland

*J. P. Maher lbw b Moss	72	– c White b Lewis	0
C. T. Perren c Berry b Lewis	40	– lbw b Lewis	32
S. G. Law c Hussey b White	18	– (4) b White	72
C. P. Simpson lbw b White	8	– (5) c Berry b Lewis	15
J. R. Hopes lbw b White	5	– (6) c White b Harvey	31
M. L. Love not out	65	– (3) lbw b Lewis	14
†C. D. Hartley lbw b Moss	0	– not out	31
A. J. Bichel lbw b White	19	– c Elliott b Lewis	3
A. A. Noffke c Lewis b Moss	13	– lbw b McDonald	13
N. M. Hauritz b McDonald	0	– c Lewis b McDonald	33
J. H. Dawes b Harvey	21	– c Berry b Lewis	2
B 3, l-b 5, n-b 6	14	B 4, n-b 4	8

(105.5 overs, 418 mins) 275   (68.3 overs, 269 mins) 254
Fall: 85 122 132 148 157 157 201 228 229 275   Fall: 0 31 56 86 152 174 177 211
                                                     249 254

Bowling: *First Innings*—Wise 10–4–21–0; Harvey 14.5–3–41–1; Lewis 24–10–66–1; McDonald 16–4–55–1; White 30–6–66–4; Moss 11–4–18–3. *Second Innings*—Lewis 17.3–4–59–6; Harvey 14–4–43–1; McDonald 15–5–34–2; Moss 5–2–19–0; White 13–1–83–1; Hodge 4–1–12–0.

Umpires: P. D. Parker and R. L. Parry.

DOMESTIC COMPETITION RECORDS

STATISTICS, 2003-04

	M	Runs Scored	Wickets Lost	Batting Avge	Runs Conceded	Wickets Taken	Bowling Avge
New South Wales	10	6,056	160	37.85	6,248	153	40.83
Queensland	11	6,257	163	38.38	6,202	159	39.00
South Australia	10	4,953	183	27.06	5,300	157	33.75
Tasmania	10	5,695	155	36.74	6,088	152	40.05
Victoria	11	6,344	138	45.97	5,726	195	29.36
Western Australia	10	6,760	167	40.47	6,501	150	43.34

OVERS BOWLED AND RUNS SCORED, 2003-04

	Overs bowled per hour	Runs scored/ 100 balls
New South Wales	15.16	63.31
Queensland	15.25	58.34
South Australia	15.28	54.11
Tasmania	15.66	54.95
Victoria	15.24	56.68
Western Australia	15.18	61.77

LEADING BATTING AVERAGES, 2003-04

(Qualification: 500 runs)

	M	I	NO	R	HS	100s	50s	Avge	S-R
M. G. Bevan (NSW)	3	6	1	507	216	2	2	101.40	47.43
S. M. Katich (NSW)	6	12	3	896	182*	3	5	99.56	70.61
M. T. G. Elliott (Vic)	11	20	3	1,381	182	7	3	81.24	52.85
J. Moss (Vic)	11	17	3	930	172*	1	7	66.43	52.19
S. G. Law (Qld)	11	20	4	1,053	203	2	6	65.81	66.52
M. W. Goodwin (W Aust)	10	20	2	1,183	201*	4	5	65.72	64.93
J. L. Langer (W Aust)	6	11	1	622	163*	1	4	62.20	61.28
B. J. Hodge (Vic)	10	19	3	984	125	4	4	61.50	58.78
D. J. Hussey (Vic)	11	16	2	857	212*	4	2	61.21	69.85
M. L. Love (Qld)	10	18	3	893	300*	2	5	59.53	53.15

LEADING BOWLING AVERAGES, 2003-04

(Qualification: 15 wickets)

	M	O	Mdns	R	W	BB	5W/i	10W/m	Avge	S-R
J. N. Gillespie (S Aust)	2	86	21	192	11	5-54	1	0	17.45	46.91
S. J. Jurgensen (Qld)	3	122.2	35	301	13	4-52	0	0	23.15	56.46
M. S. Kasprowicz (Qld)	5	196.1	54	559	24	5-84	1	0	23.29	49.04
A. B. Wise (Vic)	10	284	88	801	33	5-47	2	0	24.27	51.64
N. W. Bracken (NSW)	4	162	60	396	16	5-38	1	0	24.75	60.75
A. B. McDonald (Vic)	10	255.1	61	846	32	6-67	1	0	26.44	47.84
D. G. Wright (Tas)	9	362.5	101	980	37	5-43	1	0	26.49	58.84
P. C. Rofe (S Aust)	9	308.5	76	946	35	7-66	2	0	27.03	52.94
J. Moss (Vic)	11	163	49	514	19	4-60	0	0	27.05	51.47
M. L. Lewis (Vic)	9	312.3	74	947	34	6-59	2	0	27.85	55.15

MOST CATCHES, 2003-04

	M	Ct
C. L. White (Vic)	10	20
M. E. K. Hussey (W Aust)	9	14
M. J. Di Venuto (Tas)	9	12
M. T. G. Elliott (Vic)	11	11
D. J. Marsh (Tas)	10	11
M. J. Cosgrove (S Aust)	8	10
S. A. Deitz (S Aust)	9	10
M. L. Love (Qld)	10	10
M. E. Waugh (NSW)	10	10

MOST DISMISSALS, 2003-04

	M	Ct	St	Total
W. A. Seccombe (Qld)	8	41	1	42
S. G. Clingeleffer (Tas)	10	28	4	32
G. A. Manou (S Aust)	10	31	0	31
R. J. Campbell (W Aust)	10	23	7	30
D. S. Berry (Vic)	6	20	3	23
B. J. Haddin (NSW)	6	18	4	22
P. J. Roach (Vic)	5	17	0	17
N. S. Pilon (NSW)	4	12	0	12
C. D. Hartley (Qld)	3	9	2	11

AUSTRALIAN DOMESTIC FIRST-CLASS COMPETITION WINNERS

Sheffield Shield

1892-93	Victoria		1935-36	South Australia
1893-94	South Australia		1936-37	Victoria
1894-95	Victoria		1937-38	New South Wales
1895-96	New South Wales		1938-39	South Australia
1896-97	New South Wales		1939-40	New South Wales
1897-98	Victoria		1940-41	–
1898-99	Victoria		1941-42	–
1899-00	New South Wales		1942-43	–
1900-01	Victoria		1943-44	–
1901-02	New South Wales		1944-45	–
1902-03	New South Wales		1945-46	–
1903-04	New South Wales		1946-47	Victoria
1904-05	New South Wales		1947-48	Western Australia
1905-06	New South Wales		1948-49	New South Wales
1906-07	New South Wales		1949-50	New South Wales
1907-08	Victoria		1950-51	Victoria
1908-09	New South Wales		1951-52	New South Wales
1909-10	South Australia		1952-53	South Australia
1910-11	New South Wales		1953-54	New South Wales
1911-12	New South Wales		1954-55	New South Wales
1912-13	South Australia		1955-56	New South Wales
1913-14	New South Wales		1956-57	New South Wales
1914-15	Victoria		1957-58	New South Wales
1915-16	–		1958-59	New South Wales
1916-17	–		1959-60	New South Wales
1917-18	–		1960-61	New South Wales
1918-19	–		1961-62	New South Wales
1919-20	New South Wales		1962-63	Victoria
1920-21	New South Wales		1963-64	South Australia
1921-22	Victoria		1964-65	New South Wales
1922-23	New South Wales		1965-66	New South Wales
1923-24	Victoria		1966-67	Victoria
1924-25	Victoria		1967-68	Western Australia
1925-26	New South Wales		1968-69	South Australia
1926-27	South Australia		1969-70	Victoria
1927-28	Victoria		1970-71	South Australia
1928-29	New South Wales		1971-72	Western Australia
1929-30	Victoria		1972-73	Western Australia
1930-31	Victoria		1973-74	Victoria
1931-32	New South Wales		1974-75	Western Australia
1932-33	New South Wales		1975-76	South Australia
1933-34	Victoria		1976-77	Western Australia
1934-35	Victoria		1977-78	Western Australia

1978-79	Victoria	1994-95	Queensland
1979-80	Victoria	1995-96	South Australia
1980-81	Western Australia	1996-97	Queensland
1981-82	South Australia	1997-98	Western Australia
1982-83	New South Wales	1998-99	Western Australia

1978-79 .... Victoria
1979-80 .... Victoria
1980-81 .... Western Australia
1981-82 .... South Australia
1982-83 .... New South Wales
1983-84 .... Western Australia
1984-85 .... New South Wales
1985-86 .... New South Wales
1986-87 .... Western Australia
1987-88 .... Western Australia
1988-89 .... Western Australia
1989-90 .... New South Wales
1990-91 .... Victoria
1991-92 .... Western Australia
1992-93 .... New South Wales
1993-94 .... New South Wales

1994-95 .... Queensland
1995-96 .... South Australia
1996-97 .... Queensland
1997-98 .... Western Australia
1998-99 .... Western Australia

Pura Milk Cup
1999-00 .... Queensland

Pura Cup
2000-01 .... Queensland
2001-02 .... Queensland
2002-03 .... New South Wales
2003-04 .... Victoria

Note: The Sheffield Shield was not played during World Wars I and II.

FINALS

1982-83 .... Western Australia lost to New South Wales at Perth by 54 runs.
1983-84 .... Western Australia defeated Queensland at Perth by four wickets.
1984-85 .... New South Wales defeated Queensland at Sydney by one wicket.
1985-86 .... New South Wales drew with Queensland at Sydney.
1986-87 .... Western Australia drew with Victoria at Perth.
1987-88 .... Western Australia defeated Queensland at Perth by five wickets.
1988-89 .... Western Australia drew with South Australia at Perth.
1989-90 .... New South Wales defeated Queensland at Sydney by 345 runs.
1990-91 .... Victoria defeated New South Wales at Melbourne by eight wickets.
1991-92 .... Western Australia defeated New South Wales at Perth by 44 runs.
1992-93 .... New South Wales defeated Queensland at Sydney by eight wickets.
1993-94 .... New South Wales defeated Tasmania at Sydney by an innings and 61 runs.
1994-95 .... Queensland defeated South Australia at Brisbane by an innings and 101 runs.
1995-96 .... South Australia drew with Western Australia at Adelaide.
1996-97 .... Western Australia lost to Queensland at Perth by 160 runs.
1997-98 .... Western Australia defeated Tasmania at Perth by seven wickets.
1998-99 .... Queensland lost to Western Australia at Brisbane by an innings and 131 runs.
1999-00 .... Queensland drew with Victoria at Brisbane.
2000-01 .... Queensland defeated Victoria at Brisbane by four wickets.
2001-02 .... Queensland defeated Tasmania at Brisbane by 235 runs.
2002-03 .... Queensland lost to New South Wales at Brisbane by 246 runs.
2003-04 .... Victoria defeated Queensland at Melbourne by 321 runs.

Note: Since 1982-83 the winner of the season's competition has been decided by the two top teams playing a final at the top-of-the-table side's choice of venue.

MATCH RESULTS, 1892-93 TO 2003-04

Opponent	Played	Won	Lost	Drawn	Tied
South Australia	699	198	311	189	1
New South Wales	709	303	199	206	1
Victoria	702	263	201	237	1
Queensland	593	169	205	218	1
Western Australia	477	163	137	177	0
Tasmania	248	46	89	113	0
Total	1,714	1,142	1,142	570	2

PLACINGS

	1st	2nd	3rd	4th	5th	6th	Seasons
South Australia	13	21	32	12	19	5	102
New South Wales	43	22	18	10	6	3	102
Victoria	26	33	22	7	7	7	102
Queensland	5	16	15	23	12	1	72
Western Australia	15	7	11	15	9	0	57
Tasmania	0	3	4	5	4	11	27
Total	102	102	102	72	57	27	102

LAST TEN YEARS' PLACINGS

	94-95	95-96	96-97	97-98	98-99	99-00	00-01	01-02	02-03	03-04
South Australia ...	2	1	6	6	4	4	6	4	4	6
New South Wales ..	5	5	3	4	6	6	3	6	1	5
Victoria	3	6	5	5	3	2	2	5	3	1
Queensland	1	3	1	3	2	1	1	1	2	2
Western Australia .	4	2	2	1	1	3	5	3	5	4
Tasmania	6	4	4	2	5	5	4	2	6	3

1,000 RUNS IN A SEASON

		M	I	NO	R	HS	100s	50s	Avge
M. T. G. Elliott (Vic).	2003-04	11	20	3	1,381	182	7	3	81.24
G. N. Yallop (Vic).	1982-83	10	18	0	1,254	246	4	5	69.66
M. G. Bevan (NSW)	1993-94	11	20	5	1,240	203*	5	7	82.67
W. H. Ponsford (Vic)	1927-28	5	8	0	1,217	437	4	1	152.12
D. M. Jones (Vic)	1994-95	10	19	3	1,216	324*	4	3	76.00
M. W. Goodwin (W Aust).	2003-04	10	20	2	1,183	201*	4	5	65.72
G. S. Blewett (S Aust).	2000-01	9	18	1	1,162	260*	3	6	68.35
J. Cox (Tas).	1996-97	10	20	1	1,149	143	4	7	60.47
B. A. Richards (S Aust).	1970-71	8	13	2	1,145	356	4	3	104.09
S. M. Katich (W Aust)	2000-01	10	19	3	1,145	228*	6	2	71.56
J. L. Langer (W Aust)	1993-94	10	18	2	1,137	233	1	6	71.06
M. L. Hayden (Qld).	1993-94	6	12	3	1,136	173*	7	1	126.22
D. F. Hills (Tas).	1997-98	11	21	1	1,132	265	4	2	56.60
J. D. Siddons (S Aust).	1992-93	10	19	2	1,116	197	4	6	65.65
M. T. G. Elliott (Vic).	1995-96	9	17	2	1,116	203	5	3	74.40
D. M. Wellham (NSW).	1982-83	11	20	5	1,109	136*	2	10	73.93
M. L. Love (Qld).	2001-02	11	20	3	1,108	202*	6	2	65.18
D. S. Lehmann (S Aust)	1994-95	10	20	1	1,104	202*	3	6	58.11
D. S. Lehmann (S Aust)	1995-96	11	21	1	1,099	161	4	6	54.95
R. B. McCosker (NSW)	1982-83	11	21	3	1,096	124	3	9	60.88
W. H. Ponsford (Vic)	1926-27	5	8	0	1,091	352	5	2	136.37
S. G. Law (Qld).	1990-91	10	18	4	1,087	142*	3	8	77.64
J. P. Maher (Qld).	2001-02	9	17	1	1,085	209	5	3	67.81
J. Cox (Tas).	2000-01	10	19	3	1,070	160	5	3	66.88
D. S. Lehmann (S Aust)	1993-94	10	17	0	1,065	200	4	4	62.65
D. G. Bradman (S Aust)	1939-40	6	10	2	1,062	267	3	4	132.75
A. D. Ogilvie (Qld)	1977-78	9	18	2	1,060	194	6	2	66.25
S. G. Law (Qld).	2003-04	11	20	4	1,053	203	2	6	65.81
T. M. Moody (W Aust)	1988-89	11	18	1	1,038	202	4	3	61.06
M. T. G. Elliott (Vic).	1999-00	10	19	4	1,028	183*	4	4	68.53
K. C. Wessels (Qld）	1981-82	9	15	0	1,015	220	5	2	67.66
D. F. Hills (Tas).	1993-94	11	21	1	1,015	185*	3	7	50.75
D. W. Hookes (S Aust)	1987-88	10	18	1	1,014	132	3	7	59.65
G. M. Wood (W Aust).	1987-88	11	16	3	1,014	186*	3	5	78.00
G. S. Chappell (Qld)	1973-74	7	13	2	1,013	180	4	3	92.09
J. Dyson (NSW)	1983-84	10	18	3	1,006	241	3	3	67.07

		M	I	NO	R	HS	100s	50s	Avge
N. C. O'Neill (NSW)	1957-58	8	14	2	1,005	233	4	3	83.75
M. J. Slater (NSW)	1992-93	9	17	1	1,005	143	3	6	62.81

* Denotes not out.

MOST RUNS IN A CAREER

	M	I	NO	R	HS	100s	50s	Avge
D. S. Lehmann (S Aust/Vic)	125	227	14	11,467	255	38	44	53.84
J. D. Siddons (Vic/S Aust)	146	259	21	10,643	245	30	50	44.72
J. Cox (Tas)	153	279	17	10,459	245	30	44	39.92
D. M. Jones (Vic)	110	194	16	9,622	324*	31	40	54.06
D. W. Hookes (S Aust)	120	205	9	9,364	306*	26	44	47.78
R. J. Inverarity (W Aust/S Aust)	159	275	32	9,341	187	22	46	38.44
S. G. Law (Qld)	142	234	28	9,034	216	24	47	43.85
D. G. Bradman (NSW/S Aust)	62	96	15	8,926	452*	36	20	110.19
M. T. G. Elliott (Vic)	93	178	16	8,885	203	31	38	54.85
T. M. Moody (W Aust)	132	228	22	8,853	272	20	46	42.98
G. S. Chappell (S Aust/Qld)	101	173	20	8,762	194	27	44	57.27
S. C. Trimble (Qld)	123	230	13	8,647	252*	22	40	39.85
M. G. Bevan (S Aust/NSW)	99	175	33	8,512	216	33	35	59.94
A. R. Border (NSW/Qld)	108	181	19	8,497	200	19	47	52.45
L. E. Favell (S Aust)	121	220	4	8,269	164	20	43	38.28
G. S. Blewett (S Aust)	100	190	10	8,794	268	23	43	48.86
D. C. Boon (Tas)	119	203	7	8,029	227	20	43	40.96
M. L. Love (Qld)	102	176	16	7,668	300*	18	33	47.93
I. M. Chappell (S Aust)	89	157	13	7,665	205*	22	45	53.22
A. M. J. Hilditch (NSW/S Aust)	109	192	11	7,613	230	18	41	42.06
J. L. Langer (W Aust)	83	150	12	7,353	274*	22	26	53.28
M. L. Hayden (Qld)	82	149	17	7,332	234	24	30	55.13
M. R. J. Veletta (W Aust)	114	198	20	7,306	262	18	40	41.04
M. E. Waugh (NSW)	93	158	18	7,232	229*	23	30	51.66
P. J. P. Burge (Qld)	83	138	12	7,084	283	22	31	56.22
M. J. Di Venuto (Tas)	104	182	7	7,043	189	11	52	40.25
G. R. Marsh (W Aust)	100	175	12	7,009	355*	21	28	43.00

* Denotes not out.

HIGHEST PARTNERSHIPS FOR EACH WICKET

431 for 1st	M. R. J. Veletta and G. R. Marsh		
	Western Australia v South Australia at Perth		1989-90
386 for 2nd	G. S. Blewett and D. S. Lehmann		
	South Australia v Tasmania at Hobart (Bel).		2001-02
390* for 3rd	J. M. Wiener and J. K. Moss		
	Victoria v Western Australia at St. Kilda		1981-82
462* for 4th	D. W. Hookes and W. B. Phillips		
	South Australia v Tasmania at Adelaide		1986-87
464* for 5th	M. E. Waugh and S. R. Waugh		
	New South Wales v Western Australia at Perth		1990-91
332 for 6th	N. G. Marks and G. Thomas		
	New South Wales v South Australia at Sydney		1958-59
335 for 7th	C. W. Andrews and E. C. Bensted		
	Queensland v New South Wales at Sydney		1934-35
270 for 8th	V. T. Trumper and E. P. Barbour		
	New South Wales v Victoria at Sydney		1912-13
232 for 9th	C. Hill and E. A. Walkley		
	South Australia v New South Wales at Adelaide		1900-01
307 for 10th	A. F. Kippax and J. E. H. Hooker		
	New South Wales v Victoria at Melbourne		1928-29

* Denotes unbroken partnership.

MOST WICKETS IN A SEASON

		M	Balls	Mdns	R	W	BB	5W/i	10W/m	Avge
C. R. Miller (Tas)	1997-98	11	3,590	159	1,642	67	7-49	5	0	24.51
L. O. Fleetwood-Smith (Vic)	1934-35	6	2,164	25	1,137	60	8-113	8	0	18.95
P. R. Reiffel (Vic)	1999-00	11	2,552	118	982	59	5-65	1	0	16.64
C. D. Matthews (W Aust)	1987-88	11	2,553	81	1,215	56	8-101	3	0	21.70
J. Garner (S Aust)	1982-83	8	2,419	131	976	55	7-78	4	0	17.74
C. J. McDermott (Qld)	1989-90	10	1,392	100	1,375	54	8-44	4	0	25.46
A. J. Bichel (Qld)	1999-00	11	2,421	124	989	53	6-45	2	1	18.66
W. J. O'Reilly (NSW)	1939-40	6	1,766	48	705	52	8-23	6	0	13.55
G. R. A. Lock (W Aust)	1966-67	8	2,392	104	1,086	51	6-85	3	0	21.29
B. A. Williams (W Aust)	1999-00	10	2,194	94	1,151	50	6-74	5	0	23.02
A. L. Thomson (Vic)	1969-70	8	2,104	42	876	49	8-87	5	2	17.88
A. A. Mallett (S Aust)	1972-73	8	2,551	89	893	49	5-41	3	0	18.22
J. H. Dawes (Qld)	2000-01	9	2,151	101	1,003	49	7-98	3	1	20.47
G. R. J. Matthews (NSW)	1991-92	11	2,704	145	1,023	49	6-63	4	2	20.88
C. V. Grimmett (S Aust)	1934-35	6	2,214	35	1,043	49	9-180	5	3	21.29
P. R. Reiffel (Vic)	1990-91	10	2,585	118	1,053	49	6-57	3	2	21.49
M. S. Kasprowicz (Qld)	2001-02	9	2,369	85	1,082	49	5-44	2	0	22.08
C. V. Grimmett (S Aust)	1939-40	6	2,478	33	1,215	49	6-118	5	2	24.80

MOST WICKETS IN A CAREER

	M	Balls	Mdns	R	W	BB	5W/i	10W/m	Avge
C. V. Grimmett (Vic/S Aust)	79	28,465	446	12,976	513	9-180	48	13	25.29
J. Angel (W Aust)	105	22,351	1,033	10,418	419	6-35	13	0	24.86
M. S. Kasprowicz (Qld)	89	19,599	843	9,409	387	6-47	24	2	24.31
T. M. Alderman (W Aust)	97	19,288	778	9,299	384	7-28	17	3	24.21
C. G. Rackemann (Qld)	102	22,400	920	10,079	383	7-43	12	1	26.32
G. F. Lawson (NSW)	103	21,391	873	8,742	367	6-31	12	0	23.82
G. R. J. Matthews (NSW)	116	26,764	1,376	10,518	363	8-52	19	4	28.98
J. R. Thomson (NSW-Qld)	84	16,939	429	8,591	355	7-27	18	3	24.20
A. A. Mallett (S Aust)	77	20,906	673	8,173	344	7-57	19	2	23.76
D. K. Lillee (W Aust/Tas)	75	17,814	475	8,086	338	7-36	18	4	23.92
P. R. Reiffel (Vic)	86	19,137	843	8,242	318	6-57	7	2	25.92
C. D. Matthews (W Aust/Tas)	79	17,663	614	8,912	307	8-101	18	0	29.03
C. R. Miller (S Aust/Vic/Tas)	84	20,285	820	9,738	304	7-49	11	2	32.03
C. J. McDermott (Qld)	67	14,974	541	7,605	303	8-44	22	2	25.10
G. A. R. Lock (W Aust)	63	20,107	544	7,210	302	7-53	16	2	23.87
A. N. Connolly (Vic)	71	18,033	365	7,745	297	9-67	12	4	26.00
B. P. Julian (W Aust)	87	16,143	612	8,573	292	7-39	15	2	29.36
A. I. C. Dodemaide (Vic)	94	19,892	822	8,884	281	6-67	12	0	31.62
A. R. Bichel (Qld)	56	12,455	525	6,112	274	6-45	15	3	22.31
J. W. Martin (NSW/S Aust)	77	17,078	242	8,703	273	8-97	12	0	31.87
T. B. A. May (S Aust)	80	22,575	931	9,943	270	7-93	15	2	36.83
M. G. Hughes (Vic)	76	16,762	582	8,169	267	7-81	10	2	30.60
R. Benaud (NSW)	73	17,811	471	7,174	266	7-32	11	3	26.96
G. Dymock (Qld)	75	17,110	449	7,223	266	6-79	8	0	27.15
D. Tazelaar (Qld)	73	15,371	623	7,050	257	6-48	9	1	27.43
P. R. Sleep (S Aust)	127	19,467	671	9,893	254	8-133	7	0	38.94
R. J. Bright (Vic)	101	22,789	1,013	8,833	252	6-61	10	0	35.05
M. R. Whitney (NSW)	77	14,983	562	7,314	251	7-75	10	0	29.14

MOST CATCHES IN A CAREER – FIELDER

R. J. Inverarity (W Aust/S Aust)	189 in 159 matches
J. D. Siddons (Vic/S Aust)	189 in 146 matches
M. R. J. Veletta (W Aust)	138 in 114 matches
S. G. Law (Qld)	126 in 142 matches
D. W. Hookes (S Aust)	123 in 120 matches
M. A. Taylor (NSW)	120 in 85 matches
M. T. G. Elliott (Vic)	120 in 93 matches
A. R. Border (NSW/Qld)	117 in 108 matches
M. L. Love (Qld)	117 in 102 matches
I. M. Chappell (S Aust)	114 in 89 matches
T. M. Moody (W Aust)	114 in 132 matches
M. E. Waugh (NSW)	112 in 93 matches
J. P. Maher (Qld)	110 in 101 matches
D. F. Whatmore (Vic)	109 in 85 matches
G. S. Chappell (S Aust/Qld)	103 in 101 matches
G. R. J. Matthews (NSW)	102 in 116 matches
M. J. Di Venuto (Tas)	101 in 104 matches

MOST DISMISSALS IN A CAREER

	M	Ct	St	Total
D. S. Berry (S Aust/Vic)	139	499	47	546
W. A. Seccombe (Qld)	93	436	12	448
T. J. Zoehrer (W Aust)	107	331	28	359
R. W. Marsh (W Aust)	81	311	33	344
P. A. Emery (NSW)	109	298	41	339
J. A. Maclean (Qld)	86	289	24	313
T. J. Nielsen (S Aust)	92	255	29	284
A. T. W. Grout (Qld)	84	213	63	276
S. J. Rixon (NSW)	94	218	43	261
M. N. Atkinson (Tas)	84	236	25	261
A. C. Gilchrist (NSW/W Aust)	51	250	8	258
B. N. Jarman (S Aust)	77	193	57	250

MOST APPEARANCES

159	R. J. Inverarity (W Aust/S Aust)	1962-63 – 1984-85
153	J. Cox (Tas)	1987-88 – 2003-04
146	J. D. Siddons (Vic/S Aust)	1984-85 – 1999-00
142	S. G. Law (Qld)	1988-89 – 2003-04
139	D. S. Berry (S Aust/Vic)	1989-90 – 2003-04
132	T. M. Moody (W Aust)	1985-86 – 2000-01
127	P. R. Sleep (S Aust)	1976-77 – 1992-93
125	D. S. Lehmann (S Aust/Vic)	1987-88 – 2003-04
123	S. C. Trimble (Qld)	1959-60 – 1975-76
121	L. E. Favell (S Aust)	1951-52 – 1969-70
120	D. W. Hookes (S Aust)	1975-76 – 1991-92
119	D. C. Boon (Tas)	1978-79 – 1998-99
116	G. R. J. Matthews (NSW)	1982-83 – 1997-98
114	M. R. J. Veletta (W Aust)	1983-84 – 1994-95
110	D. M. Wellham (NSW/Tas/Qld)	1980-81 – 1993-94
110	D. M. Jones (Vic)	1981-82 – 1997-98
109	G. M. Wood (W Aust)	1977-78 – 1991-92
109	A. M. J. Hilditch (NSW/S Aust)	1976-77 – 1991-92
109	P. A. Emery (NSW)	1989-90 – 1998-99
108	A. R. Border (NSW/Qld)	1976-77 – 1995-96
107	H. N. Dansie (S Aust)	1949-50 – 1966-67
107	T. J. Zoehrer (W Aust)	1980-81 – 1993-94

105	T. V. Hohns (Qld)		1972-73 – 1990-91
105	J. Angel (W Aust)		1991-92 – 2003-04
104	S. Young (Tas)		1991-92 – 2001-02
104	M. J. Di Venuto (Tas)		1991-92 – 2003-04
103	G. F. Lawson (NSW)		1977-78 – 1991-92
102	C. G. Rackemann (Qld)		1979-80 – 1995-96
102	M. L. Love (Qld)		1992-93 – 2003-04
101	G. S. Chappell (S Aust/Qld)		1966-67 – 1983-84
101	R. J. Bright (Vic)		1972-73 – 1987-88
101	J. P. Maher (Qld)		1993-94 – 2003-04
100	K. D. Mackay (Qld)		1946-47 – 1963-64
100	G. R. Marsh (W Aust)		1977-78 – 1993-94
100	T. J. Barsby (Qld)		1984-85 – 1996-97
100	D. F. Hills (Tas)		1991-92 – 2001-02
100	G. S. Blewett (S Aust)		1991-92 – 2003-04

PLAYED FOR THREE OR MORE STATES

				Batting			Bowling	
			M	R	Avge	W	Avge	Ct
G. D. Watson	Vic	(1964-65 – 1970-71)	34	1,555	32.40	53	26.57	20
	W Aust	(1971-72 – 1974-75)	22	997	31.16	54	24.37	25
	NSW	(1976–77)	4	122	20.33	8	22.50	1
	Total		60	2,674	31.09	115	25.25	46
G. J. Cosier	Vic	(1971-72 & 1980-81)	4	133	22.17	2	43.00	2
	SAust	(1974-75 – 1976-77)	20	1,059	29.42	34	22.18	17
	Qld	(1977-78 – 1979-80)	22	1,295	35.97	16	36.75	22
	Total		46	2,487	31.88	52	27.46	41
T. M. Chappell	SAust	(1972-73 – 1975-76)	14	473	18.92	1	60.00	6
	W Aust	(1976-77)	4	160	40.00	–	–	2
	NSW	(1979-80 – 1984-85)	45	2,320	32.68	51	21.06	29
	Total		63	2,953	29.53	52	21.90	37
R. J. McCurdy	Tas	(1980-81)	5	45	4.50	17	34.82	3
	Vic	(1981-82 – 1983-84)	20	239	12.58	67	34.19	7
	SAust	(1984-85)	8	128	12.80	36	29.47	5
	Total		33	412	10.56	120	32.87	15
D. M. Wellham	NSW	(1980-81 – 1986-87)	59	3,812	44.33	0	–	28
	Tas	(1988-89 – 1990-91)	30	1,600	41.03	0	–	12
	Qld	(1991-92 – 1993-94)	21	1,327	39.03	0	–	13
	Total		110	6,739	42.38	0	–	53
C. R. Miller	Vic	(1985-86 – 2001-02)	10	88	7.33	27	42.46	2
	SAust	(1988-89 – 1991-92)	20	274	13.05	67	28.96	6
	Tas	(1992-93 – 1999-00)	54	783	15.35	210	31.70	17
	Total		84	1,145	13.63	304	32.03	25
G. J. Rowell	NSW	(1989-90 – 1990-91)	3	77	25.67	11	26.09	1
	Qld	(1991-92 – 1997-98)	34	400	10.81	116	29.80	18
	Tas	(1998-99)	6	12	4.00	18	25.50	3
	Total		43	489	11.37	145	28.99	22
S. J. Jurgensen	W Aust	(1998-99)	1	3	–	1	135.00	0
	Tas	(2000-01 – 2002-03)	17	228	12.67	54	28.72	1
	Qld	(2003-04)	3	6	2.00	13	23.15	1
	Total		21	237	11.29	68	29.22	2

NEW SOUTH WALES

The mighty go meekly

by TREVOR MARSHALLSEA

Pura Cup: Fifth
ING Cup: Fourth
Coach: Steve Rixon
Captain: Steve Waugh

Simon Katich

Two years ago New South Wales transformed themselves from wooden-spooners
to Pura Cup champions. Last year they
again produced a result that was almost the
direct opposite to the year before: from first
to second-last. The fact that they still had a
mathematical chance of reaching the final in the last round of Pura
Cup matches flattered them, for after a stirring first-up victory they
won only one game in their last nine. It was a disastrous defence of
their domestic double all-round, as they won only half their one-day
matches in pursuit of a fourth straight ING Cup title. As a farewell
to the Waugh twins and coach Steve Rixon – and, as it turned out,
to Michael Bevan and Michael Slater too – it was all decidedly anticlimactic.

Steve Waugh began with a couple of masterful centuries – 117
not out against Western Australia, 157 against Tasmania – in his
first three innings. He was moderate thereafter. From the moment
he decided to retire, after the second game in Hobart, he strung together only 286 runs at 26. He bowed out of first-class cricket at the
SCG, signing off with an innings of nine and a defeat to Queensland
in damp and difficult conditions.

His brother Mark displayed even fewer glimpses of his old
magic. His lifelong propensity for throwing away a good start appeared to have worsened with age, as he made only one half-century in NSW's first seven games. His subsequent 90 in Brisbane, and
a quickfire 72 which almost snatched a last-gasp win against
Queensland, were too little too late. Waugh's contribution was further marred when he was finally given a chance to captain his state,

against Victoria at the MCG, only to see the Blues docked a point for slow over-rates.

The malaise seeped into his one-day performances too; he made 197 runs at 28 in one of his worst efforts ever. The unavoidable conclusion was that the laid-back stylist who gave so much pleasure over the years had played on one summer too long. Indeed, he retired without a state hundred in either form of the game in his last two seasons.

Like the Waughs, the Blues lost their way in both competitions. A talent-packed squad who had recruited wisely, they did not win once in seven Pura Cup games between November 7 and February 17, earning only six out of a possible 42 points. It was a similar story in the ING Cup, where they won three of their first four matches then lost the next four.

So often in the Pura Cup, NSW built strong positions only to fail to deliver the killer punch at crucial moments. Twice they squandered winning positions by failing to defend luxurious second-innings leads, admittedly on magnificent batting wickets. Tasmania amassed 4 for 386 to win in Hobart and Victoria 7 for 455 in Newcastle, the second largest winning fourth-innings score in the competition's history. South Australia came tantalisingly close to recording an even bigger surprise in the penultimate round in Sydney, making 495 in pursuit of a world-record 521.

Apart from their unenviable record at defending targets, NSW suffered a lack of consistency from several leading batsmen. Many exhibited the same problem that beset the team as a whole: an inability to capitalise on sound starts. The average opening partnership was only 30, compared to the 44 of champions Victoria. Only three batsmen averaged over 40, and bigger things were required from the likes of Phil Jaques and Dominic Thornely.

In NSW's defence, they fielded a severely depleted line-up for much of the season. International demands restricted the dashing Michael Clarke to two Pura Cup games. Michael Bevan was in superb touch but played only three matches. The leading runscorer in the state's history, Bevan's switch to Tasmania during the off-season will leave a certain emptiness in both the hearts and scorebooks of Blues followers. Michael Slater also played only three games and also bid farewell during the winter, announcing his retirement because of his ongoing battle with ankylosing spondylitis, an arthritis-like disease that affects the spine.

There were patches of bright news. The opening batsman Greg Mail blossomed with three centuries. Simon Katich's Test recall in October sparked a magnificent summer for him at domestic level, topping the state's aggregate with 896 runs at 99.55. He also made two centuries in six ING Cup innings, was named state player of the year at the Allan Border Medal and collected the Steve Waugh Medal as NSW's finest.

In the bowling department Matthew Nicholson proved to be the buy of the season. Returning home from WA, and demonstrating an uncanny knack of grabbing a wicket in the first over of a new spell, he led the Pura Cup wicket-taking table with 39 scalps at 30.35. He was rewarded with Australia A selection against India in Hobart. Brett Lee took 10 wickets in two matches between bouts of ankle surgery and international commitments. Nathan Bracken, also on Australian duty for much of the season, bowled tightly for 16 wickets in his four games.

Heading the ING Cup wicket-takers list was the leg-spinner Stuart MacGill, with 20 wickets at 15.90. He also collected 25 wickets in six Pura Cup matches, although invariably at some expense. His average of 43.64 and economy-rate of 61 runs conceded per hundred balls were the highest of his interstate first-class career. The back-up spin options at NSW, once home to a factory line of slow bowlers of all varieties, remain weak. Liam Zammit, a rookie leg-spinner, managed only five wickets in three games. Eventually the selectors, in desperation, recalled the 34-year-old Adrian Tucker for his first game in a decade in the last round against Queensland.

It is tempting to report that the bowlers were more dependable than the batsmen. And yet their defence of some big targets was woeful. It is tempting, too, to suggest that it reflected badly on the otherwise superb record of their retiring captain Steve Waugh. Perhaps, overall, it is fairest to say that NSW significantly under-achieved on all fronts.

NEW SOUTH WALES RESULTS, 2003-04

All first-class matches – Played 10: Won 2, Lost 6, Drawn 2.
Pura Cup – Played 10: Won 2, Lost 6, Drawn 2.
ING Cup matches – Played 10: Won 5, Lost 4, Tied 1.

Back row: A. E. Tucker, N. S. Pilon, A. W. O'Brien, S. D. Bradstreet, P. A. Jaques, L. A. Zammit, D. A. Nash. *Middle row:* T. H. Bayliss, D. Kerr *(Room attendant)*, G. J. Mail, D. J. Thornely, G. M. Lambert, N. W. Bracken, S. R. Clark, G. D. McGrath, M. J. Nicholson, D. Bollinger, M. J. Phelps, Patrick Farhart, S. J. Rixon *(Coach)*. *Front row:* M. G. Bevan, M. J. Slater, S. R. Waugh, M. E. Waugh, M. J. Clarke, B. J. Haddin.

PURA CUP AVERAGES, 2003-04

BATTING

	M	I	NO	R	HS	100s	50s	Avge	Ct/St	S-R
M. G. Bevan	3	6	1	507	216	2	2	101.40	0	47.43
S. M. Katich	6	12	3	896	182*	3	5	99.56	6	70.61
B. Lee	2	3	1	114	74*	0	1	57.00	1	55.61
M. J. Phelps	1	2	0	101	62	0	1	50.50	0	63.92
G. J. Mail	10	18	2	754	152*	3	2	47.13	6	50.54
S. R. Waugh	8	15	1	560	157	2	2	40.00	3	70.00
B. J. Haddin	6	11	2	351	76	0	3	39.00	18/4	73.43
M. E. Waugh	10	18	2	598	90	0	3	37.38	10	62.62
P. A. Jaques	10	20	0	636	146	1	4	31.80	6	75.09
D. J. Thornely	6	12	0	343	143	1	2	28.58	4	49.93
N. S. Pilon	4	8	1	197	78	0	2	28.14	12	62.54
G. M. Lambert	2	3	0	72	38	0	0	24.00	1	71.29
M. J. Clarke	2	4	0	74	27	0	0	18.50	3	55.22
S. C. G. MacGill	6	5	3	36	13*	0	0	18.00	1	69.23
M. J. Slater	3	6	0	106	45	0	0	17.67	1	55.50
M. J. Nicholson	9	14	3	177	42	0	0	16.09	5	42.45
D. A. Nash	3	6	0	96	46	0	0	16.00	1	60.00
S. R. Clark	8	10	5	75	20	0	0	15.00	2	54.74
N. W. Bracken	4	4	1	43	27	0	0	14.33	1	71.67
A. E. Tucker	1	1	0	12	12	0	0	12.00	0	150.00
L. A. Zammit	3	4	0	32	15	0	0	8.00	4	43.84
A. W. O'Brien	1	2	0	7	7	0	0	3.50	1	41.18
G. D. McGrath	1	1	0	2	2	0	0	2.00	0	28.57
D. Bollinger	1	1	1	2	2*	0	0	–	0	8.00

* Denotes not out.

BOWLING

	O	Mdns	R	W	BB	5W/i	10W/m	Avge	S-R
N. W. Bracken	162	60	396	16	5-38	1	0	24.75	60.75
G. D. McGrath	28.1	14	60	2	2-43	0	0	30.00	84.50
M. J. Nicholson	343	64	1184	39	6-76	2	0	30.36	52.77
B. Lee	95	14	343	10	5-124	1	0	34.30	57.00
S. R. Clark	289.2	57	880	23	4-52	0	0	38.26	75.48
D. J. Thornely	94	28	279	7	3-52	0	0	39.86	80.57
S. M. Katich	59.5	3	244	6	4-42	0	0	40.67	59.83
S. C. G. MacGill	255.5	42	1091	25	5-79	2	0	43.64	61.40
D. A. Nash	79	22	265	5	2-70	0	0	53.00	94.80
M. J. Clarke	18	5	63	1	1-47	0	0	63.00	108.00
S. R. Waugh	16	0	65	1	1-23	0	0	65.00	96.00
L. A. Zammit	85.2	10	349	5	2-71	0	0	69.80	102.40
G. M. Lambert	64.5	22	212	3	2-55	0	0	70.67	129.67
D. Bollinger	23	5	87	1	1-87	0	0	87.00	138.00
G. J. Mail	39	8	177	2	2-57	0	0	88.50	117.00
A. W. O'Brien	20	1	95	1	1-54	0	0	95.00	120.00
A. E. Tucker	27	2	105	1	1-105	0	0	105.00	162.00
P. A. Jaques	2	0	10	0	–	0	0	–	–
N. S. Pilon	1	1	0	0	–	0	0	–	–
M. J. Slater	1	0	1	0	–	0	0	–	–
M. E. Waugh	45	7	159	0	–	0	0	–	–

NEW SOUTH WALES v WESTERN AUSTRALIA

At Sydney Cricket Ground, Sydney, November 4, 5, 6, 7, 2003. New South Wales won by five wickets. *Toss:* Western Australia. New South Wales 6 pts. *First-class debut:* J. J. Taylor, L. A. Zammit.

Steve Waugh started his 20th and final interstate campaign by leading his side on a stunning run-chase. On a last day when 511 runs were scored in 89.2 overs, Waugh's unbeaten hundred and a superb half-century by Simon Katich guided the Blues to their target of 303, with only 47.2 of a possible 52 overs used. In a strangely scheduled match – play on day one was halted for a 10-minute drinks break while the Melbourne Cup was run – WA's captain Justin Langer chose to bat first. His side's position would have been forlorn if not for Murray Goodwin's beautiful unbeaten 201 (434 minutes, 320 balls, 32 fours). His confidence boosted by a Test recall, Katich led the response with his first century for his adopted state as they posted a 60-run lead. Langer regained form himself with another big hundred, before declaring midway through the last day. The fast bowler Matthew Nicholson hinted at an impressive season to come in his first match since returning home to Sydney from Perth. A re-jigged NSW batting order slumped until Waugh and Phil Jaques added 99 for the fourth wicket. Their task still looked stiff when Katich, returning from hospital treatment on a damaged thumb, joined his skipper at 5 for 215 in the 36th over. Ignoring the pain, Katich cracked an astounding 71 off 45 balls, scoring the lion's share of an 88-run stand in 11.4 overs to secure victory. Waugh judged Katich's display as one of the finest run-chase knocks he had seen.

Match reports by TREVOR MARSHALLSEA.

Man of the Match: S. M. Katich.   *Attendance:* 1,963.

Close of play: First day, Western Australia (1) 8-350 (Goodwin 184, Thorp 9); Second day, New South Wales (1) 5-273 (Katich 101, Pilon 70); Third day, Western Australia (2) 1-154 (Langer 81, Casson 17).

Western Australia

*J.L. Langer c Mail b Nicholson	4	– not out	163
M.E.K. Hussey lbw b Nicholson	0	– c Jaques b S.R. Waugh	53
M.W. Goodwin not out	201	– (4) c Pilon b Nicholson	0
M.J. North lbw b Zammit	26	– (5) c Pilon b Zammit	28
†R.J. Campbell c Katich b Clark	34	– (6) b Nicholson	58
S.E. Marsh b Zammit	29	– (8) c Nicholson b Clark	14
P.C. Worthington c Katich b Mail	19	– c Jaques b Clark	11
B. Casson b Mail	5	– (3) b Nicholson	21
J.J. Taylor lbw b Nash	26	– c Clark b Nicholson	7
C.D. Thorp c and b Katich	18		
P. Wilson b Nash	0		
L-b 5, n-b 9	14	B 1, l-b 5, n-b 1	7

(108 overs, 438 mins) 376   (88 overs, 336 mins)   (8 wkts dec) 362

Fall: 4 11 80 144 196 247 265 313 375 376   Fall: 134 178 182 219 311 326 354 362

Bowling: *First Innings*—Nicholson 25–3–79–2; Nash 20–4–70–2; Clark 26–4–72–1; Mail 12–3–57–2; Zammit 17–1–71–2; Katich 8–0–22–1. *Second Innings*—Nicholson 18–4–69–4; Nash 12–4–44–0; Clark 13–3–55–2; Zammit 18–3–84–1; Katich 7–0–33–0; M.E. Waugh 10–1–33–0; S. R. Waugh 7–0–23–1; Slater 1–0–1–0; Mail 2–0–14–0.

New South Wales

M. J. Slater c Langer b Casson	45	– lbw b Thorp	17
G. J. Mail c Wilson b Marsh	38		
S. M. Katich not out	182	– (7) not out	71
*S. R. Waugh lbw b Casson	0	– not out	117
P. A. Jaques st Campbell b North	0	– c Worthington b North	43
M. E. Waugh b Casson	10	– b Casson	13
†N. S. Pilon b Marsh b Thorp	78	– (2) b Wilson	19
D. A. Nash c North b Thorp	9	– (3) c Worthington b Wilson	13
M. J. Nicholson c Hussey b Worthington	42		
S. R. Clark c and b Casson	13		
L. A. Zammit st Campbell b Marsh	0		
B 4, l-b 4, w 3, n-b 8	19	B 4, w 2, n-b 4	10

(131 overs, 489 mins)   436   (47.2 overs, 187 mins)   (5 wkts) 303

Fall: 58 90 92 93 127 285 322 406 433 436   Fall: 33 43 70 169 215

Bowling: *First Innings*—Nicholson 25–3–79–2; Nash 20–4–70–2; Clark 26–4–72–1; Mail 12–3–57–2; Zammit 17–1–71–2; Katich 8–0–22–1. *Second Innings*—Nicholson 18–4–69–4; Nash 12–4–44–0; Clark 13–3–55–2; Zammit 18–3–84–1; Katich 7–0–33–0; M. E. Waugh 10–1–33–0; S. R. Waugh 7–0–23–1; Slater 1–0–1–0; Mail 2–0–14–0.

Umpires: S. J. Davis and D. B. Hair.

At Bellerive Oval, Hobart, November 12, 13, 14, 15, 2003. NEW SOUTH WALES lost to TASMANIA by six wickets.

At Adelaide Oval, Adelaide, November 18, 19, 20, 21, 2003. NEW SOUTH WALES lost to SOUTH AUSTRALIA by five wickets.

At Melbourne Cricket Ground, Melbourne, December 12, 13, 14, 15, 2003. NEW SOUTH WALES lost to VICTORIA by two wickets.

NEW SOUTH WALES v TASMANIA

At Sydney Cricket Ground, Sydney, December 19, 20, 21, 22, 2003. Match drawn. *Toss:* Tasmania. New South Wales 2 pts.

Cricket's tendency towards the bizarre was confirmed once more as Tasmania played out a draw with scores level for the second time in 12 days – a result that had never previously occurred under the points system adopted in 1986. The game ended when Simon Katich and Nathan Pilon could run only two instead of three off Xavier Doherty's last ball. New South Wales, desperate for points after three straight defeats, were furious. Tasmania again drew accusations that they let their opponents do all the work to make a result possible. With Ricky Ponting opting not to play, the main talking point after a dull Tasmanian first innings was Brett Lee's five-wicket haul, a typically expensive one, in his second match back from ankle surgery. The Blues also took their time in their first innings, Michael Bevan becoming the first NSW player to reach 9,000 first-class runs. His 216 (484 minutes, 416 balls, 30 fours, one six) was his highest score and the fifth double-century of his long career. Meandering to a 140-run first-innings lead, NSW had Tasmania 2 for 105 on the fourth morning and a result looked unlikely. It soon looked impossible as the visitors, missing the injured Michael Di Venuto, dawdled along. Shane Watson's 157, including 26 fours, continued his impressive comeback from back stress fractures. New South Wales were left needing to make 176 in 22 overs. Thanks to Phil Jaques' 60-ball 85, they came tantalisingly close.

Man of the Match: M. G. Bevan.   *Attendance:* 3,632.
Close of play: First day, Tasmania (1) 8–270 (Clingeleffer 19, Griffith 4); Second day, New South Wales (1) 4-255 (Bevan 110, Thornely 43); Third day, Tasmania (2) 2-105 (Watson 56, Dighton 2).

Tasmania

J. Cox lbw b Lee	9	– (2) c Waugh b Lee	0
S. R. Mason c Zammit b Thornely	51	– (1) lbw b Katich	40
S. R. Watson c Jaques b Lee	30	– c Pilon b Bracken	157
M. J. Di Venuto c Zammit b Bracken	5		
M. G. Dighton c Pilon b Lee	69	– (4) b Zammit	11
*D. J. Marsh run out (Thornely)	45	– (5) c Mail b Katich	46
†S. G. Clingeleffer c Jaques b Lee	53	– (6) lbw b Bracken	20
A. G. Downton c Waugh b Lee	11	– (7) c Pilon b Bracken	2
X. J. Doherty lbw b Clark	12	– (8) lbw b Katich	21
A. R. Griffith c Mail b Zammit	20	– (9) c and b Katich	0
G. J. Denton not out	0	– (10) not out	4
B 4, l-b 2, n-b 11	17	L-b 8, n-b 6	14

(114.2 overs, 465 mins)   322   (108.1 overs, 422 mins)(9 wkts dec) 315
Fall: 12 73 87 128 201 227 244 261 322 322   Fall: 1 86 119 222 261 269 305 306 315

Bowling: *First Innings*—Lee 30–6–124–5; Bracken 33–17–58–1; Clark 18–8–33–1; Zammit 19.2–2–72–1; Thornely 12–6–24–1; Katich 2–1–5–0. *Second Innings*—Lee 21–3–67–1; Bracken 27–12–55–3; Clark 10–1–30–0; Zammit 24–4–77–1; Thornely 10–3–26–0; Katich 13.1–2–42–4; Waugh 3–0–10–0.

New South Wales

G. J. Mail lbw b Denton	11		
P. A. Jaques c Marsh b Doherty	1	– (1) st Clingeleffer b Doherty	85
M. G. Bevan c Clingeleffer b Marsh	216	– c Doherty b Denton	53
*S. M. Katich c Clingeleffer b Downton	53	– (5) not out	13
M. E. Waugh b Griffith	28		
D. J. Thornely st Clingeleffer b Doherty	81	– (2) c Marsh b Denton	0
†N. S. Pilon lbw b Downton	0	– (4) not out	19
B. Lee c Dighton b Doherty	37		
N. W. Bracken c and b Marsh	7		
S. R. Clark not out	1		
L. A. Zammit lbw b Doherty	4		
B 5, l-b 12, w 2, n-b 4	23	B 1, l-b 4	5

(135.4 overs, 508 mins)   462   (22 overs, 101 mins)   (3 wkts) 175
Fall: 18 29 99 160 323 326 426 449 457 462   Fall: 5 131 159

Bowling: *First Innings*—Denton 23–4–84–1; Griffith 26–10–78–1; Doherty 40.4–6–142–4; Downton 28–9–91–2; Cox 1–0–1–0; Marsh 17–4–49–2. *Second Innings*—Denton 9–0–71–2; Griffith 1–0–10–0; Downton 7–0–56–0; Doherty 5–0–33–1.

Umpires: B. N. J. Oxenford and S. A. Reed.

NEW SOUTH WALES v VICTORIA

At Newcastle Sports Ground, Newcastle, January 9, 10, 11, 12, 2004. Victoria won by three wickets. *Toss:* New South Wales. Victoria 6 pts, New South Wales 2 pts.

This exciting match provided a resounding vote of confidence in moving fixtures to regional centres. But what the healthy crowds saw was an absolute disaster for NSW. Aiming to defend a luxurious second-innings lead, the Blues instead watched David Hussey orchestrate the second-largest fourth-innings victory total in the competition's history. Needing an out-of-sight 452 on the last day, the Bushrangers reached the target with an incredible 14 overs to spare. Hussey was simply superb, providing both the backbone and the inspiration, on another misery strip for bowlers. His unbeaten 212 (310 minutes, 218 balls, 26 fours five sixes) helped continue an anomalous trend in Steve Waugh-led sides that have lost while defending large targets. Waugh, coming down from his Test farewell at the SCG three days earlier, would later lament a lame batting performance after winning the toss. Still, it was enough to earn them a 58-run lead, after the Victorians also turned their noses up at a fine batting pitch and Stuart MacGill collected five wickets. Simon Katich hit his sixth century of the summer and Dominic Thornely, promoted to No. 4, marked his maiden first-class hundred with 18 fours and two sixes. Although Victoria's target seemed unfairly lofty, they ground steadily towards it through a plan hatched by their coach David Hookes. In Victoria's final Pura Cup match before his death, Hookes told them to break the task into two one-dayers and chase 226 runs off two sets of 50 overs. New South Wales sniffed victory late when Thornely snared Cameron White and Andrew McDonald in the same over, leaving Victoria 6 for 383. But Peter Roach and Hussey calmed things down with a 39-run stand as the finishing line hovered into view.

Man of the Match: D. J. Hussey. *Attendance:* 17,654.

Close of play: First day, Victoria (1) 0-19 (Elliott 15, Arnberger 1); Second day, New South Wales (2) 2-23 (Katich 13, Thornely 0); Third day, Victoria (2) 0-3 (Arnberger 2, Elliott 1).

New South Wales

G. J. Mail b Lewis	8	– c Roach b Wise	5
P. A. Jaques c Roach b McDonald	56	– c Lewis b Wise	3
S. M. Katich c Lewis b White	76	– c Elliott b Lewis	126
D. J. Thornely lbw b McDonald	0	– c Lewis b Harwood	143
*S. R. Waugh c Roach b Lewis	7	– run out (Hussey)	31
M. E. Waugh c Harwood b Wise	20	– c Moss b Harwood	13
†B. J. Haddin c Moss b Lewis	50	– c Arnberger b Harwood	6
G. M. Lambert c White b Lewis	38	– c Lewis b McDonald	30
D. A. Nash b White	1	– c Hodge b McDonald	16
M. J. Nicholson b Harwood	26	– c Arnberger b Moss	6
S. C. G. MacGill not out	13	– not out	4
B 4, l-b 5, w 5, n-b 8	22	B 2, l-b 2, n-b 9	13

(83.2 overs, 335 mins)	317	(88.2 overs, 367 mins)	396
Fall: 32 101 101 125 175 196 266 269		Fall: 5 22 220 270 295 310 354	
271 317		384 384 396	

Bowling: *First Innings*—Harwood 12.2–1–42–1; Wise 13–4–40–1; Lewis 21–3–68–4; Moss 8–3–29–0; McDonald 15–4–57–2; White 14–2–72–2. *Second Innings*—Harwood 21–4–93–3; Wise 14–5–44–2; McDonald 18–2–86–2; Lewis 15–1–64–1; White 15–0–83–0; Hodge 1–0–4–0; Moss 4.2–1–18–1.

Victoria

M. T. G. Elliott c Thornely b Lambert	39	– (2) lbw b Nicholson	19
J. L. Arnberger c Haddin b Nicholson	27	– (1) b Nash	4
B. J. Hodge c Haddin b MacGill	29	– lbw b MacGill	33
J. Moss c Haddin b Nash	21	– c Thornely b MacGill	76
D. J. Hussey lbw b Lambert	51	– not out	212
*C. L. White lbw b MacGill	43	– c Haddin b Thornely	60
A. B. McDonald st Haddin b MacGill	5	– c Haddin b Thornely	0
†P. J. Roach c Thornely b Nicholson	13	– lbw b Nicholson	18
S. M. Harwood c Mail b MacGill	7	– not out	14
M. L. Lewis b MacGill	3		
A. B. Wise not out	0		
L-b 10, w 2, n-b 9	21	B 4, l-b 7, w 1, n-b 7	19

(89.1 overs, 358 mins)	259	(102 overs, 397 mins) (7 wkts) 455
Fall: 59 100 118 165 202 207 248 254 258 259		Fall: 13 37 72 248 383 383 422

Bowling: *First Innings*—Nicholson 25–5–58–2; Nash 14–5–35–1; MacGill 31.1–6–94–5; Lambert 16–4–55–2; Thornely 2–1–1–0; Katich 1–0–6–0. *Second Innings*—Nicholson 25–1–107–2; MacGill 36–2–160–2; M. E. Waugh 5–2–11–0; Nash 14–3–57–1; Lambert 11–2–45–0; Katich 5–0–37–0; Thornely 6–1–27–2.

Umpires: S. J. Davis and N. S. D. Fowler.

At WACA Ground, Perth, January 23, 24, 25, 26, 2004. NEW SOUTH WALES lost to WESTERN AUSTRALIA by 126 runs.

At Brisbane Cricket Ground, Brisbane, February 1, 2, 3, 4, 2004. NEW SOUTH WALES drew with QUEENSLAND.

NEW SOUTH WALES v SOUTH AUSTRALIA

At Sydney Cricket Ground, Sydney, February 17, 18, 19, 20, 2004. New South Wales won by 25 runs. *Toss:* New South Wales. New South Wales 6 pts.

Placed second-last coming into their penultimate match, and rock-bottom by lunch on day one, NSW needed a chain of extraordinary events to keep alive their mathematical chance of reaching the final. Sure enough, events began unfolding at an eerie rate, and by the end they were still in the race. New South Wales came perilously close to seeing yet another foe achieve a massive fourth-innings target; the 521 which SA needed would have been a first-class record. But the visitors, led by Graham Manou and Darren Lehmann's magnificent 237 (314 minutes, 238 balls, 34 fours, two sixes), fell agonisingly short. Greg Mail had earlier hit a century on each of the first two days, either side of a South Australian capitulation that featured an equal-competition record of six ducks. The young quick Shaun Tait wreaked havoc on the middle and lower order. Steve Waugh's alert declaration led to South Australia losing two wickets in the four overs before stumps on day one. The innings was quickly snuffed out the following morning, Matthew Nicholson celebrating another well-earned five-for. Waugh strangely opted against enforcing the follow-on, despite a 221-run lead, and by stumps Mail had recorded the first pair of tons for NSW since Mark Taylor in 1989-90. South Australia need to survive more than five sessions, but Lehmann and Manou laid such a strong foundation that they started to think of victory. With seven wickets in hand, 182 runs were needed on the final day. Ultimately a Stuart MacGill-inspired collapse cut the visitors down. They lost their last six wickets for 61 to surrender shortly after lunch.

Man of the Match: G. J. Mail.   *Attendance:* 2,060.

Close of play: First day, South Australia (1) 2-9 (Davison 5, Cosgrove 3); Second day, New South Wales (2) 2-242 (Mail 126, Thornely 18); Third day, South Australia (2) 3-339 (Lehmann 149, Flower 21).

New South Wales

G. J. Mail c Davison b Lehmann	128	– not out	152
P. A. Jaques c Cosgrove b Cleary	20	– c Cosgrove b Tait	28
M. J. Phelps lbw b Tait	39	– c Flower b Cleary	62
D. J. Thornely b Tait	0	– c Miller b Higgs	30
*S. R. Waugh lbw b Tait	35		
M. E. Waugh lbw b Cleary	7		
†N. S. Pilon lbw b Tait	50	– (5) c Cleary b Davison	10
M. J. Nicholson c Miller b Tait	14		
N. W. Bracken c Higgs b Cleary	27		
S. R. Clark not out	5		
B 2, l-b 14, n-b 9	25	B 11, l-b 2, n-b 4	17

(89.1 overs, 347 mins) (9 wkts dec) 350
Fall: 39 117 117 171 188 294 307 333 350

(75.4 overs, 264 mins) (4 wkts dec) 299
Fall: 60 206 272 299

S. C. G. MacGill did not bat.

Bowling: *First Innings*—Tait 17–4–85–5; Rofe 19–5–73–0; Cleary 15.1–1–60–3; Miller 12–5–31–0; Davison 11–1–48–0; Higgs 11–2–29–0; Lehmann 4–0–8–1. *Second Innings*—Tait 7–3–13–1; Rofe 4–0–16–0; Miller 13–1–52–0; Cleary 12–3–50–1; Higgs 17–4–61–1; Davison 17.4–3–76–1; Lehmann 5–1–18–0.

South Australia

B. P. Cameron lbw b Nicholson	0	– (2) c M. E. Waugh b Nicholson	0
†G. A. Manou c Jaques b Bracken	0	– (1) c S. R. Waugh b Clark	130
J. M. Davison b Nicholson	10	– (8) lbw b Nicholson	0
M. J. Cosgrove b Bracken	40	– (3) run out (Phelps)	27
*D. S. Lehmann b MacGill	20	– (4) c S. R. Waugh b MacGill	237
A. Flower c S. R. Waugh b Clark	44	– (5) c Mail b Bracken	24
M. A. Higgs c Pilon b Nicholson	0	– (6) b Nicholson	50
M. C. Miller c Mail b Nicholson	0	– (7) lbw b MacGill	0
M. F. Cleary c Pilon b Nicholson	0	– c Clark b MacGill	10
S. W. Tait not out	2	– lbw b MacGill	2
P. C. Rofe run out (Bracken)	0	– not out	0
B 4, l-b 9	13	B 3, l-b 12	15

(36.3 overs, 166 mins) 129
Fall: 0 6 34 63 86 93 93 93
434 439

(117.3 overs, 472 mins) 495
Fall: 7 76 286 370 434
129 129 464 487 495

Bowling: *First Innings*—Nicholson 14–4–36–5; Bracken 9–2–32–2; Clark 9.3–1–27–1; MacGill 4–1–21–1. *Second Innings*—Nicholson 28.3–3–126–3; Bracken 25–5–79–1; Clark 25–4–89–1; MacGill 29–7–144–4; M. E. Waugh 8–1–40–0; Thornely 1–0–2–0; Pilon 1–1–0–0.

Umpires: B. N. J. Oxenford and S. J. A. Taufel.

NEW SOUTH WALES v QUEENSLAND

At Sydney Cricket Ground, Sydney, March 4, 5, 6, 7, 2004. Queensland won by 37 runs. *Toss:* New South Wales. Queensland 6 pts. *First-class debut:* A. J. Nye.

What was potentially the Waugh twins' final first-class match might have produced a spectacular leap into the final. In the end it was the proverbial damp squib. Rain compromised both sides' prospects of making the decider, and when Victoria declared behind second-placed Tasmania in another rain-marred match in Hobart, NSW were out of the running. Queensland, however, were still in with a chance. At 7.34 p.m. on the fourth evening, under the floodlights and with six balls to spare, they were through. Glenn McGrath sealed a miserable comeback from ankle surgery by becoming the last wicket to fall, NSW stumbling badly in pursuit of 277 to win off 55 overs in difficult conditions. As early as the first morning one could sense the cards wouldn't fall the way of NSW, who recalled the leg-spinner Adrian Tucker for his first match in 10 years and 25 days. Sent in, Aaron Nye responded with a hundred on debut and Andy Bichel brought up his second first-class century. In a rainy NSW reply, Steve Waugh recorded his 97th and last first-class fifty. After a breezy nine-over second-innings from Queensland on day four, the chase was on. Bichel's party continued as he grabbed the first three wickets, and NSW looked almost out of the picture at 5 for 92. And then, at long last, Mark Waugh got going. He clattered 72 runs in 49 balls, dominating a 115-run stand with Brad Haddin. It was Bichel again who struck, removing Waugh and leaving the twins with a bizarre piece of statistical symmetry. Mark's last innings had lifted his career first-class average to 52.04, a mere one-tenth of one run more than Steve's 51.94.

Man of the Match: A.J. Bichel.   *Attendance:* 7,566.

Close of play: First day, Queensland (1) 6-282 (Nye 59, Bichel 46); Second day, New South Wales (1) 4-177 (Bevan 7, M.E. Waugh 0); Third day, New South Wales (1) 4-196 (Bevan 79, M.E. Waugh 11).

Queensland

C.P. Simpson lbw b Tucker	75	– (2) c Haddin b Nicholson	6
C.T. Perren c Haddin b Nicholson	20	– (1) not out	32
*M.L. Love c (s) D.J. Thornely b Bracken	52		
S.G. Law c (s) D.J. Thornely b Nicholson	10	– (3) not out	11
A.J. Nye lbw b McGrath	102		
J.R. Hopes lbw b Bracken	8		
†C.D. Hartley c Clarke b Bracken	0		
A.J. Bichel st Haddin b Clarke	112		
N.M. Hauritz not out	17		
D.R. MacKenzie c M.E. Waugh b McGrath	0		
L-b 22	22	W 5	5

(129.1 overs, 486 mins)   (9 wkts dec)   418   (9 overs, 36 mins)   (1 wkt dec)   54
Fall: 71 123 141 181 190 202 391 406 418   Fall: 8

J.H. Dawes did not bat.

Bowling: *First Innings*—McGrath 24.1–13–43–2; Nicholson 30–8–100–2; Bracken 24–7–56–3; Tucker 27–2–105–1; Clarke 13–4–47–1; Mail 10–3–37–0; S.R. Waugh 1–0–8–0. *Second Innings*—McGrath 4–1–17–0; Nicholson 3–0–18–1; S.R. Waugh 1–0–13–0; M.E. Waugh 1–0–6–0.

New South Wales

G.J. Mail c Love b MacKenzie	19	– c Hopes b Bichel	4
P.A. Jaques c and b Dawes	4	– b Bichel	6
M.G. Bevan not out	79	– c Simpson b Hopes	36
M.J. Clarke c Simpson b Bichel	13	– c Hartley b Bichel	27
*S.R. Waugh c Hartley b Hauritz	65	– c Love b Dawes	9
M.E. Waugh not out	11	– c and b Bichel	72
†B.J. Haddin (did not bat)		– not out	62
M.J. Nicholson (did not bat)		– c (sub) B.P. Nash b Simpson	4
A.E. Tucker (did not bat)		– st Hartley b Simpson	12
N.W. Bracken (did not bat)		– st Hartley b Nye	4
G.D. McGrath (did not bat)		– c Law b Simpson	2
W 5	5	L-b 1	1

(71 overs, 260 mins)   (4 wkts dec)   196   (54 overs, 233 mins)   239
Fall: 8 43 65 173   Fall: 4 11 61 76 92 207 216 231 236 239

Bowling: *First Innings*—Bichel 19–6–44–1; Dawes 22–11–48–1; MacKenzie 8–1–40–1; Hauritz 19–4–53–1; Simpson 3–0–11–0. *Second Innings*—Bichel 16.2–2–69–4; Dawes 16–4–33–1; Hopes 8–1–53–1; Hauritz 7–0–60–0; Simpson 4–1–8–3; Nye 3–1–15–1.

Umpires: I.H. Lock and R.L. Parry.

NSW DOMESTIC FIRST-CLASS RESULTS TABLE

	First Game	M	Won	Lost	Drawn	Tied
v South Australia	Dec 16, 1892	199	109	54	36	0
v Victoria	Dec 24, 1892	205	73	63	66	1
v Queensland	Nov 26, 1926	149	59	37	53	0
v Western Australia . .	Jan 30, 1948	106	43	31	32	0
v Tasmania	Mar 4, 1978	50	19	12	19	0
Total		709	303	199	206	1

NSW DOMESTIC FIRST-CLASS RECORDS

Highest score for:	452*	D. G. Bradman v Queensland at Sydney	. . . .	1929-30
Highest score against:	365*	C. Hill (South Australia) at Adelaide	. . . .	1900-01
Best bowling for:	9-41	W. J. O'Reilly v South Australia at Adelaide	. . . .	1937-38
Best bowling against:	10-36	T. W. Wall (South Australia) at Sydney	. . . .	1932-33
Highest total for:	918	v South Australia at Sydney	. . . .	1900-01
Highest total against:	1,107	by Victoria at Melbourne	. . . .	1926-27
Lowest total for:	56	v Western Australia at Perth	. . . .	1998-99
Lowest total against:	27	by South Australia at Sydney	. . . .	1955-56

MOST RUNS

	M	I	NO	R	HS	100s	50s	Avge
M. G. Bevan	93	163	31	8,174	216	32	33	61.92
M. E. Waugh	93	158	18	7,232	229*	23	30	51.66
S. R. Waugh	85	147	14	6,609	216*	22	24	49.69
A. F. Kippax	61	95	9	6,096	315*	23	14	70.88
M. A. Taylor	85	147	3	6,090	199	15	34	42.29
J. Dyson	82	150	16	5,648	241	11	29	42.15
K. D. Walters	91	159	16	5,602	253	17	24	39.17
G. R. J. Matthews	116	177	27	5,567	184	8	28	37.11
R. B. McCosker	70	124	15	5,280	168	17	26	48.44
B. C. Booth	81	128	14	4,943	177	10	25	43.36
M. A. Noble	51	81	9	4,896	281	19	17	68.00
M. J. Slater	69	130	3	4,890	204	12	25	38.50
N. C. O'Neill	61	104	10	4,749	233	15	21	50.52
D. G. Bradman	31	52	9	4,633	452*	17	12	107.74
R. B. Simpson	57	99	15	4,399	359	12	17	52.37
W. Bardsley	47	77	8	4,171	235	15	14	60.45
P. M. Toohey	64	109	10	4,038	158	15	14	40.79
G. Thomas	59	93	7	3,992	229	13	14	46.42
S. M. Small	66	113	3	3,984	184	5	29	36.22
D. M. Wellham	59	97	11	3,812	166	9	23	44.33

HIGHEST PARTNERSHIP FOR EACH WICKET

319	for 1st	R. B. McCosker and J. Dyson v Western Australia at Sydney	1980-81
378	for 2nd	L. A. Marks and K. D. Walters v South Australia at Adelaide	1964-65
363	for 3rd	D. G. Bradman and A. F. Kippax v Queensland at Sydney	1933-34
325	for 4th	N. C. O'Neill and B. C. Booth v Western Australia at Sydney	1957-58
464*	for 5th	M. E. Waugh and S. R. Waugh v Western Australia at Perth	1990-91
332	for 6th	N. G. Marks and G. Thomas v South Australia at Sydney	1958-59
255	for 7th	G. Thomas and R. Benaud v Victoria at Melbourne	1961-62
270	for 8th	E. P. Barbour and V. T. Trumper v Victoria at Sydney	1912-13
226	for 9th	C. Kelleway and W. A. S. Oldfield v Victoria at Melbourne	1925-26
307	for 10th	A. F. Kippax and J. E. H. Hooker v Victoria at Melbourne	1928-29

MOST WICKETS

	M	Balls	Mdns	R	W	BB	5W/i	10W/m	Avge	S-R
G. F. Lawson	103	20,933	873	8,673	367	6-31	12	0	23.82	57.04
G. R. J. Matthews	116	26,764	1,376	10,518	363	8-52	19	4	28.98	73.73
R. Benaud	73	18,106	474	7,172	266	7-32	12	3	26.96	68.07
J. W. Martin	70	15,890	239	7,949	263	8-97	12	0	30.22	60.42
M. R. Whitney	77	14,983	562	7,314	251	7-75	10	0	29.14	59.69
A. K. Davidson	62	13,425	275	5,195	246	7-31	10	0	21.12	54.57
S. C. G. MacGill	55	12,175	365	7,085	206	6-64	11	0	34.39	59.10
W. J. O'Reilly	33	10,740	363	3,472	203	9-41	18	7	17.10	52.91
R. G. Holland	60	15,435	806	6,250	193	9-83	7	1	32.38	79.97
K. J. O'Keeffe	58	11,971	315	5,065	187	6-49	11	1	27.08	64.02
L. S. Pascoe	49	9,560	279	4,895	183	8-41	8	2	26.75	52.24
A. A. Mailey	37	11,732	127	5,861	180	8-81	13	2	32.56	65.18
D. J. Colley	62	10,645	145	5,535	179	6-30	5	0	30.92	59.47
W. J. Holdsworth	52	9,204	269	5,518	164	7-41	9	1	33.65	56.12
D. A. Renneberg	46	9,759	145	4,925	161	7-33	6	1	30.59	60.61
M. A. Noble	51	8,887	430	3,587	159	7-44	7	1	22.56	55.89
W. P. Howell	36	9,548	482	3,742	157	9-52	9	1	23.83	60.82
D. W. Hourn	38	8,612	191	4,222	150	9-77	10	2	28.15	57.41
P. I. Philpott	46	9,112	137	4,235	143	7-53	7	2	29.62	63.72
R. R. Lindwall	34	7,098	97	2,904	139	7-45	5	1	20.89	51.06

MOST DISMISSALS

	M	Catches	Stumpings	Total
P. A. Emery	109	298	41	339
S. J. Rixon	94	218	43	261
H. B. Taber	64	179	32	211
W. A. S. Oldfield	51	109	70	179
D. A. Ford	56	107	51	107

MOST CATCHES

M. A. Taylor	120 in 85 matches	R. Benaud	92 in 73 matches
M. E. Waugh	110 in 93 matches	R. B. McCosker	91 in 70 matches
G. R. J. Matthews	102 in 116 matches	S. R. Waugh	80 in 85 matches

MOST APPEARANCES

116	G. R. J. Matthews	1982-83 – 1997-98	93	M. E. Waugh	1985-86 – 2003-04
109	P. A. Emery	1987-88 – 1998-99	91	K. D. Walters	1962-63 – 1980-81
103	G. F. Lawson	1977-78 – 1991-92	85	M. A. Taylor	1985-86 – 1998-99
94	S. J. Rixon	1974-75 – 1987-88	85	S. R. Waugh	1984-85 – 2003-04
93	M. G. Bevan	1990-91 – 2003-04	82	J. Dyson	1975-76 – 1988-89

QUEENSLAND

So far, so fast, so close

by STEPHEN GRAY

Pura Cup: Runners-up
ING Cup: Runners-up
Coach: Terry Oliver
Captain: Jimmy Maher

Jimmy Maher

A decade ago, two finals appearances and no silverware would have prompted the observation that Queensland always had the promise but lacked that special something needed to deliver. Yet in these relative times of plenty, encompassing five Pura Cup titles in the past decade, the hand-wringing and recriminations that might normally have followed last summer's final stutters were absent.

Not that there wasn't disappointment. The captain Jimmy Maher, as proud a Queenslander as exists, wore a brave face through a string of media conferences detailing his team's failure to breast the winner's tape after a withering second half of the season. But hosting the ING Cup final and snatching second spot from Tasmania in the Pura Cup table, courtesy of a thrilling last-gasp win in the SCG gloaming on the final day of the regular season, suggested that the Bulls' summer was not too far off the mark.

It was a summer unlike the golden days of recent times. Normally blessed with powerhouse attacks and settled batting combinations, the Bulls received a taste of how the other half lives, posing some early conundrums for the second-season coach Terry Oliver and a new-look selection panel. International commitments at the start of the season removed Matthew Hayden, Andy Bichel, Andrew Symonds, Michael Kasprowicz and Maher, while off-season injuries accounted for Ashley Noffke, Scott Brant and Nathan Hauritz. Rather than getting away to their familiar gang-busting start, Queensland's early defeats and draws made for a slow-burning summer. The fireworks came later.

Bestriding the stage all along was the inimitable figure of Stuart Law, dominating attacks across the land on his way to a farewell-season haul of more than 1,500 first-class and one-day runs. He also provided some valuable on-field tutelage to those who will now take up the cudgels, and his influence on this team cannot be undersold. A strong individual with fierce self-belief, Law's departure from the Australian scene might not have quite reached the frenzied heights of another grizzly right-hander whose internal fire burned brightly whenever he walked on to a field. But he was a giant of the age. It was fitting that Law's last encounter with Steve Waugh was at the SCG, with a Pura Cup final appearance resting on a Bulls' outright win. The two hard-bitten warriors have always enjoyed their battles in baggy maroon and blue, and it was no surprise when the match ended in near-darkness with an extraordinary Queensland victory.

Both finals losses were devastating in different ways. But the ING Cup defeat, with its moments of madness in the dying stages, was perhaps the more gut-wrenching. Queensland had barnstormed their way to the top of the table by winning their last five qualifying matches, including an incredible 207-run slaughter of the eventual champions Western Australia. They were ultimately torpedoed by a freakish combination of misfields, outbreaks of cramp in their last two bowlers – Bichel and James Hopes – and clear-eyed batting bravado from the Warriors' lower-order.

A peek behind the banana curtain reveals some important issues for the Bulls. Their much-vaunted pace attack, for so long the key factor in any equation for Queensland success, had its poorest output in nearly a decade. This can partly be attributed to the long-overdue international recognition of Kasprowicz, which reduced him to fleeting appearances for Queensland. The return of Bichel after his shoddy handling at national level provided only some relief, and Noffke's mysterious fall from grace further reduced the Bulls' firepower. Pitches Australia-wide, moreover, favoured the batsmen more often than not, with the Gabba and WACA offering less encouragement to the quicks than in previous seasons.

Only the dependable Joe Dawes reached 30 wickets. Kasprowicz and Bichel, with 24 and 21 wickets respectively, collected as many scalps between them as they normally would individually. Spin did not feature dramatically, although Hauritz and Chris Simpson both produced match-turning efforts. Hauritz again showed that the one-day game is his forte for the moment. Simpson, in his first real season of bowling off-breaks, has genuine potential and may blossom as his match experience grows. Any close examination of the Bulls' season highlights the fact that the attack failed to land the knockout blows, which was frequently the difference between six points, two points or none. Queensland gave up three outright defeats at home, which is almost unheard of.

On the flip-side their batsmen, buttressed by Law's virtuoso curtain-call, enjoyed a summer of extraordinary riches. They established a new Australian record – and equalled the world record – by producing 12 individual century-makers in a single first-class season. Martin Love made a triple and Law a double in his final first-class match at the Gabba. Hopes and Noffke recorded their maiden hundreds, while Chris Hartley, Craig Philipson and Aaron Nye all reached three figures on debut. There could have been a 13th had Hauritz not been controversially judged lbw six runs short of his maiden hundred at the WACA.

Queensland's batting bonanza was not restricted to the Pura Cup. Maher broke the domestic one-day record with his 187 in 129 balls against WA at the Gabba – part of the Bulls' astounding 4 for 405 – while Law slammed the season's swiftest fifty and the fastest hundred of all time. While Law and Love dominated the averages and aggregates, as ever, the batsman bubbling up was Clint Perren. An elegant right-hander, he scored solidly in both forms of the game, with the bulk of his Pura Cup runs coming as a fill-in opener rather than in the middle order where he initially made his mark.

"Steady as she goes" will be Queensland's mantra for 2004-05. The departure of such a dominant figure as Law would normally be the cue for a period of rebuilding or consolidation. But the off-season return of Shane Watson and the emergence of Philipson and Nye should partly fill the gap he leaves. The real challenge, perhaps, is to unearth a new generation of fast bowlers. For Scott Brant, Mitchell Johnson, Damien MacKenzie, Grant Sullivan and Nathan Rimmington, the time is ripe.

QUEENSLAND RESULTS, 2003-04

All first-class matches – Played 10: Won 3, Lost 3, Drawn 4.
Pura Cup – Played 10: Won 3, Lost 3, Drawn 4.
ING Cup matches – Played 10: Won 7, Lost 3.

Back row: D. M. Payne, A. J. Nye, S. J. Magoffin, A. A. Noffke, S. J. Jurgensen, L. A. Carseldine, S. J. Farrell. *Middle row:* D. Holder (*Coaching assistant*), T. G. Oliver (*Coach*), C. P. Simpson, D. R. MacKenzie, C. T. Perren, M. G. Johnson, C. A. Philipson, J. A. Sternes (*Technical officer*), T. Wilson (*Conditioner*). *Front row:* B. P. Nash, S. G. Law, A. J. Bichel, J. P. Maher, M. L. Love, J. H. Dawes, S. A. Brant. *Absent (inset):* N. M. Hauritz, A. Symonds, J. R. Hopes, M. S. Kasprowicz, M. L. Hayden, W. A. Seccombe, C. D. Harley.

QUEENSLAND PURA CUP AVERAGES, 2003-04

BATTING

	M	I	NO	R	HS	100s	50s	Avge	Ct/St	S-R
A. J. Nye	1	1	0	102	102	1	0	102.00	0	44.16
S. G. Law	11	20	4	1,053	203	2	6	65.81	9	66.52
M. L. Love	10	18	3	893	300*	2	5	59.53	10	53.15
C. A. Philipson	3	5	1	198	101*	1	1	49.50	2	48.18
C. D. Hartley	3	4	1	134	103	1	0	44.67	9/2	39.76
J. P. Maher	7	12	0	532	116	1	4	44.33	5	50.00
A. A. Noffke	8	12	4	326	114*	1	1	40.75	0	51.34
C. T. Perren	11	20	1	721	141	1	4	37.95	5	54.33
A. Symonds	2	3	0	112	102	1	0	37.33	0	78.32
A. J. Bichel	4	6	0	208	112	1	0	34.67	2	71.48
W. A. Seccombe	8	14	2	382	115	1	2	31.83	41/1	56.09
J. R. Hopes	10	17	0	510	111	1	2	30.00	7	56.98
N. M. Hauritz	8	10	3	196	94	0	1	28.00	3	67.12
M. S. Kasprowicz	5	5	1	96	47	0	0	24.00	3	80.00
S. J. Farrell	2	4	0	91	49	0	0	22.75	0	66.91
C. P. Simpson	6	11	0	206	83	0	2	18.73	6	55.38
J. H. Dawes	10	10	5	85	21	0	0	17.00	2	41.26
D. R. MacKenzie	2	3	0	43	30	0	0	14.33	0	50.00
M. G. Johnson	1	2	0	26	15	0	0	13.00	0	25.00
D. M. Payne	3	5	0	62	35	0	0	12.40	1	55.86
L. A. Carseldine	2	2	0	19	10	0	0	9.50	1	30.65
M. L. Hayden	1	1	0	9	9	0	0	9.00	0	56.25
S. J. Jurgensen	3	4	1	6	5	0	0	2.00	1	37.50

* Denotes not out.

BOWLING

	O	Mdns	R	W	BB	5W/i	10W/m	Avge	S-R
D. M. Payne	2	0	6	1	1-6	0	0	6.00	12.00
A. J. Nye	3	1	15	1	1-15	0	0	15.00	18.00
D. R. MacKenzie	37	5	127	8	4-43	0	0	15.88	27.75
S. J. Jurgensen	122.2	35	301	13	4-52	0	0	23.15	56.46
M. S. Kasprowicz	196.1	54	559	24	5-84	1	0	23.29	49.04
A. Symonds	36	8	97	4	3-25	0	0	24.25	54.00
A. J. Bichel	150	23	608	21	6-61	1	1	28.95	42.86
M. G. Johnson	15	0	59	2	2-59	0	0	29.50	45.00
J. H. Dawes	364.2	94	1081	30	4-89	0	0	36.03	72.87
A. A. Noffke	241	50	770	15	4-48	0	0	51.33	96.40
C. P. Simpson	124.1	28	407	7	3-8	0	0	58.14	106.43
N. M. Hauritz	274.1	60	1023	16	4-95	0	0	63.94	102.81
J. R. Hopes	262	71	853	12	4-63	0	0	71.08	131.00
S. G. Law	15.5	2	57	0	–	0	0	–	–
M. L. Love	4	1	6	0	–	0	0	–	–
C. T. Perren	22	6	75	0	–	0	0	–	–
C. A. Philipson	2	1	5	0	–	0	0	–	–

QUEENSLAND v VICTORIA

At Brisbane Cricket Ground, Brisbane, November 2, 3, 4, 5, 2003. Victoria won by five wickets. *Toss:* Victoria. Victoria 6 pts. *First-class debut:* S. J. Farrell, A. B. Wise.

The injured Victorian skipper Darren Berry was anxious not to miss his side's first Pura Cup victory in Brisbane in 20 years, and paid $500 to fly north to celebrate with his team-mates on the final day. Chasing a small target of 160, the Bushrangers were 0 for 50 when Berry taxied out of Melbourne airport; by the time he arrived they were 5 for 93. The all-rounder James Hopes had whipped up a mini-cyclone, taking 4 for 2 in 16 amazing deliveries. But Cameron White, the 20-year-old leg-spinner who was captaining Victoria in Berry's place, steered his side to safety with 38, following on from his six wickets in the match. Queensland were depleted by injuries and missing their captain Jimmy Maher on national duty, but fought hard to come back several times as the match swung back and forth. At 7 for 154 in the first innings, the former schoolboy rugby representative Chris Simpson swung hard for nine fours and five sixes in a whirlwind 83, allowing his side to post a respectable total. Victoria then gained the initiative and a 97-run first-innings lead through David Hussey and Jason Arnberger. Superb match-turning catches from Hussey and White helped restrain Queensland a second time round, and despite plenty of nervous moments Victoria savoured their first victory here since Ray Bright was in charge in 1983-84.

Match reports by BEN DORRIES.
Man of the Match: C. L. White. *Attendance:* 1,069.

Close of play: First day, Victoria (1) 1-31 (Arnberger 23, Harwood 0); Second day, Victoria (1) 6-351 (Moss 33, White 25); Third day, Queensland (2) 7-233 (Simpson 7, Johnson 0).

Queensland

D. M. Payne lbw b McDonald	35	– c White b Inness	11
C. T. Perren b Harwood	5	– lbw b White	44
*M. L. Love c White b Wise	11	– c Roach b Wise	24
S. G. Law c White b Inness	47	– c Hussey b McDonald	81
S. J. Farrell lbw b White	34	– b White	0
J. R. Hopes c Hussey b Wise	9	– c White b Inness	42
†W. A. Seccombe lbw b White	6	– c White b Inness	15
C. P. Simpson run out (White/Roach)	83	– c Arnberger b Moss	7
M. G. Johnson c Elliott b White	11	– c Roach b Moss	15
S. J. Jurgensen c and b White	1	– c Roach b Moss	5
J. H. Dawes not out	13	– not out	2
B 4, l-b 14, w 2, n-b 2	22	B 1, l-b 3, w 3, n-b 3	10
(82 overs, 328 mins)	277	(91.3 overs, 357 mins)	256

Fall: 5 51 51 129 143 152 154 206 212 277

Fall: 13 53 138 138 204 216 229 235 244 256

Bowling: *First Innings*—Harwood 12–3–60–1; Inness 21–7–64–1; Wise 17–7–48–2; McDonald 6–2–19–1; White 17–4–27–4; Moss 9–2–41–0. *Second Innings*—Harwood 9.5–2–54–0; Inness 22–12–42–3; Wise 9–1–34–1; White 16–3–44–2; Moss 21.4–7–61–3; McDonald 13–7–17–1.

Victoria

M. T. G. Elliott c Love b Johnson	6	– (2) lbw b Hopes	23
J. L. Arnberger lbw b Jurgensen	89	– (1) lbw b Hopes	27
S. M. Harwood c Seccombe b Hopes	22		
B. J. Hodge lbw b Johnson	40	– (3) c Payne b Hopes	2
A. B. McDonald c Seccombe b Jurgensen	11	– (4) not out	45
D. J. Hussey c Seccombe b Dawes	106	– (5) c and b Hopes	0
J. Moss c Love b Dawes	33	– (6) c Love b Dawes	22
*C. L. White c Perren b Dawes	30	– (7) not out	38
†P. J. Roach c Seccombe b Jurgensen	4		
M. W. H. Inness not out	10		
A. B. Wise c Seccombe b Jurgensen	4		
B 1, l-b 7, w 9, n-b 2	19	L-b 2, w 1	3

(122.4 overs, 458 mins)	374
Fall: 27 68 124 143 263 304 351 360 360 374	

(53.2 overs, 218 mins)	(5 wkts)	160
Fall: 50 53 54 54 93		

Bowling: *First Innings*—Jurgensen 33.4–13–72–4; Dawes 31–7–93–3; Johnson 15–1–59–2; Hopes 22–4–73–1; Simpson 17–5–58–0; Perren 4–1–11–0. *Second Innings*—Jurgensen 10–1–33–0; Dawes 20.2–4–54–1; Hopes 19–3–63–4; Simpson 3–0–4–0; Perren 1–0–4–0.

Umpires: I. H. Lock and D. L. Orchard.

At Junction Oval, St Kilda, November 11, 12, 13, 14, 2003. QUEENSLAND drew with VICTORIA.

QUEENSLAND v TASMANIA

At Brisbane Cricket Ground, Brisbane, November 20, 21, 22, 2003. Tasmania won by 174 runs. *Toss:* Queensland. Tasmania 6 pts.

A furious stand-in skipper Martin Love ordered some soul-searching for Queensland's batsmen, formerly so dominant, after they twice crumbled meekly against an underrated Tasmanian side. While the Tigers shot to the competition lead, rumblings that the Bulls were toothless without their absent internationals grew louder. "Our shot selection was ordinary, they need to have a think about their game and come up with a better plan," said Love. Queensland had started in promising enough fashion. The young fast bowler Damien MacKenzie, heavily courted by Tasmania during the off-season, bowled with sharp pace to take 4 for 43 against his former suitors. Belatedly picked when Ashley Noffke was ruled unfit, MacKenzie felled Adam Griffith with a brute of a ball in the final hour of the first day, but played only one more match all season. The next morning Damien Wright, in possibly the quickest spell of his life, collected 4 for 30 and left Queensland's victory hopes in ruin. Wright's embarrassment of the Bulls continued when he batted, chipping in with a valuable 60 as Tasmania set a challenging 343-run target in what had been a low-scoring game. Queensland fared little better in their second attempt, terrible shot selection bringing about the downfall of Daniel Payne, Stuart Law and James Hopes. Their defeat inside three days left them with two points from three matches and a big job ahead.

Man of the Match: D. G. Wright. *Attendance:* 1,158.

Close of play: First day, Tasmania (1) 8-224 (Griffith 7, Downton, 3); Second day, Tasmania (2) 6-144 (Di Venuto 39, Wright 39).

Tasmania

J. Cox lbw b Dawes	40	– (2) c Seccombe b Dawes	4
S. R. Mason c Seccombe b MacKenzie	27	– (1) c Seccombe b MacKenzie	32
S. R. Watson c and b Jurgensen	8	– c Seccombe b Hopes	11
M. J. Di Venuto c Seccombe b Hopes	59	– b Jurgensen	44
M. G. Dighton c Seccombe b MacKenzie	42	– c Seccombe b Jurgensen	6
*D. J. Marsh c Seccombe b Jurgensen	8	– lbw b Jurgensen	5
†S. G. Clingeleffer c Simpson b MacKenzie	10	– c Seccombe b Jurgensen	1
D. G. Wright lbw b MacKenzie	3	– b MacKenzie	60
A. R. Griffith lbw b Dawes	7	– c Law b MacKenzie	21
A. G. Downton c Seccombe b Jurgensen	10	– not out	15
G. J. Denton not out	2	– c and b Simpson	5
L-b 14, n-b 3	17	L-b 4, w 2, n-b 3	9

(101.4 overs, 408 mins)   233   (70.2 overs, 286 mins)   213
Fall: 50 67 110 156 171 200 207 208   Fall: 10 39 60 84 97 99 150 190
   231 233   197 213

Bowling: *First Innings*—Dawes 21–10–33–2; Jurgensen 28.4–8–60–3; Hopes 21–8–46–1; MacKenzie 16–3–43–4; Simpson 15–4–37–0. *Second Innings*—Jurgensen 17–4–52–4; Dawes 17–4–54–1; Hopes 14–4–39–1; MacKenzie 13–1–44–3; Perren 3–1–9–0; Simpson 6.2–2–11–1.

Queensland

D. M. Payne c Clingeleffer b Wright	0	– c Cox b Downton	16
C. T. Perren lbw b Wright	0	– c Di Venuto b Denton	0
*M. L. Love b Marsh b Wright	28	– lbw b Wright	21
S. G. Law c Cox b Griffith	15	– c Mason b Downton	10
S. J. Farrell c Di Venuto b Denton	8	– c Watson b Wright	49
J. R. Hopes b Denton	0	– c Mason b Downton	7
†W. A. Seccombe lbw b Griffith	24	– c Clingeleffer b Denton	6
C. P. Simpson c Watson b Wright	2	– lbw b Denton	4
D. R. MacKenzie c Di Venuto b Downton	13	– c Mason b Denton	30
J. H. Dawes not out	9	– b Wright	16
S. J. Jurgensen c and b Downton	0	– not out	0
B 3, l-b 2	5	B 4, w 3, n-b 2	9

(39.2 overs, 170 mins)   104   (41.5 overs, 182 mins)   168
Fall: 0 3 22 41 41 74 80 82 104 104   Fall: 4 39 45 52 68 75 89 135 164 168

Bowling: *First Innings*—Wright 12–4–30–4; Griffith 10–3–26–2; Downton 9.2–2–24–2; Denton 8–3–19–2. *Second Innings*—Wright 15–6–33–3; Denton 11.5–1–60–4; Downton 12–3–47–3; Marsh 2–1–8–0; Di Venuto 1–0–16–0.

Umpires: A. R. Craig and B. N. J. Oxenford.

At Adelaide Oval, Adelaide, November 27, 28, 29, 30, 2003. QUEENSLAND defeated SOUTH AUSTRALIA by 61 runs.

QUEENSLAND v SOUTH AUSTRALIA

At Brisbane Cricket Ground, Brisbane, December 19, 20, 21, 2003. Queensland won by an innings and 137 runs. *Toss:* South Australia. Queensland 6 pts. *First-class debut:* C. D. Hartley, A. M. Staunton.

A week before walking on to the Gabba for his first-class debut, the Queensland wicket-keeper Chris Hartley shed tears of joy when presented with his first maroon cap by his childhood hero Ian Healy. Stepping in for Wade Seccombe, who was away with the Australia A side, Hartley showed he has the makings of a future Test gloveman and became only the second Australian wicket-keeper to hit a century on debut. A diminutive figure, he began watchfully but played with growing flair as his confidence built, ultimately taking control of a flagging South Australian attack. His 103 included 15 fours and came in 244 balls. A typically debonair 102 from Andrew Symonds had earlier blunted the opposition and washed away a personal three-year century drought in the Pura Cup. Taking the lead from Symonds, Ashley Noffke – who was under an injury cloud again but allayed any fears by taking 4 for 48 on the first day – provided plenty of entertainment. Noffke's unbeaten 114, decorated with 17 fours, was his maiden first-class hundred, fulfilling a pre-season pledge to boost his batting average and become known as a genuine all-rounder. He and Hartley shared a 218-run partnership for the seventh wicket, a Queensland record against SA. It enabled Jimmy Maher to attack with a 293-run first-innings lead. Michael Kasprowicz burst through the top order and the South Australians capitulated, putting the finishing touches on an emphatic victory.

Man of the Match: A. A. Noffke.   *Attendance:* 1,788.

Close of play: First day, Queensland (1) 1-66 (Maher 36, Perren 15); Second day, Queensland (1) 6-440 (Hartley 79, Noffke 81).

South Australia

D. A. Fitzgerald c Perren b Noffke	0	– (2) c Hartley b Kasprowicz		8
S. A. Deitz c Kasprowicz b Noffke	74	– (1) lbw b Noffke		30
*G. S. Blewett lbw b Symonds	8	– c Hartley b Kasprowicz		23
A. Flower b Kasprowicz	11	– c Maher b Dawes		8
M. A. Higgs c Maher b Dawes	13	– b Kasprowicz		0
M. J. Cosgrove b Symonds	15	– b Hauritz		28
M. C. Miller c Hartley b Symonds	9	– run out (Carseldine)		33
†G. A. Manou c Perren b Kasprowicz	51	– c Hartley b Noffke		7
M. F. Cleary c Carseldine b Noffke	1	– lbw b Dawes		0
R. J. Harris c Kasprowicz b Noffke	14	– c Hauritz b Dawes		4
A. M. Staunton not out	3	– not out		1
L-b 5	5	B 8, l-b 2, w 4		14

(70.2 overs, 284 mins)   204   (66 overs, 264 mins)   156
Fall: 11 48 94 104 113 127 144 146   Fall: 20 63 79 79 100 116 135
178 204   139 143 156

Bowling: *First Innings*—Kasprowicz 18.2–4–41–2; Noffke 20–7–48–4; Dawes 12–4–38–1; Symonds 12–3–25–3; Hauritz 8–0–47–0. *Second Innings*—Kasprowicz 18–12–16–3; Noffke 15–4–37–2; Symonds 9–2–34–0; Dawes 11–3–31–3; Hauritz 13–6–28–1.

Queensland

*J. P. Maher c Manou b Miller	97	†C. D. Hartley c Miller b Harris	103
M. L. Hayden c Harris b Cleary	9	A. A. Noffke not out	114
C. T. Perren c Fitzgerald b Cleary	21	B 16, l-b 4, w 7, n-b 4	31
S. G. Law c Manou b Cleary	10		
A. Symonds c Harris b Staunton	102	(140 overs, 543 mins) (7 wkts)	497
L. A. Carseldine c Miller b Cleary	10	Fall: 23 79 89 181 225 279 497	

N. M. Hauritz, M. S. Kasprowicz and J. H. Dawes did not bat.

Bowling: Cleary 35–6–133–4; Miller 29–8–93–1; Harris 30–4–97–1; Staunton 24–4–92–1; Higgs 13–3–40–0; Blewett 6–1–10–0; Cosgrove 3–0–12–0.

Umpires: I. H. Lock and G. T. D. Morrow.

At WACA Ground, Perth, January 11, 12, 13, 14, 2004. QUEENSLAND drew with WESTERN AUSTRALIA.

At Bellerive Oval, Hobart, January 21, 22, 23, 24, 2004. QUEENSLAND drew with TASMANIA.

QUEENSLAND v NEW SOUTH WALES

At Brisbane Cricket Ground, Brisbane, February 1, 2, 3, 4, 2004. Match drawn. *Toss:* Queensland. Queensland 2 pts.

Queensland's experienced hands, Stuart Law and Jimmy Maher, struck elegant centuries as the home side built a commanding first innings. Steve Waugh had to shoulder some of the blame, dropping Maher at mid-wicket on 39. Law's outstanding farewell season continued. He hit 18 fours and two sixes in his unbeaten 146, overtaking Sam Trimble – another prodigious Queenslander who locals reckon was badly treated by the national selectors – as the state's leading first-class runscorer. The leg-spinner Stuart MacGill, a headache for the Bulls in the 2002-03 final, felt the cut of Law's blade when he was smashed out of the attack with a towering six over mid-on followed by consecutive boundaries. The Blues were in deep trouble at stumps on day two, falling to 4 for 96 when rain stopped play, after the fast bowler Ashley Noffke had sent down some almost unplayable deliveries. Only 39 minutes and 63 balls were possible on the third day due to persistent showers, but both skippers were desperate for outright points and played accordingly. Two declarations left NSW chasing 327 in 56 overs. Phil Jaques fanned their hopes with a remarkable solo hand of 146 off 147 balls, but the target proved frustratingly out of reach. Waugh later praised Jaques's thrilling innings, comprising 13 fours and two sixes, likening it to some played by Adam Gilchrist.

Man of the Match: P. A. Jaques. *Attendance:* 3,771.

Close of play: First day, Queensland (1) 4-285 (Hopes 13); Second day, New South Wales (1) 4-96 (S.R. Waugh 2, M.E. Waugh 2); Third day, New South Wales (1) 6-125 (M.E. Waugh 18, Nicholson 7).

Queensland

*J.P. Maher c Haddin b Clark	116	– st Haddin b O'Brien 20
C.T. Perren c Haddin b Clark	3	– c O'Brien b MacGill 57
M.L. Love c Haddin b Nicholson	68	– not out 34
S.G. Law not out	146	– not out 13
C.A. Philipson lbw b Bollinger	7	
J.R. Hopes c M.E. Waugh b Clark	38	
†W. A. Seccombe not out	34	
L-b 10, w 2, n-b 7	19	

(130 overs, 493 mins)	(5 wkts dec) 431	(18 overs, 56 mins)	(2 wkts dec) 124
Fall: 8 140 237 254 359		Fall: 49 103	

A. A. Noffke, N. M. Hauritz, M. S. Kasprowicz amd J. H. Dawes did not bat.

Bowling: *First Innings*—Nicholson 25–6–71–1; Clark 28–8–71–3; Thornely 12–4–27–0; Bollinger 23–5–87–1; MacGill 26–4–114–0; O'Brien 13–1–41–0; Jaques 2–0–10–0; Mail 1–1–0–0. *Second Innings*—Clark 2–0–6–0; Nicholson 2–0–16–0; MacGill 7–1–48–1; O'Brien 7–0–54–1.

New South Wales

G. J. Mail c Seccombe b Kasprowicz	2	– c Seccombe b Kasprowicz	50
P. A. Jaques b Dawes	53	– b Kasprowicz	146
†B. J. Haddin c Seccombe b Noffke	31	– c Seccombe b Kasprowicz	10
D. J. Thornely c Seccombe b Noffke	0	– c Kasprowicz b Noffke	1
*S. R. Waugh c Maher b Dawes	8	– lbw b Dawes	28
M. E. Waugh c Maher b Hopes	90	– c Philipson b Kasprowicz	5
A. W. O'Brien c Maher b Dawes	0	– (8) c Hopes b Hauritz	7
M. J. Nicholson not out	35	– (7) c Love b Dawes	2
S. R. Clark (did not bat)		– not out	12
D. Bollinger (did not bat)		– not out	2
L-b 2, w 2, n-b 6	10	B 1, l-b 8, w 1, n-b 4	14

(71 overs, 271 mins)	(7 wkts dec) 229
Fall: 16 86 90 91 111 111 229	

(56 overs, 230 mins)		(8 wkts) 277
Fall: 101 125 141 196 207 215 244 270		

S. C. G. MacGill did not bat.

Bowling: *First Innings*—Kasprowicz 22–8–43–1; Noffke 15–6–47–2; Dawes 18–3–69–3; Hopes 7–1–29–1; Hauritz 9–1–39–0. *Second Innings*—Kasprowicz 18–2–74–4; Dawes 14–1–73–2; Noffke 8–0–53–1; Hopes 9–0–50–0; Hauritz 7–2–18–1.

Umpires: J. Davis and S. D. Fry.

QUEENSLAND v WESTERN AUSTRALIA

At Brisbane Cricket Ground, Brisbane, February 15, 16, 17, 18, 2004. Western Australia won by seven wickets. *Toss:* Western Australia. Western Australia 6 pts.

At the end of the first day of a free-scoring clash, Queensland's skipper Jimmy Maher chuckled that it had been a good toss to lose. He was shocked when Justin Langer sent Queensland in on a stinking hot day, and the home side promptly amassed 362 thanks to Maher and James Hopes. By the end of the game it was Langer who had the last laugh, as blazing centuries from Chris Rogers and Murray Goodwin, racing along at almost a run a ball, carried WA past their victory target of 285. Marcus North bankrolled a huge Warriors' response in the first innings, putting Queensland's first-day efforts in the shade. The home side's predicament worsened when Maher was forced from the field with a hamstring strain after chasing down a ball in the outfield. Despite the outcome, the Gabba faithful had plenty to cheer in Queensland's second innings when the retiring favourite Stuart Law sealed his farewell to the ground with an emotional double-century. He batted just under five hours for his highest score at the Gabba, facing 233 balls and caressing 26 fours and one six. It added impetus to calls for Queensland authorities to erect a statue at the Gabba in Law's honour. With Maher and Andy Bichel, nursing a sore finger, unable to bat, Queensland were forced to declare earlier than planned. WA's victory celebrations were soured by news that they had been docked a point for a slow over-rate in an earlier game against NSW, scuppering their surprise tilt at a final berth.

Man of the Match: S. G. Law. *Attendance:* 2,548.

Close of play: First day, Western Australia (1) 0-1 (Langer 0); Second day, Western Australia (1) 5-345 (North 102, Meuleman 40); Third day, Queensland (2) 1-222 (Perren 82, Law 126).

Queensland

*J. P. Maher lbw b Meuleman	92		
C. T. Perren c Hussey b Wates	21	– (1) c Hussey b North	141
M. L. Love c Langer b Taylor	2	– (2) lbw b Wates	0
S. G. Law c Wates b Harvey	28	– (3) c Campbell b Meuleman	203
C. A. Philipson c Langer b Edmondson	63	– (4) c Campbell b Edmondson	22
J. R. Hopes b Taylor	71	– (5) b Wates	23
†W. A. Seccombe run out (Taylor)	3	– (6) c Hussey b Edmondson	13
A. J. Bichel c Meuleman b Taylor	16		
A. A. Noffke not out	24	– (8) c Campbell b Wates	1
N. M. Hauritz c Goodwin b Wates	12	– (7) c Meuleman b Wates	13
J. H. Dawes c Campbell b Harvey	18	– (9) not out	1
L-b 1, w 1, n-b 10	12	B 7, l-b 6, w 7, n-b 8	28

(92.1 overs, 390 mins) 362	(91.3 overs, 355 mins) (8 wkts dec) 445
Fall: 43 59 122 180 270 281 292 311 326 362	Fall: 0 369 371 402 419 443 444 445

Bowling: *First Innings*—Edmondson 21–1–82–1; Wates 21–4–76–2; Taylor 18–0–99–3; Harvey 19.1–5–54–2; Hussey 4–0–12–0; Meuleman 9–1–38–1. *Second Innings*—Edmondson 14–2–69–2; Wates 13.3–3–77–4; Taylor 20–4–88–0; Harvey 19–4–73–0; Meuleman 10–1–59–1; North 15–2–66–1.

Western Australia

B. M. Edmondson lbw b Bichel	0		
*J. L. Langer b Noffke	22		
M. E. K. Hussey b Noffke	49	– (1) run out (Hauritz)	23
C. J. L. Rogers c Philipson b Dawes	73	– (3) not out	119
M. W. Goodwin c Love b Hauritz	48	– (4) c (sub) C. P. Simpson b Bichel	119
M. J. North b Bichel	130		
S. W. Meuleman c and b Bichel	50	– (2) c Seccombe b Bichel	12
†R. J. Campbell c Law b Hauritz	91	– (5) not out	4
K. M. Harvey lbw b Hauritz	20		
J. J. Taylor lbw b Hauritz	4		
D. J. Wates not out	10		
B 7, l-b 6, w 1, n-b 12	26	L-b 6, w 1, n-b 3	10

(139.1 overs, 570 mins) 523	(48.5 overs, 201 mins) (3 wkts) 287
Fall: 0 42 133 153 239 389 406 484 490 523	Fall: 31 42 276

Bowling: *First Innings*—Bichel 28–6–124–3; Dawes 29–8–91–1; Noffke 29–4–96–2; Hopes 24–5–99–0; Hauritz 27.1–6–95–4; Philipson 2–1–5–0. *Second Innings*—Bichel 12–1–66–2; Dawes 12–2–49–0; Hauritz 14–0–103–0; Noffke 6–0–29–0; Hopes 3–0–28–0; Law 1.5–0–6–0.

Umpires: D. J. Harper and G. T. D. Morrow.

At Sydney Cricket Ground, Sydney, March 4, 5, 6, 7, 2004. QUEENSLAND defeated NEW SOUTH WALES by 37 runs.

FINAL

At Melbourne Cricket Ground, Melbourne, March 12, 13, 14, 15, 16, 2004. QUEENSLAND lost to VICTORIA by 321 runs. For details see section on Pura Cup final, 2003-04.

QUEENSLAND DOMESTIC FIRST-CLASS RESULTS TABLE

	First Game	M	Won	Lost	Drawn	Tied
v New South Wales ..	Nov 26, 1926	149	37	59	53	0
v Victoria	Dec 17, 1926	143	42	51	50	0
v South Australia	Dec 25, 1926	143	46	51	45	1
v Western Australia ..	Feb 6, 1948	108	26	36	46	0
v Tasmania	Feb 25, 1978	50	18	8	24	0
Total		593	169	205	218	1

QUEEENSLAND DOMESTIC FIRST-CLASS RECORDS

Highest score for:	300*	M.L. Love v Victoria at St Kilda	2003-04
Highest score against:	452*	D.G. Bradman (New South Wales) at Sydney	1929-30
Best bowling for:	10-61	P.J. Allan v Victoria at Melbourne	1965-66
Best bowling against:	9-67	A.N. Connolly (Victoria) at Brisbane	1964-65
Highest total for:	687	v New South Wales at Brisbane	1930-31
Highest total against:	7-821 dec	by South Australia at Adelaide	1939-40
Lowest total for:	49	v Victoria at Melbourne	1936-37
Lowest total against:	54	by Western Australia at Brisbane	1972-73

MOST RUNS

	M	I	NO	R	HS	100s	50s	Avge
S.G. Law...............	142	234	28	9,034	216	24	47	43.85
S.C. Trimble...........	123	230	13	8,647	252*	22	40	39.84
M.L. Love.............	102	176	16	7,668	300*	18	33	47.93
M.L. Hayden...........	83	150	17	7,332	234	24	30	55.13
P.J.P. Burge...........	83	138	12	7,084	283	22	31	56.22
A.R. Border............	87	143	19	6,779	196	15	37	54.67
J.P. Maher.............	101	179	20	6,430	209	11	33	40.44
K.D. Mackay	100	162	22	6,341	223	14	32	45.29
G.M. Ritchie..........	94	154	14	6,096	213*	14	34	43.54
T.J. Barsby	100	181	7	6,052	165	13	28	34.78
G.S. Chappell.........	52	84	11	5,037	194	17	22	69.00
R.B. Kerr	79	135	7	5,036	201*	15	24	39.34
K.C. Wessels	53	91	3	4,779	249	15	19	54.31
T.V. Hohns...........	105	170	30	3,965	103	2	25	28.32
P.H. Carlson	81	144	14	3,825	110*	5	18	29.42
A. Symonds...........	70	113	4	3,771	163	10	13	36.26
D. Tallon.............	69	124	7	3,594	193	5	17	30.72
G.R. Reynolds	50	83	9	3,518	203*	12	13	47.54
W.A. Brown............	37	65	3	3,493	215	9	17	56.34
J.A. MacLean..........	86	150	20	3,277	156	2	12	25.21

HIGHEST PARTNERSHIP FOR EACH WICKET

388 for 1st	K.C. Wessels and R.B. Kerr v Victoria at St Kilda	1982-83
368* for 2nd	M.L. Hayden and M.L. Love v Tasmania at Hobart (Bel)	1995-96
326 for 3rd	M.L. Love and S.G. Law v Tasmania at Brisbane	1994-95
295 for 4th	P.J.P. Burge and T.R. Veivers v South Australia at Brisbane	1962-63
236 for 5th	M.L. Love and J.R. Hopes v Victoria at St Kilda	2003-04
211 for 6th	T.R. Veivers and J.D. Bratchford v South Australia at Brisbane	1959-60
335 for 7th	W.C. Andrews and E.C. Bensted v New South Wales at Sydney	1934-35
146 for 8th	T.V. Hohns and G. Dymock v Victoria at Melbourne	1978-79
152* for 9th	A.T.W. Grout and W.T. Walmsley v New South Wales at Sydney	1956-57
105* for 10th	W.T. Walmsley and J.E. Childe-Freeman v New South Wales at Brisbane	1957-58

MOST WICKETS

	M	Balls	Mdns	R	W	BB	5Wi	10W/m	Avge	S-R
M. S. Kasprowicz	89	19,599	843	9,409	387	6-47	24	2	24.31	50.64
C. G. Rackemann	102	22,400	920	10,079	383	7-43	12	1	26.32	58.48
J. R. Thomson	77	15,172	410	7,927	328	7-27	17	3	24.17	46.26
C. J. McDermott	67	14,974	541	7,605	303	8-44	22	2	25.10	49.42
A. J. Bichel	56	12,455	525	6,112	274	6-45	15	3	22.31	45.46
G. Dymock	75	17,110	449	7,032	266	6-79	6	0	26.44	64.35
D. Tazelaar	73	15,371	623	7,050	257	6-49	9	1	27.43	59.81
J. H. Dawes	52	10,187	459	4,841	192	7-67	6	2	25.21	53.06
T. V. Hohns	105	16,694	680	7,330	188	6-56	8	1	38.99	88.80
A. C. Dale	44	11,857	733	4,065	184	7-40	8	1	22.09	64.44
J. N. Maguire	64	12,945	438	5,893	178	6-62	7	1	33.11	72.72
P. J. Allan	47	9,840	153	4,603	176	10-61	11	3	26.15	55.91
J. R. F. Duncan	53	11,913	221	5,253	175	8-55	7	1	30.02	68.07
L. J. Johnson	43	11,774	235	4,171	171	7-43	12	1	24.39	68.85
V. N. Raymer	56	14,595	475	5,098	168	7-100	5	1	30.35	86.88
R. K. Oxenham	46	12,075	412	3,693	167	6-48	7	1	22.11	72.31
F. M. Francke	49	9,859	244	4,324	146	6-62	7	1	29.62	67.53
P. W. Jackson	59	12,475	636	5,003	127	5-65	2	0	39.39	98.23
K. D. Mackay	100	12,757	269	4,574	123	5-15	5	0	37.19	103.72
J. D. Bratchford	52	9,155	160	3,488	118	6-57	3	0	29.56	77.58
C. L. McCool	35	9,203	117	4,078	118	7-128	8	0	34.56	77.99

MOST DISMISSALS

	M	Catches	Stumpings	Total
W. A. Seccombe	93	436	12	448
J. A. Maclean	86	289	24	313
A. T. W. Grout	84	213	63	276
R. B. Phillips	68	214	12	226
D. Tallon	67	145	61	206

MOST CATCHES

S. G. Law	126 in 142 matches	G. M. Ritchie	74 in 94 matches
M. L. Love	117 in 102 matches	T. J. Barsby	73 in 100 matches
J. P. Maher	110 in 101 matches	S. C. Trimble	72 in 123 matches
A. R. Border	99 in 87 matches	P. J. P. Burge	70 in 83 matches
M. L. Hayden	75 in 83 matches	R. B. Kerr	69 in 79 matches

MOST APPEARANCES

142	S. G. Law	1988-89 - 2003-04	101	J. P. Maher	1993-94 - 2003-04
123	S. C. Trimble	1959-60 - 1975-76	100	K. D. Mackay	1946-47 - 1963-64
105	T. V. Hohns	1972-73 - 1990-91	100	T. J. Barsby	1984-85 - 1996-97
102	C. G. Rackemann ..	1979-80 - 1995-96	94	G. M. Ritchie	1980-81 - 1991-92
102	M. L. Love	1991-92 - 2003-04	93	W. A. Seccombe ..	1993-94 - 2003-04

SOUTH AUSTRALIA

The beautiful and the damned

by BERNARD WHIMPRESS

Pura Cup: Sixth
ING Cup: Fifth
Coach: Wayne Phillips
Captain: Darren Lehmann

Shaun Tait

"There is surely some interaction between a cricket team and the ground it mainly lives on – does not the play of the side assume tone and colour from the scene?" So wrote Neville Cardus 80 years ago. If we are to believe Cardus we should expect the home side at Adelaide Oval, the most aesthetic of grounds, to provide more than its share of pretty cricket. With the eastern grandstand development completed, the oval – wonder of wonders – appeared even more beautiful than before. With a highly credentialled new coach in the personable Wayne Phillips, and a star recruit in the former Zimbabwean Test batsman Andy Flower, South Australian followers looked forward to a summer of hope.

Instead it was a summer of acute disappointment – or, as that other insightful sporting commentator John McEnroe might have put it, "the pits, man". The reasons were not hard to fathom; all you had to do was look up at that beautiful old scoreboard. Only Mark Cosgrove and Greg Blewett exceeded 500 Pura Cup runs. Only Cosgrove and Darren Lehmann averaged above 40. Greg Blewett, David Fitzgerald, Mick Miller and Ben Cameron, in a promising beginning, averaged in the 30s; Shane Deitz, Mark Higgs and Flower in the 20s.

Of the bowlers Paul Rofe, Shaun Tait and Mark Cleary each had excellent years. Jason Gillespie, the state's star fast bowler, took 11 wickets at 17.45 in his two early-season games. But Miller and the two spinners, John Davison and Mark Higgs, obtained their wickets at high cost. The attack fell away badly.

The first-class season fell away in similar fashion. It began with a bang: outright victories over Western Australia away and New South Wales at home, with an away draw against Tasmania sandwiched in between. It ended with a whimper, South Australia failing to secure a single Pura Cup point after November. The final ignominy was saved for last, when WA came to Adelaide with bottom place up for grabs. South Australia lost nine wickets for 72 to blow a strong winning position on the last day of the summer.

A realistic assessment might be that South Australia's early form flattered them. Even in those first three matches there were warning signs: batting slumps in each innings in Perth; a first-innings failure in Hobart; and a first-innings slump arrested in Adelaide. Fine as the rearguard actions were – a pair of 45s by Mark Cleary in the opening match; a top score of 58 by Cleary in the second; a thumping seventh-wicket stand of 181 between Cosgrove and Davison in the third – the batsmen needed to perform at some stage. Instead they went missing.

Lehmann was absent most of the summer with an Achilles injury. He was reduced to only four appearances and one scintillating innings of 237 in 238 balls against NSW, enough to win him back his Test spot. Blewett, the acting captain, missed the last two matches with a broken knuckle on his left hand. Both openers had poor seasons. Fitzgerald's 10-hour career-best 202 not out against Tasmania was his only notable contribution, and he subsequently lost his state contract for 2004-05. Deitz was unable to convert solid starts into sizeable scores.

For all that, the biggest concern was the middle to lower order. The failure of such experienced batsmen as Flower and Higgs was particularly disappointing, especially when they regularly made decent starts. The team often seemed unbalanced with Miller coming in at six and the wicket-keeper Graham Manou at seven, heralding the beginning of a long tail. Although Miller made some creditable scores early his form dropped off, and his place in a four-man pace attack rarely seemed necessary. Manou produced a surprisingly aggressive 130, as an opener, in the penultimate match of the season against NSW. But he also accumulated 11 single-figure scores, including five ducks.

The one batting success story was Cosgrove, the stocky teenager. He led the state's runscorers in his first full season, batting with Lehmann-like assurance during his century against NSW in

November and looking even more at home by the season's end, signing off with 144 and 88 in the last game against WA in Adelaide. The pace trio of Tait, Rofe and Cleary could also hold their heads high, each inching closer to representative honours. Tait bowled with good pace and variety and deserved his summons to replace Brett Lee as Australia's blast-out bowler in Sri Lanka in March. Rofe's lift, movement and nagging accuracy could eventually see him fill a McGrath-type role, perhaps at first change. The main bowling weakness was spin, with Davison failing to gain breakthroughs on Adelaide pitches that generally favoured the slow men on the third and fourth days.

South Australia's three ING Cup victories represented a significant improvement on the previous season when they managed only one. If anything, though, their one-day plight was even more frustrating. After six matches the Redbacks had recorded three wins, three defeats and looked a reasonable chance of making the final. But in their last four matches, batting second and chasing 260 or more on each occasion, they lost by six, six, eight and four runs.

The experiment of opening the innings with Davison, after his 2003 World Cup heroics with Canada, mostly paid off. His 257 runs were scored at a brilliant strike-rate of 127.86. Lehmann's 304 at a run-a-ball in five appearances were also a significant boost. Unfortunately Lehmann's top-edged pull off Stuart MacGill ended in the hands of the square-leg fieldsman instead of over the fence at Drummoyne Oval in the second last game; and it was his dismissal in the last, at 3 for 203 against Queensland, that sparked a mini-collapse and failure to overhaul a modest target.

Tait was comfortably the best of the bowlers with 18 wickets at 19.61, the highlight being his fabulous 8 for 43 against Tasmania in Adelaide. But apart from Davison, who took 5 for 26 in Hobart, no other bowler reached double figures.

The fact that it was youth leading experience for much of the season was one positive omen. South Australia at last have the makings of a strong leadership group for the future: Tait is 21, Rofe 23 and Cleary 24. The two precocious young batsmen, Cosgrove and Cameron, are 20 and 23 respectively. If the senior players can offer stronger support, if a recruit or two can be attracted and if a spinner such as Dan Cullen or Cullen Bailey can blossom, they might yet start playing the kind of cricket that matches the grandeur of the backdrop.

Back row: J. Siddons (*Assistant coach*), C. Ferguson, T. Kelly, J. Davison, C. Duval, P. Rofe, J. Gillespie, S. Tait, M. Miller, M. Cleary, R. Harris, B. Johnson, W. Phillips (*Coach*). *Front row:* B. Cameron, S. Deitz, M. Cosgrove, A. Flower, G. Blewett (*Vice captain*), D. Lehmann (*Captain*), G. Manou, D. Fitzgerald, M. Higgs, C. Davies.

SOUTH AUSTRALIA RESULTS, 2003-04

All first-class matches – Played 10: Won 2, Lost 6, Drawn 2.
Pura Cup – Played 10: Won 2, Lost 6, Drawn 2.
ING Cup matches – Played 10: Won 3, Lost 7.

SOUTH AUSTRALIA PURA CUP AVERAGES, 2003-04

BATTING

	M	I	NO	R	HS	100s	50s	Avge	Ct/St	S-R
D. S. Lehmann	4	8	1	372	237	1	0	53.14	4	71.94
M. J. Cosgrove	8	15	1	639	144	2	2	45.64	10	66.35
B. P. Cameron	3	6	1	199	81	0	3	39.80	0	55.12
G. S. Blewett	8	16	1	586	171	1	3	39.07	2	50.21
D. A. Fitzgerald	7	14	1	431	202*	1	0	33.15	9	37.87
M. C. Miller	7	13	2	341	84	0	3	31.00	6	43.27
S. A. Deitz	9	18	0	473	74	0	3	26.28	10	42.92
A. Flower	7	14	0	342	82	0	2	24.43	3	43.62
M. A. Higgs	7	14	0	290	71	0	2	20.71	5	52.73
J. N. Gillespie	2	4	1	58	32	0	0	19.33	2	55.77
G. A. Manou	10	18	0	331	130	1	1	18.39	31	62.45
J. M. Davison	9	16	2	253	84	0	1	18.07	4	73.55
M. F. Cleary	9	15	0	252	58	0	1	16.80	6	63.48
C. J. Davies	1	2	0	20	12	0	0	10.00	0	26.32
R. J. Harris	1	2	0	18	14	0	0	9.00	2	100.00
S. W. Tait	8	14	8	37	9*	0	0	6.17	2	17.70
P. C. Rofe	9	15	3	43	15	0	0	3.58	3	28.67
A. M. Staunton	1	2	2	4	3*	0	0	–	0	11.76

* Denotes not out.

BOWLING

	O	Mdns	R	W	BB	5W/i	10W/m	Avge	S-R
J. N. Gillespie	86	21	192	11	5-54	1	0	17.45	46.91
M. J. Cosgrove	17	5	62	3	1-0	0	0	20.67	34.00
P. C. Rofe	308.5	76	946	35	7-66	2	0	27.03	52.94
S. W. Tait	231	37	850	30	5-85	1	0	28.33	46.20
D. S. Lehmann	29	5	86	3	1-8	0	0	28.67	58.00
M. F. Cleary	261.1	45	893	30	5-102	1	0	29.77	52.23
G. S. Blewett	76	16	205	5	2-29	0	0	41.00	91.20
M. C. Miller	156.5	39	467	11	2-25	0	0	42.45	85.55
J. M. Davison	251.3	36	823	16	4-72	0	0	51.44	94.31
M. A. Higgs	125.3	21	424	7	3-36	0	0	60.57	107.57
A. M. Staunton	24	4	92	1	1-92	0	0	92.00	144.00
R. J. Harris	30	4	97	1	1-97	0	0	97.00	180.00

SOUTH AUSTRALIA v NEW SOUTH WALES

At Adelaide Oval, Adelaide, November 18, 19, 20, 21, 2003. South Australia won by five wickets. *Toss:* New South Wales. New South Wales 6 pts.

South Australia grasped the initiative early and hung on throughout to complete an entertaining win. A hot day and well-grassed pitch greeted the NSW batsmen, but Paul Rofe's Spartan line and each-way movement accounted for Michael Slater, the in-form Simon Katich and Steve Waugh in the first hour. Waugh pushed his first ball firmly off his hip only to walk off astonished by Mark Cosgrove's snare at leg-gully, which Waugh later described as the best catch he had seen to dismiss him. South Australia's wickets fell with enough regularity on the second day to suggest a scrap for first-innings points, but a middle-order stumble brought the swashbuckling John Davison in to join Cosgrove. They were together for only 116 minutes either side of tea, producing an extraordinary 181-run stand in 187 balls, a seventh-wicket record for SA against NSW. Davison's breakneck 81-ball innings contained an element of luck, but Cosgrove batted with authority beyond his 19 years. NSW showed more steel the second time out, exemplified by a stodgy Katich. But the bowlers chipped away diligently, Greg Blewett removing Mark Waugh by placing two mid-wickets and enticing a trademark flick. It cleared a path for Jason Gillespie, who docked the tail with four wickets in seven balls of fiendish reverse-swing. Set a dicey target of 135, South Australia slipped up on the final morning before Mark Higgs alleviated the pressure with a string of boundaries. His dismissal, trying for a six to win the game, allowed Cosgrove the pleasure of joining Blewett for the winning runs.

Match reports by DANIEL BRETTIG.

Man of the Match: M. J. Cosgrove. *Attendance:* 3,219.

Close of play: First day, South Australia (1) 0-26 (Fitzgerald 7, Deitz 11); Second day, New South Wales (2) 1-30 (Mail 18, Katich 12); Third day, South Australia (2) 2-38 (Blewett 20, Gillespie 3).

New South Wales

M. J. Slater b Rofe	10	– (2) lbw b Gillespie	0
G. J. Mail b Blewett	94	– (1) c Manou b Higgs	46
S. M. Katich c Manou b Rofe	5	– c Davison b Higgs	69
*S. R. Waugh c Cosgrove b Rofe	0	– c Gillespie b Cleary	31
P. A. Jaques c Manou b Cleary	23	– c Gillespie b Blewett	46
M. E. Waugh c Fitzgerald b Gillespie	34	– c Higgs b Blewett	29
†B. J. Haddin b Cleary	34	– lbw b Gillespie	21
D. A. Nash c Manou b Cosgrove	46	– lbw b Gillespie	11
M. J. Nicholson not out	3	– lbw b Gillespie	0
S. R. Clark c Deitz b Gillespie	1	– c Manou b Gillespie	0
S. C. G. MacGill c Deitz b Rofe	11	– not out	0
W 1, n-b 5	6	B 4, l-b 2, w 5, n-b 3	14
(81.2 overs, 326 mins)	**267**	(92.1 overs, 362 mins)	**267**

Fall: 11 21 21 64 117 166 250 250
254 267

Fall: 2 66 137 179 213 234 261
266 266 267

Bowling: *First Innings*—Gillespie 19–6–46–2; Rofe 17.2–3–62–4; Cleary 16–3–72–2; Davison 7–0–27–0; Higgs 12–1–44–0; Blewett 8–1–16–1; Cosgrove 2–2–0–1. *Second Innings*—Rofe 16–5–32–0; Gillespie 22.1–6–54–5; Cleary 11–1–40–1; Davison 8–3–21–0; Higgs 23–2–85–2; Blewett 12–4–29–2.

South Australia

D. A. Fitzgerald c Haddin b Clark	33	– (2) lbw b Nash	15
S. A. Deitz lbw b Nicholson	66	– (1) c M. E. Waugh b Nicholson	0
*G. S. Blewett lbw b Nicholson	25	– not out	65
A. Flower c Katich b Nicholson	21	– (5) c Haddin b Clark	2
M. A. Higgs c Haddin b Nicholson	12	– (6) c Nash b MacGill	23
M. J. Cosgrove lbw b MacGill	118	– (7) not out	0
†G. A. Manou c M. E. Waugh b MacGill	0		
J. M. Davison c Katich b Nicholson	84		
M. F. Cleary b Nicholson	0		
J. N. Gillespie not out	17	– (4) c MacGill b Clark	32
P. C. Rofe c Nicholson b MacGill	4		
B 5, l-b 2, w 6, n-b 7	20		

(94.4 overs, 382 mins)	400	(31.3 overs, 144 mins) (5 wkts) 137
Fall: 75 122 139 167 172 177 358 358 394 400		Fall: 0 35 85 91 131

Bowling: *First Innings*—Nicholson 20–3–76–6; Nash 11–4–31–0; Clark 18–3–75–1; MacGill 26.4–2–119–3; Katich 10–0–38–0; M. E. Waugh 3–0–19–0; Mail 3–0–21–0; S. R. Waugh 3–0–14–0. *Second Innings*—Nicholson 9.3–2–41–1; Clark 8–1–29–2; MacGill 6–2–39–1; Nash 8–2–28–1.

Umpires: S. D. Fry and P. D. Parker.

SOUTH AUSTRALIA v QUEENSLAND

At Adelaide Oval, Adelaide, November 27, 28, 29, 30, 2003. Queensland won by 61 runs. *Toss:* Queensland. Queensland 6 pts.

The Redbacks appeared poised to land a decisive blow for much of this match, only for Queensland to revive their season with a nervy victory. Batting first on an ideal pitch, Queensland's batsmen appeared spooked by surrendering outright points in their first two home games. A series of injudicious strokes, the worst being Stuart Law's heave at a John Davison long-hop, reduced the visitors to 9 for 252 late in the day. Perseverance from Wade Seccombe and a belligerent Michael Kasprowicz allowed Queensland to wriggle to 310. South Australia's reply was assured at first, with solid contributions from Greg Blewett and Andy Flower carrying them to within sight of the lead. But wickets fell rapidly enough to expose the tail to the second new ball. Although Graham Manou and Jason Gillespie looked capable, the last three wickets fell on an overcast third morning. SA's bowlers then made a fearful mess of Queensland's top-order. After a brief rain interruption the visitors were 4 for 15, a three-day result on the cards. Law produced his second valuable contribution but it was Andy Bichel and the irrepressible Seccombe, his 115 coming in 185 balls, who stole the initiative. Bichel and Kasprowicz made telling use of the last nine overs of the day and SA went to stumps in tatters. Flower and a streaky Mark Higgs were not parted until after lunch, and though Mark Cosgrove struck a memorable back-foot six over cover point it was merely a parting shot. Queensland finished the match with their confidence restored.

Man of the Match: W. A. Seccombe. *Attendance:* 3,658.

Close of play: First day, Queensland (1) 9-298 (Seccombe 67, Kasprowicz 36); Second day, South Australia (1) 7-283 (Manou 15, Gillespie 4); Third day, South Australia (2) 4-17 (Flower 2, Higgs 1).

Queensland

*J. P. Maher b Blewett	26	–	c Blewett b Rofe	0
C. T. Perren c Manou b Rofe	3	–	lbw b Gillespie	12
M. L. Love c Deitz b Davison	32	–	c Deitz b Rofe	2
S. G. Law c Cosgrove b Davison	75	–	c Blewett b Davison	72
A. Symonds c Tait b Rofe	10	–	c Deitz b Rofe	0
J. R. Hopes lbw b Blewett	14	–	c Manou b Tait	14
†W. A. Seccombe not out	67	–	lbw b Davison	115
A. J. Bichel c Cosgrove b Davison	14	–	c Flower b Higgs	44
A. A. Noffke c Fitzgerald b Gillespie	8	–	c Fitzgerald b Higgs	0
N. M. Hauritz b Gillespie	0	–	not out	7
M. S. Kasprowicz c Davison b Gillespie	47	–	c Deitz b Higgs	2
B 1, l-b 4, w 6, n-b 3	14		B 3, l-b 3	6

(102.5 overs, 408 mins)   310   (77.2 overs, 305 mins)   274
Fall: 10 62 62 75 110 198 220 247 252 310   Fall: 1 15 15 15 46 184 253 255 267 274

Bowling: *First Innings*—Gillespie 27.5–5–49–3; Tait 17–4–60–0; Rofe 20–4–77–2; Davison 15–1–48–3; Blewett 15.5–5–30–2; Higgs 6–0–33–0; Cosgrove 2–1–8–0. *Second Innings*—Gillespie 17–4–43–1; Rofe 12–3–53–3; Davison 18–2–83–2; Tait 14–4–40–1; Blewett 2–0–13–0; Higgs 14.2–1–36–3.

South Australia

D. A. Fitzgerald b Hauritz	24	–	(2) c Seccombe b Bichel	6
S. A. Deitz c Love b Bichel	12	–	(1) c Seccombe b Bichel	2
*G. S. Blewett b Bichel	62	–	(4) lbw b Kasprowicz	0
A. Flower c Seccombe b Bichel	82	–	(5) c Law b Kasprowicz	56
M. A. Higgs c Seccombe b Hauritz	37	–	(6) c Seccombe b Kasprowicz	71
M. J. Cosgrove c Hopes b Symonds	24	–	(7) lbw b Hauritz	31
†G. A. Manou c Love b Kasprowicz	31	–	(8) b Bichel	25
J. M. Davison lbw b Bichel	4	–	(9) c Seccombe b Bichel	3
J. N. Gillespie c Perren b Bichel	4	–	(3) c Seccombe b Kasprowicz	5
S. W. Tait b Bichel	2	–	not out	3
P. C. Rofe not out	0	–	lbw b Kasprowicz	7
B 4, l-b 4, n-b 11	19		L-b 4, w 1, n-b 8	13

(91.2 overs, 350 mins)   301   (72.3 overs, 285 mins)   222
Fall: 27 56 127 200 245 253 264 291   Fall: 7 12 14 16 119 171 191 196
     301 301   213 222

Bowling: *First Innings*—Bichel 16–1–61–6; Kasprowicz 22.2–7–85–1; Noffke 10–2–29–0; Symonds 11–2–32–1; Hauritz 24–5–74–2; Hopes 8–4–12–0. *Second Innings*—Bichel 16–3–52–4; Kasprowicz 23.3–4–84–5; Hauritz 24–7–48–1; Noffke 5–0–28–0; Symonds 4–1–6–0.

Umpires: S. J. Davis and I. H. Lock.

At Brisbane Cricket Ground, Brisbane, December 19, 20, 21, 2003. SOUTH AUSTRALIA lost to QUEENSLAND by an innings and 137 runs.

SOUTH AUSTRALIA v TASMANIA

At Adelaide Oval, Adelaide, January 11, 12, 13, 14, 2003. Tasmania won by 213 runs. *Toss:* Tasmania. Tasmania 6 pts.

    Heartening early form gave way to inconsistency, as South Australia's progress came to a shuddering halt against a disciplined Tasmanian side. Everything had looked so promising on the first day, SA's vaunted pace attack never allowing Tasmania's equally vaunted batting line-up to settle. Shaun Tait, Mark Cleary and Mick Miller all gained enough movement from a probing line to pick up wickets. Tasmania's dismissal after tea left South Australia with 22 overs in which to make a start, but David Fitzgerald and Shane Deitz dithered badly, Fitzgerald's downfall in the day's final over giving the visitors some momentum. It was pressed home on the second morning. Gerard Denton's pace proved particularly disconcerting and SA were dismissed for their lowest first-class score against Tasmania. The Tigers' second innings was unspectacular but professional, as early losses were averted and partnerships built. Shane Watson scored the first half-century of the match. South Australia looked set to chase around 350 after snaring the seventh wicket at 231, but Sean Clingeleffer – true to his name – hung around while another 103 were added. The target of 430 had become purely notional by stumps on day three, thanks to Denton's speed and some indiscriminate strokes. Mark Cosgrove was particularly culpable, wafting at Damien Wright shortly before the close, and any hope of a Darren Lehmann miracle was scotched when he guided the first ball next morning straight to gully. By early afternoon Tasmania had wrapped up a comprehensive victory.

Man of the Match: G. J. Denton.   *Attendance:* 3,366.

Close of play: First day, South Australia (1) 1-25 (Deitz 12); Second day, Tasmania (2) 3-175 (Watson 43); Third day, South Australia (2) 4-110 (Lehmann 10, Miller 5).

Tasmania

J. Cox c Cosgrove b Miller	36	– (2) c Manou b Cleary	32
S. R. Mason lbw b Tait	0	– (1) hit wicket b Cleary	43
S. R. Watson c Deitz b Miller	12	– c Manou b Rofe	61
M. G. Dighton c Manou b Cleary	36	– lbw b Cosgrove	45
*D. J. Marsh c Fitzgerald b Cleary	10	– c Fitzgerald b Davison	1
S. B. Tubb c Manou b Cleary	4	– lbw b Davison	21
†S. G. Clingeleffer b Tait	42	– c Manou b Lehmann	74
D. G. Wright c Manou b Cleary	0	– c Manou b Rofe	0
A. G. Downton c Cosgrove b Tait	19	– c Fitzgerald b Tait	14
X. J. Doherty not out	17	– run out (Cleary/Manou)	7
G. J. Denton b Davison	11	– not out	10
L–b 6, n-b 14	20	B 5, l-b 12, n-b 9	26

(71.4 overs, 295 mins) 207   (111 overs, 410 mins) 334

Fall: 3 33 86 109 113 116 116 176   Fall: 82 85 175 181 204 230 231 271
     181 207   307 334

Bowling: *First Innings*—Tait 18–2–61–3; Rofe 16–8–27–0; Cleary 15–4–41–4; Miller 9–2–25–2; Davison 12.4–0–43–1; Lehmann 1–0–4–0. *Second Innings*—Tait 16–1–78–1; Rofe 17–4–56–2; Miller 8–1–18–0; Cleary 15–2–36–2; Davison 39–9–85–2; Blewett 6–2–13–0; Lehmann 9–1–24–1; Cosgrove 1–0–7–1.

South Australia

D. A. Fitzgerald c Clingeleffer b Doherty	11	– (2) c Dighton b Denton	26
S. A. Deitz c Clingeleffer b Wright	13	– (1) c Mason b Wright	10
G. S. Blewett c Dighton b Denton	39	– b Denton	1
M. J. Cosgrove b Downton	21	– c Clingeleffer b Wright	54
*D. S. Lehmann c Cox b Wright	1	– c Mason b Wright	10
M. C. Miller not out	14	– not out	53
†G. A. Manou b Denton	0	– c Cox b Denton	9
J. M. Davison c Denton b Doherty	0	– c Watson b Wright	4
M. F. Cleary c Clingeleffer b Denton	0	– b Downton	38
S. W. Tait run out (Doherty)	2	– c Clingeleffer b Downton	3
P. C. Rofe c Denton b Doherty	4	– b Wright	0
L-b 4, w 1, n-b 2	7	L-b 8	8

(61.5 overs, 247 mins) 112   (69.5 overs, 268 mins) 216

Fall: 25 35 75 76 105 105 106 106 108 112   Fall: 14 15 91 95 110 119 126 192 215 216

Bowling: *First Innings*—Denton 20–9–34–3; Wright 19–6–29–2; Downton 12–5–22–1; Doherty 10.5–1–23–3. *Second Innings*—Wright 18.5–4–43–5; Denton 13–2–22–3; Downton 14–4–40–2; Doherty 12–3–32–0; Tubb 12–1–71–0.

Umpires: D. J. Harper and I. H. Lock.

SOUTH AUSTRALIA v VICTORIA

At Adelaide Oval, Adelaide, February 1, 2, 3, 4, 2004. Victoria won by 197 runs. *Toss:* Victoria. Victoria 6 pts.

Allan Wise and Mathew Inness ruthlessly snuffed out a tight contest, the first for the David Hookes Memorial Trophy, as South Australia were left pondering another missed opportunity. Victoria batted serenely on the first day, as the prolific Matthew Elliott and commanding Brad Hodge took the score to 2 for 276 in the day's final hour. But the Glenn McGrath-like straightness of Paul Rofe, and two wickets in as many balls from Shaun Tait, ensured the last eight wickets tumbled for only 67. Victoria's frustration at Rofe's good line was exemplified by David Hussey's dismissal to a stroke which might best be described as an attempted overhead smash. David Fitzgerald and Shane Deitz batted with considerable poise against the new ball but both fell in the 40s, a batting sin for which the locals would pay dearly. The middle order offered less than the required substance and several rash attempts to thrash the leg-spinner Cameron White presented him with flattering figures. Victoria's response was forgettable early, but Hodge and Hussey guided them away from danger and White deflated the SA attack with some muscular hitting. Greg Blewett and Darren Lehmann were in occupation at the close of day three, and past fourth-innings feats by this pair against Victoria offered some cause for hope. But Blewett pushed at Wise's angle to be caught behind and the rest folded meekly, granting Wise the pleasure of his best first-class figures.

Man of the Match: P. A. Jaques.   *Attendance:* 2,311.

Close of play: First day, Victoria (1) 5-310 (Hussey 12, McDonald 8); Second day, Victoria (2) 1-13 (Elliott 6, Lewis 0); Third day, South Australia (2) 2-75 (Blewett 38, Lehmann 22).

Victoria

M. T. G. Elliott lbw b Cosgrove	111	–	(2) c Cosgrove b Tait	28
M. P. Mott c Lehmann b Rofe	53	–	(1) lbw b Tait	6
B. J. Hodge lbw b Rofe	81	–	(4) c Lehmann b Davison	86
J. Moss c Manou b Rofe	27	–	(5) c Manou b Cleary	8
D. J. Hussey c Manou b Rofe	13	–	(6) c Miller b Cleary	41
C. L. White c Manou b Rofe	0	–	(7) c Cleary b Davison	75
A. B. McDonald c Manou b Tait	20	–	(8) lbw b Davison	8
*†D. S. Berry c Manou b Tait	0	–	(9) c Lehmann b Davison	1
M. L. Lewis c Lehmann b Rofe	14	–	(3) lbw b Rofe	2
M. W. H. Inness lbw b Rofe	0	–	c Cosgrove b Lehmann	3
A. B. Wise not out	6	–	not out	0
B 1, l-b 7, w 1, n-b 9	18		B 6, w 6, n-b 2	14

(105.1 overs, 424 mins)	343	(74.1 overs, 290 mins)	272

Fall: 102 236 276 296 296 322 322 332
 332 343

Fall: 7 22 61 91 182 194 217 227
 252 272

Bowling: *First Innings*—Tait 22–3–77–2; Rofe 29.1–9–66–7; Cleary 18–4–53–0; Davison 14–1–66–0; Miller 13–5–38–0; Cosgrove 7–2–25–1; Lehmann 2–0–10–0. *Second Innings*—Rofe 13–2–51–1; Tait 11–0–57–2; Miller 7–1–21–0; Cleary 13–2–43–2; Davison 22.1–4–72–4; Lehmann 8–3–22–1.

South Australia

D. A. Fitzgerald c Berry b Wise	47	– (2) lbw b Inness	2
S. A. Deitz lbw b Wise	46	– (1) c Berry b Wise	11
G. S. Blewett c Berry b McDonald	11	– c Berry b Wise	45
*D. S. Lehmann c McDonald b White	38	– lbw b Inness	45
M. J. Cosgrove c Berry b Lewis	27	– c Berry b Wise	4
M. C. Miller c Lewis b White	27	– c McDonald b Wise	7
†G. A. Manou lbw b White	14	– c Berry b Wise	0
J. M. Davison b White	28	– b Inness	13
M. F. Cleary b Lewis	12	– c Lewis b White	23
S. W. Tait lbw b Lewis	0	– not out	0
P. C. Rofe not out	0	– b Inness	0
B 6, l-b 2, w 1, n-b 3	12	B 4, l-b 2	6

(77.1 overs, 309 mins)	262	(49.3 overs, 205 mins)	156

Fall: 83 110 110 146 199 216 217 256
261 262

Fall: 3 29 89 99 109 109 131 132
156 156

Bowling: *First Innings*—Inness 13–2–47–0; McDonald 10–1–47–1; Lewis 15.1–3–47–3; Wise 24–8–53–2; White 14–2–43–4; Moss 1–0–17–0. *Second Innings*—Inness 12.3–5–26–4; Wise 15–5–47–5; Lewis 13–2–42–0; White 6–0–25–1; McDonald 3–1–10–0.

Umpires: B. N. J. Oxenford and J. H. Smeaton.

At Sydney Cricket Ground, Sydney, February 17, 18, 19, 20, 2004. SOUTH AUSTRALIA lost to NEW SOUTH WALES by 25 runs.

SOUTH AUSTRALIA v WESTERN AUSTRALIA

At Adelaide Oval, Adelaide, March 4, 5, 6(no play), 7, 2004. Western Australia won by 87 runs. *Toss:* Western Australia. Western Australia 6 pts.

In a game to determine bottom place, Western Australia's batting held the South Australian fast bowlers at bay and the home side crumbled under final-day pressure. Murray Goodwin threw away his hand with an ugly swipe. But Marcus North batted stylishly, his unbeaten 130 comprising 18 fours and two sixes, as SA again failed to snuff out the opposition tail. Shane Deitz made another start and the stroke-laden Mark Cosgrove, whose 144 came in only 200 balls, treated Darren Wates and Ben Edmondson with contempt. The middle order gave its best house of cards impression to surrender a lead, before Shaun Tait rebounded from his first-innings struggles with three wickets late on day three. Paul Rofe ousted North and Ryan Campbell in consecutive balls. WA's situation further deteriorated until Wates and Brad Hogg put together a match-turning partnership of 119. Wates faced 141 balls and displayed an array of shots he had seldom hinted at in the past. His dismissal, last man out going for his 100th run, was a minor tragedy. Needing 338 to win, SA's top order batted without a care in the world. Ben Cameron, who had struggled at No. 7 in the first innings after being hit in the face while fielding, unleashed a string of inspiring back-foot drives. With Cosgrove, he appeared to be announcing a new, brighter chapter in SA's batting. But his rousing innings came to an underwhelming end when he pushed Kade Harvey to cover. Next ball, any thoughts of victory were shattered with Andy Flower's stumps. Within 25 overs it was all over. SA's misery at finishing last was exacerbated by the Western Australian celebrations, their raucous singing audible all round the ground.

Man of the Match: M. J. North.   *Attendance:* 1,854.

Close of play: First day, South Australia (1) 0-13 (Manou 8, Deitz 4); Second day, Western Australia (2) 3-62 (Goodwin 37, North 8); Third day, South Australia (2) 1-106 (Cameron 48, Cosgrove 35).

Western Australia

*M. E. K. Hussey c Higgs b Cleary	28	– (2) c (sub) R. J. Harris b Tait	7
S. W. Meuleman run out (Cleary)	4	– (1) lbw b Tait	4
C. J. L. Rogers c Manou b Cleary	17	– b Tait	5
M. W. Goodwin c Manou b Tait	55	– c Higgs b Tait	48
M. J. North not out	130	– lbw b Rofe	13
†R. J. Campbell c Manou b Miller	28	– c Manou b Rofe	0
K. M. Harvey c Flower b Cleary	3	– c (sub) R. J. Harris b Miller	19
G. B. Hogg c and b Davison	6	– b Davison	75
D. J. Wates c Tait b Rofe	2	– run out (s) R. J. Harris/Manou)	99
A. K. Heal c Deitz b Rofe	33	– c and b Rofe	9
B. M. Edmondson lbw b Miller	1	– not out	4
B 4, l-b 10, w 2, n-b 11	27	B 13, l-b 3, w 2, n-b 1	19

(90.2 overs, 386 mins)	335	(90.1 overs, 362 mins)	302

Fall: 26 56 75 156 201 211 232 244 320 335

Fall: 11 12 31 71 71 83 116 235 2 68 302

Bowling: *First Innings*—Tait 16–1–81–1; Rofe 22–6–53–2; Cleary 17–7–43–3; Davison 17–1–76–1; Miller 16.2–4–58–2; Cosgrove 2–0–10–0. *Second Innings*—Tait 23–4–59–4; Rofe 25–3–70–3; Cleary 13–1–46–0; Higgs 12.1–3–49–0; Miller 7–1–27–1; Davison 10–1–35–1.

South Australia

†G. A. Manou c Campbell b Edmondson	8	– (7) c Campbell b Edmondson	16
S. A. Deitz b Heal	51	– c Rogers b Wates	20
M. J. Cosgrove c and b Hogg	144	– c Campbell b Edmondson	88
*A. Flower c Hogg b North	21	– b Harvey	0
M. A. Higgs c Campbell b Wates	0	– c Hogg b Harvey	11
M. C. Miller c Campbell b Harvey	5	– b Heal	13
J. M. Davison c Hogg b North	4	– (8) not out	9
B. P. Cameron c Wates b Edmondson	6	– (1) c Goodwin b Harvey	81
M. F. Cleary c North b Hogg	20	– b Edmondson	0
P. C. Rofe c Edmondson b Hogg	1	– b Edmondson	0
S. W. Tait not out	8	– b Edmondson	0
B 8, l-b 6, w 1, n-b 17	32	L-b 2, w 1, n-b 4, pen 5	12

(78.5 overs, 312 mins)	300	(63 overs, 256 mins)	250

Fall: 28 125 191 194 222 231 255 287 292 300

Fall: 42 178 178 196 217 241 243 244 244 250

Bowling: *First Innings*—Wates 16–2–55–1; Edmondson 17–1–54–2; Hogg 14.5–3–66–3; Harvey 9–1–43–1; Heal 12–3–51–1; North 10–2–17–2. *Second Innings*—Edmondson 18–2–90–5; Wates 12–2–53–1; Harvey 10–1–40–3; Hogg 13–2–41–0; Heal 10–3–19–1.

Umpires: S. D. Fry and J. H. Smeaton.

SOUTH AUSTRALIA FIRST-CLASS RESULTS TABLE

	First Game	M	Won	Lost	Drawn	Tied
v New South Wales ..	Dec 16, 1892	199	54	109	36	0
v Victoria	Dec 31, 1892	200	47	100	53	0
v Queensland	Dec 25, 1926	143	51	46	45	1
v Western Australia ..	Nov 14, 1947	108	29	46	33	0
v Tasmania	Feb 18, 1978	49	17	10	22	0
Total		699	198	311	189	1

SOUTH AUSTRALIA DOMESTIC FIRST-CLASS RECORDS

Highest score for:	365*	C. Hill v New South Wales at Adelaide	1900-01
Highest score against:	355*	G. R. Marsh (Western Australia) at Perth	1989-90
Best bowling for:	10-35	T. W. Wall v New South Wales at Sydney	1932-33
Best bowling against:	9-40	E. L. McCormick (Victoria) at Adelaide	1936-37
Highest total for:	7-821 dec	v Queensland at Adelaide	1939-40
Highest total against:	918	by New South Wales at Sydney	1900-01
Lowest total for:	27	v New South Wales at Sydney	1955-56
Lowest total against:	41	by Western Australia at Adelaide	1990-91

MOST RUNS

	M	I	NO	R	HS	100s	50s	Avge
D. S. Lehmann	97	179	10	9,454	255	32	34	55.94
D. W. Hookes	120	205	9	9,364	306*	26	44	47.78
G. S. Blewett	100	190	10	8,794	268	23	43	48.86
L. E. Favell	121	220	4	8,269	164	20	43	38.28
I. M. Chappell	89	157	13	7,665	205*	22	45	53.23
H. N. Dansie	107	196	6	6,692	185	17	32	35.22
A. M. J. Hilditch	91	161	11	6,504	230	17	32	43.36
C. Hill	68	126	6	6,270	365*	18	27	52.25
P. R. Sleep	127	211	37	6,106	146*	12	29	35.09
V. Y. Richardson	77	146	7	6,027	203	18	27	43.36
J. D. Siddons	82	150	10	5,940	197	17	26	42.43
G. A. Bishop	84	152	6	4,871	224*	8	26	33.36
P. C. Nobes	63	114	4	4,608	141	10	31	41.89
P. L. Ridings	76	131	12	4,501	186*	9	21	37.82
K. G. Cunningham	76	133	10	4,330	203	6	24	35.20
D. G. Bradman	31	44	6	4,293	357	19	8	112.97
J. A. Brayshaw	52	96	11	3,969	146	9	24	46.69
D. A. Fitzgerald	61	118	2	3,943	202*	12	13	33.99
B. A. Johnson	65	123	14	3,884	168	9	16	35.63
A. J. Woodcock	68	124	2	3,793	141	4	26	31.09

HIGHEST PARTNERSHIP FOR EACH WICKET

281	for 1st	L. E. Favell and J. P. Causby v New South Wales at Adelaide		1967-68
386	for 2nd	G. S. Blewett and D. S. Lehmann v Tasmania at Hobart (Bel)		2001-02
286	for 3rd	G. S. Blewett and D. S. Lehmann v Tasmania at Adelaide		1993-94
462*	for 4th	D. W. Hookes and W. B. Phillips v Tasmania at Adelaide		1986-87
281	for 5th	C. L. Badcock and M. G. Waite v Queensland at Adelaide		1939-40
260	for 6th	D. S. Lehmann and T. J. Nielsen v Queensland at Adelaide		1996-97
198	for 7th	G. A. Bishop and T. B. A. May v Tasmania at Adelaide		1990-91
222	for 8th	M. C. Miller and B. E. Young v Queensland at Adelaide		2002-03
232	for 9th	C. Hill and E. A. Walkley v New South Wales at Adelaide		1900-01
104	for 10th	L. Michael and E. I. Pynor v Victoria at Adelaide		1949-50

MOST WICKETS

	M	Balls	Mdns	R	W	BB	5W/i	10W/m	Avge	S-R
C. V. Grimmett	78	28,144	445	12,878	504	9-180	47	13	25.55	55.84
A. A. Mallett	77	20,988	673	8,171	344	7-57	19	2	23.75	61.01
T. B. A. May	80	22,575	931	9,943	270	7-93	15	2	36.82	83.61
P. R. Sleep	127	19,482	671	9,883	252	8-133	7	0	39.22	77.31
P. E. McIntyre	61	17,419	576	8,974	215	6-64	8	2	41.74	81.07
E. Jones	39	12,145	501	5,516	208	8-157	19	3	26.52	58.39
T. J. Jenner	65	13,559	245	6,312	207	7-127	8	1	30.49	65.50
G. Giffen	38	11,682	402	5,676	192	9-147	18	7	29.56	60.90
G. Noblet	38	11,156	273	3,396	190	7-29	10	2	17.87	58.72
G. R. Attenborough ...	50	11,137	280	5,371	172	7-90	8	2	31.23	64.75
N. J. N. Hawke	50	11,712	210	5,026	169	8-61	9	4	29.74	69.30
M. A. Harrity	62	12,034	418	6,513	166	5-65	2	0	39.23	72.49
W. J. Whitty	38	10,681	298	5,012	154	7-66	7	1	32.55	69.36
T. W. Wall	42	9,299	118	4,242	150	10-36	2	1	28.28	61.99
J. W. Wilson	46	13,796	474	4,780	147	6-55	5	0	32.52	93.85
J. C. Scuderi	57	11,061	478	5,158	146	7-79	8	1	35.33	75.76
R. M. Hogg	34	6,705	183	3,182	144	6-51	9	2	22.10	46.56
S. P. George	51	9,962	315	5,617	143	6-51	2	0	39.28	69.66
A. K. Zesers	40	10,131	550	3,808	136	7-67	4	0	28.00	74.49
B. E. Young	48	12,148	468	5,871	130	6-85	5	0	45.16	93.45

MOST DISMISSALS

	M	Catches	Stumpings	Total
T. J. Nielsen	92	255	29	284
B. N. Jarman	77	193	57	250
C. W. Walker	57	103	87	190
G. R. A. Langley	46	111	24	135
G. A. Manou	39	122	12	134
K. J. Wright	36	102	9	111

MOST CATCHES

D. W. Hookes .... 128 in 120 matches	P. R. Sleep .... 84 in 127 matches
I. M. Chappell ...... 113 in 89 matches	G. A. Bishop .... 60 in 84 matches
J. D. Siddons .... 113 in 82 matches	G. S. Blewett .... 60 in 100 matches
V. Y. Richardson ..... 99 in 77 matches	L. E. Favell .... 59 in 121 matches

MOST APPEARANCES

127	P. R. Sleep .... 1976-77 – 1992-93	97	D. S. Lehmann .... 1987-88 – 2003-04
121	L. E. Favell .... 1951-52 – 1969-70	92	T. J. Nielsen ...... 1990-91 – 1998-99
120	D. W. Hookes ..... 1975-76 – 1991-92	91	A. M. J Hilditch ... 1982-83 – 1991-92
107	H. N. Dansie ...... 1949-50 – 1966-67	89	I. M. Chappell .... 1961-62 – 1979-80
100	G. S. Blewett ...... 1991-92 – 2003-04	84	G. A. Bishop ..... 1982-83 – 1992-93

TASMANIA

Ire of the Tigers

by DAVID STOCKDALE

Pura Cup: Third
ING Cup: Sixth
Coach: Brian McFadyen
Captain: Dan Marsh

Shane Watson

Tasmania will look back on 2003-04 as the season that slipped away in the dark. The absence of lights at Bellerive Oval, and the impressive towers at the SCG, were crucial factors in the Tigers missing out on a Pura Cup final berth on the last evening of the home-and-away season. Queensland ultimately grabbed second spot with a last-gasp win against New South Wales when the lights were turned on, illuminating the Sydney darkness rather than enhancing what natural light remained as per the playing conditions. Or at least that was how the Tasmanian players saw it. They shook their heads in disbelief as the news came over the radio that the NSW No. 11 batsman, Glenn McGrath, had been dismissed off the final ball of the penultimate over at 7.35 p.m.

At Bellerive, where there were no bulbs to fight off the encroaching gloom, play had been abandoned an hour and a half earlier. Victoria had held on for a draw at 6 for 212, frustrating the Tasmanians in their pursuit of four wickets in 10 overs for victory. The respective results in Sydney and Hobart left Queensland and Tasmania locked in equal-second place on 24 points, the Bulls progressing to the final with a superior quotient of 1.11 to the Tigers' 0.92.

It was a dramatic end to a season of close calls and missed opportunities. The most notable slip of a bizarre campaign, which included two drawn matches with the scores tied, came at the WACA way back in December. Had Andrew Downton hit two off the last ball of the match instead of one, Tasmania would have gained six points instead of none, five more days at the MCG and a fourth tilt at a Pura Cup final.

For all the agonising about what might have been, there was much to be satisfied with from a Tasmanian perspective. Perhaps the biggest surprise, given the placid nature of the Bellerive pitch, was the fact that three of the state's shining lights were pace bowlers. Damien Wright and Downton led the charge with 37 Pura Cup wickets. Only NSW's Matthew Nicholson finished ahead of them.

Wright was rewarded for his immaculate control with a one-day cap for Australia A, but the left-armer Downton's rise from meek to menacing was the most noteworthy. Before the season he was sheepish about his modest physique and worried about taking his shirt off around team-mates. After building himself up in the gym he soon cottoned-on, bowling with more aggression and extracting seam, swing and opposition scalps.

The third member of the pace trio, sandy-haired Gerard Denton, was first reborn and then relocated. He put a long history of crippling back-related injuries behind him and bowled with fire and purpose, taking 30 Pura Cup wickets at 30.33. Then, just as Tasmania seemed to have assembled a settled attack, he announced that he had accepted an offer from Victoria and was switching to the other end of the Bass Strait. Providing variation was the left-arm orthodox spinner Xavier Doherty. His 22 Pura Cup wickets came at a costly 51.45, but he toiled hard on wickets offering him little assistance and was rewarded with his shock selection for the tour of India in October.

The biggest disappointment was Adam Griffith's anticlimactic second season. An ogre in 2002-03, Griffith missed the demons of the previous summer's pitches at Bellerive, which had been ousted by the new curator Cameron Hodgkins. He finished with nine wickets at 71.22. Offered a chance to join Western Australia in the off-season, Griffith opted to stay in Tasmania and attempt to recover the menace of his debut year.

Leading the way in an often imposing batting order was Shane Watson. Unable to bowl until late in the season as he recovered from the back problems that ruled him out of the 2003 World Cup, Watson made the most of his opportunities as a specialist batsman. Going in at No. 3, he amassed four impressive hundreds and 983 runs at 54.61, confirming – if confirmation were needed – that he is a Test star in the making. Not far behind him was Michael Dighton, enjoying the most prolific summer of his first-class life. His languid style belied his immense power as he piled up 944 runs at 55.22.

Watson and Dighton received solid support from Michael Di Venuto and the captain Dan Marsh. Di Venuto was as consistent as ever, weighing in with 649 runs at 46.35. His unbeaten 174 in November against NSW, chasing 386 for victory, was a brilliant matchwinning innings. But it remained his only century of the summer, suggesting that he is not quite making the most of his ability. Marsh led admirably and batted forcefully, hitting two centuries and averaging 57, even if his left-arm spin took a back seat to Doherty. The main underachievers were the openers, Scott Mason and Jamie Cox, who began the season with a fine 119 against South Australia but struggled thereafter. Cox has not averaged 40 in a season since the distant summer of 2000-01.

In the ING Cup, Tasmania's chronic woes continued. They have finished fifth or sixth 11 times in the past 12 summers, and spent most of last season in the all-too-familiar bottom position. The highlight was a lone, late victory over the four-day champions Victoria. Their stocks will be boosted this summer by the Zimbabwean all-rounder Andy Blignaut, a lively bowler and hard-hitting batsman, and Michael Bevan, formerly the world's foremost one-day cricketer. Bevan has also been appointed assistant coach, and his knowledge of one-day strategies should prove invaluable in a side that has previously been so lacking in them.

Will it be enough to compensate for the departure of Watson, who has followed the sun back home to Queensland? That is a question upon which Tasmania's destiny lies in 2004-05.

TASMANIA RESULTS, 2003-04

All first-class matches – Played 10: Won 3, Lost 1, Drawn 6.
Pura Cup – Played 10: Won 3, Lost 1, Drawn 6.
ING Cup matches – Won 1, Lost 8, No Result 1.

Back row: R. D. Langford (*Fitness*), B. A. McFadyen (*Coach*), S. R. Mason, X. J. Doherty, T. D. Paine, R. J. Lockyear, T. R. Birt,
D. G. Dawson, B. W. Hilfenhaus, A. W. Polkinghorne, G. T. Cunningham, A. R. Griffith, M. G. Dighton, L. R. Butterworth, K. S. Pickering,
J. Cox, S. P. Kremerskothen, G. J. Bailey, D. J. Saker (*Assistant coach*), D. F. Hills (*Assistant coach*). *Front row:* S. B. Tubb,
S. G. Clingeleffer, M. J. DiVenuto, S. R. Watson, R. T. Ponting, D. J. Marsh, B. Geeves, D. G. Wright, G. J. Denton, A. G. Downton.

TASMANIA PURA CUP AVERAGES, 2003-04

BATTING

	M	I	NO	R	HS	100s	50s	Avge	Ct/St	S-R
D. J. Marsh	10	18	5	751	111*	2	4	57.77	11	76.32
M. G. Dighton	10	18	1	944	152	3	5	55.53	5	57.46
S. R. Watson	10	19	1	983	157	4	3	54.61	9	52.20
M. J. Di Venuto	9	15	1	649	174*	1	4	46.36	12	52.04
S. G. Clingeleffer	10	16	2	434	79	0	3	31.00	28/4	44.97
S. R. Mason	10	19	0	548	126	1	3	28.84	8	49.95
G. J. Denton	8	11	8	85	34	0	0	28.33	4	45.95
J. Cox	9	17	1	415	119	1	1	25.94	5	42.39
D. G. Wright	9	13	1	260	65	0	2	21.67	2	65.82
X. J. Doherty	8	10	4	88	21*	0	0	14.67	2	32.12
S. P. Kremerskothen	1	2	0	29	24	0	0	14.50	1	78.38
S. B. Tubb	1	2	0	25	21	0	0	12.50	0	39.06
A. G. Downton	10	15	3	146	45	0	0	12.17	2	34.68
A. R. Griffith	5	7	0	78	21	0	0	11.14	0	29.66

 * *Denotes not out.*

BOWLING

	O	Mdns	R	W	BB	5W/i	10W/m	Avge	S-R
D. G. Wright	362.5	101	980	37	5-43	1	0	26.49	58.84
G. J. Denton	276.3	60	994	30	4-60	0	0	33.13	55.30
A. G. Downton	373.5	76	1353	37	5-71	1	0	36.57	60.62
X. J. Doherty	306.2	41	1132	22	6-149	1	0	51.45	83.55
S. R. Watson	58	8	215	4	2-31	0	0	53.75	87.00
D. J. Marsh	112	19	371	6	2-19	0	0	61.83	112.00
A. R. Griffith	171	38	641	9	2-26	0	0	71.22	114.00
J. Cox	30	2	104	1	1-44	0	0	104.00	180.00
M. G. Dighton	3	0	31	0	–	0	0	–	–
M. J. Di Venuto	6	0	50	0	–	0	0	–	–
S. P. Kremerskothen ..	13	1	42	0	–	0	0	–	–
S. B. Tubb	12	1	71	0	–	0	0	–	–

TASMANIA v SOUTH AUSTRALIA

At Bellerive Oval, Hobart, November 3, 4, 5, 6, 2003. Match drawn. *Toss:* South Australia. Tasmania 2 pts.

Tasmania's pace attack, led by the left-armer Andrew Downton, made the most of some early life to dismiss South Australia well before stumps on the opening day. The wicket then flattened out into a batsman's paradise. A bounty of 902 runs followed, including one double-century and three centuries, for the loss of 16 wickets. Downton, looking much fitter and more aggressive than in the previous season, caused the main damage as the visitors crumbled from 2 for 116 to 7 for 148. Damien Wright offered sterling support, keeping the screws tight with a miserly 3 for 47 from his 21 overs. The SA top six all got starts but only Shane Deitz made it to 40. It fell to the No. 9 Mark Cleary, with a meaty 58 off 62 balls, to ensure a vaguely respectable total. Tasmania benefited from the change in the pitch, Jamie Cox and Shane Watson adding 213 for the second wicket in a little under four hours. Cleary built on his impressive match by carrying an otherwise lacklustre attack. The Redbacks atoned for their first-innings shortcomings, but with Shaun Tait missing due to a torn groin muscle they made no attempt to set up a victory target. The cornerstone of their second innings was a 281-run partnership between the captain Greg Blewett and the opener David Fitzgerald, who batted 607 minutes and faced 494 balls for his highest first-class score.

Man of the Match: A.G. Downton.   *Attendance:* 1,032.
Close of play: First day, Tasmania (1) 1-39 (Cox 23, Watson 1); Second day, Tasmania (1) 8-358 (Marsh 27, Griffith 0); Third day, South Australia (2) 1-191 (Fitzgerald 99, Blewett 60).

South Australia

D.A. Fitzgerald b Griffith	32	– (2) not out	202
S.A. Deitz lbw b Doherty	40	– (1) c and b Doherty	28
*G.S. Blewett b Downton	25	– b Griffith	171
A. Flower c Di Venuto b Downton	28	– b Wright	13
C.J. Davies b Downton	12	– (6) c Marsh b Doherty	8
M.A. Higgs c Di Venuto b Downton	16	– (5) b Wright	19
†G.A. Manou b Wright	1	– run out (Dighton/Marsh)	1
J.M. Davison c Dighton b Wright	0	– not out	23
M.F. Cleary b Downton	58		
P.C. Rofe c Marsh b Wright	9		
S.W. Tait not out	9		
L-b 2, n-b 4	6	L-b 9, w 2, n-b 6	17

(75.5 overs, 309 mins)   236   (171 overs, 607 mins)   (6 wkts) 482
Fall: 67 75 116 140 143 148 148 190 210 236   Fall: 65 346 376 402 428 433

Bowling: *First Innings*—Wright 21–10–47–3; Griffith 21–3–85–1; Downton 22.5–7–71–5; Doherty 11–4–31–1. *Second Innings*—Wright 30–11–70–2; Griffith 33–8–100–1; Doherty 46–8–139–2; Downton 35–9–76–0; Di Venuto 2–0–15–0; Marsh 18–6–28–0; Cox 4–0–14–0; Dighton 3–0–31–0.

Tasmania

S.R. Mason lbw b Tait	13	X.J. Doherty b Cleary	0
J. Cox c (sub) T.P.Kelly b Higgs	119	A.R. Griffith lbw b Cleary	18
S.R. Watson c Manou b Cleary	103	A.G. Downton run out (Blewett)	4
M.J. Di Venuto c and b Rofe	50		
M.G. Dighton lbw b Cleary	21	B 3, l-b 6, w 1, n-b 1	11
*D.J. Marsh not out	76		
†S.G. Clingeleffer b Rofe	0	(133 overs, 501 mins)	420
D.G. Wright lbw b Cleary	5	Fall: 27 240 249 291 344 344 352 352 409 420	

Bowling: Tait 15–1–53–1; Rofe 34–10–99–2; Cleary 33–5–102–5; Higgs 17–5–47–1; Davison 19–1–58–0; Blewett 15–2–52–0.

Umpires: P.D. Parker and J.H. Smeaton.

TASMANIA v NEW SOUTH WALES

At Bellerive Oval, Hobart, November 12, 13, 14, 15, 2003. Tasmania won by six wickets. *Toss:* New South Wales. Tasmania 6 pts, New South Wales 2 pts.

Dan Marsh and Michael Di Venuto, with an unconquered 220-run stand on the final day, roared Tasmania to a memorable win over a classy New South Wales line-up. After a faltering start by Michael Slater and Greg Mail, NSW recovered through Simon Katich and Steve Waugh, who was in the final stages of deciding how long to prolong his international career. The pair ran amok with a ground-record 270-run partnership for the third wicket, Waugh blasting five sixes and 16 fours in his 218-ball innings. Katich's 171 occupied only 189 deliveries. Unbeaten cameos from Mark Waugh and Brad Haddin swelled the total beyond 400 and set up a 177-run first-innings lead, after only Marsh and Scott Mason passed fifty for Tasmania. The leg-spinner Stuart MacGill posed the main danger, with Matthew Nicholson helpfully removing both openers. Before long, however, NSW's batsmen found themselves in similar strife. Mail reached his century in 185 balls but the rest struggled, Damien Wright picking up four wickets. Set 386 for victory, Tasmania looked in trouble at 2 for 28. Di Venuto, with his only century of the summer, and the captain Marsh guided them home in emphatic fashion. Steve Waugh, for so long a masterful skipper, was again left puzzling over when and how to defend large fourth-innings targets.

Man of the Match: M. J. Di Venuto.　*Attendance:* 1,470.

Close of play: First day, New South Wales (1) 5-408 (M. E. Waugh 20, Haddin 18); Second day, Tasmania (1) 5-230 (Marsh 57, Clingeleffer 10); Third day, Tasmania (2) 1-26 (Cox 18, Watson 1).

New South Wales

M. J. Slater b Wright	16	– (2) c Watson b Griffith	18
G. J. Mail b Wright	21	– (1) not out	107
S. M. Katich run out (Downton/Marsh)	171	– (8) c Dighton b Downton	6
*S. R. Waugh c Di Venuto b Wright	157	– (7) lbw b Wright	0
P. A. Jaques lbw b Downton	4	– (3) c Clingeleffer b Griffith	0
M. E. Waugh not out	43	– b Wright	41
†B. J. Haddin not out	40	– (4) b Wright	16
G. M. Lambert (did not bat)		– (5) c Watson b Downton	4
M. J. Nicholson (did not bat)		– b Wright	0
S. R. Clark (did not bat)		– not out	11
L-b 1	1	L-b 4, w 1	5

(104 overs, 397 mins)	(5 wkts dec) 453	(60 overs, 247 mins)	(8 wkts dec) 208

Fall: 33 52 322 332 379　　　　　　　　　　Fall: 24 24 59 68 169 169 182 187

S. C. G. MacGill did not bat.

Bowling: *First Innings*—Wright 29–5–86–3; Griffith 29–3–159–0; Downton 26–3–118–1; Doherty 15–4–73–0; Marsh 5–1–16–0. *Second Innings*—Wright 21–4–50–4; Griffith 15–4–44–2; Downton 15–2–60–2; Doherty 6–0–31–0; Di Venuto 3–0–19–0.

Tasmania

J. Cox b Nicholson	0	– (2) lbw b MacGill	18
S. R. Mason c Haddin b Nicholson	58	– (1) lbw b Nicholson	2
S. R. Watson lbw b MacGill	37	– c M. E. Waugh b MacGill	42
M. J. Di Venuto run out (MacGill/Haddin)	36	– not out	174
M. G. Dighton c Nicholson b MacGill	26	– lbw b Clark	24
*D. J. Marsh b Lambert	68	– not out	107
†S. G. Clingeleffer not out	17		
D. G. Wright st Haddin b MacGill	8		
X. J. Doherty c Haddin b MacGill	1		
A. R. Griffith c Slater b MacGill	7		
A. G. Downton c Lambert b Katich	6		
L-b 9, w 1, n-b 2	12	B 11, l-b 6, w 1, n-b 1	19

(105.4 overs, 390 mins)	276	(106.5 overs, 421 mins)	(4 wkts) 386

Fall: 1 91 106 143 208 245 254 256 264 276　　　Fall: 17 28 131 166

Bowling: *First Innings*—Clark 18–6–31–0; Nicholson 15–3–44–2; Lambert 25–12–66–1; MacGill 32–10–79–5; M. E. Waugh 11–3–22–0; Katich 2.4–0–9–1; Mail 2–0–16–0. *Second Innings*—Clark 22–3–64–1; Nicholson 25–8–50–1; MacGill 29–5–135–2; M. E. Waugh 3–0–15–0; Lambert 12.5–4–46–0; Katich 11–0–52–0; S. R. Waugh 4–0–7–0.

Umpires: G. T. D. Morrow and J. H. Smeaton.

At Brisbane Cricket Ground, Brisbane, November 20, 21, 22, 2003. TASMANIA defeated QUEENSLAND by 174 runs.

At WACA Ground, Perth, December 7, 8, 9, 10, 2003. TASMANIA drew with WESTERN AUSTRALIA.

At Sydney Cricket Ground, Sydney, December 19, 20, 21, 22, 2003. TASMANIA drew with NEW SOUTH WALES.

At Adelaide Oval, Adelaide, January 11, 12, 13, 14, 2004. TASMANIA defeated SOUTH AUSTRALIA by 213 runs.

TASMANIA v QUEENSLAND

At Bellerive Oval, Hobart, January 21, 22, 23, 24, 2004. Match drawn. *Toss:* Tasmania. Tasmania 2 pts. *First-class debut:* C. A. Philipson.

Dan Marsh's decision to send Queensland in was thwarted by Tasmania's old bogeyman Martin Love. Love, who always seems to make runs in bulk at Bellerive, hit an even century and prompted one local fan on the hill to scribble a banner from the old Jim Capaldi hit 'Love Hurts'. He and Stuart Law put on 190 for the third wicket, Law slipping one short of his century. Led by Damien Wright, the Tasmanian attack struck back to have the Bulls struggling at 6 for 261, before some late-order defiance from Ashley Noffke and Michael Kasprowicz enabled Jimmy Maher to declare in apparent comfort. A powerhouse 127 not out by Michael Dighton, laced with 16 fours and three sixes, spearheaded an emphatic Tasmanian reply, with strong support coming from Michael Di Venuto and Marsh. Queensland looked in a hole at 3 for 54 in the second innings. Then Craig Philipson hit a century on debut and James Hopes fought hard for a deserved hundred. Set an unreachable 321 off 35 overs for victory, Tasmania's chase was halted by bad light amid a war of words between Maher and Marsh, each criticising the other's reticence to set up a result.

Man of the Match: M. G. Dighton. *Attendance:* 1,582.

Close of play: First day, Queensland (1) 6-289 (Seccombe 11, Noffke 19); Second day, Tasmania (1) 3-170 (Di Venuto 67, Dighton 4); Third day, Queensland (2) 4-140 (Philipson 23, Hopes 30).

Queensland

*J. P. Maher c Clingeleffer b Wright	26	– c Marsh b Wright	2
C. T. Perren c Clingeleffer b Downton	13	– lbw b Wright	26
M. L. Love b Denton	100	– c Marsh b Watson	11
S. G. Law c Di Venuto b Doherty	99	– b Watson	45
C. A. Philipson lbw b Wright	5	– not out	101
J. R. Hopes lbw b Wright	14	– c Mason b Denton	111
†W. A. Seccombe c Clingeleffer b Denton	34	– c Watson b Wright	4
A. A. Noffke c Di Venuto b Denton	46	– c Clingeleffer b Downton	10
N. M. Hauritz not out	20	– b Downton	0
M. S. Kasprowicz not out	40	– c Clingeleffer b Downton	5
J. H. Dawes (did not bat)		– c Cox b Downton	0
L-b 2, n-b 1	3	B 3, l-b 3, w 1	7

(121.3 overs, 452 mins)	(8 wkts dec) 400	(100.4 overs, 381 mins) 322
Fall: 36 40 230 239 259 261		Fall: 24 33 54 92 277 284 312 312
325 342		322 322

Bowling: *First Innings*—Wright 30–6–93–3; Denton 33–10–119–3; Downton 26–7–89–1; Doherty 24.3–5–70–1; Cox 6–0–19–0; Marsh 2–0–8–0. *Second Innings*—Wright 27–7–63–3; Denton 22–7–81–1; Downton 18.4–4–59–4; Watson 11–3–31–2; Doherty 14–1–63–0; Marsh 8–3–19–0.

Tasmania

J. Cox c Law b Kasprowicz	14	– (2) not out	6
S. R. Mason c Seccombe b Dawes	30	– (1) run out (Hopes)	0
S. R. Watson c Seccombe b Dawes	53	– not out	2
M. J. Di Venuto c Seccombe b Kasprowicz	91		
M. G. Dighton not out	127		
*D. J. Marsh not out	80		
L-b 5, n-b 2	7		

(127 overs, 484 mins)   (4 wkts dec) 402   (5 overs, 22 mins)   (1 wkt)   8
Fall: 38 47 140 231   Fall: 0

†S. G. Clingeleffer, D. G. Wright, A. G. Downton, X. J. Doherty and G. J. Denton did not bat.

Bowling: *First Innings*—Kasprowicz 25–6–56–2; Noffke 26–5–100–0; Hopes 26–8–73–0; Dawes 25–5–72–2; Hauritz 25–7–96–0. *Second Innings*—Kasprowicz 3–2–6–0; Noffke 2–1–2–0.

Umpires: B. W. Jackman and R. L. Parry.

TASMANIA v WESTERN AUSTRALIA

At Bellerive Oval, Hobart, February 4, 5, 6, 7, 2004. Match drawn. *Toss:* Tasmania. Western Australia 2 pts. *First-class debut:* A. K. Heal.

Three declarations on a pitch offering no help to the bowlers produced a thrilling end to a match that spawned six centuries and 1,612 runs. Western Australia were caught one wicket short of an unlikely victory, after making the most of a strange decision by Tasmania's captain Dan Marsh to send them in. The Bellerive wicket was back to its benign best and Marcus North (149 balls), Ryan Campbell (132 balls) and Kade Harvey (127 balls) all cashed in, belting three sixes each. Half-centuries to Mike Hussey and Murray Goodwin had earlier built a solid foundation. Tasmania declared 176 runs behind in the hope of setting up the game. Shane Watson was again impressive on his home ground, producing a fireworks display of 19 fours and two sixes, while Michael Dighton scored 80 of his 101 runs in boundaries as they pushed for quick runs. The Warriors gave the home side little chance, Justin Langer and North plundering the Tasmanian attack and setting their batsmen the tall order of 449 runs in 90 overs. They chased hard. Scott Mason was the mainstay, facing 194 balls for his 126. Watson narrowly missed out on a century in each innings, and Dighton and Michael Di Ventuo both registered half-centuries, before a late-order collapse forced them to hold on tight.

Man of the Match: M. J. North.   *Attendance:* 1,496.

Close of play: First day, Western Australia (1) 4-345 (North 118, Campbell 29); Second day, Tasmania (1) 3-192 (Watson 51, Dighton 63); Third day, Western Australia (2) 5-244 (North 82, Harvey 4).

Western Australia

*J. L. Langer c Clingeleffer b Downton	15	– b Downton	84
M. E. K. Hussey lbw b Downton	82	– run out (Cox/Watson/Clingeleffer)	9
C. J. L. Rogers lbw b Denton	18	– c Watson b Cox	20
M. W. Goodwin c Clingeleffer b Denton	77	– c Clingeleffer b Doherty	22
M. J. North lbw b Wright	118	– b Downton	87
†R. J. Campbell c Watson b Doherty	134	– b Doherty	13
K. M. Harvey not out	100	– not out	6
J. J. Taylor not out	9	– not out	18
L-b 4, w 2, n-b 3	9	B 5, l-b 6	11

(136 overs, 508 mins) (6 wkts dec) 562
Fall: 40 97 139 287 345 534

(57 overs, 210 mins) (6 wkts dec) 270
Fall: 28 58 85 198 239 249

D. J. Wates, A. K. Heal and B. M. Edmondson did not bat.

Bowling: *First Innings*—Wright 30–12–71–1; Denton 30–1–122–2; Downton 30–2–144–2; Watson 9–1–35–0; Doherty 27–2–124–1; Marsh 10–1–62–0. *Second Innings*—Denton 7–3–16–0; Downton 15–4–63–2; Doherty 18–0–98–2; Cox 9–1–44–1; Watson 8–0–38–0.

Tasmania

S. R. Mason c Edmondson b Taylor	19	– (2) st Campbell b North	126
J. Cox c Rogers b Taylor	24	– (1) lbw b Wates	2
S. R. Watson c Goodwin b Edmondson	139	– st Campbell b Hussey	92
M. J. Di Venuto c Rogers b Edmondson	21	– lbw b Harvey	50
M. G. Dighton lbw b North	101	– b Harvey	62
*D. J. Marsh not out	51	– c Rogers b Harvey	20
†S. G. Clingeleffer not out	4	– (8) c (sub) S. W. Meuleman b Edmondson	6
D. G. Wright (did not bat)		– (7) b Edmondson	9
A. G. Downton (did not bat)		– c Campbell b Edmondson	3
X. J. Doherty (did not bat)		– not out	3
G. J. Denton (did not bat)		– not out	0
B 4, l-b 10, w 2, n-b 9	25	B 8, l-b 10, w 2, n-b 3	23

(95.3 overs, 371 mins) (5 wkts dec) 384
Fall: 42 52 87
281 358

(92 overs, 354 mins) (9 wkts) 396
Fall: 26 215 260 343 358 379 385
391 394

Bowling: *First Innings*—Edmondson 21–4–54–2; Taylor 17–3–88–2; Wates 17–3–67–0; Heal 19–2–91–0; Harvey 15–2–62–0; North 6.3–2–8–1. *Second Innings*—Edmondson 18–2–83–3; Wates 7–1–23–1; Taylor 9–0–37–0; North 15–2–63–1; Heal 22–1–82–0; Harvey 16–2–70–3; Hussey 5–0–20–1.

Umpires: K. J. McGinniss and D. L. Orchard.

At Melbourne Cricket Ground, Melbourne, February 16, 17, 18, 19, 2004. TASMANIA lost to VICTORIA by 218 runs.

TASMANIA v VICTORIA

At Bellerive Oval, Hobart, March 4, 5, 6 (no play),7, 2004. Match drawn. *Toss:* Tasmania. Tasmania 2 pts. *First-class debut:* B. R. Joseland.

The weather, rather than the efforts of competition leaders Victoria, was chiefly to blame for dashing Tasmania's high hopes of reaching their fourth Pura Cup final. A blazing Michael Dighton, capping a season of almost 1,000 runs, gathered almost half of Tasmania's faintly disappointing first-innings total. He pounded five sixes and 19 fours in a savage 208-ball onslaught but received little help from his team-mates, four of whom fell to the first-change bowler Andrew McDonald. The second stage of the recovery was left to the wicket-keeper Sean Clingeleffer, with the last-wicket pair of Xavier Doherty and Gerard Denton lending the scoreline some respectability. Victoria's batting display was even more modest. Brad Hodge assumed the main responsibility, hitting 20 fours and a six in his 125, before Victoria declared 89 runs behind. The third day was washed out, Tasmania beginning their second innings on the fourth morning with only the slimmest of chances. Shane Watson took centre-stage, hammering a belligerent 117 off 107 balls in his farewell match for the state. Jamie Cox was the only other batsman to make double figures. Victoria were set 312 to win, and were battling at 6 for 212 when bad light again ended play. Tasmania's misery was completed soon after when Queensland, by beating New South Wales under lights at the SCG, snatched their spot in the final.

Man of the Match: M. J. North.   *Attendance:* 3,476.

Close of play: First day, Tasmania (1) 9-313 (Doherty 15, Denton 12); Second day, Victoria 7-252 (McDonald 51, Berry 22); Third day, No play (rain).

Tasmania

S. R. Mason c Berry b Wise	12	– (2) c Joseland b Inness	1
J. Cox b Inness	21	– (1) run out (Hussey)	54
S. R. Watson c Berry b McDonald	13	– c Mott b Moss	117
M. J. Di Venuto c Hussey b McDonald	16	– (5) lbw b Moss	1
M. G. Dighton c White b Wise	152	– (4) c Hodge b Moss	9
*D. J. Marsh c Berry b McDonald	0	– c Hussey b Wise	3
†S. G. Clingeleffer c Elliott b Joseland	46	– (8) c Joseland b Moss	7
D. G. Wright lbw b Inness	22	– (7) c (sub) M. L. Lewis b White	9
A. G. Downton lbw b Wise	3	– lbw b White	6
X. J. Doherty not out	21	– not out	4
G. J. Denton c Mott b McDonald	34	– not out	5
L-b 1	1	L-b 4, n-b 2	6

(108.1 overs, 423 mins) 341   (45 overs, 188 mins)   (9 wkts) 222
Fall: 12 46 46 83 83 246 278 286   Fall: 2 133 147 156 163 181 207
      286 341   213 213

Bowling: *First Innings*—Wise 25–6–73–3; Inness 27–7–61–2; McDonald 23.1–9–69–4; Moss 14–4–53–0; White 12–2–53–0; Hodge 1–0–12–0; Joseland 6–1–19–1. *Second Innings*—Wise 10–1–36–1; Inness 8–1–47–1; McDonald 8–0–41–0; Moss 14–2–60–4; White 5–0–34–2.

Victoria

M. T. G. Elliott c Marsh b Wright	1	– c and b Downton	34
M. P. Mott lbw b Denton	10	– lbw b Wright	5
B. J. Hodge b Watson	125	– c Clingeleffer b Downton	7
J. Moss lbw b Watson	22	– not out	77
D. J. Hussey c Marsh b Downton	7	– lbw b Marsh	3
C. L. White c Denton b Downton	2	– b Doherty	23
B. R. Joseland c Di Venuto b Denton	6	– c Clingeleffer b Marsh	51
A. B. McDonald not out	51	– not out	8
*†D. S. Berry not out	22		
L-b 4, w 1, n-b 1	6	L-b 2, n-b 2	4

(81 overs, 317 mins)   (7 wkts dec) 252   (55 overs, 206 mins)   (6 wkts) 212
Fall: 7 31 114 121 127 148 199   Fall: 19 36 55 73 115 188

M. W. H. Inness and A. B. Wise did not bat.

Bowling: *First Innings*—Wright 22–7–59–1; Watson 18–3–57–2; Denton 16–3–67–2; Downton 18–3–51–2; Doherty 5–0–8–0; Marsh 2–1–6–0. *Second Innings*—Wright 14–3–41–1; Denton 5–1–22–0; Downton 9–2–38–2; Doherty 14–0–63–1; Marsh 7–0–19–2; Watson 6–0–27–0.

Umpires: B. N. J. Oxenford and S. J. A. Taufel

TASMANIA DOMESTIC FIRST-CLASS RESULTS TABLE

	First Game	M	Won	Lost	Drawn	Tied
v Western Australia ..	Oct 29, 1977	50	6	21	23	0
v Victoria	Nov 18, 1977	49	10	14	25	0
v South Australia	Feb 18, 1978	49	10	17	22	0
v Queensland	Feb 25, 1978	50	8	18	24	0
v New South Wales ..	Mar 4, 1978	50	12	19	19	0
Total		248	46	89	113	0

TASMANIA DOMESTIC FIRST-CLASS RECORDS

Highest score for:	265	D. F. Hills v South Australia at Hobart (Bellerive) 1997-98
Highest score against:	306*	D. W. Hookes (South Australia) at Adelaide 1986-97
Best bowling for:	8-95	P. M. Clough v Western Australia at Perth 1983-84
Best bowling against:	8-41	L. S. Pascoe (New South Wales) at Hobart (TCA) 1981-82
Highest total for:	592	v South Australia at Adelaide 1987-88
Highest total against:	673	by South Australia at Adelaide 1987-88
Lowest total for:	76	v New South Wales at Hobart (Bellerive) 1991-92
Lowest total against:	83	by Victoria at Melbourne 1981-82

MOST RUNS

	M	I	NO	R	HS	100s	50s	Avge
J. Cox	153	279	17	10,459	245	30	44	39.92
D. C. Boon..............	119	203	7	8,029	227	20	43	40.96
M. J. Di Venuto..........	104	182	7	7,043	189	11	52	40.25
D. F. Hills	100	187	8	6,887	265	18	36	38.47
S. Young...............	104	176	29	5,565	175*	10	35	37.86
R. T. Ponting............	48	89	13	4,756	233	20	14	62.58
R. T. Tucker............	90	153	24	4,611	165	7	24	35.74
D. J. Buckingham	75	129	11	4,407	167	9	22	37.35
D. J. Marsh	81	135	22	4,198	134	7	22	37.15
R. D. Woolley...........	68	114	13	4,120	144	7	25	40.79
B. F. Davison	41	75	7	3,062	173	5	13	45.03
M. N. Atkinson	84	124	43	2,350	76*	0	6	29.01
G. A. Hughes............	35	62	3	2,244	147	2	16	38.03
M. G. Dighton...........	30	51	2	2,005	152	5	10	40.92
S. R. Watson	26	46	4	1,802	157	5	10	42.90
S. L. Saunders...........	48	76	8	1,795	138*	4	10	26.40
M. Ray.................	38	67	2	1,682	94	0	8	25.88
D. M. Wellham	30	46	7	1,600	95	0	15	41.03
P. I. Faulkner...........	36	56	8	1,503	100	1	9	31.31
R. J. Bennett	33	58	4	1,415	110	1	6	26.20

HIGHEST PARTNERSHIP FOR EACH WICKET

297	for 1st	D. F. Hills and J. Cox v Victoria at Hobart (Bellerive)	1997-98
294	for 2nd	J. Cox and M. J. Di Venuto v New South Wales at Hobart (Bellerive)	1999-00
290	for 3rd	D. F. Hills and R. T. Ponting v South Australia at Adelaide	1993-94
258	for 4th	M. D. Taylor and D. J. Buckingham v South Australia at Adelaide	1987-88
319	for 5th	R. T. Ponting and R. J. Tucker v Western Australia at Hobart (Bellerive) ..	1994-95
213	for 6th	B. F. Davison and R. D. Woolley v South Australia at Adelaide	1980-81
203*	for 7th	B. F. Davison and P. I. Faulkner v Western Australia at Perth	1983-84
148	for 8th	B. F. Davison and P. I. Faulkner v South Australia at Adelaide	1983-84
118*	for 9th	B. F. Davison and P. I. Faulkner v Queensland at Brisbane	1983-84
120	for 10th	S. L. Saunders and P. M. Clough v Western Australia at Perth	1981-82

MOST WICKETS

	M	Balls	Mdns	R	W	BB	5W/i	10W/m	Avge	S-R
C.R. Miller	54	13,846	556	6,657	210	7-49	8	2	31.70	65.93
S. Young	104	16,399	745	7,884	201	5-26	5	1	39.22	81.59
M.W. Ridgway	44	9,433	347	5,160	153	6-29	6	0	33.73	61.65
D.G. Wright	47	9,621	451	4,590	136	6-39	2	0	33.75	70.74
C.D. Matthews	35	7,922	272	4,234	119	6-89	7	0	35.57	66.57
D.J. Marsh	81	10,391	407	5,181	119	7-57	1	0	43.54	87.32
R.J. Tucker	90	9,139	316	4,561	112	4-56	0	0	40.72	81.60
D.R. Gilbert	36	7,345	247	3,513	110	7-127	5	0	31.94	66.67
P.M. Clough	28	6,142	226	2,913	102	8-95	5	0	28.56	60.22
P.T. McPhee	25	5,669	225	2,803	89	6-36	4	1	31.49	63.70
A.G. Downton	27	5,127	197	2,942	84	6-56	2	0	35.02	51.04
G.J. Denton	30	5,399	194	3,093	80	5-40	1	0	38.66	67.49
R.L. Brown	29	5,146	128	3,197	75	7-80	2	1	42.63	68.61
G.D. Campbell	27	5,618	213	2,591	72	6-80	4	0	35.99	78.03
D.J. Saker	23	4,590	180	2,232	65	5-53	2	0	34.34	70.62
P.I. Faulkner	36	7,497	301	3,326	61	4-68	0	0	54.52	122.90
J.P. Marquet	21	4,159	132	2,446	59	5-94	1	0	41.46	70.49
S.L. Saunders	48	6,012	185	3,335	58	5-114	1	0	57.50	103.66
S.J. Jurgensen	17	3,441	155	1,551	54	6-65	4	2	28.72	63.72
S.R. Watson	26	2,254	74	1,399	50	6-32	2	1	27.98	45.08

MOST DISMISSALS

	M	Catches	Stumpings	Total
M.N. Atkinson	84	237	25	262
S.G. Clingeleffer	41	119	8	127
R.D. Woolley	43	97	13	110
R.E. Soule	51	103	4	107
J.M. Holyman	9	25	1	26

MOST CATCHES

M.J. Di Venuto ...... 101 in 104 matches	J. Cox .... 72 in 153 matches
D.C. Boon .... 93 in 119 matches	D.F. Hills .... 67 in 100 matches
D.J. Marsh .... 89 in 81 matches	S. Young .... 62 in 104 matches

MOST APPEARANCES

153	J. Cox	1987-88 – 2003-04	90	R.J. Tucker	1988-89 – 1998-99
119	D.C. Boon	1978-79 – 1998-99	84	M.N. Atkinson ...	1991-92 – 1999-00
104	S. Young	1991-92 – 2001-02	81	D.J. Marsh	1996-97 – 2003-04
104	M.J. Di Venuto ...	1991-92 – 2003-04	75	D.J. Buckingham .	1983-84 – 1993-94
100	D.F. Hills	1991-92 – 2001-02	68	R.D. Woolley	1977-78 – 1987-88

VICTORIA

The year of redemption

by PETER HANLON

Pura Cup: Champions
ING Cup: Third
Coach: David Hookes, Greg Shipperd
Captain: Darren Berry

Darren Berry

For the many who view Australia's first-class calendar through an ever-narrowing media eye, Victoria's Pura Cup win was seen as a team turning tragedy into triumph. This is tabloid tosh. As sad, disturbing and unnecessary as David Hookes' death in January was, the team he left behind needed no mournful motivation to help them across the line. In all but the finality of winning the final, the work of Hookes and his coaching cohorts was already done.

For Victoria, success was met with a sigh as heavy as its heart. In the 13 years since Simon O'Donnell lifted the state's last major trophy, elements of the same script had been worked like an ageing ball on a bowler's trousers. Occasional spectacular in-fighting and not-so-occasional spectacular collapse; dreadful one year and a potent whiff but no cigar the next. In a state where the winter game steals more of summer's thunder each year Victorian cricket, the sitting duck that not even Laurie Levy could shelter, annually took shots both cheap and born of its own muddling.

Persistence, at last, was rewarded. John Scholes, eternally departed six months before Hookes, did much to build a squad well placed to meet a charter of winning "the Shield" and again producing Test cricketers. Mick O'Sullivan was a tireless caretaker and Greg Shipperd an over-qualified assistant. These were the team's nuts and bolts coaches. Hookes, with his daring and belief, finished the job. His high profile and outrageous tongue – part-iconoclast, part-unreconstructed ocker – generated interest in Victorian cricket just as it threatened to become nothing more than a diversion from footballers with December hamstring strains.

Those drawn by curiosity to have another look at their team found they were no longer an accident waiting to happen. This became evident as soon as the opening game, which brought Victoria's first outright victory at the Gabba in two decades. That they were steered to this rare feat by a 20-year-old leg-spinning captain in Cameron White, who took wickets and made second-innings runs in a tense chase, added to the theatre. With Darren Berry nursing and cursing a finger broken in a practice match, White captained the Bushrangers beyond Christmas in the Pura Cup and throughout the one-day summer. If this was not entirely a Hookes initiative, for White's brain and talents are universally rated, it was a fitting nod from a former prodigy to a future star.

Hunches were backed elsewhere with the impact of a gambler enjoying a surreal communion with the dice. Allan Wise, a lanky 25-year-old left-armer meandering through an unspectacular club career, played all but the first match and took 33 wickets at 24.27. Andrew McDonald, nearing the last of his lives as a batting all-rounder of promise, sent down almost as many overs as White and, with 32 wickets, claimed six more scalps. By season's end his bat was warm too, and McDonald was duly retained for the final despite Ian Harvey's return from Australian one-day duties.

Or more precisely, Harvey regained his place despite McDonald's retention, meaning Mathew Inness was relegated to 12th man. Inness began the summer as a Test prospect but was severely restricted by glandular fever; balanced against these were seven seasons of wholehearted commitment to his state. Playing the more gifted but less obviously enthusiastic Harvey in his stead was, for some, a rare flat note. Even resounding triumph would not be Victorian without a measure of controversy.

One perennial argument was finally settled. The remarkable batting of David Hussey, from Western Australia, and another majestic all-round return from the Sydneysider Jon Moss ensured that, at least for now, the push for an all-Victorian Victoria is off the agenda. Moss racked up 930 runs with seven half-centuries, one hundred and a growing command of his craft. Hussey was something else. Only a late-season lapse stopped him finishing alongside Matthew Elliott and Brad Hodge atop the batting aggregate.

A year earlier, Hussey had dropped a run-less Steve Waugh on debut, seen his mistake underlined by a Waugh double-ton, and been reminded of such from close range when his turn came to bat.

Back row: M. W. H. Inness, M. T. G. Elliott, A. Wise, A. B. McDonald, J. Moss, M. L. Lewis.
Front row: D. J. Hussey, B. J. Hodge, D. S. Berry, G. Shipperd (*Coach*), C. L. White, J. L. Arnberger, I. J. Harvey.

Waugh again had a prime view in 2003-04 as Hussey's four innings against NSW reaped 120, 50, 51 and 212 not out. The latter was an astonishing innings, spearheading Victoria's pursuit of 455 to win in Newcastle. Starting the final day at 0 for 3, Hookes told his batsmen to split the 100 overs in two and halve the ask, leaving two lots of 226 from 50 overs. By one-day standards this seemed a simple enough proposition. Few expected Hussey to take Hookes at his word.

The best was prised out of Elliott and Hodge too, after Hookes challenged them to score 1,000 runs each. Hodge finished 16 shy but Elliott's gluttonous return of 1,381 – he passed Graham Yallop's 21-year-old season record in the final – more than made up the shortfall. Elliott was an appropriate torchbearer. Other than a quirky cameo from Wayne Phillips, he is the only Victorian batsman to start an Australian career since the state's last four-day triumph. His pre-season declaration that he no longer thought of adding to his 20 Tests was a masterstroke. His next trick should be an announcement that he has no interest in winning the lottery.

Hodge made bold statements, as is his way, and generally backed them up, although his impromptu pre-final declaration at a media conference – "by the way, I'll make a hundred too" – proved a bridge too far. His sparkling innings ended on 89 when he was caught in the deep. Both Elliott and Hodge were rewarded with national contracts for 2004-05. Hodge's oft-repeated dream of achieving higher honours remains alive.

The final again tickled debate about the higher-placed team's right to kill the contest when Victoria, gleeful to be sent in by Queensland, batted until after lunch on the third day in amassing 710. When Berry chose not to enforce the follow-on the next afternoon a dispirited opponent suspected matters were getting personal. Ultimately the team that had played for outright results all season – and achieved six of them – duly won the title with a seventh. The mission was completed midway through the fifth day when Mick Lewis, dangerous all summer in his multitude of ways, found the edge of Joe Dawes and snuck past Wise with his 34th wicket.

Berry held the catch, the 552nd of his first-class career, and took his place as a title-winning captain. A 21-year-old greenhorn when Victoria last triumphed, he had coveted above all else this moment of team glory and the personal high of playing for his country. Seeing one achieved and realising the other never would be, he looked heavenward, saluted Hookes and retired.

VICTORIA RESULTS, 2003-04

All first-class matches – Played 12: Won 7, Lost 0, Drawn 5.
Pura Cup – Played 11: Won 7, Lost 0, Drawn 4.
ING Cup matches – Played 10: Won 6, Lost 3, Tied 1.

VICTORIA PURA CUP AVERAGES, 2003-04

BATTING

	M	I	NO	R	HS	100s	50s	Avge	Ct/St	S-R
M. T. G. Elliott	11	20	3	1,381	182	7	3	81.24	11	52.85
J. Moss	11	17	3	930	172*	1	7	66.43	5	52.19
B. J. Hodge	10	19	3	984	125	4	4	61.50	4	58.78
D. J. Hussey	11	16	2	857	212*	2	2	61.21	9	69.85
C. L. White	10	15	2	522	78	0	5	40.15	20	59.12
J. L. Arnberger	6	11	0	419	90	0	3	38.09	3	43.92
B. R. Joseland	1	2	0	57	51	0	1	28.50	2	77.03
M. P. Mott	6	10	1	218	78	0	2	24.22	6	39.35
D. S. Berry	6	7	1	139	61	0	1	23.17	20/3	67.80
A. B. McDonald	10	15	5	225	51*	0	1	22.50	7	49.23
S. M. Harwood	3	3	1	43	22	0	0	21.50	1	53.75
P. J. Roach	5	6	0	128	47	0	0	21.33	17	50.59
I. J. Harvey	3	3	0	62	62	0	1	20.67	3	54.39
S. K. Warne	1	1	0	18	18	0	0	18.00	1	69.23
A. B. Wise	10	8	6	19	7	0	0	9.50	5	34.42
M. W. H. Inness	7	6	3	28	10*	0	0	9.33	4	32.18
M. L. Lewis	9	10	1	65	16	0	0	7.22	9	29.15
B. E. McGain	1	1	1	9	9*	0	0	–	0	75.00

* Denotes not out.

BOWLING

	O	Mdns	R	W	BB	5W/i	10W/m	Avge	S-R
S. K. Warne	36	11	100	6	4-51	0	0	16.67	36.00
B. R. Joseland	6	1	19	1	1-19	0	0	19.00	36.00
I. J. Harvey	74.1	15	207	9	3-57	0	0	23.00	49.44
A. B. Wise	284	88	801	33	5-47	2	0	24.27	51.64
A. B. McDonald	255.1	61	846	32	6-67	1	0	26.44	47.84
J. Moss	163	49	514	19	4-60	0	0	27.05	51.47
M. L. Lewis	312.3	74	947	34	6-59	2	0	27.85	55.15
M. W. H. Inness	199.4	61	578	20	4-26	0	0	28.90	59.90
C. L. White	259.1	35	983	26	4-27	0	0	37.81	59.81
S. M. Harwood	82.1	13	327	7	3-93	0	0	46.71	70.43
D. J. Hussey	12	1	62	1	1-45	0	0	62.00	72.00
B. J. Hodge	17	1	74	0	–	0	0	–	–
B. E. McGain	31	4	109	0	–	0	0	–	–

At Brisbane Cricket Ground, Brisbane, November 2, 3, 4, 5, 2003. VICTORIA defeated QUEENSLAND by five wickets.

VICTORIA v QUEENSLAND

At Junction Oval, St Kilda, November 11, 12, 13, 14, 2003. Match drawn. *Toss:* Victoria. Queensland 2 pts.

On a Junction Oval wicket that might easily have been mistaken for the St Kilda Road that runs parallel to it, a staggering 1,194 runs were cultivated for 18 wickets in a contest best remembered for Martin Love's marathon 300 not out (610 minutes, 489 balls, 32 fours, one six). Watched by the chairman of selectors, Trevor Hohns, Love became the first player in Australia since Dean Jones's 324 against South Australia in 1994-95 to post a triple-century. Smothering the threat of the Victorian tearaway Mick Lewis and enjoying one apparent chance by the wicket-keeper Peter Roach, Love staged a commanding performance before finally pushing a single through the covers to reach 300. He was awarded the Spirit of Anzac medal struck to commemorate Remembrance Day, and was relieved to reach the mark just before drinks on day four because of plans to declare at the end of the over even if he was on 299. Love and Hopes, appropriately enough, hoisted a 236-run stand for the fifth wicket, an all-time Queensland record. The Victorians found batting a comfortable exercise too, Brad Hodge hitting his second century of the summer. Matthew Elliott, watched by his terminally ill brother-in-law, was dropped twice on his way to reaching three figures in the first innings and fell 21 short in the second. Love and the Victorian coach David Hookes were scathing about the pitch. Hookes sought out the curator of the ground, which is scheduled to host many more matches until the MCG is redeveloped in time for the 2006 Commonwealth Games.

Match reports by NABILA AHMED.

Man of the Match: M. L. Love.   *Attendance:* 2,613.

Close of play: First day, Victoria (1) 6-255 (Moss 20); Second day, Queensland (1) 2-183 (Love 82, Law 1); Third day, Queensland (1) 5-526 (Love 256, Seccombe 52).

Victoria

M. T. G. Elliott c Seccombe b Dawes	106	– (2) c Seccombe b Payne	79
J. L. Arnberger c Seccombe b Dawes	35	– (1) c Seccombe b Dawes	5
B. J. Hodge c Perren b Simpson	42	– not out	111
A. B. McDonald lbw b Jurgensen	4	– not out	5
D. J. Hussey b Dawes	34		
J. Moss c Seccombe b Jurgensen	80		
*C. L. White c Seccombe b Hopes	5		
†P. J. Roach c Law b Simpson	47		
M. L. Lewis c and b Dawes	9		
B. E. McGain not out	9		
B 4, l-b 3, n-b 3	10	B 1, l-b 5, w 2	8

(131.5 overs, 489 mins)   (9 wkts) 381
Fall: 54 146 150 219 236 255 340 367 381

(73 overs, 256 mins)   (2 wkts) 208
Fall: 7 203

M. W. H. Inness did not bat.

Bowling: *First Innings*—Noffke 28–11–50–0; Jurgensen 22–7–57–2; Simpson 29.5–8–116–2; Dawes 29–8–89–4; Hopes 23–11–62–1. *Second Innings*—Dawes 13–4–39–1; Jurgensen 11–2–27–0; Hopes 9–3–21–0; Simpson 18–3–49–0; Perren 11–4–29–0; Law 5–0–25–0; Love 4–1–6–0; Payne 2–0–6–1.

Queensland

D. M. Payne b Lewis	0	C. P. Simpson c Hussey b White	2
C. T. Perren lbw b McDonald	95	A. A. Noffke not out	28
*M. L. Love not out	300		
S. G. Law lbw b Lewis	5	B 5, l-b 7	12
L. A. Carseldine c Roach b McDonald	9		
J. R. Hopes c and b Hussey	97	(173 overs, 613 mins) (7 wkts)	605
†W. A. Seccombe c and b White	57	Fall: 0 173 187 206 442 539 551	

S. J. Jurgensen, J. H. Dawes did not bat.

Bowling: Lewis 39–12–92–2; Inness 26–7–83–0; Moss 3–1–11–0; White 30–2–123–2; McDonald 28–5–98–2; McGain 31–4–109–0; Hodge 6–0–32–0; Hussey 10–1–45–1.

Umpires: B. N. J. Oxenford and R. G. Patterson.

VICTORIA v WESTERN AUSTRALIA

At Junction Oval, St Kilda, November 19, 20, 21, 22, 2003. Match drawn. *Toss:* Western Australia. Victoria 2 pts.

Matthew Elliott's wish for the season – "rain and more rain", as stated in the Victorian media guide – was granted. But it was a delayed declaration that ultimately cost the Bushrangers. Most of day two was washed out after Andrew McDonald ripped a 14-ball, 4 for 2 whirlwind through the WA middle order late on the opening afternoon. WA, losing their last six wickets for 40, were restricted to 273. Darren Berry, after talking up the prospects of a result despite another batsman-friendly strip, then surprised most observers when he left his declaration until well after first-innings points had been sealed. Hodge raised another century but Victoria lost him, Jon Moss and McDonald shortly before passing WA's total, then stayed on past their welcome. Justin Langer narrowly missed out on a hundred and survived a torrid spell from Mick Lewis, who struck the Test opener "more times than I've been hit in a long time on a flat slow wicket". The rest of the WA batsmen lacked Langer's resolve. Lewis and Mathew Inness ran rampant through the middle order for a second time, eight wickets crumbling for 54 runs on the final day. Victoria needed to make 184 from 59 overs, but play was abandoned 47 overs early at 5.40 p.m. after a 90-minute rain delay.

Man of the Match: M. L. Lewis.   *Attendance:* 2,122.

Close of play: First day, Victoria (1) 0-12 (Elliott 8, Mott 4); Second day, Victoria (1) 1-78 (Elliott 32, Hodge 19); Third day, Western Australia (2) 0-100 (Hussey 45, Langer 53).

Western Australia

*J. L. Langer c Berry b Wise	20	– (2) c Mott b White	96
M. E. K. Hussey lbw b Wise	23	– (1) c Elliott b Lewis	57
C. J. L. Rogers c and b McDonald	103	– (4) c Berry b Lewis	52
M. W. Goodwin c Elliott b Inness	70	– (5) c Berry b Lewis	10
M. J. North lbw b Lewis	10	– (6) lbw b Inness	8
†R. J. Campbell lbw b McDonald	9	– (3) c McDonald b Wise	19
P. C. Worthington c White b McDonald	1	– c Wise b Inness	1
J. J. Taylor lbw b McDonald	0	– c Inness b Lewis	11
B. Casson c Berry b Wise	9	– c Berry b Lewis	1
J. Angel not out	12	– b Inness	0
P. Wilson run out (Hodge/Berry)	4	– not out	0
B 8, l-b 3, w 1	12	B 6, l-b 3, w 1	10

(89.1 overs, 343 mins)	273	(83 overs, 327 mins)	265
Fall: 48 51 187 215 233 243 243 244		Fall: 123 153 211 236 247 247 255	
269 273		259 259 265	

Bowling: *First Innings*—Lewis 18–4–41–1; Inness 14.1–5–37–1; Wise 19–4–56–3; White 18–0–72–0; Moss 4–0–21–0; McDonald 16–6–35–4. *Second Innings*—Lewis 23–5–58–5; Inness 12–5–23–3; White 16–3–65–1; Wise 11–2–39–1; Hussey 2–0–17–0; McDonald 12–3–28–0; Moss 7–1–26–0.

Victoria

M. T. G. Elliott c Goodwin b Casson	71	– (2) run out (Worthington)	2
M. P. Mott c Campbell b Taylor	22	– (1) not out	12
B. J. Hodge c Campbell b Wilson	100	– not out	20
J. Moss c Hussey b Taylor	52		
D. J. Hussey c Campbell b Taylor	24		
A. B. McDonald b Wilson	7		
C. L. White not out	58		
*†D. S. Berry b Taylor	0		
M. L. Lewis c Wilson b Casson	2		
M. W. H. Inness lbw b Worthington	5		
A. B. Wise not out	0		
L-b 7, w 2, n-b 5	14	N-b 1	1

(108 overs, 399 mins) (9 wkts dec) 355   (12 overs, 44 mins) (1 wkt) 35
Fall: 45 159 235 253 266 289 289 318 347   Fall: 3

Bowling: *First Innings*—Angel 17–2–62–0; Casson 22–4–68–2; Wilson 26–10–60–2; Taylor 19–5–70–4; North 5–1–17–0; Worthington 11–2–47–1; Hussey 8–1–24–0. *Second Innings*—Angel 6–2–13–0; Wilson 6–1–22–0.

Umpires: R. L. Parry and J. H. Smeaton.

VICTORIA v SOUTH AUSTRALIA

At Melbourne Cricket Ground, Melbourne, December 12, 13, 14, 15, 2003. Victoria won by two wickets. *Toss:* New South Wales. Victoria 6 pts. *First-class debut:* D. J. Thornely.

Mark Waugh made his first-class captaincy debut in his final match at the MCG, and Brett Lee returned from ankle surgery after two months on the sidelines. It was Victoria, though, who finished this game on top of the ladder. With Mathew Inness ruled out with glandular fever, Mick Lewis and Ian Harvey opened the bowling with devastating effect. By lunch NSW were already five down, Phil Jaques succumbing to a vicious Harvey inswinger, before Lee and Brad Haddin mounted a recovery. The trend continued when Victoria batted. They lost five wickets in the first session only for David Hussey, showing growing maturity, and the stand-in captain Cameron White to stage a 153-run fightback. White was one of three victims for Lee, who also plucked a stunning one-handed outfield catch. Mark Waugh received a standing ovation from a 400-strong crowd for his farewell innings at the ground. He was dropped on 0 and 5, then dusted off a couple of exquisite late-cuts in glorious sunshine, before again squandering his opportunity to sign off with a big score. Michael Bevan's departure triggered a collapse of 5 for 20, the left-armer Allan Wise completing his maiden five-wicket haul. Chasing 230, Victoria stumbled again, Stuart Clark and Matthew Nicholson combining to snare 3 for 1 in eight balls. They went to tea at 8 for 228, and White could barely bring himself to watch Lewis and Andrew McDonald scramble the winning runs. Waugh was given a framed picture of himself in action as a farewell gift; in another belated and less welcome present, his team were docked a point for their slow over-rate.

Man of the Match: D. J. Hussey. *Attendance:* 4,325.

Close of play: First day, Victoria (1) 0-16 (Elliott 4, Arnberger 12); Second day, New South Wales (2) 1-18 (Mail 4, Zammit 0); Third day, Victoria (2) 0-25 (Arnberger 17, Elliott 8).

New South Wales

G. J. Mail c Hussey b Harvey	0	– c Roach b Moss	16
P. A. Jaques lbw b Harvey	4	– c Roach b Wise	13
M. G. Bevan c White b McDonald	17	– (4) c White b Wise	106
M. J. Clarke c Roach b McDonald	25	– (5) b Lewis	9
*M. E. Waugh b McDonald	44	– (6) c Harvey b Lewis	58
D. J. Thornely c Elliott b Harvey	2	– (7) c Moss b Lewis	19
†B. J. Haddin c McDonald b Lewis	76	– (8) c White b Wise	5
B. Lee not out	74	– (9) c Roach b Moss	3
M. J. Nicholson c Roach b Lewis	0	– (10) c White b Wise	9
S. R. Clark c White b Moss	12	– (11) not out	0
L. A. Zammit run out (Lewis/Roach)	13	– (3) c White b Wise	15
B 2, l-b 13, n-b 5	20	B 3, l-b 6, n-b 6	15

(86 overs, 345 mins)   287   (95 overs, 374 mins)   268
Fall: 1 4 41 56 67 138 212 212   Fall: 18 45 45 62 178 248 256 256
237 287   266 268

Bowling: *First Innings*—Lewis 21–7–60–2; Harvey 21–3–57–3; Wise 12–3–49–0; McDonald 18–2–63–3; Moss 8–2–19–1; White 6–1–24–0. *Second Innings*—Lewis 29–8–79–3; Wise 27–11–59–5; Moss 14.5–5–34–2; McDonald 14–4–41–0; White 11–2–46–0.

Victoria

M. T. G. Elliott c Jaques b Lee	15	– (2) c Waugh b Nicholson	33
J. L. Arnberger c Lee b Clark	21	– (1) c Nicholson b Clark	41
B. J. Hodge c Clarke b Nicholson	1	– b Clark	10
J. Moss lbw b Thornely	19	– c Nicholson b Clark	63
D. J. Hussey c Haddin b Clark	120	– lbw b Nicholson	50
I. J. Harvey c Zammit b Thornely	0	– c Haddin b Clark	0
*C. L. White c Zammit b Lee	78	– c Clarke b Lee	12
A. B. McDonald b Lee	1	– not out	16
†P. J. Roach c Haddin b Thornely	46	– run out (Mail/Haddin)	0
M. L. Lewis b Clark	4	– not out	0
A. B. Wise not out	1		
B 7, l-b 7, n-b 6	20	L-b 3, n-b 2	5

(94.4 overs, 392 mins)   326   (65 overs, 268 mins)   (8 wkts) 230
Fall: 31 39 45 76 76 229 231 320 320 326   Fall: 68 83 94 200 200 201 221 228

Bowling: *First Innings*—Lee 25–4–83–3; Clark 24.4–6–62–3; Nicholson 17–3–71–1; Mail 4–1–11–0; Thornely 15–4–52–3; Clarke 4–1–11–0; Zammit 5–0–22–0. *Second Innings*—Lee 19–1–69–1; Clark 14–1–52–4; Nicholson 18–4–55–2; Thornely 11–5–23–0; Clarke 1–0–5–0; Zammit 2–0–23–0.

Umpires: P. D. Parker and R. L. Parry.

At WACA Ground, Perth, December 20, 21, 22, 2003. VICTORIA defeated WESTERN AUSTRALIA by an innings and 158 runs.

At No.1 Sports Ground, Newcastle, January 9, 10, 11, 12, 2004. VICTORIA defeated NEW SOUTH WALES by three wickets.

At Adelaide Oval, Adelaide, February 1, 2, 3, 4, 2004. VICTORIA defeated SOUTH AUSTRALIA by 197 runs.

VICTORIA v SOUTH AUSTRALIA

At Melbourne Cricket Ground, Melbourne, February 8, 9, 10, 11 (no play), 2004. Match drawn. *Toss:* South Australia. Victoria 2 pts. *First-class debut:* B. P. Cameron.
     A match re-scheduled because of the death of Victoria's coach, David Hookes, passed

virtually unnoticed thanks to Shane Warne's comeback a few miles down the road for the 2nd XI. But it was a significant game for Victoria; they retained the David Hookes Memorial Trophy and secured their first home final since their Sheffield Shield-winning season of 1990-91. Having triumphed in spectacular fashion in Adelaide a week earlier, after a brief sympathy break as players from both sides grappled with their grief, only the weather prevented the Bushrangers from completing a fifth consecutive victory. In searing, energy-sapping heat, Shane Deitz fell on the second ball of the first day and sparked the kind of collapse that was SA's batting hallmark throughout the season. The debutant Ben Cameron helped hold the innings together. Mick Miller further salvaged the situation, sharing a 47-run partnership for the ninth wicket with Shaun Tait, who batted 57 minutes for an unbeaten duck. Victoria's chase was engineered as usual by Matthew Elliott, who drove beautifully and overcame a scratchy beginning to post his 28th century for the state. He guided them to the first-innings points they needed with a boundary over the vacant slips cordon. On day three the Redbacks endeavoured fruitlessly to build a target. Cameron and Deitz put on the state's first century opening stand of the summer, but rain stopped play soon after lunch. Victoria's caretaker coach Greg Shipperd warned his players, in between card games, of the dangers of complacency leading into the final.

Man of the Match: M. T. G. Elliott.   *Attendance*: 2,867.

Close of play: First day, Victoria (1) 1-48 (Elliott 23, Hodge 22); Second day, South Australa (2) 0-3 (Cameron 3, Deitz 0); Third day, South Australia (2) 2-122 (Cameron 58).

South Australia

S. A. Deitz c McDonald b Inness	0	– (2) st Berry b White	48
B. P. Cameron c Berry b Wise	54	– (1) not out	58
G. S. Blewett c Moss b Inness	4	– lbw b White	8
*D. S. Lehmann c White b McDonald	21	– not out	0
M. J. Cosgrove c Berry b Wise	18		
M. C. Miller b Lewis	84		
†G. A. Manou c Hodge b Wise	9		
J. M. Davison c Wise b Moss	30		
M. F. Cleary c Wise b Moss	0		
S. W. Tait not out	0		
P. C. Rofe c Elliott b Lewis	0		
L-b 3, w 1, n-b 1	5	B 4, l-b 2, w 2	8

(77.4 overs, 295 mins) 225   (41.1 overs, 165 mins)   (2 wkts) 122
Fall: 0 15 68 91 100 116 178 178 225 225   Fall: 100 122

Bowling: *First Innings*—Inness 13–3–44–2; Wise 18–6–45–3; Moss 11–6–19–2; McDonald 12–3–39–1; Lewis 12.4–1–36–2; White 11–3–39–0. *Second Innings*—Lewis 12–3–37–0; Inness 10–3–29–0; Wise 9–3–19–0; McDonald 3–0–14–0; White 6.1–1–14–2; Moss 1–0–3–0.

Victoria

M. T. G. Elliott not out	154	M. L. Lewis c Deitz b Miller	16
M. P. Mott b Rofe	0	M. W. H. Inness not out	0
B. J. Hodge c Manou b Miller	73		
J. Moss c and b Cleary	46		
D. J. Hussey c Deitz b Tait	1	B 2, l-b 2, w 2, n-b 11	18
C. L. White c Cosgrove b Tait	5		
A. B. McDonald c Miller b Tait	2	(106 overs, 423 mins) (8 wkts dec) 331
*†D. S. Berry b Davison	16	Fall: 7 116 211 227 232 237 265 326

A. B. Wise did not bat.

Bowling: Tait 20–3–55–3; Rofe 24–2–91–1; Cleary 21–1–75–1; Davison 22–1–58–1; Miller 17–5–30–2; Blewett 2–0–17–0.

Umpires: A. R. Craig and D. L. Orchard.

VICTORIA v TASMANIA

At Melbourne Cricket Ground, Melbourne, February 16, 17, 18, 19, 2004. Victoria won by 218 runs. *Toss:* Victoria. Victoria 6 pts.

What was supposed to be a dress rehearsal for the Pura Cup final started horribly for Tasmania, Matthew Elliott and Brad Hodge each bringing up 1,000 first-class runs for the season in a demoralising 251-run partnership. Elliott capped his fourth 1,000-run season with a stunning unbeaten century, reaching three figures with a straight-hit six over the sightscreen. It was one of two sixes to go with the 18 fours in his innings; a pull shot off Xavier Doherty sailed over mid-wicket and out of the MCG through a gate in the Southern Stand. If Elliott was untouchable, Hodge was uncharacteristically earthly, contributing only 26 runs of the first 100 they put on. He lifted his game after tea, driving, cutting and pulling authoritatively. Shane Warne, returning from his 12-month drugs suspension, tossed down a mixed bag of all his variations in a sharp and accurate 13-over spell. He deceived Shane Watson then had Michael Di Venuto caught at short leg, before going wicketless in 10 overs the next day. Tasmania, conceding first-innings points when they declared 245 runs behind, ran into a rampant Elliott for a second time. He reeled off 12 fours and two sixes in his sixth century of the season, a Victorian record. After the match Elliott expressed his desire to add to his 20 Test matches. Tasmania tried to chase 440 at almost six an over but wickets fell steadily. They were even more disappointed a fortnight later, Queensland sneaking an unlikely win over NSW to steal second spot and Tasmania's place in the final.

Man of the Match: M. T. G. Elliott   *Attendance:* 3,150.

Close of play: First day, Victoria (1) 1-312 (Elliott 162, Hodge 115); Second day, Tasmania (1) 4-99 (Dighton 12, Marsh 15); Third day, Victoria (2) 2-104 (Elliott 63, Moss 28).

Victoria

M. T. G. Elliott run out (Dighton/Clingeleffer)	166	– not out	102
M. P. Mott c Watson b Doherty	32	– b Denton	0
B. J. Hodge c Di Venuto b Denton	121	– c Wright b Denton	9
J. Moss c Mason b Downton	35	– not out	79
D. J. Hussey c Di Venuto b Doherty	19		
C. L. White c Di Venuto b Marsh	39		
*†D. S. Berry b Doherty	39		
S. K. Warne c Kremerskothen b Doherty	18		
M. L. Lewis st Clingeleffer b Doherty	4		
M. W. H. Inness not out	10		
A. B. Wise st Clingeleffer b Doherty	7		
L-b 2, n-b 2	4	B 2, l-b 2	4

(151.2 overs, 569 mins)   494   (52 overs, 188 mins)   (2 wkts dec) 194
Fall: 71 322 323 345 403 429 458 473 478 494   Fall: 1 33

Bowling: *First Innings*—Wright 25–6–65–0; Denton 30–10–95–1; Kremerskothen 13–1–42–0; Downton 32–5–103–1; Doherty 42.2–5–149–6; Marsh 9–0–38–1. *Second Innings*—Denton 13–4–26–2; Watson 6–1–27–0; Doherty 15–2–53–0; Marsh 6–0–25–0; Downton 7–0–24–0; Wright 5–1–35–0.

Tasmania

S. R. Mason c Wise b Lewis	8	– lbw b Inness	21
S. P. Kremerskothen c Elliott b Inness	5	– (6) c Inness b Warne	24
S. R. Watson c Inness b Warne	23	– (4) c White b Inness	11
M. J. Di Venuto c Mott b Warne	33	– (2) c Hodge b Wise	17
M. G. Dighton c Mott b White	50	– st Berry b Warne	54
*D. J. Marsh c Elliott b Wise	40	– (3) b Warne	48
†S. G. Clingeleffer b Lewis	34	– b Moss	11
D. G. Wright not out	45	– c Warne b Moss	29
A. G. Downton not out	3	– run out (Moss/Berry)	1
X. J. Doherty (did not bat)		– st Berry b Warne	2
G. J. Denton (did not bat)		– not out	0
B 1, l-b 6, w 1	8	B 1, l-b 1, n-b 1	3

(102 overs, 391 mins)	(7 wkts dec) 249	(41 overs, 174 mins) 221
Fall: 13 25 65 78 133		Fall: 25 47 66 99 145 184 206
195 201		215 219 221

Bowling: *First Innings*—Lewis 24–7–65–2; Inness 14–4–32–1; Warne 23–8–49–2; Wise 18–8–36–1; White 13–2–38–1; Moss 5–2–8–0; Hodge 5–0–14–0. *Second Innings*—Inness 7–0–43–2; Lewis 6–0–50–0; Wise 6–1–36–1; White 6–1–32–0; Warne 13–3–51–4; Moss 3–0–7–2.

Umpires: I. H. Lock and R. L. Parry.

At Bellerive Oval, Hobart, March 4, 5, 6, 7, 2004. VICTORIA drew with TASMANIA.

FINAL

At Melbourne Cricket Ground, Melbourne, March 12, 13, 14, 15, 16, 2004. VICTORIA defeated QUEENSLAND by 321 runs. For details see section on Pura Cup final, 2003-04.

VICTORIA DOMESTIC FIRST-CLASS RESULTS TABLE

	First Game	M	Won	Lost	Drawn	Tied
v New South Wales ..	Dec 24, 1892	205	65	73	66	1
v South Australia	Dec 31, 1892	200	100	47	53	0
v Queensland	Dec 17, 1926	143	51	42	50	0
v Western Australia ..	Dec 5, 1947	105	33	29	43	0
v Tasmania	Nov 18, 1977	49	14	10	25	0
Total		702	263	201	237	1

VICTORIA DOMESTIC FIRST-CLASS RECORDS

Highest score for:	437	W. H. Ponsford v Queensland at Melbourne	1927-28
Highest score against:	357	D. G. Bradman (South Australia) at Melbourne	1935-36
Best bowling for:	9-40	E. L. McCormick v South Australia at Adelaide	1936-37
Best bowling against:	10-44	I. J. Brayshaw (Western Australia) at Perth	1967-68
Highest total for:	1,107	v New South Wales at Melbourne	1926-27
Highest total against:	815	by New South Wales at Sydney	1908-09
Lowest total for:	31	v New South Wales at Melbourne	1906-07
Lowest total against:	49	by Queensland at Melbourne	1936-37

MOST RUNS

	M	I	NO	R	HS	100s	50s	Avge
D. M. Jones	110	194	16	9,622	324*	31	40	54.06
M. T. G. Elliott	93	178	16	8,885	203	31	38	54.85
W. M. Lawry.............	85	139	14	6,615	266	17	41	52.92
B. J. Hodge	98	180	18	6,544	183	18	29	40.40
G. N. Yallop	76	137	11	5,881	246	18	31	46.67
A. L. Hassett	58	97	10	5,535	229	18	27	63.62
W. H. Ponsford	43	70	5	5,413	437	21	14	83.28
D. F. Whatmore...........	85	150	7	5,235	170	10	31	36.61
I. R. Redpath	76	132	11	5,222	261	11	28	43.16
W. W. Armstrong	59	106	7	4,997	250	17	17	50.47
J. D. Siddons	64	109	11	4,703	245	13	24	47.99
J. Ryder	60	104	12	4,613	295	12	22	50.14
J. Potter	73	120	14	4,608	221	12	24	43.47
P. A. Hibbert	71	121	9	4,321	163	8	23	38.58
J. L. Arnberger	60	114	10	4,144	214	8	22	39.85
R. N. Harvey	52	85	3	4,116	209	11	21	50.20
R. M. Cowper	56	85	13	4,040	195*	10	21	56.11
K. E. Rigg	59	97	8	3,938	167*	11	20	44.25
D. S. Berry	129	198	29	3,816	166*	4	10	22.58
K. R. Stackpole	61	100	6	3,660	145	5	24	38.94

HIGHEST PARTNERSHIP FOR EACH WICKET

375	for	1st	W. M. Woodfull and W. H. Ponsford v New South Wales at Melbourne ... 1926-27
314	for	2nd	W. H. Ponsford and H. S. T. L. Hendry v Queensland at Melbourne 1927-28
390*	for	3rd	J. M. Wiener and J. K. Moss v Western Australia at St Kilda 1981-82
309*	for	4th	J. Moss and D. J. Hussey v Western Australia at Perth 2003-04
316*	for	5th	L. D. Harper and G. B. Gardiner v South Australia at Carlton 1997-98
290	for	6th	M. T. G. Elliott and D. S. Berry v New South Wales at Sydney 1996-97
185	for	7th	P. A. Hibbert and R. J. Bright v New South Wales at Melbourne 1985-86
215	for	8th	R. L. Park and W. W. Armstrong v South Australia at Melbourne 1919-20
143	for	9th	G. R. Hazlitt and A. Kenny v South Australia at Melbourne 1910-11
211	for	10th	M. Ellis and T. J. Hastings v South Australia at Melbourne 1902-03

MOST WICKETS

	M	Balls	Mdns	R	W	BB	5W/i	10W/m	Avge	S-R
P. R. Reiffel	86	19,137	843	8,242	318	6-57	7	2	25.92	60.18
A. N. Connolly	71	17,973	365	7,745	297	9-67	12	4	26.08	60.52
A. I. C. Dodemaide ...	94	19,892	822	8,884	281	6-67	12	0	31.62	70.79
M. G. Hughes	76	16,762	582	8,169	267	7-81	10	2	30.60	62.78
R. J. Bright	101	22,890	1,013	8,821	252	6-61	10	0	35.00	90.87
L. O. Fleetwood-Smith	41	11,576	119	6,034	246	9-135	25	8	24.53	47.06
J. D. Higgs	75	14,961	376	7,202	240	8-66	12	2	30.01	62.34
D. W. Fleming	67	14,648	657	6,675	221	7-90	7	1	30.20	66.28
M. H. N. Walker	62	15,011	429	6,476	220	6-49	11	0	29.44	68.23
H. Ironmonger	44	14,594	432	5,290	215	7-13	16	4	24.60	67.87
J. V. Saunders	37	10,209	375	5,129	196	8-106	18	4	26.17	52.09
M. W. H. Inness	53	10,056	485	4,550	185	7-19	5	2	24.59	54.36
I. W. Johnson	51	10,996	258	4,387	180	6-46	11	2	24.37	61.09
W. W. Armstrong	59	11,030	462	4,270	177	6-66	5	0	24.12	62.32
A. G. Hurst	44	9,717	159	4,687	177	8-84	6	1	26.48	54.90
D. T. Ring	50	11,614	190	5,277	172	6-41	4	1	30.69	67.52
D. J. Saker	45	10,551	482	4,888	166	7-32	2	1	29.45	63.56
I. J. Harvey	69	10,973	463	5,374	161	7-44	3	0	33.38	68.16
H. Trumble	30	9,386	488	3,327	159	8-39	10	4	20.92	59.03
I. W. Callen	36	7.673	173	3,903	153	8-42	6	1	25.51	50.15

MOST DISMISSALS

	M	Catches	Stumpings	Total
D. S. Berry	129	468	44	512
R. D. Robinson	68	213	26	239
R. C. Jordon	70	199	31	230
M. G. D. Dimattina	60	149	19	168
J. L. Ellis	49	111	45	156

MOST CATCHES

M. T. G. Elliott	120 in 93 matches	J. D. Siddons	76 in 64 matches
D. F. Whatmore	110 in 85 matches	W. W. Armstrong	68 in 59 matches
D. M. Jones	96 in 110 matches	G. N. Yallop	66 in 76 matches

MOST APPEARANCES

129	D. S. Berry	1990-91 – 2003-04	86	P. R. Reiffel	1987-88 – 2000-01
110	D. M. Jones	1981-82 – 1997-98	85	W. M. Lawry	1955-56 – 1971-72
101	R. J. Bright	1972-73 – 1987-88	85	D. F. Whatmore	1975-76 – 1988-89
98	B. J. Hodge	1993-94 – 2003-04	76	G. N. Yallop	1972-73 – 1984-85
94	A. I. C. Dodemaide	1983-84 – 1997-98	76	M. G. Hughes	1981-82 – 1994-95
93	M. T. G. Elliott	1992-93 – 2003-04	76	I. R. Redpath	1961-62 – 1975-76

WESTERN AUSTRALIA

The need for speed

by KEN CASELLAS

Pura Cup: Fourth
ING Cup: Champions
Coach: Wayne Clark
Captain: Adam Gilchrist

Murray Goodwin

In an extraordinary and eventful season, Western Australia won the ING Cup and badly underachieved in the Pura Cup. The most bizarre moment occurred in December when the Queenslander Ben Edmondson appeared almost miraculously on the final day against Tasmania and played a vital role in the outcome. Edmondson was a resident of Perth for five days who had previously struggled to make Queensland's 2nd XI; he had never played a first-class match and wasn't even included in WA's original 12. He was picked within the Cricket Australia guidelines as a last-session stand-in for Brad Williams, who had been called up to join the Australian squad. The move triggered howls of protest from some former players, who believed that if anyone was to step up it should have been the 12th man Peter Worthington. The selection of Edmondson, they said, tarnished the integrity of the game.

What the Edmondson situation did do was highlight the paucity of fast-bowling stocks in a traditional pace state. The left-armer Michael Clark, the state's most successful bowler the previous season, was laid low by back problems and restricted to two limited-overs matches. Jo Angel at last gave in to his wonky knees and hung up his size-13s, with three first-class matches remaining and 419 wickets to his name, second only to Clarrie Grimmett in Sheffield Shield-Pura Cup history. Another veteran Paul Wilson, saddened that he was not offered a renewed contract, called it quits at summer's end. John Taylor returned to Melbourne in a bid to break into the Victorian side. And to make matters worse Beau Casson, the promising left-arm wrist-spinner, sustained a freak injury to his bowling hand and missed the second half of the summer.

There was significant off-field turmoil too. Kath White resigned as the WACA's chief executive and was succeeded by Tony Dodemaide, the former Victorian and Australian all-rounder, whose appointment was met with almost universal approval. Dodemaide, however, had barely settled when it was discovered that at least $300,000 were missing from the association's funds, resulting in the dismissal of a senior employee who was later charged with stealing. Then came news of a plot by a band of former Test players, headed by Graeme Wood, Dennis Lillee, Craig Serjeant, Sam Gannon and known as the Cricket Reform Group, to wrest control of the board. The most heartening development, after two years of unrest during Mike Veletta's coaching reign, was the return of joie de vivre under the prodigal Wayne Clark. The players' passion and enjoyment of each other's successes bodes well for the future.

But WA will not return to the top in four-day cricket until they can find a couple of quality fast bowlers. Their search, both at home and interstate, for genuinely fast men who can be considered legitimate strike bowlers has assumed never-ending proportions in recent years. Edmondson, spotted in a 2nd XI game in Brisbane, has been identified to lead the attack. Raw but athletic, with a smooth approach and fluent action, he excelled in his seven Pura Cup matches with 28 wickets at 31.61. The next best bowler was a spinner, Casson, who took 17 wickets in four matches before undergoing surgery on damaged hand ligaments, sustained while diving forward in an unsuccessful attempt to catch NSW's Aaron O'Brien.

The search goes on, meanwhile, for quicks to partner Edmondson. The arrival of Sean Ervine, the talented Zimbabwean all-rounder, and Steve Magoffin, another recruit from Queensland's 2nd XI, should add depth to the ranks in 2004-05. But it is imperative to have Clark back and firing. Late in the season a screw was inserted into one of his vertebrae, and hopes of him making a full recovery are bright. Of the 22 players who played Pura Cup matches in 2004-05, Taylor, Worthington, Darren Wates, Kade Harvey and Michael Thistle all had moderate success. Sadly none can be classed as an enforcer, someone capable of creating fear and indecision in the minds of opposition batsmen. Andrew James and Steven Jacques appear the best-credentialled of the promising locals.

The most pleasing aspect of WA's season was their revitalised approach and greater commitment. The players responded grandly to the passion and professionalism of the captain Justin Langer, with Mike Hussey proving an inspiring stand-in when Langer was

Back row: R. J. Campbell, P. C. Worthington, J. L. Langer, A. C. Voges, J. J. Taylor, C. D. Thorp, C. J. Rogers, M. W. Clark. S. W. Meuleman, S. W. Jacques, K. M. Harvey, D. J. Wates, M. J. North, A. K. Heal, M. J. Thistle, J. Angel, W. M. Clark (*Coach*), M. E. Hussey, B. D. Jones, L. Ronchi. *Front row:* C. J. Simmons, A. James, B. Casson, S. E. Marsh. *Absent (inset):* A. C. Gilchrist, M. W. Goodwin, G. B. Hogg, D. R. Martyn, B. A. Williams, P. Wilson.

on Test duty. The Warriors made a disappointing start to the season and were sitting on the bottom of the Pura Cup ladder with only two points after six matches. But a stirring finishing burst, with outright victories in three of their final four matches, helped them to fourth.

The batting was consistently of a high calibre. Few batsmen in the world are as nimble as Murray Goodwin, the former Zimbabwean Test player, who led the way with a state-record 1,183 runs at 65.72. He and Chris Rogers hit four centuries each and Marcus North three in a season where 16 were registered, a record for WA in qualifying matches, beating the 15 in 1997-98. Six players ended the first-class season with more than 600 runs. But runs alone do not win matches – or competitions. Strong batting can disguise weaknesses in four-day cricket but never hide them.

In the helter-skelter of limited-overs games, however, deficiencies in bowling can be overcome. It was WA's aggressive batting and splendid fielding that played the major part in their ING Cup triumph. They led the field comfortably before suffering a huge battering by Queensland in their penultimate qualifying match. They then returned to the Gabba a fortnight later and avenged their humiliation in a dramatic final. Harvey emerged as the hero, following up his 4 for 28 with a cool-headed unbeaten 53 from 42 balls.

There is no quick fix for the terrible void in WA's pace stocks. But Rob Langer, the general manager of cricket operations, has restructured the department and the long-term future appears rosy. A full-time fitness coordinator has been appointed. Squads of emerging players have been created and constantly updated. Peter Philpott, the former Test leg-spinner, hosted a wrist-spinning clinic in February. A series of swing-bowling clinics were headed by Terry Alderman, Mick Malone, Jim Hubble and Peter Capes. After the chaos of the previous two years, when Veletta was sacked and quality players such as Simon Katich and Matthew Nicholson defected unhappily, WA cricket is back on the rails and looking ahead to cheerier days.

WESTERN AUSTRALIA RESULTS, 2003-04

*All first-class matche*s – Played 11: Won 3, Lost 3, Drawn 5.
Pura Cup – Played 10: Won 3, Lost 3, Drawn 4.
ING Cup matches – Played 10: Won 6, Lost 3, No result 1.

WA PURA CUP AVERAGES, 2003-04

BATTING

	M	I	NO	R	HS	100s	50s	Avge	Ct/St	S-R
M. W. Goodwin	10	20	2	1,183	201*	4	5	65.72	4	64.93
J. L. Langer	6	11	1	622	163*	1	4	62.20	4	61.28
C. J. L. Rogers	8	16	1	864	142	4	3	57.60	8	66.62
M. J. North	10	19	1	984	130*	3	5	54.67	8	54.85
K. M. Harvey	5	9	4	219	100*	1	0	43.80	1	52.64
M. E. K. Hussey	9	18	0	752	138	1	6	41.78	14	48.42
R. J. Campbell	10	19	2	664	134	1	5	39.06	23/7	91.08
D. J. Wates	5	6	1	194	99	0	1	38.80	3	62.38
S. W. Meuleman	3	6	0	230	106	1	2	38.33	2	45.82
G. B. Hogg	3	6	1	135	75	0	1	27.00	5	52.33
A. K. Heal	2	2	0	42	33	0	0	21.00	0	46.67
B. Casson	4	8	3	101	28*	0	0	20.20	2	28.53
J. J. Taylor	6	9	2	132	50	0	1	18.86	3	88.00
S. E. Marsh	4	8	0	135	47	0	0	16.88	3	78.03
P. C. Worthington	4	8	0	98	50	0	1	12.25	3	49.25
B. A. Williams	1	1	0	9	9	0	0	9.00	1	60.00
C. D. Thorp	3	4	0	31	18	0	0	7.75	1	29.52
M. J. Thistle	1	2	0	14	14	0	0	7.00	0	73.68
P. Wilson	5	7	4	18	7*	0	0	6.00	2	34.62
J. Angel	4	6	2	20	12*	0	0	5.00	1	24.10
C. J. Simmons	1	2	0	8	7	0	0	4.00	0	44.44
B. M. Edmondson	7	7	3	12	4*	0	0	3.00	2	19.05

* Denotes not out.

BOWLING

	O	Mdns	R	W	BB	5W/i	10W/m	Avge	S-R
B. A. Williams	38	4	155	6	4-115	0	0	25.83	38.00
S. E. Marsh	11	0	52	2	2-20	0	0	26.00	33.00
P. C. Worthington	93.4	20	339	12	6-59	1	0	28.25	46.83
B. M. Edmondson	212.2	24	885	28	5-90	1	0	31.61	45.50
B. Casson	150	16	580	17	5-109	1	0	34.12	52.94
J. Angel	133.4	34	428	12	3-48	0	0	35.67	66.83
K. M. Harvey	143.1	22	573	14	3-40	0	0	40.93	61.36
D. J. Wates	129.4	25	497	12	4-77	0	0	41.42	64.83
S. W. Meuleman	19	2	97	2	1-38	0	0	48.50	57.00
C. D. Thorp	92	15	344	7	3-59	0	0	49.14	78.86
J. J. Taylor	136	18	615	12	4-70	0	0	51.25	68.00
M. J. North	112.3	17	419	8	2-17	0	0	52.38	84.38
M. E. K. Hussey	33	7	114	2	1-20	0	0	57.00	99.00
G. B. Hogg	95.5	14	371	6	3-66	0	0	61.83	95.83
P. Wilson	162	54	483	6	2-60	0	0	80.50	162.00
A. K. Heal	63	9	243	2	1-19	0	0	121.50	189.00
J. L. Langer	0.2	0	5	0	–	0	0	–	–
C. J. L. Rogers	3	0	12	0	–	0	0	–	–
C. J. Simmons	1	0	4	0	–	0	0	–	–
M. J. Thistle	22	2	103	0	–	0	0	–	–

WESTERN AUSTRALIA v SOUTH AUSTRALIA

At WACA Ground, Perth, October 19, 20, 21, 22, 2003. South Australia won by 56 runs.
Toss: Western Australia. South Australia 6 pts.

Wayne Clark's first match back at the helm after coaching Yorkshire proved a miserable affair. "All of us should be quite embarrassed; our fielding was quite terrible and we've simply got to take stock and improve," was how he summed it up. To make matters worse, Paul Wilson was fined half his match fee for using abusive language towards John Davison after dismissing him in the first innings. Wilson was then unable to bowl in the second innings, suffering a hairline fracture on the left side of the jaw when he ducked into a lifter from Mick Miller. Darren Wates was also unfit in the second innings after straining an abdominal muscle; later, while batting with considerable aplomb, he received a fractured big toe when struck by a Shaun Tait yorker. The much-awaited debut of the former Zimbabwe batsman Andy Flower proved a fizzer. He offered no shot to his first three deliveries before pushing forward to the next and popping a bat-pad catch to short leg. It fell to Greg Blewett to rescue SA from 4 for 50 in their first innings. At the height of his knock he plundered 25 runs in 12 deliveries, uncoiling elegant strokes all round the wicket, including successive straight sixes off the left-arm wrist-spinner Beau Casson. The young SA fast bowler Paul Rofe enhanced his reputation with eight wickets, the result of tight bowling and excellent bounce.

Match reports by KEN CASELLAS.

Man of the Match: P. C. Worthington. *Attendance:* 1,570.

Close of play: First day, South Australia (1) 9-316 (Cleary 36, Tait 2); Second day, South Australia (2) 4-101 (Higgs 33, Miller 13); Third day, Western Australia (2) 5-144 (North 35, Casson 0).

South Australia

D. A. Fitzgerald c Rogers b Wates	24	– (2) lbw b Angel	1
S. A. Deitz c Campbell b Worthington	18	– (1) c Hussey b Worthington	4
*G. S. Blewett st Campbell b Casson	85	– b Worthington	14
A. Flower c Marsh b Worthington	0	– lbw b Angel	32
M. A. Higgs c Campbell b Worthington	0	– b Worthington	38
M. C. Miller c Campbell b Angel	79	– lbw b Worthington	17
†G. A. Manou b Casson	0	– c North b Hussey	29
J. M. Davison c Angel b Wilson	35	– lbw b Worthington	6
M. F. Cleary b Angel	45	– c Worthington b Angel	45
P. C. Rofe c Hussey b Angel	3	– b Worthington	15
S. W. Tait not out	3	– not out	3
B 6, l-b 16, w 2, n-b 11	35	B 4, l-b 5, w 2, n-b 6	17
	327		221

(99.4 overs, 389 mins)   327   (79.4 overs, 306 mins)   221
Fall: 40 50 50 50 215 215 263 279   Fall: 7 8 43 72 105 116 135 169
    304 327   213 221

Bowling: *First Innings*—Wilson 25–10–61–1; Wates 15–1–55–1; Angel 21.4–8–48–3; Worthington 21–8–56–3; Casson 13–3–55–2; Hussey 4–1–30–0. *Second Innings*—Angel 28–9–76–3; Worthington 23.4–3–59–6; Hussey 11–5–25–1; Rogers 3–0–12–0; Casson 13–2–35–0; North 1–0–5–0.

Western Australia

*M. E. K. Hussey c Manou b Rofe	20	– (2) b Cleary	30
C. J. L. Rogers b Tait	5	– (1) lbw b Miller	38
M. W. Goodwin c Higgs b Miller	89	– c Manou b Cleary	9
M. J. North lbw b Rofe	0	– c Manou b Rofe	80
S. E. Marsh b Tait	15	– b Rofe	15
†R. J. Campbell c Cleary b Tait	13	– lbw b Tait	11
P. C. Worthington c Cleary b Rofe	1	– (8) c and b Rofe	50
B. Casson not out	10	– (7) c Fitzgerald b Tait	15
D. J. Wates lbw b Miller	10	– c Cleary b Rofe	48
J. Angel lbw b Tait	5	– c Fitzgerald b Rofe	0
P. Wilson retired hurt	0	– not out	7
B 1, l-b 8, n-b 1	10	L-b 7, n-b 4	11

(47.3 overs, 207 mins)	(9 wkts dec) 178	(109.2 overs, 416 mins) 314

Fall: 18 66 72 107 129 152 152
172 177

Fall: 49 79 80 118 138 207 207 307
307 314

Bowling: *First Innings*—Rofe 14–5–31–3; Tait 13–0–61–4; Miller 12.3–3–43–2; Cleary 8–2–34–0.
Second Innings—Rofe 26.2–7–89–5; Tait 22–7–70–2; Miller 13–3–31–1; Cleary 19–3–65–2; Davison
19–8–27–0; Blewett 10–1–25–0.

Umpires: S. J. Davis and R. L. Parry.

At Sydney Cricket Ground, Sydney, November 4, 5, 6, 7, 2003. WESTERN
AUSTRALIA lost to NEW SOUTH WALES by five wickets.

At Junction Oval, St Kilda, November 19, 20, 21, 22, 2003. WESTERN AUSTRALIA
drew with VICTORIA.

WESTERN AUSTRALIA v TASMANIA

At WACA Ground, Perth, December 7, 8, 9, 10, 2003. Match drawn. *Toss:* Tasmania.
Western Australia 2 pts. *First-class debut:* B. M. Edmondson.

This high-scoring encounter ended in dramatic fashion, each side finishing with 766
runs and some of the Tasmanians thinking they had earned three points for a tie. But the
contest was a draw, with WA taking the only points – their first in four matches – for a
first-innings lead. Other noteworthy occurrences in a game that averaged 383 runs a day
included a century in a session by Chris Rogers, Mike Hussey's first Pura Cup hundred
in two years – while becoming the eighth Western Australian to reach 6,000 runs – and
Sean Clingeleffer's seven first-innings catches, equalling the Tasmanian record set by
Joe Holyman in 1991-92. Most extraordinary of all, though, was the unexpected
appearance by the former Queensland 2nd XI bowler Ben Edmondson, summoned on
the final day as a replacement for Brad Williams, who left to join the Test side in
Adelaide. Edmondson played a vital part in the last session, bowling with considerable
pace to take three wickets. Until then, Tasmania's hopes had appeared bright during a
breezy 128-run stand in 73 minutes between Dan Marsh and Michael Dighton. Marsh
continued his onslaught until seven runs were needed off Edmondson's final over. In the
first three balls Marsh swung and missed twice and edged into his helmet. On the fourth
he got a bottom edge for a boundary, then glided a single to third-man. Needing two off
the last delivery, Andrew Downton scooped the ball round to deep backward square leg
but could manage only one. Had Tasmania been all out, instead of seven wickets down,
they would have gained those three points. It would later prove crucial.

Man of the Match: M. E. K. Hussey.   *Attendance:* 3,050.

Close of play: First day, Western Australia (1) 3-351 (North 70, Marsh 38); Second day, Tasmania (1) 6-216 (Clingeleffer 15, Wright 38); Third day, Western Australia (2) 1-231 (Rogers 116, Goodwin 50).

Western Australia

*M. E. K. Hussey c Clingeleffer b Wright	138	– (2) c Denton b Marsh	61
C. J. L. Rogers c Clingeleffer b Griffith	24	– (1) c Wright b Downton	120
M. W. Goodwin c Clingeleffer b Downton	72	– not out	104
M. J. North c Clingeleffer b Denton	90	– run out (Dighton/Clingeleffer)	4
S. E. Marsh c Mason b Wright	47	– c Clingeleffer b Downton	9
†R. J. Campbell c Clingeleffer b Griffith	6	– b Downton	19
G. B. Hogg c Clingeleffer b Denton	21	– not out	8
J. J. Taylor c Clingeleffer b Denton	7		
C. D. Thorp c Marsh b Downton	8		
B. A. Williams b Denton	9		
P. Wilson not out	5		
L-b 8, n-b 2	10	L-b 2, n-b 2	4

(124.4 overs, 484 mins)	437	(64 overs, 254 mins) (5 wkts dec)	329

Fall: 43 190 301 369 380 399 410 415 427 437

Fall: 94 235 253 266 294

B. M. Edmondson did not bat.

Bowling: *First Innings*—Wright 30–4–110–2; Denton 21.4–2–94–4; Griffith 28–5–87–2; Downton 23–5–85–2; Marsh 14–2–37–0; Cox 8–1–16–0. *Second Innings*—Wright 14–5–55–0; Griffith 8–2–52–0; Downton 14–0–92–3; Marsh 12–0–56–1; Denton 14–0–62–0; Cox 2–0–10–0.

Tasmania

J. Cox b Thorp	25	– (2) lbw b Williams	11
S. R. Mason hit wicket b Williams	52	– (1) lbw b Williams	13
S. R. Watson c North b Thorp	26	– c Thorp b Edmondson	46
M. J. Di Venuto c North b Williams	4	– c and b Hogg	48
M. G. Dighton b Thorp	21	– c (sub) Worthington b Wilson	88
*D. J. Marsh st Campbell b Hogg	32	– not out	111
†S. G. Clingeleffer c Marsh b Taylor	79	– c North b Edmondson	30
D. G. Wright c Hussey b Williams	65	– c Rogers b Edmondson	5
A. R. Griffith c Campbell b Williams	5		
A. G. Downton c Williams b Hogg	45	– (9) not out	4
G. J. Denton not out	14		
B 4, l-b 3, n-b 5	12	B 16, l-b 9, w 2, n-b 3	30

(114 overs, 464 mins)	380	(75 overs, 308 mins) (7 wkts)	386

Fall: 49 95 99 127 144 163 279 295 354 380

Fall: 15 24 106 166 294 358 372

Bowling: *First Innings*—Williams 27–2–115–4; Thorp 22–4–59–3; Wilson 21–6–50–0; Taylor 20–4–75–1; Hogg 23–4–71–2; Hussey 1–0–3–0. *Second Innings*—Williams 11–2–40–2; Thorp 10–1–45–0; Taylor 8–0–67–0; Wilson 14–5–43–1; Hogg 19–3–96–1; Edmondson 9–0–47–3; North 4–0–23–0.

Umpires: S. D. Fry and I. H. Lock.

WESTERN AUSTRALIA v VICTORIA

At WACA Ground, Perth, December 20, 21, 22, 2003. Victoria won by an innings and 158 runs. *Toss:* Victoria. Victoria 6 pts. *First-class debut:* C. J. Simmons, M. J. Thistle.

A dominant Victorian side humbled a pathetic WA inside three days in one of the most one-sided contests ever witnessed in Perth. Records tumbled as the stand-in skipper, Jon Moss, led a super-confident, all-conquering outfit against a woeful, undermanned opponent. Murray Goodwin's first match as captain was a nightmare. After the early losses of Goodwin and the debutant opener Craig Simmons, Marcus North and the recalled Scott Meuleman helped WA recover to 2 for 93. But with the ball swinging disconcertingly, the final eight wickets crashed for 58. The home attack was then thrashed, Victoria losing only three wickets in amassing their highest total in 105 Sheffield Shield/Pura Cup matches against WA. The effervescent David Hussey pulled, cut and drove with tremendous power and precision during his 183-ball innings, Moss joining in the fun against one of the greenest Warriors attacks in years. Their unbroken 309-run stand was the seventh-best for the fourth wicket in the competition's history. Matthew Elliott, dropped on 43, had earlier pulverised the bowlers with fluent driving, 93 of his runs coming in an arc between mid-on and extra cover. His delightful 182 occupied only 258 balls. The demoralised hosts then crashed to defeat, Andrew McDonald taking 6 for 67 in a fine exhibition of controlled swing bowling. The match was, at least, a watershed for the 23-year-old Meuleman, who had averaged only 14 in his first 12 matches. He built on his first-innings half-century with a maiden hundred in the second, facing 214 balls and hitting 15 fours.

Man of the Match: M. T. G. Elliott. *Attendance:* 2,048.

Close of play: First day, Victoria (1) 1-168 (Elliott 102, Mott 45); Second day, Victoria (1) 3-550 (Moss 149, Hussey 121).

Western Australia

S. W. Meuleman lbw b McDonald	53	– (2) lbw b Moss	106
C. J. Simmons c McDonald b Harvey	7	– (1) b Harvey	1
*M. W. Goodwin c Roach b Harwood	4	– lbw b McDonald	38
M. J. North c Mott b McDonald	31	– c Harvey b McDonald	33
S. E. Marsh c Elliott b Wise	6	– c Moss b McDonald	0
†R. J. Campbell not out	28	– c Roach b McDonald	54
G. B. Hogg c Roach b Wise	0	– c Roach b McDonald	25
P. C. Worthington c Wise b Harvey	13	– c Harvey b Harwood	2
C. D. Thorp run out (Hussey)	1	– c Hussey b McDonald	4
B. M. Edmondson b Lewis	0	– (11) not out	4
M. J. Thistle c Roach b Lewis	0	– (10) c Lewis b Harvey	14
L-b 6, n-b 2	8	B 6, l-b 7, w 6, n-b 4	23

(54.1 overs, 218 mins)   151   (90.2 overs, 368 mins)   304

Fall: 12 19 93 106 106 106 125 141   Fall: 2 93 162 162 220 263 267
141 151   275 283 304

Bowling: *First Innings*—Harwood 7–0–23–1; Harvey 10–2–34–2; Wise 15–5–35–2; Moss 6–3–8–0; Lewis 7.1–2–19–2; McDonald 9–1–26–2. *Second Innings*—Harvey 14.2–3–32–2; Harwood 20–3–55–1; Lewis 15–2–64–0; Wise 12–4–31–0; Moss 13–4–42–1; McDonald 16–2–67–6.

Victoria

M. T. G. Elliott lbw b Thorp	182	
J. L. Arnberger b Edmondson	8	B 5, l-b 1, w 2, n-b 5 13
M. P. Mott c Campbell b Worthington	78	
*J. Moss not out	172	(147 overs, 571 mins) (3 wkts dec) 613
D. J. Hussey not out	160	Fall: 30 209 304

I. J. Harvey, M. L. Lewis, A. B. McDonald, S. M. Harwood, †P. J. Roach and A. B. Wise did not bat.

Bowling: Edmondson 28–0–135–1; Thorp 36–7–123–1; Thistle 22–2–103–0; Worthington 19–3–78–1; Hogg 26–2–97–0; Simmons 1–0–4–0; North 11–2–35–0; Marsh 4–0–32–0.

Umpires: A. R. Craig and S. D. Fry.

WESTERN AUSTRALIA v QUEENSLAND

At WACA Ground, Perth, January 11, 12, 13, 14, 2003. Match drawn. *Toss:* Western Australia. Queensland 2 pts.

Stifling heat and a lifeless pitch made bowling a chore in a contest notable for the fact that four batsmen were dismissed in the 90s and only one, Murray Goodwin, scored a century. Goodwin, surviving chances on 120 and 142, made the most of the ideal batting conditions as he savaged a wilting attack under a 40-degree sun. The cut was his most productive shot against the faster men and his quicksilver footwork against Nathan Hauritz's off-spin was a delight. After scoring 104 in the final session of the first day, moving from 100 to 150 in 33 balls, he departed attempting to sweep Hauritz. Michael Kasprowicz, hampered by a leg strain, battled manfully and bowled with tremendous heart for his four wickets. Jimmy Maher, Clint Perren, Martin Love and Stuart Law got Queensland away to a flying start. But Beau Casson and Ben Edmondson, who conceded 73 runs including five successive Love boundaries in his first 10 overs, struck back. Queensland looked in trouble at 7 for 275, but Hauritz and Ashley Noffke's stirring eighth-wicket partnership of 134 – a record between the two states – guided them to first-innings points. Each batsman was dropped by Mike Hussey at second slip off Jo Angel. Hauritz was the last man out, seemingly poised for his maiden first-class century until the umpire Andrew Craig adjudged him leg-before to an Edmondson delivery that appeared clearly to be missing leg stump. Casson frequently bewildered the batsmen with his wrong'un and deserved his five wickets. An ultra-negative Queensland were never interested in chasing a victory target of 306 in 49 overs.

Man of the Match: B. Casson. *Attendance:* 2,430.

Close of play: First day, Western Australia (1) 6-378 (Harvey 4, Casson 0); Second day, Queensland (1) 7-280 (Noffke 4, Hauritz 0); Third day, Western Australia (2) 2-148 (Langer 88, Goodwin 5).

Western Australia

*J. L. Langer	c Hopes b Kasprowicz	20	– c Simpson b Kasprowicz	92
M. E. K. Hussey	c Law b Dawes	10	– c Simpson b Hopes	15
C. J. L. Rogers	c Seccombe b Kasprowicz	94	– c Seccombe b Hauritz	32
M. W. Goodwin	st Seccombe b Hauritz	156	– c Seccombe b Kasprowicz	25
M. J. North	run out (Perren)	67	– run out (Noffke/Seccombe)	37
†R. J. Campbell	lbw b Noffke	6	– c Hauritz b Dawes	50
K. M. Harvey	c Love b Kasprowicz	12	– not out	30
B. Casson	not out	28	– not out	12
J. Angel	c Seccombe b Hopes	3		
P. Wilson	c Hopes b Kasprowicz	2		
B. M. Edmondson	not out	3		
	B 4, l-b 10, w 1, n-b 11	26	B 9, l-b 4, n-b 6	19

(119 overs, 497 mins)	(9 wkts dec) 427	(85 overs, 336 mins) (6 wkts) 312
Fall: 34 43 190 363 368 373 397 406 423		Fall: 49 125 153 188 241 281

Bowling: First Innings—Kasprowicz 28–8–74–4; Noffke 29–3–89–1; Hopes 19–7–51–1; Dawes 15–4–51–1; Hauritz 20–4–84–1; Simpson 6–0–47–0; Perren 2–0–17–0. *Second Innings*—Kasprowicz 18–1–80–2; Noffke 17–3–58–0; Hopes 17–5–37–1; Dawes 14–1–45–1; Hauritz 19–5–79–1.

Queensland

*J. P. Maher c Campbell b Angel	60	– c Campbell b Edmondson	21
C. T. Perren lbw b Harvey	95	– c Rogers b Casson	61
M. L. Love c Langer b Casson	66	– lbw b Harvey	63
S. G. Law b Casson	39	– not out	54
C. P. Simpson c Campbell b Edmondson	4	– c Casson b Harvey	0
J. R. Hopes c Campbell b Edmondson	3	– st Campbell b Casson	23
†W. A. Seccombe lbw b Casson	0	– c Campbell b Casson	4
A. A. Noffke c Harvey b Casson	55	– not out	14
N. M. Hauritz lbw b Edmondson	94		
M. S. Kasprowicz lbw b Casson	2		
J. H. Dawes not out	3		
L-b 4, w 2, n-b 7	13	B 4, l-b 1, n-b 2	7

(124.2 overs, 492 mins) 434 Fall: 109 207 252 270 271 271 275 409 415 434

(49 overs, 210 mins)   (6 wkts) 247 Fall: 34 106 174 174 207 211

Bowling: *First Innings*—Wilson 24–7–83–0; Edmondson 23.2–6–89–3; Angel 23–3–83–1; Harvey 22–5–66–1; Casson 32–3–109–5. *Second Innings*—Angel 7–1–37–0; Wilson 6–3–14–0; Edmondson 11–1–55–1; Casson 16–1–90–3; Harvey 9–0–46–2.

Umpires: A. R. Craig and B. N. J. Oxenford.

WESTERN AUSTRALIA v NEW SOUTH WALES

At WACA Ground, Perth, January 23, 24, 25, 26, 2004. Western Australia won by 126 runs. *Toss:* New South Wales. Western Australia 6 pts.

Dreams do come true, and there was a fairytale finish to Jo Angel's magnificent career. The giant fast bowler took 5 for 109 and played a significant part in his state's first outright success of the season. As he approached the centre for the final time the New South Welshmen, in a sincere tribute, hurled their caps and sun hats into the air. Bowling at a considerably slower pace than on his debut against NSW in 1991-92, Angel proved a formidable competitor until the last ball, securing the wicket of Stuart MacGill in his final over. Steve and Mark Waugh each scored a century in Angel's debut match but didn't fare so well in their last first-class appearance in Perth. A succession of missed chances allowed WA to reach a sizeable total, the NSW bowlers squandering helpful conditions by bowling too wide of off stump. Rogers enjoyed plenty of luck in his 252-ball innings; by the time he notched his century he had played and missed 36 times. Simon Katich's polished 82 was the highlight of a solid NSW reply, Steve Waugh declaring 107 runs behind to set up an exciting finish. WA accepted the challenge. Justin Langer showed the way before falling to a fine piece of bowling from Nathan Bracken, who unsettled him with the short ball. When Bracken removed Murray Goodwin he had snapped up 4 for 14 in 40 deliveries. Chasing 387, NSW were 5 for 208 at tea with the Waugh twins still together. But when both fell at 222 – Steve caught behind and Mark slashing to third-man – the end was in sight.

Man of the Match: M. E. K. Hussey.   *Attendance:* 7,895.

Close of play: First day, Western Australia (1) 3-278 (Rogers 142, North 7); Second day, New South Wales (1) 2-204 (Katich 71, Thornely 28); Third day, Western Australia (2) 5-223 (Taylor 23, Harvey 0).

Western Australia

*J. L. Langer c Thornely b Bracken	12	– b Bracken	94
M. E. K. Hussey c Pilon b Thornely	76	– b Bracken	71
C. J. L. Rogers b Clark	142	– b Bracken	2
M. W. Goodwin lbw b Clark	16	– c Pilon b Bracken	20
M. J. North c Bracken b Clark	87	– lbw b Bracken	5
†R. J. Campbell b MacGill	87		
K. M. Harvey not out	28	– c M. E. Waugh b Nicholson	1
J. J. Taylor (did not bat)		– (6) c Pilon b Nicholson	50
D. J. Wates (did not bat)		– (8) c Pilon b Nicholson	25
J. Angel (did not bat)		– (9) not out	0
B. M. Edmondson (did not bat)		– (10) c Pilon b Nicholson	0
B 14, l-b 8, w 1, n-b 3	26	B 2, l-b 3, w 5, n-b 1	11

(133.1 overs, 518 mins)   (6 wkts dec) 474   (67 overs, 276 mins)   (9 wkts dec) 279
Fall: 16 195 264 281   Fall: 157 161 189 196 223 235 268
      399 474   279 279

Bowling: *First Innings*—Bracken 27–10–78–1; Nicholson 29–7–105–0; Clark 36.1–8–104–3; Thornely 18–4–56–1; Mail 5–0–21–0; MacGill 18–0–88–1. *Second Innings*—Bracken 17–7–38–5; Nicholson 14–0–62–4; Clark 17–0–80–0; MacGill 11–2–50–0; M.E. Waugh 1–0–3–0; Thornely 7–0–41–0.

New South Wales

G. J. Mail lbw b Angel	37	– c Hussey b Angel	16
P. A. Jaques c Hussey b Edmondson	45	– lbw b Harvey	56
S. M. Katich c Taylor b Angel	82	– (4) c Rogers b Angel	42
D. J. Thornely c Hussey b Edmondson	59	– (5) c Hussey b Wates	8
*S. R. Waugh c Hussey b Edmondson	51	– (6) c Hussey b Harvey	21
M. E. Waugh b Edmondson	44	– (7) c North b Taylor	36
†N. S. Pilon c Taylor b Wates	16	– (8) c Wates b Taylor	5
M. J. Nicholson not out	0	– (3) c North b Edmondson	36
S. R. Clark (did not bat)		– c Taylor b North	20
N. W. Bracken (did not bat)		– (11) not out	5
S. C. G. MacGill (did not bat)		– (10) b Angel	8
B 6, l-b 10, w 1, n-b 16	33	L-b 2, w 1, n-b 4	7

(93.1 overs, 388 mins)   (7 wkts dec) 367   (58 overs, 237 mins)   260
Fall: 98 116 217 294 311   Fall: 44 80 152 163 166 222 222
      367 367   229 248 260

Bowling: *First Innings*—Angel 18–8–42–2; Wates 18.1–4–71–1; Edmondson 22–3–78–4; North 9–1–57–0; Taylor 16–1–61–0; Harvey 10–1–42–0. *Second Innings*—Angel 13–1–67–3; Edmondson 10–2–49–1; Wates 10–5–20–1; Harvey 14–1–77–2; Taylor 9–1–30–2; North 2–0–15–1.

Umpires: I. H. Lock and R. W. Patterson.

At Bellerive Oval, Hobart, February 4, 5, 6, 7. WESTERN AUSTRALIA drew with TASMANIA.

At Brisbane Cricket Ground, Brisbane, February 15, 16, 17, 18, 2004. WESTERN AUSTRALIA defeated QUEENSLAND by seven wickets.

At Adelaide Oval, Adelaide, March 4, 5, 6, 7, 2004. WESTERN AUSTRALIA defeated SOUTH AUSTRALIA by 87 runs.

WA DOMESTIC FIRST-CLASS RESULTS TABLE

	First Game	M	Won	Lost	Drawn	Tied
v South Australia	Nov 14, 1947	108	46	29	33	0
v Victoria	Dec 5, 1947	105	29	33	43	0
v New South Wales ..	Jan 30, 1948	106	31	43	32	0
v Queensland	Feb 6, 1948	108	36	26	46	0
v Tasmania	Oct 29, 1977	50	21	6	23	0
Total		477	163	137	177	0

WA DOMESTIC FIRST-CLASS RECORDS

Highest score for:	355*	G. R. Marsh v South Australia at Perth	1989-90
Highest score against:	356	B. A. Richards (South Australia) at Perth	1970-71
Best bowling for:	10-44	I. J. Brayshaw v Victoria at Perth	1967-68
Best bowling against:	8-66	J. D. Higgs (Victoria) at Melbourne	1974-75
Highest total for:	654	v Victoria at Perth	1986-87
Highest total against:	4-601 dec	by New South Wales at Perth	1990-91
Lowest total for:	41	v South Australia at Adelaide	1989-90
Lowest total against:	52	by Queensland at Perth	1982-83

MOST RUNS

	M	I	NO	R	HS	100s	50s	Avge
T. M. Moody	132	228	22	8,853	272	20	46	42.98
J. L. Langer	83	150	12	7,353	274*	22	26	53.28
M. R. J. Veletta	114	198	20	7,306	262	18	40	41.04
G. R. Marsh	100	175	12	7,009	355*	21	28	43.00
G. M. Wood	109	174	25	6,904	186*	20	32	46.34
R. J. Inverarity	108	188	18	6,888	187	20	29	40.52
D. R. Martyn	93	163	16	6,705	203*	20	33	45.61
M. E. K. Hussey	91	166	8	6,471	187	13	33	40.96
B. K. Shepherd	75	127	13	4,934	219	11	26	43.28
R. J. Campbell	71	125	4	4,496	203	8	30	37.16
R. W. Marsh	86	139	9	4,412	168*	6	23	33.94
W. S. Andrews	82	126	12	4,292	139	5	29	37.65
T. J. Zoehrer	107	157	19	4,248	168	7	22	30.78
G. Shipperd	62	107	14	4,025	167*	9	21	43.28
R. Edwards	64	110	14	3,939	158	10	19	41.03
K. J. Hughes	57	96	3	3,925	183	11	20	42.20
I. J. Brayshaw	91	145	20	3,771	104	1	24	30.17
D. Chadwick	59	106	8	3,651	137	9	13	37.26
M. T. Vernon	65	111	4	3,631	173	7	19	33.93
S. M. Katich	46	83	10	3,498	228*	11	15	47.92

HIGHEST PARTNERSHIP FOR EACH WICKET

431	for 1st	M. R. J. Veletta and G. R. Marsh v South Australia at Perth	1989-90
254	for 2nd	G. R. Marsh and M. R. J. Veletta v Queensland at Brisbane	1985-86
330	for 3rd	G. M. Wood and G. R. Marsh v New South Wales at Sydney	1983-84
369	for 4th	C. J. L. Rogers and M. J. North v New South Wales at Perth	2002-03
301*	for 5th	R. B. Simpson and K. D. Meuleman v New South Wales at Perth	1959-60
244	for 6th	J. T. Irvine and R. Edwards v New South Wales at Sydney	1968-69
204	for 7th	G. Shipperd and T. J. Zoehrer v New South Wales at Perth	1982-83
242*	for 8th	T. J. Zoehrer and K. H. MacLeay v New South Wales at Perth	1990-91
168*	for 9th	K. H. MacLeay and V. J. Marks v New South Wales at Perth	1986-87
91	for 10th	I. J. Brayshaw and J. B. Gannon v Queensland at Brisbane	1969-70

MOST WICKETS

	M	Balls	Mdns	R	W	BB	5W/i	10W/m	Avge	S-R
J. Angel	105	22,351	1,033	10,418	419	6-35	13	0	24.86	53.34
T. M. Alderman	97	20,482	778	9,299	384	7-28	17	3	24.22	53.34
D. K. Lillee	70	16,617	439	7,544	323	7-36	18	4	23.36	51.45
G. A. R. Lock	66	20,107	544	7,210	302	7-53	16	2	23.87	66.58
B. P. Julian	87	16,143	612	8,573	292	7-39	15	2	29.36	55.28
G. D. McKenzie	73	16,566	287	7,322	232	6-100	7	0	31.56	71.40
K. H. MacLeay	90	17,761	836	7,033	229	6-93	5	0	30.71	77.56
T. M. Moody	132	14,431	673	6,297	220	7-38	5	1	28.62	65.60
C. D. Matthews	44	9,741	342	4,678	188	8-101	11	0	24.88	51.81
A. L. Mann	68	12,627	329	5,729	181	6-94	5	0	31.65	69.76
B. A. Reid	49	11,520	496	4,980	181	6-54	7	1	27.51	63.65
D. E. Hoare	49	9,834	182	4,637	176	8-98	9	1	26.35	55.88
I. J. Brayshaw	91	10,961	295	4,096	167	10-44	7	2	24.53	65.63
B. Yardley	52	9,698	387	4,131	159	7-44	11	2	25.98	60.99
M. F. Malone	37	8,283	288	3,422	139	6-33	7	0	24.62	59.59
T. G. Hogan	47	11,737	547	4,786	139	6-57	6	0	34.43	84.44
W. M. Clark	41	9,673	313	3,893	133	6-39	4	0	29.27	72.73
L. C. Mayne	29	7,206	103	3,672	118	7-75	5	0	31.12	61.07
P. A. Capes	37	7,527	273	3,670	115	5-69	3	1	31.91	65.45
M. J. Nicholson	35	7,138	259	3,651	115	5-49	2	0	31.75	62.07

MOST DISMISSALS

	M	Catches	Stumpings	Total
T. J. Zoehrer	107	331	28	359
R. W. Marsh	81	311	33	344
A. C. Gilchrist	51	250	8	258
B. L. Buggins	57	131	18	149
R. J. Campbell	36	132	8	140

MOST CATCHES

R. J. Inverarity	138 in 108 matches		D. R. Martyn	89 in 93 matches
M. R. J. Veletta	138 in 114 matches		M. E. K. Hussey	86 in 91 matches
T. M. Moody	114 in 132 matches		G. A. R. Lock	80 in 66 matches
I. J. Brayshaw	95 in 91 matches		T. M. Alderman	80 in 97 matches

MOST APPEARANCES

132	T. M. Moody	1985-86 – 2000-01	100	G. R. Marsh	1977-78 – 1993-94
114	M. R. J. Veletta	1983-84 – 1994-95	97	T. M. Alderman ...	1974-75 – 1992-93
109	G. M. Wood	1977-78 – 1991-92	93	D. R. Martyn	1990-91 – 2002-03
108	R. J. Inverarity	1962-63 – 1978-79	91	I. J. Brayshaw	1960-61 – 1977-78
107	T. J. Zoehrer	1980-81 – 1993-94	91	M. E. K. Hussey ...	1994-95 – 2003-04
105	J. Angel	1991-92 – 2003-04	90	K. H. MacLeay ...	1981-82 – 1991-92

ING Cup, 2003-04

by PETER ENGLISH

Like the 1,500 m swimmers who thought they would never break the 15-minute barrier, the 2003-04 ING Cup started with a wall of seemingly untouchable milestones. But as one fell, so did another, and by season's end a surge of performers were sucked through in the slipstream. For swimming's Housman, Perkins, Kowalski and Hackett, read the ING Cup's Law, Tait, Maher and Queensland.

The standout performance was the run riot by Jimmy Maher's Queenslanders against Western Australia at the Gabba, where they reached a massive 4 for 405. Passing 400 in a 50-over innings used to be the sport's four-minute mile, but this was the third time it had been broken worldwide in two years. Along the way, Maher himself sailed into unchartered personal territory with a competition-best 187 off 129 balls, beating Murray Goodwin's 2000-01 mark by 20 runs. He shared an opening partnership with Stuart Law of 194 in 22.4 overs, and was in clear sight of a double-century until he got out in the 44th. Winning by 207 runs, Queensland became the first team to claim two bonus points for doubling their opponents' score.

Lolling in fifth position after five matches, the Bulls thundered through the remaining preliminary games to top the table, only for WA to avenge their earlier humiliation in a gripping final. The freedom of a farewell tour proved a relaxing tonic for the 35-year-old Law, who had announced that this was to be his Australian swansong. He smashed a 69-ball century against Tasmania at Bellerive Oval, eclipsing by five deliveries the old record he had shared with Brad Haddin and Justin Langer, who had scooted to a century in 74 balls against Queensland only a fortnight earlier. Law's fifty came up in 26 balls, the speediest of the season, and he finished with more runs than anyone else too, 570 at a strike-rate of 108. It was a memorable way of saying goodbye.

The law-makers also flirted with a couple of firsts. They took a deep breath before copying an innovation from county cricket: the rule that offers batsmen a free hit as punishment for a front foot no-ball. This introduced an unruly backyard element which the fans seemed to enjoy, although it also brought bouts of confusion.

Victoria's Matthew Elliott stood behind the stumps to face one such delivery. Spectators and commentators were often unaware of the previous indiscretion, and were subsequently bewildered to see a slogging batsman get out caught or bowled only to stand his ground.

Meanwhile umpires wore microphones for the first time, treating TV viewers to the spectacle of not only hearing them call "no-ball" but "new ball" too, in instances where the original had become too scuffed. An unprecedented four players – Andy Flower, Graham Manou, Callum Ferguson and Matthew Nicholson – collected $50,000 each in the Hit The Sign competition. If crowd numbers were anything to go by the innovations proved highly popular, with a record 162,708 people attending the 31 matches. This figure, though, should be kept in some perspective; the everybody-plays-everybody-twice format has been in place only four years.

While Maher and Law were completing their Bob Beamonesque leaps into batting folklore, South Australia's Shaun Tait ensured the bowlers did not go home empty-handed either. Carl Rackemann took 7 for 34 in 9.2 overs against South Australia in 1988-89 and was not even named Man of the Match. Everyone took notice of Tait when he edged Rackemann out of the record books with 8 for 43 against Tasmania, also at Adelaide Oval, including three wickets – all bowled – in his 10th over. He finished the summer with 18 one-day wickets, the Best New Talent and Bradman Young Cricketer of the Year awards, and a place on the fringes of the Test squad.

The previous season's Bradman winner, Queensland's off-spinner Nathan Hauritz, again displayed the flight and turn that have won him international recognition. His 18 wickets played an important part in carrying Queensland into the final at the Gabba, where cramps to Andy Bichel and James Hopes in the closing stages helped let WA off the hook. Chasing 245 to win Kade Harvey, who had already taken 4 for 28 with the ball, blasted an unbeaten 53 in 42 balls to sneak WA home by four wickets.

Competition frontrunners in the early stages, WA's main batting pillars were Marcus North and Mike Hussey, who also picked up seven wickets – while going for seven runs an over – with his medium-pacers. WA recovered from a late-season slump to win their 11th trophy in 35 years. New South Wales, the next best-performed side, have won eight times.

Matthew Elliott and Brad Hodge have made a tradition out of propping up an under-achieving Victorian side in recent seasons.

They again scored heavily last summer, Hodge hitting three hundreds in nine matches, but also received some quality back-up in the shape of David Hussey and Jonathan Moss. The willingness of Allan Wise and Cameron White, their 20-year-old leg-spinning captain, to carry the bowling helped lift the Bushrangers to bronze-medal status.

It still seems unthinkable that a NSW one-day team featuring both Waugh twins for all but one game could stumble so frequently. While Steve Waugh was consistent, Mark Waugh appeared to extend his career one season too far. The Waughs' win-everything mantra that had been so successful for state and country dissolved. Stuart MacGill's leg-spin was effervescent and his 20 wickets at 15.90 led the competition. The downside of his take-wickets-at-any-cost bowling was an economy rate of 5.13, which worried the national selectors more than impatient batsmen.

South Australia finished fifth, a promising beginning undone by four tense defeats in a row – by six, six, eight and four runs. Darren Lehmann missed the first five games with an Achilles injury, eventually recovering and amassing 304 runs at 60.80. For Tasmania the season was a disaster – one win in 10 matches – due to a lack of bowling penetration and batting application.

Shane Watson's ability to play as a specialist batsman while his back healed, and then to bowl quickly with a remodelled action once it had, drew Tasmania's biggest smile. But as early as April even that had disappeared, Watson announcing he was moving back home to the Sunshine State. It capped a season where everything seemed to happen in record time for Queensland, a season of several silver linings but no silverware.

2003-04 POINTS TABLE

	Played	Won	Lost	No Result	Bonus Points	Points	Net Run-Rate
Queensland	10	7	3	0	4	32	0.7035
Western Australia	10	6	3	0	4	29	0.1402
Victoria	10	6	3	1	3	28	0.1173
New South Wales	10	5	4	1	2	23	0.1310
South Australia	10	3	7	0	2	13	-0.2940
Tasmania	10	1	8	0	0	6	-0.8635

Net run-rate was calculated by subtracting runs conceded per over from runs scored per over.

ING CUP FINAL, 2003-04

QUEENSLAND v WESTERN AUSTRALIA

At Brisbane Cricket Ground, Brisbane, February 28, 2004. Western Australia won by four wickets. *Toss:* Queensland. *Competition Debut:* C.D. Hartley.

Kade Harvey twice rescued Western Australia in a gripping final, leading them to a thrilling and redemptive victory with two deliveries to spare. First with the ball and then, more importantly, with the bat, Harvey almost single-handedly prevented a second disaster at the Gabba from unfolding. Fifteen days earlier Queensland had hammered 405 and crushed WA by a humiliating 207 runs, and a repeat effort looked on the cards when Jimmy Maher and Stuart Law raced to a 100-run opening stand in 12.3 overs. Harvey was brought on and soon dismissed both of them, Maher dragging on and Law holing out to mid-off. The match turned for the first time. The visitors, inspired by their lumbering veteran Paul Wilson and some suffocating fielding, successfully clamped the Bulls' run-flow and the innings slowed to a crawl.

WA's pursuit of 245 did not start promisingly. Despite Scott Meuleman's efforts, hitting nine fours in his best one-day innings for WA, the top order failed to master a valiant Queensland attack. Limping at mid-wicket after re-tearing his hamstring, Maher marshalled his forces as the Warriors sank to 6 for 173, needing 72 off their last 10 overs. But Harvey again stood tall. Joined by Darren Wates in the 41st over, the pair launched a cool-headed rescue mission. The target was whittled down to 32 off three overs, 17 off two and then eight off the last. The Bulls were hobbling badly. Both Andy Bichel, bowling his last two overs at half-pace, and the specialist closing seamer James Hopes suffered severe cramps. "I don't know where that sniper who was nailing everyone in the leg was sitting," said Maher afterwards, "but he kept hitting the target."

In Hopes' absence, the part-timer Clint Perren was left to bowl the last five balls of the 48th over, which went for 11 runs, and then the 50th. Harvey began the final over with a single. Wates swung wildly at the next delivery, shutting his eyes, then opening them to see the ball sailing high into the grandstand. A clip to mid-wicket two balls later completed an extraordinary comeback and sealed WA's 11th domestic one-day trophy. It was the fourth summer in a row, bizarrely, that the away team had triumphed in the final. "This is the perfect day," said Harvey. His 42-ball explosion, including two fours and two seismic sixes, made it all possible. –JOHN TOWNSEND

Man of the Match: K.M. Harvey. *Attendance:* 13,092.

Queensland

*J. P. Maher b Harvey	46	(43)	N. M. Hauritz c Rogers b Harvey	2	(4)
S. G. Law c Wates b Harvey	50	(40)	A. A. Noffke run out (Heal)	1	(5)
M. L. Love c Hussey b Edmondson	21	(37)	S. A. Brant b Harvey	0	(1)
C. T. Perren c Wilson b North	57	(89)	L-b 1, w 2, n-b 7	10	
C. A. Philipson c Wates b Wilson	10	(19)			
J. R. Hopes c Heal b North	19	(28)	(49.1 overs, 205 mins)	244	
†C. D. Hartley c Meuleman b Wilson	14	(15)	Fall: 100 103 140 168 212 215 235		
A. J. Bichel not out	14	(17)	240 244 244		

Bowling: Wates 7–0–59–0; Edmondson 10–0–57–1; Harvey 9.1–2–28–4; Wilson 10–1–39–2; Heal 10–0–43–0; North 3–0–17–2.

Western Australia

C.J.L. Rogers c (sub) C.P. Simpson
          b Brant .. 20 (34)
D.J. Wates not out 29 (27)
M.J. North st Hartley b Hauritz 32 (54)
M.W. Goodwin run out (Noffke/Hartley) 12 (16)
*M.E.K. Hussey c Hopes b Hauritz .. 6 (15)
†R.J. Campbell c Perren b Noffke ... 21 (26)

K.M. Harvey not out 53 (42)
S.W. Meuleman st Hartley b Hopes . 71 (85)

       L-b 1, w 2, n-b 1 4

(49.4 overs, 221 mins)   (6 wkts) 248
Fall: 67 111 126 133 156 173

B.M. Edmondson, A.K. Heal and P. Wilson did not bat.

Bowling: Bichel 10–0–39–0; Brant 10–0–46–1; Noffke 10–1–54–1; Hopes 8.1–0–31–1; Hauritz 10–0–55–2; Perren 1.3–0–22–0.

Umpires: D.J. Harper and S.J.A. Taufel
TV Umpire: B.N.J. Oxenford.

STATISTICS, 2003-04

	M	Runs Scored	Overs Batted	Run-Rate	Runs Conceded	Overs Bowled	Run-Rate
Queensland	11	2,853	532.2	5.35	2,521	525.3	4.79
Western Australia	11	2,543	479	5.30	2,694	512.3	5.25
Victoria	10	2,288	459	4.94	2,371	487	4.86
New South Wales	10	2,359	449	5.25	2,487	491.4	5.05
South Australia	10	2,471	483.5	5.10	2,604	490.2	5.31
Tasmania	10	2,161	485	4.45	1,998	383.1	5.21

MOST RUNS, 2003-04

	M	I	NO	R	HS	100s	50s	Avge	S-R
S.G. Law (Qld)	11	11	1	570	113*	1	5	57.00	107.95
B.J. Hodge (Vic).	9	9	2	540	114	3	3	77.14	83.46
C.T. Perren (Qld)	11	11	3	514	94*	0	5	64.25	69.84
M.T.G. Elliott (Vic)....	10	10	1	493	117*	1	4	54.78	78.25
J.P. Maher (Qld)	7	7	0	429	187	2	0	61.29	96.40
M.E.K. Hussey (W Aust)	9	8	1	426	106	1	4	60.86	89.68
M.J. North (W Aust)....	11	9	5	387	84*	0	4	96.75	82.34
S.R. Waugh (NSW)	9	9	2	378	101*	1	2	54.00	78.26
S.R. Watson (Tas)	10	10	0	375	78	0	4	37.50	76.06
M.L. Love (Qld)	11	11	1	369	110*	1	0	36.90	85.22
M.W. Goodwin (W Aust)	11	10	2	350	80*	0	3	43.75	90.91
S.M. Katich (NSW)	6	6	1	345	136*	2	0	69.00	99.14
M.G. Dighton (Tas)	10	10	0	340	113	1	1	34.00	64.15
J.L. Langer (W Aust) ...	9	8	0	318	115	2	0	39.75	77.75
M.J. Di Venuto (Tas) ...	8	8	0	316	125	1	1	39.50	76.89
D.J. Thornely (NSW)...	10	10	1	305	78	0	2	33.89	62.37
P.A. Jaques (NSW).....	8	8	0	305	75	0	2	38.13	107.77
D.S. Lehmann (S Aust) .	5	5	0	304	83	0	3	60.80	99.35
S.A. Deitz (S Aust).....	8	8	0	278	60	0	2	34.75	66.51
C.J.L. Rogers (W Aust).	9	9	2	272	117*	1	1	38.86	74.52

    * *Denotes not out.*

MOST WICKETS, 2003-04

	M	O	Mdns	R	W	BB	5W/i	Avge	RPO
N. M. Hauritz (Qld)	10	85	2	415	18	4-39	0	23.06	4.88
S. W. Tait (S Aust)	8	71.4	5	353	18	8-43	1	19.61	4.93
M. J. Nicholson (NSW) . . .	9	83.4	7	438	18	3-34	0	24.33	5.24
K. M. Harvey (W Aust) . . .	9	78.3	3	380	17	4-28	0	22.35	4.84
S. R. Clark (NSW)	10	88.5	8	434	16	4-44	0	27.13	4.89
J. R. Hopes (Qld)	11	99.2	6	478	14	3-20	0	34.14	4.81
P. C. Worthington (W A) .	7	57	2	309	12	3-45	0	25.75	5.42
M. S. Kasprowicz (Qld) . .	5	50	3	174	11	4-19	0	15.82	3.48
J. J. Taylor (W Aust)	7	56	5	247	11	3-27	0	22.45	4.41
C. L. White (Vic)	9	75	5	363	10	3-25	0	36.30	4.84
A. B. Wise (Vic)	8	59	1	287	10	2-31	0	28.70	4.86
A. R. Griffith (Tas)	9	75	3	428	10	3-40	0	42.80	5.71
M. L. Lewis (Vic)	6	58	2	248	9	2-33	0	27.56	4.28
J. Moss (Vic)	10	69	4	333	8	3-52	0	41.63	4.83
A. A. Noffke (Qld)	8	79	7	382	8	2-27	0	47.75	4.84
M. F. Cleary (S Aust)	10	90.3	5	472	8	2-34	0	59.00	5.22
J. M. Davison (S Aust) . . .	9	46	0	250	8	5-26	1	31.25	5.43
R. J. Harris (S Aust)	4	38	1	207	8	3-51	0	25.88	5.45

AUSTRALIAN DOMESTIC LIMITED-OVERS WINNERS

Australasian (V & G) Knock-Out Competition

Season	Winner	Runner-up	Season	Winner	Runner-up
1969-70	New Zealanders	Victoria	1970-71	Western Australia	Queensland

Australasian (Coca-Cola) Knock-Out Competition

1971-72	Victoria	South Australia	1972-73	New Zealanders	Queensland

Gillette Cup

1973-74	Western Australia	New Zealanders	1976-77	Western Australia	Victoria
1974-75	New Zealanders	Western Australia	1977-78	Western Australia	Tasmania
1975-76	Queensland	Western Australia	1978-79	Tasmania	Western Australia

McDonald's Cup

1979-80	Victoria	New South Wales	1984-85	New South Wales	South Australia
1980-81	Queensland	Western Australia	1985-86	Western Australia	Victoria
1981-82	Queensland	New South Wales	1986-87	South Australia	Tasmania
1982-83	Western Australia	New South Wales	1987-88	New South Wales	South Australia
1983-84	South Australia	Western Australia			

FAI Insurance Cup

1988-89	Queensland	Victoria	1990-91	Western Australia	New South Wales
1989-90	Western Australia	South Australia	1991-92	New South Wales	Western Australia

Mercantile Mutual Cup

1992-93	New South Wales	Victoria	1997-98	Queensland	New South Wales
1993-94	New South Wales	Western Australia	1998-99	Victoria	New South Wales
1994-95	Victoria	South Australia	1999-00	Western Australia	Queensland
1995-96	Queensland	Western Australia	2000-01	New South Wales	Western Australia
1996-97	Western Australia	Queensland			

ING Cup

2001-02	New South Wales	Queensland	2003-04	Western Australia	Queensland
2002-03	New South Wales	Western Australia			

MATCH RESULTS, 1969-70 TO 2002-04

	M	W	L	NR	T	Won Batting First	Won Batting Second
Australian Capital Territory ..	18	3	15	0	0	16.67%	16.67%
New South Wales	151	89	58	1	3	53.57%	69.84%
New Zealanders	10	7	3	0	0	60.00%	80.00%
Queensland	149	85	60	4	0	52.63%	65.22%
South Australia	143	56	86	0	1	41.18%	37.84%
Tasmania	130	35	91	3	1	27.12%	28.36%
Victoria	147	63	77	5	2	39.24%	53.33%
Western Australia	168	107	55	5	1	64.71%	67.02%
Total	458	445	445	9	4	46.74%	53.26%

RESULTS AT EACH VENUE

	First Game	M	NR	T	Won Batting First	Won Batting Second
MCG (Melbourne)	1969-70	60	1	1	43.10%	56.90%
Perth	1969-70	90	3	1	45.35%	55.29%
Sydney	1969-70	47	1	0	36.96%	63.04%
Adelaide Oval (Adelaide) ..	1970-71	74	0	1	46.58%	53.42%
Gabba (Brisbane)	1970-71	76	2	0	40.54%	59.46%
Launceston	1970-71	7	1	0	66.67%	33.33%
TCA (Hobart)	1973-74	12	0	0	66.67%	33.33%
Waverley (Melbourne)	1979-80	1	0	0	100.00%	–
St Kilda (Melbourne)	1981-82	1	0	0	–	100.00%
Devonport	1984-85	6	0	1	60.00%	40.00%
Football Park (Adelaide) ...	1986-87	2	0	0	50.00%	50.00%
Bellerive (Hobart)	1988-89	34	1	0	54.55%	45.45%
North Sydney	1989-90	16	0	0	62.50%	37.50%
Carlton (Melbourne)	1992-93	2	0	0	50.00%	50.00%
Canberra	1997-98	10	0	0	70.00%	30.00%
Bendigo	1997-98	1	0	0	100.00%	–
Richmond (Melbourne)	1999-00	5	0	0	20.00%	80.00%
Albion (Brisbane)	1999-00	2	0	0	50.00%	50.00%
Bankstown (Sydney)	2000-01	3	0	0	66.67%	33.33%
Coffs Harbour	2001-02	2	0	0	50.00%	50.00%
Ballarat	2002-03	1	0	0	–	100.00%
Drummoyne (Sydney)	2002-03	1	0	0	100.00%	–
Homebush (Sydney)	2002-03	2	0	0	50.00%	50.00%
Bowral	2003-04	1	0	0	0.00%	100.00%

LAST TEN YEARS' PLACINGS

	94-95	95-96	96-97	97-98	98-99	99-00	00-01	01-02	02-03	03-04
Australian Capital Territory	–	–	–	6	6	7	–	–	–	–
New South Wales .	6	3	3	2	2	3	1	1	1	4
Queensland	4	1	2	1	3	2	4	2	3	2
South Australia ...	2	4	6	4	4	4	3	3	6	5
Tasmania	5	5	5	5	7	6	5	6	4	6
Victoria	1	6	4	7	1	5	6	5	5	3
Western Australia .	3	2	1	3	5	1	2	4	2	1

HIGHEST INNINGS SCORES

187	J. P. Maher	Queensland v Western Australia at Brisbane	2003-04
167	M. W. Goodwin	Western Australia v New South Wales at Perth	2000-01
164	R. B. McCosker	New South Wales v South Australia at Sydney	1981-82
159	S. G. Law	Queensland v Tasmania at Brisbane	1993-94
152*	M. L. Hayden	Queensland v Victoria at Melbourne	1998-99
151	C. J. Richards	New South Wales v Western Australia at Perth	2001-02
146	J. L. Langer	Western Australia v South Australia at Perth	1999-00
142*	D. S. Lehmann	South Australia v Tasmania at Adelaide	1994-95
140*	P. C. Nobes	South Australia v Western Australia at Perth	1994-95
140	D. R. Martyn	Western Australia v Tasmania at Hobart (Bellerive)	1997-98
139*	D. M. Jones	Victoria v New South Wales at Sydney	1986-87

* Denotes not out.

FASTEST HALF-CENTURIES

Balls

21	D. W. Hookes	South Australia v Western Australia at Perth	1990-91
24	D. A. Nash	New South Wales v Western Australia at North Sydney . .	2000-01
26	S. G. Law	Queensland v Tasmania at Hobart (Bellerive)	2003-04
27	I. J. Harvey	Victoria v Tasmania at Hobart (Bellerive)	1998-99
28	D. S. Berry	Victoria v New South Wales at North Sydney	1997-98
29	G. A. Manou	South Australia v Tasmania at Adelaide	2002-03
30	M. G. Bevan	New South Wales v Victoria at Sydney	1992-93
31	R. W. Marsh	Western Australia v South Australia at Adelaide	1983-84
31	B. J. Hodge	Victoria v Tasmania at Hobart (Bellerive)	1998-99
31	M. A. Higgs	New South Wales v Queensland at Sydney	2001-02
32	S. G. Law	Queensland v Tasmania at Brisbane	1993-94
32	R. J. Campbell	Western Australia v Victoria at Perth	1996-97

FASTEST CENTURIES

Balls

69	S. G. Law	Queensland v Tasmania at Hobart (Bellerive)	2003-04
74	S. G. Law	Queensland v Tasmania at Brisbane	1998-99
74	B. J. Haddin	New South Wales v Tasmania at Bankstown	2001-02
74	J. L. Langer	Western Australia v Queensland at Perth	2003-04
82	R. J. Campbell	Western Australia v Queensland at Perth	1999-00
83	D. S. Lehmann	South Australia v Victoria at Adelaide	2000-01
84	J. P. Maher	Queensland v Western Australia at Brisbane	2003-04
86	D. J. Marsh	Tasmania v New South Wales at Bankstown	2001-02
88	J. P. Maher	Queensland v Western Australia at Perth	1999-00
89	S. M. Katich	New South Wales v Tasmania at Hobart (Bellerive)	2003-04

MOST RUNS

	M	I	NO	R	HS	100s	50s	Avge	S-R
J. P. Maher (Qld)	73	73	9	3,137	187	7	17	49.02	77.73
D. S. Lehmann (S Aust/Vic)	75	74	10	3,095	142*	6	22	48.36	86.45
J. L. Langer (W Aust)	78	74	6	2,815	146	6	19	41.40	69.08
G. S. Blewett (S Aust)	79	77	7	2,740	109*	3	17	39.14	66.78
B. J. Hodge (Vic)	75	73	8	2,643	118*	6	16	40.66	73.62
S. G. Law (Qld)	85	78	7	2,534	159	6	10	35.69	93.06
M. G. Bevan (S Aust/NSW)	60	60	20	2,478	135*	1	22	61.95	73.05
M. L. Love (Qld)	78	75	10	2,315	127*	4	9	35.62	76.99
S. R. Waugh (NSW)	55	54	10	2,269	131	5	13	51.57	84.26
M. T. G. Elliott (Vic)	68	66	6	2,247	118*	6	12	37.45	70.44
M. L. Hayden (Qld)	51	51	9	2,231	152*	8	11	53.12	72.18

	M	I	NO	R	HS	100s	50s	Avge	S-R
M. E. K. Hussey (W Aust)	65	61	10	2,220	106	3	17	43.53	75.98
D. M. Jones (Vic)	55	52	10	2,122	139*	4	12	50.52	74.12
M. J. Di Venuto (Tas)	75	73	7	2,020	129*	3	9	30.61	77.60
T. M. Moody (W Aust)	75	71	12	2,004	102*	2	14	33.97	72.22
M. E. Waugh (NSW)	64	60	6	1,984	123	3	10	36.74	80.55
D. R. Martyn (W Aust)	53	50	7	1,880	140	3	13	43.72	74.07
J. Cox (Tas)	75	73	4	1,879	99	0	14	27.23	64.31
S. M. Katich (W Aust/NSW)	55	53	7	1,851	136*	4	10	40.24	75.21
D. C. Boon (Tas)	55	52	4	1,725	116	1	16	35.94	66.19

* Denotes not out.

HIGHEST PARTNERSHIP FOR EACH WICKET

253	for 1st	R. B. McCosker and J. Dyson, New South Wales v South Australia at Sydney	1981-82
260	for 2nd	M. L. Hayden and S. G. Law, Queensland v Tasmania at Brisbane	1993-94
257	for 3rd	M. W. Goodwin and M. E. K. Hussey, Western Australia v NSW at Perth	2000-01
180	for 4th	G. C. Rummans and S. Lee, New South Wales v Queensland at Brisbane	1999-00
180	for 5th	J. P. Maher and C. T. Perren, Queensland v South Australia at Brisbane	2003-04
173*	for 6th	M. E. K. Hussey and G. B. Hogg, Western Australia v Victoria at Melbourne	1999-00
124	for 7th	G. T. Cunningham and C. M. Smart, ACT v Victoria at Richmond	1999-00
106*	for 8th	A. C. Gilchrist and B. P. Julian, Western Australia v NSW at Sydney	1995-96
96*	for 9th	S. M. Thompson and S. D. Bradsteeet, NSW v Queensland at North Sydney	1998-99
54	for 10th	B. E. McNamara and G. R. Robertson, NSW v South Australia at Adelaide	1996-97

* Denotes unbroken partnership.

HIGHEST INNINGS TOTALS

Batting First

4-405	Queensland v Western Australia at Brisbane	2003-04
4-397	New South Wales v Tasmania at Bankstown	2001-02
6-325	South Australia defeated Tasmania at Hobart (TCA)	1986-87
5-325	Western Australia defeated New South Wales at Perth	2000-01
4-320	Queensland defeated Tasmania at Brisbane	1993-94
7-319	New South Wales defeated South Australia at North Sydney	1997-98
8-311	Tasmania defeated Victoria at Melbourne	2002-03
4-310	New South Wales defeated South Australia at Sydney	1981-82
5-310	New South Wales defeated Victoria at North Sydney	1991-92
6-310	Western Australia defeated Tasmania at Hobart (Bellerive)	1997-98

Batting Second

7-327	Tasmania lost to New South Wales at Bankstown	2001-02
3-298	Western Australia defeated Queensland at Perth	2003-04
9-288	South Australia lost to New South Wales at Drummoyne	2003-04
8-287	South Australia lost to Victoria at Adelaide	2003-04
7-284	Western Australia defeated Victoria at Perth	1990-91
7-284	Queensland defeated Western Australia at Perth	1997-98
282	South Australia lost to New South Wales at North Sydney	1997-98
5-282	South Australia defeated Victoria at Adelaide	2000-01
6-281	South Australia defeated Western Australia at Perth	1994-95
4-280	Victoria defeated Queensland at Melbourne	1998-99

LOWEST COMPLETED INNINGS TOTALS

Total	Overs		
51	(28)	South Australia v Tasmania at Hobart (Bellerive)	2002-03
59	(21.3)	Western Australia v Victoria at Melbourne	1969-70
62	(20.3)	Queensland v Western Australia at Perth	1976-77
65	(30.4)	Victoria v Queensland at Ballarat	2002-03
76	(26.1)	Western Australia v New Zealanders at Melbourne	1974-75
77	(22.5)	Western Australia v Queensland at Perth	1976-77
78	(42.1)	Victoria v Queensland at Brisbane	1989-90
79	(23.5)	Queensland v Western Australia at Melbourne	1970-71
80	(34.3)	Tasmania v New South Wales at Devonport	1984-85
83	(21)	South Australia v Queensland at Brisbane	2002-03

MOST WICKETS

	M	O	Mdns	R	W	BB	5W/i	Avge	RPO
J. Angel (W Aust)	74	614.2	52	2525	94	5-16	2	26.86	4.11
S.C.G. MacGill (NSW)	46	387.5	21	2007	93	5-40	3	21.58	5.17
K.M. Harvey (W Aust)	70	499.2	30	2388	87	4-8	0	27.45	4.78
P. Wilson (S Aust/W Aust)	65	592.4	56	2339	83	4-23	0	28.18	3.95
M.S. Kasprowicz (Qld)	66	567.5	42	2346	80	4-19	0	29.33	4.13
T.M. Moody (W Aust)	75	534.1	41	2131	70	4-30	0	30.44	3.99
I.J. Harvey (Vic)	61	427.1	24	1909	70	5-34	1	27.27	4.47
S.A. Prestwidge (Qld)	45	364.5	18	1755	67	5-59	1	26.19	4.81
S.R. Clark (NSW)	53	467.3	37	1874	65	4-26	0	28.83	4.01
B.P. Julian (W Aust)	54	386.2	19	1779	59	4-41	0	30.15	4.60
B.E. McNamara (NSW)	42	334.1	22	1281	57	6-25	1	22.47	3.83
M.A. Harrity (S Aust)	40	338.2	26	1551	57	5-42	1	27.21	4.58
J.R. Hopes (Qld)	37	305.3	24	1349	55	5-29	1	24.53	4.42
N.M. Hauritz (Qld)	34	259.4	4	1184	54	4-39	0	21.93	4.56
S. Lee (NSW)	59	359.1	13	1695	54	4-59	0	31.39	4.72
K.H. MacLeay (W Aust)	38	316	32	1165	53	5-30	1	21.98	3.69
D.W. Fleming (Vic/S Aust)	49	432.3	45	1695	53	3-25	0	31.98	3.92
N.W. Bracken (NSW)	38	327.2	31	1412	52	5-38	1	27.15	4.31
D.G. Wright (Tas)	42	376	38	1393	51	4-23	0	27.31	3.70
G.S. Blewett (S Aust)	79	349	12	1783	51	4-33	0	34.96	5.11

HAT-TRICKS

A.G. Hurst	Victoria v Western Australia at Perth	1978-79
R.M. Baker	Western Australia v Australian Capital Territory at Perth	1999-00
N.W. Bracken	New South Wales v Victoria at Melbourne	2001-02

BEST BOWLING FIGURES

8-43	S.W. Tait	South Australia v Tasmania at Adelaide	2003-04
7-34	C.G. Rackemann	Queensland v South Australia at Adelaide	1988-89
6-18	J.R. Thomson	Queensland v South Australia at Brisbane	1978-79
6-25	B.E. McNamara	New South Wales v Tasmania at Sydney	1996-97
5-15	D.L. Boyd	Western Australia v Victoria at Perth	1982-83
5-16	J. Angel	Western Australia v Victoria at Perth	2001-02
5-20	G.D. Watson	Victoria v Western Australia at Melbourne	1969-70
5-22	H.J. Howarth	New Zealanders v New South Wales at Sydney	1969-70
5-23	R.J. McCurdy	South Australia v Western Australia at Adelaide	1984-85
5-23	J.P. Marquet	Tasmania v Queensland at Hobart (Bellerive)	1995-96

MOST CATCHES IN A MATCH

5	B. E. Young	South Australia v Tasmania at Launceston	2001-02
4	W. J. Scholes	Victoria v New Zealanders at Melbourne	1971-72
4	I. M. Chappell	South Australia v New Zealanders at Adelaide	1972-73
4	M. A. Taylor	New South Wales v Queensland at Sydney	1998-99
4	J. D. Siddons	South Australia v A.C.T. at Canberra	1999-00

MOST CATCHES

M. E. K. Hussey (W Aust)	40 in 65 matches		D. J. Marsh (S Aust/Tas)	32 in 72 matches
M. E. Waugh (NSW)	37 in 64 matches		J. D. Siddons (Vic/S Aust)	31 in 62 matches
J. P. Maher (Qld)	36 in 73 matches		S. Lee (NSW)	31 in 59 matches
S. G. Law (Qld)	35 in 85 matches		A. R. Border (NSW/Qld)	30 in 49 matches
M. J. Di Venuto (Tas)	35 in 75 matches		B. J. Hodge (Vic)	30 in 75 matches
J. L. Langer (W Aust)	34 in 78 matches		D. M. Jones (Vic)	29 in 55 matches

MOST DISMISSALS IN A MATCH

6	(all ct)	K. J. Wadsworth	New Zealanders v New South Wales at Sydney	1969-70
6	(5ct, 1st)	B. J. Haddin	New South Wales v Western Australia at Perth	2001-02
6	(5ct, 1st)	R. J. Campbell	Western Australia v New South Wales at Perth	2000-01
6	(all ct)	R. J. Campbell	Western Australia v Tasmania at Perth	2000-01
5	(all ct)	R. Edwards	Western Australia v New Zealanders at Perth	1970-71
5	(all ct)	I. A. Healy	Queensland v Tasmania at Hobart (Bellerive)	1995-96
5	(all ct)	R. J. Campbell	Western Australia v NSW at Coffs Harbour	2002-03
5	(4ct, 1st)	S. G. Clingeleffer	Tasmania v Victoria at Hobart (Bellerive)	2002-03
5	(5ct)	A. C. Gilchrist	Western Australia v Victoria at Perth	2003-04

MOST DISMISSALS

	M	Catches	Stumpings	Total
D. S. Berry (S Aust/Vic)	87	105	29	134
W. A. Seccombe (Qld)	69	92	20	112
B. J. Haddin (ACT/NSW)	53	73	19	92
R. J. Campbell (W Aust)	46	80	6	86
P. A. Emery (NSW)	58	70	11	81
A. C. Gilchrist (NSW/W Aust)	38	64	6	70
G. A. Manou (S Aust)	45	59	3	62
T. J. Nielsen (S Aust)	45	54	3	57
I. A. Healy (Qld)	29	47	7	54
R. W. Marsh (W Aust)	33	50	1	51

MOST APPEARANCES

87	D. S. Berry (S Aust/Vic)	1989-90 – 2003-04	75	T. M. Moody (W Aust)	1985-86 – 2000-01
85	S. G. Law (Qld)	1988-89 – 2003-04	75	J. Cox (Tas)	1988-89 – 2003-04
79	G. S. Blewett (S Aust)	1992-93 – 2003-04	75	D. S. Lehmann (SA/Vic)	1988-89 – 2003-04
78	J. L. Langer (W Aust)	1992-93 – 2003-04	75	B. J. Hodge (Vic)	1993-94 – 2003-04
78	M. L. Love (Qld)	1993-94 – 2003-04	75	M. J. Di Venuto (Tas)	1997-98 – 2003-04

NEW SOUTH WALES ING CUP RESULTS, 2003-04

Played 10: Won 5, Lost 4, Tied 1. *Finished fourth.*

NSW RUNSCORERS

	M	I	NO	R	HS	100s	50s	Avge	Ct/St	S-R
S. R. Waugh	9	9	2	378	101*	1	2	54.00	2	78.26
S. M. Katich	6	6	1	345	136*	2	0	69.00	3	99.14
D. J. Thornely	10	10	1	305	78	0	2	33.89	8	62.37
P. A. Jaques.	8	8	0	305	75	0	2	38.13	0	107.77
M. E. Waugh.	10	8	1	197	41*	0	0	28.14	5	89.14
A. W. O'Brien	7	5	3	150	62*	0	1	75.00	2	76.53
M. J. Phelps	2	2	0	144	136	1	0	72.00	0	99.31
B. J. Haddin	7	7	1	76	22	0	0	12.67	8/1	71.70
M. G. Bevan	1	1	0	72	72	0	1	72.00	0	66.67
M. J. Nicholson.	9	5	0	56	25	0	0	11.20	4	94.92
D. A. Nash	3	1	0	46	46	0	0	46.00	0	102.22
M. J. Clarke.	3	3	0	44	40	0	0	14.67	2	58.67
M. J. Slater	3	3	1	38	27	0	0	19.00	0	79.17
S. C. G. MacGill	7	4	3	23	13	0	0	23.00	2	74.19
S. R. Clark	10	4	0	22	14	0	0	5.50	1	59.46
N. W. Bracken	5	3	1	20	11	0	0	10.00	0	110.50
G. M. Lambert	2	2	0	8	7	0	0	4.00	1	88.89
D. Bollinger	1	1	0	5	5	0	0	5.00	1	55.56
N. S. Pilon.	3	1	0	3	3	0	0	3.00	5/3	60.00
S. D. Bradstreet.	2	1	0	0	0	0	0	0.00	3	0.00
B. Lee	1	1	1	0	0*	0	0	–	0	0.00
L. A. Zammit	1	0	–	–	–	–	–	–	0	–

Denotes not out

NSW WICKET-TAKERS

	O	Mdns	R	W	BB	5W/i	Avge	RPO
S. C. G. MacGill	62	4	318	20	4-42	0	15.90	5.13
M. J. Nicholson.	83.4	7	438	18	3-34	0	24.33	5.24
S. R. Clark.	88.5	8	434	16	4-44	0	27.13	4.89
D. A. Nash	29	4	130	5	3-34	0	26.00	4.48
D. J. Thornely	40	0	186	5	1-17	0	37.20	4.65
A. W. O'Brien.	46.1	5	213	3	2-14	0	71.00	4.61
N. W. Bracken	45	3	229	3	2-58	0	76.33	5.09
G. M. Lambert	19	0	100	3	2-43	0	33.33	5.26
M. J. Clarke.	8	0	42	2	2-37	0	21.00	5.25
D. Bollinger	9	1	43	1	1-43	0	43.00	4.78
M. E. Waugh.	12	0	64	1	1-13	0	64.00	5.33
B. Lee	10	2	41	0	–	0	–	4.10
S. D. Bradstreet.	12	0	53	0	–	0	–	4.42
S. R. Waugh	2	0	8	0	–	0	–	4.00
L. A. Zammit	4	0	17	0	–	0	–	4.25
S. M. Katich	21	0	114	0	–	0	–	5.43

NEW SOUTH WALES v VICTORIA

At Bradman Oval, Bowral, October 26, 2003. New South Wales won by seven wickets. *Toss:* Victoria. New South Wales 4 pts.

Simon Katich continued the glowing form that had followed his Test recall with another authoritative performance, the Blues scurrying to victory with 18 balls to spare. Katich hit 14 fours and five sixes in 129 balls. It must have given him special pleasure to do so against the team coached by David Hookes, after Hookes had earlier alleged that Katich was a less than deserving benefactor of bias towards New South Welshmen at the Test selection table. Victoria's youthful captain Cameron White chose to bat first and his team soon slumped to 4 for 55 in the 15th over, the top order struggling to handle the early life in the pitch. Brad Hodge took control, his 101 speckled with 11 fours and a six, but he needed more support than Jon Moss's aggressive 64, laden with three sixes. Katich calmly piloted the Blues home, sharing in three partnerships of similar dimensions with Dominic Thornely, Steve Waugh and Phil Jaques. NSW's quest for a fourth straight one-day title had begun in impressive style.

Match reports by TREVOR MARSHALLSEA.

Man of the Match: S. M. Katich.   *Attendance:* 4,869.

Victoria

M. T. G. Elliott c Pilon b Clark	12 (33)	†D. S. Berry not out	18 (13)
N. Jewell c Pilon b Nash	4 (6)	S. M. Harwood c Thornely b Nicholson	0 (1)
B. J. Hodge b Clark	101(115)	M. W. H. Inness not out	1 (5)
A. B. McDonald c Nicholson b Nash ..	1 (4)		
D. J. Hussey c Pilon b Nicholson	14 (17)	B 1, l-b 2, w 2	5
J. Moss b Nash	64 (73)		
C. L. White c Pilon b Thornely	1 (5)	(50 overs, 193 mins) (9 wkts)	244
B. R. Joseland c Pilon b Nicholson ...	23 (28)	Fall: 9 29 30 55 171 174 213 230 235	

Bowling: Clark 10–2–35–2; Nash 10–1–34–3; Thornely 10–0–50–1; Nicholson 9–0–60–3; Katich 6–0–31–0; O'Brien 5–0–31–0.

New South Wales

D. J. Thornely lbw b White	33 (54)		
S. M. Katich not out ....136(129)		B 1, l-b 1, w 4	6
*S. R. Waugh c McDonald b Hussey ..	38 (58)		
P. A. Jaques lbw b Harwood	31 (30)	(47 overs, 178 mins) (3 wkts)	246
M. J. Slater not out	2 (11)	Fall: 77 162 239	

M. E. Waugh, A. W. O'Brien, D. A. Nash, †N. S. Pilon, M. J. Nicholson and S. R. Clark did not bat.

Bowling: Harwood 10–0–49–1; Inness 10–2–31–0; Moss 4–1–27–0; White 10–2–42–1; McDonald 4–0–22–0; Hussey 5–0–37–1; Joseland 4–0–36–0.

Umpires: D. B. Hair and S. J. Davis.
TV Umpire: N. S. D. Fowler.

NEW SOUTH WALES v WESTERN AUSTRALIA

At North Sydney Oval, North Sydney, November 2, 2003. New South Wales won by four wickets (D/L Method). *Toss:* Western Australia. New South Wales 4 pts. *Competition debut:* J. J. Taylor.

WA's batsmen dawdled as though stuck on a minefield at times, registering a competitive but far from overwhelming total on this small ground. Justin Langer's ponderous 15, spread over 50 balls, started his side on the wrong foot. Chris Rogers and Michael Hussey (11 fours, one six) tried to get the Warriors going, before Murray Goodwin smashed four sixes and 34 runs in a crucial 15-ball cameo. A Blues line-up boasting a mix of young talent and wise old heads was undaunted. On a wild, windy day at North Sydney, their target was revised to 246 off 41 overs following a 50-minute rain break. It took a lone hand from the captain to get them there, Steve Waugh hitting 13 fours, one six and becoming the second NSW batsman to reach 2,000 one-day runs. Waugh made sure of the win with 15 balls in hand and timed his innings to perfection, reaching his century three deliveries before the end.

Man of the Match: S. R. Waugh.   *Attendance:* 4,141.

Western Australia

†R. J. Campbell c Haddin b Nicholson	27	(37)	M. J. North not out	11	(3)
*J. L. Langer c Haddin b Thornely	15	(50)			
C. J. L. Rogers run out (Jaques/Haddin)	75	(100)	B 1, l-b 4, w 5, n-b 1	11	
M. E. K. Hussey run out (Nicholson)	106	(94)			
M. W. Goodwin c O'Brien b Nicholson	34	(15)	(50 overs, 196 mins) (5 wkts)	280	
P. C. Worthington not out	1	(2)	Fall: 43 54 211 268 268		

B. Casson, C. D. Thorp, M. J. Thistle and J. J. Taylor did not bat.

Bowling: Clark 9–0–64–0; Nash 10–2–39–0; Nicholson 10–0–63–2; Thornely 4–0–19–1; Katich 8–0–39–0; O'Brien 9–0–51–0.

New South Wales

D. J. Thornely c North b Worthington	17	(34)	†B. J. Haddin c North b Hussey	18	(12)
S. M. Katich c Langer b Thistle	30	(28)	A. W. O'Brien not out	12	(12)
*S. R. Waugh not out	101	(94)	L-b 5, w 4, n-b 1	10	
P. A. Jaques c Campbell b Taylor	27	(23)			
M. J. Slater c Casson b Taylor	27	(20)	(38.3 overs, 157 mins) (6 wkts)	249	
M. E. Waugh c Langer b Hussey	7	(9)	Fall: 49 59 116 155 171 208		

D. A. Nash, M. J. Nicholson, S. R. Clark did not bat.

Bowling: Thorp 8–1–45–0; Taylor 9–0–48–2; Worthington 7–0–45–1; Thistle 8–0–54–1; Hussey 5.3–0–38–2; North 1–0–14–0.

Umpires: S. J. Davis and S. A. Reed.
TV Umpire: N. S. D. Fowler.

At Adelaide Oval, Adelaide, November 23, 2003. NEW SOUTH WALES lost to SOUTH AUSTRALIA by 61 runs.

At Bellerive Oval, Hobart, November 29, 2003. NEW SOUTH WALES beat TASMANIA by six wickets.

At Melbourne Cricket Ground, Melbourne, December 7, 2003. NEW SOUTH WALES tied with VICTORIA.

NEW SOUTH WALES v QUEENSLAND

At Olympic Stadium, Homebush, January 17, 2004. Day/night game. Queensland won by two wickets. *Toss:* New South Wales. Queensland 4 pts. *Competition debut:* C. A. Philipson.

The second match staged at the Olympic venue produced a thrilling contest, even if the local fans went home disappointed. The NSW batsmen had only themselves to blame, with the top five all making starts and failing to capitalise. Matthew Nicholson at least left the ground $50,000 richer after hitting an ING sign. The off-spinner Nathan Hauritz again showed his one-day value, although Stuart MacGill's four wickets under lights proved more telling. Queensland were cruising at the halfway point with Jimmy Maher, Stuart Law and Clint Perren – who hit five fours and three sixes – all making brisk runs. They then staggered towards the finish, losing 4 for 17 and relying on Ashley Noffke and Michael Kasprowicz to see them across the line with two balls to spare. A crowd of 26,190, the largest for an interstate one-dayer in NSW and the second biggest in the competition's history, was an impressive advertisement for more fixtures at the stadium. But the pitch and slippery outfield, which almost injured Simon Katich when he kicked up a massive divot while sliding to stop the ball, were criticised by both captains. "It's been a great trial and excellent experience for all the players," said Steve Waugh. "But they've got to get fair dinkum with it next year."

Man of the Match: C. T. Perren. *Attendance:* 26,190.

New South Wales

P. A. Jaques c Philipson b Noffke	19 (29)	N. W. Bracken lbw b Hauritz	11 (10)
D. J. Thornely c Philipson b Noffke	30 (49)	S. R. Clark st Seccombe b Hauritz	1 (3)
S. M. Katich c Kasprowicz b Hauritz	46 (58)	S. C. G. MacGill not out	1 (3)
*S. R. Waugh c Love b Hopes	48 (72)		
M. E. Waugh c Maher b Kasprowicz	37 (31)	L-b 5, w 9, n-b 7	21
†B. J. Haddin c Law b Hauritz	3 (13)		
A. W. O'Brien b Philipson	4 (13)	(50 overs, 203 mins)	246
M. J. Nicholson run out (Kasprowicz)	25 (22)	Fall: 50 54 151 160 169 192 218 235 237 246	

Bowling: Kasprowicz 10–1–50–1; Noffke 10–2–27–2; MacKenzie 8–0–51–0; Hopes 10–2–49–1; Hauritz 10–1–52–4; Philipson 1–0–2–1; Perren 1–0–10–0.

Queensland

*J. P. Maher lbw b MacGill	48 (58)	A. A. Noffke not out	13 (16)
S. G. Law c M. E. Waugh b MacGill	57 (47)	N. M. Hauritz b Bracken	2 (4)
M. L. Love lbw b O'Brien	0 (3)	M. S. Kasprowicz not out	6 (4)
C. T. Perren run out (Thornely)	75 (94)	L-b 6, w 3	9
C. A. Philipson st Haddin b MacGill	3 (19)		
J. R. Hopes c M. E. Waugh b Bracken	34 (52)	(49.4 overs, 187 mins) (8 wkts)	247
†W. A. Seccombe c Thornely b MacGill	0 (1)	Fall: 112 113 115 129 219 221 227 236	

D. R. MacKenzie did not bat.

Bowling: Bracken 9–1–58–2; Clark 6–0–43–0; Nicholson 5.4–0–37–0; MacGill 10–0–42–4; O'Brien 10–3–21–1; M. E. Waugh 6–0–28–0; Thornely 3–0–12–0.

Umpires: S. A. Reed and S. J. A. Taufel.

At WACA Ground, Perth, January 21, 2004. Day/night game. NEW SOUTH WALES lost to WESTERN AUSTRALIA by 23 runs.

At Brisbane Cricket Ground, Brisbane, January 30, 2004. Day/night game. NEW SOUTH WALES lost to QUEENSLAND by 25 runs.

NEW SOUTH WALES v SOUTH AUSTRALIA

At Drummoyne Oval, Drummoyne, February 15, 2004. New South Wales won by eight runs. *Toss:* New South Wales. New South Wales 4 pts. *Competition debut:* B. P. Cameron.

Three straight defeats had already dashed NSW's chances of making the final. But they salvaged some pride and tickled the crowd at this pleasant alternative venue with a close, hard-fought finale. Matthew Phelps, given few chances to shine on the big stage during the season, took full advantage of this late-summer opportunity. His 136 comprised three sixes and 11 thunderous fours, providing the cornerstone of a NSW innings that always looked likely to exceed 300. They were grateful, perhaps, for the injury-enforced absence of the in-form Shaun Tait. The South Australians were also missing Greg Blewett after he hurt a finger while fielding, but set off gamely in pursuit of the big target. At 4 for 256 in the 44th over the Redbacks looked poised to win, before imploding spectacularly against the combined might of Matthew Nicholson and Stuart MacGill. They lost four wickets, and the match, in the last four overs.

Man of the Match: M. J. Phelps.   *Attendance:* 5,574.

New South Wales

M. J. Phelps c Cameron b Miller	136	(140)	M. J. Nicholson c Davison b Lehmann 11	(11)
P. A. Jaques c Manou b Harris	 43	(35)	N. W. Bracken not out 0	(0)
D. J. Thornely b Harris	 9	(14)		
*S. R. Waugh c Harris b Cleary	 14	(15)	B 2, l-b 3, w 5, n-b 1 11	
M. E. Waugh b Harris	 20	(26)		
A. W. O'Brien not out	 49	(55)	(50 overs, 196 mins) (7 wkts) 296	
†N. S. Pilon c Higgs b Miller	 3	(5)	Fall: 92 106 125 170 262 269 290	

S. R. Clark, S. C. G. MacGill did not bat.

Bowling: Rofe 7–1–36–0; Miller 10–1–51–2; Harris 10–0–51–3; Cleary 7–1–41–1; Higgs 3–0–28–0; Davison 3–0–26–0; Lehmann 8–0–45–1; Cosgrove 2–0–13–0.

South Australia

J. M. Davison b Clark	 17	(9)	R. J. Harris b Nicholson	 1	(2)
B. P. Cameron b Clark	 66	(85)	P. C. Rofe b Nicholson	 0	(2)
M. J. Cosgrove st Pilon b Thornely	... 42	(44)	G. S. Blewett not out	 0	(1)
†G. A. Manou st Pilon b MacGill	 30	(34)		
*D. S. Lehmann c Thornely b MacGill	63	(63)	B 2, l-b 7, w 4 13	
M. A. Higgs c Thornely b Nicholson	.. 42	(42)		
M. C. Miller c S. R. Waugh b MacGill	4	(8)	(50 overs, 208 mins) .... (9 wkts) 288	
M. F. Cleary not out	 10	(10)	Fall: 19 97 147 180 256 273 285 286 286	

Bowling: O'Brien 6–0–35–0; Clark 10–0–62–2; Nicholson 10–2–34–3; Thornely 5–0–17–1; Bracken 8–0–54–0; MacGill 7–0–54–3; M. E. Waugh 4–0–23–0.

Umpires: S. J. A. Taufel and R. J. Tucker.
TV Umpire: N. S. D. Fowler.

NEW SOUTH WALES v TASMANIA

At Sydney Cricket Ground, Sydney, February 22, 2004. New South Wales won by eight wickets. *Toss:* Tasmania. New South Wales 5 pts.

Had it not been the Waugh twins' final one-dayer at the SCG, this match would have been even more inconsequential than the previous one. With both sides unable to qualify for the final, Steve Waugh decided to rock Tasmania's confidence in the hope of derailing their progress in the Pura Cup. On that premise, the Blues delivered an emphatic victory. Tasmania never stood a realistic chance of winning once the increasingly impressive Matthew Nicholson, and then Stuart MacGill, tore through their batting order. Shane Watson, with a defiant 56 in 62 balls, offered the main resistance. The Blues strolled to their target in only 26.1 overs. Phil Jaques (12 fours, one six), Dominic Thornely (12 fours) and Steve Waugh (eight fours, one six) scored almost at will in a winning goodbye to their title defence. Waugh brought up his half-century, and his final runs in coloured clothing, with a crunching pull shot off Adam Griffith.

Man of the Match: P. A. Jaques. *Attendance:* 4,632.

Tasmania

M. G. Dighton b Nicholson	15 (42)	†S. G. Clingeleffer not out	12 (19)
M. J. Di Venuto b Nicholson	46 (61)	X. J. Doherty b Clark	5 (5)
L. R. Butterworth c (sub)		A. R. Griffith lbw b Clark	0 (1)
G. M. Lambert b Thornely	18 (25)		
S. R. Watson b Nicholson	56 (62)	L-b 5, w 4	9
*D. J. Marsh c Nicholson b MacGill	3 (22)		
G. J. Bailey c M. E. Waugh b MacGill	3 (11)	(49.4 overs, 204 mins)	210
S. B. Tubb st Pilon b MacGill	37 (39)	Fall: 43 74 89 106 110 171 181	
S. P. Kremerskothen c Clark b MacGill	6 (11)	199 210 210	

Bowling: Bracken 10–1–28–0; Clark 8.4–2–23–2; Nicholson 9–1–45–3; Thornely 9–0–34–1; MacGill 10–0–55–4; O'Brien 3–0–20–0.

New South Wales

M. J. Phelps lbw b Watson	8 (5)	L-b 5, w 4	9
P. A. Jaques b Watson	75 (44)		
D. J. Thornely not out	70 (64)	(26.1 overs, 113 mins)　(2 wkts)	212
*S. R. Waugh not out	50 (44)	Fall: 8 115	

M. E. Waugh, A. W. O'Brien, †N. S. Pilon, M. J. Nicholson, N. W. Bracken, S. R. Clark and S. C. G. MacGill did not bat.

Bowling: Watson 7–0–53–2; Griffith 8–0–53–0; Doherty 6.1–0–55–0; Butterworth 2–0–26–0; Tubb 3–0–20–0.

Umpires: N. S. D. Fowler and B. N. J. Oxenford.

NSW DOMESTIC LIMITED-OVERS RESULTS

	First Game	M	Won	Lost	Drawn	Tied
v Queensland	Dec 6, 1969	33	19	14	0	0
v New Zealanders	Dec 30, 1969	1	0	1	0	0
v Western Australia	Nov 27, 1971	35	17	17	0	1
v Victoria	Dec 17, 1972	31	16	13	1	1
v Tasmania	Dec 17, 1973	25	21	3	0	1
v South Australia	Nov 23, 1975	23	13	10	0	0
v Australian Capital Territory	Dec 14, 1997	3	3	0	0	0
Total		151	89	58	1	3

RECORDS

Highest score for:	164	R. B. McCosker v South Australia at Sydney	1981-82
Highest score against:	165	M. W. Goodwin (Western Australia) at Perth	2000-01
Best bowling for:	6-25	B. E. McNamara v Tasmania at Sydney	1996-97
Best bowling against:	5-22	H. J. Howarth (New Zealanders) at Sydney	1969-70
Highest total for:	4-397	v Tasmania at Bankstown	2001-02
Highest total against:	7-327	by Tasmania at Bankstown	2001-02
Lowest total for:	92	v Queensland at Brisbane	1972-73
Lowest total against:	80	by Tasmania at Devonport	1984-85

MOST RUNS

	M	I	NO	R	HS	100s	50s	Avge	S-R
M. G. Bevan	58	58	19	2,400	135*	1	21	61.54	73.24
S. R. Waugh	55	54	10	2,269	131	5	13	51.57	84.26
M. E. Waugh	64	60	6	1,984	123	3	15	36.74	80.55
S. Lee	59	53	6	1,412	115	2	7	30.04	87.11
M. A. Taylor	38	38	0	1,218	84	0	12	32.05	59.33

	M	I	NO	R	HS	100s	50s	Avge	S-R
C.J. Richards	47	44	4	1,172	151	2	6	29.30	70.31
B.J. Haddin	44	43	1	1,029	120	1	8	24.50	96.35
M.J. Slater	50	47	2	1,023	96	0	7	22.73	67.13
R. Chee Quee	22	22	1	860	131	1	5	40.95	66.62
R.B. McCosker	21	21	2	847	164	2	5	44.58	63.99

HIGHEST PARTNERSHIP FOR EACH WICKET

253	for 1st	R.B. McCosker and J. Dyson, v South Australia at Sydney	1981-82
199	for 2nd	R. Chee Quee and M.G. Bevan, v Western Australia at Sydney	1993-94
240	for 3rd	S.R. Waugh and M.E. Waugh, v Victoria at North Sydney	1991-92
180	for 4th	G.C. Rummans and S. Lee, v Queensland at Brisbane	1999-00
156	for 5th	K.J. Roberts and R. Chee Quee, v South Australia at Sydney	1995-96
105	for 6th	M.G. Bevan and G.R.J. Matthews, v Western Australia at Perth	1990-91
105*	for 6th	S.R. Waugh and M.A. Higgs, v Queensland at Sydney	2001-02
116	for 7th	C.J. Richards and B.J. Haddin, v South Australia at North Sydney	2000-01
90	for 8th	B.E. McNamara and P.A. Emery, v Tasmania at Sydney	1992-93
96*	for 9th	S.M. Thompson and S.D. Bradstreet, v Victoria at North Sydney	1998-99
54	for 10th	B.E. McNamara and G.R. Robertson, v South Australia at Adelaide	1996-97

MOST WICKETS

	M	Balls	Mdns	R	W	BB	5Wi	Avge	RPO
S.C.G. MacGill	46	2,327	21	2,007	93	5-40	3	21.58	5.17
S.R. Clark	53	2,805	37	1,874	65	4-26	0	28.83	4.01
B.E. McNamara	42	2,005	22	1,281	57	6-25	1	22.47	3.83
S. Lee	59	2,155	13	1,695	54	4-59	0	31.39	4.72
N.W. Bracken	38	1,964	31	1,412	52	5-38	1	27.15	4.31
G.R.J. Matthews	50	2,302	25	1,500	49	3-29	0	30.61	3.91
M.R. Whitney	36	1,926	36	1,188	41	4-30	0	28.98	3.70
G.F. Lawson	35	1,811	38	1,053	39	4-31	0	27.00	3.49
S.D. Bradstreet	39	1,403	15	1,128	36	4-23	0	31.33	4.08
S.R. Waugh	55	1,104	18	853	34	4-32	0	25.09	4.64

MOST DISMISSALS

	M	Ct	St	Total
B.J. Haddin	42	64	19	83
P.A. Emery	58	70	11	81
S.J. Rixon	25	25	6	31
H.B. Taber	6	8	1	9
N.S. Pilon	4	6	3	9

MOST CATCHES

M.E. Waugh	37 in 64 matches	G.R.J. Matthews	15 in 50 matches
S. Lee	31 in 59 matches	R. Chee Quee	14 in 22 matches
M.A. Taylor	24 in 38 matches	M.A. Higgs	14 in 28 matches
S.R. Waugh	19 in 55 matches	M.G. Bevan	14 in 58 matches
C.J. Richards	18 in 47 matches	S.D. Bradstreet	13 in 41 matches

MOST APPEARANCES

64	M.E. Waugh	1985-86 – 2003-04	53	S.R. Clark	1997-98 – 2003-04
59	S. Lee	1992-93 – 2002-03	50	G.R.J. Matthews	1982-83 – 1997-98
58	P.A. Emery	1987-88 – 1998-99	50	M.J. Slater	1992-93 – 2003-04
58	M.G. Bevan	1990-91 – 2003-04	47	C.J. Richards	1996-97 – 2002-03
55	S.R. Waugh	1984-85 – 2003-04	42	B.E. McNamara	1989-90 – 1999-00

QUEENSLAND ING CUP RESULTS, 2003-04

Played 11: Won 7, Lost 4. *Finished second.*

QUEENSLAND RUNSCORERS

	M	I	NO	R	HS	100s	50s	Avge	Ct/St	S-R
S. G. Law	11	11	1	570	113*	1	5	57.00	2	107.95
C. T. Perren	11	11	3	514	94*	0	5	64.25	3	69.84
J. P. Maher	7	7	0	429	187	2	0	61.29	7	96.40
M. L. Love	11	11	1	369	110*	1	0	36.90	4	85.22
J. R. Hopes	11	9	2	170	46	0	0	24.29	3	73.91
W. A. Seccombe	10	8	4	159	67*	0	2	39.75	11/7	94.64
D. M. Payne	3	3	0	82	52	0	1	27.33	1	67.77
C. A. Philipson	5	5	1	80	48	0	0	20.00	2	62.50
A. J. Bichel	3	3	1	76	41	0	0	38.00	0	93.83
N. M. Hauritz	10	5	2	75	39*	0	0	25.00	0	90.36
L. A. Carseldine	4	4	0	61	42	0	0	15.25	0	59.80
C. P. Simpson	5	4	1	38	15	0	0	12.67	1	73.08
D. R. MacKenzie . . .	3	2	2	29	23*	0	0	–	0	96.67
A. Symonds	1	1	0	21	21	0	0	21.00	0	116.67
A. A. Noffke	8	3	1	17	13*	0	0	8.50	2	56.67
C. D. Hartley	1	1	0	14	14	0	0	14.00	0/2	93.33
M. S. Kasprowicz . . .	5	2	1	9	6*	0	0	9.00	1	112.50
S. J. Farrell	1	1	0	8	8	0	0	8.00	0	72.73
S. A. Brant	3	1	0	0	0	0	0	0.00	0	0.00
J. H. Dawes	3	0	–	–	–	–	–	–	1	–
M. G. Johnson	2	0	–	–	–	–	–	–	0	–
S. J. Jurgensen	3	0	–	–	–	–	–	–	1	–

*Denotes not out

QUEENSLAND WICKET-TAKERS

	O	Mdns	R	W	BB	5W/i	Avge	RPO
N. M. Hauritz . . . . :	85	2	415	18	4-39	0	23.06	4.88
J. R. Hopes	99.2	6	478	14	3-20	0	34.14	4.81
M. S. Kasprowicz	50	3	174	11	4-19	0	15.82	3.48
A. A. Noffke	79	7	382	8	2-27	0	47.75	4.84
C. P. Simpson	30.2	0	150	5	3-45	0	30.00	4.95
M. G. Johnson	20	2	87	4	4-37	0	21.75	4.35
A. Symonds	9.4	0	37	3	3-37	0	12.33	3.83
S. A. Brant	23	0	110	3	2-31	0	36.67	4.78
S. J. Jurgensen	27.4	2	116	2	2-31	0	58.00	4.19
A. J. Bichel	29	0	126	2	2-37	0	63.00	4.34
D. R. MacKenzie	26	1	132	2	1-37	0	66.00	5.08
J. H. Dawes	17	0	99	1	1-42	0	99.00	5.82
C. A. Philipson	2	0	12	1	1-2	0	12.00	6.00
S. G. Law	3	0	21	1	1-21	0	21.00	7.00
C. T. Perren	19.3	0	115	0	–	0	–	5.90
D. M. Payne	3	0	26	0	–	0	–	8.67

QUEENSLAND v TASMANIA

At Brisbane Cricket Ground, Brisbane, October 25, 2003. Queensland won by four wickets. *Toss:* Queensland. Queensland 4 pts. *Competition debut:* M. G. Johnson.

Mitchell Johnson, the Townsville schoolboy discovered almost accidentally by Dennis Lillee, returned after two years of injuries and uncertainties to set up a Bulls victory with a thunderous spell. Aged 21, and making his comeback match after debilitating back stress fractures, Johnson had the Tasmanian top order hopping in fear with his fast, left-arm, short-of-a-length deliveries. He had to wait until his fourth over for a wicket, beating Scott Kremerskothen with consecutive deliveries then trapping him in front with a bullet yorker. The Tigers failed to produce any substantial partnerships, although the tailender Xavier Doherty salvaged some credibility when he worked the ball around to steer the total past 200. Queensland's top three batsmen succumbed to ill-judged shots before Wade Seccombe, as so often before, launched a rescue mission. He smashed Doherty into the grandstand over long-on en route to his highest one-day score, and was still at the crease when the winning runs were struck in the 48th over.

Match reports by BEN DORRIES.

Man of the Match: W. A. Seccombe.   *Attendance:* 2,560.

Tasmania

M. J. Di Venuto c Seccombe b Johnson	11	(23)	X. J. Doherty b Hauritz	37	(37)
M. G. Dighton c Love b Johnson	10	(31)	B. Geeves not out	4	(5)
S. R. Watson c Seccombe b Jurgensen	14	(22)	A. R. Griffith not out	4	(1)
J. Cox c Dawes b Jurgensen	9	(14)			
*D. J. Marsh c Payne b Hopes	33	(53)	B 1, l-b 2, w 21	24	
S. P. Kremerskothen lbw b Johnson	18	(34)			
†S. G. Clingeleffer run out (Payne)	38	(51)	(50 overs, 203 mins) (9 wkts)	219	
D. G. Wright c Seccombe b Johnson	17	(29)	Fall: 30 32 59 59 105 123 162 192 215		

Bowling: Dawes 5–0–31–0; Johnson 10–1–37–4; Jurgensen 10–1–31–2; Hauritz 10–0–58–1; Hopes 10–1–38–1; Perren 5–0–21–0.

Queensland

D. M. Payne lbw b Griffith	8	(16)	†W. A. Seccombe not out	67	(57)
S. G. Law c Doherty b Griffith	23	(53)	N. M. Hauritz not out	6	(12)
*M. L. Love c Di Venuto b Wright	4	(5)	L-b 3, w 6	9	
C. T. Perren lbw b Geeves	60	(98)			
L. A. Carseldine c Clingeleffer b Griffith	42	(59)	(48 overs, 198 mins) (6 wkts)	221	
J. R. Hopes c and b Doherty	2	(8)	Fall: 20 34 40 114 125 206		

M. G. Johnson, J. H. Dawes and S. J. Jurgensen did not bat.

Bowling: Wright 10–0–44–1; Griffith 10–1–52–3; Geeves 10–0–31–1; Kremerskothen 10–0–54–0; Doherty 8–0–37–1.

Umpires: P. D. Parker and R. L. Parry.

QUEENSLAND v VICTORIA

At Brisbane Cricket Ground, Brisbane, October 31 2003. Day/night game. Victoria won by eight wickets. *Toss:* Queensland. Victoria 4 pts. *Competition debut:* A. B. Wise.

Matthew Elliott and Brad Hodge stamped their class with twin centuries as the Bushrangers, in a pre-cursor to their drought-breaking Pura Cup victory a few days later, romped home easily. The early signs were not good for Queensland, their batsmen failing to capitalise on a vintage half-century from Stuart Law. Things got worse when their spinner Nathan Hauritz collapsed with a hamstring strain while batting. That they managed to set a competitive target was down largely to sloppy fielding. Wade Seccombe was given four lives – all off the bowling of the left-armer Allan Wise. Victoria lost an early wicket but Elliott (13 fours, one six) and Hodge (15 fours) then monstered the attack. Their 221-run partnership was a Victorian record for any wicket. Hodge recovered quickly after being struck flush on the chin by a Mitchell Johnson bouncer when he was eight, while Elliott's night would have been $50,000 sweeter had a lusty six off James Hopes not missed an ING sign by centimetres.

Man of the Match: M. T. G. Elliott.   *Attendance:* 9,178.

Queensland

D. M. Payne c Harwood b Moss	 22	(47)	†W. A. Seccombe not out 50 (58)
S. G. Law c White b Moss	 55	(56)	N. M. Hauritz not out 39 (34)
*M. L. Love c Roach b Wise	 39	(50)	W 3, n-b 1 4
C. T. Perren c Roach b Moss	 5	(5)	
L. A. Carseldine c Hussey b White	... 4	(13)	(50 overs, 200 mins) (6 wkts) 235
J. R. Hopes c White b Wise	 17	(38)	Fall: 65 90 98 105 137 164

M. G. Johnson, J. H. Dawes and S. J. Jurgensen did not bat.

Bowling: Inness 6–0–27–0; Harwood 8–1–35–0; Moss 10–0–52–3; Wise 10–0–34–2; White 8–0–41–1; McDonald 2–0–15–0; Hussey 6–0–31–0.

Victoria

M. T. G. Elliott not out	117	(116)	L-b 2, w 3, n-b 3 8
J. Moss c Jurgensen b Dawes	 0	(3)	
B. J. Hodge b Hopes	107	(123)	(40.4 overs, 185 mins) (2 wkts) 236
A. B. McDonald not out	 4	(5)	Fall: 7 228

D. J. Hussey, *C. L. White, B. R. Joseland, A. B. Wise, S. M. Harwood, M. W. H. Inness and †P. J. Roach did not bat.

Bowling: Johnson 10–1–50–0; Dawes 6–0–42–1; Jurgensen 8.4–1–39–0; Hopes 8–0–53–1; Perren 5–0–24–0; Payne 3–0–26–0.

Umpires: D. L. Orchard and B. N. J. Oxenford.

At Melbourne Cricket Ground, Melbourne, November 16, 2003. QUEENSLAND lost to VICTORIA by seven wickets.

QUEENSLAND v SOUTH AUSTRALIA

At Brisbane Cricket Ground, Brisbane, December 17, 2003. Day/night game. Queensland won by 99 runs. *Toss:* South Australia. Queensland 5 pts.

Despite a punchy century from Jimmy Maher in his first domestic one-day appearance of the season, Queensland produced a contrasting performance with the bat. The top order misfired, slipping to 4 for 70 against the pace of Shaun Tait and Mark Cleary. But Maher, back from national duty in India, stood tall. He and Clint Perren combined for an imposing 180-run partnership, eclipsing Jamie Cox and Dan Marsh's competition record for the fifth wicket. Perren's innings was punctuated with some exciting aerial hitting, his last 44 coming in only 17 balls. After struggling early, scoring 97 off the first 25 overs, Queensland plundered 117 runs in a frenetic final 10. One over from Ben Johnson went for 21. Canada's World Cup hero, John Davison, joined in the big-hitting extravaganza as SA chased 284. His blazing 32-ball half-century rocketed the visitors past 100 in the 16th over. But Davison's run-out triggered a grim collapse, the self-destructing Redbacks handing the Bulls a vital bonus point. The off-spinners Nathan Hauritz and Andrew Symonds turned the screws on the tail as the match ground to an uneventful conclusion.

Man of the Match: J. P. Maher.   *Attendance:* 5,849.

Queensland

*J. P. Maher c Miller b Tait	.........107 (135)	†W. A. Seccombe c and b Johnson	.. 10 (3)
S. G. Law c Cosgrove b Tait	.... 11 (12)	J. R. Hopes not out	.... 4 (4)
M. L. Love c Miller b Tait	.... 4 (11)	B 2, l-b 8, w 12, n-b 2	 24
A. Symonds c Manou b Cleary	...... 21 (18)		—
L. A. Carseldine c Manou b Cleary	... 8 (21)	(50 overs, 212 mins)	(6 wkts) 283
C. T. Perren not out	.... 94 (98)	Fall: 20 28 59 70 250 267	

N. M. Hauritz, A. A. Noffke and M. S. Kasprowicz did not bat.

Bowling: Rofe 7–1–35–0; Tait 10–1–48–3; Cleary 9–1–57–2; Miller 10–0–42–0; Johnson 8–0–56–1; Davison 6–0–35–0.

South Australia

J. M. Davison run out (Perren/Symonds) 55 (34)		M. F. Cleary c Noffke b Symonds	... 10 (26)
S. A. Deitz c Seccombe b Hopes	..... 41 (63)	S. W. Tait lbw b Hauritz	.... 0 (5)
†G. A. Manou b Symonds	.... 19 (27)	P. C. Rofe not out	.... 6 (6)
*G. S. Blewett c Hopes b Noffke	..... 18 (48)	L-b 1, w 7	 8
A. Flower c Maher b Symonds	...... 4 (13)		—
M. J. Cosgrove b Hauritz	.... 8 (14)	(44.4 overs, 177 mins)	184
B. A. Johnson c Seccombe b Kasprowicz 12 (24)		Fall: 96 101 129 137 149	
M. C. Miller st Seccombe b Hauritz	... 3 (8)	149 155 168 169 184	

Bowling: Noffke 10–1–53–1; Kasprowicz 10–1–25–1; Hopes 8–1–45–1; Symonds 9.4–0–37–3; Hauritz 7–0–23–3.

Umpires: T. P. Laycock and J. F. Torpey.

At WACA Ground, Perth, January 9, 2004. QUEENSLAND lost to WESTERN AUSTRALIA by seven wickets.

At Olympic Stadium, Homebush, January 17, 2004. Day/night game. QUEENSLAND defeated NEW SOUTH WALES by two wickets.

At Bellerive Oval, Hobart, January 26, 2004. QUEENSLAND defeated TASMANIA by six wickets.

QUEENSLAND v NEW SOUTH WALES

At Brisbane Cricket Ground, Brisbane, January 30, 2004. Day/night game. Queensland won by 25 runs. *Toss:* Queensland. Queensland 4 pts.

A result looked impossible as waves of water rolled across the Gabba and the curator Kevin Mitchell, like a human sandbag, braved lightning strikes to lay covers across a sodden pitch. A fierce electrical storm plunged the stadium into darkness, twisting advertising signs and sending frightened spectators scurrying. Amazingly, play was halted for only 76 minutes and no overs lost. Upon the resumption NSW looked on course for victory until Ashley Noffke, erratic with the ball, inspired the home side with a spark of fielding brilliance. He stooped low to pick up a Mark Waugh drive in his follow–through, switched the ball from left hand to right and threw down the stumps at the striker's end. It turned the game. Michael Kasprowicz produced an economical three-wicket spell and the under-rated seamer James Hopes spoiled Steve Waugh's farewell trip to Brisbane by eliciting a faint edge. Stuart Law's 75 in 83 balls, which had earlier shored up an unconvincing Queensland batting display, proved crucial. But the storm was the main talking point afterwards, Mitchell rating it the worst he had seen and revealing that his ground staff had feared for their safety.

Man of the Match: M. S. Kasprowicz. *Attendance:* 7,222.

Queensland

*J. P. Maher c Thornely b Clark	 5	(20)	N. M. Hauritz run out		
S. G. Law c O'Brien b MacGill	 75	(83)	(Thornely/Lambert)	. 26	(29)
M. L. Love c Haddin b Bollinger	 39	(48)	M. S. Kasprowicz c Lambert		
D. R. MacKenzie not out	 6	(11)	b M. E. Waugh	 3	(4)
C. T. Perren c Bollinger b Clark	 33	(46)			
C. A. Philipson run out (Jaques)	 19	(26)	L-b 4, w 2	 6	
J. R. Hopes c M. E. Waugh b MacGill	. 1	(7)			
†W. A. Seccombe b Lambert	 13	(17)	(50 overs, 192 mins)	229	
A. A. Noffke c Haddin b Clark	 3	(9)	Fall: 13 101 130 171 173 177 183 207 213 229		

Bowling: O'Brien 10–1–41–0; Clark 10–1–43–3; Lambert 9–0–57–1; Bollinger 9–1–43–1; MacGill 10–1–28–2; M. E. Waugh 2–0–13–1.

New South Wales

P. A. Jaques b MacKenzie	 61	(67)	S. R. Clark b Kasprowicz	 7	(14)
S. M. Katich c Seccombe b Kasprowicz	14	(20)	D. Bollinger b Hopes	 5	(9)
D. J. Thornely c Seccombe b Kasprowicz	31	(51)	S. C. G. MacGill not out	 7	(6)
†B. J. Haddin lbw b Hopes	 5	(8)			
*S. R. Waugh c Seccombe b Hopes	... 16	(31)	L-b 4, w 4	 8	
M. E. Waugh run out (Noffke)	 20	(28)			
A. W. O'Brien b Hauritz	 23	(42)	(47.1 overs, 209 mins)	204	
G. M. Lambert st Seccombe b Hauritz	7	(7)	Fall: 41 89 100 129 140 159 175 186 192 204		

Bowling: Kasprowicz 10–0–38–3; Noffke 10–0–58–0; MacKenzie 9–1–44–1; Hopes 8.1–1–20–3; Hauritz 10–0–40–2.

Umpires: N. S. McNamara and B. N. J. Oxenford.

QUEENSLAND v WESTERN AUSTRALIA

At Brisbane Cricket Ground, Brisbane, February 13, 2004. Day/night game. Queensland won by 207 runs. *Toss:* Queensland. Queensland 6 pts. *Competition debut:* B. M. Edmondson, C. D. Hartley.

Queensland scaled the Mt Everest of limited-overs cricket, breaking the 400-run barrier and smashing an array of scarcely believable records. Jimmy Maher, the forgotten Australian one-day batsman, batted explosively in a cyclonic, unprecedented innings of 187 in 129 balls. It was the highest individual score in the competition's 35-year history, splattered with 26 fours and three sixes. His 194-run opening stand with Stuart Law was rustled up in a mere 22.4 overs. Maher should have been caught at point on 105; he was already walking towards the pavilion when the catch was muffed by Murray Goodwin. It was Goodwin's record of 167 against NSW in 2000-01 that he subsequently overtook, eclipsing Goodwin's mark in fine style with successive fours off Mike Hussey. A double-century looked a real possibility until he was dismissed by Ben Edmondson in the 44th over. Queensland's gigantic total, which included 49 fours and eight sixes, was the fifth highest in limited-overs matches worldwide. "It just goes to show what you can do if you apply yourself individually and as a team," said an exhausted Maher. He subsequently pouched three catches. It was truly a black Friday for WA, who never looked like getting anywhere near the victory target once Justin Langer and Chris Rogers departed. They slumped to the second heaviest defeat in domestic one-day history and conceded the first double bonus point.

Man of the Match: J. P. Maher.   *Attendance:* 5,636.

Queensland

*J.P. Maher c Langer b Edmondson	..187	(129)	C.P. Simpson not out	14 (10)
S.G. Law c Goodwin b Heal	 95	(69)	L-b 4, w 1, n-b 4	9
A.J. Bichel c Edmondson b Hussey	.. 41	(45)		—
M.L. Love lbw b Wilson	 38	(34)	(50 overs, 207 mins) (4 wkts)	405
C.T. Perren not out	 21	(17)	Fall: 194 290 349 386	

†W.A. Seccombe, J.R. Hopes, A.A. Noffke, N.M. Hauritz and S.A. Brant did not bat.

Bowling: Wilson 10–1–53–1; Wates 5–0–56–0; Edmondson 8–0–72–1; Harvey 8–0–81–0; Heal 10–1–71–1; North 5–0–32–0; Hussey 4–0–36–1.

Western Australia

*J.L. Langer c Maher b Bichel	 0	(6)	A.K. Heal c (sub) C.A. Philipson	
C.J.L. Rogers lbw b Brant	 3	(5)	b Simpson ..	2 (8)
M.J. North st Seccombe b Brant	 20	(33)	P. Wilson c (sub) C.A. Philipson	
B.M. Edmondson not out	 2	(7)	b Simpson ..	5 (18)
M.E.K. Hussey c Maher b Hauritz	 66	(83)		
M.W. Goodwin c Maher b Hopes	 18	(26)	L-b 6, w 5, n-b 1	12
†R.J. Campbell b Hopes	 15	(21)		—
K.M. Harvey c Simpson b Noffke	 43	(59)	(48.2 overs, 207 mins)	198
D.J. Wates c Seccombe b Bichel	 12	(25)	Fall: 1 10 33 77 101 170 187 189 194 198	

Bowling: Bichel 10–0–37–2; Brant 7–0–31–2; Hauritz 10–0–50–1; Hopes 10–0–44–2; Noffke 9–2–24–1; Simpson 2.2–0–6–2.

Umpires: D.J. Harper and T.P. Laycock.

At Adelaide Oval, Adelaide, February 22, 2004. QUEENSLAND defeated SOUTH AUSTRALIA by four runs.

QUEENSLAND DOMESTIC LIMITED-OVERS RESULTS

	First Game	M	Won	Lost	Drawn	Tied
v New South Wales	Dec 7, 1969	33	14	19	0	0
v South Australia	Dec 6, 1970	26	21	5	0	0
v Western Australia	Feb 6, 1971	32	14	16	2	0
v Victoria	Dec 5, 1971	26	14	11	1	0
v Tasmania	Dec 31, 1972	28	19	8	1	0
v New Zealanders	Jan 21, 1973	1	0	1	0	0
v Australian Capital Territory ..	Jan 31, 1998	3	3	0	0	0
Total		149	85	60	4	0

QUEENSLAND RECORDS

Highest score for:	187	J.P. Maher v Western Australia at Brisbane	.2003-04
Highest score against:	131	S.R. Waugh (New South Wales) at Brisbane	1992-93
Best bowling for:	7-34	C.G. Rackemann v South Australia at Adelaide	1988-89
Best bowling against:	5-23	J.P. Marquet (Tasmania) at Hobart (Bellerive)	1995-96
Highest total for:	4-405	v Western Australia at Brisbane	.2003-04
Highest total against:	6-301	by Western Australia at Perth	1999-00
Lowest total for:	62	v Western Australia at Perth	1976-77
Lowest total against:	65	by Victoria at Ballarat	2002-03

MOST RUNS

	M	I	NO	R	HS	100s	50s	Avge	S-R
J. P. Maher	73	73	9	3,137	187	7	17	49.02	77.73
S. G. Law	85	78	7	2,534	159	6	10	35.69	93.06
M. L. Love	78	75	10	2,315	127*	4	9	35.62	76.99
M. L. Hayden	51	51	9	2,231	152*	8	11	53.12	72.18
C. T. Perren	47	41	10	1,391	96	0	12	44.87	66.65
A. Symonds	55	51	6	1,152	91	0	5	25.60	95.60
T. J. Barsby	42	41	2	1,145	101	1	10	29.36	61.10
A. R. Border	43	40	8	1,049	97	0	9	32.78	72.60
G. M. Ritchie	27	24	4	825	114	1	5	41.25	74.93
W. A. Seccombe	69	51	15	731	67*	0	3	20.31	81.04

HIGHEST PARTNERSHIP FOR EACH WICKET

250	for 1st	M. L. Hayden and J. P. Maher, v Australian Capital Territory at Canberra ..	1999-00
260	for 2nd	M. L. Hayden and S. G. Law, v Tasmania at Brisbane	1993-94
187	for 3rd	J. M. Thomas and S. G. Law, v Western Australia at Brisbane	1993-94
173	for 4th	M. L. Love and C. T. Perren, v Tasmania at Brisbane	2001-02
180	for 5th	J. P. Maher and C. T. Perren, v South Australia at Brisbane	2003-04
108	for 6th	A. Symonds and J. R. Hopes, v New South Wales at North Sydney	2002-03
91	for 7th	J. N. Langley and J. A. Maclean, v South Australia at Brisbane	1975-76
55*	for 8th	S. A. Prestwidge and A. J. Bichel, v New South Wales at Sydney	1997-98
55*	for 8th	J. P. Maher and A. J. Bichel, v Tasmania at Brisbane	2001-02
62	for 9th	S. A. Prestwidge and M. S. Kasprowicz, v New South Wales at Brisbane ..	1997-98
33	for 10th	M. L. Love and C. G. Rackemann, v New South Wales at Brisbane	1993-94

MOST WICKETS

	M	Balls	Mdns	R	W	BB	5Wfi	Avge	RPO
M. S. Kasprowicz	66	3,407	42	2,346	80	4-21	0	29.33	4.13
S. A. Prestwidge	45	2,189	18	1,755	67	5-59	1	26.19	4.81
J. R. Hopes	37	1,833	24	1,349	55	5-29	1	24.53	4.42
N. M. Hauritz	34	1,558	4	1,184	54	4-39	0	21.93	4.56
C. G. Rackemann	36	1,975	38	1,249	48	7-34	1	26.02	3.79
A. J. Bichel	46	2,362	27	1,710	47	4-45	0	36.38	4.34
G. Dymock	23	1,300	26	749	39	5-27	1	19.21	3.46
A. C. Dale	27	1,451	20	842	36	4-26	0	23.39	3.48
A. A. Noffke	34	1,775	26	1,390	36	4-32	0	38.61	4.71
J. R. Thomson	25	1,273	19	821	35	6-19	1	23.46	3.87

MOST DISMISSALS

	M	Ct	St	Total
W. A. Seccombe	69	92	20	112
I. A. Healy	29	47	7	54
J. A. Maclean	19	32	1	33
R. B. Phillips	18	22	0	22
P. W. Anderson	6	4	0	4

MOST CATCHES

J. P. Maher	36 in 73 matches	M. L. Hayden	16 in 51 matches
S. G. Law	35 in 85 matches	C. T. Perren	16 in 47 matches
M. L. Love	28 in 78 matches	A. J. Bichel	14 in 46 matches
A. R. Border	26 in 43 matches	M. S. Kasprowicz	14 in 66 matches
A. Symonds	26 in 55 matches	G. S. Chappell	13 in 20 matches

MOST APPEARANCES

85	S. G. Law .... 1988-89 – 2003-04	55	A. Symonds ...... 1993-94 – 2003-04
78	M. L. Love .... 1993-94 – 2003-04	51	M. L. Hayden ..... 1992-93 – 2001-02
73	J. P. Maher .... 1993-94 – 2003-04	47	C. T. Perren ...... 1997-98 – 2003-04
69	W. A. Seccombe ... 1994-95 – 2003-04	46	A. J. Bichel ...... 1992-93 – 2003-04
66	M. S. Kasprowicz .. 1989-90 – 2003-04	45	S. A. Prestwidge .. 1992-93 – 2000-01

SOUTH AUSTRALIA ING CUP RESULTS, 2003-04

Played 10: Won 3, Lost 7. *Finished fifth.*

SA RUNSCORERS

	M	I	NO	R	HS	100s	50s	Avge	Ct/St	S-R
D. S. Lehmann	5	5	0	304	83	0	3	60.80	1	99.35
S. A. Deitz.	8	8	0	278	60	0	2	34.75	1	66.51
J. M. Davison	9	9	0	257	59	0	2	28.56	4	127.86
G. A. Manou	10	10	4	234	63	0	1	39.00	10/2	88.97
M. J. Cosgrove	9	9	0	223	55	0	2	24.78	2	75.08
G. S. Blewett.	9	9	1	221	98	0	1	27.63	4	63.87
M. A. Higgs	7	7	0	154	42	0	0	22.00	1	78.97
A. Flower	6	6	0	152	74	0	2	25.33	2	87.36
M. F. Cleary	10	10	5	125	70	0	1	25.00	2	77.11
M. C. Miller	6	6	1	120	51	0	1	24.00	3	74.53
B. A. Johnson	5	5	0	86	43	0	0	17.20	1	72.27
B. P. Cameron	2	2	0	78	66	0	1	39.00	1	72.90
C. J. Ferguson	3	3	0	68	58	0	1	22.67	1	100.00
J. N. Gillespie	1	1	0	19	19	0	0	19.00	0	57.58
P. C. Rofe	7	5	3	11	6*	0	0	5.50	4	47.83
R. J. Harris	4	3	2	10	9*	0	0	10.00	2	76.34
S. W. Tait	8	3	1	5	4*	0	0	2.50	1	17.86
T. P. Kelly.	1	–	–	–	–	–	–	–	0	–

*Denotes not out

SA WICKET-TAKERS

	O	Mdns	R	W	BB	5W/i	Avge	RPO
S. W. Tait	71.4	5	353	18	8-43	1	19.61	4.93
M. F. Cleary	90.3	5	472	8	2-34	0	59.00	5.22
J. M. Davison	46	0	250	8	5-26	1	31.25	5.43
R. J. Harris	38	1	207	8	3-51	0	25.88	5.45
P. C. Rofe	60	6	244	7	3-33	0	34.86	4.07
D. S. Lehmann	30	0	151	7	2-24	0	21.57	5.03
M. C. Miller	56	4	263	5	2-46	0	52.60	4.70
B. A. Johnson	35	0	212	4	2-67	0	53.00	6.06
J. N. Gillespie	8	1	20	1	1-20	0	20.00	2.50
T. P. Kelly.	8	0	38	0	–	0	–	4.75
M. J. Cosgrove	5.1	0	33	0	–	0	–	6.39
M. A. Higgs	28	0	194	0	–	0	–	6.93
G. S. Blewett.	14	0	99	0	–	0	–	7.07

At WACA Ground, Perth, October 24, 2003. Day/night game. SOUTH AUSTRALIA lost to WESTERN AUSTRALIA by 99 runs.

At Bellerive Oval, Hobart, November 1, 2003. SOUTH AUSTRALIA defeated TASMANIA by 27 runs.

SOUTH AUSTRALIA v WESTERN AUSTRALIA

At Adelaide Oval, Adelaide, November 9, 2003. Western Australia won by seven wickets. *Toss:* Western Australia. Western Australia 4 pts.

In 2002-03, South Australia's batsmen struggled to compile competitive totals. In this match, Murray Goodwin and Mike Hussey ensured their bowlers were unable to defend one. Greg Blewett and John Davison, the reinvented batting bomb, raced to 50 in 49 balls through a combination of full-blooded strokeplay and fortuitous edges. Davison eventually succumbed to a breathtaking catch by Hussey at extra cover, Andy Flower and the teenager Mark Cosgrove carrying SA to a presentable total. Flower's effortless sweep off Marcus North's amiable off-spin hit the sponsor's sign at mid-wicket and netted him $50,000 – half of which was shared with the team. Paul Rofe then seamed back the first ball of WA's reply to trap Ryan Campbell lbw, the opener's animated protest costing him 15% of his match fee. An uneasy Justin Langer scratched around before lifting Davison into the outfield, where Cosgrove held his second brilliant catch, and when Davison spun past North the Redbacks seemed to hold sway. But Goodwin and Hussey, on a plum batting surface, sprinted to the finish line before the home side could do much about it. Goodwin's 38–ball half-century was particularly fluent; Flower called him "unstoppable".

Match reports by DANIEL BRETTIG.

Man of the Match: M. W. Goodwin. *Attendance:* 4,336.

South Australia

J. M. Davison c Hussey b Wilson	36	(23)	†G. A. Manou not out	7	(6)
*G. S. Blewett c Marsh b Thorp	49	(70)	M. F. Cleary not out	2	(9)
S. A. Deitz c North b Worthington	14	(21)			
A. Flower c Goodwin b Harvey	74	(73)	L-b 2, w 7, n-b 1	10	
M. A. Higgs b Harvey	0	(6)			
M. J. Cosgrove run out (Goodwin)	50	(75)	(50 overs, 204 mins) (7 wkts)	262	
B. A. Johnson c Goodwin b Harvey	20	(19)	Fall: 51 102 102 106 213 252 252 ..		

P. C. Rofe, T. P. Kelly did not bat.

Bowling: Wilson 10–0–44–1; Thorp 10–0–53–1; Worthington 10–1–42–1; Harvey 10–1–39–3; Casson 2–0–16–0; Hussey 4–0–29–0; North 4–0–37–0.

Western Australia

†R. J. Campbell lbw b Rofe	0	(1)	L-b 2, w 5	7	
*J. L. Langer c Cosgrove b Davison	31	(67)			
M. J. North st Manou b Davison	63	(78)			
M. E. K. Hussey not out	84	(94)	(47.1 overs, 189 mins) (3 wkts)	265	
M. W. Goodwin not out	80	(63)	Fall: 0 87 112		

S. E. Marsh, P. C. Worthington, B. Casson, C. D. Thorp, K. M. Harvey and P. Wilson did not bat.

Bowling: Rofe 10–2–26–1; Kelly 8–0–38–0; Cleary 7–0–54–0; Davison 10–0–52–2; Johnson 5–0–34–0; Higgs 4–0–30–0; Blewett 3–0–25–0; Cosgrove 0.1–0–4–0.

Umpires: S. D. Fry and D. J. Harper.
TV Umpire: K. D. Perrin.

SOUTH AUSTRALIA v NEW SOUTH WALES

At Adelaide Oval, Adelaide, November 23, 2003. South Australia won by 61 runs. *Toss:* New South Wales. South Australia 5 pts.

Carefree lower-order batting and a burst of express pace from Shaun Tait gave SA their first limited-overs win at home in seven matches. On a pitch as juicy as any Adelaide Oval wicket of recent seasons, Steve Waugh had little hesitation inserting the home side. With the ball darting about, they soon found themselves 6 for 85. John Davison's nerveless approach seemed the best option, and his rapid knock kept the runs coming even as Stuart Clark and Don Nash were scything through the top order. Davison's aggression rubbed off on Graham Manou and Mark Cleary, who played their shots while Waugh kept the field up. Together they added 111 – a seventh-wicket record for SA – in only 17 overs. Manou clumped six fours and two sixes, while Cleary showed a high front elbow and immaculate placement, driving crisply through the off-side. The

Blues' target jumped from tantalising to distant in Tait's first over. An inswinger pinned Simon Katich and a shuffling Brad Haddin was palpably late on his first ball. During the next few overs Waugh and Dominic Thornely struggled to lay a bat on the 20-year-old. Waugh eventually scrapped his way to fifty but remained impressed: "I'd heard he was quick, but not that quick."

   Man of the Match: M. F. Cleary.   *Attendance:* 4,608.

South Australia

J. M. Davison c Katich b Nicholson	.. 48	(41)	J. N. Gillespie lbw b Clark 19	(33)
S. A. Deitz c Haddin b Clark	 13	(15)	S. W. Tait c M.E. Waugh b MacGill . 1	(12)
*G. S. Blewett c S. R. Waugh b Clark	. 0	(2)	P. C. Rofe not out 0	(2)
A. Flower c Haddin b Clark	 7	(15)		
M. J. Cosgrove b MacGill b Nash	 5	(3)	B 3, l-b 6, w 9, n-b 1 19	
B. A. Johnson b Nash	 0	(3)		
†G. A. Manou hit wicket b MacGill	.. 63	(60)	(43.1 overs, 184 mins) 245	
M. F. Cleary run out (Thornely/			Fall: 27 27 63 77 77 85	
S. R. Waugh) 70		(74)	196 232 245 245	

Bowling: Clark 9.1–2–44–4; Nash 9–1–57–2; Nicholson 10–2–54–1; Thornely 5–0–33–0; MacGill 7–1–35–2; Clarke 1–0–5–0; S. R. Waugh 2–0–8–0.

New South Wales

D. J. Thornely c Manou b Cleary	 8	(34)	M. J. Nicholson b Gillespie 14	(13)
S. M. Katich lbw b Tait	 1	(5)	S. R. Clark c Flower b Cleary 0	(4)
†B. J. Haddin lbw b Tait	 0	(1)	S. C. G. MacGill not out 2	(6)
*S. R. Waugh c Davison b Rofe	 55	(96)		
M. J. Clarke c Blewett b Rofe	 3	(16)	L-b 6, w 4 10	
M. J. Slater c Cleary b Rofe	 9	(17)		
M. E. Waugh c Blewett b Johnson	 36	(36)	(45.3 overs, 193 mins) 184	
D. A. Nash run out (Deitz)	 46	(45)	Fall: 4 4 35 46 62 89 142 176 177 184	

Bowling: Gillespie 8–1–20–1; Tait 8–2–16–2; Rofe 10–1–33–3; Cleary 9.3–1–43–2; Blewett 5–0–33–0; Johnson 5–0–33–1.

Umpires: P. D. Parker and K. D. Perrin.
TV Umpire: S. D. Fry.

At Brisbane Cricket Ground, Brisbane, December 17, 2003. Day/night game. SOUTH AUSTRALIA lost to QUEENSLAND by 99 runs.

SOUTH AUSTRALIA v TASMANIA

At Adelaide Oval, Adelaide, January 9, 2004. Day/night game. South Australia won by 3 wickets. *Toss:* Tasmania. South Australia 4 pts.

   This match was so speckled with brilliance that its outstanding individual, Shaun Tait, was all but overshadowed by the outrageous conclusion. The SA skipper Darren Lehmann returned from a career-threatening Achilles tear and, after bowling with typical thrift, switched Tait to the Cathedral End for his final two overs. Starting the last over with five wickets, Tait scattered the stumps of George Bailey, Xavier Doherty and Adam Griffith to complete the best bowling analysis in Australian one-day history, surpassing Carl Rackemann's 7 for 34 in Adelaide in 1988-89. It was hardly a controlled display; Tait's failed hat-trick ball to Griffith was one of his nine wides for the day, accompanied by four no-balls. SA's reply stuttered badly but a limping Lehmann, who plundered eight fours and a six, settled in and found a willing ally in Mick Miller. With 10 runs needed off the final over, Doherty's cool direct hit from long-off accounted for Miller and gave Tasmania the advantage. Graham Manou's response was definitive – a murderous flat pull that slammed into the ING sign at mid-wicket, his second $50,000 six in two years. The winning runs were duly knocked off. Barely a week after New Year, it would prove SA's last victory of the season.

Man of the Match: S. W. Tait.   *Attendance:* 3,447.

Tasmania

M. G. Dighton lbw b Lehmann 87 (112)	†S. G. Clingeleffer not out 0	(2)
T. R. Birt c Manou b Tait 5 (18)	X. J. Doherty b Tait 0	(1)
S. P. Kremerskothen lbw b Tait 1 (5)	A. R. Griffith b Tait 0	(1)
S. R. Watson c (sub) C. J. Ferguson		
b Tait .. 78 (110)	L-b 7, w 17, n-b 8 32	
*D. J. Marsh c (sub) C. J. Ferguson b Tait 6 (16)		
S. B. Tubb lbw b Tait 26 (26)	(49.3 overs, 208 mins) 250	
G. J. Bailey b Tait 14 (9)	Fall: 18 30 171 185 228 237 249	
D. G. Wright c Davison b Lehmann .. 1 (3)	249 249 250	

Bowling: Tait 9.3–1–43–8; Rofe 6–0–30–0; Cleary 10–0–52–0; Miller 7–1–29–0; Higgs 7–0–36–0; Blewett 3–0–18–0; Davison 2–0–11–0; Lehmann 5–0–24–2.

South Australia

J. M. Davison c Dighton b Wright 17 (11)	†G. A. Manou not out 14	(6)
G. S. Blewett b Wright 0 (2)	M. F. Cleary not out 0	(0)
S. A. Deitz c Clingeleffer b Doherty .. 41 (73)		
M. A. Higgs c Dighton b Wright 11 (21)	B 3, l-b 2, w 11, n-b 1 17	
M. J. Cosgrove c Clingeleffer b Griffith 20 (41)		
*D. S. Lehmann c Bailey b Wright ... 83 (88)	(49.5 overs, 188 mins) (7 wkts) 254	
M. C. Miller run out (Doherty) 51 (58)	Fall: 1 27 53 94 106 236 242	

P. C. Rofe, S. W. Tait did not bat.

Bowling: Wright 10–4–51–4; Griffith 9–0–56–1; Kremerskothen 2.5–0–22–0; Doherty 10–0–28–1; Tubb 8–0–44–0; Marsh 10–0–48–0.

Umpires: J. S. Booth and I. H. Lock.

At Melbourne Cricket Ground, Melbourne, January 18, 2004. SOUTH AUSTRALIA lost to VICTORIA by six runs.

SOUTH AUSTRALIA v VICTORIA

At Adelaide Oval, Adelaide, January 30, 2004. Day/night game. Victoria won by 6 runs. *Toss:* Victoria. Victoria 4 pts.

Victoria's first match after the death of David Hookes was played on his former home ground. This tough contest made for an ideal tribute. David Hussey, on the day his brother Mike was selected for Australia, opened his account with a rasping six over gully as he and Brad Hodge tore the attack to shreds. The pair's 227-run union set a new one-day record for Victoria, and the eventual total of 293 was the state's best limited-overs score. The teenagers Callum Ferguson and Mark Cosgrove went on the attack after the crucial early departure of John Davison. Unbelievably, Ferguson's smoothly on-driven six sailed into the ING sign for SA's third $50,000 prize of the season. The bustling Victorian quick Mick Lewis was held back until the score reached a dangerous 2 for 124, at which point he scuppered Ferguson's impressive stay with his second ball and bowled Mark Higgs with his fourth. After Darren Lehmann and Mick Miller righted the ship, Jon Moss bowled Greg Blewett and Mark Cleary with full-length deliveries. Lewis, given 12 runs to defend in the final over, conceded a frugal five. Lehmann joked that at least his men could now afford a more ambitious end-of-season destination than Victor Harbour.

Man of the Match: D. J. Hussey.   *Attendance:* 3,018.

Victoria

J. Moss c Cleary b Miller	7	(13)	A. B. McDonald run out (Cleary/Manou)	1 (2)
M. T. G. Elliott c Ferguson b Miller	16	(23)	†D. S. Berry not out	7 (10)
B. J. Hodge lbw b Harris	114	(122)		
D. J. Hussey c Tait b Lehmann	113	(108)	L-b 6, w 8	14
I. S. L. Hewett run out (Harris/Manou)	0	(0)		
G. C. Rummans not out	18	(16)	(50 overs, 207 mins) (7 wkts)	293
*C. L. White b Harris	3	(6)	Fall: 25 25 252 253 266 277 279	

M. L. Lewis, A. B. Wise did not bat.

Bowling: Tait 10–0–69–0; Miller 10–0–46–2; Cleary 10–0–42–0; Harris 9–0–52–2; Davison 4–0–26–0; Higgs 3–0–25–0; Lehmann 4–0–27–1.

South Australia

J. M. Davison c McDonald b Moss	13	(9)	†G. A. Manou not out	31 (25)
M. J. Cosgrove c Lewis b Wise	35	(40)	M. F. Cleary b Moss	4 (3)
C. J. Ferguson c Berry b Lewis	58	(50)	R. J. Harris not out	9 (11)
M. A. Higgs b Lewis	16	(13)	L-b 3, w 8, n-b 1	12
*D. S. Lehmann run out (Hussey/Berry)	39	(53)		
M. C. Miller run out (Hodge/White)	44	(66)	(50 overs, 209 mins) (8 wkts)	287
G. S. Blewett b Moss	26	(31)	Fall: 16 87 124 125 197 233 261 265	

S. W. Tait did not bat.

Bowling: Hewett 10–1–62–0; Moss 8–0–54–3; Wise 4–0–30–1; White 9–1–58–0; McDonald 9–0–45–0; Lewis 10–0–35–2.

Umpires: J. S. Booth and J. H. Smeaton.

At Drummoyne Oval, Sydney, February 15. SOUTH AUSTRALIA lost to NEW SOUTH WALES by eight runs.

SOUTH AUSTRALIA v QUEENSLAND

At Adelaide Oval, Adelaide, February 22, 2004. Queensland won by four runs. *Toss:* South Australia. Queensland 4 pts.

South Australia surrendered a commanding position to hand Queensland a spot in the final. The game-breaker was Nathan Hauritz, who produced an aggressive yet miserly exhibition of one-day off-spin that Peter Taylor might have been proud of. It was SA's bowlers who controlled the early proceedings but a series of useful contributions by Clint Perren, Craig Philipson and James Hopes hoisted Queensland to 268. An aggressive Graham Manou helped SA to the quick start they needed, and a super-confident Darren Lehmann then joined Shane Deitz for a stand of 120 in 22 overs. Lehmann's innings suggested a batsman in his very best form, and his sliced drive off Hauritz that sailed straight to long-off seemed to come from nowhere. Hauritz was gaining just enough turn to deceive Deitz with a straight one two balls later, and when he did the same to Mark Cosgrove in his next over Queensland had wrested the initiative. South Australia's lower order could not muster the big hits required to win from there. An annoyed Lehmann complained afterwards that he was sick of carrying the team.

Man of the Match: N. M. Hauritz.   *Attendance:* 1,647.

Queensland

C. P. Simpson lbw b Tait	4	(6)	A. J. Bichel b Harris	21	(19)
S. G. Law c Tait b Harris	28	(31)	†W. A. Seccombe not out	2	(3)
*M. L. Love c (sub) J. M. Davison					
b Miller	43	(63)	L-b 12, w 17	29	
C. T. Perren lbw b Cleary	53	(79)			
C. A. Philipson lbw b Lehmann	48	(63)	(50 overs, 189 mins) (6 wkts)	268	
J. R. Hopes not out	40	(36)	Fall: 4 70 99 189 221 260		

A. A. Noffke, N. M. Hauritz and S. A. Brant did not bat.

Bowling: Tait 5–0–21–1; Miller 10–2–43–1; Cleary 10–0–49–1; Harris 10–0–67–2; Higgs 4–0–29–0; Cosgrove 3–0–16–0; Lehmann 8–0–31–1.

South Australia

†G. A. Manou b Hopes	46	(63)	M. C. Miller not out	17	(18)
B. P. Cameron c Hopes b Noffke	12	(22)	M. F. Cleary not out	1	(1)
S. A. Deitz lbw b Hauritz	57	(93)			
*D. S. Lehmann c Noffke b Hauritz	75	(59)	L-b 6, w 10	16	
A. Flower c Perren b Hauritz	12	(14)			
M. J. Cosgrove lbw b Hauritz	7	(11)	(50 overs, 199 mins) (7 wkts)	264	
M. A. Higgs st Seccombe b Hopes	21	(19)	Fall: 53 83 203 203 214 236 260		

R. J. Harris, S. W. Tait did not bat.

Bowling: Bichel 9–0–50–0; Brant 6–0–33–0; Noffke 10–1–47–1; Hopes 10–0–50–2; Hauritz 10–1–39–4; Perren 3–0–22–0; Simpson 2–0–17–0.

Umpires: S. D. Fry and D. J. Harper.
TV Umpire: J. S. Booth.

SA DOMESTIC LIMITED-OVERS RESULTS

	First Game	M	Won	Lost	Drawn	Tied
v Western Australia	Nov 30, 1969	35	12	23	0	0
v Victoria	Oct 18, 1970	30	10	19	0	1
v Queensland	Dec 6, 1970	26	5	21	0	0
v Tasmania	Nov 14, 1971	24	16	8	0	0
v New Zealanders	Jan 14, 1973	2	0	2	0	0
v New South Wales	Nov 23, 1975	23	10	13	0	0
v Australian Capital Territory	Nov 2, 1997	3	3	0	0	0
Total		143	56	86	0	1

SA RECORDS

Highest score for:	142	D. S. Lehmann v Tasmania at Adelaide	1994-95
Highest score against:	164	R. B. McCosker (New South Wales) at Sydney	1981-82
Best bowling for:	8-43	S. W. Tait v South Australia at Adelaide	2003-04
Best bowling against:	7-34	C. G. Rackemann (Queensland) at Adelaide	1988-89
Highest total for:	6-325	v Tasmania at Hobart (TCA)	1986-87
Highest total against:	7-310	by New South Wales at North Sydney	1997-98
Lowest total for:	51	v Tasmania, Hobart (Bellerive)	2002-03
Lowest total against:	119	by Queensland at Adelaide	1993-94

MOST RUNS

	M	I	NO	R	HS	100s	50s	Avge	S-R
D. S. Lehmann	64	64	9	2,903	142*	6	21	52.78	87.86
G. S. Blewett	79	77	7	2,740	109*	3	17	39.14	66.78
J. D. Siddons	42	40	4	1,169	102	1	8	32.47	78.77
D. A. Fitzgerald	40	40	1	1,160	114	2	7	29.74	68.97
D. W. Hookes	38	38	1	1,149	101	1	6	31.05	80.07
B. A. Johnson	58	57	7	1,117	83	0	3	22.34	68.57
C. J. Davies	38	37	1	970	125	1	5	26.94	65.06
P. R. Sleep	30	28	4	846	90	0	4	35.25	65.58
P. C. Nobes	27	27	4	745	140*	1	4	32.39	58.43
G. A. Bishop	26	25	1	708	119*	2	2	29.50	66.48

HIGHEST PARTNERSHIP FOR EACH WICKET

217*	for 1st	D. S. Lehmann and P. C. Nobes, v Tasmania at Adelaide	1994-95
145	for 2nd	B. A. Richards and I. M. Chappell, v Queensland at Adelaide	1970-71
153	for 3rd	C. J. Davies and D. S. Lehmann, v Victoria at Adelaide	2000-01
125	for 4th	G. S. Chappell and K. G. Cunningham, v Western Australia at Perth	1972-73
133*	for 5th	A. M. J. Hilditch and M. D. Haysman, v Queensland at Brisbane	1984-85
130	for 6th	D. S. Lehmann and M. C. Miller, v Tasmania at Adelaide	2003-04
111	for 7th	G. A. Manou and M. F. Cleary, v New South Wales at Adelaide	2003-04
64*	for 8th	D. S. Lehmann and B. A. Swain, v Australian Capital Territory at Canberra	1999-00
61*	for 9th	M. Hendrick and A. A. Mallett, v Western Australia at Perth	1974-75
32	for 10th	T. B. A. May and C. J. Owen, v Tasmania at Adelaide	1991-92

MOST WICKETS

	M	Balls	Mdns	R	W	BB	5W/i	Avge	RPO
P. Wilson	46	2,540	42	1,676	70	4-23	0	23.94	3.96
M. A. Harrity	40	2,030	26	1,551	57	5-42	1	27.21	4.58
G. S. Blewett	79	2,094	12	1,783	51	4-33	0	34.96	5.11
B. E. Young	42	1,671	6	1,390	38	4-24	0	36.58	4.99
J. N. Gillespie	23	1,330	24	868	38	4-46	0	35.00	3.92
J. C. Scuderi	37	1,759	13	1,357	32	3-36	0	42.41	4.63
S. P. George	20	1,049	7	881	29	4-33	0	30.28	3.99
B. N. Wigney	26	1,318	23	876	29	3-24	0	30.21	5.04
T. B. A. May	24	1,318	18	818	27	4-9	0	30.30	3.72
B. A. Johnston	58	902	4	803	24	3-46	0	33.46	5.34

MOST DISMISSALS

	M	Ct	St	Total
G. A. Manou	45	59	3	62
T. J. Nielsen	45	55	3	58
W. B. Phillips	13	18	0	18
K. J. Wright	14	15	3	18
D. S. Berry	4	5	2	7

MOST CATCHES

G. S. Blewett	26 in 79 matches	D. S. Lehmann	17 in 64 matches
B. E. Young	25 in 42 matches	D. A. Fitzgerald	15 in 40 matches
D. W. Hookes	22 in 38 matches	C. J. Davies	12 in 38 matches
B. A. Johnson	21 in 58 matches	J. M. Vaughan	11 in 23 matches
J. D. Siddons	20 in 42 matches	R. J. Harris	11 in 17 matches

MOST APPEARANCES

79	G. S. Blewett	1992-93 – 2003-04
64	D. S. Lehmann	1988-89 – 2003-04
58	B. A. Johnson	1994-95 – 2003-04
46	P. Wilson	1993-94 – 2001-02
45	T. J. Nielsen	1991-92 – 1989-99
45	G. A. Manou	1999-00 – 2003-04
42	J. D. Siddons	1991-92 – 1999-00
42	B. E. Young	1996-97 – 2002-03
40	D. A. Fitzgerald	1997-98 – 2002-03
40	M. A. Harrity	1995-96 – 2002-03

TASMANIA ING CUP RESULTS, 2003-04

Played 10: Won 1, Lost 8, Drawn 1. *Finished sixth.*

TASMANIA RUNSCORERS

	M	I	NO	R	HS	100s	50s	Avge	Ct/St	S-R
S. R. Watson	10	10	0	375	78	0	4	37.50	1	76.06
M. G. Dighton	10	10	0	340	113	1	1	34.00	4	64.15
M. J. Di Venuto	8	8	0	316	125	1	1	39.50	4	76.89
D. J. Marsh	10	10	0	196	46	0	0	19.60	2	61.06
S. B. Tubb	6	6	0	165	79	0	1	27.50	0	93.22
S. G. Clingeleffer . . .	10	10	5	147	48	0	0	29.40	8	63.06
G. J. Bailey	6	6	1	112	52*	0	1	22.40	2	77.78
D. G. Wright	7	7	2	84	29	0	0	16.80	1	68.29
L. R. Butterworth . . .	4	4	0	65	23	0	0	16.25	0	80.25
X. J. Doherty	7	5	0	58	37	0	0	11.60	4	75.32
S. P. Kremerskothen .	7	7	0	53	18	0	0	7.57	3	50.48
T. R. Birt	4	4	0	50	28	0	0	12.50	1	54.95
J. Cox	3	3	0	18	9	0	0	6.00	0	26.87
A. G. Downton	2	2	1	15	9	0	0	15.00	0	71.43
R. T. Ponting	1	1	0	12	12	0	0	12.00	1	92.31
B. Geeves	5	4	1	9	4*	0	0	3.00	0	47.37
A. R. Griffith	9	7	4	9	4*	0	0	3.00	0	64.29
G. J. Denton	1	1	1	2	2*	0	0	–	1	100.00

*Denotes not out

TASMANIA WICKET-TAKERS

	O	Mdns	R	W	BB	5W/i	Avge	RPO
A. R. Griffith	75	3	428	10	3-40	0	42.80	5.71
D. G. Wright	53.2	6	255	7	4-51	0	36.43	4.78
S. P. Kremerskothen	44.5	3	204	6	3-35	0	34.00	4.55
D. J. Marsh	42	2	201	4	2-44	0	50.25	4.79
S. R. Watson	14	1	70	4	2-15	0	17.50	5.00
L. R. Butterworth	17.2	1	98	4	3-33	0	24.50	5.65
B. Geeves	40	2	195	3	1-19	0	65.00	4.88
X. J. Doherty	41.1	1	217	3	1-28	0	72.33	5.27
G. J. Denton	8.2	0	63	2	2-63	0	31.50	7.56
A. G. Downton	7	1	36	1	1-36	0	36.00	5.14
M. J. Di Venuto	2	0	8	0	–	0	–	4.00
G. J. Bailey	4.4	0	19	0	–	0	–	4.07
R. T. Ponting	5	0	24	0	–	0	–	4.80
S. B. Tubb	28.3	1	130	0	–	0	–	4.56

At Brisbane Cricket Ground, Brisbane, October 25, 2003. TASMANIA lost to QUEENSLAND by four wickets.

TASMANIA v SOUTH AUSTRALIA

At Bellerive Oval, Hobart, November 1, 2003. South Australia won by 27 runs. *Toss:* South Australia. South Australia 4 pts.

As he showed for Canada in the 2003 World Cup, John Davison can be as cyclonic with the bat as he appears innocuous with the ball. In this match he ravaged Tasmania with both, leading his adopted state to a comfortable victory. He hit eight fours in an opening stand of 54 with the captain Greg Blewett. After a couple of run-outs and a messy middle-order slump of 4 for 11, Mark Higgs and Ben Johnson rebuilt the innings while Mark Cleary gave the tail some wag. Tasmania's reply was dominated by a superb 113 in 139 balls from Michael Dighton, including 10 fours and two sixes. But only his skipper Dan Marsh offered any support. Davison weaved his best performance of the season with his off-breaks, picking up five wickets to complete a masterly all-round display.

Match reports by DAVID STOCKDALE.

Man of the Match: J. M. Davison. *Attendance:* 1,080.

South Australia

J. M. Davison c Di Venuto b Griffith .	59	(63)
*G. S. Blewett b Geeves	24	(36)
S. A. Deitz run out (Marsh)	29	(41)
A. Flower run out (Kremerskothen) . .	1	(5)
M. A. Higgs c Di Venuto b Kremerskothen	41	(65)
M. J. Cosgrove lbw b Griffith	1	(5)
B. A. Johnson run out (Wright)	43	(48)

†G. A. Manou c and b Kremerskothen	5	(6)
M. F. Cleary not out	28	(31)
P. C. Rofe not out	2	(3)
L-b 2, w 1, n-b 3	6	
(50 overs, 205 mins) (8 wkts)	239	
Fall: 54 115 116 123 126 181 194 221		

S. W. Tait did not bat.

Bowling: Wright 10–0–42–0; Griffith 10–0–47–2; Geeves 10–1–60–1; Doherty 3–0–18–0; Kremerskothen 10–0–35–2; Marsh 5–0–27–0; Di Venuto 2–0–8–0.

Tasmania

M. G. Dighton st Manou b Davison . . .	113	(139)
M. J. Di Venuto b Rofe	0	(1)
S. R. Watson c Davison b Tait	10	(17)
J. Cox lbw b Rofe	2	(5)
*D. J. Marsh c Manou b Davison	46	(62)
S. P. Kremerskothen c Deitz b Davison	5	(12)
D. G. Wright run out (Manou)	2	(8)
†S. G. Clingeleffer c Blewett b Davison	9	(15)

X. J. Doherty b Davison	10	(20)
B. Geeves lbw b Tait	3	(8)
A. R. Griffith not out	0	(3)
B 1, l-b 2, w 8, n-b 1	12	
(48.1 overs, 191 mins)	212	
Fall: 1 24 28 149 158 161 182 204 212 212		

Bowling: Rofe 10–1–37–2; Tait 9.1–0–44–2; Cleary 10–0–58–0; Higgs 4–0–22–0; Johnson 7–0–22–0; Davison 8–0–26–5.

Umpires: B. W. Jackman and J. H. Smeaton.
TV Umpire: K. J. McGinniss.

TASMANIA v NEW SOUTH WALES

At Bellerive Oval, Hobart, November 29, 2003. New South Wales won by six wickets. *Toss:* Tasmania. New South Wales 4 pts. *Competition debut:* T. R. Birt.

Michael Di Venuto and Simon Katich matched each other with outstanding innings on a day that started with a toss between the retiring Australian captain Steve Waugh and his would-be successor Ricky Ponting. Ponting won the toss and Di Venuto pressed home the advantage, accumulating only nine fours in his 125 off 135 balls. Once again, finding supplementary contributors proved a problem for the Tasmanians. Shane Watson maintained the momentum with a dashing 43 but Dan Marsh was the only other batsman to offer any real assistance. On another benign Bellerive track, Matthew Nicholson was the pick of the bowlers with 3 for 49. Katich, in contrast to Di Venuto, received vigorous support right from the start. He and Dominic Thornely stormed their way to a 168-run opening stand, Thornely heaving eight fours and three sixes. It left the middle order with a relatively simple task, Mark Waugh's unbeaten 41 off 49 balls smoothing the way home.

Man of the Match: S. M. Katich. *Attendance:* 3,377.

Tasmania

M. J. Di Venuto c Katich b Nicholson	.125	(135)
M. G. Dighton b Nicholson	19	(35)
*R. T. Ponting b MacGill	12	(13)
T. R. Birt c Thornely b MacGill	15	(12)
S. R. Watson c Katich b Clark	43	(39)
D. J. Marsh run out (M. E. Waugh/Nicholson)	34	(43)
S. P. Kremerskothen c Bradstreet b Nicholson	11	(15)
D. G. Wright not out	3	(4)
†S. G. Clingeleffer not out	2	(4)
B 2, l-b 2, w 4	8	
(50 overs, 210 mins) (7 wkts)	272	

Fall: 67 83 104 172 241 266 266

A. R. Griffith, B. Geeves did not bat.

Bowling: Bracken 10–0–55–0; Clark 8–0–38–1; Nicholson 10–0–49–3; Bradstreet 7–0–24–0; MacGill 8–0–58–2; Katich 7–0–44–0.

New South Wales

D. J. Thornely c Wright b Marsh	78	(105)
S. M. Katich c Ponting b Wright	.118	(108)
*S. R. Waugh c (sub) G. J. Denton b Marsh	14	(15)
M. J. Clarke run out (Watson)	1	(1)
M. E. Waugh not out	41	(49)
†B. J. Haddin not out	10	(13)
L-b 4, w 6, n-b 1	11	
(48.2 overs, 190 mins) (4 wkts)	273	

Fall: 168 196 199 252

S. D. Bradstreet, M. J. Nicholson, N. W. Bracken, S. R. Clark and S. C. G. MacGill did not bat.

Bowling: Wright 9.2–2–54–1; Griffith 8–0–59–0; Geeves 9–0–54–0; Kremerskothen 7–0–34–0; Marsh 10–0–44–2; Ponting 5–0–24–0.

Umpires: K. J. McGinniss and J. H. Smeaton.
TV Umpire: B. W. Jackman.

At WACA Ground, Perth, December 5, 2003. Day/night game. TASMANIA lost to WESTERN AUSTRALIA by three wickets.

TASMANIA v VICTORIA

At Devonport Oval, Devonport, January 4, 2004. Victoria won by eight wickets. *Toss:* Victoria. Victoria 5 pts.

Victoria gave the home side a lesson in how to build partnerships with bat and ball, in a rare Tasmanian day-trip away from Bellerive Oval. The Tasmanians began encouragingly enough after being sent in, with Michael Dighton and the newcomer Travis Birt putting on 59 for the first wicket. Birt lasted just over an hour in his debut knock, hitting two fours and a six. It was nearly all downhill from there. Dan Marsh and Shane Watson, who belted two sixes during his fleeting stay, were the only other notables as the Tigers were skittled for 162. Victoria's captain Cameron White was the most successful of the bowlers but it was the left-armer Allan Wise who made the crucial early inroads, dismissing Dighton and Scott Kremerskothen when Tasmania had appeared well set. Victoria coasted to victory on the back of a pair of 60s from Matthew Elliott and Brad Hodge and the game was all over with 12.2 overs to spare. Tasmania's task became more difficult when the Australia A paceman Damien Wright suffered a leg injury after three overs, exposing the attack's lack of one-day depth.

Man of the Match: C. L. White. *Attendance:* 1,715.

Tasmania

T. R. Birt c Harwood b Hewett	28	(50)	D. G. Wright not out		8	(14)
M. G. Dighton c Roach b Wise	33	(59)	A. R. Griffith lbw b White		1	(4)
S. P. Kremerskothen c White b Wise	6	(19)	B. Geeves lbw b Harvey		2	(5)
S. R. Watson b White	32	(43)	L-b 8, w 3, n-b 2		13	
*D. J. Marsh b White	27	(46)			—	
S. B. Tubb c Elliott b McDonald	5	(10)	(43 overs, 176 mins)		162	
G. J. Bailey c Elliott b McDonald	7	(9)	Fall: 59 72 75 126 138 148 148			
†S. G. Clingeleffer run out (McDonald)	0	(0)	148 154 162			

Bowling: Harwood 7–1–21–0; Harvey 8–2–24–1; McDonald 10–1–24–2; Hewett 5–0–27–1; Wise 7–0–33–2; White 6–1–25–3.

Victoria

M. T. G. Elliott run out (Dighton/Clingeleffer)	65	(92)	L-b 4, w 5, n-b 1	10	
I. J. Harvey c Clingeleffer b Kremersketen	12	(11)		—	
B. J. Hodge not out	63	(96)	(37.4 overs, 136 mins)　(2 wkts)	166	
J. Moss not out	16	(28)	Fall: 35 141		

D. J. Hussey, *C. L. White, A. B. McDonald, †P. J. Roach, I. S. L. Hewett, S. M. Harwood and A. B. Wise did not bat.

Bowling: Wright 3–0–10–0; Griffith 6–0–31–0; Geeves 5–1–31–0; Kremerskothen 5–0–24–1; Marsh 6–0–25–0; Tubb 8–0–22–0; Bailey 4.4–0–19–0.

Umpires: B. W. Jackman and J. H. Smeaton.

At Adelaide Oval, Adelaide, January 9, 2004. Day/night game. TASMANIA lost to SOUTH AUSTRALIA by three wickets.

TASMANIA v QUEENSLAND

At Bellerive Oval, Hobart, January 26, 2004. Queensland won by six wickets. *Toss:* Tasmania. Queensland 5 pts. *Competition debut:* L. R. Butterworth.

Stuart Law, in his farewell innings in Hobart, made a mess of Tasmania in a one-sided and record-breaking affair. Law dashed off the fastest century in domestic limited-overs history, racing to three figures in only 69 balls and eclipsing the old record – shared among Brad Haddin, Justin Langer and himself – by five deliveries. His fifty came up in only 26 balls, making it the speediest of the season. He hit 15 fours and batted 127 minutes. With freewheeling donations from Clinton Perren and Martin Love, the Bulls easily knocked off the runs after Michael Kasprowicz had done the damage with the ball. Kasprowicz ripped through Michael Dighton, Dan Marsh and Shane Watson cheaply to reduce Tasmania to 4 for 33. Michael Di Venuto, witnessing the carnage from the non-striker's end, survived Kasprowicz's burst and lingered for a patient half-century. He and the spinner-turned-batsman Shannon Tubb, who hit 10 fours and a six in his 75-ball 79, pushed the home side towards what they thought was a respectable score. Law had other ideas, leaving his Tasmanian admirers with a memorable goodbye.

Man of the Match: S. G. Law.　*Attendance:* 1,696.

Tasmania

M. J. Di Venuto c Love b Hauritz	 54	(96)	A. G. Downton st Seccombe b Simpson 9 (13)
M. G. Dighton b Kasprowicz	 4	(9)	X. J. Doherty b Simpson 6 (14)
*D. J. Marsh c Maher b Kasprowicz	4	(14)	A. R. Griffith not out 1 (1)
S. R. Watson lbw b Kasprowicz	 0	(8)	
G. J. Bailey c Maher b Noffke	 0	(3)	B 1, l-b 6, w 3 10
S. B. Tubb b Hopes	 79	(75)	──
†S. G. Clingeleffer c Love b Kasprowicz 19	(39)	(49.4 overs, 194 mins)	209
L. R. Butterworth b Simpson	 23	(26)	Fall: 11 29 32 33 127 161 190 192 208 209

Bowling: Kasprowicz 10–1–19–4; Noffke 10–0–41–1; Hopes 10–1–53–1; Hauritz 10–0–34–1; Simpson 8.4–0–45–3; Philipson 1–0–10–0.

Queensland

*J. P. Maher c Dighton b Downton	... 1	(7)	C. A. Philipson not out 0 (1)
S. G. Law not out	113	(85)	
C. P. Simpson c Bailey b Doherty	 15	(25)	
M. L. Love c Watson b Marsh	 37	(27)	(35.3 overs, 127 mins) (4 wkts) 212
C. T. Perren b Doherty b Butterworth	. 46	(69)	Fall: 1 65 122 206

†W. A. Seccombe, J. R. Hopes, A. A. Noffke, N. M. Hauritz and M. S. Kasprowicz did not bat.

Bowling: Griffith 5–0–40–0; Downton 7–1–36–1; Doherty 9–1–49–1; Butterworth 6–0–39–1; Marsh 3–0–19–1; Tubb 5.3–0–29–0.

Umpires: K. J. McGinniss and R. L. Parry.

TASMANIA v WESTERN AUSTRALIA

At NTCA Ground, Launceston, February 1, 2004. No result. *Toss:* Tasmania. Tasmania 2 pts, Western Australia 2 pts. *Competition debut:* A. K. Heal.

A match destined for a wet finish had a bright beginning, with Michael Dighton and Michael Di Venuto racking up a 79-run stand inside 19 overs. Di Venuto hit eight fours in his 48 but no other batsman made a significant contribution; it was the story of Tasmania's one-day summer. At least a few others made starts on this occasion, the pinch-hitter Damien Wright and George Bailey the best of them. WA's left-arm finger spinner Aaron Heal made an impressive debut, having Di Venuto caught at long-on with his sixth ball and later bowling Dan Marsh. The innings finished two overs early because of rain, which then dominated proceedings for most of the afternoon. The visitors needed six runs when torrential rain, thunder and lightning stopped play.

Man of the Match: No award. *Attendance:* 2,166.

Tasmania

M. G. Dighton c Ronchi b Taylor	 48	(74)	L. R. Butterworth b Harvey 6 (8)
M. J. Di Venuto c Clark b Heal	 25	(39)	†S. G. Clingeleffer not out 8 (9)
D. G. Wright c Rogers b Clark	 29	(43)	A. G. Downton not out 6 (8)
*D. J. Marsh b Heal	 16	(21)	L-b 6, w 8 14
S. R. Watson c Ronchi b Clark	 16	(31)	
G. J. Bailey c Goodwin b North	 36	(39)	(48 overs, 173 mins) (8 wkts) 215
S. B. Tubb c Langer b North	 11	(16)	Fall: 79 83 121 141 149 176 195 203

X. J. Doherty did not bat.

Bowling: Wilson 8–0–20–0; Clark 9–1–43–2; Harvey 10–0–39–1; Taylor 5–0–36–1; Heal 10–0–34–2; North 6–0–37–2.

Western Australia

C. J. L. Rogers not out	....	2 (8)
J. J. Taylor not out	....	0 (4)
L-b 2, w 2	....	4

(2 overs, 9 mins)   (0 wkt)   6

*J. L. Langer, M. J. North, M. W. Goodwin, S. W. Meuleman, K. M. Harvey, †L. Ronchi, M. W. Clark, A. K. Heal and P. Wilson did not bat.

Bowling: Wright 1–0–2–0; Watson 1–0–2–0.

Umpires: B. W. Jackman and D. L. Orchard.

At Melbourne Cricket Ground, Melbourne, February 14, 2004. TASMANIA defeated VICTORIA by three wickets.

At Sydney Cricket Ground, Sydney, February 22, 2004. TASMANIA lost to NEW SOUTH WALES by eight wickets.

TASMANIA DOMESTIC LIMITED-OVERS RESULTS

	First Game	M	Won	Lost	Drawn	Tied
v Victoria	Nov 22, 1969	22	9	12	1	0
v Western Australia	Nov 4, 1970	27	5	21	1	0
v South Australia	Nov 14, 1971	24	8	16	0	0
v Queensland	Dec 31, 1972	28	8	19	1	0
v New South Wales	Dec 17, 1973	25	3	21	0	1
v New Zealanders	Jan 17, 1975	1	0	1	0	0
v Australian Capital Territory ...	Nov 16, 1997	3	2	1	0	0
Total		130	35	91	3	1

TASMANIA RECORDS

Highest score for:	129*	M. J. Di Venuto v South Australia at Hobart (Bellerive) 1996-97
Highest score against:	159	S. G. Law (Queensland) at Brisbane 1993-94
Best bowling for:	5-23	J. P. Marquet v Queensland at Hobart (Bellerive) 1995-96
Best bowling against:	8-43	S. W. Tait (South Australia) at Adelaide 2003-04
Highest total for:	7-327	v New South Wales at Bankstown. 2001-02
Highest total against:	4-397	by New South Wales at Bankstown. 2001-02
Lowest total for:	80	v New South Wales at Devonport 1984-85
Lowest total against:	51	by South Australia at Hobart (Bellerive) 2002-03

MOST RUNS

	M	I	NO	R	HS	100s	50s	Avge	S-R
M. J. Di Venuto	75	73	7	2,020	129*	3	9	30.61	77.60
J. Cox..............	75	73	4	1,879	99	0	14	27.23	64.33
D. C. Boon...........	55	52	4	1,725	116	1	16	35.94	66.22
D. J. Marsh	61	56	10	1,432	101*	2	5	31.13	74.62
S. Young	64	56	6	1,428	96	0	9	28.56	65.59
D. F. Hills	42	39	3	1,137	81	0	8	31.58	56.40
R. T. Ponting	32	32	4	942	102	1	6	33.64	77.92
R. J. Tucker	39	38	2	869	75	0	6	24.14	76.56
M. G. Dighton	26	25	0	803	96	0	7	29.74	65.71
S. R. Watson	26	35	0	805	113	1	6	32.20	68.34

HIGHEST PARTNERSHIP FOR EACH WICKET

210	for 1st	J. Cox and D.C. Boon, v New South Wales at Hobart (Bellerive)	....	1998-99
137	for 2nd	M. J. Di Venuto and R. T. Ponting, v South Australia at Adelaide	....	2000-01
152	for 3rd	G. W. Goodman and J. H. Hampshire, v Queensland at Brisbane	....	1978-79
121	for 4th	M. G. Dighton and D. J. Marsh, v South Australia at Hobart (Bellerive)	...	2003-04
158	for 5th	J. Cox and D.J. Marsh, v Queensland at Hobart (Bellerive)	....	2002-03
95	for 6th	D.J. Marsh and G. T. Cunningham, v New South Wales at Bankstown	....	2001-02
96*	for 7th	T. W. Docking and J. Simmons, v Western Australia at Hobart (TCA)	....	1978-79
58	for 8th	J. Cox and S.P. Kremerskothen, v New South Wales at Devonport	....	2002-03
67	for 9th	G. T. Cunningham and D. J. Saker, v Western Australia at Perth	....	2000-01
28	for 10th	M. G. Farrell and M. W. Ridgway, v Western Australia at Hobart (Bellerive)		1996-97
28	for 10th	S. G. Clingeleffer and S. B. Tubb, v South Australia at Adelaide	....	2001-02

MOST WICKETS

	M	Balls	Mdns	R	W	BB	5Wfi	Avge	RPO
D. G. Wright	42	1,936	38	1,393	51	4-23	0	27.31	3.70
S. Young	64	2,642	39	1,864	43	3-16	0	43.35	4.23
D. J. Marsh	61	1,741	4	1,409	36	3-33	0	39.14	4.86
R. J. Tucker	39	1,461	4	1,263	34	4-31	0	37.15	5.19
C. R. Miller	33	1,843	31	1,267	34	4-48	0	37.26	4.12
M. W. Ridgway	21	1,170	22	868	28	4-37	0	31.00	4.12
M. G. Farrell	28	1,224	3	885	27	4-51	0	32.78	4.34
A. R. Griffith	19	1,019	13	779	25	3-14	0	31.16	4.59
J. P. Marquet	16	862	7	674	24	5-23	1	28.08	4.69
S. P. Kremerskothen	38	917	5	831	24	3-33	0	34.63	5.44

MOST DISMISSALS

	M	Ct	St	Total
M. N. Atkinson	35	43	7	50
S. G. Clingeleffer	40	39	3	42
R. D. Woolley	22	16	1	17
R. E. Soule	11	9	0	9
B. R. Doolan	7	6	1	7

MOST CATCHES

M. J. Di Venuto	35 in 75 matches	S. P. Kremerskothen .	14 in 38 matches
D. J. Marsh	28 in 61 matches	R. J. Tucker	13 in 39 matches
S. Young	23 in 64 matches	R. T. Ponting	13 in 32 matches
J. Cox	19 in 75 matches	D. F. Hills	10 in 42 matches
D. C. Boon	16 in 55 matches	M. G. Dighton	10 in 26 matches

MOST APPEARANCES

75	J. Cox	1988-89 – 2003-04	42	D. F. Hills	1992-93 – 2001-02
75	M. J. Di Venuto ...	1992-93 – 2003-04	42	D. G. Wright	1997-98 – 2003-04
64	S. Young	1990-91 – 2001-02	40	S. G. Clingeleffer ..	2000-01 – 2003-04
61	D. J. Marsh	1996-97 – 2003-04	39	R. J. Tucker	1987-88 – 1998-99
55	D. C. Boon	1978-79 – 1998-99	38	S. P. Kremerskothen	1998-99 – 2003-04

VICTORIA ING CUP RESULTS, 2003-04

Played 10: Won 6, Lost 3, Tied 1. *Finished third.*

VICTORIA RUNSCORERS

	M	I	NO	R	HS	100s	50s	Avge	Ct/St	S-R
B. J. Hodge	9	9	2	540	114	3	3	77.14	3	83.46
M. T. G. Elliott	10	10	1	493	117*	1	4	54.78	5	78.25
J. Moss	10	10	1	271	64	0	3	30.11	1	73.44
D. J. Hussey	10	8	1	230	113	1	0	32.86	4	83.03
G. C. Rummans	6	6	1	150	53	0	2	30.00	2	76.14
A. B. McDonald	9	8	2	146	55*	0	1	24.33	2	66.67
D. S. Berry	5	4	3	98	64	0	1	98.00	3	102.08
C. L. White	9	6	0	77	37	0	0	12.83	3	66.96
B. R. Joseland	4	2	0	38	23	0	0	19.00	1	86.36
M. L. Lewis.	6	3	1	29	19	0	0	14.50	2	64.44
P. J. Roach	5	3	1	22	14*	0	0	11.00	4	84.62
I. J. Harvey	3	3	0	21	12	0	0	7.00	1	60.00
N. Jewell.	2	2	0	15	11	0	0	7.50	0	44.12
I. S. L. Hewett	3	2	1	15	15*	0	0	15.00	0	135.14
S. K. Warne	2	2	0	9	7	0	0	4.50	0	56.25
M. W. H. Inness	4	1	1	1	1*	0	0	–	0	20.00
S. M. Harwood	4	1	0	0	0	0	0	0.00	0	0.00
B. A. Knowles	1	1	1	0	0*	0	0	–	0	0.00
A. B. Wise.	8	2	1	0	0*	0	0	0.00	0	0.00

Denotes not out

VICTORIA WICKET-TAKERS

	O	Mdns	R	W	BB	5W/i	Avge	RPO
C. L. White	75	5	363	10	3-25	0	36.30	4.84
A. B. Wise.	59	1	287	10	2-31	0	28.70	4.86
M. L. Lewis.	58	2	248	9	2-33	0	27.56	4.28
J. Moss	69	4	333	8	3-52	0	41.63	4.83
A. B. McDonald	65	4	313	7	2-24	0	44.71	4.82
I. S. L. Hewett.	22	1	130	4	3-41	0	32.50	5.91
I. J. Harvey	28	2	103	3	1-24	0	34.33	3.68
S. M. Harwood	32.5	2	129	2	1-24	0	64.50	3.93
B. A. Knowles.	10	2	42	2	2-42	0	21.00	4.20
S. K. Warne	20	1	91	2	1-43	0	45.50	4.55
M. W. H. Inness	28	3	132	2	2-46	0	66.00	4.71
D. J. Hussey	13	0	91	1	1-37	0	91.00	7.00
B. R. Joseland	7	0	60	1	1-24	0	60.00	8.57
B. J. Hodge	0.1	0	0	0	–	0	–	0.00

At Bradman Oval, Bowral, October 26, 2003. VICTORIA lost to NEW SOUTH WALES by seven wickets.

At Brisbane Cricket Ground, Brisbane, October 31, 2003. Day/night game. VICTORIA defeated QUEENSLAND by eight wickets.

VICTORIA v QUEENSLAND

At Melbourne Cricket Ground, Melbourne, November 16, 2003. Victoria won by seven wickets. *Toss:* Victoria. Victoria 4 pts. *Competition debut:* S. J. Farrell, C. P. Simpson.
  Victoria's coach David Hookes blamed inexperience and the MCG wicket – the ball

would "stop, hit the pitch, stop and balloon" – for his side's failure to secure a bonus point that would have lifted them to the top of the table. Although ultimately restricted to a sub-par total of 212, Queensland began in a blaze of boundaries by Stuart Law and Daniel Payne. Mathew Inness was banished from the attack only three overs into his spell, but after Payne's dismissal the Bulls slowed to a crawl. They added only 115 in the remaining 29.5 overs, including an 86-ball patch without a boundary. Victoria's chase started dreamily with Matthew Elliott and Jon Moss registering a century partnership. Moss, a key contributor with the ball, struck two fours and two huge sixes in consecutive overs. Hodge and Elliott, playing their best one-day cricket in years this summer, added another 63 runs to end Queensland's chances. Then Elliott, admitting to a "brain fade" 11 runs short of his hundred, was stumped chasing a wide ball from the part-timer Law. Hodge and David Hussey pushed Victoria past the post but they sloppily missed a bonus point by seven overs.

Match reports by NABILA AHMED.
Man of the Match: J. Moss. *Attendance:* 1,894.

Queensland

D. M. Payne c Hussey b McDonald	52	(58)	J. R. Hopes c Berry b Lewis 7 (20)	
S. G. Law c Hodge b Moss	24	(26)	D. R. MacKenzie not out 23 (19)	
*M. L. Love run out (Moss)	34	(55)		
S. J. Farrell b Lewis	8	(11)	B 1, l-b 7, w 3 11	
C. T. Perren not out	35	(78)		
†W. A. Seccombe b Wise	13	(22)	(50 overs, 190 mins) (7 wkts) 212	
C. P. Simpson run out (Elliott/White)	5	(11)	Fall: 39 97 114 129 153 163 182	

J. H. Dawes, S. J. Jurgensen did not bat.

Bowling: Moss 10–1–33–1; Inness 3–0–28–0; Wise 10–1–43–1; McDonald 7–0–35–1; Lewis 10–0–33–2; White 10–0–32–0.

Victoria

M. T. G. Elliott st Seccombe b Law	89	(118)	
J. Moss b MacKenzie	47	(70)	L-b 3, w 5 8
B. J. Hodge not out	50	(62)	
A. B. McDonald c Seccombe b Hopes	17	(30)	(47 overs, 189 mins) (3 wkts) 215
D. J. Hussey not out	4	(2)	Fall: 102 165 211

B. R. Joseland, *C. L. White, †D. S. Berry, M. L. Lewis, M. W. H. Inness and A. B. Wise did not bat.

Bowling: Jurgensen 9–0–46–0; Hopes 7–0–36–1; Dawes 6–0–26–0; Simpson 10–0–31–0; MacKenzie 9–0–37–1; Perren 3–0–15–0; Law 3–0–21–1.

Umpires: R. G. Patterson and J. D. Ward.

VICTORIA v NEW SOUTH WALES

At Melbourne Cricket Ground, Melbourne, December 7, 2003. Match tied. *Toss:* Victoria. Victoria 2 pts, New South Wales 2 pts. *Competition debut:* L. A. Zammit.

Four wickets in seven balls of a hectic finale allowed Victoria to escape with a tie – the fourth in Australian domestic limited-overs history – after a couple of dreadful errors nearly cost them the match. Requiring six runs from three deliveries to pass the home team's seemingly inadequate 235, NSW were in trouble with the fast bowler Matthew Nicholson on strike. He took two to long-off, two more to deep mid-wicket, then drove the final ball just wide of Mathew Inness, the desperately diving bowler. Inness succeeded only in spraying the ball further away, but the captain Cameron White executed a cool pick-up-and-throw and Nicholson was caught short attempting the second winning run. White had earlier feared he might have lost the match for his team when he dropped the ice-cool Michael Bevan en route to a typically composed 72. The Bushrangers were also generous to Mark Waugh, who managed to slip through Matthew Elliott's fingers on 28. He was picked up eight runs later by a clever Brad Hodge catch on the mid-off boundary. Running around close to the rope Hodge took the ball just inside and, feeling himself lose balance, tossed it in the air, went over the rope and jumped back in time to snare it on the second attempt.

Man of the Match: M. G. Bevan.   *Attendance:* 3,574.

Victoria

M. T. G. Elliott c Bradstreet b Clarke	30	(33)	†P. J. Roach not out 14	(11)
J. Moss c Nicholson b Clark	10	(19)	M. L. Lewis not out 4	(9)
B. J. Hodge b Nicholson	47	(59)		
I. J. Harvey c Bradstreet b Clarke	9	(18)	B 1, l-b 4, w 6, n-b 1 12	
D. J. Hussey b Nicholson	19	(27)	———	
G. C. Rummans run out (Clarke)	53	(71)	(50 overs, 215 mins) (7 wkts) 235	
*C. L. White c and b Thornely	37	(54)	Fall: 15 51 64 106 121 211 215	

M. W. H. Inness, A. B. Wise did not bat.

Bowling: Lee 10–2–41–0; Clark 10–1–44–1; Nicholson 10–1–41–2; Clarke 7–0–37–2; Zammit 4–0–17–0; Bradstreet 5–0–29–0; Thornely 4–0–21–1.

New South Wales

D. J. Thornely c Harvey b Wise	11	(29)	B. Lee not out 0	(0)
P. A. Jaques lbw b Wise	41	(39)	M. J. Nicholson run out (White/Roach) 5	(3)
M. G. Bevan b Harvey	72	(108)		
M. J. Clarke c Elliott b Lewis	40	(58)	L-b 4, w 4 8	
*M. E. Waugh c Hodge b Lewis	36	(41)	———	
†B. J. Haddin c Lewis b Inness	22	(21)	(50 overs, 224 mins) (8 wkts) 235	
S. D. Bradstreet b Inness	0	(1)	Fall: 40 64 133 189 228 230 230 235	

S. R. Clark, L. A. Zammit did not bat.

Bowling: Harvey 10–0–34–1; Inness 9–1–46–2; Wise 5–0–31–2; Moss 10–1–30–0; Lewis 10–0–56–2; White 6–0–34–0.

Umpires: G. T. D. Morrow and A. J. Soulsby.

At WACA Ground, Perth, December 18, 2003. Day/night game. VICTORIA lost to WESTERN AUSTRALIA by 101 runs.

At Devonport Oval, Devonport, January 4, 2004. VICTORIA defeated TASMANIA by eight wickets.

VICTORIA v SOUTH AUSTRALIA

At Melbourne Cricket Ground, Melbourne, January 18, 2004. Victoria won by six runs. *Toss:* Victoria. Victoria 4 pts.

The all-rounder Ian Hewett, recovering from a mid-pitch collision and two dropped catches to claim three wickets in six balls, consigned SA to defeat in a match destined to be remembered as the last coached by David Hookes. Victoria batted first and posted a challenging 8 for 260, bolstered by brisk half-centuries to Jon Moss and Graeme Rummans, the two former Sydneysiders. Cameron White and Andrew McDonald, who intercepted Greg Blewett on 98, then bowled tightly in the crucial stages to restrict SA. It was Hewett who put the game out of reach, trapping Darren Lehmann lbw – though the batsman was far from happy with the decision – when eight runs were needed off the final three balls. Hookes's faith in his team remained firm throughout the match. They entered it, he later revealed, with the theme "win from any position", inspired by their massive Pura Cup run-chase against NSW a week earlier. After celebrating the win in the dressing room, Hookes and a handful of players headed out with Lehmann and the Redbacks coach Wayne Phillips to a St Kilda hotel. Later that night Hookes was punched outside the venue, sustaining injuries that resulted in his death the following day.

Man of the Match: G.S. Blewett. *Attendance:* 3,831.

Victoria

J. Moss c Manou b Cleary	59	(69)	
M.T.G. Elliott c Miller b Cleary	22	(33)	
B.J. Hodge c Lehmann b Harris	3	(11)	
D.J. Hussey c Manou b Tait	32	(46)	
G.C. Rummans c Blewett b Davison	51	(58)	
*C.L. White b Lehmann	21	(28)	
A.B. McDonald c Harris b Lehmann	28	(39)	

I.S.L. Hewett not out	15	(11)	
†P.J. Roach lbw b Tait	7	(10)	
B 1, l-b 4, w 12, n-b 5	22		
(50 overs, 204 mins) (8 wkts)	260		

A.B. Wise, S.M. Harwood did not bat.

Fall: 61 72 100 139 168 233 239 260

Bowling: Tait 10–1–57–2; Miller 9–0–52–0; Cleary 8–1–34–2; Harris 9–1–37–1; Lehmann 5–0–24–2; Davison 7–0–33–1; Blewett 2–0–18–0.

South Australia

J.M. Davison c Hodge b Harwood	8	(9)	
G.S. Blewett lbw b McDonald	98	(131)	
S.A. Deitz lbw b Wise	23	(34)	
M.J. Cosgrove b White	55	(64)	
*D.S. Lehmann lbw b Hewett	44	(43)	
C.J. Ferguson lbw b McDonald	6	(12)	
M.C. Miller c Hussey b Hewett	1	(3)	

†G.A. Manou not out	4	(4)	
M.F. Cleary c Rummans b Hewett	0	(1)	
R.J. Harris not out	0	(0)	
B 1, l-b 7, w 6, n-b 1	15		
(50 overs, 213 mins) (8 wkts)	254		

S.W. Tait did not bat.

Fall: 8 57 179 212 232 235 253 253

Bowling: Harwood 7.5–0–24–1; Moss 8–0–42–0; Wise 7–0–37–1; Hodge 0.1–0–0–0; Hewett 7–0–41–3; White 10–0–47–1; McDonald 10–0–55–2.

Umpires: G.T.D. Morrow and A.J. Soulsby.

At Adelaide Oval, Adelaide, January 30, 2004. Day/night game. VICTORIA defeated SOUTH AUSTRALIA by six runs.

VICTORIA v TASMANIA

At Melbourne Cricket Ground, Melbourne, February 14, 2004. Tasmania won by three wickets. *Toss:* Victoria. Victoria 4 pts.

This was the day Shane Warne returned to state cricket and forgot to appeal. In stifling conditions Warne showed most of his powers remained intact, but Victoria's surprise defeat all but dashed their hopes of making the final. Things unravelled from the moment Cameron White elected to bat, with the top three back in the rooms within half an hour. Shane Watson, back at the bowling crease after his recent back troubles, was dangerous early on a moist wicket as Victoria collapsed to 6 for 83. Andrew McDonald and a pugnacious Darren Berry, hitting five fours and two sixes, salvaged a semi-respectable score from the wreckage. But handy contributions from Michael Di Venuto, Watson and George Bailey ensured that Tasmania coasted to their only one-day victory of the summer. Warne's performance was the main positive for Victoria, even though he was twice smacked for 12 runs in an over, including a four and six in successive balls by Watson. Showing he had lost none of his theatricality, Warne took his first wicket – that of Dan Marsh, dubiously lbw – with his second ball back, despite an uncharacteristic decision not to appeal. A disbelieving Berry joked that perhaps

Warne, after 12 months on the sidelines, was unfamiliar with a new rule that the batsman must be given out if the ball hits his feet on the full.

Man of the Match: S. R. Watson.   *Attendance:* 1,720.

Victoria

J. Moss lbw b Griffith	9	(18)
M. T. G. Elliott c Marsh b Watson	11	(9)
B. J. Hodge c Doherty b Watson	3	(11)
D. J. Hussey c Di Venuto b Kremerskothen	25	(52)
G. C. Rummans c Clingeleffer b Butterworth	9	(23)
*C. L. White b Clingeleffer b Butterworth	12	(18)
A. B. McDonald c and b Kremerskothen	40	(73)
†D. S. Berry c Clingeleffer b Marsh	64	(63)
S. K. Warne c and b Kremerskothen	7	(12)
M. L. Lewis lbw b Butterworth	19	(16)
A. B. Wise not out	0	(1)
L-b 8, w 11	19	
(49.2 overs, 188 mins)	218	

Fall: 24 29 31 63 83 83
      179 191 214 218

Bowling: Griffith 10–1–50–1; Watson 6–1–15–2; Butterworth 9.2–1–33–3; Kremerskothen 10–3–35–3; Doherty 5–0–30–0; Marsh 5–0–32–1; Tubb 4–0–15–0.

Tasmania

M. J. Di Venuto run out (Hussey)	45	(45)
M. G. Dighton run out (Rummans)	5	(20)
L. R. Butterworth b Lewis	18	(22)
S. R. Watson c Elliott b Lewis	63	(71)
*D. J. Marsh lbw b Warne	5	(17)
G. J. Bailey not out	52	(73)
S. B. Tubb c Hussey b White	7	(11)
S. P. Kremerskothen b White	6	(9)
†S. G. Clingeleffer not out	11	(14)
L-b 6, w 1	7	
(47 overs, 200 mins) (7 wkts)	219	

X. J. Doherty, A. R. Griffith did not bat.

Fall: 30 75 75 90 184 195 206

Bowling: Wise 6–0–25–0; McDonald 7–0–35–0; Moss 4–0–23–0; Lewis 10–1–41–2; White 10–1–41–2; Warne 10–1–48–1.

Umpires: R. L. Parry and P. R. Reiffel.
TV Umpire: R. G. Patterson.

VICTORIA v WESTERN AUSTRALIA

At Melbourne Cricket Ground, Melbourne, February 21, 2004. Victoria won by two wickets. *Toss:* Victoria. Victoria 5 pts. *Competition debut:* B. A. Knowles.

John Taylor, the former Victorian, kept his old team's ultra-slim finals dream alive with a fumble at mid-off, allowing the Bushrangers to collect the two runs they needed to claim a bonus point. WA were sent in and lost four wickets inside the first 10 overs. Brad Knowles bowled quickly and impressively on debut, securing the crucial dismissal of Justin Langer. The spirit of cricket was tested late in the innings. Peter Worthington walked halfway to the dressing room believing he had been run out when Shane Warne got a finger to Marcus North's drive on its way to the stumps. But the third umpire Geoff Morrow ruled he was safe and Worthington returned. The visitors shrugged off the controversy to set a sizeable target, with Murray Goodwin and North posting fifties. But a Victorian win was never in serious doubt once Matthew Elliott and Jon Moss had combined for a century opening stand, and the bonus point was secured in the nick of time – on the last ball of the 40th over. It mattered naught. Victoria, having drawn level with Queensland, slipped behind them again the next day when the Bulls beat South Australia.

Man of the Match: B. A. Knowles.   *Attendance:* 2,265.

Western Australia

C. J. L. Rogers c Berry b Lewis	0	(5)	K. M. Harvey lbw b White	0	(2)
†R. J. Campbell c Rummans b McDonald	22	(15)	P. C. Worthington b Knowles	.26	(26)
*J. L. Langer c Elliott b Knowles	19	(29)	A. K. Heal not out	17	(20)
J. J. Taylor lbw b McDonald	0	(6)	L-b 7, w 13, n-b 1	21	
M. E. K. Hussey b Warne	28	(47)			
M. W. Goodwin lbw b White	64	(71)	(50 overs, 211 mins)　　(8 wkts)	251	
M. J. North not out	54	(80)	Fall: 2 45 47 47 109 167 167 218		

P. Wilson did not bat.

Bowling: Lewis 10–1–42–1; McDonald 9–1–51–2; Knowles 10–2–42–2; Warne 10–0–43–1; White 6–0–43–2; Moss 5–0–23–0.

Victoria

J. Moss c Hussey b Harvey	54	(62)	†D. S. Berry not out	9	(10)
M. T. G. Elliott c (sub) S. W. Meuleman			S. K. Warne c Goodwin b Harvey	2	(4)
b Hussey	72	(67)	B. A. Knowles not out	0	(0)
B. J. Hodge c Campbell b Worthington	52	(48)			
D. J. Hussey c Campbell b Heal	23	(22)	B 4, l-b 11, w 6, n-b 1	22	
G. C. Rummans c Wilson b Worthington	15	(19)			
*C. L. White b Wilson	3	(4)	(40 overs, 168 mins)　　(8 wkts)	252	
A. B. McDonald c Rogers b Worthington	0	(5)	Fall: 141 146 187 229 241 241 245 248		

M. L. Lewis did not bat.

Bowling: Taylor 4-0-25-0; Wilson 10–1–53–1; Worthington 7-0-45-3; Heal 7-0-45-1; North 3-0-20-0; Harvey 7-0-32-2; Hussey 2-0-17-1.

Umpires: I. H. Lock and J. D. Ward.
TV Umpire: G. T. D. Morrow.

VICTORIA DOMESTIC LIMITED-OVERS RESULTS

	First Game	M	Won	Lost	Drawn	Tied
v Tasmania	Nov 22, 1969	22	12	9	1	0
v Western Australia	Dec 30, 1969	33	6	25	2	0
v New Zealanders	Jan 1, 1970	2	1	1	0	0
v South Australia	Oct 18, 1970	30	19	10	0	1
v Queensland	Dec 5, 1971	26	11	14	1	0
v New South Wales	Dec 17, 1972	31	13	16	1	1
v Australian Capital Territory	Nov 23, 1997	3	1	2	0	0
Total		147	63	77	5	2

VICTORIA RECORDS

Highest score for:	139*	D. M. Jones v New South Wales at Sydney	1986-87
Highest score against:	150*	M. L. Hayden (Queensland) at Melbourne	1998-99
Best bowling for:	5-20	G. D. Watson v Western Australia at Melbourne	1969-70
Best bowling against:	5-15	D. L. Boyd (Western Australia) at Perth	1982-83
Highest total for:	7-293	v South Australia at Adelaide	2003-04
Highest total against:	5-310	by New South Wales at North Sydney	1991-92
Lowest total for:	51	v Queensland at Ballarat	2002-03
Lowest total against:	59	by Western Australia at Melbourne	1969-70

MOST RUNS

	M	I	NO	R	HS	100s	50s	Avge	S-R
B. J. Hodge	75	73	8	2,643	118*	6	16	40.66	73.62
M. T. G. Elliott	68	66	6	2,247	118*	6	12	37.45	70.44
D. M. Jones	55	52	10	2,122	139*	4	12	50.52	74.07
I. J. Harvey	61	56	4	1,061	72	0	6	20.40	82.38
J. M. Wiener	20	20	2	1,003	108*	1	10	55.72	66.52
D. S. Berry	83	63	21	767	64*	0	2	18.26	68.36
M. Klinger	25	25	4	591	80*	0	4	28.14	60.99
G. M. Watts	19	19	0	590	85	0	6	31.05	51.39
G. N. Yallop	24	24	2	586	91	0	3	26.64	68.50
J. Moss	30	25	2	507	64*	0	4	22.04	66.97

HIGHEST PARTNERSHIP FOR EACH WICKET

194	for 1st	M. T. G. Elliott and G. R. Vimpani, v New South Wales at North Sydney ..	1999-00
221	for 2nd	M. T. G. Elliott and B. J. Hodge, v Queensland at Brisbane	2003-04
227	for 3rd	B. J. Hodge and D. J. Hussey, v South Australia at Adelaide	2003-04
127	for 4th	G. N. Yallop and J. K. Moss, v Western Australia at Perth	1978-79
124*	for 5th	B. J. Hodge and S. A. J. Craig, v Australian Capital Territory at Canberra ..	1998-99
92	for 6th	B. J. Hodge and P. R. Reiffel, v New South Wales at North Sydney	1997-98
98*	for 7th	T. J. Laughlin and R. J. Bright, v New South Wales at Sydney	1976-77
73*	for 8th	A. M. Smith and A. I. C. Dodemaide, v Queensland at Melbourne	1996-97
73	for 9th	R. C. Jordon and R. K. Rowan, v South Australia at Adelaide	1970-71
30	for 10th	D. W. Fleming and D. J. Saker, v Western Australia at Melbourne	1995-96

MOST WICKETS

	M	Balls	Mdns	R	W	BB	5W/i	Avge	RPO
I. J. Harvey	61	2,563	24	1,909	70	5-34	1	27.27	4.47
D. W. Fleming	46	2,433	43	1,584	48	3-25	0	33.00	3.91
M. L. Lewis	37	1,770	29	1,342	46	4-41	0	29.17	4.55
P. R. Reiffel	40	1,844	35	1,201	37	4-14	0	32.46	3.91
S. K. Warne	24	1,265	17	941	37	5-35	1	25.43	4.46
A. I. C. Dodemaide	38	2,019	34	1,268	35	3-11	0	36.23	3.77
M. G. Hughes	30	1,523	26	1,147	33	4-34	0	34.76	4.52
I. S. L. Hewett	22	985	12	763	29	4-22	0	26.31	4.65
D. J. Saker	27	1,344	32	869	27	4-35	0	32.19	3.88
J. Moss	30	985	9	747	25	5-47	1	29.88	4.55

MOST DISMISSALS

	M	Ct	St	Total
D. S. Berry	83	100	27	127
M. G. D. Dimattina	18	16	2	18
R. D. Robinson	17	11	4	15
P. G. Sacristani	4	8	0	8
N. M. Carlyon	3	6	1	7

MOST CATCHES

B. J. Hodge	30 in 75 matches	J. D. Siddons	11 in 20 matches
D. M. Jones	29 in 55 matches	M. G. Hughes	10 in 30 matches
M. T. G. Elliott	28 in 68 matches	S. K. Warne	10 in 24 matches
I. J. Harvey	19 in 61 matches	M. L. Lewis	10 in 37 matches
P. R. Reiffel	12 in 40 matches	D. W. Fleming	9 in 46 matches

MOST APPEARANCES

83	D. S. Berry	1990-91 – 2003-04	40	P. R. Reiffel	1987-88 – 2000-01
75	B. J. Hodge	1993-94 – 2003-04	38	A. I. C. Dodemaide	1983-84 – 1997-98
68	M. T. G. Elliott	1992-93 – 2003-04	37	M. L. Lewis	1999-00 – 2003-04
61	I. J. Harvey	1993-94 – 2003-04	30	M. G. Hughes	1981-82 – 1994-95
55	D. M. Jones	1981-82 – 1997-98	30	J. Moss	2000-01 – 2003-04
46	D. W. Fleming	1988-89 – 2001-02	27	D. J. Saker	1994-95 – 1999-00

WA ING CUP RESULTS, 2003-04

Played 11: Won 7, Lost 3, Drawn 1. *Finished first.*

WA RUNSCORERS

	M	I	NO	R	HS	100s	50s	Avge	Ct/St	S-R
M. E. K. Hussey	9	8	1	426	106	1	4	60.86	6	89.68
M. J. North	11	9	5	387	84*	0	4	96.75	5	82.34
M. W. Goodwin	11	10	2	350	80*	0	3	43.75	7	90.91
J. L. Langer	9	8	0	318	115	2	0	39.75	7	77.75
C. J. L. Rogers	9	9	2	272	117*	1	1	38.86	3	74.52
R. J. Campbell	10	10	0	210	42	0	0	21.00	13	85.71
K. M. Harvey	9	6	2	140	53*	0	1	35.00	2	91.50
S. W. Meuleman	2	1	0	71	71	0	1	71.00	1	83.53
D. J. Wates	3	3	1	63	29*	0	0	31.50	2	74.12
P. C. Worthington . . .	7	4	3	57	30*	0	0	57.00	2	111.55
J. J. Taylor	7	4	1	34	34	0	0	11.33	0	97.14
G. B. Hogg	2	1	0	26	26	0	0	26.00	0	72.22
A. K. Heal	4	2	1	19	17*	0	0	19.00	1	67.86
S. E. Marsh	2	1	0	11	11	0	0	11.00	1	64.71
M. W. Clark	2	1	1	10	10*	0	0	–	3	52.63
P. Wilson	8	1	0	5	5	0	0	5.00	2	27.78
B. M. Edmondson . . .	2	1	1	2	2*	0	0	–	1	28.57
B. Casson	5	1	0	1	1	0	0	1.00	2	7.69
D. R. Martyn	1	1	0	1	1	0	0	1.00	0	11.11
A. C. Gilchrist	1	1	0	0	0	0	0	0.00	5	0.00
J. Angel	1	0	–	–	–	–	–	–	0	–
L. Ronchi	1	0	–	–	–	–	–	–	2	–
M. J. Thistle	2	0	–	–	–	–	–	–	0	–
C. D. Thorp	3	0	–	–	–	–	–	–	0	–

*Denotes not out

WA WICKET-TAKERS

	O	Mdns	R	W	BB	5W/i	Avge	RPO
K. M. Harvey	78.3	3	380	17	4-28	0	22.35	4.84
P. C. Worthington	57	2	309	12	3-45	0	25.75	5.42
J. J. Taylor	56	5	247	11	3-27	0	22.45	4.41
M. E. K. Hussey	27.3	0	202	7	2-38	0	28.86	7.35
P. Wilson	78	5	308	6	2-39	0	51.33	3.95
G. B. Hogg	17.2	0	56	4	3-21	0	14.00	3.23
M. W. Clark	17	1	85	4	2-42	0	21.25	5.00
A. K. Heal	37	1	193	4	2-34	0	48.25	5.22
M. J. Thistle	16.1	1	86	4	3-32	0	21.50	5.32
B. Casson	25	1	134	4	4-31	0	33.50	5.36
M. J. North	30	0	192	4	2-17	0	48.00	6.40
D. J. Wates	22	1	138	2	2-23	0	69.00	6.27
B. M. Edmondson	18	0	129	2	1-57	0	64.50	7.17
C. D. Thorp	28	3	140	1	1-53	0	140.00	5.00
J. Angel	5	0	38	0	–	0	–	7.60

WESTERN AUSTRALIA v SOUTH AUSTRALIA

At WACA Ground, Perth, October 24, 2003. Day/night game. Western Australia won by 99 runs. *Toss:* Western Australia. Western Australia 5 pts. *Competition debut:* A. Flower, M. J. Thistle.

Two balls was all it took for Michael Thistle to make an impact, as WA gambled on one of their least experienced attacks in years. His first ball of SA's innings was slashed by John Davison for four. His second had Davison, Canada's buccaneering hero of the 2003 World Cup, caught at gully. In his fourth over he dismissed the dangerous Greg Blewett, flashing to slip, and WA were well on the way to defending their imposing 5 for 293. Bowling downwind at sharp pace, Thistle finished with an impressive 3 for 32. Meanwhile Beau Casson, the highly promising chinaman bowler, harried the middle order with his controlled flight to secure the best figures of his brief career. Ordinarily, either performance might have been worthy of Man of the Match honours. But that award went to the rapidly maturing Mike Hussey, whose busy 61-ball innings set WA on the path to the fourth highest score at the WACA. The former Zimbabwe captain Andy Flower hit a poised run-a-ball fifty in his first appearance for his adopted state. Sadly, it was to prove the early peak of a season that promised significantly more than it delivered.

Match reports by JOHN TOWNSEND.
Man of the Match: M. E. K. Hussey.   *Attendance:* 2,958.

Western Australia

J. L. Langer c Manou b Rofe	11	(19)	M. J. North not out	25	(22)
†R. J. Campbell c Manou b Johnson	42	(65)			
C. J. L. Rogers run out (Cleary)	40	(52)	B 1, l-b 11, w 8	20	
*M. E. K. Hussey run out (Johnson)	67	(61)			
M. W. Goodwin c Flower b Johnson	58	(62)	(50 overs, 202 mins) (5 wkts)	293	
P. C. Worthington not out	30	(23)	Fall: 21 103 103 221 250		

B. Casson, C. D. Thorp, M. J. Thistle and J. Angel did not bat.

Bowling: Tait 10–0–55–0; Rofe 10–0–47–1; Cleary 10–1–42–0; Johnson 10–0–67–2; Davison 6–0–41–0; Higgs 3–0–24–0; Blewett 1–0–5–0.

South Australia

J. M. Davison c North b Thistle	4	(2)	M. F. Cleary c Hussey b Casson	0	(7)
*G. S. Blewett c Langer b Thistle	6	(25)	P. C. Rofe run out (Angel)	3	(10)
S. A. Deitz c Worthington b Casson	60	(78)	S. W. Tait not out	4	(11)
A. Flower c Campbell b Worthington	54	(54)			
M. A. Higgs b Casson	23	(29)	L-b 7, w 2, n-b 1	10	
C. J. Ferguson c Campbell b Worthington	4	(6)			
B. A. Johnson b Casson	11	(25)	(46.1 overs, 178 mins)	194	
†G. A. Manou c Campbell b Thistle	15	(32)	Fall: 4 20 122 142 146 168 173 175 187 194		

Bowling: Thistle 8.1–1–32–3; Thorp 10–2–42–0; Angel 5–0–38–0; Worthington 7–0–31–2; Casson 10–0–31–4; North 6–0–13–0.

Umpires: J. K. Brookes and A. R. Craig.

At North Sydney Oval, Sydney, November 2, 2003. WESTERN AUSTRALIA lost to NEW SOUTH WALES by four wickets (D/L method).

At Adelaide Oval, Adelaide, November 9, 2003. WESTERN AUSTRALIA defeated SOUTH AUSTRALIA by seven wickets.

WESTERN AUSTRALIA v TASMANIA

At WACA Ground, Perth, December 5, 2003. Day/night game. Western Australia won by three wickets. *Toss:* Tasmania. Western Australia 5 pts.

Boosted by the return of three vastly experienced one-day performers – Kade Harvey, Brad Hogg and Paul Wilson – WA produced their most workmanlike effort of the summer. Wilson was miserly, Harvey probing and Hogg, in his customary containing role in the last 20 overs of the innings, as frenetic as a spinner can be. Only the talented Shane Watson and the wicket-keeper Sean Clingeleffer resisted the attack for an extended period. The pair added 70 for the sixth wicket, the powerful Watson restricted to only four fours, as Tasmania struggled to keep the score at around four runs an over. WA's nerves were jangling when Ryan Campbell, Mike Hussey and Murray Goodwin departed in the space of 25 balls. But Marcus North, determined to consolidate his spot in the team in his fifth season, shepherded the all-rounders home. He hit 12 fours and a six in his best one-day innings.

Man of the Match: M. J. North.   *Attendance:* 3,722.

Tasmania

M. G. Dighton c North b Wilson	6 (9)	B. Geeves lbw b Harvey	0 (1)
M. J. Di Venuto c Campbell b Taylor	10 (11)	A. R. Griffith not out	3 (3)
J. Cox c Campbell b Worthington	7 (48)	G. J. Denton not out	2 (2)
T. R. Birt c Hussey b Taylor	2 (11)		
S. R. Watson c Goodwin b Worthington	63 (90)	L-b 3, w 3	6
*D. J. Marsh b Hogg	22 (27)		
†S. G. Clingeleffer b Harvey	48 (80)	(50 overs, 207 mins) (9 wkts) 193	
D. G. Wright c Worthington b Harvey	24 (22)	Fall: 10 16 20 38 73 143 181 182 189	

Bowling: Wilson 10–1–24–1; Taylor 10–2–32–2; Harvey 10–0–49–3; Worthington 10–1–50–2; Hogg 10–0–35–1.

Western Australia

C. J. L. Rogers c and b Denton	14 (18)	K. M. Harvey c Clingeleffer b Griffith	0 (3)
†R. J. Campbell c Dighton b Griffith	42 (42)	P. C. Worthington not out	0 (0)
M. J. North not out	75 (98)		
*M. E. K. Hussey lbw b Geeves	0 (4)	L-b 17, w 10	27
M. W. Goodwin c Marsh b Griffith	2 (6)		
S. E. Marsh c Birt b Wright	11 (17)	(36.2 overs, 165 mins) (7 wkts) 197	
G. B. Hogg b Denton	26 (36)	Fall: 49 82 89 100 120 188 193	

J. J. Taylor, P. Wilson did not bat.

Bowling: Wright 10–0–52–1; Denton 8.2–0–63–2; Geeves 6–0–19–1; Griffith 9–1–40–3; Marsh 3–2–6–0.

Umpires: B. Bennett and A. R. Craig.

WESTERN AUSTRALIA v VICTORIA

At WACA Ground, Perth, December 18, 2003. Day/night game. Western Australia won by 101 runs. *Toss:* Western Australia. Western Australia 5 pts.

Adam Gilchrist and Damien Martyn made their only, largely unmemorable, state appearances of the summer. Gilchrist poked the first ball of the match from Ian Harvey to mid-off and Martyn nudged a single before playing Jon Moss on. Justin Langer did not miss the chance to show up his Test team-mates, hitting 13 fours and a six as he eased to his fifth domestic one-day century. He added 104 with Murray Goodwin for the fourth wicket and another 86 with Marcus North for the fifth. North hammered 11 fours and a six in his hour and a half at the wicket, his unbeaten 84 occupying only 63 balls. The unflappable Matthew Elliott held firm while John Taylor and Peter Worthington gutted Victoria's top and middle order. They slid from 1 for 52 to 5 for 64 in five overs, making the outcome a formality despite some late resistance from Andrew McDonald. Brad Hogg cleaned up the tail and Gilchrist at last found something to cherish, pouching five catches for the first time in WA's colours.

Man of the Match: J. L. Langer.   *Attendance:* 4,627.

Western Australia

†A. C. Gilchrist c Joseland b Harvey ..	0	(1)	K. M. Harvey not out	21	(19)
R. J. Campbell run out (Hussey/Moss)	0	(3)			
*J. L. Langer c Moss b Joseland	115	(145)	L-b 3, w 6, n-b 1	10	
D. R. Martyn b Moss	1	(9)		—	
M. W. Goodwin c Roach b Wise	39	(66)	(50 overs, 207 mins) (5 wkts)	270	
M. J. North not out	84	(63)	Fall: 0 5 19 123 209		

G. B. Hogg, P. C. Worthington, J. J. Taylor and P. Wilson did not bat.

Bowling: Harvey 10–0–45–1; Moss 10–1–49–1; Wise 10–0–54–1; McDonald 7–2–31–0; Lewis 8–0–41–0; Hussey 2–0–23–0; Joseland 3–0–24–1.

Victoria

M. T. G. Elliott c Langer b Hogg	59	(106)	†P. J. Roach c Gilchrist b Hogg	1	(5)
*J. Moss c Goodwin b Taylor	5	(14)	M. L. Lewis c Campbell b Worthington	6	(20)
N. Jewell c Gilchrist b Taylor	11	(28)	A. B. Wise lbw b Hogg	0	(7)
I. J. Harvey c Harvey b Worthington ..	0	(6)			
D. J. Hussey c Gilchrist b Taylor	0	(3)	L–b 3, w 10	13	
G. C. Rummans c Gilchrist b Worthington	4	(10)			
B. R. Joseland c Gilchrist b Harvey ...	15	(16)	(44.2 overs, 188 mins)	169	
A. B. McDonald not out	55	(61)	Fall: 16 52 53 54 64 94 118 129 150 169		

Bowling: Taylor 10–2–27–3; Wilson 10–1–35–0; Worthington 10–0–47–3; Harvey 7–0–36–1; Hogg 7.2–0–21–3.

Umpires: B. Bennett and J. K. Brookes.

WESTERN AUSTRALIA v QUEENSLAND

At WACA Ground, Perth, January 9, 2004. Day/night game. Western Australia won by seven wickets. *Toss:* Queensland. Western Australia 4 pts.

Perhaps comprehending that his dream of playing one-day cricket for Australia again had finally evaporated, an unusually relaxed demeanour underpinned the most extraordinary limited-overs innings of Justin Langer's life. He crashed five fours and a six in his first dozen deliveries, as his bat found the ball without conscious effort. He scooted to his century in 74 deliveries – equalling the then domestic record, only for Stuart Law to break it a fortnight later. "For the first time in my life I'm not worrying about my technique but just going with the flow," said Langer. He faced 80 balls in all, hitting 16 fours and two sixes. Chris Rogers's maiden ton was ludicrously patient by comparison, yet still he hummed along at nearly a run a ball. Their efforts enabled WA to achieve the biggest successful run-chase in 35 years of Australian one-day matches, overhauling Queensland's 5 for 297 with a full 22 balls to spare. Previously no team had failed to defend more than 283. Jimmy Maher and Stuart Law had earlier hammered out a rapid opening stand of 75, before the stylish Martin Love crafted an effortless unbeaten hundred.

Man of the Match: J. L. Langer. *Attendance:* 5,097.

Queensland

*J.P. Maher c Campbell b Taylor	.... 35 (53)	†W. A. Seccombe not out	.... 4 (7)
S. G. Law c Harvey b Taylor	.... 39 (46)		
M. L. Love not out	...............110(100)	B 2, l-b 4, w 14, n-b 1 21	
C. T. Perren b Hussey	.... 35 (63)		
L. A. Carseldine c Campbell b Harvey	7 (9)	(50 overs, 203 mins) (5 wkts) 297	
J. R. Hopes run out (Rogers/Campbell)	46 (37)	Fall: 75 86 183 196 278	

A. A. Noffke, N. M. Hauritz, M. S. Kasprowicz and C. P. Simpson did not bat.

Bowling: Taylor 8–0–45–2; Wilson 10–0–40–0; Worthington 6–0–49–0; Casson 8–1–52–0; Harvey 9–0–42–1; North 2–0–22–0; Hussey 7–0–41–1.

Western Australia

C. J. L. Rogers not out	............117(125)		
†R. J. Campbell c Law b Kasprowicz	. 23 (20)	L-b 3, w 6 9	
J. J. Taylor c Perren b Noffke	.... 0 (5)		
*J. L. Langer c Seccombe b Kasprowicz	106 (80)	(46.2 overs, 185 mins) (3 wkts) 298	
M. W. Goodwin not out	.... 43 (54)	Fall: 41 42 202	

M. E. K. Hussey, K. M. Harvey, P. C. Worthington, B. Casson, M. J. North and P. Wilson did not bat.

Bowling: Kasprowicz 10–0–42–2; Noffke 10–0–78–1; Simpson 7.2–0–51–0; Hopes 10–0–59–0; Hauritz 8–0–64–0; Perren 1–0–1–0.

Umpires: J. K. Brookes and B. N. J. Oxenford.

WESTERN AUSTRALIA v NEW SOUTH WALES

At WACA Ground, Perth, January 21, 2004. Day/night game. Western Australia won by 23 runs. *Toss:* New South Wales. Western Australia 4 pts.

The latest chapter in the Waugh farewell tour ensured a record WACA crowd for a domestic one-dayer. But a warm and generous public valedictory did not guarantee a dream ending. Driven by a watchful Mike Hussey, a rare pinch-hitting cameo from John Taylor and a flurry of late hitting, WA were sent in to bat and scraped together 237. The NSW batsmen encountered similar difficulties grappling with the bounce and seam. The left-armer Michael Clark, making a rare appearance between crippling back injuries, put a clamp on the middle order. As if to demonstrate that his lumbar fractures were well and truly out of mind, however briefly, he completed a superb athletic catch on the fine-leg fence to dismiss Matthew Nicholson. "Welcome back to cricket," roared the ground announcer. Mostly, though, this was about farewells. Mark Waugh, unpredictable to the end, was promoted to his old spot of opener. He was out first ball, wafting at Darren Wates and smartly caught by Justin Langer at slip. For Steve Waugh, the light of battle did not die without a final flicker. He found himself cast in the familiar role of rescuer, walking out in the 10th over with NSW reeling at 3 for 31. He produced a typically stout-hearted display, lingering 89 minutes and giving his team a sniff of victory, before being adjudged caught behind off a feather-edge. He departed with a scowl, a shake of the head and a brisk march off centre-stage.

Man of the Match: M. E. K. Hussey. *Attendance:* 16,987.

Western Australia

C.J.L. Rogers b Clark 1 (18)
†R.J. Campbell c Haddin b Bracken . . 18 (15)
J.J. Taylor c Haddin b MacGill 34 (20)
M.E.K. Hussey c Thornely b Nicholson 69 (97)
*J.L. Langer b Lambert 21 (13)
M.W. Goodwin c Clark b Lambert . . . 0 (6)
M.J. North c and b MacGill 23 (39)
K.M. Harvey lbw b MacGill 23 (28)
D.J. Wates b O'Brien. 22 (33)

B. Casson c Nicholson b O'Brien . . . 1 (13)
M.W. Clark not out 10 (19)

L-b 7, w 8 15
—
(49.1 overs, 202 mins)   237
Fall: 12 24 68 95 108 164 196 210
213 237

Bowling: Bracken 8–1–34–1; Clark 8–0–38–1; MacGill 10–2–46–3; Lambert 10–0–43–2; Nicholson 10–1–55–1; O'Brien 3.1–1–14–2.

New South Wales

M.E. Waugh c Langer b Wates 0 (1)
†B.J. Haddin b Taylor 18 (38)
M.J. Nicholson c Clark b Wates 1 (10)
D.J. Thornely c Hussey b Clark 18 (55)
*S.C. Waugh c Campbell b Hussey . . 42 (58)
P.A. Jaques c Casson b Clark 8 (16)
A.W. O'Brien not out 62 (74)
G.M. Lambert c Clark b Harvey 1 (2)

N.W. Bracken run out (Hussey/Campbell)9 (8)
S.R. Clark c Campbell b Hussey 14 (16)
S.C.G. MacGill b Harvey 13 (16)

L-b 5, w 22, n-b 1 28
—
(46.2 overs, 199 mins)   214
Fall: 0 8 31 73 95 114 119 137 178 214

Bowling: Wates 10–1–23–2; Clark 8–0–42–2; Taylor 10–1–34–1; Harvey 8.2–0–34–2; Hussey 5–0–41–2; Casson 5–0–35–0.

Umpires: B. Bennett and G. Patterson.

At NTCA Ground, Launceston, February 1, 2004. WESTERN AUSTRALIA and TASMANIA no result.

At Brisbane Cricket Ground, Brisbane, February 13, 2004. Day/night game. WESTERN AUSTRALIA lost to QUEENSLAND by 207 runs.

At Melbourne Cricket Ground, Melbourne, February 21, 2004. WESTERN AUSTRALIA lost to VICTORIA by two wickets.

WA DOMESTIC LIMITED-OVERS RESULTS

	First Game	M	Won	Lost	Drawn	Tied
v South Australia	Nov 22, 1969	35	23	12	0	0
v Victoria	Dec 30, 1969	33	25	6	2	0
v Tasmania	Nov 4, 1970	27	21	5	1	0
v New Zealanders	Jan 31, 1971	3	2	1	0	0
v Queensland	Feb 6, 1971	32	16	14	2	0
v New South Wales	Nov 27, 1971	35	17	17	0	1
v Australian Capital Territory . .	Jan 2, 1998	3	3	0	0	0
Total		168	107	55	5	1

WA RECORDS

Highest score for:	167	M. W. Goodwin v New South Wales at Perth	2000-01
Highest score against:	187	J. P. Maher (Queensland) at Brisbane	2003-04
Best bowling for:	5-15	D. L. Boyd v Victoria at Perth	1982-83
Best bowling against:	5-23	R. J. McCurdy (South Australia) at Adelaide	1984-85
Highest total for:	5-325	v New South Wales at Perth	2000-01
Highest total against:	4-405	by Queensland at Brisbane	2003-04
Lowest total for:	59	v Victoria at Melbourne	1969-70
Lowest total against:	62	by Queensland at Perth	1976-77

MOST RUNS

	M	I	NO	R	HS	100s	50s	Avge	S-R
J. L. Langer	78	74	6	2,815	146	6	19	41.40	69.08
M. E. K. Hussey	65	61	10	2,220	106	3	17	43.53	75.98
T. M. Moody	75	71	12	2,004	102*	2	14	33.97	72.22
D. R. Martyn	53	50	7	1,880	140	3	13	43.72	73.90
G. R. Marsh	38	37	7	1,596	110	3	12	53.20	62.30
R. J. Campbell	69	67	1	1,464	108	1	6	22.18	85.12
M. W. Goodwin	40	36	7	1,251	167	1	9	43.14	86.04
S. M. Katich	38	37	3	1,178	118	2	8	34.65	71.31
M. R. J. Veletta	42	39	8	1,077	105*	1	8	34.74	62.18
A. C. Gilchrist	36	33	3	980	115	1	7	32.67	87.34

HIGHEST PARTNERSHIP FOR EACH WICKET

171	for 1st	G. R. Marsh and M. W. McPhee, v Queensland at Perth		1990-91
188*	for 2nd	J. L. Langer and D. R. Martyn, v Victoria at Melbourne		1997-98
257	for 3rd	M. W. Goodwin and M. E. K. Hussey, v New South Wales at Perth		2000-01
167	for 4th	M. E. K. Hussey and S. M. Katich, v Victoria at Perth		2001-02
129	for 5th	J. L. Langer and W. S. Andrews, v Queensland at Brisbane		1992-93
173	for 6th	M. E. K. Hussey and G. B. Hogg, v Victoria at Melbourne		1999-00
111*	for 7th	R. W. Marsh and B. Yardley, v New South Wales at Sydney		1973-74
106*	for 8th	A. C. Gilchrist and B. P. Julian, v New South Wales at Sydney		1995-96
57	for 9th	D. R. Martyn and B. P. Julian, v Queensland at Brisbane		1997-98
43	for 10th	P. C. Worthington and M. W. Clark, v New South Wales at Perth		2002-03

MOST WICKETS

	M	Balls	Mdns	R	W	BB	5Wi	Avge	RPO
J. Angel	74	3,686	52	2,525	94	5-16	2	26.46	4.11
K. M. Harvey	70	2,996	30	2,388	87	4-8	0	27.45	4.78
T. M. Moody	75	3,205	41	2,131	70	4-30	0	30.40	3.99
B. P. Julian	54	2,318	19	1,779	59	4-41	0	30.15	4.60
K. H. MacLeay	38	1,896	32	1,165	53	5-30	1	21.98	3.69
D. K. Lillee	26	1,505	32	766	48	4-21	0	15.96	3.05
B. A. Williams	26	1,319	14	970	43	4-29	0	22.56	4.41
G. B. Hogg	59	1,410	4	1,167	43	4-50	0	27.14	4.97
T. M. Alderman	35	1,938	34	1,169	40	4-14	0	29.23	3.62
J. Stewart	32	1,564	9	1,117	36	4-34	0	31.03	4.29

MOST DISMISSALS

	M	Ct	St	Total
R. J. Campbell	46	80	6	86
A. C. Gilchrist	36	64	6	70
R. W. Marsh	33	50	1	51
T. J. Zoehrer	35	40	4	44
M. J. Cox	5	10	0	10

MOST CATCHES

M. E. K. Hussey	40 in 65 matches	M. R. J. Veletta	17 in 40 matches
J. L. Langer	34 in 78 matches	B. P. Julian	16 in 54 matches
G. B. Hogg	27 in 59 matches	D. R. Martyn	16 in 53 matches
T. M. Moody	27 in 75 matches	R. J. Inverarity	14 in 19 matches
G. R. Marsh	20 in 38 matches		

MOST APPEARANCES

78	J. L. Langer	1991-92 – 2003-04	64	M. E. K. Hussey	1996-97 – 2003-04
75	T. M. Moody	1985-86 – 2000-01	59	G. B. Hogg	1993-94 – 2003-04
74	J. Angel	1992-93 – 2003-04	54	B. J. Julian	1991-92 – 2000-01
70	K. M. Harvey	1994-95 – 2003-04	53	D. R. Martyn	1991-92 – 2003-04
69	R. J. Campbell	1992-93 – 2003-04	43	M. R. J. Veletta	1983-84 – 1994-95

Australian Cricket Academy, 2003-04

by DAMIEN FLEMING

At the age of 15, after a fruitful and largely trouble-free upbringing, the Australian Cricket Academy packed its bags and moved out of home in 2003-04. The relocation from Adelaide to Brisbane was the first step towards the establishment of Cricket Australia's Centre of Excellence, expected to be fully operational in the next two or three years. Based at Allan Border Field in Albion, it consists of four core departments: a player development unit; a sports science and medicine unit; an information resource centre; and a coaching, umpiring, administration and curator unit.

Other changes were also afoot. Long-time coaches Wayne Phillips and Troy Cooley accepted positions with South Australia and England respectively, and were replaced by Damien Fleming and John Harmer, the former England women's coach. The Academy now takes on 22 scholars a year, rather than an elite dozen or so. The programme is much shorter, running from April to August, incorporating two six-week blocks and culminating in a three-week assimilation tour of India. The first block is tailored to encompass technical, skill and physical development. In the second block scholars put what they have learned into practice in simulated game scenarios.

The standout player among last year's batch of scholars was South Australia's Shaun Tait, a big fast bowler who swings the new ball out, the old ball in and was rewarded with selection in the Australian Test squad against Sri Lanka. At 21, his pace is almost in the express range and he will only get quicker with experience. Tait is a real slinger of the ball, making it difficult for batsmen to pick up the ball in flight. He is working on becoming more efficient in his run-up and more compact in his gather. A laid-back character, he listens closely and works hard.

His state team-mate Mark Cleary is more of a hit-the-deck type than a swing bowler. His explosive delivery action gives him good bounce and pace, although he can sometimes get into trouble if he jumps too close to the stumps. Cleary reads the game particularly well and might be one of the few fast-bowling captains in later life. As with a couple of other South Australians, Callum Ferguson and Trent Kelly, a deceptively hard work ethic lurks beyond his rock-star looks.

Kelly was probably the most popular player among the group. He bowls outswingers at a fastish medium, and is working to develop more variety in his armoury. He can also hustle as a batsman when on song, and was a budding footballer before deciding to channel his energies into cricket. Ferguson, a right-hand batsman, continued to blossom in his second year with the Academy despite injuring his knee in a warm-up game for the Under-19 World Cup and being sent home. Mature beyond his years, he is another player who has the makings of a future captain.

Two other Academy scholars who broke through at first-class level were Western Australia's Scott Meuleman and Queensland's Aaron Nye. Meuleman, the son and grandson of former WA batsmen, is a determined individual who likes to score square of the wicket. Nye, a right-hand batsman and off-spin bowler, lacks nothing in confidence. Once he matures and learns to be patient at the crease until well set, he should start amassing big scores.

Another player who made his interstate debut was Luke Butterworth, the tall Tasmanian all-rounder. Butterworth bowls outswingers from a side-on position, but has a habit of kicking out with his back foot and taking the ball behind his head. If he can get his bowling arm and feet jumping to the target he will both add a few yards and become more reliable in his direction. He is a relaxed but competitive individual, whether with a cricket ball or football.

The scholars for 2003 were: Luke Butterworth (Tas), Daniel Christian (NSW), Mark Cleary (S Aust), Adam Crosthwaite (Vic), Chris Duval (S Aust), Callum Ferguson (S Aust), Mathew Gale (Vic), Stewart Heaney (ACT), Ben Hilfenhaus (Tas), Matthew Innes (Vic), Shane Jones (Vic), Trent Kelly (S Aust), Jason Krejza (NSW), Nick Kruger (Qld), Rhett Lockyear (NSW), Steven Magoffin (Qld), Scott Meuleman (W Aust), Aaron Nye (Qld), Tim Paine (Tas), Luke Ronchi (W Aust), Shaun Tait (S Aust), Callum Thorpe (W Aust), Simon Williams (NSW), Peter Worthington (W Aust).

Shane Watson, the Australian one-day all-rounder, was the first of a new category of cricketers – called "special needs" players – to spend time at the Academy last summer. The idea is that the states can send a player to the Academy to work on specific skills. In Watson's case, he worked mainly on building up his stability as part of his rehabilitation from back stress fractures. Towards the end of the summer he returned to the bowling crease, at state and international level, with a remodelled bowling action.

Twelve of the players flew to India in July-August 2003, a journey repeated in 2004, to take part in the KSCA All-India Invitation Tournament in Bangalore. The Academy side were eliminated from the competition after their two one-day matches but stayed on for an assortment of one- and two-day games. The aim of the trip was to expose scholars to the challenges of the subcontinent, to identify those players who have the qualities to succeed there, and to introduce them to a variety of cultural and social experiences. The aim of the strategic reforms that have transformed the Academy is to ensure that its initiatives are cutting-edge and to maintain Australia's position as one of the leading cricket nations.

Damien Fleming, a swing bowler, took 75 wickets in 20 Tests for Australia from 1994 to 2001. He is now a coach at the Centre of Excellence.

KSCA MRF TROPHY, 2003-04

Australian Cricket Academy Touring Squad: P.C. Worthington (*captain*) (W Aust), A.C. Crosthwaite (Vic), C.J. Duval (S Aust), C.J. Ferguson (S Aust), M.L. Innes (Vic), S.M. Jones (Vic), T.P. Kelly (S Aust), R.J.G. Lockyear (Tas), A.J. Nye (Qld), S.J. Magoffin (Qld), S.W. Meuleman (W Aust), L. Ronchi (W Aust).

RAILWAY SPORTS PROMOTION BOARD XI
v AUSTRALIAN CRICKET ACADEMY

At KSCA Palace Ground (1), July 31, August 1, 2003. *Toss:* Australian Cricket Academy. Match drawn. Australian Cricket Academy 9 dec 363 (S.W. Meuleman 56, M.L. Innes 52, R.J.G. Lockyear 110, C.J. Ferguson 29, P.C. Worthington 42, L. Ronchi 22; J.P. Yadav 2-50, S.R. Saxena 2-48, Y. Goud 2-60, M. Vinod 2-25); Railway Sports Promotion Board XI 6 for 364 (R. Rai 125, B.J. Thakar 32, J.P. Yadav 119, A.A. Pagnis 46*; S.M. Jones 2-69).

OIL & NATURAL GAS CORPORATION XI
v AUSTRALIAN CRICKET ACADEMY

At KSCA Palace Ground (2), August 4, 5, 2003. *Toss:* Australian Cricket Academy. Match drawn. Oil & Natural Gas Corporation XI 292 (S. Sharma 75, M. Manhas 38, A. Jadeja 28, A. Sharma 38, A. Ratra 41; S.J. Magoffin 4-38, T.P. Kelly 4-35); Australian Cricket Academy 222 (S.W. Meuleman 22, M.L. Innes 26, R.J.G. Lockyear 28, C.J. Ferguson 31, S.J. Magoffin 43, S.M. Jones 21*; J. Singh 2-28, A. Uniyal 3-46, S. Singh 3-76, R. Sanghui 2-51).

Cricket Australia Cup, 2003-04

by KEN PIESSE

The familiar figure at first slip started to do some stretching exercises and the Junction Oval press box suddenly emptied. A procession of cricket writers, TV reporters and photographers trailed down the creaky old wooden stairs of the Blackie-Ironmonger Stand to obtain a more informed view from directly behind the bowler's arm. It wasn't just any arm, mind you. It was Shane Warne's. And this, his drug-ban finally over, was his first serious bowl in 12 months.

For a state 2nd XI match, between Victoria and the Queensland Academy of Sport, an extraordinarily large crowd had assembled. Despite ashen skies and a lengthy rain delay, as many as 800 people had stayed on at this historic venue, not far from the seaside, and home to St Kilda Cricket Club since 1856. It was standing room only behind the scorecard at the northern end, the journos gathered five deep, all eyes trained on one man. Apart from one secret practice session earlier in the week, this was Warne's first centre-wicket appearance since the 2003 World Cup trials in Johannesburg.

It was 4.38 p.m. on February 11, 2004. Warne handed his cap to the umpire Paul Reiffel with a smile, later saying he did not know whether to call his old team-mate 'Paul', 'Pistol' or 'Chopper'. Even the ice-cream vendor paused as Warne started his familiar walk-in steps. He began with a near-wide down the leg side, which so surprised the keeper Peter Roach that he fumbled and it went behind him for a bye. Warne smiled again and landed the next five balls bang on line, each of them met with a cautious dead bat from Queensland's captain Aaron Nye.

Warne bowled 16 consecutive overs that evening, exhibiting little of his famous side-spin but a hint of drift and an immaculate line. Chris Simpson, looking for a story to tell his grandkids, smacked one ball from Warne over the mid-wicket fence to go from 94 to 100. The rest were mostly defended.

His first wicket came in his 10th over, Nye lashing at a slider and bottom-edging it to Roach. Two overs later Steve Farrell was leg-before and it was as if Warne had never been away. Of his 96 balls, 92 had been virtually spot-on. Two were long-hops, one was over-pitched and there was that widish one first-up. "It was like Christmas Day as a kid playing again," said Warne, with that trademark wide smile of his.

Apart from being a stepping stone for Australia's young fringe talents, the 2003-04 Cricket Australia Cup was also something of a comeback trail for Australia's old returning legends. Glenn McGrath's route back to competitive cricket after ankle surgery came via the New South Wales 2nd XI. His comeback game, attracting rather less feverish scrutiny than Warne's, was against Victoria at the MCG. He took 2 for 26 and 4 for 30, winning praise from the Victorian opener Jason Arnberger for extracting bounce and hitting the seam "almost every ball" on an otherwise innocuous wicket.

New South Wales's nine-wicket victory in that match was enough to clinch the title for them. They finished with four outright wins and a draw from their six games. South Australia came second, Queensland third and Australian Capital Territory fourth.

Among the less ancient brigade, the standout individual performance was the SA teenager Mark Cosgrove's 260 against the ACT at Adelaide Oval No. 2. A jaw-dropping 502 runs were hammered on the second day, with Cosgrove and Callum Ferguson sharing a fourth-wicket stand of 371. Ferguson batted with rare polish for 158 while Cosgrove, a left-hander built along expansive lines, was expansive in his strokeplay too. While the Adelaide No. 2 ground is noted for its short square boundaries, straight-hit sixes are a rarity. Cosgrove lifted four of them in all, to go with his 33 fours.

Another South Australian, Shaun Tait, accomplished the rare trick of starting the season in the state 2nd XI and finishing it in the Australian Test squad. On one dramatic morning in October he and Paul Rofe had the visiting Victorian batsmen tottering at 3 for 8, before they eventually recovered to win by 106 runs. The competition's leading wicket-taker was Darren McNees, the ACT medium-pacer, whose 26 wickets earned him a spot in an Australian development squad that toured India during the winter. McNees's opening partner, Evan Kellar, was second on the list with 23 victims.

But it was batsmen who dominated for the most part. A handful of fringe players became Pura Cup regulars on the back of some monumental mastery in the 2nd XI: Victoria's David Hussey averaged 187 in two matches; his team-mate Matthew Mott 100 in two; and NSW's Dominic Thornely 92 in three. There were one or two high-profile strugglers too. The dynamic young Western Australian batsman Shaun Marsh, relegated to the 2nd XI to find form, averaged only 17 in his four games.

CRICKET AUSTRALIA CUP POINTS TABLE, 2003-04

	Played	WO	WI	D	LI	LO	T	Points	Quotient
New South Wales Second XI ..	6	4	0	1	0	1	0	24	1.447
South Australia Second XI	6	3	1	0	0	2	0	20	1.334
Queensland Academy	6	3	0	0	1	0	0	18	0.966
Australian Capital Territory ...	6	3	0	0	0	3	0	18	0.795
Victoria Second XI	6	2	1	0	0	3	0	16	1.087
Western Australia Second XI ..	6	1	1	1	1	2	0	8	0.855
Tasmania Second XI	6	1	0	0	1	4	0	6	0.745

Quotient equals runs per wicket scored divided by runs per wicket conceded.

MOST RUNS

	M	I	NO	R	HS	100s	50s	Avge	S-R
A. J. Nye (Qld)	6	11	0	534	140	1	3	48.55	51.30
M. J. Cosgrove (S Aust)	3	5	0	485	260	1	2	97.00	76.74
C. J. Ferguson (S Aust)	5	9	1	394	158	2	1	49.25	63.86
S. B. Tubb (Tas)	5	10	2	385	96	0	3	48.13	67.31
B. P. Cameron (S Aust).............	5	8	1	371	132	1	2	53.00	66.25
D. J. Thornely (NSW).............	3	5	1	371	158	2	0	92.75	64.41
D. G. Dawson (Tas)...............	6	12	1	370	101*	1	2	33.64	35.20
A. G. Rhynehart (ACT).............	6	12	1	366	93	0	3	33.27	68.16
B. R. Joseland (Vic)	4	6	1	354	139*	1	2	70.80	63.44
S. P. Heaney (ACT)................	6	11	2	354	160*	1	2	39.33	42.60
S. P. Kremerskothen (Tas)	4	8	0	340	157	2	0	42.50	57.53
A. W. O'Brien (NSW)	5	8	1	336	119	1	1	48.00	96.83
R. J. G. Lockyear (Tas)	6	11	1	326	87	0	2	32.60	43.47
C. R. A. McLeod (ACT)	6	10	2	325	73*	0	3	40.63	51.67
C. P. Simpson (Qld)	3	6	0	324	118	1	3	54.00	64.67
R. A. Broad (Qld)	5	8	1	316	143	2	0	45.14	53.38
C. A. Philipson (Qld)	4	7	0	310	109	1	2	44.29	60.31
M. P. Mott (Vic)	2	4	1	302	114	1	2	100.67	60.16
S. W. Meuleman (W Aust)	4	8	0	301	79	0	3	37.63	55.84
K. M. Harvey (W Aust).............	3	6	0	300	89	0	3	50.00	51.90

MOST WICKETS

	O	Mdns	R	W	BB	5W/i	10W/m	Avge	S-R
D. A. McNees (ACT)	202.4	51	691	26	5-63	1	0	26.58	46.77
E. Kellar (ACT)	221.2	61	613	23	5-18	2	0	26.65	57.74
D. A. Nash (NSW)	126	37	349	18	4-35	0	0	19.39	42.00
R. J. Harris (S Aust)	117.5	25	415	17	5-46	1	0	24.41	41.59
D. J. Cullen (S Aust)	165.1	38	507	17	5-97	1	0	29.82	58.29
A. C. Bird (NSW)	83.2	19	268	14	4-34	0	0	19.14	35.71
A. C. L. James (W Aust)	140	26	540	14	3-23	0	0	38.57	60.00
M. A. Hatton (ACT)	182	36	579	14	4-73	0	0	41.36	78.00
M. A. Cameron (NSW)	90.5	23	258	13	4-32	0	0	19.85	41.92
L. A. Zammit (NSW)	116	32	389	13	3-45	0	0	29.92	53.54
S. G. Howman (W Aust)	65.5	23	166	12	6-36	1	0	13.83	32.92
B. D. Harrop (Vic)	63	11	173	12	5-24	1	0	14.42	31.50
C. D. Thorp (W Aust)	115.3	29	306	12	4-96	0	0	25.50	57.75
A. M. Staunton (S Aust)	77	9	309	12	3-38	0	0	25.75	38.50
G. M. Lambert (NSW)	108.3	21	366	12	5-75	1	0	30.50	54.25
S. J. Magoffin (Qld)	138.2	36	410	12	4-63	0	0	34.17	69.17
A. R. Griffith (Tas)	39.1	15	92	11	6-45	2	1	8.36	21.36
G. J. Denton (Tas)	39	12	149	11	6-84	2	1	13.55	21.27
T. P. Kelly (S Aust)	85.5	12	296	11	4-25	0	0	26.91	46.82
A. W. Polkinghorne (Tas)	104.2	27	342	11	4-69	0	0	31.09	56.91
S. J. Karppinen (ACT)	113	33	343	11	3-69	0	0	31.18	61.64
L. R. Butterworth (Tas)	110	29	369	11	3-64	0	0	33.55	60.00
S. J. Jurgensen (Qld)	138	41	370	11	4-79	0	0	33.64	75.27
G. J. Sullivan (Qld)	93	12	416	11	3-13	0	0	37.82	50.73

SOUTH AUSTRALIA SECOND XI v VICTORIA SECOND XI

At Adelaide Oval No 2, Adelaide, October 7, 8, 9, 10, 2003. Victoria Second XI won by 106 runs. *Toss:* South Australia Second XI.

Close of play: First day, South Australia Second XI (1) 1-10 (Deitz 10, Davies 0); Second day, Victoria Second XI (2) 5-163 (Klinger 6, Hussey 20); Third day, South Australia Second XI (2) 3-154 (Vaughan 15, Cosgrove 11).

Victoria Second XI

N. Jewell c Johnson b Rofe	0	– (2) lbw b Rofe	13
L. G. L. Buchanan c Cosgrove b Tait	5	– (1) c Deitz b Rofe	0
G. C. Rummans lbw b Tait	0	– lbw b Kelly	31
A. B. McDonald b Cullen	76	– run out (Kelly)	49
B. R. Joseland b Rofe	83	– lbw b Johnson	28
M. Klinger c Cameron b Cullen	0	– b Johnson	34
*C. L. White c Rofe b Duval	59	– (8) c Deitz b Kelly	87
T. H. Welsford c Kelly b Rofe	51	– (9) c Kelly b Cullen	3
†A. J. Crosthwaite c Ferguson b Kelly	24	– (10) not out	22
B. D. Harrop not out	0	– (11) c Deitz b Cullen	25
W. N. Carr b Rofe	0		
D. J. Hussey (did not bat)		– (7) c Deitz b Rofe	20
L-b 4, w 1, n-b 10	15	B 4, l-b 9, w 1, n-b 11	25
(78.5 overs, 322 mins)	313	(96.5 overs, 403 mins)	337

Fall: 0 2 8 133 143 207 265 312
312 313

Fall: 0 32 68 133 133 163
239 252 291 337

Bowling: First Innings—Rofe 15.5-3-50-4; Tait 12-2-56-2; Duval 10-0-57-1; Kelly 14-1-40-1; Cullen 23-6-89-2; Johnson 4-1-17-0. *Second Innings*—Rofe 23-9-48-3; Tait 23-6-91-0; Duval 13-5-47-0; Kelly 13-2-49-2; Cullen 16.5-2-60-2; Johnson 8-1-29-2.

South Australia Second XI

†S. A. Deitz lbw b Harrop	19	– (2) c Klinger b Joseland	61
B. A. Johnson c Crosthwaite b Harrop	0	– (1) c Crosthwaite b Harrop	3
*C. J. Davies c Klinger b Carr	1	– c Hussey b White	53
J. M. Vaughan c Jewell b Harrop	12	– lbw b Harrop	50
M. J. Cosgrove c McDonald b White	44	– c Rummans b McDonald	71
C. J. Ferguson c Crosthwaite b Harrop	100	– lbw b White	4
B. P. Cameron lbw b White	19	– lbw b Carr	9
T. P. Kelly c and b White	7	– b Harrop	11
C. J. Duval lbw b White	0	– c Klinger b McDonald	6
D. J. Cullen b Harrop	1	– lbw b White	13
P. C. Rofe not out	11	– not out	19
B 1, l-b 7, n-b 6	14	B 4, l-b 7, w 1, n-b 4	16
(56 overs, 220 mins)	228	(105.1 overs, 396 mins)	316

Fall: 10 13 32 41 108 166 195 199
　　208 228

Fall: 22 122 133 222 229 258
　　268 280 288 316

S. W. Tait did not bat.

Bowling: *First Innings*—Carr 14–2–56–1; Harrop 11–4–24–5; McDonald 6–1–34–0; White 17–3–60–4; Welsford 3–0–17–0; Hussey 5–1–29–0. *Second Innings*—Harrop 21–3–64–3; Welsford 8–2–30–0; McDonald 28–9–69–2; Carr 17–3–45–1; White 27.1–4–88–3; Joseland 2–1–2–1; Hussey 2–0–7–0.

Umpires: A. Collins and A. Willoughby.

QUEENSLAND ACADEMY OF SPORT v NEW SOUTH WALES SECOND XI

At Allan Border Field, Albion, October 13, 14, 15, 2003. New South Wales Second XI won by an innings and 60 runs. *Toss:* Queensland Academy of Sport.

Close of play: First day, New South Wales (1) 2-165 (Phelps 79, Maraziotis 39); Second day, Queensland Academy of Sport (2) 2-92 (Nye 2, Simpson 1).

Queensland Academy of Sport

D. M. Payne lbw b Bracken	14	– lbw b Zammit	70
B. P. Nash b Nash	3	– c Nicholson b Zammit	16
A. J. Nye c Lambert b Bracken	0	– b Clark	13
C. P. Simpson c Phelps b Bollinger	13	– lbw b Nicholson	50
S. J. Farrell lbw b Bracken	8	– b Nicholson	70
C. A. Philipson c Phelps b Zammit	52	– c O'Brien b Nicholson	7
†C. D. Hartley lbw b Nash	8	– c Pilon b Nicholson	6
*N. M. Hauritz c O'Brien b Bollinger	17	– b Nicholson	0
R. N. Le Loux c Lambert b Clark	0	– not out	12
M. G. Johnson not out	5	– st Pilon b O'Brien	4
D. R. MacKenzie c Zammit b Bollinger	9	– c Maraziotis b Lambert	16
B 1, l-b 2, n-b 7	10	B 1, l-b 3, w 1, n-b 7	12
(55 overs, 223 mins)	139	(64 overs, 268 mins)	276

Fall: 19 19 30 38 54 88 114 117
　　128 139

Fall: 87 90 116 216 228 234 234
　　241 255 276

S. J. Jurgensen did not bat.

Bowling: *First Innings*—Nash 11–4–25–2; Bracken 14–6–33–3; Clark 12–3–24–1; Bollinger 8–1–26–3; Zammit 10–1–28–1. *Second Innings*—Nicholson 14–4–73–5; Nash 10–3–41–0; Clark 11–5–22–1; Bollinger 1–0–18–0; Zammit 17–4–70–2; O'Brien 8–1–29–1; Lambert 3–0–19–1.

New South Wales Second XI

*M. J. Phelps c Hartley b Johnson	122	D. A. Nash not out	51
P. A. Jaques c Hartley b MacKenzie	30	M. J. Nicholson b Hauritz	0
G. M. Lambert c MacKenzie b Johnson	10		
P. Maraziotis c and b Hauritz	191	L-b 5, n-b 5	10
A. W. O'Brien c and b Le Loux	5		
D. J. Thornely c Hauritz b Nye	20	(120.3 overs, 417 mins) (8 wkts dec)	475
†N. S. Pilon c Farrell b Hauritz	36	Fall: 42 73 256 280 368 394 475 475	

S. R. Clark, L. A. Zammit, D. Bollinger, M. J. Nicholson and N. W. Bracken did not bat.

Bowling: Johnson 21–4–98–2; Jurgensen 14–4–53–0; MacKenzie 23–4–101–1; Hauritz 30.3–6–87–3; Philipson 3–0–19–0; Le Loux 14–2–53–1; Simpson 8–0–36–0; Nye 7–0–23–1.

Umpires: N. S. McNamara and T. P. Laycock.

WESTERN AUSTRALIA SECOND XI v VICTORIA SECOND XI

At Richardson Park, Perth, October 13, 14, 15, 16, 2003. Match drawn. *Toss:* Western Australia Second XI.

Close of play: First day, Victoria Second XI (1) 0-18 (Rummans 10, Mott 8); Second day, Western Australia Second XI (1) 0-5 (Rogers 9, Mott 15); Third day, Victoria Second XI (2) 0-28 (Rummans 9, Mott 15).

Victoria Second XI

G. C. Rummans c Ronchi b Taylor	14	– c Casson b Taylor	9
M. P. Mott c North b Casson	40	– c Marsh b North	114
M. Klinger c Ronchi b James	68	– b Casson	50
D. J. Hussey not out	167		
*A. B. McDonald lbw b Thorp	71		
L. G. L. Buchanan not out	31	– (4) c Rogers b North	35
†P. J. Roach (did not bat)		– (5) not out	15
T. H. Welsford (did not bat)		– (6) not out	2
L-b 5, n-b 4	9	B 1, l-b 2, n-b 5	8
(100.5 overs, 393 mins) (4 wkts dec)	400	(56 overs, 208 mins) (4 wkts dec)	233
Fall: 28 85 196 330		Fall: 29 125 192 224	

M. R. Albers, B. E. McGain, S. R. Pietersz, A. B. Wise did not bat.

Bowling: *First Innings*—Clark 5–3–4–0; Thorp 24–5–70–1; Taylor 20–4–61–1; James 14–0–78–1; Casson 21–1–96–1; North 6–1–19–0; Voges 5–0–32–0; Rogers 3.5–0–20–0; Marsh 2–0–15–0. *Second Innings*—Taylor 15–1–66–1; James 10–0–43–0; Casson 9–2–29–1; North 17–1–64–2; Harvey 5–0–28–0.

Western Australia Second XI

C.J.L. Rogers c Hussey b Albers	108	– (2) c Mott b McGain	75
*S.W. Meuleman c Hussey b McGain	28	– (1) c Klinger b Wise	35
M.W. Goodwin c Hussey b Wise	0	– c Hussey b Albers	96
M.J. North c McDonald b McGain	12	– c McDonald b Hussey	58
S.E. Marsh lbw b McGain	4	– b Wise	17
A.C. Voges run out (McGain/Roach)	1	– lbw b McDonald	32
K.M. Harvey c Klinger b Welsford	27	– c Hussey b Albers	5
†L. Ronchi c Roach b Pietersz	15	– c Wise b Albers	14
B. Casson not out	21	– (10) not out	4
J.J. Taylor c Hussey b Wise	35	– (9) c Welsford b Albers	6
A.C.L. James not out	10	– not out	0
B 2, l-b 1	3	L-b 3	3

(109 overs, 403 mins) (9 wkts dec) 264
Fall: 78 81 114 124 126 176 197
197 234

(60 overs, 249 mins) (9 wkts) 345
Fall: 84 136 249 277 290 299
334 339 345

C.D. Thorp, M.W. Clark did not bat.

Bowling: *First Innings*—Pietersz 21–9–37–1; Albers 9–3–28–1; Welsford 19–1–75–1; Wise 20–11–29–2; McGain 30–8–72–3; McDonald 9–3–17–0; Hussey 1–0–3–0. *Second Innings*—Pietersz 6–0–39–0; McDonald 7–1–46–1; Welsford 3–0–30–0; Wise 19–2–91–2; McGain 15–2–67–1; Hussey 3–0–29–1; Albers 7–0–40–4.

Umpires: J.K. Brookes and P.R. Pease.

NEW SOUTH WALES SECOND XI
v SOUTH AUSTRALIA SECOND XI

At Bankstown Memorial Oval, Bankstown, October 27, 28, 29, 30, 2003. New South Wales Second XI won by six wickets. *Toss:* South Australia Second XI.

Close of play: First day, New South Wales Second XI (1) 0-7 (Phelps 5, Catalano 2); Second day, New South Wales Second XI (1) 7–467 (Thornely 144, Bird 6); Third day, South Australia Second XI (2) 8-285 (Plant 33).

South Australia Second XI

L. Williams c Zammit b Cameron	0	– (2) lbw b Zammit	28
*B.A. Johnson lbw b Cameron	11	– (1) c Jaques b Cameron	3
J.M. Vaughan b Cameron	0	– b Zammit	117
B.P. Cameron run out	92	– c Pilon b Lambert	10
M.J. Cosgrove c Lambert b Bird	84	– c Pilon b Bird	26
C.J. Ferguson b Zammit	19	– lbw b Lambert	54
†J.W. Plant c Zammit b Cameron	46	– not out	38
O.C. Thomas lbw b O'Brien	6	– c Jaques b Lambert	0
T.P. Kelly c Catalano b Nupier	44	– b Lambert	0
C.J. Duval c Jaques b Nupier	17	– c Pilon b Cameron	5
D.J. Cullen not out	0	– b Lambert	4
L-b 10, w 1, n-b 2	13	L-b 7, n-b 7	14

(88.2 overs, 328 mins) 332
Fall: 0 0 15 182 196 212 227 295 332 332

(90 overs, 330 mins) 299
Fall: 9 72 89 158 213 285 285 285
294 299

M. Sheikh did not bat.

Bowling: *First Innings*—Cameron 17–7–46–4; Bird 17–4–62–1; Lambert 20–1–83–0; Nupier 12.2–2–57–2; Zammit 17–1–63–1; O'Brien 5–1–11–1. *Second Innings*—Cameron 18–6–43–2; Bird 12–2–64–1; Lambert 22–4–75–5; Zammit 22–9–59–2; Nupier 4–0–33–0; O'Brien 12–7–18–0.

New South Wales Second XI

*M. J. Phelps c Vaughan b Duval	5	– lbw b Kelly	12
N. J. Catalano c Vaughan b Duval	10	– c Cullen b Thomas	3
P. A. Jaques c Plant b Kelly	71	– c Sheikh b Thomas	7
P. Maraziotis lbw b Duval	0	– c Johnson b Cullen	20
A. W. O'Brien b Sheikh	79	– not out	37
D. J. Thornely b Duval	158	– not out	43
G. M. Lambert c Cullen b Kelly	108		
†N. S. Pilon b Cosgrove	31		
A. C. Bird run out	18		
L. A. Zammit run out	11		
M. A. Cameron not out	1		
B 2, l-b 8, w 3, n-b 2	15	B 4, l-b 1	5

(111.1 overs, 426 mins)   507   (31.4 overs, 121 mins)   (4 wkts) 127
Fall: 7 30 30 131 197 399 457 485 504 507   Fall: 12 22 22 61

C. K. L. Nupier did not bat.

Bowling: *First Innings*—Kelly 31–2–148–2; Duval 27.1–2–124–4; Thomas 16–3–85–0; Johnson 10–2–32–0; Sheikh 11–1–49–1; Cullen 11–2–38–0; Cosgrove 5–1–21–1. *Second Innings*—Kelly 7–2–17–1; Thomas 6–1–28–2; Sheikh 9–2–41–0; Cullen 9.4–1–36–1.

Umpires: R. D. Goodger and R. J. Tucker.

WESTERN AUSTRALIA SECOND XI v TASMANIA SECOND XI

At WACA Ground, Perth, October 27, 28, 29, 30, 2003. Match drawn. *Toss:* Western Australia Second XI.

Close of play: First day, No play; Second day, Western Australia Second XI (1) 0-77 (Meuleman 41, Simmons 29); Third day, Tasmania Second XI 3-178 (Birt 107, Dawson 21).

Tasmania Second XI

*S. R. Mason c James b Taylor	24	– (2) c Ronchi b Mascarenhas	19
T. R. Birt lbw b Howman	1	– (1) c Simmons b Taylor	107
†D. G. Dawson c Taylor b Howman	40	– (5) not out	101
R. J. G. Lockyear c Meuleman b James	5	– lbw b Howman	16
S. P. Kremerskothen c James b Mascarenhas	10	– (3) lbw b James	7
G. J. Bailey lbw b Howman	4	– c Voges b Taylor	8
G. T. Cunningham c and b Jones	59	– c Voges b Howman	42
T. D. Paine c Simmons b Taylor	39	– c Thistle b Taylor	27
S. B. Tubb c Voges b Jones	14	– not out	16
A. W. Polkinghorne b Taylor	2		
G. J. Denton not out	6		
B 4, l-b 13, w 1, n-b 9	27	B 5, l-b 15, w 1, n-b 3	24

(88.2 overs, 342 mins)   231   (103 overs, 378 mins) (7 wkts dec) 367
Fall: 2 40 52 72 89 110 179 202 209 231   Fall: 35 45 72 178 188 270 334

A. G. Downton did not bat.

Bowling: *First Innings*—Thistle 12–1–34–0; Howman 15–6–36–3; James 17–3–62–1; Taylor 18.2–6–45–3; Mascarenhas 18–10–18–1; Jones 8–2–19–2. *Second Innings*—Taylor 20–5–49–3; Howman 18–6–55–2; Mascarenhas 17–10–19–1; James 18–4–83–1; Thistle 14–0–62–0; Jones 10–2–34–0; Simmons 2–1–2–0; Voges 4–0–43–0.

Western Australia Second XI

*S. W. Meuleman c Dawson b Denton	44	–	(2) c Bailey b Denton	8
C. J. Simmons b Denton	31	–	(1) lbw b Denton	0
S. E. Marsh b Downton	9	–	c Tubb b Denton	0
K. M. Harvey c Paine b Denton	43	–	b Denton	89
A. C. Voges lbw b Denton	0	–	c Cunningham b Denton	3
†L. Ronchi c Kremerskothen b Denton	0	–	c Birt b Denton	8
B. D. Jones c Dawson b Kremerskothen	22	–	b Downton	23
J. J. Taylor c and b Kremerskothen	8	–	b Lockyear	70
A. D. Mascarenhas run out (Mason)	26	–	b Downton	18
S. G. Howman c Paine b Polkinghorne	36	–	not out	3
M. J. Thistle not out	18	–	not out	4
L-b 13, w 1, n-b 5	19		L-b 2, w 1	3

(72 overs, 288 mins)	256	(65 overs, 248 mins) (9 wkts)	229
Fall: 82 88 100 101 101 146 172 172 208 256		Fall: 0 6 9 15 32 81 192 211 223	

A. C. L. James did not bat.

Bowling: *First Innings*—Denton 21–7–65–5; Downton 25–6–86–1; Polkinghorne 13–3–35–1; Tubb 3–0–17–0; Kremerskothen 10–1–40–2. *Second Innings*—Denton 18–5–84–6; Downton 23–9–50–2; Lockyear 8–2–23–1; Polkinghorne 2–0–13–0; Tubb 10–2–35–0; Paine 4–0–22–0.

Umpires: B. Bennett and R. R. Pease.

SOUTH AUSTRALIA SECOND XI
v AUSTRALIAN CAPITAL TERRITORY

At Adelaide Oval No 2, Adelaide, November 10, 11, 12, 2003. South Australia Second XI won by an innings and 250 runs. *Toss:* Australian Capital Territory.

Close of play: First day, South Australia Second XI (1) 3-137 (Ferguson 33, Cosgrove 8); Second day, South Australia Second XI (1) 6-639 (Cameron 66, Kelly 36).

Australian Capital Territory

A. G. Rhynehart b Kelly	10	–	(2) c Hutchinson b Harris	13
*C. Brown b Higgs	32	–	(1) c Vaughan b Staunton	26
S. R. Cameron b Kelly	0	–	lbw b Harris	0
D. M. Jeffrey lbw b Staunton	6	–	c Cameron b Staunton	3
S. P. Heaney c Ferguson b Higgs	4	–	c Johnson b Harris	2
C. R. A. McLeod c Hutchinson b Higgs	50	–	c Vaughan b Staunton	8
†S. A. Holcombe c Kelly b Higgs	23	–	not out	69
S. E. Frost not out	11	–	b Harris	0
M. A. Hatton lbw b Kelly	1	–	lbw b Kelly	4
D. D. Mowbray lbw b Higgs	5	–	c Higgs b Harris	1
D. A. McNees b Kelly	4	–	st Hutchinson b Higgs	95
L-b 5, n-b 5	10		L-b 5, w 1, n-b 4	10

(48.5 overs, 191 mins)	158	(69.3 overs, 248 mins)	231
Fall: 23 29 40 56 69 135 137 140 145 158		Fall: 38 38 42 45 56 60 60 73 80 231	

E. Kellar did not bat.

Bowling: *First Innings*—Kelly 11.5–3–25–4; Harris 8–1–33–0; Staunton 7–2–18–1; Higgs 14–5–25–5; Burr 8–0–52–0. *Second Innings*—Kelly 9–2–17–1; Harris 14–2–46–5; Staunton 11–3–38–3; Burr 16–3–47–0; Higgs 12.3–2–45–1; Johnson 7–0–33–0.

South Australia Second XI

J. M. Vaughan lbw b Hatton	57	R. J. Harris c Jeffrey b McNees	14
*B. A. Johnson c Cameron b Kellar	19	T. P. Kelly not out	36
M. A. Higgs c Holcombe b McNees	11	B 1, l-b 8, n-b 9	18
C. J. Ferguson c Brown b McNees	158		
M. J. Cosgrove c Jeffrey b McNees	260	(141 overs, 521 mins) (6 wkts dec)	639
B. P. Cameron not out	66	Fall: 51 67 121 492 532 562	

L. Williams, †B. R. Hutchinson, M. R. Burr and A. M. Staunton did not bat.

Bowling: McNees 29–3–153–4; Kellar 31–9–143–1; Hatton 37–7–138–1; Mowbray 9.5–1–44–0; Jeffrey 18.1–4–70–0; Frost 16–1–82–0.

Umpires: A. Collins and K. D. Perrin.

QUEENSLAND ACADEMY OF SPORT v WESTERN AUSTRALIAN SECOND XI

At Allan Border Field, Albion, November 17, 18, 19, 20, 2003. Queensland Academy of Sport won by 136 runs. *Toss:* Western Australia Second XI.

Close of play: First day, Queensland Academy of Sport (1) 4-299 (Nye 118, Paulsen 6); Second day, Western Australian Second XI (1) 3-252 (Harvey 76, Voges 30); Third day, Queensland Academy of Sport (2) 7-251 (Le Loux 48, Swan 5).

Queensland Academy of Sport

B. P. Nash c Voges b Thistle	11	– (2) b Thorp	38
L. M. Stevens c Thorp b Jacques	36	– (1) lbw b Thistle	18
*A. J. Nye c Jones b Thorp	140	– c Thistle b Thorp	33
C. A. Philipson c Heal b Thorp	109	– lbw b Thorp	28
S. J. Farrell c Ronchi b Jacques	8		
S. J. Paulsen c Jones b Thorp	31	– c Harvey b Heal	65
†C. D. Hartley c Ronchi b Thorp	0	– c Ronchi b Jacques	2
R. N. Le Loux c Simmons b James	14	– not out	60
D. R. MacKenzie c Heal b Mascarenhas	7		
S. J. Magoffin not out	3	– c Meuleman b Harvey	2
C. R. Swan not out	3	– (9) c Jacques b Heal	5
G. J. Sullivan (did not bat).		– c Thorp b Heal	1
R. A. Broad (did not bat).		– (5) c Ronchi b Harvey	7
L-b 8, n-b 4	12	L-b 2, w 5	7

(115 overs, 432 mins)	(9 wkts dec) 374	(79 overs, 290 mins)	266
Fall: 47 59 265 274 328 334 357		Fall: 34 71 117 122 140 148	
361 369		236 252 259 266	

B. M. Edmondson did not bat.

Bowling: *First Innings*—Thorp 31–7–96–4; James 23–3–102–1; Mascarenhas 17–8–32–1; Thistle 15–2–39–1; Jacques 14–5–48–2; Harvey 10–2–34–0; Heal 5–1–15–0. *Second Innings*—Thorp 15–2–40–3; Mascarenhas 20–6–65–0; James 5–1–29–0; Thistle 8–4–20–1; Harvey 9–2–26–2; Heal 15–2–54–3; Jacques 3–0–13–1; Jones 4–1–17–0.

Western Australia Second XI

S. W. Meuleman c Hartley b Magoffin	50	– (2) b Magoffin	1
C. J. Simmons b Nash	80	– (1) c Hartley b Magoffin	23
B. D. Jones lbw b Swan	0	– c Nye b Magoffin	0
*K. M. Harvey c Hartley b Swan	79	– lbw b Stevens	57
A. C. Voges c Philipson b Magoffin	37	– lbw b Sullivan	35
†L. Ronchi b Edmondson	14	– b Stevens	15
A. D. Mascarenhas not out	23	– c Magoffin b Sullivan	7
A. K. Heal c Nye b Sullivan	4	– c Nash b Swan	26
M. J. Thistle b Edmondson	1	– c Hartley b Sullivan	0
A. C. L. James lbw b Edmondson	0	– (11) not out	3
S. W. T. Jacques b Edmondson	4	– (10) c Paulsen b Magoffin	18
L-b 4, n-b 17	21	L-b 2, n-b 4	6

(96 overs, 372 mins)	313	(59.3 overs, 242 mins)	191

Fall: 121 132 162 256 268 286 298 299 299 313

Fall: 1 11 38 110 126 140 145 145 183 191

C. D. Thorp did not bat.

Bowling: *First Innings*—MacKenzie 14–4–54–0; Magoffin 24–5–80–2; Sullivan 10–0–63–1; Swan 21–9–35–2; Nash 4–1–18–1; Stevens 7–2–17–0; Le Loux 7–3–11–0; Philipson 5–1–15–0; Edmondson 4–0–16–4. *Second Innings*—Magoffin 16–5–63–4; Swan 11.3–2–41–1; Edmondson 7–2–23–0; Sullivan 9–4–13–3; Le Loux 7–2–29–0; Stevens 9–1–20–2.

Umpires: G. N. Cubit and T. P. Laycock.

NEW SOUTH WALES SECOND XI v WESTERN AUSTRALIA SECOND XI

At Alan Davidson Oval, St Peters, November 24, 25, 26, 27, 2003. Match abandoned without a ball bowled.

TASMANIA SECOND XI v SOUTH AUSTRALIA SECOND XI

At Bellerive Oval, Hobart, November 24, 25, 26, 27, 2003. South Australia Second XI won by 36 runs. *Toss:* South Australia Second XI.

Close of play: First day, South Australia Second XI (1) 8-322 (Plant 9, Staunton 19); Second day, South Australia Second XI (2) 0-32 (Williams 19, Vaughan 13); Third day, Tasmania Second XI (2) 2-151 (Paine 81, Kremerskothen 49).

South Australia Second XI

J. M. Vaughan lbw b Geeves	0	– (2) c Cunningham b Hilfenhaus	...	19
L. Williams lbw b Polkinghorne	10	– (1) b Kremerskothen		51
B. P. Cameron lbw b Polkinghorne	132			
*C. J. Davies c Dawson b Geeves	48	– c Geeves b Polkinghorne		42
C. J. Ferguson c Tubb b Kremerskothen	30	– not out		11
N. T. Adcock b Polkinghorne	5	– (3) c Dawson b Polkinghorne		103
M. Weeks c Bailey b Geeves	30			
R. J. Harris c Bailey b Geeves	36			
†J. W. Plant c Birt b Polkinghorne	38			
A. M. Staunton not out	57			
C. B. Bailey run out (Birt)	4			
L-b 3	3	B 1, l-b 1, n-b 1		3

(136 overs, 473 mins) 393   (61.2 overs, 225 mins) (4 wkts dec) 229
Fall: 0 25 119 213 223 232 279 294 376 393   Fall: 48 108 215 229

D. J. Cullen did not bat.

Bowling: *First Innings*—Geeves 18–6–38–4; Hilfenhaus 26–4–96–0; Polkinghorne 30–10–104–4; Butterworth 21–7–63–0; Kremerskothen 13–7–21–1; Tubb 28–8–68–0. *Second Innings*—Hilfenhaus 21–4–63–1; Polkinghorne 20.2–2–85–2; Butterworth 3–3–0–0; Lockyear 2–1–5–0; Tubb 10–1–48–0; Kremerskothen 5–2–26–1.

Tasmania Second XI

T. D. Paine c Davies b Harris	0	– (2) c Plant b Bailey	105
T. R. Birt c Ferguson b Weeks	19	– (1) lbw b Harris	0
†D. G. Dawson b Harris	7	– c Vaughan b Staunton	14
S. P. Kremerskothen c Weeks b Staunton	0	– c Plant b Staunton	128
R. J. G. Lockyear lbw b Bailey	21	– b Harris	21
*G. T. Cunningham lbw b Harris	38	– c Staunton b Cullen	16
G. J. Bailey lbw b Cullen	3	– b Weeks	9
S. B. Tubb lbw b Harris	0	– c Williams b Staunton	92
A. W. Polkinghorne c Plant b Staunton	5	– b Bailey	41
L. R. Butterworth not out	34	– lbw b Bailey	12
B. Geeves lbw b Cullen	2		
B. W. Hilfenhaus (did not bat).		– not out	1
L-b 2, n-b 1	3	B 2, l-b 7, n-b 6	15

(48.4 overs, 173 mins) 132   (138 overs, 498 mins) 454
Fall: 0 8 9 36 80 91 91 91 127 132   Fall: 2 59 201 268 281 301 303
                                                          400 438 454

Bowling: *First Innings*—Harris 17–4–53–4; Staunton 10–1–32–2; Weeks 7–2–13–1; Cullen 11.4–6–20–2; Bailey 3–1–12–1. *Second Innings*—Harris 31–9–89–2; Staunton 24–2–75–3; Weeks 23–3–82–1; Cullen 25.4–4–68–1; Bailey 24–1–105–3; Ferguson 11–4–26–0.

Umpires: K. J. McGinniss and B. J. Muir.

NEW SOUTH WALES SECOND XI v AUSTRALIAN CAPITAL TERRITORY

At Hurstville Oval, Hurstville, December 1, 2, 3, 4, 2003. New South Wales Second XI won by 41 runs. *Toss:* Australian Capital Territory.

Close of play: First day, New South Wales Second XI (1) 311; Second day, New South Wales Second XI (2) 6-111 (Newman 15, Thornely 0); Third day, Australian Capital Territory (2) 7-266 (Radford 35, McNees 6).

New South Wales Second XI

*M. J. Phelps b McNees		0	– c Holcombe b Kellar	0
E. J. M. Cowan b McNees		9	– c Holcombe b Jones	27
G. M. Lambert c Heaney b Jones		7	– c Holcombe b McNees	0
P. Maraziotis c Hatton b Kellar		9	– c Holcombe b McNees	5
A. W. O'Brien b McNees		3	– lbw b Divin	30
D. J. Thornely c Heaney b Kellar		117	– (8) c Holcombe b Jones	33
†N. S. Pilon c McLeod b Kellar		1	– (6) c Heaney b McNees	22
S. D. Bradstreet not out		147	– (9) not out	22
B. J. Newman c Brown b McNees		1	– (7) c Holcombe b Kellar	28
D. A. Nash c Brown b Kellar		1	– not out	17
L. A. Zammit c Holcombe b Kellar		0		
L-b 8, w 1, n-b 7		16	L-b 7, w 1, n-b 4	12

(91.5 overs, 355 mins)   311
Fall: 0 7 26 26 33 34 276 294 309 311

(62 overs, 249 mins)   (8 wkts dec)   196
Fall: 7 8 22 69 69 109 131 179

M. A. Cameron did not bat.

Bowling: *First Innings*—McNees 26–7–66–4; Jones 18–2–74–1; Kellar 22.5–5–53–5; Divin 13–3–42–0; Hatton 12–1–68–0. *Second Innings*—McNees 19–6–58–3; Kellar 20–5–39–2; Jones 12–1–49–2; Divin 11–3–43–1.

Australian Capital Territory

*C. Brown b Nash		4	– c Thornely b Nash	61
A. G. Rhynehart c Pilon b Lambert		93	– c and b Thornely	53
S. R. Cameron b Nash		2	– lbw b Cameron	10
S. P. Heaney b Cameron		4	– c Newman b Cameron	0
M. A. Divin c Maraziotis b Cameron		13	– lbw b Zammit	31
C. R. A. McLeod lbw b Cameron		6	– c Pilon b Zammit	36
†S. A. Holcombe c Pilon b Nash		13	– lbw b Zammit	16
P. B. Radford c Pilon b Nash		0	– c Phelps b Lambert	45
D. A. McNees c Maraziotis b Lambert		3	– b Nash	7
M. A. Hatton not out		4	– b Nash	0
A. D. Jones b Cameron		0	– not out	33
L-b 4, w 3, n-b 3		10	B 6, l-b 8, n-b 8	22

(48.5 overs, 208 mins)   152
Fall: 4 8 18 63 74 98 110 139 149 152

(92.3 overs, 382 mins)   314
Fall: 86 116 131 146 193 204 231 268 268 314

E. Kellar did not bat.

Bowling: *First Innings*—Nash 15–5–35–4; Lambert 10–3–28–2; Cameron 12.5–3–32–4; Thornely 4–0–19–0; Zammit 7–0–34–0. *Second Innings*—Nash 25–8–76–3; Cameron 24–6–74–2; Lambert 12.3–3–41–1; Thornely 8–1–29–1; Bradstreet 5–1–22–0; Newman 5–2–13–0; Zammit 13–5–45–3.

Umpires: G. J. Lill and T. J. Keel.

VICTORIA SECOND XI v TASMANIA SECOND XI

At Albert Ground, South Melbourne, December 1, 2, 3, 4, 2003. Victoria Second XI won by 10 wickets. *Toss:* Victoria Second XI.

Close of play: First day, Victoria Second XI (1) 0-6 (Pinniger 0, Mott 5); Second day, Victoria Second XI (1) 8-270 (Lindsay 30, Brede 0); Third day, Tasmania Second XI (2) 3-132 (Lockyear 18, Tubb 34).

Tasmania Second XI

G. T. Cunningham lbw b Harwood	11	– (3) c Brede b Harrop	29
G. J. Bailey c McGain b Lindsay	17	– (1) b Harrop	41
†D. G. Dawson c Brede b Harwood	30	– (2) lbw b Hewett	3
R. J. G. Lockyear c Blizzard b Hewett	17	– c Brede b Harrop	27
*S. B. Tubb c McGain b Shanahan	96	– not out	71
R. J. Dilger b Harwood	2	– (7) run out (Joseland/Brede)	0
A. W. Polkinghorne b Harwood	0	– (8) c Brede b Lindsay	1
X. J. Doherty c and b Lindsay	3		
L. R. Butterworth b Hewett	26	– (6) c Harwood b Hewett	3
B. W. Hilfenhaus b Harwood	17	– (9) c Pinniger b Lindsay	1
L. C. Swards not out	0	– (10) c Harrop b Shanahan	10
V. G. Kay (did not bat)		– c Lindsay b Harwood	0
L-b 4, n-b 2	6	B 2, l-b 3, n-b 6	11

(85.1 overs, 334 mins) 225 (79.4 overs, 321 mins) 197
Fall: 14 39 66 104 150 150 181 183 Fall: 24 71 78 154 159 159 167
225 225 171 196 197

Bowling: *First Innings*—Harwood 25–6–57–5; Hewett 17.1–4–34–2; Lindsay 17–3–45–2; Harrop 6–1–14–0; Joseland 4–2–8–0; Shanahan 10–2–31–1; McGain 6–1–32–0. *Second Innings*—Harwood 19.4–4–48–1; Hewett 17–7–33–2; Lindsay 13–4–24–2; McGain 8–0–42–0; Harrop 13–1–36–3; Shanahan 7–4–8–1; Mott 2–1–1–0.

Victoria Second XI

M. S. Pinniger c Bailey b Tubb	64	– not out	73
M. P. Mott c Cunningham b Tubb	95	– not out	53
B. R. Joseland c Butterworth b Tubb	28		
N. Jewell b Doherty	17		
A. C. Blizzard lbw b Tubb	11		
D. R. Shanahan b Polkinghorne	17		
G. P. Lindsay c Dawson b Polkinghorne	37		
*S. M. Harwood c Dawson b Polkinghorne	0		
I. S. L. Hewett b Polkinghorne	0		
†D. C. Brede not out	13		
B. D. Harrop b Tubb	6		
B 2, l-b 2, w 1, n-b 3	8	L-b 1	1

(128 overs, 427 mins) 296 (23.1 overs, 85 mins) (0 wkt) 127
Fall: 162 168 207 215 223 265 265 265 285 296 Fall:

B. E. McGain did not bat.

Bowling: *First Innings*—Polkinghorne 30–10–69–4; Hilfenhaus 11–3–17–0; Doherty 32–11–66–1; Butterworth 6–0–21–0; Swards 8–2–21–0; Tubb 30–8–80–5; Kay 11–6–18–0. *Second Innings*—Polkinghorne 9–2–36–0; Hilfenhaus 3–0–9–0; Kay 2–0–18–0; Tubb 7–0–26–0; Butterworth 1–0–14–0; Swards 1.1–0–23–0.

Umpires: A. J. Barrow and A. P. Ward.

AUSTRALIAN CAPITAL TERRITORY v QUEENSLAND ACADEMY OF SPORT

At Manuka Oval, Canberra, December 15, 16, 17, 18, 2003. Australian Capital Territory won by three wickets. *Toss:* Queensland Academy of Sport.

Close of play: First day, Queensland Academy of Sport (1) 7-339 (Simpson 2, Swan 0); Second day, Australian Capital Territory (1) 4-271 (Divin 55, McLeod 8); Third day, Queensland Academy of Sport (2) 4-158 (Simpson 20, Le Loux 5).

Queensland Academy of Sport

D. M. Payne c Holcombe b McNees		41	– b Karppinen	18
R. A. Broad b Hatton		118	– (8) not out	17
A. J. Nye c Heaney b Kellar		67	– c and b Hatton	45
C. A. Philipson lbw b Hatton		21	– b Hatton	13
L. M. Stevens run out (Rhynehart)		32	– (2) c Holcombe b Divin	52
R. N. Le Loux c McLeod b Karppinen		34	– c Brown b Hatton	13
C. P. Simpson c Divin b Kellar		7	– (5) b Karppinen	55
†D. Wallace c Holcombe b McNees		11	– (7) c Heaney b Hatton	20
C. R. Swan b Kellar		2	– b Karppinen	8
N. J. Rimmington not out		24	– not out	1
S. J. Magoffin c Rhynehart b McNees		17		
B 4, l-b 4, w 1, n-b 8		17	B 7, l-b 10	17
(114 overs, 433 mins)		391	(73 overs, 260 mins) (8 wkts dec)	259

Fall: 74 229 243 261 318 327 339 341 349 391

Fall: 19 85 123 145 184 227 231 253

G. J. Sullivan did not bat.

Bowling: *First Innings*—McNees 23–4–99–3; Kellar 34–7–90–3; Karppinen 29–11–81–1; Divin 14–3–61–0; Hatton 14–4–52–2. *Second Innings*—Kellar 9–1–23–0; Karppinen 18–2–93–3; Hatton 29–7–73–4; McNees 9–1–35–0; Divin 8–1–18–1.

Australian Capital Territory

A. G. Rhynehart c Wallace b Sullivan		42	– (2) c Le Loux b Magoffin	4
D. J. Richards c Stevens b Le Loux		54	– (1) c and b Swan	2
*C. Brown c Rimmington b Stevens		83	– c Wallace b Swan	4
S. P. Heaney c Payne b Le Loux		1	– c Magoffin b Stevens	63
M. A. Divin run out (Sullivan)		63	– lbw b Le Loux	88
C. R. A. McLeod not out		73	– not out	43
S. J. Karppinen lbw b Sullivan		14	– b Nye	0
†S. A. Holcombe b Rimmington		7	– lbw b Nye	0
P. B. Radford c Nye b Simpson		9	– not out	24
D. A. McNees lbw b Le Loux		2		
M. A. Hatton c Swan b Simpson		5		
B 10, l-b 29, n-b 5		44	B 17, l-b 7, n-b 2	26
(116.2 overs, 431 mins)		397	(73 overs, 247 mins) (7 wkts)	254

Fall: 77 138 142 250 306 328 348 359 384 397

Fall: 4 13 13 156 201 201 207

E. Kellar did not bat.

Bowling: *First Innings*—Magoffin 12–1–50–0; Swan 10–1–50–0; Sullivan 14–2–41–2; Rimmington 17–3–71–1; Stevens 19–6–43–1; Le Loux 16–1–54–3; Nye 8–4–12–0; Philipson 5–1–14–0; Simpson 15.2–7–23–2. *Second Innings*—Magoffin 6–3–10–1; Swan 6–1–19–2; Simpson 17–5–45–0; Stevens 16–5–36–1; Le Loux 9–0–45–1; Sullivan 2–0–15–0; Philipson 4–1–17–0; Rimmington 4–0–17–0; Nye 9–3–26–2.

Umpires: S. Balchin and D. B. Harris.

AUSTRALIAN CAPITAL TERRITORY v VICTORIA SECOND XI

At Manuka Oval, Canberra, January 3, 4, 5, 6, 2004. Australian Capital Territory won by nine wickets. *Toss:* Australian Capital Territory.

Close of play: First day, Australian Capital Territory (1) 0-15 (Rhynehart 5, Richards 7); Second day, Australian Capital Territory (1) 8-300 (Heaney 96, Hatton 23); Third day, Victoria (2) 224 all out.

Victoria Second XI

L. G. L. Buchanan c Holcombe b Kellar	8	– c Holcombe b McNees	11
M. S. Pinniger c Holcombe b Kellar	36	– c McLeod b Hatton	25
M. Klinger c Rhynehart b McNees	37	– c Nason b Hatton	32
A. C. Blizzard c Holcombe b Kellar	20	– (6) run out	0
D. R. Shanahan c Heaney b Hatton	36	– lbw b Nason	19
T. H. Welsford c Holcombe b Kellar	0	– (4) b Nason	11
G. P. Lindsay c Richards b Nason	69	– c Rhynehart b Nason	17
†A. J. Crosthwaite st Holcombe b Nason	40	– not out	49
B. A. Knowles not out	14	– c Hatton b McNees	50
*M. W. H. Inness c McLeod b McNees	18	– c Rhynehart b McNees	2
S. R. Pietersz not out	3		
J. P. Mangan (did not bat).		– run out	0
B 8, l-b 8, w 1, n-b 8	25	B 1, l-b 3, n-b 4	8

(89 overs, 349 mins)   (9 wkts dec) 306
Fall: 15 71 102 115 119 167 258
   263 293

(63.3 overs, 246 mins)   224
Fall: 12 66 71 84 84 105 123 206
   224 224

Bowling: *First Innings*—McNees 20–6–52–2; Kellar 19–5–49–4; Divin 11–0–62–0; Hatton 28–6–82–1; Nason 11–2–45–2. *Second Innings*—McNees 12–3–58–3; Kellar 14.3–4–41–0; Hatton 20–3–60–2; Nason 17–4–61–3.

Australian Capital Territory

A. G. Rhynehart c Crosthwaite b Pietersz	38	– (2) c Klinger b Mangan	16
D. J. Richards lbw b Lindsay	29	– (1) not out	55
*C. Brown b Mangan	30	– not out	19
S. P. Heaney not out	160		
M. A. Divin c and b Inness	1		
C. R. A. McLeod c Knowles b Pietersz	9		
†S. A. Holcombe c Pietersz b Lindsay	31		
P. B. Radford b Inness	23		
D. A. McNees lbw b Inness	0		
M. A. Hatton lbw b Mangan	35		
E. Kellar not out	50		
B 9, l-b 10, n-b 10	29	B 1, l-b 6, n-b 1	8

(135 overs, 527 mins)   (9 wkts dec) 435
Fall: 72 72 117 128 138 195 237 244 345

(27.3 overs, 110 mins)   (1 wkt) 98
Fall: 66

M. W. Nason did not bat.

Bowling: *First Innings*—Inness 26–7–72–3; Knowles 25–4–97–0; Lindsay 17–3–49–2; Pietersz 19–4–50–2; Welsford 16–2–58–0; Mangan 26–10–60–2; Shanahan 6–1–30–0. *Second Innings*—Inness 6–0–14–0; Pietersz 7–2–23–0; Mangan 8.3–3–26–1; Knowles 6–0–28–0.

Umpires: W. F. Ruse and A. Shelley.

QUEENSLAND ACADEMY OF SPORT v SOUTH AUSTRALIA SECOND XI

At Allan Border Field, Albion, January 12, 13, 14, 15, 2003. Match drawn. *Toss:* South Australia Second XI.

Close of play: First day, South Australia Second XI (1) 6-324 (Plant 22, Harris 53); Second day, Queensland Academy of Sport (1) 4-158 (Philipson 64, Farrell 59); Third day, South Australia Second XI (2) 3-28 (Davies 12, Johnson 0).

South Australia Second XI

L. Williams lbw b Jurgensen	26		
*C. J. Davies c Paulsen b Le Loux	81	– not out	12
B. P. Cameron c Farrell b Jurgensen	41	– c Sullivan b Brant	2
M. A. Higgs c Farrell b Le Loux	0	– c Hartley b Brant	0
B. A. Johnson st Hartley b Nye	78	– not out	0
C. J. Ferguson c Farrell b Nye	5	– (1) c Broad b Brant	13
†T. C. Plant c Hartley b Philipson	82		
R. J. Harris c Sullivan b Magoffin	54		
A. M. Staunton not out	71		
D. J. Cullen c Nye b Jurgensen	8		
C. J. Duval not out	21		
L-b 9, n-b 11	20	L-b 1	1

(148 overs, 563 mins)	(9 wkts dec) 487	(10 overs, 41 mins)	(3 wkts) 28

Fall: 82 147 147 165 183 241 325 416 456 ....   Fall: 22 24 24

C. B. Bailey did not bat.

Bowling: *First Innings*—Jurgensen 35–11–96–3; Brant 11–6–14–0; Magoffin 27–10–79–1; Sullivan 19–2–74–0; Le Loux 16–2–81–2; Nye 19–6–58–2; Paulsen 10–3–32–0; Philipson 11–1–44–1. *Second Innings*—Brant 5–2–15–3; Jurgensen 5–0–12–0.

Queensland Academy of Sport

D. M. Payne c Plant b Harris	31	S. J. Jurgensen c and b Duval	2
R. A. Broad c Plant b Duval	0	S. A. Brant c Plant b Staunton	2
*A. J. Nye c Plant b Harris	12	S. J. Magoffin not out	36
C. A. Philipson c Cameron b Staunton	80		
S. J. Paulsen b Staunton	8	L-b 1, w 4, n-b 5	10
S. J. Farrell run out (Cameron)	75		
†C. D. Hartley c Bailey b Harris	72	(108.5 overs, 399 mins)	369
R. N. Le Loux c Plant b Harris	41	Fall: 6 44 44 64 204 212 285 292 295 369	

G. J. Sullivan did not bat.

Bowling: *First Innings*—Harris 21.5–4–96–4; Duval 18–3–50–2; Staunton 16–1–81–3; Cullen 23–7–68–0; Higgs 7–2–26–0; Johnson 11–6–12–0; Bailey 12–4–35–0.

Umpires: T. P. Laycock and N. S. McNamara.

AUSTRALIAN CAPITAL TERRITORY v TASMANIA SECOND XI

At Manuka Oval, Canberra, January 12, 13, 14, 15, 2004. Australian Capital Territory won by eight wickets. *Toss:* Australian Capital Territory.

Close of play: First day, Tasmania Second XI (1) 6-320 (Bailey 22, Sharman 0); Second day, Australian Capital Territory (1) 6-221 (Karppinen 10, Radford 0); Third day, Tasmania Second XI (2) 7-94 (Lockyear 22, Sharman 1).

Tasmania Second XI

*†T. D. Paine c Hatton b Karppinen	5	– (2) c McLeod b Kellar	5
T. R. Birt c Rhynehart b Karppinen	0	– (1) c Divin b Kellar	5
S. P. Kremerskothen lbw b McNees	157	– (6) c Brown b Hatton	1
D. G. Dawson c McLeod b Karppinen	23	– c McLeod b Karppinen	8
R. J. G. Lockyear c Divin b McNees	87	– not out	36
G. J. Bailey c McLeod b Kellar	26	– (3) c Richards b Nason	43
J. G. J. Selby lbw b McNees	19	– b Hatton	0
G. W. Sharman c Hatton b McNees	5	– (9) c McLeod b Kellar	10
L. R. Butterworth c Rhynehart b Kellar	1	– (8) c Divin b Hatton	1
J. Bean c b McNees	0		
B. Smith not out	2	– c McLeod b Kellar	0
B. W. Hilfenhaus (did not bat).		– b Kellar	0
L-b 5, w 2	7	B 5, l-b 3, w 2	10

(109.4 overs, 432 mins) 332
Fall: 4 13 81 277 278 314 324 330 330 332

(57 overs, 216 mins) 119
Fall: 14 15 48 83 84 84 92 117 118 119

Bowling: *First Innings*—Karppinen 25–7–69–3; Kellar 30–8–83–2; McNees 28.4–9–63–5; Divin 12–3–45–0; Hatton 7–0–26–0; Nason 7–0–41–0. *Second Innings*—Karppinen 15–4–30–1; Kellar 12–6–18–5; McNees 10–6–13–0; Hatton 11–4–17–3; Nason 9–0–33–1.

Australian Capital Territory

D. J. Richards c Sharman b Butterworth	71	– c Kremerskothen b Butterworth	8
A. G. Rhynehart b Hilfenhaus	4	– (1) not out	70
*C. Brown lbw b Hilfenhaus	12		
S. P. Heaney b Butterworth	88	– not out	10
M. A. Divin c Birt b Smith	11		
†C. R. A. McLeod lbw b Bean	12		
S. J. Karppinen c Kremerskothen b Smith	12	– (3) c Paine b Butterworth	0
P. B. Radford c Kremerskothen b Butterworth	59		
D. A. McNees c Sharman b Bean	0		
M. A. Hatton not out	42		
E. Kellar lbw b Bean	18		
B 2, l-b 13, w 3, n-b 11	29	B 4, l-b 2, w 1, n-b 2	9

(124.5 overs, 460 mins) 358
Fall: 4 29 178 189 203 210 232 232 321 358

(14.3 overs, 57 mins) (2 wkts) 97
Fall: 53 53

M. W. Nason did not bat.

Bowling: *First Innings*—Smith 19–4–61–2; Hilfenhaus 22–6–62–2; Butterworth 24–4–64–3; Bean 23.4–4–70–3; Sharman 15.1–6–34–0; Kremerskothen 11–2–27–0; Selby 2–0–9–0; Lockyear 8–4–16–0. *Second Innings*—Smith 4–0–30–0; Hilfenhaus 4–0–13–0; Sharman 2–0–15–0; Butterworth 3–1–14–2; Bean 1.3–0–19–0.

Umpires: P. Chapman and G. Clifton.

TASMANIA SECOND XI v NEW SOUTH WALES SECOND XI

At TCA Ground, Hobart, February 9, 10, 11, 2004. Tasmania Second XI won by 45 runs.
Toss: Tasmania Second XI.

Close of play: First day, New South Wales Second XI (1) 4-66 (O'Brien 35, Wallace 14); Second day, Tasmania Second XI (2) 7-159 (Tubb 21).

Tasmania Second XI

T. R. Birt lbw b Bird	9	– (2) c Cameron b Lambert	14
S. H. Clarke c Maraziotis b Nash	0	– (1) lbw b Bird	1
†D. G. Dawson c Maraziotis b Nash	62	– b Lambert	28
S. P. Kremerskothen c Wallace b Nash	17	– c Bird b O'Brien	20
R. J. G. Lockyear c Wallace b O'Brien	60	– lbw b Zammit	28
*G. J. Bailey c Pilon b Cameron	7	– run out	31
S. B. Tubb c Krejza b Nash	36	– c Cameron b Nash	27
L. R. Butterworth c Maraziotis b Krejza	24	– c Pilon b Bird	10
G. W. Sharman c Wallace b Bird	1	– lbw b Bird	0
A. R. Griffith c Krejza b Bird	0	– c and b Bird	3
B. W. Hilfenhaus not out	0		
K. S. Pickering (did not bat)		– not out	0
L-b 4, w 2, n-b 2	8	L-b 4, w 2, n-b 1	7
(72.1 overs, 297 mins)	224	(64.1 overs, 252 mins)	169

Fall: 8 18 40 120 136 194 202 220
224 224

Fall: 1 33 58 68 112 148 159 159
169 169

Bowling: *First Innings*—Bird 16.1–4–39–3; Nash 20–6–48–4; Cameron 10–1–37–1; Lambert 13–2–40–0; Zammit 3–0–17–0; Krejza 7–1–27–1; O'Brien 3–0–12–1. *Second Innings*—Nash 13–3–27–1; Bird 13.1–3–34–4; Cameron 9–0–26–0; Lambert 13–3–42–2; O'Brien 11–4–20–1; Zammit 5–2–16–1.

New South Wales Second XI

*M. J. Phelps c Bailey b Griffith	1	– lbw b Griffith	4
G. M. Lambert lbw b Griffith	4	– c Pickering b Butterworth	7
E. J. M. Cowan c Kremerskothen b Griffith	6	– b Griffith	31
A. W. O'Brien c Dawson b Butterworth	37	– lbw b Sharman	26
P. Maraziotis b Griffith	0	– lbw b Griffith	16
D. P. Wallace c Clarke b Butterworth	27	– lbw b Pickering	32
J. J. Krejza c Dawson b Griffith	16	– b Griffith	3
†N. S. Pilon lbw b Griffith	22	– c Dawson b Pickering	32
D. A. Nash c Sharman b Hilfenhaus	1	– lbw b Pickering	4
A. C. Bird not out	38	– b Griffith	1
L. A. Zammit c Hilfenhaus b Tubb	19	– not out	1
B 1, l-b 7, w 1, n-b 2	11	L-b 6, n-b 3	9
(53.5 overs, 221 mins)	182	(52.1 overs, 223 mins)	166

Fall: 7 10 19 23 77 82 107 123
125 182

Fall: 6 24 73 78 101 107 151 157
164 166

M. A. Cameron did not bat.

Bowling: *First Innings*—Griffith 21–8–45–6; Hilfenhaus 11–3–48–1; Pickering 7–1–29–0; Sharman 2–0–14–0; Butterworth 7–4–13–2; Kremerskothen 4–2–12–0; Tubb 1.5–0–13–1. *Second Innings*—Griffith 18.1–7–47–5; Hilfenhaus 5–1–8–0; Butterworth 9–2–37–1; Pickering 9–1–25–3; Sharman 7–1–31–1; Kremerskothen 1–0–1–0; Tubb 3–0–11–0.

Umpires: K. J. McGinniss and B. J. Muir.

VICTORIA SECOND XI v QUEENSLAND ACADEMY OF SPORT

At Junction Oval, St Kilda, February 9, 10, 11, 12, 2004. Queensland Academy of Sport won by three wickets. *Toss:* Victoria Second XI.

Close of play: First day, Victoria Second XI (1) 3-290 (Joseland 100, Jewell 103); Second day, Queensland Academy of Sport (1) 1-87 (Simpson 66, Nye 4); Third day, Queensland Academy of Sport (1) 4–217 (Carseldine 20, Hartley 6).

Victoria Second XI

R. G. Marcy c Hartley b Sullivan	34	– (2) c Hauritz b Jurgensen	5
M. Klinger c Nye b Brant	0	– (1) b Jurgensen	5
G. C. Rummans c Hartley b Sullivan	34	– b Nye	69
B. R. Joseland not out	139		
N. Jewell st Hartley b Hauritz	137		
S. K. Warne c Hartley b Magoffin	11	– not out	0
A. C. Blizzard lbw b Magoffin	1	– (4) not out	101
*†P. J. Roach (did not bat).		– (5) run out (Magoffin–Simpson)	4
L-b 4, n-b 19	23	B 3, l-b 2, n-b 3	8

(120.1 overs, 470 mins)	(6 wkts dec) 379	(41 overs, 159 mins) (4 wkts dec) 192
Fall: 1 80 81 354 373 379		Fall: 10 11 159 188

B. A. Knowles, G. A. Lalor, M. G. Gale and D. J. Groves did not bat.

Bowling: *First Innings*—Brant 24–2–78–1; Jurgensen 27–8–69–0; Sullivan 17–1–90–2; Magoffin 21.1–8–52–2; Hauritz 28–6–68–1; Paulsen 3–0–18–0. *Second Innings*—Jurgensen 10–3–18–2; Sullivan 5–0–37–0; Magoffin 7–2–14–0; Simpson 11–0–69–0; Nye 8–1–49–1.

Queensland Academy of Sport

C. P. Simpson c Knowles b Lalor	118	– b Knowles	81
R. A. Broad c Warne b Knowles	17	– lbw b Knowles	0
*A. J. Nye c Roach b Warne	46	– c Roach b Gale	37
L. A. Carseldine not out	54	– c Knowles b Warne	33
S. J. Farrell lbw b Warne	2	– b Warne	39
†C. D. Hartley lbw b Knowles	21	– b Knowles	51
S. J. Paulsen (did not bat)		– c Groves b Warne	0
N. M. Hauritz (did not bat)		– not out	54
S. J. Jurgensen (did not bat)		– not out	4
B 4, l-b 2, n-b 2	8	B 3, l-b 1, n-b 3	7

(62.4 overs, 236 mins)	(5 wkts dec) 266	(57.5 overs, 229 mins) (7 wkts) 306
Fall: 63 184 187 193 266		Fall: 6 76 157 157 2627 227 295

S. A. Brant, G. J. Sullivan, S. J. Magoffin did not bat.

Bowling: *First Innings*—Groves 13–1–78–0; Lalor 16–4–51–1; Knowles 9.4–0–54–2; Gale 7–1–41–0; Warne 16–4–32–2; Rummans 1–0–4–0. *Second Innings*—Knowles 13–2–50–3; Lalor 8–1–41–0; Gale 11–2–42–1; Joseland 3–1–19–0; Warne 19.5–4–120–3; Groves 2–0–19–0; Blizzard 1–0–11–0.

Umpires: P. R. Reiffel and A. J. Soulsby.

SOUTH AUSTRALIA SECOND XI v WESTERN AUSTRALIA SECOND XI

At Adelaide Oval, Adelaide, February 9, 10, 11, 12, 2004. South Australia Second XI won by six wickets. *Toss:* Western Australia Second XI.

Close of play: First day, South Australia Second XI (1) 3-41 (Fitzgerald 0); Second day, South Australia Second XI (1) 7-393 (Harris 100, Staunton 63); Third day, South Australia Second XI (2) 1-11 (T.C. Plant 5, Staunton 2).

Western Australia Second XI

*S. W. Meuleman lbw b Johnson	79	–	(2) c T.C. Plant b Cullen	56
C.J. Simmons c Higgs b Harris	28	–	(1) c Higgs b Duval	20
S. E. Marsh c and b Cullen	9	–	c Davies b Cullen	25
A.C. Voges c Fitzgerald b Duval	16	–	c Davies b Bailey	30
S.A. Glew lbw b Harris	13	–	c T.C. Plant b Bailey	31
C.J. Heron c J.W. Plant b Duval	1	–	not out	45
†L. Ronchi c J.W. Plant b Johnson	59	–	c Johnson b Cullen	14
P.C. Worthington c Higgs b Cullen	53	–	c T.C. Plant b Cullen	4
A.K. Heal lbw b Cullen	21	–	lbw b Bailey	13
C.D. Thorp c Johnson b Cullen	4	–	st J.W. Plant b Bailey	0
J. P. Coetzee not out	0	–	c Davies b Cullen	0
L-b 6, n-b 8	14		L-b 7, n-b 4	11

(78 overs, 296 mins) 297
Fall: 101 121 125 143 146 184 244 283 293 297

(74 overs, 256 mins) 249
Fall: 39 95 114 168 175 203 207 244 244 249

A.C.L. James did not bat.

Bowling: *First Innings*—Duval 9-2-25-2; Weeks 8-0-43-0; Staunton 7-0-48-0; Harris 16-3-62-2; Johnson 17-3-48-2; Cullen 13-4-31-4; Bailey 5-2-20-0; Higgs 3-0-14-0. *Second Innings*—Duval 4-1-16-1; Weeks 3-0-21-0; Staunton 2-0-17-0; Harris 10-2-36-0; Cullen 32-6-97-5; Johnson 6-1-22-0; Bailey 17-7-33-4.

South Australia Second XI

T.C. Plant c Heron b James	21	–	c Marsh b Voges	42
*C.J. Davies c Ronchi b Worthington	15	–	lbw b James	2
†J.W. Plant b Worthington	1			
D.A. Fitzgerald c Ronchi b James	12	–	c Glew b Thorp	51
M.A. Higgs c Ronchi b Worthington	9	–	not out	12
B.A. Johnson c Ronchi b Worthington	130	–	not out	20
M. Weeks c Heron b Thorp	20			
R.J. Harris c Marsh b James	101			
A.M. Staunton c Glew b Coetzee	75	–	(3) c Marsh b Thorp	3
C.J. Duval b Thorp	3			
D.J. Cullen not out	0			
B 3, l-b 9, w 2, n-b 11	25		B 4, l-b 4	8

(125.1 overs, 504 mins) 412
Fall: 36 40 41 51 86 162 262 397 412 412

(40.2 overs, 157 mins) (4 wkts) 138
Fall: 7 22 100 104

C.B. Bailey did not bat.

Bowling: *First Innings*—Thorp 33.1-10-67-2; Coetzee 19-3-86-1; Worthington 24-4-79-4; James 19-4-60-3; Heal 23-4-75-0; Voges 2-0-7-0; Simmons 4-0-25-0; Glew 1-0-1-0. *Second Innings*—James 7-2-27-1; Heal 2-0-3-0; Worthington 8-3-14-0; Thorp 12.2-5-33-2; Voges 10-1-46-1; Coetzee 1-0-7-0.

Umpires: A. Collins and K.D. Perrin.

VICTORIA SECOND XI v NEW SOUTH WALES SECOND XI

At Melbourne Cricket Ground, Melbourne, February 23, 24, 25, 2004. New South Wales Second XI won by nine wickets. *Toss:* New South Wales Second XI.

Close of play: First day, New South Wales Second XI (1) 0-28 (Lambert 9, Wallace 16); Second day, Victoria Second XI (2) 3-29 (Rummans 10, Jewell 2).

Victoria Second XI

G. C. Rummans lbw b Nash	1	– b McGrath	66
J. L. Arnberger c Maraziotis b Bird	11	– c Maraziotis b McGrath	1
B. R. Joseland c O'Brien b Nash	60	– c O'Brien b Bird	16
A. B. McDonald c Smith b McGrath	22	– c McGrath b Bird	0
N. Jewell c Smith b Bird	43	– b McGrath	2
A. C. Blizzard c Maraziotis b Zammit	34	– c Bollinger b Nash	5
*†P. J. Roach c Krejza b McGrath	24	– c Zammit b McGrath	51
T. H. Welsford c Smith b Bird	0	– c Wallace b Lambert	14
C. J. McKay c O'Brien b Bollinger	8	– b Zammit	13
B. D. Harrop c Smith b Nash	17	– not out	5
D. J. Groves not out	2	– c Krejza b Zammit	4
L-b 5, n-b 7	12	L-b 5, n-b 3	8

(84.3 overs, 341 mins) 234
Fall: 1 41 80 114 171 179 184 202
  230 234

(72 overs, 298 mins) 185
Fall: 3 27 27 29 44 136 153 176
  178 185

D. P. Nannes did not bat.

Bowling: *First Innings*—McGrath 14.3–5–26–2; Nash 19–5–48–3; Bollinger 11–3–30–1; Bird 15–6–35–3; Krejza 9–2–36–0; Lambert 7–1–27–0; Zammit 9–4–27–1. *Second Innings*—McGrath 18–7–30–4; Nash 13–3–49–1; Bollinger 10–3–26–0; Bird 10–0–34–2; Zammit 13–6–30–2; Lambert 8–4–11–1.

New South Wales Second XI

G. M. Lambert lbw b Groves	9	– (2) not out	101
D. P. Wallace lbw b Groves	20	– (1) c and b Harrop	24
E. J. M. Cowan c Roach b Welsford	22	– not out	39
A. W. O'Brien c Welsford b Nannes	119		
P. Maraziotis c Roach b Welsford	1		
J. J. Krejza c Joseland b McKay	31		
†D. Smith c Roach b Welsford	5		
D. A. Nash c McDonald b Welsford	0		
A. C. Bird b McKay	20		
L. A. Zammit c Roach b McKay	0		
G. D. McGrath not out	6		
B 3, l-b 10, n-b 9	22	L-b 4	4

(80.5 overs, 318 mins) 255
Fall: 28 37 101 106 184 191 193 220 220 255

(33.1 overs, 129 mins) (1 wkt) 168
Fall: 47

D. Bollinger did not bat.

Bowling: *First Innings*—Nannes 16.5–4–49–1; Groves 18–5–34–2; McKay 18–3–66–3; Welsford 19–3–57–4; Harrop 6–1–15–0; McDonald 3–0–21–0. *Second Innings*—Nannes 3–0–21–0; Groves 5–0–31–0; Rummans 4–1–26–0; McDonald 7–3–10–0; Harrop 6–1–20–1; Welsford 3–0–25–0; McKay 5–0–27–0; Joseland 0.1–0–4–0.

Umpires: G. A. Abood and J. D. Ward.

TASMANIA SECOND XI v QUEENSLAND ACADEMY OF SPORT

At TCA Ground, Hobart, February 23, 24, 25, 26, 2004. Queensland Academy of Sport won by 282 runs. *Toss:* Queensland Academy of Sport.

Close of play: First day, Queensland Academy of Sport (1) 5-351 (Paulsen 77); Second day, Tasmania Second XI (1) 7-251 (Butterworth 49, Pickering 8); Third day, Tasmania Second XI (2) 0-17 (Harris 9, Birt 5).

Queensland Academy of Sport

B. P. Nash c Dawson b Butterworth	18	–	(2) c Pickering b Tubb	35
R. A. Broad c Swards b Pender	143	–	(1) lbw b Swards	14
*A. J. Nye c Dawson b Stewart	86	–	c Swards b Stewart	55
S. J. Paulsen c Pender b Butterworth	92	–	(6) not out	37
S. J. Farrell run out	7	–	c Doolan b Swards	31
R. N. Le Loux b Birt b Pender	5	–	(7) c Pickering b Bailey	11
L. A. Carseldine c Doolan b Tubb	15	–	(4) c Doolan b Harris	114
†D. L. Wallis c Birt b Butterworth	1	–	c Doolan b Tubb	33
D. R. MacKenzie lbw b Tubb	4	–	not out	9
S. J. Jurgensen not out	20			
S. J. Magoffin c Lockyear b Stewart	2			
B 1, l-b 3, w 2, n-b 19	25		L-b 3, w 1, n-b 6	10

(113.5 overs, 435 mins)	418	(70 overs, 275 mins)　　　(7 wkts) 349
Fall: 41 224 298 334 351 387 389 389 407 418		Fall: 31 72 178 246 267 280 336

G. J. Sullivan did not bat.

Bowling: *First Innings*—Pickering 19–4–66–0; Stewart 19.5–4–60–2; Butterworth 24–5–88–3; Swards 14–4–41–0; Pender 12–0–75–2; Tubb 19–4–56–2; Harris 4–0–18–0; Lockyear 2–0–10–0. *Second Innings*—Butterworth 12–3–55–0; Stewart 14–3–63–2; Pender 9–1–38–0; Swards 10–0–58–1; Tubb 9–0–48–2; Bailey 8–0–38–1; Harris 8–0–46–1.

Tasmania Second XI

R. J. G. Lockyear c Carseldine b MacKenzie	8			
B. L. Harris c Carseldine b Jurgensen	35	–	(1) b Jurgensen	9
†D. G. Dawson c Wallis b MacKenzie	54	–	lbw b Jurgensen	0
*G. J. Bailey b MacKenzie	24	–	(5) run out	0
T. R. Birt c Nash b Sullivan	11	–	(2) lbw b Nye	37
A. J. Doolan b Jurgensen	44	–	(4) b Sullivan	19
S. B. Tubb b Le Loux	10	–	(6) c Wallis b Sullivan	23
L. R. Butterworth c Carseldine b MacKenzie	81	–	(7) not out	66
K. S. Pickering lbw b Jurgensen	12	–	(8) run out	6
L. C. Swards b Jurgensen	0	–	(9) c Nye b MacKenzie	10
A. J. Pender not out	13	–	(10) lbw b Magoffin	0
M. W. Stewart (did not bat)		–	c Nye b Magoffin	0
B 4, w 2, n-b 3	9		B 1, l-b 7, w 1, n-b 5	14

(88 overs, 355 mins)	301	(59.1 overs, 250 mins) 184
Fall: 16 69 122 135 142 157 226 268		Fall: 19 19 52 52 91 108 149 179
275 301		180 184

Bowling: *First Innings*—MacKenzie 25–6–91–4; Jurgensen 28–9–79–4; Magoffin 13–2–32–0; Sullivan 11–3–48–1; Le Loux 11–2–47–1. *Second Innings*—MacKenzie 14–4–40–1; Jurgensen 19–6–43–2; Magoffin 12.1–0–30–2; Sullivan 6–0–35–2; Nye 8–2–28–1.

Umpires: B. J. Muir and J. H. Smeaton.

WESTERN AUSTRALIA SECOND XI v AUSTRALIAN CAPITAL TERRITORY

At Richardson Park, Perth, February 23, 24, 25, 2004. Western Australia Second XI won by an innings and 89 runs. *Toss:* Australian Capital Territory.

Close of play: First day, Western Australia Second XI (1) 4-240 (Voges 67, Glew 9); Second day, Australian Capital Territory (2) 8-166 (Hatton 1, McNees 2).

Western Australia Second XI

C.J. Simmons c Rhynehart b Hatton	70	D.J. Wates not out	37
C.J. Heron c Heaney b Karppinen	3	A.K. Heal c Rhynehart b Karppinen	15
B.J. Lillis c McLeod b McNees	21	B.R. Dorey not out	43
S.E. Marsh c McLeod b McNees	56	B 5, l-b 16, n-b 1	22
*A.C. Voges c McLeod b Divin	124		
S.A. Glew c McLeod b Kellar	21	(131 overs, 495 mins) (8 wkts dec)	424
†L. Ronchi c McLeod b Karppinen	12	Fall: 23 101 109 212 271 325 325 344	

S.G. Howman, A.C.L. James, D.C. Bandy and T.A. Hopes did not bat.

Bowling: Karppinen 26–9–70–3; Kellar 29–10–74–1; McNees 26–6–94–2; Divin 20–4–79–1; Hatton 24–4–63–1; Nason 6–1–23–0.

Australian Capital Territory

D.J. Richards c Ronchi b Howman	0	– (2) c Ronchi b James	8
A.G. Rhynehart c Voges b Howman	13	– (1) b Howman	10
*C. Brown c Glew b Wates	4	– c Ronchi b James	11
S.P. Heaney b James	14	– c Ronchi b Dorey	6
M.A. Divin c Lillis b Howman	6	– c Ronchi b James	21
†C.R.A. McLeod c Dorey b James	64	– c Heron b Voges	24
S.J. Karppinen c Ronchi b Howman	13	– (8) c Ronchi b Bandy	9
P.B. Radford c Ronchi b James	34	– (7) lbw b Bandy	16
M.A. Hatton not out	2	– not out	21
D.A. McNees c Lillis b Howman	2	– c Voges b Bandy	6
E. Kellar c Lillis b Howman	0		
M.W. Nason (did not bat)		– c Ronchi b Hopes	28
L-b 7, w 2, n-b 6	15	L-b 3, w 2, n-b 3	8
(64.5 overs, 260 mins)	167	(69.2 overs, 254 mins)	168
Fall: 0 18 19 30 67 93 152 161 118 168		Fall: 11 27 32 51 69 99 103 112	

Bowling: *First Innings*—Howman 19.5–9–36–6; Wates 13–3–31–1; James 15–5–33–3; Dorey 10–4–28–0; Heal 7–0–32–0. *Second Innings*—Dorey 17–6–43–1; Howman 13–2–39–1; Bandy 14–4–38–3; James 12–4–23–3; Hopes 8.2–2–16–1; Voges 5–3–6–1.

Umpires: B. Bennett and R.R. Pease.

CRICKET AUSTRALIA CUP COMPETITION WINNERS

CRICKET AUSTRALIA CUP TEAM RESULTS

	First Game	M	W	L	D	% Won
Australian Cricket Academy ...	Sep 27, 1999	26	9	13	4	34.61
Queensland Academy of Sport ..	Sep 27, 1999	25	13	7	5	52.00
South Australia Second XI	Oct 5, 1999	29	10	15	4	34.48
Australian Capital Territory	Oct 25, 1999	26	7	17	2	26.92
Western Australia Second XI ...	Nov 1, 1999	28	15	7	6	53.57
Victoria Second XI	Nov 8, 1999	29	14	8	7	48.28
New South Wales Second XI ...	Nov 15, 1999	25	15	6	4	60.00
Tasmania Second XI	Nov 15, 1999	28	8	18	2	28.57

MOST RUNS

	M	I	NO	R	HS	100s	50s	Avge	S-R
L. Williams (ACA/S Aust/Tas)	31	49	6	1,981	201*	5	11	46.07	43.38
A. C. Voges (W Aust/ACA)	27	40	6	1,455	144	4	5	42.79	52.93
C. J. L. Rogers (W Aust)	16	27	4	1,396	151*	3	10	60.70	57.57
M. Klinger (W Aust/Vic)	20	32	3	1,307	138	1	12	45.07	57.22
D. G. Dawson (ACT)	17	34	3	1,227	124	2	7	39.58	37.18
S. A. Deitz (S Aust)................	16	27	0	1,177	140	3	8	43.59	51.15
S. R. Mason (Tas/ACA)	18	31	0	1,088	153	2	6	35.10	43.60
C. Brown (ACT)...................	17	32	1	1,086	136	2	6	35.03	50.21
G. C. Rummans (NSW/Vic)	15	24	3	1,080	210	2	6	51.43	60.38
M. J. North (ACA/W Aust).........	18	31	2	1,030	101	2	8	35.52	51.60
G. T. Cunningham (ACT/Tas)	20	36	0	1,006	85	0	7	27.94	62.98
P. A. Jaques (NSW/ACA)...........	22	34	1	989	135	3	3	29.97	56.64
M. J. Phelps (NSW)...............	16	26	5	952	122	4	3	45.33	57.70
C. J. Davies (S Aust)	9	17	3	933	233*	2	6	66.64	64.66
A. B. McDonald (ACA/Vic).........	21	33	4	923	122	1	4	31.83	63.06
D. J. Harris (S Aust/ACA)...........	26	43	1	922	102	1	4	21.95	38.15
N. T. Adcock (S Aust/ACA).........	17	26	2	908	170*	2	7	37.83	56.51
S. W. Meuleman (W Aust/ACA)	15	29	1	896	94	0	7	32.00	47.76
L. A. Carseldine (Qld)	9	15	3	869	230*	2	5	72.42	69.52
S. E. Marsh (W Aust/ACA).........	14	24	1	862	129	2	6	37.48	58.09

MOST WICKETS

	M	O	Mdns	R	W	BB	5W/i	10W/m	Avge	S-R
E. Kellar (ACT)	20	768.2	210	2,000	70	6–41	5	1	28.57	65.86
A. G. Downton (ACA/Tas) ..	17	505	124	1,575	68	7–46	4	2	23.16	44.56
P. C. Rofe (ACA/S Aust) ...	16	416.4	90	1,205	58	6–63	2	1	20.78	43.10
G. M. Lambert (NSW)	16	348.5	67	1,178	51	6–52	3	0	23.10	41.04
S. J. Magoffin (ACA/Qld) ...	13	407.5	95	1,204	50	5–31	1	0	24.08	48.94
M. D. Pascoe (Qld/ACA/Tas)	14	399.5	108	1,094	49	5–31	3	0	22.33	48.96
D. A. Nash (NSW)	8	253.5	76	667	47	6–61	3	1	14.19	32.40
S. J. Karppinen (W Aust/ACT)	16	433	110	1,321	46	5–44	1	0	28.72	56.48
A. B. McDonald (ACA/Vic) .	21	395	109	1,273	39	4–26	0	0	32.64	60.77
M. A. Harrity (S Aust)	8	216.4	57	596	36	6–31	2	1	16.56	36.11
S. J. Jurgensen (Tas)	15	385	93	1,182	36	5–66	1	0	32.83	64.17
A. C. L. James (ACT/ACA/WA)	11	301	50	1,211	34	5–57	1	0	35.62	53.12
A. W. Polkinghorne (SA/Tas)	15	342.4	74	1,226	34	4–69	0	0	36.06	60.47
C. D. Thorp (W Aust)	12	307.3	67	808	32	4–52	0	0	25.25	57.66
S. B. Tubb (Tas)	25	441.3	84	1,509	32	6–55	2	0	47.16	82.78
M. J. Thistle (W Aust)	11	276.3	53	927	30	5–61	2	0	30.90	55.30
L. A. Zammit (NSW)	10	282.4	68	998	30	3–45	0	0	33.27	58.53
G. J. Denton (Tas)	5	141.1	31	470	29	6–84	3	1	16.21	29.21
A. R. Griffith (Tas/ACA) ...	14	323.1	79	1,041	29	6–45	2	1	36.24	66.86

HIGHEST INDIVIDUAL SCORES

260	M. J. Cosgrove	South Australia v ACT at Adelaide	2003-04
239	B. P. Van Deinsen	New South Wales v Victoria at St Kilda	2001-02
233*	C. J. Davies	South Australia v ACT at Adelaide	2001-02
230*	L. A. Carseldine	Queensland v ACT at Canberra	2001-02
210	G. C. Rummans	Victoria v Queensland at Albion	2002-03
208	L. G. Buchanan	Victoria v ACT at St Kilda	2002-03
201*	L. Williams	Cricket Academy v South Australia at Adelaide	2000-01
196*	A. J. Sainsbury	New South Wales v ACT at Boomanulla	2000-01
191	P. Maraziotis	New South Wales v Queensland at Albion	2003-04
189	C. J. Richards	New South Wales v Queensland at Albion	2001-02

BEST BOWLING IN AN INNINGS

9–67	J. M. Davison	Victoria v South Australia at Adelaide	2001-02
8–73	B. E. Young	South Australia v ACT at Canberra	2002-03
7–46	A. G. Downton	Cricket Academy v Victoria at South Melbourne	1999-00
6–29	A. G. Downton	Tasmania v Queensland at Albion	2002-03
6–31	M. A. Harrity	South Australia v Queensland at Adelaide	2000-01
6–35	J. Moss	Victoria v Queensland at Albion	2000-01
6–36	S. G. Howman	Western Australia v ACT at Perth	2003-04
6–37	S. J. Magoffin	Queensland v ACT at Albion	2002-03
6–41	S. M. Harwood	Victoria v Tasmania at Camberwell	2001-02
6–41	E. Kellar	ACT v Cricket Academy at Canberra	2000-01

MOST WICKETS IN A MATCH

14–146	B. E. Young	South Australia v ACT at Canberra	2002-03
12–101	A. G. Downton	Cricket Academy v Tasmania at South Melbourne	1999-00
11–92	A. R. Griffith	Tasmania v New South Wales at Hobart	2003-04
11–149	G. J. Denton	Tasmania v Western Australia at Perth	2003-04
10–35	D. A. Nash	New South Wales v South Australia at Adelaide	2002-03
10–111	P. C. Rofe	Cricket Academy v Victoria at South Melbourne	2000-01
10–139	A. G. Downton	Tasmania v Queensland at Albion	2002-03
10–140	E. Kellar	ACT v Cricket Academy at Canberra	2000-01
10–163	M. A. Harrity	South Australia v Tasmania at Adelaide	2000-01

HIGHEST WICKET PARTNERSHIPS

1st	198	M. J. Phelps and N. J. Catalano	NSW v ACT at Canberra	2002-03
2nd	302	L. Williams and P. A. Jaques	ACA v S Aust at Adelaide	2000-01
3rd	277	L. G. Buchanan and C. J. Peake	Vic v S Aust at Adelaide	2002-03
4th	371	C. J. Ferguson and M. J. Cosgrove	S Aust v ACT at Adelaide	2003-04
5th	221	A. J. Sainsbury and M. G. Betsey	NSW v ACT at Boomanulla	2000-01
6th	202	D. J. Thornely and G. M. Lambert	NSW v S Aust at Bankstown	2003-04
7th	242	D. J. Thornely and S. D. Bradstreet	NSW v ACT at Hurstville	2003-04
8th	157	R. J. Tucker and D. C. Brede	ACT v NSW at Bankstown	1999-00
9th	107	S. D. Stanton and A. R. Crook	ACA v W Aust at Perth	1999-00
10th	151	S. A. Holcolme and D. A. McNees	ACT v S Aust at Adelaide	2003-04

SYDNEY GREGORY CUP, 2003-04

QUEENSLAND COLTS v NEW SOUTH WALES COLTS

At Allan Border Field, Albion, October 20, 21, 22, 23, 2003. *Toss:* New South Wales Colts. New South Wales Colts won by 36 runs.

Close of play: First day, New South Wales Colts (1) 7-203 (Zammit 57, Cameron 29); Second day, New South Wales Colts (2) 0-34 (Cowan 19, Williams 13); Third day, New South Wales Colts (2) 4-358 (Christian 73, Hunt 44).

New South Wales Colts

S. P. Williams c Summers b Glass	20	–	(2) c Philipson b Simpson		29
E. J. M. Cowan c Hartley b Glass	30	–	(1) b Simpson		19
*A. W. O'Brien c Philipson b Glass	1	–	c Hartley b Simpson		87
B. J. Rohrer c Simpson b Summers	28	–	c Hartley b Glass		101
D. T. Christian c Paulsen b Le Loux	6	–	not out		107
G. I. Hunt c Hartley b Rimmington	5	–	run out (Rimmington)		52
A. C. Bird c Hartley b Rimmington	15	–	b Rimmington		0
L. A. Zammit lbw b Glass	67	–	not out		4
M. A. Cameron b Simpson b Glass	41				
†J. B. Allsopp not out	2				
C. K. L. Nupier c Paulsen b Glass	6				
L-b 2, w 10	17		L-b 2, w 1, n-b 2		5
	238		(129 overs, 453 mins) (6 wkts dec)		**404**

(97.2 overs, 353 mins)
Fall: 41 46 65 81 90 102 114 227 230 238

Fall: 34 82 176 281 381 381

B. G. Drew did not bat.

Bowling: *First Innings*—Rimmington 26–6–75–2; Glass 28.2–10–48–6; Summers 16–9–30–1; Le Loux 12–4–46–1; McCabe 4–1–9–0; Simpson 11–3–23–0. *Second Innings*—Rimmington 26–5–107–1; Glass 24–7–61–1; Simpson 44–18–82–3; Le Loux 15–1–63–0; McCabe 4–0–28–0; Philipson 1–0–3–0; Summers 12–4–45–0; Paulsen 3–0–13–0.

Queensland Colts

A. P. Maynard b Cameron	0	–	(2) c and b Cameron		28
*C. P. Simpson c Christian b Bird	17	–	(1) c Rohrer b Bird		0
C. A. Philipson c Allsopp b Zammit	70	–	lbw b Zammit		127
R. A. Broad c Nupier b Cameron	39	–	b Drew		11
S. J. Paulsen c Drew b Zammit	12	–	c Cameron b Zammit		115
†C. D. Hartley c Rohrer b O'Brien	0	–	c Hunt b Zammit		54
P. J. Reimers c Cameron b Zammit	15	–	run out (Christian)		11
R. N. Le Loux c and b Zammit	48	–	run out (Rohrer)		7
C. R. Glass c Allsopp b O'Brien	9	–	c Cameron b Zammit		0
N. J. Rimmington c and b Zammit	4	–	(11) not out		4
C. Summers not out	6				
C. J. McCabe (did not bat)		–	(10) b Zammit		0
L-b 4, w 6	10		B 5, l-b 6, w 2, n-b 6		19
	230		(82.3 overs, 315 mins)		**376**

(74.1 overs, 251 mins)
Fall: 10 23 104 139 140 161 161 180 205 230

Fall: 11 50 74 277 304 336 366 368 369 376

Bowling: *First Innings*—Bird 14–2–49–1; Cameron 10–2–36–2; Zammit 24.1–7–69–5; Nupier 5–1–24–0; Drew 3–0–24–0; O'Brien 18–10–24–2. *Second Innings*—Bird 8–1–37–1; Cameron 19–5–70–1; Zammit 32.3–6–124–5; Drew 4–1–18–1; O'Brien 10–0–62–0; Williams 3–0–18–0; Nupier 6–0–36–0.

Umpires: G. N. Cubit and A. Curran.

Australian Under-19s, 2003-04

by GREG McKIE

New South Wales won a fiercely contested Australian Under-19s championship after four teams entered the final round with a shot at the title. Victoria blew their chances by losing to South Australia. Western Australia needed to beat Tasmania outright but could manage only a comfortable first-innings victory. NSW began the last round of matches holding the competition lead. Seeking to guarantee top spot with an outright victory, they declared the moment they eclipsed Queensland's total of 167 with four wickets in hand. Ultimately they ran out of time to mount a run-chase and had to be content with first-innings points. It proved enough to hand them the championship.

Last summer's carnival was held in Brisbane. For the second year in a row, all eight states and territories played against each other, starting with four one-day matches and climaxing with three two-day games. Consistency was the key for NSW. Sam Hinton and Ahilen Beadle were the leading batsmen but most of their team-mates averaged over 20. It was similarly a team effort with the ball. Beadle, Scott Coyte, Peter Forrest and Moises Henriques all took their wickets economically and at a healthy strike-rate, with Coyte's 5 for 22 against Victoria the best figures. Not surprisingly, five members of Australia's 14-man squad for the Under-19s World Cup in Bangladesh hailed from NSW: Beadle, Coyte, Henriques, Shane Wallace and Stephen O'Keefe.

South Australia, courtesy of their thumping last-round win over Victoria, finished runners-up for the second year in a row. They finished only one point behind NSW. Callum Ferguson, the talented right-hander who broke through at ING Cup level late in the season, was named Player of the Series for his 380 runs at 63.33.

Along the way he made history by extending his career record at under-age level, in four years of Under-17s and Under-19s championships, to 1,799 runs at 48.62. No other batsman in history has scored so many. Batting was undoubtedly SA's strength, with John Pratt and Mark Littlewood each hitting centuries and Lachlan Oswald-Jacobs chipping in with three fifties. The left-armer Gary Putland was the pick of the attack with 14 wickets, enough to earn him World Cup selection, and he received good support from Daniel Franco with 10 wickets. The other bowlers were expensive.

Western Australia moved three places up the ladder to finish third, winning their last four games straight on the back of some hefty scoring. Theo Doropoulos hit 163 against the Northern Territory. Rhys May made 162 against the Australian Capital Territory followed by 161 in his next innings against Tasmania. Luke Pomersbach had earlier racked up 147 against SA. Sam Hogg, with 10 wickets, and Cory Verco, with nine, were WA's best bowlers.

The defending champions Victoria slipped to fourth, losing their last two games largely because of the inability of their bowlers to make breakthroughs. The leg-spinner Josh Mangan was their leading bowler for the second year in a row with 16 wickets. Cameron Huckett, with 11, was the only other Victorian to finish with more than five wickets. Their batting line-up was similarly inconsistent. Their highest team effort was a relatively lowly 245 against SA, and only two players – the wicket-keeper Adam Crosthwaite (299) and James Wild (209) – exceeded 200 runs for the championship.

The Northern Territory, by contrast, enjoyed their highest position ever at Under-19 level. The cornerstone of their success, as he has been for years, was Ken Skewes. In his fourth and final Under-19s carnival he colleted four fifties, 322 runs at 64.40 and finished as the competition's all-time leading runscorer: 941 runs at 55.35. His combined record at Under-19 and Under-17 level stands at 1,656 runs at 55.20, only 143 runs fewer than Ferguson. He was soundly supported this time round by Michael Barry, who scored 173 runs, and Reece McDonald, who hit 103 against the ACT. And in Paul Cook, Rob McCard, Richie Hodgson and Skewes, the NT fielded perhaps the tightest attack in their history.

Queensland dropped two places to finish sixth, principally because of their lack of batting depth. Nathan Reardon and Lyndon Hoffman were consistent but received little support; only Reardon reached 200 runs and no one averaged 40. Their bowling was far stronger. The medium-pacer David Marriott took 5 for 49 against Victoria and was solidly backed up by Cavan Ditchmen, Adam Lavis and Michael Salerno.

Despite boasting several excellent individual performers, Tasmania were relegated to seventh position. Tim Paine stood out as their leading batsman with 268 runs, and was subsequently named captain of the Under-19s World Cup squad. Paine also effected 15 dismissals, the most by any keeper. Paul Ancher, courtesy of a string of not outs, finished with a tournament average of 172. Jason Shelton and Gordon Kerr were the pick of the bowlers with 11 wickets each.

The best figures of the championship belonged to Daniel Poidevin, the ACT left-arm medium-pacer, who snared 6 for 50 against the NT. His team-mate Michael Shaw took 11 wickets but the ACT were badly let down by their batting and failed to win a game. Nobody averaged 22 or reached 60 in an individual innings. Their nadir came against Victoria when they were bowled out for 39, the ACT's lowest tally ever at under-age level.

The Under-19s championship celebrated a momentous milestone last summer when Nathan Bracken became the 100th Test player to emerge from the competition in its 35-year history. No fewer than a dozen of the present Test line-up came through the Under-19s: Adam Gilchrist, Michael Kasprowicz, Justin Langer, Stuart MacGill, Brett Lee, Matthew Hayden, Darren Lehmann, Damien Martyn, Ricky Ponting, Jason Gillespie, Martin Love and Simon Katich.

ROUND ONE

South Australia 7 for 285 (L. G. Oswald-Jacobs 95, C. J. Ferguson 60) defeated Western Australia 9 for 284 (L. Pomersbach 147; G. D. Putland 4-28, D. J. Franco 3-53) by one run.

Queensland 150 (N. Reardon 50; R. Hodgson 4-34, P. A. W. Cook 4-22) defeated Northern Territory 142 (M. P. Barry 33; N. Fitzpatrick 3-36) by eight runs.

Tasmania 7 for 217 (T. D. Paine 118; J. P. Mangan 3-29) lost to Victoria 5 for 218 (J. Wild 77*, A. J. Crosthwaite 70) by five wickets.

New South Wales 9 for 231 (A. Beadle 45; D. Poidevin 3-36) defeated Australian Capital Territory 165 (D. Goodsell 59; S. Cook 3-15) by 66 runs.

ROUND TWO

Victoria 8 for 223 (A. J. Crosthwaite 90, A. Finch 69; C. R. Verco 3-30, C. Lagana 3-40) defeated Western Australia 127 (L. Powis 45*; J. Mangan 4-44, C. S. Huckett 3-27) by 96 runs.

Northern Territory 9 for 200 (P. Brown 32; S. N. J. O'Keefe 3-23) lost to New South Wales 1 for 204 (A. Beadle 113*, P. Forrest 53*) by nine wickets.

South Australia 313 (J. P. Pratt 109, L. D. Oswald-Jacobs 51; M. E. L. Shaw 3-46) defeated Australian Capital Territory 162 (S. L. Gaskin 38; L. Pastyn 3-19, D. J. Franco 3-28) by 151 runs.

Queensland 115 (L. Hoffman 37; P. Doherty 3-23, J. Shelton 3-28) lost to Tasmania 3 for 116 (D. Anderson 61*) by seven wickets.

ROUND THREE

Western Australia 9 for 245 (M. J. Johnston 49; A. Lavis 3-44) defeated Queensland 224 (N. Reardon 59; S. Hogg 4-37, J. Goodall 3-28) by 21 runs.

South Australia 255 (C. J. Ferguson 132; P. A. W. Cook 3-30) defeated Northern Territory 7 for 182 (K. J. Skewes 83*, G. D. Putland 3-38, M. Littlewood 3-47) by 73 runs.

Victoria 5 for 234 (A. J Crosthwaite 67) defeated Australian Capital Territory 39 (J. Mangan 4-7, C. Salm 4-9) by 195 runs.

New South Wales 7 for 284 (T. Cooper 79, S. J. Hinton 55*; J. Shelton 3-59) defeated Tasmania 9 for 229 (T. D. Paine 82; P. Forrest 3-28) by 55 runs.

ROUND FOUR

All matches were abandoned because of rain.

ROUND FIVE

Western Australia 9 for 375 (T. P. Doropoulos 163; R. Hodgson 3-57, K. J. Skewes 3-61) defeated Northern Territory 276 (S. J. Regan 67, K. J. Skewes 61; J. M. Goodall 3-45) by 99 runs.

Victoria 8 for 191 (J. Wild 70; S. Coyte 5-22) defeated New South Wales 123 (S. J. Hinton 33; C. S. Huckett 3-35) by 68 runs.

Australian Capital Territory 180 (D. Poidevin 58; W. Quarrell 3-33) lost to Tasmania 9 for 184 (W. Quarrell 40; D. Goodsell 3-35) by one wicket.

Queensland 148 (E. *Ross 23; D. J. Franco 3-31) lost to South Australia 7-149 (C. J. Ferguson 42) by three wickets.

ROUND SIX

Victoria 210 (P. M. Nevill 84; D. J. Marriott 5-49, A. Lavis 3-40) lost to Queensland 4 for 283 (L. Hoffman 96, N. Reardon 62*) on first innings.

New South Wales 7 for 331 declared (S. J. Hinton 114, S. N. J. O'Keefe 77) defeated South Australia 162 (C. J. Ferguson 45; A. Beadle 3-5) and 3 for 118 (J. P. Pratt 44) on first innings.

Australian Capital Territory 164 (D. Goodsell 34; C. R. Verco 3-25) and 4 for 157 (C. A. Johnston 57) lost to Western Australia 6 for 343 (R. May 162, T. P. Doropoulos 62) on first innings.

Tasmania 9 for 299 (P. Ancher 60, M. Wade 57; R McCard 4-73) lost to Northern Territory 9 for 301 (K. J. Skewes 68, M. P. Barry 64, D. K. Richards 50; G. S. Kerr 4-83, N. Cashion 3-54) on first innings.

ROUND SEVEN

Tasmania 214 (P. Ancher 85*; R. Phillimore 3-25) lost to Western Australia 6 for 390 (R. May 161, L. Pomersbach 83, T. P. Doropoulos 75) on first innings.

South Australia 7 for 356 declared (M. Littlewood 155*, L. D. Oswald-Jacobs 75, M. Crook 54*) defeated Victoria 245 (T. Evans 85; C. B. Bailey 4-51, S. Smith 3-25) and 2 for 59 (A. J. Crosthwaite 31*) on first innings.

Queensland 167 (E. Rose 47; A. Beadle 4-17) and 7 for 187 declared (P. Keys 61*; S. Cook 3-69) lost to New South Wales 6 for 170 declared (S. Coyte 35*, G. Clarence 35*; N. Fitzpatrick 3-67) and 1 for 25 on first innings.

Northern Territory 280 (R. J. McDonald 103, K. J. Skewes 82; D. Poidevin 6-50, M. E. L. Shaw 3-49) defeated Australian Capital Territory 194 (W. Hay 43; R. J. McDonald 4-13, R. McCard 3-40) on first innings.

UNDER-19S CHAMPIONSHIP, 2003-04

POINTS TABLE

	P	W	L	D	Bonus Points	Quotient	Points
New South Wales	7	5	1	1	1	1.552	25
South Australia	7	5	1	1	2	1.161	24
Western Australia	7	4	2	1	1	1.505	21
Victoria	7	4	2	1	4	0.205	20
Northern Territory	7	2	4	1	2	0.833	12
Queensland	7	2	4	1	0	0.904	10
Tasmania	7	2	4	1	2	0.846	10
Australian Capital Territory	7	0	6	1	0	0.513	0

MOST RUNS

	M	I	NO	R	HS	100s	50s	Avge
C. J. Ferguson (S Aust)	6	7	1	380	132	1	1	63.33
R. May (W Aust)	5	5	0	376	162	2	0	75.20
T. P. Doropoulos (W Aust)	6	6	0	352	163	1	2	58.66
L. Pomersbach (W Aust)	6	6	0	324	147	1	1	54.00
K. J. Skewes (NT)	6	6	1	322	83*	0	4	64.40
A. J. Crosthwaite (Vic)	6	7	1	299	90	0	3	49.83
T. D. Paine (Tas)	6	6	0	286	118	1	1	47.66
L. G. Oswald-Jacobs (S Aust)	6	7	0	279	95	0	3	39.85
S. J. Hinton (NSW)	6	5	1	265	114	1	1	66.25
A. Beadle (NSW)	6	7	1	243	113*	1	0	40.50

MOST WICKETS

	M	O	Mdns	R	W	BB	5W/i	Avge	RPO
J. P. Mangan (Vic) 6		96.5	30	257	16	4-7	0	16.06	2.65
G. D. Putland (S Aust) 6		72	14	237	14	4-28	0	16.92	3.29
M. E. L. Shaw (ACT) 6		84.2	18	276	11	3-46	0	25.09	3.27
C. S. Huckett (Vic) 6		70	11	238	11	3-27	0	21.63	3.40
G. S. Kerr (Tas) 6		66.5	7	272	11	4-83	0	24.72	4.06
R. McCard (NT) 6		64	2	282	11	4-72	0	25.63	4.40
J. Shelton (Tas) 6		61	8	291	11	3-28	0	26.45	4.77
D. J. Marriott (Qld) 4		58	13	169	10	5-49	1	16.90	2.91
S. Coyte (NSW) 6		58	10	179	10	5-22	1	17.90	3.08
S. Hogg (W Aust) 5		67	11	240	10	4-37	0	24.00	3.58
D. J. Franco (S Aust) 6		59	7	252	10	3-28	0	25.20	4.27
S. Cook (NSW) 5		58	5	267	10	3-15	0	26.70	4.60
D. Poidevin (ACT) 6		33	5	160	10	6-50	1	16.00	4.84

UNDER-19S CHAMPIONSHIP RECORDS

CHAMPIONSHIP WINNERS

Series	Venue	Winner	Player of the Year
1969-70	Melbourne	Victoria	no award
1970-71	Sydney	Victoria	no award
1971-72	Adelaide	Victoria	R. Wallace (Qld)
1972-73	Canberra	New Zealand	G. C. Hughes (NSW)
1973-74	Melbourne	South Australia	D. W. Hookes (SAust)
1974-75	Brisbane	Victoria	D. Brown (Qld)
1975-76	Perth	New South Wales	D. M. Wellham (NSW)
1976-77	Hobart	New Zealand	J. J. Crowe (NZ)
1977-78	Christchurch	New South Wales	P. S. Clifford (NSW)
1978-79	Sydney	Western Australia	R. J. Thomas (NZ)
1979-80	Adelaide	Western Australia/Victoria	M. D. Crowe (NZ)
1980-81	Brisbane	Victoria	D. Knox (NSW)
1981-82	Canberra	Victoria	M. R. J. Veletta (WAust)
1982-83	Perth	Victoria	I. A. Healy (Qld)
1983-84	Melbourne	South Australia	S. R. Waugh (NSW)
1984-85	Hobart	Victoria	J. K. Pyke (ACT)
1985-86	Sydney	Queensland/New South Wales	J. C. Scuderi (Qld)
1986-87	Adelaide	New South Wales	G. R. Parker (Vic)
1987-88	Brisbane	Western Australia	R. C. Kelly (WAust)
1988-89	Canberra	New South Wales	M. G. Bevan (ACT)
1989-90	Melbourne	New South Wales	J. E. R. Gallian (NSW)
1990-91	Sydney	South Australia	A. C. Gilchrist (NSW)
1991-92	Perth	Western Australia	A. D. McQuire (NSW)
1992-93	Brisbane	Victoria	J. P. Bray (NSW)
1993-94	Melbourne	Western Australia	J. L. Cassell (Qld)
1994-95	Sydney	Queensland/New South Wales	B. A. Clemow (NSW)
1995-96	Adelaide	Victoria	P. A. Sutherland (NSW)
1996-97	Canberra	New South Wales	D. J. McLauchlan (NSW)
1997-98	Melbourne	South Australia	G. A. Manou (SAust)
1998-99	Adelaide	New South Wales	M. Klinger (Vic)
1999-00	Perth	Victoria/Queensland	L. Buchanan (Vic)
2000-01	Hobart	Queensland	B. Casson (WAust)
2001-02	Newcastle	New South Wales	A. J. Crosthwaite (Vic)
2002-03	Canberra	Victoria	M. J. Cosgrove (SAust)
2003-04	Brisbane	New South Wales	C. J. Ferguson (S Aust)

LAST TEN YEARS' PLACINGS

	94-95	95-96	96-97	97-98	98-99	99-00	00-01	01-02	02-03	03-04
Australian Capital Territory	8	7	6	7	6	7	7	8	7	8
New South Wales .	1	2	1	2	1	3	4	1	3	1
Northern Territory	7	8	8	8	8	8	8	7	8	5
Queensland	1	3	5	3	2	1	1	2	4	6
South Australia . . .	6	5	3	1	4	5	5	6	2	2
Tasmania	5	6	7	6	7	4	6	3	5	7
Victoria	3	1	2	5	3	1	2	4	1	4
Western Australia .	4	4	4	4	5	6	3	5	6	3

HIGHEST INDIVIDUAL SCORES

244	G. H. Armstrong, Australian Capital Territory v Queensland at Brisbane	1987-88
242	R. J. Davison, New South Wales v Northern Territory at Brisbane	1987-88
222*	M. P. Mott, Queensland v Northern Territory at Perth	1991-92
215*	G. S. Milliken, New South Wales v Tasmania at Perth	1982-83
214	D. A. Tuckwell, Queensland v Northern Territory at Sydney	1985-86
206*	M. L. Love, Queensland v South Australia at Brisbane	1992-93
205*	B. Zacny, ACT v Northern Territory at Perth	1997-98
202*	G. S. Blewett, South Australia v Northern Territory at Melbourne	1989-90
201	R. Bowden, Northern Territory v Australian Capital Territory at Sydney	1990-91
200	J. J. Krejza, New South Wales v South Australia at Newcastle	2001-02

HIGHEST PARTNERSHIP FOR EACH WICKET

318	for 1st	V. W. Williams and D. S. Wotherspoon, NSW v South Australia at Canberra	1996-97
224	for 2nd	J. Allenby and S. E. Marsh, Western Australia v Northern Territory at Hobart	2000-01
339	for 3rd	M. Armstrong and S. P. Heaney, ACT v Northern Territory at Perth	1999-00
240	for 4th	A. I. C. Dodemaide and A. Grant, Victoria v South Australia at Perth	1982-83
231	for 5th	{ D. M. Wellham and M. Cox, NSW v Australian Capital Territory at Perth .	1975-76
		{ M. L. Love and A. Walduck, Queensland v Tasmania at Perth	1991-92
226	for 6th	K. J. Skewes and L. Mauger, Northern Territory v Tasmania at Newcastle .	2001-02
251	for 7th	C. Mason and K. M. Harvey, Western Australia v Queensland at Melbourne .	1993-94
144	for 8th	A. J. Heading and A. C. L. James, ACT v Northern Territory at Hobart	2000-01
121	for 9th	C. D. Hartley and N. J. Rimmington, Queensland v New South Wales at Hobart	2000-01
98*	for 10th	S. Bannerman and J. Cooper, ACT v South Australia at Melbourne	1989-90

BEST BOWLING IN AN INNINGS

9-11	D. J. McLauchlan, New South Wales v South Australia at Canberra	1996-97
9-70	M. C. Dolman, South Australia v Western Australia at Sydney	1978-79
8-13	C. P. Simpson, Queensland v Northern Territory at Melbourne	1997-98
8-25	M. Reidy-Crofts, Western Australia v ACT at Adelaide	1979-80
8-31	S. Hill, Western Australia v New Zealand at Sydney	1978-79
8-41	M. L. Clews, ACT v South Australia at Melbourne	1969-70
8-46	I. Woolf, Victoria v South Australia at Adelaide	1971-72
8-49	R. J. Thomas, New Zealand v ACT at Sydney	1978-79
8-58	P. Walker, ACT v Tasmania at Adelaide	1971-72
8-78	M. White, ACT v South Australia at Sydney	1978-79
8-84	S. P. Davis, Victoria v Tasmania at Christchurch	1977-78

BEST BOWLING IN A MATCH

14-15 D.J. McLauchlan, New South Wales v South Australia at Canberra 1996-97
13-18 C.P. Simpson, Queensland v Northern Territory at Melbourne 1997-98
11-54 M.J. Bright, New South Wales v Tasmania at Canberra 2002-03
10-43 D.W. Fleming, Victoria v Northern Territory at Canberra 1988-89
10-59 A.J. De Winter, Tasmania v Western Australia at Sydney 1985-86

HAT-TRICKS

D.A. Johnston, South Australia v Tasmania at Canberra 1972-73
R. Bucholz, Queensland v Victoria at Adelaide 1979-80
H.V. Hammelman, Queensland v South Australia at Perth 1982-83
A.J. De Winter, Tasmania v Western Australia at Sydney 1985-86
M.G. Bevan, ACT v New South Wales at Adelaide 1986-87
I. Connell, Tasmania v ACT at Brisbane 1992-93
J. Southam, Northern Territory v South Australia at Adelaide 1995-96
S.G. Busbridge, South Australia v ACT at Canberra 1996-97
P.D. Waite, Western Australia v Queensland at Canberra 1996-97
D.R. Mackenzie, Queensland v South Australia at Adelaide 1998-99

Australian Under-17s, 2003-04

by GREG McKIE

Although the final was drawn, Victoria were deemed winners of the national Under-17s carnival in Adelaide because of their undefeated record in the preliminary matches. Confronted by a strong New South Wales line-up in the final, Victoria batted them out of the game by carrying their innings on well into the second and last day. They finished with a competition-record total of 506 after Brett Deledio and Jack McNamara added 134 for the ninth wicket. NSW, left with only 89 overs to bat, ended on 2 for 285. Tom Cooper, the Player of the Series, played out time with an excellent unbeaten hundred.

The championship again consisted of five rounds of two-day matches. This longer version of the game gave batsmen the chance to plan their innings and, as a result, many large scores were amassed. However, a lack of batting urgency was sometimes evident. Three games were drawn when the team batting first delayed their declaration until the second day because runs were coming too slowly.

Victoria were the most imposing batting side of all, and were not bowled out until the final. They warmed up for the final with 6 for 416 against South Australia, Shaun Dean scoring 202 not out in just under six hours and putting on 163 for the sixth wicket with Marc Murphy. Dean followed up with another century in the final, and five of their players amassed more than 200 runs for the tournament. This was just as well because their attack was thin, with the exception of Stephen Gilmour – quick and economical – and Shannon Malone. Deledio was surely the best No. 9 to have appeared at national Under-17 level, scoring 51 not out, 78, 22 and 85 in his four innings.

New South Wales were also strong in batting, Cooper hitting two centuries. Against SA, he and Greg Clarence added a competition-record 252 for the third wicket. Phillip Wells, batting at No. 7, finished with an average of 199. He and Patrick Darwen added an unbroken 186 for the seventh wicket against Queensland in even time. Their bowlers often proved expensive, however, with only Jackson Bird returning respectable figures.

Western Australia possessed the leading bowler in Chris Hansberry, a slow and economical left-armer, who finished the carnival with 16 wickets. His best performance came in WA's final match against SA when he picked up 5 for 57 off 37 tight overs. Despite the fact that no WA batsmen reached three figures, they recorded three victories and only one defeat to finish third. Tom Barratt and Greg Beresi were the best of their batsmen.

Queensland won twice, lost twice and finished fourth for the second year in a row. Several batsmen hovered around the 200-run mark, with Andrew Greig (199) and Ben Gledhill (208) the best of them. Greig was their sole centurion, against NSW, when he and Ben Dunk added 142 for the fifth wicket. Michael Gould and Joel Hughes were the only reliable wicket-takers while Gledhill, with 15 dismissals, was the most prolific keeper. South Australia won their first game against Queensland but faded thereafter. Their batsmen never reached 220 and their bowlers proved expensive, hammered twice by NSW and once by Victoria.

The Australian Capital Territory faded after winning their first three games. They had three consistent batsmen in Wade Irvine, Adam Blacka and Dean Johnson. Their batting really clicked against Tasmania. Despite Tasmania batting into the second day before declaring, ACT were untroubled in passing the required total and finished on 7 for 346. Robbie Van Aalst was the pick of their attack but lacked consistent support, although Clinton Mathis secured the championship's best analysis of 5 for 53 against WA.

Tasmania held on against WA in the consolation round to finish seventh. Though no player averaged 40, they were well-served in the batting department by Matthew Lister and John Wells. Their lower order almost salvaged a thriller in the opening match against WA. Reduced to 6 for 75 at one stage, they fought back to make 277. WA were set for victory at 7 for 277 when Tom Friend took two wickets in consecutive balls, WA staggering to a first-innings victory with a wicket to spare.

The Northern Territory relied heavily on the batting of Adam Dilley, while Chris Watt was their main bowler. Dilley's tournament aggregate of 306 runs was more than twice the team's next best. He also set an all-time carnival record for the highest individual innings by an NT batsman when he made 152 not out against WA. The innings, sadly, was a mixed blessing; the NT did not allow themselves sufficient time to bowl their opponents out and let a struggling WA side off the hook.

ROUND ONE

Northern Territory 245 (A. Dilley 76; A. Blacka 3-23) lost to Australian Capital Territory 6 for 342 (A. Blacka 87, D. Johnson 78, J. Rogers 51, N. Death 50*; C. Watt 4-62) on first innings.

New South Wales 318 (T. Cooper 88, L. Eldridge 63; S. Malone 3-29) lost to Victoria 7 for 324 (N. Lynch 101*, A. Finch 69, B. Deledio 51*; M. Sykes 3-60) on first innings.

Tasmania 277 (M. Lister 97; G. Smith 3-30) and 1 for 9 lost to Western Australia 278 (T. Barratt 77; S. Nichols 3-44) on first innings.

Queensland 192 (G. Skennar 35) lost to South Australia 9 for 210 (A. Carey 56, G. Rao 50) on first innings.

ROUND TWO

Victoria 9 for 269 declared (B. Deledio 78; J. Hughes 3-17) defeated Queensland 207 (A. Greig 55; A. Finch 4-20, S. Gilmour 3-30) on first innings.

South Australia 173 (A. Carey 49; J. Bird 4-14) lost to New South Wales 325 (P. Wells 90, L. Eldridge 64, G. Clarence 55) on first innings.

Western Australia 177 (C. Tomlinson 63; C. Mathis 5-53, R. Van Aalst 3-19) lost to Australian Capital Territory 4 for 180 (S. Rooney 61, A. Blacka 58) on first innings.

Northern Territory 164 (T. Scollay 34; T. Friend 4-30) defeated Tasmania 137 (S. Nichols 44*) on first innings.

ROUND THREE

Queensland 8 for 359 declared (A. Greig 116, B. Dunk 67, B. Gledhill 65; M. Sykes 3-62) drew with New South Wales 6 for 333 (P. Darwen 104*, P. Wells 76*, G. Clarence 50).

South Australia 169 (T. Moffatt 66; S. Gilmour 4-40) lost to Victoria 6 for 416 (S. Dean 202*, M. Murphy 79; R. Sawade 3-55) on first innings.

Tasmania 9 for 295 declared (J. Wells 70; N. Death 4-86) lost to Australian Capital Territory 7 for 346 (D. Johnson 88, A. Blacka 73, S. Rooney 64, W. Irvine 58) on first innings.

Northern Territory 9 for 340 declared (A. Dilley 152*; C. Hansberry 4-72) drew with Western Australia 8 for 220 (G. Beresi 57).

POINTS TABLE

Group A	P	WO	W1	D	L1	LO	T	Points	Quotient
Victoria	3	0	3	0	0	0	0	18	1.983
New South Wales	3	0	1	1	1	0	0	6	1.096
South Australia	3	0	1	0	2	0	0	6	0.530
Queensland	3	0	0	1	2	0	0	0	0.800
Group B									
Australian Capital Territory	3	0	3	0	0	0	0	18	2.051
Northern Territory	3	0	1	1	1	0	0	6	0.887
Western Australia	3	0	1	1	1	0	0	6	0.718
Tasmania	3	0	0	0	3	0	0	0	0.826

Quotient equals runs per wicket scored divided by runs per wicket conceded.

QUALIFYING FINALS

Victoria 9 for 343 declared (M. Murphy 103*, D. Finch 71; R. Van Aalst 4-55) defeated Australian Capital Territory 181 (J. Rogers 33; S. Malone 4-10) on first innings.
New South Wales 7 for 445 declared (T. Cooper 137, G. Clarence 122; R. Sawade 3-61) defeated South Australia 216 (G. Rao 50; P. Darwen 4-57, P. Wells 3-12) on first innings.

Western Australia 293 (T. Barratt 67, C. Tomlinson 60, R. Fairchild 52; A. Dilley 4-59) and 4 for 93 (P. Mollinari 47; P. White 3-11) defeated Northern Territory 185 (T. Devereux 71; T. Whitlock 4-23, C. Hansberry 4-25) on first innings.

Queensland 7 for 319 declared (D. Pearce 68, B. Dunk 67, G. Skennar 66; B. Dicken 3-43) defeated Tasmania 169 (J. Wells 75; G. Skennar 3-36) on first innings.

CONSOLATION FINALS

Queensland 267 (B. Wilde 73, J. Hughes 52*; R. Van Aalst 3-55) defeated Australian Capital Territory 231 (W. Irvine 87; M. Gould 4-41, J. Hughes 3-28) on first innings.

Western Australia 253 (G. Beresi 92; R. Sawade 3-48, T. Pascoe 3-61) defeated South Australia 210 (T. Moffatt 44; C. Hansberry 5-57, M. Ardagh 3-20) on first innings.

Tasmania 314 (S. Clark 64, M. Lister 59; T. Devereux 3-29) defeated Northern Territory 249 (A. Dilley 42) on first innings.

FINAL

NEW SOUTH WALES v VICTORIA

At St Peter's College, Adelaide, January 15, 16, 2004. *Toss:* Victoria. Match drawn.

Victoria

T. Stray c Beaven b Bird	6	S. Malone c Beaven b Bird	39
T. Donnell c Beaven b Darwen	34	J. McNamara c Keen b Sykes	71
J. Stevenson run out	50	D. King not out	0
*A. Finch c Beaven b Warner	34		
†N. Lynch c Beaven b Sykes	46	B 5, l-b 6, n-b 1	12
S. Dean c Eldridge b Darwen	126		
M. Murphy c Warner b Bird	3	(142 overs)	506
B. Deledio c Cooper b Darwen	85	Fall: 10 68 115 143 259 261 332 370 504 506

Bowling: Bird 22–3–82–4; Darwen 28–6–74–3; Warner 23–4–65–1; Sykes 11.2–2–23–1; Eldridge 3–0–13–0; Clarence 5–2–11–0; Keen 22–5–76–0; Wells 15–1–78–0; Day 13–1–74–0.

New South Wales

L. Eldridge c Stray b Deledio	50	B 6, l-b 6, w 1	13
S. Cazzulino c Stray b Gilmour	11		
T. Cooper not out	168	(89 overs)	(2 wkts) 285
G. Clarence not out	43	Fall: 22 166

J. Bird, S. Keen, M. Day, P. Wells, P. Darwen, †R. Beaven, M. Sykes and D. Warner did not bat.

Bowling: Deledio 14-3-36-1; Gilmour 13-3-36-1; Finch 9-0-33-0; Dean 1-0-7-0; Murphy 7-2-25-0; Malone 8-2-27-0; McNamara 17-9-29-0; King 20-3-79-0.

Umpires: W. Hendricks and A. Ward.

UNDER 17s CHAMPIONSHIP, 2003-04

MOST RUNS

	M	I	NO	R	HS	100s	50s	Avge
T. Cooper (NSW)	5	5	1	426	168*	2	1	106.50
S. Dean (Vic)........	4	4	1	380	202*	2	0	126.66
A. Dilley (NT).	5	5	1	306	152*	1	1	76.50
G. Clarence (NSW)...	5	5	1	270	122	1	2	67.50
A. Blacka (ACT).....	5	5	0	263	87	0	3	52.60
B. Deledio (Vic)	5	4	1	236	85	0	3	78.66
N. Lynch (Vic)	5	5	1	229	101*	1	0	57.25
A. Finch (Vic).......	5	5	0	222	71	0	2	44.40
G. Beresi (W Aust) ...	5	5	0	209	92	0	2	41.80
D. Johnson (ACT)....	5	4	0	208	88	0	2	52.00

MOST WICKETS

	M	O	Mdns	R	W	BB	5W/i	Avge	RPO
C. Hansberry (W Aust) .	5	117.2	40	256	16	5-57	1	16.00	2.18
R. Van Aalst (ACT) ...	4	57	8	172	12	4-55	0	14.33	3.01
J. Gilmour (Vic)	5	68.3	15	180	10	4-40	0	18.00	2.02
J. Bird (NSW)	5	66.3	12	224	10	4-14	0	22.40	3.36
R. Sawade (S Aust) ...	4	57	6	228	10	3-46	0	22.80	4.00
S. Malone (Vic).......	4	41	17	86	9	4-10	0	9.55	2.04
J. Hughes (Qld)	5	75	19	199	9	3-17	0	22.11	2.65
C. Watt (NT)	4	53.2	20	152	9	4-62	0	16.88	2.85
A. Dilley (NT)	5	74	18	216	9	4-59	0	24.00	2.91

UNDER-17S CHAMPIONSHIP RECORDS

CHAMPIONSHIP WINNERS

Series	Venue	Winner	Player of the Year
1986-87	Melbourne	New South Wales	M. Galbraith (Vic)
1987-88	Launceston	New South Wales	J. C. Young (NSW)
1988-89	Sydney	South Australia	M. J. P. Minagall (SA)
1989-90	Adelaide	Victoria	T. F. Corbett (Vic)
1990-91	Brisbane	New South Wales	J. P. Maher (Qld)
1991-92	Canberra	New South Wales	B. J. Hodge (Vic)
1992-93	Hobart	New South Wales	B. A. Clemow (NSW)
1993-94	Adelaide	New South Wales	M. D. Pascoe (Qld)
1994-95	Perth	New South Wales	D. J. Thornely (NSW)
1995-96	Melbourne/Geelong	Queensland	M. J. North (WAust)
1996-97	Brisbane	New South Wales	L. Williams (SAust)
1997-98	Hobart	Victoria	A. J. Kent (Vic)
1998-99	Sydney	New South Wales	E. J. M. Cowan (NSW)
1999-00	Brisbane	Victoria	P. Boraston (Vic)
2000-01	Brisbane	South Australia	C. J. Borgas (S Aust)
2001-02	Melbourne	New South Wales	C. J. Ferguson (S Aust)
2002-03	Perth	New South Wales	D. N. Porter (W Aust)
2003-04	Adelaide	Victoria	T. Cooper (NSW)

LAST TEN YEARS' PLACINGS

	94-95	95-96	96-97	97-98	98-99	99-00	00-01	01-02	02-03	03-04
Australian Capital Territory	6	7	7	7	5	7	7	8	7	6
New South Wales	1	6	1	6	1	2	2	1	1	2
Northern Territory	8	8	8	4	7	8	8	5	8	8
Queensland	1	1	2	8	2	4	4	3	4	4
South Australia	4	2	4	5	8	3	1	2	3	5
Tasmania	5	5	6	3	6	6	5	7	5	7
Victoria	3	3	5	1	4	1	3	4	2	1
Western Australia	7	4	3	2	3	5	6	6	6	3

HIGHEST INDIVIDUAL SCORES

258*	C. J. Ferguson, South Australia v Queensland	....	2001-02
255*	A. J. Kent, Victoria v New South Wales	....	1997-98
225*	L. Williams, South Australia v Northern Territory	....	1996-97
218*	E. J. M. Cowan, New South Wales v Australian Capital Territory	....	1998-99
206	B. A. Clemow, New South Wales v Australian Capital Territory	....	1992-93
204	A. Symonds, Queensland v South Australia	....	1991-92
202	S. Dean, Victoria v South Australia	....	2003-04

HIGHEST PARTNERSHIP FOR EACH WICKET

1st	324	E. J. M. Cowan and A. Alley	New South Wales v Australian Capital Territory	1998-99
2nd	208	R. Hadley and S. E. Marsh	Western Australia v Australian Capital Territory	1998-99
3rd	252	T. Cooper and G. Clarence	New South Wales v South Australia	2003-04
4th	282	M. Galbraith and D. Shinkfield	Victoria v Western Australia	1985-86
5th	207	A. M. Rowe and S. R. Watson	Queensland v South Australia	1996-97
6th	168	M. Labrizzi and G. Matthews	Western Australia v Victoria	1987-88
7th	211	J. Lalich and K. M. Harvey	Western Australia v Australian Capital Territory	1992-93
8th	219*	A. J. Kent and G. Turner	Victoria v New South Wales	1997-98
9th	134	B. Deledio and J. McNamara	Victoria v New South Wales	2003-04
10th	125	D. A. Nash and C. Davis	New South Wales v Victoria	1994-95

BEST BOWLING IN AN INNINGS

10-28	D. Davidson, New South Wales v South Australia	1957-58
9-20	A. A. Mallett, Western Australia v New South Wales	1957-58
9-68	P. Ryan, Queensland v Victoria	1978-79
8-33	M. Smith, Queensland v New South Wales	1956-57
8-36	I. McMullen, Victoria v Western Australia	1964-65
8-49	J. Reynolds, South Australia v Western Australia	1963-64
7-8	J. Dooley, Queensland v Northern Territory	1986-87

BEST BOWLING IN A MATCH

17-78	D. Davidson, New South Wales v South Australia	1957-58
12-80	G. Crispe, Queensland v Western Australia	1964-65
13-36	S. Bell, New South Wales v Western Australia	1963-64
13-43	B. Walton, South Australia v New South Wales	1954-55
12-45	A. A. Mallett, Western Australia v New South Wales	1957-58
11-47	P. Siddle, Victoria v South Australia	2001-02
11-72	W. J. Scholes, Victoria v Queensland	1964-65

HAT-TRICKS

F. Speare	Queensland v South Australia	1954-55
R. W. Bulger	Australian Capital Territory v Tasmania	1997-98
M. J. Cosgrove	South Australia v Western Australia	2000-01

ACT First-Grade, 2003-04

by ADAM MOREHOUSE

Tuggeranong Valley ran out convincing winners of the ACT first-grade premiership, losing only one match all season in both the two-day and one-day competitions. Their single defeat, sadly for them, was in the Konica Cup limited-overs final, where North Canberra–Gungahlin won their first first-grade title in either form of the game since 1979-80.

Ball dominated bat all season, resulting in one of the closest competitions in years. The make-up of the semi-finals was not known until late on the final day of regular season competition, with Ginninderra and Wests striving for an outright result. Tuggeranong's dominance was built around a well-balanced side. Four batsmen – Justin Haywood, the captain David Jeffrey, Steve Lang and Stewart Heaney – figured among the top 10 runscorers. Tuggeranong's attack was led by their pace duo of Evan Kellar and Ben Dennett, with 36 and 38 wickets respectively, backed up by the medium-pace of Jeffrey with 30. They also unearthed a young quick bowler late in the season in Adam Ritchard, who took 15 wickets.

North Canberra–Gungahlin were the big improvers. Their success was founded on the steady improvement of their batsmen and the quality of their spinners, Matt Nason and the captain Heath Axelby. Nason was the competition's leading wicket-taker, finishing with 39 victims, while Axelby took 35. They were helped by the return from Western Australia of Stuart Karppinen, who took 22 wickets and scored 375 runs. Scott Cameron, Scott Smith and Trevor Power all passed 500 runs.

Weston Creek failed to win their fourth successive title and only scraped into the semi-finals after Ginninderra snatched an exciting outright victory over Western District. Weston Creek lost only four matches all season but these were at crucial times. They were strong in batting but depleted in bowling compared with previous seasons. The ACT Comets captain Cade Brown, with 562 runs at 46, and

Christian Hanna, 504 runs at 42, were the leading runscorers. Adam Rhynehart was the unexpected star. He forced his way into the ACT side after scoring two centuries in two days early in the season. His second century came off only 59 balls. Daniel Mowbray, with 21 wickets, was the only bowler to break 20 wickets.

Eastlake started the season strongly but faded. Their captain, Michael Kavanagh, was the batsman of the season, amassing 848 runs at 84.80 and passing 7,000 career runs in the process. No other Eastlake player reached 400 runs. Their bowling was based on the leg-spin of Matt Ramage and the pace of Darren McNees, who took 36 and 25 wickets respectively. Ginninderra–West Belconnen came closer to reaching the finals than they have in many seasons. Their young side started to mature, guided by a handful of experienced players and the acquisition of the wicket-keeper Cameron McLeod from Queensland. McLeod was their leading scorer with 552 runs, while the captain Luke Bulkeley and the leg-spinner Sam Gaskin were the leading wicket-takers with 27 apiece.

Western District also came close to winning a place in the finals, but their poor start to the season ultimately proved too much to overcome. Darren Richards was the only batsman to top 400 runs, with 407 at 31.46. The bowling was stronger with Mark Hatton, the captain Andrew Jones and Jacob Boyle all exceeding 20 wickets.

ANU avoided the wooden spoon for the first time in several seasons, fading to seventh after a promising start. Stephen Sorbello was their leading runscorer with 453 runs, while no bowler took more than 20 wickets. Their captain Matthew William became a first-class player during the off-season when he played for Malaysia against Nepal in the ICC Continental Cup. Queanbeyan finished at the foot of the table, winning only two matches overall in both competitions. Their captain Stephen Frost passed 6,000 first-grade runs during the season, only the sixth player in the history of the competition to do so.

Weston Creek and Western District both qualified for the final series of the Country Cup. Weston Creek were eliminated in their first match against the Newcastle side Merewether. Western District made it through to the quarter-finals by easily beating Lismore, before suffering a heavy defeat to Tamworth.

ACT FIRST-GRADE TABLE, 2003-04

	M	WO	WI	D	TI	LI	LO	T	Points	Quotient
Tuggeranong Valley	9	0	7	2	0	0	0	0	42	1.8061
North Canberra-Gungahlin	9	2	3	1	0	3	0	0	38	1.1423
Eastlake	9	0	4	2	0	2	1	0	24	1.1107
Weston Creek	9	0	4	3	0	2	0	0	24	0.9860
Ginninderra West Belconnen	9	2	1	2	0	4	0	0	22	0.8853
Western District	9	1	1	1	0	5	1	0	20	1.0920
Australian National University . .	9	0	3	1	0	4	1	0	18	0.7174
Queanbeyan	9	0	1	2	0	4	2	0	6	0.6227

BATTING AVERAGES, 2003-04

(Qualification: 300 runs)

	M	I	NO	R	HS	100s	50s	Avge
M. J. Kavanagh (Eastlake)	14	16	6	848	179	3	3	84.80
M. A. Divin (Eastlake)	14	12	1	571	171*	2	2	51.90
S. P. Heaney (Tuggeranong Valley).	12	12	1	525	195	2	0	47.72
C. Brown (Weston Creek)	13	12	0	562	159	2	1	46.83
P. B. Radford (Ginninderra West Belconnen) .	13	13	3	464	98	0	3	46.40
J. M. Haywood (Tuggeranong Valley).	16	16	1	673	186	2	2	44.86
D. M. Jeffrey (Tuggeranong Valley)	16	16	3	570	87	0	4	43.84
C. R. A. McLeod (Ginninderra West Belconnen)	12	14	1	552	104	2	3	42.46
C. D. Hanna (Weston Creek)	14	14	2	504	107*	1	3	42.00
T. Power (North Canberra-Gungahlin)	12	15	2	512	112	2	2	39.38

* Denotes not out.

BOWLING AVERAGES, 2003-04

(Qualification: 20 wickets)

	M	O	Mdns	R	W	BB	5W/i	10W/m	Avge
M. A. Hatton (Western District) . .	11	193.3	48	398	37	6-25	2	1	10.75
M. McGann (Western District) . . .	9	128.4	29	298	22	4-27	0	0	13.54
D. M. Jeffrey (Tuggeranong Valley)	16	230	60	449	30	3-24	0	0	14.96
M. H. Ramage (Eastlake)	12	177.1	34	563	36	6-48	3	0	15.63
E. Kellar (Tuggeranong Valley) . .	16	267.3	36	598	36	5-23	1	0	16.61
N. Madsen (Queanbeyan)	11	203	37	576	33	5-30	2	0	17.45
D. A. McNees (Eastlake)	12	186.2	48	445	25	4-61	0	0	17.80
L. J. Bulkeley (Ginninderra West Belconnen) .	11	177.1	22	499	27	4-53	0	0	18.48
H. R. Axelby (North Canberra-Gungahlin) . . .	17	238.3	45	649	35	5-72	1	0	18.54
S. L. Gaskin (Ginninderra West Belconnen)	12	141	22	520	27	5-59	1	0	19.25

ACT FIRST-GRADE SEMI-FINALS, 2003-04

TUGGERANONG VALLEY v WESTON CREEK

At Kingston Oval, Kingston, March 20, 21, 22, 2004. *Toss:* Tuggeranong Valley. Tuggeranong won on first innings. Tuggeranong Valley 448 (S. P. Heaney 195, J. D. Evans 91, S. Lang 40, D. M. Jeffrey 35; M. W. Oliver 3-67, S. E. Mowbray 3-85, D. D. Mowbray 3-86); Weston Creek 295 (S. L. Maxwell 63, C. D. Hanna 57, C. Brown 36; D. M. Jeffrey 3-50).

NORTH CANBERRA–GUNGAHLIN v EASTLAKE

At Manuka Oval, Manuka, March 20, 21, 22, 2004. *Toss:* Eastlake. North Canberra–Gungahlin won on first innings. Eastlake 221 (M. A. Divin 75; H. R. Axelby 3-23, M. W. Nason 3-80); North Canberra–Gungahlin 1 for 223 (S. R. Cameron 124*, T. Power 49, M. W. Nason 33*).

ACT FIRST-GRADE FINAL, 2003-04

TUGGERANONG VALLEY v NORTH CANBERRA–GUNGAHLIN

At Manuka Oval, March 27, 28, 29, 2004. Tuggeranong Valley won by 10 wickets. *Toss:* North Canberra–Gungahlin.

Tuggeranong Valley, the minor premiers, took on an improving North Canberra–Gungahlin side in unseasonably warm weather for the ACT first-grade premiership. Tuggeranong were looking for their first two-day premiership since 1999-2000, while Norths had not won since 1979-80. Norths won the toss and elected to bat on a grassy wicket, a gamble which failed to pay off as they collapsed to 5 for 30 in the first session. The fast bowler Ben Dennett tore the heart out of the strong Norths batting line-up. Mark Shackel top-scored in the lower order with a lusty 41. It looked to be too little too late.

By stumps on the first day, Tuggeranong had already passed Norths' total. Norths hit back on the second day, dismissing Tuggeranong for 274 after they had been cruising at 3 for 202 at one stage. Sven Holcombe went on to an even century, receiving sound support from Steve Lang, Stewart Heaney and Justin Haywood. The spin of Heath Axelby accounted for the lower order. Led by Scott Cameron, Norths had wrested back an overall lead by stumps, but could add only a further 70 runs on the third and final day. Dennett and Evan Kellar, Tuggeranong's reliable pace pair, took seven wickets between them. They were left with a target of 113 for their fourth two-day premiership. Lang and Holcombe made batting look easier than it had at any time in the match, and were still at the wicket when the winning runs were scored.

Greg Irvine Medal: S. A. Holcombe.

Close of Play: First day, Tuggeranong Valley (1) 2-129 (Holcombe 56, Heaney 13); Second day, North Canberra–Gungahlin (2) 4-178 (Cameron 70, Borgelt 27).

North Canberra–Gungahlin

T. Power c Holcombe b Dennett	2	– (2) lbw b Dennett	8
S. R. Cameron lbw b Dennett	2	– (1) b Dennett	86
M. W. Nason b Males b Ritchard	0	– c Haywood b Dennett	47
S. A. Smith c Haywood b Ritchard	11	– (5) c Haywood b Kellar	0
S. J. Karppinen b Kellar	0	– (4) c Heaney b Kellar	15
B. S. Borgelt lbw b Jeffrey	5	– run out (Jeffrey)	34
D. Wilson c Holcombe b Jeffrey	14	– st Holcombe b Kellar	23
M. Shackel c Lang b Jeffrey	42	– b Kellar	5
*H. R. Axelby not out	13	– c Heaney b Ritchard	10
†P. S. Coe c Males b Dennett	3	– not out	8
S. Cluff b Dennett	0	– run out (Haywood)	6
B 9, l-b 18, w 1, n-b 8	36	B 4, l-b 9, w 1, n-b 2	16

(54.3 overs)	128	(72 overs)	258
Fall: 6 7 7 12 30 36 86 115 128 128		Fall: 13 114 137 145 190 221	
		231 232 246 258	

Bowling: *First Innings*—Dennett 15.3–7–23–4; Ritchard 12–5–34–2; Kellar 15–9–20–1; Jeffrey 12–3–24–3. *Second Innings*—Dennett 25–5–89–3; Kellar 28–4–82–4; Ritchard 8–1–32–1; Jeffrey 8–1–24–0; Males 3–0–18–0.

Tuggeranong Valley

†S. A. Halcombe c (sub)A. Eichholzer b Axelby	... 100	– (2) not out	66
S. Lang c Coe b Nason	43	– (1) not out	41
*D. M. Jeffrey c Coe b Nason	7		
S. P. Heaney c Coe b Cluff	36		
J. M. Haywood b Shackel	32		
J. D. Evans c Coe b Cluff	2		
A. Blacka c Wilson b Axelby	0		
C. J. Males not out	28		
E. Kellar c Coe b Shackel	7		
B. W. Dennett c Cameron b Axelby	4		
A. Ritchard lbw b Shackel	2		
L-b 4, w 2, n-b 7	13	B 3, l-b 1, n-b 2	6
(89 overs)	274	(29 overs) (0 wkt)	113

Fall: 76 94 196 202 217 226 230 245 258 274

Bowling: *First Innings*—Karppinen 6–1–17–0; Shackel 18–4–51–3; Borgelt 12–3–24–0; Cluff 13–3–45–2; Axelby 25–7–71–3; Nason 15–1–62–2. *Second Innings*—Shackel 6–1–16–0; Borgelt 6–2–15–0; Axelby 4–0–12–0; Cluff 3–0–28–0; Cameron 2–0–9–0; Power 1–0–5–0; Nason 7–0–34–0.

Umpires: G. R. Clifton and A. I. Shelley.

ACT FIRST-GRADE RECORDS

ALL-TIME LEADING BATSMEN

	Runs	Club
P. J. Solway	9,285	Qbn, ANU, Elk
M. J. Kavanagh	7,509	SC, SCE, Elk
M. J. Frost	6,806	Qbn, WC
L. Maloney	6,766	Ain, Hall
G. R. Irvine	6,721	WC, ANU
S. E. Frost	6,091	Qbn
L. Lees	5,944	Nbn
B. D. Bretland	5,745	SW, WV, SC, TV
S. Smith	5,613	Nbn, WD
S. L. Maxwell	5,459	WC

ALL-TIME LEADING BOWLERS

	Wickets	Club
G. J. Smith	864	Tur, Ain, NS, Ginn
W. C. Tickner	775	Dun, Hall, Nbn
D. A. Moore	622	EC, NS, WD
K. V. McCarty	556	Ain, Nbn, Tur, City
G. J. Samuels	510	Turn, City, ANU, Qbn
A. J. Macdonald	462	Ain, City, WD
L. Lees	454	Nbn, Ain
K. L. Bone	430	Wod, WC
F. Nash	414	Qbn
M. J. Howell	408	ANU
D. B. Robin	404	Mka, King

Sydney First-Grade, 2003-04

by ADRIAN WARREN

A resurgent Eastern Suburbs became the first club to win the Sydney grade, limited-overs and state challenge titles in the same season. The club's first ever first-innings win over local rivals Randwick–Petersham in the grade final proved the perfect finale to a season of unprecedented success. Easts defeated Sydney University by four wickets to win their first limited-overs title, becoming the first side since St George in 1968-69 to do the double, and added the state challenge trophy to their collection with an 83-run victory over Country Cup champions Southern Zone.

Easts also created history by becoming the first club to win the competition after losing a finals match. Beaten by UTS–Balmain in a qualifying final, Easts defeated Bankstown in the semi-finals, thereby scuttling any hope of a swansong appearance in a club final by one or both of the retiring Waugh twins.

Easts served early notice of their intentions to win an eighth first-grade title in round three when they reached an all-time competition record target of 467 against Western Suburbs. The team's success was down to a range of contributors. Five batsmen scored over 500 runs and four bowlers took 30 or more wickets. Jeff Cook, back from another county season with Northamptonshire, topped the batting aggregate with 744 runs at 39.15. Brad Haddin, in his first season with the club, hit three centuries and averaged 52.54. Andrew Jeffrey also racked up three hundreds among his 740 runs, while Jason Swift amassed 686 runs, saving his one and only century of the summer for the final. The skipper Mark Patterson, the only remaining member of the club's last premiership side in 1991-92, contributed 620 runs. Michael Maclennan, the hero of the final, finished with 488.

The veteran leg-spinner Adrian Tucker, with 42 wickets at 19.26, added guile and variety to a pace attack led by Paul Byrom (47 wickets), Justin Dery (42) and the Jamaican Kirk Powell (30). Easts had fielded another West Indian fast bowler, the late Malcolm Marshall, in their last premiership-winning team.

Easts, who had finished in a distant 11th position the previous summer, were not the only team to go ahead leaps and bounds in 2003-04. Bankstown jumped from 13th to first in the points table, Randwick–Petersham from seventh to third and Mosman from 10th to fourth. Of the 2002-03 finalists, only UTS-Balmain (down from fourth to fifth) and Penrith (second to sixth) remained in the top six. UTS have now made the finals the last six summers in a row.

The three leading teams of 2002-03 fared badly. Champions Sydney University slumped to eighth, minor premiers Manly fell to 12th and Northern District slid from third to ninth. University boasted two of the competition's four most prolific batsmen in Ed Cowan (885 runs) and their new signing Matthew Phelps (840). But the loss of Andrew Staunton robbed the attack of its edge, and no bowler took more than 25 wickets.

Blacktown, admitted to the competition in 2002-03, finished bottom again, although they doubled the number of victories they achieved in their inaugural campaign. Gordon finished in the bottom three for a seventh straight season despite the successful return of Matthew Nicholson, who snared 25 victims at 12.72 in his nine appearances.

With the weather far less benevolent than the previous season the number of draws rose. Individual performances failed to reach the same heights of the remarkable 2002-03 season. There were nonetheless some exceptional efforts. St George's teenage speedster Moises Henriques became the youngest player in the competition's history, at age 16, to take a 10-wicket match haul. The Portuguese-born Australian Under-19s representative claimed 10 for 74 against Blacktown. His season tally of 28 wickets at 18.03 included the prize scalp of Simon Katich and earned him a state rookie contract.

Bankstown's highly regarded fast bowler Aaron Bird underlined his immense promise with 68 wickets, the most in the competition. Warwick Adlam, the Gloucestershire new-ball bowler Jon Lewis and the young leg-spinner Liam Zammit were the only others to finish with more than 50 wickets. Grant Lambert, the Fairfield–Liverpool all-rounder, enjoyed another eyecatching campaign with 675 runs at 56.25 and 30 wickets at 18.66.

The evergreen Randwick–Petersham batsman Richard Chee Quee topped the run aggregates with 907. Six batsmen exceeded 800 runs, including UTS–Balmain's Greg Hayne, whose tally of 814 lifted his career total to 11,220 – fifth on the all-time list and only 900 runs away from eclipsing the record held by Warren Bardsley. The winner of the O'Reilly Medal was Mosman's Trent Johnston, who chalked up 33 wickets at 16.69 and 558 runs at 39.85. He subsequently headed off to Ireland in a bid to represent that country in the 2007 World Cup.

SYDNEY FIRST-GRADE TABLE, 2003-04

	M	WO	WI	D	LI	LO	T	Points	Quotient
Bankstown	19	2	12	1	4	0	0	92	1.3614
Eastern Suburbs	19	1	11	1	5	0	1	79	1.4324
Randwick-Petersham	19	0	13	0	6	0	0	78	1.2733
Mosman	19	1	10	2	6	0	0	70	1.1707
UTS-Balmain	19	0	11	1	6	0	1	69	1.0805
Penrith	19	0	11	4	4	0	0	66	1.1521
Fairfield-Liverpool	19	1	9	3	6	0	0	64	1.1216
Sydney University	19	0	10	3	6	0	0	60	1.3650
Northern District	19	0	10	1	8	0	0	60	1.2070
North Sydney	19	0	8	3	6	1	1	51	0.9618
Parramatta	19	0	8	4	6	1	0	48	1.0594
Manly-Warringah	19	0	7	2	9	1	0	42	0.8701
Campbelltown-Camden	19	0	7	1	10	1	0	42	0.8209
Western Suburbs	19	0	6	5	7	0	1	39	0.8395
St George	19	1	4	1	13	0	0	30	0.8419
Sutherland	19	0	5	3	11	0	0	30	1.0248
University of NSW	19	0	5	4	9	1	0	30	0.8460
Gordon	19	0	5	3	11	0	0	30	0.7297
Hawkesbury	19	0	2	7	10	0	0	12	0.6614
Blacktown	19	0	2	3	13	1	0	12	0.5990

BATTING AVERAGES, 2003-04

(Qualification: 300 runs)

	M	I	NO	R	HS	100s	50s	Avge
D. J. Thornely (Northern District)	10	10	2	484	144*	2	1	60.50
G. M. Lambert (Fairfield-Liverpool)	12	12	0	675	166	2	3	56.25
M. N. Atkinson (Manly)	18	20	5	832	120	2	5	55.46
G. J. Mail (UTS-Balmain)	12	12	1	587	159	3	1	53.36
B. J. Haddin (Eastern Suburbs)	12	13	2	578	115	3	1	52.54
M. A. Phelps (Sydney University)	18	21	5	840	167	3	3	52.50
P. A. Jaques (Sutherland)	9	9	1	415	151	1	2	51.87
P. A. Burkhart (Western Suburbs)	18	19	5	695	164*	2	3	49.64
M. Maclennan (Eastern Suburbs)	21	19	9	488	133	1	2	48.79
R. Chee Que (Randwick-Petersham)	22	24	5	907	111	1	4	47.73

Denotes not out.

BOWLING AVERAGES, 2003-04

(Qualification: 20 wickets)

	M	O	Mdns	R	W	BB	5Wi	10W/m	Avge
M. J. Nicholson (Gordon)	9	136.5	40	318	25	7-55	2	0	12.72
S. R. Clark (Sutherland)	7	102.4	21	285	22	6-45	2	0	12.95
D. A. Nash (Fairfield-Liverpool) .	13	206.1	47	590	41	5-34	2	0	14.39
J. Lewis (Randwick-Petersham) . .	19	338.3	93	795	52	7-35	3	0	15.28
W. J. Adlam (Mosman)	21	333.2	83	946	57	7-41	3	1	16.59
D. T. Johnston (Mosman)	18	188.1	41	551	33	6-17	2	0	16.69
S. M. Thompson (Bankstown) . . .	22	283.3	62	846	47	6-26	1	0	18.00
M. Henriques (St George)	12	145.5	22	505	28	7-40	1	1	18.03
T. Keirath (Sydney University) . .	12	120.3	18	406	22	3-23	0	0	18.45
C. P. Eve (Northern District)	19	263.3	56	798	43	5-52	0	1	18.55

SYDNEY FIRST-GRADE QUALIFYING FINALS, 2003-04

BANKSTOWN v PENRITH

At Bankstown Memorial Oval, Bankstown, March 20, 21, 2004. Match drawn. Bankstown 405 (C. W. Parkinson 125, P. Maraziotis 76, A. C. Bird 72*, M. G. Betsey 60; M. A. W. Goldsmith 3-77, L. A. Zammit 3-109); Penrith 6 for 330 (D. A. Turner 81, G. I. Hunt 76, A. C. Beadle 70, K. J. Geyer 43).

EASTERN SUBURBS v UTS–BALMAIN

At Waverley Oval, Waverley, March 20, 21, 2004. UTS-Balmain won on first innings. UTS-Balmain 9 dec 234 (R. R. T. Burton 103*, T. Sparke 81; J. Dery 4-42); Eastern Suburbs 175 (B. J. Haddin 41, K. Powell 30; J. J. Krejza 4-76).

RANDWICK–PETERSHAM v MOSMAN

At Coogee Oval, Coogee, March 20, 21, 2004. Randwick–Petersham won on first innings. Mosman 234 (J. Vero 120, W. J. Adlam 35; J. Lewis 4-60, N. Rosser 3-49); Randwick–Petersham 7 for 236 (R. Chee Quee 95, U. Khawaja 63, J. V. Hill 32).

SYDNEY FIRST-GRADE SEMI-FINALS, 2003-04

BANKSTOWN v EASTERN SUBURBS

At Bankstown Memorial Oval, Bankstown, March 27, 28, 2004. Eastern Suburbs won on first innings. Bankstown 155 (S. M. Thompson 38; K. Powell 3-22, A. E. Tucker 3-33); Eastern Suburbs 3 for 170 (N. Berry 65, A. Jeffrey 48, B. J. Haddin 34*).

RANDWICK–PETERSHAM v UTS–BALMAIN

At Coogee Oval, Coogee, March 27, 28, 2004. Match drawn. UTS–Balmain 5 for 318 dec (G. J. Mail 159, B. P. Schutz 86); Randwick–Petersham 5 for 310 (P. G. Toole 68*, D. W. Parmenter 58*, U. Khawaja 42, R. Stafford 34, R. Chee Quee 33; N. W. Bracken 3-66).

SYDNEY FIRST-GRADE FINAL, 2003-04

RANDWICK–PETERSHAM v EASTERN SUBURBS

At Coogee Oval, Coogee, April 2, 3, 4, 2004. Eastern Suburbs won on first innings. *Toss:* Randwick–Petersham.

Randwick–Petersham's prospects of winning a maiden first-grade title in only their third season were dealt two blows before the match had even started. Simon Katich declared himself unavailable because of injury and Jon Lewis, the club's spearhead who had taken 52 wickets at 15.28, had to return to Gloucestershire after the qualifying final. A first-day recovery by Eastern Suburbs and an amazing innings from the middle-order batsman Michael Maclennan ultimately proved decisive. The former Easts bowler Glen Farquharson had his old side on the ropes at 5 for 15 in the early stages, before Maclennan and Jason Swift revived the innings with a sixth-wicket stand of 152. Maclennan, who had never scored a first-grade century, then added 76 with Justin Dery. He struck 17 fours and faced 231 balls, bringing up his first ever hundred with a six.

Randwick–Petersham regularly lost wickets in reply, but a stout innings from the 17-year-old opener Usman Khawaja kept them in the game. Easts grabbed the initiative thanks to the guile and experience of their leg-spinner Adrian Tucker. A defiant last-wicket stand of 28 threatened to rob Easts of a precious first-innings advantage until Andrew Harrison was run out in unusual circumstances. His partner, Farquharson, appeared to be caught and Harrison moved outside his crease to commiserate with his team-mate. He did not realise a no-ball had been called and was run out at the bowler's end.

Easts started shakily again in their second innings, Harrison taking the first three wickets in four balls. Swift and Nick Berry steadied the ship with a partnership of 81. Swift then combined with Mark Patterson, the only member of the side to play in the club's last premiership team 12 years earlier, to clinch the Belvidere Cup with an unbroken 94-run stand.

Benaud Medal: M. Maclennan.

Close of play: First day, Randwick-Petersham (1) 0-1 (Phillips 0, Khawaja 0); Second day, Eastern Suburbs (2) 0-7 (Berry 7, Jeffrey 0).

Eastern Suburbs

A. Jeffrey c Hill b Farquharson	0	– lbw b Harrison	1
N. Berry c Toole b Farquharson	6	– c Harrison b Stafford	23
J. W. Cook b Farquharson	1	– c Hill b Harrison	0
†B. J. Haddin c Parmenter b Harrrison	3	– b Harrison	4
J. J Swift c Hunter b Stafford	71	– not out	101
*M. W. Patterson c Farquharson b Rosser	0	– not out	55
M. Maclennan lbw b Harrison	133		
J. Dery run out	21		
K. Powell b Farquharson	8		
A. E Tucker c Toole b Farquharson	1		
P. J. Byrom not out	18		
B 2, l-b 5, w 1, n-b 3	11	B 2, n-b 1	3

(88.5 overs, 361 mins)	273	(43.3 overs, 187mins) (4 wkts)	187
Fall: 0 4 12 14 15 167 243 245 256 273		Fall: 8 8 12 93	

Bowling: *First Innings*—Farquharson 21.5–6–44–5; Harrison 17–3–62–2; Rosser 16–4–44–1; Stafford 19–4–62–1; Hunter 9–0–36–0; Khawaja 6–1–18–0. *Second Innings*—Farquharson 11–0–51–0; Harrison 9–1–28–3; Rosser 4–1–20–0; Khawaja 5–0–29–0; Stafford 12.3–1–54–1; Hunter 2–1–3–0.

Randwick–Petersham

R. Phillips c Patterson b Tucker 20	R. Stafford c Swift b Powell 3
U. Khawaja c Haddin b Tucker 67	G. W. Farquharson not out 28
R. Chee Quee c Maclennan b Tucker 10	A. Harrison run out 15
J. V. Hill lbw b Tucker 0	
*P. G. Toole lbw b Tucker 16	L-b 3, w 1, n-b 13 17
†D. W Parmenter lbw b Byrom 15	
B. S. Hunter c Powell b Byrom 35	(94.2 overs, 390 mins) 234
N. Rosser c Jeffrey b Tucker 8	Fall: 35 62 62 117 124 175 178 181 206 234

Bowling: Powell 16–5–47–1; Dery 13–5–25–0; Byrom 15–4–43–2; Tucker 28–6–66–6; Cook 21.2–6–40–0; Maclennan 1–0–1–0.

Umpires N. S. D. Fowler and R. J. Tucker.

SYDNEY FIRST-GRADE RECORDS

ALL-TIME LEADING BATSMEN

	Runs	Club	Duration
W. Bardsley	12,119	Glebe, Western Suburbs	1898–1933
T. J. E. Andrews	11,672	Petersham	1909–43
S. J. Carroll	11,314	Gordon	1939–66
J. W. Burke	11,231	Manly, Northern District	1946–72
G. J. Hayne	11,220	UTS Balmain, Gordon	1987–
R. J. Bower	11,219	Bankstown, Penrith, Balmain	1977–98
A. Alderson	10,705	Cumberland, Sydney University	1941–68
B. C. Booth	10,674	St George	1952–77
J. W. Chegwyn	10,455	Randwick	1926–56
P. H. Marks	10,413	Balmain, Manly-Warringah, N Sydney	1979–2001

ALL-TIME LEADING BOWLERS

	Wickets	Club	Duration
H. C. Chilvers	1,153	Northern District	1925–52
K. C. Gulliver	1,028	Mosman	1930–63
W. J. O'Reilly	962	North Sydney, St George	1926–49
O. P. Asher	861	Sydney, Paddington	1910–33
R. Aitken	774	Parramatta, Sydney	1960–88
R. M. Pearce	771	Balmain	1937–57
D. M. Chardon	762	Petersham-Marrickville, Sydney	1967–90
K. Hall	752	Bankstown, Hawkesbury, Penrith	1975–2002
R. H. Guy	717	Gordon	1953–75
W. A. Wellham	684	Western Suburbs	1950–78

Brisbane First-Grade, 2003-04

by STEPHEN GRAY

The Brisbane first-grade competition continues to produce its share of talented young players to help keep Queensland cricket in rude health. In 2003-04, you only had to witness the smooth elevations of Aaron Nye, Craig Philipson and Chris Hartley to the Queensland side, as well as Ben Edmondson in Western Australia. All four had spent many a Brisbane summer's day maturing at club level as they waited for opportunity to knock.

The leading runscorer and wicket-taker of the 2003-04 season were also young men who appear destined for bigger things. Wynnum–Manly's Ryan Broad, a 22-year-old right-hand opener, and Sandgate–Redcliffe's Nathan Rimmington, a 21-year-old right-arm fast bowler, both showed their class at regular intervals throughout the season. Rimmington, the star of the first-grade final, finished with 49 wickets and added his name to the healthy list of current and potential Queensland speedsters. A whippy fast bowler, he became the second-youngest winner of the Peter Burge Medal for the best-and-fairest first-grade player, pipping the much-improved Toombul all-rounder Derek Tate by only two points.

The hard-hitting Broad scored nearly 1,500 runs in all forms of cricket, including 696 premiership runs and 314 in the Cricket Australia Cup. One of his trio of spectacular individual innings came in the one-day competition, when he clouted 206 against Beenleigh–Logan. He hit 16 sixes that day, including five in an over off the part-time leg-spin of Rod Davision, his second hundred arriving in only 40 balls.

Remarkably, Broad's 206 was not the highest limited-overs innings of the summer. Lance Kahler, the former Queensland left-hander, had smashed 211 not out the week before against South–East Queensland, as Souths amassed 3 for 369 from their 50 overs. A week after Broad's pyrotechnics, Matthew Hayden made the most of a rare club outing for Valley to turn on the fireworks against Toombul. He scored 167 from 152 balls, dotting the court-yards of several townhouses near the Ken Mackay Oval with massive sixes.

The one-day competition was eventually won by the University of Queensland, the students claiming back-to-back titles in the competition by defeating Gold Coast at Allan Border Field. Lachlan Stevens, back in Brisbane after a stint with South Australia and working as a sports administrator with the university, top-scored with 128 and took 4 for 19 to provide a useful talking point for his next performance review.

Among the positives to emerge in the first-grade competition was the continued improvement of Beenleigh–Logan under the direction of last season's premiership coach Greg Campbell, who switched from Gold Coast during the off-season, and the re-emergence of Toombul after several years in the doldrums. Toombul led the competition for most of the season before faltering. The youthful Redlands side also acquitted themselves well, finishing third.

Andrew Francey's 165 for Sandgate–Redcliffe was the highest individual score, just ahead of the Gold Coast opener Andrew Robinson's 163. Derek Tate's 8 for 82 was the best solo effort with the ball. There were also eyecatching returns from Valley's fast bowler Andrew Barlow, a former Australian Under-17s player making his return to the game, who took 7 for 25; the Sunshine Coast off-spinner Craig Grant (7 for 35); the Souths leg-spinner Mathew James (7 for 53); and Nathan Hauritz (7 for 123). Tate, for good measure, also chipped in with 7 for 28 on another occasion.

The list of noteworthy retirees was led by the Wests trio of Greg Rowell, Dean Tuckwell and Ross Lupton. Valley bid farewell to their captain Brett Neill and the big-hitting Brendan Shinnick. Rowell, still capable at 37 of holding his own at first-class level, was denied the fairytale finish of a premiership in his last game, courtesy of a matchwinning performance by Rimmington in the final.

Western Suburbs were the club champions, despite Valley's feat of winning four of the five lower-grade premierships. Wests swept all before them in the women's competition. They claimed the first-grade and second-grade premierships – despite a tie with Wynum–Manly in the first-grade final – before clean-sweeping the available team awards with the inaugural women's Spirit of Cricket trophy. The University of Queensland won the men's equivalent. For the second season in a row Trish Brown won the Kath Smith Medal for the outstanding women's player, scoring 746 runs and taking 23 wickets for Wynnum–Manly.

BRISBANE FIRST-GRADE TABLE, 2003-04

	M	WO	WI	D	LI	LO	Points
Sandgate-Redcliffe	11	1	6	2	2	0	157.32
Western Suburbs	11	0	8	2	1	0	152.30
Redlands	11	1	5	2	3	0	137.56
Toombul	11	0	5	4	2	0	131.26
Northern Suburbs	11	0	6	2	3	0	117.74
Wynnum-Manly	11	0	4	2	3	2	107.46
Gold Coast	11	0	4	3	4	0	105.13
Beenleigh-Logan	11	1	3	1	6	0	98.94
University of Queensland	11	0	3	1	7	0	93.25
South Brisbane	11	0	2	5	4	0	84.35
Sunshine Coast	11	0	1	1	8	1	70.08
Valley	11	0	1	5	5	0	63.40

MOST RUNS, 2003-04

(Qualification: 200 runs)

	M	I	NO	R	HS	100s	Avge
R. Broad (Wynnum-Manly)	11	14	1	696	162*	3	53.54
R. J. Davison (Beenleigh-Logan)	11	17	5	660	132	2	55.00
A. Robinson (Gold Coast)	11	14	0	601	163	3	42.93
A. D. Francey (Sandgate-Redcliffe)	11	14	2	574	165	2	47.83
G. Batticciotto (Sandgate-Redcliffe)	11	14	0	515	118	1	34.33
S. J. Paulsen (Western Suburbs)	11	13	2	491	97	0	44.64
N. Reardon (University)	11	14	2	481	141*	2	40.08
L. W. Kahler (Souths Brisbane)	11	14	3	460	99	0	41.81
B. P. Nash (Northern Suburbs)	11	13	2	445	142	2	40.45
D. M. Payne (Redlands)	9	12	1	444	94	0	37.63

MOST WICKETS, 2003-04

(Qualification: 20 wickets)

	M	O	Mdns	R	W	BB	5W/i	Avge
N. J. Rimmington (Sandgate-Redcliffe)	10	279.3	65	864	49	5-23	4	17.63
D. Tate (Toombul)	11	256.4	72	688	41	8-82	3	16.78
M. A. George (Beenleigh-Logan)	11	256	65	756	40	5-34	3	18.90
M. A. Anderson (Sandgate-Redcliffe)	11	238.2	74	631	31	4-40	0	20.35
M. James (South Brisbane)	11	225	45	673	27	7-53	2	24.92
R. T. Watts (Wynnum-Manly)	10	170.2	38	527	27	n-a	0	19.52
M. J. Petrie (Redlands)	11	212	72	499	25	6-40	2	19.96
G. M. Schossow (Western Suburbs)	11	128.1	28	382	25	5-67	1	15.28
W. G. Aspeling (Redlands)	11	169.1	56	427	24	n-a	0	17.79
S. J. Jurgensen (Sandgate-Redcliffe)	9	176.2	63	392	24	3-27	0	16.33
K. Jeffs (Toombul)	11	189.4	53	546	24	n-a	0	22.75
N. Dever (University)	10	170	34	506	24	5-30	2	21.08
B. R. Teece (Wynnum-Manly)	10	147.1	21	668	24	n-a	0	27.83

BRISBANE FIRST-GRADE SEMI-FINALS, 2003-04

SANDGATE–REDCLIFFE v TOOMBUL

At Ian Healy Oval. No play possible due to wet ground. Sandgate–Redcliffe went through to the final as minor premiers.

WESTERN SUBURBS v REDLANDS

At Tigers, Graceville No.1. Redlands 124 (D. M. Payne 51; R. Lupton 4-16, C. Glass 3-18) and 8 dec 101 (S. J. Magoffin 5-45) lost on first innings to Western Suburbs 137 (R. Lupton 36, D. Tuckwell 31, G. J. Rowell 31; W. G. Aspeling 4-31, R. Leloux 3-20) and 6 for 68 (D. M Payne 3-2).

BRISBANE FIRST-GRADE FINAL, 2003-04

SANDGATE–REDCLIFFE v WESTERN SUBURBS

At Allan Border Field, Albion, March 13, 14, 20, 2004. *Toss:* Western Suburbs.

Ever since winning their inaugural premiership in 1997-98, Sandgate–Redcliffe have established themselves as a powerhouse of the competition. Aside from a lacklustre showing in 2002-03, the 'Gators' have been either premiers or contenders for the title each year. They looked poised to suffer a comprehensive defeat in the 2003-04 final, until the mother of all batting collapses on an extraordinary final morning guaranteed their fifth premiership victory in seven seasons.

Until that disastrous last morning Western Suburbs, denied by Sandgate–Redcliffe in the 2001-02 final, looked on track to claim their first premiership since 1987-88. They promptly produced a second-innings batting performance that verged on collective hysteria. Needing only 84 to win, Wests were bundled out in 11.1 overs for 31, six batsmen making ducks. Nathan Rimmington, swinging the ball prodigiously at high speed under an overcast sky, took 6 for 15 in six overs. Shane Jurgensen, the ideal foil, took the other four.

Wests had dominated the first three days despite missing their captain Aaron Nye on the opening weekend because of the Pura Cup final. After Jerry Cassell and Glen Batticciotto put on 80 for the first wicket, Sandgate–Redcliffe gradually subsided to be all out for 220. Wests then built a first-innings lead of 112, their stand-in skipper Steve Paulsen leading the way with 91. Dean Tuckwell enjoyed his cameo as Nye's replacement, making quick runs with Steve Magoffin towards the end.

The evergreen wicket-keeper Gavin Fitness, whose 38 dismissals made him the summer's leading gloveman, did his best to give Sandgate–Redcliffe a fighting chance. Coming in at 6 for 74, still 38 runs behind, he raced to 64 in 65 balls. Greg Rowell, in his last match for Wests, bowled with customary menace to take seven wickets. But Fitness, with the help of the tail, ensured Sandgate at least had some sort of total to defend. That it proved enough for victory was little short of miraculous.

Close of play: First day, Western Suburbs (1) 1-68; Second day, Sandgate–Redcliffe (2) 3-33.

Sandgate–Redcliffe

A. A. Francey c Lane b Rowell	7	– b Magoffin	6
G. Batticciotto c Paulsen b Rowell	37	– b Rowell	19
*J. L. Cassell b Lupton	56	– (6) run out	25
G. Hughes lbw b Rowell	0	– (3) c Paulsen b Rowell	0
M. C. Goggin c Moore b Magoffin	21	– (7) c Lane b Schossow	25
†G. A. J. Fitness c Lane b Magoffin	40	– (8) run out	64
P. D. Pink c Moore b Schossow	5	– (5) c Nielsen b Rowell	3
S. J. Jurgensen c Robynson b Schossow	9	– (9) c Magoffin b Lupton	23
M. A. Anderson c Lane b Schossow	6	– (4) hit wicket b Magoffin	1
N. J. Rimmington not out	6	– c Nye b Lupton	15
J. Loader c Lane b Rowell	1	– not out	0
B 1, l-b 9, w 3 n-b 19	32	L-b 4, n-b 10	14

(63.5 overs, 282 mins)   220   (42.1 overs, 192 mins)   195
Fall: 1 115 115 119 156 169 181 197 213 220   Fall: 15 25 30 33 37 74 93 145 190 195

Bowling: *First Innings*—Magoffin 11–2–39–1; Rowell 15.5–3–60–4; Schossow 18–4–61–4; Glass 4–0–16–0; Lupton 6–2–19–1; Paulsen 9–3–15–0. *Second Innings*—Magoffin 11–2–41–2; Rowell 15–1–60–3; Schossow 5–0–36–1; Glass 2–0–28–0; Lupton 6.1–1–25–2; Paulsen 1–1–0–0; Lane 2–1–1–0.

Western Suburbs

A. Robynson c Fitness b Rimmington	5	– (2) c Goggin b Rimmington	4
J. Neilson c Francey b Loader	47	– (1) lbw b Jurgensen	5
*S. Paulsen c Fitness b Loader	91	– (4) c Goggin b Jurgensen	12
M. Lane c Fitness b Loader	13	– (5) c Fitness b Jurgensen	0
R. Lupton c Fitness b Anderson	1	– (6) c Cassell b Rimmington	0
D. Tuckwell c Batticciotto b Rimmington	84		
G. J. Rowell c Goggin b Anderson	14	– b Rimmington	2
S. J. Magoffin lbw b Anderson	39	– lbw b Rimmington	0
†A. Moore c Fitness b Rimmington	11	– b Rimmington	0
C. Glass c Fitness b Loader	4	– c Anderson b Rimmington	6
G. Schossow not out	14	– not out	0
*A. J. Nye (did not bat)		– (3) c Fitness b Jurgensen	0
L–b 2, n–b 7	9	L–b 1, n–b 1	2

(91.4 overs, 375 mins)   332   (11.1 overs, 53 mins)   31
Fall: 17 127 159 160 161 194 282 303 312 332   Fall: 5 9 9 9 10 17 25 25 31 31

Bowling: *First Innings*—Jurgensen 27–4–118–0; Rimmington 18.4–6–74–3; Pink 4–1–13–0; Anderson 22–9–38–3; Loader 20–7–87–4. *Second Innings*—Jurgensen 5.1–2–15–4; Rimmington 6–1–15–6.

Umpires: N. S. McNamara and B. N. J. Oxenford.

Adelaide A-Grade, 2003-04

by LAWRIE COLLIVER

Despite finishing second on the table in the minor round, Adelaide showed they were the best team in the competition by twice beating Tea Tree Gully in the finals series to win the 2003-04 premiership. The teams met three times during the summer, the Buffaloes winning by two wickets, 33 runs and 42 runs respectively. Ben Johnson was Adelaide's outstanding player, averaging 35 with the bat and dominating with the ball, his accurate medium-pacers tying up even the best batsmen. The captain, Jack Smith, scored heavily to lead by example, while the opener Luke Williams was also reliable. The off-spinner Dan Cullen underlined his exciting potential, taking 40 wickets at 19.37. He will be hoping for similar success at first-class level in 2004-05.

Tea Tree Gully played with great heart. Ben Cameron and Wes Thomas dominated with the bat, Cameron breaking into the South Australian side late in the summer. The captain, Garry Chillingworth, had a superb season with the ball and, as always, held some brilliant catches at slip. Travis Borlace has developed into an all-rounder of great quality.

The previous year's winners, Kensington, were not prepared to give up the title without a fight, almost stealing victory in a dramatic preliminary final against Tea Tree Gully. Their batting was strong when Greg Blewett was available but fragile without him. John Lee contributed a couple of centuries, but it was the bowling of Ben Johnswood (39 wickets at 19.20) and John Campbell (33 at 21.75) that kept Kensington competitive and enabled them to make the four.

University scraped into the finals. Nathan Adcock, their skipper, carried his fine batting form into the semi-final against Kensington. His dismissal for 82, succumbing to a reckless shot, proved the crucial wicket. The former West Indies captain Carl Hooper failed to make much impact and left before the finals, apparently deciding he would rather watch the formula one grand prix in Melbourne. Chris

Slattery, the talented Australian Rules footballer, emerged as a seam bowler to watch in coming seasons.

Prospect endured an inconsistent season, finishing fifth for the second time in a row. The captain, Jeff Vaughan, led the batting with his only real support coming from Sam Ellicott. The left-hander Paul Duffett retired from A-grade cricket after a moderate season. Mike Harden, who took 38 wickets at 21.02, passed 200 A-grade wickets for the club. Sturt rose from 11th in 2002-03 to finish in the top half, their veteran Matthew Golding having a fine all-round season. The promising Mark Littlewood accumulated 353 runs at 39.22, but Andy Flower's only score of note was his 160 against Port Adelaide in his first match.

Glenelg fell out of the top four, despite David Fitzgerald's three centuries after being dropped from the state side. Ben Hook continues to be a fine all-rounder after more than 10 seasons, scoring 450 runs at 40.90 and taking 22 wickets at 14.40. The popular fast bowler Tarque Williamson (23 wickets at 15.04) made a welcome return. Shane Deitz had an outstanding season when available, becoming Southern Districts's first Bradman Medallist. But he lacked batting support. Brett Bevan again contributed with the ball, as did the New South Wales recruit Andrew Staunton, who headed back home before the end of the season.

Woodville relied heavily on the outstanding form of their all-rounder Mick Miller, who was runner-up in the Bradman Medal by one vote. Ken Skewes, from Darwin, showed promise and the seam bowler Andrew Eime was again named in the team of the year. West Torrens started well but fell away, although they did win the limited-overs competition. Ben Higgins was their star player. Jesse Lewis came over from Adelaide Turf and scored useful runs. Brad Young and Mark Harrity announced their retirements.

Port Adelaide managed to win three games, riding on the back of Matthew Weeks's all-round performances. A question mark remains over whether they will stay in the competition; they must win at least five games in 2004-05 to do so. Northern Districts were the season's most disappointing team, despite some good innings by Mark Cosgrove. Chris Duval looks a bowler of the future after a fine grade season and some promising state 2nd XI performances. East Torrens finished last, even though the veterans Craig Bradbrook and Cosi Lanzoni made runs consistently.

The A-grade Team of the Year, announced on Bradman Medal night, was: David Fitzgerald, Shane Deitz, Jeff Vaughan (captain), Nathan Adcock, Ben Higgins, Mick Miller, Matthew Weeks, Garry Chillingworth, Travis Borlace, Andrew Eime, Dan Cullen and Mike Harden.

ADELAIDE A-GRADE TABLE, 2003-04

	M	WO	W	D	T	L	LO	Match Points	Bonus Points	O/rate Points	Total Points
Tea Tree Gully	12	0	9	1	0	2	0	142.50	71.43	0	213.93
Adelaide	12	0	8	1	0	3	0	127.50	75.97	0	203.47
Kensington	12	1	6	0	0	5	0	110	82.01	0	192.01
University	12	1	6	1	0	4	0	117.50	73.92	0	191.42
Prospect	12	0	7	1	0	3	1	112.50	68.41	0	180.91
Sturt	12	0	6	1	1	4	0	105	66.22	0	171.22
Glenelg	12	1	5	1	0	5	0	102.50	67.57	0	170.07
Southern Districts ..	12	0	6	1	0	4	1	97.50	67.10	0.25	164.35
Woodville	12	0	5	1	0	6	0	82.50	69.17	0	151.67
West Torrens	12	0	4	0	0	8	0	60	77.29	0	137.29
Port Adelaide	12	0	3	1	0	8	0	52.50	65.87	0	118.37
East Torrens	12	0	1	0	1	9	1	22.50	59.25	1.75	80.00

BATTING AVERAGES, 2003-04

(Qualification: 400 runs)

	M	I	NO	R	HS	100s	50s	Avge
S. A. Deitz (Southern Districts)	8	8	3	565	129*	2	4	113.00
G. S. Blewett (Kensington)...........	7	7	2	412	126	1	2	82.00
M. C. Miller (Woodville)	7	7	1	400	132	1	2	66.67
J. M. Vaughan (Prospect)	12	13	1	762	164	2	4	63.50
W. D. Thomas (Tea Tree Gully)......	14	17	2	876	168	2	6	58.40
B. H. Higgins (West Torrens)........	11	16	3	730	127	2	4	56.15
N. T. Adcock (University)	13	15	2	713	153*	1	6	54.84
D. A. Fitzgerald (Glenelg)	12	13	0	704	153	3	3	54.15
B. P. Cameron (Tea Tree Gully)......	14	15	1	705	134	3	3	50.35
J. K. Smith (Adelaide).............	13	17	2	739	116	3	1	49.26

* Denotes not out.

BOWLING AVERAGES, 2003-04

(Qualification: 25 wickets)

	M	O	Mdns	R	W	BB	5W/i	10W/m	Avge
B. A. Johnson (Adelaide)	13	274	87	638	41	6-26	3	0	15.56
C. Slattery (University)	13	193.4	42	569	35	5-43	2	0	16.25
G. A. Chillingworth (Tea Tree Gully) .	15	306.3	63	938	55	6-49	3	1	17.05
N. Job (Adelaide).................	14	232.2	85	633	36	5-38	2	0	17.58
B. Bevan (Southern Districts)	10	188	47	583	33	4-26	0	0	17.66
M. C. Miller (Woodville)	7	135	25	467	26	7-104	3	0	17.96
N. Rowe (Glenelg)	11	228.1	59	587	32	7-70	1	0	18.34
C. Duval (Northern Districts)	10	223.4	55	573	31	6-33	1	0	18.48
T. G. R. Borlace (Tea Tree Gully)	15	315.3	73	912	49	6-37	2	1	18.61
A. M. Staunton (Southern Districts) ..	9	166.4	36	505	27	5-38	1	0	18.70

ADELAIDE A-GRADE FINALS SERIES, 2003-04

MAJOR SEMI-FINAL
TEA TREE GULLY v ADELAIDE

At Pertaringa Oval, March 13, 14, 2004. *Toss:* Adelaide. Tea Tree Gully won on first innings. Adelaide 9 for 354 (J. K. Smith 116, B. A. Johnson 90, M. Crook 50; T. G. R. Borlace 4-93); Tea Tree Gully 321 (W. D. Thomas 168, S. Stolcman 84; B. A. Johnson 4-54, N. Job 3-90).

KNOCKOUT SEMI-FINAL
KENSINGTON v UNIVERSITY

At Parkinson Oval, March 13, 14, 2004. *Toss:* Kensington. Kensington won on first innings. Kensington 280 (M. F. Cleary 102, S. Turner 69; C. Slattery 4-73, M. J. Smith 3-82); University 256 (N. T. Adcock 82, B. Hutchinson 74; J. Panelli 5-70).

PRELIMINARY FINAL
TEA TREE GULLY v KENSINGTON

At Adelaide Oval, March 20, 21, 2004. *Toss:* Kensington. Tea Tree Gully won by four wickets. Kensington 74 (D. P. Waugh 42; T. G. R. Borlace 6-37, J. Haberfield 3-14) and 188 (J. Lee 91; T. G. R. Borlace 4-55, W. D. Thomas 3-45); Tea Tree Gully 118 (B. Johnswood 7-29) and 6 for 145 (G. Harvey 45, S. Stolcman 42; J. Morgan 3-25).

ADELAIDE A-GRADE FINAL, 2003-04

TEA TREE GULLY v ADELAIDE

At Adelaide Oval, March 27, 28, 29, 2004. Adelaide won on first innings. *Toss:* Adelaide.

After a batting collapse on the first day, Adelaide dug deep to win a hard-fought grand final. In ideal batting conditions they slumped to 5 for 67 before lunch on the opening day. But a superb 215-run partnership for the sixth wicket between Ben Johnson and Chris Davies, in just under three hours, pulled the match around. Johnson played his shots from the start and was particularly severe on anything short or on his pads. Davies batted steadily at first before unleashing a full array of strokes on both sides of the wicket. His first fifty arrived in 85 balls; his second took only 39. Davies hit two memorable sixes, dancing down to the off-spinner Chillingworth and cover-driving him over the fence, then slog-sweeping Wright from well outside off stump over mid-wicket and into the new Eastern Stand. But the last five wickets fell cheaply, leaving Tea Tree Gully to chase a gettable target on a good pitch.

They began in the worst possible fashion, Harvey edging via his thigh pad to short leg and Stolcman edging an attempted drive. From 2 for 18, Thomas and Cameron steered the game the Gullies' way. They hoisted a 187-run partnership in three hours, running smartly between wickets and hitting forcefully when the bowlers' length strayed. Thomas's fine knock ended with a needless glide that ended up in the wicket-keeper's gloves. With skies threatening, Wright attempted to cut and fell to a questionable caught-behind decision. Two balls later, with Tea Tree Gully needing 87 runs and Adelaide six wickets, the rain came. Monday dawned clear, and Tea Tree Gully added 16 runs before Cameron tried to pull Johnson over the short eastern boundary and was caught just inside the fence. From that point Adelaide's bowlers dominated, mopping up the last six wickets for 28 runs in 17 overs.

David Hookes Medal: B. A. Johnson.

Close of play: First day, Adelaide (1) 321; Second day, Tea Tree Gully (1) 4-247 (Cameron 118, Borlace 2).

Adelaide

L. Williams c Stapledon b Haberfield 28	S. M. Maraun b Borlace 6
M. Crook c Cameron b Borlace 6	D. J. Cullen lbw b Chillingworth 6
D. Agars lbw b Thomas 13	N. Job not out 0
*J. K. Smith c Stapledon b Haberfield 8	
B. A. Johnson c Cameron b Chillingworth ..131	B 1, l-b 3, w 4, n-b 4 12
S. Williams c Cameron b Thomas 0	
C. J. Davies c Borlace b Pahl 110	(90.3 overs, 353 mins) 333
†J. L. McLean c Stapledon b Pahl 13	Fall: 12 49 53 67 67 282 315 322 333 333

Bowling: Pahl 25–5–75–2; Borlace 24.3–5–93–2; Haberfield 10–1–33–2; Thomas 10–3–30–2; Chillingworth 17–0–69–2; Wright 4–0–29–0.

Tea Tree Gully

S. Stolcman c McLean b Johnson 5	V. Lee c L. Williams b Maraun 6
G. Harvey c S. Williams b Johnson 3	†T. Stapledon not out 6
W. D. Thomas c McLean b Job 86	J. Haberfield c L. Williams b Maraun 0
B. P. Cameron c S. Williams b Johnson 129	
G. J. Wright c McLean b Cullen 19	B 5, l-b 3, w 1, n-b 7 16
T. G. R. Borlace lbw b Johnson 14	
*G. A. Chillingworth b Maraun 4	(90.3 overs, 352 mins) 291
B. J. Pahl run out (S. Williams/McLean) ... 3	Fall: 7 18 205 245 263 274 274 282 289 291

Bowling: Maraun 17.3–5–68–3; Johnson 36–10–91–4; Cullen 25–4–85–1; Job 9–2–29–1; S Williams 3–1–10–0.

Umpires: S. J. Davis and S. D. Fry.

ADELAIDE A-GRADE RECORDS

ALL-TIME LEADING RUNSCORERS

Wayne Bradbrook	9,619	V. Y. Richardson	7,326
R. J. Zadow	9,318	B. J. Hook	7,240
M. P. Faull	9,093	C. E. Pellew	7,154
N. R. Fielke	7,616	Craig Bradbrook	6,656
J. C. Reedman	7,346	A. P. Kimber	6,610

ALL-TIME LEADING WICKET-TAKERS

N. L. Williams	894	D. J. Lambert	636
J. P. F. Travers	819	R. J. Stratfold	624
A. T. W. Sincock	762	R. M. O'Shannassy	621
G. Giffen	744	B. M. Hurn	615
G. C. Clarke	724	R. M. Sharpe	587

TCA First-Grade, 2003-04

by BRETT STUBBS

For more than 100 years, no Tasmanian batsman had scored a first-grade triple-century. In 2003-04 it happened twice in eight days. In a season dominated by Clarence, these two individual performances and the controversy surrounding allegations of pitch doctoring for financial reward stood out.

Shane Watson single-handedly altered the shape of the finals with what turned out to be his final performance for a Tasmanian-based team. In the final round, captaining bottom side Lindisfarne against a North Hobart line-up that included Dan Marsh, Michael Dighton, Sean Clingeleffer, Adam Griffith and the English all-rounder Jon Dakin, Watson scored 228 on the opening day. He declared the following day after bringing up his 300 in only 259 balls, having plundered 27 fours and 10 sixes. When North Hobart put all nine fieldsmen in the deep to try to limit his scoring to singles, Watson continually lifted the ball over the TCA ground boundary. He then took the new ball and destroyed the opposition, finishing with 7 for 29 off 14.2 overs. Watson's feat lifted Lindisfarne off the bottom of the ladder and knocked North Hobart, who were considered Clarence's biggest threat, out of the finals.

Watson's innings was the highest TCA score since Charles Eady made 566 for Break O'Day against Wellington in 1901-02. Yet it was eclipsed the following Saturday in the semi-finals when Clarence's all-rounder Shannon Tubb made 342 against New Town at Bellerive. Tubb hit 307 on the first day and was eventually dismissed the following morning. He hit 52 fours, four sixes and faced 314 deliveries in the highest score in TCA finals history. He was the beneficiary of a fine piece of sportsmanship on 242, when he charged down the wicket only to miss the ball and see the New Town wicket-keeper Craig Stockdale take off the bails. Tubb was heading to the pavilion when Stockdale called him back, admitting to the square-leg umpire that he did not have control of the ball when he broke the stumps.

Clarence's eventual grand final opponents were again Glenorchy. First, though, Glenorchy had to overcome allegations of financial offers for pitch doctoring. During the season the new club captain, Vaughan Williams, and another member of Glenorchy offered money to the club's curators at the King George V Oval. The curators were employees of the Glenorchy City Council, and when the offer was leaked to the council and passed on to the TCA, an inquiry was held into whether or not the offer represented an incentive for the curators to doctor the pitch.

Williams vehemently denied the allegation. He made the offer, he said, out of frustration with sub-standard pitches. The investigation group – consisting of the TCA chief executive David Johnston, the grade cricket committee chairman Ray Brown and the manager of grade cricket Scott Godfrey – ruled that the actions of the pair were not a bribe to doctor wickets but an incentive for the curators to improve the wicket for all teams at the KGV Oval. They found that the club was unaware of the offer but said no action should be taken, while advising the pair that their behaviour was inappropriate, naive and should not be repeated. The investigation group also recommended that Bellerive's head curator, Cameron Hodgkins, should advise the curators on how to improve the standard of their wickets.

TEN BIGGEST INNINGS IN TCA HISTORY

566	C.J. Eady	Break O'Day v Wellington	1901-02
365*	K.E. Burn	Wellington v Derwent	1898-99
361	K.E. Burn	Wellington v Derwent	1899-00
342	**S.B. Tubb**	**Clarence v New Town**	**2003-04**
300*	**S.R. Watson**	**Lindisfarne v North Hobart**	**2003-04**
278	S. Young	North Hobart v Kingborough	1998-99
274	H. Myers	West Hobart v East Hobart	1914-15
271*	D. Green	South Hobart-Sandy Bay v New Town	1991-92
268	S.G. Hookey	North Hobart v Kingborough	1989-90
262*	K.E. Burn	Derwent v Wellington	1892-93

Note: Eady's 566 remains the highest innings in senior competition anywhere in the world. He took 7 for 87 with the ball in that same match.

For the first time in four seasons, the South Hobart–Sandy Bay captain-coach Adam Polkinghorne did not walk away with the TCA Medal. With only three votes separating the top eight place-getters, Clarence's veteran medium-pacer Mark Colegrave tied with the University batsman Graeme Cunningham. While Colegrave was one of the favourites, Cunningham's win was a surprise. He scored

432 runs at 33.23 with a top score of 82, and did not even force his
way into the first-grade team of the year.

Clarence dominated the season, holding top position on the
ladder from round two onwards. University made a brief return to
the finals after missing out the previous year, but were soundly
beaten by Glenorchy in the semis. They had better luck in the limited-overs competition, the Kookaburra Cup, reaching the final and
tying with Launceston when the game was washed out.

Qualifying games for the Kookaburra Cup were incorporated into
the TCA season to reduce the number of Saturday–Sunday fixtures
and make the roster less demanding on players. The games counted
toward both the first-grade and Kookaburra Cup tables, and saw the
introduction of coloured clothes, white balls and limited-overs rules
in TCA first-grade games for the first time.

TCA FIRST-GRADE TABLE, 2003-04

	M	WO	W1	D	Ll	LO	Points	Bonus Points
Clarence	14	3	4	5	2	0	50	49.06
University	14	0	8	3	3	0	38	39.84
Glenorchy	14	1	5	3	5	1	35.60*	46.38
†New Town	14	1	5	3	6	0	34	44.45
†North Hobart	14	2	3	3	8	0	32	41.44
South Hobart-Sandy Bay	14	0	5	3	6	2	24	38.58
Lindisfarne	14	0	4	4	4	2	20	37.51
Kingborough	14	0	4	4	5	2	18	36.75

*Glenorchy penalised .40 due to slow over-rate.

*†New Town and North Hobart both had outright wins after trailing on the first innings against
South Hobart-Sandy Bay and Glenorchy respectively.*

BATTING AVERAGES

(Qualification: 300 runs)

	M	I	NO	R	HS	100s	50s	Avge
S. R. Watson (Lindisfarne)	5	6	3	526	300*	1	2	175.33
A. J. Dykes (Clarence)	11	9	6	443	111*	2	2	147.67
S. R. Mason (Clarence)	9	8	1	366	128*	1	1	52.29
A. W. Polkinghorne (Sth Hobart-Sandy Bay)	14	15	1	612	118	2	3	43.71
L. R. Butterworth (Glenorchy)	12	14	2	475	136*	1	1	39.58
D. R. McConnon (Glenorchy)	10	11	2	335	94	0	2	37.22
D. G. Dawson (Kingborough)	12	14	2	432	102	1	1	36.00
G. J. Bailey (Sth Hobart-Sandy Bay)	13	14	1	464	97	0	3	35.69
R. J. G. Lockyear (University)	13	14	2	427	77	0	4	35.58
T. R. Birt (Glenorchy)	12	13	3	341	79	0	4	34.10

* Denotes not out.

BOWLING AVERAGES

(Qualification: 20 wickets)

	M	O	Mdns	R	W	BB	5W/i	10W/m	Avge
M. D. Colegrave (Clarence)	10	156.3	68	283	32	6-18	4	1	8.84
L. A. Nosworthy (New Town) ...	12	126.1	37	346	26	3-5	0	0	13.31
J. M. Dakin (North Hobart)	14	188.3	36	570	38	5-24	2	0	15.00
A. W. Polkinghorne (Sth Hobart-Sandy Bay) .	14	167.3	47	407	25	5-34	1	0	16.28
V. G. Kay (New Town)	13	155.2	44	441	27	5-27	1	0	16.33
K. S. Pickering (Glenorchy)	12	184.2	36	567	34	5-23	3	0	16.68
M. J. Stirling (Clarence)	13	167.5	30	518	29	7-28	1	0	17.86
B. W. Hilfenhaus (University) ...	13	254.1	67	619	32	5-38	1	0	19.34
L. R. Butterworth (Glenorchy) ...	12	184.3	40	530	27	5-73	1	0	19.63
L. Swards (Kingborough)	13	178.4	34	550	27	6-78	1	0	20.37

TCA FIRST-GRADE SEMI-FINALS, 2003-04

CLARENCE v NEW TOWN

At Bellerive Oval, Bellerive, March 20, 21, 2004. Match drawn. Clarence proceeded to the final owing to their higher position on the table. *Toss:* Clarence. Clarence 6 for 549 (S. B. Tubb 342, M. Wade 89) drew with New Town 8 for 259 (S. P. Kremerskothen 56, D. J. Saker 45*, A. Roussow 42).

UNIVERSITY v GLENORCHY

At University Oval, University, March 20, 21, 2004. Glenorchy won on first innings. *Toss:* University. Glenorchy 9 for 246 (V. M. Williams 61, T. R. Birt 57, D. R. McConnon 45*; G. Kerr 3-53); University 90 (M. J. Shelton 3-17, L. R. Butterworth 3-18).

TCA FIRST-GRADE FINAL, 2003-04

CLARENCE v GLENORCHY

At Bellerive Oval, Bellerive, March 26, 27, 28, 2004. Clarence won on first innings. *Toss:* Clarence.

For the second year running, Clarence thrashed Glenorchy to take the TCA premiership. In the final session of the second afternoon, with more than a day's play remaining, Glenorchy's captain Vaughan Williams told the umpires his side were conceding defeat. The Clarence captain, Andrew Dykes, admitted he was surprised at the announcement but happy to accept the trophy.

Dykes had no hesitation in batting after winning the toss, knowing that the longer his side batted the more pressure would be placed on Glenorchy, who had to win in order to take the flag after finishing lower on the table. Scott Mason was dismissed early but Clarence built a substantial total on an excellent batting wicket around Ben Harris. Harris, who had scored 70 in the previous season's final, shared partnerships of 56 with Shannon Tubb, 86 with Matthew Wade and 87 with Damien Wright. He brought up his second century of the summer off 199 balls with 11 fours. The second new ball triggered a Glenorchy fightback, led by the pace bowler Kelby Pickering. He found himself on a hat-trick before the game took yet another dramatic turn, Wayne Quarrell and Wright counterattacking with 74 runs in the final 54 minutes to carry Clarence to a strong position. Glenorchy cleaned up the tail quickly next day, but by then Clarence had amassed a formidable 412.

Glenorchy's reply faltered early. Nathan Matthews ran himself out in a mix-up with Phil Mustard, then Mustard and Robbie Dilger fell to Mark Colegrave, leaving the challengers tottering at 3 for 16. Luke Butterworth was the only batsman to offer any real resistance, and when he fell to the part-time off-spin of Harris the game was as good as over. Tubb finished things off by snaring his best return of the season with his chinamen, Glenorchy losing their last five wickets for 24.

Man of the Match: B. L. Harris.

Close of play: First day, Clarence (1) 6-363 (Wright 81, Quarrell 36).

Clarence

S. R. Mason b Pickering	6	†M. J. Clingeleffer c McConnon b Pickering 0
B. L. Harris c McConnon b Dilger	116	M. D. Colegrave lbw b Shelton 9
S. B. Tubb b N. G. Butterworth	22	G. J. Denton not out 6
M. Wade c Pickering b N. G. Butterworth	47	
D. G. Wright lbw b Pickering	93	B 4, l-b 12, n-b 13 29
*A. J. Dykes c McGann b Pickering	27	
G. Costelloe c McGann b Pickering	0	(123.5 overs, 444 mins) 410
W. Quarrell b Shelton	55	Fall: 15 71 157 244 289 389 389 405 412

M. J. Stirling did not bat.

Bowling: L. R. Butterworth 25–7–78–0; Pickering 23–3–77–5; N. G. Butterworth 16–3–63–2; Shelton 31.5–10–81–2; Cartledge 10–1–51–0; Dilger 18–7–46–1.

Glenorchy

P. Mustard c Dykes b Colegrave	9	†N. A. McGann c Costelloe b Tubb 6
N. D. Matthews run out (Wade)	1	B. A. Cartledge c and b Tubb 6
R. J. Dilger lbw b Colegrave	3	N. G. Butterworth not out 2
*V. M. Williams c Clingeleffer b Wright	18	
L. R. Butterworth c Colegrave b Harris	90	L-b 4, n-b 4 8
T. R. Birt st Clingeleffer b Tubb	24	
D. R. McConnon c Wright b Tubb	25	(63.5 overs, 242 mins) 193
K. S. Pickering c Wright b Tubb	1	Fall: 6 11 16 60 129 169 174 175 184 193

M. J. Shelton did not bat.

Bowling: Wright 17–4–65–1, Colegrave 11–4–24–2, Denton 13–3–26–0, Stirling 6–0–21–0, Tubb 15.5–2–49–5, Harris 1–0–4–1.

Umpires: J. H. Smeaton and S. J. Maxwell.

Victorian Premier Cricket, 2003-04

by KEN WILLIAMS

St Kilda continued their recent dominance of Melbourne grade cricket by winning their third premiership in four years. To do so, they overcame a strong challenge from Hawthorn–Monash University in a tense final that took four days to produce a first-innings result. St Kilda and Northcote had earlier fought out a tight battle for the minor premiership, Northcote winning more matches but St Kilda's three outright triumphs enabling them to head the ladder.

The two best-performed teams in the seven one-day rounds played off for the limited-overs title. Northcote, undefeated in these contests, beat Melbourne University with 19.3 overs to spare in a one-sided final at the MCG. Ian Harvey was the star, capturing 3 for 11 in his 10 overs and then smashing 65 off 56 balls.

The state's ongoing dry weather meant that only two matches were abandoned. The number of centuries struck rose from 61 the previous year to 71, and only two bowlers – both from North Melbourne – captured 50 wickets. Significantly for Victoria, not one of the 18 bowlers to capture 30 or more wickets was a spinner.

St Kilda's batting line-up, the strongest in the competition, was headed by Michael Klinger, who compiled a club-record 875 runs. Good support came from Nick Jewell (794), Graeme Rummans (719) and Shawn Craig (635). Their pace attack was less settled, Dan Horsley missing the entire season through illness and Will Carr and Jamie Murch breaking down early on. Grant Lalor (37 wickets) and Justin Gale (34) were also injured late in the season, but both played in the final. The leading wicket-taker, as in 2002-03, was the hard-working Adrian Jones with 48, while the newcomer Oliver Oostermeyer also impressed with 32 wickets. The keeper Damon Rowan effected a club-record 59 dismissals, only three short of the competition record set by Michael Butera for Carlton in 1998-99. Tim O'Sullivan again led the side capably.

Hawthorn–Monash University's achievement in upsetting Northcote to reach the final was noteworthy, for they had finished second-last in 2002-03. Their leading light was the left-armer Dirk Nannes, who captured 43 wickets, including the season's best figures of 7 for 5 against South Melbourne. He was capably backed by fellow left-armer Grant Swift (34 wickets) and David Shepard (29). Their batting struggled for consistency, with the exception of Simon Dart (747 runs). Peter Roach, in his eighth year as captain, led the side with his customary skill and made a fine hundred in the final.

Northcote enjoyed an excellent season despite the loss of several leading players and the regular absence of Harvey, Darren Berry and Mick Lewis. It was marred only by their semi-final defeat. The batting was headed by the consistent Travis Gloury (821 runs) and Rob Bartlett (737). Tim Welsford made 510 runs and captured 28 wickets. Melbourne University were best served by their new skipper Brendan Joseland, who hit 732 runs and took 25 wickets. Leigh Murphy, one of three brothers in the team, made 626 runs while Ashley Robertson took 33 wickets and Nick Williams 30.

North Melbourne's steep ascent from 16th to fifth was attributable to the return of Adam Dale after 10 illustrious years in Queensland. With 61 wickets at 12.37, he was easily the leading bowler in the competition. His new-ball partner, Shannon Waters, took 51, including 7 for 11 against Prahran. Gene Maurice collected 559 runs and the young keeper Lindsay Scown 46 dismissals. Frankston Peninsula depended heavily on their captain Matthew Mott, the competition's leading batsman with 876 runs. Luke Walker (519 runs) and opening bowlers James Miller (47 wickets) and Darren Groves (40) all had good seasons.

Dandenong rose eight places to finish seventh. The 38-year-old Warren Ayres made 838 runs to lift his career aggregate to 12,605, only 328 short of Gary Watts's record. He has now made 35 centuries, a total exceeded by Jack Ryder (37). Footscray–Victoria University were well served by another veteran in Michael O'Keefe (627 runs) and their new skipper Dale McDonald (609), but lacked penetration in attack. Geelong improved three places to finish ninth. Their captain Clinton Peake made 634 runs, while Damien Koliba (660 runs) and Trent Walerys (33 wickets) also did well.

Camberwell Magpies fell to 17th despite an excellent season from Damien Shanahan (790 runs and 28 wickets). Another team in decline was Melbourne. The frequent absences of Brad Hodge and Andrew McDonald weakened the batting, while fast bowlers Rob Cassell and Simon Cook missed several matches through injury. Richmond slipped from sixth to 12th. Their skipper Ian Hewett scored 544 runs but, still troubled by injury, captured only 10 wickets. High hopes are held for the 19-year-old left-hander Aiden Blizzard (788 runs), who won the Robert Rose Scholarship as young cricketer of the year. Fitzroy–Doncaster, minor premiers the previous season, slumped to 11th despite the best efforts of David Plumpton (571 runs) and Ben Waterman (33 wickets and 329 runs).

Prahran dropped from ninth to 15th. Adam Warren captured 35 wickets, while Bryce McGain's 29 victims represented the season's best haul by a leg-spinner. Essendon fell two places to 13th, despite Craig Berger's 739 runs and 22 wickets. Two newcomers impressed: the off-spinner Rohan Obst, who took 29 wickets at 18.48, and the left-hand batsman Tom van den Berg. Carlton, for whom the opener Ben O'Brien made 631 runs, failed to improve on the previous season's 14th. Ringwood's batsmen struggled, scoring not one century, while Craig Howard headed the wicket-takers with 26. South Melbourne, who have not finished higher than 11th in the past 12 seasons, came last for the second year in a row, despite heavy scoring from Leicestershire's Darren Stevens, whose 712 runs included the season's highest score of 178 not out, and Steven Spoljaric.

The Ryder Medal was shared for the second time in its 32-year history, with Bartlett and Dale each polling 36 votes. Matthew Mott was third, followed by dual winner Warren Ayres. The following 12 players were named in the Premier Team of the Season: Matthew Mott (captain), Rob Bartlett, Warren Ayres, Brendan Joseland, Aiden Blizzard, Damian Shanahan, Craig Berger, James Miller, Glenn Lalor, Damon Rowan, Shannon Waters and Adam Dale.

Players to announce their retirements included Brendan Joyce, who made 7,442 career runs for Fitzroy–Doncaster, and Chris Harris, who hit 5,131 runs for Collingwood, Camberwell and Northcote. The fast bowler Simon Cook called time on a career truncated by injury, finishing with 212 wickets for Melbourne. The former Victorian leg-spinner Craig Howard, who turned successfully to off-spin after injury blighted his career, also announced that this was to be his last summer. Meanwhile Mott has moved to Sydney and Dale is expected to transfer to sub-district ranks.

VICTORIAN PREMIER CRICKET TABLE, 2003-04

	M	WO	Wl	Tl (10)	LO (6)	Ll (3)	D	A	Points
St Kilda	17	3	8	1	0	4	1	0	81
Northcote	17	0	13	0	0	3	1	0	78
Melbourne University	17	0	12	0	0	5	0	0	72
Hawthorn-Monash Uni	17	1	10	0	0	4	2	0	70
North Melbourne	17	1	9	1	0	6	0	0	67
Frankston Peninsula	17	1	8	0	0	8	0	0	58
Dandenong	17	0	9	0	0	8	0	0	54
Footscray-Victoria Uni	17	0	8	1	0	7	1	0	51
Geelong	17	0	8	0	0	7	2	0	48
Melbourne	17	2*	5	0	0	10	0	0	46
Fitzroy-Doncaster	17	0	7	0	1	8	0	1	46
Richmond	17	0	7	0	0	10	0	0	42
Essendon	17	0	7	0	1	9	0	0	42
Carlton	17	0	6	0	0	11	0	0	36
Prahran	17	0	6	0	1	8	1	1	36
Ringwood	17	0	5	1	1	8	1	1	33
Camberwell Magpies	17	0	5	0	1	9	1	1	29.8†
South Melbourne	17	0	3	0	3	11	0	0	18

*Note: * Melbourne won one match outright after trailing on the first innings (6 points).*

Fitzroy-Doncaster obtained 4 points for leading on the first innings in a match lost outright.

†Camberwell Magpies were penalised 0.2 points for slow over-rates.

BATTING AVERAGES, 2003-04

(Qualification: 500 runs)

	M	I	NO	R	HS	100s	50s	Avge
M. P. Mott (Frank Peninsula)	13	14	3	876	157	3	4	79.63
W. G. Ayres (Dandenong)	17	19	4	838	126*	3	5	55.86
I. S. L. Hewett (Richmond)	12	13	3	544	125	2	3	54.40
C. A. C. Berger (Essendon)	17	19	5	739	123	1	6	52.78
M. Klinger (St Kilda)	19	21	4	875	154	3	3	51.47
B. R. Joseland (Melb Univ)	18	18	3	732	152*	1	4	48.80
T. P. Gloury (Northcote)	20	20	2	821	96	0	7	45.61
C. J. Peake (Geelong)	17	17	3	634	131*	1	5	45.28
G. C. Rummans (St Kilda)	19	20	4	719	151*	2	3	44.93
B. R. Fletcher (Essendon)	15	18	5	575	100*	1	3	44.23

* Denotes not out.

BOWLING AVERAGES, 2003-04

(Qualification: 25 wickets)

	M	O	Mdns	R	W	BB	5W/i	10W/m	Avge
A. C. Dale (North Melb)	17	395.2	126	755	61	7-34	5	2	12.37
G. A. Lalor (St Kilda)	17	256.2	85	482	37	5-19	3	0	13.02
D. P. Nannes (Haw-Mon U)	16	251.3	57	665	43	7-5	1	1	15.46
A. P. S. Robertson (Melb Univ)	17	260.4	78	558	33	4-27	0	0	16.90
R. A. Obst (Essendon)	13	177.3	43	536	29	6-37	3	0	18.48
T. A. Walerys (Geelong)	12	194	40	593	33	7-59	2	0	17.96
B. J. Waterman (Fitz-Donc)	15	191.4	24	601	33	6-34	2	0	18.21
D. J. Groves (Frank Pen)	17	312	86	733	40	5-36	1	0	18.32
S. B. Waters (North Melb)	18	337.2	72	966	51	7-11	3	0	18.94
S. A. McTaggart (Northcote)	16	139.1	18	474	25	5-33	1	0	18.96

LIMITED OVERS FINAL, 2003-04

MELBOURNE UNIVERSITY v NORTHCOTE

At Melbourne Cricket Ground, March 8, 2004 (50-over match). Northcote won by eight wickets. Melbourne University 9 for 156 (T. J. Grant 51; I. J. Harvey 3-11, S. A. McTaggart 3-31); Northcote 2 for 157 (I. J. Harvey 65, T. H. Welsford 57*).

VICTORIAN PREMIER CRICKET QUALIFYING FINALS, 2003-04

MELBOURNE UNIVERSITY v HAWTHORN–MONASH UNIVERSITY

At Melbourne University Oval, Parkville, March 13, 14, 2004. Hawthorn–Monash University won on first innings. Hawthorn–Monash University 189 (H. S. H. Alles 44, P. J. Roach 41; B. D. Harrop 4-36, B. R. Joseland 3-33); Melbourne University 186 (B. R. Joseland 94; D. P. Nannes 4-49, G. A. Swift 3-40, H. S. H. Alles 3-45).

NORTHCOTE v NORTH MELBOURNE

At Bill Lawry Oval, Northcote, March 13, 14, 2004. Northcote won on first innings. Northcote 7 for 331 (T. H. Welsford 109, S. T. Collins 63, M. D. Allen 53; S. B. Waters 3-137); North Melbourne 146 (S. A. McTaggart 3-22, W. C. Hansen 3-30).

ST KILDA v FRANKSTON PENINSULA

At St Kilda Cricket Ground, March 13, 14, 2004. St Kilda won on first innings. St Kilda 6 for 366 (M. Klinger 129, G. C. Rummans 65, N. Jewell 50; J. F. Miller 3-87); Frankston Peninsula 242 (L. Walker 57*; A. P. Jones 4-76, N. Jewell 3-40).

VICTORIAN PREMIER CRICKET SEMI-FINALS, 2003-04

NORTHCOTE v HAWTHORN–MONASH UNIVERSITY

At Bill Lawry Oval, Northcote, March 20, 21, 2004. Hawthorn–Monash University won on first innings. Hawthorn–Monash University 258 (S. P. Dart 114; I. J. Harvey 4-23); Northcote 194 (C. J. Harris 57*, T. P. Gloury 47; D. J. Shepard 4-41, D. P. Nannes 3-66).

ST KILDA v MELBOURNE UNIVERSITY

At St Kilda Cricket Ground, March 20, 21, 2004. St Kilda won on first innings. Melbourne University 9 for 278 (B. A. Lodding 96; J. A. J. Gale 3-66); St Kilda 4 for 279 (M. Klinger 114*, N. Jewell 63).

VICTORIAN PREMIER CRICKET FINAL, 2003-04

ST KILDA v HAWTHORN–MONASH UNIVERSITY

At St Kilda Cricket Ground, March 26, 27, 28, 29, 2004. St Kilda won on first innings. *Toss:* Hawthorn–Monash University.

Batting first on a pitch that played well throughout, Hawthorn–Monash University made slow progress on the opening day, dawdling along to 6 for 184 in 100 overs. John Wilson, a 27-year-old playing only his fourth game, helped Simon Dart put on 77 in three hours for the second wicket. Adrian Jones dismissed James Court and Dart with the second new ball, before Graeme Rummans's seemingly innocent left-arm slows removed Daniel Nash and the nightwatchman Dirk Nannes in the last over. Next day Hawthorn–Monash University regained the initiative through a fine partnership by Peter Roach and Craig Entwistle. Their stand of 150 was a seventh-wicket record for a final. Roach recorded his 10th Premier hundred in a chanceless display, facing 243 balls and hitting 15 fours. Rummans's five wickets doubled his number of scalps in two whole seasons with St Kilda.

Rummans and Shawn Craig safely negotiated the 22 overs before stumps. They lifted their opening stand to 158 before Nannes, the left-arm fast bowler, captured 4 for 3 in 21 balls. Obtaining reverse-swing with the old ball, he dismissed Rummans and Michael Klinger – fresh from centuries in the qualifying and semi-finals – with successive deliveries. With the game in the balance Nick Jewell and Tim O'Sullivan, whose previous highest score for the season was 33, put on 100 by the close.

Despite overnight rain play began on time on the last day, with St Kilda needing a further 116 runs. When Jewell and O'Sullivan were dismissed in fairly quick succession, 71 were still needed with four wickets standing. Roach swung his bowlers around, switched the field and made Grant Lalor and Justin Gale, batting with a runner because of an injured back, scrap hard for every run. But they held firm for two and a half tense hours, guiding St Kilda to their 16th premiership, two fewer than Melbourne. Rummans was named Player of the Final for the second year in a row, and so became the inaugural winner of the John Scholes Medal.

John Scholes Medal: G. C. Rummans.

Close of play: First day, Hawthorn–Monash University (1) 6-184 (Roach 13); Second day, St Kilda (1) 0-65 (Rummans 38, Craig 23); Third day, St Kilda (1) 4-267 (Jewell 46, O'Sullivan 53).

Hawthorn–Monash University

A. H. Powell c Jewell b Lalor	6		G. A. Swift st Rowan b Rummans	2
J. L. Wilson lbw b Oostermeyer	42		H. S. H. Alles not out	12
S. P. Dart c Rowan b Jones	69		D. J. Shepard c Craig b Rummans	8
J. P. Court b Jones	24			
D. T. Nash st Rowan b Rummans	11		B 5, l-b 4, w 1, n-b 11	21
* †P. J. Roach lbw b Oostermeyer	114			—
D. P. Nannes b Rummans	0		(178 overs, 631 mins)	383
C. T. Entwistle lbw b Rummans	74		Fall: 13 90 154 160 184 184 334 348 368 383	

Bowling: Jones 36-13-80-2; Lalor 31-14-40-1; Gale 22-10-41-0; Oostermeyer 29-10-75-2; Rummans 21-7-43-5; Jewell 19-9-28-0; Craig 13-0-39-0; Quiney 7-1-28-0.

St Kilda

G. C. Rummans lbw b Nannes	75		G. A. Lalor not out	46
S. A. J. Craig b Nannes	74		J. A. J. Gale not out	28
M. Klinger lbw b Nannes	0		B 1, l-b 11, w 2, n-b 15	29
N. Jewell c Dart b Shepard	62			—
R. J. Quiney b Nannes	2		(168.1 overs, 660 mins) (6 wkts)	384
* T. D. B. O'Sullivan lbw b Alles	68		Fall: 158 158 163 167 295 313	

†D. N. Rowan, A. P. Jones and O. V. Oostermeyer did not bat.

Bowling: Nannes 41.4–14–84–4; Swift 27–7–77–0; Alles 29–5–75–1; Shepard 33–15–65–1; Entwistle 23–7–38–0; Dart 13–2–27–0; Wilson 2–1–6–0.

Umpires: R. L. Parry and G. Patterson.

Perth First-Grade, 2003-04

by KEN CASELLAS

WACA officials will debate long and hard the playing conditions for first-grade finals matches after widespread dissatisfaction arose from the 2003-04 series. In a farcical situation, the champions Melville won their elimination final and semi-final without bowling a single delivery. Had they won the toss and batted first in the two-day final against Bayswater–Morley, they could conceivably have won the title without any of their bowlers sending down a ball in three finals matches.

What Melville did do in those first two finals was bat their opponents into submission. They amassed 410 against University and a club-record 511 against South Perth. Each time they batted throughout the first day and continued until after lunch on day two, leaving the other side less than two sessions to overhaul these massive totals. Both University and South Perth conceded without batting.

The conditions stipulate that a minimum of 100 overs must be bowled on each day of all finals. There is no compulsory declaration, and therefore it is possible that a team could bat for the entire two days. Sides that finish higher on the premiership table need only to draw an elimination or semi-final to advance, and the team with the higher finishing position is in the same boat in the final. Many pundits argue that this gives them a too generous advantage. A sensible alternative would be that the team batting first should have the option of batting on for, say, eight or 10 overs on the second day before being forced to declare. This would ensure more enterprising cricket than was seen in the Melville walkovers.

Melville's heavy scoring underlined the general dominance of batsmen during the season. Most club pitches were placid, hardly the ideal conditions to nurture young fast bowlers. Once again, the scarcity of promising fast men was of grave concern to Western Australian officials. Batsmen scored a record total of 58 centuries. Among those to cash in were Subiaco–Floreat's Steven Glew (223 against Perth), his club-mate Murray Goodwin (198), Craig Simmons (190) and Mike Hussey (182). The Claremont–Nedlands pair of Robbie Morgan (199) and Jim Allenby (169) put on a club-record third-wicket partnership of 264 against Rockingham–Mandurah.

The 21-year-old Allenby had a superb season, becoming the first player in the 118-year history of the competition to score 800 runs and take 40 wickets. A solidly built right-hand batsman and medium-pacer, Allenby was the competition's leading runscorer with 805 at an average of 50.31. His 40 wickets came at 17.70. However, Claremont–Nedlands faded after a flying start and finished 11th. They missed the left-hand batsman Geoff Cullen, who left to lead University, and fast bowler Joe Barnes, who returned to Bayswater–Morley.

Allenby and the Scarborough all-rounder David Bandy were joint winners of the Olly Cooley Medal for the fairest-and-best player. Each polled 15 votes to finish ahead of the towering Fremantle fast-medium bowler Brett Dorey (48 wickets at 11.46), Melville's captain Adam Voges (863 runs at 66.38) and the Mount Lawley medium-pacer Garrick Yandle (34 wickets at 18.09), each of whom polled 13 votes.

The Subiaco–Floreat swing bowler Sam Howman was the competition's leading wicket-taker, picking up 56 wickets at 18.20 with a best of 7 for 17 against South Perth. It gave Howman 151 wickets in the past three seasons, and he further enhanced his reputation with some good performances for the WA 2nd XI. His club Subiaco–Floreat, aiming for their fourth successive title, faltered at the first hurdle when they lost a tight elimination final to Bayswater–Morley. The loss of strike bowlers Gavin Swan and the injured Michael Clark weakened them considerably.

Scarborough finished comfortably on top of the table after the qualifying matches only to lose their way in the finals. It was a miserable finish for Scarborough, who also lost to Joondalup in the final of the Sunday League competition. They piled up 270 in their 50 overs, then had Joondalup on the ropes at 8 for 194 and again at 9 for 236. An unbeaten 63 by Mick Swart, with great support from the No. 11 Aubrey Steyn, got them home. Steyn hit Bandy for the winning four off the final ball.

PERTH FIRST-GRADE TABLE, 2003-04

	M	WO	W1	D	L1	LO	T	Points
Scarborough	13	0	12	0	0	1	0	189.92
Melville	13	0	10	1	2	0	0	170.07
Subiaco-Floreat	13	0	9	1	3	0	0	159.06
Bayswater-Morley	13	1	7	0	5	0	0	146.90
University	13	0	8	1	4	0	0	144.93
South Perth	13	0	8	1	4	0	0	144.45
Fremantle	13	1	6	0	6	0	0	137.21
Midland-Guildford	13	0	6	0	7	0	0	126.26
Perth	13	1	4	1	7	0	0	124.99
Willetton	13	0	5	0	7	1	0	111.42
Claremont-Nedlands	13	1	3	1	8	0	0	108.29
Rockingham-Mandurah	13	0	4	2	6	1	0	103.94
Mount Lawley	13	1	3	1	8	0	0	102.61
Wanneroo	13	0	4	0	9	0	0	101.01
Joondalup	13	0	3	1	8	1	0	89.90
Gosnells	13	0	2	0	1		0	81.82

BATTING AVERAGES, 2003-04

(Qualification: 300 runs)

	M	I	NO	R	HS	100s	50s	Avge
M. E. K. Hussey (Wanneroo)	5	5	1	360	182	1	2	90.00
A. C. Voges (Melville)	15	17	4	863	151	3	4	66.38
G. I. Cullen (University)	14	14	2	629	132*	2	3	52.42
G. A. Wates (South Perth)	15	14	2	618	99	0	6	51.50
J. F. Allenby (Claremont-Ned)	13	17	1	805	169	3	4	50.31
B. J. Lillis (Melville)	15	19	2	850	150	4	1	50.00
H. F. Brown (South Perth)	15	17	2	731	123*	2	3	48.73
M. W. Goodwin (Subiaco-Floreat)	7	8	0	388	198	1	1	48.50
P. C. Worthington (Midland-Guild)	10	11	0	530	120	1	4	48.18
C. T. Pivac (Midland-Guild)	13	17	2	693	156	1	4	46.20

* Denotes not out.

BOWLING AVERAGES, 2003-04

(Qualification: 25 wickets)

	M	O	Mdns	R	W	BB	5W/i	10W/m	Avge
D. C. Bandy (Scarborough)	15	187.1	46	452	41	6-33	1	0	11.02
B. R. Dorey (Fremantle)	11	251	72	550	48	7-22	3	0	11.46
C. D. Thorp (Wanneroo)	8	217.3	67	432	30	5-44	2	0	14.40
M. A. Woodhead (Fremantle)	11	248.4	66	648	41	5-25	2	0	15.80
P. Siljeg (Willetton)	12	167	49	414	25	5-35	2	0	16.56
J. P. Coetzee (Scarborough)	15	239	50	715	42	5-48	2	0	17.02
J. F. Allenby (Claremont-Ned)	13	247.3	78	719	40	6-21	3	0	17.97
T. P. McDonald (Claremont-Ned)	11	202	54	741	41	8-53	3	0	18.07
G. F. Yandle (Mount Lawley)	13	270.4	91	615	34	5-31	3	0	18.09
S. G. Howman (Subiaco-Floreat)	13	409.4	126	1,019	56	7-17	4	1	18.20

PERTH FIRST-GRADE ELIMINATION FINALS, 2003-04

SCARBOROUGH v SOUTH PERTH

At WACA Ground, Perth, March 13, 14, 2004. South Perth won on first innings. Scarborough 203 (K. Lawrence 40; C. S. Higgins 5-28, B. M. Edmondson 4-48); South Perth 1 for 207 (H. F. Brown 123*).

MELVILLE v UNIVERSITY

At Tompkins Park, Melville, March 13, 14, 2004. Melville won on forfeit – University conceded without batting. Melville 410 (A.C. Voges 151, S.W. Meuleman 87, A.G. Greig 62*, P. Wilson 56; M.R. Healey 4-50).

SUBIACO–FLOREAT v BAYSWATER–MORLEY

At Floreat Oval, Floreat Park, March 13, 14, 2004. Bayswater–Morley won on first innings. Subiaco–Floreat 211 (K. Kapinkoff 59; R.E. Phillimore 3-37, M.J. Thistle 3-57); Bayswater–Morley 8 for 214 (M.J. North 59; T.G. Silinger 4-52).

PERTH FIRST-GRADE SEMI-FINALS, 2003-04

SCARBOROUGH v BAYSWATER–MORLEY

At WACA Ground, Perth, March 20, 21, 2004. Bayswater–Morley won on first innings. Bayswater–Morley 255 (R.A. May 40; J.P. Coetzee 5-49); Scarborough 167 (L.M. Davis 51, J.P. Coetzee 40).

MELVILLE v SOUTH PERTH

At Fletcher Park, Carlisle, March 20, 21, 2004. Melville won on forfeit – South Perth conceded without batting. Melville 511 (A.D. Mascarenhas 160, S.C. Russell 61*, A.C. Voges 54, B.J. Lillis 49, C.N. Wood 40; C.S. Higgins 3-79).

PERTH FIRST-GRADE FINAL, 2003-04

MELVILLE v BAYSWATER–MORLEY

At WACA Ground, Perth, March 27, 28, 2004. Drawn. *Toss:* Bayswater–Morley.

In a tense final session the young left-hander Shawn Gillies curbed his natural flamboyant instincts and ground out an unbeaten century to guide Melville to the first-grade premiership. At stumps, Gillies was unconquered on 103 and Melville had held out for a draw, giving them the flag over Bayswater–Morley because they had finished higher in the qualifying rounds. Bayswater–Morley, the underdogs, had earlier recovered from a poor start against the experienced attack of Paul Wilson and Duncan Spencer. An unbroken eighth-wicket partnership of 103 in 75 minutes between Dan Weston and Michael Thistle rescued them from a precarious 7 for 181, and they eventually declared late on the first day.

A comfortable Melville victory looked likely after Scott Meuleman and Adam Voges guided them to 1 for 99 at lunch on day two. But the fast bowlers Thistle and Joe Barnes struck in devastating fashion, five wickets crashing for 28 runs to leave Melville wobbling at 6 for 127. Gillies was then joined by the 17-year-old left-hander Chris Wood, who bats in a similar style to his famous father Graeme, the former Test opener. Wood held firm with a painstaking 14 in a fighting stand of 35.

His dismissal left Melville vulnerable but Gillies and Steve Russell defied a vibrant attack in the final session, adding an unconquered 101 for the eighth wicket in 172 minutes. Gillies straight-drove Thistle for four to reach his century off 219 deliveries in just under four hours. He had managed only one fifty in his previous 21 innings.

Melville, led by Voges and their first-year coach Brad Thompson, celebrated only the second premiership in their 37th season in the first-grade competition. Dennis Lillee was captain-coach and Graeme Wood hit a century in their first, when Melville crushed North Perth in a four-day final in 1979-80.

Close of play: First day, Bayswater–Morley (1) 7-284 (D. J. Weston 50, M. J. Thistle 51).

Bayswater–Morley

C. G. Hall c Lillis b Russell	13		†D. J. Weston not out	50
J. L. Cantrill c Putland b Wilson	9		M. J. Thistle not out	51
R. A. May hit wkt b Spencer	55			
R. E. Phillimore lbw b Spencer	17		B 7, l-b 6, n-b 8, w 5	26
*N. D. Pishos lbw b Wilson	0			
A. J. Warren c Spencer b Wilson	42		(90 overs, 341 mins) (7 wkts dec)	284
R. T. Ford c Putland b Wilson	21		Fall: 9 36 81 82 145 171 181	

R. F. Scali and J. W. Barnes did not bat.

Bowling: Wilson 25–7–59–4; Mascarenhas 23–6–75–0; Russell 16–4–53–2; Spencer 13–2–42–2; Gillies 3–1–12–0; Voges 10–0–30–0.

Melville

S. W. Meuleman c Phillimore b Barnes	42		C. N. Wood c Phillimore b Pishos	14
B. J. Lillis c Pishos b Thistle	24		S. C. Russell not out	29
*A. C. Voges c Pishos b Thistle	32			
W. S. Gillies not out	103		B 5, l-b 5, n-b 2, w 1	13
D. N. Porter c Weston b Thistle	0			
A. D. Mascarenhas c Thistle b Barnes	2		(103 overs, 419 mins) (7 wkts)	263
D. J. Spencer c Pishos b Barnes	4		Fall: 57 99 111 111 123 127 162	

P. Wilson and †M. T. Putland did not bat.

Bowling: Thistle 32–10–64–3; Barnes 27–11–50–3; Phillimore 11–0–52–0; Scali 11–2–45–0; Pishos 8–3–14–1; Ford 11–5–21–0; May 3–0–7–0.

Umpires: A. R. Craig and I. H. Lock.

PERTH FIRST-GRADE RECORDS

ALL-TIME LEADING RUNSCORERS

S. H. D. Rowe	12,035	H. C. Howard	9,448
J. P. McGuire	10,003	A. R. Edwards	9,106
D. C. McKenzie	9,792	H. W. H. Rigg	9,095
L. H. Bandy	9,458	I. R. Dick	9,054
G. J. Ireland	9,453	M. T. Vernon	9,050

ALL-TIME LEADING WICKET-TAKERS

A. H. Christian	1,002	R. B. Strauss	724
R. A. Selk	959	W. A. Evans	718
A. L. Mann	933	C. W. Puckett	668
H. G. Bevan	805	A. G. Zimbulis	663
E. G. Bishop	735	J. S. Everett	632

Newcastle First-Grade, 2003-04

by JACK BROWN

It was a familiar story in 2003-04 as Merewether and Hamilton–Wickham, the top two sides, faced off in the grand final for the fourth season in a row. This time it was Hamilton–Wickham who triumphed in yet another disappointingly low-scoring final. It was the Ham–Wicks' sixth straight final appearance, equalling Hamilton's feat way back in the 1950s before they joined forces with Wickham. It was their third flag in those six years and they thoroughly deserved it, having recorded nine victories to Merewether's seven during the regular season.

But both sides had to win hard-fought semi-finals to get there. Merewether hung on by two wickets against Belmont and Hamilton–Wickham eventually beat Waratah–Mayfield by 44 runs, a victory that was never quite so comfortable as it might have looked. Their matchwinner was the No. 7 batsman Steve Cowen, who hit an unbeaten 103 off 140 balls after finishing the minor rounds with consecutive ducks.

The points table finished with a somewhat similar appearance to 2002-03. Charlestown dropped from third to sixth and Lambton, feeling the loss of several experienced players, fell from sixth to 11th. Charlestown were badly affected by rain, depriving them of several days' play when they looked to be in winning positions. Stockton had the highest collective batting average and appeared certain to reach the semi-finals, missing out in the final round when they were bowled out for 63 by lowly Southern Lakes. But this was essentially a two-horse race: a nine-point gap separated the two perennial finalists and the rest.

Although seven days of play were lost to rain, a record number of centuries were scored – 34 – including seven each by Stockton and Hamilton–Wickham batsmen. Two of them were double-hundreds: Charlestown's skipper Steve Mace hit 204 not out against Cardiff, his 15th first-grade century; and the Hamilton–Wickham youngster Joe Price made an unbeaten 208 against Lambton.

Merewether's skipper Simon Moore amassed four centuries and easily topped the aggregates, with 663 runs at 82.88, despite missing matches while on Newcastle representative duty. He led the New South Wales country side at the Australian Country Championships in Mount Gambier, where his performances earned him the captaincy of the Australian Country XI. Moore also led Merewether to a comfortable victory in the Tom Locker Cup limited-overs competition. They beat Belmont in the final, Moore proving the decisive influence with an innings of 104 in 120 balls.

Amid all the washouts, it was hardly surprising that no bowler claimed 30 wickets. The medium-pacers often did most of the damage, with Waratah's Nick Bower – who finished the summer with 26 wickets at 14.31 – the only prominent spinner. Cardiff's opening bowler Paul Coleman captured 8 for 48 against Southern Lakes, and Belmont's young medium-pacer Ryan Mannix took 7 for 27 against Lambton. The competition's leading wicket-taker was Hamilton–Wickham's Darren Herbert, with 28 scalps in 10 matches at 14.71.

Newcastle once again hosted a Pura Cup match with great success. The NSW versus Victoria game was played on a magnificent pitch and outfield, with 17,654 spectators watching Victoria tally 455 in the fourth innings to win a gripping contest. Another highlight of the summer came when Hamilton–Wickham won the final of the statewide One-Day Country Cup (formerly the NRMA Cup) in Newcastle, beating the Central Coast side Narara–Wyoming.

Simon Moore won the Players' Player Award. Waratah's young opening bowler Sam Gilmour, son of the former Test all-rounder Gary Gilmour, was named Cricketer of the Season. His 26 first-grade wickets came at an average of 13.69 and included match figures of 10 for 47 against University. Cardiff–Boolaroo's Scott Montgomery was the leading wicket-keeper with 28 dismissals.

The continuing dominance of Merewether, Hamilton–Wickham and to a lesser extent Stockton, who won the club championship, reflects admirably on those clubs. But it does not add up to a healthy situation for cricket in Newcastle as a whole. It is to be hoped that the competition will even out, and soon, making it more competitive and providing better quality experience for local players dreaming of representative honours.

NEWCASTLE FIRST-GRADE TABLE, 2003-04

	M	WI	WO	L1	LO	D	Points	Quotient
Merewether	13	5	2	1	0	5	47	2.132
Hamilton-Wickham	13	8	1	1	0	3	47	1.735
Waratah-Mayfield	13	5	1	2	1	4	38	1.388
Belmont	13	6	0	4	0	3	34	0.911
Stockton	13	5	0	3	0	5	33	1.069
Charlestown	13	4	0	3	0	6	31	1.080
Cardiff	13	4	0	5	0	4	29	1.080
Wallsend	13	3	0	6	0	4	26	0.888
Newcastle City	13	3	0	6	0	4	26	0.736
Southern Lakes	13	2	0	6	1	4	22	0.824
Lambton-New Lambton	13	2	0	8	0	3	22	0.706
University	13	2	0	4	2	5	22	0.604

BATTING AVERAGES, 2003-04

(Qualification: 300 runs)

	M	I	NO	R	HS	100s	50s	Avge
S. Moore (Merewether)	9	9	1	663	183	4	0	82.88
D. Mason (Waratah)	9	10	4	420	109*	1	3	70.00
S. Mace (Charlestown)	6	6	1	338	204*	1	2	67.60
M. Gerits (Newcastle City)	8	8	1	439	105*	1	4	62.71
S. Cowen (Hamilton-Wickham)	12	11	4	430	116*	1	2	61.43
B. Crosdale (Stockton)	9	9	1	487	135	2	2	60.88
J. Whithead (Stockton)	8	8	1	380	126*	2	1	54.29
R. Faraday (University)	10	12	3	467	82*	0	5	51.89
J. Price (Stockton)	8	8	1	361	208*	1	0	51.57
S. Hughes (Hamilton-Wickham)	9	10	0	504	113	2	1	50.40

* Denotes not out.

BOWLING AVERAGES, 2003-04

(Qualification: 20 wickets)

	M	O	Mdns	R	W	BB	5W/i	10W/m	Avge
C. White (Merewether)	12	132	41	24	256	5-27	1	0	10.67
S. Gilmour (Waratah)	12	144.2	28	26	356	5-19	2	1	13.69
N. Bower (Waratah)	12	128	29	26	372	5-26	1	0	14.31
D. Herbert (Hamilton-Wickham)	10	153.4	35	28	412	6-50	2	0	14.71
S. Threadgold (Charlestown)	11	152	37	24	430	6-51	1	0	17.92
R. Mannix (Belmont)	10	153.5	37	22	460	7-27	1	0	20.91
G. Geise (Wallsend)	10	147	27	24	469	5-56	2	0	21.32
B. Kneller (Cardiff)	12	126.1	18	20	427	4-52	0	0	21.35
P. Coleman (Cardiff)	12	168.3	34	27	602	8-48	1	1	22.30
B. Bannister (Belmont)	8	196.1	44	26	586	6-74	2	0	22.54

NEWCASTLE FIRST-GRADE SEMI-FINALS, 2003-04

MEREWETHER v BELMONT

At No. 1 Sports Ground, Newcastle, March 20, 21, 2004. Merewether won on first innings. Merewether 8 for 204 (N. Crittenden 48, T. Goodwin 42; M. Dries 3-63); Belmont 201 (B. Bannister 56, M. Dries 47; C. White 3-21, D. McIlveen 3-57).

HAMILTON–WICKHAM v WARATAH–MAYFIELD

At Cahill Oval, Belmont, March 20, 21, 2004. Hamilton–Wickham won on first innings. Hamilton–Wickham 288 (S. Cowen 103*, T. Campbell 77; S. Finlay 3-70, S. Gilmour 3-29); Waratah–Mayfield 244 (A. Weekes 76, M. Christie 52; R. Soper 4-37, K. Mullard 3-43).

NEWCASTLE FIRST-GRADE FINAL, 2003-04

MEREWETHER v HAMILTON–WICKHAM

At Newcastle No. 1 Sports Ground, March 27, 28, 2004. Hamilton–Wickham won on first innings. *Toss:* Merewether.

Disaster struck immediately for Merewether when Neil Crittenden was trapped leg-before in the first over. It set the pattern for the rest of the game. The left-arm quick Darren Herbert proved especially troublesome as wickets tumbled steadily, the keeper Michael Jordan pouching four catches. Simon Moore, Merewether's captain, applied himself for 63 balls and 82 minutes. But his downfall for 18 left his side tottering at 5 for 39. They eventually recovered a little, Michael Hogan and Chad White cobbling together a last-wicket stand of 38 – the best of the innings – in 6.1 overs.

With 44 overs still remaining, Hamilton–Wickham looked a distinct chance of wrapping up the winning runs on the first day. But they too lost early wickets, collapsing to 3 for 13 in the eighth over. The captain Todd Campbell then joined the opener Steve Mudford, the pair steadying the innings with a 49-run stand off 95 balls. But Campbell's departure triggered another clatter of wickets, and at 7 for 80 the match was hovering in the balance. With tensions running high, Mudford and Kirk Mullard saw Hamilton–Wickham through until stumps, eight runs away from a first-innings lead. They quickly passed their target next morning and carried on to a matchwinning partnership of 52. Mudford was rock-solid to the end, first man in and last man out, batting four hours and facing 170 balls.

With 72 overs still to be played, and trailing by only 31, Merewether set after quick runs in the outside hope of forcing an outright victory. They began in spectacular fashion, Crittenden and Moore blasting a 90-run opening partnership in 48 balls. They were all out for 204 in only 20.4 overs. Hamilton–Wickham were left needing to bat out 51 overs or make 174 to win. They had safely reached 77 without loss in 23 overs when the match was called off. After going 28 years without a flag, Hamilton–Wickham had now won three of the last five.

Close of play: First day, Hamilton–Wickham (1) 7-103.

Merewether

N. Crittenden lbw b Herbert	0	– c Hughes b Webber	41
G. Weller c Jordan b Soper	4	– (10) run out	2
*S. Moore b Webber	18	– (2) st Jordan b Mitchell	66
T. Goodwin c Jordan b Herbert	3	– (6) c Jordan b K. Mullard	2
T. Griffith c Soper b Herbert	3	– (7) run out	2
M. Irwin c K. Mullard b Soper	7	– (3) b K.Mullard	63
E. Flowers c Jordan b Herbert	5	– (8) c Cowen b K. Mullard	4
A. Wight c Mudford b K.Mullard	16	– (4) b Mitchell	6
C. White lbw b Herbert	22	– (5) c Mudford b K. Mullard	0
D. McIlveen c Jordan b K.Mullard	0	– (11) not out	3
M. Hogan not out	14	– (9) run out	0
B 5, n-b 13	18	L-b 5, w 5, n-b 6	15

(40.1 overs, 172 mins) 110
Fall: 1 11 14 31 39 51 72 72 72 110

(20.4 overs, 204 mins) 204
Fall: 90 126 146 150 175 188
194 194 198 204

Bowling: *First Innings*—Herbert 14.1–3–25–5; Soper 11–3–30–2; Webber 9–2–21–1; Mullard 6–1–29–2. *Second Innings*—Herbert 4–0–46–0; Soper 3–0–35–0; Webber 2–0–15–1; Mullard 6.4–0–54–4; Mitchell 5–0–50–2.

Hamilton–Wickham

S. Hughes c Flowers b McIlveen	0	– not out	53
S. Mudford lbw b Hogan	59	– not out	21
A. Mullard c and b Crittenden	1		
R. Soper c Moore b Crittenden	5		
*T. Campbell lbw b White	31		
D. Herbert b Hogan	0		
S. Cowen c Goodwin b White	12		
†M. Jordan c Griffith b White	0		
K. Mullard c Moore b White	27		
S. Webber c Moore b White	1		
T. Mitchell not out	0		
L-b 5	5	L-b 3	3

(56.4 overs, 237 mins) 141
Fall: 0 3 13 62 62 80 80 132 141 141

(23 overs, 80 mins)   (0 wkt) 77

Bowling: *First Innings*—McIlveen 17–6–49–1; Crittenden 7–1–19–2; Wight 3–0–10–0; White 20.4–6–33–5; Hogan 8–2–22–2; Irwin 1–0–3–0. *Second Innings*—McIlveen 3–0–9–0; Crittenden 3–0–21–0; Hogan 9–1–30–0; White 4–2–5–0; Irwin4–2–9–0.

Umpires: K. Bourke and M. Jones.

NEWCASTLE FIRST-GRADE RECORDS

ALL-TIME LEADING RUNSCORERS

	Runs	Club	Duration
Jack Mayes	14,028	Waratah	1932-63
Reg Beatty	11,064	various	1929-54
Greg Geise	10,228	Wallsend	1976-2003
Ron Camps	9,500	Wickham	1936-57
Jim De Courcy	9,424	Lambton	1941-67
Mark Curry	9,326	Charlestown, Belmont	1975-2003
Jack Anderson	9,023	Hamilton	1937-58
Ken Hill	8,988	Lambton	1934-63
Mick Hill	8,496	various	1961-89
Wal Moy	8,200	various	1901-35
Greg Arms	8,041	Waratah	1974-98

ALL-TIME LEADING WICKET TAKERS

	Wickets	Club	Duration
Ken Hill	1,128	Lambton	1934-63
Bob Holland	799	Southern Lakes	1961-2000
Reg Woolston	772	Wickham, Waratah	1920-46
Harry Hodges	731	Stockton	1924-47
Wal Moy	724	various	1903-35
Arch Frazer	667	Waratah	1934-54
Mick Hill	650	various	1961-89
Percy Lee	632	Hamilton	1929-57
Ernie O'Brien	626	Merewether	1924-35
Jack Bull	505	Wickham	1940-69
Neil Budden	451	Waratah	1971-89

Darwin A-Grade, 2003

by ANDREW HYDE

The 2003 season will be remembered as the most seismic in Darwin's sporting history: the year Test cricket came to town. It was not as if it had seemed a long time coming. Darwin had never hosted even a first-class game before. Turf pitches remained a comparatively recent phenomenon. The Northern Territory had produced precious few first-class cricketers and only one Test player, Damien Martyn, who moved to Perth as a three-year-old when Cyclone Tracy blew through town. Many locals could hardly believe Test cricket had arrived so soon.

If playing conditions are any criteria, it should be here to stay. A visiting English reporter took up his position in the Marrara Oval press box, curiously positioned square of the wicket, and was heard to sigh: "Delightful, surely there are no more perfect conditions in the world for Test cricket." There was not a cloud to be seen for 500 kilometres and more chance of Bangladesh winning by an innings than the onset of precipitation. Darwin's traditionally mild, mid-dry season climate has a charm all its own.

Had that same scribe been present a few weeks earlier, at round one of the Darwin & Districts A-grade competition, his impression may have been less glowing. An unseasonably late wet season had brought lush outfields and humidity levels of around 90%. Temperatures had more in common with Mumbai than Melbourne, although some of the pitches – damp and unpredictable – bore a striking resemblance to the MCG wicket of the early 1980s.

As is often the case in Darwin, ball held the upper hand over bat in the early rounds. There was a noticeably heightened intensity to the competition, with players battling for a rare chance for higher honours: a spot in the NT Chief Minister's XI to meet Bangladesh in the pre-Test warm-up game. Terry Bayly, the promising young Palmerston tearaway, and Waratahs' Ryan Green were the most eyecatching of the local bowlers. Yet it was the two interstate imports, South Australia's Mick Miller and the Sydneysider Nick Berry, who really relished the conditions. They finished the season with almost identical figures, Miller winning the private contest 44 wickets to 43 at an average 0.07 runs superior.

Their respective teams held sway too, Palmerston and Pint dropping only two games apiece all season. Palmerston went on to win a tightly fought final and achieve a hat-trick of flags. Their depth was underlined by the fact that Darren Treumer and Ken Vowles, two of the competition's all-time leading runscorers, came in at Nos. 7 and 8 in the grand final. Both enjoyed typically stellar seasons. The signing of Vowles, playing for his sixth local club, was a particularly shrewd off-season coup. Another veteran, Anthony Dent, ensured they invariably got off to sound starts.

Pint's season was underpinned by the 22-year-old Berry. Aside from his bowling heroics he was also the dominant batsman in town, racking up three hundreds and 793 runs at 72. Mitchell O'Connor had a consistent year with the bat, and his wonderful 118 in the preliminary final was instrumental in his team's victory over a gallant NT Institute of Sport side.

As the tropical conditions of the early rounds gave way to fast outfields and reliable pitches, one of the tightest competitions in recent years took shape. The NTIS, Nightcliff, Southern Districts and Waratahs scrapped it out for the last two finals positions. The performance of the NTIS side was particularly encouraging, their attack benefiting from the presence of their nominated mentor player Brad Hatton. Brad's brother Mark, the former Tasmanian left-arm spinner, was a solid contributor at Nightcliff as usual, although he proved slightly more menacing with bat than ball. The Tigers eventually secured fourth place, edging out Southern Districts and Waratahs on percentage. In a sign of changing times the competition's three traditional powerhouses – Waratahs, Tracy Village and Darwin – occupied the bottom three positions.

The incentive of a place in the Chief Minister's XI undoubtedly made for a more combative season. But the biggest legacy of international cricket's arrival in the Top End was the inspiring visits made by several Australian players to outlying communities. A local competition has been announced in the Tiwi Islands, and there is now some semblance of hope that cricket's stocks might one day be enriched by Aboriginal skills in the same way that the football codes have been. The absence of Aboriginal spectators at Darwin's two Tests matches, against Bangladesh and Sri Lanka, was a timely reminder of just how much work needs to done in promoting cricket in this part of the country.

DARWIN A-GRADE TABLE, 2003-04

	M	Won	Lost	Draw	Match Points	Bonus Points	Total Points
Pint	14	12	2	0	75.00	45.22	120.22
Palmerston	14	12	2	0	71.25	44.53	115.78
NT Institute of Sport	14	8	6	0	40.75	32.25	73.00
Nightcliff	14	6	8	0	36.00	33.24	69.24
Southern Districts	14	6	8	0	32.75	35.27	68.02
Waratahs	14	6	8	0	33.00	33.10	66.10
Tracy Village	14	4	9	1	26.00	31.14	57.14
Darwin	14	2	11	1	15.75	31.46	47.21

BATTING AVERAGES, 2003-04

(Qualification: 300 runs)

	M	I	NO	R	HS	100s	50s	Avge
N. L. Berry (Pint)	14	15	4	793	204*	3	3	72.09
K. E. Vowles (Palmerston)	10	7	1	390	88	0	4	65.00
D. L. Treumer (Palmerston)	13	17	7	524	147	2	1	52.40
M. M. Brown (Pint)	14	15	3	620	110*	1	5	51.67
N. J. Allen (Tracy Village)	13	17	3	553	138*	1	2	39.50
A. C. Dent (NTIS)	14	18	1	663	116	1	6	39.00
M. A. Hatton (Nightcliff)	14	17	3	538	82	0	4	38.43
M. O'Connor (Pint)	13	16	3	499	104	1	4	38.38
B. R. Sharp (Tracy Village)	14	18	2	609	86	0	5	38.06
M. R. Richardson (Waratahs)	14	15	0	528	121	2	3	35.20

* Denotes not out.

BOWLING AVERAGES, 2003-04

(Qualification: 20 wickets)

	M	O	Mdns	R	W	BB	5W/i	10W/m	Avge
R. J. Green (Waratahs)	14	170	43	445	37	6-68	2	0	12.02
P. J. Hills (Palmerston)	9	117	34	272	20	5-19	1	0	13.60
M. C. Miller (Palmerston)	13	185	24	668	44	8-40	2	1	15.18
N. L. Berry (Pint)	14	221	50	656	43	6-24	3	0	15.25
D. J. King (Pint)	11	101	21	310	20	3-24	0	0	15.50
A. C. Dent (NTIS)	14	139	19	457	29	5-22	3	0	15.75
R. Corfield (Darwin)	8	167	50	409	24	5-51	1	0	17.04
T. J. Knox (Tracy Village)	13	121	14	416	24	4-43	0	0	17.33
P. R. Cooper (Waratahs)	13	176	53	418	24	5-38	1	0	17.41
I. Redpath (Southern Districts)	14	194	53	523	30	4-11	0	0	17.43

DARWIN A-GRADE SEMI-FINALS, 2003

NIGHTCLIFF v NT INSTITUTE OF SPORT

At Nightcliff, September 13, 2003. Northern Territory Institute of Sport won on first innings. Nightcliff 161 (J. S. Hatton 34, D. Bradmore 22, M. A. Hatton 62; B. J. Hatton 5-27); Northern Territory Institute of Sport 4 for 173 (M. Barry 41, S. J. Regan 82; M. A. Hatton 2-48).

PALMERSTON v PINT

At Marrara No. 1 Sports Ground, September 13, 2003. Palmerston won on first innings. Pint 107 (B. J. Coady 26, N. L. Berry 21; K. E. Vowles 8-25); Palmerston 7 for 195 (A. C. Dent 32, S. J. Chatto 46, D. L. Treumer 34*, T. G. Bayly 35; N. L. Berry 4-49).

DARWIN A-GRADE PRELIMINARY FINAL, 2003

PINT v NT INSTITUTE OF SPORT

At Marrara No. 1 Sports Ground, September 20, 2003. Pint won on first innings. Pint 257 (M. O'Connor 118, A. Edis 45, D. J. King 21*; B. J. Hatton 5-51); Northern Territory Institute of Sport 115 (S. Mitchell 38; N. L. Berry 2-22, R. Hodgson 3-35, D. J. King 4-24).

DARWIN A-GRADE FINAL, 2003

PALMERSTON v PINT

At Marrara No. 1 Ground, Darwin, September 27, 28, 2004. Palmerston won on first innings by three wickets. *Toss:* Palmerston.

Once considered the poor rural cousins of Darwin cricket, Palmerston entered this match as strong favourites to win their third consecutive premiership. Their side boasted six members of the NT Chief Minister's squad that played Bangladesh two months earlier. Despite the absence of their leading wicket-taker, Mick Miller, they elected to bowl upon winning the toss. The left-armer Anthony Dent made immediate inroads, Brendan Coady caught by Terry Bayly off the second ball of the innings. Nick Berry and Mark Griffin steadied things with a 79-run stand, before the run-out of Griffin triggered a mini-collapse of 4 for 31. Witnessing the clatter of wickets, unflustered at the non-striker's end, was Berry. He put on 65 for the sixth wicket with his captain Matt Crawley, then proceeded to dominate a succession of handy lower-order partnerships. By the end he had carried his bat for a patient 153, made from 293 balls and comprising 16 fours and three sixes. The other 10 batsmen made 120 between them. Pint's total of 284 looked highly competitive after being sent in, especially when Palmerston lost their opener Craig Field, bowled first ball by Richie Hodgson, in the four overs before stumps. They slid to 3 for 78 the next day, before a 90-run stand between Ashley Williams and Shane Chatto restored the balance. On a twisting, turning afternoon, Williams, Bayly and Chatto fell in quick succession as Pint wrested back the initiative. Now, though, Darren Treumer and Ken Vowles, the two giants of modern Darwin cricket, were together at the wicket. They duly cobbled together a nerveless 98-run partnership in a little over 20 overs. By the time Treumer fell, edging behind off David King, victory was within sight. Vowles finished unbeaten on 71 off 78 balls, having swiped 13 crucial fours. Fittingly it was Vowles who hit the winning runs, a gratifying moment for the man who had switched to Palmerston during the off-season in pursuit of the premiership triumph that had always eluded him.

Close of play: First day, Palmerston (1) 1-18 (Denton 14, Cook 4).

Pint

B. J. Coady c Bayly b Dent	0	S. Clode b Williams	14
N. L. Berry not out	153	R. Hodgson st Treumer b Williams	14
M. Griffin run out	39	C. Leek c Hills b Cook	8
†M. M. Brown c Treumer b Dent	7		
M. O'Connor c Williams b Cook	9	B 2, l-b 5, w 2 n-b 2	11
A. Edis c Treumer b Bayly	0		—
*M. Crawley lbw b Vowles	29	(100 overs)	284
D. J. King c Treumer b Bayly	0	Fall: 0 79 88 104 110 175 180 220 261 284

Bowling: Dent 14–2–49–2; Hills 17–6–47–0; Bayly 11.1–4–22–2; Vowles 20–8–39–1; Cook 21.5–6–66–2; Williams 14–4–44–2; Drummond 2–0–10–0.

Palmerston

A. C. Dent lbw b King	50	*K. E. Vowles not out	71
C. R. Field b Hodgson	0	C. J. Whitaker not out	0
P. A. Cook c Berry b Hodgson	13		
A. N. Williams c Brown b Berry	57	B 2, l-b 6, n-b 4	12
S. J. Chatto c Brown b O'Connor	41		—
T. G. Bayly st Brown b O'Connor	8	(79.5 overs) (7 wkts)	287
†D. L. Treumer c Brown b King	35	Fall: 5 47 78 168 180 181 279

N. Drummond, P. J. Hills did not bat.

Bowling: Hodgson 16–0–83–2; King 15–3–45–2; Berry 24.5–7–68–1; Edis 8–1–38–0; O'Connor 5–0–18–2; Leek 11–2–27–0.

Umpires: J. Martin and P. Creek.

National Country Championships, 2003-04

By WARWICK TORRENS

After promising so much for so many years, Victoria at last achieved their second triumph – and their first in 13 summers – at the National Country Championships in the South Australian town of Mount Gambier. Winning all five of their matches, Victoria led the points table from start to finish. New South Wales threw out a late challenge but their unexpected defeat to South Australia in the second round ensured the odds were always stacked against them.

It was a year of bold and dramatic change for the two-week tournament. The Australian Capital Territory chose not to enter a side and to concentrate their efforts on improving their cricket elsewhere. In order to avoid a bye a new team was sought. After various options were considered the organisers accepted the nomination of a mixed team from the East Asia Pacific region.

Ten of the players came from Papua-New Guinea, two from the Cook Islands and one each from Fiji and Japan. The team had the backing of the International Cricket Council and it is hoped their participation will boost the game throughout the region. Although they did not win a match they played attractive, competitive cricket. Jamie Brazier hit both the first century and the highest score of the entire championships, making 162 – out of 209 added while he was at the crease – against Victoria. In the final round the Cook Islander Chris Brown, batting at No. 8, hit 120 as East Asia Pacific went within two wickets of upsetting Western Australia.

They were just two out of several notable performances throughout the series. Two hat-tricks were recorded, a feat that is known to have happened only once before. Queensland's Daryl Bridgeman took the first against Western Australia, and Victoria's Paul Bradley the second against SA. In the second round, Queensland's Boyd Williams and Jason Stein bowled unchanged through the first innings as East Asia Pacific were knocked over for 52. Stein followed up with 6 for 84 in the second innings, becoming the first bowler in the history of the championships to secure a 10-wicket haul. Victoria's Michael Lewis and Chris Hopper also bowled unchanged through SA's paltry second innings of 67 in the final round.

The defending champions Western Australia, who had triumphed so emphatically in Bundaberg, were disappointing. They tied their opening game with last year's runners-up Queensland on the first innings, then lost their next three. They were humbled by NSW in Penola, rolled for 92 and 102 on their way to an outright defeat. The biggest letdown of all was the form of Glen Dehring: 14 runs in six innings was a poor return from such a prolific runscorer.

Queensland, who invariably end up somewhere around the top of the table, also had an off-key championships. They finished fourth and were badly let down by their batsmen. Brian May, the competition's leading all-time runscorer, managed only one half-century against East Asia Pacific. Their best batsman was the debutant Scott Allen from Toowoomba. Finding the wickets difficult, Allen decided there was only one way to play – and that was to go after the ball. For him the theory worked well; for others it failed miserably.

It was a series of mixed fortunes for the hosts South Australia, who finished in third position. They won their first two matches but lost two of their last three. Their outstanding player was Michael Silvy, a local left-armer with first-grade experience in Adelaide. He exploited the helpful conditions and finished with 17 wickets at an exceptional average of 11.41.

The over-reliance on pace and neglect of spin bowlers was one of the reasons behind the downfall of several sides. Victoria, though, had two experienced slow bowlers in the leg-spinner Bradley and left-armer Hopper. The pair had batsmen in considerable difficulty almost every time they came on, and this was undoubtedly a major factor in Victoria's long-awaited victory. Hopper finished the series with the most wickets in the championship's history – 24 – one more than the previous record set by Queensland's Michael Warden in Toowoomba in 1996-97.

This was a bowler's year. Stein, the Queenslander, equalled Warden's old record of 23 wickets, while three others finished in the high-teens. Teams were bowled out for under 100 on four occasions. Only Victoria, in a low-scoring tournament, topped 400; NSW's 337 against East Asia Pacific, who replied with a gallant 297, was the next best.

Victoria's dominance is perhaps best summed up by the fact that in the previous 19 years they had won only one batting trophy, one bowling trophy and one Player of the Series trophy. This time around they won all three. Only the New South Welshmen Randall Starr, who won his second fielding trophy, stood in the way of a Victorian clean sweep.

Player of the Series: B.L. Campbell (Vic) and C.F. Hopper (Vic)
Don Bradman Batting Trophy: B.L. Campbell (Vic)
Bill O'Reilly Bowling Trophy: C.F. Hopper (Vic)
Fieldsman of the Series: R. Starr (NSW)

ROUND ONE

At McDonald Park, Mount Gambier, January 4, 5, 2004. Victoria won on first innings. New South Wales 9 for 242 (A.E. Alley 61; C.F. Hopper 3-50); Victoria 8 for 247 (B. L. Campbell 87, D.J. Herbert 3-73).

At Frew Park, Mount Gambier, January 4, 5, 2004 (no play on first day – rain). Match tied on first innings. Queensland 9 for 143; Western Australia 143 (D. Bridgeman 3-20, T.P. Maher 4-14).

At McCorquindale Park, Penola, January 4, 5, 2004. South Australia won on first innings. South Australia 113 (T. Gaudi 4-29, A. Norri 3-6) and 3 dec 132; East Asia Pacific 48 (M.J. Silvy 5-8) and 6 for 82.

ROUND TWO

At Marist Park, Mount Gambier, January 6, 7, 2004. Queensland won on first innings. East Asia Pacific 52 (B.O. Williams 4-14, J.C. Stein 4-37) and 8 for 279 (J. Brazier 113; J.C. Stein 6-84); Queensland 4 dec 156 (B.K.D. May 58*, S.M. Allen 58*).

At Frew Park, Mount Gambier, January 6, 7, 2004. South Australia won on first innings. New South Wales 134 (B.P.J. Nott 50; T.K. Bahr 4-31, D. Thomson 3-39) and 2 for 213 (A.E. Alley 74*, S.G. Moore 79); South Australia 180 (D. McIlveen 3-31).

At Blue Lake Sports Club, Mount Gambier, January 6, 7, 2004. Victoria won on first innings. Victoria 9 for 416 (B.I. Patrick 65, B.L. Campbell 82, J. Brown 66; C.A. Waddingham 3-87); Western Australia 169 (P. Bradley 4-48, C.F. Hopper 4-51) and 1 for 75.

ROUND THREE

At Frew Park, Mount Gambier, January 9, 10, 2004. Victoria won on first innings. East Asia Pacific 193 (I. Morea 59; B. Hauenstein 4-32, C.F. Hopper 4-44) and 9 for 222 (J. Brazier 162; M. Lewis 3-32); Victoria 8 for 322 (G.D. Pearse 74, B.I. Patrick 59, B.L. Campbell 74; R. Dikana 3-68, D. Eliaba 3-71).

At McCorquindale Park, Penola, January 9, 10, 2004. New South Wales won by 147 runs. New South Wales 172 (M.J. Gerits 80; C.G.R. Tonkin 5-43, D.A. Ellis 4-50) and 7 dec 169 (M.D. Head 3-67); Western Australia 92 (D. McIlveen 4-35, J. Ditton 3-23) and 102 (S.G. Moore 3-29, B. Bannister 5-16).

At Marist Park, Mount Gambier, January 9, 10, 2004. Queensland won on first innings. South Australia 256 (R. Reid 72; J.C. Stein 4-84); Queensland 9 for 270 (S.M. Allen 142*; D. Thomson 3-82).

ROUND FOUR

At Blue Lake Sports Park, Mount Gambier, January 12, 13, 2004. New South Wales won on first innings. East Asia Pacific 297 (M. Dai 98, J Ovia 92; D. McIlveen 4-75, B. Bannister 3-69); New South Wales 337 (M.D. Walters 147, D.J. Herbert 72; D. Eliaba 3-83, J. Brazier 3-29).

At McCorquindale Park, Penola, January 12, 13, 2004. Victoria won on first innings. Victoria 254 (B.L. Campbell 63; J.C. Stein 5-69, T.P. Maher 3-40); Queensland 117 (P. Bradley 3-26, C.F. Hopper 5-15) and 1 for 58.

At McDonald Park, Mount Gambier, January 12, 13, 2004. South Australia won on first innings. Western Australia 232 (L.G. Burns 50, L.B. Hardie 52; B.H. Steele 3-59, S.J. Merkel 3-25); South Australia 7 for 254 (A. Willis 101*; C. White 4-27).

ROUND FIVE

At Marist Park, Mount Gambier, January 14, 15, 2004. Western Australia won on first innings. East Asia Pacific 262 (C. Brown 120; C.G.R. Tonkin 4-56); Western Australia 8 for 264 (L.G. Burns 121*; T. Gaudi 4-90).

At Frew Park, Mount Gambier, January 14, 15, 2004. New South Wales won on first innings. Queensland 183 (D. McIlveen 4-17); New South Wales 6 for 185 (S.G. Moore 64; J.C. Stein 4-59).

At Blue Lake Sports Park, Mount Gambier, January 14, 15, 2004. Victoria won on first innings. South Australia 155 (P. Bradley 5-44) and 67 (M. Lewis 5-28, C.F. Hopper 5-34); Victoria 183 (B.L. Campbell 53; M.J. Silvy 5-65).

POINTS TABLE, 2003-04

	P	*WO*	*WI*	*D*	*LI*	*LO*	*T*	*Points*
Victoria Country	5	0	5	0	0	0	0	65.22
New South Wales Country	5	1	2	0	2	0	0	53.92
South Australia Country	5	0	3	0	2	0	0	46.67
Queensland Country	5	0	2	0	2	0	1	40.47
Western Australia Country	5	0	1	0	2	1	1	35.37
East Asia Pacific	5	0	0	0	5	0	0	27.25

MOST RUNS, 2003-04

	M	I	NO	R	HS	100s	50s	Avge
B. L. Campbell (Vic)	5	5	0	359	87	0	5	71.80
J. Brazier (EAP)	5	8	0	326	162	2	0	40.75
S. M. Allen (Qld)	5	5	2	233	142*	1	1	77.66
S. G. Moore (NSW)	5	7	0	233	79	0	2	33.28
J. Ovia (EAP)	5	8	1	221	92	0	1	31.57
L. G. Burns (W Aust)	5	6	1	201	121*	1	1	40.20
M. J. Gerits (NSW)	5	7	1	196	80	0	1	32.66
K. N. Elliot (W Aust)	5	7	1	189	44	0	0	31.50
A. Willis (S Aust)	5	7	2	188	101*	1	0	37.60
R. Reid (S Aust)	5	6	0	180	72	0	1	30.00
B. I. Patrick (Vic)	5	5	0	179	65	0	2	35.80

MOST WICKETS, 2003-04

	M	O	Mdns	R	W	BB	5Wi	Avge
C. F. Hopper (Vic)	5	118.2	36	265	24	5-15	2	11.04
J. C. Stein (Qld)	5	144.2	34	372	23	6-84	2	16.17
D. McIlveen (NSW)	5	120.3	39	259	19	4-17	0	13.63
M. J. Silvy (S Aust)	5	86	26	194	17	5-8	2	11.41
P. Bradley (Vic)	5	127.4	46	275	17	5-44	1	16.17
C. G. R. Tonkin (W Aust)	5	112.5	32	252	12	5-43	1	21.00
T. K. Bahr (S Aust)	5	95	23	221	11	4-31	0	20.09
M. Lewis (Vic)	4	54	9	154	10	5-28	1	15.40
R. Dikana (EAP)	5	67	18	202	10	3-68	0	20.20
D. Eliaba (EAP)	5	88	17	239	10	3-71	0	23.90

CHAMPIONSHIP WINNERS

Season	Venue	Winner	Player of the Series
1984-85	Beenleigh, Qld	New South Wales	R. T. Staff (Qld)
1985-86	Riverland, S Aust	New South Wales	S. J. Scuderi (Qld)
1986-87	Dubbo, NSW	Australian Capital Territory	G. R. Irvine (ACT)
1987-88	Canberra, ACT	Queensland	L. D. Mason (Qld)
1988-89	Bunbury, W Aust	New South Wales	A. M. Fort (NSW)
1989-90	Bendigo, Vic	New South Wales	M. S. Curry (NSW)
1990-91	Townsville, Qld	Victoria	M. S. Curry (NSW)
1991-92	Riverland, S Aust	New South Wales	M. S. Curry (NSW)
1992-93	Newcastle, NSW	New South Wales	A. M. Stuart (NSW)
1993-94	Canberra, ACT	Australian Capital Territory	P. L. Evans (ACT)
1994-95	Albany-Mt Barker, W Aust	Queensland	I. F. Sartori (Vic)
1995-96	Sale-Maffra, Vic	New South Wales	M. J. Warden (Qld)
1996-97	Toowoomba, Qld	Queensland	M. J. Warden (Qld)
1997-98	Mount Gambier, S Aust	Western Australia	M. J. Warden (Qld)
1998-99	Barooga, NSW	Queensland	B. J. Smith (Qld)
1999-00	Canberra, ACT	Queensland	B. K. D. May (Qld)
2000-01	Albany-Mt Barker, W Aust	New South Wales	B. K. D. May (Qld)
2001-02	Warrnambool, Vic	Queensland	D. R. Else (Qld)
2002-03	Bundaberg, Qld	Western Australia	D. A. Burns (W Aust)
2003-04	Mount Gambier, S Aust	Victoria	B. L. Campbell (Vic)

PLAYER TROPHY WINNERS

Season	Player of Series	Batting	Bowling	Fielding
1984-85	R. T. Staff (Qld)	–	–	–
1985–86	S. J. Scuderi (Qld)	S. J. Scuderi (Qld)	M. A. Polzin (Qld)	–
1986–87	G. R. Irvine (ACT)	G. R. Irvine (ACT)	D. J. Francis (WA)	–
1987–88	L. D. Mason (Qld)	L. D. Mason (Qld)	D. F. Benson (Vic)	–
1988–89	A. M. Fort (NSW)	A. M. Fort (NSW)	G. P. Williams (SA)	–
1989–90	M. S. Curry (NSW)	S. J. Scuderi (Qld)	E. L. Nix (ACT)	–
1990–91	M. S. Curry (NSW)	B. P. Inwood (Qld)	M. J. Warden (Qld)	–
1991–92	M. S. Curry (NSW)	P. J. Solway (ACT)	G. A. Bush (ACT)	–
1992–93	A. M. Stuart (NSW)	D. R. W. Temple (Qld)	A. M. Stuart (NSW)	–
			R. H. Menasse (WA)	
1993-94	P. L. Evans (ACT)	P. L. Evans (ACT)	P. S. Nemes (ACT)	–
			M. J. Warden (Qld)	
1994-95	I. F. Sartori (Vic)	G. R. O'Sullivan (NSW)	M. J. Warden (Qld)	A. K. D. Gray (WA)
1995-96	M. J. Warden (Qld)	N. D. Tatterson (Vic)	M. J. Warden (Qld)	M. T. Hegarty (ACT)
1996-97	M. J. Warden (Qld)	J. R. Mosey (SA)	M. J. Warden (Qld)	K. N. Spencer (WA)
1997-98	M. J. Warden (Qld)	G. J. Dehring (WA)	M. J. Warden (Qld)	B. K. D. May (Qld)
1998-99	B. J. Smith (Qld)	G. A. Grimmond (NSW)	D. K. Wrixon (NSW)	S. A. Sweet (SA)
1999-00	B. K. D. May (Qld)	B. K. D. May (Qld)	M. J. Warden (Qld)	S. A. Baker (Qld)
2000-01	B. K. D. May (Qld)	A. D. McQuire (ACT)	D. A. Ellis (WA)	R. Starr (NSW)
				B. D. Ward (WA)
2001-02	D. R. Else (Qld)	B. K. D. May (Qld)	D. A. Hughes (NSW)	S. A. Baker (Qld)
2002-03	D. A. Burns (WA)	M. J. Gerits (NSW)	P. J. Toohey (Qld)	S. A. Baker (Qld)
2003-04	B. L. Campbell (Vic)	B. L. Campbell (Vic)	C. F. Hopper (Vic)	R. Starr (NSW)
	C. F. Hopper (Vic)			

Imparja Cup, 2003-04

by BARRY NICHOLLS

The Paul Kelly song, "From Little Things Big Things Grow", tells of the day Vincent Lingiari led his Gurindji people off Wave Hill cattle station, thus beginning the Aboriginal land rights movement. It could easily become the anthem for the Imparja Cup. Australia's first indigenous cricket carnival started life a decade ago as a one-off match between two towns. Now a fully-fledged national competition, staged every autumn in Alice Springs, Queensland cruised unbothered and undefeated through last season's tournament to run out convincing winners.

It all started with a debate between two brothers, Shane and Mervyn Franey, and their friend, Ross Jakamar Williams, about whether Alice Springs or Tennant Creek had the best Aboriginal cricketers. In 1994 this hypothetical match was staged. Alice Springs won, a dispute was settled and a concept born.

Five years later players from the town of Borroloola, in the Northern Territory's gulf country, were invited to join in. Control of the tournament passed from the original custodians to the Northern Territory Cricket Association. In 2000-01, when Jimmy Adams's West Indies trekked to Alice Springs, the Cup got its first big kick-along. Aboriginal delegates from Western Australia and the NT met with Australian Cricket Board officials, and it was agreed that all states and territories should be invited to take part.

Tasmania went on to win that year but it remained a largely regional affair, bolstered by the inclusion of Darwin, Katherine and the Tiwi Islands. In 2001-02 the competition was split into two divisions, comprising six states and six regional sides. Last season it blossomed into a truly national event, featuring all eight states and territories for the first time. Cricket Australia backed the 2003-04 Imparja Cup to the tune of $25,000 and the board's chairman, Bob Merriman, officially welcomed all the players. Matches were 25-overs-a-side, culminating in a 40-over final.

Shane Franey, one of those original custodians, is stunned by how quickly the concept has taken off. "It is unreal now," he says. "We had a five-year plan about how the competition would develop; now it's at a stage that we thought might have been reached after 25 years. The original idea was that it might lead to the setting up of some coaching clinics for indigenous people, and we thought that one day we might get the states involved."

Queensland's victory was made all the more remarkable by the fact that they had never before competed in the Imparja Cup. It was the first time a Queensland Aboriginal side had embraced players from across the length and breadth of the state, including the Torres Strait Islands. Captained by Barry Weare, they dominated at every turn, shrugging aside the NT by 10 wickets in their opening match and never looking back. The Australian Capital Territory crumbled to be all out for 28 in only 11 overs. The defending champions New South Wales were comfortably blown away, as were Victoria. Queensland then sealed the tournament in emphatic fashion, crushing Tasmania by 10 wickets under lights at Traegar Park.

In five matches they lost only 10 wickets while hurtling along at more than seven runs an over. But the architects of Queensland's domination were their bowlers, led by Aaron Holt, Martin Rush and Damian Watts, who headed the wickets table with nine wickets at 7.77. Their middle-order batsmen were seldom required, but openers Keith Charles and Brett Smith – who finished with a staggering tournament average of 276 – made the most of their opportunities.

Beaten finalists Tasmania were also impressive in the early stages, winning all four preliminary matches if not in quite the same runaway style as Queensland. Their captain Sean Gower stood out as an all-rounder, averaging 39 with the bat and 10.83 with the ball. Bernie Lamont was their leading batsman. His unbeaten 120 in 65 balls against Victoria, including 10 fours and six sixes, was the highest score of the tournament. The only other centurion was the NSW opener John Duckett, who hit 115 against the ACT and averaged 55 for the carnival, his side winning three of their four games.

Western Australia finished in fourth place, with Jermaine Davis and Clinton Dann both averaging in the sixties, and the NT fifth. It was a slightly disappointing performance from the hosts, who won only one of their four matches. The much-travelled Ian Redpath was their leading runscorer but star fast bowler Adrian McAdam, a gifted all-round sportsman who enjoyed a fleeting but fabulous AFL football career with North Melbourne, managed only two wickets. Last year's grand finalists South Australia also disappointed. Their solitary victory came against bottom side ACT, who finished winless.

Four separate competitions were held concurrently. Regional teams competed in two divisions, with Alice Springs beating Tennant Creek by seven wickets in the division one final and Normanton trumping Melville Island by two wickets to take out division two. The Lord's Taverners women's competition was won by Tennant Creek, who beat Katherine by 23 runs in the final. Alice Springs High School won the schoolboys championship, edging out Callistemon College by three runs.

Cricket Australia's involvement in the Imparja Cup reflects its belated awareness of the need to sell the game beyond its traditional player base. Jason Gillespie remains the only Aboriginal player ever to have worn the baggy green. Precious few others have broken into first-class ranks. In remote communities across the NT the abiding sporting passion is for Australian Rules football. The challenge is to spread the word until cricket bats rival footballs and basketballs as a major source of entertainment.

Slowly but surely, progress is being made. The Tiwi Islands, best known for their vibrant football scene, recently announced a three-team cricket competition featuring Milikapati, Garden Point and Nguiu. Much credit was given to the former Test captain Steve Waugh, who has travelled to the islands and Katherine in the past two summers, and his all-conquering team-mates. A nod of thanks should also be extended to the original custodians of the Imparja Cup.

PRELIMINARY GAMES

At Traeger Park, February 26, 2004. Northern Territory 7 for 160 (P. Lake 22, S. Angeles 30, A. McAdam 61; S. Gower 3-14, G. McLean 2-29) lost to Tasmania 4 for 164 (B. Lamont 46, S. Gower 24, N. Kopper 36*, G. Grey 23*; D. Lowe 2-24) by six wickets.

At Treager Park, February 27, 2004. Western Australia 2 for 183 (C. Dann 42, A. Taylor 24, J. Davis 75*, G. Beresi 21*) defeated South Australia 9 for 134 (K. Thomas 31, R. Johncock 51, S. Gepp 23*; J. Bennell 3-20, G. Ugle 3-22, J. McGuire 2-2) by 49 runs.

At Albrecht Oval, February 27, 2004. Tasmania 4 for 211 (B. Lamont 120*, S. Gower 67; D. Nelson 2-35) defeated Victoria 6 for 163 (M. Hoye 34, S. Kelly 46, D. Nelson 27*) by 48 runs.

At Traeger Park, February 27, 2004. New South Wales 4 for 243 (J. Duckett 115, A. Gorgon 78; G. Murray 2-74) defeated Australian Capital Territory 9 for 72 (B. Appo 22; S. Williams 2-8, P. Cooley 3-19) by 171 runs.

At Albrecht Oval, February 27, 2004. Northern Territory 99 (A. McAdam 47; D. Watts 3-18, M. Rush 2-42, K. Gibbs 3-15) lost to Queensland 0 for 100 (K. Charles 47*, B. Smith 41) by 10 wickets.

At Traeger Park, February 27, 2004. New South Wales 5 for 152 (J. Duckett 33, R. Champion 29, B. Woods 26, J. Deal 29*; G. Taylor 2-18) defeated South Australia 8 for 81 (K. Thomas 14, P. Thomas 14*; A. Shepard 2-8, A. Gordon 2-13, G. Wellington 2-16) by 71 runs.

At Albrecht Oval, February 27, 2004. Tasmania 8 for 136 (D. Harris 27, N. Kopper 35; T. Collard 2-18, J. Davis 2-20, T. Dann 2-30) defeated Western Australia 9 for 123 (T. Dann 78*; N. Kopper 3-18, C. Nickolai 3-13) by 13 runs.

At Traeger Park, February 28, 2004. Australian Capital Territory 28 (T. Greer 11; D. Watts 4-7, M. Rush 3-14, A. Holt 3-6) lost to Queensland 1 for 29 (B. Smith 19*) by nine wickets.

At Albrecht Oval, February 28, 2004. New South Wales 6 for 162 (B. Champion 34, J. Duckett 27, A. Gordon 20, N. Levy 41; S. Angeles 3-30) defeated Northern Territory 8 for 137 (I. Redpath 57, A. Fett 24; P. Cooley 3-34, P. Jones 3-28) by 25 runs.

At Traeger Park, February 28, 2004. Western Australia 3 for 162 (C. Dann 79*, J. Davis 45, G. Beresi 23) defeated Victoria 86 (G. Nelson 15; J. Davis 3-20, J. Bennell 2-28, G. Ugle 2-17, T. Collard 2-14) by 76 runs.

At Albrecht Oval, February 28, 2004. Tasmania 7 for 212 (C. Lamont 29, D. Harris 20, B. Lamont 47, S. Gower 50, J. Wells 22; R. Bulger 2-44, P. Thomas 2-19) defeated South Australia 95 (N. Hartman 36, K. Thomas 23; S. Gower 2-20, G. Medcraft 2-2, D. Gardner 2-12) by 117 runs.

At Traegar Park, February 28, 2004. New South Wales 7 for 129 (B. Champion 25, J. Duckett 45, A. Gordon 20; B. Weare 2-13, G. Martin 2-9) lost to Queensland 2 for 133 (B. Smith 92*, D. Morrison 23*) by 8 wickets.

At Albrecht Oval, February 28, 2004. Australian Capital Territory 114 (T. Greer 48; D. Lowe 2-22, S. Angeles 2-20, G. Rosas 4-18) lost to Northern Territory 2 for 115 (I. Redpath 42, P. Lake 44) by 8 wickets.

At Traeger Park, February 28, 2004. Victoria 8 for 132 (J. Day 26, D. Nelson 43, G. Nelson 21; K. Thomas 3-14) lost to South Australia 4 for 137 (S. Gepp 31, R. Bulger 43*; M. Hoye 2-23) by 6 wickets.

At Albrecht Oval, February 29, 2004. Western Australia 6 for 175 (G. Ryder 54*, J. Bennell 59; M. Towney 3-19, B. Appo 2-30) defeated Australian Capital Territory 91 (J. Lanke 23, T. Greer 24; T. Collard 2-20, J. McGuire 2-12) by 84 runs.

At Albrecht Oval, February 29, 2004. Queensland 7 for 207 (B. Smith 84, J. Marsh 30, K. Gibbs 39*; G. Nelson 3-34, T. Perry 2-25) defeated Victoria 100 (N. Firebrace 20; C. Mosby 2-27, K. Charles 2-6) by 107 runs.

POINTS TABLE, 2003-04

	Played	Won	Lost	Points	Net Run-Rate
Queensland	4	4	0	8	2.90
Tasmania	4	4	0	8	2.04
New South Wales	4	3	1	6	2.41
Western Australia	4	3	1	6	1.71
Northern Territory	4	1	3	2	-0.45
South Australia	4	1	3	2	-2.08
Victoria	4	0	4	0	-2.74
Australian Capital Territory	4	0	4	0	-4.36

Net run-rate was calculated by subtracting runs conceded per over from runs scored per over.

MOST WICKETS, 2003-04

	M	O	Mdns	R	W	BB	Avge	RPO
D. Watts (Qld)	5	23	0	70	9	4-7	7.77	3.04
A. Holt (Qld)	5	12	1	49	8	4-12	6.12	4.08
K. Gibbs (Qld)	5	22	1	79	8	3-15	9.87	3.59
M. Rush (Qld)	5	28	1	149	8	3-14	18.62	5.32
G. Ugle (W Aust)	4	19	1	82	7	3-22	11.71	4.59
S. Gower (Tas)	4	17	1	65	6	3-14	10.83	3.82
P. Cooley (NSW)	4	10	0	67	6	3-19	11.16	6.70
T. Collard (W Aust)	4	19	0	77	6	2-14	12.83	4.05

IMPARJA CUP FINAL, 2003-04

QUEENSLAND v TASMANIA

At Traegar Park, Alice Springs, February 29, 2004. Queensland won by 10 wickets.
Toss: Tasmania.

Eddie Gilbert, the Queensland fast bowler of the 1930s, would have been a proud man if he were still alive. An Aboriginal side from Queensland had won the Imparja Cup for the first time and indigenous cricketers, better late than never, were receiving recognition on the national stage. How times had changed, he might have thought, since the days when his own career was stalled by laws incarcerating Aborigines under the Queensland Aboriginal Protection Act; when he had to get permission just to leave the Barambah mission in order to play cricket.

This year's final was almost over before the new lights at Traeger Park, part of a $5 million upgrade of Alice Springs's premier sporting facility, were even switched on. With the temperature hovering in the high 30s, Tasmania made a respectable start and were cruising at 4 for 92 at one point. Bernie Lamont lasted only three balls but the rest of the top order made useful starts. The match swung on the downfall of Nathan Kopper. The medium-pacer Aaron Holt tore through the lower order and Tasmania's last five batsmen, having spent little time at the crease during the previous couple of days, continued the trend by managing only three runs between them. The openers Keith Charles and Brett Smith eased past the meagre target in 13 overs replete with 14 boundaries.

Tasmania

C. Lamont c Smith b Rush	12
D. Harris run out	11
B. Lamont c Weare b Watts	1
*S. Gower c Watts b Gibbs	15
N. Kopper c Holt b Gibbs	34
†G. Grey lbw b Holt	11
J. Wells c Morrison b Holt	3
G. Medcraft c Martin b Holt	0
G. McLean lbw b Holt	0
C. Nickolai c Morrison b Gibbs	0
J. Green not out	0
L-b 2, w 5, n-b 1	8
(28 overs)	95

Fall: 22 27 27 62 92 92 92 92 93 95

Bowling: Watts 6–0–16–1; Rush 8–1–32–1; Gibbs 8–1–33–3; Holt 6–1–12–4.

Queensland

K. Charles not out	45
B. Smith not out	40
L-b 2, w 6, n-b 4	12
(13.3 overs)	(0 wkt) 97

B. Weare, J. Marsh, D. Rudd, †D. Morrison, G. Martin, K. Gibbs, D. Watts, A. Holt and M. Rush did not bat.

Bowling: Gower 5–0–24–0; Medcraft 4–0–42–0; McLean 2–0–17–0; Kopper 2–0–8–0; B. Lamont 0.3–0–4–0.

MOST RUNS, 2003-04

	M	I	NO	R	HS	100s	50s	Avge
B. Smith (Qld)	5	5	4	276	92*	0	2	276.00
J. Duckett (NSW)	4	4	-	220	115	0	1	55.00
B. Lamont (Tas)	5	5	1	217	120*	1	0	54.25
S. Gower (Tas)	4	4	0	156	67	0	2	39.00
J. Davis (W Aust)	4	3	1	126	75*	0	1	63.00
C. Dann (W Aust)	4	3	1	121	79*	0	1	60.50
A. Gordon (NSW)	4	4	0	118	78	0	1	29.50
I. Redpath (NT)	4	4	0	117	57	0	1	29.25
K. Charles (Qld)	4	4	2	114	47*	0	0	57.00
N. Kopper (Tas)	5	5	1	112	36*	0	0	28.00

Women's Cricket, 2003-04

By ERICA SAINSBURY

The summer of 2003-04 was a time of drawing breath in women's cricket, after the previous summer's World Series and ahead of next year's World Cup in South Africa. Limited-overs matches were the only fixtures to grace the international calendar, with Australia comprehensively beating New Zealand 5-1 to retain the Rose Bowl. On the domestic scene the title-holders Victoria relinquished their crown to a rejuvenated New South Wales.

In a move that surprised many, the veteran wicket-keeper Julia Price was replaced by NSW's Leonie Coleman in the national team. Price has not given up hope of regaining her place and the selectors will have a difficult task separating the pair, as Coleman did all that was asked of her in her debut series. Belinda Clark, Karen Rolton and Melanie Jones led the batting charge, Cathryn Fitzpatrick continued to exert her dominance with the ball and Lisa Sthalekar grew in confidence and impact as a genuine all-rounder.

Despite such resounding success one note of caution continues to sound; Australia's reliance on Fitzpatrick, the phenomenal bowling spearhead, masks a dearth in pace-bowling talent. At 36, Fitzpatrick shows little sign of slowing down but she cannot keep going forever. Emma Twining is a potential heir but did not have the best of seasons, and the most promising up-and-comers are still in their teens or early 20s and short on experience. On a brighter note, Kate Blackwell and Leah Poulton were rewarded for their consistency in the youth series with selection in the senior Australian squad, from which the 2005 World Cup side will be selected.

The season also marked the culmination of the Cricket Australia amalgamation process. The men's and women's operations are now fully integrated, with many benefits flowing to the elite women's teams as a result. All grassroots development programs now include girls as full participants, and under-age interstate girls competitions are flourishing. NSW almost completed an under-age clean sweep, taking out the Under-15s, Under-19s and 2nd XI Cricket Australia

Cup prizes, with Queensland winning the Under-17s competition. The Australian youth team enjoyed a successful tour, running out 3-1 winners in the one-day series against New Zealand A, whose team included five former senior NZ representatives. Their success was founded on several exceptional batting performances, which augurs well for the future.

This summer Australia will tour India, take part in the annual Rose Bowl fixtures and then travel to South Africa for the eight-nation World Cup, where they will probably start favourites. The tournament will mark the integration of men's and women's organisations at international level, as the ICC merges with the IWCC to create a single body.

AUSTRALIAN PLAYER PROFILES

ALEX BLACKWELL *Right-hand bat, right-arm medium-pacer*   NSW

After surprising herself with national selection the previous season, 2003-04 was a year of consolidation for the Bradman scholar Blackwell. Despite limited opportunities she played some useful innings and maintained an exceptional standard in the field. At 21, she is expected to be at the forefront of the next generation of Australian players and is being given every chance to learn from the experience of team-mates Belinda Clark, Karen Rolton and Cathryn Fitzpatrick. Blackwell was delighted to be joined by her twin sister Kate in the senior Australian squad at the end of the season. Both are talented all-rounders and potential leaders.

	M	I	NO	Runs	HS	100s	50s	Avge	Ct	St	W	Avge	BB
Test	2	4	1	84	54	0	1	28.00	0	0	0	–	–
Int'l limited-overs	8	5	3	91	27	0	0	45.50	0	0	4	10.00	2-8

KRIS BRITT *Right-hand bat, right-arm leg-spinner*   SA

Increased opportunities allowed Britt to re-affirm her position in the Australian team after an unusual debut season in 2002-03. As an established member of the attack, she grew in confidence and regularly captured important wickets with her well-flighted leg-breaks. She had fewer chances to contribute with the bat but was prepared to do whatever was required of her in any situation. Britt, like her South Australian team-mate Karen Rolton, is not afraid to loft the ball in search of the boundary and displays a full range of elegantly crafted strokes. She has safe hands in the field and her exuberance – both on and off the field – is infectious. At 21, she should have many years ahead of her in the national team. Exactly how her role in the side will evolve remains to be seen.

	M	I	NO	Runs	HS	100s	50s	Avge	Ct	St	W	Avge	BB
Test	1	2	0	8	5	0	0	4.00	0	0	1	40.00	1-17
Int'l limited-overs	9	7	2	67	34*	0	0	13.40	9	0	9	15.66	4-16

BELINDA CLARK *Right-hand bat* **Victoria**

Celebrating her 10th anniversary as Australian captain with another highly productive international campaign, Clark also enjoyed personal success at domestic level. Despite Victoria's failure to retain the national title, she again led by example with the bat. Now 34, Clark has perhaps lost some of the belligerent shotplay of her early days, when she was named *Wisden Australia*'s inaugural Cricketer Of The Year back in 1998. Her game these days is built around solid defence, fluent driving, pinpoint placement and aggressive running. Her will to win is unrivalled and her shrewd captaincy brings out the best in her team-mates. Regaining the World Cup she lost in 2000 is a clear focus in the lead-up to South Africa 2005. But in an era of increasing professionalism for elite women cricketers, there seem few reasons why her career will not extend well beyond the tournament.

	M	I	NO	Runs	HS	100s	50s	Avge	Ct	St	W	Avge	BB
Test	13	21	5	899	136	2	6	56.18	3	0	1	23.00	1-10
Int'l limited-overs	95	92	11	4,291	229*	5	28	52.97	38	0	2	21.50	2-7

LEONIE COLEMAN *Wicket-keeper, right-hand bat* **NSW**

Finally stepping out of the shadow of Julia Price, Coleman carried out her duties with a minimum of fuss and maximum efficiency. Unusually short for a keeper, her outstanding agility and glovework allows her to stand tall behind the stumps, and her chirpy on-field enthusiasm is a constant encouragement to bowlers and fielders. Although rarely called on to bat in recent times, Coleman is more than capable. She has a first-class half-century to her credit and is able to lift the scoring rate when needed. At 25, she appears set for a long and productive career with the national team. But she has Price, who still figures in the selectors' considerations, to watch out for.

	M	I	NO	Runs	HS	100s	50s	Avge	Ct	St	W	Avge	BB
Int'l limited-overs	5	1	1	11	11*	0	0	–	2	3	0	–	–

SHANNON CUNNEEN *Right-hand bat* **NSW**

Cunneen's surprise selection for the New Zealand tour was a reward for several seasons of consistent run accumulation in the National League. A middle-order bat in an exceptionally strong line-up, she had limited opportunities to impress but made the most of her chance when invited to open in the final Rose Bowl game. She is occasionally a slow starter, and needs to overcome this tendency if she is to become a regular fixture in the side. Once set, her strokeplay is wide-ranging and forceful. Cunneen is not afraid to hit over the field and is one of the few Australian players likely to hit a six. She began her career as a wicket-keeper – and occasionally fills in during an emergency – and is an outstanding fielder both in the air and on the ground.

	M	I	NO	Runs	HS	100s	50s	Avge	Ct	St	W	Avge	BB
Int'l limited-overs	4	3	0	49	39	0	0	16.33	1	0	0	–	–

CATHRYN FITZPATRICK *Right-arm fast bowler* **Victoria**

It is impossible to underestimate Fitzpatrick's contribution to Australia's success over the past decade. Still acknowledged as the fastest woman in the world at 36, she continues to be a decisive influence on most matches. Once again she was the leading wicket-taker in last summer's Rose Bowl, as well as in the National League, but her value cannot be measured by statistics alone. Fitzpatrick's dominance over the New Zealand top order and her ability to control the end of the innings are major psychological weapons. She is also a reliable bat in a crunch, and has regularly steered her side to victory in difficult conditions. Recognised as the Women's International Cricketer of the Year, Fitzpatrick will be judged by history as one of the game's greats of any age.

	M	I	NO	Runs	HS	100s	50s	Avge	Ct	St	W	Avge	BB
Test	10	4	0	40	18	0		10.00	5	0	47	17.48	5-29
Int'l limited-overs	73	32	11	237	30	0		11.28	17	0	125	15.25	5-14

JULIE HAYES *Right-arm medium-pacer, right-hand bat* **NSW**

Hayes is the quiet achiever of the Australian side. Her versatile bowling – she can open or tie down the opposition in the middle stages – combined with her immaculate fielding and adaptable approach to batting make her an invaluable asset. Her trademark is the speed with which she bowls her overs, usually in less than two minutes, and she rarely strays in line or length. Often bowling in tandem with Lisa Sthalekar, Hayes's role is to manufacture situations whereby the opposition must take risks in the closing stages. She is also an adept partnership-breaker. Although her chances with the bat are often limited, she is capable of lifting the run-rate through deft placement and speed between the wickets.

	M	I	NO	Runs	HS	100s	50s	Avge	Ct	St	W	Avge	BB
Test	3	4	1	35	18*	0	0	11.66	3	0	7	19.85	3-9
Int'l limited-overs	29	11	5	103	44	0	0	17.16	4	0	37	18.70	4-31

MELANIE JONES *Right-hand bat* **Victoria**

A successful season for Victoria and Australia culminated in Jones's matchwinning innings in the final game of the Rose Bowl. Of West Indian descent, she is flamboyant with the bat and in the field, where her enthusiasm is contagious. Her fluent strokeplay conceals her power and her arrow-like returns continue to reap run-out rewards. At 32, Jones's recent batting performances have been notable for a consistency lacking in her early days. She perhaps needs to further temper her approach if she is to go beyond the forties and fifties she regularly produces.

	M	I	NO	Runs	HS	100s	50s	Avge	Ct	St	W	Avge	BB
Test	5	8	1	251	131	1	1	35.85	3	0	0	–	–
Int'l limited-overs	44	39	5	819	58	0	3	24.08	11	0	0	–	–

LISA KEIGHTLEY *Right-hand bat, right-arm off-spinner* **NSW**

After a season in retirement, Keightley returned to international competition and regained her place in time for the Rose Bowl. Alternating between the top and middle order, she enjoyed only modest success but offered valuable experience as part of the team's brains trust. Used extensively as an off-spinner in the National League, the 33-year-old Keightley was not required to repeat her exploits for Australia. Her long-term future remains unclear; while she would be an asset in the World Cup squad, the ambiguity of her potential role may weigh against her at the selection table. She won the inaugural Belinda Clark Medal as NSW's Player of the Year.

	M	I	NO	Runs	HS	100s	50s	Avge	Ct	St	W	Avge	BB
Test	7	10	0	362	90	0	3	36.20	4	0	0	–	–
Int'l limited-overs	59	56	12	1,867	156*	3	13	42.43	18	0	0	–	–

KAREN ROLTON *Left-hand bat, left-arm medium-pacer* **SA**

Acknowledged by most judges as the world's foremost woman cricketer, Rolton is the player most likely to turn a match with either bat or ball. She dominated last summer's Rose Bowl, finishing with a batting average of 197, and it was no accident that her lowest score – of 26 – coincided with Australia's only defeat. Rolton refined her game during the season. Her penchant for attacking the bowling early in her innings was replaced with a more patient philosophy that involved accumulating steadily before launching a final-overs onslaught. A key member of the bowling armoury, she was often asked to slow the momentum and break partnerships when the New Zealand batters were in full flow – a task she relished and usually achieved.

	M	I	NO	Runs	HS	100s	50s	Avge	Ct	St	W	Avge	BB
Test	9	13	4	685	209*	2	2	76.11	7	0	8	29.50	2-6
Int'l limited-overs	73	67	21	2,672	154*	5	20	58.08	13	0	56	21.83	3-9

CLEA SMITH *Right-arm medium-pacer*   **Victoria**

Smith had a quiet international season, going wicketless in the Rose Bowl but growing in guile and accuracy with her medium-pace. She is capable of bowling long spells and once into rhythm she can be truly miserly, forcing opposition batters to take risks in order to lift the run-rate. Her challenge now is to develop more variety, so that she can bowl effectively at the end of an innings as well as the beginning. When she can do this she will become a vital and effective cog in the Australian machine. Her astute cricket brain has already been rewarded with the vice-captaincy of Victoria.

	M	I	NO	Runs	HS	100s	50s	Avge	Ct	St	W	Avge	BB
Int'l limited-overs	15	3	1	17	6	0	0	8.50	3	0	12	27.00	3-17

LISA STHALEKAR *Right-arm off-spinner, right-hand bat*   **NSW**

Born in India, Sthalekar matured into an all-rounder during the season, though it was still her bowling that took centre-stage on most occasions. Sthalekar's control of flight, drift and pace variations often entices mistimed strokes, tempting batters to hit out in frustration. Preferring to bowl her 10 overs in a single spell, she rarely fails to take at least one wicket and routinely concedes fewer than three runs an over. She is dynamic in the field, manufacturing catches where no apparent chance exists. Doubt surrounds her ideal position in the batting order, particularly since the return of Lisa Keightley, and this uncertainty has perhaps reduced her effectiveness. However, she is likely to remain an integral part of the Australian team and to play a major part in the World Cup.

	M	I	NO	Runs	HS	100s	50s	Avge	Ct	St	W	Avge	BB
Test	2	4	1	144	120*	1	0	48.00	1	0	3	23.66	1-8
Int'l limited-overs	23	21	4	356	59	0	3	20.94	10	0	22	27.77	2-19

EMMA TWINING *Left-arm fast bowler*   **NSW**

By her own standards Twining had a disappointing international season, culminating in her relegation from opening the bowling to 12th or 13th man. Usually known for her nagging accuracy, Twining struggled to maintain line and length and was punished by the New Zealand batting line-up for even the smallest error. Her confidence suffered as frustration at her inconsistency grew. After a winter of reflection and training, Twining's determination to succeed will help her as she tries to force her way back into the team as the foil and, ultimately, heir to Cathryn Fitzpatrick.

	M	I	NO	Runs	HS	100s	50s	Avge	Ct	St	W	Avge	BB
Test	2	2	1	0	0*	0	0	0.00	0	0	6	13.50	3-32
Int'l limited-overs	16	3	2	2	2*	0	0	2.00	0	0	12	38.50	3-31

AUSTRALIAN WOMEN'S NATIONAL
CRICKET LEAGUE, 2003-2004

It was business as usual for the dominant players in the domestic competition, as Victoria and New South Wales asserted their superiority with a third consecutive top-two finish. The best-of-three title play-off was again held at the MCG, and for the first time in the eight-year competition a decider was needed. In a thrilling finish NSW wrested back the title they lost the previous year to win their seventh national championship. In the process they grabbed the lion's share of places in the Australian side.

South Australia maintained third place, thanks largely to the efforts of Karen Rolton and Kris Britt, while Western Australia managed their first victories in more than two seasons to finish fourth. Paul Wilson, the big-hearted former Australian Test fast bowler, has been named WA's coach for 2004-05. The most disappointing side were

Queensland, who finished winless for the first time under their rookie captain Melissa Bulow.

NSW's Lisa Sthalekar underlined her all-round versatility with strong performances with bat and ball, while the Victorians Belinda Clark and Cathryn Fitzpatrick finished top of the batting and bowling aggregates. NSW's Lisa Keightley, the veteran opener, added a new string to her bow with the introduction of nagging off-breaks. Her team-mate Shannon Cunneen forced her way into the national side on the back of some consistent efforts in the top order.

PRELIMINARY GAMES

At Allan Border Field, Albion, November 22, 2003. Victoria won by eight wickets. *Toss:* Victoria. Queensland 123 (C.R. Smith 2-13, N. Wood 2-18, C.L. Fitzpatrick 2-23, L.C. Broadfoot 2-25); Victoria 6 for 124 (B.J. Clark 51*, L.C. Broadfoot 36).

At WACA Ground, Perth, November 22, 2003. New South Wales won by 82 runs. *Toss:* New South Wales. New South Wales 6 for 266 (S.B. Cunneen 72, L.C. Sthalekar 59, M.A.J. Goszko 43; L.N. Stammers 2-44, C. Wong 2-52, A.J. Fahey 2-56); Western Australia 7 for 184 (D. Holden 76*, Z.J. Goss 36; L.C. Sthalekar 3-34, B.L. Calver 2-35).

At Allan Border Field, Albion, November 23, 2003. Victoria won by 63 runs (D/L method, revised target 179). *Toss:* Victoria. Victoria 8 for 177 (M. Pauwels 53, K.M. Applebee 30; M.L. White 2-36, L.J. Randall 2-49); Queensland 115 (J.C. Price 36; J. Dean 3-27, C.L. Fitzpatrick 2-17).

At WACA Ground, Perth, November 23, 2003. New South Wales won by 145 runs. *Toss:* New South Wales. New South Wales 8 for 284 (L.C. Sthalekar 108, L.M. Keightley 76; C. Wong 3-47); Western Australia 9 for 139 (E.P. Campbell 36; B.L. Calver 2-25, J. Hayes 2-26, L.C. Sthalekar 2-28).

At Bradman Oval, Bowral, December 6, 2003. New South Wales won by six wickets. *Toss:* New South Wales. South Australia 5 for 143 (K.L. Rolton 75; J. Hayes 2-18); New South Wales 4 for 144 (S.B. Cunneen 49, L.M. Keightley 49; E.M. Sampson 2-27).

At Princes Park No. 2, Melbourne, December 6, 2003. Victoria won by 72 runs. *Toss:* Victoria. Victoria 7 for 265 (B.J. Clark 104, L.C. Broadfoot 65; C. Kross 3-42); Western Australia 6 for 193 (Z.J. Goss 65, A. Gray 42).

At Bradman Oval, Bowral, December 7, 2003. South Australia won by 10 runs. *Toss:* South Australia. South Australia 5 for 165 (K.L. Rolton 72, K.L. Britt 35; E. Twining 2-30); New South Wales 155 (A.J. Blackwell 70*; K.L. Rolton 3-20, K.L. Britt 2-29).

At Princes Park No. 2, Melbourne, December 7, 2003. Western Australia won by two wickets. *Toss:* Victoria. Victoria 142 (B.J. Clark 32; D. Holden 4-17, C. Kross 3-37, P. Berthold 2-26); Western Australia 8 for 146 (L.N. Stammers 39).

At Allan Border Field, Albion, December 13, 2003. Western Australia won by five wickets. *Toss:* Queensland. Queensland 7 for 197 (J.C. Price 54, M.J. Bulow 42, T.E. Brown 33); Western Australia 5 for 198 (E.P. Campbell 93, Z.J. Goss 67; R.G. Browne 2-28).

At Allan Border Field, Albion, December 14, 2003. No result. *Toss:* Queensland. Queensland 178 (J. C. Price 44; C. Kross 3-27, C. Wong 2-22, R. Chappell 2-34); Western Australia 5 for 116 (Z. J. Goss 31; B. Matheson 3-19).

At A. H. Butler Oval, Frankston, December 20, 2003. Match tied. *Toss:* Victoria. New South Wales 8 for 144 (S. B. Cunneen 63; J. Franklin 2-19, C. R. Smith 2-25); Victoria 7 for 144 (B. J. Clark 43, L. C. Broadfoot 39; J. Hayes 2-25, S. J. Andrews 2-30).

At Adelaide Oval, Adelaide, December 20, 2003. South Australia won by six runs. *Toss:* South Australia. South Australia 8 for 157 (L. J. Randall 3-33); Queensland 9 for 151 (J. M. Purves 39, J. C. Price 33; O. J. Magno 3-18, K. L Rolton 2-30).

At A. H. Butler Oval, Frankston, December 21, 2003. Victoria won by four wickets. *Toss:* New South Wales. New South Wales 9 for 178 (L. M. Keightley 52; L. C. Broadfoot 2-32); Victoria 6 for 179 (B. J. Clark 61, M. Jones 38; E. Twining 2-44).

At Adelaide Oval, Adelaide, December 21, 2003. Match abandoned. *Toss:* South Australia. South Australia 1 for 5 v Queensland.

At Scott Reserve, Perth, January 3, 2004. South Australia won by seven wickets. *Toss:* Western Australia. Western Australia 9 for 167 (E. P. Campbell 69; O. J. Magno 2-18, K. L. Rolton 2-23); South Australia 3 for 168 (K. L. Rolton 49, J. L. Woerner 32, K. L. Britt 30*).

At Scott Reserve, Perth, January 4, 2004. South Australia won by 40 runs. *Toss:* South Australia. South Australia 3 for 225 (K. L. Rolton 102*, J. L. Woerner 45, K. L Britt 35*); Western Australia 9 for 185 (L. N. Stammers 70; O. J. Magno 4-19).

At Hurstville Oval, Sydney, January 17, 2004. New South Wales won by five wickets. *Toss:* Queensland. Queensland 106 (J. M. Purves 34; B. L. Calver 2-10, L. C. Sthalekar 2-14, L. M. Keightley 2-16); New South Wales 5 for 107 (L. M. Keightley 47; R. G. Browne 2-9).

At Kensington Oval, Pembroke, January 17, 2004. Victoria won by 25 runs. *Toss:* Victoria. Victoria 2 for 222 (B. J. Clark 98*, M. Jones 87*); South Australia 7 for 197 (K. L. Britt 66, O. J. Magno 32, J. L. Woerner 30; C. L. Fitzpatrick 3-37, J. Franklin 2-12).

At Olympic Stadium, Homebush, January 18, 2004. New South Wales won by five wickets. *Toss:* Queensland. Queensland 6 for 141 (M. L. White 35*, M. J. Bulow 33; L. M. Keightley 2-14 , L. C. Sthalekar 2-16); New South Wales 5 for 142 (L. C. Sthalekar 46, M. A. Winch 41; B. Matheson 2-20).

At Kensington Oval, Pembroke, January 18, 2004. Victoria won by 43 runs. *Toss:* Victoria. Victoria 162 (K. M. Applebee 33, M. Jones 32, L. C. Broadfoot 32; L. K. Ebsary 2-19, K. L. Britt 2-35); South Australia 119 (K. L. Britt 42; J. Dean 2-15, J. Franklin 2-40).

POINTS TABLE

	Played	Won	Lost	Tied	No Result	Bonus Points	Points	Net run-rate
Victoria	8	6	1	1	0	4	30	0.719
New South Wales	8	5	2	1	0	5	27	0.973
South Australia	8	4	3	0	1	0	18	-0.025
Western Australia	8	2	5	0	1	0	10	-0.836
Queensland	8	0	6	0	2	0	4	-0.857

Bonus points were awarded for scoring at a rate in excess of 25% faster than the opposition.

A second bonus point was awarded for scoring at a rate more than double that of the opposition.

FIRST FINAL
VICTORIA v NEW SOUTH WALES

At Melbourne Cricket Ground, Melbourne, January 31, 2004. Victoria won by six wickets. *Toss:* Victoria.

Victoria took a clear psychological advantage into the replay of the previous two seasons' finals, having remained unbeaten in their past five encounters with NSW – including the first National League tie in December. Against the backdrop of ground reconstruction work, a feeble batting effort from the visitors produced their lowest total in three seasons. Only Lisa Keightley, eighth out with the score on 125, provided any steel in a patient innings. As usual Cathryn Fitzpatrick made the early breakthroughs, but it was the left-arm spin of Jodie Dean and the leg-breaks of Megan Pauwels (née Foster) that tied the middle-order in knots and their feet to the crease. Victoria's reply was equally painstaking – only 76 runs were on the board after 35 overs – but the target was well within reach. An enterprising partnership between Fitzpatrick and Kelly Applebee, combining judicious running with big hitting, complemented a stoic display from Belinda Clark.

New South Wales

S. Cunneen b Fitzpatrick	4
L. M. Keightley c Clark b Pauwels	60
L. C. Sthalekar lbw b Fitzpatrick	5
M. A. Winch c and b Dean	19
A. J. Blackwell c A. Hunter b Dean	0
K. Blackwell run out (A. Hunter)	5
*J. Hayes st A. Hunter b Pauwels	7
†L. Coleman c A. Hunter b Pauwels	0

E. Twining lbw b Fitzpatrick	3
S. Millanta not out	1
B. L. Calver run out (Jones/A. Hunter)	0
B 5, l-b 4, w 15	24
	—
(45.1 overs)	128

S. Andrews did not bat.

Fall: 4 21 69 86 99 115 120 125 128 128

Bowling: Fitzpatrick 8–3–13–3; Smith 6–1–20–0; J. Hunter 4–1–14–0; Dean 10–0–27–2; Broadfoot 10–1–29–0; Franklin 3–0–9–0; Pauwels 4.1–0–7–3.

Victoria

*B. J. Clark c Millanta b Sthalekar	38
S. Edwards run out (Twining/Coleman)	3
L. C. Broadfoot run out (K. Blackwell/Sthalekar)	19
M. Jones c K. Blackwell b Sthalekar	6
K. Applebee not out	21

C. L. Fitzpatrick not out	27
B 6, w 7, n-b 2	15
	—
(48.3 overs)	(4 wkts) 129

Fall: 24 67 76 76

C. R. Smith, J. A. Franklin, †A. Hunter, J. Dean, M. Pauwels and J. Hunter did not bat.

Bowling: Twining 7–1–24–0; Andrews 5–1–18–0; Millanta 6–1–14–0; Hayes 7–1–18–0; Keightley 10–5–16–0; Sthalekar 10–5–19–2; Calver 3.3–0–14–0.

Umpires: A. J. Barrow and A. S. Ward.

SECOND FINAL
VICTORIA v NEW SOUTH WALES

At Melbourne Cricket Ground, Melbourne, February 1, 2004. New South Wales won by five wickets. *Toss:* New South Wales.

New South Wales took the series to a third game for the first time in the competition's history with a morale-boosting victory under overcast skies. Both captains tried new opening combinations with bat and ball, however Victoria struggled to maintain a healthy run-rate against a tight medium-pace and spin attack. Belinda Clark and Melanie Jones were cautious but persistent, the home side keeping wickets up their sleeve for a final flurry. But the middle and lower orders were unable to take full advantage of the platform. NSW's reply was anchored by Shannon Cunneen, but the highlight was an unbeaten 46-run partnership in 53 balls between the 20-year-old twins Alex and Kate Blackwell. Kate, the younger by several minutes, took heavy toll of Clea Smith, plundering three boundaries in two overs. Until then wickets had fallen steadily – four out of five to run-outs – but the target was reached off a rare wayward delivery from Cathryn Fitzpatrick.

Victoria

*B. J. Clark c Cunneen b Calver	52	J. Dean lbw b Twining	2
J. A. Franklin lbw b Andrews	5	S. Edwards c Hayes b Calver	1
L. C. Broadfoot c and b Andrews	0	C. R. Smith not out	4
M. Jones lbw b Sthalekar	39	B 2, l-b 6, w 2, n-b 2	12
K. Applebee run out (Sthalekar)	18		
C. L. Fitzpatrick b Calver	18	(50 overs) (8 wkts)	162
M. Pauwels not out	11	Fall: 22 25 104 108 134 148 151 154	

†A. Hunter, J. Hunter did not bat.

Bowling: Andrews 10–2–28–2; Hayes 7–2–15–0; Twining 10–3–29–1; Keightley 4–0–15–0; Sthalekar 10–1–30–1; Calver 9–0–37–3.

New South Wales

L. M. Keightley lbw b Fitzpatrick	1	A. J. Blackwell not out	13
S. Cunneen run out (Fitzpatrick)	48	L-b 6, w 16	22
L. C. Sthalekar run out (Jones/Broadfoot)	24		
M. A. Winch run out (Clark/Pauwels)	25	(48 overs) (5 wkts)	163
K. Blackwell not out	29	Fall: 4 42 105 113 117	
L. Poulton run out (Jones/Pauwels)	1		

†L. Coleman, E. Twining, B. L. Calver, *J. Hayes and S. Andrews did not bat.

Bowling: Fitzpatrick 9–5–18–1; Smith 9–3–28–0; Dean 7–0–33–0; J. Hunter 2–0–10–0; Broadfoot 6–0–24–0; Franklin 10–3–23–0; Pauwels 5–0–21–0.

Umpires: A. J. Barrow and A. S. Ward.

THIRD FINAL
VICTORIA v NEW SOUTH WALES

At Melbourne Cricket Ground, Melbourne, February 2, 2004. New South Wales won by three wickets. *Toss:* Victoria.

The deciding final was the best of the three, with both sides producing improved batting displays. A series of determined partnerships centred around Belinda Clark took Victoria comfortably passed the 200 mark, with the NSW attack looking strangely ineffectual on a wearing track. But they stuck to their task and some sharp fielding was rewarded with two excellent run-outs. The NSW innings also began solidly, Shannon Cunneen and Lisa Keightley bringing up their century opening stand in good time, and the middle order chipped in with sensible shot placement and clever running. Cathryn Fitzpatrick fought hard to swing the game back Victoria's way, but hers was a largely solitary effort, and the target was overhauled with eight balls to spare.

Victoria

L. C. Broadfoot run out (Cunneen/Coleman)	35	M. Pauwels not out	2
*B. J. Clark c Coleman b Keightley	115	B 3, l-b 4, w 2, n-b 3	12
M. Jones c Winch b Sthalekar	6		
K. Applebee run out (A.J. Blackwell/Coleman)	23	(50 overs)	(4 wkts) 217
C. L. Fitzpatrick not out	24	Fall: 85 115 167 215	

I. Noack, J. A. Franklin, †A. Hunter, N. Wood, C. R. Smith and J. Dean did not bat.

Bowling: Andrews 3–1–17–0; Hayes 10–1–36–0; Twining 8–1–41–0; Sthalekar 10–1–27–1; A.J. Blackwell 5–0–26–0; Keightley 8–0–26–1; Calver 6–0–37–0.

New South Wales

S. Cunneen lbw b Pauwels	54	*J. Hayes b Fitzpatrick	10
L. M. Keightley c Clark b Broadfoot	75	†L. Coleman not out	3
L. C. Sthalekar c Jones b Pauwels	3		
M. A. Winch run out (A Hunter/Broadfoot)	9	B 4, l-b 4, w 12, n-b 1	21
K. Blackwell lbw b Fitzpatrick	16		
L. Poulton b Fitzpatrick	11	(48.4 overs)	(7 wkts) 218
A. J. Blackwell not out	16	Fall: 119 128 150 160 178 189 204	

B. L. Calver, E. Twining and S. Andrews did not bat.

Bowling: Fitzpatrick 9.4–2–38–3; Smith 7–0–20–0; Dean 3–0–15–0; Broadfoot 8–0–46–1; Franklin 4–0–22–0; Wood 7–1–38–0; Pauwels 10–0–31–2.

Umpires: A.J. Barrow and A.S. Ward.

MOST RUNS, 2003-04

	M	I	NO	R	HS	100s	50s	Avge	S-R
B. J. Clark (Vic)	11	11	2	622	115	2	4	69.11	63.99
L. M. Keightley (NSW)	11	11	0	394	76	0	4	35.82	55.97
S. Cunneen (NSW)	11	11	0	336	72	0	3	30.55	55.81
L. C. Sthalekar (NSW)	11	11	0	313	108	1	1	28.45	73.82
K. L. Rolton (SAust)	8	8	2	302	102*	1	2	50.33	65.65
E. P. Campbell (WAust)	8	8	0	281	93	0	2	35.13	54.88
L. C. Broadfoot (Vic)	11	11	0	262	65	0	1	23.82	53.47
M. Jones (Vic)	11	11	1	248	87*	0	1	24.80	60.19
K. L. Britt (SAust)	8	7	1	235	66	0	1	39.17	56.63
Z. J. Goss (WAust)	8	8	0	234	67	0	2	29.25	62.23
D. Holden (WAust)	8	8	1	203	76*	0	1	29.00	54.42

MOST WICKETS, 2003-04

	M	O	Mdns	R	W	BB	5W/i	Avge	RPO
C. L. Fitzpatrick (Vic)	11	96	21	275	19	3-13	0	14.47	2.86
L. C. Sthalekar (NSW)	11	97	17	267	14	3-34	0	19.07	2.75
B. L. Calver (NSW)	10	72.2	12	226	12	3-37	0	18.83	3.12
C. Wong (W Aust)	8	72.1	8	297	12	3-47	0	24.75	4.11
C. G. Kross (W Aust)	6	59	12	225	11	3-27	0	20.45	3.81
O.J. Magno (S Aust)	8	34	8	84	9	4-19	0	9.33	2.47
C. R. Smith (Vic)	11	95.5	25	262	9	2-25	0	29.11	2.73
K. L. Rolton (S Aust)	8	69	16	190	9	3-20	0	21.11	2.75
E. Twining (NSW)	11	96	17	314	9	2-30	0	34.89	3.27

AUSTRALIA v NEW ZEALAND
ROSE BOWL SERIES, 2003-04

Twelve months out from the 2005 World Cup, this series was critical for both sides as they looked to fine-tune their combinations and game-plans. The Australian selectors dropped two bombshells, omitting the long-term wicketkeeper Julia Price in favour of Leonie Coleman, and summoning Shannon Cunneen from outside the national squad. Both performed creditably, Cunneen underlying her versatility by deputising for Coleman when the latter suffered food poisoning. Lisa Keightley renounced her retirement and was reinstated, but did not immediately resume her opening partnership with Belinda Clark.

The series was comprehensively won 5-1 by Australia. It was contested on a home-and-away basis, beginning in New Zealand and concluding in Sydney, Melbourne and Hobart. Dominant performances came from the stalwarts Clark, Karen Rolton, Melanie Jones and Cathryn Fitzpatrick. They received good support from the younger brigade, most notably Alex Blackwell and Kris Britt. New Zealand relied heavily on the all-rounder Haidee Tiffen, particularly during the Australian leg.

AUSTRALIAN SQUAD

B. J. Clark (Vic) *(captain)*, K. L. Rolton (S Aust) *(vice-captain)*, A. J. Blackwell (NSW), K. L. Britt (ACT/SAust), L. A. Coleman (NSW), S. B. Cunneen (NSW), C. L. Fitzpatrick (Vic), J. Hayes (NSW), M. Jones (Vic), L. M. Keightley (NSW), C. R. Smith (Vic), L. C. Sthalekar (NSW), E. Twining (NSW).

BATTING

	M	I	NO	R	HS	100s	50s	Avge	Ct	S-R
K. L. Rolton (Aust)	6	6	4	394	102*	1	3	197.00	1	73.64
B. J. Clark (Aust)	6	6	0	214	120	1	0	35.67	1	66.05
M. Jones (Aust)	6	6	1	206	57	0	2	41.20	0	79.84
H. M. Tiffen (NZ)	6	6	2	195	60*	0	2	48.75	1	60.00
A. L. Mason (NZ)	6	6	0	142	33	0	0	23.67	2	78.45
M. A. M. Lewis (NZ)	6	6	0	114	33	0	0	19.00	2	40.71
M. F. Fahey (NZ)	6	6	0	106	41	0	0	17.67	3	33.65
E. C. Drumm (NZ)	5	5	0	104	28	0	0	20.80	0	57.78
R. J. Rolls (NZ)	6	6	0	84	42	0	0	14.00	2/1	64.62
L. C. Sthalekar (Aust)	6	5	0	68	35	0	0	13.60	5	45.95
K. L. Britt (Aust)	6	5	2	67	34*	0	0	22.33	6	74.44
N. J. Browne (NZ)	4	4	1	60	24	0	0	20.00	0	52.17
B. H. McNeill (NZ)	5	5	2	55	25	0	0	18.33	2	42.64
S. B. Cunneen (Aust)	4	3	0	49	39	0	0	16.33	1	44.95
L. M. Keightley (Aust)	5	3	0	40	20	0	0	13.33	2	35.71
A. J. Blackwell (Aust)	3	2	2	37	22*	0	0	–	0	80.43
L. E. Milliken (NZ)	6	4	3	30	14*	0	0	30.00	0	45.45
H. M. Watson (NZ)	3	3	1	28	23*	0	0	14.00	2	77.78
S. K. Burke (NZ)	5	3	2	11	8*	0	0	11.00	1	84.62
L. A. Coleman (Aust)	5	1	1	11	11*	0	0	–	1/2	35.48
C. L. Fitzpatrick (Aust)	6	2	1	10	9	0	0	10.00	1	29.41
C. R. Smith (Aust)	3	1	0	6	6	0	0	6.00	0	46.15
R. J. Steele (NZ)	6	1	0	2	2	0	0	2.00	2	40.00
J. Hayes (Aust)	6	1	0	1	1	0	0	1.00	2	5.88
A. J. Green (NZ)	2	1	0	0	0	0	0	0.00	0	0.00
E. Twining (Aust)	4	0	–	–	–	–	–	–	0	–

BOWLING

	M	O	Mdns	R	W	BB	5W/i	Avge	RPO
C. L. Fitzpatrick (Aust)	6	58	7	178	15	4-11	0	11.87	3.07
L. C. Sthalekar (Aust)	6	57	8	166	9	2-19	0	18.44	2.91
J. Hayes (Aust)	6	57	10	154	8	4-31	0	19.25	2.70
B. H. McNeill (NZ)	5	42	4	165	5	2-42	0	33.00	3.93
K. L. Britt (Aust)	6	27	3	116	5	3-26	0	23.20	4.30
L. E. Milliken (NZ)	6	46	4	214	5	2-21	0	42.80	4.65
R. J. Steele (NZ)	6	59	7	189	4	2-27	0	47.25	3.20
K. L. Rolton (Aust)	6	37	7	135	4	2-22	0	33.75	3.65
S. K. Burke (NZ)	5	44	4	166	4	1-26	0	41.50	3.77
A. L. Mason (NZ)	6	44.5	4	187	3	1-19	0	62.33	4.17
H. M. Watson (NZ)	3	22.2	0	106	3	2-19	0	35.33	4.75
E. Twining (Aust)	4	35	3	148	2	1-26	0	74.00	4.23
A. J. Green (NZ)	2	15	1	71	1	1-44	0	71.00	4.73
N. J. Browne (NZ)	4	11	0	64	1	1-13	0	64.00	5.82
A. J. Blackwell (Aust)	3	2	0	6	0	–	0	–	3.00
C. R. Smith (Aust)	3	23	6	70	0	–	0	–	3.04

NEW ZEALAND v AUSTRALIA

First Limited-Overs International

At Eden Park Outer Oval, Auckland, February 11, 2004. Australia won by 78 runs. *Toss:* Australia. *Limited-overs international debut:* L. A. Coleman, S. B. Cunneen.

The venue was different but the outcome familiar as Australia took the early initiative in the six-match series. For the first time in four years the Rose Bowl returned to the North Island, but the move did not stop the tourists from maintaining the superiority they have held over the world champions for the past three seasons. Karen Rolton led the way with her third century against New Zealand. She hit 11 fours in what was a measured performance, determined to keep her wicket intact and work the ball around as the pivot of the innings. Belinda Clark and Melanie Jones were the perfect foils and Kris Britt added the finishing touches, helping Rolton blast 73 in the final nine overs. Cathryn Fitzpatrick once again mesmerised the Kiwi top order, dismissing the dangerous Rebecca Rolls and Emily Drumm, and the home side never looked threatening. Britt completed a fine double when she demolished the middle order, Fitzpatrick coming back to finish with four wickets.

Australia

*B. J. Clark c Rolls b Mason	29	K. L. Britt not out	34
L. C. Sthalekar c Fahey b Milliken	14	L-b 2, w 4, n-b 2	8
K. L. Rolton not out	102		
M. Jones c Rolls b Burke	36	(50 overs, 188 mins) (4 wkts)	225
S. B. Cunneen c Lewis b Green	2	Fall: 19 86 149 152	

L. M. Keightley, J. Hayes, †L. A. Coleman, E. Twining and C. L. Fitzpatrick did not bat.

Bowling: Milliken 9–1–68–1; Burke 10–1–38–1; Browne 2–0–12–0; Green 9–0–44–1; Steele 10–1–20–0; Mason 10–1–41–1.

New Zealand

†R. J. Rolls c Coleman b Fitzpatrick	7	L. E. Milliken not out	5
M. F. Fahey b Sthalekar	4	R. J. Steele b Fitzpatrick	2
E. C. Drumm b Fitzpatrick	12	A. J. Green lbw b Fitzpatrick	0
M. A. M. Lewis run out (Hayes/Coleman)	33		
H. M. Tiffen b Britt	39	B 1, l-b 3, w 10	14
A. L. Mason c Clark b Britt	26		
N. J. Browne st Coleman b Hayes	5	(46 overs, 165 mins)	147
S. K. Burke c Cunneen b Britt	0	Fall: 11 11 32 79 122 135 139 139 147 147	

Bowling: Fitzpatrick 8–3–11–4; Twining 7–1–33–0; Sthalekar 10–1–45–1; Hayes 9–1–21–1; Rolton 6–0–7–0; Britt 6–1–26–3.

Umpires: D. B. Cowie and P. D. Jones.
TV Umpire: I. W. Shine.

NEW ZEALAND v AUSTRALIA
Second Limited-Overs International

At Westpac Park, Hamilton, February 15, 2004. Australia won by eight wickets. *Toss:* New Zealand. *Limited-overs international debut:* B. H. McNeill.

Despite losing two players to food poisoning and New Zealand managing to bat out their full allotment of overs, Australia strolled past the home side. Shannon Cunneen deputised more than competently for the ill keeper Leonie Coleman, while Kate Blackwell became an unlikely 12th man in place of her twin sister Alex, whom she had come to watch. Batting first on a slow-paced pitch, New Zealand's top-order batters made starts but only Maia Lewis reached 30, preventing the build-up of any momentum. For the most part the pace of Cathryn Fitzpatrick and spin of Lisa Sthalekar held sway. The early loss of Belinda Clark was nothing more than a hiccup in the Australian chase, which was again anchored by Karen Rolton, and they cruised to victory 11.1 overs early.

New Zealand

†R. J. Rolls b Twining	19	B. H. McNeill lbw b Fitzpatrick	6
M. F. Fahey b Sthalekar	24	L. E. Milliken b Fitzpatrick	0
E. C. Drumm c Britt b Sthalekar	26	S. K. Burke not out	3
*M. A. M. Lewis b Fitzpatrick	30	B 3, l-b 4, w 4	11
H. M. Tiffen b Hayes	0		
A. L. Mason run out (Sthalekar)	21	(50 overs) (8 wkts)	152
N. J. Browne not out	12	Fall: 35 63 73 84 122 131 147 147	

R. J. Steele did not bat.

Bowling: Fitzpatrick 10–0–35–3; Twining 9–1–26–1; Smith 5–2–13–0; Sthalekar 10–3–20–2; Hayes 8–3–20–1; Britt 4–0–23–0; Rolton 4–1–8–0.

Australia

L. C. Sthalekar lbw b Browne	35	L-b 7, w 8, n-b 2	17
*B. J. Clark b Milliken	1		
K. L. Rolton not out	60	(38.5 overs) (2 wkts)	153
M. Jones not out	40	Fall: 4 87	

K. L. Britt, L. M. Keightley, †S. B. Cunneen, C. L. Fitzpatrick, J. Hayes, C. R. Smith and E. Twining did not bat.

Bowling: Milliken 7–1–26–1; Burke 8–1–16–0; Mason 4.5–0–20–0; Steele 9–0–45–0; McNeill 6–0–26–0; Browne 4–0–13–1.

Umpires: K. Cross and D. M. Quested.

NEW ZEALAND v AUSTRALIA
Third Limited-Overs International

At Westpac Park, Hamilton, February 17, 2004. Australia won by 83 runs. *Toss:* New Zealand.

Australia completed a clean sweep of the New Zealand leg, Karen Rolton remaining unbeaten for the third consecutive innings and Australia racking up their third-highest total against the Kiwis. This time Rolton took second stage to a rejuvenated Belinda Clark, who was caught at deep square leg in the second last over for an elegant, confident century. The pair were merciless and precise in their demolition of an attack which struggled to exploit the favourable conditions. Clark hit 13 fours in her 148-ball knock. Cathryn Fitzpatrick again did the damage at the top of the New Zealand order, and at 6 for 84 in the 30th over the game was effectively up. The lower order refused to capitulate so easily, adding some respectability to the final total. But the Rose Bowl would stay in Australia's hands for another season.

Australia

*B. J. Clark c Fahey b Burke	120		
L. M. Keightley c and b McNeill	20	L-b 4, w 12, n-b 2	18
K. L. Rolton not out	80		
M. Jones b McNeill	2	(50 overs)	(3 wkts) 241
K. L. Britt not out	1	Fall: 39 233 237	

L. C. Sthalekar, A. J. Blackwell, C. L. Fitzpatrick, J. Hayes, †L. A. Coleman and E. Twining did not bat.

Bowling: Milliken 8–0–35–0; Burke 10–1–51–1; McNeill 9–1–42–2; Steele 10–2–41–0; Mason 10–1–43–0; Browne 3–0–25–0.

New Zealand

†R. J. Rolls c Britt b Fitzpatrick	15	B. H. McNeill b Twining	25
M. F. Fahey b Fitzpatrick	0	L. E. Milliken not out	14
E. C. Drumm b Rolton	28	S. K. Burke not out	8
*M. A. M. Lewis c and b Hayes	23	B 5, l-b 7, n-b 1	13
H. M. Tiffen b Rolton	0		
A. L. Mason b Sthalekar	13	(50 overs)	(8 wkts) 158
N. J. Browne c Sthalekar b Britt	19	Fall: 1 34 52 60 84 84 110 146	

R. J. Steele did not bat.

Bowling: Fitzpatrick 10–2–23–2; Twining 9–0–46–1; Hayes 10–2–19–1; Rolton 6–2–22–2; Sthalekar 7–1–21–1; Britt 6–0–16–1; Blackwell 2–0–6–0.

Umpires: K. Cross and D. M. Quested.

AUSTRALIA v NEW ZEALAND
Fourth Limited-Overs International

At Bankstown Oval, Sydney, February 21, 2004. New Zealand won by 20 runs. *Toss:* New Zealand.

The trophy was out of reach but New Zealand reminded Australia they could not afford to relax, snatching a hard-fought victory in the first match of the return leg. Such an outcome had seemed unlikely until late in the second innings. Both sides accumulated disappointing totals on an unresponsive pitch; the key difference lay in the spirited innings of Haidee Tiffen. She was the inspiration as the Kiwis piled up 45 runs – almost a third of their total – in the final five overs. Tiffen was particularly severe on Karen Rolton, whose last two overs cost 21 runs, and even the usually unflappable Cathryn Fitzpatrick was dealt with harshly. Belinda Clark showed a rare lapse in concentration, pulling a long-hop to mid-wicket first ball, but Lisa Keightley and Rolton re-asserted Australia's ascendancy with a 51-run stand. The subsequent batters failed to hang on to the initiative, perhaps succumbing to an expectation that the later order would push them through. The required run-rate did not climb above four an over until the final 10. But by then the Australians had lost too many wickets and run out of steam.

New Zealand

†R. J. Rolls c Britt b Fitzpatrick	1	H. M. Watson b Fitzpatrick		4
M. F. Fahey st Coleman b Sthalekar	14	B. H. McNeill not out		9
E. C. Drumm c Sthalekar b Hayes	25	B 1, w 4		5
*M. A. M. Lewis c Britt b Sthalekar	8			
H. M. Tiffen not out	52	(50 overs, 162 mins)	(6 wkts)	151
A. L. Mason c Sthalekar b Fitzpatrick	33	Fall: 2 41 43 54 108 119		

L. E. Milliken, S. K. Burke and R. J. Steele did not bat.

Bowling: Fitzpatrick 10–0–35–3; Smith 10–3–19–0; Hayes 10–2–31–1; Sthalekar 10–2–19–2; Rolton 7–3–33–0; Britt 3–1–13–0.

Australia

L. M. Keightley b Watson	19	J. Hayes lbw b Milliken		1
*B. J. Clark c Watson b Burke	0	†L. A. Coleman not out		11
K. L. Rolton c Fahey b Steele	26	C. R. Smith c McNeill b Watson		6
M. Jones c Steele b Mason	17			
K. L. Britt lbw b McNeill	19	L-b 4, w 4, n-b 3		11
L. C. Sthalekar c Lewis b Milliken	4			
S. B. Cunneen run out (Watson/McNeill)	8	(46.4 overs, 169 mins)		131
C. L. Fitzpatrick run out (Drumm)	9	Fall: 0 51 51 79 87 100 100 106 114 131		

Bowling: Milliken 10–2–21–2; Burke 7–0–26–1; Mason 6–2–19–1; McNeill 7–1–10–1; Steele 10–3–32–1; Watson 6.4–0–19–2.

Umpires: S. A. Reed and R. J. Tucker.

AUSTRALIA v NEW ZEALAND
FIFTH LIMITED-OVERS INTERNATIONAL

At Albert Ground, Melbourne, February 25, 2004. Australia won by 40 runs. *Toss:* Australia.

Another much-improved performance had New Zealand poised to win their second game in a row, but the Australians ultimately held their nerve to take an unbeatable 4-1 lead. Batting first, as is their preference, Australia reached their fourth-highest total against New Zealand with Karen Rolton narrowly missing out on a second century of the series. She added 116 for the third wicket with Melanie Jones and was joined by Alex Blackwell for a sparkling cameo at the end. Rolton had continued her anchorwoman role for most of the innings, before flinging off her self-imposed shackles in the final 10 overs. By the end her unbeaten 95 had occupied only 108 balls, with five fours and a six. New Zealand's reply began promisingly with their first half-century opening partnership of the series. But the momentum soon slowed, with Maria Fahey and Nicola Browne tied down by an accurate attack. With 12 overs left the asking rate had jumped to almost 10 an over. Aimee Mason and Haidee Tiffen launched an assault of 46 runs off only 30 balls, before crucial breakthroughs by Julie Hayes and Rolton halted the Kiwi challenge.

Australia

*B. J. Clark st Rolls b Mason	38	A. J. Blackwell not out	15
L. C. Sthalekar lbw b McNeill	11		
K. L. Rolton not out	95	L-b 4, w 11	15
M. Jones c Mason b Steele	57		
K. L. Britt c and b Steele	7	(50 overs, 191 mins) (5 wkts)	239
L. M. Keightley run out (Fahey)	1	Fall: 48 69 185 198 204	

C. L. Fitzpatrick, J. Hayes, †L. A. Coleman and C. R. Smith did not bat.

Bowling: Milliken 6–0–35–0; Green 6–1–27–0; Steele 10–0–27–2; McNeill 10–1–52–1; Mason 7–0–37–1; Watson 9–0–43–0; Browne 2–0–14–0.

New Zealand

†R. J. Rolls c Britt b Hayes	42	H. M. Watson b Hayes	1
M. F. Fahey c Keightley b Sthalekar	23	L. E. Milliken not out	11
H. M. Tiffen c Keightley b Fitzpatrick	44		
*M. A. M. Lewis c Britt b Hayes	1	B 3, l-b 4, w 4, n-b 1	12
N. J. Browne c Fitzpatrick b Sthalekar	24		
A. L. Mason b Hayes	30	(50 overs) (7 wkts)	199
B. H. McNeill not out	11	Fall: 64 73 74 126 172 174 181	

A. J. Green, R. J. Steele did not bat.

Bowling: Fitzpatrick 10–0–37–1; Smith 8–1–38–0; Sthalekar 10–1–38–2; Hayes 10–2–31–4; Britt 5–1–19–0; Rolton 7–1–29–0.

Umpires: P. R. Reiffel and A. J. Soulsby.

AUSTRALIA v NEW ZEALAND
Sixth Limited-Overs International

At Bellerive Oval, Hobart, February 27, 2004. Australia won by four wickets. *Toss:* New Zealand.

Again New Zealand were competitive, but again Australia's all-round strength and versatility were enough to secure a comfortable victory and 5-1 series margin. After Rebecca Rolls succumbed to Cathryn Fitzpatrick's third ball, the victim of an excellent diving catch by Lisa Sthalekar, Haidee Tiffen once more led the way for the Kiwis with a punishing knock. Julie Hayes and Sthalekar kept scoring to a minimum during the middle stages, but Tiffen – with good support from Aimee Mason and Helen Watson – lifted the run-rate in the closing stages. New Zealand fell only four runs short of the psychologically important 200 barrier. Australia promoted Shannon Cunneen to open the batting and, while initially slow, she grew in confidence as the innings progressed. Melanie Jones was the star, her stylish half-century completing a successful series with the bat. She and Alex Blackwell steered the Australians home with eight balls to spare.

Player of the Series: K. L. Rolton.

New Zealand

†R. J. Rolls c Sthalekar b Fitzpatrick	0	B. H. McNeill c and b Rolton	4
M. F. Fahey st L. C. Coleman b Britt	41	H. M. Watson not out	23
E. C. Drumm c L. C. Coleman b Fitzpatrick	13	L-b 6, w 11	17
*M. A. M. Lewis c and b Sthalekar	19		
H. M. Tiffen not out	60	(50 overs, 174 mins) (6 wkts)	196
A. L. Mason c Hayes b Rolton	19	Fall: 0 22 59 100 129 145	

L. E. Milliken, R. J. Steele and S. K. Burke did not bat.

Bowling: Fitzpatrick 10–2–37–2; Twining 10–1–43–0; Sthalekar 10–0–23–1; Hayes 10–0–32–0; Britt 3–0–19–1; Rolton 7–0–36–2.

Australia

*B. J. Clark lbw b McNeill	26	A. J. Blackwell not out	22
S. B. Cunneen c Tiffen b Steele	39	C. L. Fitzpatrick not out	1
K. L. Rolton c Watson b Millken	31	L-b 3, w 7, n-b 4	14
M. Jones c Burke b Watson	54		
K. L. Britt c Mason b Burke	6	(48.4 overs, 187 mins) (6 wkts)	197
L. C. Sthalekar run out (Watson/Rolls)	4	Fall: 38 101 110 124 132 196	

J. Hayes, †L. A. Coleman and E. Twining did not bat.

Bowling: Milliken 6–0–29–1; Burke 9–1–35–1; McNeill 10–1–35–1; Steele 10–1–24–1; Watson 6.4–0–44–1; Mason 7–0–27–0.

Umpires: B. W. Jackman and K. J. McGinniss.

AUSTRALIAN UNDER-23s IN NEW ZEALAND, 2003-04

The next generation of Australian players dominated their biennial joust with New Zealand's 2nd XI on the South Island, while the senior team were duplicating their efforts in the north. The 3-1 series margin was built on consistent batting and a buccaneering run-rate of more than four an over throughout the tour. Kate Blackwell, Leah Poulton and Julie Woerner led the way, with useful contributions from Kelly Applebee, Jodie Purves, Sarah Andrews and Sarah Aley. Andrews, Aley and Kirsten Pike proved the most effective with the ball. Poulton continued to grow in confidence and shrewdness as captain. She and Blackwell won promotion to the senior squad – and it should not be too long before several of their young team-mates join them.

AUSTRALIAN UNDER-23s TOURING PARTY:

L. J. Poulton (NSW) (*captain*), S. E. Aley (NSW), S. J. Andrews (NSW), K. M. Applebee (Vic), K. A. Blackwell (NSW), R. G. Browne (Qld), L. K. Ebsary (S Aust), K. E. Pike (Qld), J. M Purves (Qld), L. J. Randall (Qld), E. M. Sampson (S Aust), L. N. Stammers (W Aust), J. L. Woerner (NT/S Aust).

At Bert Sutcliffe Oval, Lincoln, February 8, 2004. Australia Youth won by 13 runs (D/L method). *Toss:* New Zealand A. Australia Youth 7 for 242 (K. A. Blackwell 69; S. Tsukigawa 2-31, H. M. Watson 2-38); New Zealand A 7 for 229 (H. M. Watson 85*, K. L. Pulford 30; L. K. Ebsary 2-34, L. J. Randall 2-40).

At Bert Sutcliffe Oval, Lincoln, February 9, 2004. Australia Youth won by 106 runs. *Toss:* Australia Youth. Australia Youth 5 for 276 (L. J. Poulton 75, J. L. Woerner 71, S. E. Aley 40, K. A. Blackwell 34; S. Tsukigawa 2-55); New Zealand A 170 (P. B. Flannery 31; S. E. Aley 3-29, L. G. Randall 2-26, R. G. Browne 2-36).

At Bert Sutcliffe Oval, Lincoln, February 11, 2004. Australia Youth won by six wickets. *Toss:* New Zealand A. New Zealand A 8 for 144 (H. M. Watson 39*; K. E. Pike 3-14, S. J. Andrews 2-25); Australia Youth 4 for 145 (K. A. Blackwell 36; K. L. Pulford 3-38).

At Bert Sutcliffe Oval, Lincoln, February 12, 2004. New Zealand A won by six wickets. *Toss:* Australia Youth. Australia Youth 214 (S. J. Andrews 54, J. M. Purves 47; K. L. Pulford 3-44); New Zealand A 4 for 215 (P. B. Flannery 76*, R. Kember 71; K. A. Blackwell 2-41).

AUSTRALIAN WOMEN'S UNDER-19s, 2003-04

New South Wales easily defeated Queensland to win the Betty Wilson Shield in Hobart for the seventh time in eight years. They were clearly the outstanding team, seldom in trouble and not losing a wicket until the fifth round. Laura Wright was involved in consecutive century opening partnerships – with Kirsty Riley and Kate Owen – and went on to average 224 for the tournament. Victoria, who finished third, compiled a competition-record 6 for 389 against the Australian Capital Territory, with Claire Lavery hitting the only century of the championships.

Batters did not have it all their own way. Victoria demolished Western Australia for 27, then passed their minuscule target inside four overs. NSW bettered that by dismissing Tasmania for 24, while the ACT were tottering at 9 for 15 against Queensland before being rescued from complete humiliation by the last-wicket pair. The Queensland off-spinner Laura Bates was the competition's leading bowler with 13 wickets. The Victorian Rachel Haynes, who averaged 53 with the bat and took 6 for 13 against WA with her left-arm mediums, was the outstanding all-rounder. Wright and Queensland's Kasee Marxsen were named joint players of the series. –GREG McKIE

ROUND ONE

Australian Capital Territory 6 for 144 (E. Howell 38; N. Iles 2-21) lost to South Australia 4 for 146 (J. Woerner 74*; J. Livesay 2-21) by six wickets.

Tasmania 9 for 80 (L. Telha 13; K. Pike 2-7) lost to Queensland 1 for 83 (K. Marxsen 47) by nine wickets.

Western Australia 27 (R. Haynes 6-13) lost to Victoria 0 for 29 by 10 wickets.

ROUND TWO

Australian Capital Territory 9 for 101 (M. Clisby 18; L Shave 4-12) lost to Western Australia 2 for 102 (L. Stammers 37*) by eight wickets.

South Australia 9 for 187 (E. Sampson 37; C. Hulett 3-37) lost to Victoria 7 for 188 (E. Byrnes 27; F. McDonald 4-23) by three wickets.

Tasmania 24 (R. Farrell 4-1) lost to New South Wales 0 for 25 by 10 wickets.

ROUND THREE

Australian Capital Territory 101 (J. Moyes 18; S. Coote 4-8) lost to New South Wales 0 for 102 (L. Wright 51*, K. Riley 36*) by 10 wickets.

Queensland 9 for 131 (D. Hollis 37; B. Binch 3-19) defeated Victoria 111 (J. Ronalds 13; L. Hinze 3-17, L. Bates 3-23) by 20 runs.

Western Australia 232 (L. Stammers 55, H. Andrews 43; E. Fitzgerald 2-24) defeated Tasmania 97 (L. Telha 31; C. Brough 6-17) by 135 runs.

ROUND FOUR

Victoria 5 for 159 (R. Haynes 45*; K. Riley 2-29) lost to New South Wales 0 for 161 (K. Owens 80*, L. Wright 68*) by 10 wickets.

Queensland 7 for 247 (D. Hollis 78, K. Marxsen 64; M. Flett 3-39) defeated Australian Capital Territory 37 (L. Bates 4-12, K. Pike 2-0) by 210 runs.

Tasmania 92 (L. Telha 26; N. Iles 6-20) lost to South Australia 2 for 93 (K. Murphy 39*) by eight wickets.

ROUND FIVE

Australian Capital Territory 109 (E. Howell 25; K. Beams 6-21) lost to Tasmania 3 for 113 (J. McKenzie 30*; M. Clisby 3-39) by seven wickets.

South Australia 88 (J. Woerner 34; L. Bates 3-8) lost to Queensland 4 for 89 (K. Marxsen 46) by six wickets.

New South Wales 4 for 222 (S. Hungerford 60*, C. Hall 55*) defeated Western Australia 162 (L. Shaw 30; R. Farrell 4-19) by 60 runs.

ROUND SIX

Tasmania 49 (E. Nadj 2-2, D. Bromley 2-3) lost to Victoria 1 for 51 by nine wickets.
South Australia 138 (J. Woerner 50; C. Hall 4-18) lost to New South Wales 1 for 141 (L. Wright 87*) by nine wickets.

Queensland 5 for 225 (A. Christie 69, L. Bates 68*, K. Marxsen 44; H. Hyder 3-38) defeated Western Australia 82 (H. Andrews 15; C. McRae 2-4, J. Rowlands 2-13, K. Pike 2-25) by 143 runs.

ROUND SEVEN

Victoria 6 for 389 (C. Lavery 110, R. Haynes 88; A. Jason-Jones 2-28) defeated Australian Capital Territory 75 (E. Howell 17; J. de Tarczynski 3-22) by 314 runs.

South Australia 122 (E. Sampson 32; C. Brough 4-23, H. Hyder 3-15) lost to Western Australia 6 for 124 (L. Shave 50*; E. Sampson 3-11) by four wickets.

Queensland 9 for 132 (S. Harris 27*; K. Riley 3-28) lost to New South Wales 4 for 133 (R. Farrell 36, K. Owen 35) by six wickets.

POINTS TABLE

	Played	Won	Lost	Tied	No Result	Bonus Points	Points	Net Run-Rate
New South Wales	6	6	0	0	0	9	33	2.230
Queensland	6	5	1	0	0	8	28	1.880
Victoria	6	4	2	0	0	6	22	2.075
Western Australia	6	3	3	0	0	4	16	-0.343
South Australia	6	2	4	0	0	3	11	-0.277
Tasmania	6	1	5	0	0	1	5	-2.270
Australian Capital Territory	6	0	6	0	0	0	0	-3.560

MOST RUNS

	M	I	NO	R	HS	100s	50s	Avge	S-R
L. Wright (NSW)	6	5	4	224	87*	0	3	224.00	77.24
K. Marxsen (Qld)	6	6	0	205	64	0	1	34.16	83.33
J. Woerner (S Aust)	6	6	1	182	74*	0	2	36.40	60.86
R. Haynes (Vic)	6	4	1	159	88	0	1	53.00	63.60
C. Lavery (Vic)	6	4	1	150	110	1	0	50.00	82.41

MOST WICKETS

	M	O	Mdns	R	W	BB	5W/i	Avge	RPO
L. Bates (Qld)	6	49.1	8	111	13	4-12	0	8.53	2.25
K. Riley (NSW)	6	45.3	10	101	12	3-28	0	8.41	2.21
R. Haynes (Vic)	6	46	4	129	12	6-13	1	10.75	2.80
R. Farrell (NSW)	6	38	3	105	11	4-1	0	9.54	2.00
C. Brough (WAust)	6	42	5	133	11	6-17	0	12.09	3.50

AUSTRALIAN WOMEN'S UNDER-17s, 2003-04

Victoria crept unbeaten through the early rounds of the Australian Under-17s championships in Adelaide, only to lose the final – and the tournament – to Queensland. After the Banana Benders posted a competitive total, everything hinged on the performance of Tammy Norquay, Victoria's captain, who had held their batting together in the previous matches. She fell cheaply and Victoria tumbled to defeat. Norquay was named Player of the Series and won the Australian Cricketers' Association's inaugural youth development award; her prize was the opportunity to spend time at the Centre of Excellence in Brisbane.

Jessica Rowlands played a major part in Queensland's success, taking 12 wickets and giving away only 1.92 runs an over. A competition highlight was the performance of the ACT's Vanessa Picker, only 13 years old, who batted for well over an hour on one occasion in a valiant attempt to rescue her side. Twelve girls also played in the Under-19 competition, which finished three days earlier. Three of those players – Rowlands, her Queensland team-mate Sarah Harris and SA's Fiona McDonald – enjoyed success at both levels and clearly have the potential to one day play at a higher grade.

ROUND ONE

Queensland 8 for 178 (S. Harris 36; E. Rogers 3-16) defeated Australian Capital Territory 9 for 62 (J. Rowlands 4-6) by 116 runs.

South Australia 8 for 91 (E. Pender 2-12) lost to Western Australia 3 for 92 (A. Gilmour 21*; H. Hyder 2-8) by seven wickets.

New South Wales 6 for 141 (E. Rixon 50; B. Evans 3-23) lost to Victoria 7 for 143 (T. Norquay 32) by three wickets.

ROUND TWO

South Australia 9 for 89 (T. McPharlin 23; J. Rowlands 2-13) lost to Queensland 5 for 91 (S. Harris 26; T. Rowbottom 3-29) by five wickets.

Victoria 8 for 181 (T. Norquay 74*; N. Ayres 2-38) defeated Western Australia 97 (E. Pender 19; E. Villani 3-19) by 84 runs.

New South Wales 5 for 222 (N. Honeysett 71, C. Ryan 63*) defeated Australian Capital Territory 7 for 69 (E. Rogers 17; E. Burns 2-9) by 153 runs.

ROUND THREE

New South Wales 114 (A. Smith 36; L. Hinze 3-14, J. Rowlands 3-23) lost to Queensland 3 for 115 (S Harris 37*) by seven wickets.

South Australia 8 for 90 (C. Fiebig 17; B. Evans 3-7) lost to Victoria 2 for 91 (T. Norquay 34*) by eight wickets.

Western Australia 8 for 210 (A. Williams 55; C. Rawstron 3-35) defeated Australian Capital Territory 92 (M. Hull 16; M. Chappell 4-25, J Wilson 3-11) by 118 runs.

ROUND FOUR

Australian Capital Territory 68 (F. McDonald 4-8) lost to South Australia 2 for 69 (F. McDonald 24*) by eight wickets.

New South Wales 6 for 152 (N. Honeysett 43; N. Ayres 2-30) defeated Western Australia 73 (H. Hyder 15; A Smith 5-23) by 79 runs.

Queensland 83 (T Norquay 2-10) lost to Victoria 8 for 84 (T. Norquay 30; L. Hinze 3-15) by two wickets.

FINALS

South Australia 6 for 231 (J. Weidenhofer 70; K. Page 2-18) defeated Australian Capital Territory 6 for 144 (C. Rawstron 35; F. McDonald 2-5) by 87 runs.

Queensland 5 for 148 (C. Reibelt 33; B. Evans 2-40) defeated Victoria 117 (J. Cameron 17; L. Kidd 4-19) by 31 runs.

Western Australia 9 for 82 (E. Burns 2-11) lost to New South Wales 3 for 83 (T. Kurzdlo 32; H. Hyder 3-14) by seven wickets.

POINTS TABLE

	Played	Won	Lost	Tied	No Result	Bonus Points	Points
Queensland	5	4	1	0	0	4	20
Victoria	5	4	1	0	0	3	19
New South Wales	5	3	2	0	0	4	16
Western Australia	5	2	3	0	0	4	12
South Australia	5	2	3	0	0	2	10
Australian Capital Territory	5	0	5	0	0	0	0

MOST RUNS

	M	I	NO	R	HS	100s	50s	Avge	S-R
T. Norquay (Vic)	5	5	2	188	74*	0	1	62.67	67.85
S. Harris (Qld)	5	5	1	120	37*	0	0	30.00	51.72
N. Honeysett (NSW)	4	4	0	119	71	0	1	29.75	77.27
A. Williams (WA)	4	4	0	98	55	0	1	19.60	40.66

MOST WICKETS

	M	O	Mdns	R	W	BB	5W/i	Avge	RPO
J. Rowlands (Qld)	5	38	10	73	12	4-6	1.92	6.08	1.92
B. Evans (Vic)	5	32.4	7	82	12	3-7	2.51	6.83	2.51
L. Kidd (Qld)	5	27.1	4	61	9	4-19	2.24	6.77	2.24
T. Rowbottom (SA)	5	32.5	1	138	9	3-29	4.20	15.33	4.20

SPEED WITHOUT HASTE

In February 2004, Don Bradman's 254 against England at Lord's in 1930 was voted the best innings ever played by an Australian. The poll was conducted among 30 cricket experts and former Test players encompassing every decade since the 1940s. It was published in *The Greatest*, a special collector's edition of *Inside Edge* magazine. In his ode to the winning innings, Gideon Haigh described Bradman's 254 as "the pinnacle of efficiency to which he himself always aspired: speed without noticeable haste, risk without obvious recklessness".

1.	D. G. Bradman	254 v England, Lord's, 1930
2.	S. J. McCabe	232 v England, Trent Bridge, 1938
3.	D. G. Bradman	334 v England, Headingley, 1930
4.	D. M. Jones	210 v India, Chennai, 1986-87
5.	K. J. Hughes	100* v West Indies, MCG, 1981-82
6.	A. C. Gilchrist	149* v Pakistan, Hobart, 1999-2000
7.	S. R. Waugh	200 v West Indies, Kingston, 1994-95
8.	S. J. McCabe	187* v England, SCG, 1932-33
9.	M. E. Waugh	116 v South Africa, Port Elizabeth, 1996-97
10.	M. L. Hayden	380 v Zimbabwe, WACA, 2003-04
11.	W. M. Lawry	130 v England, Lord's, 1961
12.	R. N. Harvey	151* v South Africa, Durban, 1949-50
13.	G. S. Chappell	131 v England, Lord's, 1972
14.	A. R. Border	98* + 100* v West Indies, Port-of-Spain, 1983-84
15.	R. N. Harvey	167 v England, MCG, 1958-59
16.	S. R. Waugh	102 v England, SCG, 2002-03
17.	R. N. Harvey	96 v Pakistan, Dacca, 1959-60
18.	S. R. Waugh	120* v South Africa, Headingley, 1999 (ODI)
19.	A. C. Gilchrist	204* v South Africa, Johannesburg, 2001-02
20.	N. C. O'Neill	181 v West Indies, Gabba, 1960-61
21.	W. B. Phillips	120 v West Indies, Bridgetown, 1983-84
22.	D. G. Bradman	103* v England, MCG, 1932-33
23.	I. M. Chappell	156 v West Indies, WACA, 1975-76
24.	D. G. Bradman	270 v England, MCG, 1936-37
25.	A. R. Morris	182 v England, Headingley, 1948
26.	I. M. Chappell	97 v West Indies, Port-of-Spain, 1972-73
27.	K. R. Miller	185 v England, Lord's, 1945 (Dominions match)
28.	G. S. Chappell	247* + 133* v New Zealand, Wellington, 1973-74
29.	M. A. Taylor	334* v Pakistan, Peshawar, 1998-99
30.	R. T. Ponting	140* v India, Johannesburg, 2003 (ODI)
31.	M. G. Bevan	78* v West Indies, SCG, 1995-96 (ODI)
32.	M. E. Waugh	126 v West Indies, Kingston, 1994-95
33.	V. T. Trumper	135* v England, Lord's, 1899
34.	J. L. Langer	127 v Pakistan, Hobart, 1999-2000
35.	K. D. Walters	242 + 103 v West Indies, SCG, 1968-69
36.	K. D. Walters	250 v New Zealand, Christchurch, 1976-77
37.	R. N. Harvey	112 v England, Headingley, 1948
38.	V. T. Trumper	104 v England, Old Trafford, 1902
39.	R. N. Harvey	92* v England, SCG, 1954-55
40.	G. M. Ritchie	106 v Pakistan, Faisalabad, 1982-83
41.	S. R. Waugh	108 + 116 v England, Old Trafford, 1997
42.	M. J. Slater	176 v England, Gabba, 1994-95
43.	R. N. Harvey	133 v West Indies, Kingston, 1954-55
44.	B. M. Laird	122 v West Indies, Port-of-Spain, 1978-79 (WSC Supertest)
45.	J. R. Thomson	21 v England, MCG, 1982-83
46.	K. D. Walters	112 v West Indies, Port-of-Spain, 1972-73
47.	M. L. Hayden	119 v India, Mumbai, 2000-01
48.	I. M. Chappell	196 v Pakistan, Adelaide, 1972-73
49.	K. D. Mackay	62* v West Indies, Adelaide, 1960-61
50.	R. B. McCosker	25 v England, MCG, 1976-77

Opposite TWIN FREAKS: Muttiah Muralidaran and Shane Warne, friendly rivals and Test history's leading wicket-takers, scooped up 54 between them in the three-Test series in Sri Lanka.
Picture by Hamish Blair/Getty Images.

6

Australians Abroad

Australia in Sri Lanka, 2004

by PETER ROEBUCK

Australia had not prevailed on the Spice Island since 1992-93, and then by a whisker, so this was a promising start to Ricky Ponting's tenure. In his first series as Test captain he led his side to a comprehensive victory. He was helped by the solidity of his own men and the frailty of opponents who kept climbing halfway up the hill before falling back in disarray.

The Australians started badly and occasionally stumbled but on each occasion had the resolution required to restore their position. Ponting provided the drive and had sufficient authority to overcome the mistakes made by a captain still learning the ropes. His leadership resembled his batting: it was adventurous, vulnerable in the early stages and ultimately productive. By the end of the tour decisive wins had been secured in both forms of the game.

Although the three-nil victory in the Tests was a team effort, several players asserted themselves during a tightly packed series played in generally steamy conditions. Once again Matthew Hayden revelled on subcontinental pitches, pounding away at the bowling in the manner of a cannon upon a castle wall. After a slow start Jason Gillespie produced bursts of incisive pace when they were needed. Most of all Shane Warne returned to representative cricket with a familiar combination of skill, cunning, perseverance and panache.

Warne was the difference between the sides. During the series he became the second man in history to take 500 wickets in Test cricket. By the end of it he was two wickets short of Courtney Walsh's world record. Throughout he outbowled Muttiah Muralidaran, who was not as influential as expected. Murali took more wickets, 28 to 26, but a high proportion were tailenders or tiring batsmen with big scores beside their names. He troubled the Australians in the first innings in Galle and faded thereafter.

Murali was handicapped by defensive field placements. Worse, his doosra – the leg-break that looks like an off-break – was reported by Chris Broad, the match referee. Broad waited till the series had been completed before announcing that he regarded this delivery as suspect. Yet Murali had been bowling the doosra for years. Arjuna Ranatunga and others smelt a white conspiracy to stop their man taking the world record. Broad, in truth, was merely putting into effect a process that gives a bowler a chance to correct a fault without experiencing the sort of public execution Murali suffered at the MCG on Boxing Day, 1995.

By way of consolation, Murali could celebrate taking his own 500th wicket one match after Warne, during the Second Test in Kandy. His other deliveries all passed muster and some observers thought he was actually more dangerous without the doosra, a surprise weapon upon which too much reliance had been placed.

Australia made a wayward start to their campaign in Galle, a southern seaside town and the scene of many local victories. Before the match the pitch provoked consternation among the more paranoid tourists, but it remained slow and full of runs. Australia's poor first innings owed more to a desire to dominate than any unreliability in the wicket.

Sri Lanka batted carefully and took a substantial lead but their innings petered out on a third morning that determined the fate of both match and series. Reprieved, the Australians counterattacked through Hayden, Damien Martyn and Darren Lehmann. Emerging from a bad patch, Martyn reasserted his right to bat at second wicket down with a methodical display. Lehmann's innings was an emotional renewal by a man devastated by the sudden death of his friend David Hookes. Torn between pursuing a remote target and saving the match, the Lankans capitulated on the final day. Warne marked an inspired return by taking his 500th wicket. Although the margin of victory was emphatic the contest had been close for long periods. Much the same could be said of the series.

Australia began badly again in Kandy, and from that moment the match was utterly compelling. Despite the dampness of a pitch that had spent days under canvas, Ponting and the touring selectors did not change their winning side, preferring to play two spinners and retain Andrew Symonds on the grounds that his bowling might be useful. Accordingly they were more or less obliged to bat upon winning the toss. A collapse followed as the top order subsided in the face of clever swing bowling by the estimable Chaminda Vaas. In the event Symonds did not bowl a ball, Stuart MacGill was flogged and the extra batsman and third fast bowler were missed. Oh, yes; and Australia still won.

It was a close call. Volunteering to bat at No. 3 in the second innings because Ponting had hurt his back, Adam Gilchrist responded with a dashing century. Martyn constructed another craftsmanlike knock full of back-foot drives, and Australia were able to set an apparently intimidating target on a pitch that, like a plum, had dried as it aged. Nothing daunts Sanath Jayasuriya, who met the challenge in characteristically robust fashion, and after numerous twists and turns Sri Lanka were left needing to score 51 runs on the last morning with three wickets remaining.

Much to the dismay of a small crowd boosted by boys from Murali's old school, the locals lost their heads and went down by 27 runs. Ponting spread his field and there were more singles around than at a Desperate & Dateless Ball. His strategy worked; Vaas swung recklessly and the rest went with a whimper. By the skin of their teeth Australia had taken an impregnable lead.

Colombo provided heat and a gruelling contest. It featured centuries from Lehmann, Marvan Atapattu and Justin Langer and, towards the end, the sight of Australia's elderly spinners trying to remove defiant batsmen as the Lankans declined to chase a remote target. Ponting's reluctance to throw the game open suggested he intends to play tighter cricket on the fifth day than did a predecessor unable to find any merit in preying upon his opponents in the latter stages of a long contest.

Sri Lanka struggled to save the match on an even-tempered pitch. Again they wilted in the face of a tougher and more intense opponent, with wickets lost to injudicious strokes. They failed by eight deliveries to avoid the clean sweep. Lehmann and Warne took the wickets whereupon the Australians celebrated in the style of men who had endured many hardships and close shaves along the way.

Since the Australians had been stretched in every match, the final margin of victory might seem unjust. Yet the locals had only themselves to blame. Australia were stronger in the mind. Afterwards the tale was told. Ponting and Warne were able to celebrate notable performances. Meanwhile Hashan Tillakaratne was handing in his resignation as captain and Murali was facing the prospect of further examination of his action.

About the only black mark against Australia was some unacceptable appealing on the last day of the final Test. Apart from these excesses the series was fairly contested, with players and officials from both sides making a point of congratulating Warne and Murali upon their extraordinary achievements. Ponting's team adapted well to the conditions and went home with the spoils and renewed confidence that India, too, can be beaten on their own patch.

AUSTRALIAN TEST SQUAD

R. T. Ponting (*captain*), A. C. Gilchrist (*vice-captain*), J. N. Gillespie, M. L. Hayden, M. .S Kasprowicz, S. M. Katich, J. L. Langer, D. S. Lehmann, S. C. G. MacGill, D. R. Martyn, W. A. Seccombe, A. Symonds, S. K. Warne and B. A. Williams.

B. Lee was replaced on March 11 by S. R. Tait due to injury.

Manager: S. R. Bernard. *Coach:* J. M. Buchanan. *Performance analyst/assistant coach:* T. J. Nielsen. *Physiotherapist:* A. Kontouri. *Masseur:* Ms L. Frostick. *Physical performance manager:* J. A. Campbell. *Media manager:* J. Rose.

AUSTRALIAN TOUR RESULTS

Test matches – Played 3: Won 3, Lost 0.
First-class matches – Played 4: Won 4, Lost 0.
Wins – Sri Lanka (3), Sri Lanka Cricket President's XI.
International limited-overs – Played 5: Won 3, Lost 2.
Other non-first-class matches: Played 2: Won 1. *Win:* Sri Lanka Cricket President's XI.

TEST BATTING AVERAGES

	M	I	NO	R	HS	100s	50s	Avge	Ct/St	S-R
D. S. Lehmann (Aus)	3	6	0	375	153	2	1	62.50	0	57.87
D. R. Martyn (Aus)......	3	6	0	333	161	2	0	55.50	2	45.49
S. M. Katich (Aus)	1	2	0	100	86	0	1	50.00	1	40.16
S. T. Jayasuriya (SL)	3	6	0	294	131	1	2	49.00	2	77.78
T. T. Samaraweera (SL)..	2	4	1	145	53	0	1	48.33	2	39.62
M. L. Hayden (Aus).....	3	6	0	283	130	1	1	47.17	7	64.03
A. C. Gilchrist (Aus)	3	6	1	201	144	1	0	40.20	11/3	69.79
J. L. Langer (Aus).......	3	6	0	241	166	1	0	40.17	3	44.96
W. P. U. J. C. Vaas (SL) ..	3	6	2	156	68*	0	1	39.00	1	57.56
M. S. Atapattu (SL)	3	6	0	212	118	1	0	35.33	1	43.44
U. D. U. Chandana (SL)..	1	2	0	70	43	0	0	35.00	1	60.87
H. P. Tillakaratne (SL)...	3	6	1	172	74*	0	1	34.40	2	36.06
R. T. Ponting (Aus)	3	6	0	198	92	0	1	33.00	1	55.93
D. P. M. D. Jayawardene (SL)	3	6	0	185	68	0	1	30.83	6	44.90
T. M. Dilshan (SL)......	3	6	0	184	104	1	0	30.67	1	60.93
S. C. G. MacGill (Aus)...	2	3	2	25	17*	0	0	25.00	0	86.21
K. C. Sangakkara (SL)...	3	6	0	112	29	0	0	18.67	7/4	60.87
K. S. Lokuarachchi (SL) .	1	2	0	31	16	0	0	15.50	0	48.44
M. Muralidaran (SL)	3	6	2	55	43	0	0	13.75	4	112.24
A. Symonds (Aus)	2	4	0	53	24	0	0	13.25	4	44.54
S. K. Warne (Aus)	3	6	0	79	32	0	0	13.17	3	39.50
D. A. Gunawardene (SL).	1	2	0	22	13	0	0	11.00	0	52.38
J. N. Gillespie (Aus).....	3	6	2	35	11*	0	0	8.75	1	39.33
M. S. Kasprowicz (Aus)..	3	6	1	19	8	0	0	3.80	2	59.38
H. D. P. K. Dharmasena (SL)	1	2	0	6	6	0	0	3.00	1	31.58
D. N. T. Zoysa (SL)	2	4	0	8	4	0	0	2.00	1	25.00
B. A. Williams (Aus).....	1	2	1	2	2	0	0	2.00	0	28.57
H. M. R. K. B. Herath (SL).	1	2	0	3	3	0	0	1.50	1	6.52

* Denotes not out.

TEST BOWLING AVERAGES

	O	Mdns	R	W	BB	5W/i	10W/m	Avge	S-R
D. S. Lehmann (Aus)...	38	4	101	6	3-42	0	0	16.83	38.00
S. K. Warne (Aus).....	168	37	521	26	5-43	4	2	20.04	38.77
M. Muralidaran (SL)...	209.1	37	649	28	6-59	4	1	23.18	44.82
M. S. Kasprowicz (Aus)	107.5	20	302	12	4-83	0	0	25.17	53.92
J. N. Gillespie (Aus) ...	110	26	316	10	4-76	0	0	31.60	66.00
W. P. U. J. C. Vaas (SL).	130.2	22	377	11	3-93	0	0	34.27	71.09
D. N. T. Zoysa (SL)....	64.3	15	233	6	4-54	0	0	38.83	64.50
H. M. R. K. B. Herath (SL)	47.2	6	167	4	4-92	0	0	41.75	71.00
S. C. G. MacGill (Aus) .	55.2	7	232	5	4-74	0	0	46.40	66.40
S. T. Jayasuriya (SL)...	35.3	3	96	2	1-27	0	0	48.00	106.50
H. D. P. K. Dharmasena (SL)	44	5	152	2	2-52	0	0	76.00	132.00
T. T. Samaraweera (SL)	29.3	5	78	1	1-38	0	0	78.00	177.00
U. D. U. Chandana (SL)	38.3	3	161	2	1-59	0	0	80.50	115.50
A. Symonds (Aus).....	24	4	85	1	1-68	0	0	85.00	144.00
K. S. Lokuarachchi (SL)	12	2	33	0	–	0	0	–	–
S. M. Katich (Aus).....	12	1	44	0	–	0	0	–	–
B. A. Williams (Aus)...	24	5	67	0	–	0	0	–	–
T. M. Dilshan (SL)	8	4	15	0	–	0	0	–	–

Note: Matches in this section that were not first-class are signified by a dagger.

SRI LANKA CRICKET PRESIDENT'S XI v AUSTRALIANS

At Colombo Cricket Club Ground, Colombo, March 2, 3, 4, 2004. Australia won by 245 runs. *Toss:* Sri Lanka Cricket President's XI.

In an age when tour games are seen increasingly as an anachronism, this was a pre-Test warm-up with a genuine edge to it. Apart from the spectacle of Shane Warne's first ball for Australia since his 12-month ban for taking diuretics, a handful of Test places were seemingly up for grabs. The pace shootout was at least partly resolved in unfortunate circumstances, Brett Lee leaving the field abruptly on the final day with what was later revealed to be a broken foot. He was taken to hospital and eventually flew back to Australia. It was the worst possible timing for Lee, who had swung the ball at high speed and looked to be returning to something like his sizzling best. None of the three competing batsmen – Simon Katich, Darren Lehmann or Andrew Symonds – hurt their Test prospects, all three making hundreds at just under a run a ball to set up a comfortable victory. Symonds continued his blistering one-day form, hitting one ball out of the ground and into a neighbouring house, never to be seen again. As for Warne, he captured his first wicket, that of Ruchira Perera, with his 38th delivery. Both he and Stuart MacGill bowled with enough loop and accuracy to suggest that the selectors might abandon their normal policy and take both leggies into the First Test.

Close of play: First day, Australians (1) 6-484 (Symonds 45); Second day, Australians (2) 4-250 (Symonds 119, Kasprowicz 15).

Australians

J. L. Langer b Herath	35	– lbw b Fernando	63
*R. T. Ponting st de Silva b Herath	116		
S. M. Katich st de Silva b Samaraweera	116		
D. S. Lehmann c Perera b Fernando	134		
A. Symonds not out	45	– (3) not out	119
†W. A. Seccombe lbw b Fernando	0	– (2) lbw b Perera	6
S. K. Warne lbw b Herath	8	– (4) lbw b Lokuarachchi	31
B. Lee		– (5) c Samaraweera b Lokuarachchi	2
M. S. Kasprowicz		– (6) not out	15
B 6, l-b 6, w 1, n-b 17	30	B 2, l-b 9, w 1, n-b 2	14

(89.5 overs)	(6 wkts dec) 484	(50 overs)	(4 wkts dec) 250
Fall: 117 204 385 465 467 484 0		Fall: 9 148 202 208	

S. C. G. MacGill and B. A. Williams did not bat.

Bowling: *First Innings*—Perera 11–0–69–0; Wijesiriwardene 10–0–48–0; Ramyakumara 12–2–54–0; Herath 24.5–0–132–3; Lokuarachchi 12–1–64–0; Samaraweera 12–0–70–1; Arnold 3–0–20–0; Fernando 5–0–15–2. *Second Innings*—Perera 9–1–46–1; Wijesiriwardene 8–3–20–0; Herath 16–0–83–0; Fernando 5–0–26–1; Ramyakumara 2–0–13–0; Lokuarachchi 10–1–51–2.

Sri Lanka Cricket President's XI

R. P. Arnold lbw b Lee	0	– c Williams b Warne	25
D. A. Gunawardene lbw b MacGill	70	– c Katich b Lee	11
W. S. Jayantha b Lee	0	– c Seccombe b MacGill	45
S. I. Fernando b Kasprowicz	12	– c Seccombe b Williams	10
*T. T. Samaraweera c Ponting b Lee	2	– c Warne b Kasprowicz	50
†S. K. L. de Silva c Seccombe b Lee	14	– c Langer b Lehmann	92
W. M. G. Ramyakumara b Kasprowicz	5	– c Seccombe b MacGill	67
K. S. Lokuarachchi c Seccombe b MacGill	17	– lbw b Warne	11
H. M. R. K. B. Herath b MacGill	8	– c Kasprowicz b Symonds	4
O. L. A. Wijesiriwardene not out	5	– c Katich b MacGill	0
P. D. R. L. Perera st Seccombe b Warne	6		
B 4, l-b 10, n-b 13	27	B 2, l-b 3, n-b 3	8

(36.2 overs)	166	(85.2 overs)	323
Fall: 0 0 28 41 76 83 115 152		Fall: 30 53 66 108 209 278 301 323	
153 166		323 323	

Bowling: *First Innings*—Lee 7–1–29–4; Kasprowicz 7–1–46–2; Williams 5–2–22–0; MacGill 11–4–34–3; Warne 6.2–1–21–1. *Second Innings*—Lee 3.4–0–18–1; Kasprowicz 10–1–43–1; Lehmann 9.2–2–25–1; Warne 23–5–79–2; Williams 10–3–31–1; MacGill 13–1–57–3; Katich 8–0–38–0; Symonds 8.2–0–27–1.

Umpires: R. Martinesz and B. B. J. Nandakumar.

SRI LANKA v AUSTRALIA

First Test Match

by GEOFF LAWSON

At Galle International Stadium, Galle, March 8, 9, 10, 11, 12, 2004. Australia won by 197 runs. *Toss:* Australia. *Test debut:* A. Symonds.

Australia's first Test of the post-Waugh era was an epic contest, twisting and turning – especially turning – through all five days. Conditions were tailor-made for the hosts, or so it seemed. The Sri Lankans, conscious of their biggest strength, picked four spinners and only one seamer in Chaminda Vaas. The Australians, suspicious of the wicket, went in with Stuart MacGill plus two new tweakers: Andrew Symonds, who was also capable of scoring fast and bowling medium, and Shane Warne, back from suspension and wearing the baggy green for the first time in 15 months.

It was not a game where you wanted to get caught batting last. Ricky Ponting's opening act as Test captain, without a nanosecond's hesitation, was to bat first. For 40 minutes no wickets fell and Justin Langer and Matthew Hayden made comfortable progress. Half an hour after tea the Australians were out in the field amid talk of a Sri Lankan rout. They had crashed from 3 for 148 in the 44th over to all out for 220 in the 69th. The much-admired Australian philosophy of all-out aggression, pioneered by Steve Waugh, was again in evidence. Except that this time there was no Waugh and it looked more like indiscipline.

Kumar Dharmasena set the tone for the series when he opened the bowling with his off-breaks. He took the wicket of Langer, cutting and bottom-edging, and then Hayden departed in typically buccaneering fashion, top-edging an attempted sweep off Muttiah Muralidaran. When Ponting was lured out of his ground by a looping, almost Warnesque leg-break from Upul Chandana the series portents for Australia looked dire. Then came the first of two substantial partnerships, Darren Lehmann hoisting 72 for the fourth wicket with Damien Martyn and 52 for the seventh with Warne.

COME IN SPINNER

First slow bowler to:

100 wickets	Johnny Briggs (Eng)	February 1, 1895	....	25th Test
200 wickets	Clarrie Grimmett (Aus)	February 17, 1936	....	36th Test
300 wickets	Lance Gibbs (WI)	December 12, 1975	....	75th Test
400 wickets	Shane Warne (Aus)	August 25, 2001	....	92nd Test
500 wickets	Shane Warne (Aus)	March 10, 2004	....	108th Test

---

Returning after a long lay-off from an Achilles injury, Lehmann looked assured in his footwork and largely untroubled in reading Murali's doosra. The rest of the top order had a vague idea, and the tail none. The last four wickets fell for five runs as Murali, turning the ball prodigiously, charged fleetingly past Warne in the race to 500. Only a tiny crowd was in attendance but the commemorative T-shirt makers went into overdrive.

Sri Lanka's reply was steady rather than spectacular, on a pitch that seemed to be improving rather than deteriorating. Warne, though as accurate as ever, lacked penetration early in his comeback spell, causing some furrowed brows among Australian team-mates, fans and selectors. Mahela Jayawardene batted sweetly before donating Symonds his first Test wicket, thrashing at a full ball outside off and spooning Hayden, Symonds's fishing buddy, a simple catch at point.

The rest of the innings was built around a patient Tillakaratne Dilshan. He was content to kick away a big-turning MacGill and an increasingly threatening Warne, while latching on to anything loose between times. By stumps on day two Sri Lanka were six down and 132 ahead, with a chance to lock the cupboard on the Australians and throw away the key. Their tail, however, fared little better than the visitors'. Rapidly closing in on his mesmerising best, Warne scooped up three of the last four wickets and it was a different game.

Certainly it looked a different Australian top order second time round. Dogged defence, crafty footwork and precise shot selection were their watchwords. Hayden, Martyn and Lehmann produced wonderful hundreds which all three, given the turning pitch and perilous match situation, may consider their finest. Immunity to Murali's doosra was built up as exposure to it increased. The more he bowled it, the more adept the Australians grew at picking it.

Hayden eventually succumbed to mental exhaustion as much as anything, sweeping at Murali for the umpteenth time and toe-ending it to slip. Until then he had run hard and hoicked inventively, with scant regard for his team's troublesome predicament. If Hayden's hundred was the most significant, laying the groundwork for Australia's fightback, Martyn's was surely the most personally rewarding. It was his first Test century in 25 months and it almost certainly rescued his place in the side. He was rarely fluent but rarely troubled either, batting with unwavering patience for five and a half hours in sapping heat and humidity.

Lehmann's innings, meanwhile, was the most emotional. He was dropped on nought but savaged the spinners thereafter, charging down the pitch and alternately pulling them over mid-wicket or sweeping them in front of square. As he entered the nineties, he later admitted, his thoughts started to dwell on David Hookes, his idol and close friend who had died two months earlier. Upon reaching three figures Lehmann raised his arms and stared at the sky. "He would have been proud," said Lehmann at the press conference that night.

So telling was Australia's turnaround that Ponting, against all odds, found himself declaring on the fourth evening and giving his bowlers three overs before stumps. Sri Lanka survived those unscathed and were given a reasonable chance of batting out the last day, if not of making 352 to win. Their hopes were shattered by Warne's last 14 balls before lunch. A pair of leg-breaks ousted Marvan Atapattu and Jayawardene, both caught by Hayden, and then Dilshan fell leg-before pushing forward to the Warne flipper.

When Hashan Tillakaratne launched into an uncharacteristically audacious sweep, only to be caught by Symonds at mid-wicket, Warne became the second man and first spinner to reach 500 Test wickets. After his indiscretions of the past, it was a scenario many thought they would never live to see. "Throughout my life things have always been a drama," said the man himself, "so today leaves me very happy and proud."

It was all over with hours to spare. Warne took 10 wickets in his comeback game. The experiment of bowling him and MacGill in tandem worked wonders. Hayden caught Dharmasena for his seventh catch of the match, equalling the all-time fielding record. And a terrific Test ended with a stirring come-from-behind victory, Ponting describing the last two days as "some of the best Test cricket Australia have played in a long time". All that without Steve Waugh.

Man of the Match: S. K. Warne.

Close of play: First day, Sri Lanka (1) 1-81 (Atapattu 29, Sangakkara 16); Second day, Sri Lanka (1) 6-352 (Samaraweera 21, Chandana 20); Third day, Australia (2) 2-193 (Hayden 106, Martyn 10); Fourth day, Sri Lanka (2) 0-3 (Atapattu 0, Sangakkara 3).

Australia

	R	B	4/6		R	B	4/6
J.L. Langer c Sangakkara b Dharmasena	12	36	1	– lbw b Jayasuriya	32	106	4
M.L. Hayden c Chandana b Muralidaran	41	46	6	– c Jayawardene b Muralidaran	130	211	12[2]
*R.T. Ponting st Sangakkara b Chandana	21	39	4	– run out (Chandana/Sangakkara)	28	78	2
D.R. Martyn c Jayawardene b Dharmasena	42	81	3	– c (sub) K.S. Lokuarachchi b M'daran	110	251	10
D.S. Lehmann b Muralidaran	63	113	6[1]	– c and b Muralidaran	129	213	16[1]
A. Symonds c Jayawardene b Muralidaran	0	15	0	– st Sangakkara b Muralidaran	24	18	4
†A.C. Gilchrist c Dharmasena b Muralidaran	4	7	1	– lbw b Chandana	0	7	0
S.K. Warne c Sangakkara b Vaas	23	63	4	– st Sangakkara b Muralidaran	0	6	0
J.N. Gillespie not out	4	7	1	– not out	11	18	2
M.S. Kasprowicz b Muralidaran	1	3	0	– not out	3	6	0
S.C.G. MacGill lbw b Muralidaran	0	1	0				
B 3, l-b 6	9			B 15, l-b 28, n-b 2	45		

(68.3 overs, 263 mins) 220

Fall: 31 62 76 148 153 163 215 219
220 220

(152 overs, 612 mins) (8-dec) 512

Fall: 91 175 245 451 480 498
498 498

Bowling: *First Innings*—Vaas 12-2-39-1; Dharmasena 20-4-52-2; Muralidaran 21.3-5-59-6; Chandana 14-1-59-1; Jayasuriya 1-0-2-0. *Second Innings*—Vaas 27-3-67-0; Dharmasena 24-1-100-0; Muralidaran 56-9-153-5; Dilshan 6-3-9-0; Jayasuriya 14.3-2-38-1; Chandana 24.3-2-102-1.

Sri Lanka

	R	B	4/6		R	B	4/6
M.S. Atapattu b Gillespie	47	113	7	– c Hayden b Warne	16	60	2
S.T. Jayasuriya lbw b Warne	35	56	4	– (5) c Hayden b MacGill	5	12	1
†K.C. Sangakkara c and b Kasprowicz	22	40	2[1]	– (2) lbw b Kasprowicz	7	13	1
D.P.M. Jayawardene c Hayden b Symonds	68	102	8	– (3) c Hayden b Warne	21	47	3
T.M. Dilshan c Langer b Kasprowicz	104	188	12[1]	– (4) lbw b Warne	6	6	1
*H.P. Tillakaratne lbw b Warne	33	97	4	– c Symonds b Warne	25	43	4
T.T. Samaraweera not out	36	120	6	– b MacGill	15	37	1
U.D.U. Chandana c Gilchrist b Warne	27	81	2	– c Langer b MacGill	43	34	7
W.P.U.J.C. Vaas c Hayden b MacGill	0	9	0	– not out	10	14	2
H.D.P.K. Dharmasena c Hayden b Warne	6	13	1	– c Hayden b Warne	0	6	0
M. Muralidaran c and b Warne	0	2	0	– st Gilchrist b MacGill	0	1	0
B 2, n-b 1	3			B 4, w 1, n-b 1	6		

(136.4 overs, 533 mins) 381

Fall: 53 92 123 198 298 323 369 372
381 381

(45.2 overs, 188 mins) 154

Fall: 14 41 49 56 56 89 119 153
153 154

Bowling: *First Innings*—Gillespie 28-9-61-1; Kasprowicz 23-3-56-2; Warne 42.4-9-116-5; Symonds 19-3-68-1; MacGill 22-4-69-1; Lehmann 2-0-9-0. *Second Innings*—Warne 15-5-43-5; Gillespie 9-2-20-0; Kasprowicz 5-1-13-1; MacGill 16.2-2-74-4.

Umpires: R.E. Koertzen (South Africa) and D.R. Shepherd (England).
TV Umpire: M.G. Silva.
Referee: B.C. Broad (England).

SRI LANKA v AUSTRALIA

Second Test Match

by PAUL COUPAR

At Asgiriya Stadium, Kandy, March 16, 17, 18, 19, 20, 2004. Australia won by 27 runs.
Toss: Australia.

Victory in Kandy gave Australia an unassailable two-nil lead in the series less than a fortnight after it began. Ricky Ponting's happy-go-lucky grin might have replaced Steve Waugh's gum-chewing scowl but Australia's dominance appeared to carry on regardless. By one measure Ponting had even surpassed his predecessor. Waugh's last Kandy Test, in 1999, ended with a series-deciding defeat and a broken nose, smashed in a sickening collision with Jason Gillespie.

But nothing about this win was ever clear cut. Australia flirted with defeat against an inferior side, with glimpses of both old strengths and unfamiliar weaknesses. There was an unusually feckless Australian first innings of 120 on a manageable pitch, their lowest since 1997 when Phil Tufnell routed them for 104 on a crumbling Oval wicket. There was a gritted-teeth fightback Allan Border would have been proud of, and a Sri Lankan counterattack led by the blazing bat of Sanath Jayasuriya, rekindling memories of the 1996 World Cup win. And finally, on a gripping last morning, there was the familiar sight of Shane Warne keeping cool when it mattered most. Australia gave Sri Lanka chances to win but, unlike India in the summer, they lacked the composure or self-belief to hammer home the advantage.

It was a bittersweet game for Muttiah Muralidaran. He became only the third man in 127 years to take 500 Test wickets. But his hometown party fell flat, partly because Warne had got there first in Galle and partly because "Murali 500" had been over-hyped by sponsors and the penurious home board. Partly, too, it was because Murali, despite taking nine wickets, looked a beaten man. He retreated to bowling round the wicket to defensive leg-side fields. Economy was one explanation for this; another was the need to bowl a middle-and-off line for his doosra. By emphasising the variation he neglected the attacking methods which had brought him his success in the first place. Australia's nimble-footed batsmen won the contest decisively.

The match began in fast forward. By the time a small crowd were opening their curry lunch-packets on day two, both first innings were over. The pitch helped seamers, batsmen and spinners in turn, but never excessively. It certainly didn't look too bad; Ponting had chosen to bat, after all, though he may have been influenced by an ill-suited Australian attack containing two leg-spinners and no third seamer. As the ball nipped around, two of his top seven swished fatally. Two padded up to straight ones. Darren Lehmann was bowled leg stump trying to glance, which summed up the impatient approach.

A total of 120 looked paltry. Sri Lankan smiles were doubly broad because Murali had reached 500, bowling Michael Kasprowicz through the gate. Firecrackers exploded, banners were unfurled, children in white shorts from Murali's old school cheered. The story made front pages of local papers, pushing aside electoral politics and confusing the *Daily News*, who mistook Tillakaratne Dilshan for the Sri Lankan prime minister in an embarrassingly prominent caption.

If Sri Lanka's morning was joyous, their afternoon was a shocker. By the close they were 7 for 92 and Australia were out of jail. Shots across the line exposed a middle order flummoxed by Warne, who combined hypnotic drift and precise control of the degree of spin. Sri Lanka had given much more than an inch; unusually Australia did not take a mile. On a surreal second morning they bowled as if wickets would fall automatically. That, and an odd decision to give Kasprowicz a long spell in search of a trophy fifth wicket, allowed the classical Chaminda Vaas and the comical Murali to pinch 79, a national record for the last wicket. Sri Lanka gratefully snatched a 91-run lead.

If that failure to land the killer blow seemed distinctly un-Australian, the hundreds by Adam Gilchrist and Damien Martyn on days two and three were the distilled essence of baggy green: unyielding, impervious to pressure, sensibly attacking and ultimately matchwinning. Gilchrist's 144 was marginally the better innings, because Martyn was dropped three times – once on nought – and because Gilchrist was under more pressure. His form had been awful, and rumours festered of cool relations with some team-mates. He responded by volunteering to bat at No. 3, for Ponting had cricked his back in the field, and by hitting mercilessly straight and hard. Meanwhile Martyn stockpiled as busily as a squirrel in autumn. They added 200 and Australia took a lead of 351.

But was 351 enough? In January, on a similar, increasingly placid Kandy pitch, Central Province had successfully chased 512 in the fourth innings, a record in first-class cricket. And on a sunny, spectacular fourth afternoon, Jayasuriya kept Sri Lanka's series alive. After struggling with cramp he largely gave up on singles, smashing straight drives in a shot-a-ball 131. But Australia kept heart, Sri Lanka lost three late wickets and both sides endured a nervous fourth night. Sri Lanka needed 51 runs, Australia three wickets.

A bigger crowd filed in on the last morning, expecting a close finish and hoping for a home win. They got neither. The agonising test of nerves lasted only three overs. Australia's plan was to give Vaas the single and attack the junior partner. Vaas increased the tension with three early boundaries. Trying for a third he swiped Warne, relentlessly accurate, towards the jungle beyond mid-wicket. The four men on the leg-side rope made it a reckless gamble. It failed. With Vaas went his side's last realistic hope of saving the series. The travelling fans broke into "Advance Australia Fair" and that smile of Ponting's seemed wider than ever, not least because it was tinged with relief.

Man of the Match: S. K. Warne.

Close of play: First day, Sri Lanka (1) 7-92 (Vaas 16, Zoysa 0); Second day, Australia (2) 2-221 (Gilchrist 140, Martyn 64); Third day, Australia (2) 5-320 (Martyn 104, Symonds 6); Fourth day, Sri Lanka (2) 7-301 (Vaas 30, Lokuarachchi 13).

Australia

	R	B	4/6		R	B	4/6
J. L. Langer lbw b Zoysa	3	39	0	– c Sangakkara b Zoysa	9	31	1
M. L. Hayden lbw b Muralidaran	54	99	7 1	– c and b Vaas	5	9	1
*R. T. Ponting lbw b Vaas	10	11	2	– (6) c Sangakkara b Vaas	27	49	2 1
D. R. Martyn lbw b Muralidaran	1	6	0	– st Sangakkara b Muralidaran	161	347	21 1
D. S. Lehmann b Zoysa	8	16	2	– lbw b Vaas	21	36	4
A. Symonds c Tillakaratne b Zoysa	6	14	0	– (7) lbw b Muralidaran	23	72	2
†A. C. Gilchrist c Sangakkara b Zoysa	0	2	0	– (3) lbw b Muralidaran	144	185	19 3
S. K. Warne c Muralidaran b Vaas	18	31	3	– c Zoysa b Muralidaran	6	26	1
J. N. Gillespie c Jayawardene b M'daran	8	24	1	– c Atapattu b Muralidaran	11	25	1
M. S. Kasprowicz b Muralidaran	0	2	0	– c Jayawardene b Zoysa	8	10	0 1
S. C. G. MacGill not out	8	10	2	– not out	17	18	4
B 1, l-b 3	4			B 2, l-b 7, n-b 1	10		
(42.2 overs, 200 mins)	120			(134.3 overs, 575 mins)	442		

Fall: 25 47 50 60 84 84 86 100
106 120

Fall: 11 26 226 255 304 360
376 393 408 442

Bowling: *First Innings*—Vaas 11.2–5–14–2; Zoysa 16–3–54–4; Muralidaran 15–4–48–4. *Second Innings*—Vaas 33–6–103–3; Muralidaran 50.3–8–173–5; Zoysa 33–11–102–2; Lokuarachchi 12–2–33–0; Jayasuriya 5–0–16–0; Dilshan 1–0–6–0.

Sri Lanka

	R	B	4/6		R	B	4/6
M. S. Atapattu c Gilchrist b Kasprowicz	9	37	1	– lbw b Gillespie	8	11	2
S. T. Jayasuriya lbw b Kasprowicz	1	4	0	– c Gilchrist b Gillespie	131	145	17 2
D. A. Gunawardene lbw b Kasprowicz	13	23	2	– lbw b Kasprowicz	9	19	2
†K. C. Sangakkara c Symonds b Gillespie	5	19	0	– c and b Warne	29	46	4
D. P. M. Jayawardene c Symonds b Warne	17	46	2	– c Gilchrist b Gillespie	13	45	2
*H. P. Tillakaratne c Gilchrist b Warne	16	60	1	– (7) c Ponting b Warne	7	15	1
T. M. Dilshan lbw b Warne	0	1	0	– (6) b Warne	43	62	6
W. P. U. J. C. Vaas not out	68	126	9 1	– c Langer b Warne	45	53	8
D. N. T. Zoysa c Gilchrist b Kasprowicz	4	8	1	– (10) c Gilchrist b Gillespie	0	6	0
K. S. Lokuarachchi c Kasprowicz b Warne	15	30	3	– (9) lbw b Warne	16	34	3
M. Muralidaran c Symonds b Warne	43	28	5 3	– not out	4	4	1
B 8, l-b 9, n-b 3	20			B 4, l-b 14, n-b 1	19		

(63.1 overs, 268 mins)	211	
Fall: 6 34 39 49 67 67 88 111		
132 211		

(73.1 overs, 332 mins)	324	
Fall: 17 36 98 174 218 239 274		
319 320 324		

Bowling: *First Innings*—Gillespie 12–4–25–1; Kasprowicz 24–5–83–4; Warne 20.1–3–65–5; Symonds 2–1–1–0; MacGill 5–1–20–0. *Second Innings*—Kasprowicz 17–1–55–1; Gillespie 20–1–76–4; Warne 21.1–2–90–5; Symonds 3–0–16–0; MacGill 12.0–0–69–0.

Umpires: S. A. Bucknor (West Indies) and D. L. Orchard (South Africa).
TV Umpire: T. H. Wijewardene.
Referee: B. C. Broad (England).

SRI LANKA v AUSTRALIA

Third Test Match

by JIM MAXWELL

At Sinhalese Sports Club Ground, Colombo, March 24, 25, 26, 27, 28, 2004. Australia won by 121 runs. *Toss:* Australia.

Australia achieved an historic series whitewash when Michael Kasprowicz trapped Rangana Herath leg-before with eight balls remaining. For the third time Sri Lanka's hopes of rescuing a spirited contest had been dashed by a combination of rash strokes, faltering concentration and Australian perseverance in wearying heat; and by the decisive, spectacular intervention of Shane Warne.

At tea on the final day, Sri Lanka were 4 for 186 and well placed to save the game. If not conquered, Warne had at least been nullified, reduced to two wickets in the first innings and none in the second. Perversely it was Darren Lehmann who winkled out three top-order batsmen, underlining Australia's dearth of a specialist finger-spinner. Meanwhile Warne probed and spun his leg-break, unlucky but undaunted. Pitching into the rough outside off, he denied the aggressive Kumar Sangakkara any errant offering. Reverting to survival mode, Sangakkara flung his pads at a full-pitched leg-break wide of off stump. His method betrayed him and the ball spun from pads to stumps.

Tillakaratne Dilshan opted for counterattack, the captain Hashan Tillakaratne for grim defence. There was no calculation to Dilshan's play. He smeared Warne for an off-driven four, then lobbed another just short of Damien Martyn at mid-off. Another invitingly flung leg-break brought a leading edge, this time drifting into Martyn's overhead grasp. Ricky Ponting claimed the new ball and the final 15-over countdown began with four wickets needed. Jason Gillespie immediately hit his length and struck Tillakaratne in front. Australia were swarming.

Gillespie and Kasprowicz strained persistently outside off, testing the judgement of Chaminda Vaas and Nuwan Zoysa. With the overs ticking Ponting called back his strike weapon. Zoysa, the tallest man on the ground, failed to reach far enough to cover a floating leg-break and was bowled. Vaas played back instead of forward and Warne leapt round in excitement. Umpire Bucknor had been rejecting optimistic appeals all afternoon, but Vaas's misjudgement elicited the characteristic Bucknor nod. It was Warne's 517th wicket. Muttiah Muralidaran, four wickets behind, survived the last three balls of the over. Kasprowicz crashed emphatically into Herath's pads in the next.

The match gyrated intriguingly over five days after Ponting maintained his unblemished record with the coin. Brad Williams replaced Stuart MacGill while Simon Katich, after much public clamouring and scores of 125 and 77 not out in his most recent Test, was reinstated ahead of Andrew Symonds. Sri Lanka also made two changes, Thilan Samaraweera coming in for Avishka Gunawardene and the left-armer Herath for Kaushal Lokuarachchi.

Some enterprising batting from Lehmann and Ponting finally enabled Australia to mount a competitive first-innings total, something which had again looked unlikely after the openers departed playing injudicious shots. Ponting contributed 92 of their dazzling 121-run partnership, racing effortlessly towards his first century as captain. He clouted Vaas for two magnificent fours then attempted a third, last ball before tea, and succeeded only in slapping a straightforward catch to mid-off. Ponting's aggression deserved the accolades of a full house. Instead the stands were almost empty, a lonely group of Australian supporters playing their own game on the vacant mound beneath the scoreboard.

DEAD-RUBBER BLUES

The record of selected Australian captains in Tests where the series outcome – win or lose – has already been decided.

	M	W	L	D	Won %
Ricky Ponting	1	1	–	–	100
Steve Waugh	12	9	3	–	75
Mark Taylor	7	2	4	1	28
Allan Border	12	8	1	3	66
Kim Hughes	3	–	2	1	0
Greg Chappell	5	2	1	2	40
Ian Chappell	4	2	1	1	50
Lindsay Hassett	5	3	1	1	60
Don Bradman	3	3	–	–	100
Bill Woodfull	5	3	2	–	60
Warwick Armstrong	4	2	–	2	50

Lehmann attacked Murali with defiant and precise footwork. He survived a difficult chance to Mahela Jayawardene at slip on 20, but the error did nothing to disrupt the flow of powerful drives and innovative deflections. He danced down and across the pitch, seeking to break up the bowlers' defensive line, and felt sufficiently at home to comment afterwards that he had been "a little bit bored". Murali again worked his way through the lower order, with only Warne lingering, eventually claiming his fourth five-wicket bag of the series.

The Sri Lankan openers responded vigorously. Marvan Atapattu was erect and efficient; Sanath Jayasuriya erupted. He pounced on some loose new-ball bowling, frequently hammering the fence with his signature cuts and cover-drives. Lehmann's first delivery, a friendly full toss, was thumped for four. Attempting more of the same next ball, Jayasuriya miscued an on-drive and Gillespie held a fine running catch in the deep. Atapattu carried on craftily for his hundred and Sri Lanka were comfortably placed at 2 for 239.

The third morning began sensationally, Gillespie pinning Jayawardene to the crease and having him caught behind off his third ball of the day. His fourth, an almost unplayable leg-cutter, cuffed the top of a bewildered Dilshan's off stump. Kasprowicz followed up with an equally immaculate off-cutter and suddenly Atapattu's off stump was bent back too. Tillakaratne, his captaincy under fire and his position under scrutiny, dug in. He was still there four and a half stoic hours later, enough to secure a narrow first-innings lead but too little too late to salvage either his leadership or his spot.

He had earlier, in bizarre circumstances, survived a belated hit-wicket appeal. TV replays showed an aberrant Justin Langer walking between Tillakaratne and the stumps as he crossed the pitch, flicking off a bail as he went. Langer told a code-of-conduct hearing he was unaware he had done it. The match referee, Chris Broad, accepted his amnesic explanation and Langer was let off with a reminder not to do it again.

Perhaps he had been mulling over his poor form: 75 runs in five innings. Certainly his determination to make amends next morning was obvious. Australia were precariously poised at 3 for 80, prompting chortles about whether dead-rubber syndrome – that occasional recent affliction – might raise its ugly head under Ponting too. Langer and Katich restored Australia's nerve with a 218-run stand. Langer, battling leg cramps and assisted by a runner, carved out a memorable century, while Katich's serene batting re-emphasised the sin of his earlier omission. Australia were all out shortly before stumps with a day to play, time enough for them to snatch a third consecutive come-from-behind victory.

Murali's three wickets gave him a total of 28. But Warne's 26 were more telling, making him a worthy man of the series. Meanwhile Ponting joined Warwick Armstrong, Lindsay Hassett and Bill Lawry as the only Australian captains to win their first three Tests in charge. Part one of his mission to improve Australia's record on the subcontinent had been accomplished.

Man of the Match: D. S. Lehmann.   *Man of the Series*: S. K. Warne.

Close of play: First day, Australia (1) 6-314 (Lehmann 104, Warne 7); Second day, Sri Lanka (1) 2-239 (Atapattu 109, Jayawardene 29); Third day, Australia (2) 3-80 (Langer 29); Fourth day, Sri Lanka (2) 0-18 (Atapattu 5, Jayasuriya 13).

Australia

	R	B	4/6		R	B	4/6
J. L. Langer c Dilshan b Vaas	19	29	3	– b Vaas	166	295	13 [2]
M. L. Hayden c (s) U. D. U. Chandana							
b S'weera	25	46	3	– lbw b Vaas	28	31	5
*R. T. Ponting c Muralidaran b Vaas	92	141	11 [1]	– c Samaraweera b Herath	20	36	2
D. R. Martyn c Sangakkara b Vaas	14	41	2	– (5) lbw b Herath	5	6	0
D. S. Lehmann c Jayasuriya b Muralidaran	153	267	14 [2]	– (6) c Sangakkara b Muralidaran	1	3	0
S. M. Katich c and b Muralidaran	14	36	2	– (7) lbw b Muralidaran	86	213	7 [1]
†A.C. Gilchrist c Jayasuriya b Muralidaran	22	46	2	– (8) not out	31	41	0 [2]
S. K. Warne lbw b Muralidaran	32	71	2	– (9) c Samaraweera b Herath	0	3	0
J. N. Gillespie c Tillakaratne b Muralidaran	0	10	0	– (4) c Jayawardene b Muralidaran	1	5	0
M. S. Kasprowicz b Jayasuriya	4	5	1	– run out (Jayasuriya)	3	6	0
B. A. Williams not out	0	3	0	– c and b Herath	2	4	0
B 13, l-b 9, n-b 4	26			B 11, l-b 11, w 4, n-b 6	32		

(115.1 overs, 487 mins)	401	(106.2 overs, 467 mins)	375

Fall: 43 60 96 217 244 299 376 380   Fall: 40 79 80 89 98 316 341 346
387 401   368 375

Bowling: First Innings—Vaas 26–3–93–3; Zoysa 3.3–1–23–0; Samaraweera 14.3–1–38–1; Muralidaran 37.1–6–123–5; Herath 23–5–75–0; Jayasuriya 11–1–27–1. *Second Innings*—Vaas 21–3–61–2; Zoysa 12–0–54–0; Muralidaran 29–5–93–3; Herath 24.2–1–92–4; Samaraweera 15–4–40–0; Jayasuriya 4–0–13–0; Dilshan 1–1–0–0.

Sri Lanka

	R	B	4/6		R	B	4/6
M. S. Atapattu b Kasprowicz	118	219	19	– b Kasprowicz	14	48	1
S. T. Jayasuriya c Gillespie b Lehmann	71	78	9 1	– c Katich b Lehmann	51	83	7
†K. C. Sangakkara c Gilchrist b Lehmann	22	39	3	– (5) b Warne	27	27	4
D. P. M. Jayawardene c Gilchrist b Gillespie	29	72	4	– c Gilchrist b Lehmann	37	100	4 1
T. M. Dilshan b Gillespie	0	1	0	– (6) c Martyn b Warne	31	44	5
*H. P. Tillakaratne not out	74	201	10	– lbw b Gillespie	17	61	3
T. T. Samaraweera c Gilchrist b Gillespie	41	84	8	– (3) st Gilchrist b Lehmann	53	125	7
W. P. U. J. C. Vaas b Warne	24	31	5	– lbw b Warne	9	38	1
D. N. T. Zoysa st Gilchrist b Lehmann	3	3	0	– b Warne	1	15	0
H. M. R. K. B. Herath c Martyn b Warne	3	26	0	– lbw b Kasprowicz	0	20	0
M. Muralidaran c Warne b Kasprowicz	8	11	1	– not out	0	3	0
B 4, l-b 7, w 1, n-b 2	14			B 4, l-b 1, w 1, n-b 2	8		

(127.1 overs, 530 mins)	407	(93.4 overs, 403 mins)	248

Fall: 134 175 240 240 256 327 378 381 390 407

Fall: 45 92 156 181 191 231 245 247 248 248

Bowling: *First Innings*—Gillespie 23–4–96–3; Kasprowicz 22.1–5–58–2; Williams 19–5–48–0; Warne 36–7–115–2; Lehmann 19–2–50–3; Katich 8–0–29–0. *Second Innings*—Gillespie 18–6–38–1; Kasprowicz 16.4–5–37–2; Warne 33–11–92–4; Williams 5–0–19–0; Lehmann 17–2–42–3; Katich 4–1–15–0.

Umpires: S. A. Bucknor (West Indies) and D. L. Orchard (South Africa).
TV Umpire: P. T. Manuel.
Referee: B. C. Broad (England).

ONE-DAY SERIES

by CHARLIE AUSTIN

Australia displayed no hint of their alleged frailties on the subcontinent during the five-match one-day series against Sri Lanka that preceded the Tests. Dusty pitches, oven-like temperatures, shirt-drenching humidity and an opposition attack bursting with spinning options – it mattered little. Australia's batsmen were spin-savvy and streetwise. The reward was a comfortable 3-2 win, their first one-day tournament victory in Sri Lanka.

On their last two visits, for the Aiwa Cup in 1999 and the Champions Trophy in 2002, Australia had come unstuck against spin bowling on excruciatingly slow pitches. Strangely it was often the part-timers – Aravinda de Silva, Russel Arnold, Sanath Jayasuriya – who unravelled Australia's top order. Sri Lanka cooked up a similar strategy this time round, with curators encouraged to produce biscuit-dry wickets and six spinners given a bowl during one game in Dambulla.

But the Australians came fully prepared. The gum-chewing, chest-pouting bravado of their one-day cricket back home, where they had ruthlessly quelled a spirited Indian rebellion in the VB Series, was replaced with a more tempered and calculated approach. Although positive, the batsmen were patient too, employing delicate wristwork to milk the spinners. Ricky Ponting led from the front with four consecutive fifties, each coming at a good lick. But the star was Andrew Symonds, bowling and batting himself ever closer to a Test debut. His off-breaks captured vital wickets at key moments, while his strokeplay was always cool-headed and often brutal.

Sri Lanka looked a little ring-rusty after playing only a single one-dayer in the previous eight months. Still, they had their moments: some fine death bowling from

Chaminda Vaas to snatch a one-run win in Dambulla; Kumar Sangakkara's exhilarating 101 under the lights at Premadasa; Nuwan Zoysa's surprise heroics with bat and ball to steal the final match. But at the pivotal moments it was the Australians who held their nerve and the Sri Lankans who self-destructed. In the opening game they looked on target for victory only to lose their last seven wickets for 33. In the fourth match, well on their way to levelling the series, eight wickets tumbled for 50.

Most importantly, the Australians had done their homework on Muttiah Muralidaran. His new and improved doosra, which spat in the opposite direction to his stock off-break, had triggered panic in the England camp before Christmas. Australia's batsmen decoded much of its mystery. Although Murali remained dangerous it was Sri Lanka's seamers who presented the greatest threat. It boded well for the Test matches ahead.

AUSTRALIAN LIMITED-OVERS SQUAD

R. T. Ponting (*captain*), A. C. Gilchrist (*vice-captain*), M. G. Bevan, M. J. Clarke, J. N. Gillespie, B. J. Haddin, I. J. Harvey, M. L. Hayden, G. B. Hogg, M. S. Kasprowicz, S. M. Katich, B. Lee, D. R. Martyn, A. Symonds and B. A. Williams.

RUNSCORERS

	M	I	NO	R	HS	100s	50s	Avge	Ct/St	S-R
R. T. Ponting (Aus)	4	4	0	257	69	0	4	64.25	1	78.35
K. C. Sangakkara (SL)	5	5	0	250	101	1	1	50.00	2	75.76
D. P. M. Jayawardene (SL)	5	5	0	225	80	0	2	45.00	3	66.77
A. Symonds (Aus)	5	5	3	211	53	0	1	105.50	0	85.08
M. L. Hayden (Aus)	4	4	0	151	93	0	1	37.75	2	75.88
D. R. Martyn (Aus)	5	5	0	133	62	0	1	26.60	0	61.29
A. C. Gilchrist (Aus)	5	5	0	98	66	0	1	19.60	9/1	83.05
M. J. Clarke (Aus)	5	5	1	83	36	0	0	20.75	3	68.60
T. M. Dilshan (SL)	5	5	1	83	30	0	0	20.75	3	62.88
M. G. Bevan (Aus)	5	5	1	83	24*	0	0	20.75	2	60.58
S. T. Jayasuriya (SL)	5	5	0	76	55	0	1	15.20	1	78.35
M. S. Atapattu (SL)	5	5	0	70	47	0	0	14.00	2	47.62
U. D. U. Chandana (SL)	5	5	0	64	34	0	0	12.80	2	64.65
D. N. T. Zoysa (SL)	3	3	2	48	47*	0	0	48.00	2	101.91
G. B. Hogg (Aus)	5	3	2	37	35*	0	0	37.00	1	67.27
R. P. Arnold (SL)	3	3	1	37	23*	0	0	18.50	1	35.92
W. P. U. J. C. Vaas (SL)	4	4	0	29	24	0	0	7.25	2	80.56
H. D. P. K. Dharmasena (SL)	3	3	1	26	24*	0	0	13.00	0	118.18
W. S. Jayantha (SL)	2	2	0	24	23	0	0	12.00	1	77.42
K. S. Lokuarachchi (SL)	1	1	0	18	18	0	0	18.00	0	94.74
S. M. Katich (Aus)	1	1	0	13	13	0	0	13.00	1	86.67
B. J. Haddin (Aus)	1	1	0	9	9	0	0	9.00	1	42.86
J. N. Gillespie (Aus)	4	1	1	8	8*	0	0	–	0	53.33
I. J. Harvey (Aus)	3	1	0	4	4	0	0	4.00	0	100.00
M. Muralidaran (SL)	5	3	2	4	2*	0	0	4.00	2	80.00
R. S. Kaluwitharana (SL)	2	2	0	2	2	0	0	1.00	0/1	18.18
B. Lee (Aus)	3	1	1	1	1*	0	0	–	2	100.00
K. M. D. N. Kulasekara (SL)	2	1	0	1	1	0	0	1.00	0	33.33
M. S. Kasprowicz (Aus)	1	0	0	0	0	0	0	0.00	0	0.00
B. A. Williams (Aus)	2	0	–	–	–	–	–	–	1	–

* Denotes not out.

WICKET-TAKERS

	O	Mdns	R	W	BB	5W/i	Avge	RPO
G. B. Hogg (Aus)	43.1	2	193	9	5-41	1	21.44	4.47
M. S. Kasprowicz (Aus)	28	5	102	8	5-45	1	12.75	3.64
M. Muralidaran (SL)	49	2	201	7	3-44	0	28.71	4.10
W. P. U. J. C. Vaas (SL)	32	2	146	7	3-34	0	20.86	4.56
U. D. U. Chandana (SL)	41.4	0	198	7	3-37	0	28.29	4.75
J. N. Gillespie (Aus)	31	5	106	5	3-36	0	21.20	3.42
A. Symonds (Aus)	48.5	3	214	5	2-34	0	42.80	4.38
M. J. Clarke (Aus)	24.5	0	112	5	5-35	1	22.40	4.51
D. N. T. Zoysa (SL)	25.1	3	111	4	3-34	0	27.75	4.41
B. A. Williams (Aus)	14	1	57	1	1-29	0	57.00	4.07
H. D. P. K. Dharmasena (SL)	26.5	0	120	1	1-40	0	120.00	4.47
K. S. Lokuarachchi (SL)	8	0	40	1	1-40	0	40.00	5.00
S. T. Jayasuriya (SL)	34	1	172	1	1-66	0	172.00	5.06
I. J. Harvey (Aus)	22	0	101	2	1-34	0	50.50	4.59
B. Lee (Aus)	23	2	122	2	1-31	0	61.00	5.30
R. P. Arnold (SL)	2	0	9	0	–	0	–	4.50
T. M. Dilshan (SL)	14.3	0	73	0	–	0	–	5.03
K. M. D. N. Kulasekara (SL)	13	0	68	0	–	0	–	5.23

†SRI LANKA CRICKET PRESIDENT'S XI v AUSTRALIANS

At De Zoysa Stadium, Moratuwa, February 17, 2004. Australians won by five wickets. Sri Lanka Cricket President's XI 8 for 283 (W. S. Jayantha 50, J. Mubarak 56, R. P. Arnold 35, W. M. G. Ramyakumara 33*; G. B. Hogg 2-46); Australians 5 for 284 (A. C. Gilchrist 43, M. L. Hayden 35, R. T. Ponting 57, D. R. Martyn 41, A. Symonds 47).

†SRI LANKA v AUSTRALIA

First Limited-Overs International

At Rangiri Dambulla International Stadium, Dambulla, February 20, 2004. Day/night game. Australia won by 84 runs. *Toss:* Australia.

The potential risks of Sri Lanka's spin-obsessed strategy, which involved the production of two bone-dry surfaces in Dambulla, were graphically exposed. Australia won the toss, savoured the best of the batting conditions and galloped past the previous ground record – Pakistan's 9 for 203 in 2002-03. The tone of both the innings and tour was set by an authoritative 104-run stand in 114 balls between Matthew Hayden and Adam Gilchrist. Ricky Ponting and Damien Martyn maintained the momentum in the middle overs, before Andrew Symonds provided an exhilarating late flourish. Forty-four of Australia's 50 overs had been bowled by spinners. Sri Lanka started disastrously, with Romesh Kaluwitharana then Sanath Jayasuriya run out after sloppy running. Mahela Jayawardene and Kumar Sangakkara first batted the hosts back into the match, then put them briefly on course for victory. But a hostile second spell from Brett Lee brought about Sangakkara's downfall and Jayawardene followed soon afterwards, inside-edging a fizzing off-break from Symonds on to his stumps. The lower order panicked upon the introduction of Brad Hogg, who finished with career-best figures. His left-arm chinamen, largely unfamiliar to Sri Lankans, gained plenty of encouragement from a rapidly wearing pitch.

Man of the Match: G. B. Hogg.

Australia

†A.C. Gilchrist c Atapattu b Chandana	66	(63)	M.J. Clarke lbw b Muralidaran	0	(3)
M.L. Hayden run out (Atapattu)	40	(58)	G.B. Hogg not out	2	(6)
*R.T. Ponting c Dilshan b Jayasuriya	58	(82)			
D.R. Martyn c and b Chandana	27	(38)	L-b 5, w 5, n-b 1	11	
M.G. Bevan st Kaluwitharana					
b Muralidaran	21	(31)	(50 overs, 194 mins) (6 wkts)	262	
A. Symonds not out	37	(20)	Fall: 104 114 189 207 239 239		

B. Lee, J.N. Gillespie and B.A. Williams did not bat.

Bowling: Vaas 3–0–19–0; Kulasekara 3–0–18–0; Dharmasena 10–0–49–0; Dilshan 5–0–28–0; Muralidaran 10–2–30–2; Chandana 10–0–47–2; Jayasuriya 9–0–66–1.

Sri Lanka

S.T. Jayasuriya run out (Lee/Gilchrist)	8	(10)	K.M.D.N. Kulasekara b Hogg	1	(3)
†R.S. Kaluwitharana run out (Ponting)	2	(8)	M. Muralidaran c Lee b Hogg	0	(2)
*M.S. Atapattu b Gillespie	1	(9)			
K.C. Sangakkara c Gilchrist b Lee	58	(91)			
D.P.M. Jayawardene b Symonds	61	(90)	B 1, l-b 2, w 13, n-b 4	20	
T.M. Dilshan not out	18	(29)			
U.D.U. Chandana lbw b Hogg	9	(13)	(43.3 overs, 189 mins)	178	
W.P.U.J.C. Vaas c Hayden b Hogg	0	(8)	Fall: 12 13 24 145 147 166 170		
H.D.P.K. Dharmasena st Gilchrist			170 178 178		
b Hogg	0	(2)			

Bowling: Gillespie 6–2–14–1; Lee 8–1–31–1; Williams 5–0–28–0; Hogg 9.3–1–41–5; Clarke 5–0–21–0; Symonds 10–0–40–1.

Umpires: B.F. Bowden (New Zealand) and E.A.R. De Silva.
TV Umpire: P.T. Manuel.
Referee: M.J. Procter (South Africa).

†SRI LANKA v AUSTRALIA

Second Limited-Overs International

At Rangiri Dambulla International Stadium, Dambulla, February 22, 2004. Sri Lanka won by one run. *Toss:* Sri Lanka.

The curator abandoned plans to use two pitches and instead patched up the surface used in the opening game. Sri Lanka's selectors gambled too, picking only one fast bowler, and were counting their blessings when Marvan Atapattu won the toss. He and Sanath Jayasuriya cantered along at a run a ball before Ricky Ponting conjured the breakthrough with a superb pick-up and diving underarm flick. At 2 for 192 with 12 overs left, Sri Lanka were dreamily poised. But Michael Clarke's flattish left-armers secured regular wickets and disrupted the expected slogathon. Promoted to opener, Clarke's day soured with his second third-ball duck in a row. The mini-reshuffle appeared to upset Adam Gilchrist's rhythm for the rest of the series, but Australia looked in control so long as Ponting and Matthew Hayden were together. The pitch was deteriorating, however, and the middle order struggled to get going. There was controversy when Andrew Symonds, on 10, was adjudged leg-before and walked halfway to the pavilion, believing he had edged the ball on to his pad. The non-striker Gilchrist threw down his gloves in disgust – a gesture for which he was fined half his match fee – and Symonds was belatedly recalled when the umpire Peter Manuel had second thoughts. Symonds and Michael Bevan then carried Australia to the brink of victory, requiring only eight runs from Chaminda Vaas's last over. Vaas permitted two singles, followed up with dot-balls, and held his nerve right to the end.

Man of the Match: W.P.U.J.C. Vaas.

Sri Lanka

*M. S. Atapattu run out (Ponting)	 47	(68)	W. P. U. J. C. Vaas c Lee b Clarke	... 5 (5)
S. T. Jayasuriya lbw b Symonds	 55	(65)	H. D. P. K. Dharmasena run out (Ponting) 2 (5)	
K. C. Sangakkara c Bevan b Harvey	.. 39	(58)	M. Muralidaran not out	.... 2 (2)
D. P. M. Jayawardene c Ponting b Clarke 38		(61)	B 1, l-b 16, w 8, n-b 7 32	
T. M. Dilshan b Clarke	 11	(18)		
†R. S. Kaluwitharana run out (Hayden)	0	(3)	(49.5 overs, 210 mins)	245
U. D. U. Chandana c Gilchrist b Clarke	4	(6)	Fall: 121 122 192 216 220 225 226	
R. P. Arnold lbw b Clarke	 10	(13)	236 242 245	

Bowling: Gillespie 7–0–36–0; Lee 6–0–39–0; Harvey 9–0–38–1; Symonds 10–0–45–1; Hogg 10–1–35–0; Clarke 7.5–0–35–5.

Australia

M. J. Clarke c Chandana b Vaas	 0	(3)	†A. C. Gilchrist c and b Vaas	.... 0 (2)
M. L. Hayden c Jayawardene			M. G. Bevan not out	.... 24 (21)
	b Dharmasena	... 93 (116)	B 1, l-b 7, w 9 17	
*R. T. Ponting c Vaas b Chandana	... 69	(93)		
D. R. Martyn c Atapattu b Vaas	 5	(13)	(50 overs, 215 mins)	(5 wkts) 244
A. Symonds not out	 36	(52)	Fall: 0 148 170 190 192	

I. J. Harvey, G. B. Hogg, B. Lee and J. N. Gillespie did not bat.

Bowling: Vaas 10–0–48–3; Dilshan 6–0–32–0; Dharmasena 10–0–40–1; Muralidaran 10–0–49–0; Chandana 9–0–40–1; Arnold 2–0–9–0; Jayasuriya 3–0–18–0.

Umpires: B. F. Bowden (New Zealand) and P. T. Manuel.
TV Umpire: M. G. Silva.
Referee: M. J. Procter (South Africa).

†SRI LANKA v AUSTRALIA

Third Limited-Overs International

At R. Premadasa Stadium, Colombo, February 25, 2004. Day/night game. Australia won by five wickets. *Toss:* Sri Lanka.

With the series level, the teams left Sri Lanka's central drylands and returned to the seaside capital of Colombo, The Premadasa pitch normally favours batsmen during the first innings of day/night games, but Jason Gillespie located some early new-ball venom on a steamy afternoon. Operating from a short run, he uncorked the top three with his extra bounce, aiming short and sharp at the batsmen's bodies. Sanath Jayasuriya poked a tame catch to gully fifth ball of the innings, Marvan Atapattu chopped on to his stumps and Kumar Sangakkara edged to slip. The hard-working Mahela Jayawardene led a partial recovery with his highest score in more than two years. But 226 looked way too modest despite a wobbly Australian start, Matthew Hayden driving straight to cover and Adam Gilchrist edging a curling outswinger. Ricky Ponting's purple patch continued with support from an acquisitive Damien Martyn, whose 62 included only three fours. The dismissal of both in consecutive overs gave Sri Lanka a sniff, but Andrew Symonds and Michael Clarke finished things off with a flourish.

Man of the Match: J. N. Gillespie.

Sri Lanka

*M. S. Atapattu b Gillespie	3	(16)
S. T. Jayasuriya c Clarke b Gillespie	0	(2)
†K. C. Sangakkara c Hayden b Gillespie	15	(30)
D. P. M. Jayawardene run out (Hogg)	80	(112)
R. P. Arnold c Clarke b Hogg	4	(26)
T. M. Dilshan c Gilchrist b Symonds	30	(38)
U. D. U. Chandana run out (Hogg)	34	(40)

W. P. U. J. C. Vaas c Hogg b Kasprowicz	24	(21)
H. D. P. K. Dharmasena not out	24	(15)
D. N. T. Zoysa not out	0	(0)
B 1, l-b 8, w 3	12	

(50 overs, 204 mins)   (8 wkts) 226

Fall: 1 10 34 54 112 170 182 218

M. Muralidaran did not bat.

Bowling: Gillespie 10–1–36–3; Kasprowicz 10–2–37–1; Harvey 6–0–29–0; Hogg 10–0–41–1; Clarke 5–0–26–0; Symonds 9–0–48–1.

Australia

†A. C. Gilchrist c Jayawardene b Vaas	0	(9)
M. L. Hayden c Muralidaran b Vaas	3	(5)
*R. T. Ponting b Vaas	63	(75)
D. R. Martyn run out (Jayasuriya)	62	(97)
A. Symonds not out	45	(52)
M. G. Bevan run out (Jayawardene)	10	(18)

M. J. Clarke not out	31	(36)
L-b 4, w 8, n-b 1	13	

(48.3 overs, 205 mins)   (5 wkts) 227

Fall: 3 4 133 136 159

I. J. Harvey, G. B. Hogg, M. S. Kasprowicz and J. N. Gillespie did not bat.

Bowling: Vaas 9–2–34–3; Zoysa 7.1–0–37–0; Dharmasena 6.5–0–31–0; Muralidaran 10–0–43–0; Chandana 7–0–36–0; Jayasuriya 8–0–40–0; Dilshan 0.3–0–2–0.

Umpires: B. F. Bowden (New Zealand) and E. A. R. De Silva.
TV Umpire: M. G. Silva.
Referee: M. J. Procter (South Africa).

†SRI LANKA v AUSTRALIA

Fourth Limited-Overs International

At R. Premadasa Stadium, Colombo, February 27, 2004. Day/night game. Australia won by 40 runs. *Toss:* Australia. *Limited-overs international debut:* W. S. Jayantha.

Sri Lanka squandered a golden winning position and Australia wrapped up the series with a game to spare. On a drier, re-used surface, Australia's smallish 233 was built around Ricky Ponting's 67 and boosted late in the innings by Michael Clarke's quick-fire 36. It shouldn't have been enough; it wouldn't have been but for a vigorous 10 overs from Michael Kasprowicz, opening the bowling in preference to Brett Lee. He nailed the early wicket of Sanath Jayasuriya, before Kumar Sangakkara snatched back the initiative with a thrilling counter-assault. He played himself in carefully, as Kasprowicz and Jason Gillespie threatened, then swung on to the offensive with a flood of off-side boundaries, working the 30,000 spectators into a frenzy. At 2 for 143 with 18 overs left, Sri Lanka were cruising. But local celebrations proved premature. Gillespie, brought back for one last blast, found Mahela Jayawardene's edge and started the freefall. Kasprowicz eventually had Sangakkara caught behind, moments after he had raised the only century of the series, then ran through the lower order as Sri Lanka lost their last eight wickets for 50. Gilchrist finished with six catches – equalling the one-day world record he already shared. Kasprowicz took his first five-for. With the Tests a week away, his timing was impeccable.

Man of the Match: M. S. Kasprowicz.

Australia

†A. C. Gilchrist c Sangakkara b Zoysa 14 (18)
M. L. Hayden c Zoysa b Vaas 15 (20)
*R. T. Ponting lbw b Muralidaran 67 (78)
D. R. Martyn c Zoysa b Lokuaracchi . 1 (6)
A. Symonds c Jayantha b Muralidaran 53 (77)
M. G. Bevan c and b Muralidaran 14 (34)
M. J. Clarke c Dilshan b Chandana ... 36 (32)
I. J. Harvey run out (Atapattu/Muralidaran) 4 (4)
G. B. Hogg lbw b Chandana 0 (1)

M. S. Kasprowicz c Sangakkara
               b Chandana..   0   (6)
J. N. Gillespie not out 8 (15)

L-b 3, w 12, n-b 6 21
                                  ——
(47.4 overs, 211 mins)   233
Fall: 28 42 62 136 177 201 205
      205 206 233

Bowling: Vaas 10–0–45–1; Zoysa 8–0–40–1; Lokuaracchi 8–0–40–1; Muralidaran 10–0–44–3; Jayasuriya 4–0–24–0; Chandana 7.4–0–37–3.

Sri Lanka

*M. S. Atapattu c Bevan b Hogg 19 (44)
S. T. Jayasuriya c Gilchrist b Kasprowicz 0 (1)
†K. C. Sangakkara c Gilchrist
               b Kasprowicz ..101(110)
D. P. M. Jayawardene c Gilchrist
               b Gillespie ... 25 (44)
W. S. Jayantha c Gilchrist b Harvey .. 1 (4)
T. M. Dilshan run out (Symonds/Ponting) 9 (9)
U. D. U. Chandana c Gilchrist
               b Kasprowicz ... 13 (22)

K. S. Lokuaracchi lbw b Kasprowicz 18 (19)
W. P. U. J. C. Vaas c Gilchrist
               b Kasprowicz ...   0   (2)
D. N. T. Zoysa lbw b Hogg 1   (5)
M. Muralidaran not out 2   (1)
L-b 2, w 2   4

(43.4 overs, 192 mins)   193
Fall: 0 78 143 148 150 158 189 189
      190 193

Bowling: Gillespie 8–2–20–1; Kasprowicz 9–1–45–5; Harvey 7–0–34–1; Symonds 10–1–47–0; Hogg 6.4–0–32–2; Clarke 3–0–13–0.

Umpires: B. F. Bowden (New Zealand) and T. H. Wijewardene.
TV Umpire: P. E. Manuel.
Referee: M. J. Procter (South Africa).

†SRI LANKA v AUSTRALIA

Fifth Limited-Overs International

At Sinhalese Sports Club Ground, Colombo, February 29, 2004. Sri Lanka won by three wickets. *Toss:* Australia.

With the series settled, Australia decided to rest several key players and the fans seemed similarly disinterested. The grassy banks in front of the giant scoreboard were quiet and empty all day long. And yet this was a taut contest with a fine finish, featuring a starring all-round role by Nuwan Zoysa. Playing his first international series in almost two years, Zoysa bogged down Australia's makeshift top order with a fine new-ball burst. But for another defiant contribution from Andrew Symonds, Australia would have posted far fewer than their below-par 198. Still, it looked more than enough when Sri Lanka slumped to 7 for 136. They reckoned without Zoysa, playing on his home ground, who chose this moment to produce the innings of his life. Dropped early, he went on to race Sri Lanka to victory, dominating a 66-run stand for the eighth wicket with Russel Arnold. Earlier in the day Michael Bevan, long regarded as the world's pre-eminent limited-overs batsman, capped a personally miserable series when he struggled to 14. He was subsequently dropped from the team and lost his national contract, virtually ensuring that this was to be the final one-day international of a glorious career.

Man of the Match: D. N. T. Zoysa. *Man of the Series:* A. Symonds.

Australia

*†A. C. Gilchrist lbw b Zoysa	18	(26)
B. J. Haddin c Jayasuriya b Zoysa	9	(21)
M. J. Clarke c Dilshan b Muralidaran	16	(47)
S. M. Katich run out (Zoysa/Sangakkara)	13	(15)
D. R. Martyn b Chandana	38	(63)
M. G. Bevan c Jayawardene b Muralidaran	14	(33)
A. Symonds c Arnold b Zoysa	40	(47)
G. B. Hogg not out	35	(48)
B. Lee not out	1	(1)
L-b 6, w 7, n-b 1	14	

(50 overs, 205 mins)   (7 wkts) 198

Fall: 23 34 55 86 117 120 196

M. S. Kasprowicz and B. A. Williams did not bat.

Bowling: Zoysa 10–3–34–3; Kulasekara 10–0–50–0; Chandana 8–0–38–1; Dilshan 3–0–11–0; Jayasuriya 10–1–24–0; Muralidaran 9–0–35–2.

Sri Lanka

*M. S. Atapattu b Kasprowicz	0	(10)
S. T. Jayasuriya c Williams b Lee	13	(19)
†K. C. Sangakkara b Hogg	37	(41)
D. P. M. Jayawardene c Clarke b Williams	21	(30)
W. S. Jayantha b Kasprowicz	23	(27)
T. M. Dilshan b Symonds	15	(38)
R. P. Arnold not out	23	(64)
U. D. U. Chandana c Katich b Symonds	4	(18)
D. N. T. Zoysa not out	47	(42)
L-b 6, w 11, n-b 2	19	

(47.5 overs, 210 mins)   (7 wkts) 202

Fall: 2 25 85 91 117 126 136

K. M. D. N. Kulasekara and M. Muralidaran did not bat.

Bowling: Lee 9–1–52–1; Kasprowicz 9–2–20–2; Williams 9–1–29–1; Hogg 7–0–44–1; Clarke 4–0–17–0; Symonds 9.5–2–34–2.

Umpires: B. F. Bowden (New Zealand) and E. A. R. De Silva.
TV Umpire: T. H. Wijewardene.
Referee: M. J. Procter (South Africa).

Australia in Zimbabwe, 2004

by CHLOE SALTAU

The surreal quality of the Test series that never was is captured in the official team photograph. It was taken moments after Cricket Australia's chairman Bob Merriman announced, with not a Zimbabwe Cricket Union official in sight, that the two boards had agreed to call off the two Test matches due to the unlikelihood of a meaningful contest. And so the Australians posed by the swimming pool (*see opposite*) at their Harare hotel, thus immortalising one of the strangest tours in the game's history.

Shane Warne is barefoot in the back row, ready to leap out of his whites, jump into a car to the airport and fly back to England, where he would resume his captaincy duties with Hampshire. Standing beside him is the junior leg-spinner Cameron White, a Bairnsdale boy with spiky blond hair, looking only marginally less bewildered than he had a few weeks earlier when he was unexpectedly called up as a replacement for Stuart MacGill. White's nine days in Africa amounted to eight overs in a tour match, four rounds of golf and a couple of in-house movies. He was due to fly home the next day along with the other Tests-only players, Justin Langer and Simon Katich. With a click of the camera their tour was over. Warne was gone.

The swiftness of his exit reflected the mood of a tour on which golf form was discussed as earnestly as cricket. Profoundly confused cricketers tried to prepare normally in conditions that were screamingly abnormal. MacGill had pulled out on the eve of the tour because he wanted to "maintain a clear conscience", making his announcement shortly after 15 white Zimbabwean players, led by Heath Streak, went on strike in protest against teams being selected on the basis of race. They were subsequently sacked. A resolution between the 15 rebels and the Zimbabwe Cricket Union moved closer one hour and further away the next. Meanwhile none of the Australian players seemed quite sure what they were doing there.

SNAP AND DASH: The Australians gather poolside for the official tour photo, with the Tests aborted and the Tests-only players preparing to board aeroplanes.

According to the Australian Cricketers' Association this was a
reluctant touring party, uninterested in playing an emasculated
Zimbabwe side but beholden to Cricket Australia's obligation to
tick this box on the international touring blueprint and move on. The
players' goodwill was articulated by Matthew Hayden. "We are
cricketers, not politicians," he said shortly after passing Zimbabwe's all-rounder Sean Ervine, on his way to Perth to start a new
career, at Johannesburg airport.

As for the moral implications of the tour, it was difficult to know
how the Australian players felt. Beyond supporting MacGill's right
to make an individual decision, they were not inclined to publicly
discuss the ethics of it. Adam Gilchrist wrote in his newspaper diary
that he was "really, really confused. Having arrived in Zimbabwe
several days ago … I'm no more certain as to what is a right or
wrong decision." What was certain was that once the Tests were
called off, many players privately could see no point in remaining in
Harare for three essentially meaningless one-day matches.

As the saga grew more protracted, the Australians grew more
frustrated and restless. One day Katich and Brad Williams caught a
helicopter to a game park, describing it as the most breathtaking part
of the tour. Glenn McGrath went hunting, Hayden and Jason
Gillespie went fishing, and the rest played yet another round of golf.
The only direct inkling they had of the local political climate was
when they were told to stay close to the team hotel during street
demonstrations by supporters of Robert Mugabe's ruling Zanu-PF
party, after a white opposition MP was assaulted in parliament by
two government officials.

Ultimately the Tests were postponed indefinitely, the one-day
series brought forward and Bulawayo sliced out of the itinerary.
Australia's specialist one-day players were rushed into Harare, and
Zimbabwe were captained by the impressive 21-year-old wicket-
keeper Tatenda Taibu. He and his side fought gamely to cope without 15 of the country's best players, not to mention the likes of
Andy Flower, Murray Goodwin and Neil Johnson, who had long
since given up on playing cricket in Zimbabwe.

Of the other Australian players in that historic photo, Williams'
days were numbered too. He aggravated his lower back during the
first one-day match and flew home early. Gillespie, Australia's wild
and mullet-haired fast bowler, took seven wickets at 12.85 and was
judged Man of the Series. Michael Clarke was the only batsman to

score a century, his first in international cricket. Australia won three-nil and did so predictably and convincingly. But they did not dismember Zimbabwe in the ruthless way the world champions generally gobble up lesser teams. "It's been a really frustrating few weeks for everyone," Gilchrist admitted.

AUSTRALIAN TEST SQUAD

R. T. Ponting (*captain*), A. C. Gilchrist (*vice-captain*), J. N. Gillespie, M. L. Hayden, S. M. Katich, M. S. Kasprowicz, D. R. Martyn, G. D. McGrath, J. L. Langer, D. S. Lehmann, S. K. Warne, C. L. White, B. A. Williams.

AUSTRALIAN LIMITED-OVERS SQUAD

R. T. Ponting (*captain*), A. C. Gilchrist (*vice-captain*), M. J. Clarke, J. N. Gillespie, G. B. Hogg, I. J. Harvey, M. L. Hayden, M. S. Kasprowicz, D. R. Martyn, G. D. McGrath, D. S. Lehmann, A. Symonds, S. R. Watson, B. A. Williams.

Manager: S. R. Bernard. *Coach:* J. M. Buchanan. *Assistant coach:* T. J. Nielsen. *Physiotherapist:* A. Kontouri. *Masseur:* Ms L. Frostick. *Physical performance manager:* J. A. Campbell. *Performance manager:* B. Romalus. *Media manager:* J. Rose.

LIMITED-OVERS RUNSCORERS

	M	I	NO	R	HS	100s	50s	Avge	Ct/St	S-R
M. J. Clarke (Aus) ..	3	3	2	126	105*	1	0	126.00	1	96.18
B. R. M. Taylor (Zim)	3	3	0	125	65	0	2	41.67	1	63.45
R. T. Ponting (Aus)	3	2	0	101	91	0	1	50.50	3	98.06
D. R. Martyn (Aus)..	3	2	1	94	74*	0	1	94.00	0	80.34
A. C. Gilchrist (Aus)	3	3	0	90	44	0	0	30.00	2	113.92
M. L. Hayden (Aus)	2	2	0	87	87	0	1	43.50	1	85.29
T. Taibu (Zim)	3	3	0	85	57	0	1	28.33	0/1	63.91
E. Chigumbura (Zim)	1	1	0	77	77	0	1	77.00	0	85.56
D. S. Lehmann (Aus)	2	1	0	67	67	0	1	67.00	2	97.10
M. A. Vermeulen (Zim)	3	3	0	62	25	0	0	20.67	0	112.73
M. L. Nkala (Zim) ..	2	2	0	47	47	0	0	23.50	0	58.02
V. Sibanda (Zim) . . .	3	3	0	43	23	0	0	14.33	2	39.45
S. Matsikenyeri (Zim)	3	3	0	39	27	0	0	13.00	1	46.99
J. N. Gillespie (Aus).	3	1	1	33	33*	0	0	–	2	206.25
G. B. Hogg (Aus) . . .	2	1	0	26	26	0	0	26.00	0	96.30
A. Maregwede (Zim)	3	3	1	24	18*	0	0	12.00	0	58.54
I. J. Harvey (Aus) . . .	2	1	0	22	22	0	0	22.00	0	100.00
A. Symonds (Aus) ..	2	1	0	20	20	0	0	20.00	0	90.91
S. R. Watson (Aus)..	1	1	1	18	18*	0	0	–	1	54.55
T. Panyangara (Zim)	2	2	1	15	14*	0	0	15.00	1	78.95
D. D. Ebrahim (Zim)	2	2	0	9	8	0	0	4.50	0	45.00
T. Mupariwa (Zim) .	3	3	0	7	4	0	0	2.33	2	29.17
M. S. Kasprowicz (Aus)	3	1	1	2	2*	0	0	–	0	66.67
E. C. Rainsford (Zim)	1	1	1	1	1*	0	0	–	0	100.00
W. Mwayenga (Zim)	2	2	0	1	1	0	0	0.50	2	9.09
D. T. Hondo (Zim) ..	2	1	1	0	0*	0	0	–	0	0.00
B. A. Williams (Aus)	1	0	–	–	–	–	–	–	0	–
G. D. McGrath (Aus)	3	0	–	–	–	–	–	–	3	–

* Denotes not out.

LIMITED-OVERS WICKET-TAKERS

	O	Mdns	R	W	BB	5W/i	Avge	RPO
J. N. Gillespie (Aus)	28	6	90	7	5-32	1	12.86	3.21
M. S. Kasprowicz (Aus) . . .	29	4	76	5	2-23	0	15.20	2.62
D. S. Lehmann (Aus)	10.3	1	39	5	4-7	0	7.80	3.71
G. B. Hogg (Aus)	16.5	1	93	5	3-37	0	18.60	5.52
T. Mupariwa (Zim)	26.3	1	159	4	2-48	0	39.75	6.00
T. Panyangara (Zim)	15.4	1	82	3	2-48	0	27.33	5.23
S. Matsikenyeri (Zim)	21	0	109	2	2-43	0	54.50	5.19
D. T. Hondo (Zim)	16.3	1	87	2	1-40	0	43.50	5.27
G. D. McGrath (Aus)	26	3	87	1	1-35	0	87.00	3.35
B. A. Williams (Aus)	5	0	31	1	1-31	0	31.00	6.20
W. Mwayenga (Zim)	12	2	83	1	1-61	0	83.00	6.92
B. R. M. Taylor (Zim)	5	0	42	1	1-42	0	42.00	8.40
S. R. Watson (Aus)	8	0	38	0	–	0	–	4.75
I. J. Harvey (Aus)	5	0	25	0	–	0	–	5.00
M. L. Nkala (Zim)	10	1	51	0	–	0	–	5.10
E. C. Rainsford (Zim)	7	0	36	0	–	0	–	5.14
A. Symonds (Aus)	15	0	82	0	–	0	–	5.47
V. Sibanda (Zim)	4	0	37	0	–	0	–	9.25
E. Chigumbura (Zim)	2.4	0	27	0	–	0	–	10.13

Note: *Matches in this section were not first-class.*

ZIMBABWE A v AUSTRALIANS

At Country Club, Harare, May 17, 18, 2004. Match drawn. *Toss:* Zimbabwe A.

This two-day tour match was lost in the atmosphere of uncertainty surrounding the scheduled Test series. Glenn McGrath's first overs for Australia in 10 months, Cameron White's first overs for Australia ever, and some polished batting from Justin Langer and Ricky Ponting proved far less compelling than the politics being played out behind the scenes. Around the same time as Zimbabwe's A side were skittled for 151, the ICC chief executive Malcolm Speed landed at Harare airport. He was greeted by Vince Hogg, an increasingly worried managing director of the Zimbabwe Cricket Union, and told him: "There is concern about the integrity of Test cricket." Judging by the mismatch unfolding back at the Country Club, Speed's fears were well-founded. Only Vusi Sibanda, a young batsman of unfettered strokeplay, was unintimidated by the Australian attack, hooking Michael Kasprowicz for six before becoming White's first victim in Australian company. The Australians cruised untroubled to 448 and, with nothing more to be gained from the lopsided affair, the match was abandoned before tea on the second day. Meanwhile an agitated Speed boarded a plane back to London after the ZCU board refused to meet him. A meeting of ICC member presidents was scheduled for the following Friday; the status of the Test series was the only item on the agenda. At least the Country Club setting was delightful, with its thatched-roof pavilion and accompanying golf course. Some of the banned 15 rebel white players pedalled exercise bikes in the nearby open-air gymnasium. But by now the Tests were doomed and Zimbabwe's credibility in tatters.

Zimbabwe A 151 (V Sibanda 48; J. N. Gillespie 4-25, M. S. Kasprowicz 2-26, C. L. White 2-14, S. K. Warne 2-14); Australians 448 (J. L. Langer 84, M. L. Hayden 61, R. T. Ponting 87, D. R. Martyn 49, S. M. Katich 48, A. C. Gilchrist 36; A. Maungwa 2-88, I. M. Chinyoka 2-47, T. P. Ruswa 2-99).

ZIMBABWE v AUSTRALIA

First Limited-Overs International

At Harare Sports Club Ground, Harare, May 25, 2004. Australia won by seven wickets.
Toss: Zimbabwe.

The Australians dropped catches, a little-known opener plodded to a half-century and Matthew Hayden was out for a golden duck. Zimbabwe refused to be world cricket's bad joke and the crowd, populated mainly by uniformed schoolchildren, was briefly in rapture. The natural order was soon restored but Tatenda Taibu's young men, robbed of the nation's most accomplished cricketers, held their heads high. With memories of their capitulation to Sri Lanka for a world-record low of 35 still painfully fresh, they bravely chose to bat first. Their aim was simply to weather 50 overs, and they did it. Brendan Taylor was a picture of patience and resilience, while Taibu demonstrated solid technique and a healthy dose of daring. Glenn McGrath made a modest return after his long lay-off with ankle problems. He experimented with and then discarded a clearly uncomfortable shorter run-up, and the wicket of Visu Sibanda was his only scalp all series. The Zimbabweans gathered in a jubilant huddle after Hayden's dismissal. But their dreams of an upset disappeared with the arrival of Ricky Ponting, in brisk and brutal touch, and Damien Martyn, who played with his usual creativity through the off side. Two of the three Australians wickets fell to stunning outfield catches by Sibanda.

Man of the Match: R.T. Ponting.

Zimbabwe

S. Matsikenyeri c Gilchrist b Gillespie	8	(16)	T. Panyangara not out		14	(15)
B.R.M. Taylor c Ponting b Lehmann	59	(101)	T. Mupariwa run out (Symonds)		3	(9)
V. Sibanda b McGrath	18	(45)	D.T. Hondo not out		0	(0)
D.D. Ebrahim b Williams	8	(16)				
*†T. Taibu c Ponting b Kasprowicz	57	(76)	B 2, l-b 5, w 4, n-b 2		13	
M.A. Vermeulen c Ponting b Kasprowicz	20	(15)				
A. Maregwede c Clarke b Gillespie	5	(8)	(50 overs, 203 mins) (9 wkts)		205	
M.L. Nkala run out (Kasprowicz)	0	(1)	Fall: 9 46 64 125 172 184 184 188 204			

Bowling: McGrath 10–1–35–1; Gillespie 10–4–21–2; Kasprowicz 10–2–26–2; Williams 5–0–31–1; Lehmann 6–0–32–1; Symonds 9–0–53–0.

Australia

†A.C. Gilchrist c Sibanda b Hondo	26	(29)			
M.L. Hayden c Mupariwa b Panyangara	0	(1)	L-b 4, w 7	11	
*R.T. Ponting c Sibanda b Panyangara	91	(93)			
D.R. Martyn not out	74	(96)	(39.4 overs, 169 mins) (3 wkts)	207	
M.J. Clarke not out	5	(18)	Fall: 1 53 197		

D.S. Lehmann, A. Symonds, J.N. Gillespie, M.S. Kasprowicz, B.A. Williams and G.D. McGrath did not bat.

Bowling: Hondo 7–0–40–1; Panyangara 9.4–1–48–2; Nkala 5–1–24–0; Mupariwa 10–1–47–0; Matsikenyeri 6–0–31–0; Sibanda 2–0–13–0.

Umpires: S.A. Bucknor (West Indies) and K.C. Barbour.
TV Umpire: R.B. Tiffin.
Referee: B.C. Broad (England).

ZIMBABWE v AUSTRALIA

Second Limited-Overs International

At Harare Sports Club Ground, Harare, May 27, 2004. Australia won by 139 runs. *Toss:* Zimbabwe.

Darren Lehmann, almost single-handedly, exposed Zimbabwe's gaping inexperience. His inventive batting underpinned a hefty Australian total and his deceptive left-arm spinners, seemingly gentle but destructive in effect, befuddled the Zimbabwean tail. The highlight of his robust knock was an extremely fine reverse-sweep for four, which was all the more striking for its ridiculousness and the fact that it nearly decapitated the wicket-keeper Tatenda Taibu. Thankfully Taibu kept his head and later pulled off a brilliant stumping to dismiss Ricky Ponting, batting down the order to offer his team-mates some time in the middle. Matthew Hayden, restrained early, finished with a sweetly struck 87 and Jason Gillespie walloped three clean sixes on the way to his highest one-day score. Zimbabwe's mountainous chase began slowly as Brendan Taylor, resisting temptation, accumulated his second consecutive fifty. Visu Sibanda and Mark Vermeulen chipped in with more adventurous cameos, and then Lehmann ambled in. Zimbabwe lost both opening bowlers to injury, Douglas Hondo hit on the side of the face during his follow-through by a full-blooded drive from Ponting. He was cleared of a fracture but sat out the rest of the series with concussion. Horribly undermanned already, it was the last thing Zimbabwe needed.

Man of the Match: D. S. Lehmann.

Australia

†A. C. Gilchrist c Mwayenga b Hondo	20	(23)	*R. T. Ponting st Taibu b Mwayenga	10 (10)
M. L. Hayden c Taylor b Mupariwa ..	87	(101)	J. N. Gillespie not out	33 (16)
M. J. Clarke b Panyangara	16	(11)	M. S. Kasprowicz not out	2 (3)
D. S. Lehmann b Matsikenyeri	67	(69)	B 1, l-b 7, w 9, n-b 3	20
I. J. Harvey c Mupariwa b Matsikenyeri	22	(22)		
G. B. Hogg c Matsikenyeri b Taylor ..	26	(27)	(50 overs, 209 mins) (8 wkts)	323
D. R. Martyn c Panyangara b Mupariwa	20	(21)	Fall: 25 43 180 219 233 274 276 314	

G. D. McGrath did not bat.

Bowling: Hondo 9.3–1–47–1; Panyangara 6–0–34–1; Mwayenga 9–1–61–1; Mupariwa 8.3–0–64–2; Matsikenyeri 10–0–43–2; Sibanda 2–0–24–0; Taylor 5–0–42–1.

Zimbabwe

S. Matsikenyeri c Hayden b Kasprowicz	27	(53)	T. Panyangara c and b Lehmann	1 (4)
B. R. M. Taylor c Gillespie b Hogg ...	65	(93)	T. Mupariwa c McGrath b Lehmann .	0 (3)
V. Sibanda c Lehmann b Kasprowicz .	23	(47)	W. Mwayenga c McGrath b Lehmann	0 (9)
M. A. Vermeulen c McGrath b Lehmann	25	(25)	B 4, l-b 8, w 10, n-b 1	23
*†T. Taibu run out (McGrath/Lehmann)	1	(1)		
A. Maregwede not out	18	(29)	(44.3 overs, 180 mins) (9 wkts)	184
D. D. Ebrahim lbw b Hogg	1	(4)	Fall: 48 108 163 164 164 168 179 180 184	

D. T. Hondo did not bat.

Bowling: McGrath 8–1–24–0; Gillespie 8–0–37–0; Harvey 5–0–25–0; Kasprowicz 9–1–23–2; Hogg 10–1–56–2; Lehmann 4.3–1–7–4.

Umpires: S. A. Bucknor (West Indies) and I. D. Robinson.
TV Umpire: R. B. Tiffin.
Referee: B. C. Broad (England).

ZIMBABWE v AUSTRALIA

Third Limited-Overs International

At Harare Sports Club Ground, Harare, May 29, 2004. Australia won by eight wickets. *Toss:* Zimbabwe. *Limited-overs international debut:* E. C. Rainsford.

Sensing a swift kill, Jason Gillespie brought back fleeting visions of Zimbabwe's disastrous 35 all-out against Sri Lanka. He trapped Brendan Taylor dead in front, tempted Stuart Matsikenyeri into an ill-fated hook and coaxed Visu Sibanda to flutter a catch to the keeper. From 3 for 10, Zimbabwe recovered to a slightly more respectable 6 for 61. It fell to Elton Chigumbura, an 18-year-old all-rounder playing his sixth match, to stave off the carnage. He had been a star of the recent Under-19s World Cup; now he produced a free-spirited 77, hitting nine fours and two sixes and dominating a 114-run stand with Mluleki Nkala. Australia's chase was lit up by their own prodigy, Michael Clarke, the talented young punk of Australian cricket. In the first match he had fumbled catches and not looked his usual cool and collected self. Challenged to open the innings, he responded with some calm but dazzling batsmanship, hitting hard, straight and often. His maiden hundred was festooned with 16 crisp fours and a six. With him at the end was Shane Watson, playing his first game since back stress fractures derailed his international progress. In a further hint of changing times Michael Kasprowicz, after bowling irresistibly all tour, relegated a sluggish Glenn McGrath to first change.

Man of the Match: J. N. Gillespie. *Man of the Series:* J. N. Gillespie.

Zimbabwe

S. Matsikenyeri c Watson b Gillespie	4	(14)		T. Mupariwa run out (Harvey/Gilchrist)	4	(12)
B. R. M. Taylor lbw b Gillespie	1	(3)		W. Mwayenga lbw b Hogg	1	(2)
V. Sibanda c Gilchrist b Gillespie	2	(17)		E. C. Rainsford not out	1	(1)
*†T. Taibu lbw b Kasprowicz	27	(56)				
M. A. Vermeulen c and b Gillespie	17	(15)		L-b 5, w 8, n-b 1	14	
A. Maregwede b Gillespie	1	(4)				
E. Chigumbura b Hogg	77	(90)		(48.5 overs, 196 mins)	196	
M. L. Nkala b Hogg	47	(80)		Fall: 4 9 10 42 50 61 175 194 195 196		

Bowling: Gillespie 10–2–32–5; Kasprowicz 10–1–27–1; McGrath 8–1–28–0; Watson 8–0–38–0; Hogg 6.5–0–37–3; Symonds 6–0–29–0.

Australia

†A. C. Gilchrist b Mupariwa	44	(27)		L-b 4, w 8	12
M. J. Clarke not out	105	(102)			—
A. Symonds c Mwayenga b Mupariwa	20	(22)		(30.4 overs, 133 mins) (2 wkts)	199
S. R. Watson not out	18	(33)		Fall: 68 115	

*R. T. Ponting, D. R. Martyn, I. J. Harvey, G. B. Hogg, J. N. Gillespie, M. S. Kasprowicz and G. D. McGrath did not bat.

Bowling: Nkala 5–0–27–0; Mwayenga 3–1–22–0; Mupariwa 8–0–48–2; Rainsford 7–0–36–0; Matsikenyeri 5–0–35–0; Chigumbura 2.4–0–27–0.

Umpires: S. A. Bucknor (West Indies) and I. D. Robinson.
TV Umpire: R. B. Tiffin.
Referee: B. C. Broad (England).

TVS Cup in India, 2003-04

by GEOFF LAWSON

Seldom in the past decade have Australia entered a tournament as underdogs. This month-long sojourn to the subcontinent was framed as one such occasion. For various reasons, mostly injuries of various descriptions, the world champions were without their entire frontline attack – Glenn McGrath, Brett Lee, Jason Gillespie and Shane Warne. Meanwhile India possessed a side long on batting riches and bowling variety, a line-up built to excel on low, slow, wearing pitches. The much-trumpeted depth of Australian cricket was about to be tested on hostile foreign soil.

It passed with flying colours. Ricky Ponting's men lost their opening match but won their last six, culminating in a pulsating 37-run victory over India before an estimated 100,000 fans at Eden Gardens, Kolkata. The tournament was hyped as India's big chance to avenge their World Cup final humiliation of seven months earlier. The games between Australia and Stephen Fleming's New Zealanders were treated almost as a sideshow, relegated to early-morning starts in the backblocks of Indian cricket: Faridabad, Pune, Guwahati. Yet it was the Kiwis who most bothered the undermanned Australians, aside from their first-up defeat to India when they had just touched down in the country and looked distinctly unprepared.

All of the batsmen contributed at various times. Ponting, Adam Gilchrist and Damien Martyn each produced memorable hundreds. Michael Bevan was as cool as ever in a crisis, marshalling the tail and digging Australia out of tight spots in Pune and Guwahati. Michael Clarke grew in authority and influence with every game, taking crucial wickets and blazing away effortlessly with the bat. History might remember this tournament for Clarke's arrival as a genuine all-round force on the international stage.

But it was the even lesser known fast bowlers who turned out to be the real stars of Australia's success. With the household names recuperating back home, Nathan Bracken, Brad Williams and Ian Harvey grasped the chance to state their credentials. Williams was fast and aggressive, forever growing in confidence. Harvey's pace variations verged on undetectable at times, most notably when he bewitched four wickets in his last eight balls to swing a tense, twisting final Australia's way.

Best of all was the left-armer Bracken. He was accurate, wobbled the ball about menacingly, consistently grabbed early wickets and finished as the tournament's leading wicket-taker. He dismissed the dangerous Indian opener Virender Sehwag every time he came up against him – for 0, 0 and 5 – and should have been named Man of the Series. That gong ultimately went to Sachin Tendulkar, for his 466 runs at 77, thus confirming that one-day cricket is still seen by the decision-makers as a batsman's game.

The only Australian bowler to have a tough time of it was the only one who went to India with an international reputation: Andy Bichel. He captured a mere five wickets, while going for a hefty 5.21 runs an over, in his seven matches. Yet it was Bichel who provided the burning memory of the whole elongated tour, a terrific off-cutter that cleaned up Tendulkar in the final and brought complete silence from 100,000 spectators.

AUSTRALIAN SQUAD

R. T. Ponting (*captain*), A. C. Gilchrist (*vice-captain*), A. J. Bichel, M. G. Bevan, N. W. Bracken, M. J. Clarke, I. J. Harvey, M. L. Hayden, G. B. Hogg, J. P. Maher, D. R. Martyn, A. Symonds.

B. Lee and J. N. Gillespie withdrew before the start of the tour and were replaced by M. S. Kasprowicz and B. A. Williams.

Manager: S. R. Bernard. *Coach:* J. M. Buchanan. *Performance analyst/assistant coach:* T. J. Nielsen. *Physiotherapist:* E. L. Alcott. *Physical performance manager:* J. A. Campbell. *Media manager:* J. Rose.

RUNSCORERS

	M	I	NO	R	HS	100s	50s	Avge	Ct/St	S-R
S. R. Tendulkar (Ind)	7	7	1	466	102	2	2	77.67	0	89.27
A. C. Gilchrist (Aus)	6	6	0	296	111	1	1	49.33	6	107.64
R. T. Ponting (Aus)	7	7	1	257	108*	1	1	42.83	4	79.32
D. R. Martyn (Aus)..	7	7	2	250	100	1	2	50.00	1	80.91
M. G. Bevan (Aus)..	7	5	2	234	84*	0	2	78.00	0	72.22
R. S. Dravid (Ind)...	7	6	1	227	59	0	2	45.40	1/1	94.19
V. V. S. Laxman (Ind)	7	7	0	222	102	1	0	31.71	2	76.29
V. Sehwag (Ind)....	6	6	0	205	130	1	0	34.17	0	88.36
S. B. Styris (NZ). ...	6	5	0	183	68	0	3	36.60	6	78.21
M. L. Hayden (Aus)..	6	6	1	170	51*	0	1	34.00	3	79.44
C. D. McMillan (NZ)	6	5	1	126	82*	0	1	31.50	3	64.62
M. J. Clarke (Aus) ..	5	4	1	118	70	0	1	39.33	1	94.40
A. Symonds (Aus) ..	7	5	1	114	48	0	0	28.50	6	76.51
B. B. McCullum (NZ)	6	5	2	113	51*	0	1	37.67	5	71.52
Yuvraj Singh (Ind)..	7	7	1	113	44	0	0	18.83	3	93.39
J. D. P. Oram (NZ)..	6	5	0	112	81	0	1	22.40	2	78.32
M. Kaif (Ind)	6	5	2	98	64	0	1	32.67	3	66.22

	M	I	NO	R	HS	100s	50s	Avge	Ct/St	S-R
S. P. Fleming (NZ) ..	5	4	0	95	40	0	0	23.75	0	54.60
H. K. Badani (Ind) ..	2	2	0	71	41	0	0	35.50	1	87.65
S. C. Ganguly (Ind) .	2	2	0	70	37	0	0	35.00	0	112.90
A. B. Agarkar (Ind) .	6	4	1	57	26*	0	0	19.00	1	111.76
C. Z. Harris (NZ) ...	6	5	0	54	38	0	0	10.80	2	41.54
C. L. Cairns (NZ) ...	3	2	0	50	27	0	0	25.00	0	76.92
I. J. Harvey (Aus)...	6	3	0	48	25	0	0	16.00	3	100.00
Zaheer Khan (Ind) ..	7	4	2	40	33*	0	0	20.00	2	160.00
A. J. Bichel (Aus) ...	7	4	1	39	15*	0	0	13.00	3	79.59
G. B. Hogg (Aus) ...	4	3	1	38	29	0	0	19.00	1	63.23
D. L. Vettori (NZ) ..	6	4	0	37	19	0	0	9.25	1	82.04
L. Vincent (NZ)	6	5	0	36	22	0	0	7.20	1	42.35
C. J. Nevin (NZ)....	5	5	0	32	29	0	0	6.40	1	49.23
A. R. Kumble (Ind)..	5	2	1	18	12*	0	0	18.00	1	45.00
P. A. Patel (Ind)	3	1	0	16	16	0	0	16.00	0/2	51.61
B. A. Williams (Aus)	6	2	2	14	11*	0	0	–	0	70.00
Harbhajan Singh (Ind)	5	3	0	13	6	0	0	4.33	1	72.22
K. D. Mills (NZ)....	3	2	1	11	7*	0	0	11.00	1	57.89
S. V. Bahutule (Ind)	1	1	0	11	11	0	0	11.00	0	84.62
P. A. Hitchcock (NZ)	2	1	0	10	10	0	0	10.00	0	52.63
N. W. Bracken (Aus)	6	1	1	7	7*	0	0	–	2	70.00
M. Kartik (Ind).....	4	3	2	6	4*	0	0	6.00	0	42.86
D. R. Tuffey (NZ)...	6	4	3	4	3*	0	0	4.00	1	21.05
J. P. Maher (Aus) ...	1	1	0	3	3	0	0	3.00	3	30.00
A. M. Salvi (Ind)....	1	1	0	0	0	0	0	0.00	0	0.00
A. Nehra (Ind)	1	0	–	–	–	–	–	–	0	–
M. S. Kasprowicz (Aus)	2	0	–	–	–	–	–	–	1	–

Denotes not out.

WICKET-TAKERS

	O	Mdns	R	W	BB	5W/i	Avge	RPO
N. W. Bracken (Aus)	54.3	8	195	14	4-29	0	13.93	3.58
B. A. Williams (Aus)	49.4	3	235	11	5-53	1	21.36	4.73
D. R. Tuffey (NZ)	49.4	5	267	11	4-30	0	24.27	5.38
I. J. Harvey (Aus)	43.5	3	194	10	4-21	0	19.40	4.43
Zaheer Khan (Ind)	50	2	288	10	3-30	0	28.80	5.76
A. B. Agarkar (Ind)	37	2	198	8	4-37	0	24.75	5.35
D. L. Vettori (NZ)	39	0	180	7	2-20	0	25.71	4.62
S. B. Styris (NZ)	36	2	172	7	3-38	0	24.57	4.78
M. J. Clarke (Aus)........	28	1	149	7	4-42	0	21.29	5.32
A. Symonds (Aus)	45	2	229	6	3-42	0	38.17	5.09
A. R. Kumble (Ind).......	37	3	174	5	2-28	0	34.80	4.70
A. J. Bichel (Aus)	53	0	276	5	1-21	0	55.20	5.21
M. Kartik (Ind)	40	4	153	4	2-38	0	38.25	3.83
Harbhajan Singh (Ind)	40	1	162	4	1-34	0	40.50	4.05
K. D. Mills (NZ)	26	0	141	4	2-36	0	35.25	5.42
G. B. Hogg (Aus)	25.2	0	114	3	2-39	0	38.00	4.50
V. Sehwag (Ind)	24	0	135	3	2-36	0	45.00	5.63
M. S. Kasprowicz (Aus)...	18	0	65	2	1-28	0	32.50	3.61
C. Z. Harris (NZ).........	17.5	0	92	2	1-15	0	46.00	5.16
C. L. Cairns (NZ)	20	0	111	2	1-16	0	55.50	5.55
Yuvraj Singh (Ind)	19	1	106	1	1-36	0	106.00	5.58
S. R. Tendulkar (Ind)	21	0	125	1	1-39	0	125.00	5.95
J. D. P. Oram (NZ)	49.5	1	309	1	1-31	0	309.00	6.20
S. C. Ganguly (Ind).......	2	0	10	0	–	0	–	5.00
P. A. Hitchcock (NZ)	5	0	25	0	–	0	–	5.00

	O	Mdns	R	W	BB	5W/i	Avge	RPO
H. K. Badani (Ind)........	8.3	0	44	0	–	0	–	5.18
A. M. Salvi (Ind).........	3	0	23	0	–	0	–	7.67
S. V. Bahutule (Ind)	3	0	24	0	–	0	–	8.00
A. Nehra (Ind)..........	10	0	80	0	–	0	–	8.00

Note: *Matches in this section were not first-class.*

INDIA v NEW ZEALAND

At M. A. Chidambaram Stadium (Chepauk), Chennai, October 23, 2003. Day/night game. No result. *Toss:* India.
   Man of the Match: No award.

India

V. Sehwag b Cairns 31 (29)	Yuvraj Singh not out 29 (38)
S. R. Tendulkar not out 48 (66)	W 3, n-b 1 4
V. V. S. Laxman c (sub)	
K. D. Mills b Styris .. 25 (23)	(26.5 overs, 119 mins) (3 wkts) 141
*R. S. Dravid c Styris b Vettori 4 (6)	Fall: 53 88 93

M. Kaif, A. R. Kumble, †P. A. Patel, Harbhajan Singh, A. B. Agarkar and Zaheer Khan did not bat.

Bowling: Tuffey 4–0–26–0; Oram 6–0–31–0; Cairns 3–0–16–1; Hitchcock 3–0–17–0; Styris 4–0–19–1; Vettori 4–0–21–1; Harris 2.5–0–11–0.

New Zealand

*S. P. Fleming, †B. B. McCullum, L. Vincent, S. B. Styris, C. D. McMillan, C. L. Cairns, C. Z. Harris, J. D. P. Oram, D. L. Vettori, D. R. Tuffey, P. A. Hitchcock.

Umpires: D. R. Shepherd (England) and A. V. Jayaprakash.
TV Umpire: I. Sivaram.
Referee: R. S. Madugalle (Sri Lanka).

INDIA v AUSTRALIA

At Captain Roop Singh Stadium, Gwalior, October 26, 2003. Day/night game. India won by 37 runs. *Toss:* India.
   India's pursuit of World Cup revenge began in dreamlike fashion at the Maharaja of Scindia's boutique ground. Sachin Tendulkar and V. V. S. Laxman made first and significant use of a hard flat pitch. It gradually slowed and crumbled, and threatened to be carried away by invading insects once the lights were switched on. India missed the chance to push past 300, their run-rate dipping as Tendulkar and Laxman seemed more concerned with reaching three figures than the team's total. Tendulkar's first fifty came at a run a ball and was lit up by nine fours; his second took 67 deliveries, containing one six and not a single four. A score of 5 for 283 looked far from unassailable, especially when Adam Gilchrist and Matthew Hayden despatched the new ball far and wide. But Gilchrist fell to an undisciplined swipe and the rest laboured against accurate spin, a softening ball and Zaheer Khan's reverse swing. Australia's uncharacteristic collapse was not entirely surprising, for they had played no warm-up games and were fresh from Test matches in Perth and Sydney. But Ponting lambasted his batsmen's poor shot selection and failure to adapt to the conditions. The headline in one Indian newspaper read: "World Cup Recaptured!" Not quite.
   Man of the Match: S. R. Tendulkar.

India

V. Sehwag c Hayden b Bracken	....	0	(3)	M. Kaif not out	....	1	(1)
S. R. Tendulkar c Gilchrist b Bracken	.100	(119)		L-b 7, w 6, n-b 1	....	14
V. V. S. Laxman run out (Symonds)	..102	(134)				
Yuvraj Singh c Symonds b Williams	..	44	(33)	(50 overs, 213 mins)	(5 wkts) 283
A. B. Agarkar c Symonds b Bracken	..	22	(10)	Fall: 1 192 256 264 283

†P. A. Patel, *R. S. Dravid, Harbhajan Singh, A. R. Kumble and Zaheer Khan did not bat.

Bowling: Bracken 10–0–53–3; Williams 10–0–67–1; Bichel 7–0–39–0; Harvey 8–0–46–0; Hogg 10–0–47–0; Symonds 5–0–24–0.

Australia

†A. C. Gilchrist b Zaheer Khan	......	83	(79)	A. J. Bichel c Kaif b Zaheer Khan	...	14	(20)
M. L. Hayden st Patel b Kumble	.....	47	(76)	B. A. Williams not out	....	11	(16)
*R. T. Ponting c and b Kumble	......	2	(5)	N. W. Bracken not out	....	7	(10)
D. R. Martyn b Sehwag	....	16	(26)	L-b 4, w 4, n-b 6	....	14
A. Symonds lbw b Zaheer Khan	.....	1	(6)			
M. G. Bevan b Sehwag	....	18	(28)	(50 overs, 246 mins)	(9 wkts) 246
I. J. Harvey b Tendulkar	....	4	(10)	Fall: 132 135 140 141 176 177 185
G. B. Hogg st Patel b Harbhajan Singh	29	(30)		225 229

Bowling: Zaheer Khan 10–0–49–3; Agarkar 6–0–42–0; Kumble 10–2–28–2; Harbhajan Singh 10–0–43–1; Tendulkar 6–0–39–1; Sehwag 7–0–36–2; Yuvraj Singh 1–0–5–0.

Umpires: N. A. Mallender (England) and K. Hariharan.
TV Umpire: A. V. Jayaprakash.
Referee: R. S. Madugalle (Sri Lanka).

AUSTRALIA v NEW ZEALAND

At Nahar Singh Stadium, Faridabad, October 29, 2003. Day/night game. Australia won by eight wickets. *Toss:* New Zealand.

Australia's unheralded pace trio of Nathan Bracken, Brad Williams and Ian Harvey made the most of conditions more likely to be found in Darwin than Delhi. The Faridabad pitch offered bounce and a reasonable amount of grass – a rare sight in this part of the world – while the humid early-morning air provided further encouragement for the ball to swing about. Stephen Fleming chose to bat and the game was all over half an hour after lunch. Bracken, in particular, displayed his new-found skill of swinging into the right-handers and away from the lefties with deadly accuracy. Williams was quicker, recording the best one-day figures in the ground's history, while Harvey wobbled the ball about and offered nothing loose. New Zealand crashed to 5 for 21 before eventually scrambling to 97, a total inflated by 18 wides and 12 leg-byes. The Australian batsmen encountered no such difficulties. The openers continued their impressive form, Adam Gilchrist slaughtering 29 off 18 balls and Matthew Hayden troubled by neither swing nor seam. The match was played an hour outside Delhi, in front of a large and enthusiastic pro-Kiwi crowd, with armed troops and sniffer dogs patrolling the ground.

Man of the Match: B. A. Williams.

New Zealand

C. J. Nevin lbw b Bracken	0	(2)	D. L. Vettori lbw b Harvey	0	(5)
*S. P. Fleming c Gilchrist b Bracken	2	(17)	P. A. Hitchcock c Hayden b Williams	10	(19)
L. Vincent c Bichel b Williams	0	(11)	D. R. Tuffey not out	3	(15)
S. B. Styris c Ponting b Williams	7	(12)			
C. D. McMillan lbw b Bichel	24	(59)	L-b 12, w 18, n-b 2	32	
J. D. P. Oram c Gilchrist b Bracken	0	(3)			
C. Z. Harris lbw b Harvey	14	(48)	(33.4 overs, 166 mins)	97	
†B. B. McCullum c Martyn b Williams	5	(13)	Fall: 0 11 11 20 21 73 77 80 80 97		

Bowling: Bracken 9–2–25–3; Williams 9.4–1–22–4; Bichel 7–0–29–1; Harvey 8–2–9–2.

Australia

†A. C. Gilchrist c and b Oram	29	(18)	L-b 5, n-b 2	7	
M. L. Hayden not out	51	(53)			
*R. T. Ponting c McCullum b Tuffey	12	(27)	(16.4 overs, 67 mins)	(2 wkts)	101
D. R. Martyn not out	2	(4)	Fall: 47 90		

A. Symonds, M. G. Bevan, I. J. Harvey, G. B. Hogg, A. J. Bichel, N. W. Bracken and B. A. Williams did not bat.

Bowling: Tuffey 6.4–0–51–1; Oram 7–1–31–1; Hitchcock 2–0–8–0; Vettori 1–0–6–0.

Umpires: D. R. Shepherd (England) and S. Venkataraghavan.
TV Umpire: I. Sivaram.
Referee: R. S. Madugalle (Sri Lanka).

INDIA v AUSTRALIA

At Wankhede Stadium, Mumbai, November 1, 2003. Day/night game. Australia won by 77 runs. *Toss:* Australia.

A hard-fought contest attracting maximum hype in downtown Mumbai was ultimately won by the Australians in conditions – slow, turning and stifling – that seemed tailor-made for the Indians. Damien Martyn played a gem of an innings, deft early and aggressive towards the end, his second fifty arriving in 34 balls. Adam Gilchrist had earlier lashed a blistering 41, Rahul Dravid rueing his decision to open proceedings with the part-timer Virender Sehwag. Australia's own part-time spinner, Michael Clarke, was the unlikely hero when India set sail after a gettable 286. Sehwag was leg-before first ball, not offering a shot, as Nathan Bracken again swung the new ball prodigiously. Dravid and Sachin Tendulkar put India back on course with a determined 89-run partnership, but then Clarke intervened. He was a late inclusion in the side, coming in for Ian Harvey when Ricky Ponting took one look at the dusty pitch. Clarke boldly predicted to his captain that he would get both Tendulkar and Dravid out, and he was as good as his word. Tendulkar was caught off-balance and bowled, then Dravid indulged in an uncharacteristically reckless sweep, India's last seven wickets tumbling meekly for 56. Australia had adapted well and quickly, while India had taken the first steps on the path to self-doubt.

Man of the Match: D. R. Martyn.

Australia

†A.C. Gilchrist c Kaif b Harbhajan Singh	41	(30)
M.L. Hayden c Yuvraj Singh .... b Zaheer Khan	0	(1)
*R.T. Ponting lbw b Agarkar	31	(37)
D.R. Martyn b Agarkar 100	(119)
A. Symonds c Harbhajan Singh b Yuvraj Singh	48	(59)
M.G. Bevan c Kaif b Agarkar	42	(57)

M.J. Clarke run out (Tendulkar/Agarkar)	2	(2)
A.J. Bichel b Agarkar	1	(2)
G.B. Hogg not out	0	(0)
B 4, l-b 2, w 8, n-b 7	21	
(50 overs, 210 mins) (8 wkts)	286	

N.W. Bracken and B.A. Williams did not bat.

Fall: 9 55 93 171 282 283 286 286

Bowling: Zaheer Khan 7-0-64-1; Sehwag 4-0-28-0; Harbhajan Singh 10-0-44-1; Kumble 8-0-50-0; Agarkar 9-0-37-4; Tendulkar 4-0-21-0; Yuvraj Singh 8-1-36-1.

India

V. Sehwag lbw b Bracken	0	(1)
S.R. Tendulkar b Clarke	68	(76)
V.V.S. Laxman c Gilchrist b Bichel ..	21	(36)
*R.S. Dravid c Bichel b Clarke	59	(70)
Yuvraj Singh c Gilchrist b Clarke	9	(15)
M. Kaif c Gilchrist b Bracken	10	(15)
A.B. Agarkar c Symonds b Bracken ..	2	(19)
†P.A. Patel c Clarke b Hogg	16	(31)

Harbhajan Singh c and b Bracken ...	6	(7)
A.R. Kumble b Clarke	6	(10)
Zaheer Khan not out	5	(8)
L-b 2, w 4, n-b 1	7	
(46.2 overs, 192 mins)	209	

Fall: 0 38 137 153 172 175 178 185 200 209

Bowling: Bracken 10-2-29-4; Williams 5-0-20-0; Bichel 6-0-31-1; Symonds 10-0-57-0; Hogg 5.2-0-28-1; Clarke 10-0-42-4.

Umpires: N.A. Mallender (England) and A.V. Jayaprakash.
TV Umpire: K. Hariharan.
Referee: R.S. Madugalle (Sri Lanka).

AUSTRALIA v NEW ZEALAND

At Nehru Stadium, Pune, November 3, 2003. Australia won by two wickets. *Toss:* Australia.

    Australia had the last laugh in the delightful university city of Pune, birthplace of Spike Milligan, winning a breathtaking match with a ball to spare. The circumstances were distinctly comical. With three balls left they needed two runs. Brad Williams got a thick edge, Brendon McCullum dropped it and the batsmen crossed for one. Next ball Symonds crashed to mid-wicket, Scott Styris put down the chance and the batsmen hurtled home for the winning single. Symonds was the hero, clubbing Daniel Vettori for a four and a six off the last two balls of the penultimate over. But he had earlier been dropped on one – a simple chance to Lou Vincent – in a game New Zealand let slip through their butterfingers. Australia had slumped to 4 for 65 before a 108-run salvage job by Michael Clarke and Michael Bevan put them in with a chance. On a pitch with ample bounce and a grassy Gabba-like sheen, New Zealand also struggled early. McCullum and Jacob Oram had to work and hit hard after Williams uprooted their first four wickets in eight overs. Seemingly quicker and more confident with each outing, he improved on his career-best figures of six days earlier.

    Man of the Match: B.A. Williams.

New Zealand

C. J. Nevin lbw b Williams	0	(8)		†B. B. McCullum not out	51	(47)
*S. P. Fleming c Harvey b Symonds	40	(97)		D. L. Vettori b Harvey	18	(15)
L. Vincent c Ponting b Williams	1	(5)		D. R. Tuffey not out	1	(1)
S. B. Styris lbw b Williams	0	(1)				
C. D. McMillan b Williams	0	(6)				
C. L. Cairns lbw b Bichel	27	(29)		L-b 4, w 32, n-b 2	38	
J. D. P. Oram b Symonds	81	(87)				
C. Z. Harris c Harvey b Williams	1	(6)		(50 overs, 225 mins) (9 wkts)	258	

Fall: 3 10 11 21 68 130 151 219 246

Bowling: Bracken 10–3–39–0; Williams 10–1–53–5; Bichel 9–0–59–1; Harvey 9–1–33–1; Symonds 10–2–56–2; Clarke 2–0–14–0.

Australia

†A. C. Gilchrist c Vettori b Tuffey	25	(31)		I. J. Harvey c Styris b Vettori	19	(19)
M. L. Hayden c Styris b Tuffey	9	(15)		A. J. Bichel c McCullum b Vettori	9	(9)
*R. T. Ponting b Styris	16	(24)		B. A. Williams not out	3	(4)
D. R. Martyn b Tuffey	10	(7)		L-b 2, w 8, n-b 1	11	
M. J. Clarke b Tuffey	70	(80)				
M. G. Bevan c Harris b Cairns	50	(72)		(49.5 overs, 216 mins) (8 wkts)	259	
A. Symonds not out	37	(39)				

Fall: 34 40 54 65 173 204 231 244

N. W. Bracken did not bat.

Bowling: Tuffey 10–2–30–4; Oram 9.5–0–65–0; Cairns 10–0–48–1; Styris 7–1–31–1; Vettori 8–0–59–2; Harris 5–0–24–0.

Umpires: D. R. Shepherd (England) and K. Hariharan.
TV Umpire: A. V. Jayaprakash.
Referee: R. S. Madugalle (Sri Lanka).

INDIA v NEW ZEALAND

At Barabati Stadium, Cuttack, November 6, 2003. Day/night game. New Zealand won by four wickets. *Toss:* India.
   Man of the Match: S. B. Styris.

India

V. V. S. Laxman c and b Styris	31	(46)		Harbhajan Singh b Tuffey	5	(7)
S. R. Tendulkar lbw b Mills	14	(14)		Zaheer Khan not out	33	(13)
M. Kaif b Styris	64	(108)		M. Kartik not out	1	(2)
*†R. S. Dravid c Styris b Vettori	31	(41)				
Yuvraj Singh c Mills b Vettori	0	(3)		B 4, l-b 2, w 2	8	
H. K. Badani c McCullum b Tuffey	41	(45)				
S. V. Bahutule lbw b Styris	11	(13)		(50 overs, 224 mins) (9 wkts)	246	
A. B. Agarkar c McMillan b Tuffey	7	(8)				

Fall: 27 77 136 136 169 193 205 206 223

Bowling: Tuffey 10–1–31–3; Mills 8–0–51–1; Oram 10–0–68–0; Styris 10–0–38–3; Vettori 10–0–39–2; Harris 2–0–13–0.

New Zealand

C. J. Nevin c Yuvraj Singh b Harbhajan Singh	29	(45)		J. D. P. Oram run out (Kaif/Dravid)	6	(16)
*S. P. Fleming lbw b Agarkar	24	(14)		†B. B. McCullum not out	19	(16)
C. Z. Harris lbw b Zaheer Khan	0	(4)				
L. Vincent b Zaheer Khan	1	(10)		B 1, l-b 6, w 12, n-b 1	20	
S. B. Styris lbw b Kartik	68	(89)				
C. D. McMillan not out	82	(92)		(47.3 overs, 226 mins) (6 wkts)	249	

Fall: 39 40 44 68 195 214

D. L. Vettori, D. R. Tuffey and K. D. Mills did not bat.

Bowling: Zaheer Khan 9–1–49–2; Agarkar 8–0–41–1; Harbhajan Singh 10–0–41–1; Kartik 10–1–34–1; Tendulkar 3–0–25–0; Bahutule 3–0–24–0; Badani 3.3–0–21–0; Yuvraj Singh 1–0–7–0.

Umpires: N. A. Mallender (England) and A. V. Jayaprakash.
TV Umpire: I. Sivaram.
Referee: R. S. Madugalle (Sri Lanka).

AUSTRALIA v NEW ZEALAND

At Nehru Stadium, Guwahati, November 9, 2003. Australia won by 44 runs. *Toss:* New Zealand.

The far northeast state of Assam was the scene of Australia's sixth straight victory over New Zealand. The players assembled in the dawn gloom to make it to the ground in time for an 8.30 a.m. start, and the heavy covering of dew persuaded Stephen Fleming to send Australia in. The absence of Matthew Hayden and Adam Gilchrist, both being rested, may also have influenced his thinking. Jimmy Maher and Ian Harvey opened the batting in an interesting experiment that ultimately proved unsuccessful. Ricky Ponting and Michael Bevan were Australia's mainstays, the rest struggling against the swing of Kyle Mills and some high-class slow bowling from Daniel Vettori. With the outfield drying a total of 225 looked chaseable, but only Scott Styris found any rhythm against some tight bowling and suffocating fielding. Michael Kasprowicz, standing in for an ailing Brad Williams, justified his slightly contentious selection with a quality exhibition of swing and seam. Bevan's cool-headed 84 not out on a sluggish wicket won him the match award, but Nathan Bracken's contribution – helping Australia defend a modest total – was the more valuable.

Man of the Match: M. G. Bevan.

Australia

I. J. Harvey c Nevin b Tuffey	25	(19)	G. B. Hogg c Styris b Harris	9	(30)
†J. P. Maher lbw b Tuffey	3	(10)	A. J. Bichel not out	15	(18)
*R. T. Ponting c McMillan b Vettori	52	(84)			
D. R. Martyn c McCullum b Mills	0	(3)	L-b 9, w 7, n-b 1	17	
A. Symonds c McCullum b Mills	18	(25)			
M. G. Bevan not out	84	(97)	(50 overs, 208 mins) (7 wkts)	225	
M. J. Clarke c McMillan b Vettori	2	(15)	Fall: 33 33 34 61 139 141 164		

M. S. Kasprowicz and N. W. Bracken did not bat.

Bowling: Tuffey 10–1–60–2; Mills 8–0–36–2; Oram 10–0–47–0; Vettori 10–0–20–2; Styris 9–1–38–0; Harris 3–0–15–1.

New Zealand

C. J. Nevin c Ponting b Bracken	2	(6)	D. L. Vettori run out (Bichel/Kasprowicz)	0	(0)
*S. P. Fleming c and b Harvey	29	(46)	K. D. Mills b Maher b Bracken	4	(9)
L. Vincent c Hogg b Bracken	12	(27)	D. R. Tuffey not out	0	(1)
S. B. Styris c Ponting b Hogg	54	(83)			
C. D. McMillan c Maher b Bichel	0	(2)	B 4, l-b 6, w 9, n-b 2	21	
J. D. P. Oram lbw b Hogg	14	(21)			
C. Z. Harris run out (Ponting)	38	(68)	(45.3 overs, 195 mins)	181	
†B. B. McCullum c Maher b Kasprowicz	7	(13)	Fall: 7 38 66 68 88 143 169 170 181 181		

Bowling: Bracken 7.3–0–34–3; Kasprowicz 8–0–28–1; Bichel 7–0–21–1; Harvey 4–0–14–1; Hogg 10–0–39–2; Symonds 4–0–14–0; Clarke 5–0–21–0.

Umpires: D. R. Shepherd (England) and K. Hariharan.
TV Umpire: I. Sivaram.
Referee: R. S. Madugalle (Sri Lanka).

INDIA v AUSTRALIA

At M. Chinnaswamy Stadium, Bangalore, November 12, 2003. Day/night game.
Australia won by 61 runs. *Toss:* Australia.

Aside from the stress that comes from having a billion countrymen willing them
through every game, India were under even greater pressure to win this game after their
surprise loss to New Zealand in Cuttack. They never came close in what was a virtual
repeat of the 2003 World Cup final massacre in Johannesburg. Back then, Australia
batted first and piled up 2 for 359; this time, they managed 2 for 347. As in
Johannesburg, Adam Gilchrist got Australia off to a flier, then Ricky Ponting and
Damien Martyn carried the match away from India's bowlers. Gilchrist flayed the new
ball to all parts of a packed Chinnaswamy Stadium, swiping 13 runs off Ashish Nehra's
opening over, racing to his fifty in 42 balls and his hundred in 94. Ponting was no less
spectacular. Quite astonishingly, he pummelled seven sixes and only one four, his
second fifty coming in 31 deliveries. Both batsmen were let off by India's part-time
keeper Rahul Dravid, Gilchrist on 15 and Ponting on 25. The Indian chase started with
a bang but Sachin Tendulkar's downfall, playing Ian Harvey on to his stumps, ended any
vague victory ambitions. Now they were under real pressure: fail to beat New Zealand
in Hyderabad and they would miss out on a berth in the final.

Man of the Match: A. C. Gilchrist.

Australia

†A. C. Gilchrist c Zaheer Khan b Kumble ...111 (105)	B 1, l-b 9, w 12, n-b 1 23	
M. L. Hayden run out (Ganguly/Dravid) 44 (45)		
*R. T. Ponting not out 108 (102)	(50 overs, 210 mins) (2 wkts) 347	
D. R. Martyn not out 61 (49)	Fall: 119 198	

M. J. Clarke, M. G. Bevan, A. Symonds, I. J. Harvey, M. S. Kasprowicz, A. J. Bichel and
B. A. Williams did not bat.

Bowling: Nehra 10–0–80–0; Zaheer Khan 10–0–67–0; Kumble 9–0–60–1; Sehwag 5–0–36–0; Kartik
10–2–51–0; Ganguly 2–0–10–0; Yuvraj Singh 4–0–33–0.

India

V. Sehwag b Harvey 39 (53)	Zaheer Khan run out (Bichel/Gilchrist) 2 (3)	
S. R. Tendulkar b Harvey 89 (91)	A. R. Kumble not out 12 (30)	
V. V. S. Laxman c Symonds b Clarke . 18 (22)	M. Kartik not out 4 (8)	
*S. C. Ganguly c Bichel b Symonds .. 37 (31)	B 4, l-b 7, w 11, n-b 1 23	
†R. S. Dravid c and b Kasprowicz 34 (33)		
Yuvraj Singh lbw b Symonds 20 (16)	(50 overs, 216 mins) (8 wkts) 286	
M. Kaif b Symonds 8 (15)	Fall: 103 148 172 217 254 254 258 277	

A. Nehra did not bat.

Bowling: Williams 8–0–43–0; Kasprowicz 10–0–37–1; Bichel 9–0–46–0; Symonds 9–0–42–3; Harvey
10–0–71–2; Clarke 4–0–36–1.

Umpires: D. R. Shepherd (England) and A. V. Jayaprakash.
TV Umpire: K. Hariharan.
Referee: R. S. Madugalle (Sri Lanka).

INDIA v NEW ZEALAND

At Lal Bahadur (Fateh Maidan) Stadium, Hyderabad, November 15, 2003. Day/night game. India won by 145 runs. *Toss:* India.
Man of the Match: V. Sehwag.

India

V. Sehwag c Vincent b Styris	......130(134)	M. Kaif not out	.... 15 (9)
S. R. Tendulkar c Oram b Harris	.....102 (91)		
*S. C. Ganguly c Tuffey b Styris	.... 33 (31)	L-b 6, w 6, n-b 1	 13
Yuvraj Singh c Harris b Mills	.... 7 (10)		
†R. S. Dravid not out	.... 50 (22)	(50 overs, 222 mins) (5 wkts)	353
V. V. S. Laxman c b Tuffey	.... 3 (4)	Fall: 182 256 283 284 303	

A. B. Agarkar, A. R. Kumble, M. Kartik and Zaheer Khan did not bat.

Bowling: Tuffey 9–1–69–1; Mills 10–0–54–1; Oram 7–0–67–0; Cairns 7–0–47–0; Styris 6–0–46–2; Vettori 6–0–35–0; Harris 5–0–29–1.

New Zealand

C. J. Nevin b Agarkar	.... 1 (4)	K. D. Mills not out	.... 7 (10)
L. Vincent lbw b Zaheer Khan	.... 22 (32)	D. R. Tuffey lbw b Zaheer Khan	.... 0 (2)
C. Z. Harris lbw b Agarkar	.... 1 (4)		
S. B. Styris c Agarkar b Kartik	.... 54 (49)		
C. D. McMillan c Dravid b Kumble	.. 20 (36)		
*C. L. Cairns c Zaheer Khan b Kumble	23 (36)	B 2, l-b 9, w 7, n-b 1	 19
J. D. P. Oram st Dravid b Kartik	..... 11 (16)		
†B. B. McCullum lbw b Zaheer Khan	. 31 (69)	(47 overs, 185 mins)	208
D. L. Vettori run out		Fall: 8 25 48 110 118 136 154 187	
(Yuvraj Singh/Tendulkar)	... 19 (25)	208 208	

Bowling: Zaheer Khan 8–1–30–3; Agarkar 6–0–28–2; Tendulkar 8–0–40–0; Kumble 10–1–36–2; Kartik 10–0–38–2; Yuvraj Singh 5–0–25–0.

Umpires: D. R. Shepherd (England) and K. Hariharan.
TV Umpire: I. Sivaram.
Referee: R. S. Madugalle (Sri Lanka).

FINAL

INDIA v AUSTRALIA

At Eden Gardens, Kolkata, November 18, 2003. Day/night game. Australia won by 37 runs. *Toss:* Australia.

If Australia started this tournament as underdogs, their sterling form and India's lack of self-belief ensured they entered the final as overwhelming favourites. But they had to work hard on a turning wicket in front of a full Eden Gardens house of around 100,000 spectators. Another 40,000 or so surrounded the venue outside, listening to the roars as Australia uncharacteristically struggled to reach 235 from their 50 overs. The batsmen's patience and techniques were tested by India's four-man spin attack. A busy 65-run partnership in the last nine overs between Michael Bevan and Michael Clarke eventually carried them to a defendable total, but by no means a secure one. Australia might count themselves fortunate to have made that many. V. V. S. Laxman held two catches and dropped four, prompting Ricky Ponting to speculate afterwards about India's apparent frailty under pressure. It materialised again with the bat. Andy Bichel bowled Sachin Tendulkar with a superb off-cutter, instantly silencing 100,000 spectators, but India looked to be in control again at 4 for 159 after 34 overs. The Australians fielded magnificently, however, and never gave up. India lost their rudder with the departure of Rahul Dravid, Clarke's second crucial victim in consecutive overs, and the door was ajar. It was all Ian Harvey needed. Unfurling his trademark grab-bag of yorkers and slower balls he nailed the last four wickets, three of them bowled, in eight balls. Suddenly India were all out, 37 runs short with a wasteful 49 balls up their sleeves. It was poor cricket by them but brilliant stuff from the baggy golds, triumphing in a hostile environment with the crowd, the pitch and the momentum against them. The stage was now set for a titanic Test series in Australia.

Man of the Match: M. J. Clarke. *Man of the Series:* S. R. Tendulkar.

Australia

†A. C. Gilchrist b Agarkar	7	(12)	M. J. Clarke not out	44	(28)
M. L. Hayden c Laxman b Zaheer Khan	19	(24)			
*R. T. Ponting c Laxman b Kartik	36	(45)	B 4, l-b 7, w 7	18	
D. R. Martyn c Yuvraj Singh b Sehwag	61	(101)			
A. Symonds c Badani b Harbhajan Singh	10	(20)	(50 overs, 205 mins) (5 wkts)	235	
M. G. Bevan not out	40	(70)	Fall: 16 32 112 129 170		

I. J. Harvey, A. J. Bichel, N. W. Bracken and B. A. Williams did not bat.

Bowling: Agarkar 8–2–50–1; Zaheer Khan 6–0–29–1; Salvi 3–0–23–0; Kartik 10–1–30–1; Harbhajan Singh 10–1–34–1; Sehwag 8–0–35–1; Badani 5–0–23–0.

India

S. R. Tendulkar b Bichel	45	(65)	Zaheer Khan b Harvey	0	(1)
V. Sehwag c and b Bracken	5	(12)	Harbhajan Singh c Symonds b Harvey	2	(4)
V. V. S. Laxman b Williams	22	(26)	A. M. Salvi b Harvey	0	(4)
*†R. S. Dravid b Clarke	49	(69)	B 4, l-b 5, w 5	14	
Yuvraj Singh c Hayden b Symonds	4	(6)			
H. K. Badani c Symonds b Clarke	30	(36)	(41.5 overs, 195 mins)	198	
A. B. Agarkar not out	26	(23)	Fall: 8 36 99 110 159 168 186 186		
M. Kartik b Harvey	1	(4)	198 198		

Bowling: Bracken 8–1–15–1; Williams 7–1–30–1; Bichel 8–0–51–1; Harvey 4.5–0–21–4; Symonds 7–0–36–1; Clarke 7–1–36–2.

Umpires: D. R. Shepherd (England) and A. V. Jayaprakash.
TV Umpire: K. Hariharan.
Referee: R. S. Madugalle (Sri Lanka).

Australians in County Cricket, 2003

by CATHERINE HANLEY

Twenty Australians graced the English county scene in 2003 – some for barely a week, others for the duration – as chaos theory ruled once more. Each county was again permitted to register two overseas players at a time and up to four a season. The result was a merry-go-round. No fewer than 51 overseas players came and went, several on very short contracts, with counties reluctant to go more than a few days without a high-profile import. Australian representation was actually down on the previous summer, when 23 made the journey across, but it remained a distinctly more Aussie circuit than the one frequented by the likes of Ted McDonald and Bill Alley. The figure of 20 does not include the ever-growing number of Australian-born players – Phil Jaques, Matthew Mason and Mark Harrity among them – armed with British parents or passports.

The Frizzell County Championship was again supplemented by three one-day tournaments: the National League (NL), the knockout Cheltenham & Gloucester (C & G) Trophy and the glitzy new Twenty20 Cup, which replaced the tired and increasingly unloved Benson & Hedges Cup. Speed was of the essence in Twenty20, with the teams limited to 20 frantic overs each and the spectators having an equally breathless time of it: jacuzzis, bouncing castles, fairground rides and boy bands were all part of the package. Traditionalists complained but crowds flocked. An unheard-of 16 days were sellouts.

SCOTT BRANT (Essex)
A lively Queensland left-armer, Brant turned in some fine performances with the ball until his season was cut short in July by a knee injury. The highlight was his aggressive 6 for 45 at Trent Bridge as Nottinghamshire were skittled for 79. It could have been worse for Notts; they were 7 for 8 at one stage, with the lowest ever first-class total of 12 under threat. Brant's batting was less of a feature, his best effort an unbeaten one

against Lancashire as Essex held out for a tense draw. It made little difference in the end. Essex have been either promoted or relegated in each of the four years since the Championship was split into two divisions, and they promptly went down again.

	M	I	NO	Runs	HS	100s	50s	Avge	Ct	St	W	Avge	BB
First-class	11	14	6	37	23	0	0	4.62	3	0	37	30.18	6-45
County Championship	10	14	6	37	23	0	0	4.62	3	0	36	29.44	6-45
C&G	2		0				–		–		–		–
–	–	–	0		0			5			19.18		3-54
NL	7	3	2	20	14*	0	0	20.00	4	0	13	22.61	4-25
Twenty20	5	2	1	1	1*	0	0	1.00	2	0	6	30.33	2-34

JAMIE COX (Somerset)

Cox's 126 against Derbyshire in May must have come as some relief: it was his first century in his past 44 first-class innings. The shackles broken, he began to play with something resembling his old fluency – certainly he looked more confident than he had in 2002, when he averaged only 31 in the Championship. Being freed of the responsibility of captaincy seemed to focus his mind. He passed 1,000 first-class runs for the season thanks to an unbeaten 88 against the students of Loughborough, and milked his favourite opponents Hampshire – against whom he averages 81.55 – for yet another century. His slight renaissance did little for Somerset's fortunes. They finished two places off the bottom in the Championship's second division and only the minnows of Scotland trailed them in the National League.

	M	I	NO	Runs	HS	100s	50s	Avge	Ct	St	W	Avge	BB
First-class	15	27	3	1,087	160	3	5	45.29	10	0	0	–	–
County Championship	14	26	2	999	160	3	4	41.62	10	0	0	–	–
C&G	2	2	1	46	39*	0	0	46.00	0	0	0	–	–
NL	16	14	0	479	130	2	1	34.21	5	0	0	–	–
Twenty20	4	4	0	128	53	0	1	32.00	2	0	0	–	–

JOE DAWES (Middlesex)

Dawes was a solid, enthusiastic but far from spectacular contributor. Signed as a replacement for fellow Queenslander Ashley Noffke, his first-class performances were adequate at best: only one five-wicket haul and an average of 31.50. In his defence, the poverty of Middlesex's attack meant he was consistently overbowled in the four-day game. There was little excuse for his National League form, which might be politely described as disastrous: he averaged a wicket every three games at a cost of 112 runs apiece. And although he was not recruited for his strokeplaying capabilities, Middlesex may have been expecting more than a highest score of two.

	M	I	NO	Runs	HS	100s	50s	Avge	Ct	St	W	Avge	BB
First-class	10	12	5	97	32*	0	0	13.85	3	0	34	31.50	5-46
County Championship	9	12	5	97	32*	0	0	13.85	3	0	32	31.50	5-46
C&G	1	0		–	–	–	–	–	0	0	2	15.00	2-30
NL	12	5	2	5	2	0	0	1.66	3	0	4	112.75	1-22
Twenty20	1	1	0	0	0	0	0	0.00	0	0	0	–	–

MICHAEL DI VENUTO (Derbyshire)

In another miserable season for Derbyshire, who finished rock bottom of the Championship for the second time in three years, Di Venuto's performance stood out like a beacon. His 1,520 first-class runs were more than one-fifth of his team's entire tally, underlining the shambolic support he received. He started with a flourish, cruising to 121 and 61 against Glamorgan and racking up a further four hundreds and seven fifties before the season was out. All too often, though, they were in a losing cause.

Add weak bowling, dressing-room unrest and a flurry of incoming and outgoing overseas players, and it is easy to understand why Derbyshire hoped to get even more out of Di Venuto when they appointed him captain for 2004. Unfortunately for them, he injured his back at the end of the Australian season and didn't return.

	M	I	NO	Runs	HS	100s	50s	Avge	Ct	St	W	Avge	BB
First-class	16	31	0	1,520	150	5	8	49.03	25	0	0	–	–
County Championship	16	31	0	1,520	150	5	8	49.03	25	0	0	–	–
C&G	3	3	0	76	51	0	1	25.33	2	0		–	–
NL	15	14	0	655	130	3	3	46.78	5	0	–	–	–
Twenty20	5	5	2	198	67	0	2	66.00	0	0	5	17.60	3-19

MURRAY GOODWIN (Sussex)

Goodwin's fantastic season climaxed on September 18, 2003, when he pulled the runs that gave Sussex the points for their first Championship crown. It had been 164 years in the making. As if to emphasise the momentousness of the occasion, and after an eight-minute delay for rejoicing, Goodwin carried on to a magnificent unbeaten 335, the highest score of the season and his first triple-century. He had already bettered his own best score a month earlier when he stroked his way to 210 in Colchester. His performance in the final game was all the more remarkable given the events of the previous match against title-challengers Lancashire. He was felled by a bouncer, received on-field treatment, carried his bat for 118 – out of a team total of 251 – then had seven stitches inserted over his eye. His one-day form was hardly less striking, although his team finished eighth in the National League's second division. After the Championship heroics, though, nobody cared.

	M	I	NO	Runs	HS	100s	50s	Avge	Ct	St	W	Avge	BB
First-class	17	29	3	1,545	335*	4	5	59.42	12	0	0	–	–
County Championship	16	28	3	1,496	335*	4	5	59.84	10	0	0	–	–
C&G	2	2	0	53	32	0	0	26.50	0	0	0	–	–
NL	18	18	3	731	129*	4	2	48.73	5	0	0	–	–
Twenty20	5	5	0	66	38	0	0	13.20	2	0	0	–	–

BRAD HODGE (Leicestershire)

It was a season of ups and downs for Hodge. The ups revolved around his own form, as he blasted 1,495 first-class runs including a career-best (and county record) 302 not out at Trent Bridge. He was his club's highest runscorer in the National League and the country's highest in the Twenty20 Cup, where he was the only man to pass 300 runs. But the Twenty20 also accounted for one of his downs, when he considered taking legal action after being publicly called a "cheat" by Derbyshire's Dominic Cork. In celebrating a catch, Hodge had carried the ball over the boundary to show it to the crowd, prompting Cork to claim the catch was illegal. The incident was taken no further but left a nasty taste in the mouth. Further lows were provided by Leicestershire's form, relegated in both the Championship and National League. Only victory in the penultimate game saved them from finishing winless for the first time in their Championship history.

	M	I	NO	Runs	HS	100s	50s	Avge	Ct	St	W	Avge	BB
First-class	16	26	2	1,495	302*	5	3	62.29	12	0	7	39.14	3-35
County Championship	15	25	1	1,293	302*	4	3	53.87	10	0	4	59.75	1-12
C&G	3	3	0	5	4	0	0	1.66	1	0	0	–	–
NL	16	16	0	475	104	1	2	29.68	6	0	6	42.66	3-34
Twenty20	6	6	0	301	97	0	3	50.16	3	0	6	14.83	3-6

MICHAEL HUSSEY (Northamptonshire)

Commentators are starting to run out of superlatives when describing the county performances of Hussey over the past three years. No matter, for the statistics speak for themselves: 1,697 first-class runs, an average of 89 and five consecutive first-class hundreds including the obligatory triple-century, his third, which broke his own county record. The only surprise was that his unbeaten 331 came against Somerset rather than his usual whipping boys Gloucestershire, although he did manage 264 against them in June. Hussey's 820 runs in the National League were a county record and he recorded the second-highest Twenty20 aggregate in the land, proving that brains could be just as effective as brawn. The feature setting 2003 apart from his previous years, however, was that this time his efforts were rewarded by team success. Northamptonshire were promoted in both the Championship and National League. It was with great consternation that they received the news he was not coming back in 2004.

	M	I	NO	Runs	HS	100s	50s	Avge	Ct	St	W	Avge	BB
First-class	14	21	2	1,697	331*	6	5	89.31	17	0	1	52.00	1-5
County Championship	14	21	2	1,697	331*	6	5	89.31	17	0	1	52.00	1-5
C&G	1	1	0	5	5	0	0	5.00	1	0	0	–	–
NL	18	18	3	820	123	3	6	54.66	8	0	1	44.00	1-12
Twenty20	5	5	1	279	88	0	3	69.75	5	0	0	–	–

MICHAEL KASPROWICZ (Glamorgan)

Not since Jim Laker in 1956 had a bowler taken nine wickets in an innings twice during an English season. Kasprowicz emulated him in 2003. His 9 for 36 and 9 for 45 – both, coincidentally, against Durham – were the two best analyses of the summer. His accuracy was highlighted by the fact that 14 of these 18 wickets were bowled or leg-before. Kasprowicz's season haul of 77 first-class wickets was second only to Sussex's Pakistani leg-spinner Mushtaq Ahmed. He chipped in with another 20 in the National League, helping Glamorgan retain their first-division status. Kasprowicz's batting was also more than useful. In a season where Glamorgan's last five wickets often outscored their first five, his consistent efforts from No. 9 earned him the Wetherell award for being the outstanding all-rounder in the first-class game.

	M	I	NO	Runs	HS	100s	50s	Avge	Ct	St	W	Avge	BB
First-class	15	26	4	556	78	0	2	25.27	7	0	77	21.15	9-36
County Championship	15	26	4	556	78	0	2	25.27	7	0	77	21.15	9-36
C&G	2	2	0	37	19	0	0	18.50	1	0	4	25.75	3-43
NL	16	11	5	146	35*	0	0	24.33	4	0	20	29.20	3-20
Twenty20	5	5	1	63	31	0	0	15.75	1	0	4	32.25	2-25

SIMON KATICH (Hampshire)

In a mixed season for Hampshire, bringing one-day promotion but four-day misery, the dependability of Katich was one of the few high points. He amassed more than 700 National League runs and over a thousand in the Championship, while collecting handy wickets with his left-arm chinamen. It was tough going, though, with his fluency often curtailed by the fact that he was batting in desperate rearguard situations in the fight to salvage a draw. It was not until the final Championship game in Derby that a Katich century helped bring about victory for his team. His commanding contributions were enough, at least, to ensure his side avoided the wooden spoon.

	M	I	NO	Runs	HS	100s	50s	Avge	Ct	St	W	Avge	BB
First-class	13	22	3	1,143	143*	4	6	60.15	15	0	17	34.76	4-21
County Championship	13	22	3	1,143	143*	4	6	60.15	15	0	17	34.76	4-21
C&G	1	1	0	82	82*	0	1	–	1	0	0	–	–
NL	18	18	1	728	106	2	6	42.82	13	0	6	30.66	2-25
Twenty20	5	5	2	179	59*	0	2	59.66	1	0	0	–	–

STUART LAW (Lancashire)

An English season wouldn't be a season these days if it didn't involve Stuart Law averaging well over 50 and pummelling more than a thousand runs. In 2003 he did it in particular style, sustaining a phenomenal 90-plus average across 16 games. His 1,820 first-class runs were 123 more than the next best in the land – his countryman Hussey – managed. A highlight was his sparkling 236 not out against Warwickshire, which he followed up with 186 in the next game against Leicestershire. He and fellow import Carl Hooper shared a 360-run partnership at Edgbaston – an all-time fifth-wicket record for Lancashire – and he needs only a hundred against his old side Essex to become the third man to collect centuries against all 18 counties. Surprisingly subdued in the Twenty20 competition, Law's consistency in the National League helped Lancashire top the second division. Small wonder that he was named the county's player of the year.

	M	I	NO	Runs	HS	100s	50s	Avge	Ct	St	W	Avge	BB
First-class	16	24	4	1,820	236*	7	6	91.00	17	0	0	–	–
County Championship	16	24	4	1,820	236*	7	6	91.00	17	0	0	–	–
C&G	4	3	0	92	59	0	1	30.66	2	0	0	–	–
NL	18	17	2	586	98	0	4	39.06	4	0	0	–	–
Twenty20	5	5	0	59	29	0	0	11.80	1	0	0	–	–

STUART MacGILL (Nottinghamshire)

MacGill was one of the few standout performers in a torrid year for Nottinghamshire, his 42 wickets helping them out of many a tight spot. But some inexcusable top-order batting meant that he seldom bowled with the security of a large total on the board, and so was less damaging than he might have been. The county finished second-last in the Championship, were mid-table also-rans in the National League's second division, and exited early from the C&G and Twenty20 tournaments. MacGill did, however, find himself the unlikeliest of heroes against Essex in May. Coming in at No. 11, with his team 9 for 19 and headed for one of the lowest first-class tallies on record, MacGill thrashed 27 in six overs as they scraped together a marginally more respectable total of 79.

	M	I	NO	Runs	HS	100s	50s	Avge	Ct	St	W	Avge	BB
First-class	11	18	6	112	27	0	0	9.33	2	0	42	33.52	6-117
County Championship	11	18	6	112	27	0	0	9.33	2	0	42	33.52	6-117
C&G	1	1	0	0	0	0	0	0.00	1	0	0	–	–
NL	12	4	2	12	5*	0	0	6.00	2	0	17	24.64	3-26
Twenty20	5	2	1	13	8*	0	0	13.00	1	0	6	24.00	3-42

JIMMY MAHER (Glamorgan)

Returning to Glamorgan for the second half of 2003 – they had intended to sign only one overseas player but found they could not manage without another – Maher failed to live up to his 2001 exploits. A meagre 491 runs in eight Championship matches left him sitting in 129th position in the national first-class averages. His one-day form was also below par. He showed only one tantalising glimpse of what he could do, lashing an aggressive 142 in Cardiff – encompassing a 181-run opening stand with Robert Croft – as Glamorgan steamrollered Essex by eight wickets.

	M	I	NO	Runs	HS	100s	50s	Avge	Ct	St	W	Avge	BB
First-class	8	16	0	491	95	0	4	30.68	7	0	0	–	–
County Championship	8	16	0	491	95	0	4	30.68	7	0	0	–	–
C&G	0	–	–	–	–	–	–	–	–	–	–	–	–
NL	10	10	0	295	142	1	1	29.50	5	0	3	9.66	3-29
Twenty20	0	–	–	–	–	–	–	–	–	–	–	–	–

ANDREW SYMONDS (Kent)

After an uninspiring beginning, things looked up for Kent with the arrival of Symonds in June. He hit 54 in his first innings, albeit in a losing cause, and his unbeaten 103 in 81 balls against Nottinghamshire a month later was instrumental in his side's first Championship victory. After that, neither Symonds nor Kent looked back. The county won five of their remaining seven games to finish a respectable fourth in the

Championship's first division, and Symonds was an integral figure in them avoiding one-day relegation. It was in the new Twenty20 Cup, however, that he really came into his own. The other counties must have felt profoundly relieved when Kent were knocked out in the early stages, thus avoiding further shell-shock from the marauding bat of Symonds. His 170 runs came at the astonishing strike-rate of 226.66.

	M	I	NO	Runs	HS	100s	50s	Avge	Ct	St	W	Avge	BB
First-class	10	16	2	659	121	2	4	47.07	6	0	16	32.31	3-38
County Championship	10	16	2	659	121	2	4	47.07	6	0	16	32.31	3-38
C&G	0	–	–	–	–	–	–	–	–	–	–	–	–
NL	9	9	2	375	93*	0	3	53.57	4	0	11	26.00	2-33
Twenty20	5	5	1	170	96*	0	1	42.50	3	0	3	43.33	2-35

Heading the list of Australians who shone more fleetingly on the county circuit was **Martin Love**, who snuck in a flying visit to Durham in between Australia's series against West Indies and Bangladesh. He had time enough to break a thumb and blast a county-record 273 against Hampshire, bettering his own 251 at Lord's the previous season. **Damien Wright**'s time at Northamptonshire was even briefer; he took seven wickets in two outings and contributed handily with the bat. **Greg Blewett** was initially signed by Kent as cover for Symonds, but ended up playing alongside his fellow Australian for several games. Blewett was the less spectacular of the pair: he averaged 31, with a best of 71, in six first-class matches.

Others had their seasons cut short by injury. **Ashley Noffke** often looked uncomfortable in accumulating 21 wickets at 35.90 in seven Championship matches for Middlesex, before flying home with a back problem. **Michael Clark**, the Western Australian left-armer, played only one first-class game for Warwickshire before he too succumbed to a back injury. It was a triumphant but turbulent time for **Ian Harvey**, who had the distinction of clattering the first Twenty20 century with his unbeaten 100 in 50 balls, comprising 13 fours and four sixes, against Warwickshire. He helped Gloucestershire to yet another one-day cup – the C&G Trophy this time – before severing ties with the county he has played for since 1999. Harvey's contribution to Gloucestershire, the limited-overs kings of modern times, was acknowledged by his selection as one of worldwide *Wisden*'s Five Cricketers of the Year.

Damien Martyn, meanwhile, had a short but remarkable end-of-season stint at Yorkshire. Upon reaching 87 in his debut innings, he top-edged a hook into his face and was taken to hospital with a broken nose. Undeterred, he played in the final Championship match against Gloucestershire, scorching his way to the fastest first-class hundred of the season – in only 65 balls – and carrying on to a spectacular, career-best 238 in 159 deliveries. He hit seven sixes and 38 fours. Martyn's 17 in the second innings proved something of a letdown, reducing his first-class average for the season to 171.

Under-19s World Cup, 2003-04

by DAVID WISEMAN

The fifth Under-19s World Cup was a tournament some of the Australians might like to forget. They began with high hopes of defending the title they had won two years earlier in New Zealand, when they stormed unbeaten through the tournament with a four-man spin attack consisting of two left-arm finger-spinners, a leg-spinner and a chinaman bowler. This year's performance was altogether less memorable. Australia failed to qualify for the Super League stage, for the first time in the cup's history, and were then narrowly beaten in the consolation final by hosts Bangladesh in front of 15,000 cheering, drum-beating locals.

In Australia's absence, Pakistan beat West Indies by 25 runs to be crowned World Cup champions. The final was played under lights in Dhaka, with around 35,000 spectators looking on. "Can't imagine this anywhere else in the world," Pakistan's coach Aqib Javed said afterwards. "A full house for an Under-19 match ... this is amazing." The cricket-mad hosts put on a great show all through the tournament, helping cement the standing of this important show-case event.

England and India were the other semi-finalists. The Indian left-hander Shikhar Dhawan was the runaway leading batsman, amassing 505 runs at 84, while Bangladesh's left-arm spinner Enamul Haque headed the wicket-takers with 22 scalps at 10. His best figures were his crucial 5 for 31 in the Plate Championship final, as Australia fell eight runs short of Bangladesh's 9 for 257.

The Australians will be better players for the experience. Coached by Bennett King, it was a less highly credentialled squad than previous Australian sides, boasting not a single first-class match between them. Still they played some polished cricket. Wickets were shared between Gary Putland, Moises Henriques, Steve O'Keefe and Cameron Huckett, while the Victorian wicket-keeper

Adam Crosthwaite's 13 dismissals were a tournament equal-high. Batting was Australia's Achilles heel. In eight matches only Theo Doropoulos passed fifty more than once.

They began impressively enough, Doropoulos heaving 11 fours and a six in a run-a-ball 57, as Australia overcame Canada by six wickets. Being dismissed for 73 was the last thing they would have expected in their next match against Zimbabwe. Only Doropoulos and Tim Paine, the captain, reached double figures. The middle- and lower-order batsmen had no answer to the fast bowlers Tinashe Panyangara and Elton Chigumbura, who found themselves in Zimbabwe's embattled Test side a couple of months later.

The massive defeat left Australia's net run-rate reeling, and they had to win comfortably in their final group match against Sri Lanka to have any chance of qualifying for the Super League stage. They won the battle but lost the war. After cobbling together 9 for 186, thanks to a defiant effort from the tail, Australia needed to restrict Sri Lanka to 97. At 4 for 10 they looked a chance, but Sri Lanka recovered sufficiently to be all out for 184 in the final over.

Finishing third in their group, and relegated to the Plate Championship between the bottom eight sides, Australia took their frustrations out on Scotland. The Scots were rolled for 22 – extras top-scoring with 10 – in 22.3 overs. Putland took 4 for 9, Huckett 4 for 7 and Australia raced to victory in 23 balls. They cruised past Papua New Guinea and Nepal by nine and six wickets respectively, then ran into Ireland in the plate semi-final. Australia plundered 5 for 340, Victoria's Matthew Harrison leading the way with 91 in 78 balls, but the Irish replied gamely with 9 for 291.

Requiring 258 to topple Bangladesh in the plate final, Australia looked to have little hope at 5 for 108 in the 28th over. A 125-run partnership between Ahilen Beadle, born in Bahrain, and O'Keefe, born in Malaysia, tilted the pendulum Australia's way. Beadle made 54 runs in 54 balls and O'Keefe 65 in 66. Within 25 runs of victory, they collapsed in a bizarre heap. Beadle was run out on the last ball of the 47th over, O'Keefe was run out on the second ball of the 48th and then Scott Coyte departed – yet another run-out – one delivery later.

"It was a high-pressure situation and it could have gone either way," King said afterwards. "We have several promising players but they've still got a lot to learn."

AUSTRALIAN TOURING PARTY

T. D. Paine (Tas) (*captain*), A. R. Beadle (NSW), S. J. Coyte (NSW), A. J. Crosthwaite (Vic), T. P. Doropoulos (W Aust), C. J. Ferguson (S Aust), M. Henriques (NSW), C. S. Huckett (Vic), J. P. Mangan (Vic), S. N. J. O'Keefe (NSW), L. Oswald-Jacobs (S Aust), G. D. Putland (S Aust), K. J. Skewes (NT), S. Wallace (NSW).

C. J. Ferguson was replaced by M. M. Harrison when he suffered cruciate ligament strain to his right knee in a warm-up game on February 14.

Manager: B. Freedman. *Coach:* B. King. *Assistant coach:* D. J. A. Moore. *Physiotherapist:* M. Pfitzner.

AUSTRALIAN BATTING

	M	I	NO	R	HS	100s	50s	Avge	Ct/St	S-R
T. P. Doropoulos	8	8	1	238	83	0	2	34.00	4	101.70
A. J. Crosthwaite	8	6	2	175	50*	0	1	43.75	9/4	89.28
A. R. Beadle	8	6	2	155	54	0	1	38.75	5	67.98
M. M. Harrison	5	4	1	146	91	0	1	48.66	4	73.36
T. D. Paine	8	8	2	142	45	0	0	23.66	2	62.83
M. Henriques	8	6	1	95	44	0	0	19.00	0	75.39
S. N. J. O'Keefe	8	3	0	76	65	0	1	25.33	3	79.16
K. J. Skewes	8	5	1	75	37	0	0	18.75	2	55.97
J. P. Mangan	7	3	3	23	21*	0	0	–	1	76.66
L. Oswald-Jacobs	3	2	0	15	8	0	0	7.50	0	31.91
C. S. Huckett	7	2	0	5	4	0	0	2.50	0	21.73
G. D. Putland	6	1	0	2	2	0	0	2.00	2	100.00
S. J. Coyte	3	2	0	1	1	0	0	0.50	0	20.00
S. Wallace	1	0	–	–	–	–	–	–	0	–

* Denotes not out.

AUSTRALIAN BOWLING

	O	Mdns	R	W	BB	5W/i	Avge	RPO
M. Henriques	60.2	7	212	11	2-10	0	19.27	3.51
G. D. Putland	40	5	158	11	4-9	0	14.36	3.95
S. N. J. O'Keefe	50.3	5	156	10	2-1	0	15.60	3.08
C. S. Huckett	44.1	9	151	10	4-7	0	15.10	3.41
T. D. Paine	39	3	156	7	2-24	0	22.28	4.00
J. P. Mangan	56	8	213	6	4-30	0	35.50	3.80
S. J. Coyte	20	2	84	4	3-42	0	21.00	4.20
A. R. Beadle	9	0	52	3	2-26	0	17.33	5.77

GROUPS

Group A	Group B	Group C	Group D
Australia	England	Bangladesh	Ireland
Canada	Nepal	India	Pakistan
Sri Lanka	South Africa	New Zealand	Papua New Guinea
Zimbabwe	Uganda	Scotland	West Indies

PRELIMINARY ROUNDS

RESULTS SUMMARY Group A

Sri Lanka v Zimbabwe

At Bogra District Stadium, Bogra, February 15, 2004. Zimbabwe 161 (S. C. Williams 47, C. de Grandhomme 41; M. F. Maharoof 4-28, A. D. Mathews 2-27) lost to Sri Lanka 8 for 162 (G. T. de Silva 33, C. K. B. Kulasekara 37; E. C. Rainsford 2-37, T. Panyangara 2-41, E. Chigumbura 3-37) by two wickets.

Australia v Canada

At Rajshahi Divisional Stadium, Rajshahi, February 16, 2004. Australia won by six wickets. *Toss:* Australia. *Man of the Match:* T. P. Doropoulos.

Canada

M. Qazi c Crosthwaite b Coyte	1	A. Baksh lbw b Paine	0
G. Bastiampillai c Beadle b Coyte	37	†K. Carto b O'Keefe	4
T. Bastiampillai c Beadle b Coyte	6	K. Patel run out (O'Keefe)	1
K. Jethi c Crosthwaite b Henriques	0		
S. Keshvani b Henriques	0	B 4, l-b 5, w 23, n-b 2	34
S. Anjaria st Crosthwaite b Paine	50		—
*U Bhatti not out	30	(45.1 overs)	164
D. Soraine run out (Paine)	1	Fall: 7 19 21 21 113 147 151 153 163 164	

Bowling: Henriques 6.1–0–18–2; Coyte 10–1–42–3; Huckett 7–0–30–0; Mangan 6–1–20–0; Paine 10–0–29–2; O'Keefe 6–0–16–1.

Australia

*T. D. Paine lbw b Jethi	22	M. Henriques not out	2
T. P. Doropoulos st Carto b Anjaria	57	L-b 2, w 7, n-b 4	13
A. R. Beadle b Baksh	2		
K. J. Skewes c and b Keshvani	37	(28.4 overs) (4 wkts)	165
†A. J. Crosthwaite not out	32	Fall: 56 76 104 157	

S. N. J. O'Keefe, S. J. Coyte, L. Oswald-Jacobs, C. S. Huckett and J. P. Mangan did not bat.

Bowling: Bhatti 3–0–26–0; Soraine 2–0–28–0; Jethi 7–1–25–1; Baksh 4–0–20–1; Anjaria 4–0–22–1; Patel 3–0–14–0; Keshvani 3.4–0–20–1; Qazi 2–0–8–0.

Umpires: K. Hariharan (India) and Mahbub-ur-Rahman.
Referee: Sultan Rana (Pakistan).

Canada v Sri Lanka

At Rajshahi Divisional Stadium, Rajshahi, February 17, 2004. Canada 81 (M. F. Maharoof 2-20, C. K. B. Kulasekara, 5-27, M. M. M. Suraj 2-6) lost to Sri Lanka 1 for 84 (H. E. Vithana 52*) by nine wickets.

Australia v Zimbabwe

At Bogra District Stadium, Bogra, February 18, 2004. Zimbabwe won by seven wickets. *Toss:* Australia. *Man of the Match:* T. Panyangara.

Australia

*T. D. Paine b Chigumbura	19	S. J. Coyte c Taylor b Panyangara	1
T. P. Doropoulos b Panyangara	26	C. S. Huckett c Williams b Chigumbura	1
A. R. Beadle c Taylor b Panyangara	3	J. P. Mangan not out	1
K. J. Skewes c Taylor b Panyangara	1		
†A. J. Crosthwaite c Taylor b Panyangara	0	B 1, l-b 4, w 5 n-b 1	11
M. Henriques b Chigumbura	3		
S. N. J. O'Keefe b Chigumbura	0	(19 overs)	73
L. Oswald-Jacobs c Rainsford b Panyangara	7	Fall: 37 51 53 53 56 56 60 63 67 73	

Bowling: Rainsford 5–0–20–0; Panyangara 9–1–31–6; Chigumbura 5–1–17–4.

Zimbabwe

†B. R. M. Taylor b Coyte	0		
J. G. Cameron c Doropoulos b Henriques	0	B 1, l-b 4, w 13, n-b 1	19
S. C. Williams not out	37		
*T. M. K. Mawoyo c Skewes b Huckett	18	(17.1 overs)	(3 wkts) 74
C. R. Ervine not out	0	Fall: 0 5 68	

E. Chigumbura, C. de Grandhomme, T. Panyangara, P. Utseya, A. G. Cremer and E. C. Rainsford did not bat.

Bowling: Coyte 5–1–18–1; Henriques 6–1–16–1; Mangan 4–0–18–0; Huckett 2.1–0–17–1.

Umpires: M. R. Benson (England) and Mahbub-ur-Rahman.
Referee: Sultan Rana (Pakistan).

Canada v Zimbabwe

At Bogra District Stadium, Bogra, February 19, 2004. Canada 9 for 180 (A. Keshvani 63, T. Bastiampillai 38; P. Utseya 4-41) lost to Zimbabwe 2 for 183 (J. G. Cameron 84*, S. C. Williams 35) by eight wickets.

Australia v Sri Lanka

At Rajshahi Divisional Stadium, Rajshahi, February 20, 2004. Australia won by two runs. *Toss:* Sri Lanka. *Man of the Match:* M. F. Maharoof.

Australia

*T. D. Paine lbw b Maharoof	4	S. N. J. O'Keefe c Tharanga b Ratnayake	11
T. P. Doropoulos lbw b Chanaka	0	J. P. Mangan not out	21
L. Oswald-Jacobs lbw b Maharoof	8	C. S. Huckett c Kularatne b Suraj	4
M. Henriques c Chanaka b Suraj	30	B 4, l-b 16, w 19, n-b 2	41
K. J. Skewes c Maharoof b Kulasekara	5		
†A. J. Crosthwaite run out	26	(50 overs)	(9 wkts) 186
A. R. Beadle c Kularatne b Suraj	36	Fall: 6 12 34 52 79 113 137 172 186	

G. D Putland did not bat.

Bowling: Maharoof 10–1–31–2; Chanaka 10–1–35–1; Kulasekara 7–3–25–1; Suraj 10–0–37–3; Ratnayake 8–2–20–1; Vithana 5–0–18–0.

Sri Lanka

W. U. Tharanga c Crosthwaite b Putland	... 0	M. M. M. Suraj run out	8
A. D. C. Kularatne lbw b Huckett	0	R. S. R. de Zoysa not out	0
H. E. Vithana lbw b Putland	1	P. U. M. Chanaka c O'Keefe b Henriques	.. 0
R. W. M. G. A. Ratnayake c Doropoulos			
b Putland	... 2		
J. K. Silva b Paine	46	B 2, l-b 6, w 9	17
*M. F. Maharoof b O'Keefe	56		
†G. T. de Silva c Mangan b O'Keefe	24	(49.1 overs)	184
C. K. B. Kulasekara run out	30	Fall: 1 1 6 10 106 118 170 184 184 184	

Bowling: Putland 6–1–16–3; Huckett 6–1–23–1; Henriques 9.1–0–48–1; Mangan 10–3–26–0; Paine 8–1–31–1; O'Keefe 10–1–32–2.

Umpires: M. R. Benson (England) and K. Hariharan (India).
Referee: Sultan Rana (Pakistan).

POINTS TABLE Group A

	Played	Won	Lost	Points	Net Run-Rate
Sri Lanka	3	2	1	4	1.268
Zimbabwe	3	2	1	4	1.039
Australia	3	2	1	4	–0.306
Canada	3	0	3	0	–2.500

Net run-rate was calculated by subtracting runs conceded per over from runs scored per over.

RESULTS SUMMARY Group B

February 15	Chittagong	Nepal 8 for 191 lost to England 2 for 192 by eight wickets
February 16	Chittagong	Uganda 125 lost to South Africa 2 for 126 by eight wickets
February 17	Chittagong	England 7 for 259 defeated Uganda 46 by 213 runs
February 18	Chittagong	South Africa 156 lost to Nepal 9 for 158 by one wicket
February 19	Chittagong	Uganda 194 lost to Nepal 5 for 195 by five wickets
February 20	Chittagong	England 189 lost to South Africa 9 for 190 by one wicket

POINTS TABLE Group B

	Played	Won	Lost	Points	Net Run-Rate
England	3	2	1	4	1.581
South Africa	3	2	1	4	0.607
Nepal	3	2	1	4	–0.110
Uganda	3	0	3	0	–2.164

Net run-rate was calculated by subtracting runs conceded per over from runs scored per over.

RESULTS SUMMARY Group C

February 15	Dhaka	Bangladesh 202 lost to New Zealand 8 for 204 by two wickets
February 16	Dhaka	India 3 for 425 defeated Scotland 8 for 155 by 270 runs
February 17	Dhaka	Scotland 95 lost to Bangladesh 1 for 96 by nine wickets
February 18	Dhaka	India 215 defeated New Zealand 146 by 69 runs
February 19	Savar	New Zealand 2 for 389 defeated Scotland 149 by 240 runs
February 20	Dhaka	India 7 for 309 defeated Bangladesh 178 by 131 runs

POINTS TABLE Group C

	Played	Won	Lost	Points	Net Run-Rate
India	3	3	0	6	3.133
New Zealand	3	2	1	4	1.175
Bangladesh	3	1	2	2	0.166
Scotland	3	0	3	0	−5.441

Net run-rate was calculated by subtracting runs conceded per over from runs scored per over.

RESULTS Group D

February 15	Khulna	Papua New Guinea 60 lost to Pakistan 2 for 63 by eight wickets
February 16	Khulna	West Indies 8 for 265 defeated Ireland 9 for 259 by six runs
February 17	Khulna	Ireland 142 lost to Pakistan 2 for 146 by eight wickets
February 18	Khulna	West Indies 3 for 371 defeated Papua New Guinea 219 by 152 runs
February 19	Khulna	Ireland 212 defeated Papua New Guinea 142 by 70 runs
February 20	Khulna	Pakistan 9 for 251 defeated West Indies 88 by 163 runs

POINTS TABLE Group D

	Played	Won	Lost	Points	Net Run-Rate
Pakistan	3	3	0	6	3.168
West Indies	3	2	1	4	0.033
Ireland	3	1	2	2	−0.326
Papua New Guinea	3	0	3	0	−2.819

Net run-rate was calculated by subtracting runs conceded per over from runs scored per over.

SUPER LEAGUE AND CHAMPIONSHIP GROUPS

Super League Group 1	*Super League Group 2*	*Plate Championship Group 1*	*Plate Championship Group 2*
India	England	Australia	Bangladesh
South Africa	New Zealand	Nepal	Canada
Sri Lanka	Pakistan	Papua New Guinea	Ireland
West Indies	Zimbabwe	Scotland	Uganda

RESULTS SUPER LEAGUE GROUP 1

February 22	Dhaka (Day/night)	South Africa 5 for 226 defeated India 223 by three runs
February 22	Dhaka	West Indies 7 for 200 defeated Sri Lanka 181 by 19 runs
February 24	Dhaka (Day/night)	India 9 for 253 defeated West Indies 157 by 96 runs
February 24	Dhaka	Sri Lanka 5 for 277 defeated South Africa 248 by 29 runs
February 26	Dhaka (Day/night)	India 5 for 316 defeated Sri Lanka 260 by 56 runs
February 26	Dhaka	West Indies 6 for 284 defeated South Africa 250 by 34 runs

POINTS TABLE Super League Group 1

	Played	Won	Lost	Points	Net Run-Rate
India	3	2	1	4	0.993
West Indies	3	2	1	4	−0.287
Sri Lanka	3	1	2	2	−0.307
South Africa	3	1	2	2	−0.400

RESULTS SUPER LEAGUE GROUP 2

February 23 Dhaka (Day/night). England 2 for 306 defeated New Zealand 209 by 97 runs
February 23 Savar .... Zimbabwe 141 lost to Pakistan 1 for 143 by nine wickets
February 25 Savar .... Zimbabwe 9 for 218 lost to England 4 for 219 by six wickets
February 25 Dhaka (Day/night). New Zealand 8 for 181 lost to Pakistan 2 for 184 by eight wickets
February 27 Dhaka........... England 196 defeated Pakistan 191 by five runs
February 27 Dhaka (Day/night). Zimbabwe 8 for 272 defeated New Zealand 180 by 92 runs

POINTS TABLE Super League Group 2

	Played	Won	Lost	Points	Net Run-Rate
England	3	3	0	6	0.719
Pakistan	3	2	1	4	1.077
Zimbabwe	3	1	2	2	0.005
New Zealand	3	0	3	0	−1.872

RESULTS PLATE GROUP 1

Australia v Scotland

At M. A. Aziz Stadium, Chittagong, February 22, 2004. Australia won by 10 wickets.
Toss: Scotland. *Man of the Match:* C. S. Huckett.

Scotland

I. D. K. Young c Putland b Huckett	5	G. Goudie b Putland	0
M. M. Iqbal lbw b Putland	0	C. R. Anderson st Crosthwaite b O'Keefe .	1
K. Farid b Putland	0	G. M. Allan not out	0
*K. J. Coetzer c Crosthwaite b Huckett	0		
†R. O. Hussain c Harrison b Huckett	0	L-b 3, w 6, n-b 1	10
S. Weeraratna c Putland b O'Keefe	5		
I. S. Brand c O'Keefe b Huckett	1	(22.3 overs)	22
R. T. Lyons b Putland	0	Fall: 7 9 10 10 11 12 13 15 20 22	

Bowling: Putland 9–3–9–4; Huckett 8–5–7–4; Henriques 3–2–2–0; O'Keefe 2.3–1–1–2.

Australia

*T. D. Paine not out	2
T. P. Doropoulos not out	16
W 4, n-b 1	5
(3.5 overs) (0 wkt)	23

M. Henriques, M. M. Harrison, †A. J. Crosthwaite, A. R. Beadle, K. J. Skewes, S. N. J. O'Keefe,
S. Wallace, C. S. Huckett and G. D. Putland did not bat.

Bowling: Anderson 2–0–15–0; Goudie 1.5–0–8–0.

Umpires: M. R. Benson (England) and I. L. Howell (South Africa).
Referee: Sultan Rana (Pakistan).

Nepal v Papua New Guinea

At Chittagong Divisional Stadium, Chittagong, February 22, 2004. Papua New Guinea
9 for 168 (V. Kila 35, C. R. Amini 34; M. Shrestha 3-33, L. Lama 4-51) lost to Nepal
3 for 169 (K. Chaugai 90*, S. Vesawkar 36; M. Tamasi 2-27) by seven wickets.

Australia v Papua New Guinea

At Chittagong Divisional Stadium, Chittagong, February 24, 2004. Australia won by nine wickets. *Toss:* Australia. *Man of the Match:* J. P. Mangan.

Papua New Guinea

M. D. Dai lbw b Putland	0	†J. Vare c Harrison b Huckett		3
W. Harry c Doropoulos b Huckett	9	L. Davai run out (Beadle)		0
V. Kila b Henriques	32	V.Vali not out		0
J. Gavera c Paine b Mangan	14			
*C. R. Amini lbw b Mangan	4	L-b 3, w 8, n-b 1		12
K. Amini c Crosthwaite b Mangan	4			
K. Arua b Henriques	5	(35 overs)		83
M. Tamasi b Mangan	0	Fall: 0 14 51 62 70 76 78 81 83 83		

Bowling: Putland 6–1–26–1; Huckett 10–3–13–2; Mangan 10–2–30–4; Henriques 7–2–10–2; O'Keefe 2–1–1–0.

Australia

*T. D. Paine not out		26
T. P. Doropoulos b Davai		34
M. M. Harrison not out		10
L-b 4, w 9, n-b 2		15
(18.2 overs)	(1 wkt)	85
Fall: 57		

M. Henriques, †A. J. Crosthwaite, A. R. Beadle, K. J. Skewes, S. N. J. O'Keefe, J. P. Mangan, C. S. Huckett and G. D. Putland did not bat.

Bowling: Vali 5–0–24–0; Tamasi 5–0–25–0; Davai 3–0–18–1; Harry 4–1–6–0; K. Amini 1.2–0–8–0.

Umpires: K. Hariharan (India) and Showkat-ur-Rahman.
Referee: Sultan Rana (Pakistan).

Nepal v Scotland

At M. A. Aziz Stadium, Chittagong, February 24, 2004. Nepal 9 for 200 (S. Vesawkar 51; C. R. Anderson 2-30, G. Goudie 3-37, M. M. Iqbal 2-34) lost to Scotland 7 for 204 (M. M. Iqbal 67, S. Weeraratna 34*; R. Rauniyar 2-32) by three wickets.

Australia v Nepal

At Chittagong Divisional Stadium, Chittagong, February 26, 2004. Australia won by six wickets. *Toss:* Nepal. *Man of the Match:* A. R. Beadle.

Nepal

K. Chaugai c Crosthwaite b Henriques	9	†M. Katuwal not out		16
B. Regmi c Beadle b O'Keefe	14	L. Lama b Huckett		7
*S.P. Gauchan c Crosthwaite b O'Keefe	6	R. Shrestha not out		0
S. Vesawkar c Beadle b Henriques	0			
P. Khadka c Doropoulos b Paine	33	L-b 8, w 23		31
P. Chaudhary c Skewes b Beadle	19			
M. Shrestha c Crosthwaite b Paine	11	(50 overs)	(9 wkts)	154
R. Rauniyar b Huckett	8	Fall: 22 48 48 52 101 105 115 140 154		

Bowling: Putland 3–0–12–0; Huckett 6–0–30–2; Henriques 9–1–26–2; O'Keefe 10–2–22–2; Mangan 10–2–19–0; Paine 9–2–24–2; Beadle 3–0–13–1.

Australia

*T. D. Paine c Katuwal b M. Shrestha 13	A. R. Beadle not out 49
T. P. Doropoulos lbw b M. Shrestha 17	W 4 4
M. M. Harrison c Katuwal b Lama 16	
M. Henriques c Katuwal b M. Shrestha ... 9	(36.2 overs) (4 wkts) 158
†A. J. Crosthwaite not out 50	Fall: 23 30 44 62

K. J. Skewes, S. N. J. O'Keefe, J. P. Mangan, C. S. Huckett and G. D. Putland did not bat.

Bowling: M. Shrestha 9–1–46–3; Khadka 4–0–23–0; Gauchan 6.2–1–17–0; Lama 9–0–33–1; R. Shrestha 4–0–26–0; Rauniyar 4–0–13–0.

Umpires: K. Hariharan (India) and A. F. M. Akhtaruddin.
Referee: Dipu Roy Chowdhury.

Papua New Guinea v Scotland

At M. A. Aziz Stadium, Chittagong, February 26, 2004. Papua New Guinea 114 (V. Kila 34; G. Goudie 2-30, K. J. Coetzer 2-20, M. M. Iqbal 2-25, R. T. Lyons 3-33) lost to Scotland 3 for 115 (I. D. K. Young 30, M. M. Iqbal 30) by seven wickets.

POINTS TABLE Plate Championship Group 1

	Played	Won	Lost	Points	Net Run-Rate
Australia	3	3	0	6	2.820
Scotland	3	2	1	4	–0.550
Nepal	3	1	2	2	–0.139
Papua New Guinea	3	0	3	0	–1.942

RESULTS PLATE GROUP 2

February 23	Chittagong	Canada 136 lost to Bangladesh 6 for 139 by four wickets
February 23	Chittagong	Ireland 9 for 329 defeated Uganda 206 by 123 runs
February 25	Chittagong	Uganda 78 lost to Bangladesh 6 for 79 by four wickets
February 25	Chittagong	Ireland 9 for 265 defeated Canada 110 by 155 runs
February 27	Chittagong	Ireland 141 lost to Bangladesh 2 for 143 by eight wickets
February 27	Chittagong	Canada 231 lost to Uganda 5 for 235 by five wickets

POINTS TABLE Plate Championship Group 2

	Played	Won	Lost	Points	Net Run-Rate
Bangladesh	3	3	0	6	1.897
Ireland	3	2	1	4	1.369
Uganda	3	1	2	2	–1.810
Canada	3	0	3	0	–1.655

SEMI FINALS

First Plate Championship Semi-Final

Australia v Ireland

At M. A. Aziz Stadium, Chittagong, February 29, 2004. Australia won by 49 runs. *Toss:* Australia. *Man of the Match:* M. M. Harrison.

Australia

*T. D. Paine c Wilson b Thompson	45	K. J. Skewes not out	0
T. P. Doropoulos c Wilson b Thompson	83		
M. M. Harrison c Porterfield b O'Brien	91	B 4, l-b 6, w 8, n-b 1	19
M. Henriques c Porterfield b Coulter	44		
†A. J. Crosthwaite c Thompson b O'Brien	47	(50 overs) (5 wkts)	340
A. R. Beadle not out	11	Fall: 131 138 213 307 330	

S. N. J. O'Keefe, J. P. Mangan, C. S. Huckett and G. D. Putland did not bat.

Bowling: Riddles 5–0–31–0; Morgan 10–0–77–0; O'Brien 10–0–70–2; Thompson 10–0–48–2; Kidd 10–0–55–0; Coulter 5–0–49–1.

Ireland

*W. Porterfield c Paine b O'Keefe	44	G. Kidd run out	0
†G. Wilson b Putland	48	G. J. Thompson b Henriques	6
E. J. G. Morgan c Harrison b Putland	65	A. Coulter not out	38
K. O'Brien lbw b O'Keefe	1		
S. Wells st Crosthwaite b Paine	9	L-b 7, w 10, n-b 2	19
R. J. Rankin c Harrison b Putland	13		
P. Blakeney c (sub) b Mangan	19	(50 overs) (9 wkts)	291
A. Riddles not out	29	Fall: 75 117 122 147 176 186 216 223 230	

Bowling: Putland 10–0–71–3; Huckett 5–0–31–0; Mangan 10–0–61–1; Henriques 10–1–45–1; O'Keefe 10–0–29–2; Paine 4–0–34–1; Beadle 1–0–13–0.

Umpires: M. R. Benson (England) and B. G. Jerling (South Africa).
Referee: Dipu Roy Chowdhury.

Second Plate Championship Semi-Final

Bangladesh v Scotland

At Chittagong Divisional Stadium, Chittagong, March 1, 2004. Bangladesh won by 91 runs. *Toss:* Bangladesh. *Man of the Match:* Nazmul Hossain.

Bangladesh

Nafis Iqbal c Brand b Coetzer	21	Rubaiyat Huq c Lyons b Goudie	14
Naeem Islam c Farid b Anderson	21	Nazmul Hossain not out	14
Aftab Ahmed run out (Lyons)	10	Enamul Haque jnr run out	4
*Ashiq-ur-Rahman c Coetzer b Iqbal	28		
Nazimuddin c Iqbal b Lyons	14	L-b 3, w 5, n-b 1	9
†Dhiman Ghosh b Young	23		
Abul Bashar run out (Lyons)	29	(49.5 overs)	197
Nadif Chowdhury c Iqbal b Coetzer	10	Fall: 37 52 58 79 113 149 153 170 183 197	

Bowling: Anderson 8–2–32–1; Goudie 8.5–2–29–1; Lyons 10–1–26–1; Coetzer 9–1–35–2; Iqbal 10–0–49–1; Young 4–0–23–1.

Scotland

I. D. K. Young b Nazmul Hossain	1	R. K. P. Cannon b Enamul Haque jnr	0
M. M. Iqbal b Nazmul Hossain	8	R. T. Lyons b Nadif Chowdhury	15
K. Farid c Rubaiyat Huq b Nazmul Hossain	9	G. Goudie b Nazmul Hossain	0
*K. J. Coetzer run out (Abul Bashar)	41	C. R. Anderson not out	4
†R. O. Hussain b Enamul Haque jnr	8	L-b 4, w 6	10
S. Weeraratna b Abul Bashar	9		
I. S. Brand c Nadif Chowdhury		(33.3 overs)	106
b Enamul Haque jnr	1	Fall: 4 14 25 43 56 65 65 102 102 106	

Bowling: Nazmul Hossain 6.3–0–11–4; Rubaiyat Huq 8–1–22–0; Abul Bashar 10–4–28–1; Enamul Haque jnr 7–1–31–3; Nadif Chowdhury 2–0–10–1.

Umpires: K. Hariharan (India) and I. L. Howell (South Africa).
Referee: Sultan Rana (Pakistan).

First Super League Championship Semi-Final

India v Pakistan

At Bangabandhu National Stadium, Dhaka, February 29, 2004 (Day/night). Pakistan won by five wickets. *Toss:* India. *Man of the Match:* Tariq Mahmood.

India

A. R. Uthappa c Mansoor Amjad b Salman Qadir	33
S. Dhawan c Khalid Latif b Ali Imran	8
P. Waghela lbw b Riaz Afridi	0
R. K. Solanki run out (Riaz Afridi)	21
S. Raina c Zulqarnain Haider b Tariq Mahmood	17
*†K. K. D. Karthik c Khalid Latif b Salman Qadir	7
Sunny Singh b Mansoor Amjad	25
Gaurav Dhiman c Salman Qadir b Tariq Mahmood	14
A. Sharma not out	21
P. Gupta b Ali Imran	3
R. P. Singh c Salman Qadir b Riaz Afridi	1
L-b 6, w 9, n-b 4	19
(47.3 overs)	169

Fall: 23 24 73 80 92 113 135 147 166 169

Bowling: Riaz Afridi 8.3–0–31–2; Ali Imran 9–0–38–2; Mansoor Amjad 10–0–33–1; Salman Qadir 10–0–27–2; Tariq Mahmood 10–2–34–2.

Pakistan

*Khalid Latif lbw b Gaurav Dhiman	1
Adnan Zaheer c Sharma b Gupta	18
Jahangir Mirza lbw b Singh	9
Usman Saeed b Sharma	19
Salman Qadir c Karthik b Singh	24
Tariq Mahmood not out	45
Fawad Alam not out	43
L-B 7, w 3, n-b 2	12
(44.5 overs) (5 wkts)	171

Fall: 3 20 48 68 83

†Zulqarnain Haider, Mansoor Amjad, Ali Imran and Riaz Afridi did not bat.

Bowling: Gaurav Dhiman 8–0–34–1; Singh 10–2–25–2; Gupta 7–2–24–1; Raina 10–1–34–0; Sharma 8.5–1–43–1; Solanki 1–0–4–0.

Umpires: B. Doctrove (West Indies) and J. W. Lloyds (England).
TV Umpire: Mahbub-ur-Rahman.
Referee: R. S. Mahanama (Sri Lanka).

Second Super League Championship Semi-Final

England v West Indies

At Bangabandhu National Stadium, Dhaka, March 2, 2004 (Day/night). West Indies won by 94 runs. *Toss:* West Indies. *Man of the Match:* D. Ramdin.

West Indies

X. M. Marshall c Lawson b Wright	45	Z. Khan not out		60
T. Maraj run out (Bopara)	0	R. Rampaul not out		1
L. M. P. Simmons lbw b Harrison	5	B 1, l-b 7, w 5		13
A. B. Fudadin b Harrison	51			
*†D Ramdin c New b Bresnan	72		(6 wkts)	249
J. C. Augustus b Harrison	2	Fall: 4 30 69 137 146 233		

L. A. Sebastien, R. Bachan and M. Matthew did not bat.

Bowling: Bresnan 10–0–52–1; Harrison 10–0–28–3; Stiff 6–0–41–0; Patel 10–0–50–0; Wright 6–0–38–1; Lawson 8–0–32–0.

England

*A. N. Cook b Rampaul	33	A. J. Harrison run out (Ramdin/Bachan)		2
R. S. Bopara c Sebastien b Rampaul	10	D. A. Stiff not out		2
S. M. Davies st Ramdin b Simmons	4	M. A. K. Lawson run out (Simmons)		1
L. J. Wright c Marshall b Simmons	3			
T. T. Bresnan run out (Ramdin/Khan)	41	L-b 3, w 10, n-b 3		16
S. R. Patel c Bachan b Khan	8			
J. C. Hildreth c Ramdin b Rampaul	27	(39.1 overs)		155
†T. J. New run out (Khan/Bachan)	8	Fall: 32 45 57 86 112 114 150 152 153 155		

Bowling: Rampaul 7.1–1–27–3; Matthew 7–1–24–0; Simmons 7–0–18–2; Khan 10–0–45–1; Bachan 8–0–38–0.

Umpires: Nadeem Ghauri (Pakistan) and P. D. Parker (Australia).
TV Umpire: A. F. M. Akhtaruddin.
Referee: J. F. M. Morrison (New Zealand).

PLATE CHAMPIONSHIP FINAL

Bangladesh v Australia

At Fatullah Cricket Stadium, Dhaka, March 4, 2004. Bangladesh won by 8 runs. *Toss:* Bangladesh. *Man of the Match:* Enamul Haque jnr.

Bangladesh

Nafis Iqbal c and b O'Keefe	59	Nazmul Hossain c (sub) S. Wallace b Mangan		2
Naeem Islam c Crosthwaite b Paine	66	Enamul Haque not out		3
Aftab Ahmed st Crosthwaite b Beadle	57	Shahadat Hossain not out		1
Nazimuddin b Beadle	18			
†Dhiman Ghosh c Beadle b Henriques	6	B 1, l-b 3, w 15, n-b 2		21
Abul Bashar run out	5			
Nadif Chowdhury b Henriques	11	(50 overs)	(9 wkts)	257
*Ashiq-ur-Rahman run out	8	Fall: 124 152 204 215 225 229 247 252 253		

Bowling: Coyte 5–0–24–0; Putland 6–0–24–0; Mangan 6–0–39–1; Henriques 10–0–47–2; O'Keefe 10–0–55–1; Paine 8–0–38–1; Beadle 5–0–26–2.

Australia

T. P. Doropoulos b Shahadat Hossain		5
K. J. Skewes b Enamul Haque jnr		32
M. M. Harrison run out		29
M. Henriques b Enamul Haque jnr		7
†A. J. Crosthwaite c Dhiman Ghosh b Enamul Haque jnr		20
A. R. Beadle run out		54
S. N. J. O'Keefe run out		65
S. J. Coyte run out		0

*T. D. Paine c Ashiq-ur-Rahman b Enamul Haque jnr		11
J. P. Mangan not out		1
G. D. Putland st Dhiman Ghosh b Enamul Haque jnr		2
B 2, l-b 3, w 17, n-b 1		23
(49.3 overs)		249

Fall: 19 63 73 103 108 233 235 235 247 249

Bowling: Nazmul Hossain 4.4–0–24–0; Shahadat Hossain 10–1–47–1; Aftab Ahmed 0.2–0–4–0; Abul Bashar 10–2–35–0; Enamul Haque jnr 9.3–1–31–5; Nadif Chowdhury 10–0–56–0; Naeem Islam 5–0–47–0.

Umpires: B. Doctrove (West Indies) and I. L. Howell (South Africa).
Referee: R. S. Mahanama (Sri Lanka).

FINAL

Pakistan v West Indies

At Bangabandhu National Stadium, Dhaka, March 5, 2004 (Day/night). Pakistan won by 25 runs. *Toss:* Pakistan. *Man of the Match:* Asif Iqbal. *Man of the Series:* S. Dhawan (India).

Pakistan

*Khalid Latif st Ramdin b Bachan		20
Adnan Zaheer b Bachan		33
Jahangir Mirza c Ramdin b Khan		11
Tariq Mahmood st Ramdin b Bachan		10
Asif Iqbal run out (Bachan)		54
Salman Qadir c Matthew b Sebastien		42
Fawad Alam c Augustus b Rampaul		10
†Zulqarnain Haider not out		23

Riaz Afridi b Matthew		1
Mansoor Amjad c Ramdin b Matthew		9
Ali Imran not out		5
L-b 3, w 6, n-b 3		12
(50 overs)		230

Fall: 53 58 79 81 178 179 195 197 211

Bowling: Rampaul 10–0–54–1; Matthew 10–2–35–2; Simmons 2–0–25–0; Bachan 10–0–34–3; Khan 10–0–35–1; Sebastien 8–0–44–1.

West Indies

X. M. Marshall c Zulqarnain b Tariq		26
T. Maraj run out (Zulqarnain/Mansoor)		32
L. M. P. Simmons lbw b Jahangir		5
A. B. Fudadin c Salman b Jahangir		13
*†D. Ramdin lbw b Riaz Afridi		36
J. C. Augustus run out (Fawad)		25
Z. Khan c Zulqarnain b Tariq		10
R. Rampaul not out		24

L. A. Sebastien run out (Zulqarnain)		0
M. Matthew c Zulqarnain b Tariq		2
R. Bachan run out (Jahangir/Mansoor)		1
B 4, l-b 16, w 9, n-b 2		31
(47.1 overs)		205

Fall: 69 72 84 94 144 169 197 200 203 205

Bowling: Riaz Afridi 6–0–39–1; Ali Imran 5–0–23–0; Salman Qadir 10–1–33–0; Mansoor Amjad 9.1–1–27–0; Tariq Mahmood 10–1–34–3; Jahangir Mirza 7–0–29–2.

Umpires: J. W. Lloyds (England) and P. D. Parker (Australia).
TV Umpire: B. G. Jerling (South Africa).
Referee: J. F. M. Morrison (New Zealand).

THE PRICEWATERHOUSECOOPERS RATINGS

Introduced in 1987 as the Deloitte Ratings, and known from 1990 to 1998 as the Coopers and Lybrand Ratings, the PricewaterhouseCoopers Ratings rank Test and limited-overs cricketers on a scale up to 1,000. A rating of 900 points is outstanding and rarely achieved. The ratings take into account performances, playing conditions, the quality of the opposition and the result of matches. A player cannot get a full Test rating until he has played 40 innings or taken 100 wickets. The leading 10 batsmen and bowlers in the world, as of September 6, 2004, were:

Tests

Batsmen	Rating		Bowlers	Rating
1. Rahul Dravid (Ind)	892		1. Steve Harmison (Eng)	875
2. Matthew Hayden (Aus)	885		2. Muttiah Muralidaran (SL)	867
3. Brian Lara (WI)	845		3. Shaun Pollock (SAf)	854
4. Ricky Ponting (Aus)	832		4. Shoaib Akhtar (Pak)	826
5. Jacques Kallis (SAf)	807		5. Glenn McGrath (Aus)	805
6. Inzamam-ul-Haq (Pak)	785		6. Shane Warne (Aus)	762
7. Sachin Tendulkar (Ind)	784		7. Anil Kumble (Ind)	751
8. Virender Sehwag (Ind)	782		8. Jason Gillespie (Aus)	740
9. Herschelle Gibbs (SAf)	764		9. Chaminda Vaas (SL)	706
10. Mark Richardson (NZ)	761		10. Makhaya Ntini (SAf)	674

Limited-overs internationals

Batsmen	Rating		Bowlers	Rating
1. Sachin Tendulkar (Ind)	772		1. Chaminda Vaas (SL)	885
2. Jacques Kallis (SAf)	764		2. Muttiah Muralidaran (SL)	863
3. Ricky Ponting (Aus)	758		3. Jason Gillespie (Aus)	855
4. Adam Gilchrist (Aus)	754		4. Shaun Pollock (SAf)	851
5. Andrew Flintoff (Eng)	741		5. Jacob Oram (NZ)	801
6. Chris Gayle (WI)	734		6. Glenn McGrath (Aus)	785
7. Stephen Fleming (NZ)	725		7. Brett Lee (Aus)	748
8. Matthew Hayden (Aus)	715		8. Andrew Flintoff (Eng)	736
9. Ramnaresh Sarwan (WI)	710		9. Heath Streak (Zim)	721
10. Kumar Sangakkara (SL)	707		10. Harbhajan Singh (Ind)	713

Opposite STILL THE ONE: Richie Benaud, pictured here in 1961, witnessed his 500th Test – more than anyone else in history – when England played New Zealand at Lord's in May 2004.

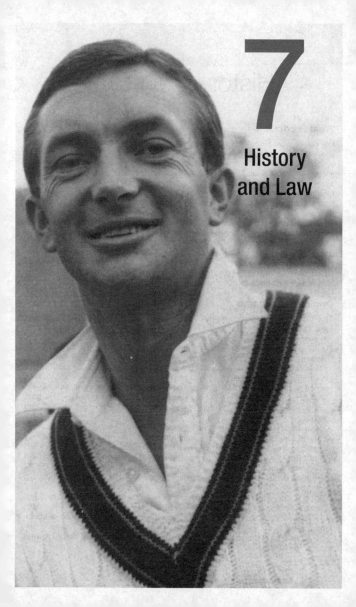

7

History
and Law

History of Cricket

What is cricket?

Cricket is a game played between two teams, generally of 11 members each. In essence, it is single combat, in which an individual batsman does battle against an individual bowler, who has helpers known as fielders. The bowler propels the ball with a straight arm from one end of the 22-yard pitch in an attempt to dismiss the batsman by hitting a target known as the wicket at the other end, or by causing the batsman to hit the ball into the air into a fielder's grasp, or by inducing one of a number of other indiscretions. The batsman attempts to defend the wicket with the bat and to score runs – the currency of the game – by striking the ball to the field boundary, or far enough from the fielders to allow the batsman to run to the other end of the pitch before the ball can be returned. At least two bowlers must take turns, from alternating ends; also, there are always two batsmen on the field, each to take a turn as required. When all but one of the batting team have been dismissed – or after an agreed period – the teams' roles are reversed. After all the players required to bat on both sides have done so either once or twice (which can take from a few hours to five days) the total number of runs accumulated determines the winner. But sometimes there isn't one.

Origins of the game

The origins of cricket lie somewhere in the Dark Ages – probably after the Roman Empire, almost certainly before the Normans invaded England, and almost certainly somewhere in Northern Europe. All research concedes that the game derived from a very old, widespread and uncomplicated pastime by which one player served up an object, be it a small piece of wood or a ball, and another hit it with a suitably fashioned club.

How and when this club-ball game developed into one where the hitter defended a target against the thrower is simply not known. Nor is there any evidence as to when points were awarded dependent upon how far the hitter was able to despatch the missile; nor when helpers joined the two-player contest, thus beginning the evolution into a team game; nor when the defining concept of placing wickets at either end of the pitch was adopted.

Etymological scholarship has variously placed the game in the Celtic, Scandinavian, Anglo-Saxon, Dutch and Norman-French traditions; sociological historians have variously attributed its mediaeval development to high-born country landowners, emigré Flemish cloth-workers, shepherds on the close-cropped downland of south-east England and the close-knit communities of iron- and glass-workers deep in the Kentish Weald. Most of these theories have a solid academic basis, but none is backed with enough evidence to establish a watertight case. The research goes on.

What is agreed is that by Tudor times cricket had evolved far enough from club-ball to be recognisable as the game played today; that it was well established in many parts of Kent, Sussex and Surrey; that within a few years it had become a feature of leisure time at a significant number of schools; and – a sure sign of the wide acceptance of any game – that it had become popular enough among young men to earn the disapproval of local magistrates.

Dates in cricket history

*c.*1550	Evidence of cricket being played in Guildford, Surrey.
1598	Cricket mentioned in Florio's Italian-English dictionary.
1611	Randle Cotgrave's French-English dictionary translates the French word "crosse" as a cricket staff.
	Two youths fined for playing cricket in Sidlesham, Sussex.
1624	Jasper Vinall becomes first man known to be killed playing cricket: hit by a bat while trying to catch the ball, at Horsted Green, Sussex.
1676	First reference to cricket being played outside Britain, by British residents in Aleppo, Syria.
1709	First recorded inter-county match: Kent v Surrey.
1729	Date of earliest surviving bat, belonging to John Chitty, now in the pavilion at The Oval, London.
1771	Width of bat limited to 4$^{1}/4$ inches, where it has remained ever since.
1774	LBW law devised.
1776	Earliest known scorecards, at the Vine Club, Sevenoaks, Kent.
1780	The first six-seamed cricket ball, manufactured by Dukes of Penshurst, Kent.
1788	First revision of the Laws of Cricket by Marylebone Cricket Club (MCC).
1795	First recorded case of a dismissal "leg before wicket".
1804	First cricket match in Australia by officers and crew of HMS *Calcutta* at Hyde Park, Sydney.
1807	First mention of "straight-armed" (i.e. round-arm) bowling: by John Willes of Kent.
1814	Lord's ground opened on its present site, in St John's Wood, London.
*c.*1836	Batting pads invented.
1838	Melbourne Cricket Club formed. Oldest surviving cricket club in Australia.
1844	First official international match: Canada v United States.
*c.*1850	Wicket-keeping gloves first used.
1851	Initial first-class match in Australia: Tasmania v Victoria at Launceston Racecourse.
1854	First match at MCG: Melbourne Cricket Club v Geelong.
1856	First Victoria v NSW match at MCG. NSW won by three wickets.
1857	First first-class match in Sydney at The Domain.
1858	First recorded instance of a hat being awarded to a bowler taking three wickets with consecutive balls.
1861	First touring team to visit Australia, captained by Heathfield Stephenson, all matches against odds.
1864	"Overhand bowling" authorised by MCC.
	John Wisden's *The Cricketer's Almanack* first published.
1868	Team of Australian Aborigines tour England.
1877	First Test match: Australia beat England by 45 runs in Melbourne.
1880	First Test match in England: England beat Australia by five wickets at The Oval.
1882	First Test match at SCG: Australia beat England by five wickets.

	Following England's first defeat by Australia in England, an "obituary notice" to English cricket in the *Sporting Times* leads to the tradition of The Ashes.
1884	First Test match at Adelaide Oval: England defeat Australia by eight wickets.
1887-88	Charles Turner the only bowler to take 100 wickets in an Australian first-class season: 106 in 12 matches.
1889	Declarations first authorised, but only on the third day, or in a one-day match.
1891	George Giffen scores 271 and takes 16 for 166 versus Victoria at Adelaide Oval, the greatest all-round performance in first-class cricket.
1892-93	Sheffield Shield competition begins with three competing colonies: NSW, Victoria and South Australia. Won by Victoria.
1894-95	George Giffen scores 902 runs and captures 93 wickets in 11-game season.
1899	A. E. J. Collins scores 628 not out in a junior house match at Clifton College, England, the highest individual score in any match.
	Green and gold colours first worn by Australian Test team on English tour.
	George Beldam takes his photograph of Victor Trumper stepping out to drive.
1900	Bernard Bosanquet, an English leg-spinner, invents the googly.
1905	Australian Board of Control for International Cricket, now called Cricket Australia, is formed.
1909	Imperial Cricket Conference (now the International Cricket Council) set up, with England, Australia and South Africa the original members.
1910	Six runs given for any hit over the boundary, instead of only for a hit out of the ground.
1911	Adelaide Oval scoreboard opened. Oldest functioning mechanical board.
1912	The "Big Six" – Clem Hill, Victor Trumper, Warwick Armstrong, Tibby Cotter, Hanson Carter and Vernon Ransford – refuse to tour England because of a dispute over player rights.
1915	Victor Trumper dies, aged 37.
	W. G. Grace dies, aged 67.
1920-21	Warwick Armstrong's team defeat England 5–0: remains the only whitewash in Ashes history.
1926-27	Queensland becomes the fourth state to enter the Sheffield Shield.
	Victoria score 1,107 v NSW in Melbourne, the record total for a first-class innings.
1928-29	First Test match at Brisbane Exhibition Ground: England defeat Australia by 675 runs.
	Don Bradman scores 1,690 runs in a season, still a record for an Australian season.
1930	Bradman scores 452 not out for NSW v Queensland at the SCG, which remains the highest first-class innings by an Australian.
	Bradman's first tour of England: he scores 974 runs in the five Ashes Tests, still a record for any Test series.
1931	First Test match at the Gabba: Australia defeat South Africa by an innings and 163 runs.
1932-33	The Bodyline tour of Australia in which England bowl at batsmen's bodies with a packed leg-side field to neutralise Bradman's scoring.

Tim Wall captures 10 for 36 for SA v NSW at the SCG, the best figures in first-class cricket in Australia.

1934   Jack Hobbs retires with 197 centuries and 61,237 first-class runs, both records.

First women's Test: Australia v England in Brisbane.

1935   MCC condemn and outlaw Bodyline.

1935-36 Clarrie Grimmett takes 44 wickets at 14.59 against South Africa, the highest number of wickets in a Test series for Australia. He is never selected again.

1936-37 A total of 954,290 spectators, the most for any series, watch Australia come back from 2–0 down to beat England 3–2.

1938   A Test is broadcast on TV for the first time: England v Australia at Lord's.

1947-48 Western Australia enters the Sheffield Shield on a restricted basis and wins the trophy.

1948   Bradman concludes Test career with a second-ball duck at The Oval and a batting average of 99.94 — four runs short of 100. His team go through England undefeated and become known as The Invincibles.

1953   England regain the Ashes after a 19-year gap, the longest ever.

1956   Jim Laker of England takes 19 for 90 v Australia in Manchester, the best match analysis in first-class cricket.

1957   Declarations authorised at any time.

1960   First tied Test, Australia v West Indies in Brisbane.

1962-63 Garry Sobers becomes the first player to achieve the double of 1,000 runs and 50 wickets in an Australian season.

1963   Distinction between amateur and professional cricketers abolished in English cricket.

Ian Meckiff called for throwing four times in one over against South Africa at the Gabba. He retires instantly.

1963-64 Sobers repeats the double and remains the only player to do so.

1969-70 Domestic one-day cricket begins in Australia.

1970   South Africa excluded from international cricket because of their government's apartheid policies.

First Test match at the WACA: Australia draws match against England.

1971   First one-day international: Australia v England in Melbourne, won by Australia.

1972   Bob Massie takes 16 for 137 on his Test debut at Lord's, the best match figures by an Australian.

1975   First World Cup: West Indies beat Australia in final at Lord's.

1977   Centenary Test in Melbourne, with identical result to the first match: Australia beat England by 45 runs.

Australian media tycoon Kerry Packer signs 51 of the world's leading players in defiance of the cricketing authorities.

1977-78 Tasmania enters the Sheffield Shield on a restricted basis.

1978   Graham Yallop wears a protective helmet to bat in a Test match, the first player to do so.

1979   Packer and official cricket agree on a peace deal. Channel Nine broadcasts a Test match for the first time.

1980	Eight-ball over abolished in Australia, making the six-ball over universal.
1981	Trevor Chappell, under instruction from his brother Greg, bowls an underarm delivery to the New Zealand tailender Brian McKechnie.
	England beat Australia in Leeds Test after following on, with bookmakers offering odds of 500 to 1 against them winning.
1982	The first electronic scoreboard, complete with TV replays and ads, makes its Test debut at the MCG.
1984	Dennis Lillee, Greg Chappell and Rod Marsh play their farewell Test against Pakistan at the SCG.
1986	Second tied Test, India v Australia in Chennai.
1987	Australia win the World Cup for the first time, defeating England in the final at Eden Gardens, Kolkata.
1988	The Cricket Academy opens in Adelaide.
1991	South Africa return to international cricket, with a one-day series in India.
1993	The ICC ceases to be administered by MCC, becoming an independent organisation with its own chief executive.
	Shane Warne bowls his first delivery in England. A huge leg-break, it bowls Mike Gatting and is proclaimed the ball of the century.
1994	Allan Border retires after setting world Test record of 11,174 runs and captaining Australia in 93 Test matches.
	Brian Lara becomes the only player to pass 500 in a first-class innings: 501 not out for Warwickshire v Durham.
1999–2000	Pura Milk sponsors interstate cricket, signifying the end of the Sheffield Shield as the major domestic competition.
2000	South Africa's captain Hansie Cronje banned from cricket for life after admitting receiving bribes from bookmakers in match-fixing scandal.
2001	Don Bradman dies, aged 92.
	Steve Waugh's Australian side ends 16-Test winning streak when defeated by India at Eden Gardens, Kolkata.
2003	First Test match at Marrara Cricket Ground, Darwin: Australia defeat Bangladesh by an innings and 132 runs.
	First Test match at Cazaly's Stadium, Cairns: Australia defeat Bangladesh by an innings and 98 runs.
	Matthew Hayden hits 380 against Zimbabwe at the WACA, the highest Test score by an Australian.
2004	Steve Waugh retires after world-record 168 Test appearances.
	Brian Lara of West Indies becomes the only player to reach 400 in a Test innings: 400 not out v England.
	Richie Benaud attends his 500th Test, more than any living person.
	Shane Warne equals Muttiah Muralidaran's record of 527 wickets in the Cairns Test against Sri Lanka.

Cricket Organisations

INTERNATIONAL CRICKET COUNCIL

On June 15, 1909, representatives of cricket in England, Australia and South Africa met at Lord's and founded the Imperial Cricket Conference. Membership was confined to the governing bodies of cricket in countries within the British Commonwealth where Test cricket was played. India, New Zealand and West Indies were elected as members on May 31, 1926, Pakistan on July 28, 1952, Sri Lanka on July 21, 1981, Zimbabwe on July 8, 1992 and Bangladesh on June 26, 2000. South Africa ceased to be a member of ICC on leaving the British Commonwealth in May, 1961, but was elected as a Full Member on July 10, 1991.

On July 15, 1965, the Conference was renamed the International Cricket Conference and new rules were adopted to permit the election of countries from outside the British Commonwealth. This led to the growth of the Conference, with the admission of Associate Members, who were each entitled to one vote, while the Foundation and Full Members were each entitled to two votes, on ICC resolutions. On July 12, 13, 1989, the Conference was renamed the International Cricket Council and revised rules were adopted.

On July 7, 1993, ICC ceased to be administered by MCC and became an independent organisation with its own chief executive, the headquarters remaining at Lord's. The category of Foundation Member, with its special rights, was abolished. On October 1, 1993, Sir Clyde Walcott became the first non-British chairman of ICC. On June 16, 1997, ICC became an incorporated body, with an executive board and a president instead of a chairman.

Officers

President: Ehsan Mani (2003–05). *Chief Executive:* M. W. Speed.
Chairmen of Committees: Cricket – Management: M. W. Speed; *Cricket – Playing:* S. M. Gavaskar; *Development:* M. W. Speed; *Audit Committee:* Sir John Anderson.
Executive Board: The president and chief executive sit on the board and all committees *ex officio*. They are joined by Ali Asghar (Bangladesh), Sir John Anderson (New Zealand), P. Chingoka (Zimbabwe), J. Dalmiya (India), E. H. C. Griffith (West Indies), R. F. Merriman (Australia), F. D. Morgan (England), J. Rayani (Kenya), Shaharyar Khan (Pakistan), P. H. F. Sonn (South Africa), T. Sumathipala (Sri Lanka), HRH Tunku Imran (Malaysia), R. van Ierschot (Netherlands). *General Manager – Cricket:* D. J. Richardson. *Cricket Operations Manager:* C. D. Hitchcock. *Umpires and Referees Manager:* C. S. Kelly. *Development Manager:* M. R. Kennedy. *General Manager – Corporate Affairs:* B. F. Clements. *Commercial Manager:* D. C. Jamieson. *Chief Finance Officer:* F. Hasnain. *In-house Lawyer:* U. Naidoo.

Constitution

President: Each Full Member has the right, by rotation, to appoint ICC's president. In 1997, India named J. Dalmiya to serve until June 2000, when M. A. Gray of Australia took over. Ehsan Mani of Pakistan succeeded Gray in June 2003; he and subsequent presidents will serve for two years.

Chief Executive: Appointed by the Council. M. W. Speed was appointed in June 2001.

Membership

Full Members: Australia, Bangladesh, England, India, New Zealand, Pakistan, South Africa, Sri Lanka, West Indies and Zimbabwe.

Associate Members*: Argentina (1974), Bermuda (1966), Canada (1968), Cayman Islands (2002), Denmark (1966), East and Central Africa (1966), Fiji (1965), France (1998), Germany (1999), Gibraltar (1969), Hong Kong (1969), Ireland (1993), Israel (1974), Italy (1995), Kenya (1981), Malaysia (1967), Namibia (1992), Nepal (1996), Netherlands (1966), Nigeria (2002), Papua New Guinea (1973), Scotland (1994), Singapore (1974), Tanzania (2001), Uganda (1998), United Arab Emirates (1990), USA (1965), Zambia (2003).

Affiliate Members*: Afghanistan (2001), Austria (1992), Bahamas (1987), Bahrain (2001), Belgium (1991), Belize (1997), Bhutan (2001), Botswana (2001), Brazil (2002), Brunei (1992), Chile (2002), Cook Islands (2000), Costa Rica (2002), Croatia (2001), Cuba (2002), Cyprus (1999), Czech Republic (2000), Finland (2000), Gambia (2002), Ghana (2002), Greece (1995), Indonesia (2001), Iran (2003), Japan (1989), Kuwait (1998), Lesotho (2001), Luxembourg (1998), Malawi (2003), Maldives (2001), Malta (1998), Morocco (1999), Mozambique (2003), Norway (2000), Oman (2000), Panama (2002), Philippines (2000), Portugal (1996), Qatar (1999), Rwanda (2003), St Helena (2001), Samoa (2000), Saudi Arabia (2003), Sierra Leone (2002), South Korea (2001), Spain (1992), Suriname (2002), Sweden (1997), Switzerland (1985), Thailand (1995), Tonga (2000), Turks & Caicos Islands (2002) and Vanuatu (1995).

* Year of election shown in parentheses.

The following governing bodies for cricket shall be eligible for election.

Full Members: The governing body for cricket recognised by the ICC of a country, or countries associated for cricket purposes, or a geographical area, from which representative teams are qualified to play official Test matches.

Associate Members: The governing body for cricket recognised by the ICC of a country, or countries associated for cricket purposes, or a geographical area, which does not qualify as a Full Member but where cricket is firmly established and organised.

Affiliate Members: The governing body for cricket recognised by the ICC of a country, or countries associated for cricket purposes, or a geographical area (which is not part of one of those already constituted as a Full or Associate Member) where the ICC recognises that cricket is played in accordance with the Laws of Cricket. Affiliate Members have no right to vote or to propose or second resolutions at ICC meetings.

CRICKET AUSTRALIA

Officers

Chairman: R. Merriman AM. *Chief Executive:* J. Sutherland.

Board of Directors: R. Merriman (*chairman*), J. Clarke, W. Edwards, B. F. Freedman OAM, R. E. Horsell, W. J. Jocelyn, I. M. McLachlan AO, D. G. Mullins SC, F. C. O'Connor, A. R. Border AO, B. Paulsen, T. Steele, T. Harrison, G. L. Tamblyn.

AUSTRALIAN CRICKETERS' ASSOCIATION

The Australian Cricketers' Association was incorporated in February 1997. It represents the collective voice of all first-class cricketers in Australia. The ACA has recently completed negotiating a Memorandum of Understanding with Cricket Australia, which formalises remuneration and welfare issues between the players and their respective cricket boards within Australia. The ACA is actively involved in protecting and providing benefits to all members, particularly in the area of professional advice and secular career training.

President: I. Healy. *Chief Executive Officer:* T. B. A. May.

ADDESSES

INTERNATIONAL CRICKET COUNCIL

M. W. Speed, The Clock Tower, Lord's Ground, London NW8 8QN (44 20 7266 1818; fax 44 20 7266 1777; website www.icc.cricket.org; email icc@icc.cricket.org).

Full Members

AUSTRALIA: Cricket Australia, J. Sutherland, 60 Jolimont Street, Jolimont, Victoria 3002 (03 9653 9999; fax 03 9653 9900; website www.cricket.com.au).

BANGLADESH: Bangladesh Cricket Board, Arafat Rahman, Navana Tower (5th floor), 45 Gulshan Avenue, Dhaka 10 (880 2 966 6805; fax 880 2 956 3844; email bcb@bangla.net).

ENGLAND: England and Wales Cricket Board, T. M. Lamb, Lord's Ground, London NW8 8QZ (44 20 7432 1200; fax 44 20 7289 5619; website www.ecb.co.uk).

INDIA: Board of Control for Cricket in India, Kairali, GHS Lane, Manacaud, Trivandrum 695009 (91 471 245 3307; fax 91 471 246 4620; email secbcci@sify.com).

NEW ZEALAND: New Zealand Cricket Inc., M. C. Snedden, PO Box 958, 109 Cambridge Terrace, Christchurch (64 3 366 2964; fax 64 3 365 7491; website www.nzcricket.org.nz).

PAKISTAN: Pakistan Cricket Board, C. Mujahid, Gaddafi Stadium, Ferozepur Road, Lahore 54600 (92 42 571 7231; fax 92 42 571 1860).

SOUTH AFRICA: United Cricket Board of South Africa, M. G. Majola, PO Box 55009, North Street, Illovo, Northlands 2116 (27 11 880 2810; fax 27 11 880 6578; website www.ucbsa.cricket.org; email ucbsa@ucb.co.za).

SRI LANKA: Board of Control for Cricket in Sri Lanka, L. R. D. Mendis, 35 Maitland Place, Colombo 7 (94 1 691439/689551; fax 94 1 697405; email: cricket@sri.lanka.net).

WEST INDIES: West Indies Cricket Board, R. Braithwaite, Factory Road, PO Box 616 W, Woods Centre, St John's, Antigua (1 268 481 2450; fax 1 268 481 2498; email wicb@candw.ag).

ZIMBABWE: Zimbabwe Cricket Union, V. Hogg, PO Box 2739, Josiah Tongogara Avenue, Harare (263 4 704616; fax 263 4 729370; website www.zcu.cricket.org; email zcu@mweb.co.zw).

Associate and Affiliate Members

Afghanistan Allah Dad Noori, afghan_cricket_fed@yahoo.com
Argentina R. Lord, cricarg@hotmail.com
Austria A. Simpson-Parker, simpson-parker@chello.at
Bahamas G. T. Taylor, firstslip@hotmail.com
Bahrain M. M. Osman, Osman@ramsis.com.bh
Belgium T. Vorzanger, t.vorzanger@skynet.be
Belize E. R. V. Wade Jr, juniorbest@btl.net
Bermuda R. Pearman, rpearman@logic.bm
Bhutan T. Tashi, bhutan_cricket_association@hotmail.com
Botswana E. A. Bhamjee, chico@botsnet.bw
Brazil J. N. Landers, john.landers@apis.com.br
Brunei M. B. Ahmad, mirbash@brunet.bn
Canada G. Edwards, Geoffed01@cs.com
Cayman Islands C. Myles, cicaadmin@candw.ky
Chile A. Adams, aadams@britanico.cl
Cook Islands V. Henry, lily@oyster.net.ck
Costa Rica R. Illingworth, trillingworth@yahoo.co.uk
Croatia J. Butkovic, croatia@cricinfo.com
Cuba L. I. Ford, leona@inder.co.uk
Cyprus S. Carr, carrs@cylink.com.cy
Czech Republic D. Talacko, talacko@vol.cz
Denmark C. B. S. Hansen, dcf@cricket.dk
East and Central Africa syusuf@globmw.net
Fiji S. Yaqona, fijicrick@connect.com.fj
Finland A. Armitage, fcachairman@cricketfinland.com
France O. Dubaut, Olivier.dubaut@paris.pref.gouv.fr
Gambia T. Manly-Rollings, sonnyann@qanet.gm
Germany C. Hoefinghoff, hoefinghoff@adfontes.net
Ghana W. Hackman, whackman@africaonline.com.gh
Gibraltar T. J. Finlayson, gibarchives@gibnynex.gi
Greece G. Sagiadinou, cricketadm@otenet.gr
Hong Kong J. A. Cribbin, hkca@hkabc.net
Indonesia M. K. Suresh, mksuresh1@yahoo.com
Iran Mohammed B. Zolfagharian, mbzbaseballir@hotmail.com
Ireland J. Wright, johnpwright@eircom.net
Israel S. Perlman, israel@cricket.org
Italy S. Gambino, segreteria@cricketitalia.org
Japan T. Lto, takaoo804@aol.com
Kenya H. Shah, kcricket@iconnect.co.ke
Lesotho P. Maliehe, lesothosportcommission@ilesotho.com
Luxembourg R. Fyfe, LCF@cricket.lu
Malawi Shiraz Yusuf, syusuf@globemw.net
Malaysia C. Sivanandan, crickmal@tm.net.my

Maldives Ahmed Hassan Didi, ccbm@avasmail.com.mv
Malta P. Naudi, maltacricket@yahoo.co.uk
Morocco M. Boujil, marocricket@caramail.com
Mozambique Angela Melo, fmc.moz@webmail.co.za
Namibia L. Pieters, cricket@iway.na
Nepal P. R. Pandey, prpandey52@hotmail.com
Netherlands A. de la Mar, cricket@kncb.nl
Nigeria John Abebe, segun_adeuk@yahoo.co.uk
Norway R. Gibb, bobgibb@c2i.net
Oman Madhu Sampat, latmad@omanteal.net.om
Panama Ismael Patel, aptecpa@cwpanama.net
Philippines C. Hartley, cjh@dls.com.ph
Portugal P. D. Eckersley, mail@portugalcricket.org
Qatar Manzoor Ahmad, afx@qatar.net.qa
Rwanda Charles Haba, rwandacricket@yahoo.fr
St Helena B. A. George, barbara@sainthelena.gov.sh
Samoa U. L. Apelu, laki@samoa.ws
Saudi Arabia Hasan Kabir, saudicricket@sps.net.sa
Scotland C. Carruthers, admin@scottishcricket.co.uk
Sierra Leone G. Fewry, hallelujahg@yahoo.com
Singapore A. Kalaver, cricket@singnet.co.sg
South Korea H. S. Kim, haksu@mac.com
Spain K. Sainsbury, ksainsby@dragonet.es
Suriname R. Hiralal, deloitte@sr.net
Sweden J. Govindarajah, mohan_Sweden@hotmail.com
Switzerland A. D. MacKay, alex.mackay@swisscricket.ch
Tanzania Z. Rehmtulla, wizards@cats-net.com
Thailand R. Sehgal, ravisehgall@hotmail.com
Tonga S. Puloka, pmotrain@kalianet.to
Turks & Caicos Islands H. Coalbrooke, mpapt@tciway.tc
Uganda J. Bagabo, ugandacricket@utlonline.co.ug
United Arab Emirates Mazhar Khan, cricket@emirates.net.ae
USA G. Dainty, smxrefaie@aol.com
Vanuatu M. Stafford, bdo@vanuatu.com.vu
Zambia R. M. Patel, acricket@zamtel.zm

Note: Full contact details for all Associate and Affiliate Members are available from the ICC.

UK ADDRESSES

ENGLAND AND WALES CRICKET BOARD: T. M. Lamb, Lord's Ground, London NW8 8QZ (44 20 7432 1200; fax 44 20 7289 5619; website www.ecb.co.uk).

MARYLEBONE CRICKET CLUB: R. D. V. Knight, Lord's Ground, London NW8 8QN (44 20 7289 1611; fax 44 20 7289 9100. Tickets 44 20 7432 1066; fax 44 20 7432 1061).

AUSTRALIAN STATE CRICKET ASSOCIATION ADDRESSES

AUSTRALIAN CAPITAL TERRITORY: ACT Cricket, PO Box 3379, Manuka, Australian Capital Territory 2603 (02 6239 6002; fax 02 6295 7135).

NEW SOUTH WALES: Cricket NSW, PO Box 333, Paddington, New South Wales 2021 (02 9339 0999; fax 02 9360 6877). *Chief Executive:* D. R. Gilbert. *Chairman:* R. E. Horsell.

QUEENSLAND: Queensland Cricket, PO Box 575, Albion, Queensland 4010 (07 3292 3100; fax 07 3262 9160). *Chief Executive:* G. J. Dixon. *Chairman:* D. Mullins SC. *Coach:* T. G. Oliver.

SOUTH AUSTRALIA: South Australian Cricket Association, Adelaide Oval, North Adelaide, South Australia 5006 (08 8300 3800; fax 08 8231 4346). *Chief Executive:* M. J. Deare. *President:* I. M. McLachlan AO. *State Manager of Cricket:* W. Phillips.

TASMANIA: Tasmanian Cricket Association, PO Box 495, Rosny Park, Tasmania 7018 (03 6211 4000; fax 03 6244 3924). *Chief Executive:* D. A. Johnston. *Chairman:* B. Palfreyman.

VICTORIA: Cricket Victoria, VCA House, 86 Jolimont Street, Jolimont, Victoria 3002 (03 9653 1100; fax 03 9653 1196). *Chief Executive Officer:* K. W. Jacobs. *Chairman:* R. F. Merriman.

WESTERN AUSTRALIA: Western Australian Cricket Association, PO Box 6045, East Perth, Western Australia 6892 (08 9265 7222; fax 08 9221 1823). *Chief Executive Officer:* K. White. *President:* P. B. Rakich.

Other Bodies

ASSOCIATION OF CRICKET UMPIRES AND SCORERS: G. J. Bullock, PO Box 399, Camberley, Surrey, GU16 5ZJ, UK (44 1276 27962; fax 44 1276 62277; website www.acus.cricket.org; email admin@acus.org.uk).

AUSTRALIAN CRICKETERS' ASSOCIATION: T. B. A. May, Level 4, 424 St Kilda Road, Melbourne, Victoria 3004 (03 9828 0700).

AUSTRALIAN SCHOOLS' CRICKET COUNCIL INC: A. A. K.Gifford, 29 George Street, Avalon, New South Wales 2107 (02 9918 3103; fax 02 9918 7211).

BRADMAN MUSEUM: R. Mulvaney, PO Box 9994, Bowral, NSW 2576 (02 4862 1247; fax 02 4861 2536).

CRUSADERS, THE: Swan Richards, 69 Victoria Parade, Collingwood, Victoria, 3066 (03 9415 6924; fax 03 9417 6911; website www.crusaderscricket.com.au; email newberry@bigpond.net.au).

CRICKET ASSOCIATIONS AND SOCIETIES

AUSTRALIAN CRICKET SOCIETY INC., Mr Ken Penaluna (secretary), Suite 15, 47 Bourke Street, Melbourne, Victoria 3000 (03 9639 6530). There are branches of the Society in each state.

The Laws of Cricket

As updated in 2003. World copyright of MCC and reprinted by permission of MCC. Copies of the "Laws of Cricket" may be obtained from Lord's Cricket Ground or from the MCC website at www.lords.org

INDEX TO THE LAWS

THE PREAMBLE – THE SPIRIT OF CRICKET

Cricket is a game that owes much of its unique appeal to the fact that it should be played not only within its Laws but also within the Spirit of the game. Any action which is seen to abuse this spirit causes injury to the game itself. The major responsibility for ensuring the spirit of fair play rests with the captains.

1. There are two Laws which place the responsibility for the team's conduct firmly on the captain.

   Responsibility of captains
   The captains are responsible at all times for ensuring that play is conducted within the Spirit of the game as well as within the Laws.

   Player's conduct
   In the event of a player failing to comply with instructions by an umpire, or criticising by word or action the decisions of an umpire, or showing dissent, or generally behaving in a manner which might bring the game into disrepute, the umpire concerned shall in the first place report the matter to the other umpire and to the player's captain, and instruct the latter to take action.

2. Fair and unfair play
   According to the Laws the umpires are the sole judges of fair and unfair play.
   The umpires may intervene at any time and it is the responsibility of the captain to take action where required.

3. The umpires are authorised to intervene in cases of:
   • time wasting
   • damaging the pitch
   • dangerous or unfair bowling
   • tampering with the ball
   • any other action that they consider to be unfair

4. The spirit of the game involves respect for:
   • your opponents
   • your own captain and team
   • the role of the umpires
   • the game's traditional values

5. It is against the spirit of the game:
   • to dispute an umpire's decision by word, action or gesture
   • to direct abusive language towards an opponent or umpire
   • to indulge in cheating or any sharp practice, for instance:
     a) to appeal knowing that the batsman is not out
     b) to advance towards an umpire in an aggressive manner when appealing
     c) to seek to distract an opponent either verbally or by harassment with persistent clapping or unnecessary noise under the guise of enthusiasm and motivation of one's own side

6. Violence
   There is no place for any act of violence on the field of play.

7. Players
   Captains and umpires together set the tone for the conduct of a cricket match. Every player is expected to make an important contribution to this.

The players, umpires and scorers in a game of cricket may be of either gender and the Laws apply equally to both. The use, throughout the text, of pronouns indicating the male gender is purely for brevity. Except where specifically stated otherwise, every provision of the Laws is to be read as applying to women and girls equally as to men and boys.

LAW 1.   THE PLAYERS

1. Number of Players

A match is played between two sides, each of 11 players, one of whom shall be captain. By agreement a match may be played between sides of more or less than 11 players, but not more than 11 players may field at any time.

2. Nomination of Players

Each captain shall nominate his players in writing to one of the umpires before the toss. No player may be changed after the nomination without the consent of the opposing captain.

3. Captain

If at any time the captain is not available, a deputy shall act for him.

(a) If a captain is not available during the period in which the toss is to take place, then the deputy must be responsible for the nomination of the players, if this has not already been done, and for the toss. See 2 above and Law 12.4 (The Toss).

(b) At any time after the toss, the deputy must be one of the nominated players.

4. Responsibilities of Captains

The captains are responsible at all times for ensuring that play is conducted within the spirit and traditions of the game as well as within the Laws. See The Preamble – The Spirit of Cricket and Law 42.1 (Fair and Unfair Play – Responsibility of Captains).

LAW 2. SUBSTITUTES AND RUNNERS; BATSMAN OR FIELDER LEAVING THE FIELD; BATSMAN RETIRING; BATSMAN COMMENCING INNINGS

1. Substitutes and Runners

(a) If the umpires are satisfied that a player has been injured or become ill after the nomination of the players, they shall allow that player to have:

(i) a substitute acting instead of him in the field

(ii) a runner when batting.

Any injury or illness that occurs at any time after the nomination of the players until the conclusion of the match shall be allowable, irrespective of whether play is in progress or not.

(b) The umpires shall have discretion, for other wholly acceptable reasons, to allow a substitute for a fielder, or a runner for a batsman, at the start of the match or at any subsequent time.

(c) A player wishing to change his shirt, boots, etc. must leave the field to do so. No substitute shall be allowed for him.

2. Objection to Substitutes

The opposing captain shall have no right of objection to any player acting as substitute on the field, nor as to where the substitute shall field. However no substitute shall act as wicket-keeper. See 3 following.

3. Restrictions on the Role of Substitutes

A substitute shall not be allowed to bat or bowl nor to act as wicket-keeper or as captain on the field of play.

4. A Player for whom a Substitute has Acted

A player is allowed to bat, bowl or field even though a substitute has previously acted for him.

5. Fielder Absent or Leaving the Field

If a fielder fails to take the field with his side at the start of the match or at any later time, or leaves the field during a session of play:

(a) The umpire shall be informed of the reason for his absence.

(b) He shall not thereafter come on to the field during a session of play without the consent of the umpire. See 6 following. The umpire shall give such consent as soon as is practicable.

(c) If he is absent for 15 minutes or longer, he shall not be permitted to bowl thereafter, subject to (i), (ii) or (iii) below, until he has been on the field for at least that length of playing time for which he was absent.

    (i) Absence or penalty for time absent shall not be carried over into a new day's play.

    (ii) If, in the case of a follow-on or forfeiture, a side fields for two consecutive innings, this restriction shall, subject to (i) above, continue as necessary into the second innings but shall not otherwise be carried over into a new innings.

    (iii) The time lost for an unscheduled break in play shall be counted as time on the field for any fielder who comes onto the field at the resumption of play. See Law 15.1 (An Interval).

6. Player Returning Without Permission

If a player comes onto the field of play in contravention of 5(b) above and comes into contact with the ball while it is in play:

    (i) the ball shall immediately become dead and the umpire shall award five penalty runs to the batting side. See Law 42.17 (Penalty Runs). The ball shall not count as one of the over.

    (ii) the umpire shall inform the other umpire, the captain of the fielding side, the batsmen and, as soon as practicable, the captain of the batting side of the reason for this action.

    (iii) the umpires together shall report the occurrence as soon as possible to the Executive of the fielding side and any Governing Body responsible for the match, who shall take such action as is considered appropriate against the captain and player concerned.

7. Runner

The player acting as a runner for a batsman shall be a member of the batting side and shall, if possible, have already batted in that innings. The runner shall wear external protective equipment equivalent to that worn by the batsman for whom he runs and shall carry a bat.

8. Transgression of the Laws by a Batsman Who has a Runner

    (a) A batsman's runner is subject to the Laws. He will be regarded as a batsman except where there are specific provisions for his role as a runner. See 7 above and Law 29.2 (Which is a Batsman's Ground).

    (b) A batsman with a runner will suffer a penalty for any infringement of the Laws by his runner as though he himself had been responsible for the infringement. In particular he will be out if his runner is out under any of Laws 33 (Handled the Ball), 37 (Obstructing the Field) or 38 (Run Out).

    (c) When a batsman with a runner is striker he remains himself subject to the Laws and will be liable to the penalties that any infringement of them demands. Additionally if he is out of his ground when the wicket is put down at the wicket-keeper's end he will be out in the circumstancs of Law 38 (Run Out) or Law 39 (Stumped) irrespective of the position of the non-striker or the runner. If he is thus dismissed, runs completed by the runner and the other batsman before the dismissal shall not be scored. However, the penalty for a No Ball or a Wide shall stand, together with any penalties to either side that may be awarded when the ball is dead. See Law 42.17 (Penalty Runs).

    (d) When a batsman with a runner is not the striker:

        (i) he remains subject to Laws 33 (Handled the Ball) and 37 (Obstructing the Field) but is otherwise out of the game.

        (ii) he shall stand where directed by the striker's end umpire so as not to interfere with play.

        (iii) he will be liable, notwithstanding (i) above, to the penalty demanded by the Laws should he commit any act of unfair play.

9. Batsman Leaving the Field or Retiring

A batsman may retire at any time during his innings. The umpires, before allowing play to proceed, shall be informed of the reason for a batsman retiring.

    (a) If a batsman retires because of illness, injury or any other unavoidable cause, he is entitled to resume his innings subject to (c) below. If for any reason he does not do so, his innings is to be recorded as "Retired – not out".

(b) If a batsman retires for any reason other than as in (a) above, he may only resume his innings with the consent of the opposing captain. If for any reason he does not resume his innings it is to be recorded as "Retired – out".

(c) If after retiring a batsman resumes his innings, it shall only be at the fall of a wicket or the retirementr of another batsman.

10. Commencement of a Batsman's Innings

Except at the start of a side's innings, a batsman shall be considered to have commenced his innings when he first steps onto the field of play, provided "Time" has not been called. The innings of the opening batsmen, and that of any new batsman at the resumption of play after a call of "Time", shall commence at the call of "Play".

LAW 3.   THE UMPIRES

1. Appointment and Attendance

Before the match, two umpires shall be appointed, one for each end, to control the game as required by the Laws, with absolute impartiality. The umpires shall be present on the ground and report to the Executive of the ground at least 45 minutes before the scheduled start of each day's play.

2. Change of Umpires

An umpire shall not be changed during the match, other than in exceptional circumstances, unless he is injured or ill. If there has to be a change of umpire, the replacement shall act only as the striker's end umpire unless the captains agree that he should take full responsibility as an umpire.

3. Agreement with Captains

Before the toss the umpires shall:

(a) ascertain the hours of play and agree with the captains:

    (i) the balls to be used during the match. See Law 5 (The Ball).

    (ii) times and durations of intervals for meals and times for drinks intervals. See Law 15 (Intervals).

    (iii) the boundary of the field of play and allowances for boundaries. See Law 19 (Boundaries).

    (iv) any special conditions of play affecting the conduct of the match.

(b) inform the scorers of the agreements in (ii), (iii) and (iv) above.

4. To Inform Captains and Scorers

Before the toss the umpires shall agree between themselves and inform both captains and both scorers:

(i) which clock or watch and back-up time piece is to be used during the match.

(ii) whether or not any obstacle within the field of play is to be regarded as a boundary. See Law 19 (Boundaries).

5. The Wickets, Creases and Boundaries

Before the toss and during the match, the umpires shall satisfy themselves that:

(i) the wickets are properly pitched. See Law 8 (The Wickets).

(ii) the creases are correctly marked. See Law 9 (The Bowling, Popping and Return Creases).

(iii) the boundary of the field of play complies with the requirements of Law 19.2 (Defining the Boundary – Boundary Marking).

6. Conduct of the Game, Implements and Equipment

Before the toss and during the match, the umpires shall satisfy themselves that:

(a) the conduct of the game is strictly in accordance with the Laws.

(b) the implements of the game conform to the requirements of Laws 5 (The Ball) and 6 (The Bat), together with either Laws 8.2 (Size of Stumps) and 8.3 (The Bails) or, if appropriate, Law 8.4 (Junior Cricket).

(c)   (i)   no player uses equipment other than that permitted. See Appendix D.

(ii)   the wicket-keeper's gloves comply with the requirements of Law 40.2 (Gloves).

7. Fair and Unfair Play

The umpires shall be the sole judges of fair and unfair play.

8. Fitness of Ground, Weather and Light

The umpires shall be the final judges of the fitness of the ground, weather and light for play. See 9 below and Law 7.2 (Fitness of the Pitch for Play).

9. Suspension of Play for Adverse Conditions of Ground, Weather of Light

(a)   (i)   All references to ground include the pitch. See Law 7.1 (Area of Pitch).

(ii)   For the purpose of this Law and Law 15.9 (b)(ii) (Intervals for Drinks) only the batsmen at the wicket may deputise for their captain at any appropriate time.

(b) If at any time the umpires together agree that the condition of the ground, weather or light is not suitable for play, they shall inform the captains and, unless:

(i)   in unsuitable ground or weather conditions both captains agree to continue, or to commence, or to restart play, or

(ii)   in unsuitable light the batting side wish to continue, or to commence, or to restart play, they shall suspend play, or not allow play to commence or to restart.

(c)   (i)   After agreeing to play in unsuitable ground or weather conditions, either captain may appeal against the conditions to the umpires before the next call of Time. The umpires shall uphold the appeal only if, in their opinion, the factors taken into account when making their previous decision are the same or the conditions have further deteriorated.

(ii)   After deciding to play in unsuitable light, the captain of the batting side may appeal against the light to the umpires before the next call of Time. The umpires shall uphold the appeal only if, in their opinion, the factors taken into account when making their previous decision are the same or the condition of the light has further deteriorated.

(d) If at any time the umpires together agree that the conditions of ground, weather or light are so bad that there is obvious and foreseeable risk to the safety of any player or umpire, so that it would be unreasonable or dangerous for play to take place, then notwithstanding the provisions of (b)(i) and (b)(ii) above, they shall immediately suspend play, or not allow play to commence or to restart. The decision as to whether conditions are so bad as to warrant such action is one for the umpires alone to make. The fact that the grass and the ball are wet and slippery does not warrant the ground conditions being regarded as unreasonable or dangerous. If the umpires consider the ground is so wet or slippery as to deprive the bowler of a reasonable foothold, the fielders of the power of free movement, or the batsmen of the ability to play their strokes or to run between the wickets, then these conditions shall be regarded as so bad that it would be unreasonable for play to take place.

(e) When there is a suspension of play it is the responsibility of the umpires to monitor the conditions. They shall make inspections as often as appropriate, unaccompanied by any of the players or officials. Immediately the umpires together agree that conditions are suitable for play they shall call upon the players to resume the game.

(f) If play is in progress up to the start of an agreed interval then it will resume after the interval unless the umpires together agree that conditions are or have become unsuitable or dangerous. If they do so agree, then they shall implement the procedure in (b) or (d) above, as appropriate, whether or not there had been any decision by the captains to continue, or any appeal against the conditions by either captain, prior to the commencement of the interval.

10. Exceptional Circumstances

The umpires shall have the discretion to implement the procedures of 9 above for reasons other than ground, weather or light if they consider that exceptional circumstances warrant it.

11. Position of Umpires

The umpires shall stand where they can best see any act upon which their decision may be required.

Subject to this over-riding consideration the umpire at the bowler's end shall stand where he does not interfere with either the bowler's run up or the striker's view.

The umpire at the striker's end may elect to stand on the off side instead of the on side of the pitch, provided he informs the captain of the fielding side, the striker and the other umpire of his intention to do so.

12. Umpires Changing Ends

The umpires shall change ends after each side has had one completed innings. See Law 14.2 (Forfeiture of an Innings).

13. Consultation between Umpires

All disputes shall be determined by the umpires. The umpires shall consult with each other whenever necessary. See also Law 27.6 (Consultation by Umpires).

14. Signals

(a) The following code of signals shall be used by umpires.

(i) Signals made while the ball is in play:

Dead Ball	– by crossing and re-crossing the wrists below the waist.
No-ball	– by extending one arm horizontally.
Out	– by raising the index finger above the head. If not out, the umpire shall call "Not out".
Wide	– by extending both arms horizontally.

(ii) When the ball is dead, the signals above, with the exception of the signal for Out, shall be repeated to the scorers. The signals listed below shall be made to the scorers only when the ball is dead.

Boundary 4	– by waving an arm from side to side finishing with the arm across the chest.
Boundary 6	– by raising both arms above the head.
Bye	– by raising an open hand above the head.
Commencement of Last Hour	– by pointing to a raised wrist with the other hand.
Five Penalty Runs to be Awarded to the batting side	– by repeated tapping of one shoulder with the opposite hand.
Five Penalty Runs to be Awarded to the fielding side	– by placing one hand on the opposite shoulder.
Leg-bye	– by touching a raised knee with the hand.
New Ball	– by holding the ball above the head.
Revoke last signal	– by touching both shoulders, each with the opposite hand.
Short Run	– by bending one arm upwards and touching the nearer shoulder with the tips of the fingers.

(b) The umpires shall wait until each signal to the scorers has been separately acknowledged by a scorer before allowing play to proceed.

14. Correctness of Scores

Consultation between umpires and scorers on doubtful points is essential. The umpires shall satisfy themselves as to the correctness of the number of runs scored, the wickets that have fallen and, where appropriate, the number of overs bowled. They shall agree these with the scorers at least at every interval, other than a drinks interval, and at the conclusion of the match. See Laws 4.2 (Correctness of Scores), 21.8 (Correctness of Result) and 21.10 (Result not to be Changed).

LAW 4.   THE SCORERS

1. Appointment of Scorers

Two scorers shall be appointed to record all runs scored, all wickets taken and, where appropriate, number of overs bowled.

2. Correctness of Scores

The scorers shall frequently check to ensure that their records agree. They shall agree with the umpires, at least at every interval, other than a drinks interval, and at the conclusion of the match, the runs scored, the wickets that have fallen and, where appropriate, the number of overs bowled. See Law 3.15 (Correctness of Scores).

3. Acknowledging Signals

The scorers shall accept all instructions and signals given to them by the umpires. They shall immediately acknowledge each separate signal.

LAW 5.   THE BALL

1. Weight and Size

The ball, when new, shall weigh not less than 5½ oz/155.9g, nor more than 5¾ oz/163g; and shall measure not less than 8¹³⁄₁₆ in/22.4cm, nor more than 9 in/22.9cm in circumference.

2. Approval and Control of Balls

(a) All balls to be used in the match, having been approved by the umpires and captains, shall be in the possession of the umpires before the toss and shall remain under their control throughout the match.

(b) The umpire shall take possession of the ball in use at the fall of each wicket, at the start of any interval and at any interruption of play.

3. New Ball

Unless an agreement to the contrary has been made before the match, either captain may demand a new ball at the start of each innings.

4. New Ball in Match of More than One Day's Duration

In a match of more than one day's duration, the captain of the fielding side may demand a new ball after the prescribed number of overs has been bowled with the old one. The Governing Body for cricket in the country concerned shall decide the number of overs applicable in that country, which shall not be less than 75 overs.

The umpires shall indicate to the batsmen and the scorers whenever a new ball is taken into play.

5. Ball Lost or Becoming Unfit for Play

If, during play, the ball cannot be found or recovered or the umpires agree that it has become unfit for play through normal use, the umpires shall replace it with a ball which has had wear comparable with that which the previous ball had received before the need for its replacement. When the ball is replaced the umpires shall inform the batsmen and the fielding captain.

6. Specifications

The specifications, as described in 1 above, shall apply to men's cricket only. The following specifications will apply to

(i)   *Women's cricket*

Weight: from 4¹⁵⁄₁₆ oz/140g to 5⁵⁄₁₆ oz/151g.

Circumference: from 8¼ in/21.0cm to 8⁷⁄₈ in/22.5cm.

(iii) *Junior cricket*

Weight: from 4^1_{16} oz/133g to 5^1_{16} oz/144g.

Circumference: 8^1_{16} in/20.5cm to 8^{11}_{16} in/22.0cm.

LAW 6.   THE BAT

1. Width and Length

The bat overall shall not be more than 38 in/96.5cm in length. The blade of the bat shall be made solely of wood and shall not exceed 4 ¼ in/10.8cm at the widest part.

2. Covering the Blade

The blade of the bat may be covered with material for protection, strengthening or repair. Such material shall not exceed ¹⁄₁₆ in/1.56mm in thickness, and shall not be likely to cause unacceptable damage to the ball.

3. Hand or Glove to Count as Part of Bat

In these Laws,

(a) reference to the bat shall imply that the bat is held by the batsman.

(b) contact between the ball and either

(i)   the striker's bat itself, or

(ii) the striker's hand holding the bat, or

(iii) any part of a glove worn on the striker's hand holding the bat

shall be regarded as the ball striking or touching the bat, or being struck by the bat.

LAW 7.   THE PITCH

1. Area of Pitch

The pitch is a rectangular area of the ground 22 yds/20.12m in length and 10ft/3.05m in width. It is bounded at either end by the bowling creases and on either side by imaginary lines, one each side of the imaginary line joining the centres of the two middle stumps, each parallel to it and 5ft/1.52m from it. See Laws 8.1 (Width and Pitching) and 9.2 (The Bowling Crease).

2. Fitness of the Pitch for Play

The umpires shall be the final judges of the fitness of the pitch for play. See Laws 3.8 (Fitness of Ground, Weather and Light) and 3.9 (Suspension of Play for Adverse Conditions of Ground, Weather or Light).

3. Selection and Preparation

Before the match, the Ground Authority shall be responsible for the selection and preparation of the pitch. During the match, the umpires shall control its use and maintenance.

4. Changing the Pitch

The pitch shall not be changed during the match unless the umpires decide that it is unreasonable or dangerous for play to continue on it and then only with the consent of both captains.

5. Non-turf Pitches

In the event of a non-turf pitch being used, the artificial surface shall conform to the following measurements:

Length: a minimum of 58 ft/17.68m.

Width: a minimum of 6 ft/1.83m.

See Law 10.8 (Non-turf Pitches).

LAW 8.   THE WICKETS

1. Width and Pitching

Two sets of wickets shall be pitched opposite and parallel to each other at a distance of 22 yds/20.12m between the centres of the two middle stumps. Each set shall be 9 in/ 22.86cm wide and shall consist of three wooden stumps with two wooden bails on top.

2. Size of Stumps

The tops of the stumps shall be 28 in/71.1cm above the playing surface and shall be dome shaped except for the bail grooves. The portion of a stump above the playing surface shall be cylindrical, apart from the domed top, with circular section of diameter not less than 1⅜ in/3.49cm nor more than 1½ in/3.81cm.

3. The Bails

(a) The bails, when in position on top of the stumps,

  (i)   shall not project more than ½ in/1.27cm above them.

  (ii) shall fit between the stumps without forcing them out of the vertical.

(b) Each bail shall conform to the following specifications

Overall length:	4⅛ in/10.95cm
Length of barrel:	2⅛ in/5.40cm
Longer spigot:	1⅜ in/3.49cm
Shorter spigot:	1³⁄₁₆ in/2.06cm

4. Junior Cricket

In junior cricket, the same definitions of the wickets shall apply subject to the following measurements being used.

Width:	8 in/20.32cm
Pitched for Under-13:	21 yds/19.20m
Pitched for Under-11:	20 yds/18.29m
Height above playing surface:	27 in/68.58cm
Each stump	
Diameter:	not less than 1¼ in/3.18cm
	nor more than 1⅜ in/3.49cm
Each bail	
Overall length:	3¹³⁄₁₆ in/9.68cm
Length of barrel:	1¹³⁄₁₆ in/4.60cm
Longer spigot:	1¼ in/3.18cm
Shorter spigot:	¾ in/1.91cm

5. Dispensing with bails

The umpires may agree to dispense with the use of bails, if necessary. If they so agree then no bails shall be used at either end. The use of bails shall be resumed as soon as conditions permit.

See Law 28.4 (Dispensing with Bails).

LAW 9.   THE BOWLING, POPPING AND RETURN CREASES

1. The Creases

A bowling crease, a popping crease and two return creases shall be marked in white, as set out in 2, 3 and 4 below, at each end of the pitch.

2. The Bowling Crease

The bowling crease, which is the back edge of the crease marking, shall be the line through the centres of the three stumps at that end. It shall be 8ft 8 in/2.64m in length, with the stumps in the centre.

3. The Popping Crease

The popping crease, which is the back edge of the crease marking, shall be in front of and parallel to the bowling crease and shall be 4ft/1.22m from it. The popping crease shall be marked to a minimum of 6ft/1.83m on either side of the imaginary line joining the centres of the middle stumps and shall be considered to be unlimited in length.

4. The Return Creases

The return creases, which are the inside edges of the crease markings, shall be at right angles to the popping crease at a distance of 4ft 4 in/1.32m either side of the imaginary line joining the centres of the two middle stumps. Each return crease shall be marked from the popping crease to a minimum of 8ft/2.44m behind it and shall be considered to be unlimited in length.

LAW 10. PREPARATION AND MAINTENANCE OF THE PLAYING AREA

1. Rolling

The pitch shall not be rolled during the match except as permitted in (a) and (b) below.

(a) Frequency and Duration of Rolling
During the match the pitch may be rolled at the request of the captain of the batting side, for a period of not more than seven minutes, before the start of each innings, other than the first innings of the match, and before the start of each subsequent day's play. See (d) below.

(b) Rolling After a Delayed Start
In addition to the rolling permitted above, if, after the toss and before the first innings of the match, the start is delayed, the captain of the batting side may request to have the pitch rolled for not more than seven minutes. However, if the umpires together agree that the delay has had no significant effect on the state of the pitch, they shall refuse the request for the rolling of the pitch.

(c) Choice of Rollers
If there is more than one roller available the captain of the batting side shall have the choice.

(d) Timing of Permitted Rolling
The rolling permitted (maximum seven minutes) before play begins on any day shall be started not more than 30 minutes before the time scheduled or rescheduled for play to begin. The captain of the batting side may, however, delay the start of such rolling until not less than ten minutes before the time scheduled or rescheduled for play to begin, should he so desire.

(e) Insufficient Time to Complete Rolling
If a captain declares an innings closed, or forfeits an innings, or enforces the follow-on, and the other captain is prevented thereby from exercising his option of the rolling permitted (maximum seven minutes), or if he is so prevented for any other reason, the extra time required to complete the rolling shall be taken out of the normal playing time.

2. Sweeping

(a) If rolling is to take place the pitch shall first be swept to avoid any possible damage by rolling in debris. This sweeping shall be done so that the 7 minutes allowed for rolling is not affected.

(b) The pitch shall be cleared of any debris at all intervals for meals, between innings and at the beginning of each day, not earlier than 30 minutes nor later than 10 minutes before the time scheduled or rescheduled for play to begin. See Law 15.1 (An Interval).

(c) Notwithstanding the provisions of (a) and (b) above, the umpires shall not allow sweeping to take place where they consider it may be detrimental to the surface of the pitch.

3. Mowing

(a) The Pitch
The pitch shall be mown on each day of the match on which play is expected to take place, if ground and weather conditions allow.

(b) The Outfield

In order to ensure that conditions are as similar as possible for both sides, the outfield shall be mown on each day of the match on which play is expected to take place, if ground and weather conditions allow.

If, for reasons other than ground and weather conditions, complete mowing of the outfield is not possible, the ground authority shall notify the captains and umpires of the procedure to be adopted for such mowing during the match.

(c) Responsibility for Mowing

All mowings which are carried out before the match shall be the responsibility of the ground authority.

All subsequent mowings shall be carried out under the supervision of the umpires.

(d) Timing of Mowing

(i) Mowing of the pitch on any day of the match shall be completed not later than 30 minutes before the time scheduled or rescheduled for play to begin on that day.

(ii) Mowing of the outfield on any day of the match shall be completed not later than 15 minutes before the time scheduled or rescheduled for play to begin on that day.

4. Watering

The pitch shall not be watered during the match.

5. Re-marking Creases

The creases shall be re-marked whenever either umpire considers it necessary.

6. Maintenance of Footholes

The umpires shall ensure that the holes made by the bowlers and batsmen are cleaned out and dried whenever necessary to facilitate play. In matches of more than one day's duration, the umpires shall allow, if necessary, the re-turfing of footholes made by the bowler in his delivery stride, or the use of quick-setting fillings for the same purpose.

7. Securing of Footholds and Maintenance of Pitch

During play, the umpires shall allow the players to secure their footholds by the use of sawdust provided that no damage to the pitch is caused and that Law 42 (Fair and Unfair Play) is not contravened.

8. Non-turf Pitches

Wherever appropriate, the provisions set out in 1 to 7 above shall apply.

LAW 11. COVERING THE PITCH

1. Before the Match

The use of covers before the match is the responsibility of the Ground Authority and may include full covering if required. However, the Ground Authority shall grant suitable facility to the captains to inspect the pitch before the nomination of their players and to the umpires to discharge their duties as laid down in Laws 3 (The Umpires), 7 (The Pitch), 8 (The Wickets), 9 (The Bowling, Popping and Return Creases) and 10 (Preparation and Maintenance of the Playing Area).

2. During the Match

The pitch shall not be completely covered during the match unless provided otherwise by regulations or by agreement before the toss.

3. Covering Bowlers' Run-ups

Whenever possible, the bowlers' run ups shall be covered in inclement weather, in order to keep them dry. Unless there is agreement for full covering under 2 above the covers so used shall not extend further than 5ft/1.52m in front of each popping crease.

4. Removal of Covers

(a) If after the toss the pitch is covered overnight, the covers shall be removed in the morning at the earliest possible moment on each day that play is expected to take place.

(b) If covers are used during the day as protection from inclement weather, or if inclement weather delays the removal of overnight covers, they shall be removed promptly as soon as conditions allow.

LAW 12.   INNINGS

1. Number of Innings

(a) A match shall be one or two innings of each side according to agreement reached before the match.

(b) It may be agreed to limit any innings to a number of overs or by a period of time. If such an agreement is made then:

   (i) in a one-innings match it shall apply to both innings.

   (ii) in a two-innings match it shall apply to either   the first innings of each side or the second innings of each side or both innings of each side.

2. Alternate Innings

In a two-innings match each side shall take their innings alternately except in the case provided for in Law 13 (The Follow-on) or Law 14.2 (Forfeiture of an Innings).

3. Completed Innings

A side's innings is to be considered as completed if:

   (a) the side is all out, or

   (b) at the fall of a wicket, further balls remain to be bowled, but no further batsman is available to come in, or

   (c) the captain declares the innings closed, or

   (d) the captain forfeits the innings, or

   (e) in the case of an agreement under 1(b) above, either

      (i) the prescribed number of overs has been bowled or

      (ii) the prescribed time has expired.

4. The Toss

The captains shall toss for the choice of innings on the field of play not earlier than 30 minutes, nor later than 15 minutes, before the scheduled or any rescheduled time for the match to start. Note, however, the provisions of Law 1.3 (Captain).

5. Decision to be Notified

The captain of the side winning the toss shall notify the opposing captain of his decision to bat or to field, not later than 10 minutes before the scheduled or any rescheduled time for the match to start. Once notified the decision may not be altered.

LAW 13.   THE FOLLOW-ON

1. Lead on First Innings

(a) In a two innings match of 5 days or more, the side which bats first and leads by at least 200 runs shall have the option of requiring the other side to follow their innings.

(b) The same option shall be available in two innings matches of shorter duration with the minimum required leads as follows:

   (i) 150 runs in a match of three or four days;

(ii) 100 runs in a two-day match;

(iii) 75 runs in a one-day match.

2. Notification

A captain shall notify the opposing captain and the umpires of his intention to take up this option. Law 10.1(e) (Insufficient Time to Complete Rolling) shall apply.

3. First Day's Play Lost

If no play takes place on the first day of a match of more than one day's duration, 1 above shall apply in accordance with the number of days remaining from the actual start of the match. The day on which play first commences shall count as a whole day for this purpose, irrespective of the time at which play starts.

Play will have taken place as soon as, after the call of "Play", the first over has started. See Law 22.2 (Start of an Over).

LAW 14.   DECLARATION AND FORFEITURE

1. Time of Declaration

The captain of the batting side may declare an innings closed, when the ball is dead, at any time during a match.

2. Forfeiture of an Innings

A captain may forfeit either of his side's innings. A forfeited innings shall be considered as a completed innings.

3. Notification

A captain shall notify the opposing captain and the umpires of his decision to declare or to forfeit an innings. Law 10.1(e) (Insufficient Time to Complete Rolling) shall apply.

LAW 15.   INTERVALS

1. An Interval

The following shall be classed as intervals.

(i) The period between close of play on one day and the start of the next day's play.

(ii) Intervals between innings.

(iii) Intervals for meals.

(iv) Intervals for drinks.

(v) Any other agreed interval.

All these intervals shall be considered as scheduled breaks for the purposes of Law 2.5 (Fielder Absent or Leaving the Field).

2. Agreement of Intervals

(a) Before the Toss:

(i)   the hours of play shall be established.

(ii)   except as in (b) below, the timing and duration of intervals for meals shall be agreed.

(iii)   the timing and duration of any other interval under 1(v) above shall be agreed.

(b) In a one-day match no specific time need be agreed for the tea interval. It may be agreed instead to take this interval between the innings.

(c) Intervals for drinks may not be taken during the last hour of the match, as defined in Law 16.6 (Last hour of match – number of overs). Subject to this limitation the captains and umpires shall agree the times for such intervals, if any, before the toss and on each subsequent day not later than 10 minutes before play is scheduled to start. See also Law 3.3 (Agreement with Captains).

3. Duration of Intervals

(a) An interval for lunch or for tea shall be of the duration agreed under 2(a) above, taken from the call of "Time" before the interval until the call of "Play" on resumption after the interval.

(b) An interval between innings shall be ten minutes from the close of an innings to the call of "Play" for the start of the next innings, except as in 4, 6 and 7 below.

4. No Allowance for Interval Between Innings

In addition to the provisions of 6 and 7 below:

(a) if an innings ends when ten minutes or less remain before the time agreed for close of play on any day, there will be no further play on that day. No change will be made to the time for the start of play on the following day on account of the ten minutes between innings.

(b) if a captain declares an innings closed during an interruption in play of more than ten minutes duration, no adjustment shall be made to the time for resumption of play on account of the ten minutes between innings, which shall be considered as included in the interruption. Law 10.1(e) (Insufficient Time to Complete Rolling) shall apply.

(c) if a captain declares an innings closed during any interval other than an interval for drinks, the interval shall be of the agreed duration and shall be considered to include the ten minutes between innings. Law 10.1(e) (Insufficient Time to Complete Rolling) shall apply.

5. Changing Agreed Time for Intervals

If for adverse conditions of ground, weather or light, or for any other reason, playing time is lost, the umpires and captains together may alter the time of the lunch interval or of the tea interval. See also 6, 7 and 9(c) below.

6. Changing Agreed Time for Lunch Interval

(a) If an innings ends when ten minutes or less remain before the agreed time for lunch, the interval shall be taken immediately. It shall be of the agreed length and shall be considered to include the ten minutes between innings.

(b) If, because of adverse conditions of ground, weather or light, or in exceptional circumstances, a stoppage occurs when ten minutes or less remain before the agreed time for lunch then, notwithstanding 5 above, the interval shall be taken immediately. It shall be of the agreed length. Play shall resume at the end of this interval or as soon after as conditions permit.

(c) If the players have occasion to leave the field for any reason when more than ten minutes remain before the agreed time for lunch then, unless the umpires and captains together agree to alter it, lunch will be taken at the agreed time.

7. Changing Agreed Time for Tea Interval

(a)　(i) If an innings ends when 30 minutes or less remain before the agreed time for tea, then the interval shall be taken immediately. It shall be of the agreed length and shall be considered to include the ten minutes between innings.

(ii) If, when 30 minutes remain before the agreed time for tea, an interval between innings is already in progress, play will resume at the end of the ten-minute interval.

(b)　(i) If, because of adverse conditions of ground, weather or light, or in exceptional circumstances, a stoppage occurs when 30 minutes or less remain before the agreed time for tea, then unless either there is an agreement to change the time for tea, as permitted in 5 above, or the captains agree to forgo the tea interval, as permitted in 10 below, the interval shall be taken immediately. The interval shall be of the agreed length. Play shall resume at the end of this interval or as soon after as conditions permit.

(ii) If a stoppage is already in progress when 30 minutes remain before the time agreed for tea, 5 above will apply.

8. Tea Interval – Nine Wickets Down

If either nine wickets are already down when two minutes remain to the agreed time for tea, or the ninth wicket falls within these two minutes or at any later time up to and including the final ball of the over in progress at the agreed time for tea, then not withstanding the provisions of Law 16.5 (b) (Completion of an over) tea will not be taken until the end of the over in progress 30 minutes after the originally agreed time for tea, unless the players have cause to leave the field of play or the innings is completed earlier.

9. Intervals for Drinks

(a) If on any day the captains agree that there shall be intervals for drinks, the option to take such intervals shall be available to either side. Each interval shall be kept as short as possible and in any case shall not exceed five minutes.

(b)   (i) Unless both captains agree to forgo any drinks interval, it shall be taken at the end of the over in progress when the agreed time is reached. If, however, a wicket falls within five minutes of the agreed time then drinks shall be taken immediately. No other variation in the timing of drinks intervals shall be permitted except as provided for in (c) below.

   (ii) For the purpose of (i) above and Law 3.9(a)(ii) (Suspension of Play for Adverse Conditions of Ground, Weather or Light) only, the batsmen at the wicket may deputise for their captain.

(c) If an innings ends or the players have to leave the field of play for any other reason within 30 minutes of the agreed time for a drinks interval, the umpires and captains together may rearrange the timing of drinks intervals in that session.

10. Agreement to Forgo Intervals

At any time during the match, the captains may agree to forgo the tea interval or any of the drinks intervals. The umpires shall be informed of the decision.

11. Scorers to be Informed

The umpires shall ensure that the scorers are informed of all agreements about hours of play and intervals, and of any changes made thereto as permitted under this Law.

LAW 16. START OF PLAY; CESSATION OF PLAY

1. Call of "Play"

The umpire at the bowler's end shall call "Play" at the start of the match and on the resumption of play after any interval or interruption.

2. Call of "Time"

The umpire at the bowler's end shall call "Time" on the cessation of play before any interval or interruption of play and at the conclusion of the match. See Law 27 (Appeals).

3. Removal of Bails

After the call of "Time", the bails shall be removed from both wickets.

4. Starting a New Over

Another over shall always be started at any time during the match, unless an interval is to be taken in the circumstances set out in 5 below, if the umpire, after walking at his normal pace, has arrived at his position behind the stumps at the bowler's end before the time agreed for the next interval, or for the close of play, has been reached.

5. Completion of an Over

Other than at the end of the match:

(a) if the agreed time for an interval is reached during an over, the over shall be completed before the interval is taken except as provided for in (b) below.

(b) when less than two minutes remain before the time agreed for the next interval, the interval will be taken immediately if either

    (i) a batsman is out or retires, or

    (ii) the players have occasion to leave the field

whether this occurs during an over or at the end of an over. Except at the end of an innings, if an over is thus interrupted it shall be completed on resumption of play.

6. Last Hour of Match – Number of Overs

When one hour of playing time of the match remains, according to the agreed hours of play, the over in progress shall be completed. The next over shall be the first of a minimum of 20 overs which must be bowled, provided that a result is not reached earlier and provided that there is no interval or interruption in play. The umpire at the bowler's end shall indicate the commencement of this 20 overs to the players and the scorers. The period of play thereafter shall be referred to as the last hour, whatever its actual duration.

7. Last Hour of Match – Interruptions of Play

If there is an interruption in play during the last hour of the match, the minimum number of overs to be bowled shall be reduced from 20 as follows.

(a) The time lost for an interruption is counted from the call of "Time" until the time for resumption of play as decided by the umpires.

(b) One over shall be deducted for every complete three minutes of time lost.

(c) In the case of more than one such interruption, the minutes lost shall not be aggregated; the calculation shall be made for each interruption separately.

(d) If, when one hour of playing time remains, an interruption is already in progress:

    (i) only the time lost after this moment shall be counted in the calculation.

    (ii) the over in progress at the start of the interruption shall be completed on resumption of play and shall not count as one of the minimum number of overs to be bowled.

(e) If, after the start of the last hour, an interruption occurs during an over, the over shall be completed on resumption of play. The two part-overs shall between them count as one over of the minimum number to be bowled.

8. Last Hour of Match – Intervals Between Innings

If an innings ends so that a new innings is to be started during the last hour of the match, the interval starts with the end of the innings and is to end ten minutes later.

(a) If this interval is already in progress at the start of the last hour, then to determine the number of overs to be bowled in the new innings, calculations are to be made as set out in 7 above.

(b) If the innings ends after the last hour has started, two calculations are to be made, as set out in (c) and (d) below. The greater of the numbers yielded by these two calculations is to be the minimum number of overs to be bowled in the new innings.

(c) Calculation based on overs remaining:

    (i) At the conclusion of the innings, the number of overs that remain to be bowled, of the minimum in the last hour, to be noted.

    (ii) If this is not a whole number it is to be rounded up to the next whole number.

    (iii) Three overs to be deducted from the result for the interval.

(d) Calculation based on time remaining:

    (i) At the conclusion of the innings, the time remaining until the agreed time for close of play to be noted.

(ii) Ten minutes to be deducted from this time, for the interval, to determine the playing time remaining.

(iii) A calculation to be made of one over for every complete three minutes of the playing time remaining, plus one more over for any further part of three minutes remaining.

9. Conclusion of Match

The match is concluded:

(a) as soon as a result, as defined in sections 1, 2, 3 or 4 of Law 21 (The Result), is reached.

(b) as soon as both

(i) the minimum number of overs for the last hour are completed, and

(ii) the agreed time for close of play is reached unless a result has been reached earlier.

(c) if, without the match being concluded either as in (a) or in (b) above, the players leave the field, either for adverse conditions of ground, weather or light, or in exceptional circumstances, and no further play is possible thereafter.

10. Completion of Last Over of Match

The over in progress at the close of play on the final day shall be completed unless either

(i) a result has been reached, or

(ii) the players have occasion to leave the field. In this case there shall be no resumption of play, except in the circumstances of Law 21.9 (Mistakes in Scoring), and the match shall be at an end.

11. Bowler Unable to Complete an Over During Last Hour of Match

If, for any reason, a bowler is unable to complete an over during the last hour, Law 22.8 (Bowler Incapacitated or Suspended During an Over) shall apply.

LAW 17. PRACTICE ON THE FIELD

1. Practice on the Field

(a) There shall be no bowling or batting practice on the pitch, or on the area parallel and immediately adjacent to the pitch, at any time on any day of the match.

(b) There shall be no bowling or batting practice on any other part of the square on any day of the match, except before the start of play or after the close of play on that day. Practice before the start of play:

(i) must not continue later than 30 minutes before the scheduled time or any rescheduled time for play to start on that day.

(ii) shall not be allowed if the umpires consider that, in the prevailing conditions of ground and weather, it will be detrimental to the surface of the square.

(c) There shall be no practice on the field of play between the call of "Play" and the call of "Time", if the umpire considers that it could result in a waste of time. See Law 42.9 (Time-Wasting by the Fielding Side).

(d) If a player contravenes (a) or (b) above he shall not be allowed to bowl until either at least one hour later than the contravention or until there has been at least 30 minutes of playing time since the contravention, whichever is sooner. If an over is in progress at the contravention he shall not be allowed to complete that over.

2. Trial Run-Up

No bowler shall have a trial run-up between the call of "Play" and the call of "Time" unless the umpire is satisfied that it will not cause any waste of time.

LAW 18. SCORING RUNS

1. A Run

The score shall be reckoned by runs. A run is scored:

(a) so often as the batsmen, at any time while the ball is in play, have crossed and made good their ground from end to end.

(b) when a boundary is scored. See Law 19 (Boundaries).

(c) when penalty runs are awarded. See 6 below.

(d) when "Lost ball" is called. See Law 20 (Lost Ball).

2. Runs Disallowed

Notwithstanding 1 above, or any other provisions elsewhere in the Laws, the scoring of runs or awarding of penalties will be subject to any disallowance of runs provided for within the Laws that may be applicable.

3. Short Runs

(a) A run is short if a batsman fails to make good his ground on turning for a further run.

(b) Although a short run shortens the succeeding one, the latter if completed shall not be regarded as short. A striker taking stance in front of his popping crease may run from that point also without penalty.

4. Unintentional Short Runs

Except in the circumstances of 5 below:

(a) if either batsman runs a short run, unless a boundary is scored the umpire concerned shall call and signal "Short run" as soon as the ball becomes dead and that run shall not be scored.

(b) if, after either or both batsmen run short, a boundary is scored, the umpire concerned shall disregard the short running and shall not call or signal "Short run".

(c) if both batsmen run short in one and the same run, this shall be regarded as only one short run.

(d) if more than one run is short then, subject to (b) and (c) above, all runs so called shall not be scored.

If there has been more than one short run the umpire shall inform the scorers as to the number of runs scored.

5. Deliberate Short Runs

(a) Notwithstanding 4 above, if either umpire considers that either or both batsmen deliberately run short at his end, the following procedure shall be adopted:

    (i) The umpire concerned shall, when the ball is dead, warn the batsmen that the practice is unfair, indicate that this is a first and final warning and inform the other umpire of what has occurred. This warning shall continue to apply throughout the innings. The umpire shall so inform each incoming batsman

    (ii) The batsmen shall return to their original ends.

    (iii) Whether a batsman is dismissed or not, the umpire at the bowler's end shall disallow all runs to the batting side from that delivery other than the penalty for a No ball or Wide, or penalties under Laws 42.5 (Deliberate Distraction or Obstruction of Batsman) and 42.13 (Fielders Damaging the Pitch), if applicable.

    (iv) The umpire at the bowler's end shall inform the scorers as to the number of runs scored.

(b) If there is any further instance of deliberate short running by any batsman in that innings, when the ball is dead the umpire concerned shall inform the other umpire of what has occurred and the procedure set out in (a)(ii) and (iii) above shall be repeated. Additionally, the umpire at the bowler's end shall:

    (i) award five penalty runs to the fielding side. See Law 42.17 (Penalty Runs).

    (ii) inform the scorers as to the number of runs scored.

    (iii) inform the batsmen, the captain of the fielding side and, as soon as practicable, the captain of the batting side of the reason for this action.

    (iv) report the occurrence, with the other umpire, to the Executive of the batting side and any governing body responsible for the match, who shall take such action as is considered appropriate against the captain and player or players concerned.

6. Runs Scored for Penalties

Runs shall be scored for penalties under 5 above and Laws 2.6 (Player Returning Without Permission), 24 (No-ball), 25 (Wide Ball), 41.2 (Fielding the Ball), 41.3 (Protective Helmets Belonging to the Fielding Side) and 42 (Fair and Unfair Play).

7. Runs Scored for Boundaries

Runs shall be scored for boundary allowances under Law 19 (Boundaries).

8. Runs Scored for Lost Ball

Runs shall be scored when "Lost ball" is called under Law 20 (Lost Ball).

9. Batsman Dismissed

When either batsman is dismissed:

(a) any penalties to either side that may be applicable shall stand but no other runs shall be scored, except as stated in 10 below.

(b) 12(a) below will apply if the method of dismissal is Caught, Handled the Ball or Obstructing the Field. 12(a) will also apply if a batsman is Run Out, except in the circumstances of Law 2.8 (Transgression of the Laws by a Batsman Who Has a Runner) where 12(b) below will apply.

(c) the not out batsman shall return to his original end except as stated in (b) above.

10. Runs Scored When a Batsman is Dismissed

In addition to any penalties to either side that may be applicable, if a batsman is

(a) dismissed Handled the Ball, the batting side shall score the runs completed before the offence.

(b) dismissed Obstructing the Field, the batting side shall score the runs completed before the offence.

If, however, the obstruction prevents a catch from being made, no runs other than penalties shall be scored.

(c) dismissed Run Out, the batting side shall score the runs completed before the dismissal.

If, however, a striker with a runner is himself dismissed Run Out, no runs other than penalties shall be scored. See Law 2.8 (Transgression of the Laws by a Batsman Who Has a Runner).

11. Runs Scored When a Ball Becomes Dead

(a) When the ball becomes dead on the fall of a wicket, runs shall be scored as laid down in 9 and 10 above.

(b) When the ball becomes dead for any reason other than the fall of a wicket, or is called dead by an umpire, unless there is specific provision otherwise in the Laws, the batting side shall be credited with:

    (i) all runs completed by the batsmen before the incident or call, and

    (ii) the run in progress if the batsmen have crossed at the instant of the incident or call. Note specifically, however, the provisions of Laws 34.4(c) (Runs Permitted From Ball Lawfully Struck More Than Once) and 42.5(b)(iii) (Deliberate Distraction or Obstruction of Batsman), and

    (iii) any penalties that are applicable.

12. Batsman Returning to Wicket he has Left

(a) If, while the ball is in play, the batsmen have crossed in running, neither shall return to the wicket he has left, except as in (b) below.

(b) The batsmen shall return to the wickets they originally left in the cases of, and only in the cases of:

    (i) a boundary.

    (ii) disallowance of runs for any reason.

    (iii) the dismissal of a batsman, except as in 9(b) above.

LAW 19.   BOUNDARIES

1. The Boundary of the Field of Play

(a) Before the toss, the umpires shall agree the boundary of the field of play with both captains. The boundary shall if possible be marked along its whole length.

(b) The boundary shall be agreed so that no part of any sight-screen is within the field of play.

(c) An obstacle or person within the field of play shall not be regarded as a boundary unless so decided by the umpires before the toss. See Law 3.4(ii) (To Inform Captains and Scorers).

2. Defining the Boundary – Boundary Marking

(a) Wherever practicable the boundary shall be marked by means of a white line or a rope laid along the ground.

(b) If the boundary is marked by a white line:

    (i) the inside edge of the line shall be the boundary edge.

    (ii) a flag, post or board used merely to highlight the position of a line marked on the ground must be placed outside the boundary edge and is not itself to be regarded as defining or marking the boundary. Note, however, the provisions of (c) below.

(c) If a solid object is used to mark the boundary, it must have an edge or a line to constitute the boundary edge.

    (i) For a rope, which includes any similar object of curved cross section lying on the ground, the boundary edge will be the line formed by the innermost points of the rope along its length.

    (ii) For a fence, which includes any similar object in contact with the ground, but with a flat surface projecting above the ground, the boundary edge will be the base line of the fence.

(d) If the boundary edge is not defined as in (b) or (c) above, the umpires and captains must agree, before the toss, what line will be the boundary edge. Where there is no physical marker for a section of boundary, the boundary edge shall be the imaginary straight line joining the two nearest marked points of the boundary edge.

(e) If a solid object used to mark the boundary is disturbed for any reason during play, then if possible it shall be restored to its original position as soon as the ball is dead. If this is not possible, then:

    (i) if some part of the fence or other marker has come within the field of play, that portion is to be removed from the field of play as soon as the ball is dead.

    (ii) the line where the base of the fence or marker originally stood shall define the boundary edge.

3. Scoring a Boundary

(a) A boundary shall be scored and signalled by the umpire at the bowler's end whenever, while the ball is in play, in his opinion:

    (i) the ball touches the boundary, or is grounded beyond the boundary.

  (ii) a fielder, with some part of his person in contact with the ball, touches the boundary or has some part of his person grounded beyond the boundary.

(b) The phrases "touches the boundary" and "touching the boundary" shall mean contact with either

  (i) the boundary edge as defined in 2 above, or

  (ii) any person or obstacle within the field of play which has been designated a boundary by the umpires before the toss.

(c) The phrase "grounded beyond the boundary" shall mean contact with either

  (i) any part of a line or a solid object marking the boundary, except its boundary edge, or

  (ii) the ground outside the boundary edge, or

  (iii) any object in contact with the ground outside the boundary edge.

4. Runs Allowed for Boundaries

(a) Before the toss, the umpires shall agree with both captains the runs to be allowed for boundaries. In deciding the allowances, the umpires and captains shall be guided by the prevailing custom of the ground.

(b) Unless agreed differently under (a) above, the allowances for boundaries shall be six runs if the ball having been struck by the bat pitches beyond the boundary, but otherwise four runs. These allowances shall still apply even though the ball has previously touched a fielder. See also (c) below.

(c) The ball shall be regarded as pitching beyond the boundary and six runs shall be scored if a fielder:

  (i) has any part of his person touching the boundary or grounded beyond the boundary when he catches the ball.

  (ii) catches the ball and subsequently touches the boundary or grounds some part of his person beyond the boundary while carrying the ball but before completing the catch. See Law 32 (Caught).

5. Runs Scored

When a boundary is scored:

(a) the penalty for a No Ball or a Wide, if applicable, shall stand together with any penalties under any of Laws 2.6 (Player Returning Without Permission), 18.5(b) (Deliberate Short Runs) or 42 (Fair and Unfair Play) that apply before the boundary is scored.

(b) the batting side, except in the circumstances of 6 below, shall additionally be awarded whichever is the greater of:

  (i) the allowance for the boundary.

  (ii) the runs completed by the batsmen, together with the run in progress if they have crossed at the instant the boundary is scored. When these runs exceed the boundary allowance, they shall replace the boundary for the purposes of Law 18.12 (Batsman Returning to Wicket He Has Left).

6. Overthrow or Wilful Act of Fielder

If the boundary results either from an overthrow or from the wilful act of a fielder the runs scored shall be:

  (i) the penalty for a No-ball or a Wide, if applicable, and penalties under any of Laws 2.6 (Player Returning Without Permission), 18.5(b) (Deliberate Short Runs) or 42 (Fair and Unfair Play) that are applicable before the boundary is scored, and

  (ii) the allowance for the boundary, and

  (iii) the runs completed by the batsmen, together with the run in progress if they have crossed at the instant of the throw or act.

Law 18.12(a) (Batsman Returning to Wicket He Has Left) shall apply as from the instant of the throw or act.

LAW 20.   LOST BALL

1. Fielder to Call "Lost Ball"

If a ball in play cannot be found or recovered, any fielder may call "Lost ball". The ball shall then become dead. See Law 23.1 (Ball is Dead). Law 18.12(a) (Batsman Returning to Wicket He Has Left) shall apply as from the instant of the call.

2. Ball to be Replaced

The umpires shall replace the ball with one which has had wear comparable with that which the previous ball had received before it was lost or became irrecoverable. See Law 5.5 (Ball Lost or Becoming Unfit for Play).

3. Runs Scored

(a) The penalty for a no-ball or a wide, if applicable, shall stand, together with any penalties under any of Laws 2.6 (Player Returning Without Permission), 18.5(b) (Deliberate Short Runs) or 42 (Fair and Unfair Play) that are applicable before the call of "Lost ball".

(b) The batting side shall additionally be awarded, either

      (i) the runs completed by the batsmen, together with the run in progress if they have crossed at the instant of the call, or

      (ii) six runs,

whichever is the greater.

4. How Scored

If there is a one-run penalty for a no-ball or for a wide, it shall be scored as a no-ball extra or as a wide as appropriate. See Laws 24.13 (Runs Resulting from a No-ball – How Scored) and 25.6 (Runs Resulting from a Wide – How Scored). If any other penalties have been awarded to either side, they shall be scored as penalty extras. See Law 42.17 (Penalty Runs).

Runs to the batting side in 3(b) above shall be credited to the striker if the ball has been struck by the bat, but otherwise to the total of byes, leg byes, no-balls or wides as the case may be.

LAW 21.   THE RESULT

1. A Win – Two-Innings Match

The side which has scored a total of runs in excess of that scored in the two completed innings of the opposing side shall win the match. Note also 6 below. A forfeited innings is to count as a completed innings. See Law 14 (Declaration and Forfeiture).

2. A Win – One-Innings Match

The side which has scored in its one innings a total of runs in excess of that scored by the opposing side in its one completed innings shall win the match. Note also 6 below.

3. Umpires Awarding a Match

(a) A match shall be lost by a side which either

      (i) concedes defeat, or

      (ii) in the opinion of the umpires refuses to play and the umpires shall award the match to the other side.

(b) If an umpire considers that an action by any player or players might constitute a refusal by either side to play then the umpires together shall ascertain the cause of the action. If they then decide together that this action does constitute a refusal to play by one side, they shall so inform the captain of that side. If the captain persists in the action the umpires shall award the match in accordance with (a)(ii) above.

(c) If action as in (b) above takes place after play has started and does not constitute a refusal to play

(i) playing time lost shall be counted from the start of the action until play commences, subject to Law 15.5 (Changing Agreed Times for Intervals).

(ii) the time for close of play on that day shall be extended by this length of time, subject to Law 3.9 (Suspension of Play for Adverse Conditions of Ground, Weather or Light).

(iii) if applicable, no overs shall be deducted during the last hour of the match solely on account of this time.

4. A Tie

The result of a match shall be a tie when the scores are equal at the conclusion of play, but only if the side batting last has completed its innings.

5. A Draw

A match which is concluded, as defined in Law 16.9 (Conclusion of a Match), without being determined in any of the ways stated in 1, 2, 3 or 4 above, shall count as a draw.

6. Winning Hit or Extras

(a) As soon as a result is reached, as defined in 1, 2, 3 or 4 above, the match is at an end. Nothing that happens thereafter, except as in Law 42.17 (b), shall be regarded as part of it. Note also 9 below.

(b) The side batting last will have scored enough runs to win only if its total of runs is sufficient without including any runs completed before the dismissal of the striker by the completion of a catch or by the obstruction of a catch.

(c) If a boundary is scored before the batsmen have completed sufficient runs to win the match, then the whole of the boundary allowance shall be credited to the side's total and, in the case of a hit by the bat, to the striker's score.

7. Statement of Result

If the side batting last wins the match without losing all its wickets, the result shall be stated as a win by the number of wickets still then to fall. If the side batting last has lost all its wickets but, as the result of an award of five penalty runs at the end of the match, has scored a total of runs in excess of the total scored by the opposing side, the result shall be stated as a win to that side by penalty runs. If the side fielding last wins the match, the result shall be stated as a win by runs.

If the match is decided by one side conceding defeat or refusing to play, the result shall be stated as "Match conceded" or "Match awarded" as the case may be.

8. Correctness of Result

Any decision as to the correctness of the scores shall be the responsibility of the umpires. See Law 3.15 (Correctness of Scores).

9. Mistakes in Scoring

If, after the umpires and players have left the field in the belief that the match has been concluded, the umpires discover that a mistake in scoring has occurred which affects the result, then, subject to 10 below, they shall adopt the following procedure.

(a) If, when the players leave the field, the side batting last has not completed its innings, and either

(i) the number of overs to be bowled in the last hour has not been completed, or

(ii) the agreed finishing time has not been reached,

then unless one side concedes defeat the umpires shall order play to resume.

If conditions permit, play will then continue until the prescribed number of overs has been completed and the time remaining has elapsed, unless a result is reached earlier. The number of overs and/or the time remaining shall be taken as they were when the players left the field; no account shall be taken of the time between that moment and the resumption of play.

(b) If, when the players leave the field, the overs have been completed and time has been reached, or if the side batting last has completed its innings, the umpires shall immediately inform both captains of the necessary corrections to the scores and to the result.

10. Result Not to Be Changed

Once the umpires have agreed with the scorers the correctness of the scores at the conclusion of the match – see Laws 3.15 (Correctness of Scores) and 4.2 (Correctness of Scores) – the result cannot thereafter be changed.

LAW 22.   THE OVER

1. Number of Balls

The ball shall be bowled from each wicket alternately in overs of six balls.

2. Start of an Over

An over has started when the bowler starts his run-up or, if he has no-run up, his delivery action for the first delivery of that over.

3. Call of "Over"

When six balls have been bowled other than those which are not to count in the over and as the ball becomes dead – see Law 23 (Dead Ball) – the umpire shall call "Over" before leaving the wicket.

4. Balls Not to Count in the Over

(a) A ball shall not count as one of the six balls of the over unless it is delivered, even though a batsman may be dismissed or some other incident occurs before the ball is delivered.

(b) A ball which is delivered by the bowler shall not count as one of the six balls of the over:

   (i)   if it is called dead, or is to be considered dead, before the striker has had   an opportunity to play it. See Law 23 (Dead Ball).

   (ii) if it is a no-ball. See Law 24 (No-Ball).

   (iii) if it is a wide. See Law 25 (Wide Ball).

   (iv) if it is called dead in the circumstances of Laws 23.3(b)(vi) (Umpire Calling and Signalling "Dead ball")

   (v)   When five penalty runs are awarded to the batting side under any of Laws 2.6 (Player Returning Without Permission), 41.2 (Fielding the Ball), 42.4 (Deliberate Attempt to Distract Striker) or 42.5 (Deliberate Distraction or Obstruction of Batsman).

5. Umpire Miscounting

If an umpire miscounts the number of balls, the over as counted by the umpire shall stand.

6. Bowler Changing Ends

A bowler shall be allowed to change ends as often as desired, provided only that he does not bowl two overs, or parts thereof, consecutively in the same innings.

7. Finishing an Over

(a) Other than at the end of an innings, a bowler shall finish an over in progress unless he is incapacitated, or he is suspended under any of Laws 17.1 (Practice on the Field), 42.7 (Dangerous and Unfair Bowling – Action By the Umpire), 42.9 (Time-Wasting by the Fielding Side), or 42.12 (Bowler Running on the Protected Area After Delivering the Ball).

(b) If for any reason, other than the end of an innings, an over is left uncompleted at the start of an interval or interruption of play, it shall be completed on resumption of play.

8. Bowler Incapacitated or Suspended During an Over

If for any reason a bowler is incapacitated while running up to bowl the first ball of an over, or is incapacitated or suspended during an over, the umpire shall call and signal "Dead ball". Another bowler shall complete the over from the same end, provided that he does not bowl two overs, or parts thereof, consecutively in one innings.

LAW 23.   DEAD BALL

1. Ball is Dead

(a) The ball becomes dead when:

(i)   it is finally settled in the hands of the wicket-keeper or the bowler.

(ii)   a boundary is scored. See Law 19.3 (Scoring a Boundary).

(iii)   a batsman is dismissed.

(iv)   whether played or not it becomes trapped between the bat and person of a batsman or between items of his clothing or equipment.

(v)   whether played or not it lodges in the clothing or equipment of a batsman or the clothing of an umpire.

(vi)   it lodges in a protective helmet worn by a member of the fielding side.

(vii)   there is a contravention of either of Laws 41.2 (Fielding the Ball) or 41.3 (Protective Helmets Belonging to the Fielding Side).

(viii)   there is an award of penalty runs under Law 2.6 (Player Returning Without Permission).

(ix)   "Lost ball" is called. See Law 20 (Lost Ball).

(x)   the umpire calls "Over" or "Time".

(b) The ball shall be considered to be dead when it is clear to the umpire at the bowler's end that the fielding side and both batsmen at the wicket have ceased to regard it as in play.

2. Ball Finally Settled

Whether the ball is finally settled or not is a matter for the umpire alone to decide.

3. Umpire Calling and Signalling "Dead Ball"

(a) When the ball has become dead under 1 above, the bowler's end umpire may call "Dead ball", if it is necessary to inform the players.

(b) Either umpire shall call and signal "Dead ball" when:

(i)   he intervenes in a case of unfair play.

(ii)   a serious injury to a player or umpire occurs.

(iii)   he leaves his normal position for consultation.

(iv)   one or both bails fall from the striker's wicket before he has the opportunity of playing the ball.

(v)   he is satisfied that for an adequate reason the striker is not ready for the delivery of the ball and, if the ball is delivered, makes no attempt to play it.

(vi)   the striker is distracted by any noise or movement or in any other   way while he is preparing to receive or receiving a delivery. This shall apply whether the source of the distraction is within the game or outside it. Note, however, the provisions of Law 42.4 (Deliberate Attempt to Distract the Striker). The ball shall not count as one of the over.

(vii)   the bowler drops the ball accidentally before delivery.

(viii)   the ball does not leave the bowler's hand for any reason other than an attempt to run out the non-striker before entering his delivery stride. See Law 42.15 (Bowler Attempting to Run out Non-striker Before Delivery).

(ix)   he is required to do so under any of the Laws.

4. Ball Ceases to Be Dead

The ball ceases to be dead – that is, it comes into play – when the bowler starts his run up or, if he has no run up, his bowling action.

5. Action on Call of "Dead Ball"

(a) A ball is not to count as one of the over if it becomes dead or is to be considered dead before the striker has had an opportunity to play it.

(b) If the ball becomes dead or is to be considered dead after the striker has had an opportunity to play the ball, except in the circumstances of 3(vi) above and Law 42.4 (Deliberate Attempt to Distract Striker), no additional delivery shall be allowed unless "No-ball" or "Wide" has been called.

LAW 24.   NO-BALL

1. Mode of Delivery

(a) The umpire shall ascertain whether the bowler intends to bowl right-handed or left-handed, and shall so inform the striker. It is unfair if the bowler fails to notify the umpire of a change in his mode of delivery. In this case the umpire shall call and signal "No-ball".

(b) Underarm bowling shall not be permitted except by special agreement before the match.

2. Fair Delivery – The Arm

For a delivery to be fair in respect of the arm the ball must not be thrown. See 3 below.

Although it is the primary responsibility of the striker's end umpire to ensure the fairness of a delivery in this respect, there is nothing in this Law to debar the bowler's end umpire from calling and signalling "No-ball" if he considers that the ball has been thrown.

(a) If, in the opinion of either umpire, the ball has been thrown, he shall

  (i) call and signal "No-ball".

  (ii) caution the bowler, when the ball is dead. This caution shall apply throughout the innings.

  (iii) inform the other umpire, the batsmen at the wicket, the captain of the fielding side and, as soon as practicable, the captain of the batting side of what has occurred.

(b) If either umpire considers that after such caution a further delivery by the same bowler in that innings is thrown, the umpire concerned shall repeat the procedure set out in (a) above, indicating to the bowler that this is a final warning. This warning shall also apply throughout the innings.

(c) If either umpire considers that a further delivery by the same bowler in that innings is thrown:

  (i) the umpire concerned shall call and signal "No-ball". When the ball is dead he shall inform the other umpire, the batsmen at the wicket and, as soon as practicable, the captain of the batting side of what has occurred.

  (ii) the umpire at the bowler's end shall direct the captain of the fielding side to take the bowler off forthwith. The over shall be completed by another bowler, who shall neither have bowled the previous over nor be allowed to bowl the next over. The bowler thus taken off shall not bowl again in that innings.

  (iii) the umpires together shall report the occurrence as soon as possible to the Executive of the fielding side and any governing body responsible for the match, who shall take such action as is considered appropriate against the captain and bowler concerned.

3. Definition of Fair Delivery – The Arm

A ball is fairly delivered in respect of the arm if, once the bowler's arm has reached the level of the shoulder in the delivery swing, the elbow joint is not straightened partially or completely from that point until the ball has left the hand. This definition shall not debar a bowler from flexing or rotating the wrist in the delivery swing.

4. Bowler Throwing Towards Striker's End Before Delivery

If the bowler throws the ball towards the striker's end before entering his delivery stride, either umpire shall call and signal "No-ball". See Law 42.16 (Batsmen Stealing a Run). However, the procedure stated in 2 above of caution, informing, final warning, action against the bowler and reporting shall not apply.

5. Fair Delivery – The Feet

For a delivery to be fair in respect of the feet, in the delivery stride:

    (i) the bowler's back foot must land within and not touching the return crease.

    (ii) the bowler's front foot must land with some part of the foot, whether grounded or raised, behind the popping crease.

If the umpire at the bowler's end is not satisfied that both these conditions have been met, he shall call and signal "No-ball".

6. Ball Bouncing More Than Twice or Rolling Along the Ground

The umpire at the bowler's end shall call and signal "No-ball" if a ball which he considers to have been delivered, without having previously touched the bat or person of the striker, either

    (i) bounces more than twice, or

    (ii) rolls along the ground

before it reaches the popping crease.

7. Ball Coming to Rest in Front of Striker's Wicket

If a ball delivered by the bowler comes to rest in front of the line of the striker's wicket, without having touched the bat or person of the striker, the umpire shall call and signal "No-ball" and immediately call and signal "Dead ball".

8. Call of "No-Ball" for Infringement of Other Laws

In addition to the instances above, an umpire shall call and signal "No-ball" as required by the following Laws.

    Law 40.3 – Position of wicket-keeper,
    Law 41.5 – Limitation of on-side fielders,
    Law 41.6 – Fielders not to encroach on the pitch,
    Law 42.6 – Dangerous and unfair bowling,
    Law 42.7 – Dangerous and unfair bowling – action by the umpire,
    Law 42.8 – Deliberate bowling of high full pitched balls.

9. Revoking a Call of "No-Ball"

An umpire shall revoke the call of "No-ball" if the ball does not leave the bowler's hand for any reason.

10. No-Ball to Over-ride Wide

A call of "No-ball" shall over-ride the call of "Wide ball" at any time. See Law 25.1 (Judging a Wide) and 25.3 (Call and Signal of "Wide Ball").

11. Ball Not Dead

The ball does not become dead on the call of "No-ball".

12. Penalty for a No-Ball

A penalty of one run shall be awarded instantly on the call of "No-ball". Unless the call is revoked, this penalty shall stand even if a batsman is dismissed. It shall be in addition to any other runs scored, any boundary allowance and any other penalties awarded.

13. Runs Resulting from a No Ball – How Scored

The one run penalty for a no-ball shall be scored as a no-ball extra. If other penalty runs have been awarded to either side, these shall be scored as in Law 42.17 (Penalty Runs). Any runs completed by the batsmen or a boundary allowance shall be credited to the striker if the ball has been struck by the bat; otherwise they also shall be scored as no-ball extras. Apart from any award of a five-run penalty, all runs resulting from a no-ball, whether as no-ball extras or credited to the striker, shall be debited against the bowler.

14. No-Ball Not to Count

A no-ball shall not count as one of the over. See Law 22.4 (Balls Not to Count in the Over).

15. Out from a No-Ball

When "No-ball" has been called, neither batsman shall be out under any of the Laws except 33 (Handled the Ball), 34 (Hit the Ball Twice), 37 (Obstructing the Field) or 38 (Run Out).

LAW 25.   WIDE BALL

1. Judging a Wide

(a) If the bowler bowls a ball, not being a no-ball, the umpire shall adjudge it a wide if according to the definition in (b) below, in his opinion, the ball passes wide of the striker where he is standing and would also have passed wide of him standing in a normal guard position.

(b) The ball will be considered as passing wide of the striker unless it is sufficiently within his reach for him to be able to hit it with his bat by means of a normal cricket stroke.

2. Delivery Not a Wide

The umpire shall not adjudge a delivery as being a wide

(a) if the striker, by moving, either

   (i) causes the ball to pass wide of him, as defined in 1(b) above, or

   (ii) brings the ball sufficiently within his reach to be able to hit it with his bat by means of a normal cricket stroke.

(b) if the ball touches the striker's bat or person.

3. Call and Signal of "Wide Ball"

(a) If the umpire adjudges a delivery to be a wide he shall call and signal "Wide ball" as soon as the ball passes the striker's wicket. It shall, however, be considered to have been a wide from the instant of delivery, even though it cannot be called wide until it passes the striker's wicket.

(b) The umpire shall revoke the call of "Wide ball" if there is then any contact between the ball and the striker's bat or person.

(c) The umpire shall revoke the call of "Wide ball" if a delivery is called a "No-ball". See Law 24.10 (No-Ball to Over-ride Wide).

4. Ball Not Dead

The ball does not become dead on the call of "Wide ball".

5. Penalty For a Wide

A penalty of one run shall be awarded instantly on the call of "Wide ball". Unless the call is revoked (see 3 above), this penalty shall stand even if a batsman is dismissed, and shall be in addition to any other runs scored, any boundary allowance and any other penalties awarded.

6. Runs Resulting From a Wide – How Scored

All runs completed by the batsmen or a boundary allowance, together with the penalty for the wide, shall be scored as wide balls. Apart from any award of a five-run penalty, all runs resulting from a wide ball shall be debited against the bowler.

7. Wide Not to Count

A wide shall not count as one of the over. See Law 22.4 (Balls Not to Count in the Over).

8. Out From a Wide

When "Wide ball" has been called, neither batsman shall be out under any of the Laws except 33 (Handled the Ball), 35 (Hit Wicket), 37 (Obstructing the Field), 38 (Run Out) or 39 (Stumped).

LAW 26.   BYE AND LEG-BYE

1. Byes

If the ball, not being a no-ball or a wide, passes the striker without touching his bat or person, any runs completed by the batsmen or a boundary allowance shall be credited as byes to the batting side.

2. Leg-Byes

(a) If the ball delivered by the bowler first strikes the person of the striker, runs shall be scored only if the umpire is satisfied that the striker has either

(i)   attempted to play the ball with his bat, or

(ii)   tried to avoid being hit by the ball.

If the umpire is satisfied that either of these conditions has been met, and the ball makes no subsequent contact with the bat, runs completed by the batsmen or a boundary allowance shall be credited to the batting side as in (b). Note, however, the provisions of Laws 34.3 (Ball Lawfully Struck More Than Once) and 34.4 (Runs Permitted From Ball Lawfully Struck More Than Once).

(b) The runs in (a) above shall

(i)   if the delivery is not a no-ball, be scored as leg-byes.

(ii)   if no-ball has been called, be scored together with the penalty for the no-ball as no-ball extras.

3. Leg-Byes Not to Be Awarded

If in the circumstances of 2(a) above, the umpire considers that neither of the conditions (i) and (ii) has been met, then leg-byes will not be awarded. The batting side shall not be credited with any runs from that delivery apart from the one-run penalty for a no-ball if applicable. Moreover, no other penalties shall be awarded to the batting side when the ball is dead. See Law 42.17 (Penalty Runs).

The following procedure shall be adopted.

(a) If no run is attempted but the ball reaches the boundary, the umpire shall call and signal "Dead ball", and disallow the boundary.

(b) If runs are attempted and if:

(i)   neither batsman is dismissed and the ball does not become dead for any other reason, the umpire shall call and signal "Dead ball" as soon as one run is completed or the ball reaches the boundary. The batsmen shall return to their original ends. The run or boundary shall be disallowed.

(ii)   before one run is completed or the ball reaches the boundary, a batsman is dismissed, or the ball becomes dead for any other reason, all the provisions of the Laws will apply, except that no runs and no penalties shall be credited to the batting side, other than the penalty for a no-ball if applicable.

LAW 27.   APPEALS

1. Umpire Not to Give Batsman Out Without an Appeal

Neither umpire shall give a batsman out, even though he may be out under the Laws, unless appealed to by the fielding side. This shall not debar a batsman who is out under any of the Laws from leaving his wicket without an appeal having been made. Note, however, the provisions of 7 below.

2. Batsman Dismissed

A batsman is dismissed if either

(a) he is given out by an umpire, on appeal, or

(b) he is out under any of the Laws and leaves his wicket as in 1 above.

3. Timing of Appeals

For an appeal to be valid it must be made before the bowler begins his run-up or, if he has no run-up, his bowling action to deliver the next ball, and before "Time" has been called.

The call of "Over" does not invalidate an appeal made prior to the start of the following over provided "Time" has not been called. See Laws 16.2 (Call of Time) and 22.2 (Start of an Over).

4. Appeal "How's That?"

An appeal "How's That?" covers all ways of being out.

5. Answering Appeals

The umpire at the bowler's end shall answer all appeals except those arising out of any of Laws 35 (Hit Wicket), 39 (Stumped) or 38 (Run Out) when this occurs at the striker's wicket. A decision "Not out" by one umpire shall not prevent the other umpire from giving a decision, provided that each is considering only matters within his jurisdiction.

When a batsman has been given not out, either umpire may, within his jurisdiction, answer a further appeal provided that it is made in accordance with 3 above.

6. Consultation by Umpires

Each umpire shall answer appeals on matters within his own jurisdiction. If an umpire is doubtful about any point that the other umpire may have been in a better position to see, he shall consult the latter on this point of fact and shall then give his decision. If, after consultation, there is still doubt remaining the decision shall be "Not out".

7. Batsman Leaving his Wicket Under a Misapprehension

An umpire shall intervene if satisfied that a batsman, not having been given out, has left his wicket under a misapprehension that he is out. The umpire intervening shall call and signal "Dead ball" to prevent any further action by the fielding side and shall recall the batsman.

8. Withdrawal of an Appeal

The captain of the fielding side may withdraw an appeal only with the consent of the umpire within whose jurisdiction the appeal falls and before the outgoing batsman has left the field of play. If such consent is given the umpire concerned shall, if applicable, revoke his decision and recall the batsman.

9. Umpire's Decision

An umpire may alter his decision provided that such alteration is made promptly. This apart, an umpire's decision, once made, is final.

LAW 28.   THE WICKET IS DOWN

1. Wicket Put Down

(a) The wicket is put down if a bail is completely removed from the top of the stumps, or a stump is struck out of the ground by:

  (i) the ball.

  (ii) the striker's bat, whether he is holding it or has let go of it.

  (iii) the striker's person or by any part of his clothing or equipment becoming detached from his person.

  (iii) a fielder, with his hand or arm, providing that the ball is held in the hand or hands so used, or in the hand of the arm so used.

The wicket is also put down if a fielder pulls a stump out of the ground in the same manner.

(b) The disturbance of a bail, whether temporary or not, shall not constitute its complete removal from the top of the stumps, but if a bail in falling lodges between two of the stumps this shall be regarded as complete removal.

2. One Bail Off

If one bail is off, it shall be sufficient for the purpose of putting the wicket down to remove the remaining bail, or to strike or pull any of the three stumps out of the ground, in any of the ways stated in 1 above.

3. Remaking the Wicket

If the wicket is broken or put down while the ball is in play, the umpire shall not remake the wicket until the ball is dead. See Law 23 (Dead Ball). Any fielder, however, may

(i) replace a bail or bails on top of the stumps.

(ii) put back one or more stumps into the ground where the wicket originally stood.

4. Dispensing with Bails

If the umpires have agreed to dispense with bails, in accordance with Law 8.5 (Dispensing with Bails), the decision as to whether the wicket has been put down is one for the umpire concerned to decide.

(a) After a decision to play without bails, the wicket has been put down if the umpire concerned is satisfied that the wicket has been struck by the ball, by the striker's bat, person, or items of his clothing or equipment separated from his person as described in 1(a)(ii) or 1(a)(iii) above, or by a fielder with the hand holding the ball or with the arm of the hand holding the ball.

(b) If the wicket has already been broken or put down, (a) above shall apply to any stump or stumps still in the ground. Any fielder may replace a stump or stumps, in accordance with 3 above, in order to have an opportunity of putting the wicket down.

LAW 29.   BATSMAN OUT OF HIS GROUND

1. When Out of His Ground

A batsman shall be considered to be out of his ground unless his bat or some part of his person is grounded behind the popping crease at that end.

2. Which is a Batsman's Ground?

(a) If only one batsman is within a ground:

(i) it is his ground.

(ii) it remains his ground even if he is later joined there by the other batsman.

(b) If both batsmen are in the same ground and one of them subsequently leaves it, (a)(i) above applies.

(c) If there is no batsman in either ground, then each ground belongs to whichever of the batsmen is nearer to it, or, if the batsmen are level, to whichever was nearer to it immediately prior to their drawing level.

(d) If a ground belongs to one batsman, then, unless there is a striker with a runner, the other ground belongs to the other batsman irrespective of his position.

(e) When a batsman with a runner is striker, his ground is always that at the wicket-keeper's end. However, (a), (b), (c) and (d) above will still apply, but only to the runner and the non-striker, so that that ground will also belong to either the non-striker or the runner, as the case may be.

3. Position of Non-Striker

The batsman at the bowler's end should be positioned on the opposite side of the wicket to that from which the ball is being delivered, unless a request to do otherwise is granted by the umpire.

LAW 30.   BOWLED

1. Out Bowled

(a) The striker is out *Bowled* if his wicket is put down by a ball delivered by the bowler, not being a no-ball, even if it first touches his bat or person.

(b) Notwithstanding (a) above he shall not be out Bowled if before striking the wicket the ball has been in contact with any other player or with an umpire. He will, however, be subject to Laws 33 (Handled the Ball), 37 (Obstructing the Field), 38 (Run Out) and 39 (Stumped).

2. Bowled to Take Precedence

The striker is out *Bowled* if his wicket is put down as in 1 above, even though a decision against him for any other method of dismissal would be justified.

LAW 31.   TIMED OUT

1. Out Timed Out

(a) Unless "Time" has been called, the incoming batsman must be in position to take guard or for his partner to be ready to receive the next ball within three minutes of the fall of the previous wicket. If this requirement is not met, the incoming batsman will be out, *Timed Out*.

(b) In the event of protracted delay in which no batsman comes to the wicket, the umpires shall adopt the procedure of Law 21.3 (Umpires awarding a match). For the purposes of that Law the start of the action shall be taken as the expiry of the three minutes referred to above.

2. Bowler Does Not Get Credit

The bowler does not get credit for the wicket.

LAW 32.   CAUGHT

1. Out Caught

The striker is out *Caught* if a ball delivered by the bowler, not being a no-ball, touches his bat without having previously been in contact with any member of the fielding side and is subsequently held by a fielder as a fair catch before it touches the ground.

2. Caught to Take Precedence

If the criteria of 1 above are met and the striker is not out Bowled, then he is out Caught, even though a decision against either batsman for another method of dismissal would be justified. Runs completed by the batsmen before the completion of the catch will not be scored. Note also Laws 21.6 (Winning Hit or Extras) and 42.17(b) (Penalty Runs).

3. A Fair Catch

A catch shall be considered to have been fairly made if:

(a) throughout the act of making the catch:

(i)   any fielder in contact with the ball is within the field of play. See 4 below.

(ii)   the ball is at no time in contact with any object grounded beyond the boundary.

The act of making the catch shall start from the time when a fielder first handles the ball and shall end when a fielder obtains complete control over the ball and over his own movements.

(b) the ball is hugged to the body of the catcher or accidentally lodges in his clothing or, in the case of the wicket-keeper, in his pads. However, it is not a fair catch if the ball lodges in a protective helmet worn by a fielder. See Law 23 (Dead Ball).

(c) The ball does not touch the ground, even though the hand holding it does so in effecting the catch.

(d) a fielder catches the ball after it has been lawfully struck more than once by the striker, but only if the ball has not touched the ground since first being struck.

(e) a fielder catches the ball after it has touched an umpire, another fielder or the other batsman. However, it is not a fair catch if the ball has touched a protective helmet worn by a fielder, although the ball remains in play.

(f) a fielder catches the ball in the air after it has crossed the boundary provided that:

(i)   he has no part of his person touching, or grounded beyond, the boundary at any time when he is in contact with the ball.

(ii)   the ball has not been grounded beyond the boundary. See Law 19.3 (Scoring a Boundary).

(g) the ball is caught off an obstruction within the boundary, provided it has not previously been decided to regard the obstruction as a boundary.

4. Fielder Within the Field of Play

(a) A fielder is not within the field of play if he touches the boundary or has any part of his person grounded beyond the boundary. See Law 19.3 (Scoring a Boundary).

(b) six runs shall be scored if a fielder:

   (i) has any part of his person touching, or grounded beyond, the boundary when he catches the ball.

   (ii) catches the ball and subsequently touches the boundary or grounds some part of his person over the boundary while carrying the ball but before completing the catch.

See Laws 19.3 (Scoring a Boundary) and 19.4 (Runs Allowed for Boundaries).

5. No Runs to Be Scored

If the striker is dismissed Caught, runs from that delivery completed by the batsmen before the completion of the catch shall not be scored, but any penalties awarded to either side when the ball is dead, if applicable, will stand. Law 18.12(a) (Batsman Returning to Wicket He Has Left) shall apply from the instant of the catch.

LAW 33.   HANDLED THE BALL

1. Out Handled the Ball

Either batsman is out *Handled the Ball* if he wilfully touches the ball while in play with a hand or hands not holding the bat unless he does so with the consent of the opposing side.

2. Not Out Handled the Ball

Notwithstanding 1 above, a batsman will not be out under this Law if:

   (i) he handles the ball in order to avoid injury.

   (ii) he uses his hand or hands to return the ball to any member of the fielding side without the consent of that side. Note, however, the provisions of Law 37.4 (Returning the Ball To a Member of the Fielding Side).

3. Runs Scored

If either batsman is dismissed under this Law, any runs completed before the offence, together with any penalty extras and the penalty for a no-ball or wide, if applicable, shall be scored. See Laws 18.10 (Runs Scored When a Batsman is Dismissed) and 42.17 (Penalty runs).

4. Bowler Does Not Get Credit

The bowler does not get credit for the wicket.

LAW 34.   HIT THE BALL TWICE

1. Out Hit the Ball Twice

(a) The striker is out *Hit The Ball Twice* if, while the ball is in play, it strikes any part of his person or is struck by his bat and, before the ball has been touched by a fielder, he wilfully strikes it again with his bat or person, other than a hand not holding the bat, except for the sole purpose of guarding his wicket. See 3 below and Laws 33 (Handled the Ball) and 37 (Obstructing the Field).

(b) For the purpose of this Law, "struck" or "strike" shall include contact with the person of the striker.

2. Not Out Hit the Ball Twice

Notwithstanding 1(a) above, the striker will not be out under this Law if:

(i) he makes a second or subsequent stroke in order to return the ball to any member of the fielding side. Note, however, the provisions of Law 37.4 (Returning the Ball to a Member of the Fielding Side).

(ii) he wilfully strikes the ball after it has touched a fielder. Note, however, the provisions of Law 37.1 (Out Obstructing the Field).

3. Ball Lawfully Struck More Than Once

Solely in order to guard his wicket and before the ball has been touched by a fielder, the striker may lawfully strike the ball more than once with his bat or with any part of his person other than a hand not holding the bat.

Notwithstanding this provision, the striker may not prevent the ball from being caught by making more than one stroke in defence of his wicket. See Law 37.3 (Obstructing a Ball from Being Caught).

4. Runs Permitted from Ball Lawfully Struck More Than Once

When the ball is lawfully struck more than once, as permitted in 3 above, only the first strike is to be considered in determining whether runs are to be allowed and how they are to be scored.

(a) If on the first strike the umpire is satisfied that either

    (i) the ball first struck the bat, or

    (ii) the striker attempted to play the ball with his bat, or

    (iii) the striker tried to avoid being hit by the ball

then any penalties to the batting side that are applicable shall be allowed.

(b) If the conditions in (a) above are met then, if they result from overthrows, and only if they result from overthrows, runs completed by the batsmen or a boundary shall be allowed in addition to any penalties that are applicable. They shall be credited to the striker if the first strike was with the bat. If the first strike was on the person of the striker they shall be scored as leg-byes or no-ball extras, as appropriate. See Law 26.2 (Leg-Byes).

(c) If the conditions of (a) above are met and there is no overthrow until after the batsmen have started to run, but before one run is completed:

    (i) only subsequent completed runs or a boundary shall be allowed. The first run shall count as a completed run for this purpose only if the batsmen have not crossed at the instant of the throw.

    (ii) if in these circumstances the ball goes to the boundary from the throw then, notwithstanding the provisions of Law 19.6 (Overthrow or Wilful Act of Fielder), only the boundary allowance shall be scored.

    (iii) if the ball goes to the boundary as the result of a further overthrow, then runs completed by the batsmen after the first throw and before this final throw shall be added to the boundary allowance. The run in progress at the first throw will count only if they have not crossed at that moment; the run in progress at the final throw shall count only if they have crossed at that moment. Law 18.12 (Batsman Returning to Wicket He Has Left) shall apply as from the moment of the final throw.

(d) If, in the opinion of the umpire, none of the conditions in (a) above have been met then, whether there is an overthrow or not, the batting side shall not be credited with any runs from that delivery apart from the penalty for a no-ball if applicable. Moreover, no other penalties shall be awarded to the batting side when the ball is dead. See Law 42.17 (Penalty Runs).

5. Ball Lawfully Struck More Than Once – Action By The Umpire

If no runs are to be allowed, either in the circumstances of 4(d) above, or because there has been no overthrow and:

(a) if no run is attempted but the ball reaches the boundary, the umpire shall call and signal "Dead ball" and disallow the boundary.

(b) if the batsmen run and:

    (i) neither batsman is dismissed and the ball does not become dead for any other reason, the umpire shall call and signal Dead Ball as soon as one run is completed or the ball reaches the boundary. The batsmen shall return to their original ends. The run or boundary shall be disallowed.

(ii) a batsman is dismissed, or if for any other reason the ball becomes dead before one run is completed or the ball reaches the boundary, all the provisions of the Laws will apply except that the award of penalties to the batting side shall be as laid down in 4(a) or 4(d) above as appropriate.

6. Bowler Does Not Get Credit

The bowler does not get credit for the wicket.

LAW 35.   HIT WICKET

1. Out Hit Wicket

(a) The striker is out *Hit Wicket* if, after the bowler has entered his delivery stride and while the ball is in play, his wicket is put down either by the striker's bat or person as described in Law 28.1(a)(ii) and (iii) (Wicket Put Down) either:

(i) in the course of any action taken by him in preparing to receive or in receiving a delivery, or

(ii) in setting off for his first run immediately after playing, or playing at, the ball, or

(iii) if he makes no attempt to play the ball, in setting off for his first run, providing that in the opinion of the umpire this is immediately after he has had the opportunity of playing the ball, or

(iv) in lawfully making a second or further stroke for the purpose of guarding his wicket within the provisions of Law 34.3 (Ball Lawfully Struck More Than Once).

(b) If the striker puts his wicket down in any of the ways described in Law 28.1(a)(ii) and (iii) (Wicket Put Down) before the bowler has entered his delivery stride, either umpire shall call and signal "Dead ball".

2. Not Out Hit Wicket

Notwithstanding 1 above, the batsman is not out under this Law should his wicket be put down in any of the ways referred to in 1 above if:

(a) it occurs after he has completed any action in receiving the delivery, other than as in 1(a)(ii), (iii) or (iv) above.

(b) it occurs when he is in the act of running, other than in setting off immediately for his first run.

(c) it occurs when he is trying to avoid being run out or stumped.

(d) it occurs while he is trying to avoid a throw-in at any time.

(e) the bowler, after entering his delivery stride, does not deliver the ball. In this case either umpire shall immediately call and signal "Dead ball". See Law 23.3 (Umpire Calling and Signalling "Dead ball").

(f) the delivery is a no-ball.

LAW 36.   LEG BEFORE WICKET

1. Out LBW

The striker is out *LBW* in the circumstances set out below.

(a) The bowler delivers a ball, not being a no-ball and

(b) the ball, if it is not intercepted full pitch, pitches in line between wicket and wicket or on the off side of the striker's wicket, and

(c) the ball not having previously touched his bat, the striker intercepts the ball, either full-pitch or after pitching, with any part of his person, and

(d) the point of impact, even if above the level of the bails, either

    (i) between wicket and wicket, or

    (ii) is either between wicket and wicket or outside the line of the off stump, if the striker has made no genuine attempt to play the ball with his bat, and

(e) but for the interception, the ball would have hit the wicket.

2. Interception of the Ball

(a) In assessing points (c), (d) and (e) in 1 above, only the first interception is to be considered.

(b) In assessing point (e) in 1 above, it is to be assumed that the path of the ball before interception would have continued after interception, irrespective of whether the ball might have pitched subsequently or not.

3. Off Side of Wicket

The off side of the striker's wicket shall be determined by the striker's stance at the moment the ball comes into play for that delivery.

LAW 37. OBSTRUCTING THE FIELD

1. Out Obstructing the Field

Either batsman is out *Obstructing the Field* if he wilfully obstructs or distracts the opposing side by word or action. It shall be regarded as obstruction if either batsman wilfully, and without the consent of the fielding side, strikes the ball with his bat or person, other than a hand not holding the bat, after the ball has touched a fielder. See 4 below.

2. Accidental Obstruction

It is for either umpire to decide whether any obstruction or distraction is wilful or not. He shall consult the other umpire if he has any doubt.

3. Obstructing a Ball from Being Caught

The striker is out should wilful obstruction or distraction by either batsman prevent a catch being made.

This shall apply even though the striker causes the obstruction in lawfully guarding his wicket under the provisions of Law 34.3 (Ball lawfully struck more than once).

4. Returning the Ball to a Member of the Fielding Side

Either batsman is out under this Law if, without the consent of the fielding side and while the ball is in play, he uses his bat or person to return the ball to any member of that side.

5. Runs Scored

If a batsman is dismissed under this Law, runs completed by the batsmen before the offence shall be scored, together with the penalty for a no-ball or a wide, if applicable. Other penalties that may be awarded to either side when the ball is dead shall also stand. See Law 42.17(b) (Penalty Runs).

If, however, the obstruction prevents a catch from being made, runs completed by the batsmen before the offence shall not be scored, but other penalties that may be awarded to either side when the ball is dead shall stand. See Law 42.17(b) (Penalty Runs).

6. Bowler Does Not Get Credit

The bowler does not get credit for the wicket.

LAW 38. RUN OUT

1. Out Run Out

(a) Either batsman is out *Run Out*, except as in 2 below, if at any time while the ball is in play

    (i) he is out of his ground and

    (ii) his wicket is fairly put down by the opposing side.

(b) (a) above shall apply even though "No-ball" has been called and whether or not a run is being attempted, except in the circumstances of Law 39.3(b) (Not Out Stumped).

2. Batsman Not Run Out

Notwithstanding 1 above, a batsman is not out Run out if:

(a) he has been within his ground and has subsequently left it to avoid injury, when the wicket is put down.

(b) the ball has not subsequently been touched again by a fielder, after the bowler has entered his delivery stride, before the wicket is put down.

(c) the ball, having been played by the striker, or having come off his person, directly strikes a helmet worn by a fielder and without further contact with him or any other fielder rebounds directly on to the wicket. However, the ball remains in play and either batsman may be Run out in the circumstances of 1 above if a wicket is subsequently put down.

(d) he is out Stumped. See Law 39.1(b) (Out Stumped).

(e) he is out of his ground, not attempting a run and his wicket is fairly put down by the wicket-keeper without the intervention of another member of the fielding side, if "No-ball" has been called. See Law 39.3(b) (Not Out Stumped).

3. Which Batsman is Out

The batsman out in the circumstances of 1 above is the one whose ground is at the end where the wicket is put down. See Laws 2.8 (Transgression of the Laws by a Batsman Who Has a Runner) and 29.2 (Which is a Batsman's Ground).

4. Runs Scored

If a batsman is dismissed Run Out, the batting side shall score the runs completed before the dismissal, together with the penalty for a no-ball or a wide, if applicable. Other penalties to either side that may be awarded when the ball is dead shall also stand. See Law 42.17 (Penalty Runs).

If, however, a striker with a runner is himself dismissed Run Out, runs completed by the runner and the other batsman before the dismissal shall not be scored. The penalty for a no-ball or a wide and any other penalties to either side that may be awarded when the ball is dead shall stand. See Laws 2.8 (Transgression of the Laws by a Batsman Who Has a Runner) and 42.17(b) (Penalty Runs).

5. Bowler Does Not Get Credit

The bowler does not get credit for the wicket.

LAW 39. STUMPED

1. Out Stumped

(a) The striker is out *Stumped* if

    (i)   he is out of his ground, and

    (ii) he is receiving a ball which is not a no-ball, and

    (iii) he is not attempting a run, and

    (iv) his wicket is put down by the wicket-keeper without the intervention of another member of the fielding side. Note Law 40.3 (Position of Wicket-Keeper).

(b) The striker is out Stumped if all the conditions of (a) above are   satisfied, even though a decision of Run Out would be justified.

2. Ball Rebounding from Wicket-Keeper's Person

(a) If the wicket is put down by the ball, it shall be regarded as having been put down by the wicket-keeper if the ball

    (i)   rebounds on to the stumps from any part of his person or equipment, other than a protective helmet, or

    (ii) has been kicked or thrown on to the stumps by the wicket-keeper.

(b) If the ball touches a helmet worn by the wicket-keeper, the ball is still in play but the striker shall not be out Stumped. He will, however, be liable to be Run Out in these circumstances if there is subsequent contact between the ball and any member of the fielding side. Note, however, 3 below.

3. Not Out Stumped

(a) If the striker is not out Stumped, he is liable to be out Run Out if the conditions of Law 38 (Run Out) apply, except as set out in (b) below.

(b) The striker shall not be out Run Out if he is out of his ground, not attempting a run, and his wicket is fairly put down by the wicket-keeper without the intervention of another member of the fielding side, if "No-ball" has been called.

LAW 40.   THE WICKET-KEEPER

1. Protective Equipment

The wicket-keeper is the only member of the fielding side permitted to wear gloves and external leg guards. If he does so, these are to be regarded as part of his person for the purposes of Law 41.2 (Fielding the Ball). If by his actions and positioning it is apparent to the umpires that he will not be able to discharge his duties as a wicket-keeper, he shall forfeit this right and also the right to be recognised as a wicket-keeper for the purposes of Laws 32.3 (A Fair Catch), 39 (Stumped), 41.1 (Protective Equipment), 41.5 (Limitation of On Side Fielders) and 41.6 (Fielders Not to Encroach on the Pitch).

2. Gloves

If, as permitted under 1 above, the wicket-keeper wears gloves, they shall have no webbing between fingers except joining index finger and thumb, where webbing may be inserted as a means of support. If used, the webbing shall be:

(a) a single piece of non-stretch material which, although it may have facing material attached, shall have no reinforcement or tucks.

(b) such that the top edge of the webbing:

> (i) does not protrude beyond the straight line joining the top of the index finger to the top of the thumb.

> (ii) is taut when a hand wearing the glove has the thumb fully extended.

3. Position of Wicket-Keeper

The wicket-keeper shall remain wholly behind the wicket at the striker's end from the moment the ball comes into play until

(a) a ball delivered by the bowler either:

> (i) touches the bat or person of the striker, or

> (ii) passes the wicket at the striker's end

> or

(b) the striker attempts a run.

In the event of the wicket-keeper contravening this Law, the umpire at the striker's end shall call and signal "No-ball" as soon as possible after the delivery of the ball.

4. Movement By the Wicket-Keeper

It is unfair if a wicket-keeper standing back makes a significant movement towards the wicket after the ball comes into play and before it reaches the striker. In the event of such unfair movement by the wicket-keeper, either umpire shall call and signal "Dead ball". It will not be considered a significant movement if the wicket-keeper moves a few paces forward for a slower delivery.

5. Restriction on Actions of Wicket-Keeper

If in the opinion of either umpire the wicket-keeper interferes with the striker's right to play the ball and to guard his wicket, Law 23.3(b)(vi) (Umpire Calling and Signalling "Dead Ball") shall apply. If, however, the umpire concerned considers that the interference by the wicket-keeper was wilful, then Law 42.4 (Deliberate Attempt to Distract Striker) shall apply.

6. Interference with Wicket-Keeper by Striker

If, in playing at the ball or in the legitimate defence of his wicket, the striker interferes with the wicket-keeper, he shall not be out, except as provided for in Law 37.3 (Obstructing a Ball from Being Caught).

LAW 41. THE FIELDER

1. Protective Equipment

No member of the fielding side other than the wicket-keeper shall be permitted to wear gloves or external leg guards. In addition, protection for the hand or fingers may be worn only with the consent of the umpires.

2. Fielding the Ball

A fielder may field the ball with any part of his person but if, while the ball is in play he wilfully fields it otherwise:

> (a) the ball shall become dead and 5 penalty runs shall be awarded to the batting side. See Law 42.17 (Penalty Runs). The ball shall not count as one of the over.

> (b) the umpire shall inform the other umpire, the captain of the fielding side, the batsmen and, as soon as practicable, the captain of the batting side of what has occurred.

> (c) the umpires together shall report the occurrence as soon as possible to the Executive of the fielding side and any governing body responsible for the match who shall take such action as is considered appropriate against the captain and player concerned.

3. Protective Helmets Belonging to the Fielding Side

Protective helmets, when not in use by fielders, shall only be placed, if above the surface, on the ground behind the wicket-keeper and in line with both sets of stumps. If a helmet belonging to the fielding side is on the ground within the field of play, and the ball while in play strikes it, the ball shall become dead. Five penalty runs shall then be awarded to the batting side. See Laws 18.11 (Runs Scored When Ball Becomes Dead) and 42.17 (Penalty Runs).

4. Penalty Runs Not Being Awarded

Notwithstanding 2 and 3 above, if from the delivery by the bowler the ball first struck the person of the striker and if, in the opinion of the umpire, the striker neither

> (i) attempted to play the ball with his bat, nor

> (ii) tried to avoid being hit by the ball,

then no award of five penalty runs shall be made and no other runs or penalties shall be credited to the batting side except the penalty for a "No-ball" if applicable. See Law 26.3 (Leg-Byes Not to Be Awarded).

5. Limitation of On-Side Fielders

At the instant of the bowler's delivery there shall not be more than two fielders, other than the wicket-keeper, behind the popping crease on the on side. A fielder will be considered to be behind the popping crease unless the whole of his person, whether grounded or in the air, is in front of this line. In the event of infringement of this Law by the fielding side, the umpire at the striker's end shall call and signal "No-ball".

6. Fielders Not to Encroach on the Pitch

While the ball is in play and until the ball has made contact with the bat or person of the striker, or has passed the striker's bat, no fielder, other than the bowler, may have any part of his person grounded on or extended over the pitch. In the event of infringement of this Law by any fielder other than the wicket-keeper, the umpire at the bowler's end shall call and signal "No-ball" as soon as possible after the delivery of the ball. Note, however, Law 40.3 (Position of Wicket-Keeper).

7. Movement by Fielders

Any significant movement by any fielder after the ball comes into play and before the ball reaches the striker is unfair. In the event of such unfair movement, either umpire shall call and signal "Dead ball". Note also the provisions of Law 42.4 (Deliberate Attempt to Distract Striker).

8. Definition of Significant Movement

(a) For close fielders anything other than minor adjustments to stance or position in relation to the striker is significant.

(b) In the outfield, fielders are permitted to move in towards the striker or striker's wicket, provided that 5 above is not contravened. Anything other than slight movement off line or away from the striker is to be considered significant.

(c) For restrictions on movement by the wicket-keeper see Law 40.4 (Movement By Wicket-Keeper).

LAW 42.   FAIR AND UNFAIR PLAY

1. Fair and Unfair Play – Responsibility of Captains

The responsibility lies with the captains for ensuring that play is conducted within the spirit and traditions of the game, as described in The Preamble – The Spirit of Cricket, as well as within the Laws.

2. Fair and Unfair Play – Responsibility of Umpires

The umpires shall be the sole judges of fair and unfair play. If either umpire considers an action, not covered by the Laws, to be unfair, he shall intervene without appeal and, if the ball is in play, shall call and signal "Dead-ball" and implement the procedure as set out in 18 below. Otherwise the umpires shall not interfere with the progress of play, except as required to do so by the Laws.

3. The Match Ball – Changing Its Condition

(a) Any fielder may:

    (i)   polish the ball provided that no artificial substance is used and that such polishing wastes no time.

    (ii)   remove mud from the ball under the supervision of the umpire.

    (iii)   dry a wet ball on a towel.

(b) It is unfair for anyone to rub the ball on the ground for any reason, interfere with any of the seams or the surface of the ball, use any implement, or take any other action whatsoever which is likely to alter the condition of the ball, except as permitted in (a) above.

(c) The umpires shall make frequent and irregular inspections of the ball.

(d) In the event of any fielder changing the condition of the ball unfairly, as set out in (b) above, the umpires after consultation shall:

    (i)   change the ball forthwith. It shall be for the umpires to decide on the replacement ball, which shall, in their opinion, have had wear comparable with that which the previous ball had received immediately prior to the contravention.

    (ii)   inform the batsmen that the ball has been changed.

    (iii)   award five penalty runs to the batting side. See 17 below.

    (iv)   inform the captain of the fielding side that the reason for the action was the unfair interference with the ball.

    (v)   inform the captain of the batting side as soon as practicable of what has occurred.

    (vi)   report the occurrence as soon as possible to the executive of the fielding side and any governing body responsible for the match, who shall take such action as is considered appropriate against the captain and team concerned.

(e) If there is any further instance of unfairly changing the condition of the ball in that innings, the umpires after consultation shall:

    (i)   repeat the procedure in (d)(i), (ii) and (iii) above.

    (ii)   inform the captain of the fielding side of the reason for the action taken and direct him to take off forthwith the bowler who delivered the immediately preceding ball. The bowler thus taken off shall not be allowed to bowl again in that innings.

    (iii)   inform the captain of the batting side as soon as practicable of what has occurred.

(iv) report the occurrence as soon as possible to the executive of the fielding side and any governing body responsible for the match, who shall take such action as is considered appropriate against the captain and team concerned.

4. Deliberate Attempt to Distract Striker

It is unfair for any member of the fielding side deliberately to attempt to distract the striker while he is preparing to receive or receiving a delivery.

(a) If either umpire considers that any action by a member of the fielding side is such an attempt, at the first instance he shall:

    (i) immediately call and signal "Dead ball".

    (ii) warn the captain of the fielding side that the action is unfair and indicate that this is a first and final warning.

    (iii) inform the other umpire and the batsmen of what has occurred. Neither batsman shall be dismissed from that delivery and the ball shall not count as one of the over.

(b) If there is any further such deliberate attempt in that innings, by any member of the fielding side, the procedures, other than warning, as set out in (a) above shall apply. Additionally, the umpire at the bowler's end shall:

    (i) award five penalty runs to the batting side. See 17 below.

    (ii) inform the captain of the fielding side of the reason for this action and, as soon as practicable, inform the captain of the batting side.

    (iii) report the occurrence, together with the other umpire, as soon as possible to the executive of the fielding side and any governing body responsible for the match, who shall take such action as is considered appropriate against the captain and player or players concerned.

5. Deliberate Distraction or Obstruction of Batsman

In addition to 4 above, it is unfair for any member of the fielding side, by word or action, wilfully to attempt to distract or to obstruct either batsman after the striker has received the ball.

(a) It is for either one of the umpires to decide whether any distraction or obstruction is wilful or not.

(b) If either umpire considers that a member of the fielding side has wilfully caused or attempted to cause such a distraction or obstruction he shall

    (i) immediately call and signal "Dead ball".

    (ii) inform the captain of the fielding side and the other umpire of the reason for the call.

Additionally,

    (iii) neither batsman shall be dismissed from that delivery.

    (iv) five penalty runs shall be awarded to the batting side. See 17 below. In this instance, the run in progress shall be scored, whether or not the batsmen had crossed at the instant of the call. See Law 18.11 (Runs Scored When Ball Becomes Dead).

    (v) the umpire at the bowler's end shall inform the captain of the fielding side of the reason for this action and, as soon as practicable, inform the captain of the batting side.

    (vi) the ball shall not count as one of the over.

    (vii) the batsmen at the wicket shall decide which of them is to face the next delivery.

    (viii) the umpires shall report the occurrence as soon as possible to the executive of the fielding side and any governing body responsible for the match, who shall take such action as is considered appropriate against the captain and player or players concerned.

6. Dangerous and Unfair Bowling

(a) Bowling of Fast Short-Pitched Balls

    (i) The bowling of fast short-pitched balls is dangerous and unfair if the umpire at the bowler's end considers that by their repetition and taking into account their length, height and direction they are likely to inflict physical injury on the striker, irrespective of the protective equipment he may be wearing. The relative skill of the striker shall be taken into consideration.

    (ii) Any delivery which, after pitching, passes or would have passed over head height of the striker standing upright at the crease, although not threatening physical injury, shall be included with bowling under (i) both when the umpire is considering whether the bowling of fast short-pitched balls has become dangerous and unfair and after he has so decided. The umpire shall call and signal "No-ball" for each such delivery.

(b) Bowling of High Full-Pitched Balls

    (i) Any delivery, other than a slow paced one, which passes or would have passed on the full above waist height of the striker standing upright at the crease is to be deemed dangerous and unfair, whether or not it is likely to inflict physical injury on the striker.

    (ii) a slow delivery which passes or would have passed on the full above shoulder height of the striker standing upright at the crease is to be deemed dangerous and unfair, whether or not it is likely to inflict physical injury on the striker.

7. Dangerous and Unfair Bowling – Action by the Umpire

(a) As soon as the umpire at the bowler's end decides under 6(a) above that the bowling of fast short-pitched balls has become dangerous and unfair, or, except as in 8 below, there is an instance of dangerous and unfair bowling as defined in 6(b) above, he shall call and signal "No-ball" and, when the ball is dead, caution the bowler, inform the other umpire, the captain of the fielding side and the batsmen of what has occurred. This caution shall continue to apply throughout the innings.

(b) If there is any further instance of such dangerous and unfair bowling by the same bowler in the same innings, the umpire at the bowler's end shall repeat the above procedure and indicate to the bowler that this is a final warning. Both the above caution and final warning shall continue to apply even though the bowler may later change ends.

(c) Should there be any further repetition by the same bowler in that innings, the umpire shall:

    (i) call and signal "No-ball".

    (ii) direct the captain, when the ball is dead, to take the bowler off forthwith. The over shall be completed by another bowler, who shall neither have bowled the previous over nor be allowed to bowl the next over. The bowler thus taken off shall not be allowed to bowl again in that innings.

    (iii) report the occurrence to the other umpire, the batsmen and, as soon as practicable, the captain of the batting side.

    (iv) report the occurrence, with the other umpire, as soon as possible to the Executive of the fielding side and to any governing body responsible for the match, who shall take such action as is considered appropriate against the captain and bowler concerned.

8. Deliberate Bowling of High Full-Pitched Balls

If the umpire considers that a high full pitch which is deemed to be dangerous and unfair, as defined in 6(b) above, was deliberately bowled, then the caution and warning prescribed in 7 above shall be dispensed with. The umpire shall:

(a) call and signal "No-ball".

(b) direct the captain, when the ball is dead, to take the bowler off forthwith.

(c) implement the remainder of the procedure as laid down in 7(c) above.

9. Time-Wasting by the Fielding Side

It is unfair for any member of the fielding side to waste time.

(a) If the captain of the fielding side wastes time, or allows any member of his side to waste time, or if the progress of an over is unnecessarily slow, at the first instance the umpire shall call and signal "Dead ball" if necessary and

    (i) warn the captain, and indicate that this is a first and final warning.

    (ii) inform the other umpire and the batsmen of what has occurred.

(b) If there is any further waste of time in that innings, by any member of the fielding side, the umpire shall either

    (i) if the waste of time is not during the course of an over, award five penalty runs to the batting side. See 17 below, or

    (ii) if the waste of time is during the course of an over, when the ball is dead, direct the captain to take the bowler off forthwith. If applicable, the over shall be completed by another bowler, who shall neither have bowled the previous over nor be allowed to bowl the next over. The bowler thus taken off shall not be allowed to bowl again in that innings.

    (iii) inform the other umpire, the batsmen and, as soon as practicable, the captain of the batting side of what has occurred.

    (iv) report the occurrence, with the other umpire, as soon as possible to the executive of the fielding side and to any governing body responsible for the match, who shall take such action as is considered appropriate against the captain and team concerned.

10. Batsman Wasting Time

It is unfair for a batsman to waste time. In normal circumstances the striker should always be ready to take strike when the bowler is ready to start his run-up.

(a) Should either batsman waste time by failing to meet this requirement, or in any other way, the following procedure shall be adopted. At the first instance, either before the bowler starts his run-up or when the ball is dead, as appropriate, the umpire shall:

    (i) warn the batsman and indicate that this is a first and final warning. This warning shall continue to apply throughout the innings. The umpire shall so inform each incoming batsman.

    (ii) inform the other umpire, the other batsman and the captain of the fielding side of what has occurred.

    (iii) inform the captain of the batting side as soon as practicable.

(b) if there is any further time wasting by any batsman in that innings, the umpire shall, at the appropriate time while the ball is dead:

    (i) award five penalty runs to the fielding side. See 17 below.

    (ii) inform the other umpire, the other batsman, the captain of the fielding side and, as soon as practicable, the captain of the batting side of what has occurred.

    (iii) report the occurrence, with the other umpire, as soon as possible to the executive of the batting side and to any governing body responsible for the match, who shall take such action as is considered appropriate against the captain and player or players and, if appropriate, the team concerned.

11. Damaging the Pitch – Area to be Protected

(a) It is incumbent on all players to avoid unnecessary damage to the pitch. It is unfair for any player to cause deliberate damage to the pitch.

(b) An area of the pitch, to be referred to as "the protected area", is defined as that area contained within a rectangle bounded at each end by imaginary lines parallel to the popping creases and 5ft/1.52m in front of each and on the sides by imaginary lines, one each side of the imaginary line joining the centres of the two middle stumps, each parallel to it and 1ft/30.48cm from it.

12. Bowler Running on the Protected Area After Delivering the Ball

(a) If the bowler, after delivering the ball, runs on the protected area as defined in 11(b) above, the umpire shall at the first instance, and when the ball is dead:

  (i) caution the bowler. This caution shall continue to apply throughout the innings.

  (ii) inform the other umpire, the captain of the fielding side and the batsmen of what has occurred.

(b) If, in that innings, the same bowler runs on the protected area again after delivering the ball, the umpire shall repeat the above procedure, indicating that this is a final warning.

(c) If, in that innings, the same bowler runs on the protected area a third time after delivering the ball, when the ball is dead the umpire shall:

  (i) direct the captain of the fielding side to take the bowler off forthwith. If applicable, the over shall be completed by another bowler, who shall neither have bowled the previous over nor be allowed to bowl the next over. The bowler thus taken off shall not be allowed to bowl again in that innings.

  (ii) inform the other umpire, the batsmen and, as soon as practicable, the captain of the batting side of what has occurred.

  (iii) report the occurrence, with the other umpire, as soon as possible to the executive of the fielding side and to any governing body responsible for the match, who shall take such action as is considered appropriate against the captain and bowler concerned.

13. Fielder Damaging the Pitch

(a) If any fielder causes avoidable damage to the pitch, other than as in 12(a) above, at the first instance the umpire shall, when the ball is dead:

  (i) caution the captain of the fielding side, indicating that this is a first and final warning. This caution shall continue to apply throughout the innings.

  (ii) inform the other umpire and the batsmen.

(b) If there is any further avoidable damage to the pitch by any fielder in that innings, the umpire shall, when the ball is dead:

  (i) award five penalty runs to the batting side. See 17 below.

  (ii) inform the other umpire, the batsmen, the captain of the fielding side and, as soon as practicable, the captain of the batting side of what has occurred.

  (iii) report the occurrence, with the other umpire, as soon as possible to the executive of the fielding side and any governing body responsible for the match, who shall take such action as is considered appropriate against the captain and player or players concerned.

14. Batsman Damaging the Pitch

(a) If either batsman causes avoidable damage to the pitch, at the first instance the umpire shall, when the ball is dead:

  (i) caution the batsman. This caution shall continue to apply throughout the innings. The umpire shall so inform each incoming batsman.

  (ii) inform the other umpire, the other batsman, the captain of the fielding side and, as soon as practicable, the captain of the batting side.

(b) If there is a second instance of avoidable damage to the pitch by any batsman in that innings:

  (i) the umpire shall repeat the above procedure, indicating that this is a final warning.

  (ii) additionally he shall disallow all runs to the batting side from that delivery other than the penalty for a no-ball or a wide, if applicable. The batsmen shall return to their original ends.

(c) If there is any further avoidable damage to the pitch by any batsman in that innings, the umpire shall, when the ball is dead:

    (i) disallow all runs to the batting side from that delivery other than the penalty for a no-ball or a wide, if applicable.

    (ii) additionally award five penalty runs to the fielding side. See 17 below.

    (iii) inform the other umpire, the other batsman, the captain of the fielding side and, as soon as practicable, the captain of the batting side of what has occurred.

    (iv) report the occurrence, with the other umpire, as soon as possible to the executive of the batting side and any governing body responsible for the match, who shall take such action as is considered appropriate against the captain and player or players concerned.

15. Bowler Attempting to Run Out Non-striker Before Delivery

The bowler is permitted, before entering his delivery stride, to attempt to run out the non-striker. The ball shall not count in the over. The umpire shall call and signal "Dead ball" as soon as possible if the bowler fails in the attempt to run out the non-striker.

16. Batsmen Stealing a Run

It is unfair for the batsmen to attempt to steal a run during the bowler's run up. Unless the bowler attempts to run out either batsman – see 15 above and Law 24.4 (Bowler Throwing Towards Striker's End Before Delivery) – the umpire shall:

    (i) call and signal "Dead ball" as soon as the batsmen cross in any such attempt.

    (ii) return the batsmen to their original ends.

    (iii) award five penalty runs to the fielding side. See 17 below.

    (iv) inform the other umpire, the batsmen, the captain of the fielding side and, as soon as practicable, the captain of the batting side of the reason for the action taken.

    (v) report the occurrence, with the other umpire, as soon as possible to the executive of the batting side and any governing body responsible for the match, who shall take such action as is considered appropriate against the captain and player or players concerned.

17. Penalty Runs

(a) When penalty runs are awarded to either side, when the ball is dead the umpire shall signal the penalty runs to the scorers as laid down in Law 3.14 (Signals).

(b) Notwithstanding the provisions of Law 21.6 (Winning Hit or Extras), penalty runs shall be awarded in each case where the Laws require the award. Note, however, that the restrictions on awarding penalty runs in Laws 26.3 (Leg-Byes Not to Be Awarded), 34.4(d) (Runs Permitted From Ball Struck Lawfully More Than Once) and Law 41.4 (Penalty Runs Not to Be Awarded) will apply.

(c) When five penalty runs are awarded to the batting side, under either Law 2.6 (Player Returning Without Permission) or Law 41 (The Fielder) or under 3, 4, 5, 9 or 13 above, then:

    (i) they shall be scored as penalty extras and shall be in addition to any other penalties.

    (ii) they shall not be regarded as runs scored from either the immediately preceding delivery or the following delivery, and shall be in addition to any runs from those deliveries.

    (iii) the batsmen shall not change ends solely by reason of the five-run penalty.

(d) When five penalty runs are awarded to the fielding side, under 18.5(b) (Deliberate Short Runs), or under 10, 14 or 16 above, they shall be added as penalty extras to that side's total of runs in its most recently completed innings. If the fielding side has not completed an innings, the five penalty extras shall be added to its next innings.

18. Players' Conduct

If there is any breach of the Spirit of the Game by a player failing to comply with the instructions of an umpire, or criticising his decisions by word or action, or showing dissent, or generally behaving in a manner which might bring the game into disrepute, the umpire concerned shall immediately report the matter to the other umpire.

The umpires together shall:

(i) inform the player's captain of the occurrence, instructing the latter to take action.

(ii) warn him of the gravity of the offence, and tell him that it will be reported to higher authority.

(iii) report the occurrence as soon as possible to the executive of the player's team and any governing body responsible for the match, who shall take such action as is considered appropriate against the captain and player or players, and, if appropriate, the team concerned.

REGULATIONS OF THE INTERNATIONAL CRICKET COUNCIL

Extracts

1. Standard Playing Conditions

In 2001, the ICC Cricket Committee amended its standard playing conditions for all Tests and one-day internationals to include the new Laws of Cricket. The following playing conditions were to apply for three years from September 1, 2001:

Duration of Test Matches

Test matches shall be of five days' scheduled duration and of two innings per side. The two participating countries may:

(a) Provide for a rest day during the match, and/or a reserve day after the scheduled days of play.

(b) Play on any scheduled rest day, conditions and circumstances permitting, should a full day's play be lost on any day prior to the rest day.

(c) Play on any scheduled reserve day, conditions and circumstances permitting, should a full day's play be lost on any day. Play shall not take place on more than five days.

(d) Make up time lost in excess of five minutes in each day's play due to circumstances outside the game, other than acts of God.

Hours of Play, Intervals and Minimum Overs in the Day

1. Start and cessation times shall be determined by the home board, subject to there being six hours scheduled for play per day (Pakistan a minimum of five and a half hours).

(a) Play shall continue on each day until the completion of a minimum number of overs or until the scheduled or rescheduled cessation time, whichever is the later. The minimum number of overs to be completed, unless an innings ends or an interruption occurs, shall be:

(i) on days other than the last day - a minimum of 90 overs (or a minimum of 15 overs per hour).

(ii) on the last day - a minimum of 75 overs (or 15 overs per hour) for playing time other than the last hour when a minimum of 15 overs shall be bowled. All calculations with regard to suspensions of play or the start of a new innings shall be based on one over for each full four minutes. If, however, at any time after 30 minutes of the last hour have elapsed both captains (the batsmen at the wicket may act for their captain) accept that there is no prospect of a result to the match, they may agree to cease play at that time.

(iii) Subject to weather and light, except in the last hour of the match, in the event of play being suspended for any reason other than normal intervals, the playing time on that day shall be extended by the amount of time lost up to a maximum of one hour. The minimum number of overs to be bowled shall be in accordance with the provisions of this clause (i.e. a minimum of 15 overs per hour).

(iv) If any time is lost and cannot be made up under (a)(iii), additional time of up to a maximum of one hour per day shall be added to the scheduled playing hours for the next day, and subsequent day(s) as required. Where appropriate, the first 30 minutes (or less) of this additional time shall be added before the scheduled start of the first session and the remainder to the last session. Where it is not possible to add this time before the scheduled start, the timing of the lunch and tea intervals will be adjusted to provide a scheduled two-and-a-half-hour session time. On any day's play, except the last day, when the scheduled hours have been completed but the required number of overs have not been bowled, and weather or bad light causes play to be abandoned, the remaining overs shall be made up on the next or subsequent days. On any one day, a maximum of 15 additional overs shall be permitted.

(b) When an innings ends, a minimum number of overs shall be bowled from the start of the new innings. The number of overs to be bowled shall be calculated at the rate of one over for each full four minutes to enable a minimum of 90 overs to be bowled in a day. The last hour of the match shall be excluded from this calculation (see (a) (ii)).

Where a change of innings occurs during a day's play, in the event of the team bowling second being unable to complete its overs by the scheduled cessation time, play shall continue until the required number of overs have been completed.

2. The umpires may decide to play 30 minutes (a minimum eight overs) extra time at the end of any day (other than the last day) if requested by either captain if, in the umpires' opinion, it would bring about a definite result on that day. If the umpires do not believe a result can be achieved, no extra time shall be allowed. If it is decided to play such extra time, the whole period shall be played out even though the possibility of finishing the match may have disappeared before the full period has expired. Only the actual amount of playing time up to the maximum 30 minutes' extra time by which play is extended on any day shall be deducted from the total number of hours of play remaining and the match shall end earlier on the final day by that amount of time.

Use of Lights

If, in the opinion of the umpires, natural light is deteriorating to an unfit level, they shall authorise the ground authorities to use the available artificial lighting so that the match can continue in acceptable conditions. The lights are only to be used to enable a full day's play to be completed as provided for in Clause 1 above. In the event of power failure or lights malfunction, the existing provisions of Clause 1 shall apply.

Dangerous and Unfair Bowling: The Bowling of Fast, Short-Pitched Balls: Law 42.6

1.   (a) A bowler shall be limited to two fast, short-pitched deliveries per over.

(b) A fast, short-pitched ball is defined as a ball which passes or would have passed above the shoulder height of the batsman standing upright at the crease, but not clearly above the batsman's head so that it is so high it prevents him from being able to hit it with his bat by means of a normal cricket stroke.

(c) The umpire at the bowler's end shall advise the bowler and the batsman on strike when each fast short-pitched ball has been bowled.

(d) For the purpose of this regulation, a ball that passes clearly above head height, other than a fast, short-pitched ball, that prevents the batsman from being able to hit it with his bat by means of a normal cricket stroke shall be a no-ball.

(e) Any fast, short-pitched delivery called no-ball under this condition shall count as one of the allowable short-pitched deliveries in that over.

2. In the event of a bowler bowling more than two fast, short-pitched deliveries in an over, the umpire at the bowler's end shall call and signal "no-ball" on each occasion. The umpire shall call and signal "no-ball" and then tap the head with the other hand.

If a bowler delivers a third fast, short-pitched ball in one over, the umpire must call no-ball and then invoke the procedures of caution, final warning, action against the bowler and reporting as set out in Law 42.7. The umpires will report the matter to the ICC referee who shall take such action as is considered appropriate against the captain and bowler concerned. The above Regulation is not a substitute for Law 42.6 (as amended below), which umpires are able to apply at any time:

The bowling of fast, short-pitched balls is unfair if the umpire at the bowler's end considers that, by their repetition and taking into account their length, height and direction, they are likely to inflict physical injury on the striker, irrespective of the protective clothing and equipment he may be wearing. The relative skill of the striker shall also be taken into consideration.

The umpire at the bowler's end shall adopt the procedures of caution, final warning, action against the bowler and reporting as set out in Law 42.7. The ICC referee shall take any further action considered appropriate against the captain and bowler concerned.

New Ball: Law 5.4

The captain of the fielding side shall have the choice of taking a new ball any time after 80 overs have been bowled with the previous ball. The umpires shall indicate to the batsmen and the scorers whenever a new ball is taken into play.

Ball Lost or Becoming Unfit for Play: Law 5.5

The following shall apply in addition to Law 5.5:

> However, if the ball needs to be replaced after 110 overs for any of the reasons above, it shall be replaced by a new ball. If the ball is to be replaced, the umpires shall inform the batsmen.

Judging a Wide: Law 25.1

Law 25.1 will apply, but in addition:

> For bowlers attempting to utilise the rough outside a batsman's leg stump, not necessarily as a negative tactic, the strict limited-overs wide interpretation shall be applied. For bowlers whom umpires consider to be bowling down the leg side as a negative tactic, the strict limited-overs wide interpretation shall be applied.

Practice on the Field: Law 17

In addition to Law 17.1:

> The use of the square for practice on any day of any match will be restricted to any netted practice area on the square set aside for that purpose.

Fieldsman Leaving the Field: Law 2.5

If a fielder fails to take the field with his side at the start of the match or at any later time, or leaves the field during a session of play, the umpire shall be informed of the reason for his absence, and he shall not thereafter come on to the field during a session without the consent of the umpire. The umpire shall give such consent as soon as practicable. If the player is absent from the field for more than eight minutes, he shall not be permitted to bowl in that innings after his return until he has been on the field for at least that length of playing time for which he was absent. In the event of a follow-on, this restriction will, if necessary, continue into the second innings. Nor shall he be permitted to bat unless or until, in the aggregate, he has returned to the field and/or his side's innings has been in progress for at least that length of playing time for which he has been absent or, if earlier, when his side has lost five wickets. The restrictions shall not apply if he has suffered an external blow (as opposed to an internal injury such as a pulled muscle) while participating earlier in the match and consequently been forced to leave the field, nor if he has been absent for exceptional and acceptable reasons (other than injury or illness).

ICC CODE OF CONDUCT

1. Players and/or team officials shall at all times conduct play within the spirit of the game as well as within the Laws of cricket, and the captains are responsible at all times for ensuring that this is adhered to.

2. Players and/or team officials shall at no time engage in conduct unbecoming to their status which could bring them or the game of cricket into disrepute.

3. Players and/or team officials shall be required to report to the captain and/or team manager or to a senior board official or to the Anti-Corruption and Security Unit any approach made to them by a bookmaker or any other corrupt approach or knowledge of such approach made to any other player or team official.

4. Players and/or team officials shall not bet on matches nor otherwise engage in any conduct of the nature described in the paragraphs below. For conduct in breach of this rule, the penalties to be considered are set out below, for individuals who have:

> i. Bet on any match or series of matches, or on any connected event, in which such player, umpire, referee, team official or administrator took part or in which the Member country or any such individual was represented (penalty (a));

> ii. Induced or encouraged any other person to bet on any match or series of matches or on any connected event or to offer the facility for such bets to be placed (penalty (b));

> iii. Gambled or entered into any other form of financial speculation on any match or on any connected event (penalty (a));

> iv. Induced or encouraged any other person to gamble or enter into any other form of financial speculation on any match or any connected event (penalty (b));

v. Was a party to contriving or attempting to contrive the result of any match or the occurrence of any connected event (penalty (c));

vi. Failed to perform on his merits in any match owing to an arrangement relating to betting on the outcome of any match or on the occurrence of any connected event (penalty (c));

vii. Induced or encouraged any other player not to perform on his merits in any match owing to any such arrangement (penalty (c));

viii. Received from another person any money, benefit or other reward (whether financial or otherwise) for the provision of any information concerning the weather, the teams, the state of the ground, the status of, or the outcome of, any match or the occurrence of any connected event unless such information has been provided to a newspaper or other form of media in accordance with an obligation entered into in the normal course and disclosed in advance to the cricket authority of the relevant Member country (penalty (b));

ix. Received any money, benefit or other reward (whether financial or otherwise) which could bring him or the game of cricket into disrepute (penalty (d));

x. Provided any money, benefit or other reward (whether financial or otherwise) which could bring the game of cricket into disrepute (penalty (d));

xi. Received any approaches from another person to engage in conduct such as that described above, and has failed to disclose the same to his captain or team manager, or to a senior board official or to the Anti-Corruption and Security Unit (penalty (e)); or

xii. Is aware that any other player or individual has engaged in conduct, or received approaches, such as described above, and has failed to disclose the same to his captain or team manager, or to a senior board official or to the Anti-Corruption and Security Unit (penalty (e));

xiii. Has received or is aware that any other person has received threats of any nature which might induce him to engage in conduct, or acquiesce in any proposal made by an approach, such as described above, and has failed to disclose the same to his captain or team manager, or to a senior board official or to the Anti-Corruption and Security Unit (penalty (e));.

xiv. Has engaged in any conduct which, in the opinion of the Executive Board, relates directly or indirectly to any of the above paragraphs (i to xiii) and is prejudicial to the interests of the game of cricket (penalty (e)).

Penalties:

(a) Ban for a minimum of two years and a maximum of five years. In addition, a fine may be imposed, the amount to be assessed in the circumstances.

(b) Ban for a minimum of two years and a maximum of five years if a bet was placed directly or indirectly for the benefit of the individual; otherwise, a ban for a minimum of 12 months. In addition, a fine may be imposed, the amount to be assessed in the circumstances.

(c) Ban for life (a minimum of 20 years).

(d) Ban for a minimum of two years and a maximum of life. In addition, a fine may be imposed, the amount to be assessed in the circumstances.

(e) Ban for a minimum of one year and a maximum of five years. In addition, a fine may be imposed, the amount to be assessed in the circumstances.

5. A valid defence may be made to a charge in respect of any prohibited conduct in paragraphs 4 (xi) to (xiii) above if a person proves that this conduct was the result of an honest and reasonable belief that there was a serious threat to the life or safety of himself or any member of his family.

6. Players and/or team officials shall not use or in any way be concerned in the use or distribution of illegal drugs. Illegal drugs shall mean those drugs which are classified as unlawful in the player's or team official's home country or in the country in which he is touring. Any such conduct shall constitute behaviour prohibited under paragraph 2 and shall be dealt with as such. Players and team officials shall also be subject to any doping policy which is applied by their home board and such policies which are introduced for ICC events. Any breach of such doping policy shall be dealt with under the terms of such policy itself and not under this code.

CRICKET AUSTRALIA
PLAYING CONDITIONS, 2003-04

Note: This section is an abridged version of the full Playing Conditions Booklet of Cricket Australia. Some parts have been omitted.

TEST MATCH
PLAYING CONDITIONS

Except as modified for one-day internationals and in the section on other tour matches, these playing conditions shall apply to all tour matches.

1. Laws of Cricket

Except as varied hereunder the Laws of Cricket (2000 Code 2nd Edition – 2003) shall apply.

2. Duration of Matches

Test matches shall be of five days' scheduled duration, and of two innings per side. The two participating countries may:

    (a)   Provide for a rest day during the match, and/or a reserve day after the scheduled days of play.

    (b)   Play on any scheduled rest day, conditions and circumstances permitting, should a full day's play be lost on any day prior to the rest day.

    (c)   Play on any scheduled reserve day, conditions and circumstances permitting, should a full day's play be lost on any day. Play shall not take place on more than five days.

    (d)   Make up time lost in excess of five minutes in each day's play due to circumstances outside the game other than acts of God.

Other tour matches shall be as scheduled as in the tour program authorised by Cricket Australia.

3. Hours of Play, Intervals and Minimum Overs in the Day

3.1   Start and Cessation Times

3.1.1   Test Series

Australia v Zimbabwe

Western Australia

10.00 a.m.–12.00 p.m.	Session 1
12.00 p.m.–12.40 p.m.	Lunch
12.40 p.m.–2.40 p.m.	Session 2
2.40 p.m.–3.00 p.m.	Tea
3.00 p.m.–5.00 p.m.	Session 3

New South Wales

10.30 a.m.–12.30 p.m.	Session 1
12.30 p.m.–1.10 p.m.	Lunch
1.10 p.m.–3.10 p.m.	Session 2
3.10 p.m.–3.30 p.m.	Tea
3.30 p.m.–5.30 p.m.	Session 3

Australia vs India
New South Wales, South Australia, Victoria

11.00 a.m.–1.00 p.m.	Session 1
1.00 p.m.–1.40 p.m.	Lunch
1.40 p.m.–3.40 p.m.	Session 2
3.40 p.m.–4.00 p.m.	Tea
4.00 p.m.–6.00 p.m.	Session 3

Queensland

10.00 a.m.–12.00 p.m.	Session 1
12.00 p.m.–12.40 p.m.	Lunch
12.40 p.m.–2.40 p.m.	Session 2
2.40 p.m.–3.00 p.m.	Tea
3.00 p.m.–5.00 p.m.	Session 3

3.2   Other Tour Matches

Wherever possible, the above conditions shall apply to all matches. However, the home board with the agreement of the visiting country's board may provide for local variations for matches other than Test and One Day International matches. In the case of one-day matches, starting and finishing times (and interval times) may be altered on any scheduled playing day with the prior approval of the State authority, the Cricket Australia and the touring team Manager.

State players shall be bound by the terms of the Cricket Australia Code of Behaviour. Touring team players shall be bound by Law 42.18 and/or the terms of the ICC Code of Conduct for Players and Team Officials.

The local State Association shall appoint a representative to meet with the umpires and captains prior to the commencement of the match to secure uniform interpretation of these playing conditions and to adjudicate, if necessary, should there be any dispute.

The following playing times for tour matches will apply for the 2003–04 season:

3–5 October	**Zimbabwe vs Western Australia**	**Perth**
10.30 a.m.–12.30 p.m.	Session 1	
12.30 p.m.–1.10 p.m.	Lunch	
1.10 p.m.–3.10 p.m.	Session 2	
3.10 p.m.–3.30 p.m.	Tea	
3.30 p.m.–5.30 p.m.	Session 3	

25–27 November	**India vs Victoria**	**Melbourne**
11.00 a.m.–1.00 p.m.	Session 1	
1.00 p.m.–1.40 p.m.	Lunch	
1.40 p.m.–3.40 p.m.	Session 2	
3.40 p.m.–4.00 p.m.	Tea	
4.00 p.m.–6.00 p.m.	Session 3	

29 November–1 December	**India vs Queensland Academy XI**	**Brisbane**
10.00 a.m.–12.00 p.m.	Session 1	
12.00 p.m.–12.40 p.m.	Lunch	
12.40 p.m.–2.40 p.m.	Session 2	
2.40 p.m.–3.00 p.m.	Tea	
3.00 p.m.–5.00 p.m.	Session 3	

15–17 November	**Australia A vs India**	**Hobart**
11.00 a.m.–1.00 p.m.	Session 1	
1.00 p.m.–1.40 p.m.	Lunch	
1.40 p.m.–3.40 p.m.	Session 2	
3.40 p.m.–4.00 p.m.	Tea	
4.00 p.m.–6.00 p.m.	Session 3	

1 January	**Australia A vs Zimbabwe**	**Perth**
1.30 p.m.–5.00 p.m.	Session 1	
5.00 p.m.–5.45 p.m.	Interval	
5.45 p.m.–9.15 p.m.	Session 2	

4 January	WA vs Zimbabwe	Perth
2.30 p.m.–6.00 p.m.	Session 1	
6.00 p.m.–6.45 p.m.	Interval	
6.45 p.m.–10.15 p.m.	Session2	

7 January	Australia A vs Zimbabwe	Adelaide
1.45 p.m.–5.15 p.m.	Session 1	
5.15 p.m.–6.00 p.m.	Interval	
6.00 p.m.–9.30 p.m.	Session 2	

28 January	India vs Prime Minister's XI	Canberra
10.00 a.m.–1.30 p.m.	Session 1	
1.30 p.m.–2.15 p.m.	Interval	
2.15 p.m.–5.45 p.m.	Session 2	

4. Law 5 – The Ball

ICC regulations shall apply as regards to the ball. The Kookaburra "Turf" brand red ball has been approved by Cricket Australia.

VB SERIES
PLAYING CONDITIONS

Test Match Playing Conditions and the Laws of Cricket (2000 Code 2nd Edition – 2003) shall apply, except as varied below.

1. Duration of Matches

One-day international matches shall be of one day's scheduled duration. The participating countries in a series may provide for a reserve day on which an incomplete match may be replayed (but not continued from the scheduled day). The matches will consist of one innings per side and each innings will be limited to 50 six-ball overs. A minimum of 25 overs per team shall constitute a match.

2. Hours of Play and Intervals

2.1 Start and Cessation Times

Day Matches

Tasmania

10.00 a.m.–1.30 p.m.	Session 1
1.30 p.m.–2.15 p.m.	Interval
2.15 p.m.–5.45 p.m.	Session 2

Western Austalia

10.30 a.m.–2.00 p.m.	Session 1
2.00 p.m.–2.45 p.m.	Interval
2.45 p.m.–6.15 p.m.	Session 2

Day/Night Matches

Queensland

1.15 p.m.–4.45 p.m.	Session 1
4.45 p.m.–5.30 p.m.	Interval
5.30 p.m.–9.00 p.m.	Session 2

Western Australia

1.30 p.m.–5.00 p.m.	Session 1
5.00 p.m.–5.45 p.m.	Interval
5.45 p.m.–9.15 p.m.	Session 2

South Australia

1.45 p.m.–5.15 p.m.	Session 1
5.15 p.m.–6.00 p.m.	Interval
6.00 p.m.–9.30 p.m.	Session 2

New South Wales, Victoria

2.15 p.m.–5.45 p.m.	Session 1
5.45 p.m.–6.30 p.m.	Interval
6.30 p.m.–10.00 p.m.	Session 2

3.2 Extra Time

Subject to agreement by the participating countries, provision has been made for up to 15 minutes of extra playing time in day matches and up to 45 minutes in day/night matches.

4. The Ball

Cricket Australia shall provide cricket balls of an approved standard for One Day International cricket and spare used balls for changing during a match, which shall also be of the same brand. Kookaburra "Turf" brand white balls as approved by Cricket Australia will be used in all matches.

5. Finals Series

The two teams with highest number of points at the completion of the preliminary matches shall play in the finals series.

In the event of a drawn final, the prizemoney will be shared equally between the two competing teams.

In the best of three final series, a third match will always be played where neither team has a clear two match advantage after the scheduled completion of the second match.

For the determination of the final series no reference will be made to preliminary match results, wins or run rates. In the event of a tied final series, the prizemoney will be shared equally between the two competing teams.

PURA CUP
PLAYING CONDITIONS

1. Laws of Cricket

Except as varied hereunder the Laws of Cricket (2000 Code 2nd Edition – 2003) shall apply.

2. Duration of Matches

Matches shall be four days scheduled duration.

3. Hours of Play and Intervals

3.1 Start and Cessation Times

New South Wales, South Australia, Tasmania, Victoria, Western Australia

11.00 a.m.–1.00 p.m.	Session 1
1.00 p.m.–1.40 p.m.	Lunch
1.40 p.m.–3.40 p.m.	Session 2
3.40 p.m.–4.00 p.m.	Tea
4.00 p.m.–6.00 p.m.	Session 3

Queensland

10.00 a.m.–12.00 p.m.	Session 1
12.00 p.m. –12.40 p.m.	Lunch
12.40 p.m.–2.40 p.m.	Session 2
2.40 p.m.–3.00 p.m.	Tea
3.00 p.m.–5.00 p.m.	Session 3

The following playing times shall apply in these matches.

4–7 March   Western Australia vs South Australia

10.30 a.m.–12.30 p.m.	Session 1
12.30 p.m.–1.10 p.m.	Lunch
1.10 p.m.–3.10 p.m.	Session 2
3.10 p.m.–3.30 p.m.	Tea
3.30 p.m.–5.30 p.m.	Session 3

3.2 Daylight Saving Time

Daylight saving will commence on 27 October 2002 and finish on 30 March 2003.

3.3 Hours of Play

Any state wishing to change the hours of play must first obtain approval from Cricket Australia.

4. Minimum Overs in the Day

(a) Play shall continue on each day until the completion of a minimum number of overs or until the scheduled or re-scheduled cessation time, whichever is the later.

The minimum number of overs to be completed, unless an innings ends or an interruption occurs, shall be:

(i) on days other than the last day – a minimum of 96 overs (or a minimum of 16 overs per hour).

(ii) on the last day – a minimum of 80 overs (or a minimum of 16 overs per hour) for playing time other than the last hour of the match when Clause (e) below shall apply.

(iii) Additional Hour: Subject to weather and light, except in the last hour of the match, in the event of play being suspended for any reason other than normal intervals, the playing time on that day shall be extended by the amount of time lost up to a maximum of one hour. In these circumstances, the minimum number of overs to be bowled shall be in accordance with the provisions of this clause i.e. a minimum of 16 overs per hour and the cessation time shall be rescheduled accordingly.

(iv) If play has been suspended for 30 minutes or more prior to the commencement of the scheduled or rescheduled tea interval, the tea interval shall be delayed for half an hour.

(v) If any time and overs are lost and cannot be made up under (iii) above, additional time and overs of up to a maximum of one hour per day (16 overs) shall be added to the scheduled playing hours for the next day, and subsequent day(s) as required (to make up as much lost time as possible). Where appropriate the first 30 minutes (or less) of this additional time shall be added prior to the scheduled start of the first session, and the remainder shall be added to the last session.

In circumstances where it is not possible to add this additional time prior to the scheduled start of the first session, the timing of the lunch and tea intervals will be adjusted to provide a scheduled two hour session and not affect the start time.

On any day's play, except the last day, when the scheduled hours of play have been completed, but the required number of overs have not been bowled and weather or bad light causes play for that day to be abandoned, the remaining overs on that day shall be made up on the next or subsequent days (refer (v) above for timings). On any one day, a maximum of 16 additional overs shall be permitted.

When additional time is added to subsequent day(s), no scheduled days play shall exceed 7 hours. The length of each session of play is subject to the provisions of Law 15.

Under Law 15.5 timings can be altered at any time on any day if playing time is lost, not necessarily on that day. The captains, umpires and the local State Association can agree different timings under those circumstances before play starts on any day.

(b) When an innings ends a minimum number of overs shall be bowled from the start of the new innings. The last hour of the match shall be excluded from this calculation when Clause (e) shall apply.

Where there is a change of innings during a day's play (except at lunch or tea or when play is suspended due to unfit ground, weather or light conditions or for exceptional circumstances), 2 overs will be deducted from the minimum number of overs to be bowled.

(c) Except in the last hour of the match, for which Clause (e) makes provision, if play is suspended due to adverse weather or light for more than one hour in aggregate on any day, the minimum number of overs shall be reduced by one over for each full 3.75 minutes of the aggregate playing time lost on that day.

(d) On the last day, if any of the minimum of 80 overs, or as recalculated, have not been bowled when one hour of scheduled playing time remains, the last hour of the match for the purposes of Clause (e) shall be the hour immediately following the completion of those overs.

(e) Laws 16.6, 16.7 and 16.8 will apply except that a minimum of 16 overs shall be bowled in the last hour and all calculations with regard to suspensions of play or the start of a new innings shall be based on one over for each full 3.75 minutes (refer (i) below). If, however, at any time after 30 minutes of the last hour have elapsed both Captains (the batsmen at the wicket may act for their Captain) accept that there is no prospect of a result to the match, they may agree to cease play at that time.

(f) Notwithstanding any other provision, there shall be no further play on any day, other than the last day, if a wicket falls or a batsman retires or if the players have occasion to leave the field during the last minimum over within 2 minutes of the scheduled or re-scheduled cessation time or thereafter.

(g) An over completed on resumption of a new day's play shall be disregarded in calculating minimum overs for that day.

(h) Except on the final day, if in the event of ground, weather or light conditions causing a suspension of play and/or if the players are already off the field at the re-scheduled cessation time or any time thereafter, stumps shall be drawn.

(i) Fractions are to be ignored in all calculations re the number of overs except where there is a change of innings in a day's play, when the over in progress at the conclusion shall be rounded up.

(j) The scoreboard shall show:
   – the total number of overs bowled with the ball currently in use: and
   – the minimum number of overs remaining to be bowled in a day;
   – the number of overs above or below the target overs for the innings.

(k) Penalties shall apply for not achieving over rates.

Subject to the provisions of Clause 4 (Minimum Overs in the Day), over rates shall be assessed on 16 overs per hour, ie a minimum of 96 overs in a six hour day, subject to the following deductions:

1 minute	for every wicket taken
4 minutes	for one drinks break taken in any session
actual time	where treatment by authorised medical personnel is required on the ground and/or for a player leaving the field due to serious injury.

Overs will be calculated at the end of the match. For each over short of the target number 0.5 shall be deducted from the team's match points.

For the purpose of calculation of penalties.

   (a) the scheduled last hour of the match, as defined in clause 4 (e) shall be excluded
   (b) a maximum allowance of 20 overs in any hour shall apply

In the event of a match finishing within 3 scheduled playing days, penalties for not achieving the required over rates shall not apply, regardless of the hours played on those days.

A Commissioner appointed by Cricket Australia will hear and determine all appeals against penalties imposed.

For the purpose of determining whether the fielding side has fallen short of the target number of overs, umpires may take into account any factor they consider relevant including whether inclement weather has adversely affected the ability of the fielding side to comply with the required over rate.

Appeals shall be lodged within 14 days of the completion of the match.

The onus shall be on the appellant to prove that the umpires have erred in their assessment of time allowances. Video evidence where available may be produced by the appellant in support of the appeal.

Umpires will be required to record all delays and stoppages on the appropriate form.

5. Extra Time

The umpires may decide to play 30 minutes (a minimum of eight overs) extra time at the end of any day (other than the last day) if requested by either captain if, in the umpires' opinion, it would bring about an outright result on that day (this is in addition to the maximum one hour's extra time provided for in 4(a) (iii) above). If the umpires do not believe an outright result can be achieved, no extra time shall be allowed.

If it is decided to play such extra time on one or more of these days, the whole period (30 minutes or a minimum of eight overs) shall be played out even though the possibility of finishing the match may have disappeared before the full period has expired.

Only the actual amount of playing time up to the maximum 30 minutes extra time by which play is extended on any day shall be deducted from the total number of hours of play remaining, and the match shall end earlier on the final day by the amount of time by which play was previously extended under this clause.

6. Use of Lights

If in the opinion of the umpires, natural light is deteriorating to an unfit level, they shall authorise the ground authorities to use the available artificial lighting so that the match can continue in acceptable conditions. If natural light improves, the artificial lights may be turned off. The lights are only to be used to enable a full day's play to be completed as provided in clauses 3, 4 and 5.

7. Luncheon Interval

Law 15.6 shall apply and the luncheon interval shall be of 40 minutes duration.

8. Tea Interval

A tea interval of 20 minutes duration will be taken from or at the conclusion of the over in progress at the agreed time for the tea interval subject to the provisions of Law 15.

9. Intervals for Drinks

The provisions of Law 15.9 shall be strictly observed except that under conditions of extreme heat the umpires may permit extra intervals for drinks.

An individual player may be given a drink either on the boundary edge or at the fall of a wicket, on the field, provided that no playing time is wasted. If individual drinks have been brought onto the field at the fall of a wicket, the fielding side must be ready to continue play as soon as the new batsman reaches the wicket. No other drinks shall be taken onto the field without the permission of the umpires.

Any player taking drinks onto the field shall be dressed in approved clothing and equipment as described in Cricket Australia Rule 11 – Wearing Apparel of Players and Umpires.

10. Time Keeping

The umpires must notify the local State Association which clock is to be followed, so that the spectators and representatives of the media may be informed. If the clock on the ground is out of order, the watches of the umpires shall determine the time.

11. Law 1.3 – Captain

The following shall apply in addition to Law 1.3 (a): The deputy must be one of the nominated players.

12. Appointment of Umpires

Cricket Australia shall appoint all umpires from its panel of umpires. The umpires for the final shall be appointed by Cricket Australia and must be members of the ICC Elite or Cricket Australia National Panels.

Cricket Australia shall also appoint a third umpire from its panel of umpires who shall act as the emergency umpire and officiate in regard to TV replays in all televised matches where the technology is available. The third umpire will officiate in regard to TV replays only when the umpires on the field have referred a decision to him in regard to hit wicket, run out and stumping appeals.

Either the on-field or third umpire shall be entitled to call for a TV replay to assist him in making a decision about whether the fieldsman had any part of his person in contact with the ball when he touched or crossed the boundary edge or whether a four or six had been scored (refer to Regulation of ICC Umpires Code of Conduct).

13. Nomination of Players

Law 1.2 shall apply except that the players nominated shall include the selected emergency fieldsman.

Subject to advice being given by the home State to the visiting State or its Team Manager, the emergency fieldsman of the home State may be released to play with his Club team, in which case the home State shall supply another emergency fieldsman to act in his stead if required.

13.1 Replacement Player

Should any player during a match be required by Cricket Australia for playing duties elsewhere, that requirement shall take precedence.

(a) The player's State Association will then be able to select a like player as the replacement for the remainder of the match concerned.

(b) The player's State Association will submit nominations for the replacement player to the opposing team captain for approval that must not be unreasonably withheld.

(c) If after a replacement player has been chosen, the replaced player's services are no longer required by Cricket Australia, the player may resume his place in the team only if his replacement has not either batted or bowled in his absence. Otherwise the player may take no further part in the match and the replacement player must continue in his stead.

14. Substitutes

14.1 Law 2.5 – Fielder Absent or Leaving the Field – Shall Apply as Modified:

(a) If a fielder fails to take the field with his side at the start of the match or at any later time, or leaves the field during a session of play, the umpire shall be informed of the reason for his absence, and he shall not thereafter come onto the field during a session of play without the consent of the umpire (See Law 2.6 as modified). The umpire shall give such consent as soon as practicable. If the player is absent from the field for longer than eight minutes:

  (i)   the player shall not be permitted to bowl in that innings after his return until he has been on the field for at least that length of playing time for which he was absent. In the event of a follow-on, this restriction will, if necessary, continue into the second innings.

  (ii)   The player shall not be permitted to bat unless or until, in the aggregate, he has returned to the field and/or his side's innings has been in progress for at least that length of playing time for which he has been absent or, if earlier, when his side has lost five wickets.

(b) The restriction in (i) and (ii) above shall not apply if the player has suffered an external blow (as opposed to an internal injury such as a pulled muscle) whilst participating earlier in the match and consequently been forced to leave the field. Nor shall it apply if the player has been absent for very exceptional and wholly acceptable reasons (other than injury or illness).

(c) This restriction shall not apply at the commencement of a new day's play.

(d) In the event of a fieldsman already being off the field at the commencement of an interruption in play through ground, weather or light conditions, he shall be allowed to count any such stoppage time as playing time, provided that he personally informs the umpires that he is fit enough to take the field had play been in progress and then takes the field on resumption of play.

14.2 Law 2.6 – Player Returning Without Permission

Law 2.6 shall apply except that the reference to "Governing Body" shall be replaced by Cricket Australia.

14.3 Injury to Player or Umpire

(a) An injured batsman who has temporarily retired, and is unable to return after the fall of the ninth wicket shall be recorded in the scorebooks as "retired – not out" and the innings shall be deemed closed.

(b) Where an injury occurs to a batsman involved in a tenth wicket partnership, a maximum of five minutes will be allowed in order for the batsman to obtain treatment. If the injury occurs within 30 minutes of a scheduled interval, the interval shall be taken immediately if the batsman is unable to resume after the five minutes. If the batsman is unable to resume after the five minutes or after the early interval, he shall be recorded in the scorebooks as "retired – not out", as described above.

(c) Where an injury occurs to an umpire, and he must leave the field for treatment, the other umpire shall officiate at the bowler's end. The local State Association shall provide a competent person to stand at the striker's end until the injured umpire is able to resume or a suitable replacement has been appointed.

15. Law 3.8 and Law 3.9 – Fitness of Ground, Weather and Light

15.1 Add the following to Law 3.8:

If conditions during a rain stoppage improve and the rain is reduced to drizzle, the umpires must consider if they would have suspended play in the first place under similar conditions. If the on-field umpires agree that the current drizzle would not have caused a stoppage, then play shall resume immediately. In these circumstances the provisions of Laws 3.9 (b) (i) and 3.9 (c) (i) shall not apply. However, should the umpires be of the opinion that a resumption of play under these circumstances would contribute to worsening ground conditions, they will resume play only with the approval of both captains.

15.2 In addition, attention is drawn to Law 3.9 (d) with regards to application of clause 15.1.

"The fact that the grass and ball are wet and slippery does not warrant the ground conditions being regarded as unreasonable or dangerous. If the umpires consider the ground is so wet or slippery as to deprive the bowler of a reasonable foothold, the fielders the power of free movement, or the batsmen the ability to play their shots and run between the wickets, then these conditions shall be regarded as so bad that it would be unreasonable for play to take place."

15.3 The umpires shall disregard any shadow on the pitch from the stadium or from any permanent object on the ground.

If a shadow from the fielder falls across the striker's half of the pitch, the fielder must remain stationary from the time the bowler commences his run-up until the striker has received the ball. In the event of a fielder moving before the striker receives the ball, the umpire shall call and signal "Dead ball" if he considers the striker has been disadvantaged by the action. The provisions of Law 23.5(a) & (b) shall apply as to whether any additional delivery is to be allowed.

16. The Ball

16.1 First quality balls approved by Cricket Australia shall be used in Pura Cup matches.

Note: The Kookaburra "Turf" brand red ball has been approved. Law 5.4 shall apply except that the fielding captain may demand a new ball after 80 overs have been bowled with the old one.

16.2 The umpires shall retain possession of the match ball(s) throughout the duration of the match when play is not actually taking place. During play, umpires shall periodically and irregularly inspect the condition of the ball and shall retain possession of it at the fall of a wicket, a drinks interval or any other disruption in play.

16.3 In the event of a ball becoming wet and soggy as a result of play continuing in inclement weather or it being affected by dew, and in the opinion of the umpires being unfit for play, the ball shall be replaced by a ball that has had a similar amount of wear, even though it has not gone out of shape. Either bowler or batsmen may raise the matter with the umpires and the umpires' decision as to a replacement or otherwise will be final.

16.4 Ball Lost or Becoming Unfit for Play

The following shall apply in addition to Law 5.5. However, if the ball needs to be replaced after 110 overs for any of the reasons above, it shall be replaced by a new ball. If the ball is to be replaced, the umpire shall inform the batsmen.

16.5 Law 5.6 Specifications, shall not apply.

17. Law 6 – The Bat

In addition to Law 6.1 the blade of the bat shall have a conventional flat face.

18. Law 7 – The Pitch

18.1 In addition to Law 7.3, the following will apply:

Captains, umpires and ground staff shall co-operate to ensure that, prior to the start of any day's play, no one bounces a ball on the pitch or strikes it with a bat to assess its condition or for any other reason, or causes damage to the pitch in any other way.

18.2 Prior to the start of play on any day, only the captain and team coach may walk on the pitch to assess its condition. Spiked footwear is not permitted.

18.3 Prior to the commencement of a day's play and during the lunch and tea intervals, one TV commentator and camera crew of the official licensed TV broadcaster/s (but not news crew) may be permitted to inspect the pitch and surrounds (without walking on the pitch or interfering with pitch preparation) subject to the following:

– a ball must not be bounced on the pitch
– a key or knife may only be inserted in the pitch in the area between the popping and bowling creases

18.4 In the event of any dispute, the local State Association will rule and their ruling will be final.

19. Law 7.4 – Changing the Pitch

19.1 Law 7.4 will not apply. In the event of a match being abandoned because of negligent pitch and/or ground preparation it is considered that the match be awarded to the visiting team.

19.2 For the purposes of this clause, the local State Association will be deemed to have been negligent if the match is abandoned as a direct or indirect result of the local State Association (or any of its employees, contractors or agents) failing to take proper precautions in the circumstances to ensure that:

(a) The pitch was properly prepared; or

(b) The pitch was properly protected against the elements or other acts of God, vandalism or foul play, machinery or equipment failure or other reasonably foreseeable events.

19.3 Cricket Australia Cricket Operations Department shall arrange and ensure that a thorough investigation of the circumstances into the abandonment of the match is conducted and that a report be presented to a forum (to be determined) for decision and penalty if appropriate.

19.4 Law 7.5 Non-Turf Pitches Shall Not Apply.

20. Law 8 – The Wickets

The following shall apply in addition to Law 8.2:

For televised matches, the local State Association may provide a slightly larger stump to accommodate the stump camera. When the larger stump is used, all three stumps must be exactly the same size.

21. Law 9.3 – The Popping Crease

Law 9.3 shall apply, except that the reference to "a minimum of 6 ft" shall be replaced by "a minimum of 15 yards".

22. Law 10 – Preparation and Maintenance of the Playing Area

22.1 Mowing the Outfield – The outfield shall be mown daily before play begins.

22.2 Maintenance of Footholds – Law 10.6 will apply but add:

The umpires shall see that wherever possible and whenever it is considered necessary, action is taken during all intervals in play to do whatever is practicable to improve the bowlers' footholds. As soon as possible after the conclusion of each day's play, bowlers' footholds will be repaired.

22.3 Watering the Outfield

In order that the condition of the outfield can be maintained throughout the duration of a match, oval managers/curators must first be granted approval by both captains and umpires to water the outfield after any day's play. Similarly, the oval manager/curator may wish to lightly water a pitch under preparation for an upcoming match. Agreement must be reached prior to the commencement of the match before any such watering will be permitted.

23. Law 11 – Covering the Pitch – Before and During a Match

In place of Laws 11.2, 11.3 and 11.4, the following shall apply:

23.1 In all matches, the pitch shall be entirely protected against rain up to the commencement of play and for the duration of the period of the match. It shall be wholly covered at the termination of each day's play or providing the weather is fine, within a period of two hours thereafter.

23.2 The covers shall be removed no earlier than 5.00 a.m. and no later than 7.00 a.m. on each morning of the match provided it is not raining at the time, but they will be replaced if rain falls prior to the commencement of play.

Note: The covers must totally protect the pitch and also the pitch surroundings to a minimum of five metres either side of the pitch and any worn or soft areas in the outfield, as well as the bowlers' run-ups to a distance of at least 10 x 10 metres.

Attention is drawn to Clause 15.

24. Drying of Pitch and Ground

24.1 Prior to tossing for choice of innings, the artificial drying of the pitch and outfield shall be at the discretion of the groundsman. Thereafter and throughout the match the drying of the outfield may be undertaken at any time by the groundsman, but the drying of the affected area of the pitch shall be carried out only on the instructions and under the supervision of the umpires. The umpires shall be empowered to have the pitch dried without reference to the captains at any time they are of the opinion that it is unfit for play.

24.2 The umpires may instruct the groundsman to use any available equipment, including any roller for the purpose of drying the pitch and making it fit for play.

Note: an absorbent roller may be used to remove water from the covers including the cover on the match pitch.

25. Law 12 – Innings

Law 12.1 (a) shall apply as modified:

(a) A match shall be two innings per side subject to the provisions of Law 13.1.

Law 12.1 (b) and 12.3 (e) shall not apply.

26. Law 13 – The Follow-On

Add the following to Law 13.1:

If the provision of clause 4 (a) (v) is applied, the additional time is regarded as part of that day's play for the purpose of Law 13.3, i.e. it is the number of days remaining and not the total number of hours available.

27. Law 17 – Practice on the Field

Add the following to Law 17.1:

The use of the square for practice on any day of any match will be restricted to any netted practice area on the square set aside for that purpose.

28. Law 18 – Scoring Runs

Law 18.5 shall apply, except that the reference to "Governing Body" shall be replaced by Cricket Australia.

29. Law 19 – Boundaries

Add the following to Law 19.1:

29.1 All boundaries must be designated by a rope or similar object of a minimum standard as authorised by Cricket Australia from time to time. Where appropriate, the rope should be a required minimum distance (three yards) inside the perimeter fencing or advertising signs. For grounds with a large playing area, the maximum length of boundary should be used before applying the minimum three yards between the boundary and the fence.

29.2 If an unauthorised person enters the playing arena and handles the ball, the umpire at the bowler's end shall be the sole judge of whether the boundary allowance should be scored, or the ball be treated as still in play, or called Dead ball if a batsman is liable to be out as a result of the unauthorised person handling the ball. See Law 19.1 (c).

29.3 Sightscreens shall be provided at both ends of all grounds. Advertising shall be permitted on the sightscreen behind the striker, providing it is removed for the subsequent over from that end.

29.4 Attention is drawn to Law 19.2 (e). Should a rope or similar object used to mark the boundary be disturbed during play, umpires, players and ground staff should cooperate to ensure that it is restored to its original position as soon as the ball is dead.

30. The Result

30.1 Match Points

(i)	For an outright win after leading on the first innings	6 Points
(ii)	For an outright win after a tie in the first innings	6 Points
(iii)	For an outright win after being behind on the first innings	6 Points
(iv)	For a tie where both teams have completed two innings (irrespective of the first innings result)	3 Points
(v)	For a first innings lead (to be retained even if beaten outright)	2 Points
(vi)	For an outright loss after leading on the first innings	2 Points
(vii)	For a tie on the first innings (and no outright result)	1 Point each
(viii)	For an outright loss after a tie in the first innings	1 Point
(ix)	For a loss on the first innings	Nil
(x)	For an outright loss after being behind on the first innings	Nil
(xi)	Abandoned or drawn matches with no first innings result	Nil
(xii)	Abandoned match due to negligence (see Clause 19)	

30.2 Law 21 shall apply with the following:

Any query on the result of the match as defined in Law 21.1, 21.3, 21.4, 21.5, 21.8, and 21.10 shall be resolved as soon as possible and a final decision made by the umpires at the close of play.

30.3 *Note:* It is possible for a team to record a negative points tally on the Pura Cup table as a result of penalties incurred under the provisions of Clause 4.

30.4 Qualifying For The Final

The two teams which have highest aggregate of points at the end of a season shall play off in a final for the Pura Cup for that season (refer Clause 58).

In the event of an equality of points the higher number of outright wins will determine the positions on the Pura Cup table.

Should there be equality in both points and wins, the positions shall be determine by quotient calculated thus:

(i) divide the total number of runs scored by a State by the total number of wickets lost by it.

(ii) divide the total number of runs scored against a State by the total number of wickets taken by it.

(iii) divide the former (i) by the latter (ii).

(iv) The team having the higher quotient shall be considered to have the better performance.

For the purpose of the calculations and for individual averages a team declaring its innings closed shall be deemed to have lost only the number of wickets which have actually fallen.

31. Law 22 – The Over

31.1 Law 22.5 shall apply with the following:

Whenever possible the third umpire or TV umpire shall liaise with the scorers and if possible inform the on-field umpires by the use of two-way radio if the over has been or is likely to be miscounted.

31.2 Law 4.3 – The Scorers – Acknowledging Signals

Law 4.3(b) is modified as follows:

Note: In the event of multiple signals by the umpires off the same delivery, the scorers shall acknowledge all signals. The umpire at the bowler's end shall direct the attention of the scorers to the signal(s) by the umpire at the striker's end, and both umpires will wait until the scorers have acknowledged all signals before allowing the game to proceed.

31.3 Maximum Overs for Medium and Pace Bowlers

(a) Definitions

  (i) Bowling Type: Bowlers of medium pace or faster (as determined by the umpires and broadly defined as one to whom the wicket-keeper would stand back, or one who is not considered a slow bowler). The umpires shall immediately notify the captains of both sides of each bowler who they determine should be treated differently to this broad definition.

  (ii) Player's Age: The player's age shall be determined as their age on 1st September preceding each cricket season (ie. Under-19 players will be 17 or 18 on 1 September; Under-17 players will be 15 or 16 on 1st September etc.) and the appropriate bowling limitations shall apply for the entire season.

(b) Notification

The team captain must indicate to the umpires on the team sheet each player to whom this playing condition applies and indicate their age.

(c) Bowling Limitations

Bowling limitations apply at the following ages:

  (i) Under-19:
      A maximum spell of eight (8) consecutive overs
      A maximum daily allocation of twenty (20) overs

  (ii) Under-17:
      A maximum spell of six (6) consecutive overs
      A maximum daily allocation of sixteen (16) overs

  (iii) Under-15:
      A maximum spell of five (5) consecutive overs
      A maximum daily allocation of ten (10) overs

  (iv) Under-14:
      A maximum spell of four (4) consecutive overs
      A maximum daily allocation of eight (8) overs

(d) Length of Break

  (i) The break between spells is to be a minimum of 60 minutes (including the lunch and tea interval and any unscheduled breaks in play).

  (ii) A bowler who has bowled a spell of less than the maximum spell permitted for their age (defined in (iii) above) may resume bowling prior to the completion of the necessary break, but this will be considered an extension of the same spell and the maximum spell limit for that age of player shall still apply. Following the completion of the extended spell, the normal break of 60 minutes between spells will apply and the break within the spell is disregarded.

  (iii) If a change of innings occurs, and a bowler commences bowling in the new innings within 60 minutes of bowling in the previous innings, this will be considered an extension of the same spell and the maximum spell limit and daily limits for that age of player shall still apply.

(iv) If any interval or interruption in play results in an over not being completed, then that part of the over bowled after the break shall constitute one over for the purposes of calculating the bowler's spell and daily limits. If this over is completed at the start of a new day's play, the over shall be considered the first over of a new spell for that bowler and the first over of the new daily limits.

(e) Change of Bowling Type

Where a bowler changes between medium pace (or faster) and slow bowling during a day's play:

(i) if the bowler begins with medium pace (or faster), the bowler is subject to the playing condition throughout the day.

(ii) if the bowler begins with slow bowling and changes to medium pace (or faster), the playing condition applies from the time of the change, and all overs of slow bowling bowled prior to the change shall not be taken into account in either the current spell or the daily limit.

(f) Management

(i) It is the responsibility of the fielding captain to ensure that this playing condition is upheld.

(ii) If the umpires become aware of breaches of this playing condition, when the ball is dead, they shall direct the captain to take the bowler off forthwith. If applicable, the over shall be completed by another bowler who shall have neither bowled the previous over nor be allowed to bowl the next over.

(iii) Should a dispute or uncertainty regarding the application of this playing condition occur during play, the umpires shall make the final decision on its application based on information available from the scorers or other sources.

32. Law 24 – No Ball

Law 24.1 (b) shall be replaced by the following:

The bowler may not deliver the ball underarm. If a bowler bowls a ball underarm, the umpire shall call and signal No ball.

33. Law 24.2 – Fair Delivery – The Arm

Law 24.2 shall apply, except that the reference to "Governing Body" shall be replaced by Cricket Australia.

34. Law 25.1 – Judging a Wide

Law 25.1 will apply with the addition of the following:

If in the umpire's opinion the bowler is attempting to utilise the rough outside a batsman's leg stump, or is bowling down the leg side as a negative tactic, the umpire will call and signal Wide ball unless the ball passes sufficiently within the reach of the striker for him to be able to hit it with his bat by means of a normal cricket stroke. Refer to Law 25.1 Judging a Wide.

35. Helmets

The following will apply to the batsman:

A batsman may call for a helmet to be brought out to him at any time. He must then wear or carry it personally all the time while play is in progress, or can have it taken off the field at the fall of a wicket, or at the end of an over, or at any drinks interval.

In all cases, no actions involving helmets are to waste playing time. Umpires are not to hold helmets.

36. Law 41 – The Fielder

Law 41 shall apply with the following:

The exchanging of protective equipment between members of the fielding side on the field shall be permitted provided that the umpires do not consider that it constitutes a waste of playing time. A batsman may only change other items of protective equipment (e.g. batting gloves, etc.) provided that there is no waste of playing time.

37. Law 41.2 – Fielding the Ball

Law 41.2 shall apply, except that the reference to "Governing Body" shall be replaced by Cricket Australia.

38. Law 42.3 – The Match Ball – Changing its Condition

Law 42.3 shall apply, and penalty runs shall be awarded, as defined in this Law.

In addition, the umpires shall report the incident to Cricket Australia.

Law 42.3 shall apply as modified:

(a) That the reference to "Governing Body" shall be replaced by Cricket Australia.

(b) Delete Law 42.3 (e) (ii) and replace with the following:

Inform the captain of the fielding side of the reason for the action taken.

And in addition to Law 42.3:

In the event that a ball has been interfered with and requires replacement, the batsman at the wicket shall choose the replacement ball from a selection of six other balls of various degrees of usage (including a new ball) and of the same brand as the ball in use prior to the contravention.

39. Law 42.4 – Deliberate Attempt to Distract Striker

Law 42.4 shall apply, and penalty runs shall be awarded, as defined in this Law.

In addition, the umpires shall report the incident to Cricket Australia.

Law 42.4 shall apply as modified:

(a) That the reference to "Governing Body" shall be replaced by Cricket Australia.

40. Law 42.5 – Deliberate Distraction or Obstruction of Batsman

Law 42.5 shall apply, and penalty runs shall be awarded, as defined in this Law.

In addition, the umpire shall report the incident to Cricket Australia.

Law 42.5 shall apply as modified:

(a) That the reference to "Governing Body" shall be replaced by Cricket Australia.

41. Law 42.6 (a) – The Bowling of Fast Short Pitched Balls

Law 42.6 (a) (i) and (ii) shall be replaced by the following:

1.
    (a) A bowler shall be limited to two fast short pitched deliveries per over.

    (b) A fast short pitched ball is defined as a ball, which after pitching, passes or would have passed above shoulder height of the batsman standing upright in his normal guard position at the crease.

    (c) The umpire at the bowler's end shall advise the bowler and the batsman on strike when each fast short pitched delivery has been bowled.

    (d) In addition, for the purpose of this regulation, a ball that passes clearly above head height of the batsman, other than a fast short pitched ball as defined in (b) above, that prevents him from being able to hit it with his bat by means of a normal cricket stroke shall be called a Wide and will also count as one of the allowable balls above shoulder height for that over.

2.
    (a) In the event of a bowler bowling more than two fast short pitched deliveries in an over as defined in (b) above, the umpire at the bowler's end shall call and signal No ball on each occasion. A differential signal shall be used to signify a No ball for a fast short pitched delivery. The umpire shall call and signal No ball and then tap the head with the other hand.

    (b) If a bowler delivers a third fast short pitched ball in an over, the umpire, after the call of No ball and when the ball is dead, shall caution the bowler, inform the other umpire, the captain of the fielding side and the batsmen at the wicket of what has occurred. This caution shall apply throughout the innings.

(c) If there is a second instance of the bowler being no balled in the innings for bowling more than two fast short pitched deliveries in an over, the umpire shall advise the bowler that this is his final warning for the innings. The umpire will also inform the other umpire, the captain of the fielding side and the batsmen at the wicket of what has occurred.

(d) Should there be any further instance by the same bowler in that innings, the umpire shall call and signal No ball and when the ball is dead direct the captain to take the bowler off forthwith. If necessary, the over shall be completed by another bowler, who shall neither have bowled the previous over nor be allowed to bowl the next over.

(e) The bowler thus taken off shall not be allowed to bowl again in that innings.

(f) The umpire will report the occurrence to the other umpire, the batsmen at the wicket and as soon as possible to the captain of the batting side.

(g) The umpires will then report the matter to Cricket Australia which shall take such action as is considered appropriate against the captain and the bowler concerned. (Refer also to Law 42.1 Fair and Unfair Play – Responsibility of the Captains.)

The above is not a substitute for Playing Condition 42 below, which umpires are able to apply at any time.

42. Dangerous and Unfair Bowling

Law 42.7 shall be replaced by the following:

Regardless of any action taken by the umpire as a result of a breach of Clauses 41, 43 or 44, the following shall apply at any time during the match.

The bowling of fast short pitched balls is unfair if the umpire at the bowler's end considers that by their repetition and taking into account their length, height and direction, they are likely to inflict physical injury on the striker, irrespective of the protective clothing and equipment he may be wearing. The relative skill of the striker shall also be taken into consideration.

In the event of such unfair bowling, the umpire at the bowler's end shall adopt the following procedure:

(a) In the first instance the umpire shall call and signal No ball, and when the ball is dead, caution the bowler and inform the other umpire, the captain of the fielding side and the batsmen of what has occurred.

(b) If there is a second instance by the same bowler in that innings, he shall repeat the above procedure and indicate to the bowler that this is a final warning.

(c) Both the above caution and final warning shall continue to apply throughout the innings even though the bowler may later change ends.

Should there be a further instance by the same bowler in that innings, the umpire at the bowler's end shall:

(i) Call and signal No ball and when the ball is dead direct the captain to take the bowler off forthwith and to complete the over with another bowler, provided that the bowler does not bowl two overs or part thereof consecutively. See Law 22.8 (Bowler Incapacitated or Suspended during an Over).

(ii) Not allow the bowler, thus taken off, to bowl again in the same innings.

(iii) Report the occurrence to the captain of the batting side as soon as the players leave the field for an interval.

(iv) Report the occurrence to the Executive of the fielding side and to Cricket Australia, which shall take any further action which is considered to be appropriate against the captain and the bowler concerned. (Refer also to Law 42.1 Fair and Unfair Play – Responsibility of the Captains.)

43. Law 42.6 (b) – The Bowling of High Full Pitched Balls

Law 42.6 (b) shall apply as modified:

(a) Any delivery, other than a slow paced one, which passes or would have passed on the full above waist height of the striker standing upright at the crease is deemed dangerous and unfair, whether or not it is likely to inflict physical injury on the striker.

(b) A slow delivery that passes or would have passed on the full above shoulder height of the striker standing upright at the crease is to be deemed dangerous and unfair, whether or not it is likely to inflict physical injury on the striker.

(c) In the event of a bowler bowling a high full pitched ball as defined in (a) and (b) above (i.e. a beamer), the umpire at the bowler's end shall adopt the following procedure:

(d) In the first instance the umpire shall call and signal No ball and when the ball is dead, caution the bowler and issue a first and final warning. The umpire shall inform the other umpire, captain of the fielding side and the batsman of what has occurred.

(e) At the first repetition, call and signal No ball and when the ball is dead direct the captain of the fielding side to take the bowler off forthwith and to complete the over with another bowler, provided that the bowler does not bowl two overs or part thereof consecutively.

(f) Not allow the bowler, thus taken off, to bowl again in the same innings.

(g) At the first opportunity report the occurrence, with the other umpire, to the captain of the batting side and Cricket Australia which shall take any further action that is considered to be appropriate against the captain and the bowler concerned. (Refer also to Law 42.1 Fair and Unfair Play – Responsibility of the Captains.)

44. Deliberate Bowling of High Full Pitched Balls

Law 42.8 shall be replaced with the following:

If the umpire considers that a high full pitch which is deemed dangerous and unfair as defined in clause 43 (a) and (b) was deliberately bowled, then the first and final warning process shall be dispensed with. The umpire at the bowler's end shall:

(a) Call and signal No ball.

(b) When the ball is dead, direct the captain to take the bowler off forthwith.

(c) Not allow the bowler to bowl again in that innings.

(d) Complete the over with another bowler provided that the bowler does not bowl two overs or part thereof consecutively.

(e) At the first opportunity, the umpires will report the occurrence to the captain of the batting side and Cricket Australia, which shall take any further action which is considered appropriate against the captain and bowler concerned.

(Refer also to Law 42.1 Fair and Unfair Play – Responsibility of the Captains.)

45. Dangerous and Unfair Bowling – Action by the Umpires

The Bowling of Fast Short Pitched Deliveries, Dangerous and Unfair Bowling, The Bowling of High Full Pitched Balls and Deliberate Bowling of High Full Pitched Balls.
Cumulative cautions and warnings will NOT apply and each different form of dangerous and unfair bowling will be treated separately in the caution and warning process as defined in clauses 41, 42, 43 and 44.

46. Law 42.9 – Time Wasting by the Fielding Side

Law 42.9 shall apply, and penalty runs shall be awarded, as defined in this Law.
In addition, the umpires shall report the incident to Cricket Australia.
Law 42.9 shall apply as modified:

(b) If there is any further waste of time in that innings by any member of the fielding side the umpire shall:
(i) Delete Law 42.9 (b) (ii)
(ii) Call and signal Dead ball.

The reference to "Governing Body" shall be replaced by Cricket Australia …

CRICKET AUSTRALIA
CODE OF BEHAVIOUR

PREAMBLE

Cricket is a game that owes much of its unique appeal to the fact that it is to be played not only within its Laws, but also within the spirit of the game. Any action seen as abusing this spirit causes injury to the game itself.

Embracing the spirit of the game means playing fairly and exhibiting respect for opponents, fellow team members, the umpires and the game's traditional values such as graciousness in defeat and humility in victory.

Cricket has a distinct place in Australian society and history. As an element in Australia's national identity, cricket plays a significant role. This status brings with it particular responsibilities for players and officials to conform to high standards of fair play and personal behaviour on and off the field.

This Code of Behaviour is intended to protect and enshrine such important qualities and standards so that all may continue to enjoy the game of cricket now and in the future.

SECTION 1: RULES FOR BEHAVIOUR – OFFENCES

Each of the rules for behaviour has a guideline. The guidelines are intended as an illustrative guide only and in the case of any doubt as to the interpretation of the Rule, the provisions of the Rule itself shall take precedence over the provisions of the guidelines. The guidelines should not be read as an exhaustive list of offences or prohibited conduct.

1. Level 1 Offences

The Offences set out at 1.1 to 1.6 below are Level 1 Offences. The range of penalties which shall be imposed for a Level 1 Offence is set out in Section 5 of this Code. Players and, where applicable, officials must not:

1.1 Abuse cricket equipment or clothing, ground equipment or fixtures and fittings
- Includes actions outside the course of normal cricket actions such as hitting or kicking the wickets and actions which intentionally or negligently result in damage to the advertising boards, boundary fences, dressing room doors, mirrors, windows and other fixtures and fittings.

1.2 Show dissent at an umpire's decision by action or verbal abuse
- Includes excessive, obvious disappointment with an umpire's decision or with an umpire making the decision and obvious delay in resuming play or leaving the wicket.
- This Rule does not prohibit the bowler involved in the decision or a team captain from asking an umpire to provide an explanation for a decision or a Team official from making a formal complaint.

1.3 Use language that is obscene, offensive or insulting and/or the making of an obscene gesture
- This includes swearing and offensive gestures which are not directed at another person such as swearing in frustration at one's own poor play or fortune.
- This offence is not intended to penalise trivial behaviour. The extent to which such behaviour is likely to give offence shall be taken into account when assessing the seriousness of the breach.

1.4 Engage in excessive appealing
- Excessive shall mean repeated appealing when the bowler/fielder knows the batsman is not out with the intention of placing the umpire under pressure. It is not intended to prevent loud or enthusiastic appealing. However, the practice of celebrating or assuming a dismissal before the decision has been given may also come within this Rule.

1.5 Point or gesture towards the pavilion in an aggressive manner upon the dismissal of a batsman
- Self explanatory.

1.6 Breach any regulation regarding approved clothing or equipment
- This includes regulations regarding bat logos and regulations regarding other logos or advertising which may be worn or displayed.

2. Level 2 Offences

The Offences set out at 2.1 to 2.9 below are Level 2 Offences. The range of penalties which shall be imposed for a Level 2 Offence is set out in Section 5 of this Code. Players and, where applicable, officials must not:

2.1 Show serious dissent at an umpire's decision by action or verbal abuse

- Dissent should be classified as serious where the dissent is expressed by a specific action such as the shaking of the head, snatching cap from umpire, pointing at pad or inside edge, other displays of anger or abusive language directed at the umpire or excessive delay in resuming play or leaving the wicket.
- This Rule does not prohibit the bowler involved in the decision or a team captain from asking an umpire to provide an explanation for a decision or a Team official from making a formal complaint.

2.2 Engage in inappropriate and deliberate physical contact with other players or officials in the course of play

- Without limitation, players will breach this regulation if they deliberately walk or run into or shoulder another player, official or match official.

2.3 Charge or advance towards the umpire in an aggressive manner when appealing

- Self explanatory.

2.4 Deliberately and maliciously distract or obstruct another player or official on the field of play

- This does not replace clauses 39 and 40 of the Pura Cup Playing Conditions.
- Without limitation, players will breach this rule if they deliberately attempt to distract a striker by words or gestures or deliberately shepherd a batsman while running or attempting to run between wickets.

2.5 Throw the ball at or near a player or official in an inappropriate and/or dangerous manner

- This Rule will not prohibit a fielder or bowler from returning the ball to the stumps in the normal fashion.

2.6 Use language that is obscene, offensive or of a seriously insulting nature to another player, official or spectator.

- This is language or gestures which are directed at another person. See comments under Rule 1.3 above in relation to the seriousness of the breach.

2.7 Change the condition of the ball in breach of Law 42.3

- Prohibited behaviour includes picking the seam or deliberately throwing the ball into ground for the purpose of roughening it up and the application of moisture to the ball, save for perspiration and saliva.

2.8 Without limiting Rule 8, attempt to manipulate a Match in regard to the result, net run rate, bonus points or otherwise. The captain of any team guilty of such conduct shall be held responsible.

- Prohibited conduct under this rule will include incidents where a team bats in such a way as to either adversely affect its own, or improve its opponent's, bonus points, net run rate or quotient.

2.9 Seriously breach any regulation regarding approved clothing or equipment

- See guideline for Rule 1.6 above. Without limitation, a breach will be considered serious if it is done in bad faith or where it has serious commercial consequences (eg display of logo of competing CA or State sponsor)

3. Level 3 Offences

The Offences set out at 3.1 to 3.3 below are Level 3 Offences. The range of penalties which shall be imposed for a Level 3 Offence is set out in Section 5 of this Code. Players and, where applicable, officials must not:

3.1 Intimidate an umpire or referee whether by language or conduct

- Includes appealing in an aggressive or threatening manner.

3.2 Threaten to assault another player, Team official or spectator

- Self explanatory.

3.3 Use language or gestures that offend, insult, humiliate, intimidate, threaten, disparage or vilify another person on the basis of that person's race, religion, colour, descent or national or ethnic origin
 • Self explanatory.

4. Level 4 Offences

The Offences set out at 4.1 to 4.4 below are Level 4 Offences. The range of penalties which shall be imposed for a Level 4 Offence is set out in Section 5 of this Code. Players and, where applicable, officials must not:

4.1 Threaten to assault an umpire or referee
 • Self explanatory.

4.2 Physically assault another player, umpire, referee, official or spectator
 • Self explanatory.

4.3 Engage in any act of violence on the field of play
 • Self explanatory.

4.4 Use language or gestures that seriously offends, insults, humiliates, intimidates, threatens, disparages or vilifies another person on the basis of that person's race, religion, colour, descent or national or ethnic origin
 • Self explanatory.

5. Laws of Cricket and Spirit of the Game

Players must obey the Laws of Cricket and play within the spirit of the game. The captain and Team coach must use their best efforts to ensure that their Team and individual members of the Team complies with this rule
 • This is meant as a general Rule to deal with situations where the facts of or the gravity or seriousness of the alleged incident are not adequately or clearly covered by the offences set out in Rules 1 – 4 (inclusive) of the Code.
 • Conduct which will be prohibited under the clause includes using an illegal bat, time wasting and any conduct which is considered "unfair play" under Law 42 of the Laws of Cricket.
 • This Rule is not intended to punish unintentional breaches of the Laws of Cricket.
 • Reference may be made to any statement or explanation of the Spirit of Cricket published in conjunction with the Laws of Cricket.
 • Nothing in this Rule or the Code alters the onus on the captain to ensure that the Spirit of the Game is adhered to as stated and defined in the preamble to the Laws of Cricket.

6. Unbecoming Behaviour

Without limiting any other rule, players and officials must not at any time engage in behaviour unbecoming to a representative player or official that could bring the game of cricket into disrepute or be harmful to the interests of cricket
 • This is also meant as a general Rule to deal with situations where the facts of or the gravity or seriousness of the alleged incident are not adequately or clearly covered by the offences set out in Rules 1 – 4 (inclusive) of the Code.
 • It is intended to include serious or repeated criminal conduct, public acts of misconduct, unruly public behaviour and cheating during play.
 • This Rule applies in the following circumstances only (whichever is the longer):

  (a) subject to paragraph (b), participation in any Match, tour or training camp in Australia or overseas – from the time of departure from the player's or official's usual private residence prior to the tour or camp until return to that residence after the tour or camp;

  (b) participation in a Home Match or series of Home Matches – from the commencement of the day before the first day of the Match or series of Matches until the end of the day following the conclusion of the Match or series of Matches;

  (c) participation in a home training session – from the time of arrival at the venue until departure; and

(d) attendance at an official cricket function or performance of obligations under a contract with Cricket Australia or a state or territory cricket association - from the time of departure from the player's or official's usual private residence prior to the function or performance of the obligation until return to that residence afterwards.

Notwithstanding the foregoing, this Rule applies at all times where the unbecoming behaviour involves:

(i) serious or repeated criminal conduct; or

(ii) public comment or comment to or in the media.

7. Anti-Doping Policy

Players and officials must obey Cricket Australia's Anti-Doping Policy (as amended from time to time).

• Any behaviour prohibited by this Rule will be dealt with under the Anti-Doping Policy and not under the Code of Behaviour.

8. Betting, Match-fixing and Corruption

Players or officials must not, directly or indirectly, engage in the following conduct:

(a) bet, gamble or enter into any other form of financial speculation on any cricket match or on any event connected with any cricket match (for the purposes of this Rule, an Event);

(b) induce or encourage any other person to bet, gamble or enter into any other form of financial speculation on any cricket match or on any Event or to offer the facility for such bets to be placed;

(c) be a party to contriving or attempting to contrive the result of any cricket match or the occurrence of any Event in exchange for any benefit or reward (other than a benefit or reward received from his home Board);

(d) fail to attempt to perform to the best of his ability in any cricket match for any reason whatsoever (including, in particular, owing to an arrangement relating to betting on the outcome of any cricket match or on the occurrence of any Event) other than for legitimate tactical reasons in relation to that cricket match;

(e) induce or encourage any player not to attempt to perform to the best of the player's ability in any cricket match for any reason whatsoever (including, in particular, owing to an arrangement relating to betting on the outcome of any cricket match or on the occurrence of any Event) other than for legitimate tactical reasons in relation to that cricket match;

• For the purpose of this Rule:

(a) a reference to a "cricket match" includes any cricket match whatsoever played anywhere in the world and is not restricted to a cricket match in which the player or official concerned, or any Team, took part; and

(b) a reference to an "attempt" shall include an offer or an invitation.

(f) for benefit or reward (whether for the player him or herself or any other person), provide any information concerning the weather, the state of the ground, a Team or its members (including, without limitation, the Team's actual or likely composition, the form of individual players or tactics) the status or possible outcome of any cricket match or the possible occurrence of any Event other than in connection with bona fide media interviews and commitments;

(g) engage in any other form of corrupt conduct in relation to any cricket match or Event;

(h) fail to promptly disclose to the Chief Executive Officer of Cricket Australia that he or she has received an approach from another person to engage in conduct such as that described in paragraphs (a) – (g) above (such disclosure to be in writing and include full particulars of any such approach);

(i) fail to promptly disclose to the Chief Executive Officer of Cricket Australia that he or she knows or reasonably suspects that any current or former player or official or any other person has engaged in conduct, or been approached to engage in conduct, such as that described in paragraphs (a) – (g) above (such disclosure to be in writing and include full particulars of any such knowledge or suspicion);

(j) fail to promptly disclose to the Chief Executive Officer of Cricket Australia that he or she has received, or is aware or reasonably suspects that another player or official or any other person has received, actual or implied threats of any nature in relation to past or proposed conduct such as that described in paragraphs (a) – (g) above (such disclosure to be in writing and include full particulars of any such knowledge or suspicion); or

(k) engage in conduct that relates directly or indirectly to any of the conduct described in paragraphs (a) – (j) above and is prejudicial to the interests of the game of cricket.

A valid defence may be made to a charge in respect of any prohibited conduct set out in this Rules 8(h), (i) and (j) if the person charged proves that the conduct was the result of an honest and reasonable belief that there was a serious threat to the life or safety of the person charged or any member of the person's family.

9. Detrimental Public Comment

Without limiting any other rule, players and officials must not make public or media comment which is detrimental to the interests of the game

> Without limitation, players and officials will breach this rule if by making any public or media comment they:
> • publicly denigrate another player or publicly denigrate or criticise an official, umpire, referee or team against which they have played or will play, whether in relation to incidents which occurred in a match or otherwise;
> • denigrate a country in which they are or are likely to be touring or officiating;
> • denigrate the home country of a touring team against which they are or are likely to be playing or in respect of which they are or are likely to be officiating;
> • denigrate another player or official by inappropriately commenting on any aspect of his or her performance, abilities or characteristics;
> • comment on the likely outcome of a hearing or a report or an appeal;
> • criticise the outcome of a hearing or an appeal; or
> • criticise any evidence, submission or other comment made by any person at the hearing of a report or any appeal.

10. Racial and Religious Vilification Code

Without limiting Rules 3.3 and 4.4, players and officials must obey Cricket Australia's Racial and Religious Vilification Code (as amended from time to time)
> • Any behaviour prohibited by this Rule will be dealt with under the Racial and Religious Vilification Code and not under the Code of Behaviour, save where a report is made under another rule of the Code of Behaviour (in which case a player or official may also lodge a complaint under the Racial and Religious Vilification Code).

11. Anti-Harassment Policy

Players and officials must obey Cricket Australia's Anti-Harassment Policy (as amended from time to time).
> • Any behaviour prohibited by this Rule will be dealt with under the Anti-Harassment Policy and not under the Code of Behaviour, save where a report is made under another rule of the Code of Behaviour (in which case a player or official may also lodge a complaint under the Anti-Harassment Policy).

SECTION 5: PENALTIES

1. In the event the Commission decides that any person has breached any of Rules 1 – 4 (inclusive) of Section 1 of this Code of Behaviour, it will apply a penalty within the range of penalties for each level of offence set out in the table below and may also apply any or all of the penalties set out in Rule 2 of this Section (with the exception of Match bans and fines contemplated under Rules 2(a) and 2(c)).

The following rules of interpretation apply to any penalty imposed under this Rule:

(a) A "multi-day Match" means a Match of more than one days' scheduled duration and a "one-day Match" means a Match of one days' scheduled duration.

(b) The Commission must specify the type of Match or Matches in which the ban is to be served. The Commission may specify a different ban (within the applicable range) for each type of Match in respect of which the ban is to apply. For example, a player found guilty of a Level 3 offence may be banned for 4 Pura Cup Matches, 2 Test Matches, 6 ING Cup Matches and 5 One Day International Matches.

(c) In addition to any ban imposed under this Rule (and without limiting the Commission's powers with respect to Level 4 bans), the Commission may, if it deems appropriate, ban the person from participation in any club match or matches for a specified period of time.

(d) In the event that a player receives an ICC imposed international Match ban for a breach of any of the offences set out in either Level 3 or Level 4 of the ICC Code of Conduct (or their equivalent from time to time) other than a Level 3 offence under the ICC Code of Conduct for a repeat of a Level 2 offence within a twelve month period, the Senior Commissioner or the Deputy Senior Commissioner (or another Commissioner nominated by the Chief Executive Officer of Cricket Australia) will conduct a hearing to determine whether the player should receive a domestic Match ban during the period commencing on the first day of the ICC imposed ban and the last day of the ICC imposed ban, and if so, the type of Match or Matches in which the ban is to be served. As far as appropriate, the provisions of Section 4 of this Code will apply to any hearing under this paragraph (d) except that:

   (i) the hearing will be a hearing as to penalty only (and will not be a review of the guilt or innocence of the player under the ICC Code of Conduct or a rule of this Code); and

   (ii) the hearing must be convened within 10 business days of the relevant decision (or an appeal from that decision) under the ICC Code of Conduct.

When imposing any penalty under this paragraph (d) the following principles will apply:

   (i) the Commission may not impose a ban in relation to Test Matches or One Day International Matches;

   (ii) the Commission may not impose a ban which extends beyond the last day of the ICC imposed match ban;

   (iii) the number of domestic matches in a ban imposed by the Commission must not exceed the number of matches forming part of the ICC imposed match ban (for example, a player who receives a three Test Match ban may not receive a ban of more than three Pura Cup Matches); and

   (iv) the Commission may take into account any circumstance it considers relevant, including those listed in Rule 3 of this Section 5.

(e) If a player or official repeats an offence within a particular Level (excluding Level 4) within a twelve month period, the Commission will impose a penalty in line with the next highest Level. For example, if a player is found to have committed a Level 2.3 offence and six months later is found to have committed a Level 2.6 offence, the player will be penalised as if he or she had committed a Level 3 offence.

(f) In relation to a fine which is determined by reference to a 'match fee' (as referred to in the table above), the relevant match will be the match in which the offence occurred.

2. Without limiting Rule 1 of this Section, in the event the Commission decides that any person has breached any of Rules 5, 6 or 9 of Section 1 of this Code of Behaviour, it will apply one or more of the following penalties:

(a) Ban the person from participating in any Match;

(b) Ban the person from holding (or continuing to hold) any position within Cricket Australia or a State or Territory Cricket Association (including as an employee, official or officer);

(c) Fine the person an amount that accords with Rule 11 of this Section;

(d) Direct that the person make reparation for damage caused by that person to any property;

(e) Require the person to undergo counselling for a specified time;

(f) Require the person to perform voluntary service to cricket or the community; and/or

(g) Reprimand the person.

3. Without limiting Rule 1 of this Section, when imposing any penalty upon a person who has breached this Code of Behaviour, the Commission may take into account any circumstance it considers relevant, including the following:

(a) the seriousness of the breach;

(b) the harm caused by the breach to the interests of cricket;

(c) the person's seniority and standing in the game;

(d) remorse shown by the person and the prospect of further breaches;

(e) the prior record of the person in abiding by this Code, the ICC Code of Conduct and any similar code of behaviour; and

(f) the impact of the penalty on the person, including the person's capacity to pay a fine as evidenced by the proportion of the person's annual income from Cricket Australia or a state or territory cricket association that the proposed fine represents.

4. In the event the Commission decides that a person is guilty of an offence under any of Rules 1 – 4 of Section 1 of this Code and the person is not described in the table under Rule 1 above, the Commission will impose one or more of the penalties set out in Rule 2 of this Section, taking into account any circumstance which it considers relevant including those set out in Rule 3 of this Section.

5. Penalties for behaviour which contravenes the codes and policies described in Rules 7, 10 and 11 of Section 1 will be determined in accordance with the relevant code or policy.

6. Any player or official required to pay a fine or to make reparation must do so within thirty (30) days or as otherwise decided by the Commission. Any failure to meet this requirement will render the player or official ineligible for selection or official duties in any Team or Match.

7. If the Commission finds a person reported for separate incidents within a match to be guilty of more than one offence, it should impose separate penalties in respect of each offence. Penalties in such cases are cumulative and not concurrent.

8. Plea bargaining is not permitted. It is open to the Commission to find a person guilty of an offence in a level lower than that in which he or she is charged where the constituent elements of the lesser offence are the same. For example, if a player is charged with serious dissent under Rule 2.1 of Section 1, it is open to the Commission to find the player guilty of dissent under Rule 1.2 of Section 1 rather than serious dissent.

9. In the event the Commission decides that any person has breached a provision of Rule 8 of Section 1, the Commission:

(a) may impose any or all of the penalties under Rules 2(c) to (g) inclusive; and

(b) will impose the penalties under Rules 2 (a) and (b) of this Section, and will ban the person from (in the case of a player) being selected in a Team or (in the case of an official) being involved in any Team or Match, for the following periods of time:

Rule 8(a)	-	Between 2 and 5 years
Rule 8(b)	-	Between 2 and 5 years if the player or official directly benefited (or intended to directly benefit) from his or her actions; otherwise, a minimum of 1 year
Rule 8(c)	-	life
Rule 8(d)	-	life
Rule 8(e)	-	life
Rule 8(f)	-	Between 2 and 5 years if the player or official directly benefited (or intended to directly benefit) from his or her actions; otherwise, a minimum of 1 year
Rule 8(g)	-	Between 2 years and life
Rule 8(h)	-	Between 1 and 5 years
Rule 8(i)	-	Between 1 and 5 years
Rule 8(j)	-	Between 1 and 5 years
Rule 8(k)	-	Between 1 and 5 years

10. Nothing in this Section limits the Commission's ability to impose a ban and a fine in respect of a breach of Rule 8 of Section 1.

11. When the Commission imposes a fine for a breach of Rules 5, 6, 8 or 9 of Section 1, it will not exceed the amounts listed in the following table, provided that no fines will be imposed on players or officials who do not receive remuneration as a result of their playing or officiating duties:

Rule Number	Description of Offence	First Breach	Further Breach
Rule 5	Laws of Cricket and Spirit of the Game	$5,750	$11,500
Rule 6	Unbecoming Behaviour	$5,750	$11,500
Rule 8	Betting, Match Fixing and Corruption	unlimited	unlimited
Rule 9	Detrimental Public Comment	$5,750	$11,500

Opposite WILD COLONIAL BOY:
David Hookes, laconic larrikin of Australian
cricket, died in January 2004 at the age of 48.
Picture by Getty Images.

8

The Wisden Review

Obituaries

by WARWICK FRANKS

BAIRD, JAMES GEORGE, died on November 4, 2003, in the Melbourne bayside suburb of Sandringham. A multi-skilled athlete long before that gratingly ugly expression came into use, there was a period in Jim Baird's life when he spent summer playing cricket, autumn on the running track and winter at the top level of Australian Rules football. Born in the inner suburb of Parkville on November 9, 1920, he was a member of the Carlton 1st XI by the age of 19. He played 167 games for the club between 1939-40 and 1956-57, taking 374 wickets at 18.06. His value as an opening bowler lay in his sharp pace and ability to produce late-moving inswingers from a high action. In addition, his physical fitness allowed him to sustain his hostility for long periods, never giving the batsmen any respite despite a deceptively stringy (178 cm and 72 kg) frame.

It was not until 1948-49 that his effectiveness at district level finally forced the state selectors to include Baird on the trip to Tasmania. He took 2 for 28 and 4 for 44 in Launceston, enough to earn him a spot in the last Sheffield Shield match of the season against South Australia in Adelaide, replacing Harry Lambert who had left for a league appointment in England. Baird bowled effectively, taking 4 for 69 in the first innings and always asserting that he was unlucky not to get an lbw decision against Don Bradman, who was appearing in his final first-class match. A tailender who could hit to good effect, he contributed 13 not out to a last-wicket stand of 55 in 33 minutes with Bill Johnston, who slogged his way to his highest first-class score of 38.

With Johnston and Sam Loxton away in South Africa, Baird was installed as Victoria's main strike weapon with the new ball for the 1949-50 season. He responded with enthusiasm, skill and 30 wickets, his best match coming against SA in Melbourne, when he was persistently dangerous for 44 overs in returning 7 for 108 and 3 for 67. To complete a satisfying game, he made his highest first-class score of 25 not out, joining the unlikely Jack Iverson in a last-wicket stand of 45. In the next match against New South Wales in Sydney he took 3 for 76 and 3 for 50. Despite these performances, Baird was dropped to make way for the returning tourists at the beginning of 1950-51, and a subsequent injury ruled him out of further consideration. Next season the selectors continued to overlook him, even though they tried four new opening bowlers and even though Baird continued on his effective way with Carlton.

He was a versatile footballer of real class, playing 130 senior games and kicking 95 goals for Carlton between 1941 and 1951. Possessed of speed and the ability to leap effortlessly, he often played in the ruck despite his lack of real size, and could attack or defend with equal ease. Baird began his career at full-forward, booting 10 goals against Richmond in the opening round of 1943. Soon after he suffered a knee injury, which was so serious that he was ruled unfit for army service and missed the whole of the 1944 season following restorative surgery. He subsequently appeared in two winning grand final sides: in 1945, when he played in the back pocket through the mayhem of the infamous "Bloodbath" against South Melbourne; and in 1947, when he played at full-forward and kicked three goals, Carlton beating Essendon by a single point.

Immediately after the war, Baird sprang to prominence as an athlete. Filling in to complete a relay team of footballers at a charity carnival, he demonstrated such a turn of speed that he temporarily gave up cricket for professional running and made the final of the 1946 Stawell Gift. For a novice, he was given the large handicap of six and a half yards, yet still managed to run a close third. Realising that handicappers would give him little chance of success, he retired soon after. A child of the depression, he was forced to find work at the end of his education at Errol Street primary school in North Melbourne. Having made the most of his natural aptitudes, in 1948 he joined his brother, Jack, in a home-building partnership that lasted 36 years. Jack was a giant opening bowler who took 236 wickets for Carlton between 1936-37 and 1945-46, often sharing the new ball with his younger brother during the war years.

Jim Baird's sporting reputation was such that he was awarded a place in Jim Main and Russell Holmesby's celebratory football volume *Carlton: The 100 Greatest* (1994). A life member of both Carlton cricket and football clubs, he was selected in 1999 as a member of the Carlton Cricket Club's Team of the Century. A month before his death, Baird attended the Victorian players' dinner in the Long Room at the MCG, the last official function held by Cricket Victoria before the Long Room was demolished.

	M	I	NO	Runs	HS	100s	50s	Avge	Ct	St	W	Avge	BB
First-class	10	14	7	119	25*	0	0	17.00	4	0	42	24.83	7-108
Domestic first-class	8	12	5	101	25*	0	0	14.43	2	0	35	26.00	7-108

BEAMES, PERCY JAMES, died on March 28, 2004, in the Melbourne suburb of Kew. A superb example of the breadth and depth of Melbourne's sporting culture, which could never be reproduced in the northern states, Beames is the only member of both the Australian Football League and Cricket Victoria's 200 clubs. For three decades he later transformed practice into precept, rising to become chief cricket and football journalist for the Melbourne *Age*. Ron Carter, who worked for 20 years as his deputy during the football season, described him as "the best-credentialled football writer of his time" and "a peerless cricket writer", possessing an "uncanny insight" into both sports.

Born in the former goldrush city of Ballarat on July 27, 1911, and educated at Ballarat College, the diminutive (168 cm and 68 kg) Beames made such a mark in local cricket that he appeared against successive MCC teams in 1928-29 and 1929-30. In 1931-32 he switched from South Melbourne to

Never uninteresting: Percy Beames

the Melbourne club, quickly becoming one of district cricket's most attractive and consistent batsmen. He scored more than 500 runs in four successive seasons. Originally rather fragile in defence, he tightened his game without sacrificing the power of his strokes. Strong off his pads, he could also cut with facility and drive through the covers with an ease that belied his small stature. The excitement of his presence at the crease caused 'Southerner' in *The Referee* to summarise him with severe understatement as "never uninteresting".

An indication of Beames's power is reflected in a story about an innings he played against South Melbourne at the Albert Ground. He peppered the tennis court next door with so many sixes that, in an early example of occupational health and safety policy, tennis was suspended until Beames was dismissed. Notwithstanding his club prowess, for a number of years he was given only the occasional state match, mostly against Tasmania. In the first of these, in Hobart in 1933-34, he took 5 for 52 in the second innings, his four late wickets enabling Victoria to win with 17 minutes to spare.

He ran riot with the bat on the island trip of 1938-39. In Launceston he made a sedate 93, then was given out lbw only to be recalled by the local captain Ron Morrisby, who realised Beames had hit the ball. Deciding that every run from there on was a bonus, and having taken 193 minutes to make his first hundred, Beames piled on another century in an hour. His unbeaten 226, including 28 fours and a six, was made out of 338 runs scored while he was at the crease. Beames hit more exuberant runs in Hobart, his 169 not out culminating in an unbroken fifth-wicket partnership of 209 in only 106 minutes with Ian Johnson. Even so, he had to wait until the second half of the next season before getting an extended run at Sheffield Shield level. In the match against South Australia in Melbourne, Beames made a sparkling 104 in 143 minutes, playing the Test leg-spinners Clarrie Grimmett and Frank Ward with dash and poise.

He continued to score prolifically for Melbourne during the war, hitting more than 800 runs in three consecutive one-day seasons. By the time first-class cricket resumed in 1945-46, Beames was made state captain. He led the side constructively, Victoria winning four out of seven matches and not conceding a first-innings lead. His own batting remained purposeful and consistent, highlighted by a belligerent 59 against a hostile New South Wales attack in Sydney and an undefeated 94 against Queensland at the Gabba. At the end of the summer he announced his retirement from cricket in order to concentrate on his journalism, even though he was being mentioned as a possible Test candidate for the 1946-47 Ashes series. After one more match for Melbourne that season, he finished his district career with 7,850 runs at 46.44 from 189 matches, including 20 centuries, and a reputation as the best cover-point of his time in Victoria.

As a youth, Beames became known in Ballarat football as a muscular and indefatigable rover. Melbourne officials took him to the city for a trial in 1931; he delighted in recounting that the reason for his noisy first night was that the boarding establishment doubled as a brothel. The club signed him immediately and he became one of the leading footballers of his generation, gaining state selection in 1932, 1935, 1937 and 1939. He played 213 games for the Demons between 1931 and 1944, kicking 323 goals. He was a key member of the side which won three successive premierships from 1939, and ended his career with three years as captain-coach.

Upon Beames's arrival in Melbourne in the depths of the Depression, Joe Blair, president of the Melbourne Football Club and an executive at the Vacuum Oil Company, found him what Beames called "a sympathy job" in the stationery department. He stayed for 15 years. In 1946 his ability to record and analyse cricket and football gained him a position covering both sports at *The Age*. Given that television did not arrive for another decade and that Melbourne had no Sunday papers until the 1970s, his reports were vital eyewitness accounts of matches.

But Beames also established a reputation for judicious, informed commentary. He always eschewed sensationalism in favour of readable analysis, illuminated by his understanding of the skills and tactics of both games. In all, he covered 119 Tests over 25 series, both at home and abroad, before retiring from the press box at the end of the 1975-76 series against West Indies. Possibly his biggest scoop was his discovery that during the Third Test of 1954-55 the cracked Melbourne pitch had been watered in an attempt to stop further deterioration. His knowledge of football was encyclopaedic and he was saturated in its lore. Although a confidant of many coaches and players, he understood the discretion needed to maintain the confidence of his contacts. Naturally he was a much sought-after panellist on various football programmes after the advent of television.

Beames's stature is reflected in the fact that he was a member of the AFL's Hall of Fame and a life member of the Melbourne Football Club, the Melbourne Cricket Club and the Australian Football Media Association. His older brother, Norman, was a Ballarat cricketer of note and appeared with his younger brother for the local side against Douglas Jardine's Bodyline tourists in 1932-33. His daughter, Adrienne, was also gifted across a number of fields. She was Victorian squash champion for three successive years from 1966, won second prize as a mezzo-soprano in the prestigious Sun Aria competition, and forged a successful career on the road-running circuit in the United States. In 1971 she became the first woman to run a marathon in under three hours.

	M	I	NO	Runs	HS	100s	50s	Avge	Ct	St	W	Avge	BB
First-class	18	27	4	1,186	226*	3	3	51.56	8	0	7	22.42	5-52
Domestic first-class	5	9	0	302	104	1	1	33.56	2	0	0	–	–

BRIGGS, RONALD EDWARD, died on October 10, 2003, in Katoomba in the Blue Mountains of New South Wales. Ron Briggs always made a distinctive sight as an opening batsman, with his low grip and crouching stance, but he scored heavily enough in the mid-1950s to prompt as sagacious a judge as Ray Robinson to identify him as a potential Test candidate. Robinson characterised Briggs as "no stylist [but] the kind of batsman who writes his own reference with runs on the board". His state team-mate Keith Miller wrote: "There are many more attractive batsmen playing today, but there are few who can rival his watertight defence."

Miller was in a good position to judge. He had flattened Briggs with a bumper during Miller's debut season in Sydney in 1947-48, rushing to the batsman's aid and using his handkerchief to staunch the flow of blood from Briggs' gashed eyebrow. The stained and crumpled piece of cloth remained in Briggs' kit for years afterwards, as both a talisman and a reminder of a painful encounter with a young man's hero. He overcame his apprehension at the short ball, and later a couple of cracks on the head from the irrepressible Sam Loxton in a 1952-53 Sheffield Shield match, to become a ready and successful hooker. A penchant for the leg-glance and the ability to cut strongly, both in front of and behind point, completed the picture of an opener whose game was built on sure foundations but who could play with real power behind the wicket. Yet Briggs was despatched peremptorily from the state side while he still had much to offer.

Born on September 22, 1929, in the south-western Sydney suburb of Belmore, and educated at the local Central Junior Technical School, he made his first-grade debut for Marrickville at 16. He made steady enough progress to be selected in the NSW Colts team against their Queensland counterparts at the Gabba in November 1948. He responded with a determined 155, sharing a century opening stand with Graeme Hole and another for the third wicket with Jim Burke, who were both playing for Australia two years later. Later that season he appeared in a 2nd XI match against Victoria. In a corresponding fixture in Melbourne two years later, he showed his defensive capabilities for 158 minutes, contributing 58 to an opening partnership of 121 with Sid Carroll which helped avoid an innings defeat.

Briggs joined the new Bankstown–Canterbury club in 1951-52 for their inaugural grade season. He made it memorable with 964 runs at 68.85, an aggregate not surpassed until Kevin Roberts made 1,168 runs in 1993-94. His first-class opportunity came when NSW visited Western Australia while Arthur Morris was in Brisbane for the First Test against South Africa in 1952-53. In the second innings, with his side trailing by 146 runs, Briggs made the game safe with 121 in 307 minutes. His century on debut amply made up in determination what it lacked in polish, and included a third-wicket partnership of 167 with Ian Craig. His reward was to be made 12th man for the return match against WA, but he finished the season with successive innings of 80 against Victoria and 83 against South Australia.

After carrying the drinks in the opening Shield game of 1953-54, he was a model of consistency. He joined Morris in opening stands of 158 against SA in Adelaide and 166 at the MCG, missing out on a century by four runs. In Sydney, against Queensland, Briggs and Burke concluded a drawn game with an unbeaten stand of 132. He crowned the season with 136 against SA, also at the SCG, this time getting the innings started with 161 in virtually even time with the debutant Bill Watson. Briggs's 487 runs came at an average of 54.11. He was now showing an ability to bat more pugnaciously, despite his comparatively slight (175 cm and 71 kg) build.

Briggs appeared for an Australian XI against MCC early next season, top-scoring with a grinding 48 in a rain-sodden match in Melbourne. He found runs harder to come by after that, apart from a matchwinning 100 against Queensland in Sydney. His season ended on a downbeat note with a pair against Queensland in the return match, when he was out first ball of the match and lasted only one ball longer second time round. And that was that. New South Wales tried four different partners for Burke in 1955-56 but used Briggs only for the 2nd XI game. His 27 was not enough to force the selectors to reconsider him. Instead he was appointed captain of his club side, where he was popular, successful and astute. He showed he had lost none of his ability with 850 runs at 53.13 in 1957-58. The following season he led Bankstown–Canterbury to their maiden first-grade premiership.

Originally a clerical officer in the NSW Government Railways, Briggs trained as a technical education teacher and in 1960 was appointed to Casino, on the far north coast, to teach English and accountancy. He immediately made his presence felt there with two centuries. Two seasons later he took 112 off a strong Lismore attack in an inter-district match. Appointed back to Sydney in 1963, he had another season with Bankstown–Canterbury. Neither his batting nor captaincy skills had waned. In 1965 he was appointed as senior head teacher to Tamworth, in the state's north-west, ending his Sydney grade career with 6,778 runs at 39.40. He continued to play cricket during successive appointments at Gosford, on the central coast, and Wagga Wagga, where he was regional supervisor of technical education.

As a young man, Briggs was a successful table tennis player, named Australian junior champion in 1947 and a member of the state team which toured Queensland. Shortly afterwards he felt compelled to choose between his two sports, and cricket won the day. His son, Greg, was an outstanding schoolboy cricketer and was graded by Northern District at 13 years of age. He represented NSW at Under-19 level, toured Pakistan with the Australian Under-19 team in 1980-81 and subsequently transferred to his father's old club at Bankstown.

	M	I	NO	Runs	HS	100s	50s	Avge	Ct	St	W	Avge	BB
First-class	15	24	1	1,089	136	3	5	47.34	12	0	0	–	–
Domestic first-class	13	21	1	1,041	136	3	5	52.05	11	0	0	–	–

BROOKS, GORDON VICTOR, died on January 31, 2004, at the Holy Spirit Hospital, Northside, in the northern Brisbane suburb of Chermside, after a long illness. Brooks made a useful contribution to South Australian cricket over three seasons. He was a tall, slim opening bowler of peppery pace, whose restricted contributions were dictated by the predilection of his state skipper, Les Favell, for a varied spin attack. While he appeared to some to be another in the line of South Australian new-ball bowlers of the period with doubtful actions, he was never called.

Brooks was born on May 30, 1938, in Ceduna, on the far west coast of South Australia, and educated at Woodville High School in Adelaide. His sporting contribution to the school was mainly in tennis, where he captained the A team, and baseball. In 1954 he was selected in the state schoolboys' baseball team, captaining them in 1955. Baseball skills ran deep in the family; he and three of his four brothers played for the state schoolboys' side at different times, and all played major league in Adelaide. Their sporting heritage was shaped by their father, Charles, a gifted athlete in his youth who held 16 state titles across a range of events.

After some cursory appearances with both Woodville and the Colts sides in the late 1950s, Brooks suddenly appeared as a fully-formed fast bowler in the 1960-61 season. He took 24 wickets at 14.45 for Woodville that year. He spent the next three summers in the state side, where he was a consistent performer despite never taking more than four wickets in an innings or six in a match. In his first season of 1961-62 he captured 25 wickets at 30.88. His 3 for 53 against New South Wales in Adelaide comprised the wickets of Bob Simpson, Brian Booth and Richie Benaud. Shortly after, he caused mayhem among the visiting Tasmanians with three wickets in his first couple of overs on his way to 4 for 11. Next season he gained his best Sheffield Shield figures, 4 for 40 versus Victoria, again in Adelaide.

Peppery pace: Gordon Brooks

Brooks made useful contributions to South Australia's Shield-winning season of 1963-64. But his opportunities were limited by Favell's concentration on a three-pronged attack: the swing and cut of Neil Hawke; the leg-spin of Rex Sellers; and the limitless variety of Garfield Sobers. Brooks did, however, give the South African Test batsman Tony Pithey cause to remember his first visit to Adelaide Oval. Brooks had him caught behind from the opening delivery of the match against the tourists, then completed Pithey's pair by bowling him fourth ball of the second innings. Brooks was dropped from the last two matches of the season, ending both his first-class and grade days as he concentrated on his business career. He was a No. 11 of archetypal proportions, never reaching double figures in 31 first-class innings. Indeed his career yielded 20 more wickets than it did runs, although he did manage a partnership of 18 with David Sincock against NSW in 1961-62. He finished with 146 grade runs at 6.95, including a 29 in his last season, and 57 wickets at 24.31.

Brooks spent most of his working life in sales and marketing, including a period overseas with Qantas. Having lived in Western Australia for 17 years, he and his wife moved to Brisbane in the 1990s. From there, he was the moving force in organising a reunion to mark the 40th anniversary of South Australia's 1963-64 Shield win. Sadly he lost his battle with cancer on the day of the reunion. His contribution to the event was marked with warmth and appreciation by his former team-mates.

	M	I	NO	Runs	HS	100s	50s	Avge	Ct	St	W	Avge	BB
First-class	26	31	15	41	6	0	0	2.56	13	0	61	33.26	4-11
Domestic first-class	21	29	13	29	4*	0	0	2.23	9	0	43	37.12	4-40

CALVERT, DERRECK, died in Hobart on December 25, 2003, three days after his 84th birthday. Born in the small town of South Arm, situated on the eastern shore of the Derwent estuary where it meets Storm Bay, 'Snowy' Calvert was educated locally. He grew up in an area which is the historical heartland of Tasmanian cricket. It was close to the place where the first recorded game took place, and the district was dominated by such famous Tasmanian cricketing names as the Richardsons and Morrisbys – as well as the Calverts.

He enjoyed a prolific and prolonged grade career of more than two decades with the Sandy Bay, South Hobart and Clarence clubs. Calvert was a neat, well-organised batsman with a sound defence. His durability was such that he finished top of the Hobart batting averages in 1965-66. Even after retiring from grade cricket, he was still representing Rokeby at Country Week in his late forties. After army service from 1940 to 1943, he made his first appearance for South in the annual fixture against North in 1943-44, top-scoring for his side with 92 not out. He followed up with 96 next season and 100 in 1946-47, including a 147-run stand with his brother Trevor. It was enough to earn him a spot as 12th man for Tasmania's match against Victoria over New Year, when he caught Tom Tuttle off the bowling of Jules Murfett while acting as a substitute fieldsman. A fortnight later he was picked against MCC in Launceston, making two and 18 on a rain-affected pitch on the last day.

The selectors lost interest in Calvert until his continued good form obliged them to turn to him during the 1952-53 season. Against the South Africans, in a two-day non-first-class match in Hobart, Calvert played a couple of brave strokes in scoring 18 of his side's total of 35. His second-innings duck came after he again hooked at the pace of Michael Melle, and was again caught on the boundary by Roy McLean. When the teams next met in Launceston, Calvert made a determined 27 in the first innings – putting on 60 of his team's 131 with Emerson Rodwell – and a golden duck in the second. He ended the summer with 22 and 15 against the 1953 Australians in Hobart, as they prepared to leave for England.

Calvert's working life was spent in partnership with one of his brothers, Mervyn, on the family's Rokeby property, Belmont Lawn, a mixed enterprise concentrating on raising fat lambs and growing cereal crops such as barley. In his forties he took up golf so successfully that he became A-grade champion of the Richmond club nine times in the 1970s and 80s. He continued to play veterans' golf until 12 months before his death. Calvert was a man of great personal charm, remembered with universal respect for his equable and affable temperament.

	M	I	NO	Runs	HS	100s	50s	Avge	Ct	St	W	Avge	BB
First-class	3	6	0	84	27	0	0	14.00	1	0	0	–	–

CROMPTON, COLIN NEIL, died on December 11, 2003, at the Cabrini Hospital in the Melbourne suburb of Malvern, after suffering from cancer. Born in Dandenong on August 16, 1937, Neil Crompton – habitually known as 'Frog' – was another of that considerable band of Victorians who played both cricket and Australian Rules football for state. It was football that won him sporting immortality, thanks to the goal he produced from nowhere to snatch victory for Melbourne over Collingwood in the 1964 grand final.

Educated at Caulfield Technical School, Crompton played his initial district match for Melbourne at 16 and made unspectacular progress as a left-hand opening batsman. He was selected for Victoria in 1957-58 after a classic case of producing the right innings at the right moment. The state needed openers, with Colin McDonald away in South Africa and Bill Lawry still to earn regular consideration, and Crompton began the season with 150 against Footscray. It was an innings of real sparkle and flair. After a series of useful contributions, bringing 162 runs in his first seven Sheffield Shield innings, his batting flowered with two centuries and an 84 in his next six visits to the crease.

Against New South Wales in Sydney, Victoria scored a miserable 117 in reply to the home side's 531 and were left with only pride to salvage. Crompton showed the way with 124, partnering John Shaw in a second-wicket partnership of 211 which at least forced NSW to bat again. In the last match of the season, against Western Australia in Perth, his brisk 101 in 169 minutes showed the power of his wiry frame (178 cm and 79 kg) and helped build an unassailable lead. During the season Crompton proved himself an agile and versatile fieldsman close to the wicket, holding 14 catches. He took four of these in his second game, against Queensland in Melbourne, when he held three first-innings catches as part of John Edwards' leg-trap and the visitors were sent packing for 65.

Crompton had a less productive season in 1958-59, but shone with two contrasting innings against the touring Englishmen. His 73 in the first innings was replete with positive shots, whereas his 64 in the second was a stubborn but forlorn effort to hold the innings together. It was during this match that his skipper, Len Maddocks, tried a few overs of Crompton's undemanding leg-breaks. He responded with the wickets of Colin Cowdrey and Roy Swetman in quick succession, later dismissing Peter Richardson in the second innings. His deliveries were really mostly top-spinners, but the Victorian captains of his time – such as Maddocks and Jack Potter – often had moments of intuition when they would call on such apparently unlikely change bowlers as Bill Lawry. Crompton fell under this category and captured eight wickets in first-class cricket. Fourteen seasons of district cricket brought him an aggregate of only one more.

He performed steadily enough over the next three years without reaching the heights of his debut year, and was dropped from the state side after the first two matches of 1962-63. Ironically he went on to have his most productive district season, scoring 539 runs at 67.37. Crompton retired from the Melbourne club at the end of 1966-67. He had played 119 matches, amassing seven centuries and 3,314 runs at 27.84. He maintained his interest in the game and represented Victoria in the Breville Masters' Cricket Championship in Sydney in 1980. He and the former state player David Anderson cracked 73 in 40 minutes for the fourth wicket, as Victoria ran out undefeated champions.

As a footballer Crompton started as a rover, moved to the forward line and eventually became a reliable back-pocket player. His game was characterised by an unspectacular and workmanlike approach. He played 99 games and kicked 24 goals for Melbourne between 1957 and 1966, but his moment of flair and inspiration came in the 1964 grand final. Before a crowd of 104,000, Collingwood seemed to have the game in their grasp with only seconds to go. Having drifted downfield to be deliberately out of position, Crompton calmly grabbed a loose ball and kicked it through an open goal to seal his side's four-point victory. It was his first goal in eight seasons. In 1966 he made history by achieving a unique double: he was awarded provident fund payments by both the Victorian Cricket Association and the Victorian Football League. Crompton was a much-loved coach of Werribee, then a new team in the Victorian Football Association, for three years from 1967. Most of his working life was spent as an insurance salesman and consultant for AMP.

	M	I	NO	Runs	HS	100s	50s	Avge	Ct	St	W	Avge	BB
First-class	45	73	5	2,162	124	3	11	31.79	47	0	8	48.37	2-11
Domestic first-class	40	64	5	1,752	124	2	7	29.69	44	0	5	69.80	1-3

DICK, WILLIAM ALLAN, died in Melbourne on March 27, 2004. Allan Dick had an outstanding career in Melbourne district ranks as a slow-bowling all-rounder. He was known as 'The Professor', both for his bespectacled and studious demeanour and for the scholarly care with which he set his fields. It was his misfortune to come to cricketing maturity when Victoria's spin larder was well-stocked with Test representatives: Ian Johnson, Doug Ring, Jack Iverson, Jack Hill. He did, however, enjoy a late flourish in the state side during which he showed his capabilities at the top level. Yet this was only part of the picture of a man whose business acumen spurred him to a distinguished career of devoted voluntary service with the Anti-Cancer Council of Victoria.

Born in Newcastle, NSW, on October 11, 1922, Dick grew up in Melbourne, was educated at Melbourne Grammar School and studied commerce at the University of Melbourne. His studies were interrupted during World War II by his service as a warrant officer with the 3 Australian Base Supply Depot in Melbourne. After a season with Melbourne in 1939-40, he joined the University club. He was picked for his batting, which was based on the simple principles of watchful defence and a willingness to lambast anything loose. While there were no airs and graces about his batting, he was extremely effective. In 1945-46 he scored 843 runs at 93.66, setting a University record aggregate that stood for 44 years until Geoff Allardice bettered it by 25 runs in 1989-90.

When he was first selected for Victoria, against South Australia in Melbourne at the end of the 1946-47 season, it was as a specialist batsman. Two seasons earlier, however, his club had needed a spinner, so he polished up his leg-breaks. Influenced by watching the Englishman Doug Wright on tour in 1946-47, Dick lengthened his run, quickened his pace and put more body into his bowling. His stock ball was a fizzing top-spinner, delivered with enough pace and accuracy to put batsmen under constant pressure. He became a prolific wicket-taker at miserly cost.

Yet it seemed that Dick would never be anything more than a bit player at state level. He was held in enough esteem to be made captain of the 2nd XI against NSW in 1949-50 and to lead the side against Tasmania in Melbourne, where he made 53 and took 4 for 32. With Johnson and Ring away on Test duty he filled in for three games in 1951-52. But there seemed little prospect of many more state caps. In 1954-55, however, with Iverson and Ring retired and Johnson captaining Australia, the selectors turned to Dick. He made an immediate impression. Against New South Wales, in Melbourne, his figures of 5 for 31 and 3 for 66 were a crucial factor in the visitors' only defeat of the season. In a rain-ruined match against MCC, he came to the crease after Brian Statham and Trevor Bailey had reduced Victoria to 6 for 39. His 102 minutes of capable resistance brought him 41 and helped his side shuffle into three figures.

These performances were not enough to protect his spot the following summer. Dick finally got a full season in 1956-57, at the age of 34, once Johnson had retired. He made useful runs and took timely wickets, his 4 for 46 in Adelaide helping the young Lindsay Kline spin Victoria to victory. At Junction Oval, against Queensland, he contributed 45 to a seventh-wicket stand of 111 with Neil Harvey. Before the last match of the season Dick announced his first-class retirement, urging the selectors to give precedence to the younger brigade of Victorian spinners.

After captaining University in 1946-47, he moved to Hawthorn–East Melbourne next season, where he was captain for six summers from 1948-49. His tenure of office included successive flags, Dick making signal contributions both times. He captured 33 wickets at 13.12 in the 1949-50 premiership victory, then made 684 runs at 48.85 in 1950-51. His best season was 1955-56 when he took 49 wickets at 11.85. He retired two years later after 213 district matches. He scored 6,507 runs, including nine centuries, at 30.98 and took 359 wickets at 14.49, with 17 five-wicket hauls.

He had an extensive career in accountancy and at senior levels in the financial sector. At various stages, Dick became a partner with Arthur Anderson and Co. and a senior management consultant with McKinsey and Co.; he served as chairman of the Health Insurance Group, the Bank of America in Australia and Pacific Carpets International. In the late 1970s he was simultaneously chairman of the Australian Travel Industry Association and deputy chairman of the Tourist Industry Advisory Council. In 1981-82 he was a member of the Commonwealth Telecommunications Committee.

A vital dimension of his life began in 1953, when he and two Melbourne surgeons formed an informal education group which became the Anti-Cancer Council of Victoria education committee. Dick chaired it from 1955 to 1982. His vision was for a national body, which he helped to create in 1960 and served on as a Victorian delegate until 1973. He was president of the ACCV from 1982 until 1998, during which time its scope and sophistication were transformed. It extended its activities from education to patient support and oncological research. His countless hours of voluntary work were recognised in 1991 when he was made an Officer of the Order of Australia (AO) for his service to public health and education. When Paul de Jersey, president of the Australian Cancer Society, presented the society's gold medal to Dick in 1999 he described him as "an extraordinary man". "No one Australian," he said, "better exemplifies volunteerism as the foundation of cancer control in this country than Mr Allan Dick."

	M	I	NO	Runs	HS	100s	50s	Avge	Ct	St	W	Avge	BB
First-class	18	26	1	485	53	0	1	19.40	10	0	36	26.88	5-31
Domestic first-class	14	21	1	312	45	0	0	15.60	6	0	32	26.16	5-31

FOLEY, DARREN STUART, died on June 15, 2004, in Melbourne. Born in that city on December 1, 1964, Foley gave yeoman service to both the Richmond and Dandenong district clubs as an opening bowler of strength and persistence. His accuracy allowed batsmen no liberties and his venomous leg-cutter was a potent attacking weapon. His former Dandenong coach, Brendan McArdle, believed Foley was desperately unlucky to have missed state selection. He played with Richmond from 1983-84 to 1987-88 and Dandenong from 1988-89 to 1994-95, before leaving to pursue a work opportunity in Perth. His 149 games netted him 281 wickets at 23.38, the best of his seven five-wicket hauls being 7 for 25 against Collingwood in 1988-89. He was a good enough tailender to compile five fifties and 1,399 runs at 17.27. Foley, who had an outstanding reputation for passing on his knowledge and enthusiasm to younger club-mates, had been ill for more than a year with cancer. He was the brother-in-law of the Australian Test player Matthew Elliott.

GARDNER, ROY, died on April 2, 2004, at Mount Eliza on the Mornington Peninsula. After a brief playing career in Melbourne district cricket he became a benign and constructive coach, both in terms of player development and premiership success. Born on January 18, 1914, in the inner Melbourne suburb of West Hotham (now North Melbourne), Gardner was educated at West Brunswick State School and captained the Victorian schools team that played in the 1928 interstate carnival in Sydney. While playing for the Brunswick sub-district side he appeared twice for the Colts at district level in 1930-31. After one season with Carlton in 1933-34, Fitzroy claimed him on residential grounds and he spent the next four summers there. Of slight physique (173 cm and 73 kg), he had the on-side strength associated with his pronounced two-eyed stance, although his game was built on a tight defence and he could cut with delicacy.

He had a memorable season in 1935-36, hitting 117 not out against South Melbourne and contributing consistently enough to make the two-match tour of Tasmania then play in the return match in Melbourne. Gardner batted soundly in each of his five first-class innings. His best performance was his 45 and 32 on debut, sharing in opening stands of 71 and 55 with Lester Wynne. In the district semi-final against Carlton that season, he batted 404 minutes over two days to hit a match-defining 214. He ended the season with 807 runs at 53.80. Still only a young man, Gardner left Fitzroy at the end of 1937-38, having made 2,300 runs at 32.39 in a district career spanning 65 matches. He returned to Brunswick and became the competition's youngest captain-coach, winning four successive premierships between 1939-40 and 1942-43.

After three years with the RAAF as a leading aircraftsman – during which he served in New Guinea, the Pacific Islands and Borneo – Gardner returned for two final seasons at Brunswick. After 1956 he built on his reputation as a coach, first with University and then with Essendon, who responded to his influence by winning their first premiership in 1963-64. They were then runners-up in three successive seasons from 1965-66. Among those whose careers Gardner assisted were the state players John Grant, Keith Kirby and John Swanson. He had joined the Melbourne Cricket Club in 1937 and became foundation member of the club's social cricket side, the 29ers, in 1956. He attended each of their convivial annual dinners from the formation year until 2002. As a young man, Gardner had been a representative for the famous firm of Rawleighs, before joining his father and brother in the family furniture removal business.

	M	I	NO	Runs	HS	100s	50s	Avge	Ct	St	W	Avge	BB
First-class	3	5	0	146	45	0	0	29.20	0	0	0	–	–

HOOKES, DAVID WILLIAM, died on January 19, 2004, at the Alfred Hospital in the Melbourne suburb of Prahran, after suffering head injuries during an altercation outside a St Kilda hotel. A bouncer from the hotel is facing charges over Hookes's death. The violent intrusion of death into an evening of celebrations following a one-day match between South Australia and Victoria brought a shocked reaction around Australia. It provoked much discussion of the link between alcohol, sport and violence in Australian society, and sportspeople began to wonder whether they would be forced to retreat into an even more hermetically-sealed world safe from the unwanted attention of fans. Meanwhile the apparent senselessness of the incident unhinged a section of the media's sense of proportion. For several weeks, Hookes had the title of "cricket legend" conferred on him and in the process was seemingly elevated to the greatest Australian cricketer since Don Bradman. Hookes himself would have had too much salty commonsense to accept this kind of estimate.

The golden promise of 1976-77 never materialised into the fertile Test career that seemed to beckon. For a while he became the highest run-maker in Sheffield Shield history. Yet it was Hookes, ever aware of his own strengths and weaknesses, who pointed out that this simply meant that an average of 34.36 in 23 Tests had allowed him plenty of time for domestic cricket. He did, however, transform himself into something of more lasting benefit to the cricket world. As senior player, captain and, latterly, as Victorian coach, he became a nurturer of ability and an aggressively wise developer of potential. Two pages of tributes from a wide cross-section of the sporting and general community in Melbourne's *Herald-Sun* spoke of a man still making a vital impact in his sphere of influence.

It also suggested the ways in which Hookes encapsulated the qualities of the traditional Australian: laconic, direct, unpretentious, practical. He had more than a touch of the larrikin. He appealed to people because he was the genuine article, rather than merely a slick advertising concept. Alan Shiell, the former South Australian player and sportswriter who wrote the biography *Hookesy* (1993), summarised him thus: "He was such a personality. He was so good for the media long before he went into the media himself. He was a great character, full of fun, always enjoyable to be with. He knew everyone and everyone knew Hookesy, always the life of the party."

Born on May 3, 1955, in the inner Adelaide suburb of Mile End, Hookes was a prodigiously talented schoolboy cricketer. He successfully represented South Australia at the national schoolboys' carnival three years in a row while a student at Underdale High School. He was also playing for West Torrens, making his A-grade debut in 1972-73, and his aggressively fluent left-hand batting and all-purpose left-arm bowling earned him a place in the SA Colts side in 1973-74. State selection came in 1975-76; he produced a modestly consistent 395 runs at 32.91 and the promise of more to come. His biggest innings was his first, against the touring West Indians, when he batted sensibly for 138 minutes in making 55.

The summer of 1976-77 was his year of wonders. After scoring only 35 runs in four innings, then missing several matches because of university exams, Hookes exploded on to the national cricketing consciousness with five blistering centuries in six innings. All were at Adelaide Oval, and all in the space of a fortnight. Four hours of controlled power against the Victorians brought him 163, including seven sixes and 10 fours. Four of the sixes contributed to the 29 runs which came off one over from the leg-spinner Colin Thwaites. He took 185 and 105 off the Queensland attack, his second hundred occupying only 101 minutes and 90 balls. New South Wales suffered next as he made 135 and 156. The first of these innings was almost disdainful in its mastery of the attack, as he hoisted a fourth-wicket stand of 204 in 134 minutes with the opener Tony Handrickan.

Naturally he appeared in the Centenary Test, creating a defining moment in an unforgettable match. One over from Tony Greig allowed Hookes to enter Australian cricket folklore. After the occasion and the pitch had combined to send 23 wickets tumbling on the first two days, the third day was less hectic. The powerfully framed Hookes (183 cm and 83 kg) began soberly enough, before cracking five successive fours in five balls off Greig. Hookes saw this as a riposte to Greig's description of him as "just another left-hander who can't bat". The over after the fireworks he was dismissed by Derek Underwood and given a tart send-off by Greig. Hookes shot back: "At least I'm an Australian playing this game, not a fucking import." As a batsman, Hookes had begun as he would continue for the rest of his career. Footwork could be an optional extra; defence could be sketchy. But he had that thrilling combination of a hawk-like eye, explosive power and complete self-belief. It made him supremely watchable. To sit square of the boundary on the narrow Adelaide Oval was to imperil life and limb on repeated occasions during a Hookes innings.

He was a contracted Packer player when he went on the 1977 Ashes tour. The distraction of the majority of Australian players was evident in the results as cricket headed towards its brave new world. Hookes hit a century against Somerset in 81 minutes but only twice reached fifty in the Tests; a last-gasp 85 at The Oval was his best effort. He looked to be in top form in the World Series Supertests that began in Australia at the end of that year. At the Sydney Showground, he had made a rollicking 81 when an Andy Roberts bouncer broke his jaw. Even though he assured his partner, Rod Marsh, that he could still utter the copulatory verb, and even though he made consistent runs in the 1978-79 series, close observers felt the injury had dented the easy confidence on which his batting was built.

Thus began life for Hookes as a fringe dweller in the camp of Australian cricket. He was given one of the six Tests against West Indies and England in 1979-80, then sent on the subsequent tour of Pakistan. He managed only 10 runs in six first-class innings and bagged a pair in his only Test, in Karachi, thanks to the left-arm spinner Iqbal Qasim. His fortunes turned when he was appointed state captain in 1981-82, his positive approach helping South Australia win the Sheffield Shield. Next season he looked back to his best, topping the national aggregates with four centuries and 1,424 runs at 64.72. Against Victoria, in Adelaide, he made 137. Then, incensed at what he saw as Graham Yallop's churlish declaration – requiring South Australia to make 272 runs off 30 overs – he gave spectators 43 minutes of incandescence. After 10 overs the score had reached 128. Hookes sprinted to his century in 34 balls, which included three sixes and 17 fours, the fastest hundred ever recorded in first-class cricket.

His anger had not abated when the South Australians visited Melbourne. He smashed 193 in better than even time off the hapless Victorians, not appearing overly inconvenienced by a broken thumb. He regained his place for all five of that summer's Ashes Tests and batted consistently. He hit four fifties in eight innings for an average of 49.14. His 66 not out at the Gabba was a commanding innings, his unbroken fourth-wicket partnership of 107 with Kim Hughes ensuring an Australian victory. He was appointed vice-captain for the short inaugural Test tour of Sri Lanka. In the only Test, in Kandy, he took advantage of the easy conditions to hit his first and last Test century, an unconquered 143, including a hundred between lunch and tea on the second day.

Hookes then proceeded to give an example of his belief that valour was the better part of discretion, indulging in some trenchant on-air criticism of Hughes, his national captain. It probably cost him his place during the home series of 1983-84 against Pakistan. Restored to the team for the Caribbean tour, he struggled to make runs – like most of the Australians apart from Allan Border. His one innings of real achievement was his 51 in the Fourth Test at St John's, Antigua, where he joined Border in a fifth-wicket partnership of 123. He was dropped for the next Australian season but returned for the last time in 1985-86. He played four out of six Tests against New Zealand and India without getting past 42.

And so Hookes's Test career was closed, that sense of abundant potential to remain forever unfulfilled. He now entered a new phase: as a senior player on the domestic circuit and a batsman for whom caution was an obscene word. He still had a huge appetite for runs too. His 306 not out in Adelaide in 1986-87 was vintage stuff in its sustained demolition of the Tasmanian attack. He faced only 330 balls, hitting two sixes and 41 fours, and his undefeated 462-run stand for the fourth wicket with Wayne Phillips broke all previous Australian partnership records. He again passed 1,000 runs in 1987-88. The following season he led South Australia to an unsuccessful Shield final in Perth. Controversy returned again when the captaincy was removed from him at the end of 1989-90. His replacement, Andrew Hilditch, cited internal team friction as the reason for the decision, but Hookes remained flummoxed by its origins. He soldiered on for another two seasons. When he retired at the end of the 1991-92 season, he had scored more runs and taken more catches for the state than anyone else. With 90 games as captain, he was only one behind the record of Les Favell, who must have seen Hookes as a spiritual descendant.

Hookes had a substantial media profile in Adelaide, and in 1995 he raised eyebrows by moving to what seemed like the lion's den of Melbourne to work with the former footballer Gerard Healy on radio station 3AW's *Sports Today*. He was in his element, adept at providing pithy commentary across a wide range of sports. Hookes specialised in memorably colourful language and felt uninhibited by what he saw as pettifogging notions of political correctness. In October 2003, when Simon Katich was called up to the Australian side, Hookes offered this explanation: "When they give out the baggy blue cap in New South Wales, they give you a baggy green cap in a brown paper bag as well to save making two presentations."

In another surprise move, Hookes was appointed coach of Victoria in 2002-03. His influence was immediate. He infused the team with a sense of self-confidence and a willingness to play positive cricket. He expunged the diffidence and defensiveness of previous seasons, inspiring several key players to realise their potential. The advent of David Hussey, the growing stature of Jon Moss and the renaissance of Brad Hodge all have the mark of Hookes upon them. It was fitting that the side should have continued on without him to the most convincing of Pura Cup wins in 2003-04.

A week after his death, his funeral service was held at Adelaide Oval, the ground where he had played the majority of his memorable innings and whose short square boundaries had often resounded to the fusillade of his attacking strokes. Again, a huge cross-section of the community turned out. In addition to eulogies from his family, heartfelt words were spoken by his former team-mates and friends: Bob Zadow, Wayne Phillips and Ian Chappell. Hookes died on the eve of Victoria's 1,000th first-class match, against South Australia, in Melbourne. To commemorate his life, the governments of the two states combined to donate a trophy for matches between Victoria and South Australia. Fittingly, it is designed to reflect Hookes' habit of leaning his bat against the stumps and leaving his cap and gloves at their base during a break, as a silent reminder that he would soon be back to resume his innings.

	M	I	NO	Runs	HS	100s	50s	Avge	Ct	St	W	Avge	BB
First-class	178	304	16	12,671	306*	32	65	44.00	166	0	41	58.02	3-58
Domestic first-class	120	205	9	9,364	306*	26	44	47.78	128	0	26	64.46	2-22
Tests	23	41	3	1,306	143*	1	8	34.37	12	0	1	41.00	1-4
Int'l limited-overs	39	36	2	826	76	0	5	24.29	11	0	1	28.00	1-2
Domestic limited-overs	38	38	1	1,149	101	1	6	31.05	22	0	12	37.58	5-41

LANGDON, CHRISTOPHER WALTER, died at the Sir Charles Gairdner Hospital in Perth on May 2, 2004. It was men like Wally Langdon who transformed Western Australian cricket from a patronised outpost into a powerhouse of the national game. He was a key all-round factor in the heady success of the Sandgropers capturing the Sheffield Shield at their first attempt in 1947-48, then became a solid foundation as the grim reality of the early 1950s erased the euphoria. Finally, as selector and coach, he was instrumental in shaping the revival of the 1960s and the success of the 1970s.

Born on July 4, 1922, in Boulder, on the Kalgoorlie goldfields, Langdon was educated at Kalgoorlie High School and appeared in five successive Country Week carnivals in Perth. In the first of these, as a 15-year-old in short pants, he was the youngest player on show. His left-arm orthodox spinners made an immediate impression, yielding him 4 for 11 and 6 for 33 against Albany, 4 for 9 against Narrogin and 5 for 25 versus Bunbury. His batting soon flowered too. In the 1938 final against Mount Barker he made an unbeaten 147. He took 9 for 25 against Bruce Rock in 1941, and dominated North-Eastern District with 153 and 7 for 4. Langdon joined the Royal Australian Air Force in December 1942, and after extensive training in Australia and Canada was assigned to 460 Squadron, where he attained the rank of flight-lieutenant. He spent the latter part of the war as a navigator on Lancaster bombers, flying several missions over Germany.

His form for the Claremont club made him an automatic selection for the state team from 1946-47. Langdon made an important contribution to WA's inaugural Sheffield Shield match against South Australia in Perth. Bowling slow medium-pacers on a sporting pitch, he shattered the visitors' second

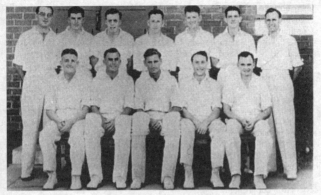

The early conquerors: WA's Shield-winners of 1947-48, including Wally Langdon (back, fourth from left) and Tom Outridge (back, second from left).

innings with 4 for 28, helping his side to an innings victory. Later in the season he showed one of the characteristic qualities of his batting by making runs against the toughest opposition. He took 70 off a strong New South Wales attack in Sydney, then 112 in a commanding display against the might of the 1948 Ashes touring team. Langdon's name was sufficiently to the fore that he was invited to take part in the Bradman testimonial match at the MCG in December 1948, contributing a pleasant 60 and 42 for Lindsay Hassett's side.

He toured India, Pakistan and Ceylon with the Commonwealth team of 1949-50. He scored five fifties in 20 innings and played in the Third and Fourth unofficial Tests, but did not make the big runs he was capable of. Back to his best in 1950-51, he was selected for an Australian XI side against MCC in Sydney. The gloss of the invitation was somewhat dulled when he was sent in at No. 7 and almost totally destroyed when he was run out for 27, having been stranded by Jim Burke. After a wretched 1951-52 season, during which he passed 20 only once in 10 innings, Langdon was in peak form the following summer and found his new office of state captain no burden to carry. He began with a circumspect 120 not out against the touring South Africans, including a third-wicket stand of 170 with Ken Meuleman, and went on to average 55 for the season. His friend Meuleman, for one, felt Langdon should have been selected for the 1953 Ashes tour. He would have been a better bet than several of the batsmen who did make the trip. His defence was organised and he had plenty of attractive strokes, particularly square of the wicket. Above all, he was an adaptable player who could defend or attack with equal facility. Test audiences never got to see it.

Langdon spent the English seasons of 1954 and 1955 playing successfully with Burnley in the Lancashire League. On his return he made his final first-class appearances on WA's two-match tour to the eastern states in 1955-56.

Two hours of calm occupation brought him 46 against South Australia, showing he had lost none of his touch. He finished his club career with Claremont–Cottesloe in 1958-59. In 126 grade matches he made 6,070 runs at 48.56, with 17 centuries, and took 192 wickets at 14.45. His best seasons were 1950-51, when he amassed 1,020 runs at 145.71, and 1951-52, when he captured 31 wickets at 14.55.

For most of the 1960s Langdon was a state selector, before becoming WA's coach in 1967-68. He understood his team well and worked with such a sense of focus that WA at last repeated their first-up Sheffield Shield triumph of 20 years earlier. Throughout the 1970s he became a familiar voice on ABC radio as an expert commentator, whose insights were clear, well-expressed and revealing. Langdon's extensive contribution was recognised in 1985 when the WACA awarded him life membership. He had trained as a teacher after the war and spent many years at John Curtin High School in Fremantle, where he coached Ross Edwards and billeted Barry Shepherd. The latter part of his career was spent as a recruitment officer for the WA education department.

	M	I	NO	Runs	HS	100s	50s	Avge	Ct	St	W	Avge	BB
First-class	45	76	6	2,502	138	5	15	35.74	24	0	27	41.00	4-28
Domestic first-class	21	39	1	1,292	138	3	5	34.00	19	0	18	45.39	4-28

MARTIN, EDMUND JOHN, died on June 9, 2004, in Perth, three months short of his 102nd birthday and content in his position as Australia's longest-lived first-class cricketer. He was born on September 26, 1902, in Eaglehawk, a suburb of the central Victorian goldrush city of Bendigo. Teddy Martin moved to Western Australia in the 1920s, playing with Subiaco–Leederville from 1927-28 to 1930-31 and then for Mount Lawley, where the influential Dick Bryant held sway, from 1931-32 to 1934-35. During 1932-33 he turned out for North–East Province in an experimental elite competition tried in Perth that season. In 99 matches he scored 1,441 runs at 15.01 and took 230 wickets with his flighted leg-spinners, which included a preponderance of googlies in addition to what he called "straight-throughers".

Martin had to wait until 1932-33 for his chance in first-class cricket. In a candid interview with John Townsend of *The West Australian* in January 2001, he felt sure that a letter he had written to that paper in the 1920s urging the selectors to adopt a youth policy was probably held against him. Playing for WA against Douglas Jardine's Bodyline tourists, he took some punishment and suffered from dropped catches, but still returned figures of 3 for 115 and 3 for 50. His victims were Herbert Sutcliffe, Bob Wyatt and the Nawab of Pataudi in the first innings, and Maurice Leyland, Freddie Brown and Hedley Verity in the second. Three days later, five batsmen from the eastern states joined the local players for the Australian XI match against MCC at the WACA. This time Martin received a real lashing, his 16 wicketless overs going for 126 runs before the visitors declared at 7 for 583. He might have taken some comfort that this was the only game in which Don Bradman conceded more than 100 runs in an innings, although he did take two wickets. Martin was unimpressed with the wise men from the east. He

Golden oldie: Ted Martin, who survived two first-class matches against Douglas Jardine's Bodyline tourists and lived on to 101.

felt they held themselves aloof from the lowly Sandgropers, apart from Vic Richardson, whose bluffness came across as self-important bombast.

After starting work as an office boy with a firm of Perth solicitors, Martin became a skilled accountant, eventually filling a senior role with BP where he worked until he was 72. He remained alert and interested in the modern game, asserting that, compared with his day, Shane Warne should be labelled a medium-pacer. He lived in his own home at Applecross, in the southern suburbs of Perth, comfortably and self-sufficiently until less than two years before his death.

	M	I	NO	Runs	HS	100s	50s	Avge	Ct	St	W	Avge	BB
First-class	2	2	0	3	2	0	0	1.50	0	0	6	48.50	3-50

McDONALD, STANLEY JAMES, died on June 8, 2003, in the Perth suburb of Floreat Park. Born in East Perth on March 24, 1916, McDonald was Western Australia's oldest first-class umpire. He took up umpiring after World War II, having been a player of moderate ability in local suburban cricket. In a career which lasted until 1973-74 he umpired 360 pennant matches, of which 260 were in first-grade. He stood in matches against New South Wales in 1963-64 and South Australia the following season. On both occasions his partner was Alan Mackley, for whom he deputised after lunch on the second day against Victoria in 1964-65 when Mackley was struck by a return from the outfield and suffered a gashed head. McDonald was awarded life membership of the WA Cricket Umpires' Association in 1972.

MULLINS, JOHN ROSS, died on October 26, 2003, at his home in Longueville on Sydney's lower North Shore. A respected and experienced journalist, Mullins came to cricket writing late in his career, spending the decade until his retirement in 1988 as chief cricket writer for Australian Associated Press. During this time, apart from his coverage of cricket at home, he reported on two tours to New Zealand and one to Pakistan. He quickly gained a reputation for balanced, lucid writing which aimed to analyse and report the game without sensation or exaggeration. In 1948 Mullins joined Lane Cove Cricket Club in the Sydney municipal and shires competition. He acted as player, captain, selector, committeeman and secretary, a breadth and depth of service which resulted in the club making him a life member. He was also a member of the New South Wales Cricket Association's media and publicity committee, and a director of the Cricketers' Club of NSW.

Born in the Sydney suburb of Chatswood on January 2, 1923, he was educated at Marist Brothers' School in nearby North Sydney, until his father's premature death in 1939 caused Mullins to follow in his footsteps at the John Fairfax newspaper group. During World War II he served with the Australian army in an anti-aircraft battery in Darwin, before joining the British occupation forces in Borneo and Labuan. He was concerned that those who fought in and defended Darwin should be officially recognised, and conducted a campaign that lasted nearly half a century. It bore fruit in 1994 when the Australian government belatedly sanctioned that personnel from that theatre of war should be eligible for the award of the 1939-45 Star. After leaving the Fairfax group in 1964, he worked in a number of media areas before his late blooming as a cricket correspondent.

OUTRIDGE, THOMAS MICHAEL, died on July 21, 2003, in Bunbury, in the south-west of Western Australia. A left-hand batsman who also indulged in left-arm wrist-spin, Outridge was born in Subiaco on September 8, 1927. He made his first-grade debut for East Perth at 16 while still a student at Aquinas College. He hit his maiden first-grade century soon after transferring to Subiaco in 1945-46, establishing himself as a forceful yet stylish batsman. Continued good form resulted in his selection for the WA Colts team which played MCC in Fremantle in October 1946. A state spot, however, proved difficult to secure. He eventually forced his way in for the last two games of the 1947-48 season – against the touring Indians and Don Bradman's 1948 Australian XI – after making successive club centuries. He then waited another two seasons for his next appearance, against South Australia in Perth, top-scoring with a solid 49 in WA's first innings.

Outridge made a spectacular 92 in WA's opening game of 1950-51 against MCC. After WA were set an unlikely 320 to win in 170 minutes, Outridge lifted three sixes off Brian Close and hit nine fours in his two hours at the crease, dominating a fourth-wicket partnership of 134 with Ron Frankish. His rumbustious approach that day was in contrast to the more careful methods he usually adopted at state level. Next season, for example, against South Australia in Perth, he joined Alan Edwards in a sixth-wicket partnership of

181, a record at the time for WA. But Outridge's 93 occupied 285 minutes. He closed his first-class career in 1952-53 with a fighting 50 in 145 minutes against Victoria in Melbourne. His caution on that occasion may be partly explained by the fact that he had made ducks in his previous three innings.

For some time his bowling was neglected at state level. He was given only 32 overs in his first eight games, waiting until his ninth match in 1951-52 to capture a wicket. He suddenly became an important member of the attack the following season, taking 2 for 40 and 4 for 80 against New South Wales in Perth, and 5 for 78 against Victoria in Melbourne. Until then he had relied mainly on prodigious spin from over the wrist, but he now developed a subtle and effective wrong'un. Despite bowling with his left hand, Outridge threw with his right hand. At the end of that season he moved to Bunbury, where his accountancy skills were used in the family hotel. He finished his Perth career by spending four seasons with Claremont–Cottesloe. In 115 first-grade games with his three clubs, he scored 3,377 runs at 28.38 and took 106 wickets at 24.41.

In Bunbury, he represented WA Country against the 1954-55 MCC team, capturing the first wicket of the tour against them when he bowled Len Hutton for 59. That summer Outridge received an offer to play with Lowerhouse in the Lancashire League, but was unable to accept for business reasons. He continued to be a prolific player locally and represented Bunbury at seven Country Week tournaments, five of which produced wins for his side. He made three centuries in four innings in the 1958-59 carnival, three not outs helping him to an average of 323. Despite a natural diffidence and quietness of demeanour, he was generous in his support for and encouragement of local cricketers. Outridge came from an impeccable sporting background. His father, also Thomas, played first-grade with West Perth and Subiaco but was best known as one of Perth's leading Australian Rules footballers. A ruckman for Subiaco, he was the inaugural Sandover Medallist in 1921, awarded to Perth's best and fairest footballer. To complete his accomplishments, he was a member of the state rowing team which contested the King's Cup in 1920.

	M	I	NO	Runs	HS	100s	50s	Avge	Ct	St	W	Avge	BB
First-class	19	36	1	724	93	0	4	20.68	8	0	21	45.57	5-78
Domestic first-class	12	23	1	458	93	0	3	20.82	5	0	18	37.78	5-78

PERROTT, THOMAS JAMES, died on May 14, 2003, at the St John of God Hospital in the Perth suburb of Subiaco. In 1980, Perrott's old friend Bernie Prindiville became president of the WACA. Wanting to push the association towards a more pro-active business approach, Prindiville invited Perrott to join the executive because of his business expertise. He became president in 1990 and returned the office to a more ceremonial function after the turbulence of the business-cricket split of the Prindiville years. During Perrott's time in office, the WACA was transformed in appearance, with new light towers and the Lillee-Marsh Stand. He was made a life member in 1995 and stood down from office in 1997.

Born in North Perth on September 3, 1920, Perrott was educated at Aquinas College where he was a member of the 1st XI. He qualified as an accountant and in 1957 took over his father's painting business, which he developed into an international company. His achievements were recognised when he was named Citizen of the Year in 1986 for his services to WA commerce and industry. He suffered from hearing problems and became well-known for his philanthropic contributions to community services for the disabled. He was made a Member of the Order of Australia (AM) for this work in 1982.

RADFORD, ROBERT MICHAEL, died on February 28, 2004, at his home in Cremorne on the northern side of Sydney Harbour. Bob Radford was utterly individual as a cricket administrator. He was too flamboyant to be one of the puritans of the past, yet his sense of the game's history and his fascination with people made him temperamentally unfitted to join the bean-counter brigade of the contemporary world. Born on October 18, 1943, in the northern Sydney suburb of Epping, he was educated at the Sydney Church of England Grammar School, known as Shore, where he played in the 1st XI. He played a little with the North Sydney club but spent most of his playing days with Lane Cove, in the municipal and shires competition, where he mixed many ducks with a few centuries at the top of the order. Yet he was a good enough sportsman to represent his state at baseball in the 1960s.

After spending several years as a clerical officer at Lane Cove Municipal Council, Radford became assistant secretary to Alan Barnes at the New South Wales Cricket Association in 1970, succeeding him on his retirement in 1976. In 1984 his title was changed to executive director, a position he held until retiring in 1995. His approach to the job was more informal than his predecessors. He cultivated a wide circle of contacts, often at his own expense, throughout the community and used them to cricket's benefit. Don Bradman dubbed him the best cricket administrator in Australia – before lunch – and the comment catches the contradictions of Radford's personality. He loved the tradition and lore of cricket, yet could behave outrageously; he was a stickler for form and ceremony, yet was impatient of those who took themselves too seriously. While his mode of living was self-destructive, his approach to his job and his wide vision were the essence of constructiveness.

A memorial gathering at the SCG was alive with Radford stories. Many of those present had been on the famous cruise on Sydney Harbour in 2000, when he invited 200 friends to a lunch excursion which had more than a touch of the epic to it. Others remembered him remonstrating with Greg Chappell over what Radford saw as the iniquities of vegetarianism; Chappell responded by asserting that Radford would not reach 60 unless he adopted a less bibulous lifestyle. The consequent bet resulted in Chappell consuming a huge steak at the Mosman Rowing Club when Radford reached the requisite age in 2003. Yet his administration was careful and intelligent, with a steady focus on the players, spectators and the advancement of the game itself. He sought out and welcomed old state players and tended to the needs of the contemporary side. From 1993 to 1997 he chaired the Bradman Foundation, seeing its work as a crucial way of linking the past with the future of

A legend before lunch: Bob Radford with Keith Miller, left, and Neil Harvey, right.

Australian cricket. His services to the game were recognised when he was made a Member of the Order of Australia (AM) in 1992.

At the gathering referred to above, the former state player and administrator Neil Maxwell told of how Radford would issue them with a copy of Philip Derriman's history of the NSWCA, *True to the Blue*, then test them on it after a few months in the job. Readers of this section owe him a debt of gratitude because of his commitment to the value of the game's history. He was instrumental in turning the idea of an association library into a reality, and actively supported the production of such books as Derriman's history (1985) and the printing of Jas Scott's *Early Cricket in Sydney, 1803–1856* (1991). Under his watchful eye, the library was fostered with appropriate facilities and resources, which made it a first-rate research site. Would that there were more administrators like him.

THOMS, GEORGE RONALD, died on August 29, 2003, in Melbourne. Although his cricketing fame rests on one prolific season, Thoms gave decades of service through his skills as a gynaecologist, forsaking the world of fashionable practice to return to the western suburbs of Melbourne, the world from which he had come and to which he was professionally and personally committed.

Born in Footscray on March 22, 1927, Thoms was educated at Williamstown High School and gained an engineering diploma at the Royal Melbourne Institute of Technology. He joined Essendon in 1944-45 and his dour, unflappable approach as an opener brought him successive centuries early in the 1946-47 season. It was enough to win him a place in the Victorian side against Queensland, standing in for Ken Meuleman who was away with the Australian team. Thoms made 37 competent runs but had to wait almost five years for a repeat invitation. It came after a golden district season for University, which produced 727 runs at 80.77. Returning to the side in 1951-52, this time at Meuleman's expense, he repaid the selectors' endorsement with a resolute six-hour innings of 150 against Western Australia in Perth. Although he hit only 10 fours, he kept one end safe until he was sixth out at 357, setting Victoria well on the road to an innings victory.

This innings was the foundation of a consistent season. He hit another century against Queensland and a 64 in Sydney. Bill O'Reilly wrote approvingly of Thoms's patience and temperament, which was "mature enough to allow him to keep on concentrating on his job". His batting was built around a sound defence and good judgment of what to leave alone, together with the occasional neat leg-glance and an even more occasional hefty drive. He formed a consistent partnership with his club-mate Colin McDonald, the pair racking up two century stands plus two more partnerships of 96. The selectors turned to them for the Fifth Test against West Indies in Sydney, when Jack Moroney was dropped and Arthur Morris was unavailable because of an injured thigh. It was a unique occurrence of the same pair opening for club, state and country in the same season.

Oppressively humid conditions and a Sydney greentop made the first day a cut-price excursion for swing bowlers. By day's end, West Indies were 9 for 64 in reply to Australia's 116. In this context, Thoms and McDonald had resisted gamely in putting on 39 in 63 minutes, Thoms lingering for another 22 minutes before being dismissed for 16. Next day, they spent 94 minutes eking out 55 before Thoms trod on his stumps on 28. Time was as important as runs, however, as they occupied the crease while the sting left the pitch, paving the way for Australia to compile an unreachable 377. Thoms's Test batting contribution was therefore spread over three hours and was all over by lunch on the second day of his only match.

Next season he experienced a much leaner time, starting with a pair in Victoria's opening game against the South Africans. In 14 innings he managed only two fifties, both against South Australia, and was dropped for the final two matches. In 1953-54 he appeared in the two games against Tasmania; in the first, in Hobart, he made an unusually sprightly 140, sharing hundred partnerships with Bert Numa and Dave Kerr. These games turned out to be his first-class farewell. Thoms had recently graduated in medicine from the University of Melbourne, and one of his senior colleagues was impressing on him the need to choose between sport and surgery. In a final flourish, after seven seasons with University, he enjoyed two productive years with Melbourne. Thoms played 120 district games in all, which yielded 4,383 runs at 37.46 and included a dozen centuries. Upon joining University in 1948-49 he became a useful change bowler of apparently innocuous medium-pacers. They harvested 31 wickets at 37.35, including a memorable 5 for 48 in 1953-54, his only wickets of that season.

From 1957 to 1962 he worked in a number of British hospitals, gaining specialist experience in gynaecology and being admitted as a Fellow of the Royal College of Gynaecologists in both England and Edinburgh. It was during this time that he met and married the English actress Felicity Young. When he returned to Australia he made a conscious decision to return to practice in Footscray, despite having initially had rooms in the prestigious environment of Collins Street. Ignoring the counsel of some of his colleagues, Thoms explained his decision thus: "One day I just said 'oh bugger it' and moved. The people here are my type of people, ordinary working-class guys – just like me." He spent 30 years at Footscray's Western Hospital and 39 years in consulting practice in the suburb. His self-effacing dedication in what was regarded by some as a less-fashionable area was recognised in 1996, when he was awarded the Medal of the Order of Australia (OAM) for his services to gynaecology, obstetrics and hospital administration.

Thoms maintained his long friendship with Colin McDonald to the end of his life. Six weeks before he died Thoms made a gallant visit to the Test cricketers' reunion held in Sydney, despite being seriously ill with leukaemia. As a young man he had excelled in a wide variety of sports. He captained both the tertiary education institutions at which he studied in Australian Rules, and was also a pennant player in squash and table tennis, a reflection of the sporting milieu in which he had grown and lived. His brother Jim played six first-grade games for Essendon and another 54 for Footscray, scoring 1,746 runs at 24.25. Jim also played 120 games of Australian Rules for Footscray as a winger, kicking 101 goals, and was an all-Australian table tennis champion. His brother-in-law Arthur Olliver was one of Footscray's most illustrious footballers; between 1935 and 1950 he played 272 games as a ruckman, kicking 354 goals.

	M	I	NO	Runs	HS	100s	50s	Avge	Ct	St	W	Avge	BB
First-class	19	32	0	1,137	150	3	5	35.53	10	0	1	14.00	1-8
Domestic first-class	13	22	0	837	150	2	4	38.05	6	0	0	–	–
Tests	1	2	0	44	28	0	0	22.00	0	0	0	–	–

TRESIDDER, PHILLIP LYLE, died on October 19, 2003, at the Prince of Wales Hospital in the south-eastern Sydney suburb of Randwick. Born in nearby Kensington on September 20, 1928, Tresidder was educated at Sydney Boys' High School and intimately identified with the Randwick Cricket Club for more than 60 years, initially as a lower grade player who captured 176 wickets with his left-arm medium-pacers. His moment of triumph came in 1951-52 when he took 9 for 18, including a hat-trick, and 7 for 39 in a fourth-grade match against Manly. He served as club president from 1991 to 2000, then as inaugural co-patron of the newly amalgamated Randwick–Petersham club. He was Randwick's delegate to the New South Wales Cricket Association from 1979 to 1985 and 1991 to 1999, and to the Sydney Cricket Association from 1986 to 1999. Randwick made him a life member in 1982 and the NSWCA followed suit in 2001. So passionate was his commitment to his club that Randwick–Petersham's president, Lyall Gardner, was more than half-serious in suggesting in his club's tribute that Tresidder would take a cut lunch if he travelled west of Anzac Parade, three kilometres from his beloved Coogee Oval.

Mr Versatile: Phil Tresidder wrote evocatively and knowledgably, whatever the ball game.

Professionally, Tresidder became one of the most respected Australian sporting journalists. He was born at a time when the narrow specialisation which marks so much of contemporary life had not yet taken hold of journalism. As a 19-year-old at the *Daily Telegraph*, he persuaded the forbidding Frank Packer to send him to England to cover the 1947-48 Australian rugby union tour, stay on for the summer to report on Bradman's farewell trip and the London Olympics, and to finish the assignment by writing about the 1948-49 Kangaroos rugby league Test series. This adaptability, together with his ability to write both economically and evocatively, was the foundation of his long career with Packer's daily and Sunday papers in Sydney.

In time, he covered not only cricket and both of the northern states' football codes, but also became a knowledgable chief golf correspondent and later editor of *Australian Golf Digest*. His golfing insights were aided by his ability to maintain a single-figure handicap throughout most of his life.

Tresidder assisted Alan Davidson in the preparation of his autobiography *Fifteen Paces* (1963) and produced an account of the 1968-69 West Indies tour of Australia, *Captains on a See-Saw* (1969). He also wrote the *The Shark Bites Back: A Portrait of Greg Norman* (1993), *Karrie Webb: The Tigress Bites Back* (2000) and *A Life Worth Living*, a collaboration with the former Australian rugby union player and Sydney lord mayor Nicholas Shehadie (2003). His work was marked by clear readable prose, whose colour never descended into sensationalism. His unobtrusive support for young sports players was another facet of his achievement. In cricket, he was particularly supportive of the future Test opener Alan Turner and was a mentor to the fast bowler Mike Whitney. It was Tresidder who insisted that Whitney's 1981 contract with English league club Fleetwood should include a release clause in case he was called up to the Ashes touring side. The move proved both fortuitous and far-sighted.

VAWSER, BRUCE FORBES, died on May 1, 2004, in Melbourne. Born on June 17, 1929, in the southern Adelaide suburb of Mitcham, Vawser grew up in Melbourne and attended Melbourne Grammar School, where he was in the 1st XI for three years. A punishing left-hand opener with South Melbourne from 1947-48 to 1961-62, he delighted in the on-drive and was a ferocious cutter, but suffered from shakiness at the start of his innings. His one chance at state level came against Tasmania in Melbourne in 1951-52. He made only three before being caught behind off Terry Cowley, whereupon double-centuries to Dick Maddocks and Jeff Hallebone transformed Victoria's 2 for 7 into 647. Next season Vawser (135) and the former state player Roy Howard took St Kilda's bowling apart in an opening stand of 245 in 168 minutes, only six runs short of a first-innings lead. His most productive season was 1956-57 when he made 516 runs at 28.66; his 126-match career brought him 3,457 runs at 23.67. A gifted golfer at the Metropolitan Club, he won the Captain's Trophy there in 1952 and 1971, and also played baseball for South Melbourne. Vawser had an extensive career as a sales executive in the furniture industry and then with ICI.

	M	I	NO	Runs	HS	100s	50s	Avge	Ct	St	W	Avge	BB
First-class	1	1	0	3	3	0	0	3.00	1	0	0	–	–

WEITEMEYER, ROLAND, died on June 10, 2004, in the Brisbane suburb of Sandgate on Moreton Bay. Known always as Ron, Weitemeyer was the leading Queensland umpire of the immediate period after World War II, and at the age of 98 was the state's oldest and longest-lived wearer of the white coat. Born in Nambour, on the hinterland of the Sunshine Coast, his grandfather was a Danish immigrant who in the early 1870s was attracted to the goldfields west of Cooktown, in the far north of the state. Weitemeyer was educated at Brisbane Grammar School and played lower grade cricket with Sandgate, although he was selected in five first-grade games in 1935-36. Soon after he turned to umpiring and quickly rose to first-class level, becoming the most regularly appointed official of his time. Between 1939-40 and 1950-51 he umpired 17 matches at the Gabba, including the state games of the MCC in 1946-47 and 1950-51 and the Indians in 1947-48. His competence during 1946-47 was such that he was appointed to the Australian umpires panel, but George Borwick and Jack Scott controlled each of the five Tests. In his final season he stood in the inaugural Sydney Gregory Cup match between the Queensland and New South Wales Colts sides.

WILLIAMS, RONALD JAMES, died on November 9, 2003, in Launceston. The label "dedicated servant of cricket" can sometimes be an easy cliché; to apply it to Ron Williams does only the palest justice to a lifetime's devotion. He played, umpired, scored, kept statistics and wrote history, all with skill and dedication and all totally without expectation of return beyond the pleasure of being involved in the game he loved.

Born on October 20, 1919, in the small town of Colebrook, north of Hobart, Williams joined the Tasmanian Government Railways during the Depression. So tough were the times that he spent his first six months as a station porter working without wages, before ultimately working in the controller's office in Launceston. It was during his service on the north-west coast in Burnie and Devonport that he came to prominence as an energetic left-arm fast-medium bowler. In Burnie, he formed a feared opening partnership with the state player Ivor Clay for the North West Tasmanian Cricket Association side. He was transferred to Launceston and joined the

Westbury club, representing North in the annual game against South several times in the early 1950s.

From 1959 to 1980 he umpired A-grade matches in Launceston; in 1979 he was awarded life membership of the Northern Tasmanian Umpires' Association. He also became the scorer for the South Launceston club, his accuracy earning him appointment to many first-class and one-day games, including the first Sheffield Shield match in Launceston in 1977-78, Launceston's one and only limited-overs international in 1985-86, and the inaugural Test at Hobart's Bellerive Oval between Australia and Sri Lanka in 1989-90. During the 1980s, Williams was the Northern Tasmanian Cricket Association's statistician. This was the decade in which he transformed his statistical knowledge and copious research into Launceston cricket into several authoritative and well-produced histories. *South Launceston Cricket Club: A History* (1982) was followed by *A Century of Northern Tasmanian Cricket* (1986); both of these organisations granted him life membership. A history of the Launceston Cricket Club followed in 1987, while in 1994 he collaborated with Rick Smith in *WG Down Under: Grace in Australia, 1873–74 and 1891–92*. Australian Rules football also attracted his attention, and in 1990 he produced *A History of North Launceston Football Club*.

Modest, self-effacing and obliging, Williams was held in the highest regard both in the sporting community and the wider world of Launceston. This was officially recognised in 1999 when he was awarded the Medal of the Order of Australia (OAM). It was also marked immediately after his death by the Tasmanian side, who wore black armbands on the first day of the match against New South Wales in Hobart. His son, Wayne, played cricket for Launceston and the NTCA side. His grandson, Michael Farrell, played 25 first-class and 28 one-day matches for Tasmania between 1989-90 and 1997-98, initially as a specialist left-hand batsman and later as an off-spinner.

Warwick Franks was the editor of Wisden Cricketers' Almanack Australia *from 2001-02 to 2003-04.*

Serfs up

by GIDEON HAIGH

Just what did happen in Pretoria on the evening of March 5, 2003? One imagines, reading the **World Cup Diary** (Random House, $29.95) of Glenn McGrath, that it was a pretty convivial evening. A few drinks, then dinner at a local steakhouse with Ricky Ponting, Andrew Symonds, fitness adviser Jock Campbell and the former Australian Cricket Board media manager Brian Murgatroyd ("a top guy even for a Welshman"). It transpires that both McGrath and Ponting – with Murgatroyd's help – have publishing contracts. But hey, the more the merrier, eh? "Even though two of us are writing tour diaries, they should make for interesting reading, with things seen from two different points of view."

Quite so: "different points of view" do make "interesting reading". For if we check the **World Cup Diary** (HarperSports, $29.95) of Ponting, we find that Australia's captain was left rather unmoved by the festivities. In fact, as Ponting remembers it, he was alone in the hotel: "I was happy to do very little this evening and just relax in my room. I haven't gone out very much in the evenings on this trip except with Rianna [his wife], and was in no mood to change that habit tonight. I think I will sleep well."

Maybe we should attempt to triangulate. Let's check Adam Gilchrist's tour diary **Walking to Victory** (Pan Macmillan, $35). But it turns out that Gilly's thoughts were elsewhere that evening, concerned instead with a newspaper article that had just appeared headlined "Million Dollar Men". "It was about how Pigeon [McGrath], Punter [Ponting] and I stood to crack a million dollars a year if we won the World Cup." He was fretting: "Whenever this sort of story appears it unnerves us all."

So unnerved, perhaps, that either: (a) McGrath failed to realise that he was dining with a Ponting clone; (b) when McGrath started droning on about pig-shooting, Ponting simply blotted out all memory of him and fantasised that he was back in his room; or (c) Gilchrist, learning that he and his cobbers were on the brink of a seven-figure jackpot, decided they should justify this by writing completely different tour diaries, and himself wrote a vivid first-hand account of a game of Russian roulette with Nelson Mandela – which his editor later took out to allow space for further stats.

Who knows? Who cares? Reading this year's crop of cricket auto-hagiographies, it occurred to me that the authors might as well start making things up. There's a story about the great baseballer Dizzy Dean – how, whenever a journalist asked him his birthdate, he would tell them a different day. "I always like to give 'em an exclusive," he explained. Almost anything would be preferable to the stupefying tedium of McGrath's apparently minute-by-minute account of Australia's 2003 World Cup progress.

To be fair, it is a work quite magisterial in its conscientiousness, starting daily with the alarm ("my alarm goes off at 6.30 a.m. for our 7 a.m. departure" … "my alarm goes off at 6.45 a.m." … "my alarm goes off at 6.30 a.m.") and exhibiting an almost fetishistic fascination with the author's luggage ("after waking up and getting ready, I take my bags downstairs at 8.45 a.m. to be checked in and identified" … "I wake and finish packing my bags" … "I finished packing my bags and put them outside my door" … "we're leaving for Port Elizabeth and our bags have to be in the foyer by 8 a.m."). But that scarcely excuses it. On the contrary, McGrath knows how boring this is and how repetitive is the nature of life on the modern cricket tour. "You'll probably be able to work out by now why we call our days 'Groundhog Day'," he says. "We're either training, playing or travelling – or a combination of all three." Then, helpfully, just in case we didn't get the reference: "Each day is similar to the one before, as it is for Bill Murray in the movie *Groundhog Day*, where he relives the same day over and over again."

The funny thing about this allusion is that, if you remember, the plot of *Groundhog Day* is devoted to Murray's efforts to resist and ultimately overthrow this mind-numbing state of affairs. McGrath just goes with it. He's got a contract, dammit, and he's gonna deliver. The bowler whose metier is the dot ball has perfected the dot day, and produced a dot diary.

Ponting's diary, if not quite so formulaic, has a similarly reductive tone. He would have prospered in the world of espionage for he lets nothing slip, whether the subject is the World Cup banquet ("there were some speeches and in the end it all went on too long for my taste") or Austin Powers's *Goldmember* ("it was solid without being brilliant"). Would he, a reporter asked, shake hands with Zimbabwe's president Robert Mugabe? "My answer was that I couldn't answer that because I haven't been put in that position." Makes John Howard look like the acme of candour. But Ponting is as used to the spin of politics as he is to the spin of cricket. He was alarmed not when Darren Lehmann racially vilified the Sri Lankans last year, but when baggygreen.com.au carried a report of Lehmann's words. "Surely we had control over that."

Control. It's a word pregnant with meanings these days. One unconsciously revealing section of Ponting's book concerns his team's preparation for playing New Zealand. Fleming? "Bowl tight in the corridor just outside off stump." McMillan? "Tight, short of a length bowling in the corridor outside the off stump." Astle? "Good, tight, short of a length bowling in the corridor outside the off stump, and spin." Styris? "Good corridor and length bowling." Cairns? "Long-hops and flippers." No, only kidding. "Tight corridor bowling." Harris? Prepare to be amazed. "Straight and tight in the corridor outside off stump." Vettori? It can't be true, can it? Yes it can. "Good tight line and length in the corridor." Doesn't anyone bowl in the vestibule anymore?

Those seeking an insight into the contrast between the new captain and the old will come away disappointed, although Ponting seems to have traded Steve Waugh's mental disintegration for what might be called the psychological squirrel grip. Of England, he gloats: "Mentally, we've got them by the balls."

Perhaps the most telling passages in Ponting's book concern Zimbabwe – if mainly in what they do not say. The impression previously conveyed was that the question of whether or not Australia should play Zimbabwe in the World Cup provoked at least some debate in Australian ranks. Ponting insists otherwise. Documenting the meeting of February 4, 2003, with the board's CEO James Sutherland and the Australian Cricketers' Association's CEO Tim May, Ponting recalls: "James is especially keen for the ACB and us, as players, to avoid going down the path of making moral pronouncements, especially as I reckon most of us would not really have much of an idea about what is going on in Zimbabwe. And while some of us might have misgivings about the regime, the safety issue seems to be the top of most people's agendas. The bottom line for me is that we are cricketers – our job is to play cricket, not get involved in politics … When it all wrapped up, after a couple of hours, we opted not to say anything to the media, preferring instead to nominate James and Tim as our spokesmen. That may seem like a cop-out, but we really do want to focus on the cricket now and leave the decision of whether or not we play in Zimbabwe to the administrators. I hope people understand that."

Yes, skipper, it does seem like a cop-out – and I'm afraid I do find it difficult to understand. For decades, Australian cricketers complained about being treated like mugs, griped that they were never consulted by administrators, and moaned that they were always serfs to the board's barons. Now they have the power, they seem not to want it. Hey, don't expect us to think: we're sportsmen!

Or was it actually like that? While it mostly lands in the same corridor of cliché as the books of McGrath and Ponting, Gilchrist's *Walking to Victory* contains some flashes of original thought. Of the same meeting over which Ponting draws a discreet veil, Gilchrist is more forthcoming: "The meeting was very confusing. No one seemed sure which way they were thinking." And the self-imposed silence irked him: "The players actually asked the ACB to put a blanket no-comment policy on the Zimbabwe issue. We were asking to be silenced. This really disappointed me. I voiced my disapproval, but I didn't hear or feel too much support around me … Aside from the fact that I felt we shouldn't hide from the Mugabe issue, I find the contractual restrictions on our freedom of speech onerous enough without us trying to slap more bans on ourselves … We're all grown-ups. Yet here we were giving up our independence and our ability to make decisions and to think."

In fact, as Gilchrist senses, this made a mockery of the courageous black-armband protests of Andy Flower and Henry Olonga, striving to exercise their right to freedom of expression in the face of a regime that wished to deprive them of it. Gilchrist was ultimately content with playing in Zimbabwe, but not without misgivings. He quotes from a post-match conversation in which Flower, looking like "a man under great strain" but someone "leaving his mark on the world", was asked why his whole team did not make a stand. "It's not in our nature to stand up against things," explained Flower. "He [the average Zimbabwean] finds it hard to really speak out and protest against anything." Rather like the average Australian, methinks.

At least Gilchrist's candour kills the spin that the issue revolved around player security. "There was a lot more to it, and everyone at some point was talking about the moral issues surrounding the regime. I wasn't alone in my desire not to go. Various players argued that it wasn't our safety, but that of spectators and protesters, that was at risk." A pity that the same players were content for the same risk to be run if administrators took responsibility for it.

When I read *Walking to Victory*, I thought it would provoke a good deal of comment, presenting as it did a courageously different version of events from that peddled by the Australian board and captain. It certainly did stimulate a response: to the passages concerned with Gilchrist's decision to walk when given not out by Rudi Koertzen during the Super Six game against Sri Lanka. These, it is true, are quite interesting, again quite candid in their muddle-headedness.

But it struck me as another instance of the media's inability to distinguish wood from trees that they devoted hectares of commentary to the ethics of walking and overlooked the ethics of playing against a country whose designated cricket authority has a criminal dictator as its patron. Funny old world, innit? I subsequently sat as co-host through an interview with Gilchrist in which a hard-hitting ABC morning radio host, known for taking it up to prime ministers and big businessmen alike, asked such questions as: "So, is it hard being a wicket-keeper?" Perhaps *Walking to Victory* would have attracted more intelligent comment if it had borne a different title, say *Truckling to Tyrants*.

No player product attracted more attention last season, of course, than that of the grandpappy of product, Steve Waugh. His 12th book **Never Say Die** (HarperSports, $29.95) focuses on his "epic hundred" against England at the SCG in January 2003 which, in case the reader was marooned in the New Guinea Highlands or confined to a punishment cell at Villawood at the time, was completed with a boundary off the second day's final delivery.

Focus is a problem with *Never Say Die*: it is not tight enough. Two-thirds of the book is a blur of bumpf – about Tests against West Indies and Bangladesh, the World Cup, the baggy green – bulking it out to sellable specifications. More, though, is less. It distracts attention from the third that does concern the innings in question, which is excellent. Apparently when he reached his hundred, Waugh's daughter Rosie told her mother: "Mummy, my heart feels funny."

I know how she felt. In its way that innings reduced us all to delighted children, and to read Waugh's retelling of it is to enjoy those sensations anew. Gilchrist's interpolations about the innings and its aftermath are, again, worth reading. "It was quite an extraordinary feeling, just the energy and emotion in that room," he recalls. "It just felt like everyone couldn't really look each other right in the eye, maybe for fear of, I don't know, crying or screaming or whatever." I'm disappointed only that the publishers did not have the courage of their conviction; if they had cut this book in half, *Never Say Die* would have been a minor classic. But that, I guess, would have entailed selling it at half the price and making half the money – and we couldn't have that, could we?

Waugh's diligent amanuensis, Geoff Armstrong, also bided his time last year by producing a fair stocking-filler called **Top 10s of Australian Test Cricket** (ABC Books, $29.95) with Ian Russell. Some of these are pretty good, even subtly reinforcing of cricket's verities. Ten Umpiring Decisions That Went Australia's Way are balanced by Ten Umpiring Decisions That Went Against Australia, as if to verify that old saw about them all evening out. Mind you, The Top Ten Bizarre Decisions By Australian Selectors is not offset by Ten Strokes Of Selection Genius – something, as chairman of selectors at the Yarras, I observed rather ruefully. On the whole there should have been more lists of this nature; the statistics get down to such a minute level as to become *de trop*. Do we really need to know the 10th best bowling figures by an Australian at Bellerive Oval?

An alternative to all this authorised product is the highly unauthorised memoir of Graham Halbish, the CEO sacked by the ACB in February 1997. **Run Out** (Lothian Books, $29.95) is unique: the first book, I believe, by a senior cricket administrator about senior cricket administration (Syd Smith's two books were both historical works). As such, it deserves to be read, and the candour of apostasy lends it colour that it might not otherwise have had. Halbish confesses, for example, that in player contract negotiations of yore, the board deliberately understated its revenues: "I suppose we cooked the pie. The books certainly weren't cooked, but the pie was from a recipe of the board's creation."

There are stories, too, that have not previously seen the light of day, such as the disclosure that the board chairman Alan Crompton went to South Africa a decade ago with a legal letter for Bob Simpson's sacking as coach. Simmo's stridency in defending Shane Warne and Merv Hughes from the fines levied after the Johannesburg Test had turned the board against him. "Their [the lawyers'] advice was that

Simmo had clearly breached his contract with the ACB," recalls Halbish, "and the letter should be signed by the chairman and handed to him immediately." A narrow squeak.

Those seeking a guide to the faultlines in Australian cricket administration over the last 20 years will find *Run Out* required reading. It is very much the voice of the old guard: not just Halbish but Crompton, Ian McDonald, Col Egar, Phil Ridings and even Darrell Hair. The villains are Denis Rogers, Bob Merriman, Malcolm Gray and Malcolm Speed – who, as an aside, we are told "did not even know the players in the Test team when he arrived". This is, of course, the book's weakness as well. For all the sympathy one might extend towards someone whose dearest achievement was suddenly denied him, Halbish is simply too thoroughgoing in his self-justification and self-exculpation to be truly convincing.

Much of *Run Out,* for instance, is devoted to rationalising the board's handling of match-fixing, especially the secret fining of Warne and Mark Waugh for their tarrying with John The Bookie. This is discussed independently of Halbish's account of the financial inducements for failure that Warne, Waugh and May allege they were offered by Salim Malik. The connection between the two – the very real probability that John's approaches were to ascertain the players' venality – is thus unmade. Furthermore, Halbish attacks the International Cricket Council for letting the Pakistan Cricket Board deal with it as an internal affair: "The matter should have become a vital, urgent issue for the game's governing body. Instead, the ICC allowed Pakistan to claim the allegation as an internal matter that it would sort out." This is at least ironic, seeing that he sought and received the same dispensation. Remember Judge Brandeis? "Sunlight is the best disinfectant."

The fact is that the board's actions, however well-intentioned, eventually proved extremely damaging to the credit of Warne and Waugh as witnesses to the Qayyum inquiry and to Australia's standing in this whole sorry affair. Halbish's beef is, essentially, that many on the board distanced themselves from the cover-up after earlier approving it – and here he might well have grounds for complaint. But this does not make the cover-up and the lengths gone to in maintaining it anything other than an unfortunate mistake.

Not being on the official payroll, Halbish is free to vent his spleen on issues confronting cricket, including what seems a rather tendentious analysis of the Muralidaran saga. "We have an incredible situation now where a man is playing Test cricket and his action has never been cleared," Halbish asserts. What's so incredible about this? For as long as the game contains Law 24, no bowler's action can be "cleared". And perhaps we should, at least momentarily, cease to wonder whether Murali's action is fair and instead wonder about our own. The fact is that Murali has hidden nothing from his accusers and consented to every official test set him, in the face of some of the most despicable calumnies ever aimed at a cricketer. The Australian response has been to repeat for 10 years: "Well, he looks like a chucker, so he must be a chucker."

This is not a simple question, and it serves no purpose pretending that it is. If you can be bothered following the findings of the biomechanists at the University of Western Australia – and Halbish clearly can't – then you will find a strong case for regarding Murali as a bowler *sui generis*. "The problem is that he continues to win accolades despite an action which is unfair," says Halbish, "and the cost of this could be borne by those who fall victim to his bowling." The same, of course, was said of the original round-arm and over-arm bowlers.

Halbish's contrast with Shoaib Akhtar's treatment is unfortunate to say the least: "Shoaib was referred to the nine-man advisory panel on illegal deliveries. This system avoided all the drama, heartaches, sensationalism, embarrassment and torment which was forced upon Hair four years earlier." Well, yes he was. He was also allowed to arrive in Australia only to be told he couldn't bowl, then unilaterally excused by the ICC president Jagmohan Dalmiya, setting the process at nought. Another triumph.

Fortunately, not every book last season was a monument to self-regard. The outstanding publication of the season by far came out with neither hype nor hoopla, entirely in keeping with both its subject and creator. And I'm not talking about *Wisden Australia*.

In his marvellous book *The Fatal Englishman*, Sebastian Faulks stops to consider the ineluctable fascination of the bright, brilliant, brief life. He conjectures that everything about such lives is naturally intensified and enriched by their brevity: "The stories of young people who delight parents and friends with their talents have a concentrated significance in their beginnings, and in their premature ends there is a natural poignancy that brutally epitomises the disappointment that is also common but less evident in longer, duller lives."

No one in cricket has struck this chord so effectively as David Frith, not only in his biographies of Archie Jackson and Drewy

Stoddart, but in his survey of suicides among the game's great and obscure. Retelling **The Ross Gregory Story** (Lothian Books, $34.95), which he considers "third in a trilogy of brilliant but ill-fated cricketers", comes naturally to him. For those who don't know, the diminutive Gregory played for Victoria while still at school. He twice represented his country, looking like a boy among men but averaging 51, only to die in aerial combat in May 1942. Though memory of Gregory has faded with the passage of time, Frith has produced a book of startling comprehensiveness, longer and deeper than the biographies of cricketers with 100 Tests or more.

It might even be thought a little too long. Frith's recapitulation of Gregory's cricket career is exhaustively, perhaps exhaustingly, thorough. "You will not mind if I do not say anything," the 20-year-old Gregory told the press when chosen for his Test debut in January 1937 – which is rather charming but little help to a biographer. Frith goes as far as he can on the sometimes cursory impressions of others, but at one stage has to confess: "Ross Gregory was clearly one of those fellows about whom it would seem pointless to search for expressions of reservation or disapproval during that stage of his life." The story obtains shade, as it were, from the penumbra of imminent tragedy. The scoreline at the end of his subject's highest Test score, Frith notes, has "no parallel in Test history in terms of future tragedy": Gregory c Verity b Farnes encompasses three men destined to die in uniform.

The coup of Frith's book is the diary Gregory kept as a Royal Australian Air Force navigator, which he started almost a year to the day of his death. Though it was this diary's purchase at auction some years ago that set Frith to writing the Gregory story, I was initially dubious of the wisdom of republishing it in its entirety. In fact, this bold choice comes off. Gregory was not a war hero. He was a cog in the military machine – the sense of which became increasingly oppressive to him. But while his diary was often pervaded by boredom, Gregory was anything but a boring writer. He was perceptive, droll, often caustic, especially where the British were concerned. "A declining nation" who were "too dumb and dogmatic", he thought, complaining of ineptitude that was "just the pommies all over" and "typical British organisation".

Frith writes that Gregory was "coarsened" by war. He certainly grew up quickly. After a while the sangfroid is almost soothing – until you read an eyewitness account of a Wellington bomber exploding, or of Gregory's pilot causing a near-terminal tailspin by passing out. "What a war!" he sighs in his last entry. In recording the casual interplay of terror and tedium, Gregory not only reveals much about himself but a good deal about combat.

Perhaps the most affecting remnant of Gregory's brief life, meanwhile, is the letter he wrote to his parents in November 1941 in case of his death. "I am absolutely certain in my own mind that you both have the courage to face the facts as they are presented, and I would be keenly disappointed if you regretted my action in doing what I consider to be my duty." And there's more, for in a village in Bangladesh, Frith even found surviving eyewitnesses to the dogfight in which Gregory's last flight ended. The publishers have done Frith's book few favours with its unprepossessing cover and production; they obscure a small but multi-faceted gem. It even contains a line sure to appeal to lovers of Johnstonia: "There was a light interlude when Badcock was struck agonisingly in the groin."

On the perplexing question of what actually took place in Pretoria on the evening of March 5, 2003, alas, no light is cast. But, as Frith reveals, cricket is a game that abounds in extraordinary untold stories.

It's make-or-flake time

by TIM LANE

The original joke was the golfer Lee Trevino's, but the late David Hookes once applied it to cricket with telling effect when asked whether he might eventually turn his hand to administration. He wouldn't be eligible, Hookes replied, because he didn't have a blue jacket and he didn't have dandruff.

Such is the image of sports officialdom. Australia's cricket administrators now have a new name, Cricket Australia, and the national board has a more youthful, less fusty look than it once did. But its reputation for the blue blazer *avec la neige* lives on. It is a stereotype fed by generations of players and reinforced by media comment, and the game would be well served if it were overcome.

One must feel some respect for those at the helm simply for their preparedness to be there. The current crop are responsible for the management of a system that has produced one of the greatest teams in the history of its sport, plus a women's side that is also a world leader. And the playing of cricket remains one of Australia's favourite pastimes, although it must be noted that soccer has recently outstripped it as the most popular participation sport in the land.

Never before, moreover, has the role of the game's administrators been so serious. As the business of sport booms globally, those managing it face an unending stream of challenges with the potential to take administrators well beyond their range of practised skills. Cricket faced such a circumstance in its deliberations over Australia's scheduled tour of Zimbabwe in May 2004. Predictably, officialdom was seen to have got it wrong. From London to Canberra, politicians, journalists, cricketers and the public berated both international and Australian cricket administrators for apparently lacking moral conscience and fortitude in determining that the tour should proceed. One player, Stuart MacGill, even staged a personal boycott. Yet from this seat, the case against the tour appeared to be short on coherence and long on selective morality and inconsistency.

Over a period of months, as various arguments were mounted for a cancellation, it became increasingly less clear what the central issue actually was. First it was the regime of Zimbabwe's president Robert Mugabe that prompted the boycott calls. Later it was the apparent government interference in cricket administration and selection policy. Finally the disarray of both the Zimbabwe Cricket Union and the team itself added to the cacophony.

In relation to the Mugabe regime people asked why, if it was once right for South Africa to have been boycotted, wasn't it now right for the tyrannical black administration in neighbouring Zimbabwe to face the same consequence? This, though, was to miss the twin points that the boycotts of South Africa were globally applied, starting with the Olympic Games in 1964 and gradually extending across a range of sports; and that by targeting sports, the anti-apartheid boycotts took aim at a vulnerable spot within the collective psyche of white South Africa.

Cricket does not provide that in relation to Zimbabwe and there is no global sports boycott of the nation. It participated, and won three medals, in the recent Athens Olympics. Where were the voices of disapproval while that was taking place? Morally, cricket was perfectly entitled to say: why us? To mount one's own crusade would, as Charlie Brown said in an old cartoon, be like wetting oneself while wearing a dark suit. There would be a warm feeling but no one would notice.

The intrusion of government ideology into selection policy provided the strongest argument against the tour but not one that could be coherently sustained. In January 2002 the South African board president, Percy Sonn, over-ruled his country's selectors on racial grounds, replacing Jacques Rudolph with Justin Ontong for the SCG Test. Should Australia have boycotted that match? Or do we make selective decisions according to whether or not we approve of national governments?

It could be argued that those final weeks of total turmoil within Zimbabwean cricket, which led to the abandonment of the two Tests and an abbreviated tour, actually validated the International Cricket Council's and Cricket Australia's position. In the end, Zimbabwe was forced to acknowledge that it wasn't able to proceed with a Test series. One hopes this will force it to face its own circumstances more sincerely and attempt to rescue the game within its borders. Forlorn a prospect as that may be, it is likely that the chances of cricket surviving in Zimbabwe are better for it not having been shunned by the game's rulers.

Of course, cricket is a minor component of a much bigger picture. But that is another reason why Australian cricket, and cricket internationally, were entitled to argue that they alone need not carry the burden as arbiter and conscience. The ICC was not only within its rights to proceed with the tour, it had an obligation under its charter – of promoting cricket as a global sport – to do so. Australian cricket, as one of its constituencies, had a duty to co-operate. What Cricket Australia could have done better during the extended period of this debate was to present its reasoning more clearly and persuasively. Those looking to the board for leadership – be they players, other sporting officials, or the general public – would have been disappointed. The constant impression was of a lack of authority on an important issue, albeit one of intimidating proportion.

Regrettably, that same lack of authority was evident in the handling of Shane Warne's return from his 12-month drug ban. Here, Cricket Australia and Cricket Victoria did not only fail their sport; in allowing Warne to make his return in a match that began before his suspension was complete, they failed sport generally on its biggest global issue.

The facts are these. Warne became eligible to resume competitive cricket on February 10, 2004. The 2nd XI match in which he returned commenced on February 9. Therefore his name could not be included on Victoria's team list at the toss, as required by the game's Laws. The match was a scheduled fixture in a competition under Cricket Australia's jurisdiction, with its own stated playing conditions. There is no condition in that competition, the Cricket Australia Cup, which allows for a player to be substituted into a team during the course of a match unless he replaces someone called up for higher duties (which clearly wasn't the case). The only Law of Cricket that permitted Warne's substitution into the match is Law 1.2, which would require the opposition captain's consent to such a move. Yet a decision had been made about Warne playing in that match a good two months before the event.

In other words, cricket administrators contrived to provide a drug offender with a premature return – either that, or they allowed themselves to be hustled. Whatever, the effect was to treat their own rules and regulations, and the spirit of the drug code, with cavalier disregard. At least we can rest assured that our Cricket Australia Cup youngsters are learning the tricks of the trade early.

Tricks, it seems, are now part of Cricket Australia's repertoire. You may have noticed the hard sell of another limited edition frame late last season, capitalising on Steve Waugh's farewell from the game. It featured a montage of photos: Steve batting, Steve bowling, Steve lying face down on the turf at The Oval in 2001 acknowledging the cheers of the crowd for another ton. And, of course, emblazoned across the face of his bat was "MRF".

But hang on. Wasn't the 2001 Ashes series the one in which the Australian skipper used an unbranded bat? The truth is that the photo had been digitally enhanced. The poster is a licensed product of Cricket Australia, which claims that the enhancement was made purely for cosmetic reasons, to bring a look of consistency to the photos that composed the montage.

That may well be true. But in an era of virtually everything being for sale – even truth, in this case – it raises some serious questions. Did anyone profit from this? What if the bat had carried the brand of an earlier sponsor? Would the same consistency-of-look defence apply? Is the blade of Don Bradman's bat now for sale in the merchandising of such products? Even if we accept the most benign explanation for what happened, one can still only conclude that this sort of low-grade chicanery on the part of a senior sports administration warrants a description once used by a couple of cricketers involved in another incident at another time: naive and stupid.

One of Cricket Australia's most significant recent achievements is its Spirit of Cricket campaign, designed to provide a guide as to how the game should be played and to celebrate what it stands for. The most obvious performance indicator as to its success is the way the national team conducts itself, and the early indications are that it's working. Cricket Australia must never forget, though, that the ultimate responsibility for the spirit of cricket in this country rests with it. The cricket world has been a murky place in recent times. For the sport to convince the public that it can completely trust it again, its administration must be transparent and beyond reproach. In that respect, Cricket Australia has room for improvement.

Tim Lane is a long-time cricket and Australian Rules commentator, now with Channel 10.

CRICKET PEOPLE, 2003-04

Beyond a boundary

by ASHLEY MALLETT

Not every old Australian cricketer winds up in the Channel Nine commentary box. Far unlikelier fates await some. **John Maclean**, the former Test keeper, now heads an engineering firm in Brisbane. **Mick Malone**, the one-Test wonder of 1977, runs a real estate business in Perth. **Eric Freeman**, until recently, was CEO of the South Australian Lacrosse Association. Down the road from him is **Max O'Connell**, umpire during the Centenary Test, who worked at the Electricity Trust in Adelaide for a while but is now gifts and bequests officer at the State Library.

It is 31 years since **Paul Sheahan**, once the coming superstar of Australian batsmanship, quit the Test arena at 27. His decision was influenced by the need to eke out enough money to complement the pittance paid in those days for playing Test cricket. So he went back to school, first as a mathematics teacher at Geelong College, then at Winchester, Geelong Grammar and St Peter's College in Adelaide. He was principal at Geelong College from 1986 to 1995 and has been headmaster at Melbourne Grammar ever since. As a batsman, Sheahan possessed a grace and charm one associates nowadays with Mark Waugh or David Gower, and a cut off the front foot reminiscent of **Keith Miller**. Miller is 84 now, living in Melbourne, fading in health but still sharp as a tack mentally.

Bob Cowper was another gloriously elegant batsman, another unfulfilled talent, who put career ahead of cricket at the age of 28. He carved out a hugely impressive record in business, starting out at John Elliott's IXL company and now in Monaco, where he has lived for two decades. **Ross Edwards** is another expat doing well in England. Edwards struggled to balance life as a top-level cricketer and accountant; he returned from Australia's 1973 tour of the West Indies with $10 in the bank. Kerry Packer asked him to speak on behalf of the impoverished at World Series Cricket's High Court skirmish in 1977 – and Edwards, in the 10-minute cab ride from hotel to court with a leading Packer executive, talked himself into a position at Channel Nine. He wound up as head of advertising, then landed a job in London, and later went to ESPN Star TV in Singapore, all on excellent salaries. He is retired now, an eccentric man with a kind heart. He plays cricket, tennis, hockey and golf, drinks red wine, smokes Petersen pipes and talks incessantly to whoever is in earshot.

Ian Redpath, the unflappable former Test opener, is still built like a whippet and still working as an antiques dealer in Geelong. **Ray 'Slug' Jordon**, battling crook knees and a dicey hip, is a talent scout for various AFL clubs. A wicket-keeper, Jordon toured India and South Africa in 1969-70, and was for many years a sporting commentator on commercial radio. So was **Ian Meckiff**, who has led an eventful existence since being no-balled out of Test cricket in 1963-64. He sold advertising for radio stations 3UZ and Sport 927, was involved in advertising sign sales at the MCG and other grounds through Boyer Sports Media, and remains an excellent golfer who recently stood down as captain of the prestigious Victoria Golf Club.

Doug Walters and **Rodney Hogg** are both regulars on the speaking circuit. Walters is amazing, telling the same jokes at the same venues every year and still going down a treat. Hogg, with a glint in his eye and a ready smile, tells a good yarn too. He also helps out with Victoria's fast bowlers after many years as a greengrocer. **Len Pascoe** is an events organiser with his own company – Len Pascoe Sports Entertainment – and arranges anything from Elvis impersonators to after-dinner speakers. "I was the dumb fast bowler, remember?" he said recently. "Well, now the dumb fast bowler is lining up speaking engagements for **Greg Chappell** and **Doug Walters**."

Chappell has also delved into the insurance business and written dietary books. His latest enterprise is The Chappell Way – check out www.chappellway.com. He describes it as "a proprietary sports training system" that maximises the natural skill of athletes by "using the knowledge and understanding of how best to train the mind and body in harmony". Pascoe, incidentally, still lives in Sydney and is a neighbour of **John Dyson**, who has taken a break from his job within the NSW Education Department to coach Sri Lanka. Pascoe's old comrade **Jeff Thomson**, in between coaching and TV commentary commitments, hosts charter fishing trips on his luxury boat. **Bruce Laird**, once a key man at the Swan Brewery and one of the bravest souls to stand up to genuine pace bowling, now lives in relative obscurity within easy range of his vegetable garden. He moved recently to Bunbury, south of Perth, where he works for Elders Insurance.

Another old cricketer who likes a chat is the former wicket-keeper **Barry Jarman**. He was for many years a partner in Rowe & Jarman, the premier sports store in Adelaide, and later became an ICC referee. Now partially retired, he runs a houseboat business on the Murray River and is a brilliant host. A day or two in one of Jar's houseboats is something to behold. Every year he catches up – either on a houseboat or at the Adelaide Test – with his old mates **Norm O'Neill**, still handsome and dashing, and **Lindsay Kline**.

And then there are the dozens still tangled up in cricket: selecting, coaching, administering, pontificating. Some are less visible than others. The former all-rounder **Graeme Watson**, who played the last of his five Tests in 1972, was a draftsman during and after his cricket. He now runs a business involved in developing sports stadiums, and is working with the ICC to design and help establish cricket grounds in developing nations. **Martin Kent**, a fabulous right-hander, is now CEO of the Queensland Cricketers' Club.

A staggering proportion of old Aussie greats are in England. **John Inverarity** has retired from teaching – his last post was as headmaster at Hale School in Perth – and is now, at 60, coaching Warwickshire. **Terry Jenner** also does most of his coaching in England these days, nurturing young leg-spinners through a new scheme established by the Brian Johnston Trust; you can pick a leggie under Jenner's influence because they all appear to have modelled their actions on him. **Jack Potter** tried his hand at selling ice creams in Glenelg once his days as foundation coach of the Australian Cricket Academy – where he taught Shane Warne how to bowl a flipper – were behind him. He now coaches at Oxford University.

Tom Moody, meanwhile, is entrenched at Worcestershire. He looms as perhaps the man mostly likely to one day replace Duncan Fletcher as England's coach. Picking the team, as one of England's national selectors, and fine-tuning their most precocious young talents at the academy in Loughborough is **Rod Marsh**. He was entitled to a share of the credit for England's apparent and belated renaissance during 2004. Come July 2005, he will be barracking for the Poms to reclaim the Ashes. Now that really is an unlikely fate.

Ashley Mallett, an off-spinner, played 38 Tests for Australia between 1968 and 1980. He now coaches young spinners and is writing a biography of Ian Chappell.

Going troppo

by PETER ENGLISH

Explorers took an age to discover Australia's Top End by land. Test cricket took considerably longer. Robert O'Hara Burke and William John Wills were the first to navigate that far north from Melbourne in 1861. Precisely 142 years later Cricket Australia, with similar feelings of apprehension and uncertainty, left its southern headquarters and ventured to the tropical north in search of adventure and new frontiers.

While Burke and Wills were satisfying their zest for discovery, Cricket Australia's motive was slightly less noble – to satisfy the convoluted playing schedule. The International Cricket Council's cluttered new home-and-away timetable compelled Australia to look for out-of-the-way venues to host out-of-season Test matches, at a time of year when southern sports followers were wrapped up in woolly coats and football. The cities of Darwin and Cairns were chosen courtesy of their warm winters and the cool response to the merits of Bangladesh. The gulf in skill levels promised to be as wide as the Gulf of Carpentaria which Burke and Wills died discovering.

On July 18, 2003, Darwin became Australia's eighth Test venue. Seven days later Cairns became the ninth. This was rapid expansion indeed. Australia had previously been reticent in welcoming new Test locations, admitting only seven in the previous 126 years, which was far fewer than the likes of India (19 in 70) or Pakistan (17 in 48). Never before had Test cricket strayed from Australia's first-class capitals.

The locals, naturally enough, were delighted, scarcely able to believe their luck. Unlike Perth and Hobart, granted Test status in 1970-71 and 1989-90 respectively, there was little sense that either Darwin or Cairns had been made to serve a long and frustrating first-class apprenticeship. Neither city had ever toasted a homegrown Test player (Damien Martyn left Darwin at three and never returned). Neither had staged an official interstate match but had instead been limited to a tour match here, a pre-season acclimatisation camp there. Any Test heritage was strictly incidental. In Darwin, the sightscreens were imported from the MCG; in Cairns, spectators sat in the Gabba's old Western Stand, which had been relocated in 1995.

Indeed Darwin had never even hosted a first-class game before, thus joining such far-flung destinations as Lucknow, Sheikhupura and Sharjah as the 11th venue in history whose maiden Test was also its first taste of first-class cricket. Big-time competition in Darwin had generally amounted to the occasional charity weekend, featuring a bunch of locals, some enthusiastic ring-ins and a handful of clapped-out former Test players. Grassy banks encircled most of the arena, which blended the country vibe of a hill with a modern grandstand. Marrara Cricket Ground, or Football Park as the locals know it, is actually an Australian Rules oval which had never previously staged as much as a local A-grade cricket match.

It is a similar story in Cairns, where the ground is named after the local Aussie Rules legend Roy Cazaly, although the city's cricketing pedigree is slightly stronger. Clive Lloyd's West Indians played the first tour game there, against a Queensland Country XI at the Showgrounds in 1975-76, when spectators got down on hands and knees to mop up the ground after heavy morning rain. West Indies returned in 1991-92, this time beating a full-strength Queensland side at Barlow Park. Pakistan stopped off for a game at Gatton Park in 1988-89 and Jimmy Maher, the region's only international player, was a member of the Queensland team that defeated Sri Lanka in 1995-96. The first international side to step on to Cazaly's were Stephen Fleming's New Zealanders of 1997-98, crushed by Queensland by an innings and 127 runs in the ground's initial first-class match.

Domestic cricket looked in new directions too. For the second year in a row only one of New South Wales's ING Cup games was at the SCG. Instead the Blues trekked north to picturesque North Sydney Oval, west to Drummoyne Oval, even further west to the Olympic Stadium in Homebush and south to beautiful Bradman Oval in Bowral. Crowds flocked in much bigger numbers than might have been expected on a typical day at the SCG, and it is an experiment other states should urgently consider. In 2003-04 the outground revolution passed by all others except Tasmania, who took matches to Devonport and Launceston. Bunbury, Bundaberg and Ballarat beckon loudly.

The most successful of NSW's alternative venues was the Olympic Stadium, which hosted its second day-nighter. Despite worries about a ropey pitch and slippery playing surface, 26,190 fans watched Queensland beat NSW – 427 more than turned up for the stadium's inaugural cricket match the previous summer. By July 2004, Cricket NSW was calling for tenders and the push was on, as of 2005-06, to switch Tests and one-day internationals from the SCG (capacity 44,000) to the Olympic Stadium (capacity 80,000). The SCG Trust, though, was digging in for the mother of all pitch battles. "There is no argument," said its chairman Rodney Cavalier, "that the SCG is one of the two finest cricket grounds in the world. Only Lord's can complete. There's a lot at stake here for cricket."

Change was also afoot at Australia's other Test venues. Adelaide Oval was gleaming like never before after a $20 million redevelopment, increasing the ground's capacity to 32,000. A new TV replay screen was built, the two Chappell Stands – named after Ian, Greg and Trevor – were opened and the southern grandstand was christened the Clem Hill Stand. Queenslanders welcomed the news that the Gabba was to go full circle – the old "horseshoe" is to be replaced by a "donut" – and that the full-house sign would eventually go up at 42,000. This entailed the demolition of the Sir Gordon Chalk Building, which houses the Lions Social Club. Construction work is expected to finish during the 2004-05 season.

But the biggest renovations were unfolding, as ever, at the MCG. The 2003-04 Boxing Day Test was played without the Ponsford Stand for a backdrop. Nor was the old pavilion, awaiting imminent demolition, used as the $435 million redesign ahead of the 2006 Commonwealth Games gathered pace. By July 2004 the new Ponsford Stand, with three levels and a corporate section, was completed. The bottom section of the new pavilion was underway and only half of the Olympic Stand, the third to be knocked down, remained.

While the magnificent MCG is transformed for the umpteenth time in readiness for more great deeds, the Test calendar's two newest outposts face a less assured future. The smallish crowds that greeted the inaugural experiment against Bangladesh were blamed on that country's low box-office appeal. But attendances were actually more disappointing a second time round. Only 13,355 Darwinites – 507 fewer – went along to see Australia play Sri Lanka in July. In Cairns the crowd rose to 20,102 – 6,823 more than the previous year. But given that Shane Warne made history and the Sri Lankans made the game last almost two days longer, this was nothing to get excited about.

With the Australians preoccupied abroad during the next two winters, no further Tests will be scheduled up north until at least 2007. Meanwhile Zimbabwe's unsettled future threatens to slow down, if only temporarily, the international merry-go-round. The fate of Darwin and Cairns might yet mirror that of Burke and Wills: a sad, lonely ending after a long and romantic discovery.

Peter English is a former assistant editor of Inside Edge *and* Wisden Cricket Monthly.

MARVELLOUS TEAM, THAT

In August 2004, the TV legend and former Australian Test captain Richie Benaud announced his Greatest XI of the 20th century. As you would expect it was a shrewd piece of selection, brimming with depth and variety. It contained three fast bowlers, one leg-spinner, one left-arm master-of-all-trades and still found room to squeeze Adam Gilchrist in at No. 8. In batting order, Benaud's team read: Jack Hobbs (England), Sunil Gavaskar (India), Don Bradman (Australia), Sachin Tendulkar (India), Viv Richards (West Indies), Imran Khan (Pakistan), Garry Sobers (West Indies), Adam Gilchrist (Australia), Shane Warne (Australia), Sydney Barnes (England) and Dennis Lillee (Australia).

Interestingly, Benaud's team contained five players who appeared in the 1980s (Gavaskar, Tendulkar, Richards, Imran, Lillee) and a further two who debuted in the 1990s (Gilchrist, Warne). Not a single player from the 1950s or 60s – Benaud's own Test-playing era – was deemed worthy. His side would surely crush the bowler-heavy, Oz-centric dreamteam allegedly picked by Don Bradman and published posthumously in a 2001 book by Roland Perry. Bradman's forgettable XI, in case you've forgotten, was: Barry Richards (South Africa), Arthur Morris (Australia), Don Bradman (Australia), Sachin Tendulkar (India), Garry Sobers (West Indies), Don Tallon (Australia), Ray Lindwall (Australia), Dennis Lillee (Australia), Alec Bedser (England), Bill O'Reilly (Australia) and Clarrie Grimmett (Australia). Benaud's Greatest XI is available on DVD, a medium undreamed of when Sydney Barnes – Benaud's choice to share the new ball with Dennis Lillee – was in his flame-flinging, turn-of-the-century pomp.

Sold, Warnie

by STEPHEN W. GIBBS

It has been a buoyant 12 months for the cricket memorabilia market in Australia, with various intriguing items coming into the public domain. Most intriguing of all was the ball with which Shane Warne dismissed Sri Lanka's Upul Chandana in Cairns to capture his record-equalling 527th Test wicket. Warne, in a generous gesture, allowed the ball to be sold through eBay in July 2004, with the proceeds going to his children's charity, the Shane Warne Foundation. The winning bid was $42,700.

Elsewhere Don Bradman, as ever, reigned supreme, although there was nothing to match the $425,000 reportedly – and amazingly – paid the previous year for Bradman's 1948 baggy green. This year the emphasis was on The Don's bats. The bat he used against England in the First Test of 1934 at Trent Bridge, when Bradman scored only 29 and 25, fetched $42,000 at a Charles Leski auction in Melbourne. It was signed by both teams and described as being in superb condition. Another bat signed and used by Bradman at the SCG in 1946-47, when he and Sid Barnes hit 234 apiece in the Second Test against England, was sold for $34,500 at a Lawson–Menzies auction in Moss Vale.

Beyond Bradman, the demand for cricket memorabilia continues to bound ahead, as collectors seek to acquire items relating to the heroes of their youth – and to earlier heroes who evoke the glory days of carefree and simpler living. The National Museum of Australia paid $14,000 at a Lawson–Menzies auction, way beyond the pre-sale estimate of $2,000 to $3,000, for an original 1867 composite photograph of the 1868 Aboriginal team that toured England. Taken by Peter Dawson of Hamilton, Victoria, it depicted the individual portraits of the 14 Aboriginal cricketers, plus two officials, who made up the touring party, and was framed in contemporary cedar with a gold-painted mount.

The museum also paid $11,000 to acquire the boomerang of one of the players – Twopenny, the better-known name of the fast bowler Murrumgunarrimin – who went on to become the first Aboriginal first-class cricketer. He topped the bowling averages on that 1868 tour and used the boomerang to provide English audiences with exhibitions of Aboriginal hunting techniques. "It's rare to get two such very early pieces that talk … about contact between cultures," said Jo Duke, senior curator of the museum.

The baggy green worn by Dennis Lillee during his 70-Test career was sold at Leski's for $13,500. It was a rare instance of a celebrated fast bowler's cap coming on to the market, and the hefty price underlined the respect and affection Lillee still commands among cricket followers. The signed baggy green of Bruce Reid – another West Australian quick who used his height to telling effect in 27 Tests from 1985 to 1993 – fetched $6,750 at Leski's.

TOP 10 SELLERS OF 2003-04

1	Shane Warne's record-equalling ball	$42,700
2	Don Bradman's 1934 bat	$42,000
3	Don Bradman's 1946-47 bat	$34,500
4	1868 Aboriginal team photograph	$14,000
5	Dennis Lillee's baggy green	$13,500
6	Victor Trumper's signed Beldam print	$11,000
7	Twopenny's boomerang	$11,000
8	Clarrie Grimmett's South Australian cap	$7,700
9	Bruce Reid's baggy green	$6,750
10	Bodyline series signed bat	$4,750

Note: all prices quoted are before the payment of the buyer's premium and GST

Leski also had on offer a magnificent half-tone offset lithograph print of George W. Beldam's famous image of Victor Trumper jumping out to drive, as depicted on the jacket of this book. Signed by both Trumper and Beldam, it sold for $11,000. Meanwhile yet another cap, the South Australian cap belonging to the champion 1930s leg-spinner Clarrie Grimmett, was bought at Cromwell's Auctioneers in Sydney for $7,700. A full-size Gradidge bat, matchused and signed by the Australian team for the fourth Bodyline Test of 1932-33, realised $4,750 at Leski's in December 2003. It was missing the signature of the captain Bill Woodfull but included that of 'Hammy' Love, playing his only Test.

Other desirable items at auction included a bat signed by both teams from Bradman's last match – for the Prime Minister's XI against MCC in Canberra in 1963. It sold via Legends Genuine Memorabilia for $3,500. Another Bodyline bat was sold by Lawson–Menzies for $3,750. This was the one used by the wicketkeeper Bert Oldfield in the infamous Adelaide Test, when Oldfield's skull was fractured by a ball from Harold Larwood, and it carried the signatures of the entire Australian squad plus 15 members of the English touring party. A 1909 Australian team autograph page, described by Leski as "extremely rare and attractive" and adorned with a dozen signatures – including those of Monty Noble, Warwick Armstrong and Syd Gregory – made $4,250.

One item which fetched a price well above the estimated sum ($80 to $100) was a Bodyline season itinerary and fixtures booklet produced by Plaster's Ship Inn, Pitt St & Circular Quay, Sydney. It sold at Cromwell's for $600. Cromwell's also sold a 1928-29 Ashes series autograph book, signed by players from both countries and in good condition, for $1,430. The minimum estimate was $800.

Non-print items continue to attract interest from bidders because of their scarcity and aesthetic character. One example was a glass bowl, 21.5 cm in diameter and crafted around 1930, with the word "Don" inscribed and an image of Bradman driving excised from the glass in the base. Estimated at $400 to $600, it was sold by Cromwell's for $1,300. A Bradman Toby jug, made by Marutomoware in Japan in the early 1930s, sold for $550 after a minimum estimate of $200.

Collector cards are another generally appreciating sector of the market. Cards which featured strongly this year included an incomplete collection – 45 of a full set of 57, including variants – of the 1901 Wills (Australia) Cricketers Series. It sold for $4,500 at Leski's in February. The 1896 Wills Cricketers set of 50 cards realised $3,750 at Leski's. At the bargain end, a set of 16 Dudgeon & Arnell 1934 Australian Test team cards sold for $200. The complete set of 14 British American Tobacco cricket badges Cameo English Cricketers, made in Australia in 1901, was sold by Leski's for $2,900 on an estimate of $1,400 to $1,600.

Over in England, meanwhile, there was an interesting postscript to Bradman's $425,000 baggy green. The cap he wore during his triumphant 1930 Ashes tour – when he amassed 974 runs in five Tests and first announced his brilliance to the world – was sold by Christie's in London in June for $95,000. This sets a more realistic market benchmark for a Bradman baggy green. But the figures generated by The Don, in death as in life, remain mighty impressive.

Stephen W. Gibbs is a cricket bibliographer, an indexer of cricket references and a player in the over-40s competition in Sydney.

Fixtures, 2004-05

CRICKET
AUSTRALIA

NEW ZEALAND, PAKISTAN AND WEST INDIES IN AUSTRALIA
2004-05 INTERNATIONAL SEASON

Tour Matches

November 11–14	NSW v New Zealand	Sydney
December 7	Chairman's XI v Pakistan	Lilac Hill, Perth
December 9–12	Western Australia v Pakistan	Perth
January 5	Victoria v West Indies (day/night)	Melbourne
January 8	Australia A v West Indies	Hobart
January 9	Australia A v West Indies	Hobart
January 12	Australia A v Pakistan	Adelaide
January 25	Prime Minister's XI v Pakistan	Canberra

Tests

November 18–22	First Test – Australia v New Zealand	Brisbane
November 26–30	Second Test – Australia v New Zealand	Adelaide
December 16–20	First Test – Australia v Pakistan	Perth
December 26–30	Second Test – Australia v Pakistan	Melbourne
January 2–6	Third Test – Australia v Pakistan	Sydney

Chappell-Hadlee Trophy

December 5	Australia v New Zealand (day/night)	Melbourne
December 8	Australia v New Zealand (day/night)	Sydney
December 10	Australia v New Zealand (day/night)	Brisbane

VB SERIES

January 14	Australia v West Indies (day/night)	Melbourne
January 16	Australia v Pakistan	Hobart
January 19	Pakistan v West Indies	Brisbane
January 21	Australia v West Indies (day/night)	Brisbane
January 23	Australia v Pakistan (day/night)	Sydney
January 26	Australia v West Indies (day/night)	Adelaide
January 28	Pakistan v West Indies	Adelaide
January 30	Australia v Pakistan (day/night)	Perth
February 1	Pakistan v West Indies	Perth
February 4	First Final (day/night)	Melbourne
February 6	Second Final (day/night)	Sydney
February 8	Third Final (if required) (day/night)	Adelaide

2004-05 PURA CUP

October 15–18	Queensland v New South Wales	Brisbane
October 16–19	South Australia v Victoria	Adelaide
October 17–20	Western Australia v Tasmania	Perth
November 2–5	New South Wales v Western Australia	NSW
November 8–11	Tasmania v Victoria	Tasmania
November 9–12	South Australia v Queensland	Adelaide
November 16–19	Tasmania v South Australia	Tasmania
November 21–24	Western Australia v Queensland	Perth
November 23–26	Victoria v New South Wales	Melbourne
December 2	Queensland v Tasmania	Brisbane
December 1–4	Victoria v Western Australia	Melbourne
December 2–5	New South Wales v South Australia	NSW
December 16–19	New South Wales v Tasmania	NSW
December 19–22	South Australia v Western Australia	Adelaide
	Queensland v Victoria	Brisbane
January 16–19	Western Australia v Victoria	Perth
January 18–21	Tasmania v Queensland	Tasmania
	South Australia v New South Wales	Adelaide
January 27–30	Victoria v South Australia	Melbourne
	New South Wales v Queensland	NSW
	Tasmania v Western Australia	Tasmania
February 24–27	Queensland v South Australia	Brisbane
	Victoria v Tasmania	Melbourne
	Western Australia v New South Wales	Perth
March 3–6	Victoria v Queensland	Melbourne
	Western Australia v South Australia	Perth
	Tasmania v New South Wales	Tasmania
March 10–13	New South Wales v Victoria	NSW
	Queensland v Western Australia	Brisbane
	South Australia v Tasmania	Adelaide
March 18–22	Final	TBC

2004-05 ING CUP

October 10	Queensland Bulls v New South Wales Blues	Brisbane
October 15	Western Warriors v Tasmanian Tigers (day/night)	Perth
October 23	Queensland Bulls v Southern Redbacks	Brisbane
October 24	New South Wales Blues v Tasmanian Tigers	NSW
October 30	Southern Redbacks v Victorian Bushrangers	Adelaide
October 31	New South Wales Blues v Western Warriors	NSW
November 6	Tasmanian Tigers v Victorian Bushrangers	Tasmania
November 7	Southern Redbacks v Queensland Bulls	Adelaide
November 14	Victorian Bushrangers v Western Warriors	Melbourne
November 19	Western Warriors v Queensland Bulls (day/night)	Perth
November 21	Victorian Bushrangers v New South Wales Blues	Melbourne
	Tasmanian Tigers v Southern Redbacks	Tasmania
December 4	Queensland Bulls v Tasmanian Tigers (day/night)	Brisbane
December 11	New South Wales Blues v Southern Redbacks	NSW
December 12	Victorian Bushrangers v Tasmanian Tigers	Melbourne
December 17	Queensland Bulls v Victorian Bushrangers (day/night)	Brisbane
	Southern Redbacks v Western Warriors (day/night)	Adelaide
January 2	Western Warriors v New South Wales Blues (day/night)	Perth
	Tasmanian Tigers v Queensland Bulls	Tasmania
	Victorian Bushrangers v Southern Redbacks	Melbourne
January 14	Western Warriors v Victorian Bushrangers (day/night)	Perth
January 15	New South Wales Blues v Queensland Bulls (day/night)	NSW
January 23	Tasmanian Tigers v Western Warriors	Tasmania
	Southern Redbacks v New South Wales Blues (day/night)	Adelaide
February 4	Western Warriors v Southern Redbacks (day/night)	Perth
February 5	Tasmanian Tigers v New South Wales Blues	Tasmania
February 6	Victorian Bushrangers v Queensland Bulls	Melbourne
February 11	Queensland Bulls v Western Warriors (day/night)	Brisbane
February 12	Southern Redbacks v Tasmanian Tigers	Adelaide
February 13	New South Wales Blues v Victorian Bushrangers	NSW
February 20	Final	TBC

AUSTRALIANS IN NEW ZEALAND, 2004-05

February 17	Twenty20 international (night)	Eden Park, Auckland
February 19	First one-day international (day/night)	Westpac Stadium, Wellington
February 22	Second one-day international(day/night)	Jade Stadium, Christchurch
February 26	Third one-day international (day/night)	Eden Park, Auckland
March 2	Fourth one-day international (day/night)	Westpac Park, Hamilton
March 5	Fifth one-day international	McLean Park, Napier
March 10–14	First Test	Jade Stadium, Christchurch
March 18–22	Second Test	Basin Reserve, Wellington
March 26–30	Third Test	Eden Park, Auckland

AUSTRALIANS IN ENGLAND, 2005

Twenty20

June 13	England v Australia	Rose Bowl

The NatWest Series

June 16	England v Bangladesh	The Oval
June 18	Australia v Bangladesh	Cardiff
June 19	England v Australia	Bristol
June 21	England v Bangladesh (day/night)	Trent Bridge
June 23	England v Australia (day/night)	Durham
June 25	Australia v Bangladesh	Old Trafford
June 26	England v Bangladesh	Headingley
June 28	England v Australia (day/night)	Edgbaston
June 30	Australia v Bangladesh	Canterbury
July 2	Final	Lord's

NatWest Challenge

July 7	England v Australia	Headingley
July 10	England v Australia	Lord's
July 12	England v Australia	The Oval

Test Series

July 21–25	First Test – England v Australia	Lord's
August 4–8	Second Test – England v Australia	Edgbaston
August 11–15	Third Test – England v Australia	Old Trafford
August 25–29	Fourth Test – England v Australia	Trent Bridge
September 8–12	Fifth Test – England v Australia	The Oval

Other tour matches not yet confirmed at time of publication

WOMEN'S NATIONAL CRICKET LEAGUE, 2004-05

October 30	New South Wales v Western Australia	Drummoyne Oval, NSW
October 31	New South Wales v Western Australia	North Sydney No. 2 Oval, NSW
November 6–7*	Queensland v South Australia	Allan Border Field, Qld
November 13–14*	Western Australia v Victoria	Settlers Hill, Baldivis, WA
November 20–21*	South Australia v New South Wales	Kensington Oval, SA (TBC)
	Victoria v Queensland	Harry Trott Oval, Vic
January 15–16*	South Australia v Western Australia	Adelaide Oval No. 2, SA
January 15	New South Wales v Victoria	Drummoyne Oval, NSW
January 16	New South Wales v Victoria	Telstra Stadium, NSW
January 22–23*	Western Australia v Queensland	TBC
January 29–30*	Queensland v New South Wales	Allan Border Field, Qld
	Victoria v South Australia	Harry Trott Oval, Vic
February 11–13	Finals series (1 v 2)	1st place to host

* *Denotes games on consecutive days.*

2005 ICC SUPER SERIES

One-Day Internationals

October 5	World XI v Number One-Ranked ODI Team	Melbourne
October 7	World XI v Number One-Ranked ODI Team	Melbourne
October 9	World XI v Number One-Ranked ODI Team	Melbourne

Tests

October 14	World XI v Number One-Ranked Test Team	Sydney

Note: At the time of publication all fixtures were correct. They are subject to change without notice.

Contributors

Nabila Ahmed writes on cricket for *The Age*, Melbourne.

Charlie Austin is Sri Lankan editor of Wisden CricInfo.

Greg Baum is chief sportswriter of *The Age*, Melbourne.

John Birmingham's books include *He Died with a Felafel in his Hand* and *Weapons of Choice*.

Tim Blair is a columnist with *The Bulletin* magazine.

Martin Blake writes on sport for *The Age*, Melbourne.

Max Bonnell is the author of *How Many More Are Coming? The Short Life of Jack Marsh*.

Daniel Brettig is a journalist with the *Advertiser* in Adelaide.

Rohit Brijnath is an *Age* journalist and former sports editor of *India Today* magazine.

Jack Brown is secretary of the Wallsend Cricket Club in Newcastle.

Ken Casellas was chief cricket writer for *The West Australian* for 27 years.

Lawrie Colliver is a sports reporter with 5AA in Adelaide.

Malcolm Conn is cricket correspondent of *The Australian* newspaper.

Paul Coupar is assistant editor of worldwide *Wisden Cricketers' Almanack*.

Charles Davis is a Melbourne-based cricket writer and scientist.

Ben Dorries writes on cricket for the *Courier-Mail*, Brisbane.

Ross Dundas is Australia's only full-time cricket statistician.

Bob Ellis's latest book is *Night Thoughts in Time of War*.

Peter English is a former assistant editor of *Inside Edge* and *Wisden Cricket Monthly*.

Ric Finlay is a Hobart statistician and the author of *Island Summers*.

Damien Fleming took 75 wickets in 20 Tests for Australia between 1994 and 2001.

Angus Fontaine, editor-at-large for ACP magazines, is a former editor of *Inside Edge*.

Warwick Franks edited *Wisden Cricketers' Almanack Australia* from 2001-02 to 2003-04.

David Frith has written 26 books on cricket. His latest is *The Ross Gregory Story*.

Stephen W. Gibbs is a cricket bibliographer and indexer of cricket references.

Stephen Gray is media manager for Queensland Cricket.

Gideon Haigh edited *Wisden Cricketers' Almanack Australia* from 1999 to 2000-01.

Catherine Hanley is a Somerset supporter and a contributor to Wisden CricInfo.

Peter Hanlon is Saturday sports editor of *The Age*, Melbourne.

John Harms is a Melbourne-based sportswriter and author of *Confessions of a Thirteenth Man*.

Andrew Hyde is a Darwin-based television producer.

Malcolm Knox, literary editor of the *Sydney Morning Herald*, is the author of *Taylor & Beyond*.

Tim Lane is a long-time cricket and Australian Rules commentator, now with Channel 10.

Geoff Lawson took 180 wickets in 46 Tests for Australia between 1980 and 1989.

Ashley Mallett took 132 wickets in 38 Tests for Australia between 1968 and 1980.

Trevor Marshallsea is cricket correspondent of the *Sydney Morning Herald*.

Jim Maxwell commentates for ABC radio and is editor of the *ABC Cricket Book*.

Greg McKie is a long-time writer and statistician on Australia under-age cricket.

Adam Morehouse is a Canberra statistician and the author of *From Country to Comets*.

Barry Nicholls is an ABC radio presenter in Alice Springs.

Kerry O'Keeffe took 53 wickets in 24 Tests for Australia between 1971 and 1977.

Ken Piesse is the author of 28 cricket books and a former editor of *Cricketer* magazine.

Dileep Premachandran is a Bangalore-based assistant editor of Wisden CricInfo.

Matt Price is a journalist in the Canberra press gallery who writes for *The Australian*.

Peter Roebuck is a cricket columnist for *The Age* and *Sydney Morning Herald*.

Christian Ryan is a former editor of *Inside Edge* and Australian editor of Wisden CricInfo.

Erica Sainsbury is a long-time scorer, statistician and writer about women's cricket.

Chloe Saltau is cricket correspondent of *The Age*, Melbourne.

Geoff Sando is a cricket historian and secretary of East Torrens Cricket Club.

Rob Steen has written biographies of David Gower, Desmond Haynes and Sonny Liston.

David Stockdale is a senior sports journalist with Hobart's *Mercury* newspaper.

Brett Stubbs is a Tasmanian cricket writer.

Warwick Torrens is a Queensland cricket historian and statistician.

John Townsend writes on cricket for *The West Australian*.

Adrian Warren is a Sydney-based sports writer.

Andrew Webster, a Sydney journalist, was formerly staff feature writer of *Inside Sport*.

Bernard Whimpress is curator of the SACA museum and the author of *Passport to Nowhere*.

Ken Williams is a Melbourne-based cricket writer and statistician.

David Wiseman is a Sydney-based cricket writer.

PICTURE CREDITS

The Advertiser pp 126, 135, 519, 522; *The Age* p 914; Cricket NSW pp 123,162, 167, 491, 494, 934; Cricket Victoria pp 145, 166, 546, 548; Christine Hall p 938; Queensland Cricket pp 134, 138, 150, 155, 157, 505, 508, 533; South Australian Cricket Association pp 132, 918; Tasmanian Cricket Association pp 124, 126, 166, 536; *The West Australian* p 931; Western Australian Cricket Association pp 140, 160, 162, 560, 562. All others picture credits given with photos.